DE JURE BELLI AC PACIS LIBRI TRES

BY

HUGO GROTIUS

THE TRANSLATION

BY FRANCIS W. KELSEY

WITH THE COLLABORATION OF

ARTHUR E. R. BOAK, HENRY A. SANDERS,

JESSE S. REEVES AND HERBERT F. WRIGHT

AND AN INTRODUCTION BY

JAMES BROWN SCOTT

With a new introduction by

William E. Butler

John Edward Fowler Distinguished Professor of Law,
Dickinson School of Law, Pennsylvania State University;
Emeritus Professor of Comparative Law, University of London (University College London);
Foreign Member, National Academy of Sciences of Ukraine and
National Academy of Legal Sciences of Ukraine

THE LAWBOOK EXCHANGE, LTD.
Clark, New Jersey

ISBN 978-1-61619-659-2

Lawbook Exchange edition 2021

The quality of this reprint is equivalent to the quality of the original work.

THE LAWBOOK EXCHANGE, LTD.
33 Terminal Avenue
Clark, New Jersey 07066-1321

Please see our website for a selection of our other publications and fine facsimile reprints of classic works of legal history:
www.lawbookexchange.com

Library of Congress Cataloging-in-Publication Data

Names: Grotius, Hugo, 1583-1645, author. | Kelsey, Francis W. (Francis Willey), 1858-1927 translator. | Scott, James Brown, 1866-1943 writer of introduction. | Butler, William Elliott, 1939- writer of new introduction.
Title: De jure belli ac pacis libri tres / by Hugo Grotius ; the tranlsation by Francis Willey Kelsey ; with the collaboration of Arthur E. R. Boak [and three others] ; and an introduction by James Brown Scott ; with a new introduction by William E. Butler.
Other titles: De jure belli ac pacis libri tres. English
Description: [Lawbook Exchange edition]. | Clark : The Lawbook Exchange, Ltd., 2021. | Includes bibliographical references and index. | Summary: "An important translation of a classic treatise on the conduct of armed conflict"-- Provided by publisher.
Identifiers: LCCN 2021046916 | ISBN 9781616196592 (hardcover)
Subjects: LCSH: International law. | War (International law) | Natural law.
Classification: LCC KZ2093.A3 J881355 2021 | DDC 341--dc23/eng/20211020
LC record available at https://lccn.loc.gov/2021046916

Printed in the United States of America on acid-free paper

THE KELSEY TRANSLATION OF HUGO GROTIUS

Hugo Grotius was a formidably productive writer whose works ranged from the law of nations to Dutch law, poetry, history, theology, philosophy, literature, and other disciplines. Throughout the remainder of the seventeenth century following his death, a veritable "Grotiana factory" devoted to translations of his works into English and the other principal European vernacular languages operated throughout Europe. Latin language editions continued to find an audience, however.

To make the writings of Grotius commercially attractive and accessible to a broader readership, publishers were prepared, usually in the form of consortiums of one species or another, to share the risks of translation costs and quality and undertake joint marketing arrangements for an agreed portion of the print run. Who took the initiative remains in most cases to be determined: did the translator(s) take the initiative and approach the publisher(s) with the idea of translating Grotius, or did the publishers see market demand and commission the translations?

When Grotius was alive, these matters would have been left to him. Were he so inclined, he probably had the necessary command of languages, in addition to the original Latin, to produce his own foreign language versions. No evidence exists that this was contemplated with respect to the *Law of War and Peace*. Translations from the Latin postdate 1645, the year that Grotius perished as a consequence of shipwreck off the Baltic coast. The third (sometimes called the fifth) Latin language edition (1646) is regarded as the last lifetime version in which he made authorial changes and, in the view of many, the definitive and preferred text.

A Note on Grotius

Hugo Grotius (1583–1645) remains after more than four and a third centuries from his birth perhaps the single most recognizable name in the history of international law. Sometimes (quite wrongly) labeled the "father of international law", his works on the subject – above all the work here considered – became classics in the field even during his lifetime.[1] In some works on the

[1] See L. E. van Holk, "Hugo Grotius, 1583–1645: A Biographical Sketch", in L. E. van Holk and C. G. Roelofson (eds.), *Grotius Reader: A Reader for Students of International Law and Legal History* (1983), pp. 23-44; J. L. de Burigny, *The Life of the Truly Eminent and Learned Hugo Grotius* (London, 1754); E. Dumbauld, *The Life and Legal Writings of Hugo Grotius* (1969); W. S. M. Knight, *The Life and Works of Hugo Grotius* (1925); S. C. Neff, "Introduction", in H. Grotius, *On the Law of War and Peace: Student Edition* (2012), pp. xiii-xxxv. Of the foregoing, the most thorough and extensive was Knight's biography, but that has now

history of international law, "Grotius" is singled out as a period in its development.[2] A first edition of *De jure belli ac pacis* (1625) in fine state brings upwards of E150,000 in 2021 and is included among the 500 most important books ever printed.[3]

Grotius was born at Delft into an influential Calvinist family of patricians. The eldest of four children, his intellectual abilities manifested themselves early on. He was educated at home by his father, Jan de Groot (1554-1640), and the Latin School in Delft, probably attending from age six to eleven. Instruction and daily discourse with classmates and teachers was obligatorily in Latin. Composing Latin verses at the age of seven (said by Eyffinger[4] to be "… the only man in world history acclaimed a child prodigy by virtue of his juvenile poetry"), he praised Maurice, Prince of Orange (1567-1625), a year later in a poem commemorating the capture of Nijmegen on 21 October 1591. Matriculating at the University of Leiden at the age of eleven, he was far from unique in pursuing learning at such a tender age; exceptional were his remarkable intellectual abilities. Nellen quoted the recollections of Isaac Casaubon (1559-1614), who related that "… Grotius' earliest attempts at poetry had struck all the scholars dumb with astonishment".[5]

Following the usual pattern of study in those days, Grotius began with the study of philosophy, including rhetoric and history, in the faculty of arts and moved on to the higher faculty of law, having chosen not to pursue the alternatives of medicine or theology. He seems to have entertained a career in the civil service and chose law as best suited to provide an appropriate grounding. He continued to perfect his command of Greek and Latin and most likely studied

been comprehensively superseded by the Grayson translation of what will be for generations to come the definitive biography. See Henk Nellen, *Hugo Grotius: A Lifelong Struggle for Peace in Church and State, 1583-1645*, transl. J. C. Grayson (2015), originally published as Nellen, *Hugo de Groot: een leven in strijd om de vrede, 1583-1645* (2007).

2 See W. E. Butler, "Periodization and International Law", in A. Orakhelashvili (ed.), *Research Handbook on the Theory and History of International Law* (2d ed.; 2020), pp. 281-295.

3 Percy H. Muir (intro.), *Printing and the Mind of Man* (2d ed. rev.; 1983), no. 125, p. 75. On the early history of the first edition, see J. S. Reeves, """The First Edition of Grotius's De Jure Belli ac Pacis, 1625", *American Journal of International Law*, XIX (1925), pp. 12-22; Reeves, "Grotius, De Jure Belli ac Pacis: A Bibliographic Account", ibid., XIX (1925), pp. 251-262.

4 A. Eyffinger, "In Quest of Synthesis: An Attempted Synopsis of Grotius's Works According to Their Genesis and Objective", *Grotiana*, IV (N.S., 1983), pp. 76-88. In 1926 he was ranked equal second in an assessment of the intelligence quotients of three hundred geniuses in world history. See C. M. Cox, *Genetic Studies of Genius: The Early Mental Traits of Three Hundred Geniuses* (1926), cited in Neff, note 1 above, p. xiv.

5 Nellen, note 1 above, p. 33.

Arabic and Hebrew. He left Leiden University at the age of fourteen, having satisfactorily performed in the fields of law, philosophy, and mathematics.

A widely-practiced way of completing one's university education in those times was to undertake a journey to a foreign land and acquire practical experience through seeing the world. Presumably Grotius' father arranged with his sometime co-investor Johan van Oldenbarnevelt (1547-1619) that Grotius should accompany a Dutch Embassy to Henry IV of France (1553-1610). Grotius was present at the first audience with Henry IV, which is presumed to be the legendary occasion when the King proclaimed "Voilà le miracle de Hollande"; later during the Embassy Grotius was among the recipients of a gold medallion presented by Henry IV.[6] The Embassy itself, designed in collaboration with the English, failed to prevent the conclusion of the Treaty of Vervins (2 May 1598) between France and Spain. While en route back to Holland, the Embassy stopped for a day at Orléans. The instructions drawn up by Jan de Groot for his son mentioned matriculation at the University of Orleans, but not promotion. Nonetheless on 5 May 1598 the degree of *Doctor utriusque juris* (Doctor of both laws, i.e., Roman and canon law) was conferred, a degree that involved a *disputatio* without the involvement of a professor as *praeses*. In those times university degrees were acquired by the payment of a fee and involved a token ceremony following a period of study; in Holland it was believed that foreign degrees, especially French and German, carried more gravitas for someone pursuing a professional career than did a Dutch degree. Grotius himself later advised Johannes Arnoldi Corvinus (1582-1650) to have his son seek a law degree in France because French titles "carried much more weight than Dutch degrees in foreign countries".[7]

Published verses in Latin and Greek kept the name of Hugo Grotius before the Dutch public. Some were designed to flatter people whom Grotius wished to cultivate, such as poems to celebrate the marriage of the Treasurer-General of the Generality, or the appointment of Professor Johannes Cuchlinus (1546-1606) as Regent of a training school for theologians in the University of Leiden. By 1598 Grotius had completed his text of the *Satyricon* in the version by Martianus Capella (fl. 410-420 AD), which he dedicated

[6] Nellen observes that these sentiments, if uttered, were not mentioned in the Report of the embassy or other contemporary sources. They first appear in the dedication of a play to Grotius written by Gerbrandt Adriaenszoon Bredero (1585-1618) in late 1616. See Nellen, note 1 above, p. 47.

[7] Nellen, note 1 above, pp. 49-50. The original diploma has been lost and no reference to the occasion survives in Grotius' letters or publications.

to Henri II de Bourbon (1588-1646), Prince of Condé, whom he befriended during the Embassy to France.[8]

A year later followed an edition of a didactic poem by Aratus of Soloi in Cilicia (c. 315/310-240 BC), which contained metrical translations by Marcus Tullius Cicero (106-43 BC), Claudius Caesar Germanicus (10 BC-54 AD), and Rufus Festus Avienus (fourth century AD).[9] These works earned him a gold medal and welcome financial support from the States-General. A biblical drama accompanied by sacred poems was well received in Holland and abroad.[10]

Admitted to legal practice at the age of sixteen, on 13 December 1599, in fact younger than the legally permitted age, he was successful in attracting clients and continued to excel at his first love, the humanities. At twenty years of age he was appointed Historiographer of Holland.[11]

His first known work on the law of nations originated in a commission from the Dutch East India Company to prepare an opinion of the legality of the seizure of a Portuguese ship, the carrack *Sta. Catarina*, by the Company flotilla during the war in February 1603 between the Netherlands and Spain.[12] A substantial manuscript was produced, one chapter of which was published in 1609 as *Mare liberum*[13] (the full text was not discovered until 1864 and published in 1868).[14] The text was also used for Grotius' later work on the law of war and peace (1625).

[8] M. Capella, *Satyricon, in quo De nuptiis Philologiae & Mercurii libri duo & De septem artibus liberalibus libri singulares,* ed. H. Grotius ([Leiden], 1599)

[9] H. Grotius, *Syntagma Arateovm: opus poeticae et astronomiae studiosis utilissimum* [(Leiden], 1600). Dedicated to the States-General.

[10] H. Grotius, *Sacra in quibus Adamus exul* (The Hague, 1601).

[11] See A. Nussbaum, *A Concise History of the Law of Nations* (rev. ed., 1954; reprint ed. Gryphon, 2008).

[12] A rich prize, the vessel and its cargo were valued at more than three million guilders. The work was commissioned by the Amsterdam Chamber of the East India Company to sustain the Company's view that it had the right to seize as lawful prize property that was owned by nations with which the Republic was at war, which in this case would have included Portugal as well as Spain.

[13] We are blessed with two recent published versions, one originally made by Richard Hakluyt but never fully published in its time. See Grotius, *The Free Sea*, transl. R. Hakluyt; ed. D. Armitage (2004); and Grotius, *Mare Liberum 1609–2009*, ed. R. Feenstra (2009), a sumptuous edition. Also see on this book W. E. Butler, "Grotius and the Law of the Sea", in H. Bull, B. Kingsbury, and A. Roberts (eds.), *Hugo Grotius and International Relations* (1990), pp. 209–220. On Hakluyt in this connection, see D. Pirillo, "Balance of Power and Freedom of the Sea: Richard Hakluyt and Alberico Gentili", in D. Carey and C. Jowitt (eds.), *Richard Hakluyt and Travel Writing in Early Modern Europe* (2012), pp. 177-186. For an account of the composition and printing, see Nellen, note 1 above, pp. 106-109.

[14] The most recent edition, attended in several instances by new supporting materials, is H. Grotius, *Commentary on the Law of Prize and Booty*, ed. & intro. Martine Julia van Irtersum (2006).

Grotius rose rapidly in the Dutch establishment, being appointed to influential legal posts (including Advocate-Fiscal in 1607) and continuing his sundry writings on history, theology, and Dutch law. His political career in Holland ended when he was sentenced to life imprisonment for his role in a dispute among Calvinists in 1619 that Prince Maurice of Orange (1567-1625) equated to treason.[15] His tenure in prison and ultimate escape were known to every schoolboy throughout Europe.[16] During two years of confinement, he wrote two major works, one an introduction to Dutch jurisprudence and the other an exposition of the central doctrines of the Christian faith intended for seafarers. He was allowed to have books in quantity and the companionship of his wife, Maria van Reigersberch (1589-1653). He trained himself to lie in a closed chest and was eventually removed clandestinely in that receptacle on 22 March 1621 to the safety of friends, who assisted him in escaping via Antwerp to France disguised as a bricklayer. There he was received by the King of France, awarded an allowance, and, during 1622–1624, commenced and completed the Latin version of the monumental *Law of War and Peace*.[17] Dedicated to Louis XIII, the book, it was hoped, might contribute to a resolution of the Thirty Years War, then fully in progress.[18]

The work, well received at the time, disappointed in that its appearance did not enable Grotius to return home or to secure a position consistent with his stature and ambition. Eventually, in 1634 he was appointed by the Court of Sweden to become the Swedish Ambassador to Paris. He held the post for a decade, but not without difficulties. In manner he was not diplomatic, and his continued preoccupations with matters of theology and literature were seen by his Swedish patrons as detracting from the proper performance of his duties.

There have been more than fifty editions of the original Latin text, including the three during Grotius' lifetime with his emendations. There are

[15] On a later assessment of the trial based on access to sealed records of the proceedings, see G. G. Brandt, *Brandts Historie van de Rechtspleging gehouden in de Jaeren 1618 en 1619. Ontrent de dry gevangene Heeren Mr. Johan van Oldenbarnevelt Mr. Rombout Hoogerbeets Mr. Hugo de Groot* (Rotterdam, 1708). On Oldenbarnevelt's defense of his conduct, see Jan van Barnevelt, *Barnevelt's Apology of Holland's Mysterie, with Marginall Castigations* (1618). Also see John L. Motley, *The Life and Death of John of Barneveld, Advocate of Holland; with a View of the Primary Causes and Movements of the Thirty Years' War* (London, 1874). 2 vols. Oldenbarnevelt was found guilty and beheaded.

[16] Recounted in Burigny, note 1 above and greatly embellished by "that literary larcenist", Charles Butler, in what one reviewer called his "indifferent life" of Grotius. See C. Butler, *The Life of Hugo Grotius with Brief Minutes of the Civil, Ecclesiastical, and Literary History of the Netherlands* (London, 1826).

[17] Intellectually, Tuck suggests, *De Iure Belli ac Pacis* really grew out of Grotius's time in prison". See R. Tuck, "Introduction", in H. Grotius, *The Rights of War and Peace* (2005), p. xv.

[18] On that War and references to Grotius, see P. H. Wilson, *The Thirty Years War: Europe's Tragedy* (2009), pp. 134, 318, 389, 463, 553, and 675.

translations into Chinese, Dutch, French, German, Japanese, Russian,[19] Spanish, Swedish, and Church Slavonic,[20] among others. Although well regarded in France and Spain, Grotius' fame was greatest in Protestant countries. The Vatican placed his book on the Index in 1626, where it remained until 1899.

The Kelsey Translation

In January 1907 James Brown Scott (1866-1943), then the Solicitor for the Department of State of the United States, wrote a letter to Robert Simpson Woodward (1849-1924), the President of the Carnegie Institution of Washington, suggesting that the Institution undertake a project to republish the "classics of international law" with new translations, annotations, and introductions.[21] Included in the proposal was a substantial list of candidates, pride of place being given to Hugo Grotius. The Project received the approbation and financial support of the Carnegie Institution and matured into the famed" Classics of International Law" series issued in 22 volumes in 40 between 1911 and 1950.[22] Scott choosing, in his capacity of initiator of the Project, to identify himself as the legal advisor to the Department of State cannot have failed to add gravitas to, if not official interest in, the suggestion.

Development of the Project. The project began expeditiously. Scott contacted his contacts among international lawyers around the world. Having the year

[19] The most comprehensive bibliography of foreign translations of Grotius is Jacob Ter Meulen and P. J. J. Diermanse, *Bibliographie des* écrits *imprimés de Hugo Grotius* (The Hague, 1950). Published more than seven decades ago, it requires some correction and augmentation. With respect to the Russian versions, for example, it is unaware of the 1902 St. Petersburg edition, which seems to be the first printed appearance of Grotius' treatise on the law of war and peace in Russia, although heavily censored. The later editions mentioned are not editions at all, but merely an enumeration of the table of contents from Grotius or extremely abbreviated extracts on certain topics (for example, ambassadorial immunity). The first full edition of Grotius in Russian appeared in 1956, after the Ter Meulen/Diermanse bibliography was published. It is entirely possible that the reaction of the Russian Orthodox Church to Grotius was not dissimilar from that of the Vatican.

[20] See W. E. Butler, "Grotius' Influence in Russia", in Bull, et al., note 13 above, pp. 257–266.

[21] See [James Brown Scott], *The Classics of International Law: Letter from James Brown Scott, Solicitor for the Department of State, to R. S. Woodward, President of the Carnegie Institution of Washington relative to a Project for the Republication of the Classics of International Law* [Washington D. C.] (Printed for the Carnegie Institution, January 1907). 13 p. A copy is held in the George Finch papers at the Archives of Georgetown University. Prepared for the Trustees of the Carnegie Institution, the "Letter" was printed on a fine handmade paper, fore-edge untrimmed, in sewn wrappers. A more elegant submission can hardly be imagined.

[22] The series has been reprinted in its entirety by Oceana Publications (1964), by Legal Classics Library (Grotius only; 1984), by William S. Hein (1995), and serially by Lawbook Exchange Ltd. The series commenced in 1911 and concluded in 1950, initially published by the Carnegie Institution of Washington. From 1 January 1917 the series was transferred to the Carnegie Endowment for International Peace.

previously acted as one of the Founders of the American Society of International Law, he was perhaps the American international lawyer best-connected with the European, Latin American, and Asian establishment of the international legal profession. Support was solicited among colleagues for the Project in principle, suggestions for works to be included and candidates to undertake the translations, annotations, and notes were requested, and agreements made with individuals – mostly professors of international law – to accept the task of producing a text for the Project.

Success was early. Professor Thomas Erskine Holland (1835-1926) was among those to answer Scott's invitation to assist in pursuing the idea of a "*Corpus Juris Gentium*". He observed that the translations in the series would demand a knowledge not only of Latin, but also of law and of the style of the period. The style of Alberico Gentili (1552-1608), he noted, was "very crabbed". Gentili's *De jure belli* was, excluding Grotius, probably the "most historically important" of all the works proposed for translation. Whewell's translation of Grotius, said Holland, was "useless".[23] He agreed to undertake Zouche and, in addition to suggesting Gentili, also suggested the inclusion of Giovanni da (Johannes de Lignano) Legnano (c, 1310-1382) in the series – a suggestion promptly endorsed by Robert S. Woodward.[24] By May 1909 an image of Hugo Grotius had been chosen to preface the planned photographic reproduction of the 1646 edition.[25] Barnum had estimated translation costs of Ayala, with notes, to be $600, and the introduction and editing to be $500; for Legnano, $250 for translation and $500 for editing; for Zouche, $500 each for translation and editing.[26]

[23] Archive of the Carnegie Endowment for International Peace, Butler Library, Columbia University, Letter of Holland to Scott, 13 April 1909 (hereinafter: CEIPA).

[24] CEIPA, Woodward to Scott, 26 April 1909. Woodward added: "I trust we may be able to get the services of Professor Holland to edit Legnano". See Woodward to Scott, 6 May 1909. Holland edited Legnano, *De Bello, de repraesaliis et de duello* (1917), published as No. 8 in the Classics of International Law, translated by J. L. Brierley. Scott enjoyed the warm and direct support of Woodward and later Elihu Root (1845-1937) for the Classics of International Law throughout their respective associations with the Carnegie Endowment. Woodward, an engineer by training, requested copies of the letters between Scott and Holland, Lassa Oppenheim (1858-1919), and John Westlake "since they will enable me to have the honor of interviews" with them and to "avail myself of all opportunities to learn the points of view and animating ideals of men whose fields of activity are different ...". CEIPA, Woodward to Scott, 18 May 1909.

[25] CEIPA, William Barnum to Scott, 3 May 1909. William Barnum was the Chief Clerk of the Carnegie Institute of Washington.

[26] CEIPA, Barnum to Scott, 7 June 1909. Holland was authorized to sub-contract the translation, which he duly did. See CEIPA, Scott to Holland, 8 June 1909.

In individual letters of same date (23 June 1909) to Emanuel von Ullmann (1841-1913), Ludwig von Bar (1836-1913), Nicolas Politis (1872-1942), Albert Geouffre de Lapradelle (1871-1955), Philipp Zorn (1850-1928), Heinrich Lammasch (1853-1920), Ferdinand von Martitz (1839-1921), Max Huber (1874-1960), Friedrich Meili (1848-1914), Tobias Michael Carel Asser (1838-1913), and others, Scott announced the Project and invited each recipient to suggest titles for the Project and possibly agree to editing and/or translating a title. Georg Jellinek (1851-1911) was authorized to undertake a single volume containing works by Jean-Jacques Rousseau (1712-1778), Immanuel Kant (1724-1804), and Jeremy Bentham (1748-1832), with the possible inclusion of the peace projects of King Henry IV (1553-1610) and William Penn (1644-1718), and to edit Christian von Wolff's (1679-1754) *Institutions*.[27] Nys was recruited as a "special advisor" to the series and in due course provided introductions to the volumes on Gentili and Victoria.[28]

By 1911, No. 1 of the series was in print following the pattern of presentation outlined in the 1907 Scott Proposal: a photographic reproduction of the first or other preferred edition of the work, with an introduction, list of errata, table of authors, and portrait of the respective international lawyer, followed by or accompanied in a second volume by a new translation commissioned by the Carnegie Endowment. The lead title was Richard Zouche (1590-1661), *Juris et judicii fecialis, sive juris inter gentes, et quaestionum de eodem explicatio*, under the editorship of Holland, with the translation by James Leslie Brierley (1881-1955) – both international lawyers in this case. Publication was in two volumes.

A year later there followed Balthazar Ayala (1548-1584), *De jure et officis bellicis et disciplina militari*, edited with an introduction by John Westlake (1828-1913), portrait of Ayala, and an accompanying translation by John Pawley Bate (1857-1921), in two volumes. Bate undertook several volumes in the series.

Early Translation of Grotius. No. 3 in the series was to be Grotius, *De jure belli ac pacis*, and its numbered place was duly reserved. The Carnegie Institution contracted, probably at once in 1907, with the Rev. Dr. John Deman Maguire (1868-1916) to undertake the translation. He was unable to complete the Grotius, as was confirmed by a cryptic sentence in a letter from Scott to Kelsey: "*Nihil de mortuis nisi bonum*. I may, however, be allowed to call your attention to

[27] CEIPA, Scott to Jellinek, 7 August 1909, in response to Jellinek letter of 12 July 1909. Scott expected Jellinek to "explain the nature and origin of the movement toward and federation of the nations and indicate the means proposed for its accomplishment". Scott agreed with Jellinek that the essays were forerunners of and the real call for the Hague Conferences.

[28] CEIPA, Scott to Nys, 7 August 1909 and 20 September 1909.

the fact that your predecessor consumed nine years in the translation, without getting it in such a shape that he was willing to submit it to us for printing".[29]

Given the central importance of Grotius to the Project and his unrivalled place in the world of international law, and the fact that three of his works were contemplated for inclusion in the series, the choice of a replacement editor/translator would have been of the greatest significance. Whatever the reality, the series continued to No. 4 (Vattel); No. 5 (Rachel); No. 6 (Textor); and No. 7 (Victoria), the translations of all but the Vattel being undertaken and completed by Bate; Charles Ghequiere Fenwick (1880-1971), translated the French text of Vattel. All four of these titles were published between 1913 and 1917.

Grotius, moreover, had another attraction: the year 1925 would mark the 300th anniversary of the first edition of his classic. Whether Scott had that jubilee in mind back in 1907 when he first proposed his Project is not clear, but as the years passed the Carnegie Endowment wanted to celebrate that anniversary with a new and what they hoped would be the "critical" edition of the work.

Having commissioned an editor/translator of Grotius, the Endowment moved at once toward producing volume one of the title: a photographic reproduction of *De jure belli ac pacis*. In an introductory Note prefacing the photographic reproduction, Scott explained the thinking of the Project in his capacity as "general editor". Three works by Grotius would be included in the Project in the order in which they were published: the *De jure praedae commentarius* (c. 1604); followed by *Mare liberum* (1609), and then the "masterpiece" entitled *De jure belli ac pacis* (1625). A single volume containing a photographic reproduction of all three proved to be unwieldy, and so too did producing merely the last with an extensive introduction explaining the relation between the three volumes. Instead, the intention was to produce "a special introduction" at a later date, "in separate form", a general introduction to the three.

Upon further consideration, it was decided that the photographic reproduction should not contain the first edition of 1625, but rather that published posthumously in 1646, the Project being guided by a statement in Dietrich Henrich Ludwig von Ompteda (1746-1803)[30] to the effect that the 1646 edi-

[29] CEIPA, Scott to Kelsey, 27 January 1922. On 15 July 1922 Scott made a similar statement: "The gentleman who originally undertook to make the translation promised to deliver it from time to time during a period of nine years … Thirteen years have passed. I do not think this is treating Grotius fairly, and I am sure it is not treating Mr. Root fairly". CEIPA, Scott to Kelsey, 15 July 1922. Whatever the identity of the individual concerned, apparently the Carnegie Endowment did not have a copy or otherwise make available the draft translation to Kelsey and his team.

[30] D. H. L. von Ompteda, *Litteratur des gesammelten sowohl natürlichen als positive Völkerrechtes* (1785), p. 394.

tion served as the basis of all subsequent versions. It was also believed to contain the last emendations made by the author and therefore the definitive version. Rather than a mirror image of the original, the photographic reproduction was enlarged slightly with generous margins. 500 copies were printed by the Oxford University Press.

Finding a New Translator of Grotius. No doubt after asking about, by mid-1918 Scott believed he had found his quarry and approached Francis Willey Kelsey (1858-1927) about undertaking the translation of Grotius.[31] Kelsey was a classicist and archaeologist. Scott approached him as an individual who appreciated the value of classics to the man of affairs. Grotius himself was a classicist who was a man of affairs. A translation of his major work in a world in which a War without precedent in scale and violence had just ended was "so much needed" and "will be in the next few years".[32] Grotius' book "made international law". The Carnegie Endowment wanted a translation "worthy in every respect of the author". The honorarium would be $1500, plus $300 for clerical assistance.

Kelsey at the time was the Professor of Latin Language and Literature at the University of Michigan. Born on a farm near Ogden, Monroe County, New York, on 23 May 1858, he received his A.B. (1880) and Ph.D. (1886) from the University of Rochester. He taught at Lake Forest University before taking a position in 1889 at the University of Michigan, at which institution he remained for the rest of his life. By coincidence, Grotius, Scott, and Kelsey happened by profession of faith to be Calvinists (Presbyterian). Kelsey's early contributions to classical scholarship took the form of publishing texts of ancient authors, accompanied by annotations and other supporting materials to aid students. His edition of Julius Caesar (100-44 BC), *Gallic War* (1886) went through more than twenty-one editions. He collaborated with the German art historian and archaeologist, Arthur Mau (1840-1909), in producing *Pompeii, Its Life and Art* (1899) and initiated and edited the Humanistic Series with support of the Faculty Senate of the University of Michigan. He combined his

[31] On Kelsey and the Grotius Project see the Kelsey Papers and Kelsey Museum of Archaeology Records held by the Bentley Historical Library at the University of Michigan, especially Boxes 30, 36, and 93-95 (hereinafter: KMA); and the CEIPA, held by The Butler Library, Columbia University. In the interests of concision, references are given to the respective Archive and the date of the materials cited. The CEIPA contains the originals of Kelsey correspondence, chiefly with James Brown Scott. The Michigan materials have all been used to advantage by John Griffiths Pedley, *The Life and Work of Francis Willey Kelsey: Archaeology, Antiquity, and the Arts* (2012), who, however, gives only a few paragraphs to Kelsey's translation of Grotius (pp. 241-242).

[32] KMA, Scott to Kelsey, 18 June 1918.

background in the Latin language and material culture to advocate vigorously in favor of including material culture into the teaching of classical languages.

Following World War I, he undertook three major expeditions in the Mediterranean region with support from the President of the Burroughs Adding Machine Co., Standish Backus (1875-1943), one of the original stockholders in the Ford Motor Company, Horace H. Rackham (1858-1933), and others. There he acquired manuscripts, papyri, and other artifacts for the University of Michigan: at the Imperial Roman colony of Pisidian Antioch in Asia Minor; at the agricultural village of Karanis in Egypt, and at Carthage in Tunisia. So significant were his acquisitions that the Kelsey Museum of Archaeology is named in his honor at the University of Michigan.

Prior to the First World War, he served as Secretary and then President of the Archaeological Institute of America and as President of the American Philological Association. Music was an abiding interest; for thirty-six years he was President of the University Musical Society and Ann Arbor School of Music and was instrumental in raising funds and spearheading the construction of an art museum, auditorium, and school of music at the University of Michigan.

Scott was clever in appealing to Kelsey's classical and humanitarian instincts. During the First World War, Kelsey had supported the work of the Near East Relief Committee after the Armenian Massacre and in Michigan acted as the Secretary of the Belgian Relief Committee, for which he was awarded a medal by the King of Belgium. In a posthumous tribute Kelsey was described as a "human dynamo working with an energy, smoothness, and precision" normally seen in men much younger.

These qualities were much in evidence in Kelsey's reply to Scott's offer. Kelsey had, he said, completed a piece of work which had taken him about four years when Scott's letter arrived and he was pondering what next to take on. Three pieces of work remained that required the consultation of material in Europe and could not be completed until after the War. As for the Grotius, Kelsey had reviewed the 1646 photographic reproduction supplied by Scott and noted that it contained not far from 700 pages of closely printed Latin. In his view, no one person could translate this amount of material in time to bring the book out before 1920.[33] However, he suggested, if one person was made responsible for the whole undertaking and would revise the literary form and interpretation of the parts he did not do himself but would commit to others, the work might be "Englished" and through press within a year from this time. The honorarium was inadequate, though; no person could be trusted to do

[33] KMA, Kelsey to Scott, 21 June 1918. The typescript reads 1921, corrected in pen to 1920.

more than four or five pages a day and produce quality work, and a competent scholar could not take time from other matters for work of this kind. He sent to Scott a bit of translation for which he had been editorially responsible.

Kelsey Translation Plan. Having slept on the invitation, Kelsey the next day, 22 June 1918, sent a further letter suggesting a plan in haste because Scott wanted to publish the Grotius translation before the end of the War and because the individuals whom Kelsey had in mind would scatter for the summer after Commencement – an immediate decision was necessary. Kelsey proposed to draw upon several former pupils who were now colleagues and competent in their mastery of Latin and in the knowledge of the historical background and use of English. Three were scholars of international standing and another was "fresh from Oxford" and doing advanced work in international law.

Kelsey believed that the preliminaries of the post-war peace negotiations would come in Autumn 1919, and the Grotius should be published about the time of the opening of the proposed or anticipated offensive of the Allies in spring 1919. The value of the Grotius under these circumstances could not be over-estimated and should appear sufficiently in advance to ensure distribution throughout the British Empire, the United States, and Western continental countries. His Plan consisted of nine points, summarized as follows:

[1] the translation work to be divided among competent men at the University of Michigan, asking them to set aside all other summer commitments to concentrate on the translation as a patriotic duty;

[2] Kelsey would translate as much of the Latin as he could manage and would revise and blend the work of younger men so as to unify English style and be responsible for the accuracy and form of the entire translation;

[3] quotations and citations of Greek and Latin authors would be verified and footnotes would give references to the standard editions;

[4] copy read for the printer would be delivered by 30 September 1918 of the first 300 pages of the Latin text and the balance, including a general and authors' index, by 30 December 1918;

[5] all translation to be paid at the rate of $2.50 per page of Latin text, payment due as the manuscript is received and approved by Scott. Given the word-count on the Latin text per page, the time required to verify the references, and the "unusual scholarship" required, Kelsey believed quality work could not be had for less;

[6] the Carnegie Endowment would supply three copies of the text and any translations in French, English, and German as the translators may require;

[7] the Carnegie Endowment to defray any expenses of travel required that were necessary in Scott's judgment to implement the plans;

[8] if the Plan were agreeable, Kelsey would be responsible for the entire work, with due acknowledgement for the work done by others and Kelsey would read the proofs. Kelsey would be paid $1,000, payable half on completion of the manuscript and the balance on finishing the proof-reading;

[9] if the Plan were acceptable, the additional details should be agreed and the parts of the Grotius text assigned to individuals by 29 June 1918, with working commencing on 1 July 1918.

Kelsey requested a response by wire and indicated a willingness to come to Washington D.C. to clear up details.

Scott received the letter of 21 June on the 25 June 1918 and accepted in principle the observations made by Kelsey, including the idea of a collaborative translation under Kelsey's leadership and guidance. As for the letter of 22 June, the post was slow, and Scott did not receive Kelsey's letter of 22 June until 27 June 1918. He accepted the Plan as "very practicable" which "meets with my entire satisfaction" and sent a telegram of confirmation: "Your letter June twenty two just received this morning your plan very satisfactory please make arrangement in accordance therewith letter follows", also followed by five copies, four unbound, of the 1646 photographic reproduction by express.

Thus was the Project of the Grotius translation agreed and Kelsey's basic Plan for achieving its completion. What was planned to be completed in time for forthcoming peace negotiations would in actuality not culminate in a final product until Spring 1928 – two decades after the original proposal approved by the Carnegie Endowment in January 1907. The Saga had commenced, would test the good will of many, would result in a false date of publication, but would be accompanied by the first thorough dissection of Grotius ever undertaken.

Assembling the Team of Translators. In a letter to Scott of 8 July 1918, Kelsey nominated his team of translators: Henry Arthur Sanders (1868-1956), Arthur Edward Romilly Boak (1888-1962), Joseph Horace Drake (1860-1947), Clarence Linton Meader (1867-1967), and Hessel Edward Yntema (1891-1966).[34] Kelsey himself agreed to undertake Book I of Grotius, and Sanders and Boak, Book II. He left Book III to see how much time the others might have available.

Although point [6] of the Kelsey Plan required that the Carnegie Endowment supply the translators with "any translations" in French, German, and

[34] The only jurist on the team, Yntema at the time was an instructor in the Department of Political Science at the University of Michigan. He is credited in the published translation of Grotius with having read and commented on the draft translation and proofs. The Yntemas were originally a Dutch family before emigrating to the United States. Indeed Kelsey noted that "Yntema is so overworked that I am not certain how much he can do". KMA, Kelsey to Scott, 8 July 1918.

English that may be required, all indications are that the Carnegie Endowment and the translators looked primarily and initially to libraries to supply these rather than the antiquarian book market. Kelsey assumed that the Carnegie Endowment had "a copy of each important edition and translation, perhaps more than one copy", which might be sent to the library of the University of Michigan. Depending on what the Carnegie Endowment was itself able to supply, Kelsey instructed the Michigan Librarian to confer with the librarians at Harvard University, Yale, and other institutions and endeavor to collect from them enough copies "to fill out at least three complete sets for the use of each of the three translators at once". The aim, Kelsey stressed, was to produce a translation that would be "final" so far as this generation is concerned. He had in view a "critical edition" that would take account collations and all differences discovered among the various versions of the book. This task of collation would commence at once upon receipt of the "edition of 1625"; that is, the first edition.

Two days later Kelsey followed with a letter containing a draft translation of the dedication to Grotius and a suggested Memorandum for the translators.[35] The Memorandum contained eight points, here summarized:

[1] the English to read smoothly and idiomatically, as if the work were written originally in English, no trace of Latin idiom remaining;

[2] the paragraphing to be frequent, averaging three or four paragraphs to a page, the close analysis of Grotius making subdivision by short paragraphs an easy matter;

[3] all "copy" to be typewritten, with wide inner margin and double spacing between lines;

[4] all titles from classical authors to be given in full, being a convenience for non-classical readers, and all references to be given to the best critical editions, with as finished a translation of quoted matter as possible;

[5] all notes to be transferred from the ends of chapters and placed at the bottom of the page;

[6] the University of Michigan Library is undertaking through loan from other libraries to supply each translator with a full set of the principal translations listed in the catalogues of the British Museum and the Library of Congress;

[7] the emendations by Barbeyrac listed in the *Epist. ad Lectorem* in his edition, reprinted by Whewell, to be noted and dealt with in each case;

[8] a memorandum on the text later, after receipt of early editions.

[35] KMA, Kelsey to Scott, 10 July 1918. The Draft Memorandum became separated in the Archive filing system but, undated and unrecognized, survives.

By 20 July 1918 Kelsey had completed a first draft translation of the first two pages of the Prolegomena of Grotius, sought comments for improvement, and offered to meet Scott in Washington D.C. or somewhere convenient in between. One issue was annotation, "which presents difficulties because Grotius, quoting from memory, did make slips" which needed correction. This Kelsey regarded as a "matter of delicacy". The second matter was a critical Latin text, which Kelsey was prepared to consider undertaking – an arduous task "because every word of the text must be compared line for line in the editions of 1625, 1631, 1646, and two later editions".[36] In a separate letter on the same day Kelsey sent a second revision of the Dedication to Grotius and explained his method of work: "… I always go over three times, first making a tentative rough draft, then a second revise having regard to both content and form, and finally the preparation of 'Copy' for the printer, based usually on the second revise and dealing entirely with literary form".[37]

Postal delays being what they were, Scott responded to the Kelsey letters of 6 and 10 July on 22 July without having received Kelsey's of later date. The letter of 22 July contained decisions of enduring moment for the Project. As regards other editions of Grotius, the Carnegie Endowment had been unable to source either the quarto or octavo editions of 1650 published at Amsterdam. Given that Grotius had made and approved his own corrections in the 1646 edition, it did not seem necessary to consider later editions unless such be those of Barbeyrac containing important emendations. As for a critical Latin edition, Scott in principle supported this idea, but not until after the translation was published, in which event he hoped that Kelsey would undertake that task. As for the 1625 first edition, Scott described it as a "very beautiful small quarto", but neither he nor the Carnegie Endowment possessed a copy. His recollection was that the copy was borrowed "from the Henry Wheaton Collection of the Library of Brown University, which I think has the most complete collection of editions of Grotius of any American library". Nor, said Scott, did the library of the Holland Society of New York appear to have a copy.

As for Scott's comments on Kelsey's draft translation of the Dedication, some were made, but not by Scott, who passed the draft on to Herbert Francis Wright (1892-1945), "formerly with the Catholic University of America but now of the Endowment's Division of International Law". Here the issue of annotations was addressed: the decision was "in general" not to add notes of "our own", but sometimes to do so and in order to distinguish them from those of Grotius, to enclose them in square brackets. Finally, in response to

36 KMA, Kelsey to Scott, 20 July 1918.

37 KMA, Kelsey to Scott, 20 July 1918 (second letter).

Kelsey's suggested style rules, Scott supplied the text of "Standardization Rules for Translations in the Classics of International Law", which might by agreement be waived or amended if the translators considered this to be advisable.[38]

Kelsey had entertained further thoughts about the Grotius translation Project and was ready to submit at a personal meeting (preferred) or letter "the complete plan for the publication of the Grotius in such a way as might perhaps meet the different aspects" of this difficult and important problem. Kelsey was increasingly convinced of the "vitality" of the "message of Grotius" and its "timeliness with reference to the conditions now confronting the world". Scott's thought of bringing this to bear on the forming of opinion precedent to the peace negotiations "is nothing short of brilliant" in Kelsey's view. He sent for Scott's judgment the full text of his translation of the Prolegomena and again laid down precepts of translation:

> It is a question of literary form, as well as of meaning. With reference to certain terms the translation is purely tentative; in point of style while it should be free from Latin idioms, it should nevertheless if possible in some degree suggest the peculiar quality of the style of Grotius which may seem to us now and then quaint but is nevertheless cogent in its development of thought.[39]

In a letter of same date from Kelsey to Wright, the latter's opinion was sought on the draft translation of the Prolegomena: whether Wright considered the translation to be "too free, or in any respects misleading in so difficult a discussion" that treats the "origin of ethics and of law so succinctly" as set out in the Prolegomena.[40]

Scott replied to both Kelsey letters of 20 July 1918 on 31 July 1918. He was content with either the first or second version of the Dedication and was confident that any third version would be more than acceptable. In other words, Scott was satisfied with Kelsey's method and final product. As for the Prolegomena, he considered the first draft to be "admirable in every way", for this was the part of Grotius "which makes the continuous and universal appeal". In the matter of annotations, Scott reiterated that the "text of Grotius will be … translated accurately, whether he makes mistakes or not …", and his mistakes should be rectified in bracket footnotes with references when Grotius quotes an author without indicating the source. In this event, the best critical editions should be cited, including to the Loeb Classical Library when possi-

[38] KMA, Scott to Kelsey, 22 July 1918.

[39] KMA, Kelsey to Scott, 30 July 1918, writing from his summer cabin at Cavanaugh Lake, near Chelsea, Michigan.

[40] KMA, Kelsey to Wright, 30 July 1918.

ble. Grotius needed to be tracked to his sources, "… as he wrote from a well stocked mind, and sometimes took liberties, as the great are wont to do, with materials he found fitted to his purpose".[41]

At this point, Scott proposed having "formal contracts drawn" in accordance with the terms agreed in the letters between Scott and Kelsey "… as this would protect you and your collaborators in case of any unforeseen hitch in carrying out the arrangements". Kelsey responded in his letter of 6 August 1918 by asking that he be sent the names of four or six men in the field of international law anywhere in the English-speaking world whose judgments on points in the Grotius treatise would be helpful. Kelsey sought by this means a consensus of criticism on three or four new translations that he wished to suggest for technical terms in Book I.[42] In another reply of 12 August 1918, also in rough copy, Kelsey felt that, if the Carnegie Endowment so desired, "some sort of Memorandum" for the work on the Grotius translation might be appropriate and asked that such be prepared. The translating, he added, would be done by Sanders, Boak, and himself; the other men named previously would be consulted on special points, as would outside staff.

Scott responded that the sample translation of the Prolegomena was "admirable in every respect"; he rejected, however, the proposal for outsiders to be invited to pass upon any technical terms for which Kelsey suggested new English equivalents. That matter, Scott said, could be handled ourselves "as we are more familiar with the subject-matter" and therefore more able to pass upon those questions than others to whom they would be largely, if not entirely, new. As for Kelsey's complete plan for the publication of Grotius (the text of which was not available in the Archive), this could be tabled for the present. As for the Prolegomena, Scott said he was contemplating a separate circulation of that portion of Grotius in pamphlet form using the Kelsey translation – a proposal that several years later would be realized.[43] Scott returned to the question of a formal contract (not a memorandum) and said a draft would be prepared in accordance with the various letters.[44]

Kelsey emphasized the need for a critical Latin edition "not too long" after the appearance of the translation. He noted that near the end of the seventh section on page 26 of the 1646 edition one "Undecimum" introduced the

[41] KMA, Scott to Kelsey, 31 July 1918.

[42] KMA, Kelsey to Scott, 6 August 1918. This text is a "copy" in Kelsey's own hand (not typed as his "stenographer" was on holiday) and is incomplete.

[43] KMA, Scott to Kelsey, 12 August 1918.

[44] KMA, Scott to Kelsey, 15 August 1918.

last argument of the section; however, in the first and second editions this is the twelfth argument introduced by Duodecimum; the eleventh argument was brief but important and, Kelsey said, there was no historical or logical reason for its omission: "did Grotius then cancel the eleventh point"? Kelsey believed not; rather, he suggested this was a typesetting error not picked up during the proofreading. He proposed that the missing section be inserted in a footnote with an explanation, but wondered whether the translation should also appear in the text. Attention was given to the physical appearance of the English version of the translation. It should be "dignified" and "attractive", with fonts of types chosen which will align perfectly and tastefully in Latin, Greek, and Hebrew words. The English text would be complicated by footnotes of two types: those of Grotius properly translated and a considerable number of footnotes correcting Grotius where necessary and introducing exact citations in place of the general references which Grotius supplied. Kelsey though the use of square brackets "disfigures" the page under the conditions encountered in the Grotius translation.[45] In an undated telegram of about the same date, Kelsey requested the Grotius editions of 1625, 1650, and three copies of translations by Barksdale, Barbeyrac, Campbell, Courtin, Kirchmann, and Whewell.

Kelsey continued to press the discussion of legal terminology and sought the opinions of Scott, Wright, and any other appropriate members of Carnegie staff. Having completed a first draft of Book I, chapters 1 and 2, of Grotius, he underscored legal terms in red on his manuscript and requested views on the proper translation. He also inserted section titles of Grotius in the text rather than massing them at the beginning of long chapters in seventeenth-century style: "in order to do justice to the thought" of Grotius, the outward form must be adapted by present conventions of arrangement and printing "just as we do in the case of the best presentation of classical authors". A "tasteful type" would set off the section titles without "the appearance of over-emphasis".

Kelsey proposed to add to the beginning of the translation a note on the word *jus*, demonstrating how this Latin word means the English "right" on the subjective side and "law" in English on the objective side, so that an interpretation of *jus* by "either term fails to supply the suggestion of the other". Similarly, he translated *jus naturae* as "natural law" rather than as "law of nature" even where the latter translation carried or suggested the connotation usually associated with that term in English. As for the earlier suggestion from Scott that quotations be inserted from the Loeb Classical Library, Kelsey noted that the translations of Grotius from the Greek are often so phrased or the quota-

[45] KMA, Kelsey to Scott, 19 August 1918.

tions from Latin are frequently so "woven into the context", that it was difficult to smoothly fit a translation borrowed from the Loeb volumes or similar versions. He preferred to translate the quotations in the context of Grotius or at least adapting them as Grotius had done.[46] The final publication of Grotius did not address this matter.

Selection of Printer. Attention turned from format and typography to the selection of a printer for the Grotius. Scott mentioned that the American Branch of the Oxford University Press "does good printing" and can be "made to do the kind of printing with which you would like your name to be connected". Their services had not been used "as with the transfer of the series from the Carnegie Institution to the Carnegie Endowment a change of publishers took place". The views of Kelsey were solicited. On 4 September 1918 Kelsey recommended the J. S. Cushing Company of Norwood, Massachusetts, observing that the Oxford Press had no printery of its own and that he had no personal (meaning financial) stake in the ultimate choice.[47] Scott was receptive to the suggestion ("my chief interest is as yours, to have the text of the Grotius well executed, and not merely imprisoned, as was the case with the author"). Oxford often used the firm of Quinn & Boden Co. for their work and some was done by a firm in Washington (unnamed); Scott saw no reason why some of the work might not be undertaken by Cushing.[48]

Kelsey was not slow in responding to the invitation. A four-page letter suggested the arrangement of the "front matter" of the Grotius, duly recognizing the name of the Peace Endowment, the name of the series, and the title of the work itself, accompanied by a complete list of the volumes in the Series at the end of the volume. If this suggestions were acceptable, Kelsey was prepared to contact the Manager of the Norwood Press "which has a display of types perfectly suited to carry out my idea".[49] In the end, the Carnegie Endowment chose the Clarendon Press of England to publish the Grotius "inasmuch as it appears to be generally considered as among the very best if not actually the best of publishers". The Clarendon Press had agreed to act as publisher to the Endowment and "it seems right and proper that we should have them under-

46 KMA, Kelsey to Scott, 2 September 1918.

47 KMA, and Scott to Kelsey, 3 September 1918; Kelsey to Scott [4] September 1918, in rough draft.

48 KMA, Scott to Kelsey, 13 September 1918.

49 KMA, Kelsey to Scott, 14 September 1918.

take the Classics". Kelsey's suggestions as to format were passed on to Oxford in due course with a view to specimen pages being prepared.[50]

"Copy" for specimen pages Kelsey submitted in the form of a "theory of typographical dress and arrangement of matter" which reorganized the Grotius as follows:

[1] front matter with own pagination, the translation beginning on page 1 with a translation of the original title-page by Grotius;

[2] the title in English should be "The Law of War and Peace" in order to adapt the universal element on Grotius to modern conditions of presentation, omitting the translation of "*De*"in the Latin title as superfluous and no greater utility than similar prepositions in biblical and other titles in common use;

[3] introduce a system of numbered sections to facilitate reference, in a modest type in the margin so as to interfere as little as possible with the appearance of the page;

[4] the numerous quotations from classical Greek authorities are translated from the Latin version of Grotius, which is often quite free in order to correlate such passages with the text;

[5] in translating the notes of Grotius the references and other additions to the notes by Kelsey were placed in brackets;

[6] Kelsey's own notes were brief and avoided all discussion of legal points, but comments were made to make the text more intelligible. When Grotius wrote, his readers were in the habit of reading Greek and Latin authors as he did and fragments of quotations were perfectly intelligible. Kelsey's method would enable the full force of Grotius's use of classical references to be realized;

[7] no previous edition of Grotius adequately solved the problem of presenting the translation, Grotius's notes, and other notes required to correct, supplement, or explain the notes of Grotius. The "progress of good taste" in printing makes this possible and produces a good effect by using a different system of reference and different sizes of type.[51]

On 4 November 1918 Kelsey submitted a statement of account for stenographic work, postage, and the like covering the period from 1 July to 31 October 1918 – this sum to be set off against the appropriation of $300 for this purpose. Of this amount, $50.35 was incurred for payments to Edwards Brothers in Ann Arbor for stenographic services from 10 July to 5 October

[50] KMA, Scott to Kelsey, 14 October 1918. Kelsey apparently had located a copy of the Whewell translation for the sum of "three dollars", which Scott agreed to reimburse "so that it will not be necessary for anybody connected with the University of Michigan to go into bankruptcy on that account".

[51] KMA, Kelsey to Scott, 26 October 1918.

at the same rate paid by the University. That firm could no longer continue with the work, whereupon Kelsey retained the services of Miss Eleanor Neil, with Edwards Brothers supplying a room and typewriter for one week. Thereafter the University furnished Kelsey with a special typewriter and the work was contracted for at the rate of forty cents per hour plus materials used. For typing from 5 to 14 October 1918, Miss Neil was paid the sum of $3.90 and another typist $6.10 for typing from 23 to 31 October 1918. Four packages of copy paper came to $2.75, and postage to $1.47.[52]

By 7 November 1918 news had been received that the War was at an end – rather earlier than had been anticipated by the Project. Kelsey confirmed that the typing of the second Book of Grotius was well under way and the remainder of Book I would be sent as soon as he had looked over the copy.[53] The draft translation of Book I, chapters four and five, were sent on 16 November and typing was advanced on Book II. By 23 November Kelsey was pressing for comments on chapters three to five to be returned to him by Wright so that the first part of the work was ready for submission to the printer.[54]

"Changed" Postwar Conditions. By 17 December Kelsey was aware that Scott had been appointed to "work abroad" with the Peace Commission and took the occasion to recommend to Scott the "erection" of an international tribunal to try "all cases of atrocities". Because no atrocities were committed on American territory, the initiative should come from England or France.[55]

Scott's absence abroad delayed organizational progress on printing, but the translation work continued.[56] Given that the War had ended and the initial reason for making the Grotius translation available had been overtaken by events, in a "watershed letter" Kelsey sought guidance on the course to be pursued "under the changed conditions". As a patriotic service, Kelsey said, he undertook this "bit of translation" on the assumption that the peace negotiations would not come until summer 1919 and had offered with the help of colleagues to have material ready for the printer. In his own plans of work, the year which is just closing had been set aside for this purpose. He had the impression that prompt publication would be acceptable to the Carnegie Endowment and printing would be done in the United States so that proofs could be rapidly corrected.

52 KMA, Kelsey to Scott, 4 November 1918.

53 KMA, Kelsey to Scott, 7 November 1918.

54 KMA, Kelsey to Scott, 23 November 1918.

55 KMA, Kelsey to Scott, 17 December 1918.

56 KMA, Kelsey to North, 10 December 1918; North to Kelsey, 14 December 1918.

When it was decided to use the Clarendon Press as the printers in England, Kelsey still assumed that the work could be completed "with rapidity", having understood that in the printery such work as the Grotius would have precedence over most publications. Kelsey and his team has persevered with the translation of the text and notes, and the entire manuscript, unrevised, lay before him and most of it had been in his hands since January. The revisions should not be undertaken until all questions of printing had been settled. The specimen pages sent in October 1918 were not received until March; when they arrived, "they were of such sort that I should not feel justified either in reading proofs with such composition, or in allowing my name to be associated with a piece of work having a display so inappropriate to the content".

The sample pages were received when about two-thirds of the year set aside for completion of the translation had elapsed, and "it was evident" that the translation could not be produced in accordance with the original intention. Further comparison of the life-time editions of Grotius strengthened the conviction that a critical Latin text should precede the final revision and publication of the translation. Kelsey visited the residual staff at the Carnegie Endowment in Washington D.C. in March 1919 to press the case for a critical Latin edition; the matter was submitted to the Executive Committee of the Carnegie Endowment, which decided to "defer the whole subject" until Scott could give it personal attention. In June 1919 Kelsey visited the printery at Norwood, Massachusetts, and had two "dummy" volumes prepared with the front matter, four pages of the Latin text, critical notes supplied by Kelsey, and blank pages filled in to show the size of each of the two volumes which would be required in this format to contain the text.

Kelsey then turned to his own future. The conclusion of the First World War made it imperative for him to carry out plans deferred by the War but alluded to in the early correspondence with Scott regarding the Grotius. The University of Michigan had received a gift of $25,000 to finance a scientific expedition under Kelsey's leadership to commence in early August 1919. Kelsey was expecting to be abroad for two years, "but the work on the Grotius could be much better done in the British Museum, or the National Library of France", than in Ann Arbor because of the handicap occasioned by the lack of access to books used by Grotius. Before he sailed, Kelsey would deposit a complete set of the manuscripts of the unrevised translation with the Endowment in Washington D.C. If the critical Latin edition were to be undertaken on the lines of the sample pages in the "dummy" sent, Kelsey would need to take the collection of editions and other materials with him for deposit in a fireproof place until he could work on them in London or Paris, or possibly

Rome – all "question of revising and issuing the translation to be deferred until the critical text is ready for the printer or actually in type".[57]

During Scott's absence abroad in Government service, his duties were assumed by an Acting Secretary, Simon Newton Dexter North (1849-1924), beginning around 1 December 1918. Kelsey anxiously awaited the "sample pages" from the Clarendon Press, copy for which he had sent to Scott on 26 October 1918, but transmission to the Press had experienced "unavoidable delay" until 4 December 1918. He prayed for a meeting in Washington D.C. in March 1919 to resolve outstanding matters with North and to prepare a memorandum for Scott which could be sent to Paris, where Scott was working on the Peace negotiations. It was noted that "there is no contract for the editorial work on the Grotius" and asked that North review the "plan of the undertaking" sent to Scott in a letter at the end of last June "and which he accepted as our working basis".[58] North accepted the request for a meeting "if you think this advisable".[59] In the meantime the specimen pages arrived from the Oxford University Press. Kelsey was disappointed in the quality: "these pages … hardly do justice to the standard of the Oxford Press".[60]

The meeting took place (Kelsey stayed at the nearby Cosmos Club), and Kelsey took the trouble to prepare a summary dated 27 March 1919 of what was concluded, in summary as follows:

[1] Kelsey and his colleagues undertook the translation of Grotius as a means of "doing our bit"; the arrangement of the armistice and the opening of peace negotiations, almost a year earlier than anticipated, released this important piece of work from need of haste;

[2] in the course of the translation work it became apparent that a new edition of the Latin text should be made, presenting the differences in readings between the editions published during Grotius' lifetime and the emendations proposed by later scholars, also indicating differences of reading in the numerous quotations from ancient authors;

[3] now that there is no longer reason for haste in printing the translation, the requirements of modern scholarship demand the publication of Grotius in the best possible way, which involved the issuing of a new edition of the text and the translation at the same time and in such form that reference can be made from one to the other;

57 KMA, Kelsey to Scott, 28 June 1919.

58 KMA, Kelsey to North, 27 February 1919.

59 KMA, North to Kelsey, 6 March 1919.

60 KMA, Kelsey to North, 18 March 1919.

[4] Kelsey was gratified to see that Scott had anticipated his conclusion in a paragraph which appeared in the note preceding the photographic reproduction of the 1646 edition: "Notes and comments of a critical kind have not been supplied and no lists of misprints or corrections of errors in the body of the work have been appended, as a critical edition of the text is contemplated";

[5] given that four-fifths of the translation is in first draft, Kelsey recommended that the preparation of the "critical edition" be undertaken at once.

Kelsey carried the day, for the moment at least. On 28 March 1919 North wrote that "authorization is given to you, *subject to the formal approval by the Executive Committee*, to proceed with the preparation of a critical edition" of Grotius as outlined in the penultimate paragraph of the Note preceding the photographic reproduction of the 1646 edition "... on the same terms as those stated in your letter of June 22, 1918". Namely, $2.50 per printed page of the edition of 1646 plus an honorarium of $1,000 for the responsible editorship ...". Authorization also was given to spend up to $75.00 for the preparation of specimen pages of the English translation and critical Latin text and title-pages for those two works.[61]

Having carried the burden of persuasion in his discussions with North, Kelsey prepared an extensive Memorandum on Publications devoted to the publication activities of the Carnegie Endowment generally. He addressed general policy, production, distribution, and consumption – all at a general and abstract level.[62] This he followed the next day by reporting a "bitter criticism" of the Classics of International Law: the Carnegie Endowment charged "... a price that puts the volumes beyond the private ownership of the average student and professor interested in the subject ...".[63]

North was not pleased by the criticism implied in the Memorandum on Publication: "It is an interesting letter, but not quite what I hoped to receive from you after our recent pleasant conferences". He invited Kelsey "at your early convenience" to supplement the letter with another in which "your own views" on each of the points stated will "be given for our benefit".[64]

Preparations for the critical Latin edition of Grotius continued. Kelsey wrote that the University of Michigan was rapidly accumulating a collection of editions of Grotius considerably larger than the British Museum possesses. Two cablegrams had been sent to The Hague "to a dealer specializing in this

[61] KMA, North to Kelsey, 28 March 1919.

[62] KMA, Kelsey to North, with attached Memorandum, 31 March 1919.

[63] KMA, Kelsey to North, 1 April 1919.

[64] KMA, North to Kelsey, 4 April 1919.

field", one directing the shipment of an entire list of Grotiana, including editions and rare works connected therewith, and another asking to send a copy of the "excessively rare first edition (1625) which seemingly just turned up". The price quoted for the first edition was 250 florins. Kelsey had been using the copy which we borrowed from the Harvard Law Library, there being no copy in the Library of Congress.[65]

The bad news came on 15 May 1919. North reminded Kelsey that the preparation of a critical Latin edition of Grotius was subject to the approval of the Executive Committee. The "matter was presented to the Executive Committee" on 12 May and, after giving the matter careful consideration, "the Committee did not feel justified in authorizing the work at the present time".[66]

Kelsey understood the decision of the Executive Committee to be one of delay, not rejection, and reacted positively for two reasons: first, intensive work on both text and translation since 26 March convinced Kelsey that neither the text nor the translation could be put in final form for publication consistent with the requirements of modern scholarship without several months work in European libraries. Second, the University of Michigan had received a grant to support an expedition in the interests of Biblical and humanistic research which would take Kelsey out of the country for a considerable period. He hoped to combine his expedition with the final version of Grotius, but could not now bind himself to any particular time for finishing the transcript of either translation or critical text. In early June Kelsey expected to deliver the manuscript of all, or at least the greater portion, of the translation, "ready for the final revision in some European library center where works, inaccessible in this country, can be found".[67]

North rejected the delay in finalization of the translation pending a critical Latin edition of Grotius. The Executive Committee, he wrote, "... is very anxiously and eagerly awaiting the publication of the translation which, as you must know, was planned among the first in the series". The Executive Committee, said North, "would look with extreme disfavor upon any undue postponement in the publication of his long-looked-for masterpiece".[68]

In early June 1919 Kelsey visited the printer in Norwood, Massachusetts, and brought with him to Washington D.C. four "dummy" volumes to illustrate the style and format which he recommended for the text of the critical Latin

65 KMA, Kelsey to North, 19 April 1919.

66 KMA, North to Kelsey, 15 May 1919.

67 KMA, Kelsey to North, 20 May 1919.

68 KMA, North to Kelsey, 27 May 1919.

edition and the translation. Two other dummies he retained for his own reference. This had been authorized up to a price of $75.00; in fact, the price came to $93.00, and the invoice was submitted for payment.[69]

Kelsey on Expedition. Thereafter, Scott remained abroad and Kelsey embarked upon his research expedition. Kelsey met Scott at Paris in February 1920 and hoped, he said, to settle down in Rome towards the end of that month and "to attack immediately" the revision of the Grotius manuscript. Scott sent the full manuscript to Rome, where it awaited Kelsey at the American Academy in Rome, but duties relating to the Expedition made further work impossible.[70] By May 1921 Scott was anxious to have work resumed on the translation. He wired Jesse Reeves in Ann Arbor to request "at earliest convenience translation of Grotius that we may consider rendering of legal terms" and asked for "any news" of Kelsey and his present address.[71] By letter of same date, Reeves reported that Kelsey was expected to return in about a month and retained the same address in Rome. Reeves wished not to be "mixed up in the matter at all"; he had merely acceded to a request by a colleague, and entered into no obligations or responsibilities whatever". No one had authority to speak or act for Kelsey.[72] Scott wired Kelsey in Rome: "Endowment most anxious to issue Grotius translation at this critical and psychological moment in international relations. Kindly let us have manuscript, making your final changes in proof".[73]

Kelsey replied to the telegram on 24 June 1921, saying that during the past twenty months had the opportunity to observe superficially conditions closely parallel to those described by Grotius in a number of passages. The only complete manuscript of the Grotius was with him in Rome, and he was not returning to Michigan until late September 1921. Each colleague in Michigan needed to read the final revision before it was sent to the printer, and about half the manuscript needed to be retyped. The final revision would commence next October.[74] Without having received his Letter, the Carnegie Endowment sent another telegram, with the authorization of Elihu Root, which would affect the Classics of International Law for the foreseeable future: "It is necessary

69 KMA, Kelsey to North, 14 June 1919, in Kelsey's hand from the Cosmos Club.

70 CEIPA, Kelsey to Scott from Rome, 29 January 1921.

71 CEIPA, Scott to Reeves, Western Union Telegram, 28 May 1921.

72 CEIPA, Reeves to Scott, 28 May 1921.

73 CEIPA, Scott to Kelsey, Western Union Telegram, 31 May 1921.

74 CEIPA, Kelsey to Scott, 24 June 1921.

for the success of the series that the Grotius appear before any others, as it is the center of the Solar System".[75]

On the assumption that Kelsey had not received the cable of 1 July, Scott wrote on 12 July to expand upon the position of the Carnegie Endowment. There are "five Classics now in press, three of which are ready for binding or nearly so". It was essential for the success of the series that the "... Grotius appear, if possible, before any others". To proceed otherwise would be to "produce 'Hamlet' minus Hamlet himself". Scott understood that Kelsey planned to return to the States shortly and might bring the Grotius translation with him when he passed through Washington.[76]

Immediately after sending the Letter of 12 July, Scott received Kelsey's letter of 24 June, to which he responded on 14 July and proposed "the best way" to expedite the publication of Grotius. First, a complete copy of the manuscript should be kept in Washington at the Carnegie Endowment whether ready for the printer or not to ensure intelligent handling of the proofs. Thereafter the copy might be released to the printer in fair sized quantities as it is prepared. Scott then disclosed that he would be abroad when Kelsey arrived in the United States and would remain so until November 1921. All, in effect, was agreed to recommence in earnest in the autumn.[77] On 20 October 1921 Scott began to apply pressure. Aware that Kelsey had returned from Europe, he suggested that it would be appropriate to have the Grotius appear during the Conference on the Limitation of Armament and the Settlement of Pacific Problems – an important psychological moment even if only a few advance copies might be bound for the delegates.[78]

Kelsey Returns from Europe. Kelsey said the shipment of the manuscript and accompanying books had been delayed, but even so it would be "impracticable" to put the manuscript of the entire work into shape for publication

[75] CEIPA, Scott to Root, 1 July 1921. The file copy bears in pencil the note: "no answer. July 11, 1921". A letter dated 10 July 1921 from Professor Ralph van Deman Magoffin (1874-1942) indicated that neither the cable nor a letter from Scott had been received by Kelsey. There was no way of getting the Grotius translation except "through Professor Kelsey". CEIPA, Magoffin to Scott, 10 July 1921.

[76] CEIPA, Scott to Kelsey, 12 July 1921.

[77] CEIPA, Scott to Kelsey, 14 July 1921. A telegram instructing Kelsey to retain the manuscript was sent the same day. The approach to publication was confirmed to Kelsey by Scott in a Letter dated 1 October 1921.

[78] CEIPA, Scott to Kelsey, 20 October 1921. His letter was followed by a telegram the following day saying that "Mr. Root is very anxious to have the translation of Grotius appear at the earliest possible moment; if possible, during the Conference. He is unwilling to have any of the Classics of International Law appear until the Grotius is out, ... that without the Grotius, the series is 'acephalos' ... or as you would ... say in Latin ... 'sine capite'". Scott requested the manuscript by express or "we will send a messenger for it". CEIPA, Scott to Kelsey, 21 October 1921.

during the Conference in Washington. Instead he offered the Prolegomena, which could be circulated as a sample of the new work.[79] And there the matter remained. Scott pressed again in two letters of 18 January, reiterating the wish of Mr. Root to have the Grotius translation and enumerating nine manuscripts in hand awaiting publication.[80] Kelsey responded that he was "… doing the best I can" and said his absences for the University would be less exacting "in the latter part of the year".[81] Scott understood the implications of this last sentence and replied at once that Kelsey's letter had been read with a "sense of disappointment bordering on heart-failure". He understood Kelsey to be saying that a completed translation could not be assured by the first of May. Scott had read the Prolegomena and found it "as literary as … it was accurate", and was assured by Wright that the entire manuscript could hardly be improved. Scott therefore felt "compelled" to ask for a definite date upon which delivery of the completed manuscript would be accomplished; otherwise, he warned, "the future of the whole series is likely to be imperiled at the forthcoming meeting of the Executive Committee". He hoped for special arrangements to be made to have the manuscript within three, or at the latest four, months.[82]

Taking the suggestion of "special arrangements" seriously, Kelsey cabled Scott on 4 February 1922 "in order to speed up Grotius work" to ask that Jesse Reeves be authorized to assist in the editing with an honorarium of $500. Two weeks later Scott reported that the Executive Committee approved this request on "condition that manuscript of Grotius is ready for press on first day of May". Kelsey was delighted with the response, said that Reeves had begun work on the "next day", and planned to have the entire manuscript "in your hands" ready for the printer by the first day of May.[83]

Scott expressed delight with this assurance. Scott felt sure that when Kelsey looked over the translation he would be of the opinion that the manuscript merely needed "slight correction", chiefly ensuring that the technical expressions of the Latin original were rendered in technical English.[84]

[79] CEIPA, Kelsey to Scott, 24 October 1921. The suggestion apparently was not taken up.

[80] CEIPA, Scott to Kelsey, 18 January 1922: "If … Grotius were out of the way, my troubles would be lessened to the extent of nine manuscripts".

[81] CEIPA, Kelsey to Scott, 24 January 1922.

[82] CEIPA, Scott to Kelsey, 27 January 1922. Kelsey in response said before the end of February he would be in a position "to give definite assurance" to the time of completion of the manuscript and in ample time for making up the budget for next year. CEIPA, Kelsey to Scott, 2 February 1922.

[83] CEIPA, Kelsey to Scott; Scott to Kelsey, and Kelsey to Scott, 4 February, 17 February, and 18 February 1922.

[84] CEIPA, Scott to Kelsey, 9 March 1922: "Do not, I beg you, allow anything to intervene …:".

On 5 May 1922 Scott cabled Kelsey: "just a word to remind you that May Day has come. Where is Grotius"?[85] Replying the following day, Kelsey welcomed Scott's "telegraphic May-day greeting" and said he had just received the "copy" for the title-page, preface, dedication, and introduction to the Grotius. Kelsey then expressed agreement with what he understood to be Scott's view that the manuscript might be sent to the printer in parts as each was ready, in which case he requested four copies of the galley proofs. He also asked Scott to mark in the manuscript any "sentences which sound to you like translation", for the purpose of translation is to make Grotius "talk English". Reeves, he said, had not yet started Book II but would commence soon, and Kelsey wanted to retain the copy of Book I a "little longer" pending the settlement of some points of vocabulary.[86]

In a letter to Reeves, Scott expressed doubts about submitting the manuscript in parts to the printer until the entire manuscript was in his hands and anxiously awaited the "balance of the copy".[87] Reeves in his reply explained what the editing process involved:

> Considering the importance of the translation every care is being taken to have the translation as nearly perfect as possible. Going over the translation from a technical point of view I have had to collate the translation with former English translations and I have also been collating with French and German translations. The result is that frequently expressions are sent back for conference to the translator and considering the fact that they have other duties to perform in connection with the University, as I have, the work is, I think, progressing with all possible speed.[88]

At about the same time, in a letter to Professor Eugene Wambaugh (1865-1940) at Harvard Law School, Scott reported that work on the Classics series had been "suspended" until the translation of Grotius was in the hands of the Carnegie Endowment and sent to the printer.[89]

Scott tried another argument in a lengthy letter of 15 June 1922. Noting that "for several years" the Carnegie Endowment had been expecting by "almost any mail" the completed translation of Grotius, it had not come. The failure to receive it had blocked the entire series and now there was a further complication which made it necessary to receive the Grotius or "… reluctantly, we try to make other arrangements". It was of a confidential nature:

[85] CEIPA, Scott to Kelsey, 5 May 1922.

[86] CEIPA, Kelsey to Scott, 6 May 1922.

[87] CEIPA, Scott to Reeves, 11 May 1922.

[88] CEIPA, Reeves to Scott, 18 May 1922.

[89] CEIPA, Scott to Wambaugh, 5 May 1922.

> Mr. Root has agreed to write a Life of Grotius to appear in a series of great Dutchmen which is, I understand, to be similar in content and format to the American Statesmen series. As President of the Endowment, it would be a scandal if he was not able to quote from the translation of Grotius, which I have assured him the Endowment has in press.[90]

Scott also invoked the agreement to appoint Reeves on condition of receiving completion of the work by 1 May. It was "now the 15th of June, and we have only received the Prolegomena", which we understand was finished several years ago. Not a line of the first, second, or third book had been received. Kelsey was requested to acknowledge the letter by telegram so that other arrangements might be made, if necessary. Kelsey did reply by telegram: "we are further along than you think. It was not possible to finish the manuscript by May First for reasons which you understand. Reeves is now half through his revision".[91]

Scott followed the telegram with a four-page letter of the same date. He had not seen the letter to Reeves of 11 May, but Kelsey in the meantime had been drawn off the translation by University "matters on the research side", mostly relating to the acquisition of early manuscripts for the University at auction. He enclosed "copy" for the first chapter of Book I and proposed another "practicable plan": to send the introductory materials and portion of Book I to the printer, with six sets of galleys to be provided, of which one set to Mr. Root, one set to Wright, and four sets to Kelsey for the individuals in Ann Arbor preparing the revised text. The first lot amounted to ca. 100 pages, as would each subsequent lot – "just about the right size to be handled by the printer advantageously". Detailed suggestions were made as to format, including: "… with few exceptions the titles of books quoted in the notes should be in English and in full and that no Greek or Latin should appear in the text except where the word is used in a connection requiring the original". The reason – "the aim of the whole undertaking is to make Grotius talk English". He repeated his position that he was not willing to have any "copy" leave "Ann Arbor unless I feel that we have done our best with it".[92]

Apart from expressing full admiration for Kelsey's translations and leaving any substantive comments to Wright over the years, Scott had refrained from offering any observations of his own. Pressed by Kelsey to do so in the latter's letter of 20 June, Scott observed:

[90] CEIPA, Scott to Kelsey, 15 June 1922.

[91] CEIPA, Kelsey to Scott, 19 June 1922. Scott replied: "Glad to receive telegram … Please consult my letter 11 May to Professor Reeves". CEIPA, 20 June 1922.

[92] CEIPA, Kelsey to Scott, 20 June 1922.

> I have but one suggestion … in section 2 of the prolegomena … the word *conditionibus*, which you have rendered 'status' in the sense of 'legal status'. From a detailed discussion of this very term in Bynkershoek's *De dominio maris*, it seems that this term in Roman law, from Cicero on, was considered synonymous with *pactionibus*, and might therefore be rendered by the word 'agreements'.[93]

Scott agreed to Kelsey's "practicable plan" on condition that Kelsey send a complete carbon copy of the manuscript, whether finally approved for the printer or not, and the printer would be supplied with portions of 100 pages or so as fast as Kelsey approved them. Scott agreed with Kelsey's insistence on quality, but noted that "there sometimes comes a time when we lose our sense of perspective and are not nearly such good judges of our work as others …".

An internal memo from the Publications Department of the Carnegie Endowment reported that 382 copies of the photographic reproduction of the 1646 edition had been received from the Carnegie Institution, an additional 48 had been bound (making 430 in total), 57 had been distributed, leaving 373 on hand.[94]

Nearly a month elapsed, and no further copy was sent on from Ann Arbor. Scott wrote on 15 July of his "serious misgivings" when he has consented to submission by 1 May "as my experience did not offer an assurance that the manuscript would be received …". Inasmuch as he was leaving for Europe on 19 August, he was "constrained" to inform Kelsey that unless the translation reaches the Endowment by 15 August, the Endowment shall consider itself "released from any arrangements, contractual or otherwise, with you and your associates", as other plans must be made.[95]

Scott wrote to Elihu Root on 16 July 1922 reporting that he had telegraphed and written to Kelsey but not yet gotten his hands on the manuscript. He had served notice on Kelsey that unless the manuscript was received by 15 August 1922 other arrangements would have to be made as "it would be a scandal for the President of the Endowment to use a translation other than the Endowment's in his proposed work on Grotius". If Kelsey did not comply, Scott said that "we shall have it translated 'by several hands' so that it will be in your own hands" within a few months, whether it be Kelsey's or another translation.

Kelsey reacted a week later and promised Scott, without consulting with his co-workers, that by about 10 August a complete carbon copy of the Gro-

93 CEIPA, Scott to Kelsey, 28 June 1922.

94 CEIPA, Memo to Wright, 6 July 1922.

95 CEIPA, Scott to Kelsey, 15 July 1922. Scott wrote to Reeves on the same day and in the same spirit. CEIPA, Scott to Reeves, 15 July 1922.

tius beyond Book II would be sent and Scott could proceed to set up matters as suggested in his Letter of 28 June. The work of revision, said Kelsey, "takes far more time than you realize" and is going as rapidly as is consistent with the standard both parties wish to maintain. Kelsey was obliged to retype every page of "copy" not because of the technical terms introduced by Reeves, but rather "the refinements of expression required in order to make the text readable". The book must "represent the best" and cannot be done like the preparation of "copy" in a newspaper office.[96] The complete carbon copy of Books II and III, unrevised, was sent by express to Scott on 4 August 1922, but without the notes because a carbon copy was not made. The corrections have been numerous, chiefly of "legal terms in order to make the terminology consistent" and of English phrasing, so a fresh copy was being made for the printer. In the meantime, Kelsey was "expecting to devote an entire month" in seclusion, probably commencing in about a week.[97]

On 15 August 1922 Scott wrote to the Clarendon Press, enclosing the entire Prolegomena of the Grotius, and said that the entire volume was to be published in approximately 850 printed pages. A specimen page was requested with an estimate for printing and binding the work. The book was said to consist of 1,700 manuscript pages, to be set in Caslon type, 30 picas wide, body type to be 11-point, with 1-point leads, quotations to be in 10-point solid, footnotes in 8-point solid; running heads in 11-point italic, with 11-point Roman figures, set off from the text by a single rule. The estimate was to be for 1,500 copies on suitable paper for an 850-page volume, including the cost of stereomolds and a sample of paper stock and cloth for the binding.[98]

At Finch's urging,[99] on 23 August 1922 Kelsey sent the rest of the manuscript for the printer up to the beginning of Book II.[100] By 8 November 1922 Kelsey had sent 347 pages in total of the manuscript to Scott for the

[96] CEIPA, Kelsey to Scott, dated 20 July 1922; sent 24 July 1922.

[97] CEIPA, Kelsey to Scott, 4 August 1922. Scott was urged to send what manuscript he had in hand to the printer, an admonition repeated "in the strongest terms" in a Letter to George Finch dated 12 August 1922.

[98] CEIPA, Scott to the Secretary of Clarendon Press, 15 August 1922.

[99] CEIPA, Finch to Kelsey, 19 August 1922. Finch was present at the interview between Root and Scott and reported that Root directed him (Finch) to send some one to Ann Arbor to get the manuscript.

[100] CEIPA, Kelsey to Finch, 25 August 1922. Kelsey described Scott as "one of the most lovable men that I ever knew", but added "from other sources we have learned that Mr. Root has become arbitrary and unreasonable in other matters ...".

printer.[101] In the meantime, the Clarendon Press had obliged with specimen page, estimate, stock, and cloth, all of which were approved by Scott on 14 October 1922 in a cable to the Press.[102] At Kelsey's prompting, Scott wrote to the Clarendon Press to alter the specifications slightly, the type measure being changed to 28 picas to accommodate side-notes in later pages.[103] Scott, in turn, pressed Kelsey for the manuscript of Book II.[104] On 11 December 1922 Scott was able to send the first set of galleys to Root[105] and two days later, two sets to Kelsey.[106] By 2 January 1923 several sets of galleys had been received from England. Scott reported to Root that the Grotius translation was "coming along fairly well" and was "the best job that Grotius has ever had done for him in this English speech of ours"; the preceding week Magoffin had sent his translation of Grotius, *De jure praedae*, to "our trembling and somewhat grasping hands".[107]

At this stage, Mrs. Kelsey's health intervened to delay matters by at least a month. Kelsey expressed pleasure with the proofs received so far ("remarkably free from mistakes"), was pleased with the style of captions in italics, recommended that the spacing of italic captions between the lines be left as in the proof, left "undecided" the choice of type for marginal references, and sought reconsideration of the insertion of page references to the 1646 edition.[108] Without awaiting a reply, Kelsey wrote again to send the manuscript of Chapter XX of Grotius in Book I, the longest chapter in the entire work, comprising about one-twelfth of the whole manuscript.

[101] CEIPA, Memorandum of Kelsey to Carnegie Endowment Publications Division, received 28 August 1922 with penciled additions.

[102] CEIPA, Telegram from Scott to Clarendon Press, 14 October 1922. Scott sought a firm date of final completion of the manuscript for the meeting of the Carnegie Endowment Executive Committee to be held on 3 November. CEIPA, Scott to Kelsey, 20 October 1922. Kelsey responded by cable, "anxiously awaiting proofs" to the end of Book I. CEIPA, Telegram from Kelsey to Scott, 25 October 1922.

[103] CEIPA, Scott to Clarendon Press, 26 October 1922. Kelsey lobbied for faster production of proofs again on 15 November 1922: "… where men are collaborating and wish to attain uniformity in the use of a technical vocabulary, sets of proofs of the earlier part of the matter will be a great convenience …:".

[104] CEIPA, Scott to Kelsey, 17 November 1922.

[105] CEIPA, Scott to Root, 11 December 1922. Root acknowledged receipt in a Note of 12 December 1922.

[106] CEIPA, Scott to Kelsey, 13 December 1922. Kelsey acknowledged receipt on 20 December 1922 and sought suggestions and criticisms of the proofs from all, "particularly if I seem to depart too far from the language of the original in an effort to make Grotius talk English".

[107] CEIPA, Scott to Root, 2 January 1923.

[108] CEIPA, Kelsey to Scott, 5 February 1923.

Kelsey Abroad Again for Extended Period. This letter marked another benchmark in the Grotius translation. Kelsey reported that he would "go abroad" for a year at the beginning of summer and wanted to expedite the preparation of proofs in galley form before they were made up into pages on account of the number of corrections.[109] Kelsey thought the system of pagination in the first and second proofs was wrong and should commence with the Dedication (that is, with the translation, and not other front matter).[110] The rest of the manuscript following Chapter 20 of Book II to the end of the book, together with the notes, was sent to Scott on 9 March 1923. The manuscript had been read four times, once by the translator, once by Reeves, and twice by Kelsey.[111] Scott now hoped that the Grotius could appear during the session of the Academy of International Law at The Hague between 14 July and 1 September 1923:[112]

> The presentation of a copy of your translation of the masterpiece of Grotius would ... be singularly appropriate on such an occasion. The Hague was the center of Grotius' activity. He was born and is buried within a gun shot of it, and he wrote the first sketch of his great work as a lawyer's brief, while in practice at The Hague. The law which the Academy will profess is the law which Grotius systematized, if he did not actually devise it.[113]

As the idea matured in Scott's mind, he pressed: "I must have a copy of the Grotius to present at the opening session of the Hague Academy ... Page proof will serve my purpose; but the book it must be".[114]

Kelsey returned to the issue of pagination. He could see no reason for giving the Prolegomena separate pagination from the body of the work "except that Grotius and his printer treated the Prolegomena in that way in ac-

[109] CEIOPA, Kelsey to Scott, 9 February 1923. Scott replied to both letters on 15 February 1923 and took no exception to the request for galleys rather than page proofs. Reeves pressed for expediting the Grotius proof as well. CEIPA, Reeves to Scott, 20 February 1923.

[110] CEIPA, Letters from Kelsey to Scott and Wright, 21 February 1923. Scott replied that the pagination in the second proof was correct and consistent with other volumes in the series. See CEIPA, Scott to Kelsey, 23 February 1923. In the meantime, the American Branch of the Oxford University Press inquired when the Grotius would be ready; the reply from Finch suggested six months. See Letters from H. V. Clulow to Finch, 24 February 1923 and reply, Finch to Clulow, 26 February 1923.

[111] CEIPA, Kelsey to Scott, 9 March 1923.

[112] CEIPA, Scott to Kelsey, 15 March 1923.

[113] CEIPA, Scott to Kelsey, 4 April 1923. Even if the volume itself could not be presented, "we could at least say that it was in press, and that we hoped to have it appear in time for the formal opening of the Academy". Kelsey said he would try. CEIPA, Kelsey to Scott, 25 April 1923.

[114] CEIPA, Scott to Kelsey, 2 May 1923.

cordance with the typographical taste of the time …". The modern point of view was different. The cogency of the Prolegomena "in the development of fundamental principles" is such that it "stands almost by itself as a basic document in international law". He believed that reference to the Prolegomena in "books and articles will be relatively as frequent and as important" as those to any other part of the work. Moreover, the patience of librarians, students, and writers would be taxed to use a two-fold system of references to any standard work, and where there are three systems, the more so. Grotius, in his view, was "bound to become a text book" and the intention should be to put the Grotius "into the form" which he would have adopted "if he were living at the present time and accustomed to the use of modern law books". Accordingly, Kelsey had broken up the involved text into shorter or longer paragraphs so "that each paragraph will present a unit of thought …".[115]

Portions of the manuscript continued to be sent. Kelsey now said the delay was with himself: "… I sometimes have to spend half an hour on a paragraph before I am satisfied with an answer to the question how old Grotius would have written it if he should be writing in English at the present moment".[116] He could not meet the deadline of 14 July but sent on portions of Book III for the printer. He then turned to what was described as a "matter of fundamental importance": "We are making so many changes in the terminology of translation that a complete index should be prepared of leading topics. There should also be an index not only of authors but of works and passages cited".[117] Scott's absence from Washington D.C. occasioned a delay in reply (no doubt he was at The Hague, but no mention was made of his whereabouts). On 7 September 1923 Kelsey sent the "end of the text of Grotius", the only portion now lacking being a portion of the first part of Book II.[118] The missing portion was sent on 15 September 1923[119] and immediately forwarded on to the printer.[120] Nonetheless, the manuscript was not quite complete. Scott pressed again;[121] Kelsey sent copy for Chapters 6-10 in Book II, which still left a small

115 CEIPA, Kelsey to Scott, 17 March 1923. The suggestion regarding pagination was accepted.

116 CEIPA, Kelsey to Scott, 12 June 1923.

117 CEIPA, Kelsey to Scott, 6 July 1923.

118 CEIPA, Kelsey to Scott, 7 September 1923.

119 CEIPA, Kelsey to Scott, 15 September 1923 – in Kelsey's hand, not typed.

120 CEIPA, Finch to Kelsey, 20 September 1923.

121 CEIPA, Scott to Kelsey, 3 November 1923.

portion unsubmitted but was expected shortly.[122] He returned to the need for an Index, suggested that Finch be recruited to make the subject index and the Wright be enlisted to undertake an index of authors and works cited. Final proofs Kelsey hoped to complete by the "middle of March" of 1924 because he was leaving the United States "for a year and possibly more".

Scott agreed that a subject index was "essential", but office duties and "his leisure time" managing the *American Journal of International Law* meant Finch would be unavailable. Wright, however, was willing to undertake all three indexes, with use being made of the Molhuysen Dutch edition to this end.[123] Kelsey countered with the possibility of involving two Michigan postgraduate students, one in residence at Oxford and the other in Ann Arbor. The work on authors and citations might be done for about $150;[124] Scott authorized the sum of $150 for the preparation of the author's index.[125] Professor James Eugene Dunlap (1889-1983) agreed to undertake the indexing. Without mentioning a name, Kelsey also sought a special honorarium for one of the translators who "is moving into a new house" and was in need of money.[126] It was decided to emulate Grotius and include the commentary on Philemon in the translation.[127] Kelsey sent on the last bits of the translation of the main work and advised that he would be leaving the country "as early as possible in 1924".[128]

Still hoping to improve the text, Kelsey offered the services of Reeves to contribute a note of six or seven pages dealing with the Grotian vocabulary of international law as conceived by Grotius in terms of Dutch and Latin equivalents. Reeves had discovered a glossary prepared by Grotius in a Dutch text with Latin equivalents of technical terms printed in the margin and reconstructed the technical vocabulary of Grotius.[129] Scott approved the suggestion, but more importantly welcomed receipt of the "last revised page" of Grotius, which means that "if you give them their way and their time, classical scholars live up to their agreements". Mr. Root, Scott hoped, would "be able to bear

[122] CEIPA, Kelsey to Scott, 7 November 1923.

[123] CEIPA, Scott to Kelsey, 21 November 1923.

[124] CEIPA, Kelsey to Scott, 27 November 1923.

[125] CEIPA, Scott to Kelsey, 1 December 1923.

[126] CEIPA, Kelsey to Scott, 8 December 1923. Dunlap required 3,000 index cards for this purpose, duly authorized by Scott.

[127] CEIPA, Scott to Kelsey, 12 December 1923.

[128] CEIPA, Kelsey to Scott, 12 December 1923.

[129] CEIPA, Kelsey to Scott, 18 December 1923. Reeves had reference to H. Grotius, *Inleiding tot de Hollandsche Rechts-geleertheyd* (1636).

the news". The book, said Scott, "will be out in time for the celebration of the 300th Anniversary of the appearance of the Latin original". He added: "… if, as Grotius himself writes, I have said anything to you during the past contrary to the principles of the Christian religion or against good morals, consider it unsaid".[130]

Still to come for the printer was the text of the Epistle to Philemon. Scott sent a version translated by Wright in case it might be of use.[131] Proofs continued to flow from Oxford, and Dunlap required a further 3,000 index cards for references to other authors. Reeves had gone to Paris for some time, having finished proofing all galleys in his possession before departure. Scott wondered if proofs might be sent directly to Reeves in France.[132] By early March, the Carnegie Endowment was chasing Kelsey for corrected galleys, not having heard from him for some time and aware of his imminent departure.[133] Kelsey expected to visit Washington and would bring proofs with him, also confirming that Reeves would read proofs in Paris.[134] This quickly changed; Kelsey sent proofs by post and delayed his visit to Washington by a week. Dunlap expected to reach 10,000 references in his Index.[135]

Kelsey met with Scott and Finch on 20 March 1924 in Washington and prepared a Memorandum regarding the handling of Grotius proofs. Some would be sent to the ship of his departure on 22 March; some would be sent to Dunlap for indexing; corrected galleys would be sent to Kelsey in London, Reeves in Paris, and Dunlap in Ann Arbor; and all galleys would be sent to Washington D.C., where they would be collated and then transmitted to the Clarendon Press.[136]

At this point a translation issue arose. Reeves wrote:

> I left the translation [of Justum] as just in c. 4 for the very reason that G. used the word justum in 2 senses. Where the sense of law is clearly indicated, I have rendered the word as lawful. Where there is a moral idea only I have left it as just, i.e. morally

[130] CEIPA, Scott to Kelsey, 22 December 1923. Kelsey responded to Scott from Boston, Massachusetts, and promised to approach Reeves about the note on terminology.

[131] CEIPA, Scott to Kelsey, 21 January 1924.

[132] CEIPA, Scott to Kelsey, 4 February 1924.

[133] CEIPA, Finch to Kelsey, 1 March 1924.

[134] CEIPA, Kelsey to Scott, 3 March 1924.

[135] CEIPA, Kelsey to Scott, 12 March 1924.

[136] CEIPA, Memorandum of 20 March 1924 prepared by Finch. Kelsey gave his own version of the meeting in a Letter of 21 March 1924, also mentioning that Wright would prepare the subject index. Finch confirmed the arrangements. Scott to Kelsey, 4 April 1924.

> *just*. The word *just* has with us no legal signification, but moral only. Not so with Grotius. His argument is to prove that wars may be and are lawful (just). Not just in the moral sense – But of course this means lawful, i.e. consonant with either jus naturale or jus gentium. *Justum* is lawful = *de droit*, or just – *de la morale*. In English our restricted use of lawful causes the trouble. If you will read the paragraph again you will see that G. uses justum in the first 2 in the sense of lawful. In the second sentence it is the moral quality (just underlying jus). I stand on this translation, though I know some may criticize it.[137]

Kelsey agreed entirely with Reeves on this matter.[138] In the interests of saving a month of time, Kelsey promptly violated the agreed Memorandum on the disposition of proofs by sending the revised proofs of Book I, chapters 3-5, directly to the Clarendon Press.[139]

As matters were progressing, the Carnegie Endowment tweaked its instructions to the Clarendon Press. The Press indicated that Japan paper might be used without having too thick a volume. The Carnegie Endowment preferred a thin paper for the Grotius rather than run the risk of having a volume so large, so thick, and so heavy as certain other international legal titles in the market. A sample was requested, for a "heavy and unserviceable volume would defeat the publication of Grotius in connection with the tercentenary of its appearance in 1625". The size of the edition would be the usual print run for the Classics of International Law series: 1,500, of which 500 are on Japan paper and 1,000 on a cheaper grade paper. Given that stereomolds were specified, it would be comparatively easy to "run off a second edition should there be a sufficient demand". Because the 1913 photographic reproduction of the 1646 edition was treated as Volume I of the title, the translation would be Volume II, with the same size trim and binding as other numbers in the series. The sample binding cloth had been approved in October 1922. Of the 373 copies of Volume I on hand and unbound, the question of a substitute title-page for Volume I to conform with Volume II needed to be discussed.[140]

Kelsey returned to the United States in late June 1924, meeting with Wright in Washington D.C. and delivering personally a substantial set of corrected proofs, together with galleys proofread by Reeves. His corrections were collated with the master set in Washington and outstanding issues resolved; for instance, all references of Plutarch *On Embassies* were to be revised and all canon law references were to be modernized and the marginal notes correctly

137 CEIPA, Reeves to Kelsey, 7 April 1924.

138 CEIPA, Kelsey to Scott, 10 April 1924.

139 CEIPA, Kelsey to Scott, 12 April 1924.

140 CEIPA, Scott to Clarendon Press, 7 May 1924.

placed.[141] Scott recommended that Wright be included as a named member of the Kelsey group of collaborators; his services have been "those of a scholar and collaborator, not of a clerk".[142] Dunlap was off to Europe for the summer, and Kelsey asked that Wright be allowed to take over the Dunlap card catalogues and data and prepare the list of authors and works.[143] This was apparently agreed, for the same day Kelsey returned to Wright certain books belonging to the Endowment and Dunlap's card indexes.[144] The following week Kelsey returned to London. By the end of July he was in Constantinople, but planned to spend the month of September in Oxford to finish correcting most of the proofs. Whether he actually did so remains inconclusive, but he did at least visit the Clarendon Press and so reported on 25 October 1924, just before his return to the United States in early November. Scott reported that Kelsey called in the Endowment and made more corrections to the master set of proofs.[145]

Kelsey returned to Europe in February 1925, having been delayed by the "illness of persons concerned in the matters at hand".[146] The Endowment renewed discussions with the Clarendon Press about the technical specifications for the Grotius. Various paper samples were considered, with a preference the Volume II should not exceed 3.5 pounds in weight or be much less than 1.5 inches in bulk – roughly the same as Volume I. The trim size, binding cloth, and in other respects Volume II was to match the other numbers in the Classics of International Law series.[147]

But it was clear to Scott that even the September date was optimistic and uncertain. In response to an inquiry as to what the American Society of International Law intended to do in order to commemorate the 300th anniver-

141 CEIPA, Memorandum of Kelsey Visit, 24 June 1924, prepared by Wright.

142 CEIPA, Scott to Kelsey, 30 June 1924.

143 CEIPA, Kelsey to Scott, 30 June 1924.

144 CEIPA, Kelsey to Reeves, 30 June 1924. The books returned included the 1631 and 1651 editions of Grotius, the Campbell translation, and the Morrice translation of 1714 ("by several hands").

145 CEIPA, Scott to Reeves, 28 November 1924.

146 CEIPA, Kelsey to Wright, 7 February 1925. The cryptic reference apparently referred to the sudden death of the President of the University of Michigan.

147 CEIPA, Finch to Clarendon Press, 19 February 1925. In response to an inquiry from the University of Leiden, Finch reported that Volume II was "in press" and would probably be ready for distribution in September 1925. CEIOPA, Finch to E. E. Molhuysen, 9 March 1925. On 21 March 1925 Scott reported to Reeves that "… a half or more is in page proof, the balance in galleys". By way of compromise, "we have had the Prolegomena struck off, with a title page, as indicating the nature of the translation". CEIPA, Scott to Reeves, 21 March 1925.

sary of the publication of Grotius, Scott said that the translation was "all in type", but the work had been "time-consuming". Whewell's translation was "abridged and rather free", and even more so with regard to Campbell's translation, republished in 1901 with an introduction by David Jayne Hill. Pending publication, Scott wrote, the Prolegomena would be distributed and promised to send a copy.[148] That very day Scott ordered by cable 500 copies of the Prolegomena to be sent to the Endowment and additional copies to the Librarian of the Peace Palace in The Hague, and 1,000 copies for the Endowment and trade use by the Oxford University Press in England and the United States.[149] The Prolegomena made quite a favorable impression.[150]

Over the summer of 1925 proofs continued to come in to the Endowment at "fairly regular intervals", as of mid-August 1925 up to page 350, which was less than half of the translation.[151] Kelsey was at his summer cabin in rural Michigan; after "some weeks of struggle", he had succeeded in clearing his desk for the Grotius work[152] and expected to remain in the United States for some months before returning to Europe. Scott was in France at the time. Finch reported that from the Endowment's perspective, the translation was over 75% completed. Scott apparently was himself at work on a Life of Grotius.[153]

Thereafter, the proofing and correction process carried on. Kelsey reported in October 1925 that Scott should soon receive the manuscript translation of the Commentary on the Epistle to Philemon.[154] In December Scott still awaited the revised preface from Kelsey with which the volume would begin. Even though the volume would not appear in 1925, the Endowment wished the translation "to bear the date 1925, even although the book will not be off the press until the New Year has begun its precarious course". As of that date,

[148] CEIPA, Scott to Edwin D. Mead, 24 March 1925.

[149] CEIPA, Telegram from Scott to Clarendon Press, 25 March 1925. The additional 1,000 copies for the Endowment were mailed by Clarendon Press to members of the American Society of International Law using mailing labels supplied. Ibid., Scott to Clarendon Press, 26 March 1925. Kelsey was supplied with 25 copies.

[150] For example, see the warm letter of thanks from Frederic René Coudert (1871-1955) to Scott, 15 May 1925.

[151] CEIPA, Finch to Kelsey, 17 August 1925.

[152] CEIPA, Kelsey to Finch, 22 August 1925.

[153] CEIPA, Finch to Scott, 24 August 1925.

[154] CEIPA, Kelsey to Scott, 16 October 1925.

notwithstanding the preface, the Endowment still had 590 pages of proofed text in hand.[155]

The 300th anniversary of the appearance of Grotius passed without the translation; there was no possibility in reality of its being completed. A year later Kelsey thanked Wright for the proofs of the "Philemon matter" and said that all other matter was being held until the last page proof of Book III was in hand, whereupon a final reading of the entire work would be undertaken.[156] A revision of the Preface was submitted on 1 May 1926, but the final proof still lacked the final fifty pages.[157] By 20 May Scott's own introduction to the translation had "gone off to the printer".[158] The Project was coming to an end. Kelsey still had time for a translation comment.[159]

Instructing the Clarendon Press. Reeves was instructed to "put into shape with all convenient speed" a list of Grotius editions to precede the List of authors cited – as "complete a list as is humanly possible".[160] As the final proofing proceeded, Kelsey distinguished between corrections "for which the mistake is chargeable to the compositor and not to the author".[161] By August attention turned to final instructions for the Clarendon Press, whose fortitude over these many years was nothing short of remarkable. Matters in Oxford were in the hands of Kenneth Sisam, Secretary to the Press. He summarized the state of play as he understood the matter:

[1] the Grotius to be in two editions, one on Japanese vellum and the cheaper edition on thin paper for libraries and students;

[2] the edition on Japanese vellum to be in three volumes, each containing a Book and each weighing about two to 2½ pounds, bulking to 1¼ inches each, adjusting the weight of the paper to the number of pages in the volume. The cheap edition would weigh not more than three pounds in sheets and the paper would in tone be something like the Japanese vellum;

[3] subject to confirmation, 500 copies of the Japanese vellum edition and 1,000 of the cheap edition;

155 CEIPA, Scott to Kelsey, 9 December 1925.

156 CEIPA, Kelsey to Wright, 25 March 1926.

157 CEIPA, Kelsey to Scott, 1 May 1926; Kelsey to Wright, 3 May 1926.

158 CEIPA, Scott to Kelsey, 20 May 1926.

159 "P.S. Among classical men *legi* or *legit*, 'I have *read*' or 'he has read', has precisely the connotation which covers the careful checking over of the manuscript by Mr. Wright, and of book I of the ms. by Professor Yntema". CEIPA, Kelsey to Scott, 29 May 1926.

160 CEIPA, Scott to Reeves, 5 June 1926.

161 CEIPA, Kelsey to Scott, 3 July 1926.

[4] paper dummies to reach Wright in Paris no later than 10 September 1926;

[5] separate title pages for each volume of the three-volume edition;

[6] the frontispiece, and whether halftone or photogravure, still to be settled, the suggestions being: (a) tomb of Grotius at Delphi; (b) statue of Grotius at Delphi.[162]

The paper issues having been resolved, the Carnegie Endowment began to release final proofs to Clarendon Press, confirmed the press run, and reiterated that the binding cloth was to be the same as other volumes in the series.[163] Kelsey in the meantime had departed for Cairo, where he expected to be until 15 March 1927 and would review final proofs there. Final corrections kept being submitted well into January 1927. Ten preliminary copies of Book I were received by the Carnegie Endowment in early February 1927, and further corrections sent in to the Press, including the correction of the date on the title page to read 1925 instead of 1927. The Clarendon Press raised questions about the announced price of volumes 1 and 2 together of the Grotius being 2.5 guineas. Volume 1 had not been published by Oxford. Scott reported that the Endowment had on hand 256 copies of the photographic reproduction for sales purposes; if any of these were ordered by customers, some might be sent to England for filling orders or drop-shipped from Washington D.C. But the expectation was that demand would be greatest for the other volumes alone. A prospectus would be issued for the entire series.[164]

* * *

An anonymous seven-page "note" entitled "The Closed Book" reposes in the Kelsey Archives at the University of Michigan which, judging from its content, was written in autumn 1927 to mark pending final publication of the Grotius translation. It would appear to originate from someone at the Clarendon Press, or someone closely connected therewith, before the completion of the printing of volume 3. The year of publication mentioned (1925), the author noted, is a "falsification", and in fact "two parts really came from the press in May and July 1927". The author continued: "The book of Grotius is not a peace book but a war book, and this translation is a war translation".

[162] CEIPA, Sisam to Wright, 18 August 1926. Actual costs of the paper were quoted on 9 September 1926. Scott agreed the paper on 17 September 1926.

[163] CEIPA, Scott to Sisam, 30 September 1926 and 12 October 1926. Copy for the back-strip die was supplied on 11 November 1926.

[164] CEIPA, Scott to Clarendon Press, 21 March 1927.

It was planned in June 1918 "so that it might be ready by the time – in 1920, so it was thought – when the world would begin to confer on the subject of peace". Peace "came one year earlier and the translation seven years later than was expected".

The anonymous author (possibly a Dutchman) asks: "what sort of fantastic men were they, across the ocean, who thought that something essential to the benefit of a renovated world could come out of this book"? And did Professor Holland share this illusion? At a banquet held in Gray's Inn Hall, one of the Inns of Court in London, to commemorate the 300th anniversary of the first edition of Grotius, a peer of the realm acting as chairman of the occasion said: "Holland lets Grotius represent her – but she rendered no other service to the cause of this book than to let it escape from Loevenstein". Up to now, continued the author, there has been no good translation. "The only comparatively agreeable and reliable translation" was that of Paul Pradier-Fodéré (1827-1904).[165] The new "Oxford translation" put an abrupt end to any evasion on "our part". It was "really outstanding, in content and style, in faithfulness to the text and in carefulness of printing":

> To translate Grotius means: to be thoroughly familiar with Latin, with the classics (including the Fathers of the Church), with ancient history, theology and law; to understand the allusions of his versatile mind and to follow his text so literally that the translation may not only read with pleasure but quoted with confidence ... it would be impossible to conceived of a better translation than this reliable work handled with such living care ... the English is fresh and clear; the bits of translated verse – scattered throughout the book – are melodious; the longer quotations and notes are printed in an exceptionally fine manner and the removal of the headings (indices to the paragraphs) which paraded in endless lines at the top of chapters in the Latin text after the beginning of the different paragraphs themselves ... makes the development of the argument much more comprehensible to the reader.[166]

Kelsey did not live to see the completed publication, which did not appear until early 1928. He passed away from "rheumatism of the heart" on 14 May 1927. For Kelsey's biographer, the publication of Grotius was a minor episode in the life and career of a remarkable classicist and archaeologist.[167] On 18 June 1928 the Carnegie Endowment sent labels to the Clarendon Press for the "general distribution" of Grotius covering 887 copies to depositary libraries and the divisional organization. The depositary labels in the United States were

165 H. Grotius, *Le droit de la guerre et de la paix*, transl. Paul Pradier-Fodéré (Paris, 1867). 3 vols. This translation was, he said, "... old fashioned in some respects, attracted no attention and gave a number of notes without those of the Latin book itself".

166 Ibid.

167 Pedley, note 31 above.

to receive the India paper edition of Books I-III in one volume, The remaining 470 labels were to be supplied with the heavier paper edition in three volumes as far as available.[168]

Kelsey's team remained remarkably intact over the decade required to bring the Project to fruition. Kelsey acted as the principal translator and ultimate editor of the final version. The title page mentioned as collaborators Boak, Sanders, and Reeves, all of the University of Michigan, and Wright, from the Carnegie Endowment. Scott produced the introduction, but used for this purpose an article originally published to mark the 300th anniversary of the Grotius on the genesis of the Grotian treatise.[169]

The delay in publication of the translation was attributed in the translators' prefatory note to the peace negotiations after the Armistice in 1918 and to the fact that "near the close of 1919 Mr. Kelsey was obliged to go abroad on a scientific mission which involved an absence of two years from the United States".[170] In fact, the matter was, as demonstrated above, vastly more complicated: several trips abroad by Kelsey and Scott, extensive commitments elsewhere, and a drive for perfection that consumed immense time and resources.

The division of work was as follows and is so recorded in the translation: Kelsey was responsible for the translation to the end of Book I and for the final form of the rest of the translation, as well as for the translation of the Commentary on the Epistle of Paul to Philemon; Sanders completed the first draft for Book II, chapters 1-20, and Book III, chapters 18-25; Boak did the first draft translation for Book II, chapters 21-26 and Book III, chapters 1-17. Reeves revised the entire manuscript with regard to choice of legal terms and phrases; Wright read the entire manuscript and proofs, verified the references in the translation, and prepared the indexes on the basis of preliminary work undertaken by James Dunlap. Yntema read portions of the manuscript. The translators' prefatory note is dated 18 March 1925 – also a fictitious date.

The original scheme had been to produce the Grotius translation within about eighteen months, as noted. When the unexpected early end to the First World War and professional obligations of both Kelsey and Scott required their extended absence from their respective bases, delays generated disenchantment and dissatisfaction with the pace of delivery of the manuscript. The Grotius translation was but one dimension of a fuller professional life for Kelsey, and in the minds of the outside world, a minor distraction in the career

168 CEIPA, Finch to Clarendon Press, 18 June 1928.

169 J. B. Scott, "La Genèse du traité du droit du la guerre et de la paix", *Revue de droit international et de législation comparée* (1925), pp. 481-527.

170 See H. Grotius, *De jure belli ac pacis libri tres*, transl. F. Kelsey (1925), p. xlv.

of an immensely successful and productive scholar and administrator. Despite the efforts on the part of the Carnegie Endowment to induce Kelsey to complete the Project – letters and cables of entreaty, "firm" deadlines, threats to replace Kelsey as translator, scheduling publication to major commemorative Grotian events (never realized), relating completion of the translation to Elihu Root's commitments to write a life of Grotius, authorizing assistance from other individuals, generously supporting additional financial commitments, absorbing what must have been high costs for authorial corrections and emendations, agreeing to complicated distributions of "copy" and proofs throughout Europe and the United States as the translators traveled about the world – the level of civility throughout in correspondence and personal encounters, especially on the part of James Brown Scott, was truly stunning. The arrangement between Kelsey and the Carnegie Endowment, despite the latter's suggestions, was never reduced to a contract. Scott was unfailingly complimentary – and sincerely so – of the quality of Kelsey's work. A consummate diplomat had met his match in a gifted procrastinator, but the latter with the best of intentions and a commitment to perfectionism. Never was breach of contract mentioned or invoked. The entire Project rested, successfully albeit slowly, on the original exchange of correspondence between Kelsey and Scott.

Comparative Analysis of Grotius Translations

The examples below are drawn from each of the full English translations (omitting later edited or abridged versions based on these, such as Tuck (based on 1738 Morrice text) and Neff (based on Kelsey text). Grotius' brief annotation to the passage in the form of a footnote is omitted. The original Latin text of Book II, Chapter XV, paragraph VIII, by Grotius was as follows (following Molhuysen):[171]

> VIII. De federibus frequens est questio, licitene ineantur cum his qui a vera religione alieni sunt: quæ res in iure naturæ dubitationem non habet. Nam id ius ita omnibus hominibus commune est, ut religionis discrimen non admittat. Sed de iure divino quæritur, ex quo hanc quæstionem tractant, non Theologi tantum, sed et Jurisconsultorum nonnulli, inter quos Oldradus et Decianus.

The passage quoted was selected at random, with criteria of brevity and topicality in mind. It does not necessarily follow that whatever this passage

[171] Hugo Grotius, *De iure belli ac pacis Libri tres, in quibus ius naturae et gentium, item iuris publici praecipua explicantur*, ed. P. C. Molhuysen (Leiden, 1919), p. 303. This was the standard critical Latin edition of the 1625 first edition incorporating the posthumous 1646 final version edited by Grotius and noting any differences from the 1632 and 1642 editions. Grotius made no changes to the paragraph quoted.

may show with respect to translation technique and practice is typical of the text as a whole.

Barksdale (p. 246):

Leagues are Covenants or Agreements made by command of the highest powers: wherein the parties are bound over to the divine wrath, in case they break their faith. It is a famous question, Whether they may be entered into with those that are aliens from true Religion: which in the Law of Nature hath no doubt or difficulty; for that Law is so cõmon to all men, that is admitted not any difference of Religion. But the question is about the Law Divine: out of which it is discussed, not by Divines only, but by some Lawyers too, and amongst them by *Oldradus* and *Decianus*.[172]

Evats (p. 184):

Concerning Leagues, it is frequently disputed, Whether they may be lawfully made with a people that are enemies to the true Religion: which if we respect the Law of nature only, is not to be doubted. For that Law is so equally indulgent to all men, that it will not admit of any difference upon the score of Religion. The question then is, whether by the Law of God, it be lawful, or not? And thus we find it often controverted, by not only the Divines, but some Lawyers, amongst whom are *Oldradus* and *Decianus*.[173]

Morrice (1715; II, p. 342):

Concerning *Leagues*, it is often disputed whether they may be *lawfully* made with those who are *Enemies* of the true *Religion*, which is, not to be doubted in Respect to the *Law of Nature* only. For that *Law* is so kind to all, that it will not allow of any Difference on the account of *Religion*; the Question is then, whether by the *Law of God* it be *lawful* or *not*, which has been the subject of frequent Controversie, not only among *Divines*, but among some *Lawyers* too, of which number are *Oldradus* and *Decianus*.

Morrice (1738; I, p. 342):

VIII. Concerning Leagues, it is often disputed whether they may be lawfully made with those who are not of the true Religion, which is not to be doubted in Respect to the Law of Nature only. For the Right of making Alliances is common to all Men, and

[172] H. Grotius, *The Illustrious Hugo Grotius of the Law of Warre and Peace with Annotations*, transl. C. Barksdale (1655; reprint ed., 2013, with Introduction by W. E. Butler), p. 246.

[173] H. Grotius, *His Three Books Treating of the Rights of War & Peace*, transl. W. Evats (1682; reprint ed., 2013, with Introduction by W. E. Butler), p. 184.

admits of no Exception on the Account of Religion. The Question is then, whether by the Law of GOD it be lawful or not? which has been the subject of frequent Controversy, not only among Divines, but among some Lawyers too, of which Number are *Oldradus* and *Decianus*.[174]

Campbell (1814; II, p. 127)

VIII. In considering treaties, it is frequently asked, whether it be lawful to make them with nations, who are strangers to the Christian religion; a question, which, according to the law of nature, admits not of a doubt. For the rights, which it establishes, are common to all men, without distinction of religion.

The gospel has made no change in this respect, but rather favours treaties, by which assistance in a just cause may be afforded even to those, who are strangers to religion. For to embrace opportunities of doing good to all men is not only permitted as laudable, but enjoined as a precept. For in imitation of God, who makes his sun to rise upon the righteous and the wicked, and refreshes them both with his gracious rain, we are commanded to exclude no race of men from their due share of our services. Yet, in equal cases, it admits of no doubt, that those within the pale of our own religious communion have a preferable claim to our support.

Whewell (II, pp. 137-138):

It is often made a question whether it is lawful to make treaties with those who are strangers to the true Religion; which point in Natural Law is open to no doubt. For that Law is so far common to all men that it recognizes no distinction of Religion. But the question is put on the ground of the Divine Law, and so treated, not only by Theologians but by Jurists, and among them, by Oldradus and Decianus.[175]

Kelsey (II, p. 397):

That treaties with those who are strangers to the true religion are permissible by the law of nature.

A question frequently raised concerning treaties is whether they are lawfully entered into with those who are strangers to the true religion.

According to the law of nature this is in no degree a matter of doubt. For the right to enter into treaties is so common to all men that it does not admit of a distinction arising from religion. There is, however, a question in regard to the teaching of

174 H. Grotius, *The Rights of War and Peace in Three Books*, transl. [J. Morrice] (1738), p. 342.

175 H. Grotius, *De jure belli et pacis*, transl. W. Whewell (1853 ; reprint ed., 2012, with Introduction by W. E. Butler), II, pp. 137-138.

the divine law, and in consequence not only the theologians but also some jurists treat the question; among these are Oldradus and Decianus.[176]

Loomis (p. 171):

8. In considering treaties, the question is often asked, whether it is lawful to make them with persons who are strangers to the true religion, a matter which, according to the law of nature, admits of no doubt. For that law is common to all men without distinction of religion ...[177]

Sakketti (p. 390)

VIII. Часто относительно договоров возникают вопрос дозволено ли их заключать с народами, чуждыми истиной веры. Положительное решение этого вопроса с точки зрения естественного права не вызвывает сомнения, ибо такое право настолько обще всем людям, что не проводит различия между вероисповеданиями. Но с точки зрения права божественного этот вопрос ставится и обсуждается не только богословами, но и некоторыми юристами, в том числе Ольдрадом и Децианом (Фома Аквинский, II, II, вопр. 10, ст. 10; Ольдрадом, «Заключения», LXXI; Дециан, «Заключения», III, 20).[178]

Comparing the English versions above, the rendering of one word is of special interest: the Latin "*alieni*". Barksdale translated this as "aliens"; Evats and Morrice (1715) as "enemies"; Morrice (1738) avoided a characterization; Campbell, Whewell, Kelsey, and Loomis as "strangers". Which choice of term is preferred makes a considerable difference to the meaning of Grotius in this passage. The Russian text by Sakketti (1881-1966), interestingly, treats the Latin noun as a verb; instead of speaking about aliens, enemies, or strangers, the Russian text refers to "... peoples who are alien to the true faith" and thereby finesses the problem dealt with variously by the English translators.

The examples of the translations of Grotius are merely an illustration of a larger comparative study that might be undertaken. Perhaps Grotius is among the supreme challenges by reason of the range of his intellect and learning and

[176] H. Grotius, *De jure belli ac pacis libri tres*, transl. F. W. Kelsey (1964 reprint ed.), II, p. 397.

[177] Hugo Grotius, *The Law of War and Peace (De Jure Belli ac Pacis)*, transl. Louise R. Loomis. Intro. P. E. Corbett (1949), p. 171. A new translation based on Molhuysen, note 297 above, and compared with Kelsey and Campbell.

[178] H. Grotius, О праве войны и мира [On the Law of War and Peace], transl. A. L. Sakketti (1956; reprint ed., 1994), p. 390. Sakketti worked from the 1646 Latin edition of Grotius using the facsimile version reproduced by James Brown Scott to accompany the Kelsey translation. Book One of the Sakketti translation was published at Moscow in 1948, but the full version not published until 1956.

of his involvement early in life in some of the burning (quite literally) issues of his time – religious strife, diplomacy and the resolution of armed conflict (Thirty Years War), litigation, and philosophical discourse. His writings, influential in their day, were to appear on various agendas for centuries following his death and, indeed, do so still.

To compare the English translations along the lines suggested here is not to address their accuracy as a rendering of the Latin original. For our purposes each of them is accepted as a version of the original in its own right and compared to determine what different translators saw in a particular passage at a certain point in time. We cannot be sure whether later translators consulted earlier translations, although indications are strong that this was done; in the case of Kelsey, we know that he did consult because he so stipulates without telling us precisely which versions.[179] Barksdale, being the first, could have consulted no other English versions. As for the others, one may merely speculate.

None of the translators were jurists. Evats was reputed to be learned in the "civil law", and may have attended lectures at Oxford on the subject or read widely in the literature. Morrice and Campbell were of the clergy. Kelsey was an archaeologist and classicist who had the assistance of international lawyers with respect to choice of terminology,[180] an understandable practice but one which may irreparably distort Grotius' original intentions and meanings beyond repair (and this version the one most accessible to the modern generation and mostly likely to be relied upon). This effectively amounts to "rewriting" Grotius with a "modernization" agenda. Whewell indicated that he did consult other translations very late in his work; he was aware of Barksdale, possibly not of Evats, probably of the Morrice versions, and no indication of Campbell. The fluency of his manuscript and his assured command of Latin and French would suggest minimal influence from earlier versions.

Grotius' work is not a normative legal act, and therefore translators have greater latitude to move away from a literal translation and to introduce elements of literary style. All of the translators seem to have taken advantage of this element of discretion. Which is closest to the original is for the reader to

[179] "The previous translations into English, French, and German have been utilized". See "Translators' Prefatory Note", in H. Grotius, *De jure belli ac pacis libri tres*, transl. F. W. Kelsey (1964 reprint ed.), p. xlv.

[180] "Mr. Reeves revised the entire manuscript with special reference to the choice of the legal terms and phrases which would most clearly express the concepts of Grotius for readers of English to-day". Ibid., pp. xlv-xlvi. The reference is to Jesse Siddall Reeves (1872-1942), who was head of the Department of Political Science, University of Michigan. During the First World War, he served in the Department of Advocate General and later as a representative of the United States on the Pan-American Commission of Jurists. From 1926 to 1927 he was the President of the American Political Science Association.

determine. Campbell took the greatest liberties with the text, interpolating his own references to post-Grotian events and writings or to British State practice and quite literally manufacturing passages that are not in the original

That clergymen should be the sole translators of Grotius' work, rather than individuals trained in the law, until James Brown Scott launched his Carnegie project devoted to the "classics of international law" is further support for the proposition that, in their eyes, Grotius was part of a religious dialogue within and between protestant churches, which one must assume cannot have failed to influence choice of terminology and approach to translation.

Editorial practices of the various translators are significant, for appreciating the original Grotius, his thought patterns, his marshaling of the evidence persuasive to him, his patterns of exposition, his powers of persuasion. This is partly what Barbeyrac complained about in the extract quoted above from his own 1724 French translation of Grotius. The marginal and footnoted observations, illustrations, and annotations are part of a larger composite picture reinforced by the typography and page layout. For the English reader, these are perhaps most handsomely preserved in the 1738 folio edition of the Morrice translation and the 2005 Tuck edition.

As for the extracts from Grotius above, there are nuanced differences in the translations sufficient to suggest that the comparative analysis of translations of doctrinal classics in public international law is a worthy endeavor in its own right as part of the re-examination of the history of international law.

Conclusions

Each English translation of Grotius from 1654 onwards has been a major achievement in its own time. None has been the product of an international lawyer; only the Kelsey translation actively enlisted international lawyers to assist with the terminology. Four of the six translations here considered were undertaken by one individual (Barksdale, Evats, Campbell, Whewell); two were the product of "several hands". All were by individuals steeped in the classics and proficient in the Latin tongue.

Each translator believed the translation of Grotius to be appropriate to the era in which the translation was undertaken, whether an era of theological dialogue and/or major events in international affairs, among them peace negotiations or military conflicts. As posthumous editions of Grotius accumulated in the principal vernacular languages of Europe, so too did the quality of the edition: annotations, notes, corrections, scholarly apparatus, indices, references to secondary literature, editorial polishing, or the desire for a critical Latin edition.

Approaches to translation, of course, varied over time. Later translations built upon earlier versions; it would not be amiss to speak of successive generations of English translations of Grotius. The two undertaken "by several hands" (Morrice, Kelsey) have commended themselves for re-issuance or re-printing on multiple occasions in the twentieth and twenty-first centuries or served as the basis of translations from English into other languages (Russian, for example). Each approach contained its own pitfalls. As the work of a single individual, the translation represented the preferences and limitations of that man (no women are known to have been involved in translating Grotius). Translation "by committee" contains its own perils, often taking the form of compromises over choices of terminology or lapses in coordination. If measured by later reprintings, however, collective translations of Grotius have been preferred to individual products.

Each translation in its own way has sought to reach a large readership – the lay public, statesmen, students, availability in libraries. Morrice distributed "author's copies" of the 1715 edition copiously; Whewell produced full and truncated versions in hopes of reaching a dual market and making a less expensive version available for instructional purposes. Abridged versions (Hill, Loomis) were intended for a general readership and inexpensive. The Kelsey translation from the earliest planning stages had in view a combination of what many saw as incompatible objects: a definitive edition of the highest scholarship accessible to a general readership, including for instructional use. The Carnegie Endowment budget for the series, original estimates and actual expenditures, were generous and commensurate with the task undertaken, reinforced by a labor of love on the part of the team of contributors.

Given the support over the decades by Andrew Carnegie (1835-1919) for the expansion of public libraries in the United States, the Peace Palace in The Hague, and other institutional collections throughout the world, it comes as no surprise that the Carnegie Endowment allocated almost 60% of the print run for donation to institutions. Realization of the Grotius and of the series generally was never conceptualized as a commercial venture based on market demand. Critics were correct to observe that this strategy embodied a pricing policy that made the series inaccessible to the ordinary household or student budget[181] – the presumption was that library access would be sufficient. Only

[181] The two-volume Grotius (Latin text and translation) was offered in the mid-1920s at $12.50 in the United States or 2½ guineas in Great Britain. Volume I was not sold separately; volume II was offered in three separately bound books at $7.50, or 1½ guineas. A student edition was finally achieved in 2012. See H. Grotius, *On the Law of War and Peace*, ed. and annotated by Stephen C. Neff (2012), whose version "... is a determined, and long overdue, effort to rescue Grotius from the consequences of his own ornately pedantic writing style" (p. xxxvii).

in the twenty-first century was a student edition based on the Kelsey translation achieved. That version excised about two-thirds of the original text, a reduction "readily justified by the very stance on natural law endorsed by Grotius".

One suspects Kelsey would have been sympathetic to the truncated student text, although the editorial policies of the series were otherwise. Kelsey had the 1919 Molhuysen critical edition to assist him; the 2012 student edition was able to rely on an improved later version.[182] Above all, Kelsey wanted to produce the critical definitive text. Although Scott had endorsed this in principle once the translation was completed, one must doubt whether Scott's experience of the translation would have inclined him to undertake another endeavor with Kelsey himself.

The distinction drawn between the ordinary Grotian vocabulary and the "technical" legal vocabulary of Grotius – a constant theme in the management of the Kelsey translation – no doubt deserves a study in its own right. A highly experienced classicist and fluent expert in the Latin language, Kelsey nonetheless felt unable to cope along with what he called the legal terminology. He was not without some legal training: as an undergraduate at Rochester University, he had taken senior-level courses in Roman law, Justinian, and constitutional law.[183] Reeves and Wright were brought on board precisely to assist and made corrections or adjustments throughout. But the distinction drawn between the two "worlds" – general classics and law – itself raises questions about the ability of the modern mind to truly have a command of Grotian thought. For Grotius these terminologies were an integrated phenomenon, not separated.

William E. Butler
September 2021

[182] See Grotius, *De Iure Belli ac Pacis Libri Tres: in quibus ius naturae et gentium item iuris publici praecipua explicantur*, ed. B. J. A. de Kanter-van Hettinga Tromp, with annotations by R. Feenstra, C. E. Persenaire, and E. Arps-de Wilde (1993).

[183] Pedley, note 31 above, p. 12.

THE CLASSICS OF INTERNATIONAL LAW

EDITED BY

JAMES BROWN SCOTT

President of the Institute of International Law
President of the American Institute of International Law

DE JURE BELLI AC PACIS LIBRI TRES

BY HUGO GROTIUS

VOL. I. A Photographic Reproduction of the Edition of 1646, with a Portrait of Grotius.

VOL. II. A Translation of the Text, by Francis W. Kelsey, with the collaboration of Arthur E. R. Boak, Henry A. Sanders, Jesse S. Reeves, and Herbert F. Wright, with an Introduction by James Brown Scott.

This volume with Volume I constitutes No. 3 of 'The Classics of International Law'. A list of the numbers already published is given at the end of this volume.

DE JURE BELLI AC PACIS LIBRI TRES

BY

HUGO GROTIUS

VOLUME TWO

THE TRANSLATION

BOOK I

BY FRANCIS W. KELSEY

WITH THE COLLABORATION OF

ARTHUR E. R. BOAK, HENRY A. SANDERS,

JESSE S. REEVES AND HERBERT F. WRIGHT

AND AN INTRODUCTION BY

JAMES BROWN SCOTT

OXFORD: AT THE CLARENDON PRESS

LONDON: HUMPHREY MILFORD

1925

Printed in England
At the OXFORD UNIVERSITY PRESS
By John Johnson
Printer to the University

CONTENTS

INTRODUCTION[1]

Huig de Groot, whom we know and venerate under the latinized name of Hugo Grotius, is not a man with one book to his credit; but lawyers of all parts of the world are celebrating the three hundredth anniversary of one work of his, *De Jure Belli ac Pacis Libri Tres.*

It appeared, it would seem, some time in the month of March 1625.

For many years it was looked upon as a *tour de force*, as an extraordinary achievement for a politician in exile and a humanist to his finger-tips to have turned off within the space of a few months a treatise on a dry and admittedly technical subject, whose principles were ill-defined and, where known, were treated with scant respect.

His preparation for the work was not obvious. It is true that a pamphlet on the freedom of the seas had been published anonymously some sixteen years before, and it was known to those who took an interest in the matter that Grotius was its author; the connexion, however, between the *Mare Liberum* of 1609 and the masterpiece of 1625 was not evident. It was a far cry from a pamphlet maintaining a special interest, to a general treatise setting forth the rights and duties of nations in war and in peace. The knowing ones would have us believe that he began the composition of the great work in 1623, upon a suggestion of the famous Frenchman, Nicholas Peiresc, 'the Maecenas of his Century and the Ornament of Provence', and a letter from Grotius himself, dated January 11, 1624, is invoked in support of Peiresc's intervention. Writing to his patron from Paris, Grotius said:

> I am not idle, but am continuing the work on the Law of Nations (De Jure Gentium), and if it proves to be such as to deserve readers, posterity will have something which it will owe to you, who summoned me to this labour by your assistance and encouragement.

It may well be, indeed, that Grotius was moved to compose the law of nations because of the encouragement which he received from Peiresc, but he would have been unable to please his patron by the production of a manuscript within two years on such a subject without elaborate preparation extending through a long period of years. The suggestion that Grotius should write something for publication may have come from Peiresc, but that it should be a treatise on the law of nations doubtless came from Grotius.

So matters stood until 1868, when another and an earlier manu-

[1] Translated from 'La Genèse du Traité du Droit de la Guerre et de la Paix' in *Revue de Droit international et de Législation comparée,* 1925, pp. 481–527.

script of Grotius was published at The Hague, not due this time to a literary patron, such as Peiresc, but to the Dutch East India Company, which had availed itself, it would appear, of Grotius's services as counsel in a case in which it was deeply interested. It was a moderate-sized octavo volume under the title of *De Jure Praedae Commentarius*. At once the relation between the booklet of 1609 and the book on the law of nations of 1625 became evident.

The tractate on the freedom of the seas was only the twelfth chapter of the manuscript *On the Law of Prize*, and the three books *On the Law of War and Peace* were the revision of the *Commentary on the Law of Prize* expanded by its author to apply to a world at war. We are no longer face to face with a professional brief in which law is pressed into the service of a client, but we are confronted with a treatise whose purpose was to bring the actions of this world at war into harmony with principles of justice and the practice of Christian peoples. The three books were the work of a lawyer, as was the *Commentarius*; they were likewise the work of a humanist, or, better still, of a humanitarian in whom the head and the heart co-operated.

The first public intimation of the existence of the *Commentarius* was contained in a catalogue of manuscript books which were stated to have once belonged to Grotius, and which, in 1864, Mr. Martinus Nijhoff, a bookseller of The Hague, was about to dispose of at public sale.

Grotius himself seems never to have mentioned the manuscript in his other books or in many letters, according to Professor Hamaker's introduction prefixed to the text of the *Commentarius*, which he edited and Nijhoff published in 1868. The manuscript was purchased by the University of Leyden, in which seat of learning Grotius had been a student and of which he is certainly one of the most illustrious graduates. It was found to be, as claimed, in the handwriting of Grotius. The *Mare Liberum* was known to be his, and it was now found, barring slight modifications to fit it for independent publication, to have formed the twelfth chapter of the *Commentarius*.

We have Grotius's own account, in his *Annales et Historiae de Rebus Belgicis ab Obitu Philippi Regis usque ad Inducias Anni 1609*,[1] of the facts which led to the composition of the *Commentary*:

The King of Jora also (this is a Kingdome in the region of Malacca), daring to rip up old injuries against the Portugueses, incited Jacob Hemskerck, then having with him two Holland Ships, to set upon a Carrack of an immense magnitude that lay in the Streights between Malacca, a Portugal colony, and Sumatra; which he accordingly did, the said King being both the author and witness of the Victory. The Hollanders, con-

[1] This work was written by Grotius in 1612, but was published for the first time in 1657, some thirteen years after the death of the illustrious author. The above quotation is taken from the English translation published at London in 1665 under the title *De Rebus Belgicis: or, The Annals and History of the Low-Countrey-Warrs*, Book XI, pp. 731–2.

tented with the booty, which was very great, spared the lives of all the persons in it, (being near seven hundred of all sexes and ages), although there yet appeared many fresh examples of Portugal cruelty. . . . Thus wealth being gotten from the publick Enemy, and great damage done to the King and Portuguese, great advantage was gotten with honour by the Hollanders both in private and publick. Yet some were found in this industrious and gain-seeking Nation, who would refuse part thereof as not convenient or fitting, being by force of Warre taken from Merchants and, as it many times happens, such as least deserve it. . . .

And from this time, a new Warre as it were arising in the East, the Indian Company began to be esteemed a great part of the Commonwealth, for that not onely a part of all booty came to the publick Treasury, but also the common Enemy was exhausted at the charge of private citizens, that daily made spoil of him, and made him be at infinite expences in his defence.[1]

According to this passage, it is evident that there is question: (1) of a capture made by Dutch vessels against the Portuguese; (2) of a prize case; and (3) of the scruples of certain Dutchmen to take a share of the booty coming to them under the law of prize.

The year in which the capture took place was 1602, and many competent persons believe that Grotius was retained by the Dutch East India Company to justify the capture of the Portuguese galleon.

The reasons which induced Grotius to write his *Commentary* are disclosed in a *Defense of the Freedom of the Sea against Welwod.*

It was not published during his life, but the manuscript was found together with the *Commentary on the Law of Prize*, to which the *Defense* is related. And it is Grotius himself who explains to us, what he withheld from his contemporaries, the circumstances surrounding the composition of the *Commentary.*

Some years ago when I saw that the commerce with India which is called East was of great importance for the security of the Fatherland, and it was apparent that this commerce could not be sufficiently maintained without arms, in view of the Portuguese obstructing it through violence and trickery, I gave my attention to arousing the spirit of our countrymen to safeguarding bravely what had been so felicitously begun, since there had been put before my eyes the justice and equity of the case itself, the source from which in my opinion originated the confidence in law which has been handed down to us by the ancients. Therefore all of the rights of war and prize and the history of those deeds of savagery and cruelty which the Portuguese had perpetrated against our countrymen and many other things relevant thereto, I had detailed in a sufficiently complete *Commentary* which up to the present I have refrained from publishing.[2]

It is to be supposed that Grotius prepared the *Commentary* either in his own professional interest in the case before the Prize Commission, or in order to satisfy the curiosity of the Dutch and foreigners interested in this *cause célèbre*, or even at the request of the East India Company, which was largely interested in the affair in a financial way. The *Commentary* appears to have been written in the winter of

[1] *Ibid.*, p. 734.

[2] Translated from the original as quoted in Professor Hamaker's preface to *Hugonis Grotii de Jure Praedae Commentarius* (1868), pp. ix–x.

1604–5, and Grotius himself stated, according to Professor Hamaker, that he 'neither changed nor added anything in the text after November 1608, at which time he ordered Chapter XII to be published separately'.[1]

In any case, it is this Company, to which Grotius had rendered professional services, which is responsible for the publication in 1609 of that chapter of the *Commentary* dealing with the *Freedom of the Seas*.

This is the reason according to the *Defense against Welwod*:

> But when, a short time thereafter,[2] some hope was extended by the Spaniards for peace or truce with our country, but any unjust condition was demanded by them, namely, that we refrain from commerce with the Indies, a part of that *Commentary*, in which it was shown that this demand rested neither upon law nor upon any probable colour of law, I determined to publish separately under the title of *Mare Liberum*, with the intention and hope that I might add courage to our countrymen not to withdraw a tittle from their manifest right and might find out whether it were possible to induce the Spaniards to treat the case a little more leniently after it had been deprived not only of its strongest arguments but of the authority of their people, both of which considerations were not without success.[3]

We do not know why Grotius refrained from publishing the complete text of the *Commentary*. 'It is probable', according to Rolin-Jaequemyns, 'that the stringent scruples of some members of the Company disappeared of themselves in less time than was needed for the author to get out his learned argument.'

We do know, however, both the circumstances surrounding the composition of the *De Jure Belli ac Pacis* and the motive which determined Grotius to make it public in 1625. He takes us into his confidence in the twenty-eighth section of the Prolegomena or introduction which he prefixed to the treatise, saying:

> •Fully convinced, . . . that there is a common law among nations, which is valid alike for war and in war, I have had many and weighty reasons for undertaking to write upon this subject.

And he continues with a passage hardly less applicable to-day than it was in the stirring times during which he spent his exile in Paris.

> Throughout the Christian world I observed a lack of restraint in relation to war, such as even barbarous races should be ashamed of; I observed that men rush to arms for slight causes, or no cause at all, and that when arms have once been taken up there is

[1] The opinion of Fruin and Hamaker is not shared, it seems, by Kosters, himself a Dutch savant, who finds it hard to believe that there could be already found in the *Commentary* of Grotius, written in 1604 and revised for the last time in 1608, 'the same distinction between the two kinds of Law of Nations that seven years later was to be revealed at Coimbra by the venerable Spanish Jesuit, Suarez, *Tractatus de legibus ac Deo legislatore*, and to become a decisive element in the development of the Law of Nations'. See *Les Fondements du Droit des Gens*, a masterly contribution to the general theory of the Law of Nations, by J. Kosters, Judge of the Supreme Court of the Netherlands, former Professor of the Law Faculty of Groningen, in *Bibliotheca Visseriana*, vol. iv (Leyden, 1925), p. 41.

[2] The composition of the *Commentary* (1604–5) referred to by Grotius in the passage cited above.

[3] Translated from the original as quoted in Professor Hamaker's preface to *Hugonis Grotii de Jure Praedae Commentarius* (1868), pp. ix–x.

no longer any respect for law, divine or human; it is as if, in accordance with a general decree, frenzy had openly been let loose for the committing of all crimes.

In the thirtieth section Grotius takes his readers still further into his confidence. 'At the same time,' he said, 'through devotion to study in private life I have wished—as the only course now open to me, undeservedly forced out from my native land, which had been graced by so many of my labours—to contribute somewhat to the philosophy of the law, which previously, in public service, I practised with the utmost degree of probity of which I was capable.' This is the reason which he gave to show his preparation for the work in question. It is followed by another, not untinged with ambition. 'Many heretofore have proposed to give to this subject a well-ordered presentation', a statement followed with the laconic observation that 'no one has succeeded'.

The impelling purpose was to show that there was a law in time of war and, by so doing, to contribute not only to its observance, but also to the philosophy of law. Lawyer by profession and having practised his profession, as he himself informs us, 'with the utmost degree of probity', he was intellectually qualified for the task. In the *Commentary on the Law of Prize* he had at hand the materials for his undertaking. But the *Commentary* was only the skeleton; it was the privilege and the immense service of Grotius, still in his early manhood, to make of it a thing of flesh and blood.

Rolin-Jaequemyns [1] thus compares the *De Jure Praedae* of 1604–5 with the *De Jure Belli ac Pacis* of 1625:

The first work has all the qualities and all the defects of youth except ignorance. We know how precocious Grotius was. The *De Jure Praedae* teems with erudition, classical, theological, philosophical, and juristic. This erudition, however, does not prevent a warm and brilliant style, rapidity of thought, nor even a certain striving for striking expressions. The defect is that throughout the work Grotius is an ardent advocate rather than an impartial judge. He has not reached that sublime severity which experience later gave him. He loves positive and paradoxical assertions (the very title, *De Jure Praedae*, has an air of defiance), and he has no idea of those famous *temperamenta*, which, in his great treatise, were to represent the progressive and humanitarian element of law. . . .

That is to say, the work of his youth has not the full ripeness nor masterly character of the author's masterpiece. None the less it is a remarkable work which alone would have sufficed to place Grotius beside Victoria, Ayala and Gentili.[2]

It is to be noted that M. Rolin-Jaequemyns mentions in this passage the great predecessors of Grotius whose works had been

[1] In a review of Hamaker's edition of Grotius's *De Jure Praedae* in *Revue de Droiti nternational et de Législation comparée*, vol. vii (1875), p. 696.

[2] *Ibid.*, p. 695. We know that Grotius, like Victoria, although a layman, was a theologian to his finger-tips; that he was interested in war and its conduct, though not an officer in the army as was Ayala; if not a professor, as was Gentilis, he was even more learned, and as an advocate he was accustomed to regard even theoretical questions from the practical point of view.

published before the composition of the *Commentary*. If we add the *Tractatus de Legibus ac Deo Legislatore* of Suarez which appeared in 1612, we have four of the names honoured by posterity as the founders of international law. By adding that of Grotius, who terminated the first period and is the point of departure for the next, we have five, of whom two, Gentilis and Grotius, were Protestants.

There are some who are prone to forget that there were great men before these two masters. Enough time has passed, it would seem, since the Reformation to be just to their predecessors, and especially should we be mindful of this in this tercentenary of the publication of the treatise of Grotius, who himself did not forget it.

International law existed before the publication of the first systematic treatise which Grotius has had the great honour of transmitting to posterity. Thomas Aquinas specialized in natural law. Victoria the Spaniard distinguished *jus naturale* and *jus inter gentes*, which Suarez had treated in a masterly passage and with final authority. Ayala, to whom Grotius referred in the Prolegomena, is also a Spaniard, and we may say that the work of this great Spanish trinity, not to mention many other Spanish notables of that epoch, would perhaps have enabled another than Grotius to combine their work systematically and to make of it the basis of his treatise.

The primary foundation of the system of the law of nations is the Roman law, the universal law, upon which was based the canon law, as universal as the Church from which it emanates.

The theologians and philosophers of the Middle Ages fused together these two systems of law, and it is quite natural that the faithful of the Church universal laid down the foundations of that universal law which is the law of nations. If we recall that Gentilis was Italian, we may say that international law is of Latin origin, as well as of Catholic origin.

In any case, as we are told very plainly by a compatriot of Grotius, Dr. Kosters, in his admirable *Fondements du Droit des Gens*,[1] who prefers the tree of science to inanimate foundations, 'we have come to the fullness of time; a hand is stretched to gather the ripened fruit'.

It was the hand of a Hollander.

* * *

In 1604 a case was tried at Amsterdam which for many reasons remains a *cause célèbre*. It appealed to the imagination of Europe, and it seemed to furnish indirectly the opportunity for composing the first systematic treatise on the law of nations.

It is thought that Hugo Grotius represented the Great United Company of the East Indies in the proceedings before the Prize Court.

[1] In *Bibliotheca Visseriana*, vol. iv (Leyden, 1925), p. 32.

The documents which could establish the fact no longer exist, having been destroyed in the last century by a fire which burnt the buildings of the Ministry of the Navy where they were preserved. We do know, however, that he had very close relations with the Company and that he represented it before the States General in 1606.

In the interval he composed the *De Jure Praedae Commentarius*, which was based on official documents and was a written brief or argument on behalf of the Company in its capture of the Portuguese galleon in the waters of the East Indies, from which the Portuguese sought to exclude the Dutch.

We also know that upon the request of the Company he detached the twelfth chapter of the *Commentary* to publish it separately in 1609 under the title of *Mare Liberum*, in order to defend the interests of the Company and to influence favourably the negotiations then in progress between Spain and Holland for peace on reciprocally acceptable bases.

The opinion of the Dutch savant, M. Robert Fruin, formerly Professor of Dutch History at the University of Leyden,[1] who has examined all the existing documents relating to the capture of the Portuguese vessel, the prize procedure before the Dutch Admiralty in 1604, and the relations of Grotius with the Company, is that it was indeed he who represented the Company before the Prize Commission and defended its interests to the world at large. Professor Fruin is firmly convinced that the *Commentary* is only a development of the professional arguments which Grotius found effective before the Prize Court. Hence it follows that the great treatise *On the Law of War and Peace*, justly considered as the first systematic treatise on international law, is the result of the professional labours of a Dutch advocate versed in international law and away from his practice: one who, as we now know, kept his *Commentary* with him and enlarged it by adding the parts concerning peace, in order to treat of war and peace for the first time in a systematic form acceptable to the nations.

Thus it is that the arguments of Grotius have made their way from the Prize Commission throughout the world, and that even in

[1] *Een Onuitgegeven Werk van Hugo de Groot*, in his *Verspreide Geschriften*, vol. iii, pp. 367–445. The text of this remarkable work appeared for the first time in 1868; an appendix was added in 1874.

An English translation entitled *An Unpublished Work of Hugo Grotius's* appears in *Bibliotheca Visseriana*, vol. v (Leyden, 1925), pp. 1–100.

Professor Hamaker, in the Preface to his edition of the *De Jure Praedae*, is in agreement with Professor Fruin. Likewise the study of Professor Fruin forms the basis of the present article, the text of which may be considered in large part a résumé of that excellent monograph.

The writer of the present article, nevertheless, asked two Ministers of Foreign Affairs of the Netherlands to have the archives of their country examined in a last effort to find, if that were still possible, official documents concerning the prize case. They stated that there was nothing more to be had. In the absence of original documents, Dr. Fruin's essay therefore has unusual value. It is almost our only source, and the one which is destined to become a classic, concerning that episode in the life of Grotius.

our own days they influence foreign offices as they formerly convinced the Dutch magistrates.

Without the fire which destroyed the arsenal and with it the original documents, it would not be necessary to cite secondary proofs; but we cannot be content with a simple statement when the practical origin of the first treatise on international law is in question.

The victorious Heemskerck arrived with his prize at Amsterdam in the summer of 1604. The cargo of the captured vessel was of a kind and value to appeal not only to the Dutch but to foreigners. The articles were of two kinds, one of them perishable. For this reason it was impossible to await the end of the case before offering them for sale. The Dutch are above all reasonable people, and are reputed to possess commercial traits which are lacking in others. Professor Fruin tells us that it was desired to take advantage of the approaching fair at Frankfort to sell the perishable goods, and we may also recall that Grotius himself later worked in haste in order to get the first copies of his treatise on sale at the Frankfort Fair.

The States-General of Holland, by a resolution of July 29, 1604, authorized the public sale, 'notwithstanding that no judgment has declared the property good prize,' and this sale was fixed for August 15 and the days following.

As Fruin has it, relying on the declarations of Grotius himself, 'an incredible multitude had come from all the countries of Europe, especially from the Hanseatic towns and the imperial cities of Swabia.' Thanks to this commercial instinct which characterized the Dutch of that time, the prospective purchasers were divided into two classes: those from Amsterdam who were given six months' credit, and foreigners who paid cash.

The hearing continued during the sale, and on September 9, 1604, the carak with its entire cargo was declared good prize. After the judgement another sale took place, on September 21, and this second sale was more widely advertized abroad than the first. Only merchants took the perishable goods; but the great of this world took an interest in the distribution of the durable property. Henry IV, through the agency of his ambassador, took some. On October 4, 1604, the French Ambassador, M. de Buzenval, wrote to M. Villeroy, the King's Minister, who was not above accepting some of the produce: 'I caused our case to be put as honourably as I could, in keeping with the dignity of Their Majesties, in behalf of that which was found therein to be the most worth while,' and with reason, for had not the great Henry called the little Grotius 'the miracle of Holland', and is it not customary to pay compliments.

Nor were the Ambassador and M. Villeroy the only signatories to accept the merchandise; the colleagues of the Minister Villeroy, the Sieurs Sillery and Rosny, better known as the Duc de Sully, appropriated their part of the prize.

It seems that France was the first to present itself, but that other nations also came forward. For example, the King of England and Scotland, the famous James Stuart, accepted a portion, although he was at that very time in the midst of negotiations for a treaty of peace with Spain, which was at war with Holland. Nor is the Margrave of Anspach to be forgotten who, by a happy chance, found himself in Holland. But the Dutchman knew his business. The beneficiaries of the prize affixed their seals to the Admiralty award, which was, on their part, a recognition both of the justice of the award and of the right of Holland to make war on independent nations and to capture their vessels.

This case appealed not only to the imagination of the great. There was at The Hague, according to Professor Fruin, a young advocate who sought glory as the lords sought profit. It was Grotius, who at that time was only twenty-one years old, but had for four years practised the profession of law and had already attracted attention at the bar. Nevertheless he was not satisfied. He envied the lot of his friend Heinsius, Professor at the University of Leyden, although he was but three years older than the young Grotius who found himself condemned to waste his time with the trials of others.

In a letter of June 21, 1603, exactly a year before the arrival of the prize and the case it occasioned, the young advocate wrote harshly of his profession. Cases, he said, required a great deal of time and trouble ; they inconvenienced those who loved to study, like these two serious young men, and besides, they brought neither gratitude nor glory. Grotius was sure that the labours of an advocate were not worth the candle.

He admitted that he had made progress at the bar, thanks to several cases which turned out well, and the poor young man was worrying because each day he had less and less time. That is to say, he was making such progress at the bar that he did not have enough time at his disposal to devote to classical studies. As very often happens, he succeeded despite his regrets.[1]

Exactly four years from the date of this doleful letter, Grotius was appointed Fiscal Advocate, that is to say, Attorney-General, of

[1] Regarding the value of the experience which Grotius had had at the bar, Professor Fruin '. . . His activity as advocate was not lost to jurisprudence. A man like de Groot could not occupy himself with any branch of knowledge without shedding light on it. . . . Trained in the school of antiquity, used to logical method, and himself of an excellently systematic turn, he already mentally classified the subject-matter which in the dungeon of Loevestein he was to expose in such a masterly manner in his *Introduction to Dutch Jurisprudence*. In later years he prided himself on having been the first to make known to the Dutch bar that jurisprudence, " that knowledge of things divine and human, that art of the equitable and the good, whose leaders are reason and the revelation of God, whose companions are all the sciences ", in all its extent and its excellence' (*op. cit.*, pp. 38–9).

Holland, and by his *Introduction to Dutch Jurisprudence*, written later, in prison, when he had but few books at his disposal, he so clearly demonstrated his mastery of the knowledge of the law of his country, that this book, still justly celebrated in Holland, is even now the basis of jurisprudence in South Africa, colonized, as we know, by his compatriots. After prolonged research and a profound analysis of the cases and the labours of Grotius in connexion with them, Professor Fruin is of the opinion that he was certainly the advocate of the victorious claimant in the prize case of 1604. There is a most interesting passage in his masterly essay [1] on the unpublished work of Grotius called the *Commentary*, in which Fruin says:

> We may imagine how happy a man like him must have felt as often as a case cropped up in his practice that could not be decided according to the common routine, but had to be settled in conformity with the higher principles of law. With joy he then consulted his favourite authors, the Roman lawyers and their worthy rivals of later times, the philosophers and even the theologians, and he meditated on what he had read and used it, but as the material which only in his hands became fit for the purpose proposed. Such a question of law now presented itself when the admiral of the East India Company captured the Portuguese ship. An ordinary practising lawyer was not able to answer it fundamentally fully. The laws of war and the law of nations had to be applied, and what barrister had ever heard of those laws? Most of them did not even know from what sources they sprang. De Groot, who was not twenty-one years old, was among all his colleagues probably the only one who knew how to tackle such a case, whence he had to borrow the principles of law which must guide him in deciding. If my conjecture is correct, and the Company entrusted the conduct of the lawsuit to him, they could not have been more fortunate in their choice.

The learned professor thinks that it would not have been necessary to prove Grotius's connexion with the case by indirect means, if the documents concerning it had not been burned in a fire. Not only were the files of the advocates who pleaded the case destroyed, but the award itself did not survive the disaster. Nevertheless the case was so celebrated that the Germans, who have a keen eye for international affairs, were interested in it to such an extent that they procured the documents, including the award. From this award, preserved by their care, the contentions of the victors are known to us and they are the same as those discussed by Grotius in his *Commentary*. It may be, as Professor Fruin says, that their similarity can be explained by the simple fact that Grotius knew the award, but he adds [2] that Grotius

> was not the man to merely repeat what others had demonstrated before him. I am more inclined to surmise that he served the company in its lawsuit as a barrister, and that he himself was the drafter or one of the drafters of the written demands about which the sentence was pronounced.

If the great Dutch historian is right, the ambition of Grotius was

[1] *Op. cit.*, p. 39.

[2] *Op. cit.*, p. 25.

satisfied. He had already found in this celebrated case the glory which more modest clients failed to bring. Grotius was, however, very difficult to satisfy. He had insatiable ambition ; he wished to achieve distinction as a statesman, and he tried to rival the great ministers of his time. He composed verses, especially in Latin, as was then the mode. He was a theologian, and was so eager to unite the sects to the Church universal that even in our day it is disputed whether he was Protestant or Catholic at heart. We may be sure that he made use of the celebrated case from a literary point of view, just as he put to profit his literary taste and even his religious sentiments. The interests of the Company were in accord with the ambitions of the advocate to connect his name for ever with an international incident. The Dutch merchants had decided to send their vessels to the East Indies. The first vessel to journey to the promised land returned with more experience than profit, but it brought the welcome news of the feebleness of the Portuguese. Therefore the merchants of Holland zealously organized the Companies for the great adventure. As competition would injure them, they were combined into one great East India Company. To make money was agreeable enough, but to make war was a very different matter ; it was over costly. They were obliged to be armed to defend themselves against the Portuguese ; they were obliged to be armed still more in order to capture them. And it was exactly at this point, as often happens elsewhere, that moral scruples cropped up.

Among the Protestants composing the great Company, there were some Mennonites and members of other peace-loving bodies whom it is customary to style Anabaptists. It cannot be doubted that their members were sincere in their opposition to war, but it seems to be human nature to protest more strongly when the pocket-book is affected. The expenses necessary to arm ships diminished by just so much the profits of trade, which requires an atmosphere of peace in order to bear fruit.

At the outset merchant vessels were authorized to defend themselves against attack. Later the States-General authorized the Company to make captures. This was privateering. Now the capture which gave rise to the case which has been described was made before the authorization given by the States-General to engage in hostilities. The judgement of the Prize Commission in favour of the Company justified the capture of the ship. The Anabaptists were shocked, as they were opposed to the use of force, and the authorization given by the States-General determined them to withdraw from a Company which evidently would not hesitate, either in its own interest or in that of the State, to wage war against the Portuguese in the East Indies. This could not be helped. If it was desired that the trade be continued, what was to be done? The chief among the Anabaptists set the example. He sold his stock, withdrew from the Company, of which he was a director, and attempted to gain profit from a peaceable trade in the same countries.

As there had been some thought of organizing an East India Company in France under the patronage of the same Henry IV, who, as we already have seen, had a liking for oriental gifts, one Peter Lijntgens, the director in question, saw in this a double protection: the Dutch Company would have the better of the Portuguese, if they had any idea of attacking the Dutch enterprise; and his Company, being organized in France, would be able, so he hoped, to trade peacably in oriental waters, since France was at peace with Portugal and its suzerain Spain.

But the Dutch were prudent. Oldenbarneveldt, at that time Grand Pensionary of the Netherlands, intervened, it seems, in an underhand way, and Henry IV died in 1610 without the Company being organized. Thereafter there was no reason for establishing the French Company, for on April the 9th of the preceding year, through the good offices of France, a truce of twelve years had been signed between the Netherlands and Spain, and of course Portugal, recognizing the right of the Dutch in the coveted waters, a truce which was transformed at length into formal peace. But at the time of the judgement the future could not be foreseen, and the United Company of Holland wished to be protected in every way against the unknown.

Here again we find Grotius.

Engaged in the prize case, he set himself immediately after the judgement to write a defence of the Company, which he finished in the spring of 1605. This is the *Commentary on the Law of Prize*, written in the interest if not at the direct suggestion of the Company. He wrote it rapidly, for two years had not elapsed between the arrival of the prize in the Dutch roadstead and the termination of the *Commentary*. There was exactly the same period of time between the beginning and the finishing of the *Law of War and of Peace*, and for the same reason. For the preparation of the *Commentary*, it seems that he had his memoranda made as advocate, the judgement rendered by the Prize Commission, and the documents of the Company. For the composition of his masterpiece a score of years later, he had at his disposal the *Commentary*, and, as Professor Fruin points out, the argumentative part alone of the *Commentary* furnished him half of the famous treatise. To justify the Company and pacify the Anabaptists it was necessary to prove that war was not opposed to the Christian religion, and that it was permitted to Christians to make what was called a 'just war'. Besides it was necessary to prove that a private company could make private war in its own defence before it had been converted into a public war. This was the double task of Grotius ; he succeeded so well and to his own satisfaction that he has likewise justified private war as well as public war in his great treatise. We are permitted to think, therefore, that the advocate of 1604 was practising his profession when he addressed himself some eighteen years afterwards to the composition of the elaborate treatise.

We are obliged to conjecture why Grotius did not publish the *Commentary*, as he himself gives no reason. There may have been several reasons. One might be that after all, since the Anabaptists had been unable to create a great French Company owing to the intervention of the Dutch authorities, it was not necessary to 'convince' them, for they had not succeeded in creating competition. Another reason might be that the business of the Company was prospering and that the losses did not materialize which had been anticipated. Business and profits continued. The capture of the Portuguese ships was a patriotic work and public opinion approved it.

Professor Fruin thinks that there was something in the character of the Dutch impelling them to attend to their business and to keep silence. He points out a passage of a letter from Grotius to his brother, written later : 'I am curious to know whether the Dutch will defend themselves in silence while keeping what they have acquired, or whether they will try to justify themselves.' This passage is laconically commented upon by his fellow-countryman Fruin. It was more simple to do what was possible than to prove what was permissible. To use the diplomatic phrase, 'we bow before the accomplished fact.'

But the Company had not finished with Grotius, although it was decided not to publish his *Commentary*. The Anabaptists were silent, but they still had influence. There was under negotiation a treaty of peace with the enemy, and Spain did not wish to recognize in the Dutch the right of navigation and commerce in the oriental waters. The Company feared that public opinion would prefer to sacrifice the individual interest of the Company rather than give up peace.

Their rights were defended in published pamphlets, and again recourse was had to Grotius. The Company asked him in a letter of November 4, 1608, to detach Chapter XII of his *Commentary*, and, after making the changes necessary for its separate publication, to give it to the public. The young advocate, who had then retired from the bar and was Attorney-General of Holland, was persuaded to do so. He worked rapidly in order that the chapter, now christened *Mare Liberum*, might make its appearance in time. It seems probable that it was published in the month of March 1609. His great treatise made its first appearance likewise in the month of March, sixteen years later. Grotius asserts that this little work, which did not bear his name on its first appearance, confirmed public opinion and influenced the Spaniards to renounce their illegal claims. And perhaps Grotius knew better than his critics, who are of the contrary opinion. In any event, a part of the *Commentary* was published. Grotius knew very well, although the world at large did not suspect until the publication of the *Commentary on the Law of Prize* in 1868, the connexion between the *Mare Liberum* and the *Commentary*, and that between the *Commentary* and its amplification which is called the *Law of War and Peace* of 1625. It may well be that the publication of a fragment of the *Commentary* created in Grotius a desire to publish it in its entirety. But in its existing state that was impossible. The war with Spain had terminated, and the denunciation of the Portuguese was better suited to a pleading than to a scientific work. The first, or theoretical part, of the *Commentary* remained intact. The third part concerning the liberty of commerce on the high seas had been published, and the second or historical part could not be made use of as it was. The anonymous author therefore waited for a more propitious moment, although the Company on September 16, 1612, had under consideration : 'whether it would not be well to have revised, for the honour and glory of the Company and of the country, the history of the trade with the East Indies by the Fiscal Advocate Grotius or some other expert ; and have this history printed at an opportune time.'

Professor Fruin thinks that Grotius was behind this resolution, and indeed that it was he who had suggested it. The Company postponed its decision because of the need of more information concerning the East Indies. Grotius was, it would seem, too much occupied with public duties to undertake this work. He had become the associate of the Grand Pensionary Oldenbarneveldt. Three years after the proposed history, he himself became the first magistrate of Rotterdam, and the necessary time was wanting. Moreover, even if his professional occupations had left him time to do so, he no longer had the inclination. The great quarrel between the Arminianists, as the liberal Calvinists were called after the name of their chief, and the Gomarists, or uncompromising Calvinists, had broken out.

Oldenbarneveldt and Grotius belonged to the moderate party. The public took the side of the conservatives, accepting unreservedly the doctrine of predestination, and Prince Maurice the Stadtholder attached himself to the popular party, finding there a good pretext for getting control of the Government and getting rid of Oldenbarneveldt and his followers, the Barneveldt who had aided his father William, Prince of Orange, and who had completed the work of the great silent statesman by securing the recognition of the independence of his country. Oldenbarneveldt was brought before a picked commission, condemned to death, and executed on May 13, 1619. Grotius, then the understudy of the great statesman, was likewise brought before this illegal commission and sentenced to what they were pleased to consider a living death: perpetual detention in the fortress of Loevestein. This took place on May the 18th. Through the intelligence and heroism of his wife, Grotius escaped on March 22, 1621, reached France, and there began and finished the composition of the three books *On the Law of War and Peace*.

In the month of November 1622 he was beginning to gather some books '*ad aliquid de jure commentandum*', and as Professor Fruin aptly says, this *aliquid* was nothing else than the plan of his masterpiece. He set himself seriously to work in April of the following year, and two years later the first systematic treatise on the law of nations was finished. Up to the publication of the *Commentary* in 1868 it could not be satisfactorily explained how Grotius had been able to write within a couple of years a systematic treatise *On the Law of War and Peace*. As a very young man he was considered a prodigy; but he would have better deserved that reputation if he had been able to begin and complete this great volume, while in exile far from his books, in the space of two years. The discovery of the manuscript of the *Commentary* and its publication in 1868 explain the miracle. We now know that Grotius devoted himself professionally in a great degree to international law during a certain number of years. His correspondence shows that, even after he withdrew from the bar and had given up the practice of his profession, he meditated upon the subject-matter of the *Commentary*, and if Professor Fruin is right, Grotius always had in mind the revision of the theoretical part of the *Commentary* and of publishing it separately, as in the case of Chapter XII, under the title of *Mare Liberum*, although the original would need to be modified and greatly enlarged.

In support of this opinion, Professor Fruin states that Grotius dealt in the same way with a book of his youth which he did not wish to publish as it stood, and which, by reason of the necessities of his profession, he had not had time to put into a more suitable shape.[1]

There is not lacking evidence that Grotius always had in mind *aliquid* concerning the law of nature and of nations, and perhaps concerning international law. In this connexion Professor C. van Vollenhoven takes the place of guide, instead of Professor Fruin, in the admirable series of observations which he made in 1924 *On the*

[1] 'About the same time, it seems, he acted likewise in connection with another product of his youth, which he had kept in his desk for years and probably had not even finished, the often quoted comparison of commonwealths: *Parallelon Rerum Publicarum libri tres.* . . . The famous *Antiquitas Reipublicae Batavae*, which saw the light in 1610, is nothing but a separate and possibly a somewhat altered edition of the second book of these Parallela' (Fruin, *op. cit.*, p. 46).

Genesis of De Jure Belli ac Pacis in a communication to the Royal Academy of Sciences of the Netherlands, and which he had the happy idea of publishing in a separate reprint.[1]

In a letter of 1614 to his younger brother William, who was taking up the study of law, written from Rotterdam where Grotius was himself Pensionary, the elder begged the younger to read carefully and to note in the margin passages concerning the natural law and the law of nations.

The following year Grotius wrote, still from Rotterdam, to his great friend du Maurier, then Ambassador of France to the Netherlands, a letter giving advice as to studies in law and especially the law of nations.

At the same time he wrote again to his brother giving him certain outlines on the subject of natural law and the law of nations, and in the autumn of the same year he wrote him still again on the same subject. The following year, that is in 1616, the last year of his brother's course as a student at the University of Leyden, he wrote again and mentioned anew, among other subjects, civil law and the law of nations. The Loevestein incident took place in 1619, and it would have put an end to such considerations had Grotius been an ordinary man. Happily for the world, he was not an ordinary man. We know from a letter written from Paris in 1623, still to his brother William, that he managed to procure in prison and to read the *De Jure Belli* and the *Advocatio Hispanica* of Gentilis.

Even before undertaking the composition of the great book he occupied himself with public law, as we gather from a letter to the brother of that noble woman who preserved him for us and for international law.

It has already been remarked that Grotius wrote in prison the *Introduction to Dutch Jurisprudence*. He was thus obliged again to consider natural law in its relation to the civil law of a country, his own.[2] As has already been suggested, it was appropriate that he should complete his studies in law by the application of natural law to nations, especially if we think of the *Commentary*, the first part of which treats precisely of this law. In doing this he gave to the world a treatise of the law of nations, which Professor Fruin assures us had always been his intention.

We should nevertheless consider the foundation of the opinion current before the publication of the *Commentary*, that it was Peiresc

[1] Amsterdam, 1924. See pp. 1–5 for the views of van Vollenhoven, and pp. 15–19 for the correspondence of Grotius; pp. 19–20 for two letters of Grotius to Peiresc and the letter of Peiresc himself regarding the *De Jure Belli* and the *De Jure Gentium*.

[2] See *The Introduction to Dutch Jurisprudence of Hugo Grotius*, now first rendered into English by Charles Herbert (London, 1845), Book I, chap. i, sect. v, vi, vii, x; chap. ii, sect. i, iv, v vi viii ix, x, xi, xii, xiii, xiv.

who suggested to Grotius the composition of the famous treatise *On the Law of War and Peace*, the French Maecenas of his time, ' one of the glories of Aix-en-Provence ' called by Bayle ' procurator of the Republic of Letters ', the friend of Malherbe, of Rubens, of Saumaise, of Galileo, of Gassendi . . . between the times when he collected medals, pictures, antique statues, gathered together one of the finest libraries of books and manuscripts, and corresponded with every one then considered by the world to be savants and men of letters.[1] Two letters of Grotius are brought to the support of this opinion, but they are not of great value when considered in connexion with the *Commentary*, whose existence was not suspected for two and a half centuries, and placed against the letters which preceded them.

The first of these letters is dated January 11, 1624 : ' I am continuing the work on the law of nations ; and if it proves to be such as to deserve readers, posterity will have something which it will owe to you, who summoned me to this labour by your assistance and encouragement.'

It may be remarked that Grotius had not finished his treatise at this date. When he had ended it, he sent to the noble gentleman a copy of the book on war and peace, excusing himself for not sending him ' Carmina ' as the poet would say, and availing himself of the occasion to say that it was thanks to Peiresc that he had written the book. Compliments were the order of the day in the seventeenth century.

In the absence of the correspondence, still unpublished, between the Maecenas and his ' poet ' from the years 1621 to 1625, it is the part of prudence not to express any opinion on its contents.

In the meantime there is a letter from Peiresc, dated July 16, 1624, and addressed to another friend of Grotius, which explains the relations between them :

> I am greatly rejoiced to learn that Grotius has finished his treatise *De Jure Belli*. This will be a great step toward the greater work *De Jure Gentium* which he promised, and which consists more in that than in anything else. I beg you to remember me to him and have him make clear that point, namely whether it is included therein, or whether he will undertake the rest.

Several observations of a technical nature are necessary in order properly to understand the import of this letter. In November 1622 Grotius commenced to procure books for his great undertaking, but it was not until April of the following year that he got to work, apparently after having obtained elsewhere the books of Ayala and Gentilis he had requested of his brother. According to what he himself told Peiresc, he worked slowly at first. But in the month

[1] Emile Henriot, in *Le Temps*, September 1, 1925.

of June 1624 he had made so much progress that his nephew, who lived with him, was already helping him with the copying. The task was almost finished. Peiresc said that Grotius had finished his treatise *De Jure Belli* in the month of July. Grotius had written to his father, on March 31, 1623, when he was revising his notes, that he intended to give his attention *ad juris opus aliquod*, and he thought first of *De Jure Belli.* It is quite possible that Peiresc knew better than the critics the nature of the work.

In any event he evidently considered as we do that war formed the nucleus of such a work, and that Grotius intended to make of it a treatise on the law of nations, adding what was necessary to the part concerning the law of war.

It may be admitted that the part concerning peace is, so to speak, interpolated in the text, and that it has more the air of an intruder than of an integral part of a project completely conceived in advance. It appears reasonable to believe that Grotius perfected the part which concerns war, which was before his eyes, and which was, according to him, the *raison d'être* of the treatise.

Peiresc could easily have encouraged Grotius without having suggested the subject to him, and indeed without even knowing just how much progress he had made at a given time.[1]

A savant like Professor Fruin insists upon the resemblance, with regard to subject-matter, between the part devoted to war, the most important of the treatise, and the first part of the *Commentary.* As Grotius had the text of the *Commentary* before his eyes, it is natural that he should enlarge it for inclusion in the new project. It remained for him only to add the sections lacking in the *Commentary*, forming almost all the second book of the treatise.

If Grotius had the manuscript of the *Commentary* before him when he commenced the revision of what was to become an independent work, it is evident that he worked rapidly after going over the *Commentary* to enlarge and add to it, in order to make of it a fairly complete treatise on the law of nations in a period of two years.

To be convinced of the use Grotius made of the work of his youth, it is only necessary to compare the *Commentary on the Law of Prize* with the treatise on international law. Professor Fruin himself made this comparison in such a way that he may be imitated but never

[1] This is the opinion which Professor van Vollenhoven develops in his pamphlet *On the Genesis of De Jure Belli ac Pacis* (*Grotius, 1625*) (Amsterdam, 1924), pp. 4–5: 'The true appreciation of Peiresc's share seems to be given in 1806 by Luden, Grotius's German biographer (*Hugo Grotius nach seinen Schicksalen und Schriften dargestellt,* 1806, p. 190): "and the encouragement of the celebrated Peiresc only advanced his decision to submit to the world the result of his researches." Hély, in 1875, also assigns to Peiresc the role of a supporter and promoter only of what sprang from Grotius's own ideas and impressions (*Etude sur le droit de la guerre de Grotius,* 1875, p. 19): "The intervention of the Councillor of Aix was not wanted at all. The fruit would have ripened without any fostering by other people (sans culture étrangère)."'

surpassed. It would be better to cite him and to give a résumé of the analysis which he has made of the relationship of these two books to each other, an analysis which has become an authority and which will, no doubt, remain a classic.

Professor Fruin states that Grotius 'found nothing essential' to modify in his *Commentary* when, after a lapse of twenty years, 'he undertook to transform his legal arguments into a manual on international law'. And the professor adds that Grotius could utilize in the treatise everything found in the *Commentary*. He seems perfectly convinced of this, and in support of his statement, 'I have compared the two carefully', he says,[1] 'and noted the corresponding passages in the margin of my copy.' It is to be regretted that we cannot have this precious copy before our eyes. Unhappily we have not, and in any event we do not share his opinion when he says that 'it would be too tedious and take too long to enumerate them all'.

But we have the summary of his conclusions: 'It may suffice to assure the reader that nearly all that occurs in the *Dogmatica* has been incorporated in the *Jus belli ac pacis*. All the juridical quotations, all the passages cited from classical authors of antiquity, and with which the *Jus Praedae* is ornamented, have been transferred to the *Jus belli*.' However, this does not mean that they are textually cited.[2]

In making use of the same ideas, Grotius gives them another form; however, they sometimes are copied word for word. And, a thing even more important, 'the legal system of both, which is the essential part, is identical.' Fruin [3] gives the following proof:

> The fundamental notion that waging war is a legal way of claiming under circumstances in which there is no court of law to pronounce sentence, and that therefore there are as many and just the same causes of war (*fontes belli*) as of legal claims—this notion is common to both books and also all that is inferred from it, especially this important consequence: that war may also be waged to punish injustice.

But this is not all. Fruin goes so far as to affirm that the only difference to be found between the *Commentary* and the treatise can be explained by the fact that the author of the latter work was older and had more experience than when he wrote the former, and that the older we are the more we reflect before making a pronouncement, and the less we are sure of ourselves. This is the case with the *Jus*

[1] *Op. cit.*, p. 58.

[2] Here is a striking example cited by Fruin (*op. cit.*, p. 58):

De Jure Praedae, pp. 148, 149: 'quod dixi aliis interdum quam militi praedam aut pecuniam ex ea redactam concedi solere, id ferme ita contigit ut his qui tributum ad bellum contulerant, tantumdem redderetur. Quin et ludos e manibiis instructos sub Regibus annotes.'	*De Jure Belli*, I, III, chap. vii, § 19: 'quod dixi aliis interdum extra milites praedum aut pecuniam e praeda redactam concedi solere, id ferme ita contigit ut his qui tributum ad bellum contulerant, tantundem redderetur. Ludos quoque ex manubiis interdum instructos notes.'

Such accurate correspondence, however, is only very rarely found.

[3] *Op. cit.*, pp. 58–9.

Belli. The tone is less assured, and in the treatise are to be found more exceptions to the rule. Of this Fruin gives examples. The doctrine of freedom of commerce is the same in both books, but to use the very words of Fruin :

> What was passed over in the older is noticed in the later, namely that there is a difference between the ocean and the sea, between larger and smaller seas, and it is conceded that, as regards the latter, the freedom of trade and fishery may be limited by treaties and custom.

It may be added that the young Grotius, like the Romans, extended natural law to beasts as well as to men, but that the Grotius of the treatise excluded therefrom ' inferior beings '.

Moreover, the difference between the two works may be explained by their object. The *Commentary* was an argument to justify the right of commerce with the Indies and the resort to hostilities incident to its enjoyment. The treatise, on the contrary, was written in the interest of justice and of peace, which is its ripened fruit.

It is often said that the radical of to-day is the conservative of to-morrow. In his case the transition was perhaps not so rapid, but it is certain that Grotius in exile was more conservative than the Grotius of 1604, who doubtless expected important positions under the Government, but had not yet obtained them.

In other words, in the work of his youth he was more a partisan of liberty, but after filling posts which he lost by an unjust process, and enduring an arbitrary imprisonment and an unjustified exile, he became more a partisan of established order. In our days he would perhaps be considered reactionary, but it is probable that his preference for established government, for kings and princes, caused his system to be more readily accepted.

In this regard there is a marked difference between the two books. There is still another which is fundamental and largely responsible for the permanent influence of the treatise. The *Commentary* was a defence of war and an encouragement to hostilities on the part of a great commercial company ; the treatise, on the contrary, was, if we may accept the declaration of Grotius, a reasoned protest against war.

It may be considered that such modifications influenced his opinions regarding law, but the system of the *Commentary* as such remains intact, because both of them form an impersonal juridical system.

To the support of his thesis of 1604, Grotius invoked his predecessors. To sustain that of 1625, he appealed to the same authorities. The materials which had entered into the construction of his systematic edifice were before him. In 1604 he made use of them with the enthusiasm of youth ; in 1625 he was the master architect. The expressions differ, and there are numerous details in the treatise which are missing in the *Commentary*. The basis is the same and it endures, and his successors, following in this his own example, made use of Grotius's materials for the construction of their own systems.

This is, according to the learned historian Fruin, the literary history of the masterpiece of Grotius. Better than any one he has collected the facts and demonstrated the relationship between the two works, of which he seems to prefer the first.

A good historian, he contents himself with showing how things happened in accordance with the scientific formula of our day. The literary origin is doubtless very interesting and would justify the profound research of the compatriot of Grotius.

Valuable in themselves and for the literature of international law, Professor Fruin's investigations are of fundamental importance to practical international law, to those who see in the very existence of nations the necessity for a law to regulate their mutual relations, a law similar to if not identical with domestic law, and in its principles overleaping national boundaries, but undergoing change in order to be adapted to the international society which law now controls, thanks to Grotius, his predecessors and successors.

Professor Fruin's essay on *An Unpublished Work of Grotius* also explains why the dissertations of his predecessors remained, so to speak, in the background. They meditated in the cloister, taught in the universities, published systems. Their works have had an indirect rather than a direct influence, because they did not spring from international needs. The *Commentary* of Grotius, on the contrary, was born of actual practice. The argument of the advocate had triumphed before the Prize Commission. The *Commentary* on a celebrated case has become more than the basis of the first systematic treatise on international law, the object of which was practical from a triple point of view. It sought to make clear that there was a law in time of war to control the actions of belligerents as well as to settle in a friendly way in time of peace the relations between nations, a text in which men of affairs could read of the questions most often arising, the principles according to which they should be decided, the reasons applicable to a greater or less degree to new problems, and upon which nations as well as individuals, and even more than they, should always rely in good faith, in time of war as in time of peace. These are the words with which Grotius ends his treatise and which Christian Powers should keep to heart.

To sum up in a word, the first systematic treatise had its birth in a court of justice ; its principles are developed like the principles of law ; they are studied in the universities of the world ; they are applied in the chancelleries, in municipal courts of justice, and in our day an international court of justice has been established to apply them to disputes between States in the royal residence of the country of which Grotius was and remains one of its chiefest glories.

In the month of March 1625 there was put on sale for the first time a volume which justly has remained celebrated.

It was an international event even in its smallest details. The volume consists of three parts—*De Jure Belli ac Pacis Libri Tres*—which together form the first treatise of the law of nations.

This work, whose international influence has been so great, was international from its origin. The professional opinion given by its author in 1604 in a case of capture between Holland and Portugal, was enlarged to embrace peace as well as war, both of which thenceforth come under the principles of law.

The work of a Dutchman, the treatise was worked out in France, written in Latin, the international language of the day, printed in Paris, which was already a cosmopolitan centre, and exposed for sale at the fair of Frankfort, a free city of that Confederation of Germanic Nations which was the Holy Roman Empire.

Grotius lived at a time when the principle of authority no longer existed. A Dutchman, he emphatically rejected the direct or indirect authority of the universal empire which we may call the temporal authority of past centuries. A Protestant, he rejected the direct or indirect authority of the Universal Church, that is to say religious authority. He sought earnestly to supplant the old principles of authority by a new principle, and he found the latter in the natural law which may be described as the laic and universal authority. It was based upon fundamental conceptions, and for that reason universal ones.

The essential elements of his system are as follows. Man is an animal, but a social animal. It is the theory of Aristotle. Men associate together and unite in society, and each society, however small or large, has need of laws for its preservation. Even brigands have need of justice, as Aristotle remarks. The law must be just.

But man, while an animal, is an intelligent being; whence it results that the law must derive its needs from men living in society. Law is as universal as society; it conforms to the social nature of man and to the general needs of society. There is a primitive law such as that whereby property exists in common. But natural law, to use the expression of Grotius, can be developed and perfected so as to satisfy new conditions, and this gives rise to the division of things hitherto held in common and to the origin of private property. But this development came about, for the most part, in the prehistoric period of humanity.

As man is an intelligent animal, his law is the product of his primitive intelligence. But man is also a reasonable animal, and law, even primitive law, has developed under the control of reason. The instinct of sociability is its origin ; preservation of society is its purpose ; justice is the means and the necessary condition for realizing this purpose ; reason, the supreme judge of application and even of intelligence.

For Grotius, the natural law is a rigid system, though susceptible of modifications.

But man even in society is, as regards his fellows, in a state of nature. It is necessary to progress beyond it, and it happens in this way according to Grotius. As a political animal, he is organized into a body politic. He forms a group with his fellows and from this group there results a political community, whether small or large. Men associate together, we may say, involuntarily, because sociability is an instinct ; they organize groups by agreement, because man is independent and in forming a group each member engages to maintain the group. The result is a political contract, the famous social contract. It is a principle of natural law to conform to the obligations of the contract, in default of which there is a sanction. We thus find ourselves face to face with the Grotian state, whether it be small or large. If the state emigrates, that is to say, leaves its territorial domain, exists, it persists, because the state is the people organized by the social contract. The form of the government makes no difference. The community is sovereign. The people may very well keep the sovereignty in its hands and exercise it directly by magistrates of its choice, responsible to it ; or the people may yield the sovereignty by contract to some particular person. In this way a personal sovereign appears, the prince or the king. But it is a question of domestic organization, for the state is sovereign from the constitutional point of view.

According to primitive natural law, men were equal and free, as having no superior. States, as such, are, according to this same natural law, free and equal, as having no superior. But, no more than individuals, can they live in isolation ; they are not sufficient unto themselves ; for their preservation they are impelled to associate. They are like individuals in the state of nature and the natural law applies to them as well as to individuals. But this primitive law may be perfected. How ? By contract between the states. The natural law which imposes itself and the law between the states which is created by custom, consent, or contract. The promise of states, like that of an individual, gives rise to an obligation and contractual law, just as natural law, executes itself. Thus we have the law of nations.

In this way we have, according to Grotius, two great systems of law : domestic law and the law between states. The first, the law proper of the state, is obligatory within ; the second, the external law or law between states, is obligatory between the states. Each of the two systems can be executed, either within or without, by suitable means and appropriate agents.

But natural law is in conformity with the divine law, although it exists of itself and without revelation ; and justice exists, without reference to revelation. God himself cannot change justice, for what is just remains so regardless of its origin ; but as God is just and the source of all justice, law, when it is revealed to us by God, is just, and it is to be supposed that He approves human justice, which is in agreement with divine justice. Thus it is that law, being separated from ethics, becomes laic but remains obligatory, as if it were of divine origin.

These are the principles of authority which Grotius sought to establish and upon which rest both national and international law. We may discuss the processes ; we cannot reject the result, and this result is a system of law of nations founded upon domestic law with modifications suitable to make it applicable to the relations between equal and independent states.

Louis XIV could well say, 'I am the State,' with the approval of his French subjects. He could not say even with their approval, 'I am the community of nations.'

This should be clearly stated. As Grotius was of the opinion that there was a law which controlled the actions of Governments in time of war, and that there was a law which regulated the actions of individuals as well as Governments in time of peace, he was forced to state, from the technical point of view, the meaning which he ascribed to the expression 'right' in the sense of justice, a moral quality which attaches to the person and authorizes him to possess as his own such and such an object. When the moral quality is perfect, the right is called a faculty. In the contrary case it is called an aptitude.

A perfect right may be maintained even by force, because he who possesses the faculty has the right to act ; but with regard to aptitude, he does not possess the right to act. However, he possesses the capacity to receive the right according to his merit or his worth, from which the right results, and at this moment the right ceases to be imperfect and becomes perfect.

In other words, the aptitude becomes a faculty. The difference from the legal point of view is that whoever possesses the faculty can protect it by all the means of procedure recognized by the state, and especially by proceedings in a court of justice.

The right creates a duty ; the violation of duty, an obligation, and to fulfil this obligation there exist organs of the state. There is this right with the sanction of the state. The faculty is the right in the strict and technical sense with which Grotius cites as an example the power, either over oneself or over others, ownership which is the faculty of exacting that which is due. There are two sorts of faculties. The first is ordinary. It is the right which a person has to require something from another, a right which exists even among individuals who are not united in society. The other is an extraordinary or superior right which belongs to the community against the persons and property of those who compose it.[1]

To employ the technical expressions used by Grotius, the faculty or the perfect right is the object of expletive justice executed or enforced by courts of justice due to the existence of a perfect right. The aptitude is the object of attributive justice—the distributive justice of Aristotle which attributes or distributes rights to persons, such as liberalities, clemency, inheritances, &c.

Right is therefore synonymous with law or statute, to make use of the exact language of Grotius:

> as a rule of moral actions imposing obligation to what is right . . . for counsels and instructions of every sort, which enjoin what is honourable indeed but do not impose an obligation, do not come under the term statute or law.

Whatever conforms to this right is just. To adopt the expression of Aristotle, there is natural law and voluntary law, a classification which Grotius considered the best, and these terms are used in the strict and technical sense of the words as creating an obligation which can be enforced and not as a counsel which may be followed or not.

Natural law is the rule of right reason which teaches us that an act is just in so far as it conforms to natural reason, and morally just or unjust and consequently forbidden or commended by God himself as the Author of nature. This natural law does not change. God Himself cannot change the scheme of things so that two and two do not make four.

The law in conformity with intelligence and the reason of man cannot be modified. To do so, it would be necessary to change human nature, which would be equivalent to overthrowing at once both the law and its object. But if we admit that natural law cannot be modified, it does not follow that the possessor of right under the law cannot renounce the consequences of the law. For example, a particular creditor can release the debtor from payment of his debt; the law exists, but renunciation is made only of the execution of the

[1] For the analysis of the Grotian system see the paragraphs which Westlake devotes to the work of Grotius in his *Chapters on International Law* (Cambridge, 1894), pp. 36–51 of *Collected Papers of John Westlake on Public International Law* (Cambridge, 1914). This study of the English savant has been translated into French by Nys in his *Etudes sur les principes du Droit international* (Brussels and Paris, 1895), pp. 40–56.

obligation. The renunciation can be made general and we have the action of creditors who renounce payment from the bankrupt or who insist upon only a part of that which is due them. In the same way those who possess property can modify the conditions of tenancy according to the circumstances of the case.

The community, acting in the interest of the whole, as the individual does for his own account, can, in a general way, renounce by law payment of debts after a fixed period of time. It may even be prescribed that a proprietor loses his right of ownership, after occupation of his property by one who has no right to it, or what amounts to the same thing, that the right to this property is acquired by continued possession during a certain period. The community, applying always its superior right, can decree a general law which would release all bankrupt debtors.

It is equally possible to change, by the intervention of the community, the relations which exist between the proprietor and his tenant, by modifying the condition of tenancy. It is possible as well to reimburse the individual for losses sustained in the interest of the community and, to use a well-known example, it is possible to impose on the members of the community a tax equivalent to a confiscation, in the interest of society.

If these acts are in the interest of society, they are just ; if not, they are termed unjust. Society is organized in the interest of individuals. Law finds its origin in the necessity of self-preservation. The law must conform to the exigencies of society composed of intelligent beings and under the control of right reason. Who must be the judge of it ? Society.

The natural law is proved *a priori* by showing the conformity of an act with the right, and *a posteriori* by its general employment, which demands a common cause or the existence of a law, and Grotius cites the admirable statement of Tertullian to this effect, that a general acceptance or acceptance by a great number is tradition rather than error.

Voluntary law finds its origin in the will of free and intelligent individuals. The principal branch of human law is the civil law, or that of a state, which is the body of free persons who are associated under the protection of law for their well-being. More extensive than civil law is what is called the law of peoples or of nations, or, as we now prefer to call it, international law, which derives its obligatory force from the will of all the nations or of a considerable number of them. As with the civil law, it is proved by continued usage and the testimony of those who are accustomed to its study and usage. It is, as St. Chrysostom says, 'the creation of time and custom'. Arbitrariness is discarded in the relations either among individuals before their union in a society, or in the society which composes a state, or even in that larger community of nations which it is attempted to organize.

Thus it is recognized, to use the language of Grotius himself, that

in such things it is meet for the nature of man, within the limitations of human intelligence, to follow the direction of a well-tempered judgement, being neither led astray by fear or the allurement of immediate pleasure, nor carried away by rash impulse.

To this exercise of judgement belongs moreover the rational allotment to each man, or to each social group, of those things which are properly theirs. . . .'

And there is a further passage of Grotius which is worthy of note because applicable to every society, be it great or small, to a state within itself or to the community of states :

This maintenance of the social order . . . is the source of law properly so-called. To this sphere of law belong the abstaining from that which is another's, the restoration to another of anything of his which we may have, together with any gain which we may have received from it ; the obligation to fulfil promises, the making good of a loss incurred through our fault, and the inflicting of penalties upon men according to their deserts.

The violation of these rights or the refusal to carry out the duties resulting from them gives rise to courts where suits may be brought to protect them and a government established to enforce them if necessary—a process in a state where the members, either by contract or by tacit consent, are united in a society and have created legal remedies for the protection of their rights.

In a society organized upon solid bases the individual is considered to have renounced his right to redress in person the violation of his rights ; the community is superior to him and has power over him. In such a state of affairs there are as many suits as there are violations of law. But states, despite centuries of effort, remain, one may say, isolated. They have no superior who can impose recourse to justice between nations to redress the violation of their rights. Nevertheless it remains true that there can be as many controversies as there are rights and as many suits as there are rights, but each state, having no superior, is obliged or authorized to conduct its own suits. Within a state it is a legal process on account of the juridical organization. Between states it is a process of force, to the extent that right precedes force between the states of the community of nations, as between the individuals of a single state.

The contents of the second book of the treatise of Grotius is very surprising, because it discusses questions relating to domestic law. The reason is simple, if Grotius's point of view is accepted and when it is remembered that he endeavoured to explain in his treatise ' the law of nature, the law of nations and the principles of public law ', or whatever concerns the public government of a state.

The violation of a principle of national law can give rise to a suit

and as Grotius assures us in the very first words of his book, immediately after the Prolegomena, that

> Controversies among those who are not held together by a common bond of municipal law are related either to times of war or to times of peace. Such controversies may arise among those who have not yet united to form a nation, and those who belong to different nations, . . .

And it is said in the very first article :

> War, however, is undertaken in order to secure peace, and there is no controversy which may not give rise to war. In undertaking to treat the law of war, therefore, it will be in order to treat such controversies, of any and every kind, as are likely to arise.

Thus, according to his conception, Grotius felt obliged to treat of those matters which could give rise to controversies, since each violation could be the ground of a suit : 'the sources from which wars arise are as numerous as those from which lawsuits spring ; for where judicial settlement fails, war begins.'

These legitimate causes—we need not consider vain pretexts—are, according to most authors, three in number : 'Defense, recovery of what belongs to us, and punishment.' Thus war begins a suit between nations and as litigation within a state cannot be begun without giving him who has caused the injury the opportunity to avoid being brought to justice, so war, which replaces the process of domestic law, should not be resorted to, if the nation violating the law proposes, as it should do, to submit the question to arbitration or any other pacific settlement.

If the immediate and ostensible object of Grotius was to subject the conduct of war to the rules of law, his other and less apparent purpose was to preserve uninterrupted the peace resulting from war.

In short, the principle of authority exists within the state and, although individuals are equal before the law, the law is superior to them and applies to the legal controversies arising between them. But in the absence of a formal engagement, each state remains the equal of every other. Therefore there is no superior among them, and as the law of nations is not self-executory. Therefore each state executes its own right against the state violating it, whence it results that controversies between nations can be regulated by force. This is war, but according to Grotius it ought not to be undertaken ' except for the enforcement of rights '. It should be carried on ' only within the bounds of law and good faith ' ; ' but in order that wars may be justified, they must be carried on with not less scrupulousness than judicial processes are wont to be '.

It is quite evident that according to Grotius war occurs only for the want of an organization among states similar to that existing among individuals, whereby the superior will of the state is imposed upon its members, who by their free consent engage to bow before the law of their own creation. But while awaiting the final victory of law, there are, he tells us, three means of avoiding war, in consequence of which 'a great many sufferings usually fall upon even innocent persons'.

The three methods which were of a kind to prevent in the future recourse to arms are: first, conferences; secondly, arbitration; and thirdly, lot. He mentions the latter method only in passing, but it is evident that he would prefer an accidental peace without bloodshed to an uncertain peace at the price of war.

For the friendly conference between the parties, he invokes the authority of his friend Cicero 'since there are two ways of settling a difference, the one by argument, the other by force. The former is characteristic', it is still Cicero speaking, 'of man, the latter of brutes'. And still according to Cicero, 'We should have recourse', he tells us, 'to the second only when it is not permitted to use the first'.

The second is arbitration, that is to say, a compromise at the hands of arbitrators for those who have not common judges. Grotius again invokes the authority of antiquity. This time it is Thucydides who holds 'it is not lawful to proceed against one who offers arbitration, just as against a wrongdoer'.

In a note to the text, Grotius gives approbation to the reply of the Gepidae to the Lombards: 'We are ready to settle our differences by recourse to an arbitration; it is wicked violently to assail those who are willing to abide by the decision of a tribunal.'

The good Christian that he was, Grotius seeks to reinforce his arguments for the employment of arbitration by examples drawn from the Holy Scriptures:

> Christian Kings and states are bound to pursue this method of avoiding wars. For if certain arbiters were established both by Jews and by Christians, in order that the sentences of strange judges might be avoided by those of the true faith and this was prescribed by Paul, how much more should this be done to avoid a far greater disadvantage, that is, war?

This is the application which Grotius wished to make of the doctrine of the Gospel to the circumstances of his own time, which unhappily remain those of our own:

> It would be advantageous, indeed in a degree necessary, to hold certain conferences of Christian powers, where those who have no interest at stake may settle the disputes of others, and where in fact, steps may be taken to compel parties to accept peace on fair terms.[1]

[1] There are writers in the international field who claim that Grotius borrowed the idea of international conferences just mentioned in the text from the *Nouveau Cynée*, the work of the Frenchman, Emeric Crucée, which appeared in Paris in 1623 and was reprinted in 1624, one year before the publication of Grotius's masterpiece. In this connexion see the analysis of van Vollenhoven, in his *On the Genesis of De Jure Belli ac Pacis* (*Grotius, 1625*), pp. 5–12.

The opinion of this Dutch savant is that the 'desire to advocate conferences to avoid war was', as he puts it, 'in the air', and if it is necessary to furnish an authority for Grotius it is rather the work

It is to be noticed that the difference must be arranged through disinterested parties, or rather by parties interested, for all powers are or should be interested in the preservation of peace as well as the powers in controversy, who, being present at the assembly, can state and defend their point of view to the others. Grotius does not enter into details and does not suggest the terms of an arrangement ; but apparently he thought that the powers in dispute could be constrained to accept the judgement of the conference. One naturally wonders if the preponderance of material power can impose the arrangement and make it accepted. Only the future can tell.

The system of international conference has been tried and has produced excellent results. To content ourselves with recent examples, the two Peace Conferences held at The Hague may be cited, and also the series of conferences of the American Republics. They are all a homage to the wisdom and foresight of Grotius.

Unfortunately, it happens only too often that a conference has been called at the end of a war to determine the conditions of peace. But nations might and should confer before the war, inasmuch as they are later obliged to do so. Should they come together before the war, it is reasonable to suppose that there would not be so many after-war conferences.

It is easy to see that Grotius was an advocate versed in active practice and a jurist to such an extent that he identified causes of action that might arise between individuals within a state with those that might happen in the international relations between states. He was not an advocate in the prize case for nothing, and, in this controversy between states before a Prize Commission, he pointed out the dawn of a system of organization among states which would substitute a court for war, legal procedure for an act of hostility, and the decision of a judge for the arbitrament of force.

We cannot say that Grotius would not have thought of the relations between nations from the legal point of view if he had not been an advocate ; but because of his legal training we see how natural it was for him to seek to apply to all nations the method of settlement through a process which could terminate the controversy between two states. For him this method was judicial procedure. He has laid down the principles of law which the wisdom of nations should complete. The advocate can play a beneficent role in the betterment of the world.

But Grotius was not a pacifist, either within or without the state. As an advocate he was peace-loving, preferring the solution of

of Luis Molina, a member of the Society of Jesus, who published his *De Justitia et Jure* in 1614, in which a suggestion is found that might have served as an inspiration to Grotius. For the text of this passage see van Vollenhoven, *op. cit.*, p. 24, Appendix E.

every difference by the application of the rules of law. He even said that the great Richelieu hated him 'for the sole reason that I loved peace', and in an intimate letter to his brother, dated May 4, 1641: 'But if Christian princes listened to my warnings, there would be no more war among them; they would prefer to abandon some of their right or to choose upright arbitrators.'

It is difficult to put a value on the direct influence of Grotius; it is impossible to trace his indirect influence. There is an example of the latter which deserves to be recalled.

There was a young man whose name was John Jay, a descendant of an American Huguenot family which, in order to escape the persecution following the revocation of the Edict of Nantes, took refuge in the New World.

Born in the English colony of New York in 1745, he studied at King's College, now become the great Columbia University. On graduating at the head of his class he delivered, as is the custom in the United States, a formal address, and he chose for his subject: 'The Advantages of Peace'. As he was destined for the bar, his teacher, one of the most eminent lawyers of the time, advised him to devote himself to the reading of the treatise of Grotius as the best introduction to the study and, eventually, to the practice of law. He spent a full year on the work.

He became successively Chief Justice of the Supreme Court of New York, President of the Congress of the Colonies in revolt, and one of the Commissioners to negotiate at Paris the Treaty of Peace with the mother country. After his return to the United States he became Secretary for Foreign Affairs of the Confederation and in 1785 he recommended the Congress for the first time, in a report which shows the influence of Grotius, to settle, by a mixed commission, boundary questions between Great Britain and his own country, so far as they were not susceptible of arrangement through diplomatic channels. Congress did not follow up this step. Later, as Chief Justice of the Supreme Court of the United States and Secretary of State ad interim until the return of Jefferson from Paris to take that post, he advised the first President of the United States, General George Washington, to submit his report again to the Senate that the differences between the two countries might be adjusted by a mixed commission. President Washington added to the report a statement to the effect that the differences of the United States with all the nations of the world should be settled in an amicable way.

The Senate did not act.

As envoy on special mission to Great Britain, with which the situation was then very serious, John Jay concluded on November 19, 1794, the treaty which appropriately bears his name and which submitted to mixed commissions the controversies between the two contracting parties.

The success of the Commission organized under Article 7 of the treaty manifested anew the importance of arbitration for the pacific settlement of the bitterest disputes. In this way arbitration was again introduced, not only in Great Britain, but also in the modern world.

May the youth of 1925 devote themselves to the study of the treatise of Grotius, and among them be found another John Jay.

The great Mirabeau, who maintained that law is the sovereign of the world and Mars the tyrant, said to the 'Batavians' on the eve of the French revolution that Grotius was the eternal honour of their nation and that 'the work of his which should forever preserve his memory, even when it shall have become entirely useless, is his book on peace and war, the first treatise ever made to reduce to a system the most beautiful and most useful of all sciences'

This is why we have a law of nations; this it why we shall have some day peace between nations; these are the services that Grotius rendered to humanity above even the nations.

The world of Grotius was small: it consisted of Europe, the country of Christianity, to the west of the frontier of Poland, and of Europe which confronted the Ottoman Empire, the home of Islam ready to profit by the internal religious strife of Christianity. The Indies were already visited and conquests made; and America, beyond the Atlantic, was visited for the purpose of planting colonies.

The world of our day is large, but Europe still remains its intellectual centre, and it is still France which holds the mandate of modern civilization; America is composed of twenty-one independent republics and a vast country which has its own government in the bosom of the British Empire; Asia is becoming conscious of its existence; Africa is emerging and Australia reveals itself a continent.

All is changed.

The nations are co-operating in the common task of civilization and they are submitting their individual wills to the rules of one law of nations. Hugo Grotius, a Dutchman exiled from his own country, has become a citizen of the world and an international legislator, and from The Hague he causes judgement to be passed on the nations through the Permanent Court of International Justice.

* * *

The treatise on the law of nations is living evidence of the fact that Grotius was a jurist of profound achievements; and we know from his earlier life and from the history of his country that he was a lawyer in active practice and of great repute. The historian Motley says in his *Life and Death of John of Barneveld*, who in his old age leaned heavily upon Grotius, that, 'At the age of seventeen he was already an advocate in full practice before the supreme tribunals of The Hague, and when twenty-three years old he was selected by Prince Maurice from a list of three candidates for the important post of Fiscal or Attorney General of Holland.' [1]

But he was not only Attorney-General, he was the Pensionary, that is Chief Magistrate of Rotterdam, and member of the States of Holland and of the States-General. We know that he was interested, and to his detriment, in the religious conflicts of the time; so that we have to deal with a lawyer of standing and in active practice, and the official legal adviser of the Province of Holland. As the Chief Magistrate of Rotterdam and as member of the States of Holland, he was deeply immersed in matters of state and in the partisan politics of the day.

Without dwelling upon his religious activity, the author of the *Commentary* and of the treatise on international law was, therefore, lawyer, statesman, and theologian; and the treatise on the law of nations is the result of his eminence in each of these walks of life. We are dealing with a practical man who, himself, was dealing with a practical subject which had been the cause of profound study and reflection on his part, and the outcome of professional activity. The treatise has held the attention of the world because of these qualities and of these qualifications; it is not a theoretical disquisition, although it is full of theory; it is not a philosophical dissertation, for Grotius was rather a logician than a philosopher; it was the amplification of a professional brief in the light of many years' experience after the case was ended. His contemporaries looked upon him as a man of affairs and as an international lawyer; and Sweden, at that time sharing with France the domination of the world, appointed him its Ambassador at the Court of France during the Thirty Years' War because of his experience in international law and with international relations. Indeed, that he wished to be looked upon as a man of affairs clearly appears in his epitaph, which he wrote himself with his own hand:

Grotius hic Hugo est: batavus, captivus et exsul,
Legatus regni, Suecia magna, tui.

The immense influence of the treatise of Grotius is doubtless due to the practical experience which he had had as a lawyer and as a man of affairs before its final composition.[2]

[1] Vol. ii (New York, 1902), pp. 403–4.

[2] In the critical biography which W. S. M. Knight has published, in this year of the tercentenary of the publication of Grotius's masterpiece, there is a passage expressing in a different and perhaps better way the reason for the pre-eminence of Grotius and the influence of his work: 'He made of Justice the foundation clearly and succinctly such of his system.... His detailed examination of public

The writings of the learned on questions of international law are entitled to respect ; the writings of the learned who have had experience are followed by nations. The contentions of nations are fought out in the chancelleries of the world. The claim of a nation is transmitted to the Ministry of Foreign Affairs, where it is examined in the light of its origin and according to the interest of the country. A principle of law is opposed to defeat the claim by the country against which it is brought. Better than principle is the practice of one or other nation in dispute, and stronger still are the precedents of many nations, which are likewise the permanent evidence of agreement upon conflicting views. It is the process of the law court on a larger scale where principle is opposed to principle, and precedent to precedent. The court is enlightened by the argument of contending counsel ; in full knowledge of the cause at issue and of the principles of law advanced as applicable it decides. A judgement is a precedent because it has been carefully considered and argued ; on the other hand, a judgement rendered without argument is treated with scant respect, and judges are wont from the bench to inform counsel who cite such a judgement as an authority, that it was decided without the benefit of argument.

Conceived in the practice of law, born in the law court, and matured in the study, the treatise on the law of nations has prevailed and still prevails, because of this extraordinary combination of theory and practice in the exposition of a subject in which nations are and must be interested, if their relations are to be decided by principles and their practical application.

It is rare that any man born of woman has a title to continued remembrance ; it is still rarer that he has more than one title ; and certainly there can be few in the annals of history who have more varied and more permanent claims to remembrance than Grotius, who in his youth was called the ' Miracle of Holland ',[1] and who has justified that title before posterity.

Great as are these titles, he is held in grateful remembrance for what many have called an incident in a busy life, but which we know was his very life, his work on the law of nations, which, written at various times, culminated in the three books on the law of war and peace.

If it is immortality to live in the lives of others, how sure must the immortality be of him who lived not merely in the lives of those with whom he came into contact when he was still a thing of flesh

and private law easily recalled to men's minds the inevitableness of Justice as both root and essence of that law. Then, almost unconsciously, they are moved on to international law, the law of war and of peace, as to a development of a similarly constituted law.' *The Life and Works of Hugo Grotius* (London, 1925), p. 210.

[1] Bynkershoek calls Grotius ὁ Μέγας in his *De Dominio Maris*, p. 374.

and blood, but who survives in the lives of subsequent centuries, and whose life has influenced nations and bids fair to control their actions for a period to which we can assign no definite bounds?

His book has become the law of nations of which it was the first systematic exposition, if, indeed, he is not the father of the system. Sir James Mackintosh,[1] a man of large and varied learning, impressionable and subject to emotion, has said, and truly, of the work of Grotius, that it 'is perhaps the most complete that the world has yet owed, at so early a stage in the progress of any science, to the genius and learning of one man'. And the judicious Hallam, who was not prone to exaggeration, and whose views are not coloured by enthusiasm, as he was a man of cold and discriminating judgement, may be considered as pronouncing the judgement of mankind upon Grotius and his services to international law when he says:

> The book may be considered as nearly original, in its general platform, as any work of man in an advanced stage of civilization and learning can be. It is more so, perhaps, than those of Montesquieu and Smith. No one had before gone to the foundations of international law so as to raise a complete and consistent superstructure; few had handled even separate parts, or laid down any satisfactory rules concerning it.[2]

Expressed differently, the views of Mackintosh and Hallam are to the effect that if everything which Grotius had written, or spoken, should pass away, leaving us only the three books *On the Law of War and Peace*, he would, indeed, have justified his existence.

It would be exaggeration, but it would be pardonable exaggeration, to say that his life and his works would alone give to his country a claim to remembrance, if the waters of oblivion should threaten it.

Perhaps the best comment upon his life and influence is that, although he gave war first place in the rights and duties of nations, any man writing to-day would give peace that predominance; in other words, the whole standard of thought has been changed, peace being in conception, and bound to be in fact, the normal state of things in any system of law; whereas war is at best an abnormal condition and as such opposed to a settlement of disputes according to any system of law which is itself derived from justice.

JAMES BROWN SCOTT.

THE HAGUE,
August 5, 1925.

[1] *A Discourse on the Study of the Law of Nature and Nations* (London, 1835), pp. 20–1.

[2] Henry Hallam, *Introduction to the Literature of Europe* (fourth edition, London, 1847), vol. ii, p. 545.

TRANSLATORS' PREFATORY NOTE

THE invitation to prepare an English translation of the *De Jure Belli ac Pacis* by Hugo Grotius was extended to Mr. Kelsey by Mr. Scott, of the Carnegie Endowment for International Peace, in June 1918. At that time the opinion was quite general that the World War would probably last for two years longer; and it was thought that if the translation could be made ready before the peace negotiations should begin, the publication would be particularly opportune. The invitation was accepted with the condition that the work might be divided, in order to facilitate progress.

The preparation of the manuscript was well under way when the Armistice came, and during the subsequent peace negotiations the undertaking was allowed to lag. Then, too, near the close of 1919, Mr. Kelsey was obliged to go abroad on a scientific mission which involved an absence of two years from the United States. Hence the delay in publication, which has now become opportune by reason of the tercentenary of the first publication of the *De Jure Belli ac Pacis* in 1625.

The translation, however, was made from the text of the edition published in Amsterdam in 1646, because this embodied the last revision of the author. In making the final draft for the printer, the translators have consulted the other editions published in the lifetime of Grotius and have had the advantage of consulting also the new edition of the text by P. C. Molhuysen, which was published in Leyden in 1919.

Of the translation it is necessary only to say that the aim has been to express the thought as Grotius might have expressed it if he had been writing in English rather than Latin. The previous translations into English, French, and German have been utilized; the one that has been found most useful is that by P. Pradier-Fodéré, to which an acknowledgement of special obligation is due.

In the division of the work, Mr. Kelsey is responsible for the translation to the end of Book I and for the final form of the remainder of the translation, also for the translation of the Commentary on the Epistle of Paul to Philemon; Mr. Sanders made the first draft of the translation for Book II, chapters 1–20, and Book III, chapters 18–25; Mr. Boak made the first draft of the translation for Book II, chapters 21–6, and Book III, chapters 1–17. Mr. Reeves revised the entire manuscript with special reference to the choice of the legal terms and phrases which would most clearly express the concepts of Grotius for readers of English to-day. Mr. Wright has collaborated in the work by reading the entire manuscript, by verifying the references in which the treatise abounds, and by correcting the proofs and preparing the indexes. Part of the manuscript was read also by Mr. H. E. Yntema, and preliminary work on the Index of Authors was done by James E. Dunlap.

In the notes as well as the text the titles of many works cited by Grotius in the Latin form are translated into English. While this is contrary to current practice, it was thought that not a few readers who are unfamiliar with the works themselves would welcome such translations as suggesting the character of the treatises to which Grotius referred. In the Index of Authors Cited, at the end of this volume, the English form of the title is in all cases followed by the Latin form which Grotius used.

A General Index to the translation appears at the end of this volume.

The translators regret that the scope of the undertaking did not permit the addition of foot-notes which should aim to throw light on Grotius's use of his sources, and thus to contribute to a better understanding of his method of work and point of view. Full references to the authors and works cited by Grotius will in most cases be found in the foot-notes in the edition of the text by Molhuysen; there still remain some references which thus far it has not been possible to verify. In this translation corrections of references given by Grotius, and additional references supplied by the translators, are set off by brackets. References to the Vulgate have been added where this differs from the Authorized Version.

The figures in heavy brackets inserted in the text and foot-notes indicate the beginnings of pages of the edition of 1646, which is photographically reproduced in Volume I.

A few other additions by the translators have been inserted in brackets.

THE TRANSLATORS.

UNIVERSITY OF MICHIGAN,
March 18, 1925.

[*The Title-Page of the Edition of 1646*]

HUGO GROTIUS

ON

THE LAW OF WAR AND PEACE

THREE BOOKS

Wherein are set forth the law of nature and of nations
Also the principles of public law

NEW EDITION

With the annotations of the author
Now much enlarged in consequence of his last revision
before his death

Whereto have been added also Notes on
THE EPISTLE OF PAUL TO PHILEMON

AMSTERDAM
JOHAN BLAEU
1646

[iii]

HUGO GROTIUS

TO THE MOST CHRISTIAN KING OF FRANCE AND NAVARRE

LOUIS XIII

Most eminent of Kings: This work presumes to inscribe your revered name in dedication because of confidence not in itself, nor in its author, but in its theme. For it has been written on behalf of justice, a virtue in so distinguishing a manner yours that in consequence, both from your own merits and from the general recognition of mankind, you have received a surname truly worthy of so great a king; you are now everywhere known by the name of Just no less than that of Louis. To the generals of ancient Rome titles drawn from the names of conquered peoples, from Crete, Numidia, Africa, Asia, and other lands, seemed the height of glory; but how much more glorious is your title, by which you are designated as an enemy everywhere, and vanquisher always, not of a nation, or of a person, but of that which is unjust!

The kings of Egypt thought it a great thing if men could say of them that one was devoted to his father, another to his mother, still another to his brothers. But of how slight moment are such particulars in the case of your title, which in its scope embraces not only such traits but all else that can be conceived as beautiful and virtuous! You are Just, when you honour the memory of your father, a king great beyond characterization, by following in his footsteps; [iv] Just, when you train your brother in all possible ways, but in no way more effectively than by your own example; Just, when you arrange marriages of the utmost distinction for your sisters; Just, when you call back to life laws that are on the verge of burial, and with all your strength set yourself against the trend of an age which is rushing headlong to destruction; Just, but at the same time merciful, when from subjects, whom a lack of knowledge of your goodness has turned aside from the path of duty, you take away nothing except the opportunity to do wrong, and when you offer no violence to souls that hold views different from your own in matters of religion; Just, and at the same time compassionate, when by the exercise of your authority you lighten the burdens of oppressed peoples and of downcast princes, and do not suffer too much to be left to Fortune.

Such extraordinary kindness, characteristic of you, and as like to that of God as the limitations of human nature permit, constrains me as an individual and on my own behalf to offer to you thanks even in this public dedication. For just as the heavenly bodies not only flood the vast expanses of the universe but suffer their force to descend to each living thing, so you, a most beneficent star upon the earth, not content to lift up princes and to succour peoples, willed to become a protection and solace also to me, who had been badly treated in my native country.

In order to complete the sum of virtues comprised in justice, to your acts of a public nature we must add the blamelessness and purity of your private life, which are worthy to be admired not alone by men but even by the spirits of heaven. For how many of the common run of mankind, how many even of [v] those who have cut themselves off from the world, are found to be as free from all faults as you are, though you occupy a station in life which is beset on all sides with innumerable enticements to wrongdoing? How great a thing it is in the midst of affairs, among the crowd, at the Court, surrounded by men who set examples of wrongdoing in so many different ways, to attain to that uprightness of character which to others, even in seclusion, comes with difficulty, and often not at all! This truly is to deserve not only the name of Just but even, while you are still living, that of Saint, which the unanimous agreement of good men conferred after death upon your ancestors Charlemagne and Louis [1]; this is to be in very truth Most Christian, not merely by a right inhering in your lineage but by a right inhering in yourself.

But while no aspect of justice is foreign to you, that nevertheless with which the matter of this work is concerned—the principles underlying war and peace—is in a peculiar sense your province because you are a king, and further, because you are King of France. Vast is this realm of yours, which stretches from sea to sea, across so many prosperous lands so great in extent; but you possess a kingdom greater than this, in that you do not covet kingdoms belonging to others. It is worthy of your devotion to duty, worthy of your exalted estate, not to attempt to despoil any one of his rights by force of arms, not to disturb ancient boundaries; but in war to continue the work of peace, and not to commence war save with the desire to end it at the earliest possible moment.

How noble it will be, how glorious, how joyful to your conscience, when God shall some day summon you to His kingdom, which alone is better than yours, to be able with boldness [vi] to

[1] [The reference is to Louis IX, who died near Tunis in 1270, while engaged in a Crusade, and was canonized in 1297; see Appendix, pages 863–4.]

say: 'This sword I received from Thee for the defence of justice, this I give back to Thee guilty of no blood rashly shed, stainless and innocent.' Hence it will come to pass that the rules which we now seek to draw from books will in the future be drawn from your acts as from a complete and perfect exemplification.

This will be a very great achievement. Yet the peoples of Christian lands are so bold as to ask of you something further, that, with the extinction of warfare everywhere, through your initiative peace may come again, not only to the nations but also to the churches, and that our time may learn to subject itself to the discipline of that age [1] which all we who are Christians acknowledge in true and sincere faith to have been Christian. Our hearts, wearied with strifes, are encouraged to such a hope by the friendship lately entered into between you and the King of Great Britain, who is most wise and singularly devoted to that holy peace; a friendship cemented by the most auspicious marriage of your sister.[2] Hard the task is by reason of partisan passions, fired by hatreds which blaze more fiercely day by day; but no task except one fraught with difficulty, except one that all others have given up in despair, is meet for so great kings.

May the God of Peace, the God of Justice, O just king, O peace-making king, heap upon your Majesty, which is nearest unto His own, not only all other blessings but with them also the distinction of having accomplished this task. MDCXXV.

[1] [The period of the Early Church, before there was a division into sects.]

[2] [In December 1624 Richelieu arranged a treaty of marriage between Henrietta Maria, sister of Louis XIII, and Charles, son of James I of England. James died in March 1625. In the following June Henrietta came to England and was married to Charles I.

PROLEGOMENA
TO THE THREE BOOKS
ON THE LAW OF WAR AND PEACE

1. The municipal law of Rome and of other states has been treated by many, who have undertaken to elucidate it by means of commentaries or to reduce it to a convenient digest. That body of law, however, which is concerned with the mutual relations among states or rulers of states, whether derived from nature, or established by divine ordinances, or having its origin in custom and tacit agreement, few have touched upon. Up to the present time no one has treated it in a comprehensive and systematic manner; yet the welfare of mankind demands that this task be accomplished.

2. Cicero justly characterized as of surpassing worth a knowledge of treaties of alliance, conventions, and understandings of peoples, kings and foreign nations; a knowledge, in short, of the whole law of war and peace. And to this knowledge Euripides gives the preference over an understanding of things divine and human; for he represents Theoclymenus as being thus addressed: [*For Balbus*, vi. 15.] [*Helena*, 928 f.]

> For you, who know the fate of men and gods,
> What is, what shall be, shameful would it be
> To know not what is just.

3. Such a work is all the more necessary because in our day, as in former times, there is no lack of men who view this branch of law with contempt as having no reality outside of an empty name. On the lips of men quite generally is the saying of Euphemus, which Thucydides quotes,[1] that in the case of a king or imperial city nothing is unjust which is expedient. Of like implication is the statement that for those whom fortune favours might makes right, and that the administration of a state cannot be carried on without injustice.

Furthermore, the controversies which arise between peoples or kings generally have Mars as their arbiter. That war is irreconcilable with all law is a view held not alone by the ignorant populace; expressions are often let slip by well-informed and thoughtful men which lend countenance to such a view. Nothing is more common than the assertion of antagonism between law and arms. Thus Ennius says: [In Gellius, xx. 10.]

> Not on grounds of right is battle joined,
> But rather with the sword do men
> Seek to enforce their claims.

[1] [xix] The words are in Book VI [VI. lxxxv]. The same thought is found in Book V [V. lxxxix], where the Athenians, who at the time of speaking were very powerful, thus address the Melians: 'According to human standards those arrangements are accounted just which are settled when the necessity on both sides is equal; as for the rest, the more powerful do all they can, the more weak endure.'

[*Art of Poetry*, 122.] Horace, too, describes the savage temper of Achilles in this wise:

> Laws, he declares, were not for him ordained;
> By dint of arms he claims all for himself.

[Lucan, I. 225.] Another poet depicts another military leader as commencing war with the words:

> Here peace and violated laws I leave behind.

[Plutarch, *Fort. of Alex.*, 330 E.] [*Apoth.*, 202 D; *Marius*, xxviii = 421 E.] Antigonus when advanced in years ridiculed a man who brought to him a treatise on justice when he was engaged in besieging cities that did not belong to him. Marius declared that the din of arms made it impossible for him to hear the voice of the laws.[1] Even Pompey, whose expression of countenance was so mild, dared to say: 'When I am in arms, am I to think of laws?'[2]

4. Among Christian writers a similar thought finds frequent expression. [*An Answer to the Jews*, vii] A single quotation from Tertullian may serve in place of many: 'Deception, harshness, and injustice are the regular business of battles.' They who so think will no doubt wish to confront us with this passage in Comedy: [Terence *Eunuch*, I. i. 16 ff.]

> [viii] These things uncertain should you, by reason's aid,
> Try to make certain, no more would you gain
> Than if you tried by reason to go mad.

5. Since our discussion concerning law will have been undertaken in vain if there is no law, in order to open the way for a favourable reception of our work and at the same time to fortify it against attacks, this very serious error must be briefly refuted. In order that we may not be obliged to deal with a crowd of opponents, let us assign to them a pleader. And whom should we choose in preference to Carneades? For he had attained to so perfect a mastery of the peculiar tenet of his Academy that he was able to devote the power of his eloquence to the service of falsehood not less readily than to that of truth.

Carneades, then, having undertaken to hold a brief against justice, in particular against that phase of justice with which we are concerned, was able to muster no argument stronger than this, that, for reasons of expediency, men imposed upon themselves laws, which vary according to customs, and among the same peoples often undergo changes as times change; moreover that there is no law of

[1] In Plutarch Lysander displaying his sword says [*Apothegms, Lysander*, iii = 190 E]: 'He who is master of this is in the best position to discuss questions relating to boundaries between countries.'

In the same author Caesar declares [*Caesar*, xxxv = 725 B]: 'The time for arms is not the time for laws.'

Similarly Seneca, *On Benefits*, IV. xxxviii [IV. xxxvii]: 'At times, especially in time of war, kings make many grants with their eyes shut. One just man cannot satisfy so many passionate desires of men in arms; no one can at the same time act the part of a good man and good commander.'

[2] This view-point of Pompey in relation to the Mamertines Plutarch expresses thus [*Pompey*, x = 623 D]: 'Will you not stop quoting laws to us who are girt with swords?' Curtius says in Book IX [IX. iv. 7]: 'Even to such a degree does war reverse the laws of nature.'

nature, because all creatures, men as well as animals, are impelled by nature toward ends advantageous to themselves; that, consequently, there is no justice, or, if such there be, it is supreme folly, since one does violence to his own interests if he consults the advantage of others.

6. What the philosopher here says, and the poet reaffirms in verse, [Horace, *Satires*, I. iii. 113.]

> And just from unjust Nature cannot know,

must not for one moment be admitted. Man is, to be sure, an animal, but an animal of a superior kind, much farther removed from all other animals than the different kinds of animals are from one another; evidence on this point may be found in the many traits peculiar to the human species. But among the traits characteristic of man is an impelling desire for society, that is, for the social life—not of any and every sort, but peaceful, and organized according to the measure of his intelligence, with those who are of his own kind; this social trend the Stoics called 'sociableness'.[1] Stated as a universal truth, therefore, the assertion that every animal is impelled by nature to seek only its own good cannot be conceded.

7. Some of the other animals, in fact, do in a way restrain the appetency for that which is good for themselves alone, to the advantage, now of their offspring, now of other animals of the same species.[2]

[1] Chrysostom, *On Romans*, Homily XXXI [Homily V, i, on chap. i, verse 31]: 'We men have by nature a kind of fellowship with men; why not, when even wild beasts in their relation to one another have something similar?'

See also the same author, *On Ephesians*, chap. i [Homily I], where he explains that the seeds of virtue have been implanted in us by nature. The emperor Marcus Aurelius, a philosopher of parts, said [V. xvi]: 'It was long ago made clear that we were born for fellowship. Is it not evident that the lower exist for the sake of the higher, and the higher for one another's sake?'

[2] There is an old proverb, 'Dogs do not eat the flesh of dogs'. Says Juvenal [*Sat.* xv. 163, 159]:

> Tigress with ravening tigress keeps the peace;
> The wild beast spares its spotted kin.

There is a fine passage of Philo, in his commentary on the Fifth Commandment, which he who will may read in Greek. As it is somewhat long, I shall here quote it only once and in Latin [Philo, *On the Ten Commandments*, xxiii, in English as follows]:

'Men, be ye at least imitators of dumb brutes. They, trained through kindness, know how to repay in turn. Dogs defend our homes; they even suffer death for their masters, if danger has suddenly come upon them. It is said that shepherd dogs go in advance of their flocks, fighting till death, if need be, that they may protect the shepherds from hurt. Of things disgraceful is not the most disgraceful this, that in return of kindness man should be outdone by a dog, the gentlest creature by the most fierce?

'But if we fail to draw our proper lesson from the things of earth, let us pass to the realm of winged creatures that make voyage through the air, that from them we may learn our duty. Aged storks, unable to fly, stay in their nests. Their offspring fly, so to say, over all lands and seas, seeking sustenance in all places for their parents; these, in consideration of their age, deservedly enjoy quiet, abundance, even comforts. And the younger storks console themselves for the irksomeness of their voyaging [xx] with the consciousness of their discharge of filial duty and the expectation of similar treatment on the part of their offspring, when they too have grown old. Thus they pay back, at the time when needed, the debt they owe, returning what they have received; for from others they cannot obtain sustenance either at the beginning of life, when they are small, or, when they have become old, at life's end. From no other teacher than nature herself have they learned to care for the aged, just as they themselves were cared for when they were young.

'Should not they who do not take care of their parents have reason to hide themselves for very

This aspect of their behaviour has its origin, we believe, in some extrinsic intelligent principle, because with regard to other actions, which involve no more difficulty than those referred to, a like degree of intelligence is not manifest in them. The same thing must be said of children. In children, even before their training has begun, some disposition to do good to others appears, as Plutarch sagely observed; thus sympathy for others comes out spontaneously at that age. The mature man in fact has knowledge which prompts him to similar actions under similar conditions,[1] together with an impelling desire for society, for the gratification of which he alone among animals possesses a special instrument, speech. He has also been endowed with the faculty of knowing and of acting in accordance with general principles. Whatever accords with that faculty is not common to all animals, but peculiar to the nature of man.

[*Consolation*, 608 D.]

8. This maintenance of the social order,[2] which we have roughly sketched, and which is consonant with human intelligence, is the source of law properly so called. To this sphere of law belong the abstaining from that which is another's,[3] the restoration to another of anything of his which we may have, together with any gain which

shame when they hear this—they that neglect those whom alone, or above all others, they ought to help, especially when by so doing they are not really called upon to give, but merely to return what they owe? Children have as their own nothing to which their parents do not possess a prior claim; their parents have either given them what they have, or have furnished to them the means of acquisition.'

In regard to the extraordinary care of doves for their young, see Porphyry, *On Abstaining from Animal Food*, Book III; concerning the regard of the parrot-fish and lizard-fish for their kind, see Cassiodorus, [*Variae*,] XI. xl.

[1] Marcus Aurelius, Book IX [IX. xlii]: 'Man was born to benefit others'; also [IX. ix]: 'It would be easier to find a thing of earth out of relation with the earth than a human being wholly cut off from human kind'. The same author in Book X [X. ii]: 'That which has the use of reason necessarily also craves civic life.'

Nicetas of Chonae [*On Isaac Angelus*, III. ix]: 'Nature has ingrained in us, and implanted in our souls, a feeling for our kin.' Add what Augustine says, *On Christian Doctrine*, III. xiv.

[2] Seneca, *On Benefits*, Book IV, chap. xviii: 'That the warm feeling of a kindly heart is in itself desirable you may know from this, that ingratitude is something which in itself men ought to flee from, since nothing so dismembers and destroys the harmonious union of the human race as does this fault. Upon what other resource, pray tell, can we rely for safety, than mutual aid through reciprocal services? This alone it is, this interchange of kindnesses, which makes our life well equipped, and well fortified against sudden attacks.

'Imagine ourselves as isolated individuals, what are we? The prey, the victims of brute beasts—blood most cheap, and easiest to ravage; for to all other animals strength sufficient for their own protection has been given. The beasts that are born to wander and to pass segregate lives are provided with weapons; man is girt round about with weakness. Him no strength of claws or teeth makes formidable to others. To man [deity] gave two resources, reason and society; exposed as he was to danger from all other creatures, these resources rendered him the most powerful of all. Thus he who in isolation could not be the equal of any creature, is become the master of the world.

'It was society which gave to man dominion over all other living creatures; man, born for the land, society transferred to a sovereignty of a different nature, bidding him exercise dominion over the sea also. Society has checked the violence of disease, has provided succour for old age, has given comfort against sorrows. It makes us brave because it can be invoked against Fortune. Take this away and you will destroy the sense of oneness in the human race, by which life is sustained. It is, in fact, taken away, if you shall cause that an ungrateful heart is not to be avoided on its own account.'

[3] Porphyry, *On Abstaining from Animal Food*, Book III [III. xxvi]: 'Justice consists in the abstaining from what belongs to others, and in doing no harm to those who do no harm.'

we may have received from it; the obligation to fulfil promises, the making good of a loss incurred through our fault, and the inflicting of penalties upon men according to their deserts.

9. From this signification of the word law there has flowed another and more extended meaning. Since over other animals man has the advantage of possessing not only a strong bent towards social life, of which we have spoken, but also a power of discrimination which enables him to [ix] decide what things are agreeable or harmful (as to both things present and things to come), and what can lead to either alternative: in such things it is meet for the nature of man, within the limitations of human intelligence, to follow the direction of a well-tempered judgement, being neither led astray by fear or the allurement of immediate pleasure, nor carried away by rash impulse. Whatever is clearly at variance with such judgement is understood to be contrary also to the law of nature, that is, to the nature of man.

10. To this exercise of judgement belongs moreover the rational allotment [1] to each man, or to each social group, of those things which are properly theirs, in such a way as to give the preference now to him who is more wise over the less wise, now to a kinsman rather than to a stranger, now to a poor man rather than to a man of means, as the conduct of each or the nature of the thing suggests. Long ago the view came to be held by many, that this discriminating allotment is a part of law, properly and strictly so called; nevertheless law, properly defined, has a far different nature, because its essence lies in leaving to another that which belongs to him, or in fulfilling our obligations to him.

11. What we have been saying would have a degree of validity even if we should concede that which cannot be conceded without the utmost wickedness, that there is no God, or that the affairs of men are of no concern to Him. The very opposite of this view has been implanted in us partly by reason, partly by unbroken tradition, and confirmed by many proofs as well as by miracles attested by all ages. Hence it follows that we must without exception render obedience to God as our Creator, to Whom we owe all that we are and have; especially since, in manifold ways, He has shown Himself supremely good and supremely powerful, so that to those who obey Him He is able to give supremely great rewards, even rewards that are eternal, since He Himself is eternal. We ought, moreover, to believe that He has willed to give rewards, and all the more should we cherish such a belief if He has so promised in plain words; that He has done this, we Christians believe, convinced by the indubitable assurance of testimonies.

[1] Ambrose treats this subject in his first book *On Duties* [I. xxx].

12. Herein, then, is another source of law besides the source in nature, that is, the free will of God,[1] to which beyond all cavil our reason tells us we must render obedience. But the law of nature of which we have spoken, comprising alike that which relates to the social life of man and that which is so called in a larger sense, proceeding as it does from the essential traits implanted in man, can nevertheless rightly be attributed to God,[2] because of His having willed that such traits exist in us. In this sense, too, Chrysippus and the Stoics used to say that the origin of law should be sought in no other source than Jupiter himself; and from the name Jupiter[3] the Latin word for law (*ius*) was probably derived.

13. There is an additional consideration in that, by means of the laws which He has given, God has made those fundamental traits more manifest, even to those who possess feebler reasoning powers; and He has forbidden us to yield to impulses drawing us in opposite directions—affecting now our own interest, now the interest of others—in an effort to control more effectively our more violent impulses and to restrain them within proper limits.

14. But sacred history, besides enjoining rules of conduct, in no slight degree reinforces man's inclination towards sociableness by teaching that all men are sprung from the same first parents. In
Dig. I. i. 3. this sense we can rightly affirm also that which Florentinus asserted from another point of view, that a blood-relationship has been established among us by nature; consequently it is wrong for a man to set a snare for a fellow-man. Among mankind generally one's parents are as it were divinities,[4] and to them is owed an obedience which, if not unlimited, is nevertheless of an altogether special kind.

15. Again, since it is a rule of the law of nature to abide by pacts (for it was necessary that among men there be some method of obligating themselves one to another, and no other natural method can be imagined), out of this source the bodies of municipal law have arisen. For those who had associated themselves with some

[1] [xxi] Hence, in the judgement of Marcus Aurelius, Book IX [IX. i]: 'He who commits injustice is guilty of impiety.'

[2] Chrysostom, *On First Corinthians*, xi. 3 [Homily XXVI, iii]: 'When I say nature I mean God, for He is the creator of nature.' Chrysippus in his third book *On the Gods* [Plutarch, *On the Contradictions of the Stoics*, ix = *Morals*, 1035 C]: 'No other beginning or origin of justice can be found than in Jupiter and common nature; from that source must the beginning be traced when men undertake to treat of good and evil.'

[3] Unless perhaps it would be more true to say that the Latin word for 'right', *ius*, is derived, by process of cutting down, from the word for 'command', *iussum*, forming *ius*, genitive *iusis*, just as the word for 'bone', *os*, was shortened from *ossum*; *iusis* afterwards becoming *iuris*, as *Papirii* was formed from *Papisii*, in regard to which see Cicero, *Letters*, Book IX. xxi [*Ad Fam.* IX. xxi. 2].

[4] Hierocles, in his commentary on the *Golden Verse* [rather *How parents should be treated*, quoted by Stobaeus, *Anthology*, tit. lxxix. 53], calls parents 'gods upon earth'; Philo, *On the Ten Commandments* [chap. xxiii], 'Visible gods, who imitate the Unbegotten God in giving life'. Next after the relationship between God and man comes the relationship between parent and child; Jerome, *Letters*, xcii [cxvii. 2]. Parents are the likenesses of gods; Plato, *Laws*, Book XI [XI. 11]. Honour is due to parents as to gods; Aristotle, *Nicomachean Ethics*, Book IX, chap. ii.

group, or had subjected themselves to a man or to men, [x] had either expressly promised, or from the nature of the transaction must be understood impliedly to have promised, that they would conform to that which should have been determined, in the one case by the majority, in the other by those upon whom authority had been conferred.

16. What is said, therefore, in accordance with the view not only of Carneades but also of others, that

> Expediency is, as it were, the mother
> Of what is just and fair,[1]

is not true, if we wish to speak accurately. For the very nature of man, which even if we had no lack of anything would lead us into the mutual relations of society, is the mother of the law of nature. But the mother of municipal law is that obligation which arises from mutual consent; and since this obligation derives its force from the law of nature, nature may be considered, so to say, the great-grandmother of municipal law.

The law of nature nevertheless has the reinforcement of expediency; for the Author of nature willed that as individuals we should be weak, and should lack many things needed in order to live properly, to the end that we might be the more constrained to cultivate the social life. But expediency afforded an opportunity also for municipal law, since that kind of association of which we have spoken, and subjection to authority, have their roots in expediency. From this it follows that those who prescribe laws for others in so doing are accustomed to have, or ought to have, some advantage in view.

17. But just as the laws of each state have in view the advantage of that state, so by mutual consent it has become possible that certain laws should originate as between all states, or a great many states; and it is apparent that the laws thus originating had in view the advantage, not of particular states, but of the great society of states. And this is what is called the law of nations, whenever we distinguish that term from the law of nature.

This division of law Carneades passed over altogether. For he divided all law into the law of nature and the law of particular countries. Nevertheless if undertaking to treat of the body of law which is maintained between states—for he added a statement in regard to war and things acquired by means of war—he would surely have been obliged to make mention of this law.

18. Wrongly, moreover, does Carneades ridicule justice as folly.

[1] In regard to this passage Acron, or some other ancient interpreter of Horace [*Sat.* I. iii. 98]: 'The poet is writing in opposition to the teachings of the Stoics. He wishes to show that justice does not have its origin in nature but is born of expediency.' For the opposite view see Augustine's argument, *On Christian Doctrine*, Book III, chap. xiv.

For since, by his own admission, the national who in his own country obeys its laws is not foolish, even though, out of regard for that law, he may be obliged to forgo certain things advantageous for himself, so that nation is not foolish which does not press its own advantage to the point of disregarding the laws common to nations. The reason in either case is the same. For just as the national, who violates the law of his country in order to obtain an immediate advantage,[1] breaks down that by which the advantages of himself and his posterity are for all future time assured, so the state which transgresses the laws of nature and of nations cuts away also the bulwarks which safeguard its own future peace. Even if no advantage were to be contemplated from the keeping of the law, it would be a mark of wisdom, not of folly, to allow ourselves to be drawn towards that to which we feel that our nature leads.

[Horace, *Satires*, I. iii. 111.]

19. Wherefore, in general, it is by no means true that

> You must confess that laws were framed
> From fear of the unjust,[2]

[*Republic*, II. ii; *Gorgias*, xxxviii.]

a thought which in Plato some one explains thus, that laws were invented from fear of receiving injury, and that men are constrained by a kind of force to cultivate justice. For that relates only to the institutions and laws which have been devised to facilitate the enforcement of right; as when many persons in themselves weak, in order that they might not be overwhelmed by the more powerful, leagued themselves together to establish tribunals and by combined force to maintain these, that as a united whole they might prevail against those with whom as individuals they could not cope.

[Plutarch, *Solon*, xv.]

And in this sense we may readily admit also the truth of the saying that right is that which is acceptable to the stronger; so that we may understand that law fails of its outward effect unless it has a sanction behind it. In this way Solon accomplished very great results, as he himself used to declare,

> [xi] By joining force and law together,
> Under a like bond.

[*Gorgias*, lxxx.]

20. Nevertheless law, even though without a sanction, is not entirely void of effect. For justice brings peace of conscience, while injustice causes torments and anguish, such as Plato describes, in the breast of tyrants. Justice is approved, and injustice condemned, by

[1] This comparison Marcus Aurelius pertinently uses in Book IX [IX. xxiii]: 'Every act of thine that has no relation, direct or indirect, to the common interest, rends thy life and does not suffer it to be one; such an act is not less productive of disintegration than he is who creates a dissension among a people.' The same author, Book XI [XI. viii]: 'A man cut off from a single fellow-man cannot but be considered as out of fellowship with the whole human race.' In effect, as the same Antoninus says [VI. liv]: 'What is advantageous to the swarm is advantageous to the bee.'

[2] As Ovid says [*Metamorphoses*, VIII. 59]:

> Strong is the cause when arms the cause maintain.

the common agreement of good men. But, most important of all, in God injustice finds an enemy, justice a protector. He reserves His judgements for the life after this, yet in such a way that He often causes their effects to become manifest even in this life, as history teaches by numerous examples.

21. Many hold, in fact, that the standard of justice which they insist upon in the case of individuals within the state is inapplicable to a nation or the ruler of a nation. The reason for the error lies in this, first of all, that in respect to law they have in view nothing except the advantage which accrues from it, such advantage being apparent in the case of citizens who, taken singly, are powerless to protect themselves. But great states, since they seem to contain in themselves all things required for the adequate protection of life, seem not to have need of that virtue which looks toward the outside, and is called justice.

22. But, not to repeat what I have said, that law is not founded on expediency alone, there is no state so powerful that it may not some time need the help of others outside itself, either for purposes of trade, or even to ward off the forces of many foreign nations united against it. In consequence we see that even the most powerful peoples and sovereigns seek alliances, which are quite devoid of significance according to the point of view of those who confine law within the boundaries of states. Most true is the saying, that all things are uncertain the moment men depart from law.

23. If no association of men can be maintained without law, as Aristotle showed by his remarkable illustration drawn from brigands,[1] [Stobaeus, x. 50.] surely also that association which binds together the human race, or binds many nations together, has need of law; this was perceived [Cicero, *On Duties*, I. xlv. 159.] by him who said that shameful deeds ought not to be committed even for the sake of one's country. Aristotle takes sharply to task[2] [*Politics*, VII. ii.]

[1] Chrysostom, *On Ephesians*, chap. iv [Homily IX, iii]: 'But how does it happen, some one will say, that brigands live on terms of peace? And when? Tell me, I pray. This happens, in fact, when they are not acting as brigands; for if, in dividing up their loot, they did not observe the precepts of justice and make an equitable apportionment, you would see them engaged in strifes and battles among themselves.'

Plutarch [*Pyrrhus*, ix = 388 A] quotes the saying of Pyrrhus, that he would leave his kingdom to that one of his children who should have the sharpest [xxii] sword, declaring that this has the same implication as the verse of Euripides in the *Phoenician Maidens* [line 68]:

That they with gory steel the house divide.

He adds, moreover, the noble sentiment: 'So inimical to the social order, and ruthless, is the determination to possess more than is one's own!'

Cicero, *Letters*, XI. xvi [*Ad Fam.* IX. xvi. 3]: 'All things are uncertain when one departs from law.' Polybius, Book IV [IV. xxix. 4]: 'This above all other causes breaks up the private organizations of criminals and thieves, that they cease to deal fairly with one another; in fine, that good faith among them has perished.'

[2] Plutarch, *Agesilaus* [xxxvii = 617 D]: 'In their conception of honour the Lacedaemonians assign the first place to the advantage of their country; they neither know nor learn any other kind of right than that which they think will advance the interests of Sparta.'

In regard to the same Lacedaemonians the Athenians declared, in Thucydides, Book V [V. cv]: 'In relations with one another and according to their conception of civil rights they are most strict those who, while unwilling to allow any one to exercise authority over themselves except in accordance with law, yet are quite indifferent as to whether foreigners are treated according to law or not.

24. That same Pompey, whom I just now quoted for the opposite view, corrected the statement which a king of Sparta had made, that that state is the most fortunate whose boundaries are fixed by spear and sword; he declared that that state is truly fortunate which has justice for its boundary line. On this point he might have invoked the authority of another king of Sparta, who gave the preference to justice over bravery in war,[1] using this argument, that bravery ought to be directed by a kind of justice, but if all men were just they would have no need for bravery in war.

Bravery itself the Stoics defined as virtue fighting on behalf of [x=p. 132 B C.] equity. Themistius in his address to Valens argues with eloquence that kings who measure up to the rule of wisdom make account not only of the nation which has been committed to them, but of the whole human race, and that they are, as he himself says, not 'friends of the Macedonians' alone, or 'friends of the Romans',[2] but 'friends of mankind'. The name of Minos [3] became odious to future ages for no other reason than this, that he limited his fair-dealing to the boundaries of his realm.

25. Least of all should that be admitted which some people imagine, that in war all laws are in abeyance. On the contrary war ought not to be undertaken except for the enforcement of rights; when once undertaken, it should be carried on only within the bounds of law and good faith. Demosthenes well said that war is directed against those who cannot be held in check by judicial processes. For judgements are efficacious against those who feel that they are too weak to resist; against those who are equally strong, or think that they are, wars [xii] are undertaken. But in order that wars may be justified, they must be carried on with not less scrupulousness than judicial processes are wont to be.

[*On the Affairs in the Chersonese*, viii. 29.]

26. Let the laws be silent, then, in the midst of arms, but only the laws of the State, those that the courts are concerned with, that

in their practice of virtue. But with respect to others, though many considerations bearing upon the subject might be brought forward, he will state the fact in a word who will say that in their view what is agreeable is honourable, what is advantageous is just.'

[1] Hearing that the king of the Persians was called great, Agesilaus remarked: 'Wherein is he greater than I, if he is not more just?' The saying is quoted by Plutarch [*Apophthegms, Agesilaus,* lxiii = *Morals,* 213 C].

[2] Marcus Aurelius exceedingly well remarks [VI. xliv]: 'As Antoninus, my city and country are Rome; as a man, the world.' Porphyry, *On Abstaining from Animal Food,* Book III [III. xxvii]: 'He who is guided by reason keeps himself blameless in relation to his fellow-citizens, likewise also in relation to strangers and men in general; the more submissive to reason, the more godlike a man is.'

[3] In regard to Minos there is a verse of an ancient poet:

Under the yoke of Minos all the island groaned.

On this point see Cyril, *Against Julian,* Book VI.

are adapted only to a state of peace; not those other laws, which are of perpetual validity and suited to all times. It was exceedingly well said by Dio of Prusa, that between enemies written laws, that is, laws of particular states, are not in force, but that unwritten laws [1] are in force, that is, those which nature prescribes, or the agreement of nations has established. This is set forth by that ancient formula of the Romans, 'I think that those things ought to be sought by means of a war that is blameless and righteous.' [*Orations*, lxxvi.] [Livy, I. xxxii. 12.]

The ancient Romans, as Varro noted, were slow in undertaking war, and permitted themselves no licence in that matter, because they held the view that a war ought not to be waged except when free from reproach. Camillus said that wars should be carried on justly no less than bravely; Scipio Africanus, that the Roman people commenced and ended wars justly. In another passage you may read: 'War has its laws no less than peace.' Still another writer admires Fabricius as a great man who maintained his probity in war—a thing most difficult—and believed that even in relation to an enemy there is such a thing as wrongdoing. [In Nonius, XII.] [Livy, V. xxvii. 6; XXX xvi. 9.] [V. xxvii. 6.] [Seneca, *Letters*, cxx. 6.]

27. The historians in many a passage reveal how great in war is the influence of the consciousness that one has justice on his side; [2] they often attribute victory chiefly to this cause. Hence the proverbs, that a soldier's strength is broken or increased by his cause; that he who has taken up arms unjustly rarely comes back in safety; that

[1] Thus King Alphonse, being asked whether he owed a greater debt to books or to arms, said that from books he had learned both the practice and laws of arms. Plutarch [*Camillus*, x = 134 B]: 'Among good men certain laws even of war are recognized, and a victory ought not to be striven for in such a way as not to spurn an advantage arising from wicked and impious actions.'

[2] Pompey well says in Appian [*Civil Wars*, II. viii. 51]: 'We ought to trust in the gods and in the cause of a war which has been undertaken with the honourable and just [xxiii] purpose of defending the institutions of our country.' In the same author Cassius [*Civil Wars*, IV. xii. 97]: 'In wars the greatest hope lies in the justice of the cause.' Josephus, *Antiquities of the Jews*, Book XV [XV. v. 3]: 'God is with those who have right on their side.'

Procopius has a number of passages of similar import. One is in the speech of Belisarius, after he had started on his expedition to Africa [*Vandalic War*, I. xii. 21]: 'Bravery is not going to give the victory, unless it has justice as a fellow-soldier.' Another is in the speech of the same general before the battle not far from Carthage [I. xii. 19]. A third is in the address of the Lombards to the Herulians, where the following words, as corrected by me, are found [*Gothic War*, II. xiv]: 'We call to witness God, the slightest manifestation of whose power is equal to all human strength. He, as may well be believed, making account of the causes of war, will give to each side the outcome of battle which each deserves.' This saying was soon afterward confirmed by a wonderful occurrence.

In the same author Totila thus addresses the Goths [*Gothic War*, III. viii]: 'It cannot, it cannot happen, I say, that they who resort to violence and injustice can win renown in fighting; but as the life of each is, such the fortune of war that falls to his lot.' Soon after the taking of Rome Totila made another speech bearing on the same point [*Gothic War*, III. xxi].

Agathias, Book II [*Histories*, II. i]: 'Injustice and forgetfulness of God are to be shunned always, and are harmful, above all, in war and in time of battle.' This statement he elsewhere proves by the notable illustrations of Darius, Xerxes, and the Athenians in Sicily [*Histories*, II. x]. See also the speech of Crispinus to the people of Aquileia, in Herodian, Book VIII [*Histories*, VIII. iii. 5, 6].

In Thucydides, Book VII [VII. xviii], we find the Lacedaemonians reckoning the disasters which they had suffered in Pylus and elsewhere as due to themselves, because they had refused a settlement by arbitration which had been offered them. But as afterward the Athenians, having committed many wicked deeds, refused arbitration, a hope of greater success in their operations revived in the Lacedaemonians.

hope is the comrade of a good cause; and others of the same purport.

No one ought to be disturbed, furthermore, by the successful outcome of unjust enterprises. For it is enough that the fairness of the cause exerts a certain influence, even a strong influence upon actions, although the effect of that influence, as happens in human affairs, is often nullified by the interference of other causes. Even for winning friendships, of which for many reasons nations as well as individuals have need, a reputation for having undertaken war not rashly nor unjustly, and of having waged it in a manner above reproach, is exceedingly efficacious. No one readily allies himself with those in whom he believes that there is only a slight regard for law, for the right, and for good faith.

28. Fully convinced, by the considerations which I have advanced, that there is a common law among nations, which is valid alike for war and in war, I have had many and weighty reasons for undertaking to write upon this subject. Throughout the Christian world I observed a lack of restraint in relation to war, such as even barbarous races should be ashamed of; I observed that men rush to arms for slight causes, or no cause at all, and that when arms have once been taken up there is no longer any respect for law, divine or human; it is as if, in accordance with a general decree, frenzy had openly been let loose for the committing of all crimes.

29. Confronted with such utter ruthlessness many men, who are the very furthest from being bad men, have come to the point of forbidding all use of arms to the Christian,[1] whose rule of conduct above everything else comprises the duty of loving all men. To this opinion sometimes John Ferus [Johann Wild] and my fellow-countryman Erasmus seem to incline, men who have the utmost devotion to peace in both Church and State; but their purpose, as I take it, is, when things have gone in one direction, to force them in the opposite direction, as we are accustomed to do, that they may come back to a true middle ground. But the very effort of pressing too hard in the opposite direction is often so far from being helpful that it does harm, because in such arguments the detection of what is extreme is easy, and results in weakening the influence of other statements which are well within the bounds of truth. For both extremes therefore a remedy must be found, that men may not believe either that nothing is allowable, or that everything is.

30. At the same time through devotion to study in private life I have wished—as the only course now open to me, undeservedly

[1] Tertullian, *On the Resurrection of the Flesh* [chap. xvi]: 'The sword which has become blood-stained honourably in war, and has thus been employed in man-killing of a better sort.'

forced out from my native land, which had been graced by so many of my labours—to contribute somewhat to the philosophy of the law, which previously, in public service, I practised with the utmost degree of probity of which I was capable. [xiii] Many heretofore have purposed to give to this subject a well-ordered presentation ; no one has succeeded. And in fact such a result cannot be accomplished unless—a point which until now has not been sufficiently kept in view—those elements which come from positive law are properly separated from those which arise from nature. For the principles of the law of nature, since they are always the same, can easily be brought into a systematic form ; but the elements of positive law, since they often undergo change and are different in different places, are outside the domain of systematic treatment, just as other notions of particular things are.

31. If now those who have consecrated themselves to true justice should undertake to treat the parts of the natural and unchangeable philosophy of law, after having removed all that has its origin in the free will of man ; if one, for example, should treat legislation, another taxation, another the administration of justice, another the determination of motives, another the proving of facts, then by assembling all these parts a body of jurisprudence could be made up.

32. What procedure we think should be followed we have shown by deed rather than by words in this work, which treats by far the noblest part of jurisprudence.

33. In the first book, having by way of introduction spoken of the origin of law, we have examined the general question, whether there is any such thing as a just war ; then, in order to determine the differences between public war and private war, we found it necessary to explain the nature of sovereignty—what nations, what kings possess complete sovereignty ; who possess sovereignty only in part, who with right of alienation, who otherwise ; then it was necessary to speak also concerning the duty of subjects to their superiors.

34. The second book, having for its object to set forth all the causes from which war can arise, undertakes to explain fully what things are held in common, what may be owned in severalty ; what rights persons have over persons, what obligation arises from ownership ; what is the rule governing royal successions ; what right is established by a pact or a contract ; what is the force of treaties of alliance ; what of an oath private or public, and how it is necessary to interpret these ; what is due in reparation for damage done ; in what the inviolability of ambassadors consists ; what law controls the burial of the dead, and what is the nature of punishments.

35. The third book has for its subject, first, what is permissible in war. Having distinguished that which is done with impunity, or even that which among foreign peoples is defended as lawful, from that which actually is free from fault, it proceeds to the different kinds of peace, and all compacts relating to war.

36. The undertaking seemed to me all the more worth while because, as I have said, no one has dealt with the subject-matter as a whole, and those who have treated portions of it have done so in a way to leave much to the labours of others. Of the ancient philosophers nothing in this field remains; either of the Greeks, among whom Aristotle had composed a book with the title *Rights of War*, or—what was especially to be desired—of those who gave their allegiance to the young Christianity. Even the books of the ancient Romans on fetial law have transmitted to us nothing of themselves except the title. Those who have made collections of the cases which are called 'cases of conscience' have merely written chapters on war, promises, oaths, and reprisals, just as on other subjects.

37. I have seen also special books on the law of war, some by theologians, as Franciscus de Victoria, Henry of Gorkum, William Matthaei;[1] others by doctors of law, as John Lupus, Franciscus Arias, Giovanni da Legnano, Martinus Laudensis. All of these, however, have said next to nothing upon a most fertile subject; most of them have done their work without system, and in such a way as to intermingle and utterly confuse what belongs to the law of nature, to divine law, to the law of nations, to civil law, and to the body of law which is found in the canons.

38. What all these writers especially lacked, the illumination of history, the very learned [xiv] Faur undertook to supply in some chapters of his *Semestria*, but in a manner limited by the scope of his own work, and only through the citation of authorities. The same thing was attempted on a larger scale, and by referring a great number of examples to some general statements, by Balthazar Ayala; and still more fully, by Alberico Gentili. Knowing that others can derive profit from Gentili's painstaking, as I acknowledge that I have, I leave it to his readers to pass judgement on the shortcomings of his work as regards method of exposition, arrangement of matter, delimitation of inquiries, and distinctions between the various kinds of law. This only I shall say, that in treating controversial questions it is his frequent practice to base his conclusions on a few examples, which are not in all cases worthy of approval, or even to follow the opinions of modern jurists, formulated in arguments of which not

[1] To these add the work of Joannes de Carthagena, published at Rome in 1609.

a few were accommodated to the special interests of clients, not to the nature of that which is equitable and upright.

The causes which determine the characterization of a war as lawful or unlawful Ayala did not touch upon. Gentili outlined certain general classes, in the manner which seemed to him best; but he did not so much as refer to many topics which have come up in notable and frequent controversies.

39. We have taken all pains that nothing of this sort escape us; and we have also indicated the sources from which conclusions are drawn, whence it would be an easy matter to verify them, even if any point has been omitted by us. It remains to explain briefly with what helps, and with what care, I have attacked this task.

First of all, I have made it my concern to refer the proofs of things touching the law of nature to certain fundamental conceptions which are beyond question, so that no one can deny them without doing violence to himself. For the principles of that law, if only you pay strict heed to them, are in themselves manifest and clear, almost as evident as are those things which we perceive by the external senses; and the senses do not err if the organs of perception are properly formed and if the other conditions requisite to perception are present. Thus in his *Phoenician Maidens* Euripides represents [494–6.] Polynices, whose cause he makes out to have been manifestly just, as speaking thus:

> Mother, these words, that I have uttered, are not
> Inwrapped with indirection, but, firmly based
> On rules of justice and of good, are plain
> Alike to simple and to wise.[1]

The poet adds immediately a judgement of the chorus, made up of women, and barbarian women at that, approving these words.

40. In order to prove the existence of this law of nature, I have, furthermore, availed myself of the testimony of philosophers,[2] historians, poets, finally also of orators. Not that confidence is to be reposed in them without discrimination; for they were accustomed to serve the interests of their sect, their subject, or their cause. But when many at different times, and in different places, affirm the same thing as certain, that ought to be referred to a universal cause; and this cause, in the lines of inquiry which we are following, must be either a correct conclusion drawn from the principles of nature,

[1] The same Euripides represents Hermione as saying to Andromache [*Andromache*, 243]:

> Not under laws barbaric do men live
> In this our city;

and Andromache as answering [ibid., 244]:

> What there is base, here too not blameless is.

[2] Why should not one avail himself of the testimony of the philosophers, when Alexander Severus constantly read Cicero *On the Commonwealth* and *On Duties*? [Lampridius, *Alexander Severus*, xxx. 2.]

or common consent. The former points to the law of nature; the latter, to the law of nations.

The distinction between these kinds of law is not to be drawn from the testimonies themselves (for writers everywhere confuse the terms law of nature and law of nations), but from the character of the matter. For whatever cannot be deduced from certain principles by a sure process of reasoning, and yet is clearly observed everywhere, must have its origin in the free will of man.

41. These two kinds of law, therefore, I have always particularly sought to distinguish from each other and from municipal law. Furthermore, in the law of nations I have distinguished between that which is truly and in all respects law, and that which produces merely a kind of outward effect simulating that primitive law, as, for example, the prohibition to resist by force, or even the duty of defence in any place by public force, in order to secure some advantage, or for [xv] the avoidance of serious disadvantages. How necessary it is, in many cases, to observe this distinction, will become apparent in the course of our work.

With not less pains we have separated those things which are strictly and properly legal, out of which the obligation of restitution arises, from those things which are called legal because any other classification of them conflicts with some other stated rule of right reason. In regard to this distinction of law we have already said something above.

42. Among the philosophers Aristotle deservedly holds the foremost place, whether you take into account his order of treatment, or the subtlety of his distinctions, or the weight of his reasons. Would that this pre-eminence had not, for some centuries back, been turned into a tyranny, so that Truth, to whom Aristotle devoted faithful service, was by no instrumentality more repressed than by Aristotle's name!

For my part, both here and elsewhere I avail myself of the liberty of the early Christians, who had sworn allegiance to the sect of no one of the philosophers, not because they were in agreement with those who said that nothing can be known—than which nothing is more foolish—but because they thought that there was no philosophic sect whose vision had compassed all truth, and none which had not perceived some aspect of truth. Thus they believed that to gather up into a whole the truth which was scattered among the different philosophers[1] and dispersed among the sects, was in reality to establish a body of teaching truly Christian.

[1] The words are those of Lactantius, *Divine Institutes*, Book VI, chap. ix [VII. vii. 4].

Justin, *First Apology* [*Second Apology*, chap. xiii]: 'Not because the teachings of Plato are altogether different from the teachings of Christ, but because they do not completely harmonize,

43. Among other things—to mention in passing a point not foreign to my subject—it seems to me that not without reason some of the Platonists and early Christians [1] departed from the teachings of Aristotle in this, that he considered the very nature of virtue as a mean in passions and actions. That principle, once adopted, led him to unite distinct virtues, as generosity and frugality, into one; to assign to truth extremes between which, on any fair premiss, there is no possible co-ordination, boastfulness, and dissimulation; and to apply the designation of vice to certain things which either do not exist, or are not in themselves vices, such as contempt for pleasure and for honours, and freedom from anger against men.

44. That this basic principle, when broadly stated, is unsound, becomes clear even from the case of justice. For, being unable to find in passions and acts resulting therefrom the too much and the too little opposed to that virtue, Aristotle sought each extreme in the things themselves with which justice is concerned. Now in the first place this is simply to leap from one class of things over into another class, a fault which he rightly censures in others; then, for a person to accept less than belongs to him may in fact under unusual conditions constitute a fault, in view of that which, according to the circumstances, he owes to himself and to those dependent on him; but in any case the act cannot be at variance with justice, the essence of which lies in abstaining from that which belongs to another.

By equally faulty reasoning Aristotle tries to make out that adultery committed in a burst of passion, or a murder due to anger, is not properly an injustice. Whereas nevertheless injustice has no other essential quality than the unlawful seizure of that which belongs to another; and it does not matter whether injustice arises from avarice, from lust, from anger, or from ill-advised compassion; or from an overmastering desire to achieve eminence, out of which instances of the gravest injustice constantly arise. For to disparage such incitements, with the sole purpose in view that human society may not receive injury, is in truth the concern of justice.

45. To return to the point whence I started, the truth is that

as the teachings of others do not [xxiv] —for example, those of the Stoics, the poets, and the writers of history. For each one of these spoke rightly in part, in accordance with the reason which had been implanted in him, perceiving what was consistent therewith.'

Tertullian [*On the Soul*, xx]: 'Seneca often on our side'; but the same writer also warns us [*An Answer to the Jews*, ix] that the entire body of spiritual teachings was to be found in no man save Christ alone.

Augustine, *Letters*, ccii [xci. 3]: 'The rules of conduct which Cicero and other philosophers recommend are being taught and learned in the churches that are increasing all over the world.' On this point, if time is available, consult the same Augustine in regard to the Platonists, who, he says, with changes in regard to a few matters can be Christians; *Letters*, lvi [cxviii. 21]; *On the True Religion*, chap. iii, and *Confessions*, Book VII, chap. ix, and Book VIII, chap. ii.

[1] Lactantius treats this subject at length in the *Institutes*, VI. xv, xvi, xvii. Says Cassiodorus [Peter of Blois, *On Friendship*, chap. *Quod affectus sine consensu non multum prosit vel obsit*]: 'It is advantageous or harmful to be moved not by feelings, but in accordance with feelings.'

some virtues do tend to keep passions under control; but that is not because such control is a proper and essential characteristic of every virtue. Rather it is because right reason, which virtue everywhere follows, in some things prescribes the pursuing of a middle course,[1] in others stimulates to the utmost degree. We cannot, for example, worship God too much; for superstition errs not by [xvi] worshipping God too much, but by worshipping in a perverse way. Neither can we too much seek after the blessings that shall abide for ever, nor fear too much the everlasting evils, nor have too great hatred for sin.

[IV. ix. 14.] With truth therefore was it said by Aulus Gellius, that there are some things of which the extent is limited by no boundaries—the greater, the more ample they are, the more excellent. Lactantius, having discussed the passions at great length, says:

[*Divine Institutes*, VI. xvi. 7.] 'The method of wisdom consists in controlling not the passions, but their causes, since they are stirred from without. And putting a check upon the passions themselves ought not to be the chief concern, because they may be feeble in the greatest crime, and very violent without leading to crime.'

Our purpose is to make much account of Aristotle, but reserving in regard to him the same liberty which he, in his devotion to truth, allowed himself with respect to his teachers.

46. History in relation to our subject is useful in two ways: it supplies both illustrations and judgements. The illustrations have greater weight in proportion as they are taken from better times and better peoples; thus we have preferred ancient examples, Greek and Roman, to the rest. And judgements are not to be slighted, especially when they are in agreement with one another; for by such statements the existence of the law of nature, as we have said, is in a measure proved, and by no other means, in fact, is it possible to establish the law of nations.

47. The views of poets and of orators do not have so great weight; and we make frequent use of them not so much for the purpose of gaining acceptance by that means for our argument, as of adding, from their words, some embellishment to that which we wished to say.

48. I frequently appeal to the authority of the books which men inspired by God have either written or approved, nevertheless

[1] Agathias, Book V, in a speech of Belisarius [*Histories*, V. xviii]: 'Of the emotions of the soul those ought in every case to be seized in which there is found, pure and unmixed, an impulse in harmony with the requirements of duty and worthy to be chosen. Those emotions, however, which have a trend and inclination toward evil, are not to be utilized in all cases, but only so far as they contribute to our advantage. That good judgement is a blessing pure and unmixed no one would deny. In anger the element of energy is praiseworthy, but what exceeds the proper limit is to be avoided, as involving disadvantage.'

with a distinction between the Old Testament and the New. There are some who urge that the Old Testament sets forth the law of nature. Without doubt they are in error, for many of its rules come from the free will of God. And yet this is never in conflict with the true law of nature; and up to this point the Old Testament can be used as a source of the law of nature, provided we carefully distinguish between the law of God, which God sometimes executes through men, and the law of men in their relations with one another.

This error we have, so far as possible, avoided, and also another opposed to it, which supposes that after the coming of the New Testament the Old Testament in this respect was no longer of use. We believe the contrary, partly for the reasons which we have already given, partly because the character of the New Testament is such that in its teachings respecting the moral virtues it enjoins the same as the Old Testament or even enjoins greater precepts. In this way we see that the early Christian writers used the witnesses of the Old Testament.

49. The Hebrew writers,[1] moreover, most of all those who have thoroughly understood the speech and customs of their people, are able to contribute not a little to our understanding of the thought of the books which belong to the Old Testament.

50. The New Testament I use in order to explain—and this cannot be learned from any other source—what is permissible to Christians. This, however—contrary to the practice of most men—I have distinguished from the law of nature, considering it as certain that in that most holy law a greater degree of moral perfection is enjoined upon us than the law of nature, alone and by itself, would require. And nevertheless I have not omitted to note the things that are recommended to us rather than enjoined, that we may know that, while the turning aside from what has been enjoined is wrong and involves the risk of punishment, a striving for the highest excellence implies a noble purpose and will not fail of its reward.

51. The authentic synodical canons are collections embodying the general principles of divine law as applied to cases which come up; they either show what the divine law enjoins, or urge us to that which God would fain persuade. And this truly is the mission of the Christian Church, to transmit those things which were transmitted to it by God, and [xvii] in the way in which they were transmitted.

Furthermore customs which were current, or were considered praiseworthy, among the early Christians and those who rose to the measure of so great a name, deservedly have the force of canons.

[1] This was perceived by Cassian [Cassiodorus] as shown by his *Institute of Holy Writ* [Preface].

Next after these comes the authority of those who, each in his own time, have been distinguished among Christians for their piety and learning, and have not been charged with any serious error; for what these declare with great positiveness, and as if definitely ascertained, ought to have no slight weight for the interpretation of passages in Holy Writ which seem obscure. Their authority is the greater the more there are of them in agreement, and as we approach nearer to the times of pristine purity, when neither desire for domination nor any conspiracy of interests had as yet been able to corrupt the primitive truth.

52. The Schoolmen, who succeeded these writers, often show how strong they are in natural ability. But their lot was cast in an unhappy age, which was ignorant of the liberal arts; wherefore it is less to be wondered at if among many things worthy of praise there are also some things which we should receive with indulgence. Nevertheless when the Schoolmen agree on a point of morals, it rarely happens that they are wrong, since they are especially keen in seeing what may be open to criticism in the statements of others. And yet in the very ardour of their defence of themselves against opposing views, they furnish a praiseworthy example of moderation; they contend with one another by means of arguments—not, in accordance with the practice which has lately begun to disgrace the calling of letters, with personal abuse, base offspring of a spirit lacking self-mastery.

53. Of those who profess knowledge of the Roman law there are three classes.

The first consists of those whose work appears in the Pandects, the Codes of Theodosius and Justinian, and the Imperial Constitutions called Novellae.

To the second class belong the successors of Irnerius, that is Accursius, Bartolus, and so many other names of those who long ruled the bar.

The third class comprises those who have combined the study of classical literature with that of law.

To the first class I attribute great weight. For they frequently give the very best reasons in order to establish what belongs to the law of nature, and they often furnish evidence in favour of this law and of the law of nations. Nevertheless they, no less than the others, often confuse these terms, frequently calling that the law of nations which is only the law of certain peoples, and that, too, not as established by assent, but perchance taken over through imitation of others or by pure accident. But those provisions which really belong to the law of nations they often treat, without distinction or discrimination, along with those which belong to the Roman law, as may be seen by reference to the title *On Captives and Postliminy*. We have therefore endeavoured to distinguish these two types from each other.

54. The second class, paying no heed to the divine law or to ancient history, sought to adjust all controversies of kings and peoples by application of the laws of the Romans, with occasional use of the canons. But in the case of these men also the unfortunate condition of their times was frequently a handicap which prevented their complete understanding of those laws, though, for the rest, they were skilful enough in tracing out the nature of that which is fair and good. The result is that while they are often very successful in establishing the basis of law, they are at the same time bad interpreters of existing law. But they are to be listened to with the utmost attention when they bear witness to the existence of the usage which constitutes the law of nations in our day.

55. The masters of the third class, who confine themselves within the limits of the Roman law and deal either not at all, or only slightly, with the common law of nations, are of hardly any use in relation to our subject. They combine the subtlety of the Schoolmen with a knowledge of laws and of canons; and in fact two of them, the Spaniards Covarruvias and Vázquez, did not refrain from treating the controversies of peoples and kings, the latter with great freedom, the former with more restraint and not without precision of judgement.

[xviii] The French have tried rather to introduce history into their study of laws. Among them Bodin and Hotman have gained a great name, the former by an extensive treatise, the latter by separate questions; their statements and lines of reasoning will frequently supply us with material in searching out the truth.

56. In my work as a whole I have, above all else, aimed at three things: to make the reasons for my conclusions as evident as possible; to set forth in a definite order the matters which needed to be treated; and to distinguish clearly between things which seemed to be the same and were not.

57. I have refrained from discussing topics which belong to another subject, such as those that teach what may be advantageous in practice. For such topics have their own special field, that of politics, which Aristotle rightly treats by itself, without introducing extraneous matter into it. Bodin, on the contrary, mixed up politics with the body of law with which we are concerned. In some places nevertheless I have made mention of that which is expedient, but only in passing, and in order to distinguish it more clearly from what is lawful.

58. If any one thinks that I have had in view any controversies

of our own times, either those that have arisen or those which can be foreseen as likely to arise, he will do me an injustice. With all truthfulness I aver that, just as mathematicians treat their figures as abstracted from bodies, so in treating law I have withdrawn my mind from every particular fact.

59. As regards manner of expression, I wished not to disgust the reader, whose interests I continually had in mind, by adding prolixity of words to the multiplicity of matters needing to be treated. I have therefore followed, so far as I could, a mode of speaking at the same time concise and suitable for exposition, in order that those who deal with public affairs may have, as it were, in a single view both the kinds of controversies which are wont to arise and the principles by reference to which they may be decided. These points being known, it will be easy to adapt one's argument to the matter at issue, and expand it at one's pleasure.

60. I have now and then quoted the very words of ancient writers, where they seemed to carry weight or to have unusual charm of expression. This I have occasionally done even in the case of Greek writers, but as a rule only when the passage was brief, or such that I dared not hope that I could bring out the beauty of it in a Latin version. Nevertheless in all cases I have added a Latin translation for the convenience of those who have not learned Greek.[1]

61. I beg and adjure all those into whose hands this work shall come, that they assume towards me the same liberty which I have assumed in passing upon the opinions and writings of others. They who shall find me in error will not be more quick to advise me than I to avail myself of their advice.

And now if anything has here been said by me inconsistent with piety, with good morals, with Holy Writ, with the concord of the Christian Church, or with any aspect of truth, let it be as if unsaid.

[1] [The English translation, of course, follows Grotius' Latin version, which sometimes differs from the original Greek.]

[1]

HUGO GROTIUS

ON

THE LAW OF WAR AND PEACE

BOOK I

CHAPTER I

WHAT IS WAR? WHAT IS LAW?

I.—*Scope of the treatise*

Controversies among those who are not held together by a common bond of municipal law are related either to times of war or to times of peace. Such controversies may arise among those who have not yet united to form a nation, and those who belong to different nations, both private persons and kings; also those who have the same body of rights that kings have, whether members of a ruling aristocracy, or free peoples.

War, however, is undertaken in order to secure peace, and there is no controversy which may not give rise to war. In undertaking to treat the law of war, therefore, it will be in order to treat such controversies, of any and every kind, as are likely to arise. War itself will finally conduct us to peace as its ultimate goal.

II.—*Definition of war, and origin of the word*

1. As we set out to treat the law of war, then, we ought to see what is war, which we are treating, and what is the law which forms the subject of our investigation.

Cicero defined war as a contending by force. A usage has gained currency, however, which designates by the word not a contest but a condition;[1] thus war is the condition of those contending by force, viewed simply as such. This general definition includes all the classes of wars which it will hereafter be necessary to discuss. For I do not exclude private war, since in fact it is more ancient than public war and has, incontestably, the same nature as public war; wherefore both should be designated by one and the same term. [*On Duties*, I. xi. 34.]

2. The origin of the word, moreover, is not inconsistent with this use. For *bellum*, 'war', comes from the old word *duellum*, as

[1] [10] Philo, *On Special Laws*, II [III. xv]: 'Not alone are they considered enemies who are actually engaged in fighting on land or sea, but those also are to be viewed as such who bring up appliances of war before harbours or walls, even if they are not yet commencing to fight.'

Servius in his comment *On the Aeneid*, Book I [Book I, line 545],

Nor mightier in war and arms than he,

remarks: '"War" (*bellum*) contains also the idea of "plan and purpose" (*consilium*); the word "arms" (*arma*) refers only to actual hostilities.' The same commentator in a note to Book VIII [line 547]: '"War" (*bellum*) extends over the whole period in which any preparation necessary for fighting is being made, or in which fighting is carried on; the word "battle" (*proelium*) is used of actual engagements.'

bonus, 'good', from an earlier *duonus*, and *bis*, 'twice', from *duis*. The word *duellum*, again, bears to *duo*, 'two', a relation in sense similar to that which we have in mind when we call peace 'union'. In like manner the Greeks derived their word for 'war' (πόλεμος) from a word meaning 'multitude'; [2] the ancients also took a word for 'faction' (λύη) from the idea of dissolution in it, just as the dissolution of the body suggested δύη, 'anguish'.

3. And usage does not reject this broader meaning of the word. If, to be sure, the term 'war' is at times limited to public war, that implies no objection to our view, since it is perfectly certain that the name of a genus is often applied in a particular way to a species, especially a species that is more prominent.

I do not include justice in my definition because this very question forms a part of our investigation, whether there can be a just war, and what kind of a war is just; and a subject which is under investigation ought to be distinguished from the object towards which the investigation is directed.

II.—*Law is considered as a rule of action, and divided into rectorial law and equatorial law*

1. In giving to our treatise the title 'The Law of War', we mean first of all, as already stated, to inquire whether any war can be just, and then, what is just in war. For law in our use of the term here means nothing else than what is just, and that, too, rather in a negative than in an affirmative sense, that being lawful which is not unjust.

Now that is unjust which is in conflict with the nature of society of beings endowed with reason. Thus Cicero declares that to take away from another in order to gain an advantage for oneself is contrary to nature; and in proof he adduces the argument that, if this should happen, human society and the common good would of necessity be destroyed. Florentinus shows that it is wrong for a man to set a snare for a fellow man, because nature has established a kind of blood-relationship among us. 'Just as all the members of the body agree with one another,' says Seneca, 'because the preservation of each conduces to the welfare of the whole, so men refrain from injuring one another because we are born for community of life. For society can exist in safety only through the mutual love and protection of the parts of which it is composed.' [1]

On Duties, III [III. v. 21].

Digest, I. i. 3.

On Anger, Book II xxxii [II. xxxi. 7].

[1] The same Seneca, *Letters*, xlviii [xlviii. 3]: 'This fellowship ought carefully and scrupulously to be cultivated; for it mingles us all with all men, and brings the conviction that there is a bond of right common to the human race.'

On this point reference may be made to Chrysostom, *On First Corinthians*, xi. 1 [Homily XXV, iii–iv.]

2. Moreover, just as there is one form of social relationship without inequality,[1] as that between brothers, or citizens, or friends, or allies; another with inequality—the 'paramount' type, in the view of Aristotle—as that between father and children, master and slave, king and subjects, God and men[2]; so there is one type of that which is lawful applying to those who live on an equality, and another type applying to him who rules and him who is ruled, in their relative positions. The latter type, if I mistake not, we shall properly call rectorial law; the former, equatorial law. [*Nicom. Ethics,* VIII. viii.]

IV.—*A body of rights in respect to quality is divided into faculties and aptitudes*

There is another meaning of law viewed as a body of rights, different from the one just defined but growing out of it, which has reference to the person. In this sense a right becomes a moral quality of a person, making it possible to have or to do something lawfully.

Such a right attaches to a person, even if sometimes it may follow a thing, as in the case of servitudes over lands, which are called real rights, in contrast with other rights purely personal; not because such rights do not also attach to a person, but because they do not attach to any other person than the one who is entitled to a certain thing.

When the moral quality is perfect we call it *facultas*, 'faculty'; when it is not perfect, *aptitudo*, 'aptitude'. To the former, in the range of natural things, 'act' corresponds; to the latter, 'potency'.

V.—*Faculties, or legal rights strictly so called, are divided into powers, property rights, and contractual rights*

A legal right (*facultas*) is called by the jurists the right to one's own (*suum*); after this we shall call it a legal right properly or strictly so called.

Under it are included power, now over oneself, which is called freedom,[3] now over others, as that of the father (*patria potestas*) and that of the master over slaves; ownership,[4] either absolute, or less than absolute, as usufruct and the right of pledge; and contractual

[1] Thus grammarians distinguish between a construction involving agreement and a construction involving subordination.

[2] On this relationship see Philo on the words 'Noah awoke' [*Genesis*, ix. 24; Philo, *On Sobriety*, x].

Plutarch has also some remarks in his *Numa* [iv = 62].

[3] The Roman jurists very properly define liberty as a 'legal right' (*facultas*).

[4] 'Right' is used to designate 'ownership' of something, according to the Scholiast on Horace [*Epist.* II. ii. 174; *Sat.* II. iii. 217].

rights, to which on the opposite side contractual obligations correspond.

VI.—*Another division of legal rights, into private and public*

Legal rights, again, are of two kinds: private, which are concerned with the interest of individuals, and public which are superior to private rights, since they are exercised by the community over its members, and the property of its members, for the sake of the common good.

Thus the power of the king has under it both the power of the father and that of the master; thus, again, for the common good the king has a right of property over the possessions of individuals greater than that of the individual owners;[1] thus [3] each citizen is under a greater pecuniary obligation to the state, for the meeting of public needs, than to a private creditor.

VII.—*What is an aptitude?*

Nicomachean Ethics, V [vi].

Aptitude is called by Aristotle ἀξία, that is, 'worthiness'.[2] Michael of Ephesus renders the idea of fairness, which according to him should come next to worthiness, as 'that which fits to' something and 'that which is fitting', that is 'that which is suitable'.

VIII.—*On expletive justice and attributive justice; that these are not properly distinguished by geometrical and arithmetical proportion, and that the latter is not concerned with public property, the former with private property*

1. Legal rights are the concern of expletive justice (*iustitia expletrix*), which is entitled to the name of justice properly or strictly so called. This is called 'contractual' justice by Aristotle, with too narrow a use of the term; for though the possessor of something

[1] Philo, *On Noah's Planting* [chap. xiii]: 'Surely silver, gold and the other treasures which are guarded by subjects, belong to those who rule rather than to those who possess them.' Pliny, *Panegyric* [xxvii. 4]: 'He, to whom belongs whatever all possess, has himself as much as all possess'; later he adds [chap. l], 'Would Caesar see anything which was not his own?' Add John of Salisbury, *Policraticus*, Book V, chap. i.

[2] Cicero, *On Duties*, I [I. xvii. 58]: 'If, however, a contrast and comparison of some sort should be made, in order to see who has the strongest moral claims upon us, first and foremost would come our country and our parents, whose services have placed us under the deepest obligation; next, our children and entire household, who look to us alone and can have no other recourse; lastly, the relatives with whom we are on good terms, who in most cases have also a common interest with us. In consequence, the support of life on the material side is due to those whom I have mentioned, above all others; but intimacy of relations in life and in living, counsel, conversation, words of encouragement and words of consolation, sometimes even reproofs, thrive best in friendship.'

See what will be said below in Book II, chap. vii, 9 and 10.

Seneca, *On Benefits*, Book IV, chap. xi, when he is treating of wills: 'We try to find those who are most worthy, in order that we may leave our property to them'; consult the passage itself.

Add Augustine, *On Christian Doctrine*, Book I, chaps. xxviii and xxix.

belonging to me may give it back to me, that does not result 'from a contract', and nevertheless the act falls within the purview of this type of justice; and so the same philosopher has more aptly termed it 'restorative' justice.

Aptitudes are the concern of attributive justice (*iustitia attributrix*). This Aristotle called 'distributive' justice. It is associated with those virtues which have as their purpose to do good to others, as generosity, compassion, and foresight in matters of government.

2. Aristotle says also that expletive justice is expressed by a simple proportion, which he calls 'arithmetical'; attributive justice, by a proportion involving comparison, which he calls 'geometrical', this having the name of a proportion only among mathematicians.[1] Such proportions are often applicable, but not always so; and in fact expletive justice differs essentially from attributive justice not in a relation expressed by such a proportion but in the matter with which it is concerned, as we have already said. Thus a partnership agreement is carried out according to a proportion based on comparison; and if only one person can be found who is fitted for a public position, the award will be made to him on the basis of a simple proportion only.

3. Not more true, again, is that which some say, that attributive justice is concerned with public property, while expletive justice is concerned with private property. On the contrary, if a man wishes to give a legacy from property belonging to him, he acts in conformity with attributive justice; and the state which pays back, from public funds, what a citizen has advanced for the public interest, is discharging the function of expletive justice.

This distinction was correctly observed by the teacher of Cyrus. For when Cyrus had given to the smaller boy a smaller tunic although it belonged to another, and on the other hand had given a larger tunic to the larger boy, his teacher thus instructed him: [Xenophon, *Training of Cyrus*, I. iii. 17.]

That would have been a proper course to pursue in case a referee had been appointed to decide what would be suitable for each; but when the question to be settled was, to which boy the tunic belonged, then only one point was to be considered, which boy was more justly entitled to it[2]—whether the object should belong to him who had violently taken it away, or to him who had made it or purchased it.

[1] [11] This is called by Cassiodorus [*On Dialectic*, p. 408, edition of 1589], a comparison in respect to mode of being. Of this proportion, which attributive justice is wont to use, there is a not inappropriate description in Homer [*Iliad*, XIV. 382]:

Excellent things to the excellent gave he, mean to the vulgar.

[2] See the same Xenophon, *Training of Cyrus*, Book II [II. ii. 18]. The law given through Moses has a similar bearing: 'Neither shalt thou favour a poor man in his cause'; *Exodus*, xxiii. 3; *Leviticus*, xix. 15. It is, in fact, necessary, as Philo says [*On the Judge*, iv], 'to separate the case itself entirely from consideration of the parties thereto.'

IX.—*Law is defined as a rule, and divided into the law of nature and volitional law*

1. There is a third meaning of the word law, which has the same force as statute [1] whenever this word is taken in the broadest sense as a rule of moral actions imposing obligation to what is right. We have need of an obligation; for counsels and instructions of every sort, which enjoin what is honourable indeed but do not impose an obligation, do not come under the term statute or law. Permission, again, is not, strictly speaking, an operation of law, but a negation of operation, except in so far as it obligates another not to put any hindrance in the way of him to whom permission is given. We said, moreover, 'imposing obligation to what is right', not merely to what is lawful, because law in our use of the term here stands related to the matter not only of justice, as we have set it forth, but also of other virtues.[2] Nevertheless that which, in accordance with this law, is right, in a broader sense is called just.

[*Nicom. Ethics*, V. x.] 2. The best division of law thus conceived is found in Aristotle, that is, into natural law and volitional law, to which he applies the term statutory, with a rather strict use of the word statute; sometimes he calls it established law.

The same distinction is to be found among the Jews who, when they expressed themselves with exactness called the law of nature, 'commandments',[3] and established law [4] 'statutes'. These terms the Greek-speaking Jews are accustomed to translate as 'duties' and 'commands'.

X.—*Definition of the law of nature, division, and distinction from things which are not properly so called*

1. The law of nature is a dictate of right reason,[4] which points out that an act, according as it is or is not in conformity with rational nature, has in it a quality of moral baseness or moral necessity; and

[1] With this meaning Horace said [*Satires*, I. iii. 111]:

> You must confess that laws were framed
> From fear of the unjust.

Elsewhere he says [*Art of Poetry*, 122]:

> Let him deny that laws were made for him,

where the Scholiast has the comment: 'Let him be a despiser of laws.'

[2] An example is to be found in a law of Zeleucus [Aelian, *Various History*, II. xxxvii], which imposed a penalty on a man who should have drunk wine against the order of a doctor.

[3] So Maimonides, *Guide of the Perplexed*, Book III, chap. xxvi.

[4] Philo, *That Every Virtuous Man is Free* [chap. vii]: 'Now the law that deceives not is right reason; and this law is not mortal as devised by this or that mortal, not lifeless as writ on leaves of paper or on columns that are without life, but incorruptible, since it has been imprinted by immortal nature on an immortal intelligence.'

Tertullian, *On the Soldier's Chaplet* [chap. vi]: 'You will ask then, for a law of God, and this you have, common throughout the world, written on nature's tablets.' Marcus Aurelius, Book II

that, in consequence, such an act is either forbidden or enjoined by the author of nature, God.

2. The acts in regard to which such a dictate exists are, in themselves, either obligatory or not permissible, and so it is understood that necessarily they are enjoined or forbidden by God. In this characteristic the law of nature differs not only from human law, but also from volitional divine law; for volitional divine law does not enjoin or forbid those things which in themselves and by their own nature are obligatory or not permissible, but by forbidding things it makes them unlawful, and by commanding things it makes them obligatory.

3. For the understanding of the law of nature, again, we must note that certain things are said to be according to this law not in a proper sense but—as the Schoolmen love to say—by reduction, the law of nature not being in conflict with them; just as we said above that things are called just which are free from injustice. Sometimes, also, by misuse of the term, things which reason declares are honourable, or better than their opposites, are said to be according to the law of nature, although not obligatory.

4. It is necessary to understand, further, that the law of nature deals not only with things which are outside the domain of the human will, but with many things also which result from an act of the human will. Thus ownership, such as now obtains, was introduced by the will of man; but, once introduced, the law of nature points out that it is wrong for me, against your will, to take away that which is subject to your ownership. Wherefore Paul the jurist said that theft is prohibited by the law of nature[1]; Ulpian, that it is by nature base; and Euripides declares that it is displeasing to God, in these verses of the *Helena*: *Digest*, XLVII. ii. 1. *Digest*, L. xvi. 42. [903 ff.]

> For God himself hates violence; he wishes
> That not by rapine but by honest toil
> We riches gain. Let wealth be scorned that not
> By right has come. Common to men the air is,
> And also earth, on which 'tis meet that each

[II. xvi]: 'The end for beings endowed with reason is to follow the law and rule of that most ancient city and state.'

Add the passage of Cicero, *On the Commonwealth*, III, which Lactantius quotes, [*Divine Institutes*,] VI. viii. There are some excellent observations which Chrysostom makes, *On the Statues*, [Homilies] XII, XIII. And the remarks of Thomas Aquinas, *Secunda Secundae*, lvii. 2, and of Duns Scotus, [*On the Sentences*,] III, Dist. 37, are by no means to be slighted.

[1] After the law which relates to acknowledging and worshipping the Deity, says Julian [*Oration* VII, 209 C, D. Cf. translation by Wright, vol. i, pp. 85–6]: 'There is a second law which in its very nature is sacred and divine. This law bids men always and everywhere to hold aloof from the property of others, and does not grant permission for them to go contrary to it either in word or in deed or in the secret thoughts of the mind.'

Cicero, *On Duties*, Book III [III. x. 42], following Chrysippus: 'So in life it is not unfair for each to try to get for himself what contributes to his advantage; but to take what belongs to another is not right.'

His home make large, if he his hands restrain
From things of others, and from violence.

5. The law of nature, again, is unchangeable—even in the sense that it cannot be changed by God. Measureless as is the power of God, nevertheless it can be said that there are certain things over which that power does not extend; for things of which this is said are spoken only, having no sense corresponding with reality and being mutually contradictory. Just as even God, then, cannot cause that two times two should not make four, so He cannot cause that that which is intrinsically evil be not evil.

[*Nicom. Ethics*, II. vi.] This is what Aristotle means when he says: 'Some things are thought of as bad the moment they are named.' For just as the being of things, from the time that they begin to exist, and in the manner in which they exist, is not dependent on anything else, so also the properties, which of necessity characterize that being; such a property is the badness of certain acts, when judged by the standard of a nature endowed with sound reason. Thus God Himself suffers Himself to be judged according to this standard, as may be seen by referring to *Genesis*, xviii. 25; *Isaiah*, v. 3; *Ezekiel*, xviii. 25; *Jeremiah*, ii. 9; *Micah*, vi. 2; *Romans*, ii. 6, iii. 6.

6. Sometimes nevertheless it happens that in the acts in regard to which the law of nature has ordained something, an appearance of change deceives the unwary, although in fact the law of nature, being unchangeable, undergoes no change; but the thing, in regard to which the law of nature has ordained, undergoes change. For example, if a creditor gives a receipt for that which I owe him, I am no longer bound to pay him, not because the law of nature has ceased [5] to enjoin upon me that I must pay what I owe, but because that which I was owing has ceased to be owed. Thus Arrian
[I. vii. 16.] in *Epictetus* reasons correctly when he says: 'To constitute an indebtedness it is not enough that a loan has been made; the obligation must remain as yet unsatisfied.' So if God should command that any one be slain, or that the property of any one be carried off, homicide or theft—words connoting moral wrong—will not become permissible; it will not be a case of homicide or theft, because the deed is done by authority of the Supreme Lord of life and property.

7. Furthermore, some things belong to the law of nature not through a simple relation but as a result of a particular combination of circumstances. Thus the use of things in common was in accordance with the law of nature so long as ownership by individuals was not introduced; and the right to use force in obtaining one's own existed before laws were promulgated.

XI.—*That the instinct common to other animals, or that peculiar to man, does not constitute another kind of law*

1. The distinction, which appears in the books of Roman law, between an unchangeable law common to animals and man, which the Roman legal writers call the law of nature in a more restricted sense, and a law peculiar to man, which they frequently call the law of nations, is of hardly any value. For, strictly speaking, only a being that applies general principles is capable of law, as Hesiod rightly observed: [*Works and Days*, 276 ff.]

> For law to man by most high Jove was given;
> The fish, the wild beasts and the winged birds
> On one another feed, for right no place
> Among them has. Justice he gave to man,[1]
> The gift most excellent.

'We do not speak of justice in the case of horses or lions,' says Cicero in the first book of his treatise *On Duties*. [I. xvi. 50.] Plutarch in his *Life of Cato the Elder* remarks: 'We have been so constituted that we avail ourselves of law and justice only in respect to men.' [v=p. 339 A.] Says Lactantius, in his fifth book: 'In all animals, which are devoid of reason, we see that there is a nature which looks out for itself. [.V xvii. 30.] For they do harm to others in order to secure advantage for themselves, since they do not know that to do harm is evil. But man, because he has a knowledge of good and evil, refrains from doing harm to another, even with disadvantage to himself.'

Polybius, having recounted the beginnings of organized society, when men had first come together, adds that if any one should have done harm to his parents [2] or benefactors, it could not possibly have happened that the rest would not be incensed at his conduct, and adds the reason: 'For since the race of men differs from the other animals in this, that it is endowed with intelligence and reason, it is quite unbelievable that an act so contrary to their nature would have been passed over by men, as by other animals, without [Book VI [VI. vi. 4].]

[1] Juvenal, *Satires*, xv [lines 143 ff.]:

> We alone have as our portion gained
> A reverential mind; we things divine
> May apprehend, we fitted are to know
> Life's arts, and practise them. [12] From heaven's height
> A heaven-born sympathy we drew, and this
> The grovelling and earth-gazing creatures lack.
> To them, when new the world, its Maker gave
> Life only, but to us a soul as well,
> That mutual kindly feeling might us prompt
> To seek and render aid, and peoples form
> From scattered dwellers.

Chrysostom, *On Romans*, vii [viii=Homily XIV, v] declares: 'Even in the case of creatures which lack reason and perception men ought not to deviate from the consideration of what is just and unjust.'

[2] An example is found in the case of Ham (*Genesis*, x [ix]. 22), where the punishment follows.

notice; such a deed must have attracted attention and have given offence.'[1]

2. If, however, a sense of justice is sometimes attributed to brute creatures,[2] that is done without proper grounds, in consequence of observing in them a shadow or trace of reason.[3] But whether an act, in regard to which the law of nature has pronounced, is common to us and other animals, as the rearing of offspring, or peculiar to us, as the worship of God, has no bearing whatever on the nature of the law.

XII.—*In what way the existence of the law of nature is proved*

1. In two ways men are wont to prove that something is according to the law of nature, from that which is antecedent and from that which is consequent. Of the two lines of proof [6] the former is more subtle, the latter more familiar.

Proof *a priori* consists in demonstrating the necessary agreement or disagreement of anything with a rational and social nature; proof *a posteriori*, in concluding, if not with absolute assurance, at least with every probability, that that is according to the law of nature which is believed to be such among all nations, or among all those that are more advanced in civilization. For an effect that is universal demands a universal cause; and the cause of such an opinion can hardly be anything else than the feeling which is called the common sense of mankind.

[*Works and Days*, 763 f.] 2. Hesiod has a saying which has been quoted by many:

> Not wholly void of truth the opinion is
> Which many peoples hold.

[Sextus Empiricus, *Against the Mathematicians*, vii. 134.] 'Those things which appear true to men generally are worthy of credence,'[4] Heraclitus used to say, judging that common acceptance

[1] Chrysostom, *On the Statues*, XIII [Homily XIII, iii]: 'We are so constituted by nature that we feel indignation along with those who have been badly treated. Whence in fact we become incensed at men who inflict wrongs, even though the wrong in no way affects us.'

The Scholiast on Horace, *Satires*, I. iii [line 97]: 'Feeling and mind experience one sort of indignation when we hear that a murder has been committed, another when we hear of a theft.'

[2] A kind of foreshadowing of justice the Elder Pliny notes in elephants, Book VIII, chap. v [*Natural History*, VIII. iv. 9].

The same author, Book X [X. lxxiv. 208], relates that there was a female asp which itself killed its own snakelet because this had caused the death of the son of the man who took care of it.

[3] Seneca, *On Anger*, Book V, chap. iii [I. iii. 4, 6], said that brutes are devoid of anger, but that they have an impulse in place of anger. 'Mute creatures', he declares, 'are without the feelings of men; but they have certain impulses similar to the impulses of men.' Thus in brutes, said Origen, *Against Celsus* [IV. xcii=p. 225], there are not faults but the appearance of faults, 'just as if a lion could get angry'. So the Peripatetics in Porphyry, *On Abstaining from Animal Food*, Book III [III. xxii=p. 309].

[4] Aristotle, *Nicomachean Ethics*, X. ii: 'What seems to all to be so, this we say is so; and he who wishes to take away this belief will himself say things in no respect more worthy of belief.' Seneca [*Letters*, XI. ii. 31=lxxxi. 31]: 'Amidst so great difference of opinions, all men with one voice, as the saying is, will declare to you that gratitude is due to those who do kindnesses.' Quintilian

is the best criterion of truth. Says Aristotle: 'The strongest proof is, if all men agree upon what we say'; Cicero, 'The agreement of all nations upon a matter ought to be considered a law of nature'; Seneca, 'The proof of truth is the fact that all hold the same view upon something'; and Quintilian, 'We consider those things certain upon which there is agreement in the common opinion of men.'

[*Eudem. Ethics*, I. vi.] *Tusculan Disputations*, I [I. xiii. 30]. [Seneca,] *Letters*, cxvii [cxvii. 6]. [*Inst. Or.*, V. x. 12.]

Not without reason did I speak of the nations 'more advanced in civilization'; for, as Porphyry rightly observes, 'Some nations have become savage and unhuman,[1] and from them it is by no means necessary that fair judges draw a conclusion unfavourable to human nature.' Andronicus of Rhodes says: 'Among men endowed with a right and sound mind there is an unchangeable law, which is called the law of nature. And if men having sick or distorted mentalities think otherwise, that has no bearing on the matter. For he who says that honey is sweet does not lie, just because to sick people it may seem otherwise.'

[*On Abstaining*, IV. xxi.] [*On Nic. Ethics*, V. x.]

Consistent with these expressions is a remark of Plutarch, in his *Life of Pompey*: 'By nature no man either is or has been a wild and unsociable animal; but man becomes brutelike when, contrary to nature, he cultivates the habit of doing wrong. By adopting different habits, however, and making a change of place and of life, he returns again to a state of gentleness.' Aristotle presents this characterization of man in the light of the qualities peculiar to him: 'Man is an animal gentle by nature.'[2]

[xxviii = p. 633 D.] *Topics*, V. ii.

[*Institutes of Oratory*, I. vi. 45]: 'The common usage of educated men I shall call custom in speech, just as in life we call the common practice of good men custom.'

Josephus, *Antiquities of the Jews*, Book XVI [XVI. vi. 8]: 'There is no nation which throughout maintains the same customs; in many instances customs differ very greatly in different towns. But the right is equally advantageous for all men, and as useful to barbarians as to Greeks. To right, at any rate, the laws of our nation pay the greatest heed, and so, if we but strictly observe them, they render us well disposed and friendly to all men. Such are the characteristics which it is fair to demand from the laws; and others ought not to think, on account of differences in institutions, that our laws, being foreign, are repugnant to them, but they ought rather to see whether these are adjusted to a standard of virtue and upright conduct. For virtue and upright conduct [13] concern all men in common, and are of themselves sufficient to safeguard the life of men.'

Tertullian, *Prescription against Heretics* [chap. xxviii]: 'That which among many is found to be one, is an offshoot not of error but of tradition.'

[1] Justin, *Dialogue with Trypho* [chap. xciii = 697 A]: 'With the exception of those who, possessed by unclean spirits, and corrupted through perverse training, bad practices and unjust laws, have lost the ideas derived from nature.' Says Philo, *That Every Virtuous Man is Free* [chap. vii]: 'Rightly then may one marvel that so dense darkness has been shed about them that they do not perceive the true characteristics of things, clear as these are.' Chrysostom, in the sermon *That Christ is God* [xi]: 'Take not thy judgement of things from those whose soul is corrupt.'

[2] The same thing is said by Chrysostom, *On the Statues*, Homily XI [XI, iv]. The thought is more fully set forth by Philo, *On the Ten Commandments* [chap. xxv]: 'Man, who was to be the most gentle of animals, nature made sociable and desirous of companionship, summoning him to live a harmonious life in society; and she gave to him speech also which would unite men by adapting their natures one to the other and leading them to a concord of feeling.' The same philosopher in his treatise *On the Indestructibility of the World* [vii = p. 495 E]: 'The gentlest of animals is man, because nature has given to him the gift of speech, by which the most unrestrained passions are soothed as by enchantment.'

Politics, I. v. In another passage he says: 'In order to find what is natural we must look among those things which according to nature are in a sound condition, not among those that are corrupt.'

XIII.—*Division of volitional law into human and divine*

We have said that another kind of law is volitional law, which has its origin in the will.

Volitional law is either human or divine.

XIV.—*Human law is divided into municipal law, law narrower in scope than municipal law, and law broader in scope than municipal law, which is the law of nations; explanation thereof, and how proved*

1. We begin with human law, because that is familiar to the greater number. Human law, then, is either municipal law, or broader in scope than municipal law, or more restricted than municipal law.

Municipal law is that which emanates from the civil power. The civil power is that which bears sway over the state. The state is a complete association of free men, joined together for the enjoyment of rights and for their common interest.

The law which is narrower in scope than municipal law, and [7] does not come from the civil power, although subject to it, is of varied character. It comprises the commands of a father, of a master, and all other commands of a similar character.

The law which is broader in scope than municipal law is the law of nations; that is the law which has received its obligatory force from the will of all nations, or of many nations.[1] I added 'of many nations' for the reason that, outside of the sphere of the law of nature, which is also frequently called the law of nations, there is hardly any law common to all nations. Not infrequently, in fact, in one part of the world there is a law of nations which is not such elsewhere, as we shall at the proper time set forth in connexion with [Book III, vii and ix.] captivity and postliminy.

2. The proof for the law of nations is similar to that for unwritten municipal law; it is found in unbroken custom and the testimony of those who are skilled in it. The law of nations, in fact, [*Orations*, lxxvi = p. 648.] as Dio Chrysostom well observes, 'is the creation of time and custom.' And for the study of it the illustrious writers of history are of the greatest value to us.

[1] Vázquez, *Controversiae*, II. liv. 4.

XV.—*Divine law is divided into universal divine law and divine law peculiar to a single people*

1. What volitional divine law is we may well understand from the meaning of the words. It is, of course, that law which has its origin in the divine will; and by this origin it is distinguished from the law of nature, which also, as we have said, may be called divine. [Prolegomena, 12.]

In the consideration of volitional divine law that is applicable which Anaxarchus [1] rather vaguely expressed, that God does not will a thing because it is lawful, but that a thing is lawful—that is obligatory—because God willed it.

2. This law, moreover, was given either to the human race, or to a single people. To the human race we find that the law was thrice given by God: immediately after the creation of man, a second time in the renewal of human kind after the Flood, lastly in the more exalted renewal through Christ.

These three bodies of divine law are beyond doubt binding upon all men, so far as they have become adequately known to men.

XVI.—*That those not of Jewish birth have never been bound by the Hebraic law*

1. Among all peoples there is one to which God vouchsafed to give laws in a special manner; that is the Jewish people, which Moses thus addresses (*Deuteronomy*, iv. 7): 'For what great nation is there, that hath a God so nigh unto them, as Jehovah our God is whensoever we call upon Him? And what great nation is there, that hath statutes and ordinances so righteous as all this law, which I set before you this day?'

Similar are the words of the psalmist (*Psalms*, cxlvii):

> He showeth his word unto Jacob,
> His statutes and his ordinances unto Israel.
> He hath not dealt so with any nation;
> As for his ordinances, they have not known them.

2. Nor should we doubt that those of the Jews are in error (among them Trypho, in his discussion with Justin) who think that even foreigners, if they wish to be saved, must pass under the yoke of the Hebraic law. An ordinance, in fact, is not binding upon those to whom it has not been given. But in the case under consideration the ordinance itself declares to whom it was given, in the words: 'Hear, O Israel,' [2] and everywhere the covenant is spoken of as made with the Jews, and they themselves are said to be chosen as

[1] The passage is in Plutarch's *Alexander* [lii = p. 695 A].

[2] Moses Maimonides held the same opinion, and supported it by *Deuteronomy*, xxxiii. 4.

the peculiar people of God. The truth of this was recognized by Maimonides, who proves it by the passage in *Deuteronomy*, xxxiii. 4.

3. Among the Jews, moreover, there always dwelt some men of foreign birth, 'devout men and that fear God,' such as the Syro-Phoenician woman (*Matthew*, xv. 22), Cornelius (*Acts*, x. 2), and
[xvii. 4.] 'the devout Greeks' (*Acts*, xviii. 4). In Hebrew we find 'the pious ones of the Gentiles', as we read in the title of the Talmud concerning the King.[1] Such is he who in the law is called 'foreigner', literally 'son of strangeness' (*Leviticus*, xxii. 25); also 'stranger or sojourner' (*Leviticus*, xxv. 47), where the Chaldean has 'uncircumcised inhabitant'.[2]

These, as the Jewish teachers themselves declare, were bound to observe the laws that had been given to Adam and Noah, to abstain from idols, from blood, and from the other things which will be mentioned below in their proper place; but they were not bound to observe also the laws which were peculiar to the Israelites. And so, while the Israelites were not permitted to eat the flesh of a creature which had died a natural death, [8] nevertheless this was allowed to foreigners who were living among them (*Deuteronomy*, xiv. 21). There were exceptions only in the case of certain laws in which it was expressly stated that sojourners should be bound by them no less than natives.

4. Again, strangers who came from outside, and were not subject to Jewish institutions, were permitted to worship God in the temple at Jerusalem, and to offer sacrifices; they must stand nevertheless in a place separate and apart[3] from that where the Israelites stood (*1 Kings*, Vulgate, *3 Kings*, viii. 41; *2 Maccabees*, iii. 35; *John*, xii. 20; *Acts*, viii. 27). And Elisha did not point out to Naaman the Syrian,[4] nor Jonah to the people of Nineveh, nor Daniel

[1] Also the title *On the Sanhedrin*, chap. xi.

[2] Reference is made to such an 'uncircumcised sojourner' also in *Exodus*, xii. 45. From him the proselyte, that is the circumcised stranger, is distinguished, as shown by comparison with a passage in *Numbers*, ix. 14. Of these pious uncircumcised persons Maimonides has much to say in his book *On Idolatry*, chap. x, 6. Also in his commentary *To Misnajoth*, and frequently elsewhere, he says that those pious persons from among the Gentiles will be sharers in the blessings of time to come.

Chrysostom, *On Romans*, chap. ii [Homily V, iii, on verse 10]: 'What Jew does he mean, and of what Greeks is he discoursing? Of those who were before the coming of Christ; for his argument has not yet been brought down to the times of grace.' Then, 'By Greeks he here means not those that worshipped idols but those that feared God, that obeyed the law of nature, that strictly kept all observances which make for piety, save only the Jewish observances.' Examples he finds in Melchizedek, Job, the Ninevites, Cornelius; later he adds [Homily VI, iv, on verse 29]: 'And again he is speaking of a Greek, not as a worshipper of idols, but god-fearing, virtuous, and free from the observances of the law.' To the same effect [14] he explains the words 'to them that are without law as without law' [*On First Corinthians*, Homily XXII, iii, on verse 21]; and *On the Statues*, Homily XII [XII, v]: 'The Greek whom he names here is not devoted to idols, but a worshipper of the one God; nevertheless one who is not bound by the constraint of Jewish observances, as, for example, the keeping of the Sabbath day, circumcision, and various purifications; yet one who meanwhile manifests devotion to wisdom and piety in all things.'

[3] See Josephus, where the history of Solomon's temple is treated [Josephus, *The Jewish War*, V. v. 6; *Antiquities of the Jews*, VIII. iv. 3].

[4] Hilary expressed the same opinion, *On Matthew*, xii.

to Nebuchadnezzar, nor the other prophets to the Tyrians, the Moabites, or the Egyptians to whom they wrote, that it was necessary for them to receive the law of Moses.

5. What I have said of the law of Moses as a whole, I wish to consider as said also with reference to circumcision, which was as it were the introduction to the law. There is only this difference, that the Israelites alone were bound by the law of Moses, while the whole posterity of Abraham was held subject to the law of circumcision; in consequence, we read in the historical writings of both Jews and Greeks that the Idumaeans adopted circumcision under compulsion of the Israelites. Wherefore we may well believe that the peoples which, besides the Israelites, practised circumcision (there are several of them, mentioned by Herodotus, Strabo, Philo, Justin, Origen, Clement of Alexandria, Epiphanius, and Jerome [1]) were descended from Ishmael, or from Esau, or from the descendants of Keturah.[2]

6. For the rest, in all cases the principle stated by Paul (*Romans*, ii. 14) was applicable:

'When Gentiles that have not the law do by nature'[3] (that is in accordance with the usages that flowed from the primitive source, unless one prefers to refer 'nature' to what precedes, in order to contrast the Gentiles with the Jews, into whom from birth the law was inculcated) 'the things of the law, these, not having the law, are the law unto themselves, in that they show the work of the law written in their hearts, their conscience bearing witness therewith, and their thoughts one with another accusing or else excusing them.'

And in the same connexion (verse 26) there is another statement: 'If the uncircumcision' (that is a man who has not been circumcised) 'keep the ordinances of the law, shall not his uncircumcision be reckoned for circumcision?' With reason, therefore, in the history by Josephus, the Jew Ananias instructed Izates of Adiabene (Tacitus calls him Ezates), that even without circumcision God can be rightly worshipped and propitiated.[4] *Antiquities of the Jews*, XX [ii. 4]. [*Annals*, XII. xiv.]

In regard to the fact that many foreigners were circumcised, and through circumcision made themselves subject to the law (as

[1] Theodoret may be added.

[2] From them apparently were descended those of the Ethiopians whom Herodotus [II. civ] reckons among the circumcised. Epiphanius [*On the Twelve Stones*] calls them Homeritae.

[3] 'By the reasonings of nature,' says Chrysostom [*On Romans*, Homily V, v, on chap. ii. 14]. Afterward he adds, 'For this reason they are to be admired, because they had no need of a law'; also [ibid., on verse 16]: 'In place of the law conscience and the use of reason suffice.'

Tertullian, *An Answer to the Jews* [chap. ii] says: 'Before the law of Moses, writ upon tablets of stone, I maintain that there was an unwritten law, which was understood by nature, and was kept by the fathers.' Not far from this is the thought of Isocrates [*Areopagiticus*, xvi = 148 A]: 'Those who wish to have a good commonwealth ought not to fill their colonnades with inscribed decrees but to carry in their hearts a regard for what is just.'

[4] Trypho himself, relaxing his uncompromising attitude, speaks thus to Justin [Justin, *Dialogue with Trypho*, viii = 493 A]: 'If you had continued in that kind of philosophy, some hope of a better state would have been left to you.'

Paul explains, *Galatians*, v. 3), they did this in part that they might acquire the right of citizenship, for proselytes, whom the Jews called foreigners of righteousness, had the same rights as the Israelites (*Numbers*, xv. 15);[1] in part that they might become sharers of the promises[2] which were not common to the human race but peculiar to the Jewish people. Nevertheless I should not deny that in the following centuries a perverse opinion was embraced by some, to the effect that there was no salvation outside the pale of Judaism.

7. From this we conclude that we are bound by no part of the Hebraic law, so far as this is law of a special kind. For, outside of the law of nature, the binding force of law comes from the will of him who makes the law; and it is not possible to discover, from any indication, that God willed that others than Israelites should be bound by that law. There is, then, no need of proof that in respect to ourselves this law has been abrogated; for a law cannot be abrogated in respect to those on whom it has never been binding. But for the Israelites its binding force was abrogated in respect to rituals, at least, the moment the law of the Gospel began to be promulgated, as was clearly revealed to the chief of the Apostles (*Acts*, x. 15). It was abrogated also in regard to other things, after the Jewish people, though the fall and [9] devastation of their city, which was destroyed without hope of restoration, ceased to be a nation.

8. What we, who are not of Jewish birth, gained from the coming of Christ, was not that we should not be bound by the laws of Moses, but that, having previously had only an obscure hope resting on the goodness of God, we are now upheld by a covenant expressed in plain words. We are therefore able to unite ourselves with the Jews, sons of the Patriarchs, in one church, since their law, by which as by a barrier they were held apart from us, has been done away with (*Ephesians*, ii. 14).

XVII.—*What arguments Christians may draw from the Hebraic law, and in what way*

1. Since the law given through the agency of Moses cannot impose direct obligation upon us, as we have already shown, let us see whether it may be useful to us in any other way, not only in this inquiry regarding the law of war but in other similar inquiries. To know this is, in fact, on many accounts important.

2. First, then, the Hebraic law shows that that which is enjoined

[1] Justin, *Dialogue with Trypho* [cxxiii = 761 A]: 'The proselyte who has been circumcised and has joined himself with the people is on a plane with the native-born [Israelite].'

[2] For this reason they were admitted to a participation in the feast of the Passover [cf. *Exodus*, xii. 19, 47, 48].

by it is not contrary to the law of nature. For since the law of nature, as we have previously said, is perpetual and unchangeable, nothing contrary to that law could be enjoined by God, who is never unjust. Further, the law of Moses is called 'pure' and 'right' (*Psalms*, xix. 8; Vulgate, xviii. 8), and the Apostle Paul calls it 'holy', 'just', and 'good' (*Romans*, vii. 12).

I am speaking of the ordinances of the law; for in regard to the things which it permits a closer distinction must be made. Now permission which is accorded by a law—we are not concerned here with a permission which involves fact merely, signifying the removal of an impediment—is either complete, which authorizes the doing of something with the fullest possible liberty, or incomplete, which only grants freedom from punishment among men, with the right of non-interference by another. From permission of the former kind, not less than from a command, it follows that that with which the law deals is not contrary to the law of nature. With permission of the second sort the case is different.[1] But inference from the law of Moses to the law of nature is rarely in order, for the reason that, when the words which express the permission are equivocal, it is more fitting for us to determine by the law of nature of which kind the permission is rather than to proceed by argument from the character of the permission to the law of nature.

3. Akin to this first observation is a second, that to those who among Christians have the sovereign power it is now permitted to make laws having the same purport as the laws which were given by the agency of Moses; exception being made of those laws whose entire content belonged to the time when Christ was still expected and the Gospel was not yet revealed, and of laws in relation to which Christ ordained the contrary, either in general or in particular. Outside of these three cases no reason can be thought of why that which was ordained by the law of Moses should now be outside the range of things which are permissible.

4. A third observation should be added. All that was enjoined by the law of Moses with reference to those virtues which Christ requires of His disciples, is just as much, or even in a greater degree, to be required of Christians now.[2] The basis of this observation is to be found in the fact that the virtues required of Christians, as humility, long-suffering, and love, are required in a higher degree[3]

[1] See Chrysostom, *On Romans*, end of chap. vii [Homily XIII, iv].

[2] Tertullian, *On Modesty* [chap. vi]: 'Liberty in Christ has done no wrong to innocence. There remains in its entirety the law of piety, truth, steadfastness, chastity, justice, mercy, kindliness, modesty.'

[3] Chrysostom, *On Virginity*, xciv [lxxxiv]: 'Now a greater degree of virtue ought to be displayed . . . because the grace of the Spirit has now been abundantly shed abroad, and because the coming of Christ is a great gift.' The same father presents similar expressions in the homily, *That*

than was the case under the Hebraic law; that, too, with good reason, because the heavenly promises are set forth in the Gospel much more clearly.

Hence the old law compared with that of the Gospel is said to have been neither 'perfect' nor 'faultless' (*Hebrews*, vii. 19; viii. 7), and Christ is said to be 'the end of the law' (*Romans*, x. 4); also, the law is spoken of as a 'tutor to lead us to Christ' (*Galatians*, iii. 25). Thus the ancient law of the Sabbath and that of tithes[1] show that Christians are bound to set apart not less than a seventh of their time for divine worship, and not less than a tenth of their income for the support of those who minister in the sacred offices, or to similar pious uses.

Faults are the Result of Neglect [= *On the Devil as Tempter,* Homily III, vii]; also, *On Fasting,* III; and *On Romans,* the passages dealing with vi. 14 [Homily XI] and vii. 5 [Homily XII; see also on verse 6].

Add Irenaeus, [*Against Heresies,*] Book IV, chap. xxvi. The writer of the *Synopsis of Holy Scriptures* [xlvii] which is found in the works [15] of Athanasius, treating the fifth chapter of Matthew, says: 'Christ here renders the "precepts of the law more strict".'

[1] Thus Irenaeus [*Against Heresies*], Book IV, chap. xxxiv, makes application of this law in respect to Christians; so does Chrysostom also, *On First Corinthians,* end of the last chapter [Homily XLIII, iv to verse 9], and *On Ephesians,* ii. 10 [Homily IV, iv, on verse 10].

CHAPTER II

WHETHER IT IS EVER LAWFUL TO WAGE WAR

I.—*That war is not in conflict with the law of nature is proved by several considerations*

1. Having seen what the sources of law are, let us come to the first and most general question, which is this: whether any war is lawful, or whether it is ever permissible to war. This question, as also the others which will follow, must first be taken up from the point of view of the law of nature.

[III. v. 17.]

Gellius, [*Attic Nights*,] XII. v.

Marcus Tullius Cicero, both in the third book of his treatise *On Ends* and in other places, following Stoic writings learnedly argues that there are certain first principles of nature—'first according to nature', as the Greeks phrased it—and certain other principles which are later manifest but which are to have the preference over those first principles. He calls first principles of nature those in accordance with which every animal from the moment of its birth has regard for itself and is impelled to preserve itself, to have zealous consideration for its own condition and for those things which tend to preserve it, and also shrinks from destruction and things which appear likely to cause destruction. Hence also it happens, he says, that there is no one who, if the choice were presented to him, would not prefer to have all the parts of his body in proper order and whole rather than dwarfed or deformed; and that it is one's first duty to keep oneself in the condition which nature gave to him, then to hold to those things which are in conformity with nature and reject those things that are contrary thereto.

2. But after these things have received due consideration [Cicero continues], there follows a notion of the conformity of things with reason,[1] which is superior to the body. Now this conformity, in which moral goodness becomes the paramount object, ought to be accounted of higher import than the things to which alone instinct first directed itself, because the first principles of nature commend us to right reason, and right reason ought to be more dear to us than those things through whose instrumentality we have been brought to it.[2]

[1] Seneca, *Letters*, cxxiv [XX. vii. 11]: 'Just as in every case a nature, unless brought to its highest perfection, does not manifest its type of good, so the good of man is not found in man unless reason has been perfected in him.'

[2] Seneca, *Letters*, lxxvi [IX. v. 8]: 'That to which each creature is born, and on account of which

Since this is true and without other demonstration would easily receive the assent of all who are endowed with sound judgement, it follows that in investigating the law of nature it is necessary first to see what is consistent with those fundamental principles of nature, and then to come to that which, though of later origin, is nevertheless more worthy—that which ought not only to be grasped, if it appear, but to be sought out by every effort.

3. According to the diversity of the matter, that which we call moral goodness at times consists of a point, so to speak, so that if you depart from it even the least possible distance you turn aside in the direction of wrong-doing; at times it has a wider range, so that an act may be praiseworthy if performed, yet if it be omitted altogether or performed in some other way no blame would attach, the distinction being generally without an intermediate stage, like the transition from being to not-being. [16] Between things opposed in a different way, however, as white and black, a mean may be found either by effecting a combination of the two or by finding an intermediate between them.

It is with this latter class of actions that both divine and human laws are wont to concern themselves, in order that those acts which were in themselves merely praiseworthy might become also obligatory. But we said above, in discussing the law of nature, that the question is this, whether an act can be performed without injustice; and injustice is understood to be that which is utterly repugnant to a rational and social nature.

4. In the first principles of nature there is nothing which is opposed to war; rather, all points are in its favour. The end and aim of war being the preservation of life and limb, and the keeping or acquiring of things useful to life, war is in perfect accord with those first principles of nature. If in order to achieve these ends it is necessary to use force, no inconsistency with the first principles of nature is involved, since nature has given to each animal strength sufficient for self-defence and self-assistance. 'All kinds of animals', says Xenophon, 'understand some mode of fighting, and they have learned this from no other source than nature.' In the fragment of the *Piscation* we read·

[*Training of Cyrus*, II. iii. 9.]
[Ovid, *Halieutica*, 7–9.]

To all has it been given
To recognize a foe, likewise to know

it is esteemed, is the best thing in it. What is the best thing in a man? Reason.' See also *Letters*, cxxi [XX. iv] and cxxviii [apparently cxxiv, cited in the previous note, is meant].

Juvenal, *Satires*, xv [lines 106–8]:

Zeno's rules to us
Give better guidance; for their teaching is
That not all things, but only certain things
We may do to save life.

Their safeguards each its own, and power and use
Each of its weapon.

Horace had said: [*Satires*, II. i. 52 f.]

With tooth the wolf, with horn the bull attacks;
And why, unless by inner feeling guided?

Lucretius presents the thought more fully: [V. 1033 ff.]

Each creature feels the strength which it can use.
Felt by the calf his horns are, ere they stand
Upon his forehead; and with them he butts
Angrily, and, threatening, forward thrusts.[1]

The same idea is thus expressed by Galen: 'We see that each animal uses for its protection that in which it is strongest. For the calf whose horns have not yet sprouted threatens with that part, and the colt kicks before its hoofs are hard, and the puppy tries to bite when its teeth are not yet strong.' Galen also remarks (*On the Use of Parts*, 1) that man is an animal born for peace and war. Weapons, to be sure, are not born with him, but he has hands suited for fashioning and handling weapons; and we see that babies of their own accord, and without being taught by any one, use their hands in place of weapons.[2] So Aristotle, too (*On the Parts of Animals*, IV. 10), says that in the case of man the hand has the place of spear, sword, and all other weapons, because he is able to take and hold everything with the hand.

5. Right reason, moreover, and the nature of society, which must be studied in the second place and are of even greater importance, do not prohibit all use of force, but only that use of force which is in conflict with society, that is which attempts to take away the rights of another. For society has in view this object, that through community of resource and effort each individual be safeguarded in the possession of what belongs to him.

[1] [37] Martial [*Epigrams*, III. lviii. 11]:

The calf with head unhorned is keen to fight.

Porphyry, *On Abstaining from Animal Food*, Book III [III. ix]: 'Each animal knows in what part it is weak, in what part strong; the former it shields, the latter it makes use of. The panther uses its teeth, the lion its claws and teeth, the horse its hoof, and the ox its horns.'

Chrysostom, *On the Statues*, XI [Homily XI, iv]: 'The animals, devoid of reason, have their weapons in the body itself; thus the ox has horns, the wild boar tusks, the lion claws. To me, on the contrary, God has not furnished weapons in the organization of my body, but outside the body, showing by this very fact that man is a gentle animal, and that I do not at all times have need of such weapons. Often, in fact, I lay my missile aside, sometimes I take it up again. Weapons, therefore, he caused to be separate and apart from my nature, in order that I might be more free and unfettered, and might not be compelled always to carry them.' The latter part of the quotation accords well with the passage of Galen quoted in the text.

[2] Cassiodorus, *On the Soul* [ix]: 'And since the body of man is able to defend itself neither with horn nor with tusk nor by means of flight' (as the other animals do), 'there were granted to him a powerful chest and arms; to the end that with the hand he might ward off attempted injury and protect himself by presenting his body—so to speak—as a kind of shield.'

It is easy to understand that this consideration would hold even if private ownership (as we now call it) had not been introduced; for life, limbs, and liberty would in that case be the possessions belonging to each, and no attack could be made upon these by another without injustice. Under such conditions the first one taking possession would have the right to use things not claimed and to consume them up to the limit of his needs, and any one depriving him of that right [17] would commit an unjust act. But now that private ownership has by law or usage assumed a definite form, the matter is much easier to understand. I shall express the thought in the words of Cicero:

On Duties, III [III. v. 22].

> Just as, in case each member of the body should have a feeling of its own, so that it might think that it could gain in vigour by drawing to itself the vigour of the nearest member, the whole body would of necessity be weakened and utterly perish, so, if every one of us should seize upon the possessions of others for himself and carry off from each whatever he could, for his own gain, human society and the community of life would of necessity be absolutely destroyed. For, since nature does not oppose, it has been granted that each prefer that whatever contributes to the advantage of life be acquired for himself rather than for another; but nature does not allow us to increase our means of subsistence, our resources, and our riches, from the spoil of others.

6. It is not, then, contrary to the nature of society to look out for oneself and advance one's own interests, provided the rights of others are not infringed; and consequently the use of force which does not violate the rights of others is not unjust. This thought also Cicero has presented: 'Since there are two ways of settling a difference, the one by argument, the other by force, and since the former is characteristic of man, the latter of brutes, we should have recourse to the second only when it is not permitted to use the first.' 'What can be done', says the same writer in another passage, 'against force without force?'

[*On Duties*, I. xi. 34.]

Letters, XII. iii [XII. iii. 1].

Digest, XLIII. xvi. 1. 27.

In Ulpian we read: 'Cassius writes that it is permissible to repel force by force, and this right is bestowed by nature. From this moreover it appears, he says, that it is permissible to repel arms by means of arms.' Ovid had said:

[*Art of Love*, III. 492.]

> The laws permit arms 'gainst armed men to bear.

II.—*That war is not in conflict with the law of nature is proved from history*

1. Our statement that not all war is in conflict with the law of nature is more fully proved from sacred history. For Abraham with his servants and allies had taken up arms and had won the victory over the four kings who had sacked Sodom; and God approved the deed through his priest Melchizedek. Thus in fact Melchizedek addressed him (*Genesis*, xiv. 20): 'Praise be to God Most High,

who has delivered thine enemies into thine hand.' But Abraham had taken up arms, as is evident from the narrative, without a special command of God; in accordance with the law of nature, therefore, did he act, a man not only most holy but also most wise—so recognized even by the testimony of foreigners, Berosus and Orpheus.

[Josephus *Antiquities of the Jews*, I. vii. 2; Clement of Alexandria, *Stromata*, V. x. 124.]

I shall not appeal to the history of the seven peoples whom God delivered to the Israelites to be destroyed; for in that case there was a special command to execute a judgement of God upon peoples guilty of the greatest crimes. These wars therefore in holy writ are properly called the wars of God, since they were undertaken by the command of God, not at the discretion of men. Having a more direct bearing on our subject is the war in which the Jews, under the leadership of Moses and Joshua, by arms repelled the Amalekites who were attacking them (*Exodus*, xvii). This act, which God had not commanded in advance, He approved afterward.

2. But further, God laid down for His own people general and perpetual laws in regard to the mode of carrying on war (*Deuteronomy*, xx. 10, 15), showing by this very act that a war can be just even without having been specifically commanded by Him. For in these passages He plainly distinguishes the case of the seven peoples from that of other peoples; and since in the same passages He presents no ordinance dealing with the just causes for undertaking war, by this very fact He shows that these are clearly enough known from nature. A just cause of war, for example, is the defence of territory, in the war of Jephthah against the Ammonites (*Judges*, xi); another is the maltreatment of envoys, in the war of David against the same people (*2 Samuel*, x).

In the same connexion we should note what the inspired writer to the Hebrews says, that Gideon, Barak, Samson, Jephthah, David, Samuel, and others 'through faith subdued kingdoms, waxed valiant in fight, turned to flight the armies of the aliens' (*Hebrews*, xi. 33, 34). In this passage, as the context makes plain, he includes in the term 'faith' the conviction that [18] what is done is pleasing to God. So also a wise woman says that David 'fights the battles of God' (*1 Samuel*, xxv. 28), that is, battles that are righteous and just.

III.—*That war is not in conflict with the law of nature is proved from general agreement*

1. Our thesis is proved also by the general agreement of all nations, and especially among the wise. Well known is the passage of Cicero in regard to force used in the defence of life, in which he bears witness to nature herself:

For Milo [iv. 10].

There is this law which is not written, but born with us; which we have not learned, have not received, have not read, but which we have caught up, have sucked in, yes have wrung out from nature herself; a law regarding which we have not been instructed, but in accord with which we have been made; to which we have not been trained, but with which we are imbued—the law that if our life has been placed in jeopardy by any snare, or violence, or weapons either of brigands or of enemies, every possible means of securing safety is morally right.[1]

[*For Milo*, xi. 30.] The same writer in another passage adds:

This law reason has enjoined upon the learned, necessity upon barbarians, custom upon nations, and nature herself upon wild beasts, that always, with whatever means of defence they possess, they ward off all violence from body, from head, from life itself.

Digest, IX. ii. 4. *Dig.*, I. i. 3. *Jewish War*, III. xxv [III. viii. 5]. The jurist Gaius says: 'Natural reason permits defence of oneself against danger'; the jurist Florentinus, 'In accordance with this law it comes about that whatever each may have done in defence of his person he is thought to have done lawfully.' 'For there is', says Josephus, 'that law of nature which applies in the case of all creatures, that they wish to live; and therein lies the reason why we consider those as enemies who clearly wish to rob us of life.'

Dig. IX. i. 1. §§ 3, 11. Add *Exodus*, xxi. 28. [*Natural History*, VII. pr.] 2. So obvious is the fairness of this principle that even among brutes which, as we have said, have not the substance of legal rights but only a shadowy appearance of them, we may distinguish between the use of force which attempts an injury and that which wards it off. For Ulpian, having said that an animal devoid of sense, that is, of the use of reason,[2] is incapable of doing what is legally wrong, nevertheless immediately adds that when rams or bulls have fought, and one has killed the other, on the authority of Quintus Mucius a distinction ought to be made. If the animal which started the fight should be killed, an action would not lie; but if the animal which had not started the fight should be killed, an action would lie. A passage of Pliny will serve to throw light on what has been said:

The fierceness of lions does not manifest itself in attacks upon lions, the bites of serpents are not directed to serpents; but if violence is attempted there is no creature which does not manifest anger, which does not possess a spirit impatient of injury and will not show a ready liveliness in defending itself if you do it harm.

[1] Seneca [*Letters*, XX. iv. 18]: 'The surest means of defence in the case of each is nearest at hand; to each the protection of itself has been committed.' Quintilian, [*Institutes of Oratory*,] VII. ii [VII. ii. 21]: 'First, in every sort of case there must be a defence, because by nature our own safety is more important to us than the destruction of an adversary.'

Well does Sophocles say in the *Trachinian Women* [lines 278, 279]:

For openly had he himself defended,
God would have pardoned him his combat just.

See also the *Law of the Visigoths*, Book VI, title i, chap. 6 [VI. iv. 6; ed. Zeumer, p. 267].

[2] In like manner, Seneca speaks of wild beasts [*On Benefits*, I. ii. 5]: 'Far as they are from the understanding and appraisal of a benefit, yet persistent repetition of kindnesses completely masters them.' See the whole passage, *On Benefits*, Book I, chap. iii, and compare our quotation from Philo in the *Prolegomena* [note 2, p. 11].

IV.—*Proof is adduced that war is not in conflict with the law of nations*

1. It is sufficiently well established, therefore, that not all wars are at variance with the law of nature; and this may also be said to be true of the law of nations.

2. That wars, moreover, are not condemned by the volitional law of nations, histories, and the laws and customs of all peoples fully teach us. Rather, Hermogenianus said that wars were introduced by the law of nations;[1] but I think that this statement ought to be understood as having a meaning slightly different from that ordinarily given to it, namely, that a definite formality in the conduct of war was introduced by the law of nations, and that particular effects follow wars waged in accordance with such formality under the law of nations. Hence arises the distinction, which we shall have to make use of later, between a war which, according to the law of nations, is formally declared and is called legal, that is a complete war; and a war not formally declared, which nevertheless does not on that account cease to be a legal war, that is according to law. For as regards other wars, provided the cause be just, the law of nations does not indeed lend them support, but it does not oppose them, as will be explained more fully later. 'It has been established by the law of nations,' says Livy, 'that arms are to be warded off by arms.' And Florentinus declares that the law of nations authorizes us to ward off violence and injury in order to protect our body.

Dig. I. i. 5.

[Book III. iii.]

Book XLIII [XLII. xli. 11]. *Dig.* I. i. 3.

V.—*Proof is adduced that war was not in conflict with the divine volitional law before the time of the Gospel, and objections are answered*

1. A greater difficulty presents itself in connexion with the divine volitional law. Let no one at this point raise the objection that the law of nature is unchangeable, and that in consequence nothing can be established by God which is contrary to it. For this holds true in respect to those things which the law of nature [19] forbids or enjoins, but not in respect to the things which by the law of nature are permissible only. Things of the latter class, since they do not properly belong to the sphere of the law of nature but are outside that sphere, can be both forbidden and enjoined.

2. First, therefore, as against war some are accustomed to bring forward the law given to Noah and his posterity, in which God thus speaks (*Genesis*, ix. 5, 6):

[1] The writer of the *Lives of Famous Men* says in *Themistocles* [Nepos, *Themistocles*, vii. 4]: 'He declared that the Athenians in accordance with his advice—as they were permitted to do by the common law of nations—surrounded with walls the gods of their state, their city, and their homes, in order that they might be able the more easily to defend these against the enemy.'

And surely your blood, the blood of your lives, will I require; from every beast will I require it; and at the hand of man, even at the hand of every man's brother, will I require the life of man. Whoso sheddeth man's blood, by man shall his blood be shed: for in the image of God made He man.

The first part of this passage, then, in which the requiring of blood is mentioned, they understand as altogether general; and they suppose that the second part, about the shedding of blood in turn, is in the nature of a menace, not an expression of approval. Neither interpretation is to me convincing. For the prohibition in regard to the shedding of blood has no wider application than the commandment, 'Thou shalt not kill'; but this commandment, it is clear, has not proved to be an obstacle either to capital punishment or to wars. The latter rule of law then, as well as the former, had in view not so much the ordaining of something new as the declaration and repetition of a rule of the law of nature which had been effaced by degenerate usage. Hence these words are to be taken in a sense which conveys the idea of a moral fault, just as by the word homicide we understand not the slaying of a man in general, but a premeditated murder of an innocent man. What follows in regard to the shedding of blood in turn seems to me to contain not a statement of a bare fact, but a provision of law.

3. I explain the matter thus. According to nature it is not unfair that each suffer to the full extent of the evil he has committed, in accordance with the principle which is called the law of Radamanthus:[1]

> If each shall suffer all that he has done,
> It will be fair and right.

[*Controversies*, X. pr. 5.] Seneca the father phrased the idea thus: 'By a most just recompense of suffering each through his own punishment undergoes what he devised for another.' In accordance with the view-point of this natural equity Cain, conscious of parricide, had said (*Genesis*, iv. 14): 'Whosoever findeth me shall slay me.'

In those first times, however, either on account of the scarcity of men or because criminals were few in number and so there was less need of an example, that which seemed to be permitted by nature God repressed by a command; He desired that contact and intercourse with a murderer be avoided, but that life be not taken from him. [*Laws*, IX. viii.] A similar regulation Plato established among his laws; that such was the practise formerly in vogue in Greece Euripides informs us in these verses: [*Orestes*, 512 ff.]

[1] The law of Radamanthus is stated by Apollodorus, in Book II [Apollodorus, *Library*, II. iv. 9]: 'The law of Radamanthus: if a man has avenged himself on one who first attempted to injure him, let him go unpunished.'

How well the prescient age of our forebears
Decreed, that whoso murder had committed
Should far from way and sight of men depart,
By flight, not death, his dreadful crime atone!

To the same point the following passage of Thucydides relates: Book III
'It is believable that in antiquity penalties were light[1] even for great [xlv].
crimes; but as these in the course of time came to be viewed with contempt, recourse was had to the death penalty.' 'Until now,' says Lactantius, 'it seemed in fact wicked to inflict the punishment Book II
of death upon criminals who, no matter how bad, are nevertheless [ix. 23].
men.'

4. Upon the one striking example was based a conclusion [20] in regard to the divine will, and this passed over into a law. Thus Lamech, having committed a similar crime,[2] in the light of that example promised himself exemption from punishment (*Genesis*, iv. 24).

5. But since already before the Flood, in the period of the giants, a general orgy of murders had prevailed, in the renewal of the human race after the Flood God judged that severer measures must be taken, in order that the same custom might not become fixed; and having done away with the mildness of the former age, He Himself permitted that the man who had killed a murderer[3] should be innocent—a measure which nature declared was not unfair. Afterward, when courts were established, for very weighty reasons this permission was restricted to judges alone. Nevertheless, a trace of the older custom remained in the right of the next of kin of a murdered man; this right was recognized even after the law of Moses, as will be more fully discussed later.

6. In favour of our interpretation we have the great authority of Abraham who, being not ignorant of the law given to Noah, took up arms against the four kings, obviously in the belief that his action was not in conflict with that law. In like manner also Moses ordered that the Amalekites, who were attacking the people, be resisted by force of arms; he made use, as we see, of the law of nature, for it

[1] [38] Servius, *On the Aeneid*, Book I [Book I, line 136], explains *luetis*, 'you shall atone for', by *persolvetis*, 'you shall pay for', and says: 'The expression arose from the use of money; among the ancients all penalties were in terms of money.' Also on Book II [Book II, line 229], explaining *expendere*, 'to expiate' [literally 'to weigh out']: 'The word is taken from the use of money; for among our ancestors it is established that penalties were in terms of money, even when, on account of the rudeness of the age, money was still weighed out; in consequence the word was applied to the death penalty.' On Book VI [Book VI, line 21], explaining 'to pay' [literally 'to weigh', in the phrase 'to pay the penalty' (*pendere poenas*)]: 'The word was taken from condemnation to a penalty in money.'

Pliny, *Natural History*, Book VII, chap. lvi [VII. lvi. 200], relates that the first sentence of death was pronounced in the Areopagus.

[2] Or rather, if he had committed a similar crime; for this is the meaning of the words recorded by Moses [*Genesis*, iv. 24].

[3] Josephus [*Antiquities of the Jews*, I. iii. 8]: 'I enjoin upon you that your hands be kept free from the shedding of men's blood; and if a man shall have committed murder, let him be punished.'

does not appear that God had been specifically consulted in regard to this act (*Exodus*, xvii. 9). Furthermore, it is clear that capital punishment was already applied not only to murderers but also to other criminals, and not merely among foreign peoples but among the favoured recipients of the holy teaching (*Genesis*, xxxviii. 24).

7. Beyond doubt interpretation of the divine will, with the help of natural reason, had proceeded from like to like, so that it seemed not unfair to apply to others who were guilty of exceptional crimes the penalty which had been appointed for the murderer. For there are certain things which are rated of equal value with life, as reputation, maidenly chastity, and conjugal fidelity; and things without which life cannot be safe, such as respect for the governing power which maintains the social order. Those who attack these things seem no better than murderers.

8. In this connexion belongs the ancient tradition which is found among the Jews, that several laws were given by God to the sons of Noah, of which not all were recorded by Moses, because it was sufficient for his purpose that these were afterwards included in the particular law of the Jews. Thus it is evident that there was an old law against incestuous marriages (*Leviticus*, xviii), although this was not mentioned by Moses in the proper place. Among the ordinances which God gave to the sons of Noah they say that the following also had a place, that not only murder but also adultery, incest, and robbery with violence should be punished with death. This is confirmed by the words of Job (xxxi. 11).

9. Now the law which was given through the agency of Moses justifies the inflicting of capital punishment by reasons which carry not less weight among other peoples than with the Jewish people; examples are to be found in *Leviticus*, xviii. 24, 25, 27, 28; *Psalms*, ci. 5; and *Proverbs*, xx. 8. Of murder it is specifically said that no expiation can be made for the land except by shedding the blood of the murderer (*Numbers*, xxxv. 31, 33). Besides, it is absurd to think that on the one hand the Jewish people were allowed to protect their moral code and the safety both of the state and of individuals by means of capital punishment and to defend themselves by war, and that, on the other hand, the same course of action was not at the same time permissible to other kings and nations, while, nevertheless, those kings or nations were never warned by the prophets, as they were frequently warned in regard to other sins, that the use of capital punishment and wars of every kind were viewed with disapproval by God.

10. Who, on the contrary, would not believe that, since the law of Moses with reference to judgements embodied a faithful expression of the divine will, the nations would have acted rightly

and fittingly in taking this as a model for themselves? It is believable that at any rate the Greeks, the Attic Greeks in particular, did this; [21] thence it came about that there is so great similarity between the ancient Attic law, together with the part of the Roman law of the Twelve Tables derived from it, and the Hebraic laws. These considerations seem sufficient to make it plain that the law given to Noah did not have the meaning attributed to it by those who on the strength of it oppose all wars.

VI.—*Preliminary considerations bearing upon the question whether war is in conflict with the law of the Gospel*

1. The arguments against war which are drawn from the Gospel have greater plausibility. In examining them I shall not assume, as many do, that in the Gospel outside of the ordinances relating to belief and to the sacraments there is nothing which does not belong to the law of nature; for I do not think that this is true, at least in the sense in which most people take it.

2. I willingly recognize the fact that in the Gospel nothing is enjoined upon us which does not have the quality of natural moral goodness; but I do not see why I should grant that we are not bound by the laws of Christ beyond the limit of obligation imposed by the law of nature of and by itself. It is amazing to see how those who think differently labour in the effort to prove that things which are forbidden by the Gospel are not permissible by the law of nature, as concubinage, divorce,[1] and polygamy. These things in fact are of such a nature that reason itself declares that it is morally better to abstain from them, but they are not such that wickedness would be manifest in them without divine law. Again, who would say that we are bound by the law of nature to do that which the law of Christ enjoins, that we expose ourselves to the danger of death for others (*1 John*, iii. 16)? Pertinent is the saying of Justin: 'To live according to nature is the problem of him who has not yet become a believer.'[2]

3. I shall not even follow those who make another by no means slight assumption, that Christ, in delivering the precepts which are found in the fifth chapter of *Matthew* and immediately thereafter, was speaking only as an expounder of the law given through the agency of Moses. Of an altogether different import are the words so often repeated: 'Ye have heard that it was said to them of old time—but I say unto you.' The contrast here, as in the Syriac and other versions, shows that the meaning is, 'to them of old time,' not

[1] To this point the passage of Jerome relates [*To Oceanus, Letters*, lxxvii. 3]: 'Different are the laws of Caesar and the laws of Christ; Papinian enjoins one thing, our Paul another.'

[2] The quotation from Justin is in the letter *To Zena* [ii]; and the same thought is found in Origen, in those extracts which are known as *Philocalia* [chap. ix].

'by them of old time'; so 'to you', not 'by you'. Now 'they of old time' were none other than those who were living in the time of Moses. For the things which are declared to have been said 'to them of old time' are not utterances of men learned in the law but of Moses, either word for word, or in substance. These utterances are:

[xx. 13.] Thou shalt not kill (*Exodus*, xx. 30);

[*Lev.*, xxiv. 21.] Whoso hath killed a man shall be held in judgement (*Leviticus*, xxi. 21; *Numbers*, xxxv. 16, 17, 30);

[xx. 14.] Thou shalt not commit adultery (*Exodus*, xx. 30);

Whoso putteth away his wife, let him give to her a bill of divorcement (*Deuteronomy*, xxiv. 1);

Thou shalt not swear falsely, but thou shalt render unto the Lord that which thou hast sworn (*Exodus*, xx. 7; *Numbers*, xxx. 2);

An eye for an eye, a tooth for a tooth—supply 'it may be permitted to demand in judgement' (*Leviticus*, xxiv. 20; *Deuteronomy*, xix. 21);

Thou shalt love thy neighbour (that is, an Israelite; *Leviticus*, xix. 18), and shalt hate thine enemy (for example, the seven peoples,[1] with whom the Israelites are forbidden to have friendship and to whom they are to show no mercy; *Exodus*, xxxiv. 11; *Deuteronomy*, vii. 1. To these the Amalekites are to be added, against whom the Jews are [*Ex.*, xvii. 16.] bidden to wage implacable war; *Exodus*, xxvii. 19; *Deuteronomy*, xxv. 19).

4. For the understanding of the words of Christ, however, we must once for all observe that the law given through the agency of Moses may be considered in two ways. First, it may be viewed in relation to that which it has in common with other laws customarily established by men, in so far, surely, as it restrains the graver crimes by the fear of visible punishments (*Hebrews*, ii. 2) and by this means holds the Jewish people in a state of civil society; from this point of view it is called 'the law of a carnal commandment' (*Hebrews*, [vii. 16.] vii. 13), and law 'of works' (*Romans*, iii. 27). Or, in the second place, the Mosaic law may be viewed in relation to that which is peculiar to divine law, in so far, at any rate, as it demands purity of soul and certain actions which can be omitted without a temporal penalty; from this point of view it is called [22] 'spiritual law' (*Romans*, vii. 14), 'restoring the soul' (*Psalms*, xix. 9; Vulgate xviii. 9). The scribes and the Pharisees, contenting themselves with the first point of view, paid small heed to the second, which is more important, and did not impress it upon the people; the truth of this statement can be shown not only from our books but also from Josephus and the learned men of the Jews.

5. Even in relation to the second point of view, however, it is important to know that the virtues required of Christians were also either commended to the Jews, or enjoined upon them; but they

[1] That the hatred of these peoples was permitted by the law is remarked by the distinguished Abrabanel, in his comment *On Deuteronomy*, xxiii. 21.

were not enjoined upon the Jews with the same emphasis and with so great breadth [1] of application as upon Christians. In both respects moreover Christ sets His teachings over against those of the old time; whence it is clear that His words do not embody a mere interpretation. Recognition of this fact is important not merely with reference to the point now under consideration, but many others as well, that we may not make use of the authority of the Hebraic law to a greater extent than is just.

VII.—*Arguments drawn from Holy Writ on behalf of the negative view, that war is not in conflict with the law of the Gospel*

1. Passing by the arguments, then, which seem to us untenable, the first and weightiest evidence by which we prove that the right to war was not completely annulled by the law of Christ, shall be that passage of Paul in *1 Timothy* (ii. 1–3):

> I exhort, therefore, first of all that supplications, prayers, intercessions, thanksgivings be made for all men; for kings and all that are in high place; that we may lead a tranquil and quiet life in all godliness and gravity.[2] This is good and acceptable in the sight of God our Saviour, who would have all men to be saved, and come to the knowledge of the truth.

In this passage we are taught three things: that it is acceptable to God that kings become Christians; also that, having become Christians, they remain kings (the thought was thus expressed by Justin Martyr: 'For this we pray, that kings and princes along with their royal power may possess a sound mind'; and in the book entitled *Constitutions of Clement* the Church prays for 'Christian authorities', that is, for Christian magistrates [3]); finally, that this also is acceptable to God, that Christian kings enable other Christians to lead a tranquil life. [*Apology*, I. xvii.]

[1] For some comments bearing upon this topic see the notes to the end of the first chapter [p. 49, note 3]. Especially fine is this passage of Chrysostom, *On Virginity*, chap. xliv:

> Formerly, so high a degree of virtue had not been demanded of us, but it was permitted to exact vengeance of him who inflicted an injury, to return abuse for abuse, and to devote oneself to amassing riches; to swear an oath free from guile, to take an eye for an eye, and to hate an enemy. Nay, more, it had not been forbidden to live luxuriously, or to give way to anger, or to cast out one wife and take another. And not even this only, but the law permitted a man to have two wives at the same time, and both in this and in other matters there was large latitude in those times. But after the coming of Christ the way of life was made much more narrow.

In the same treatise, chap. lxxxiii: 'The degree of virtue exacted from them was not the same as from us.' The same writer in the sermon *That the Son is Equal to the Father*, which is in vol. VI [*Against the Anomoeans*, Homily, X, iv], says that in the Gospel 'there is both a strengthening of the Commandments and an increase in their number'.

[2] Seneca, *Letters*, lxxiii [IX. ii], says that those who are devoted to philosophy are falsely thought to be despisers of public officials and kings. 'On the contrary', he declares [IX. ii. 1], 'none are better disposed toward them, and not without good reason; for to none do those that govern contribute more than to those to whom it is permitted to enjoy undisturbed quiet.' The letter is well worth reading, and therein is also the following [IX. ii. 5]: 'The benefits of this peace, which contributes to the advantage of all, accrue more abundantly to those who make good use of it.'

[3] [39] Unless you prefer to interpret this as 'the end of the Christian life'.

2. But how shall the ruler do this? Paul explains elsewhere (*Romans*, xiii. 4): 'For he is a minister of God to thee for good. But if thou do that which is evil, be afraid, for He beareth not the sword in vain. For he is a minister of God, an avenger for wrath to him that doeth evil.' By the right of the sword through a figure of speech every form of compulsion is understood, as also sometimes in the writings of the jurists; but in such a way, nevertheless, that the right to impose the extreme penalty, that is the actual use of the sword, is not excluded.

The second *Psalm* serves to throw not a little light upon this passage; for although it had its true application in the person of David, nevertheless it is more fully and more completely applicable to Christ, as we may learn from *Acts* (iv. 25; xiii. 33) and *Hebrews* (v. 5). This Psalm exhorts all kings to receive the Son of God with reverence; that is, that as kings they show themselves also His ministers, as St. Augustine rightly explains.

Contra Cres. Gram., III [ii. 56].

The words of Augustine on this point I quote: 'In this way kings serve God in the capacity of kings if, just as is divinely enjoined upon them, in their kingdoms they ordain good and prohibit evil, not only in respect to matters which relate to human society but also matters that concern the divine religion.' In another passage he says: 'In what way, then, do kings serve the Lord in fear, except by prohibiting and punishing with religious severity the things that are done contrary to the commandments of the Lord? For it is one thing to serve the Lord as man, another to serve Him as king.' 'Kings', he says, a little further on, 'serve the Lord in the capacity of kings when in serving Him they do those things which they cannot do except as kings.'

Letters, I [clxxxv. 19], *To Boniface*.

3. A second argument is furnished to us by that very passage
[23] of which we have quoted a portion (*Romans*, xiii), wherein the highest power, such as that of the king, is said to be from God, and is called an ordinance of God. From this follows the inference that obedience should be rendered to it, and respect paid to it—that, too, whole-heartedly—and that he who resists it is resisting God.

If by the word 'ordinance' a thing should be understood which God merely does not will to prevent, as the attitude of God is with reference to wicked actions, there would follow no obligation to pay respect or to render obedience, least of all, whole-heartedly; and the Apostle in proclaiming and in magnifying this power so earnestly would be saying nothing which would not be appropriate to acts of brigandage and thievery. It follows, therefore, that this power is understood to have been ordained by the approval of the will of God; hence the inference, since God does not will that which is contrary to Himself, that this power is not in conflict with the will of God revealed through the Gospel and binding upon all men.

4. The force of this argument, furthermore, is not weakened by the objection that those who were in authority at the time when Paul wrote were strangers to the Christian faith. For, in the first place, the statement is not unreservedly true, since Sergius Paulus, propraetor of Cyprus, had long before professed Christ (*Acts*, xiii. 12); not to speak of the ancient tradition in regard to the king of Edessa,[1] which to some extent may be tinged with falsehood, yet seems to have had its origin in truth. Then, again, the question is not whether the individuals were unrighteous but whether the function exercised by them was in itself unrighteous. That it was not, we maintain, was declared by the Apostle when, speaking even of his own time, he said that this function was ordained of God, and therefore should be honoured even in the inmost feelings of the soul, which in a proper sense are subject to God alone. Consequently both Nero, and King Agrippa, whom Paul so earnestly urges to embrace the Christian religion (*Acts*, xxvi), could have subjected themselves to Christ and have retained in the latter case a royal, in the former an imperial power, the maintenance of which without the right of the sword and of arms is inconceivable. Just as the sacrifices in the olden time were sacred according to the law even though offered by wicked priests, so sovereign power is a righteous thing even though it is held by a wicked man.[2]

5. A third argument is drawn from the words of John the Baptist. When he was earnestly asked by Jewish soldiers (from Josephus and other writers it is perfectly clear that many thousands of this race were in the military service of the Romans) what they must do to escape the wrath of God, he did not bid them withdraw from military service, as he must have done if such was the will of God, but to abstain from extortions and deceit, and to be content with their wages (*Luke*, iii. 14).

In regard to these words of the Baptist, which clearly enough imply an approval of military service, many make answer that what the Baptist enjoined differs so greatly from the precepts of Christ that it was quite possible for the Baptist to teach one thing, and Christ another. The validity of this objection I cannot admit. The gist of the doctrine which John and Christ brought to men they set forth with the same introductory plea: 'Repent, for the kingdom of heaven is at hand' (*Matthew*, iii. 2; iv. 17). Christ himself said

[1] Edessa is in Osrhoene. The name of Abgar is frequent in those regions. It appears on coins, in Tacitus and Appian; in Dio Cassius, not only the writings first published but also in the later excerpts, and in Capitolinus.

[2] This point is well developed by Chrysostom in his comment on this subject, *On Romans* [xiii. 3–4 = Homily XXIII, ii].

that the kingdom of heaven (that is, the new law, for the Jews have the custom of calling the law by the name of the kingdom) commenced to be taken by violence from the days of the Baptist (*Matthew*, xi. 12). It is said that John preached the baptism of repentance for the remission of sins (*Mark*, i. 4); the Apostles did the same, it is said, in the name of Christ (*Acts*, ii. 38). John demands fruits worthy of repentance, and threatens destruction to those who do not bring forth such fruits (*Matthew*, iii. 8 and 10). He demands works of love beyond [24] the law (*Luke*, iii 11). It is said that the law lasted until John, that is, that a more perfect doctrine began with him (*Matthew*, xi. 13). And the beginning of the Gospel is traced to John (*Mark*, i. 1; *Luke*, i. 77). John himself by this title is reckoned greater than the prophets (*Matthew*, xi. 9; *Luke*, vii. 26), since he was sent to give a knowledge of salvation to the people (*Luke*,
[i. 77.] ii. 77), to announce the Gospel (*Luke*, iii. 18).

Nowhere, in fact, does John distinguish Jesus from himself by the difference in their teachings, although the things which were taught by John in a more general and vague way, as rudiments, were clearly set forth by Christ, the true Light. The difference which John recognized between them lay rather in this, that Jesus was the promised Messiah (*Acts*, xix. 4; *John*, i. 29), the king of the Heavenly Kingdom, who would give the power of the Holy Spirit to them that believe on him (*Matthew*, iii. 11; *Mark*, i. 8; *Luke*, iii. 16).

6. The fourth argument, which seems to me to have no slight weight, is this. If the right to inflict capital punishment and to defend citizens by arms against brigands and robbers should be taken away, there would follow a riot of crimes and a deluge, so to speak, of evils, since even now, with regularly constituted courts in operation, the force of evil is with difficulty restrained.[1] Wherefore if it had been the purpose of Christ to bring about such a state of affairs as had never been heard of, beyond doubt with the most direct and explicit words he would have laid down the rules that no one should pass a sentence of death, and that no one should bear arms. We nowhere read that he did this; for the statements which are brought forward to that effect are either exceedingly general, or obscure. But fairness itself and common sense teach not only that general statements should be limited, and ambiguous expressions favourably interpreted, but even that in a degree there may be a departure from the strict signification and ordinary use of words, in order to avoid an interpretation which would involve extremely grave consequences.

[1] Chrysostom in his homily *To the Believing Father* [x]: 'For the restraint of criminals do courts exist, and laws, and punishments, and so many kinds of penalties.'

7. Fifth, by no argument can it be shown that the law of Moses relating to judgements ceased to be in force before the city of Jerusalem was destroyed, and with it alike the form of the Jewish state and the hope of its re-establishment. For neither in the law of Moses is any term set for this law, nor do Christ or the Apostles ever speak of the abolition of it, except in so far as this may seem to be included in the destruction of the state, as we have said. On the contrary Paul says that the high priest was appointed in order that he might render judgement according to the law of Moses (*Acts*, xxiv. 3). Christ himself in words introductory to his teachings [xxiii. 3.]
says that he came not to destroy the law but to fulfil (*Matthew*, v. 17).

What bearing this has on the part of the law relating to rituals is not obscure; for shadowy outlines are filled out when the perfect form of the thing is shown. But in what way can this be true of the laws relating to judgements, if Christ, as some think, by his coming did away with them? If, however, the obligation of the law remained so long as the Jewish state continued to exist, it follows that Jews, even when converted to Christianity, if they were summoned before a magistrate could not escape service, and that they were bound to judge not otherwise than as Moses had commanded.

8. Weighing all the arguments deliberately I do not find even the most trivial consideration which could have influenced any upright man, who heard those words of Christ as they were spoken, to form a different opinion. I recognize the fact that before the time of Christ some things were permitted, as a matter of external freedom from punishment or even of purity of mind—we have neither need nor leisure to deal with those details more fully here—which Christ did not permit to those who followed his doctrine; as, for example, [25] to put away a wife for any sort of offence whatsoever, and to exact vengeance in court from him who had inflicted an injury. But while between the teachings of Christ and those permissions there is indeed a difference, there is no conflict. For the man who keeps his wife, or who renounces his right as an individual to exact vengeance, does nothing contrary to the law; he does in fact what the law above all desires. Far different, on the other hand, is the case of the judge whom the law does not permit, but commands, to punish the murderer with death; if he fails in this duty, he will himself become guilty before God. If Christ forbids the judge to punish the murderer with death, he enjoins what is absolutely contrary to the law, he destroys the law.

9. The sixth argument shall be drawn from the example of Cornelius, the Centurion. He received the Holy Spirit, an infallible sign of justification, from Christ, and was baptized a Christian by

the Apostle Peter; nevertheless we do not read that he gave up his military service, or was advised by Peter that he was obliged to give it up.

Some may answer that, when Cornelius received instruction from Peter in the Christian religion we must suppose that he was at the same time instructed in regard to the abandonment of military life. These would have an argument if it were certain and beyond cavil that any prohibition of military service is to be found among the teachings of Christ. Such a prohibition in plain words nowhere appears; but surely in case Christ wished to lay down a rule opposed to current usage, it was necessary that something be said on the subject, at any rate in this connexion, where it was specially required, in order that the age to come might not be ignorant of the rules controlling its duty. And it is not the practice of Luke, when the quality of persons required some particular change in manner of life, to pass this by without mention, as may be seen in the nineteenth chapter of *Acts* (verse 19) and elsewhere.

10. The seventh argument, similar to the preceding, is taken from the case of Sergius Paulus, of whom we have already made mention. For in the record of his conversion there is no indication that he gave up his office, or was instructed to give it up. What is not mentioned when, as we have said, it would be of the utmost importance that mention be made, ought to be considered as not having happened.

11. The eighth argument is that Paul the Apostle, understanding that there was a plot [1] of the Jews against him, desired that this be reported to the tribune; and when the tribune had given him soldiers, under whose protection on his journey he would be safe against all violence, he raised no objection. He did not admonish the tribune, or the soldiers, that the repelling of force by force was not pleasing to God. And yet this was the Paul who himself never let slip any opportunity to point out one's duty, or wished that such opportunity be let slip by others (*2 Timothy*, iv. 2).

12. The ninth argument lies in this, that the proper end of a thing that is honourable and obligatory cannot be otherwise than honourable and obligatory. The payment of taxes is honourable —it is even an ordinance binding conscience, as the Apostle Paul

[1] The passage relating to Paul is cited as authority by the Council of Africa [chap. xciii]: 'Against the fury of these we are able to utilize the means of protection which are customary and not inconsistent with Scripture, since the Apostle Paul, as is known to the faithful from the *Acts of the Apostles,* also foiled a plot of zealots with the help of the military.'

The same passage is often referred to by Augustine, as in *Letters,* l [clxxxv. 28], *To Boniface*; in *Letters,* cliv [xlvii. 5], *To Publicola,* in which this appears: 'And if the wicked men had fallen upon the arms of the soldiers, in the shedding of their blood Paul would not have regarded himself as guilty of crime'; also in *Letters,* clxiv [lxxxvii. 8, *To Emeritus*]: 'Paul arranged to have an escort even of armed men given to him.'

explains; but the purpose of taxation is to provide the public administration with funds upon which it may draw in order to protect good men and check evil-doers (*Romans*, xiii. 3, 4, 6). Quite to the point Tacitus remarks: 'The peace of the nations cannot be had without arms, nor arms without pay, nor pay without taxes.' *Histories*, IV [lxxiv]. Similar is the observation of Augustine: 'We pay taxes in order that pay may be provided for the soldiery, for the necessaries of life.' *Against Faustus*, XXII. lxxiv.

13. The tenth argument is furnished by the passage in *Acts* (xxv. 11) in which Paul thus speaks: 'If I have wronged any one, and have committed anything worthy of death, I refuse not to die.'[1] Paul held the view, as I infer from this statement, that even after the publishing abroad of the law of the Gospel, there were certain crimes for which justice permitted, or even demanded, punishment by death. This is also the teaching of Peter (*1 Peter*, ii. 19, 20). If at that time it had been the will of God that capital punishment be abstained from, Paul might, to be sure, have cleared himself, but it was his duty not to leave in men's minds the belief that it was [26] then not less permissible than previously to punish criminals with death.

Now when it is once proved that the inflicting of capital punishment could be lawfully retained after the coming of Christ, it is, I think, proved at the same time that in some cases war is lawfully waged, as, for example, against criminals gathered in a great number and armed, who must be conquered in battle in order that they may be brought to trial. For while the strength of criminals and their boldness in resistance may be taken into account in prudent deliberation, the force of the law is not thereby diminished.

14. The eleventh[2] argument is based on the fact that the law of Christ did away with the law of Moses only in respect to the separation of the Gentiles from the Jews (*Ephesians*, ii. 14). But it by no means did away with the things which are honourable by nature and by the common agreement of the more civilized Gentiles; rather it included them in the general teaching of all that is honourable and virtuous (*Philippians*, iv. 8; *1 Corinthians*, xi. 13, 14). Now in

[1] So also *Acts*, xxviii. 18: 'because there was no cause of death in me.' Justin, in his *Second Apology* [I. xvi], says: 'Moreover we desire that those who do not live in consistency with those teachings, and are Christians only in name, receive punishment, and at your hands.'

[2] [In the editions of 1625, 1631, and 1632 this is the twelfth argument, and the eleventh runs as follows:

The eleventh argument is that in the prophecy of the Apocalypse certain wars of the righteous are foretold, with manifest approval (*Rev.* xviii. 6 and elsewhere).

This paragraph is omitted in the editions of 1642 and 1646, probably because struck out by the author. Yet the omission may have been due originally to haplography in composition, on account of the relative positions of the words *Undecimum* and *Duodecimum* in a page of the edition of 1631 or 1632 used as printer's copy.]

truth the punishment of crimes, and the use of arms which prevent wrongdoing, are by nature considered praiseworthy and are referred to the virtues of justice and beneficence.

Here in passing it is worth while to note an error on the part of those who maintain that the right of the Israelites to wage war came merely from the fact that God had given them the land of Canaan. This is, to be sure, a just cause, but not the only one. For before those times under the guidance of reason, righteous men carried on wars; and afterwards the Israelites themselves waged wars on account of other causes, as David did, because of the affront offered to his envoys. For the possessions which each has by human law are not less his than if God had given them to him; this right, moreover, is not taken away by the Gospel.

VIII.—*Answering of the arguments from Holy Writ on behalf of the affirmative view, that war is in conflict with the law of the Gospel*

1. Let us now see by what considerations the contrary opinion is supported, in order that the serious-minded appraiser may be able the more easily to decide which of the two views has the weight of argument in its favour.

First of all it is customary to bring forward the prophecy of Isaiah,[1] who says that it will come to pass that the people will beat their swords into mattocks and their spears into pruning-hooks; 'and nation shall not lift up sword against nation, neither shall they learn war any more' (*Isaiah*, ii. 4). But this prophecy, as many others, may be taken in a conditional sense. With such an interpretation undoubtedly we are to understand that such will be the state of affairs if all peoples receive and fulfil the law of Christ;[2] to this end God will not suffer that there be any lack of assistance on His part. It is moreover certain that if all men were Christians, and were

[1] This prophecy is interpreted by Chrysostom with reference to the peace which came to the world through the beneficent agency of the Roman Empire; in his homily *That Christ is God* [vi] he says:

> It was foretold, in fact, not only that this religion would be steadfast, immovable, and unshaken, but that with it peace would come to the world, that in the different states the rule of aristocracies, yes even of kings, would cease, and that there would be one rule over all men: of that empire the greater part would enjoy peace, a condition opposite to that which previously existed. Formerly, in fact, even craftsmen and orators put on arms and stood in line of battle. But after the coming of Christ that custom fell into disuse and the practices of war were restricted to a limited class of individuals.

Precisely the same thought you find in Eusebius's *Preparation*, Book I, chap. x [I. iv. 5].

[2] For of the Christians Justin says [*First Apology*, xxxix], 'We do not fight against enemies.' This is like what Philo says about the Essenes, in his treatise *That Every Virtuous Man is Free* [chap. xii]: 'Among them you would find no maker of javelins or arrows, of sword or helmet or coat of mail or shield, no one to fashion either arms or engines of war.'

Similar is the comment of Chrysostom, *On First Corinthians*, xiii. 3 [Homily XXXII, v]: 'If there were among men such love as there ought to be, there would be no capital punishments.'

living the Christian life, there would be no wars. This thought Arnobius expresses as follows: [*Against the Heathen*, I. vi.]

If all who consider themselves men, on the ground not of bodily shape but of the possession of reason, would be willing for a little while to lend ear to His wholesome and pacific dictates, and would not, swollen with pride and arrogance, entrust themselves to the guidance of their passions rather than of His admonitions, the whole world, having long ago turned its iron to milder uses, would be living in the most delightful tranquillity, and through mutual confidence in inviolable treaties would be united in a beneficent concord.

Lactantius speaks on this wise: [*Divine Institutes*, I. xviii. 16.]

What will happen if all men shall agree to live in perfect accord? This surely can happen, if men would only cast aside their destructive and impious fury and be willing to be innocent and just.

Or, again, the prophecy can be understood literally. If it is interpreted in this way, the facts show that it has not yet been fulfilled, but that the fulfilment of it, like the general conversion of the Jews, is to be expected. But in whichever way you interpret the prophecy, no inference can be drawn from it against the justice of wars, so long as there are men who do not suffer those that love peace to enjoy peace, but do violence to them.

2. Several arguments are ordinarily taken from the fifth chapter of *Matthew*. In order to form a proper judgement in regard to them it is necessary to recall what we said a little before, that if it had been Christ's purpose absolutely to do away with capital punishment and the right to carry on war, he would have expressed this purpose with words as plain and explicit as possible, on account of the importance of the ruling, [27] and its newness. All the more would he have been led to do this for the reason that no Jew could think otherwise than that the laws of Moses relating to judicial proceedings and public administration must retain their validity in respect to all Jews so long as their state endured. With this general observation in mind, let us discuss the bearing of the several passages in order.

3. The contrary view, then, in the second place fortifies itself with these words: 'Ye have heard that it hath been said, an eye for an eye and a tooth for a tooth; but I say unto you, Resist not him that is evil' (in Hebrew, 'the wicked man,' which the Greeks translate 'him that doeth a wrong',[1] *Exodus*, ii. 13); 'but whosoever shall smite thee on thy right cheek, turn to him the other also.' From this some infer that no injury ought to be warded off, or made the subject of a demand for requital, whether as a public or as a private matter. And yet, that is not the meaning of the words. Christ is here addressing not the magistrates, but those who are [*Matthew*, v. 38.]

[1] [40] As also Luke, in the address of Stephen [*Acts*, vii. 27]: 'He that did his neighbour wrong.'

assailed; and he is not treating of injuries in general, but of a specific sort of injury, such as a slap on the cheek; for the latter part of the statement restricts the generality of the earlier part.

[*Matthew*, v. 41.] 4. Similarly in the precept which follows, 'And if any man would go to law with thee, and take away thy coat, let him have thy cloak also',[1] not every appeal to a judge or arbitrator is forbidden. Such at any rate is the interpretation of Paul, who does not prohibit all lawsuits (*I Corinthians*, vi. 4), but does forbid Christians to sue one another in pagan court-rooms. In this he follows the example of the Jews, among whom the maxim was current that 'He who refers matters of the Israelites to strangers dishonours the name of God'. Now Christ, in order to train us in forbearance, wishes us not to go to law about things easy to replace, as a coat, or a cloak in addition to the coat if need be; but though our legal rights be absolutely perfect, he wishes us to abstain from enforcing them.

Philostratus, II. xv [*Life of Apollonius*, II. xxxix]. Apollonius of Tyana used to say that it was unworthy of a philosopher 'to engage in a lawsuit about a small sum of money'. 'The praetor', says Ulpian, 'does not disapprove the act of him who considered it worth the while to deprive himself of property that he might not have to engage too frequently in lawsuits in regard to it. This attitude of restraint, on the part of a man who has an aversion to lawsuits, is not to be criticized.' *Dig.* IV. vii. 4. 1. What Ulpian here mentions as approved by good men, Christ enjoins, selecting the matter of his teachings from the most honourable and universally approved examples.

From this, however, you would not rightly infer that it would be wrong even for a parent or guardian in case of necessity to defend before a judge that which involved the means of subsistence of children or of wards. For a coat and a cloak are one thing; entire means of subsistence is quite another. In the *Constitutions* of Clement (I. xlv [II. xlv]) it is said of the Christian, if he has a lawsuit, 'Let him try to settle it, even if thereby he be compelled to suffer some loss.' Here also that is applicable which is customarily said of things moral, that they do not consist in a point, but have a certain latitude.

[*Matthew*, v. 41.] 5. In like manner, in what follows, 'And whosoever shall

[1] The idea is thus expressed by Cyprian, *On Patience* [chap. xvi], 'That you are not to try to get back what belongs to you after it has been taken from you.' Irenaeus, Book IV, chap. xxvii [*Against Heresies*, IV. xiii. 3]: '"To him that taketh away thy coat, give thy cloak also"; but let us not grieve, as those unwilling to be defrauded, but let us rejoice as those who have given willingly. "And if anyone," He says, "shall compel thee to go a mile, go with him twain," in order that thou mayst not follow like a slave, but as a free man go before him.'

Even Libanius, who had read the Gospels, in his oration *On the Custody of Men under Accusation*, praises those who do not go to law about a coat or a cloak. Jerome, *Against Pelagius*, Dialogue I [I. xxix]: 'The Gospel teaches that to him who wishes to contend with us through judicial procedure, and by means of lawsuits and altercations wrest a coat from us, a cloak also should be given.'

compel thee to go one mile, go with him two,' our Lord did not speak of a hundred miles, a journey which would take a man too far from his business, but of one mile, and, if need be, of two, involving an amount of walking which would seem like nothing at all. The meaning, therefore, is that in matters which are not likely to inconvenience us very much we ought not to insist upon our rights, but to give up even more than is demanded, in order that our patience and kindness may become manifest to all.[1]

6. There follow the words: 'Give to him that asketh thee,[2] and from him that would borrow of thee turn not thou away.' If you should put this into practice without limitation, nothing could be more harsh. He who does not take care of those of his own house 'is worse than an unbeliever', says Paul (*1 Timothy*, v. 8). Let us then follow the same Paul, a most excellent interpreter of the law laid down by the Master. In urging the Corinthians [28] to exercise a spirit of liberality toward those that were in Jerusalem he says: 'Not that others may be eased and ye distressed, but that by equalization your abundance may be a supply for their want' [3] (*2 Corinthians*, viii. 13); that is—adopting the words of Livy in respect to a not dissimilar case—that from the superabundance of your resources you minister to the necessities of others. The same point of view appears also in Xenophon's *Cyrus*: 'Whatever I see that I have beyond my needs I use to supply the wants of my friends.' A similar principle of equalization we may apply to the interpretation of the precept which we have just quoted.

[*Matthew*, v. 42.]

[VI. xv. 9.]

[*Training of Cyrus*, VIII. ii. 22.]

7. Just as the Hebraic law favoured freedom of divorce in order that it might mitigate the harsh treatment of wives by their husbands, so also in order to restrain private vengeance, to which that nation was specially prone, it had conferred upon an injured person the right to exact retaliation from the wrongdoer, not, however, by his own hand, but before the judge. This rule the law of the Twelve Tables also followed: 'If a man breaks a limb of another, let there be like injury in turn.' But Christ, who enjoined

[1] Justin, in his *Second Apology* [I. xvi]: 'What He said has this in view, that toward all men we are to be patient, ready to render service, and altogether devoid of anger.'

[2] Justin, in the same *Apology* [I. xv]: 'With reference to the duty of sharing what we have with the needy, and that we might not do anything in order to gain glory thereby, He said this, "To everyone that asketh give," etc.' In another passage [I. xiv]: 'sharing what we have with everyone in need.'

Cyprian, *Testimonies*, Book III, chap. i: 'Alms are to be denied to none.' Also, in the same passage: 'Give to everyone that asketh thee, and from him who would borrow from thee, turn not away.'

[3] Seneca, *On Benefits*, Book II [II. xv. 1]: 'I shall give to the needy, but in such a way that I myself may not be in want.'

Chrysostom, in his note to the verse of Corinthians quoted [*On Second Corinthians*, viii. 12 = Homily XVII, i]: 'God demands according to a man's power, "according as he hath, not according as he hath not."' That this may be rightly understood, the following is added [to verse 13]: 'He praises, indeed, those' (that is among the Thessalonians) 'who had done beyond their power, but he does not force these' (the Achaeans are meant) 'to do the same thing.'

a greater degree of forbearance, so far from expressing approval of the demanding of vengeance by a man who is already the victim of an injury, wishes that some injuries be not even warded off, either by violence or by judicial procedure. But what sort of injuries? Such, we see, as are bearable—not that such action is not also praiseworthy in the case of more dreadful injuries,[1] but that Christ is satisfied with forbearance of a more restricted scope. So he took for illustration a slap on the cheek; this does not endanger life, or mutilate the person, but merely indicates a kind of contempt for us, which makes us not a whit the worse. Seneca, in his treatise *On the*
[v. 1.] *Steadfastness of the Wise Man*, distinguishes injury from insult:

'The former', Seneca says, 'is in its nature more serious; the latter is of less import, and serious only for the thin-skinned, who are not hurt by it, only offended. So great is the feebleness and emptiness of men's minds that some think nothing more bitter. Thus you may find a slave who would rather be cut with a scourge
[x. 1.] than have his ears boxed.' In another passage the same philosopher remarks: 'Insult is a lesser injury, which we can complain of rather than take into court. The laws have not thought it worthy of penalty.'

[Nonius, *De Diff. Verb.*] In Pacuvius a character says: 'Easily I suffer wrong if it is free from insult.' And in Caecilius another remarks:

[Ibid.]
> Misery I can endure if only free from injury;
> And injury as well, except when insult adds indignity.

[*Against Meidias*, xxi. 72.] Demosthenes has a similar thought: 'For freemen it is not so dreadful a thing to be scourged, dreadful though that is, as it is to be lashed with insult.' The same Seneca, of whom I have spoken, a little farther
[x. 2.] on says that the pain arising from insult is a mental disturbance produced by a sense of humiliation as the mind contracts on account of a deed or word reflecting dishonour.

8. Under such conditions, then, Christ enjoins forbearance. And that no one may urge as an objection that hackneyed maxim,
[Publilius Syrus, *Sent.*, 645.] 'By enduring a long-standing wrong you invite a new one,' he adds that it is better to suffer even a second injury[2] than to repel the first, because, of course, we receive no harm from it except that which exists in foolish imagining.[3] 'To turn the cheek to another' in Hebrew idiom means 'to suffer patiently', as is clear from *Isaiah*
[l. 6.] (xxx. 6) and *Jeremiah* (iii. 3); the phrase 'to expose one's face to
[III. xxxi.] insults'[4] Tacitus used in the third book of his *Histories*.

[1] See Chrysostom, in the passage already quoted.

[2] Chrysostom, *On Romans*, chap. vii [Homily XII, ix]: 'This is a glorious victory, to give to the offender more than he wishes, and by generous exercise of one's own patience even to pass beyond the bounds of his wicked desires.'

[3] Chrysostom, *On the Statues*, Homily I [Homily II, viii]: 'An insult is felt or comes to naught, not by the intention of him who offers it but by the disposition of those who bear it.'

[4] 'To present one's face' is found with the same meaning in the *Adelphi* of Terence [215=II. ii. 7].

9. The third argument is wont to be taken from the passage which follows in *Matthew*: 'Ye have heard that it was said, Thou shalt love thy neighbour and hate thine enemy; but I say unto you, love your enemies, bless them that curse you, pray for them that despitefully use you and persecute you.' For there are men who think that with such love and well-doing toward enemies and them that despitefully use us, both capital punishment and wars are irreconcilable. [v. 43.]

The argument, however, is easily refuted if [29] we take into consideration the precise provision of the Hebraic law. It was enjoined upon the Jews to love their neighbour, that is a Jew;[1] that the word 'neighbour' is to be taken in this sense is evident from a comparison of the seventeenth verse of the nineteenth chapter of *Leviticus*, with the eighteenth verse of the same chapter. But magistrates were none the less commanded to put to death murderers and others guilty of heinous crimes; the eleven tribes none the less attacked the tribe of Benjamin in a just war on account of a monstrous crime (*Judges*, xxi); none the less did David, who 'fought the battles of the Lord', undertake to wrest from Ishbosheth by arms, and rightly, the kingdom which had been promised to him. [xx.]

10. Let us concede, then, a broader signification of the word 'neighbour', to include all men—for all men have now been received into a common dispensation, there are no peoples doomed by God to destruction—nevertheless that will be permitted with respect to all men which was then permitted with respect to the Israelites; they were bidden to love one another, just as now all men are. And if you wish to believe also that a greater degree of love is commanded in the law of the Gospel, let this too be granted, provided also the fact is recognized that love is not due to all in the same degree,[2] but that a greater love is due to a father than to a stranger. In like manner also, in accordance with the law of a well-ordered love, the good of an innocent person should receive consideration before the good of one who is guilty, and the public good before that of the individual.

Now it is in the love of innocent men that both capital punishment and just wars have their origin. Reference may be made to the moral sentiment expressed in *Proverbs* (xxiv. 11). The teachings

[1] The proselyte was on a level with the Jew; and the laws in regard to not harming one another were extended also to the uncircumcized inhabitants who were discussed in chap. I above, § 16. So the Talmudists.

[2] Tertullian, *Against Marcion*, [41] IV [IV. xvi]: 'The second step in charity is toward strangers; the first step is toward one's neighbours.' Jerome, *Against Pelagius*, Dialogue I [I. xxx]: 'It has been enjoined upon me, to love my enemies and to pray for them that persecute me. It is not just, is it, to love them as I love my neighbours, and my kindred, so that there would be no distinction between a rival and an intimate associate?'

of Christ in regard to loving and helping men ought, therefore, to be carried into effect unless a greater and more just love stand in the way. Familiar is the old saying: 'It is as much a cruelty to spare all as to spare none.' [1]

11. There is the further consideration that we are bidden to love our enemies by the example of God, who 'maketh his sun to rise upon the unjust'. But the same God inflicts punishments upon some wicked men even in this life, and will inflict most severe punishments hereafter. The same argument meets also the difficulty presented by the injunctions laid upon Christians in regard to mercy, which are usually brought to bear upon this point. For God is called gracious, merciful, and long-suffering (*Jonah*, iv. 2; *Exodus*, xxxiv. 6). But the sacred writings in various places describe His wrath against them that set themselves against Him,[2] that is, His will to punish them (*Numbers*, xiv. 18; *Romans*, ii. 8). And of this anger the magistrate has been appointed minister (*Romans*, xiii. 4). Moses is commended for his extraordinary mercifulness; yet he inflicted punishments on the guilty, even capital punishments. The mercy and long-suffering of Christ we are everywhere bidden to imitate; yet it is Christ who inflicts the severest punishments upon the disobedient Jews [3] (*Matthew*, xxii. 7), and will condemn the wicked according to their deserts in the Day of Judgement. The mercifulness of the Master was imitated by the Apostles, who nevertheless used the power, which had been given them by God,[4] for the punishment of wrongdoers (*1 Corinthians*, iv. 21 and v. 5; *1 Timothy*, i. 20).

12. A fourth passage presented in opposition is in *Romans* (xii. 17):

'Render to no man evil for evil. Take thought for things honourable in the sight of all men. If it be possible, as much as in you lieth, live in peace with all men. Avenge not yourselves,[5]

[1] The words are those of Seneca, *On Clemency*, Book I. chap. ii. Chrysostom, *On First Corinthians*, iii. 12 ff., treating of human punishments [Homily IX, ii]: 'And men do such things not in cruelty but in kindness.' Augustine [*Letters*, cliii. 17, *To Macedonius*]: 'Just as sometimes there is a mercy that inflicts punishment, so there is also a cruelty that spares.'

The emperors Valentinian, Theodosius, and Arcadius, in the third law *On the defenders of cities*, in the *Theodosian Code* [*Cod. Theod.*, I. xxix. 3]: 'Let there be done away with all forms of protection which, by favouring the guilty and affording aid to criminals, have hastened the increase of crimes.'

Totilas in Procopius, *Gothic War*, II [III. viii]: 'To do wrong, and to prevent the punishment of those who do wrong, I consider as on the same plane.' See also what is said in Book II, xxi. 2.

[2] On this point see Cyril, *Against Julian*, Book V.

[3] Add the references: *Matthew*, xxi. 44; *Luke*, xix. 12, 14, 27.

Chrysostom, *On Romans*, chap. xiv [Homily XXV, v, on verse 13], having described the evils that fell upon the inhabitants of Jerusalem, exclaims: 'That it was Christ who did these things, hear him declaring, now by means of parables, now clearly and explicitly.' He uses similar expressions in his second oration *Against the Jews*.

[4] Chrysostom, *On First Corinthians*, iv. 21 [Homily XIV, ii, on verse 21]: 'Shall I kill, shall I maim? . . . For as there is a spirit of gentleness, so also there is a spirit of severity.'

See also Augustine, *On the Sermon of Our Lord on the Mount*, Book I, and others cited by Gratian, *Decretum*, II. xxiii. 8.

[5] The Vulgate has in this place *defendentes*, 'defending'. This expression is often taken by the

beloved, but give place unto the wrath of God, for it is written, Vengeance belongeth unto me, I will recompense, saith the Lord. But if thine enemy hunger, feed him; if he thirst, give him to drink; for in so doing thou shalt heap coals of fire on his head. Be not overcome of evil but overcome evil with good.'

Here also the same answer may be made as in the case of the preceding passage. For at the very time when it was said by God, 'Vengeance is mine, I will repay,' both the penalty of capital punishment was being imposed and laws had been written for the conduct of wars. Moreover it is ordered that kindness be shown to enemies, belonging, of course, to the same nation (*Exodus*, xxiii. 4, 5); but this nevertheless, as we have said, put no [30] obstacle in the way either of capital punishment or of lawful wars, even against the Israelites themselves. Wherefore not even now ought the same words, or similar teachings, even though given a broader application, to be violently forced into such a meaning.

Such an interpretation is the less tenable for the reason that the chapter divisions of the Biblical writings were not made by the Apostles, nor in their time, but much later, in order to break up the text and make the citation of passages easier. Hence it has come about that the words at the beginning of chapter xii, 'Let every soul be in subjection to the higher powers,' and those that follow, are to be taken with the teachings which forbid the exacting of vengeance.

13. Now in this part of his exposition Paul says that the public authorities are the ministers of God and His avengers for wrath against evil-doers, that is, for the punishment of evil-doers. In this way with perfect clearness he distinguishes between vengeance

Christian writers, however, to express the idea of vengeance. Tertullian, *On Patience* [chap. x]: 'If now you defend yourself too feebly, you will be mad; if too vigorously, you will have to take the consequences. What have I to do with vengeance, the measure of which I have not the power to regulate, on account of my inability to endure pain?'

The same writer, *Against Marcion*, II [II. xviii]: 'Now herein there is no suggestion of permission for the inflicting of mutual injury; but there is kept in view the complete restraining of violence. To a people exceedingly obdurate and lacking faith in God, it might seem irksome, or even beyond credence, to expect from God that vengeance (*defensam*) which was afterward to be declared by the prophet: "Vengeance (*defensam*) is mine, and I will repay (*defendam*), saith the Lord." In the meantime the committing of wrong was to be checked by the fear of immediate retaliation, and the permission to exact retribution was to be the prevention of provocation, to the end that cunningly devised wickedness thus might come to an end, while through permission of the second, it might be terrified by the first; and through being deterred by the first, the second might not be committed. And thereby also in other respects the fear of retaliation is more easily aroused, by reason of the savour of suffering in it; nothing is more bitter than yourself to suffer what you have inflicted upon others.'

Tertullian, again, *On Monogamy* [chap. iv]: 'The flood was provoked by other iniquities, always avenged (*defensae*), whatsoever they were, nevertheless not "seventy times seven", the vengeance that double marriages deserve.'

The passage of Paul treated in the text is explained not infelicitously by Augustine, *Letters*, cliv [xlvii. 5]: 'Moreover it has been said, "we are not to resist evil" to this end, that vengeance, which feeds the soul with another's misfortune, may not give us pleasure.'

See what is said below, II. xx. 5 and 10.

in the public interest, which is inflicted by a public authority acting in place of God, and which is to be traced back to the vengeance reserved for God; and revenge, which has as its purpose to satisfy resentment, and which he had forbidden just a little before. For if you maintain that in the prohibition of revenge is included also the vengeance which is exacted in the public interest, what would be more absurd than to add, after saying that capital punishment must be refrained from, that public authorities have been established by God, in order that they may inflict punishments in place of God?

14. A fifth passage, which some make use of, is in *2 Corinthians* (x. 3): 'For though we walk in the flesh, we do not war according to the flesh; for the weapons of our warfare are not of the flesh,[1] but mighty befo:e God to the casting down of strongholds,' and what follows.

This has no bearing on the point under discussion. For the passages which precede and follow show that by the term 'flesh' in that connexion Paul understood a weak condition of his body, of a sort that attracted attention and brought him into contempt. To this Paul opposed his own weapons, that is, the power given to him as an Apostle to restrain the refractory, such as he made use of against Elymas, against the Corinthian guilty of incest, Hymenaeus, and Alexander. This power, then, he says, is not of the flesh, that is, weak; on the contrary he declares that it is most mighty. What has this to do with the right to inflict capital punishment, or to wage war? Nothing whatever. Because the Church at that time was without the backing of public authorities, for its protection God had called forth that supernatural power; that power, again, began to fail at about the time when Christian emperors came to the support of the Church, just as the manna failed when the Jewish people reached fertile lands.

15. In the sixth place *Ephesians* (vi. 12) is quoted: 'Wherefore put ye on the whole armour of God, that we may be able to stand against the wiles of the Devil; for your wrestling is not against flesh and blood' (supply 'only', as in Hebrew idiom), 'but against principalities,' and what follows. This has reference to the warfare which Christians are obliged to wage as Christians, not the warfare which under certain conditions they may be able to wage in common with other men.

16. In the seventh place a passage of *James* (iv. 1) is brought forward:

Whence come wars and whence come fightings among you?

[1] Chrysostom on this passage [*On Second Corinthians*, x. 4=Homily XXI, ii], by 'weapons of the flesh' understands [42] 'wealth, glory, power, eloquence, craftiness, canvassing for votes, flatteries, hypocrisies'.

Come they not hence, even of your pleasures that war in your members ? Ye lust, and have not ; ye envy and covet, and cannot obtain ; ye fight and wage war, and receive not, because ye ask not ; ye ask, and receive not, because ye ask amiss, that ye may spend it in your own pleasures.

This passage contains nothing of universal application. It says only that the wars and fightings in which at that time the Jews, scattered, were wretchedly contending among themselves (a history of a part of these strifes may be found in Josephus) had their origin in causes that were not righteous ; that such a condition exists even at the present time we know, and we grieve that it is so. *Antiquities of the Jews,* XVIII. xii [XVIII. ix] and XIX.

A couplet of Tibullus contains an implication not unlike that of the passage of *James* : [I. x. 7 f.]

> [31] Curse of rich gold this is ; and wars were not
> When beechen cups beside men's victuals stood.

In Strabo you may find in several places the comment that peoples whose food is the simplest live in greatest innocency.[1] Not far from this point of view are the lines of Lucan : [IV. 373 ff.]

> O lavish luxury,
> Never with modest outlay satisfied ;
> Vainglorious craving for those viands rare
> Which quest on land and in the sea procures,
> And glamour of the sumptuous board : learn ye
> Upon how little life can be sustained,
> How little nature craves. Not high-born wine,
> Put up so long the Consul is forgot,
> Restores the sick ; from gold and crystal cups
> They drink not, but with water pure their life
> Comes back. Enough for men the stream and grain
> Of Ceres. Oh wretched men, whom wars engage !

To this may be added the statement of Plutarch in the *Contradictions of the Stoics* : 'There is no war among men which does not [= p. 1049 D.]

[1] The same thing is said by Philo, *On the Contemplative Life* [chap. ii], where he quotes from Homer this line [*Iliad,* xiii. 6] :

> Of men who live on milk, and needy are,
> A race which is most just.

Justin, in regard to the Scythians [*Histories,* II. ii. 7] : 'They do not try to get gold and silver, as other mortals do.' A little later he adds [II. ii. 10] : 'This restraint of character has also imparted justice to them, since they desire nothing that belongs to another. Certainly where there is use of riches, there is also the eager desire for them.'

Gregoras, Book II [II. iv], has a passage of similar import about the Scythians, which is worth reading.

Taxiles said to Alexander [Plutarch, *Alexander,* lix. = 698 A] : 'What need is there, Alexander, of war and fighting between us, if you have come hither with the purpose of taking away from us neither water nor necessary food ? For these are the only things for which men possessed of reason are obliged to fight.'

Pertinent in this connexion is the saying of Diogenes [Porphyry, *On Abstaining from Animal Food,* I. xlvii] : 'Neither thieves nor makers of wars, in fact, rise up from among those whose food is barley.'

Porphyry, in his second book *On Abstaining from Animal Food* [II. xiii] : 'Whatever is easy to make ready, and is of small cost, tends to perpetual piety, and that too among all men.'

originate in a fault. One is kindled by an eager desire for pleasures, another by avarice, another by an overmastering passion for public
[II. ii. 11–13.] office or supreme power.'[1] Justin, having praised the institutions of the Scythians, says: 'If only other mortals would exercise a like self-restraint, and have the same respect for the property of others! Surely in that case so many wars would not be following one after the other through all the ages in all the world, and steel and weapons would not be carrying off more men than the term of fate as fixed by nature.'
[I. xiii. 44.] In Cicero we read, in the first book *On Ends*: 'Out of passionate desires arise hatreds, disagreements, dissensions, strifes, and wars.'
[xxix. 6.] Says Maximus of Tyre: 'Now all places are full of wars. For everywhere passionate desires are rife and throughout all lands they arouse covetousness for the things which belong to others.' 'The body',
[*Protrepticon*, xiii.] says Iamblichus, 'and the passionate desires of the body cause wars, fightings, and dissensions. For wars have their origin in the effort to obtain possession of things that are useful.'

[1] This thought is absolutely true, but men seldom reflect upon it, though it has been set forth in many admirable statements by the ancients. What harm, then, to fortify it by the sayings of others, which are not less effective?

Athenaeus, the philosopher, in Diogenes Laertius [X. xii]:

> For evil things you toil, O wretched men!
> A lust of gain insatiate drives you on
> To strifes and wars.

Fabianus Papirius, in the *Controversies* of Seneca the father [II. ix]:

> Look you—armies in battle formation, often made up of fellow-citizens and kindred, have taken their positions ready to fight, and the hills are filled with horsemen on both sides; forthwith all the country round is strewn with the bodies of the slain, with a multitude of corpses of the fallen, or a multitude of despoilers.
>
> Suppose that some one shall raise the question, what cause forced man against man into wickedness? For the wild beasts do not wage wars on one another; and if they did, the same actions would not be fitting for man, a creature of peaceful disposition and very near the divine. What so great anger carries you on, being, as you are, one stock and blood? Or what furies have goaded you to mutual bloodshed? What so great evil has been inflicted upon the human race, either by chance or by fate? Was the slaughter of men worth while that banquets might be copiously furnished with cups, and ceilings glitter with gold? Great and praiseworthy should be the inducements which should lead men at such cost to prefer to gaze upon their own table and decorated panels rather than to look upon the light of day in innocence. Was it necessary to try to enslave the world in order that nothing might be denied to the stomach and to lust? Why, pray, are curse-bringing riches in such ways to be sought, if not even for this purpose, to leave them to one's children?

Philo, *On the Ten Commandments* [chap. xxviii]: [43] 'Is the love of money, or of women, or of glory, or, in fine, of any thing else that gives pleasure, the cause of merely slight and ordinary evils? By reason of this love, kindred are estranged from kindred, natural affection being changed into incurable hate; large and populous countries, furthermore, are laid waste by strifes between fellow-citizens; then, again, both land and sea are filled with disasters constantly recurring through engagements of infantry and naval forces. For those wars of the Greeks and the barbarians, whether among themselves or of Greeks against barbarians, even though sung and resung in tragedies, have all flowed from one fountain of passionate desire, whether of riches or glory or pleasure.'

Pliny, *Natural History*, Book II, chap. iii [II. lxiii. 154]: 'Yet we make such use of the too gentle earth that all the products of her bounty lead to crimes, to slaughter and to war; and we drench her with our blood, we cover her with unburied bones.'

Jerome, *Against Jovinianus*, II [II. xi]: 'Diogenes affirms that tyrants and destroyers of cities, and wars whether against foreign enemies or between fellow-citizens, have their origin not in the requirements of simple living on vegetables and fruits, but in a passionate desire for choice meats and feastings.'

Chrysostom, *On First Corinthians*, xiii. 3 [Homily XXXII. v]: 'For if all men loved one another,

17. There remains what was said to Peter: 'He that smiteth with the sword shall perish by the sword.' This relates, however, not to war in general, but specifically to private war; for Christ in not allowing a defence of himself to be made, or in neglecting to defend himself, presents as the reason that his kingdom is not of this world (*John*, xviii. 36). This will be more appropriately treated in another connexion. [I. iii. 3. 7.]

IX.—*The agreement of the early Christians in regard to the subject under discussion is examined*

1. Whenever question is raised in regard to the interpretation of a writing, great weight is commonly attributed both to subsequent usage and to the authority of wise men. This point of view ought to be maintained also in the interpretation of Holy Writ. For it is not probable that the churches which had been founded by the Apostles either suddenly, or in all cases, fell away from those teachings which, though written down in concise form, the Apostles had more fully explained by word of mouth or had even introduced into practice. Now those who oppose wars are wont to bring forward several sayings of the early Christians in regard to which I have three things to say.

2. In the first place, any inference based upon these sayings represents nothing more than the private opinion of certain individuals, not the opinion of the churches publicly expressed. Further, the authors of the sayings referred to are for the most part men who like to follow a road different from that of others and to set forth a teaching on some point in rather a lofty strain. Such are Origen and Tertullian; and these writers are, in fact, not self-consistent. For Origen says that bees were given by God [32] as an example to show 'how wars, if ever there should arise a necessity for them, should be waged in a just and orderly manner among men'; and the same Tertullian, who else- [*Against Celsus*, IV. lxxxii.]

no man would injure another; far from us would be murders, and strifes, and wars, and seditions, and lootings, and frauds, and all other evils.' The same preacher in his sermon *To the Believing Father* [ix], speaking of the rich, says: 'Through these come there not seditions, and wars, and strifes, and the destruction of cities, and kidnapping, and slavery, and captivities, and murder, and innumerable evils of life?'

Claudian [*Against Rufinus*, I. 217–19]:

> If this were known to men, we should enjoy
> The simple life. The trumpet-calls to strife
> No more would sound, no more the whistling dart
> Would fly; wind would not shatter ships
> Nor battering-ram the walls.

Agathias, *Histories*, Book I [I. i]: 'Because the souls of men of their free choice slip into greed of gain and injustice, they fill all places with wars and tumults.'

These fine sayings I shall conclude with one from Polybius [Dionysius of Halicarnassus, V. xii, quoted by Suidas, *Lexicon*, under Αὐτάρκεια]: 'A soul that is satisfied with what is necessary needs no other teacher in order to become wise.'

[*De Spectaculis*, xix.] where seems to be less in favour of capital punishment, said: 'No one denies that it is a good thing when the guilty are punished.'[1]

In regard to military service Tertullian hesitates. For in his [xix.] book *On Idolatry* he says: 'The question is raised whether the faithful can turn to military service, and whether the military can be admitted to the faith'; and in this connexion he seems inclined to a view adverse to military service. But in the book *On the Soldier's* [xi.] *Chaplet*, having presented some considerations adverse to military service, he immediately distinguishes those who were enrolled in military service before baptism from those who enlisted after they were baptized. 'Evidently', he says, 'the condition of those whom the faith finds already engaged in military service is altogether different, as was the condition of those whom John admitted to baptism, also that of the very faithful centurions, of whom one was commended by Christ, the other instructed by Peter. Nevertheless, having received the faith and having been confirmed in it,[2] either they must at once abandon the profession of arms, as many have done, or they must resort to cleverness in every possible way (that is, they must "take every precaution") that no offence be committed against God.' He recognized the fact, therefore, that the latter class remained in military service after baptism; but this they would by no means have done if they had understood that military service had been forbidden by Christ—no more than the soothsayers, the magicians, and other practisers of forbidden arts[3] were permitted to remain in the practice of [i.] their art after baptism. In the same book, praising a certain soldier, and that too a Christian, he says, 'Oh soldier, glorious before God!'

3. My second observation is that Christians have often disapproved or avoided military service on account of the condition of the times, which hardly permitted them to engage in such service without committing certain acts in conflict with Christian law. In [*Antiquities*, XIV. x. 12.] the letters of Dolabella to the Ephesians, which are found in Josephus, we see that the Jews demanded exemption from service on military expeditions, for the reason that, mingled with foreigners, they would

[1] The same Tertullian, *On the Soul* [chap. xxxiii]: 'Who would not prefer the justice of the world, which, as even the Apostle testifies, "beareth not the sword in vain," which partakes of the nature of religion when it resorts to severity in the defence of human life?' Also *To Scapula* [chap. iv], Scapula being a proconsul: 'We who do not fear are not trying to frighten you. But I would that we might be able to save all men by warning them not to fight against God! You may both discharge the duties of your office, and remember the claims of humanity, even because you also are under the sword.'

[2] The distinction which he here makes in respect to warfare he elsewhere applies to marriage, both in the treatise *On Monogamy*, and in the *Exhortation to Chastity*.

[3] Tertullian, *On Idolatry* [v]: 'They who practise the arts that the discipline of God has not accepted, are not admitted into the church.'

Augustine, *On Faith and Works* [xviii. 33]: 'Courtesans and actors, and all others whose activities involve public disgrace, [44] are not permitted to approach the sacraments of Christ unless they have cast off or broken such bonds.' For an example in the case of an actor, see Cyprian, *Letters*, lxv [lxi]; for cases of gladiatorial trainers, procurers, and purveyors of victims, see Tertullian [*On Idolatry*, chap. xi]; the case of a charioteer of the circus is to be found in Augustine [Migne, XLIII. 786 f.].

not be able properly to keep up the rites of their law, and because they would be forced to carry arms and make long marches on the Sabbath day. Josephus further informs us that for the same reasons Jews requested and obtained exemption from Lucius Lentulus. Elsewhere he relates that when the Jews were bidden to leave the city of Rome some were enrolled in military service, others were punished because they would not serve on account of respect for the laws of their forefathers, that is, for the reasons which we have mentioned. [*Antiquities*, XIV. x. 13.] [XVIII. iii. 5.]

Sometimes there was also a third reason, that they thought they would have to fight against those of their own people; but from their point of view 'to take up arms against those of their own people was a crime', especially at a time when men of their own people were risking their lives in order to keep the law of their forefathers. Whenever the Jews were able to safeguard themselves against these disadvantages, they would engage in military service even under foreign kings, but 'continuing in the practices of their forefathers [1] and living in accordance with their statutes'; and this they were accustomed to stipulate in advance, as we know on the authority of Josephus. [Josephus, *Life*, vi.]

Very similar to these hazards are those which Tertullian urges against the military service of his day. In the book *On Idolatry* he says: 'Incompatible are the oath of allegiance to God and that to man, the standard of Christ and the standard of the Devil'; the reason is that soldiers were bidden to take oath in the name of the gods of the nations, as Jupiter, Mars, and other divinities. But in the book *On the Soldier's Chaplet* he writes: 'Shall he keep guard in front of temples whose worship he has abjured, and sup in a place not acceptable to the Apostle, and defend by night those whom in the daytime he has put to flight by means of exorcisms?' A little further on he adds: 'How many other things can be descried among the offences arising from the activities of the camp, which must be regarded as transgressions?' [xix.] [xi.]

4. In the third place we note that the Christians of the earliest time were fired by so great zeal to attain to the most excellent things that [33] they often interpreted divine counsels as commands. 'The Christians', says Athenagoras, 'do not avail themselves of judicial procedure against those who seize their property.' Salvianus asserts that we are enjoined by Christ to abandon things which are the subject of a lawsuit, provided only we get rid of litigation. And yet that principle, thus broadly stated, is a matter of counsel, and a concern of the higher life; [2] it was not laid down as a command. [*Apology for the Christians*, i.] [*On the Government of God*, III. vi. 22.]

[1] The words are those of Josephus, *Antiquities of the Jews*, XI [XI. viii. 5].

[2] Fourth Council of Carthage [canon xix]: 'A bishop is not to engage in litigation on behalf of temporal interests, even when attacked.' Add Ambrose, *On Duties*, Book II. xxi, and Gregory the Great, Book II, Ind. xi, Epist. lviii.

The case is similar in respect to the taking of an oath, which most of the early Christians disapprove without making any exception, although Paul used an oath, on an important occasion. The Christian in Tatian says: 'I refuse the office of praetor'; in Tertullian we read, 'The Christian does not aspire to the aedileship.' In like manner Lactantius declares that the just man, such as he wishes the Christian to be, will not engage in war; but at the same time and in the same way he declares that the just man will not travel on the sea. How many of the early writers try to dissuade Christians from second marriages? All the things recommended are praiseworthy, excellent, and in a high degree pleasing to God; but they are not exacted of us by the required observance of any law.

[*Orations against the Greeks*, xvi.] [*Apology* xlvi.] [*Divine Institutes*] V. xviii [V. xvii. 12.]

These observations, then, will be adequate to meet the objections which are urged.

5. In order to establish our case, first, on our side there is no lack of writers, and very early writers, too, who hold the opinion that both capital punishment and war, the legitimacy of which depends on the justification of capital punishment, may be lawfully resorted to by Christians. For Clement of Alexandria says that the Christian, if he is summoned to power, as Moses was, will be for his subjects a living law, and that he will reward the good, inflict punishment on the bad. And elsewhere, describing the dress of the Christian, he says that it is seemly for a man to go barefoot, unless perchance he be in military service. In the *Constitutions*[1] which bear the name of Clement of Rome we read (Book VII, chap. iii): 'Not as though all putting to death were unlawful, but only that of an innocent person; nevertheless, even when justifiable, this has been reserved for magistrates alone.'

[*Stromata*, I. xxvi, xxvii.] [*Paedagogus*, II. xi. 116.]

6. But let us leave the expressions of opinion by individuals and come to the authoritative public practice of the church, which ought to be of very great weight. I say, then, that men engaged in military service have never been refused baptism, or excommunicated from the Church; nevertheless such action ought to have been taken, and would have been taken, if military service had been irreconcilable with the provisions of the New Covenant.

In the *Constitutions* just quoted (Book VIII, chap. xxxii), the writer treats of those who in the olden days were from time to time admitted to baptism, or excluded from it: 'Let the soldier who asks for baptism be taught to abstain from unjust acts and false accusations, and to be content with his wages. If he obey these instructions, let him be admitted.' Tertullian in his *Apology*, speaking

Chap. xlii.

[1] This book seems to have been written at the end of the second century.

in the name of the Christians, says: 'We sail with you and we engage in military service with you.' A little before he had said: 'We are not of you, and we have filled all places belonging to you, your cities, islands, fortified posts, towns, places of assembly, even your camps.' In the same book he had related that in answer to the prayers of Christian soldiers a rainstorm was sent to the Emperor Marcus Aurelius.[1] In the *Chaplet* he says that the soldier who had cast away his chaplet manifested a more steadfast courage than his brethren, and shows that the man had many fellow soldiers who were Christians. Chap. xxxvii. [Chap. v.] [i.]

7. Furthermore, there were some soldiers who, having suffered tortures and death for Christ, received from the Church the same honour as the other martyrs. Among them are mentioned three companions of Paul;[2] Cerialis under Decius, and Marinus under Valerian; fifty soldier martyrs under Aurelian; Victor, Maurus, and Valentine, a chief of soldiers, under Maximian, and about the same time Marcellus the centurion; and Severianus, under Licinius. In regard to Laurentinus and Ignatius, [34] natives of Africa, Cyprian writes: [*Letters* xxxiv. 3.]

> They once served as soldiers in the warfare of this world, but afterward as true and spiritual soldiers of God they routed the Devil by confessing Christ, and through martyrdom won the palms and glorious crowns bestowed by the Lord.

From all this it is clear what opinion the body of Christians held in regard to military service, even before there were Christian emperors.

8. It ought not to seem strange if in those times Christians did not willingly take part in criminal proceedings, since very frequently judgement was to be passed upon Christians themselves. There is the further consideration that in respect to other matters also the Roman laws were harsher than accorded with Christian lenity; this is evident enough from a single instance, the senatusconsultum Silanianum.[3] But after Constantine began to view the Christian religion with approval and advance its interests, the infliction of capital punishment did not on that account cease. Constantine himself, in fact, among other laws promulgated a law in regard to sewing up parricides in a leather bag, and this law is extant in the Code, in the title *Concerning those who have killed Parents or Children*; although, for the rest, in inflicting punishments Constantine was exceedingly mild, so that he is criticized by not a few [*Code*, IX. xvii. 1.]

[1] See also Xiphilinus in regard to this incident [Dio Cassius, *Roman History*, LXXI. viii].

[2] Add a certain soldier baptized by Cornelius, of whom Ado makes mention.

[3] The harshness of this decree [*Digest*, XXIX. v. 1, §§ 7, 21] was mitigated by Hadrian the Emperor, as we read in Spartianus [*Hadrian*, xviii]. To the harsh laws of the Romans may be added those which forbade the admission of the testimony of a slave except under torture [*Code of Justinian*, VI. 1. 4].

historical writers because of his excessive leniency.[1] Also he had in his army a great many Christians, as history teaches us, and he inscribed the name of Christ upon his banner. In consequence the military oath also was changed into the form which is found in

[II. v.] Vegetius: 'By God and Christ and the Holy Spirit, and by the Majesty of the Emperor, which, next after God, ought to be for mankind the object of love and respect.'

9. And at that time among so many bishops, of whom a number had passed through the most cruel sufferings for their religion, we do not read that there was a single one who by arousing fear of the wrath of God sought to deter either Constantine from inflicting the death penalty and engaging in war, or Christians from military service; this, too, in face of the fact that a great many of the bishops were very alert guardians of discipline, and not at all disposed to hold back any suggestion regarding the duty either of the emperors or of other persons. Such a bishop, in the time of Theodosius, was Ambrose, who in his seventh discourse speaks as follows: 'To serve as a soldier is not an offence, but to serve as a soldier in order to obtain booty is a sin'; and in his work ***On Duties*** he says, 'Bravery, which by means of war defends one's native land from barbarians, or at home protects the weak, or safeguards one's associates from brigands, is complete justice.' This argument seems to me to be of so great force that I do not need to add anything to it.

[= Augustine, *Sermones*, Appendix, lxxxii.]

I. xxvii [128].

10. Nevertheless I am not unmindful of the fact that frequently bishops[2] and Christian people by interposing their supplications have averted punishments, and death penalties especially; also that the custom had been introduced that they who had taken refuge in a church,[3] should not be given up except under a pledge that their lives would be spared, and that about Easter time[4] those who were being kept in prison on account of their crimes should be set free. But he who will take the pains to weigh all the facts cited, and others like them, will find that these are the manifestations of Christian goodness which seizes every opportunity to show mercy, not of

[1] Zonaras [*History*, XIII. v. 11; speaking of Constantine the Great]: 'He would show himself clement to those who had abandoned a wicked life, saying that a limb which was diseased and decaying must be cut off, in order not to spread contagion to parts that were healthy, but not a limb that was either already healed, or in process of healing.' See also Eusebius [*On the Life of Constantine*, IV. xxxi].

Just as you find Christians complaining of the leniency of Constantine as too great, so in Saxo the historian you may find the Danes making complaint about the leniency of their King Harold [*History of Denmark*, Book XI].

[2] Augustine [*Letters*, cliii. 1]: 'It is the duty of a priest to intercede on behalf of those under accusation.' In his letters there are many examples of such goodness.

[3] See Chrysostom, *On the Statues*, Homily XVI; [*First*] *Council of Orleans*, chap. iii; *Law of the Visigoths*, Book VI, title v, chap. 16; Book IX, title ii, chap. 3 [VI. v. 16, *If a Murderer flees for Refuge to a Church*; IX. iii. 3, *On the Penalty for dragging a Man away from a Church*; ed. Zeumer].

[4] *Code*, I. iv. 3.

a spirit that condemns all judicial proceedings involving the death penalty. Hence such kindnesses, and even intercessions, were restricted by various exceptions [1] arising from both place and time.

11. At this point in opposition to the view advocated by us some present the twelfth canon of the Council of Nicaea, which runs as follows:

> Those who, having been called by grace,[2] at first manifested their zeal and faith and laid off their soldier's belt, but afterward returned as dogs to their vomit, some even having given money and offered inducements in order to get back into military service—let them, after having been hearers for three years, remain in penitence for ten years. In the case of all of them, however, it is needful that the purpose and the manner of their repentance be kept in view. They who through fear, and tears, and long-suffering, and good works do show forth a sincere conversion shall, on completing their term as hearers, [35] be permitted to take part in the prayers, and after that it shall be permissible for the bishop to be more kindly disposed toward them. But they that have acted with indifference, and have thought that the formality of entering a church was alone sufficient for conversion, are to complete the appointed term without any reduction.

The period of thirteen years clearly enough indicates that we are here dealing not with a fault that is trivial or open to question but with a serious and undoubted offence.

12. Now the matter here dealt with is beyond doubt idolatry.[3] For the mention of the times of Licinius in the eleventh canon, which precedes, ought to be considered as silently repeated in this canon. It often happens that the meaning of canons which follow depends on the meaning of those which precede; for an example reference may be made to the eleventh canon of the Council of Elvira.

Licinius, in fact, in the words of Eusebius, 'forced men out of military service unless they would offer sacrifice to the gods.'[4] His example was afterward imitated by Julian, and for that reason Victricius and others, we read, cast away the soldier's belt for Christ. The same thing had been done previously, under Diocletian, by eleven hundred and four soldiers in Armenia, of whom mention is [*On the Life of Constantine*, I. liv.]

[1] For these exceptions see Cassiodorus [*Variae*], XI. xl; also, among other references, *Decretals*, III. xlix. 6.

[2] Simeon Magister gives an epitome of this canon:

> Those who seemed to offer resistance when violence was attempted, but who have been vanquished by impiety and have again entered military service, are to be excluded from communion for ten years.

The same meaning of this canon is expressed by Balsamon and Zonaras, and by Ruffinus, Book X, chap. vi.

[3] This as the principal crime is called by Tertullian, *On Idolatry* [chap. i], 'the highest offence chargeable against the world'; and by Cyprian, *Letters*, xii [x. 1], 'the most grave and utmost sin'.

[4] Sulpicius Severus [*Sacred History*, II. xxxiii]: 'Licinius, because he was contending with Constantine for the sovereign power, had ordered his soldiers to offer sacrifice; those who refused he rejected from military service.' For the same reason Valentinian, who afterward became emperor, left the service under Julian. Similar is the fact related by Victor of Utica [Victor Vitensis, *Persecution of the Vandals*, II. vii], that under King Huneric many abandoned the calling of arms, because it had been associated with Arianism.

made in the martyrologies, and in Egypt by Mennas and Hesychius. Under such conditions in the time of Licinius many cast away their belts; among them was Arsacius, who is named among the confessors, and Auxentius, who afterward became bishop of Mopsuestia.

In consequence, soldiers who, pricked in conscience, had once cast away their belts, could not return to military service under Licinius except by adjuring their Christian faith; and since that step was all the more reprehensible for the reason that their former act evidenced in them a fuller knowledge of the divine law, such backsliders are punished more severely even than those dealt with in the preceding canon, who had renounced Christianity without running any risk of the loss of life or of property. To interpret the canon which we have quoted as referring broadly to all military service is altogether unreasonable. History in fact plainly testifies that those who had renounced military service under Licinius, and, in order that they might not do violence to their Christian faith, had not returned to it while Licinius was in power, received from Constantine an option, to remain exempt from military service if they so desired, or to return to military service; beyond doubt many chose the latter alternative.

[Eusebius, *On the Life of Constantine,* II. xxxiii.]

13. Some urge in opposition also the letter of Leo, which says: 'It is contrary to the rules of the Church, after an act of penitence, to return to secular service of arms.' But we must know that in the case of penitents no less than in that of the clergy and ascetics there was required a mode of life not merely Christian, but of conspicuous holiness, in order that their example might be as effective for correction as it had previously been for the committing of sin.[1] Similarly in the most ancient formulated customs of the Church which, to render them more acceptable through a more impressive name, were commonly called the *Apostolic Canons*, in the eighty-second canon the rule is laid down: 'Let no bishop, priest or deacon devote himself to the profession of arms, and at the same time remain in the service of Rome and retain his priestly function. To Caesar belong the things that are Caesar's, and unto God the things that are God's.' By this very statement it is made clear that Christians who did not aspire to the honour of the clerical profession were not forbidden to engage in military service.

14. It was, furthermore, forbidden to admit to the clerical profession [2] those who, after baptism, had taken office as magistrates

[1] Leo, letter xc, *To Rusticus* [Leo the Great, *Letters*, clxvii]: 'He who asks pardon for things forbidden ought [45] also to refrain from many things which are permissible.'

In the letter of the bishops to King Louis we read: 'A man ought to cut himself off from things permissible in the degree that he remembers that he has done things which were not permissible'; in the *Capitularies* of Charles the Bald: 'Let each seek greater gains through good works in proportion as he has brought greater losses on himself through fault.'

[2] Eusebius, *Demonstrations*, Book I [chap. viii], describes the Christian life as of two types, the

or had assumed military responsibilities, as may be seen in the letters of Syricius and Innocent, and in the canons of the Council of Toledo. Candidates for orders, as we know, were chosen not from among Christians of any and every sort but only from among those who had presented an example of the most correct life. Again, the obligation imposed by military service and by some magistracies was permanent; but those who were set aside for the sacred office were not to allow themselves to be distracted by any outside responsibility or [36] daily task.[1] For this reason the sixth canon ordered that no bishop, priest or deacon should administer secular interests, the eightieth that they should not become involved in public administration. The sixth of the African canons ordered that they should not assume charge of the interests of others,[2] or the defence of others' causes. Consistently with this decree Cyprian [3] thinks it altogether wrong for these officers of the Church to be appointed guardians.

15. In support of our view we have the clearly formulated judgement of the Church in the first Council of Arles, which was held under Constantine. The third canon of that Council reads thus: 'In regard to those who cast away their arms in time of peace, it was decreed that they abstain from the communion.' This has reference to those who deserted from the army in times when there was no persecution; for that is what Christians meant by the term peace,[4] as is apparent from Cyprian and others. There is the further example of the soldiers under Julian, whose progress in Christianity was so great that they were ready to bear witness to Christ by their death. Ambrose speaks of them in these words: [*Decretum*, II. xi. 3. 94= Augustine, *Letters*, cv.]

> The Emperor Julian, although an apostate, nevertheless had Christian soldiers under him. When he said to them, 'Go into battle in defence of the state,' they were obedient to him; but when he would say to them, 'Bear arms against Christians,' they recognized as their leader the ruler of heaven.

Such spirit long before had been manifested by the Theban

one perfect, the other falling short of perfection. Christians who represent the latter type among other things 'point out to those who are engaged in just warfare what their duty is'.

[1] See the canon of the Council of Mainz in Gratian, *Decretals* III. l. 1.

[2] See the letter of Jerome *To Nepotianus* [lii].

[3] In his letter *To the Priests, Deacons, and People at Furni* [*Letters*, lxv]. Add the law, *Code*, I. iii. 51 (52).

[4] Tertullian, *On Idolatry* [xix]: 'Nay, how even in peace will the Christian render military service?' The same writer, *On Flight in Persecution* [iii]: 'What war does our peace have, excepting persecution?'

Cyprian, *Letters*, x [ix. 3]: 'When the first thing is that our mother, the Church, should first have received peace from the mercy of the Lord'; *Letters*, xxii [xxi. 2; letter of Lucian]: 'Since the Lord has begun to give peace to the Church'; *Letters*, xxxi [xxxi. 5; the Roman clergy to Cyprian]: 'That the peace of the Church must be maintained,' that is, is to be expected; *On the Lapsed* [chap. v]: 'long peace had corrupted the discipline.'

Sulpicius Severus [*Sacred History*, II. xxxii]: 'During the reign of Antoninus Pius the churches had peace'; later [xxxii. 2], 'after an interval of thirty-eight years the Christians had peace'; and in the period of Constantine [xxxiii. 3], 'since then we have been enjoying a condition of tranquillity in peace'; also, at the beginning of his *History* [I. 1. 3]: 'Tormentings of the people of Christ, and then times of peace.'

legion, which in the reign of Diocletian had received the Christian religion from Zabdas, thirtieth bishop of Jerusalem, and afterward gave an example of Christian steadfastness and long-suffering memorable for all time. To this example we shall refer later. [I. iv. 7. 10 ff.]

16. Here it may suffice to quote the utterance of the members of the Theban legion, which with compact brevity sets forth the duty of the Christian soldier:

> To oppose any foe whatsoever we offer our hands, which we deem it impious to stain with the blood of the innocent. Our right hands themselves know how to fight against wicked men and enemies; they do not know how to tear in pieces righteous men and fellow citizens. We remember that we took up arms on behalf of citizens rather than against citizens. We have always fought on behalf of justice, on behalf of loyalty, on behalf of the safety of the innocent; up to the present time this has been the reward for our dangers. We have fought on behalf of the faith; and how are we to keep our faith toward you—the words are addressed to the Emperor—if we do not show forth faith toward God?

Basil spoke thus of the Christians of the earlier time:

> Slayings in war our ancestors did not consider as murder; they considered that those who fight in defence of virtue and righteousness are absolved.

CHAPTER III

DISTINCTION BETWEEN PUBLIC AND PRIVATE WAR; EXPLANATION OF SOVEREIGNTY

I.—*Division of war into public and private*

[46] 1. THE first and most essential division of war is that into public war, private war, and mixed war. Syl., word *bellum*, I, no. 1.

A public war is that which is waged by him who has lawful authority to wage it; a private war, that which is waged by one who has not the lawful authority; and a mixed war is that which is on one side public, on the other side private. Let us deal first with private war, as the more ancient.

2. That private wars in some cases may be waged lawfully, so far as the law of nature is concerned, is, I think, sufficiently clear from what was said above, when we showed that the use of force to ward off injury is not in conflict with the law of nature. But possibly some may think that after public tribunals had been established private wars were not permissible. For although public tribunals are the creation not of nature but of man, it is, nevertheless, much more consistent with moral standards, and more conducive to the peace of individuals, that a matter be judicially investigated by one who has no personal interest in it, than that individuals, too often having only their own interests in view, should seek by their own hands to obtain that which they consider right; wherefore equity and reason given to us by nature declare that so praiseworthy an institution should have the fullest support. Says Paul the jurist, *Dig.* L. xvii. 176. 'Individuals must not be permitted to do that which the magistrate can do in the name of the state, in order that there may be no occasion for raising a greater disturbance.' 'The reason', King Theodoric[1] Cass., *Variae*, IV. iv [IV. x]. said, 'why laws were clothed with a reverential regard, was that nothing might be done by one's own hand, nothing on individual impulse. For what difference is there between tranquil peace and the hurly-burly of war, if controversies between individuals are settled by the use of force?'

The laws term it a use of force 'when an individual tries to *Digest*, IV. ii. 13. enforce his claim to what he thinks is due him without having recourse to a judge'.

[1] See the *Edict* of Theodoric, chaps. x and cxxiv.

II.—*The proposition, that according to the law of nature not all private war is unpermissible since the establishment of courts, is defended, illustrations being added*

1. It is surely beyond doubt that the licence which was prevalent before the establishment of courts has been greatly restricted. Nevertheless there are circumstances under which such licence even now holds good, that is, undoubtedly, where judicial procedure ceases to be available. For the law which forbids a man to seek to recover his own otherwise than through judicial process is ordinarily understood as applicable only where judicial process has been possible.

Now judicial procedure ceases to be available either temporarily or continuously. It ceases to be available temporarily[1] when one cannot wait to refer a matter to a judge without certain danger or loss. It ceases to be available continuously either in law or in fact: in law, if one finds himself in places without inhabitants, as on the sea, in a wilderness, or on vacant islands, or in any other places where there is no state; in fact, if those who are subject to jurisdiction do not heed the judge, or if the judge has openly refused to take cognizance.

Molina, *Disp*, 100, § dubio vero.

2. What we said, that even after the establishment of courts not all private wars were in conflict with the law of nature, can be supported also from the law which was given to the Jews; for therein through the agency of Moses God said (*Exodus*, xxii. 2): 'If the thief be found breaking in, and be smitten so that he dieth, there shall be no bloodguiltiness for him. If the sun be risen upon him, there shall be bloodguiltiness for him.'

It seems clear that this ordinance, which makes so careful a distinction, not only assures impunity but also explains the law of nature, and that it is not founded upon a special divine mandate, but grounded in common equity. Hence, we see, other nations also followed it. Well known is the provision of the Twelve Tables, undoubtedly taken from the ancient Attic law[2]: 'If a theft has been committed at night, and any one has killed the thief, be it that the thief was rightly slain.' Thus by the laws of all peoples known to us the person who in peril of his life has by means of arms defended himself against an assailant is adjudged innocent. An agreement so manifest furnishes in itself the proof that in it there is nothing in conflict with the law of nature.

[*Macrobius, Saturnalia*, I. iv. 19.]

[1] Servius, *On the Aeneid*, XI [X, line 419], on the words 'The fates laid hand upon him' (*Iniecere manum Parcae*): 'They took what was due to them. The poet here used a legal expression, for there is said to be a "laying on of the hand" when, without authority from a judge, we lay claim to a thing that is due to us.'

[2] The words of Solon [Demosthenes, *Against Timocrates*, xxiv. 113 = p. 736]: 'If any one in the daytime steal in an amount exceeding fifty drachmas, it shall be right to take him before the Eleven; but if any one steal at night, even the least thing, it shall be permitted even to kill him.'

Add what is said below in the second book, chap. xii [II. i. 12].

III.—*The proposition is defended that private war in some cases is permissible even according to the law of the Gospel, objections being met*

1. In the case of the volitional divine law in its more perfect form, that is, the law of the Gospel, [47] a greater difficulty presents itself. I do not doubt that God, Who has over our lives a more absolute right than we ourselves, might have required of us so great a degree of forbearance that, as individuals, when confronted with danger, it would be our duty to allow ourselves to be killed rather than to kill. But did God purpose to bind us in so extreme a fashion ? That is the point which we are to investigate.

On the affirmative side, two passages are commonly brought forward to which, in the discussion of the general question, we have already referred. They are : 'But I say unto you, Resist not him that is evil' (*Matthew*, v. 39) ; and 'Avenge not yourselves, beloved' (*Romans*, xii. 19), where the Latin translation has 'Defend not yourselves, beloved'. A third passage is in the words of Christ to Peter : 'Put up again thy sword into its sheath ; for all they that take the sword shall perish with the sword.' In this connexion some add also the example of Christ, who died for his enemies (*Romans*, v. 8, 10). [I. ii. 8. 3, 12.] [*Matthew*, xxvi. 52.]

2. Among the early Christians there was no lack of those who did not indeed disapprove of public war, but who thought that in the case of an individual self-defence was forbidden. The passages of Ambrose favourable to war we quoted above. Familiar to all are the statements of Augustine, which are even more numerous and more clear. But the same Ambrose says : 'And perchance He said to Peter, who offered him two swords, "It is enough," as if He had said that the use of the sword in self-defence was permissible up to the time of the Gospel ; with the implication that the teaching of the law stressed equity, while the teaching of the Gospel stressed truth.' And in another passage he adds : 'The Christian, even if he fall in the way of an armed brigand, cannot strike in turn one who strikes him, from fear that, while defending his safety, he mar his piety.' [I. ii. 9. 9.] *On Luke*, X [liii]. *On Duties*, III. iii [III. iv].

'I find no fault', says Augustine, 'with the law which permits the slaying of such people' (brigands and others who assault with violence), 'but I do not see how to justify those who put them to death.' In another connexion he declares : 'The idea of killing men in order not to be killed by them is not acceptable to me, unless, perchance, in the case of a soldier or of a public functionary acting not for himself but on behalf of others, in the exercise of a lawful *On Free Will*, I. v [12]. *Letters*, cliv [xlvii. 5], *To Publicola*.

Chaps. 43 and 55 [*Letters*, cxcix. 43]. authority.' It is plain enough, from Basil's second letter to Amphilochius, that he held the same view.[1]

3. The contrary opinion, that no such degree of forbearance is required, is certainly more common, and also seems to me more true. For in the Gospel we are bidden to love our neighbour as ourselves, not above ourselves; further, if a like evil threatens, we are not forbidden to look out for ourselves in preference to others,[2]
[I. ii. 8. 6.] as we showed above on the authority of Paul when he was explaining the rule of kindness.

Perhaps some one may press the point and say: 'Even if I may be able to give the preference to my own advantage over the advantage of my neighbour, this would not hold in the case of unequal advantages; wherefore I ought rather to give up my life than to suffer that my assailant fall into eternal damnation.' But the answer may be made that in many cases even the man who is attacked has need of time for repentance, or probably thinks he has; and the assailant also may have time for repentance before death. Further, from the point of view of morals it is not clear that that ought to be accounted a danger into which a man has thrown himself, and from which he can extricate himself.

4. Up to the very last some of the Apostles, under the eye of
[*Jewish War*, II. viii. 4.] Christ and with his knowledge, certainly seem to have made their journeys armed with swords. From Josephus we learn that other Galileans, when hastening from their country toward Jerusalem, did the same thing, because the roads were infested with highwaymen; and he has reported a similar practice on the part of the Essenes, the most inoffensive of men. Thus it came about that when Christ was saying that the time was at hand when even a garment should be sold in order to buy a sword (*Luke*, xxii. 36), the Apostles at once answered that among their company there were two swords; and in that [48] company there were none except Apostles.

What Christ said, then, does not in truth embody a command; it is, rather, a proverbial expression, indicating that extremely serious dangers threatened. This is clearly shown by the contrasting reference to the earlier time (verse 35), which had been safe and propitious. Nevertheless the words are such as plainly to suggest what was customary, and what the Apostles considered permissible.

[*For Milo*, iv. 10.] 5. Rightly did Cicero declare that 'It would surely not be

[1] Add the canon of the Council of Orleans cited by Gratian, *Decretum*, II. xiii. 2. ult.

[2] Cassiodorus, *On Friendship* [cf. Peter of Blois, *On the Love of God and Neighbour*, xi]: 'Truly no one is bound by any commandment, or any reason, to accomplish the safety of his neighbour's soul by the loss of his own soul, or the freeing of his neighbour's body by the destruction of his own body, save only when the hope of eternal salvation is at stake.'

permissible to have swords, if it were not in any way permissible to use them'. Again, the precept 'Resist not him that is evil' is not more general in its application than that which follows, 'Give to every one that asketh thee.' The latter, nevertheless, is modified by the restriction, provided that we do not overburden ourselves. Nothing is added to the precept about giving which restricts its application, and it is limited by the sense of equity alone; but the precept about not resisting carries with it an explanation in the concrete example of a slap. It is, then, to be understood that the obligation not to offer resistance is absolutely binding upon us only when the injury which threatens us is either a slap, or something in the same class. Otherwise it would have been more in accordance with what is right to say: 'Resist not him that doeth injury, but give up life itself rather than to make use of weapons.'

6. In the words of Paul to the Romans, 'Avenge not yourselves,' the Greek has the meaning 'avenge', not 'defend'; so also *Judith*, i. 11, and ii. 1; *Luke*, xviii. 7, 8, and xxi. 22; *2 Thessalonians*, i. 8; *1 Peter*, ii. 14; *Romans*, xiii. 4; *1 Thessalonians*, iv. 6. This is made perfectly plain by the context; for the injunction 'Render to no man evil for evil' had preceded, and these words are applicable only to revenge, not to defence. And in support of his contention Paul cites the sentence from *Deuteronomy*: 'Justice is [xxxii. 35.] mine, I will repay,' where the Hebrew has 'to me also vengeance'. Both the proper use of the term in Hebrew shows that vengeance is meant, and the meaning of the passage does not permit us to suppose that defence can be referred to.

7. What was said to Peter does in fact contain a prohibition of the use of the sword, but not of such use in defence. Peter did not have need to defend himself; for in regard to his disciples Christ had already said (*John*, xviii. 8, 9): 'Let these go their way, that the word might be fulfilled which he spake, of those whom thou hast given me I lost not one.' And there was no need to defend Christ, for he did not wish to be defended. So in the narrative of John Christ adds the reason for the prohibition (*John*, xviii. 11): 'The cup which the Father hath given me, shall I not drink it?' And in *Matthew* he says: 'How then should the Scriptures be [xxvi. 54.] fulfilled, that thus it must be?' Peter, then, being impetuous, was impelled by a desire for revenge, not for defence. Further, he was taking up arms against those who were coming as representatives of the public authority; whether under any circumstances resistance should be offered to those representing the public authority is a question by itself, to which we must return later.

Now the sentence which our Lord adds, 'All they that have taken up the sword shall perish by the sword,' is either a proverb taken from common usage, signifying that bloodshed is provoked by bloodshed, and that in consequence the use of weapons is never free from hazard; or, in accordance with the opinion held by Origen, Theophylactus, Titus, and Euthymius, it means, that we ought not to forestall God by taking the vengeance which He himself will sufficiently exact in His own time. Evidently of such import is the verse in *Revelation* (xiii. 10): 'If any man shall kill with the sword, with the sword must he be killed. Here is the patience and the faith of the saints.' In agreement therewith is the comment of Tertullian:

[*On Patience*, xv.] 'An all-sufficing Depositary for our patience is God. If you leave with Him a wrong, He is the avenger; if suffering, He is the physician; if death, He raises from the dead. How great is the privilege of patience, to have God as her Debtor!' At the same time, in these words of Christ [49] there seems to be a prophecy of the punishment which the sword of the Romans was to exact from the blood-guilty Jews.

8. As for the example of Christ, when we are told that He died for His enemies the rejoinder may be made that all the acts of Christ exemplify virtue in fullest measure, that it is praiseworthy to imitate them, so far as possible, and that such imitation will not fail of its reward; nevertheless not all His acts are of such a character that they proceed from a law, or themselves establish a law. For in dying for His enemies and for the ungodly Christ acted not in obedience to any law, but in accordance with a special promise and covenant, as it were, made with the Father; if He should thus die the Father promised to Him not only supreme glory but a people that should endure forever (*Isaiah*, liii. 10). That in other respects this act is as it were unique, to which scarcely any parallel can be found, Paul shows (*Romans*, v. 7). Christ, furthermore, bids us expose our lives to danger not for any and every person, but on behalf of them that share the same profession (*1 John*, iii. 16).

9. The opinions which are cited from the Christian writers seem in part to embody counsel and exhortation to a lofty purpose rather than a rigid rule; in part they are the personal views of the writers themselves, and do not reflect opinions shared by the whole

Can. xlv [lxiv]. *Decretals*, V. xxxix. 3 and V. xii. 16. Church. In fact in the most ancient canons, which are called Apostolic, only he is cut off from the communion who in a quarrel has killed his opponent with the first blow 'on account of the excess of passion'.[1] This opinion Augustine himself, whom we have quoted for the opposite view, seems to approve (*On Exodus*, qu. lxxxiv).

[1] Ambrose, *On Luke*, Book X [chap. liii]: 'Lord, why dost thou bid me purchase a sword whilst thou biddest me not to strike? Why dost thou direct that a sword be carried which thou forbiddest to have drawn? Unless, perhaps, that defence be in readiness, vengeance not necessary.'

IV.—*Division of public war into formal and less formal*

1. Public war is either formal, according to the law of nations, or less formal.

The word 'formal' I use here as equivalent to 'legal' (*iustum*) in the sense in which we speak of a legal will (*iustum testamentum*) as distinguished from codicils, and a legal marriage as distinguished from the union of slaves (*contubernium*). This does not mean that it is not permissible for any one to make codicils who may desire to do so, or for a slave to have a woman living with him (*in contubernio*);[1] but it does mean that from the point of view of the civil law the formal will and the formal marriage have certain peculiar effects. It is useful to note this distinction; for many, having a wrong understanding of the word 'legal' (*iustum*) in such a connexion think that all wars, to which the adjective 'legal' (*iusta*) is inapplicable, are under condemnation as inconsistent with justice or not permissible.

In order that a war may be formal, according to the law of nations, two conditions are requisite: first, that on both sides it be waged under the authority of the one who holds the sovereign power in the state; then, that certain formalities be observed, which we shall discuss later in the proper connexion. Since both conditions are conjointly requisite, one without the other does not suffice.

2. A less formal public war may lack the formalities referred to, may be waged against private persons, and on the authority of any public official. And surely if the matter be viewed without reference to the laws of particular states, it would seem that every public official has the right to wage war for the protection of the people entrusted to his charge, and also in order to maintain his jurisdiction if assailed by force. But because the whole state is endangered by war, provision has been made by the laws of almost every state that war may be waged only under the authority of him who holds the sovereign power in the state.

Such a provision is to be found in the last book of Plato *On Laws*. In the Roman law he is declared guilty of treason who has waged war, or made a levy, or brought together an army without the order of the emperor; the Cornelian Law, proposed by Lucius Cornelius Sulla, had said, 'without the order of the people.' In the *Code* of Justinian, there is extant an imperial constitution of Valentinian and Valens bearing on the same point: 'No person shall have

[XII. vii.] *Digest*, XLVIII. iv. 3.

[XI. xlvii. 1.]

[1] Among citizens there were certain marriages which were not 'formal' (*iusta*); children not 'legitimate' (*iusti*) according to civil law. Paul, *Sententiae*, Book II, title xix [II. xix. 6]; *Digest*, XLVIII. v. 14 (13); so also there is a kind of liberty that is not 'formal' (*iusta*). Seneca, *On the Happy Life*, chap. xxiv; Suetonius, *Octavius* [*Octavianus*], chap. xl.

the authority to inaugurate a movement of arms of any sort without our knowledge and without consulting us.' Here belongs the statement of Augustine:[1] 'The order which is according to nature and adapted to the maintenance of peace among mortals [50] demands that the authority and the decision in respect to commencing war reside in those who hold the chief authority.'

Vict., *De Iure Belli*, no. 9. Molina, *Disp.*, 100, § *idem Vict.* Bartolus, *On Dig.*, I. i. 5. Bart., *On Reprisals*, 3 principali, ad secundam, no. 6. Martinus Laud., *De Bello*, qu. 2. Livy, XXXIX [XXIV. xxxvii–xxxix].

3. But as all statements, no matter how general, are to be interpreted in the light of justice, so also is this law. For in the first place it cannot be doubted that it is permissible for a public official, who has proper authority over a district, through his subordinates to restrain by force a few that are disobedient, whenever there is no need of larger forces for the purpose, and danger does not threaten the state.

Again, if the danger is so pressing that time does not permit consultation with him who has the supreme authority in the state, in that case also necessity will make an exception. Of such a justification Lucius Pinarius, who was in command of the garrison at Enna, in Sicily, availed himself. Having learned with certainty that the people of the town were planning to revolt to the Carthaginians, he had them massacred, and so held possession of Enna. When no such necessity was present, Franciscus de Victoria presumed to ascribe to citizens of towns the right to carry on war in order to redress wrongs which the king had neglected to prosecute; but his view is deservedly rejected by others.

V.—*Whether there may be a public war waged by the authority of a public official not having sovereign power, and when*

Ayala, *De Iure Belli*, I. ii, no. 7; Sylv., word *bellum*, no. 2. Innocent, in *Decretals*, II. xiii. 12, no. 8; II. xxiv. 29, no. 5. Panor., *ibid.* Bartolus, *On Dig.*, XLIX. xv. 24.

1. The jurists, however, are by no means agreed regarding the circumstances under which minor public officials may have the right to inaugurate a movement of arms, or whether such a war should be called a public war. The affirmative view is held by some, the negative by others.

Truly if we use the word public as including whatever is done by the authority of an official, there is no doubt that such wars are public, and consequently those who under conditions of this sort oppose public officials expose themselves to the punishment awaiting men that stubbornly resist their superiors. But if the word public is understood in a higher sense as characterizing that which is done with due formality, as beyond question this word often is, such wars are not public, for the reason that both the decision of the sovereign

[1] *Against Faustus*, Book XXII, chap. lxxiv [lxxv], cited by Gratian, *Decretum*, II. xxiii. i. 4.

Among the Hebrews every war which was [not] undertaken by special command of God was called 'a war of the powers'.

power and other conditions are necessary for the fulfilment of the legal requirements involved. And I am not affected by the consideration that even in disturbances of the kind under consideration men who resist authority are ordinarily deprived of their property,[1] which may even be turned over to the soldiers. For such occurrences are not so peculiar to formal war that they may not also take place under other conditions.

Livy, as cited above.

2. This situation, moreover, may arise, whereby in an empire having a wide extent of territory, subordinate authorities may have a delegated power [2] of beginning war. If such a situation does arise, we are to consider that the war is actually being waged by virtue of the sovereign authority; for he who vests another with the right to do anything is himself regarded as doer of it.

Vict. no. 29. Cajetan, *On II. ii*, 40, art. 1. Sylv., word *bellum*, pt. 1, no. 2. Lorca, *Disp.* l, no. 12.

3. A more controverted question is whether, in case such an authorization has not been given, the presumption that such an authorization is intended will be sufficient.

The affirmative view ought not, I think, to be conceded. For it is not enough to consider what under such conditions would be acceptable to him who holds the sovereign power if he could be consulted; the real point to be considered is, what he would wish to have done without consulting him in a matter admitting delay, or of doubtful expediency, if a general law covering the case were to be passed. For although in a particular instance a consideration influencing the decision of the head of the state may seem, if examined from a particular point of view, to be inapplicable, yet, generally speaking, the consideration arising from the desire to avoid danger does not cease to apply. This general consideration cannot have its proper weight if every public official takes the decision of such questions into his own hands.

4. Not without just reason, then, was Gnaeus Manlius accused by his legionary commanders because he had made war upon the Galatians without the authorization of the Roman people. For although there had been legions of Gauls in the army of Antiochus, nevertheless, after peace had been made with Antiochus, the question, whether punishment for that offence should be visited upon the Galatians, was not for Gnaeus Manlius to decide but for the Roman people.

Livy, XLVIII [XXXVIII. xlv ff.].

Cato wished to have Julius Caesar delivered up to the Germans because he had made war on them; but I believe that he had in mind not so much the question of right as a desire to free the city

[1] To the jurists cited for this point may be added Franciscus Aretinus, *Consilia*, xiv, no. 7; Gail, *De Pace Publica*, I, chap. ii, no. 20; Cardinal Toschi, *Practicae quaestiones*, LV, letter B, word 'bellum', no. 10. Goeddaeus, *Cons. Marp.*, XXVIII, nos. 202 ff.

[2] See the law of the Emperor Frederick, in Conrad, Abbot of Ursperg [Bavaria].

from the fear of a prospective master. The Germans, in fact, [51] had helped the Gauls, who were enemies of the Roman people, and consequently they had no reason to complain that a wrong had been done to them, provided the Roman people had a just cause for making war on the Gauls. But Caesar ought to have been satisfied with driving the Germans out of Gaul, the province which had been assigned to him; he ought not to have carried war against them into their own territory without first consulting the Roman people, especially since there was no imminent danger from that source. The Germans therefore did not have the right to demand that Caesar be surrendered to them, but the Roman people had the right to punish him, on grounds clearly similar to those which the Carthaginians set forth in their answer to the Romans:

Livy, XXXI [XXI. xviii. 6].

> I consider that the question at issue is not whether Saguntum was attacked in accordance with a decision of an individual or of the state, but whether it was attacked rightfully or wrongfully. For the question whether our citizen acted in accordance with our decision, or his own, is our business, and to us belongs the punishment of a citizen of ours. The subject of discussion between you and us is merely, whether under our treaty the attack was permissible.

5. Marcus Tullius Cicero defended the action of Octavius and of Decimus Brutus in taking up arms against Antony on their own initiative. And yet, even if it were settled that Antony deserved to be treated as an enemy, they ought to have waited for the decision of the senate and the Roman people as to whether it was in the public interest to overlook the action of Antony or to avenge it; to come to terms of peace, or rush to arms. No one, in fact, is compelled to avail himself of a right of which the use frequently involves the risk of loss. Again, even if Antony were adjudged a public enemy, it was for the senate and the Roman people to decide to whom they would prefer that the conduct of the war should be entrusted. Thus, when Cassius requested auxiliary troops of the Rhodians in accordance with the treaty, they answered that they would send the forces if the Roman senate should so direct.

Appian, *Civil Wars*, IV [ix. 66].

6. This illustration—and there are many others—may serve to remind us that we are not to receive with approval everything which authors, no matter how famous, may tell us; they are under the influence often of their times, often of their feelings, and they fit 'their measuring-rule to the stone'. Wherefore in these matters we must make every effort to use a discriminating judgement and not allow ourselves rashly to seize upon something as a precedent which can be exculpated rather than praised. In the use of such a method vicious errors are commonly committed.

7. Since, then, it has been said that a public war ought not to be waged except by the authority of him who holds the sovereign

power, for the understanding both of this subject and of questions relating to formal war, and consequently for the understanding of many other questions, it will be necessary to understand what sovereignty is, and who hold it. This inquiry is all the more necessary because learned men of our own age, treating the matter from the point of view of usage under present conditions rather than from that of the truth, have added greatly to the complexity of the subject, which in itself was far from simple.

VI.—*In what the civil power consists*

1. The moral faculty of governing a state, which is ordinarily designated by the term civil power, is described by Thucydides as [V. xviii.] having three characteristics. He speaks of a state, which truly is a state, as 'having its own laws, courts, and public officials'.[1]

Aristotle distinguishes three parts in the government of a state: *Politics,* IV. iv [IV. xiv]. deliberation in regard to matters of common interest; the choice of officials; and the administration of justice. To the first he refers deliberation in regard to war, peace, the making and abrogation of treaties, and legislation. To this he adds, further, deliberation in regard to the death penalty, exile, confiscation of property, and proceedings in cases of extortion, that is, as I interpret the passage, the administration of justice in criminal cases, since previously in treating the administration of justice he has dealt with cases involving the interests of individuals only.

Dionysius of Halicarnassus notes three principal functions: Book IV [xx]. the right to create and appoint to public offices; the right to make and abrogate laws; and the right of decision regarding war and peace.[2] In another passage he adds a fourth, the right to render Book VII [lvi]. judicial decisions; elsewhere, again, he includes also the adminis- Book II [xiv]. tration of matters pertaining to worship, and the convening of assemblies of the people.

2. Now if one wishes to make an exact [52] division he will find it possible easily to include everything relating to civil power in such a way that there will be nothing omitted and nothing superfluous. For he who governs a state governs it in part through his own agency, in part through others. He governs through his own agency by devoting his attention either to general interests or to particular interests. In devoting himself to general interests he

[1] The translation 'taxes' can also be used; in this sense the Scholiast to Thucydides understood it. The word αὐτοτελῆ has a twofold meaning.

[2] [71] Servius, *On the Aeneid,* I [line 236], comments on the words 'with unlimited sway' (*omni dicione*) [literally 'with every sway']: 'more correctly "who should hold the sea and the lands with unlimited sway" than "the sea and all the lands with their sway"; purposing to convey the meaning "all power, peace, laws, war".'

concerns himself with framing and abrogating laws respecting religious matters (so far as the care of religious matters belongs to the state) as well as secular. The branch of the science of government which deals with such matters Aristotle calls architectonic, 'the architectural'.

[*Nicomachean Ethics*, vi. 8.]

The particular interests, with which he who governs concerns himself, are either exclusively public interests, or private interests which have a relation to public interests. Exclusively public interests are either actions, as the making of peace, of war, and of treaties; or things, such as taxes, and other things of a like nature, wherein the right of eminent domain, which the state has over citizens and over the property of citizens for public use, is included. The branch of the science of government which deals with such matters Aristotle designates by the general term 'political', that is 'civil', and 'deliberative'.

Private interests [as here understood] are controversies between individuals the termination of which by public authority is important for the tranquillity of the state. The branch of the science of government concerned therewith is called by Aristotle 'the judicial'.

The affairs that are administered through others are administered either through public officials, or through other responsible agents, among whom ambassadors are included.

In these things, then, the civil power consists.

VII.—*What sovereignty is*

1. That power is called sovereign whose actions are not subject to the legal control of another, so that they cannot be rendered void by the operation of another human will. When I say 'of another', I exclude from consideration him who exercises the sovereign power, who has the right to change his determinations; I exclude also his successor,[1] who enjoys the same right, and therefore has the same power, not a different power. Let us, then, see who is the subject of sovereignty.

The subject of a power is either common or special. Just as the body is a common, the eye a special subject of the power of sight, so the state, which we have defined above as a perfect association, is the common subject of sovereignty.

2. We exclude from consideration, therefore, the peoples who have passed under the sway of another people, such as the peoples of the Roman provinces. For such peoples are not in themselves a state, in the sense in which we are now using the term, but the inferior members of a great state, just as slaves are members of a household.

[1] Cacheranus, *Decisiones Pedemontanae*, cxxxix, no. 6.

Again, it happens that several peoples may have the same head, while nevertheless each of them in itself forms a perfect association. While in the case of the natural body there cannot be one head belonging to several bodies, this does not hold also in the case of a moral body. In the case of a moral body the same person, viewed in different relations, may be the head of several distinct bodies. A clear proof of this may be found in the fact that on the extinction of the reigning house, the right of government reverts to each people separately.

Vict., *De Iure Belli*, no. 7.

It may also happen that several states are bound together by a confederation, and form a kind of 'system', as Strabo in more than one passage calls it, while nevertheless the different members do not cease in each case to retain the status of a perfect state. This fact was noted by other writers, and by Aristotle also in more than one passage.

[IX. iii. 7; XIV. iii. 2.] *Politics*, II. xx [II. ii], III. ix.

3. It may be granted, then, that the common subject of sovereignty is the state, understood as we have already indicated.

The special subject is one or more persons, according to the laws and customs of each nation; 'the first power', according to Galen, in the sixth book of his treatise *On the Teachings of Hippocrates and Plato*.

VIII.—*The opinion that sovereignty always resides in the people is rejected, and arguments are answered*

1. At this point first of all the opinion of those must be rejected who hold that everywhere and without exception sovereignty resides in the people, [53] so that it is permissible for the people to restrain and punish kings whenever they make a bad use of their power. How many evils this opinion has given rise to, and can even now give rise to if it sinks deep into men's minds, no wise person fails to see. We refute it by means of the following arguments.

To every man it is permitted to enslave himself to any one he pleases for private ownership, as is evident both from the Hebraic and from the Roman Law. Why, then, would it not be permitted to a people having legal competence to submit itself to some one person, or to several persons, in such a way as plainly to transfer to him the legal right to govern, retaining no vestige of that right for itself? And you should not say that such a presumption is not admissible; for we are not trying to ascertain what the presumption should be in case of doubt, but what can legally be done.[1]

Exodus, xxi. 6. *Instit.* I. iii. 2. Gell., II. vii [II. xviii].

It is idle, too, to bring up the inconveniences which result, or

[1] Gail, *De Arrestis*, chap. vi, 22 ff.

may result, from such a procedure; for no matter what form of government you may devise, you will never be free from difficulties and dangers. Says the comedy:

[Terence, *Self-tormentor*, II. iii. 84.]

> Have this with that, then, if you choose,
> Or that with this together lose.[1]

2. Just as, in fact, there are many ways of living, one being better than another, and out of so many ways of living each is free to select that which he prefers, so also a people can select the form of government which it wishes; and the extent of its legal right in the matter is not to be measured by the superior excellence of this or that form of government, in regard to which different men hold different views, but by its free choice.[2]

3. In truth it is possible to find not a few causes which may impel a people wholly to renounce the right to govern itself and to vest this in another, as, for example, if a people threatened with destruction cannot induce any one to defend it on any other condition; again, if a people pinched by want can in no other way obtain the supplies needed to sustain life. For if the Campanians, constrained by necessity, once made themselves subject to the Roman people[3] in the manner indicated by these words: 'The people of Campania, and the city Capua, the lands, the shrines of the gods and all things of gods and men in our possession we give over, Conscript Fathers, to your dominion';[4] and if, according to Appian, some peoples desiring to make themselves subject to the Roman people were not even permitted to do so, what is there to prevent any people from giving itself up, in the same way, to one exceedingly powerful man? In Virgil we read:

[Livy, VII. xxxi. 4.] [*Preface*, vii.] [*Aeneid*, IV. 619 f.]

> Nor when, by terms of unjust peace compelled,
> Himself to sovereign power he shall subject.

It may happen, again, that the head of a house possessing great estates may be unwilling under any other conditions to allow permanent residents to come upon his lands; or that the owner of a great number of slaves may set them free upon condition that they submit to his authority and pay him taxes. For these supposed cases we do

[1] Cicero, *On Laws*, Book III [III. x. 23]: 'It is unfair in bringing forward every charge, to pass by good points, presenting only an enumeration of bad things and a selection of faults'; later, 'the good which is sought therein we should not have without the evil.'

[2] The city of Augsburg petitioned the Emperor Charles V that the decisions of the senate of their city should not become valid unless they had been approved by the ward officials; and at the same time the city Nuremberg asked just the opposite.

[3] As the Faliscans in Livy, Book V [V. xxvii], the Samnites in Book VIII [IX. xlii]. Thus the people of Epidamnus [modern Durazzo] abandoned by the people of Corcyra [modern Corfu], gave themselves over to the Corinthians, in order that they might be protected against the Taulantians and the exiles; Thucydides, Book I [I. xxv].

[4] Also the Venetians; Bembo [*History of Venice*], Book VI.

not lack concrete examples. Of the slaves of the Germans we read in Tacitus: [*Germany*, xxv.]

Each controls his own place of habitation, his own household. The master exacts from him a certain amount of grain, or live stock, or clothing, as from a tenant, and the slave renders obedience up to the limit of this requirement.

4. Further, as Aristotle said that some men are by nature slaves, that is, are suited to slavery, so there are some peoples so constituted that they understand better how to be ruled than to rule. [*Politics*, I. ii.] Such an opinion the Cappadocians seem to have entertained in regard to themselves; they preferred life under a king to the freedom offered them by the Romans, declaring that they could not live without a king. Strabo, XII [ii. 11]. Justin, XXXVIII [ii. 8]. So Philostratus, in his *Life of Apollonius*, says that it is absurd to grant to Thracians, Mysians, and Getans a freedom in which they do not have pleasure. Book VI [VII. iii].

5. Some, again, cannot fail to be impressed by the example of nations which for a number of centuries have lived happily enough under a form of government clearly monarchical.[1] According to Livy the cities which were under the rule of Eumenes[2] would not have been willing to exchange their lot for that of any free city. Book XLII [v. 3]. Sometimes the condition of a state is such that it seems possible to assure its safety only through [54] the unrestricted rule of one man;[3] such, in the view of many discerning persons, was the condition of the Roman state in the time of Augustus Caesar.

For these and similar reasons, then, it not only can happen, but actually does happen, that men make themselves subject to the rule and power of another, as Cicero also observes, in the second book of his treatise *On Duties*. [II. vi. 22.]

6. Just as private property can be acquired by means of a war that is lawful (*iustum*), according to our use of the term above, [I. iii. 4. 1.] so by the same means public authority, or the right of governing, can be acquired, quite independently of any other source. What has been said, again, must not be understood as limited to the maintenance of the rule of a monarch, when that is the type of govern-

[1] Seneca, *On Benefits*, Book II, chap. xx, speaking of Brutus [in relation to Brutus's participation in the murder of Caesar]: 'For my part, although the man was great in other things, in this he seems to me to have committed a most serious error, and not to have conducted himself in accord with Stoic doctrine. Either he was afraid of the name of king, although the best condition of a state is under a just king; or he hoped that liberty would abide there where the reward both of commanding and of serving was so great; or he thought that the state could be brought back to its former condition, although the customs of the early time had disappeared; and that there would be a just enforcement of civil right, and proper observance of laws, where he had seen so many thousands of men fighting, to determine not whether they would serve, but which leader they would serve.'

See also Bizarri, *History of Genoa*, Book XIV, p. 329.

[2] Thus, many came from the free states of Greece to Salamis, on the island of Cyprus, which was the kingdom of Evagoras, as Isocrates relates [p. 199 B = *Evagoras*, xxi. 5].

[3] Dion in Philostratus, Book V, chap. xi [*Life of Apollonius*, V. xxxiv]: 'I fear that the Romans subdued by long periods of tyrannical rule, would be unable now to endure a change.'

ment concerned; for the same right and the same course of reasoning hold good in the case of an aristocracy which governs with the exclusion of the common people. What shall I say of this fact, that no republic has ever been found to be so democratic that in it there were not some persons, either very poor people or foreigners, also women and youths, who were excluded from public deliberations?

7. Some peoples, moreover, have under their sway other peoples[1] as subject to them as if they obeyed kings. Hence the question: 'Is the people of Collatia its own master?' Thus it is said of the Campanians, after they had given themselves over to the Romans, that they had become subject to a foreign power; of Acarnania and Amphilochia, that they were under the jurisdiction of the Aetolians; of Peraea and Caunus, that they were under the sway of the Rhodians; and of Pydna, that it was given by Philip to the people of Olynthus.

When the towns which had been subject to the Spartans were delivered from Spartan domination, they received the name of Eleutherolacones, 'Free Lacedaemonians'. The city Cotyora is mentioned by Xenophon as having belonged to the people of Sinope. According to Strabo, Nice, in Italy, was assigned to the people of Marseilles, and the island of Ischia to the people of Naples. So we read in Frontinus that the town Calatis was assigned to the colony of Capua, and Caudium to the colony of Beneventum, with their territories. Otho gave the Moorish states as a present to the province of Baetica; the fact is on record in Tacitus. All these territorial adjustments must be set aside as null and void if we take the position that the right to govern is always subject to the judgement and will of those who are governed.

8. That in fact there have been kings who did not derive their power, even in a general way, from the will of the people, sacred and secular history alike bear witness. God says, addressing the people

Livy, I [xxxviii. 2]. Livy, VII [xxxi. 6]. Livy, XXVI [XXV. xxiv]. [XXXVIII. iii.] Livy, XXXII [xxxiii]. Strabo, XIV [ii. 1]. Diod. XVI [viii]. Paus., *Lac.*, [III. xxi. 6]. *Anabasis*, V [v. 3]. Book IV [i. 9]. Book V [iv. 9]. [Front., *On Colonies*.] *Histories*, I [lxxviii].

[1] Thus the island of Salamis was under the control of the Athenians from the time of Philaeus and Eurysaces, sons of Ajax, as Plutarch in his *Solon* [x = 83 D] informs us. This Salamis Augustus took away from the Athenians, as afterward Hadrian took away Cephalenia, as Xiphilinus bears witness [Dio Cassius, LXIX. xvi].

Atarneus from ancient times belonged to the people of Chios, according to Herodotus, Book I [I. clx], and the Samians held many towns on the mainland, as Strabo informs us, Book XIV [XIV. xx = 639]. Anactorium belonged in part to the Corinthians, in part to the people of Corfu, as Thucydides writes in Book I [I. lv].

In respect to peace with the Aetolians in Livy [XXXVIII. xi] this provision is recorded: 'The Oeneadae, with their city and country, shall belong to the Acarnanians.'

Pliny relates, *Natural History*, Book V, chap. xxix, that six towns were granted by Alexander the Great to Halicarnassus. In Book XXXIII, chap. iv, the same writer says that the island of Lindus belonged to the Rhodians. You find the same thing said about Caunus in Book XXXV [XXXV. x]. Cicero also bears witness to this fact in a letter to his brother [*Letters to his Brother Quintus*, I. i. 11. § 33]. To the same Rhodians, because they had helped the Romans against Antiochus, several cities were given as a present, says Eutropius, Book III [IV. ii]; these were cities of the Carians and the Lycians, which were taken away from them again by the senate. Both incidents are of record in the *Selections* of Polybius xxxvi and xciii].

of Israel, 'If thou shalt say, I will set a king over me'; and to Samuel He said: 'Show unto them the manner of king that shall reign over them.' Hence the anointed king is said to be 'over the people', 'over the Lord's inheritance', 'over Israel'; and Solomon is said to be 'king over all Israel'. Thus David gives thanks to God because he has made his people subject to him; and Christ says, 'The kings of the Gentiles have lordship over them.' Familiar are the lines of Horace:

Deut., xvii. 14. *I Sam.*, viii. 4 [9]. *I Sam.*, ix. 16, x. 1, xv. 1; *2 Sam.*, v. 2. *I Kings*, iv. 1. *Psalms*, cxliv. 2. *Luke*, xxii. 25. [*Odes*, III. i. 5 f.]

> O'er their own herds the rule of fearsome kings,
> O'er kings themselves the rule of Jove abides.

9. Seneca thus describes three types of government: 'Sometimes it is the people that we ought to fear; sometimes, if the constitution of the state is such that most of the public business is transacted by the senate, influential men in the state are feared; and sometimes individuals, upon whom the power of the people, and over the people, has been conferred.' Such are the men of whom Plutarch says that 'they have supreme power not only in accordance with the laws but also over the laws'. In Herodotus Otanes thus characterizes sovereignty in the hands of one person: 'To do whatever one pleases, without being accountable to anyone.' Dio of Prusa defines the power of the king in similar terms: 'So to rule as not to be accountable to anyone.' Pausanias, in his *Messenia*, contrasts 'the power of a king with a power which has to assume responsibility for its acts'.

Letters, xiv [7]. *Flamin.* [*Comp. of Philop. and Titus*, iii = p. 382 D]. [III. lxxx.] [liv = p. 565.] [IV. v. 10.]

10. Aristotle says that there are some kings who are vested with the same [55] powers that in other cases the nation itself has, over itself and its possessions. Thus after the Roman emperors began to make use of a power veritably royal, it was said that to these the people had transferred all their own authority and power, even over themselves, as Theophilus explains. Hence that saying of Marcus Aurelius the philosopher: 'No one but God alone can be judge of an emperor.'

Politics, III. xiv. *Instit.*, I. ii. 6. Xiphilinus, *Life of M. Antoninus*, IV [LXXI. iii].

Of such an emperor Dio says (Book LIII): 'He is free, and master of himself and of the laws, so that he both does what he wishes and does not do what he does not wish to do.' Such in ancient times at Argos, in Greece, was the royal power of the descendants of Inachus;[1]

[xxviii.]

[1] [72] These are the Anakim mentioned in *Deuteronomy*, ii. 10. Hence also the goddess called in Greek Ongka, to whom Cadmus dedicated a temple at Thebes. The Greeks called her Pallas.

Aeschylus says [*Suppliants*, 253] that the descendants of Inachus were Pelasgians, that is 'exiles', from a Syrian word. Also those who first inhabited Lacedaemon were Pelasgians, whence the Spartans used to say that they were descendants of Abraham, as we find in the history of the Maccabees [*I Maccabees*, xii. 21].

Now just as the kings of Argos exercised absolute power, following the practice of the Orient from which they had come, so also did the kings of Thebes, who were sprung from the Phoenicians. This is evident from the words attributed to Creon by Sophocles [*Antigone*, lines 516 ff., 681, 682] and to the Theban herald in the *Suppliants* of Euripides [lines 410, 411].

for in the Argive tragedy of the *Suppliants*, Aeschylus represents the people as thus addressing the king:

[370–373.]

> Thou art the city, thou the commonweal,
> A sovereign thou not subject to a judge;
> Upon thy throne, as on an altar raised,
> Thou rulest all things by thy single will.

[*Suppliants*, 404–407.] 11. In a far different way Theseus, himself a king, in Euripides speaks of the commonwealth of the Athenians:

> Not ruled
> By one man is our city, but 'tis free.
> The people rules, bestowing year by year
> Office on this or that in turn.

[*Theseus*, xxiv= p. 11.] For Theseus, as Plutarch explains, was only a military leader and guardian of the laws; in other respects he was on a level with the mass of citizens.[1]

In the light of such instances, clearly kings who are subject to the people are not properly called kings. Thus according to Polybius, [Book IV [VI. iii]. *Cleom.* [iii=p. 805 E]. *Agesil.* [i].] Plutarch, and Cornelius Nepos,[2] after the time of Lycurgus, and especially after the office of ephor was created, the kings of the Lacedaemonians were kings only in name, not in fact. This example was followed also by other peoples in Greece. Says Pausanias, in the [II. xix.] part of his work relating to Corinth: 'The Argives who, from time immemorial, had been devoted to equality and liberty, reduced the royal power to the extreme limit, with the result that they left to the sons and successors of Cisus nothing of kingly power except the name.' [*Greek Quest.* [291 F]. *Politics*, III. xii [III. xvi].] Aristotle declares that such kingships do not constitute a distinct type of government, because in reality they only form a part in a commonwealth controlled by an aristocracy or by the people.

12. Furthermore, even in the case of peoples who are not permanently subject to kings we see examples of a kind of temporary kingship[3] which is not subject to the people. Such was the power [Livy, Book II [xviii. 8]. Plutarch, *Marcel.* [xxiv= p. 312 E] Dion. Hal., V [lxx].] of the Amymones among the people of Cnidus, and of the dictator among the Romans in the earliest times, when there was no appeal to the people. Hence Livy says that an edict of the dictator was complied with as a divine decree, and that there was no resource

[1] Demophon, son of Theseus, in the *Children of Hercules*, by Euripides [lines 424–5]:

> For I rule not as do barbarian kings;
> Just my deeds are, while justly I hold sway.

[2] The words of Nepos, or of the writer, whoever it was, that wrote the *Lives of Illustrious Men*, in *Agesilaus* [chap. i]: 'That they had two kings, in name rather than in respect to governing power'; in another passage [*On the Kings*, ii]: 'Agesilaus, just as the other Spartan kings, was king in name, not in power.'

[3] Livius Salinator in his censorship put all tribes except one in the aerarian class, and thus showed that he exercised a right over the whole people [Livy, XXIX. xxxvii].

except in obedience. Cicero declares that the dictatorship was invested with royal powers. [*Philippics*, I. i. 3.]

13. The arguments which are presented on the other side [56] it is not hard to meet. For, in the first place, the assertion, that he who vests some one with authority is superior to him upon whom the authority is conferred, holds true only of a relationship the effect of which is continually dependent on the will of the constituent authority; it does not hold true of a situation brought about by an act of will, from which a compulsory relationship results, as in the case of a woman giving authority over herself to a husband, whom she must ever after obey. To the soldiers who had made him emperor and were demanding something which did not meet with his approval, the Emperor Valentinian returned this answer[1]: Sozom., *Eccles. Hist.*, XVI [VI. vi].

> Soldiers, when you chose me to be your Emperor, it was in your power to choose. But now that you have chosen me, the decision regarding that which you ask rests with me, not with you. It belongs to you, as subjects, to obey; to me, to ponder what should be done.

It is, however, not true, as is assumed, that all kings are clothed with authority by the people. This can be clearly enough understood from the illustrations given above, of the head of a house receiving strangers only under the stipulation of rendering obedience to him, and that of nations conquered in war. [I. iii. 8. 3.]

14. Another argument men take from the saying of the philosophers, that all government was established for the benefit of those who are governed, not of those who govern; from this they think it follows that, in view of the worthiness of the end they who are governed are superior to him who governs.

But it is not universally true, that all government was constituted for the benefit of the governed. For some types of governing in and of themselves have in view only the advantage of him who governs; such is the exercise of power by the master, the advantage of the slaves being only extrinsic and incidental, just as the earnings of a physician bear no relation to medicine as the art of healing. Other types of governing have in view a mutual advantage, as that of marriage. Thus some imperial governments may have been constituted for the benefit of kings, as those which have been secured through victory, and yet are not on that account to be called tyrannical, since the tyranny, at any rate as the word is now understood, connotes injustice. Some, again, may have in view as much the advantage of him who governs as of those who are governed, as when a people

[1] His words are thus reported by Theodoret, Book IV, chap. v [IV. vi]: 'It was your act, soldiers, when there was no emperor, to place in my hands the reins of this governing power. From the moment that I took them up, it became not your responsibility, but mine, to discern what the interest of the state might require.'

powerless to help itself places itself in subjection to a powerful king for its own protection.

Nevertheless I do not deny that in the case of most states the benefit of those who are governed is the primary consideration; and that this is true which Cicero said after Herodotus, and Herodotus after Hesiod, that kings received authority in order that men might enjoy justice. But it does not on that account follow, as our opponents infer, that the peoples are superior to the kings; for guardianship was instituted for the sake of the ward, and yet guardianship includes both a right and power over the ward. Furthermore there is nothing in the objection, which some may urge, that a guardian, in case he administers his trust badly, can be removed, and that, therefore, the same right ought to hold in the case of a king. In the case of a guardian, who has a superior, such procedure is obviously valid; but in the case of a government, because the series does not extend to infinity, it is absolutely necessary to stop with some person, or assembly, whose sins, because it has no judge superior to it, God takes into special consideration, as He himself bears witness. He either metes out punishment for them, if He deems punishment necessary, or tolerates them, for the chastisement or the testing of a people.

[*On Duties*, II. xii. 41.] [I. xcvi f.] [*Theogony*, 83 ff.] *Jerem.* xxv. 12.

15. 'Endure,' Tacitus very well says, 'Endure the luxury or avarice of those who govern, just as you put up with unfruitfulness or too heavy rains, and other scourges of nature. There will be faults so long as there shall be men; but they are not continuous, and are offset from time to time by better things.' Marcus Aurelius said that private persons are judged by the magistrates, magistrates by the emperor, the emperor by God.[1] There is a striking passage of Gregory of Tours, in which, himself a bishop, he thus addresses the king of the Franks:

[*Histories*, IV. lxxiv.] [*History of the Franks*, V. xix.]

> If anyone of us, O king, wishes to overstep the bounds of justice, he can be chastised by you; but if you pass beyond them, who shall chastise you? For we speak to you—if you wish, you hear; but if you do not wish to hear, who [57] shall condemn you, unless He who has declared that He is justice?

Among the dogmas of the Essenes, Porphyry relates, was this: 'The power of governing falls to the lot of no one without the special care of God.'[2] Irenaeus very aptly remarks: 'Kings, too,

[*On Abstaining*, IV. xiii.] Book V [*Against*

[1] Xiphilinus [Dio Cassius, LXXI. iii; Marcus Aurelius is quoted]: 'In regard to those who exercise the supreme power, only deity can judge.' Vitiges, the king, in Cassiodorus [*Variae*, X. xxxi] says: 'The case of royal power is to be referred to the celestial courts, since this power was sought from heaven, and to heaven alone is indebted for its innocence.' In the same writer [VI. iv] the king says: 'We cannot be made subject to others because we have not judges.'

[2] Homer [*Iliad*, II. 197]:

> From Jupiter the highest honour springs

Diodorus Siculus, Book I [I. xc], speaking of the Egyptians: 'They think, in fact, that it is not without

receive authority at the bidding of Him at whose bidding men are born; and they are fitted to rule over those who in their time are ruled by them.' The same thought appears in the *Constitutions* called Clementine: 'You will fear the king, knowing that he was chosen by the Lord.'

Heresies, V. xxiv. 3].

Book VII. xvii.

16. What we have said is in no degree invalidated by the fact that we sometimes read of people being punished on account of the sins of their kings. This happens not because the people did not punish their king, or did not restrain him, but because it connived with him in his offences, at least through silence. And yet God, even without the people, could make use of the supreme power and authority, which He has over the life and death of individuals, for the chastisement of the king, for whom it is punishment to be deprived of his subjects.

1 Kings, iv. 16 [xiv. 16]; *2 Kings*, x. 17 [xvii. 7].

IX.—*The argument that there is always a relation of mutual dependence between king and people, is refuted*

1. Some imagine that between king and people there is a relation of mutual dependence, so that the whole people ought to obey the king who governs well, while the king who governs badly should be made subject to the people. If they who hold this opinion should say that anything which is manifestly wrong should not be done because the king commanded it, they would be saying what is true and is acknowledged among all good men; but such a refusal implies no curtailing of power or any right to exercise authority. If it had been the purpose of any people to divide the sovereign power with a king (on this point something will need to be said below), surely such limits ought to have been assigned to the power of each as could easily be discerned from a difference in places, persons, or affairs.

2. The moral goodness or badness of an action, especially in matters relating to the state, is not suited to a division into parts; such qualities frequently are obscure, and difficult to analyse. In consequence the utmost confusion would prevail in case the king on the one side, and the people on the other, under the pretext that an act is good or bad, should be trying to take cognizance of the same matter, each by virtue of its power. To introduce so complete disorder into its affairs has not, so far as I know, occurred to any people.

a kind of divine providence that kings have come to have the highest authority of all men.'

Augustine, *On the City of God*, Book V [V. xxi]: 'He who' gave imperial authority, as is clear from what precedes, 'to Vespasian, either father or son, kindliest emperors, gave it also to Domitian, the most cruel; and, not to note each case, He who gave the imperial authority to Constantine, gave it to the Apostate Julian.'

Vitiges in Cassiodorus [*Variae*, X. 31]: 'Every promotion, above all, that to the position of king, must be accounted as a gift of divinity.' There was a saying of the Emperor Titus [Aurelius Victor, *Epitome*, x. 10]: 'Powers are conferred by Fate.'

X.—*Cautions are offered for the right understanding of the true opinion: the first is, in regard to the distinguishing of similar words which differ in meaning*

1. Now that the false views have been eliminated, it remains to offer some cautions which may serve to point out to us the road leading to a right decision of the question to whom, in each nation, the sovereign power belongs.

The first caution is, not to allow ourselves to be led astray by the equivocal meanings of words, or by the external appearance of things. For instance, in Latin writers the words *principatus*, 'chief authority', 'principate', and *regnum*, 'kingly power', 'monarchy', are ordinarily
[*Gallic War*, VII. iv.] used in contrast, as when Caesar says that the father of Vercingetorix had obtained the chief authority of Gaul but was put to death because
[*Annals*, II. lvii.] he aspired to the kingship. Similarly, Piso, in Tacitus, says that Germanicus is son of him who holds the principate among the Romans,
[*Caligula*, xxii.] not of a king of the Parthians; and Suetonius declares that Caligula came very near transforming the semblance of a principate into a
[II. cviii.] monarchy. Also in Velleius it is said that Maroboduus aimed to acquire not the chief authority, which rests on the will of those who render obedience, but royal power.

2. We see, nevertheless, that these two words are often confounded. For the Spartan chiefs, descendants of Hercules, after they were made subordinate to the ephors, continued to be called kings, as we just now observed. In ancient Germany there were kings of
[*Germany*, xi.] whom Tacitus says that they exercised authority through persuasion,
I [vii. 8]. not through the power to command. Of King Evander Livy says that he ruled more by personal influence than by sovereign power.
[*Politics*, II. xi.] Aristotle and Polybius called the suffete of the Carthaginians king, as
[VI. li.] Diodorus also does; in like manner Solinus [1] said that Hanno [58]
XV. lxx [XV. xv]. was king of the Carthaginians. Of the people of Scepsis in the Troad
[lvi. 12.] Strabo says that after they had taken the Milesians into their state
Book XIII [i. 52]. and had formed a democratic commonwealth, the royal title, and some degree of distinction also, remained to the descendants of the ancient kings.

3. On the other hand, when the Roman emperors had come to hold absolutely unrestricted powers of government, openly and without subterfuge, they were nevertheless called 'men holding the chief authority' (*principes*). In some free states, also, emblems of royal

[1] Thus the author of the *Life of Hannibal* [Cornelius Nepos, *Hannibal*, vii]: 'Just as at Rome consuls, so at Carthage two kings were chosen annually, to serve a year.'

[73] To those who are not properly called kings may be added also sons to whom the name of king has been given by royal fathers while still retaining the royal power. Such a king was that Darius whom, after judgement had been passed on him, his father Artaxerxes ordered put to death. Plutarch, *Artaxerxes* [xxix = 1026 C].

dignity are customarily granted to those in whose hands the chief authority rests.

4. Again, the assembly of the estates, that is, the meeting of those who represent the people as divided into classes—those, of course, of whom Gunther speaks : [*Ligurinus*, VIII. 577.]

The clergy, the nobility, and delegates of towns—

in some states at any rate serves only this purpose, that they form a greater king's council; through it the complaints of the people, which are often passed over without mention in the king's cabinet, reach the ear of the king, who is then free to determine what seems to him best to meet the case. In other states such bodies have the right to pass in review the acts of the ruler, and even to enact laws by which the ruler is bound.

5. Many think that the distinction between sovereign power, and power that is less than sovereign, ought to be made according to the mode of conferring such power, whether by election or by succession. They maintain that that alone is sovereign power which is conferred by succession, that that is not sovereign power which is conferred by election. But surely this cannot be universally true. For succession is not a title of power, which gives character to the power, but a continuation of a power previously existing. The legal right to govern which was founded by selection in a family is continued by succession; in consequence, succession confers only so much power as was granted by the first act of choice.

Among the Spartans the kingship passed to heirs, even after the office of ephor was created. To such a kingship, that is to such a holding of authority, Aristotle makes reference: 'Some kingships are conferred by right of descent, others by choice.' Such in the heroic age were most kingships in Greece,[1] as both this author and Thucydides observe. Among the Romans, on the contrary, the sovereign power continued to be conferred by election, even after all power had been taken away from the senate and the people. [*Politics*, III. xiv.] [Book I [xiii].]

XI.—*The second caution, as to distinguishing rights from the manner of possessing rights*

1. The second caution shall be this, that the distinction must be kept in mind between a thing and the mode of its possession.[2] This distinction holds not only for corporeal but also for incorporeal things. Just as a field is a thing, so rights of way over it for pedestrians,

[1] This was noted also by Dionysius of Halicarnassus, Book II [II. xii] and Book V [V. lxxiv].

[2] One who has leisure may consult Charles Dumoulin, *Ad Consuetudines Parisienses*, title I, § ii, gl. 4, nos. 16, 17.

for cattle, and for use as a road are also things. These three rights, however, are held by some with full ownership, by others as usufruct, by others still with power of temporary use. Similarly, the Roman dictator held the sovereign power by a right limited in time[1]; but most kings, both those who are the first to be chosen and those who succeed them in lawful succession, hold it as a usufruct. Some kings, however, possess the sovereign power in full right of ownership, having acquired it in lawful war, or through the submission of a people which, to avoid greater disaster, subjected itself without any reservation.

2. I am unable to agree with those who declare that the dictator was not the bearer of sovereignty because his power was not perpetual. For the character of immaterial things is recognized from their effects, and legal powers which have the same effects ought to be designated by the same name. Now the dictator during his period of office performed all acts by virtue of the same legal right[2] which a king has who possesses absolute power; and his acts could not be rendered null and void by any one. Duration, moreover, does not change the nature of a thing.

If, as we may grant, question is raised as to the prestige which is commonly called majesty, there is no doubt that this is to be found in fuller measure in him to whom the perpetual right has been given than in him upon whom a temporary right has been conferred; the manner of holding does effect prestige. [59] I maintain, further, that the same holds true of him who is made regent of a kingdom before a king has attained to his majority, or while the king is prevented from reigning by madness or captivity. Under such conditions regents are not subject to the people, and their power is not revocable before a time fixed by law.

3. We must consider as altogether different the case of those who received a power revocable at any moment, that is resting on sufferance. Such the kingship of the Vandals in Africa once was, and that of the Goths in Spain,[3] where the people deposed their kings whenever these failed to please them.[4] Single acts of such rulers can be annulled by those who conferred upon them their power

Procopius, *Vandalic War*, I [ix]. Aimoin, II. xx; IV. xxxv.

[1] An example of an emperor chosen for a limited time you will find in Gregoras at the beginning of Book IV [Gregoras Nicephorus, *History*, iv. i].

[2] To such a degree did this hold true that the people, when it wished to save Fabius Rutilianus, made supplications on his behalf to the dictator [Livy, VIII. xxix–xxxv].

[3] There is a trace of the ancient custom among the Behetrians. See Mariana, Book XVI [XVI. xvii].

[4] This was related of the Herulians by Procopius, *Gothic War*, Book II [II. xiv, xv]; of the Langobards by Paul Warnefrid [Paulus Diaconus], Books IV and VI; of the Burgundians by Ammianus Marcellinus, Book XXVIII [v. 14]; of the Moldavians by Laonicus Chalcocondylas [II]; of the king of Agade, in Africa, by John Leo, Book VII. Of the Norwegians William of Newburgh [*History of England*, III. vi] says that he who had killed the king became king over them; similar statements about the Quadi and the Iazyges you find in the *Selections* from Dio [lviii].

subject to revocation ; and as the effect is not the same, so the right is not the same.

XII.—*It is shown that in some cases the sovereign power is held absolutely, that is with right of transfer*

1. What I have said, that in some cases sovereign power is held with full proprietary right, that is in patrimony, some learned men oppose, using the argument that free men cannot be treated as property. But just as the power of the master is one thing, that of the king another, so also personal liberty is different from civil liberty, the liberty of individuals from the liberty of men in the aggregate. The Stoics said that one form of slavery was 'subjection', and in the Holy Scriptures subjects are called servants of the king. Just as personal liberty, then, excludes subjection to a master, so civil liberty excludes subjection to a king and any other form of control properly so called.

Hotman, *Cont. Ill.*, qu. 1.

Diog. Laert. [VII. cxxii]. *1 Sam.*, xxii. 18 [17] ; *2 Sam.*, x. 2. *1 Kings*, ix. 22.

Livy contrasts the two points of view thus : 'Not having yet tasted the sweetness of liberty, they were demanding a king.' The same writer elsewhere says : 'It seemed a pity that the Roman people, so long as it was in subjection under kings, was not beset by war and by enemies, and that the same people, when it had become free, was besieged by the Etruscans.' In still another passage Livy remarks : 'The Roman people was not under the power of a king, but was free.' Elsewhere, again, he contrasts nations which were in a condition of liberty with those that lived under the rule of kings.[1]

Book I [xvii. 3]. Book II [xii. 2]. [II. xv. 3.] Book XLV [xviii].

Cicero had said : 'Either the kings ought not to have been driven out, or liberty ought to have been given to the people in fact, not in words.' After the time of both Cicero and Livy Tacitus said : 'At the beginning the city of Rome was in the power of kings ; Lucius Brutus established liberty and the consulship.' And in another place he declares : 'The liberty of the Germans is a keener foe than the absolutism of Arsaces.' Arrian in his account of the peoples of India refers to 'kings and free states'. Caecina in Seneca says : 'There are royal thunderbolts, whose force smites either the spot where elective assemblies meet or the governmental headquarters of a free city ; the prognostication of such thunderbolts is that the state is threatened by the rule of a king.'[2]

On Laws, III [x. 25].

Annals, I [i].

On the Customs of the Germans [xxxvii]. [*Indica*, xi. 9.] [*Natural Questions*, II. xlix.]

[1] Thucydides [II. xxix] : 'This Teres, the father of Sitalces, was the first to increase the dominion of the Odryses, so that it extended over other kings of Thrace ; for there is also a part of the Thracians that remains independent.'

Seneca the father in the first *Suasoria* [v] : 'In a free city one's opinion is not to be spoken in the same way as under the rule of kings.' Josephus, *Antiquities of the Jews*, Book XIII [XIII. ix. 2] : 'to kings and free peoples.' Cicero, *Letters*, XV. iv [XV. iv. 3] : 'the auxiliary forces furnished by the free peoples and allied kings.'

Pliny, Book VI, chap. xx [*Natural History*, VI. xx. 74], speaking of the people of India : 'These inhabitants of the mountains who hold the seashore in a continuous tract, free and without kings.'

[2] For an example of such a portent see Bizarri, *History of Genoa*, Book XIX [p. 450].

With similar underlying thought those of the Cilicians who were not subject to kings were called Free Cilicians. Of Amisus Strabo says that it was at times free, at times under the rule of kings. In various places in the Roman laws relating to war and to proceedings of recovery foreigners are distinguished as under kings or belonging to free peoples. Here, then, the liberty of a people is concerned, not that of individuals. Moreover, just as in the case of private servitude, so also in the case of peoples in subjection, some are said to be not their own masters, not under their own control. Hence these forms of expression: 'What cities, what territories, what men once belonged to the Aetolians'; and 'Is the people of Collatia its own master?'

Book XII [iii. 14].

[*Digest*, XLIX. xv. 19.]

Livy, XXXVIII [xi. 9].

Livy, V [I. xxxviii. 2].

2. Nevertheless, when a people is transferred this is not, strictly speaking, a transfer of the individuals but of the perpetual right of governing them in their totality as a people. Similarly, when a freedman is allotted to one of the children of a patron, this is not a transfer of ownership of a free man but the transfer of a right which is valid over the man.

3. Equally devoid of foundation is the assertion that if a king has acquired any peoples in war, since he has not acquired them without blood and sweat of his citizens, they ought in consequence to be considered as acquired for the citizens rather than for the king. For it might happen that a king had supported an army from his private means,[1] or even from the income of the estate which came to him as holding the position of chief authority.[2] For a king may have over such an estate only the right of usufruct, in the same way that [60] he holds the right of ruling over the people who chose him; nevertheless the income is absolutely his own. The case is like that in the civil law, when the restitution of an inheritance has been ordered; the income is not restored, because the income is considered not as forming a part of the inheritance but as a part, rather, of the property.

Digest, XXXVI. i. 19 (18). 1.

It can happen, then, that a king may have the sovereign power in his own right[3] over certain peoples; in such cases, then, he can transfer it. Strabo says that the island of Cythera, lying over against Cape Matapan, belonged to Eurycles, a leading man among the Lacedaemonians, 'in his individual right.' Thus King Solomon

Book VIII [v. 1].

1 Kings, xii [ix. 11].

[1] Marcus Aurelius, having drained the public treasury in the war with the Marcomanni, and wishing not to impose a new tax on the people, made an auction in Trajan's Forum and thus disposed of vessels of gold, crystal and murrine cups, silken and gold-broidered garments of his wife as well as of himself, and many ornaments of precious stones. [Capitolinus, *Marcus Antoninus the Philosopher*, xvii. 4].

[2] On such grounds Ferdinand claimed for himself a half of the kingdom of Granada, as acquired from the revenues of Castile for the period of his marriage. This is set forth by Mariana, *History of Spain*, Book XXVIII [XXVIII. xiii].

[3] They who went with Baldwin to the East to wage war made the concession that there should be granted to him a half of the cities, provinces, taxes, and things taken in war.

gave to Hiram, king of the Phoenicians (Hiromos in Greek, for so he is named by Philo of Byblos, who translated the history of Sanchoniathon), twenty cities. These cities were not among those which belonged to the Jewish people; for Cabul—such is the name given to them—lay outside the Jewish territory (*Joshua*, xix. 27). They were a portion of the cities which conquered peoples, enemies of the Jews, had held up to that time; part of them had been conquered by the king of Egypt, Solomon's father-in-law, and given to Solomon as dowry, part had been vanquished by Solomon himself. That they were not at that time inhabited by Israelites is indicated by the fact that Solomon began to colonize them with Jews only after Hiram had given them back to him.

1 Kings, ix. 6, 12 [ix. 13]. *1 Chron.*, viii. 14 [*2 Chron.*, viii. 2].

4. In like manner we read that the sovereignty over Sparta, which had been captured in war, was given by Hercules[1] to Tyndareus subject to the condition that if Hercules should leave any children, it should revert to them. Amphipolis was given as dowry to Acamas, the son of Theseus. In Homer, too, Agamemnon promises that he will give seven cities to Achilles. The King Anaxagoras presented two thirds of his kingdom to Melampus.[2] Of Darius Justin speaks as follows: 'By will he left his kingdom to Artaxerxes; to Cyrus, the cities of which Cyrus was governor.' Similarly, we are to believe, the successors of Alexander,[3] each for his own part, succeeded to the full and proprietary right to rule the peoples which had been subject to the Persians, or themselves acquired sovereignty by right of victory; it is not, therefore, to be wondered at if they assumed to themselves the right of transfer.

Diod., IV [xxxiii].

[*Iliad*, IX. 149.]

Book V [xi].

[1] [74] The same Hercules, having conquered the Dryopes, who lived near Parnassus, presented them to Apollo, as Servius says *On the Aeneid*, Book IV [line 146]. Aegimus, king of the Dorians, took Hercules as an ally in the war against the Lapithae, giving him a part of his kingdom as the price of the alliance [Apollodorus, *Library*, II. vii. 7].

Cychreus, king of Salamis, having no children left his kingdom by will to Teucer. From Eurylion, king of Phthia, Peleus received a third part of his kingdom as dowry [Apollodorus, *op. cit.*, III. xii. 1]. These instances Apollodorus has. In Livy, we find in Book I [I. iii]: 'Proca bequeathed the kingdom to Numitor.'

[2] See Servius, *On Eclogues*, VI [line 48].

So in Homer, Iobates gives his daughter to Bellerophon [*Iliad*, VI. 193]:

And half the kingly honours to him gave.

This is explained by Servius on Virgil [*Aeneid*, V, line 118]: 'gave to him his daughter in marriage with a part of the kingdom.'

Of Peleus Phoenix says [*Iliad*, IX. 483 f.]:

And many peoples did he give to me
That I the part of Phthia might possess
Which holds the kingdom of the Dolopes.

Lanassa, being wedded to Pyrrhus, king of Epirus, brought to him as dower the city of Corcyra [modern Corfu], which had been captured by her father Agathocles in war; Plutarch, *Pyrrhus* [chap. ix = 387 F].

[3] Ammianus Marcellinus, speaking of Persia in Book XXII [XXIII. vi. 7], not quite in accord with the truth of history says that by will all the nation was transferred to the power of a single successor.

5. In like manner when King Attalus,[1] son of Eumenes, had by will made the Roman people heir to his property, the Roman people under the designation 'property' included also his kingdom. In regard to this procedure Florus remarks: 'After taking possession of this inheritance, the Roman people held it as a province, not by right of war or of arms but—as is fairer—by testamentary disposition.' Afterward, again, when Nicomedes,[2] king of Bithynia, dying, had made the Roman people his heir, his kingdom was reduced to the form of a province. To this Cicero refers, in his second speech Against *Rullus*: 'We have entered upon an inheritance, the kingdom of Bithynia.' Similarly a part of north-eastern Africa, the Cyrenaica,[3] was left by Apion the king to the same people by will.

Florus, Book II [xx]. *Epitome of Livy*, lviii.

[II. xv. 40.]

6. Tacitus, in the fourteenth book of his *Annals*, makes mention of the domains which had once belonged to King Apion [4] and had

[XIV. xviii.] *Epitome of Livy*, xliii.

[1] Valerius Maximus [V. ii. *Externa* 3]: 'Attalus by the fair terms of a will in gratitude bequeathed Asia to the Roman people.' On that matter Sertorius in Plutarch [*Sertorius*, xxiii = 580 E]: 'Since the Roman people with the most perfect right held that country.'

[2] See Appian, *Mithridatic Wars* [i. 7], and *Civil Wars*, Book I [I. xiii. 111].

[3] In this country were the cities Berenice, Ptolemais, and Cyrene; Eutropius, Book VI [VI. xi].

[4] Appian, *Mithridatic Wars* [xvii. 121]: 'Apion, a bastard of the family of the Lagidae, left Cyrene by will.' Ammianus Marcellinus, Book XXII [XXII. xvi. 24]: 'We acquired arid Libya by the last will of Apion the king; Cyrene with the other states of Libya Pentapolis we took over through the generosity of Ptolemy.' The king of Cyrene was in fact called both Apion and Ptolemy; see the *Epitome of Livy*, Book LXX. This same Apion had received the kingdom of Cyrene by the will of his father, according to Justin, Book XXXIX [XXXIX. v. 2]. Of another Appion, referred to by Ammianus, who had left arid Libya to the Roman people, mention is made in the *Chronicle* of Eusebius, under the year 1952.

Add also that which Procopius relates in *Buildings* [*On the Buildings of Justinian*, III. i], that, by the will of Arsaces the king, Armenia was so divided that the larger part went to his son Arsaces, the smaller part to Tigranes. From Josephus, *Antiquities of the Jews*, Books XV and XVI, we learn that Herod, after Augustus granted to him permission to leave his kingdom to whomever of his children he might choose, changed his will several times.

This custom the Goths and Vandals also had, in respect to those countries which they held by right of arms. The Vandal Gizeric disposed of Spain by will; so Procopius, *Vandalic War*, I [*History of the Wars*, III. vii. 29]. Theoderic gave Lilybaeum, in Sicily, as dowry for his sister Amalfrida, *id.* [III. viii. 13].

Among other nations the same practice was in vogue. Aquitaine, which Pippin had acquired in war, he divided among his children, [75] as Fredegarius, at the end of his *Chronicle*, bears witness. In regard to the leaving of Burgundy by will see Aymoinus [Aimoin, *History of the Franks*], III. lxviii and lxxv. The king of Fez left Fez by will to his second son, as we learn from Leo of Africa [*Description of Africa*], Book III; in regard to Bougie, see the same author, Book V.

The Sultan Aladdin bequeathed a large number of states to Osman; see Leunclavius, *Turkish History*, Book II. The king of Kermian gave to his daughter, who was about to marry Bayezid [Bayezid I], the cities of Phrygia; see the same Leunclavius, Book V. The kingdom of the Turks in Cappadocia Musa divided up among his children; see Nicetas [*Manuel Comnenus*], Book III [III. v]. The cities near the Black Sea were granted to Murad by Chuscin Bey; Leunclavius, Book I. Bayezid gave to Stephan the cities of Serbia in honour of his wife, who was a sister of Stephan; *id.*, Book VI. The Sultan Mohammed left his kingdom by will to Murad; *id.*, Book XII. Jacob Bey, ruler of Kermian, made the Sultan Murad heir of his dominion; *id.*, Book XIV. Mohammed the Turk [Mohammed I] had thought of leaving the sovereignty to his two sons, that of Europe to Amurad, that of Asia to Mustafa; the fact is recorded by Chalcocondylas, Book IV. The Emperor Basil Porphyrogenitus was made heir by David Curopalates to that region which David held in Iberia; this is related by Zonaras [XVII. vii].

I come to the Christian conquerors in the East. Michael Despota divided Thessaly among his children; this on the authority of Gregoras, Book IV [IV. ix]. The prince of Aetolia left Athens to the Venetians, and sold Boeotia to Antony; Chalcocondylas, Book IV. Messene, Ithome, and the maritime part of Arcadia were given by the prince of Arcadia as dowry to his daughter, when she was married to Thomas, son of the Greek Emperor; *id.*, Book V. Acarnania was divided by the will of

been left to the Roman people with his kingship. 'Who does not know', says Cicero in his speech *On the Agrarian Law*, 'that the kingdom of Egypt, by the will of the Alexandrian king, has been made a possession of the Roman people?' Justin represents Mithridates as saying in a speech about Paphlagonia that 'this country had come into the possession of his father not by force, not by arms, but by the acceptance of a will'. Of Orodes, king of the Parthians, the same author relates that for a long time he was in doubt which of his sons he should designate to succeed him as king. Polemon, ruler of the Tibareni and of the adjacent country, made his wife heiress of his sovereignty; the same thing had previously been done by Mausolus, in Caria, although he left brothers surviving him. [II. xvi. 41.] XXXVIII [v. 4]. XLII [iv. 14]. Strabo, XII [iii. 29]. Strabo, XIII [ii. 17].

XIII.—*It is shown that in some cases the sovereign authority is not held absolutely*

1. In the case of kingships which have been conferred by the will of the people the presumption is, I grant, that it was not the will of the people to permit the king to alienate the sovereign power.[1] Wherefore we have no reason to criticize Krantz because [61] in the case of Unguin, who had bequeathed Norway by will, he comments on such procedure as lacking precedent, if we assume that he had in mind the customs of the Germans, among whom the sovereign power is held with no such right. Charlemagne, Louis the Pious, and other kings after them, even among the Vandals and the Hungarians, did, as we read, dispose of their kingdoms by will; but such action had rather the character of a recommendation to the people than of a transfer in the true sense.[2] Of Charlemagne in particular Ado relates that he wished to have his will confirmed by the Frankish nobles. We read of a similar instance in Livy. Philip, king of Mace- *Danish History*, II. iv. Book I [XL. lvi].

Prince Charles among his illegitimate sons, and parts of Aetolia were given to blood-relations; this on the authority of Chalcocondylas whom I mentioned [Book V].

In like manner also the kingdoms of Jerusalem and Cyprus were in part bequeathed by will, in part conveyed by contracts; in regard to the transfer of Cyprus, see Bembo, *Italian History* [*History of Venice*], Book VII, and Paruta [*History of Venice*], Book I. The Genoese received as a gift the town of Castro in Sardinia, and other places, which were subject to Cagliari; Bizarri, *On the Pisan War*, Book II. Robert [Robert Guiscard] gave Durazzo and Avlona to his younger son Bohemund; Anna Comnena, [*Alexiad*,] Book V [V. iii].

Alfonso of Arragon left to his bastard son Ferdinand the kingdom of Naples, as won by conquest [Mariana, *History of Spain*, Book XXII, chap. xviii]. In the same kingdom Ferdinand bequeathed certain cities to his nephew; Mariana, Book XXX [XXX. xxvii].

[1] Vopiscus, *Tacitus* [chap. vi], says that sovereignty ought not to be left to others as lands and slaves are left. Salvianus [*Against Avarice*, I. xi]: 'He was not able to convey to the needy by will the peoples whom he ruled.'

[2] See the *Capitularies* of Charles the Bald, chap. xii, *Conventus ad Carisiacum*. To this head refer the will of Pelagius, by which he left Spain to Alfonso and Ormisind [Mariana, *History of Spain*, Book VII, chap. iii], and some facts in relation to Denmark which are noted by Saxo Grammaticus. It is not, then, to be wondered at, that some wills of rulers have been made of no effect because they were disapproved by the people, as that of Alfonso of Arragon; see Mariana, Book X [X. xv, xvi]. A similar fate befell the will of Alfonso of Leon, since he had given the preference to his daughters over his son; the same Mariana, Book XII [XII. xv].

donia, desiring to keep Perseus from the throne and to make Antigonus, his brother's son, king in place of Perseus, visited the cities of Macedonia in order to recommend Antigonus to the leading men.[1]

2. When we read that Louis the Pious gave back the city of Rome to Pope Paschal, this act has no bearing on the case. The Franks, having received from the Roman people the sovereignty over the city of Rome, could rightly restore it to the same people; and he who was at the head of the highest order was representative, as it were, of this people.

XIV.—*It is shown that in some cases intermediate governmental authority is held absolutely, that is with right of transfer*

Up to this point we have tried to show that the sovereignty must in itself be distinguished from the absolute possession of it. So true is this distinction that in the majority of cases the sovereignty is not held absolutely. Furthermore, in many cases intermediate governmental powers are held absolutely. In consequence, marquisates and earldoms are wont to be sold [2] and bequeathed by will more easily than kingdoms.

XV.—*The distinction stated is reinforced from the difference in mode of appointing regents in kingdoms*

1. Another proof of this distinction appears in the method of safeguarding royal power [3] when the king is prevented by age or by disease from performing his functions.

In the case of monarchies which are not patrimonial, the regency passes into the hands of those to whom it is entrusted by public law, or, that failing, by the consent of the people.[4] In the case of patrimonial monarchies, the regency goes to those whom the father or near relatives have chosen.[5] Thus we see that in the case of the kingship of the Epirotes, which had its origin in the consent of the people, guardians were appointed by the people for the king Aribas, who was a minor [6]; and guardians were appointed by the

Justin, XIII [ii. 4].

[1] See the similar case in Cassiodorus, Book VIII, letter viii [VIII. iii ff.]. So the agreements of Sanchez and James of Arragon in regard to reciprocal succession were confirmed by the nobles; Mariana, Book XII [XII. xvi]. The will of Henry of Navarre, by which [76] he made John his heir, was likewise confirmed; the same Mariana, Book XIII [XIII. xxii]; similarly, the will of Isabella, queen of Castile; *id.*, Book XXVIII [xi, xii].

[2] For the Principality of Urgel see Mariana, Book XII, chap. xvi.

[3] See Cothmann, vol. I, cons. xli, no. 11.

[4] See Mariana [Book VIII, chap. x] in regard to Alfonso V, king of Leon. But the will of King John in regard to the regency and administration of the kingdom was disapproved by the nobles; Mariana, Book XVIII [XVIII. xv].

[5] Ptolemy, king of Egypt, left the Roman people as guardian for his son; Valerius Maximus, Book VI, chap. vi, 1.

[6] [The remainder of this sentence is repeated in a note in the 1646 edition.]

nobles of Macedonia for the posthumous son of Alexander the Great. But in Asia Minor, which had been conquered by war, the king Eumenes assigned his brother as guardian for his son Attalus. In like manner the father Hiero, reigning in Sicily, by will designated those whom he wished as guardians for his son Hieronymus.

Justin, LXVII [xvii. 3]. Plut., *On the Love of Brothers* [489 F].

2. Whether the king be, at the same time, owner of the domain in his own right as proprietor, as the king of Egypt was after the time of Joseph, and the Indian kings [1] according to Diodorus and Strabo, or not, such ownership lies outside the realm of sovereignty and in its essence has no relation to sovereignty. Wherefore it does not constitute a separate type of sovereignty, or a different mode of possessing sovereign power.

Book II [xl]. Book XV [i. 40].

XVI.—*It is shown that sovereignty is not limited even by a promise of that which lies outside the sphere of the law of nature or of divine law*

1. A third comment is, that sovereignty does not cease to be such even if he who is going to exercise it makes promises—even promises touching matters of government—to his subjects or to God.[2] I am not now speaking of the observance of the law of nature and of divine law, or of the law of nations; observance of these is binding upon all kings, even though they have made no promise. I am speaking of certain rules, to which kings would not be bound without a promise.

That what I say is true becomes clear from the similarity of the case under consideration to that of the head of a household. If the head of a household promises that he will do for it something which affects the government of it, he will not on that account cease to have full authority over his household, so far as matters of the household are concerned. A husband, furthermore, is not deprived of the power conferred on him by marriage because he has promised something to his wife.

2. Nevertheless it must be admitted that when such a promise is made, the sovereign power is in a way limited, [62] whether the obligation affects only the exercise of the power, or even the power itself directly. In the former case an act performed contrary to the promise will be unjust, for the reason that, as we shall show elsewhere, a true promise confers a legal right upon the promisee; in the latter

[1] Diodorus Siculus, Book II [*History*, II. xl].

[2] Trajan devoted his head and his right hand to the wrath of the gods, in case he should knowingly have sworn falsely; Pliny, *Panegyric* [lxiv. 3]. The Emperor Hadrian swore that he would never punish a senator excepting in accordance with a decree of the senate [Spartianus, *Hadrian*, vii]. The Emperor Anastasius took oath that he would abide by the decrees of the Council of Chalcedon; the fact is recorded by Zonaras [XIV. iii], Cedrenus and others. The later Greek emperors made oath to the church; see the same Zonaras, in his account of Michael Rhangabe [*History*, XV. xxii], and elsewhere.
For an example also among the Gothic kings see Cassiodorus [*Variae*], X. xvi, xvii.

case, the act will be void on account of lack of power. From this, nevertheless, it does not follow that the promisor is subject to some superior; the nullification of the act in this case results not from the interposition of a superior power but from the law itself.

[*On Monarchy* = p. 826 F; *Them.*, xxvii = p. 125 C.] X [i. 2]. Val. Max., IX. v [Ext. 2]. [*Training of Cyrus*, VIII. v. 27.] [*Dan.*] vi. 8, 12, 15. [xxvii = p. 125 C]. [XVII. xxxiv.] [I. v.]

3. Among the Persians the king possessed absolute power. 'He was an autocrat, and accountable to no one,' as Plutarch says, and he was worshipped as the image of deity. According to Justin a change of kings took place only through death. A king it was who said to the Persian nobles: 'In order that I might not seem to follow only my own counsel, I have brought you together; for the rest, remember that for you the obligation is greater to obey than to advise.' The Persian king, nevertheless, on assuming royal power took an oath, as Xenophon and Diodorus Siculus observed; and it was wrong for him to change laws[1] which had been made in accordance with a certain formality, as we learn from the story of Daniel and Plutarch's *Themistocles*. To this fact Diodorus Siculus bears witness also in his seventeenth book and, after a long interval, Procopius in the first book of the *Persian War*, where there is a remarkable story bearing on the point.[2]

Book III [v]. Book I [lxx].

Diodorus Siculus relates the same thing of the kings of the Ethiopians. According to this writer, again, the kings of the Egyptians who, as other Oriental rulers, incontestably exercised absolute power, were bound to the observance of many regulations. If they disregarded these, they could not be called to account while living; but after death proceedings were brought against them,[3] and if they were found guilty the honour of ceremonious burial was denied them. In like manner the bodies of the Jewish kings[4] who had reigned badly were buried outside the place set aside for the kings (*2 Chronicles*, xxiv. 25, and xxviii. 27). This was an excellent measure, which preserved the respect due to the supreme authority and yet, through fear of a future judgement, restrained kings from violating their pledges. We learn from Plutarch's *Life of Pyrrhus*,[5] that the kings

[1] Josephus, in his account of Vashti [*Antiquities of the Jews*, XI. vi. 2]: 'By reason of the law he could not be reconciled with Vashti.' Laws of this sort were called laws of the kingdom, as Iacchiades notes, *On Daniel*, ii. 13. For the laws of the kingdoms in Spain see Mariana, Book XX, chap. iii.

[2] The same historian nevertheless in regard to the fortress of Lethe mentions a law which was changed by the king, but he does not approve [chap. vi; the story to which reference is made is in chap. v].

[3] 'The laws enjoin that the bodies of tyrants be unburied and cast outside the borders'; Appian, *Civil Wars*, Book III [II. xviii. 134]. The Emperor Andronicus deprived of burial the body of his father Michael, because Michael had begun to profess the faith of the Latin Church; Gregoras, Book VI [VI. ii].

[4] In regard to the two Jorams, one king of Jerusalem, the other king of Israel, see Josephus, Book VIII, chaps. iii and v [*Antiquities of the Jews*, IX. v. 3 and vi. 3]; also in regard to Joash, king of Jerusalem [*ibid.*, IX. viii. 4].

[5] Plutarch's words are: 'In the country of the Cassari, which forms a part of Molossia, it was customary for the kings to offer sacrifices to Jupiter Ares, and to make oath to the Epirotes. The kings took oath that they would govern in accordance with the laws; the Epirotes, that they would uphold the government of the king in accordance with the same laws' [Plutarch, *Pyrrhus*, v. 4 = 385 C].

of Epirus also were accustomed to swear that they would reign in accordance with the laws.

4. What if there should be added the condition that if the king should violate his pledge he would lose his kingship?[1] Even under such circumstances the power of the king will not cease to be supreme, but the mode of possessing it will be restricted by the condition, and it will resemble the sovereign power limited in time. Of the king of the Sabaeans Agatharchides related that he was 'accountable to no one', being possessed of the most absolute power, but that if he should go outside his palace he could be stoned. This fact was noted also by Strabo, on the authority of Artemidorus. In Photius. Book XVI [iv. 19].

Thus a landed estate, which is held in trust in pursuance of a request, is in fact legally ours not less than if possession were had in absolute ownership; but it is held on condition that it be not dissipated. A similar commissary clause is applicable not only in respect to the renunciation of governmental authority but also in other contracts. For we see that even some treaties of alliance between neighbouring states have been entered into with a similar stipulation.[2]

XVII.—*It is shown that sovereignty is sometimes divided into parts, subjective or potential*

1. In the fourth place it is to be observed that while sovereignty is a unity, in itself indivisible, consisting of the parts which we have enumerated above, and including the highest degree of authority, which is 'not accountable to any one'; nevertheless a division[3] is sometimes made into parts designated as 'potential' (*partes potentiales*) and 'subjective' (*partes subjectivas*). Thus, while the sovereignty of Rome was a unity, yet it often happened that one emperor administered the East, another the West, or even three emperors governed the whole empire in three divisions.

So, again, it may happen that a people, when choosing a king, may reserve to itself certain powers but may confer the others on the king absolutely. This does not take place, however, as we have already shown, when the king obligates himself by certain promises; it must be understood as taking place only in cases [63] where either the division of power,[4] of which we have spoken, is

[1] See an example given by Krantz, *History of Sweden*, Book IX [*Vandalica*, IX. xxxi].

[2] Either that the subjects should not aid the king if he should violate the agreement, or that they should not obey him; see Kromer, *History of Poland*, Books XIX and XXI. [77] There is also an instance given by Lambert von Aschaffenburg, in his account of Henry IV, year 1074.

[3] See Zasius, *Singularia Responsa*, Book II, chap. xxxi.

[4] Thus in the time of Probus the senate confirmed the laws made by the emperors, took cognizance of appeals, appointed proconsuls; and gave lieutenant-generals to the consuls [Vopiscus, *Probus*, chap. xiii].

See also Gail, *Observationes*, Book II, 157, no. 7; and Cardinal Mantica, *De Tacitis et Ambiguis Conventionibus*, Book XXVII, title v, no. 4.

explicitly provided for, or the people, yet free, enjoins upon the future king something in the nature of a perpetual command, or an additional stipulation is made from which it is understood that the king can be constrained or punished. A command is, in fact, the act of one having superior authority, at least in respect to that which is commanded. To constrain is not, at any rate not in all cases, the function of a superior—by nature every one has the right to constrain a debtor; yet the act of constraining is inconsistent with the position of an inferior. From the power of constraint, therefore, flows at least a recognition of parity, and in consequence a division of the supreme power.

2. Against such a state of divided sovereignty—having, as it were, two heads—objections in great number are urged by many. [I. iii. 8. 1.] But, as we have also said above, in matters of government there is nothing which from every point of view is quite free from disadvantages; and a legal provision is to be judged not by what this or that man considers best, but by what accords with the will of him with whom the provision originated.

An ancient example of divided sovereignty is given by Plato in [III. v.] the third book of the *Laws*. Since the Heraclids had founded Argos, Messene, and Sparta, the kings of these states were bound to govern within the provisions of the laws which had been laid down; so long as they should do so, the peoples were bound to leave the royal power in the hands of the kings themselves and their successors, and not to allow any one to take it away from them. To this end, then, not only did the peoples bind themselves to their kings, and kings to their peoples, but also the kings bound themselves to one another, and peoples to one another.[1] Further, the kings bound themselves to neighbouring peoples, and peoples to neighbouring kings, and they promised to render aid, each to the other.

XVIII.—*That nevertheless it is wrong to infer that there is a division of sovereignty when kings do not wish certain acts of theirs to have the force of law unless approved by some assembly*

Bohier, *On Decretum*, I. ii. 1.

1. They are greatly mistaken, however, who think that a division of sovereignty occurs when kings desire that certain acts of theirs do not have the force of law unless these are approved by a senate or some other assembly. For acts which are annulled in this way must be understood as annulled by the exercise of sovereignty on the part of the king himself, who has taken this way to protect himself in

[1] There are numerous examples in the history of the northern peoples. See John Magnus, *History of Sweden*, Books XV and XXIX; Krantz, *History of Sweden*, Book V; see also Pontanus, *History of Denmark*, Book VIII.

order that a measure granted under false representations might not be considered a true act of his will. A case in point was the rescript of King Antiochus the Third to the public officials, directing them not to obey him in case he should have given any order which was in conflict with the laws. Another instance is the law of Constantine that wards or widows should not be compelled to appear in person for legal proceedings at the emperor's court, even though a rescript of the emperor requiring their presence should be presented to them.[1]

Plut., *Apothegms* [183 F].

Code, III. xiv. 1.

2. The case under consideration, then, resembles a will to which the clause has been added that no later will would be valid; for such a clause establishes the presumption that a later will would not express the real desire of the testator. But just as in the case of such a testamentary clause, so too the analogous declaration of the king can be nullified by an explicit order and specific expression of a later act of will.

XIX.—*That other examples of wrong inference regarding the division of sovereignty are found under this head*

At this point I do not follow Polybius, who assigns the Roman republic to the class of states having a mixed government. In his time this state, if we fix our attention not on the civil acts but on the body of law behind the acts, was a pure democracy; for both the authority of the senate, which he considers as the control of an aristocracy, and that of the consuls, whom he likens to kings, were subject to the people. [VI. ix ff.]

The same statement in my view is applicable to the observations of other writers, who, dealing with matters of government, find it more to their purpose to give their attention to matters of outward form and daily administration than to the body of law which is the expression of sovereignty.

XX.—*True examples of mixed sovereignty*

1. More in point is the generalization of Aristotle, who wrote that there are certain types of monarchy intermediate between the full royal power, which he calls absolute monarchy (this is the same as the 'complete monarchy'[2] in the *Antigone* of Sophocles; it is called by Plutarch 'monarchy governing in its own right[3] and not accountable to any one', and by Strabo 'authority absolute

[*Politics*, III. xv.]

[1163.]

[*On Monarchy* = p. 826 F.]

[VI. iv. 2.]

[1] Add the law, *Code*, X. xii. 1.

[2] The writers of tragedy, as we noted in sec. 8 [8. 10], represent the Theban kingship as similar to the kingships of the Phoenicians, from whom the Theban kings traced their origin.

[3] Similarly, Dionysius of Halicarnassus, in regard to the kings of Sparta [*Roman Antiquities*, II. xiv]: 'And in fact the Spartan kings did not possess absolute power.'

in itself'), and the kingship of the Lacedaemonians, which is merely a government by leading men.

In my opinion an example of division of sovereign power may be found in the case of the Jewish kings. That in respect to most matters these kings [64] ruled with sovereign power, is, I think, beyond cavil. The people had in fact wished to have a king such as the neighbouring peoples had;[1] but Oriental peoples were ruled in a very arbitrary
[213.] way. In the *Persians* Aeschylus represents Atossa as thus speaking of the king of the Persians:

> Not to the state responsible is he.

[*Georgics*, IV. 210 ff.] Familiar is the passage of Virgil:

> Not Egypt and great Lydia, nor tribes
> Of Parthians, or Median Hydaspes,
> To their king such homage pay.

Book XXXVI [xvii. 5]. In Livy we read: 'The Syrians and the inhabitants of Asia are races born for servitude.' Not unlike this is the remark of Apollonius in
[VII. xiv.] Philostratus: 'The Assyrians and the Medes even worship despotism.' 'The Asiatics . . . endure despotic government contentedly,' says Aris-
Histories, IV [xvii]. totle, in the third book of his *Politics*, chapter fourteen. In Tacitus we find Civilis, the Batavian, saying to the Gauls: 'Syria and Asia and the Orient, accustomed to kings, might well remain in slavery';[2] for in Germany and in Gaul at that time there were kings, but, as the
[*Germany*, xi.] same Tacitus observed, they held their right to rule on sufferance and by power of persuasion, not by authority to command.

[1] The people thought—to use the words of Josephus [*Antiquities of the Jews*, VI. iii. 6]: 'It was in no respect absurd, if, when their neighbours were under the rule of kings, they themselves should receive the same form of government.'

[2] Cicero, *On the Consular Provinces* [v. 10]: 'Jews and Syrians, nations born for servitude.' Euripides in the *Helena* [line 276]:

> Among barbarians all are slaves but one.

The thought was foreshadowed by Aeschylus [*Prometheus Bound*, 50]:

> For no one liveth free, save Jupiter alone.

Similar to this is the expression of Lucan [*Pharsalia*, II. 280]:

> Caesar alone in all the world
> Will now be free.

Sallust [*Histories*, V. i], in regard to the peoples of the Orient: 'So inborn in them is veneration of the name of king'; the passage is cited by Servius [*On the Georgics*, IV, line 211] and Philargyrius in relation to the passage in the *Georgics*.

Apollonius in regard to Damis, in Philostratus, Book VII [VII. xiv]: 'Since he is an Assyrian, and dwells on the Median border, he has no exalted ideas in respect to freedom.'

Julian, writing against the Christians [Cyril, *Against Julian*, IV]: 'Why should I speak to you in detail either of the Germans, whose hearts are devoted to freedom and impatient of the yoke; or, on the other hand, of the Syrians and Parthians, who are easily led to endure the hand of a master, and all the barbarous peoples who live in the East and South, and many other nations that are content to live under kings who imitate the rule of masters over slaves?'

Claudian [*On the Fourth Consulship of Honorius*, lines 306–7]:

> [78] We have not committed to you Sabaeans taught to serve,
> Nor have we made you master of the Armenian land.

2. The entire Jewish people, as we remarked above also, was under a king: and Samuel, setting forth the rights of kings, makes it plain enough that the people had no recourse against acts of injustice on the part of the king. This conclusion coincides with the interpretation which the early commentators rightly gave to the words of the Psalm: 'Against Thee only have I sinned.' On these words Jerome has the comment, 'Because he was king, and feared no one else.'[1] The same words are thus explained by Ambrose: [*Psalms*,] li. 6. [*Defence of David*, I. x.]

He was a king, he was himself bound by no laws because kings are free from the shackles of accountability for their wrong-doings. For they are not brought by any laws to face punishment, being secure on account of the possession of supreme power.[2] David did not, therefore, sin against men, to whom he was not held accountable.

The same thing may be read in one of the *Letters* (no. 383) of Isidore of Pelusium, lately published.[3]

I see that the Jewish authorities are agreed that lashes were laid upon the king who sinned against the laws that were extant in writing in regard to the duty of kings; but in their view such blows were free from disgrace. The king, in fact, voluntarily underwent scourging as a sign of his repentance; and so he was scourged not by a particular attendant, but by some one whom he had chosen, and he himself fixed the number of stripes. The kings were so shielded from penalties of a coercive nature that in their case even the law of excalceation, which involved disgrace, was not applied. An opinion of the Jew Barnachmon is found in the sayings of the Rabbis, under the title *On Judges*: 'No creature passes judgement on the king, only God alone the Blessed.'

3. Although this is true, nevertheless I think that the judicial cognizance of some matters was taken away from the kings, and remained in the jurisdiction of the sanhedrin, composed of seventy men, which by divine command was established by Moses and lasted, with unbroken co-optation, to the time of Herod. Thus both Moses and David called the judges gods, and their judgements are called the judgements of God; the judges are further said to render judgement in place not of men but of God. *Exodus*, xxii. 8. *Psalms*, lxxxii. 1. *Deut.*, i. 17; *2 Chron.*, xix. 6, 8.

Moreover, the things of God are plainly distinguished from the things of the king, where the things of God, according to the opinion of the most learned Jews, must be understood as judgements to be rendered in accordance with the law of God. I do not deny that *1 Chron.*, xxvi. 32; *2 Chron.*, xix. 11.

[1] The same Jerome in his letter *To Rusticus On Penitence* [*Letters*, cxxii]: 'For he was a king; he feared no one else, he had no one above him.'

[2] The younger Arnobius has similar comments on the same Psalm. Vitiges in Cassiodorus [*Variae*, X. xxxi]: 'The case of royal power is to be referred to the court of heaven, since this power was sought from heaven, and to heaven alone is indebted for its innocence.'

[3] [Antwerp, 1623.]

the king of Judah on his own cognizance in certain cases passed sentences of death; in this respect Maimonides considers him as having the advantage over the king of the ten tribes of Israel. The fact is established by not a few examples, part in the Holy Scriptures, part in the writings of the Jews. On the other hand, there were certain classes of matters the cognizance of which seems not to have been entrusted to the king, as those relating to a tribe, a high priest or a prophet.[1] [65] A proof of this is in the history of the prophet
Jerem., xxxviii. 5. Jeremiah. When the princes demanded that he be put to death, the king answered: 'Behold, he is in your hand; for the king is not he that can do anything against you,' meaning, of course, in a matter of this kind.

Josephus, *Antiquities*, XIV. xvii [XIV. ix. 4]. The king, again, could not deliver from judgement a man who on any other charge had been accused before the sanhedrin. Thus Hyrcanus, being unable to hinder the passing of a sentence on Herod, evaded it by a ruse.

4. In Macedonia the kings who were descended from Caranus,
[*Anab.*, IV. xi.] as Callisthenes says in Arrian, 'obtained the right to govern the
[IV. vii. 30.] Macedonians not by force, but by law.' Curtius in his fourth book declares that 'the Macedonians were accustomed to the rule of a king, but were under the shadow of a liberty greater than that enjoyed by other nations'. In fact judgements involving sentence of death upon citizens were not in the jurisdiction of the king. The same Curtius
[VI. viii. 25.] in his sixth book says: 'In accordance with an ancient practice among the Macedonians the army took cognizance of capital crimes. In time of peace, this responsibility rested with the people. The power of the kings counted for nothing except by previous authoriza-
Book VIII [i. 18]. tion.' Further evidence of this mixed sovereignty is found in another passage of Curtius: 'In accordance with a custom of their nation the Macedonians did not allow their king to go hunting on foot, and without an escort chosen from among the leading men or friends.'

[*Germany*, xliii.] Of the Goths Tacitus says: 'They are already governed somewhat more arbitrarily than the other German nations, but not yet
[xi.] beyond the limit of liberty.' He had previously described a governmental headship resting upon power of persuasion, not on authority
[xliv.] to command. Afterward he characterizes an absolute kingship in these words: 'One man issues commands; there are no restrictions, his right to rule does not rest on sufferance.' Eustathius in a comment
[195.] on the sixth book of the *Odyssey*, where the state of the Phaeacians is described, says that it is 'a mixture of kingship and aristocracy'.[2]

[1] 'It cannot be that a prophet perish out of Jerusalem.' *Luke*, xiii. 33.

[2] Laonicus Chalcocondylas says that of this sort were the kingships of the Pannonians and Angles, Book II; of Arragon, Book V; and of Navarre, in the same book, where he says that magistrates were not appointed by the king, nor garrisons imposed, without the consent of the people, and that

5. A condition somewhat similar I note in the times of the Roman kings. In that period almost all matters were administered by the hand of the king. 'Romulus', says Tacitus, 'had ruled over us as he pleased.' 'The fact is established', Pomponius declares, 'that in our state at the beginning the kings had all the power.' Nevertheless even at this time Dionysius of Halicarnassus makes out that there were some matters which were reserved to the people. [III. xxvi.] [*Digest*, I. ii. 2, § 14.] [IV. xx.]

If, now, we concede a greater degree of reliability to the Roman writers, Seneca, basing his opinion upon the books of Cicero *On the Commonwealth*, also the pontifical books and Fenestella, averred that in certain cases there was a right of appeal from the kings to the people. Soon Servius Tullius, who had been raised to the kingship less by right than by popular favour, lessened even more the power of the kingship; in fact, as Tacitus remarks, 'He sanctioned laws which even the kings must obey.' It is, then, not surprising to find in Livy the statement that the power of the first consuls differed from the power of the kings chiefly in the fact that it was limited to one year. *Letters*, c [cviii. 31]. *Annals*, III [xxvi]. [II. i. 7.]

6. Similar was the mixture of democracy and aristocracy at Rome in an interregnum, and in the earlier part of the period of the consuls. In some matters—those that were of greater importance—a measure passed by the people had the force of law only if validated by the authority of the senate.[1] Later, when the power of the people had been increased, as Livy and Dionysius observe, this procedure remained only as an antiquated form, since the senators began to ratify in advance the uncertain issue of the assemblies of the people. Still later a trace of the mixed sovereignty remained, as the same Livy tells; so long in fact as the power of governing was in the hands [I. xvii. 9.] [II. xiv.] Book VI [xxxvii. 4].

no command was laid upon the people contrary to the customs. That some kings possessed absolute authority, while others were subject to the laws, was noted also by the Jew Ben Gerson in his comment on *1 Samuel*, viii. 4.

What Pliny writes about Taprobane, [*Natural History*] Book VI, chap. xiii [VI. xxii. 89–91], is remarkable:

> The king is chosen by the people with reference to age and mildness of disposition, and he must be without children; if afterward a child is born to him he must abdicate, that the kingship may not become hereditary. Thirty ministers are given to him by the people, and a man cannot be condemned to death except by a vote of the majority. Even under such conditions there is an appeal to the people; 70 judges are appointed. If not more than 30—for that number ought to be read here—vote to free the accused, they have no standing, they are in very deep disgrace.
>
> The dress of the king is that of father Liber [Bacchus]; the others have the costume of the Arabs. If a king does any wrong, he is punished with death; no one puts him to death, but all avoid him, refusing even to speak with him.

Servius, *On the Aeneid*, Book IV [line 682 referring to Carthage], on the words 'the people and the fathers': 'Some find here an allusion to the three parts of the body politic, the people, the optimates, and the royal power. Cato in fact says that the political organization of Carthage was composed of those three parts.'

[1] Plutarch, *Coriolanus* [xxix = 227 E]: 'The people had not the right either to enact a law or to give any order unless authorized by a previous decree of the senate.'

Chalcocondylas, Book V, notes that in his time there was a similar mixture of sovereignty in the Genoese republic.

of the patricians, that is the senate, and a means of relief lay in the hands of the tribunes, that is the people; the means of relief was, of course, the right of veto or intercession.

[*Panathenaic Oration*, cliii = p. 265 A.]

7. In like manner Isocrates makes out that in the time of Solon the Athenian state was 'an aristocracy compounded with democracy'.

Having laid down these principles, let us discuss certain questions which frequently come up in connexion with the subject.

XXI.—*It is shown that sovereignty may be vested in him who is bound by an unequal alliance; and objections are met*

1. The first question is, whether he can possess sovereign power who [66] is bound by an unequal alliance.

By an unequal alliance I mean here not an alliance entered into between states of unequal strength, such as that which the Theban state in the time of Pelopidas had with the king of Persia, and the Romans at one time with the Massilians, afterward with King Masinissa. Nor, again, do I have reference to a relation which has a temporary effect, as in the case of an enemy who is admitted to friendly terms until he pays the costs of a war, or fulfils some other condition. An unequal alliance is one which, by the very character of the treaty, gives to one of the contracting parties a permanent advantage over the other; when, for example, one party is bound to preserve the sovereignty and majesty of the other, as in the treaty of the Aetolians with the Romans—that is, to put forth every effort that its sovereignty remain secure and its prestige, which is understood by the word majesty, remain unimpaired. This is what Tacitus called 'the feeling of awe for the empire', explaining what he had in mind as follows: 'In respect to place of habitation and territories they belong on their own bank, in mind and heart they act with us.' Says Florus, 'The other peoples also, who were not under our imperial authority, felt nevertheless its greatness, and stood in awe of the Roman people as conqueror of the nations.'

[Justin, XLIII [v. 10]. Val. Max., VII. i [V. ii. *ext.* 4].]

[[*Germany*, xxix.]]

[Book IV [xii].]

Characterized by a similar inequality are certain rights which to-day are known as rights of protection, defence, and patronage; also, among the Greeks, the right of the mother cities over their colonies. As Thucydides says, the colonies in respect to legal independence were on the same plane as the mother cities, but they were under obligation 'to honour the mother city', and to manifest their feeling by 'the customary signs of respect'—a deferential attitude, undoubtedly, and certain outward marks of honour.

[Book I [xxv, xxxviii].]

2. Of the ancient treaty between the Romans, who had obtained a complete mastery over Alba, and the Latins, who were natives of

Alba, Livy says: 'In that treaty the Roman state had greatly the advantage.' Rightly did Andronicus of Rhodes, following Aristotle, say, that this is characteristic of a relation of friendship between those who are unequal, that more honour is granted to the stronger, more help to the one that is weaker. I [lii. 4]. *On Nicom. Ethics*, IX. xviii [VIII. xviii].

We know what answer Proculus gave to the question under consideration. He said that a state is independent which is not subject to the power of another, even though a stipulation may have been made in a treaty of alliance that this state shall use its good offices to maintain the dignity of another state. If, therefore, a state bound by such a treaty remains independent, if it is not subject to the power of another, the conclusion follows that it retains its sovereignty. *Digest*, XLIX. xv. 7, § 1.

The same conclusion, further, must be affirmed in the case of a king. The case of an independent state and that of a king, who truly is a king, are in this matter identical. Proculus adds that the stipulation referred to is made a part of a treaty in order that 'it may be understood that one state holds a position of superiority, not that it may be understood that the other state is not independent.' This position of superiority we ought to consider as having reference not to power (for he had just said that the lesser state was not subject to the power of another), but to influence and prestige. This is brought out by an apt comparison, in the following words: [*Digest*, XLIX. xv. 7, § 1.]

Just as we understand (says Proculus) that our clients are free men, even though they are not our equals in respect to authority, standing and legal status, so it must be understood that those also are free who are under obligation through their good offices to maintain our prestige. [*Digest*, XLIX. xv. 7, § 1.]

3. Clients are under the protection of their patrons; so lesser states[1] are by treaty placed under the protection of a state which is superior in prestige. They are 'under protection, not under domination', as Sulla says in Appian; 'under patronage, not under subjection,' as Livy expresses it. In the second book of his treatise *On Duties* Cicero, characterizing the times when the Romans were more conscientious, says that with them their allies had protection, not domination. In harmony with this is the saying of the elder Scipio Africanus, that 'The Roman people prefers to bind men to it through kindness rather than through fear, and to have foreign *Mith. Wars* [ix. 62]. Book XXXI. [II. viii. 27.] Livy, XXVI [xlix. 8].

[1] See Cardinal Toschi, *Practicae Conclusiones*, 935.

You have an example in the Dilimnites, who, being free and independent, engaged in military service under the Persians; Agathias, Book III [III. xvii]. Thus it was the design of Irene to divide the empire up among the children of her husband in such a way that she should make those who were born later 'inferior in standing, yet independent and possessing full authority'.

See Krantz, *History of Saxony*, Book X [X. iii], in regard to the cities which gave themselves over to the protection of Austria.

Herodian, Book V [VII. ii. 1]: 'Of the Osroeni and Armenians, of whom the former were subjects, the latter friends and allies.'

nations joined with it in protecting care and in alliance rather than subject to it in depressing servitude.' In harmony also is what Strabo said of the Lacedaemonians after the Romans [67] came into Greece: 'They remained free, contributing nothing except what was required by the terms of alliance.' [VIII. v. 5.]

Just as private patronage in the case of individuals does not take away individual liberty, so patronage in the case of a state does not take away independence; and independence without sovereignty is inconceivable. So in Livy you may see that the conditions 'to be under protection' and 'to be in subjection' are contrasted. According to Josephus, Augustus made the threat to Syllaeus, king of the Arabs, that if he did not refrain from injuring his neighbours, Augustus would see to it that he should become a subject instead of a friend. In the condition of subjects, in truth, the kings of Armenia were. They, as Paetus wrote to Vologeses, were under the domination of the Romans, and so were kings in name rather than in fact. Such, at an earlier time, were the kings of Cyprus and other kings who, as Diodorus says, were 'subject' to the kings of Persia. [VIII. i. end; XXXVI. xxviii. 4.] [*Antiquities*, XVI. ix. 3.] Book XVI [xlvi].

4. Contradictory, seemingly, to what we have said, is the statement which Proculus adds: 'Citizens of allied states are subject to legal proceedings among us, and if they are found guilty we punish them.' [*Digest*, XLIX. xv. 7, § 2.]

In order that this statement may be understood, it is necessary to know that there are four kinds of controversies which can arise. First, if subjects of a state or of a king who is under the protection of another are charged with having violated the treaty of alliance; in the second place, if the states or kings themselves are accused of such violation; thirdly, if allies who are under the protection of the same state or king have differences among themselves; fourthly, if subjects complain that they have suffered wrongs at the hands of those to whom they are subject.

In the first case, if the offence is evident, the king or state is bound to punish the offender, or to deliver him up to the party that suffered the wrong. This holds not only in the case of unequal alliances, but also in the case of alliances made on equal terms; also, again, in the case of those who are not bound by any alliance, as we shall show elsewhere. The king or state furthermore is bound to see to it that the losses are made good. At Rome this was the business of the board of recuperators (*recuperatores*). So Aelius Gallus, as quoted by Festus: 'There is recovery when between the Roman people and foreign kings, nations and states a law provides in what way property may be restored and recovered through the agency of the recuperator, and how men are to proceed for the adjustment of private interests between themselves.' However, one ally does not have the [II. xxi. 4.] [under the word *reciperatio*.]

right directly to seize or punish a subject of another ally. Thus the Campanian Decius Magius was placed in fetters by Hannibal and taken to Cyrene, thence deported to Alexandria; he showed that he had been placed in bonds by Hannibal in violation of the terms of alliance, and so was released from his chains. Livy, XXIII [vii–x].

5. In the second case, one ally has the right to compel the other ally to abide by the terms of the treaty, and also to punish him, in case he has failed to do so. But this, again, is not limited to unequal alliances. The same rule of right holds in the case of a treaty on equal terms. For in order to exact punishment from one who has committed an offence, it is sufficient that the party inflicting the punishment be not subject to the offender; but this point will be treated by us later. In consequence the same practice has arisen also between kings and states not in alliance. [II. xx. 3.]

6. In the third case, in unequal as in equal alliances, controversies are ordinarily referred to a conference of the allies [1] who have no interest in the matter under dispute—such, we read, was the practice among the Greeks, the early Latins, and the Germans; —otherwise, either to arbitrators, or even to the leading member of a confederation as a common arbitrator. The latter alternative is ordinarily adopted in the case of an unequal alliance, so that controversies are settled by reference to him who has the leading place in the alliance. Even this method does not disclose an authority based on sovereign power; for kings often plead before judges appointed by themselves.

7. In the last case the allies have no right of intervention. Thus when Herod on his own initiative submitted charges against his sons to Augustus, they said to him: 'You were able to punish us yourself in your own right, both as father and as king.' [68] When charges were brought against Hannibal at Rome by some of the Carthaginians, Scipio [2] declared that the senators ought not to interfere in a matter which belonged to the Carthaginian state. This is in harmony with the statement of Aristotle, that an alliance of states differs from a single state in this, that the allies are charged with preventing the commission of wrong against any one of them, not with prevention of wrong-doing among the citizens of an allied state. Josephus, XVI. vii. 8 [*Antiquities*, XVI. iv. 3]. Val. Max., IV. i. *Politics*, III. ix.

8. Another objection is often raised, that in the histories the word 'command' is sometimes used with reference to him who holds a position of vantage in an alliance, and 'obey' with reference to him who holds the inferior position. This, however, ought not

[1] Such a meeting is called a 'common court' in an ancient inscription of isopolity or treaty of reciprocal rights between the Priansians and the Hieropotamians [*Corpus Inscriptionum Graecarum*, I. 2556.58].

[2] See Polybius in *Selections on Embassies*, cv.

to disturb us. For we are here concerned either with matters that relate to the common good of the alliance, or with the particular interest of him who in the alliance holds the position of vantage. In respect to matters of common interest, except at the time of a conference of the allies, even when there is an alliance on equal terms, he who is chosen as head of the alliance—'prince of the covenant' (*Daniel*, xi. 22)—ordinarily holds the command. Thus Agamemnon commanded the Greek kings; afterward the Spartans, then the Athenians, commanded the Greeks. In the address of the Corinthians
[I. cxx.] in Thucydides we read:

> It is fitting that those who have the leading place in an alliance should arrogate to themselves no privilege in relation to their own interests, but should make themselves conspicuous above the others through their careful management of the common interests.

[*Panegyric*, civ= p. 62 c.] Isocrates says that the ancient Athenians held the military leadership, 'assuming the responsibility on behalf of all the allies, but in such a way as to leave their independence unimpaired'; [lxxx= p. 56 E.] in another passage, 'in such a way that they thought their duty was to administer the command of the war, not to bear sway'; in a third [civ= p. 62 c.] passage, he adds: 'administering their affairs in the spirit of an ally, not of a master.'

This right of the leading member of an alliance the Romans expressed by *imperare*, 'to command'; the Greeks, with greater self-constraint, by a word meaning 'to put in order', 'arrange'.
[I. xcvi.] Thus, according to Thucydides, the Athenians, having received the direction of the war against the Persians, 'arranged' (so it was said of those who were sent from Rome to Greece, that they were sent 'to arrange the affairs of free states' [1]) 'what cities should contribute money for the war against the barbarian, what cities should contribute ships'. If this, then, is done by one who is only the leading member in an alliance, it is not remarkable if the same thing is done by him who in an unequal alliance has, according to the terms of the treaty, the position of vantage. Understood in this sense, the right on the part of the leading ally to hold command, that is hegemony, does not take away the independence of the others.

Consistent with this point of view is the statement of the
XXXVII [liv. 25]. Rhodians in their speech to the Roman senate, as reported by Livy:

> In former times the Greeks by their own strength gained also the power to rule. Now they earnestly desire that the power to rule may remain permanently where it is; they count it sufficient to maintain their independence with the help of your arms, since they are not able to maintain it with their own.

Book XV [xxviii]. In the same spirit, after the citadel of Cadmus had been retaken by the Thebans, as Diodorus relates, many states of Greece joined

[1] Pliny, *Letters*, VIII. xxiv.

together, 'to the end that they might be free, but might avail themselves of the military leadership of the Athenians.' Of the Athenians themselves in the time of Philip of Macedon Dio of Prusa says that 'at this time they had lost their position of military leadership and retained only their independence'. Caesar soon names as allies the same peoples who, as he tells us, had been under the dominion of the Suevi. [*Orations*, xxi = p. 350.] [*Gallic War*, V. xxxix.]

9. In matters which affect the particular interest of him who holds the position of vantage in an unequal alliance, requests are often spoken of as commands, not rightly but in accordance with the similarity of the effect produced; in like manner the prayers of kings are often said to be commands, and sick people are said to give orders to their physicians. Says Livy (Book XLII): 'Before the time of this consul'—Gaius Postumius—'no one was ever a burden or source of expense to the allies in any matter; so the public officials were provided with mules, tents, and all other military equipment, in order that they might not requisition such material from the allies.' [XLII. i. 8.]

10. It is, nevertheless, true that in the majority of cases he who has the position of vantage in a treaty, if he [69] is greatly superior in respect to power, gradually usurps the sovereignty properly so called. This is particularly liable to happen if the treaty is perpetual, and if it contains the right to introduce garrisons into towns, as the Athenians did, when they allowed appeals to be made to them by their allies—something that the Spartans had never done. The rule of the Athenians over the allies in those times Isocrates compares to the rule of a king. With similar provocation the Latins complained that under the shadow of an alliance [1] with Rome they were experiencing subjection as slaves. Thus the Aetolians declared that there now remained to them only a vain appearance and empty name of liberty; the Achaeans, afterward, that 'What was, in appearance, an alliance, was already a slavery, dependent on another's will'. According to Tacitus, Civilis the Batavian complains of the same Romans, declaring that his people 'were no longer regarded as allies, as formerly, but as bondmen'; and in another passage, that 'A pitiable servitude is falsely called peace'. [*On Peace*, xxxvi = p. 182 D.] Hal., VI [Livy, VIII. iv. 2]. Livy, XXXIV [xxiii. 7]. [XXXIX. xxxvii. 13.] *Histories*, IV [xiv]. [IV. xvii.]

In Livy, too, Eumenes says that the allies of the Rhodians are

[1] [79] This is the very thing that Plutarch speaks of in his *Life of Aratus* [xxxviii = 1045 A], 'to make of an alliance a bondage under a mild name'; Vocula calls it 'a mild servitude' in Tacitus, *Histories*, IV [IV. lvii]. Festus Rufus [X], speaking of the Rhodians: 'At first they enjoyed liberty of action; afterward, led on by the mildness of the Romans, they gradually became accustomed to render obedience.' Those whom Caesar had previously spoken of as having a relation of friendship with the Aeduans and had called clients, in a later passage [*Gallic War*, VII. lxxv] he mentions as being under the rule of the Aeduans.

Add references, if desired, to Frederick Mindanus, *De Processibus*, Book II, chap. xiv, no. 3; Ziegler, sec. *Landsassii*, 86; Gail, *Observationes*, Book II, 54, no. 6.

See Agathias, Book I [I. ii, iii], where the Goths are warned what in the course of time they are to expect from the Franks.

XXXV [xxxi. 12] and XXXVII [liii. 4]. allies in name only, being in reality subject to the rule of another and accountable to it. The Magnesians also declared that Demetrias, though independent according to appearances, was in reality at the beck and call of the Romans.[1] Thus Polybius observes that the [IV. xiv.] people of Thessaly were in appearance independent, but in reality under the rule of Macedonia.

11. When such things happen, with the result that non-resistance on the part of the weaker passes over into the right of ruling on the part of the stronger—there will be opportunity to discuss this point elsewhere—then either those who had been allies become subjects, or there is at any rate a division of sovereignty such as, according to our previous statement, may take place.

XXII.—*That sovereignty may be held by him who pays tribute*

There are some allies who pay a definite amount,[2] either as reparation for wrong-doings, or as a contribution to secure pro- I [xix]. tection; these are 'allies subject to tribute', as Thucydides calls them. Such were the kings of the Jews,[3] and of the nations near them after the time of Antony, being 'under agreement to pay [*Civil Wars*, V. viii. 75.] tribute', as Appian says.

I see no reason for doubting that such nations may possess sovereignty, although the confession of weakness does detract somewhat from their standing.

XXIII.—*That sovereignty may be held by him who is bound by feudal law*

1. To many the problem of sovereignty in relation to feudal tenure seems more difficult; it can, however, be easily solved in the light of what has been said. In discussing this type of contract, which is peculiar to the Germanic nations and is found only where the Germans settled, two elements need to be considered, the personal obligation, and the property right.

2. The personal obligation is the same whether a person by feudal law possesses the actual right of governing, or anything else

[1] Such were the Lazi also in the time of Justinian. See Procopius, *Persian War*, II [II. xv. 1, 2].

[2] The Persians used to receive from Justinian a yearly grant; on this subject see Procopius, *Persian War*, II [II. x. 20-4], and *Gothic Wars*, IV [IV. xv]. This payment under a mild designation was called a contribution for protecting the Caspian Gates. The Turks appease the mountain Arabs with money.

[3] Josephus, Book XV [XV. iii. 8]: 'Antony declared that it was not right that the king be called upon to render an account in regard to those things which he had done as a king; that under such conditions he would in fact not even be a king. It was fair, he said, that those who had conferred the honour upon him should also permit him to use his authority in the freest possible way.'

Chrysostom, *On Alms*, ii: 'After the affairs of the Jews began to decline . . . and they were brought under the authority of the Romans, they neither enjoyed complete liberty as before, nor, nevertheless, were they altogether in subjection, as at present; but they were honoured with the title of allies, paying taxes to their kings and from these receiving magistrates. For the rest, in most matters they used their own laws, so that they themselves punished in accordance with the customs of the country those of their people who committed offences.'

even though situated in a different place. Now, as such an obligation would not deprive an individual of the right of personal liberty, so it does not deprive a king or a state of sovereignty, which is political freedom.

This is most clearly seen in the case of free fiefs, which are called frank-fiefs. These do not consist in any property rights but in a personal obligation only. Such fiefs are, in fact, only a kind of unequal alliance, which we have been treating; of the contracting parties one engages to render service to the other, the other in turn to furnish defence and protection. Suppose even that the service of the vassal had been promised against all men in the case of the fief now called a liege fief [1] (formerly the term had a wider application); that in no degree lessens his right of sovereign power over his subjects—not to speak of the fact that in such a promise there is always an unexpressed condition, provided the war be lawful, which is to be dealt with later.

3. So far as the property right is concerned, if one holds by feudal law, the right of governing may be lost on the extinction of a family, or even on account of certain crimes. But in the meantime the power of the vassal does not cease to be sovereign; for, as we have often said, the object is one thing, the manner of possession quite another. I see that a number of kings were placed in authority by the Romans with the stipulation that if the royal family should become extinct the political power should revert to them; this fact was remarked by Strabo, with reference to Paphlagonia and some Book XII
other kingdoms. [iii. 41].

[70] XXIV.—*Distinction between the right of sovereignty and the exercise of the right, with examples*

In the case of political power not less than in that of private ownership it is necessary to distinguish between the right and its exercise, or the first act and the second. For a king who is an infant possesses political power but is unable to use it. A king, again, may be insane or a captive; and a king may be in foreign territory and live in such a way that freedom of action in respect to a dominion existing elsewhere is not permitted to him.

In all these cases it is necessary to provide guardians, or regents. And so Demetrius,[2] being in the power of Seleucus, and unable to live with sufficient freedom, forbade that reliance be placed on his seal or his letters, and desired that the administration in all respects be carried on as if he were dead.

[1] See Baldus, *On Digest*, pr.; Natta, *Consilia*, 485.
[2] See Plutarch, *Demetrius* [chap. li=914 D].

CHAPTER IV

WAR OF SUBJECTS AGAINST SUPERIORS

I.—*State of the question*

[80] 1. War may be waged by private persons against private persons, as by a traveller against a highwayman; by those who have sovereign power against those who possess like power, as by David against the King of the Ammonites; by private persons against those who have sovereign power, but not over them, as by Abraham against the King of Babylon and his neighbours; and by those who have sovereign power against private persons who are either their subjects, as in the war waged by David against the party of Ishbosheth, or are not their subjects, as in the war waged by the Romans against the pirates.

2. The question to be considered here is simply this, whether it is permissible for either private or official persons to wage war against those under whose authority they are, whether this authority be sovereign or subordinate.

First of all, the point is settled beyond controversy, that arms may be taken up against subordinates by those who are armed with the authority of the sovereign power. A pertinent case is that of Nehemiah who, authorized by an edict of Artaxerxes, waged war on the petty princes near him. Similarly the Roman emperors granted to the proprietor of an estate the privilege of driving off the surveyors who make measurements for a camp. Our question, then, is to determine what action is permissible against the sovereign power, or against subordinates acting under the authority of the sovereign power.

Code, XII. xl. 5.

3. Among all good men one principle at any rate is established beyond controversy, that if the authorities issue any order that is contrary to the law of nature or to the commandments of God, the order should not be carried out. For when the Apostles said that obedience should be rendered to God rather than men, they appealed to an infallible rule of action, which is written in the hearts of all men, and which you may find in Plato expressed in about as many words. But if from any such cause, or under other conditions as a result of caprice on the part of him who holds the sovereign power, unjust treatment be inflicted on us, we ought to endure it rather than resist by force.

[*Apology*, xvii.]

II.—*That as a general rule rebellion is not permitted by the law of nature*

1. By nature all men have the right of resisting in order to ward off injury, as we have said above. But as civil society was instituted in order to maintain public tranquillity, the state forthwith acquires over us and our possessions a greater right, to the extent necessary to accomplish this end. The state, therefore, in the interest of public peace and order, can limit that common right of resistance. That such was the purpose of the state we cannot doubt, since it could not in any other way achieve its end. If, in fact, the right of resistance should remain without restraint, there will no longer be a state, but only a non-social horde, such as that of the Cyclopes, among whom— [Homer, *Odyssey*, IX. 114 f.]

> Each bears rule
> O'er wife and offspring.
> A mob confused, where none the other heeds.[1]

Eurip., *Cyclops* [120].

Such, too, were the Aborigines, whom Sallust represents as a race of men rude, without laws, without government, free and unrestrained; and such, according to the same author in another passage, were the Getulians, who were controlled neither by custom nor by the law or rule [81] of any one. [*Catilinarian War*, VI. i; *Jugurthine War*, XVIII. i.]

2. The usage of all states is as I have stated. Augustine says: 'There is a general agreement of human society to obey kings.' Says Aeschylus: [*Confessions*, III. viii.]

> Full power the king enjoys, responsible to none.

[*Prometheus Bound*, 326.]

In the words of Sophocles:

> Rulers they are—obedience must be rendered;
> And why not?

[*Ajax*, 668.]

A kindred thought is expressed by Euripides:

> Crass blundering of them who rule
> Must be endured.

[*Phoenician Maidens*, 394.]

To these quotations may be added the words of Tacitus which we quoted above, in a similar connexion, and also the following: 'To the emperor the gods have given the supreme direction of affairs; to subjects has been left the honour of rendering obedience.' Here also belongs the verse: [*Annals*, VI. xiv.] [I. iii. 8. 15.]

> Unworthy things must worthy be esteemed,
> If the king does them.

[Plautus, *Captives*, 200 f.]

[1] Valerius [*Argonauts*, IV. 102–3] has a similar characterization of the Bebrycians:

> No bonds of law they heed,
> Nor rights that stay and calm men's minds.

[*Medea*, 194.] [*Antigone*, 666 ff.] Here, again, a sentence from Seneca: 'The rule of a king, just and unjust, you must endure.' The thought was borrowed from Sophocles, who had said:

> You must obey him whom the state has placed
> In power, alike in small things and in things
> Unjust as well as just.

[*Jugurthine War*, XXXI. xxvi.] A sentence of Sallust has the same purport: 'To do whatever you wish with impunity, that is to be a king.'[1]

3. Hence it comes about that everywhere the majesty, that is, the prestige, whether of the state or of him who exercises the sovereign power, is safeguarded by so many laws, so many penalties; this cannot be maintained if licence to offer resistance be free to all. If a soldier has resisted a centurion who wishes to punish him and has laid hold of the centurion's staff, he is degraded in rank; if he has purposely broken the staff, or 'has laid a hand on the centurion he is punished with death'. In Aristotle we read, 'If he who has official authority has struck any one, he is not to be struck in return.' [*Digest*, XLIX. xvi. 13, § 4–5, Rufus, *Leg. Mil.*, xv. [*Nicomachean Ethics*, V. v.]]

III.—*That rebellion is not allowable according to Hebraic law*

Deut., xvii. 12. *Josh.*, i. 18. *1 Sam.*, viii. 11. In Hebraic law he was condemned to death who had been disobedient either to the high priest or to one that had been appointed by God out of the ordinary way as ruler of the people.

If we examine closely the passage in Samuel which deals with the right of the king, it becomes clear that on the one hand this must not be understood as setting forth a true right, that is a power to do something in a manner morally right and just (an altogether different manner of life is prescribed for the king in the part of the law which deals with the duty of the king), nor, on the other hand, is a mere fact indicated; for there is nothing in it peculiar to a king, since private persons also are wont to do wrongs to private persons. A fact is set forth, however, which has in a measure a legal effect, that is, the obligation not to offer resistance.[2] So it is added, that the people when oppressed by such wrongs should implore the help of God, because, in fact, there would be no recourse at the hands of man. That, therefore, is called a legal right in the sense that the praetor is said to 'enforce a legal right even when he gives an unjust decision'. [*Deut.*, xvii. 14.] [*Dig.* I. i. 11.]

[1] Applicable here are the words of Mark Antony which we have already quoted above, after Josephus [p. 136, note 3].

[2] Philo, *Against Flaccus* [chap. x. i, speaking of the Jews]: 'For when were we suspected of revolt? When, in the view of all men, were we thought to be other than peacefully disposed? And the practices which we maintain in our daily life: are they not beyond reproach, are they not conducive to the harmony and well-being of the state?'

IV.—*That rebellion is even less allowable according to the law of the Gospel; proof is presented from Holy Writ*

1. In the New Covenant Christ enjoined men 'to render unto Caesar the things that are Caesar's'. By this he meant that his followers owed to sovereign powers an obedience joined, if need be, with long-suffering, not less in degree, if not even greater, than that which the Jews owed to the Jewish kings. This thought the Apostle Paul, a most excellent interpreter of Christ, develops more fully. Describing in detail the duties of subjects, among other things he says: 'He that resisteth the power, withstandeth the ordinance of God; and they that withstand shall receive to themselves judgement.' A little farther on he adds: 'For he is a minister of God to thee for good'; afterward, 'Wherefore ye must needs be in subjection, not only because of the wrath, but also for conscience' sake.' *Rom.*, xiii [2–5].

Under subjection the Apostle includes the necessity of non-resistance—not the necessity only which arises from fear of a greater [82] evil but that which flows from our very sense of duty and lays upon us an obligation not only to men but also to God. He adds two reasons. The first is that God approved this constituted order of bearing rule and rendering obedience both in earlier time, under the Hebraic law, and now under the Gospel; in consequence, we are to look upon public authorities as if they had been established by God himself. For the acts to which we have given our authorization we make our own. The other reason is, that this constituted order contributes to our good.

2. And yet, an objector may say, there is no advantage in suffering wrongs. On this point some declare—with more of truth than of consistency with the Apostle's meaning, I judge—that even these wrongs are advantageous to us, because such long-suffering will not fail of its reward. It seems to me that the Apostle had in view the universal end which the constituted order had in view; this is, the maintenance of public tranquillity,[1] in which also that of individuals is comprised. Truly we cannot doubt that generally we do attain to this good through the agency of the powers of government; for no one wishes to bring harm upon himself, and the good fortune of the ruler consists in the good fortune of his subjects. 'May there be those whom you may rule,'[2] one of the ancients said. Among the Jews there is a proverb, 'If there were no public authority, men [*Pirke Aboth.*, iii.]

[1] Well does Chrysostom [*On Romans*, xiii. 4=Homily XXIII, ii] remark: 'He is co-worker with thee, he co-operates with thee,' the emperor, that is, with him who preaches the Gospel. He hews the surface which you smooth.

[2] This saying is ascribed to Sulla by Plutarch [cf. *Sulla*, xxxi=472], Florus [*Epitome*, II. ix. 25, or III. xxi], and others, from whom it was taken by Augustine, *On the City of God*, III. xxviii.

would swallow one another alive.' The same thought is found in Chrysostom: 'If there were no rulers of states, we should be living a life more wild than the life of wild beasts, not only biting one another, but devouring one another.'[1]

3. If sometimes under the influence of excessive fear or anger or other passions, rulers are turned aside so that they do not enter the straight road that leads to tranquillity, this after all must be reckoned among the things that less frequently happen; and such things, as [*Histories*, IV. lxxiv.] Tacitus remarks, are offset by the interposition of better things. Laws, again, count it sufficient to have in view what generally happens, *Dig.* I. iii. 6; V. iv. 3, end. Livy, XXXIV [iii. 5]. as Theophrastus remarked. A saying of Cato bears on the same point: 'There is no law which is sufficiently well adapted to all cases; this only is aimed at, that a law be serviceable to the majority, and of general application.'

Things which happen rather infrequently ought nevertheless to be brought together under general rules; for although the principle embodied in a law may in a special case not have a specific application, yet the principle remains of general scope, and it is right that particular cases should be determined accordingly. This is better than to live without a rule, or to suffer the rule to be left to every one's discretion. *On Benefits*, VII. xvi [3]. Quite to the point Seneca remarks: 'It was better that even a well-grounded excuse be not accepted from a few than that any and every kind of an excuse be tried by all.'

4. At this point we may quote as pertinent those words of Pericles in Thucydides,[2] which cannot be too often brought to mind:

> For my part I think that even for the individual citizens it is more advantageous that the state prosper than that, while their private interests prosper, the state as a whole should suffer. For though a man may have his private means well invested, nevertheless if the state perish he must perish with it; but the man who, in a prosperous state, has been unfortunate, is much more likely, under such a condition, to regain his footing. Since, then, a state is able to bear the misfortunes of individuals, while the individual is not able to bear the misfortunes of a state, what reason is there why all should not unite in taking counsel for the state, and for its protection, and not do as you are doing, you who, panic stricken as it were, by private losses, are abandoning the safety of the state?

[1] The quotation is from Chrysostom, *On the Statues*, Homily VI [i], in which this also is found [ii]: [94] 'Abolish the courts of justice and you will take all tranquillity out of life.' In a later passage: 'Do not speak to me of those who have abused their official positions, but look at the beauty of the institution itself, and you will admire the wisdom of him who was the originator of it.'

The same writer *On Romans* [xiii. 5=Homily XXIII, ii]: 'If you were to do away with magistrates, all things would perish; in such case cities will not remain, not the fields, not the forum, nor anything else. All things will be turned upside down, and the weaker will become the prey of the stronger.' A similar thought is expressed by the same writer, *On Ephesians*, v [Homily XX, i].

[2] Book II [II. lx]. With this the thought of Ambrose, *On Duties*, Book III [III. iv. 25], accords: 'The interest of the individual is the same as that of the general body.' And the following in a legal statement, in *Digest*, XVII. ii. 65, § 5: 'Always not that which is to the advantage of one of the partners but that which is advantageous to the partnership is to be kept in view.'

Add the next to the last section in the *Code*, VI. li. 14.

The same thought is expressed by Livy briefly in these words: XXVI [xxxvi. 9].
'A state that is in a sound condition easily safeguards the interest of individuals; in betraying the general interest you would vainly think to protect your own.' Plato had said, in the fourth book of his *Laws*: [xiii.] 'It is the common interest which binds a state together, that of individuals which rends it apart. Wherefore, it is more advantageous, both for the state and for the individual, that public interests be cared for in preference to [83] private interests.'

Xenophon presents a slightly different point of view: 'He who in war acts treacherously against his general does so at the peril of his life.' [*Anabasis*, VI. i. 29.] The words of Iamblichus bear upon the same subject: 'The private interest is not dissociated from the public interest; rather, the good of the individual is comprised in the general good. [In Stobaeus, xlvi. 74.] In states, as in the case of animals and the rest of nature, the welfare of the parts is dependent upon the welfare of the whole.'

5. Now beyond doubt the most important element in public affairs is the constituted order of bearing rule and rendering obedience, regarding which I have spoken. This truly cannot coexist with individual licence to offer resistance. The point is well set forth in a fine passage of Dio Cassius: [XLI. xxxiii.]

> For my part I think that it is not a proper thing for the ruler of a state to be overridden by his subjects, and that there is no hope of safety if the element whose function it is to obey strives to rule. Consider what kind of order there would be in a household if the elders should be scorned by the young. How would the sick recover their health if they should not obey their physicians in everything? What safety for those who travel by ship if the crew should treat with contempt the orders of the helmsmen? By nature in truth it is for men a necessity, and a means of safety, that some rule and others obey.

6. With Paul let us associate Peter as a companion. Peter's words are: *1 Peter*, ii. 12 [ii. 17–20].

> Honour the king.
>
> Servants, be in subjection to your masters with all fear; not only to the good and gentle, but also to the froward. For this is acceptable, if for conscience toward God a man endureth griefs, suffering wrongfully. For what glory is it, if, when ye sin, and are buffeted for it, we shall take it patiently? But if, when ye do well and suffer for it, ye shall take it patiently, this is acceptable with God.[1]

A little farther on Peter confirms this exposition by the example of Christ. The same thought in the *Constitutions* of Clement is [IV. xii.] expressed in these words: 'Let the servant who fears God at the same time bring goodwill to his master, no matter how ungodly, no matter how unjust.'

Two comments need to be made. First, the submission which is spoken of as due to masters, even harsh masters, must be considered as due also to kings; for what follows is based upon that as a founda-

[1] Tertullian, *On Repentance* [chap. vii]: 'Man's fear is honour to God.'

tion, and regards the duty of subjects not less than that of servants. And in the second place, the submission which is required of us carries with it the endurance of wrongs, as the saying is in regard to parents :

[Publilius Syrus, 8.]

> Your father love if he is just ; if not,
> Bear with him.[1]

[Aelian, *Var. Hist.*, IX. xxxiii.] Book XV [iii. 10]. XXVII [xxxiv. 14]. *Annals*, XVI [XII. xi]. *Histories*, VI [IV. viii].

A young man from Eretria, who for a long time had been frequenting the school of Zeno, was asked what he had learned there ; he answered, 'To endure my father's rage.' Of Lysimachus Justin said : 'With greatness of soul he bore the insulting treatment of the king as if it had been that of a father.' In Livy we read : 'Harsh treatment on the part of our country, as on the part of our parents, we must assuage by suffering and enduring.' In Tacitus, again, 'The caprices of kings are to be endured' ; and in another passage, 'We should pray for good emperors, put up with those we have.' Among the Persians, in the commendatory words of Claudian :

[*Against Eutropius*, II. 479 f.]

> Howe'er so cruel masters are,
> They are obeyed.

V.—*That rebellion is not allowable according to the practice of the early Christians*

1. From this law of the Lord the practice of the early Christians,[2] [84] which is a most excellent commentary upon the law, did not depart. Although the administration of the Roman Empire was often in the hands of extremely bad men, and there was no lack of pretenders who opposed them under the pretext of rescuing the state, the Christians never associated themselves with their attempts. In the *Constitutions* of Clement the rule is laid down, 'It is wrong to resist the authority of a king.' Says Tertullian in his *Apology* :

[xxxv.]

> Whence come men like Cassius, and men like Niger, and men like Albinus ? Whence they who beset a Caesar between the two laurels ? Whence they who practise wrestling in order to strangle him ? Whence they who in arms burst into the palace, more audacious than all the men like Sigerius[3] (this is the distinct reading of the manuscript which is in the possession of those distinguished young gentlemen the Dupuys) and Parthenius ?

[1] Terence, *Hecyra* [line 301=III. i. 21] :

> For duty, Parmeno, bids me endure
> The hurts my mother causes.

Cicero, *For Cluentius* [vi. 17] : 'Men ought not only to maintain silence in regard to wrongs done to them by their parents, but even to endure such wrongs patiently.' In regard to this maxim Chrysostom has some fine remarks, *On Second Timothy*, and *Against the Jews*, Book V [VIII. vii].

What Epictetus says [*Manual*, lxv] and after him Simplicius on the two handles, is pertinent here.

[2] To this point canon xviii of the Council of Chalcedon relates, repeated in canon iv of the Trullan Council ; also the Fourth Council of Toledo ; *Capitulary* ii of Charles the Bald, *In Villa Colonia* ; canon v of the Council of Soissons.

[3] Xiphilinus, *Domitian* [Dio Cassius, LXVII. xv] : 'Moreover Parthenius, a chamberlain, and

From among the Romans, if I mistake not, that is from among men who are not Christians.

Tertullian's allusion to the practice of wrestling refers to the murder of Commodus, which was accomplished by the hand of a wrestler acting under the orders of the prefect Aelius Laetus; yet in point of wickedness hardly any one was worse than this emperor. Parthenius, whose crime Tertullian likewise abhors, was the man responsible for the assassination of the extremely bad emperor Domitian. To these Tertullian compares the pretorian prefect, Plautianus, who had wished to kill Septimius Severus—truly a bloodthirsty emperor—in the palace. Arms had been taken up against the same Septimius Severus, under pretence of devotion to the state, by Pescennius Niger in Syria, and by Claudius Albinus in Gaul and Britain. But the action of these men also was displeasing to the Christians, as Tertullian boasts to Scapula. 'We are charged with treason,' he says; 'nevertheless among the followers of Albinus, or of Niger, or of Cassius, no Christians could ever be found.' The followers of Cassius were those who had joined Avidius Cassius, an excellent man; he took up arms in Syria, alleging as the reason that he was going to restore the state, which the neglect of Marcus Aurelius was bringing to ruin. [*To Scapula*, ii.]

2. Ambrose believed that wrong would be done not only to himself but also to his flock and to Christ, by Valentinian, son of Valentinian; yet he would not take advantage of an uprising of the people, who were thoroughly aroused, to offer resistance. 'Although under compulsion', he says, 'I know not how to make resistance.[1] I shall be able to grieve, to weep, to groan; against arms, soldiers, even the Goths, my weapons are my tears. Such are the defences of the clergy; in no other way ought I to offer resistance, in no other way can I resist.' In another passage he adds: 'The demand was made upon me that I calm the people. I made answer that it was my duty not to arouse the people; that the quieting of the people was in the hand of God.' *Against Auxentius*, V [ii; following *Letters*, xxi]. [*Letters*, xx. 10.]

The same Ambrose refused to make use of the troops of Maximus Theodoret, *Eccl. Hist.*, V. iv.

Sigerius, also one of the chamber attendants, together formed a plot to kill him.' Martial, Book IV [*Epigrams*, IV. lxxviii. 8]:

> Your talk is only of Sigerius,
> Parthenius, too, and others of that ilk.

The name was wrongly given not only in Tertullian but also in Suetonius [*Domitian*, xvii], where *Saturius* appears, and again in [Aurelius] Victor, as he is commonly called, where *Casperius* [*Epitome*, xii. 8] is read.

[1] Gratian has inserted these words, *Decretum*, II. xxiii. 8 [21]. The same Ambrose, *Letters*, xxxiii [xx]: 'Do you wish to cast me into chains? That is my desire; I shall not shield myself by means of the crowd round about me.'

Gregory the Great imitated the passage, *Letters*, Book VII. i: 'If I had wished to have a part in the death of the Lombards, to-day the Lombard nation would have neither king, nor dukes, nor counts, and would be dispersed in the utmost disorder.'

against the emperor, though the emperor was both an Arian and a persecutor of the church.

Against Julian, I [xcvi]. In illustration of the same attitude, Gregory Nazianzen declares that Julian the Apostate, while deliberating upon dreadful plans, was held back by the tears of Christians; he adds the reason, 'because this was the only resource they had against the persecutor.' And yet, the army of Julian was almost altogether made up of Christians. There [lxxv.] is the further fact that the cruelty of Julian, as the same Gregory observes, not only worked harm to the Christians but brought the state itself into very great danger. Pertinent is the comment of *Prop.,* lxxiv. Augustine, explaining the words of the Apostle to the Romans: 'For the welfare of this life it is necessary that we be submissive, not offering resistance if they (the rulers) wish to take away anything from us.'

VI.—*The view which holds that it is permissible for subordinate officials to rebel against sovereign authority is refuted, both by argument and by Holy Writ*

1. In our time there are to be met with men who possess learning, it is true, but being too much under the influence of time and place have persuaded first themselves (for so I believe), then others, that what has been said is applicable only to private individuals and not also to subordinate officials.[1] They think that subordinate officials have the right to offer resistance to wrong-doing on the part of him who holds the supreme power; further, [85] that these do wrong if under such conditions they do not offer resistance.

The validity of this opinion ought not to be admitted. Just as in logic an intermediate species,[2] from the point of view of the genus, is a species, but from the point of view of a sub-species is a genus, so subordinate officials from the point of view of officials of lower rank are persons vested with public authority, but from the point of view of those possessing higher authority are private persons. All governmental authority possessed by public officials is in fact so subordinated to the sovereign power that whatever they do contrary to the will of him who holds it is divested of authority and is, accordingly, Averroes, *On Metaph.,* V. vi. to be considered as a private act. The saying of the philosophers is here in place, that an orderly arrangement is possible only in relation to a first point.

2. They who think otherwise seem to me disposed to bring into this world such a condition of affairs as existed in heaven, according

[1] Peter Martyr, *On Judges,* chap. iii; Pareus, *On Romans,* chap. xiii; Junius Brutus; Daneau, *Politici,* Book VI; and others.

[2] [95] 'Special genus', according to Seneca, *Letters,* lviii [VI. vi. 12].

to the tale the ancients used to tell, before a sovereign power arose; for at that time, they said, the lesser gods had not yet submitted to Jupiter. But the orderly arrangement of which I spoke, and the principle of subordination,[1] are recognized not alone by the common sense of mankind. From such recognition came the verse:

> Subject to a kingship still more powerful
> Each kingship is.

[Seneca, *Thyestes*, 612.]

Likewise the words of Papinius: [*Silvae*, III. iii. 49 f.]

> In alternation all is ruled,
> And rules in turn.

Also Augustine's famous statement[2]:

> Consider the gradations of rank in human relations. If a subordinate official has given some order, the thing must be done; nevertheless if the proconsul orders the contrary, it is not to be done. A similar situation arises if the consul issues some order, and the emperor gives a different order. In such a case you do not treat official power with disrespect, but you choose to serve the higher authority; the official of lower rank ought not to be angry if preference is given to the higher.

Decretum, II. xi. 3. 97.

Of Pilate, Augustine said: 'The power which God had given to him was such that he was himself also under the power of Caesar.' *On the Gospel of John* [cxvi. 5].

3. Such subordination is proved also by divine authority. The chief of the Apostles desires that we submit ourselves in one way to the king, in another to public officials. We are to submit ourselves to the king as to the supreme authority, that is without any reservation except in regard to those things which God directly enjoins upon us; and He approves the endurance of wrong and does not forbid it. We are to submit ourselves to public officials as if they had been sent by the king, that is to those who derive their power from the king. When Paul desires that 'every soul be in subjection to the higher powers', he includes also the subordinate public officials. [*I Peter*, ii. 1 [ii. 13 f.]. [*Romans*, xiii. 1.]]

Among the Jewish people, where there were so many kings who treated with contempt divine as well as human law, the subordinate officials, among whom were very many upright and brave men, never assumed to themselves the right to oppose any force to the kings, unless they had received a special command from God, whose right over kings is supreme. On the contrary, Samuel showed what the duty of the elders was when, in the presence of the *I Sam.*, xv. 30.

[1] Thus in the household first the father, then the mother, then the children; after these, the ordinary servants; lastly the under-servants.
See Chrysostom, *On First Corinthians*, xiii. 3 [Homily XXXII, vi].

[2] Augustine has almost the same words in his *On the Words of the Lord*, VI [= *Sermones de Scripturis*, lxii. 13].

elders and the people, he treated Saul with the customary respect, although Saul already was reigning badly.

4. And so among the Jews the condition of public worship also always depended upon the will of the king and the sanhedrin. Since, after the king, the public officials at the same time with the people promised that they would be faithful to God, this must be understood to mean, so far as it would be in the power of each. We have never read that even the images of false gods, which were standing in public places, were ever thrown down except by order of the people, when the state was a free republic, or by that of the kings, when kings were in power. If sometimes violence was used against kings, the fact is reported as evidence of the interposition of divine providence which permitted the deed, not as a mark of approval of the action in the sight of men.

5. The authors who maintain the opposite view are accustomed to bring forward the saying of Trajan, when he handed a dagger to the pretorian prefect: 'Use this for me, if I govern rightly; against me, if I govern badly.' [Xiphil., LXVIII. xvi.] But the fact must be recognized, [86] as is manifest from Pliny's *Panegyric*, [lxvii. 8.] that Trajan made it his particular care to see to it that nothing suggestive of kingly power should appear, but that he should act as truly a chief magistrate,[1] subject, accordingly, to the authority of the senate and the people; their decrees the prefect was bound to carry into effect, even against the chief magistrate himself. The case of Marcus Aurelius was similar; we read of him [Dio VI [Xiphil., LXXI. xxxiii].] that he was unwilling to touch public funds unless authorized by a decree of the senate.

VII.—*What view is to be taken in case of extreme and in other respects unavoidable necessity*

1. More serious is the question whether the law of non-resistance should bind us in case of extreme and imminent peril. Even some laws of God, although stated in general terms, carry a tacit exception in case of extreme necessity. Such a limitation was put upon the law of the Sabbath by learned men in the time of the Maccabees; hence the well-known saying: 'Danger to life breaks the Sabbath.' In Synesius, [*Letters*, iv.] again, a Jew presents this excuse for having violated the law of the Sabbath: 'We were exposed to imminent danger of death.'[2]

This exception was approved by Christ, as also an exception in

[1] This course of action Pertinax and Macrinus afterward imitated; their excellent addresses you may see in Herodian [*Histories*, II. iii. 5–11; IV. xiv. 4–8].

[2] *I Maccabees*, ix. 10, 43, and 44: 'When Bacchides had heard this, he came with a large army to the banks of the Jordan on the very day of the Sabbath. But Jonathan said to his men: "Let us rise up now, and fight for our lives; for our situation now is not as it was yesterday and day before yesterday."'

the case of another law, which forbade the eating of shewbread. The Jewish rabbis, in accordance with an ancient tradition, admit a similar exception in the case of the law forbidding the use of certain articles of food, and in some other cases; and rightly so. This does not mean that God has not the right to oblige us to submit ourselves to certain death; it does mean that since there are some laws of such a nature, we are not to believe that they were given with so inflexible an intent. The same principle holds even more manifestly in the case of human laws.

2. I do not deny that even according to human law certain acts of a moral nature can be ordered which expose one to a sure danger of death; an example is the order not to leave one's post.[1] We are not, however, rashly to assume that such was the purpose of him who laid down the law; and it is apparent that men would not have received so drastic a law applying to themselves and others except as constrained by extreme necessity. For laws are formulated by men and ought to be formulated with an appreciation of human frailty.

Now this law which we are discussing—the law of non-resistance—seems to draw its validity from the will of those who associate themselves together in the first place to form a civil society; from the same source, furthermore, derives the right which passes into the hands of those who govern. If these men could be asked whether they purposed to impose upon all persons the obligation to prefer death rather than under any circumstances to take up arms in order to ward off the violence of those having superior authority, I do not know whether they would answer in the affirmative, unless, perhaps, with this qualification, in case resistance could not be made without a very great disturbance in the state, and without the destruction of a great many innocent people. I do not doubt that to human law also there can be applied what love under such circumstances would commend.

3. Some one may say that this strict obligation, to suffer death rather than at any time to ward off any kind of wrong-doing on the part of those possessing superior authority, has its origin not in human but in divine law. It must be noted, however, that in the first instance men joined themselves together to form a civil society not by command of God, but of their own free will, being influenced by their experience of the weakness of isolated households against attack. From this origin the civil power is derived, and so Peter calls this an *1 Peter,*
ordinance of man. Elsewhere, however, it is also called a divine ii. 13.
ordinance, because God approved an institution which was beneficial

[1] See Josephus, where he speaks of the guards of Saul [*Antiquities of the Jews*, VI. xiii. 9]. Polybius [Suidas, *Lexicon*, under *πρόστιμαν*]: 'Among the Romans death was the penalty inflicted upon one who left his post.'

to mankind. God is to be thought of as approving a human law, however, only as human and imposed after the manner of men.

Adv. Monarchom., III. viii; VI. xxiii, xxiv.

4. Barclay, though a very staunch advocate of kingly authority, nevertheless comes down to this point, that he concedes to the people, and to a notable portion of the people, the right of self-defence against atrocious cruelty, despite the fact that he admits that the entire people is subject to the king. I readily understand that in proportion as that which is preserved is of greater importance, the equity of admitting an exception to the letter of a law is increased. [87] But on the other hand I should hardly dare indiscriminately to condemn either individuals, or a minority which at length availed itself of the last resource of necessity in such a way as meanwhile not to abandon consideration of the common good.

I Sam., xxii. 2; xxiii. 13.

We may illustrate the point from the history of David, who, with the exception of a few deeds, is represented as having passed a life in accordance with the laws. Now David had about him first four hundred armed men, then a considerably larger number; for what purpose, except to defend himself in case violence should be attempted? But at the same time this fact should be noted, that David did not gather this force until after he had been informed by Jonathan, and had learned by numerous and sure evidences from other sources, that Saul was threatening his life. Even then, however, he did not fall upon cities, nor seize opportunities to fight; but he sought hiding-places, sometimes in places difficult of access, sometimes among foreign peoples, and with such scruple that he never did harm to those of his own nation.

5. Comparable with the conduct of David was that of the Maccabees. Their taking up of arms some, indeed, seek to justify on the ground that Antiochus was not their king, but a usurper. This view I consider untenable. For nowhere in their history do the Maccabees, and those who had espoused their cause, address Antiochus with any other title than that of king. And the title was properly applied, since for a considerable period the Jews had acknowledged the sovereignty of the Macedonians, and to their right to rule Antiochus had succeeded. For the rule of law forbidding that a foreigner should be set over the people must be understood as relating to voluntary choice; it has no bearing on that which the people were forced to do when constrained by the necessity of the times.

Others, again, declare that the Maccabees availed themselves of the right of a people entitled to self-government. This argument, however, is as devoid of foundation as the first. For the Jews were first reduced to subjection by Nebuchadnezzar, by right of conquest; and by the same right they rendered obedience to the successors of the Chaldeans, that is, the Medes and Persians, whose entire empire passed under the rule of the Macedonians.[1] Hence Tacitus calls the Jews 'the most insignificant part of those who were in subjection while the East was under the power of the Assyrians, the Medes, and the Persians'. The Jews obtained no concession whatever from Alexander and his successors, but came under their absolute power without any stipulation, just as they had previously been under the power of Darius. If from time to time the Jews were permitted openly to practise their religious rites and to follow their own laws, their right to do so was by sufferance, resting on the goodwill of the kings, not on any legal provision safeguarding their government. *Histories*, I. v [V. viii].

The Maccabees, therefore, had no justification except extreme and unavoidable danger. This justification held, at any rate, as long as they kept within the limits of self-defence, so that, following the example of David, they withdrew into places difficult of access, seeking safety; and as long as they did not use arms except when they were attacked.

6. Meanwhile the caution must be observed that even in such danger, the person of the king must be spared. Those who think that David conformed to this rule not from a sense of duty, but from a higher purpose, are mistaken. For David himself openly said, that no one who laid hands on the king could be innocent. Undoubtedly he knew that it was written in the law: 'Thou shalt not revile the gods', that is the highest judges, 'nor curse a ruler of thy people.'[2] The special mention of the higher powers in this law indicates that something noteworthy is enjoined. Wherefore Optatus of Milevis, speaking of this course of action on the part of David, says: 'A memory filled with the commandments of God held him back.'[3] And into the mouth of David he puts these words: 'I wished to vanquish my enemy; but the first duty is to keep the commandments of God.' *1 Sam.*, xxvi. 9. *Deut.*, xxii. 8 [*Exodus*, xxii. 28]. II [xxv].

7. Malicious false statements are not permissible even against a private individual; accordingly, in the case of a king malicious statements even of what is true must be refrained from, for the reason that, as the author of the *Problems* which bear the name of Aristotle says: 'He who reviles the ruler works [88] injury to the Sec. xl [xxix. 14].

[1] Justin, Book XXXVI [XXXVI. iii]: 'Xerxes, king of the Persians, was the first to conquer the Jews. Afterward along with the Persians themselves they came under the rule of Alexander the Great, and they remained a long time in the power of the Macedonians. Having revolted from Demetrius they sought the friendship of the Romans, and were the first among all the peoples of the Orient to regain their freedom, since the Romans then easily became generous at the expense of another.'

[2] Joab, son of Shimei, in Josephus [*Antiquities of the Jews*, VII. xi. 2]: 'Shall you not die, who have dared to curse him that God has established on the throne?'

[3] In regard to David, Josephus [VI. xiii. 4]: 'But immediately touched with repentance he said that it was wrong to kill his lord'; in a later passage [VI. xiii. 9]: 'He said that it was a terrible crime to slay a king, no matter how wicked; for over the head of one who did such a deed punishment, at the hands of Him who gave the king, would be suspended.'

state.'[1] If, then, harm must not be done to the ruler with speech, surely much less with the hand. Hence we read, that David was filled with penitence because he had violently laid hold of the garment of the king; so profound a sense did he have of the inviolability of the king's person! And not without reason. For since the sovereign power is inevitably exposed to the hatred of many,[2] the security of him who is charged with the exercise of it must be safeguarded in an altogether exceptional way.

1 Sam., xxiv. 6.

This the Romans determined even in the case of the tribunes of the people; they enacted that the tribunes should be safe from seizure, that is inviolable. Among the sayings of the Essenes was this, that kings are to be regarded as holy; and there is a noteworthy expression in Homer:

[*Iliad*, v. 566 f.]

> For the shepherd of the people did he fear,[3]
> Lest harm should come to him.

[X. iii. 3.] Not without reason, we read in Curtius, do 'the nations which are under the government of kings, revere the name of the king as that of a god'. Says Artaban,[4] the Persian: 'Of the many good laws which we have this is the most excellent, that we must reverence and adore the king, as the image of God who preserves all things.' 'It is neither right nor permissible', says Plutarch in his life of *Agis*, 'to lay hands on the person of a king.'

[xix= p. 804 A.]

8. It is a more difficult question to determine whether, in this matter, as much is permitted also to Christians as was permitted to David or to the Maccabees; for the Master of the Christians, on so many occasions bidding them to bear the cross, seems to exact a greater degree of long-suffering. Surely when the higher powers

[1] Julian, *Misopogon* [342 B]: 'Laws in fact are severe in the interest of rulers, so that he who has done harm to a ruler has from excess of feeling trampled the laws under foot.'

[2] Quintilian, *Declamations*, 348: 'This is the situation of all who undertake the government of a state, that in doing the things which in the highest degree concern the common safety they are obliged to subject themselves to a kind of unpopularity.'

See the words of Livia to Augustus on this point, in Xiphilinus, from Dio [Dio Cassius, *Roman History*, LV. xv].

[3] Well does Chrysostom say, *On First Timothy* [i. 1 = Homily I, i]: 'If one kills a sheep, the flock is made smaller by him; but if any one has taken the shepherd out of the midst, the whole flock is scattered by him.'

Seneca, *On Clemency*, Book I, chap. iii [I. iii. 3–5]: 'His [the king's] sleep men protect by night-watches; they press to his sides and surround him in order to defend him; they expose themselves to the dangers which threaten him. Not without reason is this universal custom on the part of the peoples and cities, to protect and love their kings, and to sacrifice themselves and all they have whenever the safety of the ruler demands it. This is not a cheapening of themselves, nor [96] madness, that so many thousands give themselves to the sword for the sake of one and with many deaths ransom a single life, not infrequently the life of one who is aged and feeble. Just as the whole body is under the domination of the mind'—what immediately follows is merely an expanding of the thought—'so this vast multitude, which environs the life of one, is ruled by his spirit, is swayed by his reason, destined to overburden itself and break up into parts unless sustained by his wisdom. Men therefore devote themselves to their own safety,' etc.

Add what is said below in II. i. 9.

[4] In Plutarch, *Themistocles* [xxvii= 125 C].

threaten death to Christians on account of their religion, Christ concedes to them the right to flee—to those, at any rate, whom the necessary discharge of duty does not bind to a particular place. Beyond the right to flee, he makes no concession. Peter, in fact, says that in suffering Christ left to us an example that we should follow; though he was free from sin, and without guile, 'when he was reviled he reviled not again; when he suffered, threatened not, but committed himself to Him that judgeth righteously.' He says also that Christians ought to return thanks to God, and rejoice, if as Christians they suffer punishment. And we read that the Christian religion waxed strong chiefly by reason of such long-suffering. *I Peter*, iv. 12–16.

9. Thus the early Christians, fresh from the teachings of the Apostles and of Apostolic men, both understood the Christian rules of conduct better, and lived up to them more fully, than did the men of later times; wherefore I think that the greatest injustice is done to them by those who think that their reason for not defending themselves, when in certain danger of death, was lack of strength, not intention. Imprudent, surely, and devoid of shame, would Tertullian have been if, in the presence of the emperors, who could not be in ignorance of the facts, he had dared with so much assurance to lie when he said: [*Apology*, xxxvii.]

> If we wished to act as open enemies, and not merely as secret avengers, should we lack the power of numbers and of forces? Are the Moors, forsooth, and the Marcomans, and even the Parthians, or all the nations which, in contrast with us, are confined to one region and hemmed in by their own boundaries—are they more numerous than we, who are spread over the whole earth? Strangers we are, and yet we have filled all places belonging to you, your cities, islands, fortified posts, towns, places of assembly, even your camps; your tribes, town-councils, palace, senate, Forum. Only your temples have we left to you. What war should we not have been capable of undertaking, and ready to undertake, even if inferior in forces—we who are so willingly slaughtered—if according to our doctrine it were not more lawful to suffer ourselves to be killed than to kill?

In this matter Cyprian, too, follows his teacher, and openly affirms: 'This is the reason why no one of us offers resistance, when he is seized, or tries to avenge himself for unjust violence on your part, albeit our people are numerous and well provided with means; sure confidence in a future vengeance makes us patient. The innocent yield to the guilty.'[1] 'For', says Lactantius, 'we put our trust [89] in the majesty of Him who is able to exact vengeance alike for contempt for Himself and for sufferings and wrongs inflicted on His servants. *To Demetrianus* [xvii]. V [xxi. 9–10].

[1] These words are in the treatise *To Demetrianus* [chap. xvii]. Elsewhere (*Letters*, I. i) the same author says: Our opponent 'understood that the soldiers of Christ are watchful, that they are sober and stand armed for battle, that they cannot be conquered, that they can die; and for this very reason they are unconquerable, because they do not fear to die, and they do not fight against those who attack them, since it is not permitted to them, although innocent, to slay one who is guilty, but they freely give both their lives and their blood.'

And so, when we are suffering outrages unspeakable, we do not resist, even with a word; but we leave vengeance to God.'

On Joshua, VI, qu. x [*On Heptateuch*, VI. x]. *Letters*, clxvi [cv. 7].

This is precisely what Augustine had in mind, when he said: 'In such circumstances let the just man above all reflect, that only he for whom it is right to wage war should commence war; for this is not right for all men.' 'Whenever the emperors', says Augustine in another passage, 'hold a mistaken view, in order to protect their delusion against the truth they establish laws through the enforcement of which the upright are tested and receive the crown.' In still another passage he writes: 'Peoples should bear with rulers, and slaves with masters, in such a way that they may sustain themselves under temporal ills through the exercise of endurance, and hope for blessings that abide forever.' Elsewhere, speaking of the example of earlier Christians, he thus characterizes it:

[*On Psalms*, cxxiv. 8.]

City of God, XXII [vi. 1].

And at that time the city of Christ, although it was still wandering over the earth and was able to muster armies of so great peoples against impious persecutors, did not fight for temporal safety, but, rather, refrained from resisting, that it might obtain eternal safety. Christians were bound, were imprisoned, were beaten, were twisted on the rack, were tortured with fire, were mangled, were slaughtered, and yet they multiplied. It was not for them to fight for safety, save only to scorn the safety of this world in comparison with salvation.

[*On John*, xviii. 10.]

10. The words of Cyril, commenting on the passage in John about the sword of Peter, are of the same import, and not less noteworthy.

The Theban legion, as the *Acts* [of martyrdom] informs us, consisted of six thousand six hundred and sixty-six soldiers, all of whom were Christians. When the emperor Maximian, being in the neighbourhood of Martigny, tried to force his army to offer sacrifice to false gods, this legion started to march to Agaunum [St. Maurice]. When the emperor sent a messenger thither to order them to come and sacrifice, the soldiers of the legion refused. Maximian thereupon ordered that every tenth man be put to death by his aids, who easily carried out the order, since no one offered resistance.

11. The ranking officer of the legion was Maurice,[1] whose name was afterwards given to the town of Agaunum. On the authority of Eucherius, bishop of Lyons, we read that at this juncture Maurice addressed his men as follows:

[1] In regard to the honours paid to this martyr among the Swiss, see Guilleman [*History of Switzerland*, I. xv and II. viii].

In an ancient account of the transfer of the relics of Saint Justin to New Corbie we read: 'Whence, in accordance with the trustworthy character of the *Chronicles*, we conclude that he suffered in that most cruel and unparalleled persecution, the tenth after the persecution under Nero. This was more terrible than the preceding persecutions in that it sent to heaven an imposing host of martyrs, among whom a notable company were the companions of Saint Maurice, and the mirror of innocence.'

On the transfer of the relics of Theban martyrs to Brunswick see Krantz, *History of Saxony*, VII. xvi.

How I did fear that some one of you—it is such an easy thing for armed men to do—under the appearance of self-defence would try to prevent these most blessed funeral rites! For my part, in order to forbid such an act I was already on the point of following the example of our Christ, who with a command uttered by his own voice put back into the sheath the sword that had been drawn out by the Apostle. Thus he teaches us that the courage which comes from trust in Christ is stronger than all arms, in order that no one may with mortal hands try to stay a mortal work; nay rather, that each may complete the work begun, through unfaltering loyalty to his faith.

After the decimation, the emperor gave the same order to the survivors as before. They all replied:

Caesar, as soldiers we belong to you, and we took up arms in order to defend the Roman state. We have never deserted in the presence of war, nor evaded the requirements of military service, nor incurred the disgrace of punishment for cowardice. We should always be obedient to your orders also, excepting that, as instructed in the rules of the Christian life, we must avoid the worship of demons and their altars always polluted with blood. We have learned that you are determined either to defile us Christians with sacrilegious acts, or to cow us by decimation. You have no need to spend longer time searching us out as if we were concealing ourselves: know that we are all Christians. You will have the bodies of us all in your power; over our souls, which look only to their Master, Christ, you will have no power.

12. Then Exsuperius, standard-bearer of the legion, it is said, addressed it thus:

Most excellent fellow-soldiers, you see that I carry standards of the wars of this world. But not to such arms do I summon you, not for such wars do I seek to arouse your spirits and courage. It is yours to choose a different kind of battle. Not through the use of these swords can you press forward to the kingdom of heaven.

Then he bade carry this message to the emperor: 'Despair, which is most brave in perils, Emperor, has not armed us against you Look, we are holding [90] our weapons, and shall resist not,[1] because we prefer to die rather than conquer, and we are more eager to perish in innocency than to live in guilt.' Afterward he said: 'We are throwing away our weapons. Your followers will find our right hands weaponless, but our hearts armed with the catholic faith.'

13. Thereupon a butchery of the unresisting men followed. In his account of it Eucherius uses these words: 'The greatness of the number did not protect these righteous men from punishment, though generally when a great number is involved in an infraction of law punishment is not enforced.' In an ancient *Martyrology* the story is thus told:

And so they were cut down indiscriminately with swords, not uttering a cry of protest; they even laid aside their weapons and offered their throats or bared bodies

[1] Similar are the words of the Alexandrian Jews addressed to Flaccus [rather, addressed by Jews of Judaea to Petronius; Philo, *On the Embassy to Gaius*, chap. xxxii]: 'Unarmed we are, as you see, and yet some bring charges against us as if we were public enemies. Even those members which nature gave to us for self-defence we have put behind us, where they can do nothing; we offer our bodies unprotected and ready to suffer the attack of those who shall wish to kill us.'

to their slayers. They were not stirred by the greatness of their number or by the movement of their weapons, to defend with steel the justice of their cause. They remembered only this, that they were confessing Him who was led to death without uttering a cry of protest; as a lamb he opened not his mouth. They, also, as a flock of sheep of the Lord suffered themselves to be torn in pieces as by wolves rushing upon them.

14. Valens [1] impiously and cruelly raged against those who, in accordance with the Holy Scriptures and the tradition of the fathers, professed the 'homoousian' doctrine. Although the number of believers was very great, they never defended themselves with arms.

1 Peter, ii. 21. *Matthew*, x. 39. *Luke*, xii. 33 [xvii. 33].

15. Surely when long-suffering is enjoined upon us, the example of Christ, we see, is often brought forward for our imitation, as we just now heard in the case of the Theban soldiers; and His long-suffering was prolonged even until death. He who thus loses his life is declared by Christ truly to have gained it.

We said that resistance cannot rightly be made to those who hold the sovereign power. There are certain points which we now ought to bring to the reader's attention, in order that he may not consider those guilty of disobeying this law who in reality are not guilty.

VIII.—*That the right to make war may be conceded against him who has the chief authority among a free people*

First, then, if rulers responsible to the people, whether such power was conferred at the beginning or under a later arrangement, as at Sparta [2]—if such rulers transgress against the laws and the state, not only can they be resisted by force, but, in case of necessity, they can be punished with death. An example is the case of Pausanias, king of the Lacedaemonians. And since the earliest kingships of Italy were of this character, it is not surprising that, after narrating the exceedingly dreadful crimes of Mezentius, Virgil adds:

> Then all Etruria in just anger rose; [3]
> The punishment of death forthwith demand
> They for their king.

[1] See the excerpts from John of Antioch, published from the manuscript of Nicholas Peiresc, a man worthy of everlasting memory.

[2] Plutarch, *Lysander* [xxx= p. 450]: 'The Spartans summoned their king to trial for his life, but he evaded it and fled to Tegea.'

The same author, *Sulla* [*Comparison of Lysander and Sulla*, ii= 476 C]: 'The Spartans took away the kingship from some of their kings, on the ground that they were not fitted to be kings, but were insignificant and of no account.'

In regard to Agis who was condemned unjustly, but nevertheless condemned, see the same Plutarch [*Agis*, xix= 803 D–F].

The Mosynoecians punished their king by starvation; Mela, Book II [I. xix].

[3] And in respect to those who were rising against Mezentius the Etruscan soothsayer said [Virgil, *Aeneid*, VIII. 500 f.]:

> Whom against the foe
> Just resentment urges.

IX.—*That the right to make war may be conceded against a king who has abdicated the sovereign power*

In the second place, if a king, or any other person, has renounced his governmental authority, or manifestly has abandoned it, after that time proceedings of every kin are permissible against him as against a private person. But he is by no means to be considered as having renounced a thing who is merely too neglectful of it.

X.—*That the right to make war may be conceded against a king who alienates his kingdom, but only so far as to prevent the transfer*

In the third place, Barclay holds the opinion that if a king alienates his kingdom, or places it in subjection to another, the kingdom is no longer his. Book IV. xvi.

I do not go so far. For an act of this character, if the kingship is conferred by election or by a law of succession, is null and void, and acts which are null and void do not have any effect in law. Nearer the truth, in my opinion, is the view of the jurists in regard to a usufructuary, to whose position, we have said, that of such a king is analogous; by alienating his right to a third person the usufructuary effects nothing. And the statement that the usufruct reverts to the owner of the property must be construed in accordance with the period fixed by law. *Instit.* II. iv, § 3. *Digest*, XXIII. iii. 66.

If, nevertheless, a king actually does undertake to alienate his kingdom, or to place it in subjection, I have no doubt that in this case he can be resisted. For the sovereign power, as we have said, is one thing, the manner of holding it is another; and a people can oppose a change in the manner of holding the sovereign power, for the reason that this is not comprised in the sovereign power itself. With this you may not ineptly compare a remark of Seneca, in respect to a case by no means dissimilar: [91] 'And if a man is bound to render obedience in all respects to his father, he is not bound to be obedient to a command through which the father ceases to be a father.' *Controversies*, II. ix [ix. 20].

XI.—*That the right to make war may be conceded against a king who openly shows himself the enemy of the whole people*

In the fourth place, says the same Barclay, the kingdom is forfeited if a king sets out with a truly hostile intent to destroy a whole people.[1]

[1] For a like reason Gracchus ingeniously maintained that he who is tribune of the people ceased by right to be such; his words are worth reading, in Plutarch [*Tiberius Gracchus*, xv = p. 831 D].

John Major, on the fourth book of the *Sentences* [of Peter Lombard], says that a people cannot [97] deprive itself of the power of deposing the prince in the event that he shows a disposition to destroy it. The principle is readily developed from what is said here.

This I grant, for the will to govern and the will to destroy cannot coexist in the same person. The king, then, who acknowledges that he is an enemy of the whole people, by that very fact renounces his kingdom. This, it is evident, can hardly occur in the case of a king possessed of his right mind, and ruling over a single people. Of course, if a king rules over several peoples, it can happen that he may wish to have one people destroyed for the sake of another, in order that he may colonize the territory thus made vacant.

XII.—*That the right to make war may be conceded against a king who has lost his kingdom in consequence of a commissory law*

Fifthly, if a kingdom be granted under the condition that upon the commission of felony against the overlord, or the violation of a clause inserted in the grant of power, that if the king do thus and so [1] the subjects are released from all duty of obedience to him, in such a case also the king reverts to the position of a private person.

XIII.—*That the right to make war may be conceded against a king who, possessing only a part of the sovereign power, seeks to possess himself of the part that does not belong to him*

Sixthly, in case the sovereign power is held in part by the king, in part by the people or senate,[2] force can lawfully be used against the king if he attempts to usurp that part of the sovereign power which does not belong to him, for the reason that this authority does not extend so far.

In my opinion this principle holds, even though it has already been said that the power to make war should be reserved to the king. For this, it must be understood, refers to external war. For the rest, whoever possesses a part of the sovereign power must possess also the right to defend his part; in case such a defence is resorted to, the king may even lose his part of the sovereign power by right of war.

XIV.—*That the right to make war is conceded against a king in case liberty to offer resistance has in certain cases been reserved*

Seventhly, if in the conferring of authority it has been stated that in a particular case the king can be resisted,[3] even though such

[1] For the kingdom of Arragon see Mariana [*History of Spain*], Book VIII.

[2] An example you find in the Genoese republic, Bizarri [*History of Genoa*], Book XVIII [p. 414]; in Bohemia in the time of Wenceslaus [Dubraw], *History*, Book X. Add Azor, *Moral Institutes*, Book X, chap. viii, and Lambert von Aschaffenburg, in regard to Henry IV.

[3] See the examples in De Thou's *History*, Book CXXXI, in the account of the year 1604, and in Book CXXXIII, in the account of the year 1605, both in relation to Hungary; in Meyer [*Annals of*

an agreement does not involve the retention of a part of the authority, some natural freedom of action, at any rate, has been reserved and exempted from the exercise of royal power. For he who alienates his own right can by agreement limit the right transferred.

XV.—*How far obedience should be rendered to a usurper of sovereign power*

1. We have spoken of him who possesses, or has possessed, the right of governing. It remains to speak of the usurper of power, not after he has acquired a right through long possession or contract, but while the basis of possession remains unlawful. Now while such a usurper is in possession, the acts of government which he performs may have a binding force, arising not from a right possessed by him, for no such right exists, but from the fact that the one to whom the sovereignty actually belongs, whether people, or king, or senate, would prefer that measures promulgated by him should meanwhile have the force of law, in order to avoid the utter confusion which would result from the subversion of laws and suppression of the courts.

Vict., *De Potest. Civ.*, no. 23; Suarez, *De Legibus*, III. x. 9. Lessius, *De Iust. et Iure*, II. xxix, dub. 5 [9], no. 73.

Cicero disapproved of the laws of Sulla as harsh toward the children of the proscribed, whom they did not permit to become candidates for public office. Nevertheless he thought that it was necessary to live up to them, asserting, as Quintilian informs us, that the welfare of the state was so bound up with these laws that if they should be done away with the state itself could not survive. Of the acts of the same Sulla, Florus says: 'Lepidus was making ready to annul the acts of this great man; and there was good reason for such procedure, provided only the result could be accomplished without bringing disaster upon the state.' A little further on he adds: 'The interest of the state, sick, as it were, and suffering from injuries, required that it have rest in any way possible, in order that the wounds might not be torn open by the application of remedies.'

[*Institutes of Oratory*,] XI. i. [85].

[III. xxiii.]

2. In the case of measures promulgated by the usurper which are not so essential, and which have as their purpose to establish him in his unlawful possession, obedience is not to be rendered unless disobedience would involve grave danger. But whether it is permissible to use violence in overthrowing such a usurper of authority, or even to put him to death, is the question before us.

Belgium] under the year 1339, on the subject of Brabant and Flanders; and under the year 1468, in relation to the treaty between the king of France and Charles of Burgundy.

Add, in regard to Poland, what Chytraeus has, *History of Saxony*, Book XXIV; and in relation to Hungary, Bonfini, [*History of Hungary*,] Decade IV, Book IX.

XVI.—*That resistance by force may be used against a usurper by virtue of a right of war still continuing*

In the first place, if the usurper has seized the governmental power by means of a war that is unlawful and not in accordance with the law of nations, and no agreement has been entered into afterward, and no [92] promise has been given to him, but possession is maintained by force alone, it would seem that the right to wage war against him still remains, and whatever is permissible against any enemy is permissible against him. Just as an enemy, so also a usurper, under such conditions, can lawfully be put to death by any one, even by an individual. 'Against men guilty of treason and against public *Apology* [ii]. enemies', says Tertullian, 'every man is a soldier.'

Code, III. xxvii. 2. Thus also, in the interest of general tranquillity, the right of enforcing public punishment against deserters from military service is granted to all.

XVII.—*That resistance by force may be used against a usurper by virtue of a pre-existing law*

[=p. 570 C D.] With Plutarch, who expresses the opinion in his book *On Fate* dedicated to Piso, I hold that the same conclusion must be accepted in the case that prior to the usurpation there was in existence a public law which conferred upon any man the right to kill a person who dared to do this or that which falls within its purview; who, for example, though a private individual, should have surrounded himself with a bodyguard and should have seized the citadel; who had put to death a citizen uncondemned, or without lawful judgement; or who had chosen public officials without regular elections.

Many such laws were in force in the Greek states, and in consequence the killing of tyrants of the sort referred to must have been thought justifiable. Such, at Athens, was the law of Solon, which was renewed after the return from the Piraeus; this was directed against those who should have done away with the popular form of government, or who, after it had been done away with, should hold office. Of similar character was the Valerian Law[1] at Rome, against any who should assume the duties of a public official without the authorization of the people. Such, again, was the consular law passed after the absolute rule of the Decemvirs, forbidding the appointment of any magistrate whose decisions should be without appeal; the man

[1] Plutarch, *Publicola* [xii= 103 B]: 'Giving permission without trial to kill him who purposed to rule as a tyrant.' Later he adds [*Comparison of Solon and Publicola*, ii= 110 C]: 'If any one should attempt to rule as a tyrant, Solon appointed a penalty only after conviction, but Publicola gave permission to kill him even before a trial.'

responsible for such an appointment might be lawfully and rightfully slain.

XVIII.—*That resistance by force may be used against a usurper by virtue of a mandate of one possessing sovereign power*

It will likewise be permissible to put a usurper to death in case the deed is explicitly authorized by the true possessor of sovereign power, whether king, or senate, or people.

To these we should add also guardians of the children of kings, such as Jehoiada was in the case of Joash, when he forced Athaliah from the kingship. *2 Chron.*, xxiii.

XIX.—*Why resistance to a usurper should be limited to the cases mentioned*

1. Outside of the cases which have been considered I cannot concede that it is permissible for a private citizen either to put down by force, or to kill, a usurper of sovereign power. For it may happen that he who holds the sovereign power by right would prefer that the usurper should be left in possession rather than that the way should be opened for dangerous and bloody conflicts, such as generally take place when those who have a strong following among the people, or friends outside the country, are treated with violence or put to death. At any rate, it is not certain that the king or the people would wish that matters should be brought to such extremities, and without their known approval the use of violence cannot be lawful.

Favonius used to say, 'Civil war is a worse evil than unlawful government.' [Plutarch, *Brutus*, xii=989 A.] 'To me', Cicero declared, 'peace on any terms between citizens seems more advantageous than civil war.' [*Philippics*, II. xv. 37.] Titus Quintius affirmed that it was better that the tyrant Nabis[1] be left in power in Sparta, for the reason that his expulsion could be accomplished only with utter ruin of the state, which through the attempt to retain its liberty would be brought to destruction. Livy, XXXIV [xlix]. Of similar purport is the thought of Aristophanes, that a lion ought not to be reared in a city; but if a lion has been so reared, the people must endure it. [*Frogs*, 1431 f.]

1 This is explained by Plutarch in the life of Titus Quintius [*T. Quintius Flamininus*, xiii=376 E] as follows: 'When he saw that the tyrant could not be destroyed without serious hurt to the other Spartans.'

Nor foreign to this subject is what Plutarch relates in his *Lycurgus* [xx=52 E], that a certain Spartan, having read the lines

> As tyranny they sought through Mars to quench,
> Mars, merciless, before Selinus' walls
> Swept them away,

made answer: 'The men met a just death; for they ought to have waited till tyranny should burn itself out.'

[*Histories*, IV. lxvii.] 2. An exceedingly weighty question it surely is, as Tacitus says, which is preferable, independence or peace; it is an extremely *Letters to Atticus*, IX. iv. difficult political problem, Cicero found, to determine 'whether, when one's country is oppressed by an unlawful exercise of power, every effort should be put forth to accomplish its abolition, even if the state should thereby be brought into extreme peril'. Yet individuals ought not to take it upon themselves to decide a question which involves the interest of the whole people. That is, then, an obviously mischievous sentiment:

[Lucan, I. 351.]

> We are taking away the masters
> From a city content to serve them.[1]

Appian, *Civil Wars*, I [vii. 57]. Thus Sulla, being asked why he was attacking his country with arms, made answer, [93] 'in order to deliver it from tyrants'.

3. Better advice was given by Plato in his letter to Perdiccas, *Letters*, I [ix. 18]. as thus expressed in Latin by Cicero: 'Your efforts in public affairs should be carried only so far as shall meet the approval of your fellow citizens; violence should not be used against either a parent or *Jugurthine War* [iii. 3]. native land.' The same thought is found also in Sallust: 'To govern one's country or one's subjects by force, even if you possess the power and may be correcting abuses, is nevertheless unsuitable, especially since all sweeping changes involve slaughter, flight, and other incidents of a hostile nature.'

Not far from this point of view is the remark of Stallius quoted [xii= p. 989 A.] by Plutarch, in his *Life of Brutus*: 'It is not fair that a man who is prudent and wise should plunge into the midst of dangers and troubles for the benefit of those who are without scruple and devoid of sense.' Not inappropriately in the same connexion you may quote the state- *On Duties*, II. ii [II. xxi. 102]. ment of Ambrose:

> This also contributes to the increase of good reputation, if you rescue a poor man from the hands of the mighty, and if you save from death a man who has been condemned, in so far as such a result can be accomplished without raising a disturbance. We must beware lest we seem to act for the sake of display rather than pity, and cause more grievous wounds while we are trying to apply remedies to wounds of less consequence.

II. ii, qu. 42, art. 2. Thomas says that the destruction of a government even though tyrannical is sometimes an act of sedition.

Judges, iii. 15; *Nehem.*, ix. 27. 4. The deed of Ehud, which he committed upon Eglon, king of Moab, ought not to incline us to the opposite view. For the sacred text plainly bears witness that Ehud was raised up by God Himself as an avenger, that is to say, under a special command. And in fact it is not clear that this king of the Moabites did not possess his right of governing by virtue of an agreement. For in the case of other kings

[1] Plutarch in *Cato the Elder* [xii=342 F], speaking of Antiochus the Great: 'He made it his pretext for war to free the Greeks, who had no lack of freedom.'

also, God caused His judgements to be executed by means of chosen servants, as in the case of Joram by the hand of Jehu. *2 Kings*, ix.

XX.—*When the right of sovereignty is in dispute private persons ought not to take it upon themselves to settle the matter*

Above all, in case of a controversy the private individual ought not to take it upon himself to pass judgement, but should accept the fact of possession.

Thus Christ bade that tribute be paid to Caesar because the coin bore Caesar's image,[1] that is because Caesar was in possession of the governing power. *Matthew*, xxii. 20.

[1] This is the most sure indication of possession; see Bizarri, *History of Genoa*, Book XVIII 423].

[98] CHAPTER V

WHO MAY LAWFULLY WAGE WAR

I.—*The efficient causes of war are in part those who wage war on their own account as principals*

As in other matters, so also in acts originating in the will, there are ordinarily three kinds of efficient causes—principal agents, auxiliary agents, and instruments.

In war the principal efficient cause is generally the person whose interest is at stake—in private war, the individual; in public war, the public power, in most cases the sovereign power. Whether war can be made by one on behalf of others who do not make war on their own account, we shall see elsewhere. Meanwhile we shall hold to this principle, that by nature every one is the defender of his own rights; that is the reason why hands were given to us.

II.—*The efficient causes of war are in part those who wage war on another's account, as auxiliary agents*

Digest, XVIII. vii. 7. Cicero, *On Duties*, II [v. 16], following Panaetius. Doctors, *On Dig.*, XLVII. ii. 7. *Code*, X. i. 5. *Rhetoric to Alexander*, iii [ii].

1. But to render service to another, so far as we can, is not only permissible, it is also honourable. Those who have written on the subject of duties rightly say that nothing is more useful to a man than another man. There are, however, various ties which bind men together and summon them to mutual aid. Thus those who are related by kinship unite to assist one another. Neighbours, too, and those who belong to the same state, call on one another for help; hence the cry 'Hither, Romans' and the word 'to call the Romans' (*quiritari*). Aristotle said that every man ought to take up arms on his own behalf, if he had suffered wrong, or on behalf of his kindred or benefactors, or of his associates, in case wrong should have been suffered by them. It was the teaching of Solon [1] that those commonwealths will be the most fortunate in which each citizen views the wrongs of others as his own.

2. But in default of all other ties, the common bond of human

[1] The words are quoted by Plutarch [*Solon*, xviii = 88 D]: 'Of cities that is the best to live in, in which those who have not suffered wrong, not less than those who have, put forth effort to punish them who attempt to do wrong.'

Pertinent are the words of Plautus, *Rudens* [III. ii. 12 = line 626]:

Wring the neck of injury
Before she reaches you.

nature is sufficiently strong. Devoid of interest to man is nothing that pertains to man. In the words of Menander[1]:

> If we our strength should all together join,
> Viewing each other's welfare as our own,
> If we should each exact full punishment
> From evil-doers for the wrongs they do,
> The shameless violence of wicked men
> Against the innocent would not prevail;
> Guarded on every hand, and forced to pay
> The penalties which their misdeeds deserve,
> They soon would cease to be, or few become.

Bartolus, *On Dig.*, I. i. 3; 7 and 8; Jason, same, 29. Castren., *On Dig.*, I. i. 1, § 4. Bartolus, *On Dig.*, XLIX. xv. 24, 9. Innocent, *On Decretals*, II. xxiv. 13, and II. xiii. 12, no. 16. Panormitanus, no. 18. Sylvester, word *bellum*, qu. 8.

Similar is this saying of Democritus[2]: 'Those who are oppressed by wrong-doing must be defended to the limit of our strength, and not neglected; for that is a work of justice and goodness.' The thought is thus developed by Lactantius:

> God, who did not impart wisdom to the other animals, made them more safe from attack and from danger by natural means of defence. But because He made man naked and weak, to the end that He might the rather equip him with wisdom, in addition to other gifts He gave to man this feeling of mutual regard, that man should defend, should love, should protect man, and should both receive and furnish help against all dangers.

Divine Institutes, VI. [x. 3].

III.—*The efficient causes of war are in part those who wage war as instruments, as servants and subjects*

When we use the word 'instruments' in this connexion we do not mean 'weapons' and similar things; we mean persons whose acts of will are dependent on the will of another.

An instrument, as we use the term here, is a son in relation to his father, viewed as by nature a part, so to speak, of the father; such an instrument also is a slave in relation to his master, a part, as it were, in a legal sense. For just as a part is a part of the whole not only in the same relation that the whole sustains to the part, but also the very thing which constitutes a part pertains to the whole, so possession becomes something [99] of the possessor. Says Democritus,[3] 'Use slaves just as parts of the body, one for one purpose, another for another.' What a slave is in the household, a subject is in the state, an instrument, accordingly, of the ruler.

Code, XI. xlviii. 22. Aristotle, *On Morals* [*Nic. Ethics*], V. x. *Code*, IX. ix. 4. Sen. I. iv.

IV.—*By the law of nature no one is enjoined from waging war*

There is no doubt that by nature all subjects may be used for purposes of war; but certain classes are exempted by special enact-

[1] [In Stobaeus, xliii. 30.]
[2] [In Stobaeus, xlvi. 43.]
[3] [In Stobaeus, lxii. 45.]

ment, as formerly slaves[1] at Rome, now men in holy orders[2] generally. Nevertheless a special enactment of this kind, as such laws generally, must be understood as subject to exception in cases of extreme necessity.

Thomas, II. ii. 40, art. 2.
Sylvester, word *bellum*, III.

Let these general statements in regard to auxiliary agents and subjects suffice; for the special questions relating to them will be treated in the proper connexion.

[1] Servius, *On the Aeneid*, IX [line 544=547].

[2] The Levites were in olden times exempt from military service, as Josephus remarked [*Antiquities of the Jews*, III. xii. 4]. For the clerics see Nicetas of Chonae, Book VI; *Capitularies* of Charles the Bald, *In Sparnaco*, xxxvii, in Gratian, *Decretum*, I. v. 5 [I. l. 5] and II. xxiii. 8. Such are the canons; but consult Anna Comnena [X. viii. 7] to see how much more strictly they were observed by the Greeks than by the Latins.

END OF BOOK I

[100]

HUGO GROTIUS

ON

THE LAW OF WAR AND PEACE

BOOK II

CHAPTER I

THE CAUSES OF WAR: FIRST, DEFENCE OF SELF AND PROPERTY

I.—*What causes of war may be called justifiable*

1. Let us proceed to the causes of war—I mean justifiable causes; for there are also other causes which influence men through regard for what is expedient and differ from those that influence men through regard for what is right.

The two kinds of causes Polybius accurately distinguishes from each other and from beginnings of war,[1] such as the [wounding of the] stag was in the war between Aeneas and Turnus. Although the distinction between these matters is clear, nevertheless the words applied to them are often confused. For what we call justifiable causes Livy, in the speech of the Rhodians, called beginnings: 'You certainly are Romans [2] who claim that your wars are so fortunate because they are just, and pride yourselves not so much on their outcome, in that you gain the victory, as upon their beginnings, because you do not undertake wars without cause.' *Histories*, III [vi f.]. [Virgil, *Aeneid*, VII. 483.] XVI [xxii. 5].

In the same sense also Aelian (in Book XII, chapter liii) speaks of the beginnings of wars, and Diodorus Siculus (Book XIV), giving an account of the war of the Lacedaemonians against the Eleans, expresses the same idea by using the words 'pretexts' and 'beginnings'.[3] [XIV xvii].

2. These justifiable causes are the special subject of our discussion. Pertinent thereto is the famous saying of Coriolanus quoted by Dionysius of Halicarnassus: 'This, I think, ought to be your first concern, that you have a cause for war which is free from reproach and just.' Similarly Demosthenes says: 'As the substructures of houses, the framework of ships, and similar things ought VIII [viii]. *Olynthiacs*, II. x [=20–1].

[1] [109] Virgil [*Aeneid*, VII. 40] calls these 'the beginnings of battle' (*exordia pugnae*).

[2] Certainly, hardly any race has remained for so long a time scrupulous in examining into the causes of war. Thus in Suidas, under the word ἐμβαίνειν, Polybius says: 'The Romans have striven earnestly for this, that they be not the first to lay violent hands upon their neighbours, but that it should always be believed that they proceeded against an enemy in order to ward off injuries.' Dio Cassius, *Excerpta Peiresciana* [Diodorus Siculus, p. 314, 316], manifests the same point of view in an excellent comparison of the Romans with Philip of Macedon and King Antiochus; and again in the *Selections on Embassies* he says: 'The ancients thus did nothing in haste, to the end that they might begin their wars justly.' And again, *Excerpta Peiresciana*, p. 341 [also Diodorus] the same author says: 'The Romans desire earnestly that the wars which they undertake be just and that they decree nothing of that sort without cause or rashly.'

[3] Procopius, *Gothic War*, III [III. xxxiv] calls these 'just occasions'. See also below, beginning of chap. xxii of this book.

to be most firm, so, in the case of actions, the causes and fundamental reasons[1] ought to be in accord with justice and truth.' Equally pertinent is the statement of Dio Cassius: [101] 'We must give the fullest consideration to justice. With justice on our side, military prowess warrants good hope; without it, we have nothing sure, even if the first successes equal our desires.' Cicero also says, 'Those wars are unjust which have been undertaken without cause'; and in another passage he criticizes Crassus because Crassus had determined to cross the Euphrates without any cause[2] for war.

XII [XLI. xxxii].

On the Commonwealth, III [xxiii. 35].

[*On Ends*, III. xxii. 75.]

3. What has been said is no less true of public than of private wars. Hence the complaint of Seneca:

Letters, xcvi [xcv. 30].

> We try to restrain murders and the killing of individuals. Why are wars and the crime of slaughtering nations full of glory? Avarice and cruelty know no bounds. In accordance with decrees of the Senate and orders of the people atrocities are committed, and actions forbidden to private citizens are commanded in the name of the state.[3]

Wars that are undertaken by public authority have, it is true, in some respects a legal effect, as do judicial decisions, which we shall need to discuss later; but they are not on that account more free from wrong if they are undertaken without cause. Thus Alexander, if he commenced war on the Persians and other peoples without cause, was deservedly called a brigand by the Scythians, according to Curtius, as also by Seneca[4]; likewise by Lucan he was styled a robber, and by the sages of India 'a man given over to wickedness', while a pirate once put Alexander in the same class with himself. Similarly, Justin tells how two kings of Thrace were deprived of their royal power by Alexander's father, Philip, who exemplified the deceit and wickedness of a brigand. In this connexion belongs the saying of Augustine: 'If you take away justice, what are empires if not vast robberies?' In full accord with such expressions is the statement of Lactantius: 'Ensnared by the appearance of empty glory, men give to their crimes the name of virtue.'

[II. iii f.]

[VII. viii. 19.] [X. 21.]

Arrian [*Anabasis of Alexander*], VII [i].

[VIII. iii. 15.]

On the City of God, IV. iv.

On the False Religion, I [*Divine Institutes*, I. xviii].

4. No other just cause for undertaking war can there be excepting injury received. 'Unfairness of the opposing side occasions just wars,' said the same Augustine, using 'unfairness' when he meant

On the City of God, IV [XIX. vii].

[1] So also Julian said 'excuse' for war in his oration *On the Praises of Constantius* [ii = p. 95 B Span.].

[2] Appian [*Civil Wars*, II. iii. 18] says that the same Crassus was forbidden by the tribunes 'to make war on the Parthians, who had been found guilty of no wrong-doing'. And Plutarch [*Crassus*, xvi = 552 E] of the same man: 'A large party arose which was displeased that any one should go to make war on men who were not only not guilty of any injustice but were protected by treaty relations.'

[3] Also Seneca, *On Anger*, II. viii [II. ix. 3]: 'Some actions are considered as glorious which, so long as they can be restrained, are held to be crimes.' See other passages from Seneca and Cyprian cited below, III. iv. 5, near the end.

[4] The citation is from *On Benefits*, I. xiii [I. xiii. 3]. Justin Martyr in his *Second Apology* [I. xii] well says: 'Rulers who place their own opinions above the truth are just as powerful as robbers in a desert.' Philo [*On the Ten Commandments*, xxvi]: 'Those who commit great thefts, who under the honourable name of government cover up actions that in reality are nothing else than robberies.'

'injury', as if he had confused the Greek words for these two concepts. In the formula used by the Roman fetial are the words, 'I call you to witness that that people is unjust and does not do what is right in making restitution.'

Sylv., word *bellum*, I, no. 2.

[Livy, I. xxxii. 10.]

II.—*Justifiable causes include defence, the obtaining of that which belongs to us or is our due, and the inflicting of punishment*

1. It is evident that the sources from which wars arise are as numerous as those from which lawsuits spring; for where judicial settlement fails, war begins. Actions, furthermore, lie either for wrongs not yet committed, or for wrongs already done.

An action lies for a wrong not yet committed in cases where a guarantee is sought against a threatened wrong, or security against an anticipated injury, or an interdict of a different sort against the use of violence. An action for a wrong committed lies where a reparation for injury, or the punishment of the wrong-doer, is sought.

These two sources of legal obligations were rightly distinguished by Plato,[1] in the ninth book of the *Laws*. Reparation is concerned either with what is or has been ours, giving rise to actions involving property interests, and certain personal actions; or with what is owed to us by contract, or in consequence of a criminal act; or by operation of law, a category to which must be referred also cases arising from implied contracts and constructive crimes. Under these subdivisions the rest of the personal actions fall. An act deserving punishment opens the way to accusation and public trial.

Bal., *On Code*, III. xxxiv. 2, no. 7

2. Authorities generally assign to wars three justifiable causes, defence, recovery of property, and punishment. All three you may find in Camillus's declaration with reference to the Gauls: 'All things which it is right to defend, to recover, and to avenge.' In this enumeration the obtaining of what is owed to us was omitted, unless the word 'recover' is used rather freely. But this was not omitted by Plato when he said that wars are waged not only in case one is attacked, or despoiled of his possessions, but also if one has been deceived. In harmony with this is a sentence of Seneca: 'Perfectly fair, and in complete accord with the law of nations, is the maxim, "Pay what you owe."' The thought was expressed also in the formula of the fetial: 'Things which they have not given, nor paid, nor done, which things ought to have been given, to have been done,

Wilh. Mat., *De Bello Iusto et Licito* [beginning].

Livy, V [xlix. 3].

Alcibiades [i. 5].

On Benefits, III. xiv.

Livy, I [xxxii. 11].

[1] [110] [Plato, *Laws*, IX. vi = 862 B.] Also before him Homer [*Odyssey*, XXII. 61 ff.]; for when the suitors of Penelope wished to pay a fine Ulysses said: 'Not if you should restore all my inherited wealth, which now you hold, and add much more besides, would I refrain from dyeing my hands in your blood, until you pay the penalty for all your sins as suitors.' Cassiodorus, *Letters*, V. xxxv, says: 'When we have not insisted on revenge, we should by no means experience loss.' See also below at the beginnings of chapters xvi and xx of this book.

[*Oration of Macer*, xvii.] to have been paid'; in the words of Sallust, in his *Histories*: 'I demand restitution in accordance with the law of nations.'

On Joshua, VI, qu. . When, however, Augustine said, 'Those wars are wont to be defined as just which avenge wrongs,'[1] he used the word 'avenge' in a rather general way [102] to mean 'exact requital for'. This is shown by what follows, for therein we find not a logical subdivision but a citation of examples: 'War, then, ought to be undertaken against that people and state which has either neglected to exact punishment for wrongs done by its members, or to return what has been wrongfully taken away.'

3. It was in accordance with this natural principle that a king [II. 18.] of India, according to Diodorus, brought against Semiramis the charge 'that she commenced war without having suffered any wrong'. Livy, V [xxxv. 5]. So also the Romans demanded of the Senones that they should not attack a people at whose hands they had received no injury. Aristotle in his *Analytics*, Book II, chapter 11, says: 'It is customary to make war on those who were the first to inflict injury.' XII [VII. vi. 11]. Of the Abians, who were Scythians, Curtius says: 'It was agreed that of barbarians they were the most just; they refrained from war unless attacked.'[2]

The first cause of a justifiable war, then, is an injury not yet inflicted, which menaces either person or property.

III.—*War for the defence of life is permissible*

We said above that if an attack by violence is made on one's person, endangering life, and no other way of escape is open, under Sylv., word *bellum*, I, no. 3, and II. such circumstances war is permissible, even though it involve the slaying of the assailant. As a consequence of the general acceptance of this principle we showed that in some cases a private war may be lawful.

This right of self-defence, it should be observed, has its origin directly, and chiefly, in the fact that nature commits to each his own Bart., *On Dig.* I. i. 3. Bal., *On Code*, VIII. iv. 1. protection, not in the injustice or crime of the aggressor. Wherefore, even if the assailant be blameless, as for instance a soldier acting in good faith, or one who mistakes me for some one else, or one who is rendered irresponsible by madness or by sleeplessness—this, we read,

[1] Servius, *On the Aeneid*, IX [IX. 52], says about the Romans: 'When they wished to declare war, the herald, that is the chief of the fetials, would proceed to the boundaries of the enemy's country; and after repeating certain customary formulas he would say, in a loud voice, that he declared war on account of certain causes, either because they had injured Roman allies, or because they did not restore stolen cattle or deliver up guilty parties.'

[2] Plutarch in his *Nicias* [xxv = 539 E] says that 'Hercules subdued all the world while defending himself from attack'. Josephus, *Antiquities of the Jews*, XVII [XVII. ix. 6]: 'Those who proceed to do violence to men who have no thought of making a hostile attack force these against their will to resort to arms in self-defence.'

has actually happened to some—the right of self-defence is not thereby taken away; it is enough that I am not under obligation to suffer what such an assailant attempts, any more than I should be if attacked by an animal belonging to another.

Báñez, *On* II. ii, 10, art. 10, dub. ult. Soto, *Disputat.*, IV. v, art. 10. Valent., *On* II. ii, disp. 5, qu. 10, par. 7.

IV.—*War in defence of life is permissible only against an actual assailant*

1. It is a disputed question whether innocent persons can be cut down or trampled upon when by getting in the way they hinder the defence or flight by which alone death can be averted. That this is permissible, is maintained even by some theologians. And certainly, if we look to nature alone, in nature there is much less regard for society than concern for the preservation of the individual. But the law of love, especially as set forth in the Gospel, which puts consideration for others on a level with consideration for ourselves, clearly does not permit the injuring of the innocent even under such conditions.

Card., I, qu. 33. Petr. Nav., II. iii, no. 147. Cajetan, *On* II. ii, qu. 2, art. 67.

2. It has been well said by Thomas—if he is rightly understood—that if a man in true self-defence kills his assailant the slaying is not intentional. The reason is not that, if no other means of safety is at hand, it is not sometimes permissible to do with set purpose that which will cause the death of the assailant; it is, rather, that in such a case the inflicting of death is not the primary intent, as it is in the case of procedure by process of law, but the only resource available at the time. Even under such circumstances the person who is attacked ought to prefer to do anything possible to frighten away or weaken the assailant, rather than cause his death.

II. ii, qu. 64, art. 1.

V.—*War in defence of life is permissible only when the danger is immediate and certain, not when it is merely assumed*

1. The danger, again, must be immediate [1] and imminent in point of time. I admit, to be sure, that if the assailant seizes weapons in such a way that his intent to kill is manifest the crime can be forestalled; for in morals as in material things a point is not to be found which does not have a certain breadth. But those who accept fear of any sort as justifying anticipatory slaying are themselves greatly deceived, and deceive others. Cicero said truly, in his first book *On Duties*, that most wrongs have their origin in fear, since he [I. vii. 24.]

[1] See an excellent use of this distinction in Agathias, IV [IV. i, ii]. In the eighth book of Thucydides [VIII. l] Phrynichus says that 'since he was put in peril of his life by them, he would be quite excusable in doing both this and anything else rather than to allow himself to be destroyed by his bitterest foes'.

who plans to do wrong to another fears that, if he does not accomplish his purpose, he may himself suffer harm. In Xenophon, Clearchus says: [103] 'I have known men who, becoming afraid of one another, in consequence of calumny or suspicion, and purposing to inflict injury before receiving injury, have done the most dreadful wrongs to those who had had no such intention, and had not even thought of such a thing.' Cato, in his speech for the Rhodians, asks: 'Shall we be the first to do what we say they wished to do?' There is a notable expression of the thought in Gellius:

[*Anab.*, II. v. 5.]

[*Attic Nights*, VI. iii. 26 and 31.]

> When a gladiator is equipped for fighting, the alternatives offered by combat are these, either to kill, if he shall have made the first decisive stroke, or to fall, if he shall have failed. But the life of men generally is not hedged about by a necessity so unfair and so relentless that you are obliged to strike the first blow, and may suffer if you shall have failed to be first to strike.

Quoted by Quintilian, V, 'On Refutation' [*Institutes of Oratory*, V. xiii. 21].

In another passage Cicero says, not less rightly: 'Who has ever established this principle, or to whom without the gravest danger to all men can it be granted, that he shall have the right to kill a man by whom he says he fears that he himself later may be killed?' In this connexion we may quote the well-known verses of Euripides:

[Frag. 459, in Gell., VI. iii. 28.]

> If, as you say, your husband wished to take
> Your life, wishing were then your part as well,
> Until the time should come.

I [xlii].

A parallel is found in Thucydides: 'The future is still uncertain, and no one, influenced by that thought, should arouse enmities which are not future but certain.' Thucydides, further, in the passage in which he sets forth the evils arising from the manifestations of party-spirit in the Greek states, reckons as a fault also this: 'The man was praised who had himself been first to commit the evil deed which another was going to commit.' 'In the effort to guard against fear,' says Livy, 'men cause themselves to be feared,[1] and we inflict upon others the injury which has been warded off from ourselves, as if it were necessary either to do or to suffer wrong.' To such men the query of Vibius Crispus, which Quintilian praised, is applicable: 'Who has permitted you to harbour so great fear?' According to Dio, Livia said that they do not escape disgrace who are first to do the deed that they fear.

III [lxxxii].

III [lxv. 11].

[*Institutes of Oratory*, VIII. v. 15.]

LV [xvi].

2. Further, if a man is not planning an immediate attack, but it has been ascertained that he has formed a plot, or is preparing an ambuscade, or that he is putting poison in our way, or that he is making ready a false accusation and false evidence, and is corrupting

[1] As Caesar, when he was seizing upon the government, kept saying that he was led to that course by fear of his enemies. There is a fine passage in Appian, *Civil Wars*, II [II. xxi. 150].

the judicial procedure, I maintain that he cannot lawfully be killed, either if the danger can in any other way be avoided, or if it is not altogether certain that the danger cannot be otherwise avoided. Generally, in fact, the delay that will intervene affords opportunity to apply many remedies, to take advantage of many accidental occurrences; as the proverb runs, 'There's many a slip 'twixt cup and lip.' There are, it is true, theologians and jurists who would extend their indulgence somewhat further; but the opinion stated, which is better and safer, does not lack the support of authorities.

Báñez, [*On II. ii,*] 64, art. 7, dub. 4. Baldus, *On Code*, VII. xvi. 17, and VIII. iv. 1. Less., II. ix, dub. 8. Soto, V. i, art. 8. Card., *On Clem.*, V. iv. 1. Covarr., *ibid.*, pt. 3, § 1, no. 2. Sylvester, word *homicidium*, III, qu. 4.

VI.—*Defence of limb against injury is also justifiable*

What shall we say about the danger of injury to a part of the body?

Truly the loss of a limb, especially if it is one of the principal limbs, is an extremely serious matter, and in a sense comparable to loss of life; further, we cannot be sure that injury to a part of the body will not bring danger of death. If, therefore, the injury cannot be avoided in any other way, I should think that he who is on the point of inflicting such injury can be rightly slain.

VII.—*The defence of chastity is in the highest degree justifiable*

That the same right to kill should be conceded also in defence of chastity is hardly open to question; not only the general opinion of men, but also the divine law puts chastity on a plane with life.[1] Thus Paul the jurist said that virtue could properly be defended by such an act.

Sent., V. iii [V. xxiii. 8].

We find an example in Cicero[2] and Quintilian; the case was that of a tribune of Marius, who was killed by a soldier. In the histories there are also some examples [104] of men who were slain by women. The killing of a man under such circumstances is called by Chariclea, in Heliodorus, 'a justifiable defence for warding off a violation of chastity.'

[*For Milo*, iv. 9.] *Declamations*, iii.

[I, beginning.]

[1] Seneca in his first book *On Benefits*, eleventh chapter [I. xi. 4]: 'In the next place come those things, such as liberty, chastity, and sanity, without which we can indeed live, but in such fashion that death is preferable.' Paul, *Sententiae*, V, tit. xxiii [V. xxiii. 8]: 'Whoever has killed a robber attempting his life or any one making an assault on chastity should not be punished; for the one in defending life, the other in defending chastity, performs a public service.' Augustine, *De Libero Arbitrio*, I [I. v. 11]: 'The law gives the right to the traveller to kill a robber, in order that he may not be killed by him, and to any man or woman to slay an assailant attempting rape, or even after the rape has been committed, if this be possible.'

[2] See also Plutarch, *Marius* [xiv = 413]. Mars also is said to have been acquitted by the judgement of the gods when he killed the one who was offering violence to his daughter. The tale is told by Apollodorus, *Library*, III [III. xiv. 2]. Add the remarkable story in the ninth book of Gregory of Tours [*History of the Franks*, IX. xvii].

VIII.—*Not to take advantage of the right of defence is permissible*

We said above, that while it is permissible to kill him who is making ready to kill, yet the man is more worthy of praise who prefers to be killed rather than to kill.

Soto, [V,] qu. i. Sylvester, word *bellum*, II, no. 5. This principle, however, is by some conceded in such a way that an exception is made in the case of a person whose life is useful to many. But I should deem it unsafe to extend this rule, which is inconsistent with long suffering, so as to include all those whose lives are necessary for others. And so I should think that the exception ought to be restricted to those whose duty it is to ward off violence from others, such as members of an escort on a journey, who were hired with that purpose in view, and public rulers, to whom the [V. 685 ff.] verses of Lucan may be applied [translation by Ridley]:

> When on thy breath so many nations hang
> For life and safety, and so great a world
> Calls thee its master, to have courted death
> Proves want of heart.[1]

IX.—*Defence is sometimes not permissible against a person useful to the state because at variance with the law of love*

1. On the other hand, it may happen that, since the life of the assailant is useful to many, he cannot be killed without wrong. And this is true, not only according to divine law, whether of the old Soto, as above. or the new dispensation—this we treated above, when we showed that the person of a king is sacred—but also by the law of nature. For the law of nature, in so far as it has the force of a law, holds in view not only the dictates of expletive justice, as we have called it, but also actions exemplifying other virtues, such as self-mastery, bravery, and prudence, as under certain circumstances not merely honourable, but even obligatory. And to such actions we are constrained by regard for others.

Cont. Illust., I. xviii [10]. 2. And I am not moved to renounce this opinion by Vázquez, when he says that a ruler who maltreats an innocent man by that very act ceases to be a ruler. A statement either less true or more dangerous than that, it would be hard to make. For just as ownership, so the exercise of sovereign power is not lost by wrong-doing, unless the law so prescribe. But a law in regard to the exercise of sovereign power containing the provision that it should cease in

[1] Curtius, Book X [IX. vi. 8]: 'But while you so eagerly expose your life to manifest dangers, forgetting that you are dragging down into ruin the lives of so many citizens.'

consequence of committing a wrong against a private individual has nowhere been, and in my opinion never will be, framed; for such a law would lead to the utmost confusion.

The foundation upon which Vázquez bases this and many other conclusions is, that all exercise of sovereign power has in view the interest of those who obey, not of those who rule. Even if this should be true in general, it would not be in point here; for a thing whose usefulness is impaired only in part does not at once cease to be of use. His further statement, that the safety of the state is desired by individuals in their own interest, and in consequence every man ought to put his individual welfare above that of the whole state, is lacking in consistency. We do desire, in our own interest, that our state be safe, yet not merely for our own sake but for the sake of others as well.

3. False, in fact, and rejected by the more sound philosophers, is the view of those who think [1] that friendship has its origin in need alone; we are drawn to friendship spontaneously, and by our own nature. Regard for others often warns me, sometimes commands me, to put the interest of many above my own. Appropriate to this connexion is a passage of Seneca: *On Clemency*, I. iv.

> It is not to be wondered at if emperors,[2] kings, and others charged with the responsibility of public administration, whatever their titles, are loved with a deeper devotion even than personal relatives. If, in fact, men of sound judgement place public above private interests, it follows that he also should be more dear who represents the state personified.

Similar is the thought of Ambrose: 'Since each one would count it a greater joy to have warded off destruction from his country than from himself.' *On Duties*, III.iii [23]. And again, Seneca, whom I mentioned, says: 'Callistratus and Rutilius, the former at Athens, the latter in Rome, were unwilling that their homes be restored to them at the price of a general disaster; for it was better that two men suffer a single injustice than that a public calamity be visited upon all.' *On Benefits*, VI. xxxvii.

[1] [111] Seneca refutes this harmful opinion in his first book *On Benefits*, chap. i, and the fourth book, chap. xvi.

[2] Plutarch, at the beginning of *Pelopidas* [i = 278 D]: 'The first work of virtue is to save the one who saves the rest.'

Cassiodorus, *On Friendship* [Peter of Blois, *On the Love of God and Neighbour*]: 'If the hand by favour of the eyes has noticed a brandished sword threatening another limb, it grasps the sword without considering its own danger in the least, and fearing more for the other than for itself.' And again: 'Therefore those who by their own death save from death their masters act rightly in this, if they take into consideration rather the safety of their own souls than the freedom of the body of another. For since conscience dictates to them that they ought to show fidelity to their masters, it seems also consistent with reason, that they ought to prefer the life of their masters to their own physical lives.' Later: 'And so a man may properly expose his body to death because of regard for others, and especially for the safety of a great number.'

[105] X.—*It is not permissible for Christians to kill in order to ward off a blow, or to avoid any indignity of like sort, or to prevent any escape*

Soto, as above. Navarrus, xv, no. 3. Sylvester, word *homicidium*, 1, qu. 5. Lud. Lopez, chap. lxii.

1. There are some who think that, if a man is in imminent danger of receiving a blow or a similar injury, he has the right to prevent it by killing his enemy. For my part, if expletive justice only be considered, I raise no objection. For although death and a blow are not on the same level, yet the man who makes ready to injure me by that very act confers on me a right, a sort of actual and unlimited moral right[1] against him, in so far as otherwise I cannot ward off the injury from myself. Furthermore, in such a case regard for others does not in itself seem to impose on us the obligation to favour the one who attempts the injury. But the law of the Gospel has made such action in self-defence altogether unpermissible; for Christ bids us submit to a blow rather than do harm to an aggressor. How much more earnestly does He forbid the slaying of an assailant in order to escape a blow!

[Covarr.] as above, § 1.

This example warns us to beware of the principle laid down by Covarruvias, that human knowledge, being not ignorant of the law of nature, does not allow anything to be permitted by natural reason which would not likewise be permitted by God, who is nature itself. For God, the creator of nature, is also able to act freely outside the realm of nature, and has the right to lay down laws for us even concerning those matters which are by nature left free and undetermined; even greater is His right to make obligatory what by nature is honourable, even though not obligatory.

Navarrus, xv, no. 4. Henr., *De Irreg.*, xi. Vict., *De Iure Belli*, no. 5.

2. Since the will of God is so clearly manifest in the Gospel, strange it is that there are to be found theologians, and Christian theologians, too, who think that a man is allowed not only to kill in order to avoid a blow, but even to recover his honour, as men say, after receiving a blow, in case the assailant flees. This seems to me entirely inconsistent with both reason and religion. For honour is a recognition of superiority; but the man who endures such an injury shows that in a superior degree he possesses the virtue of long-suffering, and thus rather increases his honour than diminishes it. And it does not make any difference if some individuals of faulty judgement turn this virtue into a vice by applying to it names which they have made up; for such faulty judgements change neither the

[1] Apollodorus, treating of Linus, II [II. iv. 9]: 'When Linus had come to Thebes and had been made a Theban citizen, he was there struck with a lyre by Hercules and killed. For Hercules was enraged because Linus had wounded him, and therefore slew Linus; and when he was brought to trial by certain persons on the charge of murder he pleaded in court the law of Rhadamanthus, by which any person is declared innocent if he has harmed a man who has previously used force against him.'

thing nor the value of the thing. The truth in this case was perceived not only by the early Christians but also by the philosophers, who said, as we have shown elsewhere, that it is characteristic of a small soul not to be able to bear an insult.

3. From this it is also clear that we ought not to accept with approval the opinion handed down by most authorities, that slaying in self-defence is permissible according to divine law (for I do not dispute the statement that it is permissible by the law of nature), even if one can escape without danger, because flight, especially in the case of a nobleman, would be disgraceful. And yet in such an act there is no disgrace; there is only a false notion of what is dishonourable, a notion deserving of contempt on the part of all true seekers after virtue and wisdom. On this point I am glad to have the support, among jurists, of Charles Dumoulin.

Soto, d. i, art. 8. Doctors, *On Dig.*, I. i. 3 and *Code*, VIII. iv. 1. Vázquez, xviii, as above, no. 13, 14. Sylvester, word *bellum*, II, no. 4.

In *Additions to Alexander's Cons.*, 119.

What I have said about a blow and flight, I wish to consider as said also about other occurrences which in reality do not in any degree affect our honour. But what if some one should spread a report about us, which, if believed, would hurt our standing in the estimation of good men? There are those who teach that such a person also can be slain. But this view is wholly erroneous, and contrary to the law of nature as well; slaying under such circumstances is not the proper means to be employed to defend one's reputation.

Petr. Navarr., II. iii, no. 376.

XI.—*By the law of nature it is permissible to kill in defence of property*

We may now come to injuries that are attempted upon property.

If we have in view expletive justice only, I shall not deny that in order to preserve property a robber can even be killed, in case of necessity. For the disparity between property and life is offset by the favourable position of the innocent party and the odious rôle of the robber, as we have said above. From this it follows, that if we have in view this right only, a thief fleeing with stolen property can be felled with a missile, if the property cannot otherwise be recovered. [106] In his speech against Aristocrates, Demosthenes exclaims: 'In the name of the gods is not this a hard and unjust thing, contrary not only to written laws but also to the law common to all men, that I am not permitted to use force against the man who, in the manner of an enemy, seizes and carries off my property?' [xxiii. 61.]

If, furthermore, we leave divine and human law out of account, regard for others, viewed as a principle of conduct, interposes no hindrance to such action, unless the stolen property is of extremely slight value and consequently worthy of no consideration. This exception is by some rightly added.

XII.—*How far defence of property is permitted by the law of Moses*

1. Let us see what the purport of the Hebraic law is; for in harmony with the Hebraic law is the ancient law of Solon which Demosthenes refers to in his speech against Timocrates, and from which a law of the Twelve Tables [1] was derived; also an ordinance [= 874 B.] proposed by Plato in the ninth book of the *Laws*.

All the laws mentioned agree in this, that they make a distinction between a thief who commits a theft by night and one who steals in the daytime. In regard to the reason for the law, however, there is doubt. Some think that the only consideration had in view was this, that at night it is impossible to determine whether the intruder is a thief or an assassin, and so he can be killed as if he were an assassin. Others hold that the distinction rests on this point, that at night, since the thief is unknown, there is less chance of recovering the property.

Soto, as above. Matesilanus, *Notab.*, 135. Jason and Gom., *On Inst.* IV. vi. pr. Covarr., as above, § 1, no. 10. Lessius, dub. 11, no. 68.

In my opinion the framers of the laws had sharply in mind neither of the considerations suggested. It was their desire, rather, to establish this principle, that no one should be killed for the sake of property merely; such a case might arise, for example, if with a missile I should strike down a thief in flight, in order that by killing him I might recover the thing stolen. If, however, I myself should be brought into peril of life, then it should be permissible for me to ward off danger from myself, even with danger to the life of another; and it should not be to my disadvantage that I should expose myself to danger through the effort to keep possession of what belonged to me, either by seizing it after it had been taken or by capturing the thief. In following such a course no accusation could be brought against me, since I should be engaged in a lawful act, and since, acting within my right, I should be doing no one an injustice.

Covarr., as above. Aug. cited in *Decretals*, V. xii. 3. Lessius, ch. ix, as above, dub. 11, no. 66.

2. The distinction, then, between the act of a thief by night and by day is founded on this fact, that at night it is difficult to procure witnesses. If, therefore, a thief is found slain, it is easy enough to give credence to the man who alleges that he killed the thief in self-defence, especially if a dangerous weapon is found with the body. The latter condition is in fact recognized in the Hebraic law, which speaks of a thief caught 'in the act of breaking in'; for this [*Exod.*, xxii. 2.] is by some translated 'while digging through', but others, perhaps better, render it 'with an instrument for digging through', the

[1] We can add the *Law of the Visigoths*, Book VII, tit. i. 15 [VII. ii. 16] and the *Capitularies* of Charlemagne, Book V, chap. cxci [V. cccxliii]. According to the law of the Lombards, one who enters the house-court of another at night can be killed unless he allows himself to be bound.

Hebrew word being thus explained also in *Jeremiah* (ii. 34) by the most learned of the Jews.

I am led to adopt the latter translation by the law of the Twelve Tables, which forbids the killing of a thief by day, but adds the exception: unless he defend himself with a weapon. The presumption against a thief at night is, therefore, that he has defended himself with a weapon. As weapons, moreover, instruments of iron, clubs, and stones are understood, as Gaius noted in connexion with this very law. Ulpian on the contrary maintained that the legal provision that the man who kills a thief at night is free from punishment must be understood to have effect only if he could not spare the life of the thief without danger to himself, while, of course, defending his property. *Digest,* XLVII. ii. 55 (54). 2. *Digest,* XLVIII. viii. 9.

3. The presumption therefore, as I said, favours the man who has killed a thief by night. If, however, there should chance to be witnesses, through whom it can be established that the man who killed the thief was not brought into peril of life, in such a case the presumption will cease to be valid and the slayer will be held on the charge of murder. The law of the Twelve Tables further required that the man who had detected a thief, whether by day or by night, should make the fact known by shouting, undoubtedly that, as we learn from Gaius, [107] magistrates or neighbours might if possible hasten to the place in order to give aid and to serve as witnesses. *Dig.* IX. ii. 4. But because people are more easily brought together by day than by night, as Ulpian notes in connexion with the passage of Demosthenes just cited, the one who alleges the endangering of life at night is more readily believed.

4. There is a similar provision in the Hebraic law,[1] which directs that the word of a maid be taken in regard to rape committed in the country, but not in a city, because in town she could, and should, have summoned help by screaming. [*Deut.,* xxii. 23 ff.]

To the considerations already presented we may add also this, that even if conditions in other respects are the same, nevertheless when things happen at night it is less easy to investigate them and find out what they are and how serious; wherefore they are more terrifying. The Hebraic law, then, as well as the Roman, enjoins upon citizens what regard for others suggests, that they should not kill a man merely because he is stealing property, but that such an act of violence becomes permissible only in case the person who has sought to safeguard his property has himself been exposed to danger.

[1] Philo gives a good explanation of this, that the place was suggested as illustrating the more common occurrence and not because on that alone the decision of a disputed fact must rest. For as he has shown, in his book *On Special Laws* [III. xiii], a girl can suffer violence in the city if her outcry is stifled, and in the country she can consent to debauchery.

Moses Maimonides remarked that for one individual to kill another is not permissible except to safeguard that of which the loss is irreparable, life and chastity.

XIII.—*Whether, and under what limitations, it is permissible, according to the law of the Gospel, to kill in defence of property*

1. What, now, shall we say in regard to the law of the Gospel? Does it permit the same that the law of Moses permitted? Or since it is more perfect in other respects than the law of Moses, does it also in this case demand more from us?

That the law of the Gospel demands more from us, I do not doubt. For if Christ bids that a tunic and a cloak be given up, and Paul, that an unjust loss be endured, rather than that recourse be had to a lawsuit—a contest without bloodshed—how much more do they wish that things also of greater value be relinquished rather than that a man, the image of God, sprung from the same blood with ourselves, should be killed! Wherefore, if a thing belonging to us can be saved in such a way that there seems to be no danger of causing death, it may rightly be defended; if not, then the thing should be given up, unless perchance it is of such a sort that our life and the life of our family is dependent on it and it cannot be recovered by process of law, since the thief is unknown, and also that there is some prospect that recovery will be made without slaughter.

Soto, as above, art. 8. Lessius, dub. 11, no. 74. Sylvester, word *bellum*, II. no. 3. *De Lib. Arb.* I [v. 13].

2. Although to-day almost all jurists and theologians teach that we have a right to kill a man in the defence of our property, even going beyond the limits within which such an act was permitted by the law of Moses and the Roman law—as, for instance, if the thief be making off with what he has stolen—nevertheless we do not doubt that the opinion which we have just set forth was held by the early Christians. And upon that matter Augustine, too, had no doubt; his words are as follows: 'How, in the presence of Divine Providence, can those be free from sin who have polluted themselves with the killing of men for the sake of things which ought to be viewed with contempt?'

Panorm., *De Homicidiis*, ii. Lessius, as above.

In this matter, undoubtedly, as in many others, discipline has become relaxed with time,[1] and little by little the interpretation of the law of the Gospel has begun to be adjusted to the customs of the age. Formerly among the clergy conformity to the ancient practice was ordinarily kept up; but finally even the clergy have been released from censure in this matter.

[1] Jerome, in his *Life of Malchus* [1]: 'After the Church began to have Christian rulers, it became greater in wealth, but weaker in virtue.' See *Decretals*, V. xii. 10, and *Decretum*, I. l. 36.

XIV.—*Whether the civil law, in permitting that life be taken in self-defence, confers a right, or merely freedom from punishment, is discussed, with a noting of distinctions*

The question is raised by some whether the civil law at any rate, since it contains the right of life and death, in permitting that a thief be killed by a private individual, does not at the same time free the act from all guilt.

In my judgement this ought by no means to be conceded. In the first place, the law does not have the right of death over all citizens for any offence whatever, but only for offences so serious that they deserve death. Altogether worthy of approval is the opinion of Scotus, that it is not right to condemn any one to death[1] except for the crimes which the law of Moses punished with death, or, in addition, for crimes which, judged by a fair standard, are equally heinous. For in this so serious matter it seems possible to obtain a knowledge of the divine will, [108] which alone gives peace of mind, from no other source than from that law, which does not with certainty appoint for the thief the penalty of death.

Furthermore, the law ought not to confer, and ordinarily does not confer, upon private individuals the right to put to death even those who have deserved death, excepting only in the case of the most atrocious crimes; otherwise the authority of the courts would have been constituted in vain. Wherefore, if the law says that a thief is killed with impunity, we are to consider that it takes away a penalty but does not also confer a right.

XV.—*When a single combat may be permissible*

From what we have said it is apparent that two conditions can arise under which individuals may engage in single combat without blame.

The first condition is, when an assailant grants to the person attacked an opportunity to fight, though determined to kill him without combat in case he does not fight. The second is, if a king or magistrate matches against each other two criminals deserving of death; in this case it will indeed be their privilege to grasp at a hope of safety. The official who has ordered such a combat, however, would seem not to have discharged his duty properly, since, if the punishment of one seemed sufficient, it would have been better to choose by lot which one should die.

[1] Against the laws which punish rustics with death for hunting, see Gregory of Tours, [*History of the Franks*,] X. x; John of Salisbury, *Policraticus*, I. iv; and Peter of Blois, *Letters*, 129.

XVI.—*Concerning defence in public war*

What has been said by us up to this point, concerning the right to defend oneself and one's possessions, applies chiefly, of course, to private war[1]; yet it may be made applicable also to public war, if the difference in conditions be taken into account.

In private war the right is, so to say, momentary; it ceases as soon as circumstances permit an approach to a judge. But since public wars do not arise except where there are no courts, or where courts cease to function, they are prolonged, and are continually augmented by the increment of fresh losses and injuries. Besides, in private war, self-defence is generally the only consideration; but public powers have not only the right of self-defence but also the right to exact punishment. Hence for them it is permissible to forestall an act of violence which is not immediate, but which is seen to be threatening from a distance; not directly—for that, as we have shown, would work injustice—but indirectly, by inflicting punishment for a wrong action commenced but not yet carried through. This point there will be an opportunity to take up later.

XVII.—*A public war is not admitted to be defensive which has as its only purpose to weaken the power of a neighbour*

Quite untenable is the position, which has been maintained by some, that according to the law of nations it is right to take up arms in order to weaken a growing power which, if it become too great, may be a source of danger.

Alb. Gent., I, xiv.

That this consideration does enter into deliberations regarding war, I admit, but only on grounds of expediency, not of justice. Thus if a war be justifiable for other reasons, for this reason also it might be deemed far-sighted to undertake the war; that is the gist of the argument which the writers cited on this point present. But that the possibility of being attacked confers the right to attack is abhorrent to every principle of equity. Human life exists under such conditions that complete security is never guaranteed to us. For protection against uncertain fears we must rely on Divine Providence, and on a wariness free from reproach, not on force.

Baldus, *On Digest*, I. viii. 3.

[1] Ammianus Marcellinus, Book XXIII [XXIII. i. 7]: 'Since in the case of an attack by a foreign foe there is one invariable law, to defend our safety in every way, unhindered by the force of custom.' Alexander Severus said in a speech to his soldiers, Herodian, V [VI. iii. 4]: 'The oné who is the first to commit unjust acts has no reasonable justification. But he who defends himself from assailants takes confidence from a clear conscience and hopes for success, because he is not acting unjustly but defending himself.'

XVIII.—*A public war is not admitted to be defensive on the part of him who has himself given just cause for war*

1. Not less unacceptable is the doctrine of those who hold that defence is justifiable on the part of those who have deserved that war be made upon them ; the reason they allege is, that few are satisfied with exacting vengeance in proportion to the injury suffered. But fear of an uncertainty cannot confer the right to resort to force ; hence a man charged with a crime, because he fears that his punishment may be greater than he deserves, does not, on that account, have the right to resist by force the representatives of public authority who desire to take him. Alb. Gent., I. xiii. Cast. *De Iustitia*, V.

2. He who has done injury to another ought first to offer satisfaction to him whom he has injured, through the arbitrament of a fair-minded man ; if such an offer of satisfaction is rejected, then his taking up of arms will be without reproach. Thus Hezekiah did not abide by the terms of the treaty which his forefathers had made with the king of Assyria ; but being attacked in war he confessed his fault, and left it to the king to determine [109] what reparation was due. Having made reparation, afterward he was attacked in war a second time ; supported now by a clear conscience he withstood the violence of the enemy, and enjoyed the favour of God. Pontius the Samnite, after restitution had been made to the Romans and the instigator of the war had been delivered up, said : *2 Kings*, xviii. 7, 14, and xix. [Livy, IX. i, iii, iv, vii, viii.]

> Whatever wrath of the gods has come upon us in consequence of our breaking of the treaty has been expiated. I am well enough assured that those gods whose pleasure it was that we be subjected to the necessity of making restitution were not pleased that the satisfaction offered for violation of the treaty was so scornfully rejected by the Romans. What more [he adds further on] do I owe to you, Roman, what more to the treaty, what more to the gods, the judges of the treaty ? Whom shall I accept as arbitrator between your anger and my punishment ? I raise objection to no one, whether people or private person.

Likewise when the Thebans had offered just satisfaction in all respects to the Lacedaemonians, but the Lacedaemonians were insisting on more, Aristides, in his first speech *On Leuctra*, said that the justice of the cause had passed to the other side.[1] [= p. 93.]

[1] [112] See Zonaras [XVII. xi] on the subject of the Prince of Chalep, who had offered peace and the unpaid tribute to the Roman Emperor Argyropolus. A similar instance concerning the crusaders is found in Kromer, Book XVII [*History of Poland*, XVII, p. 393] ; see also Philippe de Comines, Book VII, concerning the Swiss, who had offered satisfaction to Charles of Burgundy for a cart-load of sheepskins, stolen from merchants.

CHAPTER II

OF THINGS WHICH BELONG TO MEN IN COMMON

I.—*The division of that which is our own*

Next in order among the causes of war is an injury actually received; and first, an injury to that which belongs to us. Some things belong to us by a right common to mankind, others by our individual right.

Let us begin with the right which is common to all men. This right holds good directly over a corporeal thing, or over certain actions. Corporeal things are either free from private ownership, or are the property of some one. Things not in private ownership are either such as cannot become subject to private ownership, or such as can. In order to understand the distinction fully, it will be necessary to know the origin of proprietorship, which jurists call the right of ownership.

II.—*The origin and development of the right of private ownership*

1. Soon after the creation of the world, and a second time after the Flood, God conferred upon the human race a general right over things of a lower nature. 'All things', as Justin says, 'were the common and undivided possession of all men, as if all possessed a common inheritance.'[1] In consequence, each man could at once take whatever he wished for his own needs, and could consume whatever was capable of being consumed. The enjoyment of this universal right then served the purpose of private ownership; for whatever each had thus taken for his own needs another could not take from him except by an unjust act. This can be understood from the comparison used by Cicero in his third book *On Ends*[2]: 'Although the theatre is a public place, [113] yet it is correct to say that the seat which a man has taken belongs to him.'

Genesis, i. 29, 30; ix. 2. XLIII [i. 3]. [III. xx. 67.]

This primitive state might have lasted if men had continued in great simplicity, or had lived on terms of mutual affection such as rarely appears. Of these two conditions, one, exemplified in the

[1] A trace of this survived in the Saturnalia.

[2] Seneca, *On Benefits*, Book VII. xii [VII. xii. 3]: 'The equestrian seats belong to all the Roman knights; nevertheless, in those places whichever one I have occupied is mine.'

community of property [1] arising from extreme simplicity, may be seen among certain tribes in America, which have lived for many generations in such a condition without inconvenience. The second, again, exemplified in the community of property arising from affection, was formerly realized among the Essenes,[2] afterward among the first Christians at Jerusalem; at the present time, also, by a goodly number who live an ascetic life.

Evidence showing the simplicity of the state of the first men [3] who were created is to be found in their nakedness. Among them there was ignorance of vices rather than knowledge of virtue, as Trogus says of the Scythians. 'The most ancient mortals', says Tacitus, 'were yet free from wicked excess of passion, living their lives without reproach, without crime, and in consequence without punishment or restraints.' [4] In Macrobius is the statement: 'Among mankind at first there was a simplicity having no knowledge of evil, and hitherto quite devoid of guile.' This simplicity seems to be called 'incorruption' [5] by the Hebrew sage, but 'simplicity' by the Apostle Paul, who opposes to it 'craftiness', that is, crafty cunning. The only concern of these first men was the worship of God, whose symbol was the tree of life,[6] as the ancient Hebrews explain; and this interpretation is supported by a passage of the *Apocalypse*. They lived easily on the fruits which the earth brought forth of its own accord, without toil.[7]

Justin, II [ii. 15]. [*Annals*, III. xxvi. 1.] *On Scipio's Dream*, II [x. 15]. *Wisdom*, iii. 24 [ii. 23]. 2 *Corinthians*, xi. 3. *Proverbs*, iii. 18. Philo, *On the Creation of the World* [liv]. *Revelation*, xxii. 2.

[1] Horace [*Odes*, III. xxiv. 9–16]:

> The Scythians of the plains thus better live,
> Whose wandering carts their homes by custom bear;
> And so the Getae, too, of habits stern,
> For whom unmeasured acres bear the grain,
> And fruits likewise, to all the tribesmen free.
> And no one tills the ground beyond a year;
> And for the one whose labours then are done
> By equal lot another takes his turn.

[2] And from these arose the Pythagoreans; see Porphyry [*Life of Pythagoras*, xx]; Diogenes Laertius [VIII. 10]; Gellius, I. ix.

[3] Adam is the type of the human race. See Origen, *Against Celsus* [VII. xxviii]; also in point here is what Tertullian says in his book *On the Soul* [xvi]: 'What is natural must be believed to be reasonable, because it has been instilled in the soul from the very beginning by a creator possessed of reason. For what is there, which God has published by command, and still more which He has given forth by His own breath, that is not reasonable? But that which is not reasonable must be understood to be of later origin, as something which has come in at the instigation of the serpent, that is, the admission of sin; and thereafter it has taken root and grown to maturity in the soul after the likeness of nature, because it came in immediately at the beginning of nature.'

[4] Seneca, on the same subject, *Letters*, xc [xc. 46]: 'Because of ignorance they were innocent.' Then after speaking of justice, prudence, self-control, and bravery he adds: 'Their uncultured life had certain elements similar to all these virtues.' Josephus [*Antiquities of the Jews*, I. i. 4] says: 'Having their souls estranged by no care.'

[5] So also Paul, *Ephesians*, vi. 24; he spoke also of 'incorruptness', *Titus*, ii. 17 [ii. 7].

[6] The higher holiness of the Jewish Rabbis; [123] the divine wisdom of Arethas, *On Revelation* [xxii. 2]; on the subject of Paradise see *Ecclesiasticus*, xl. 17, and on the four rivers of Paradise the same book, xxiv. 35 ff.

[7] See the excellent passage of Dicaearchus on this subject, quoted by Varro, *On Farming*, Book II [I. ii]; and another from the same writer quoted by Porphyry, *On Abstaining from Animal Food*, IV [ii].

2. Men did not, however, continue to live this simple and innocent life, but turned their thoughts to various kinds of knowledge, the symbol for which was the tree of knowledge of good and evil,[1] that is, a knowledge of the things of which it is possible to make at times a good use, at times a bad use. This Philo calls the 'middle understanding'. In regard to it Solomon said: 'God made man upright,' that is, simple, 'but they have sought out many inventions.' 'Men degenerated into craftiness,' as Philo declares in the passage cited. Says Dio of Prusa in his sixth *Oration*: 'But to the men who came after the first the craft and various inventions[2] devised for the advantage of life proved not to be very useful; for men devoted their talents not so much to the cultivation of bravery and justice as to devising means of enjoyment.'

On the Creation of the World [liv]. *Ecclesiastes*, vii. 30 [29]. [=p. 92A.]

The most ancient arts, agriculture and grazing, were pursued by the first brothers, not without some interchange of commodities. From the difference in pursuits arose rivalry, and even murder; and at length, since the good were corrupted by contact with the wicked,[3] there came the kind of life ascribed to the giants, that is given over to violence, like the life of those whom the Greeks characterized as 'men that cultivate justice with the fist'.[4] After the world had been cleansed by the Deluge, that brutish life was succeeded by a passion for pleasure,[5] to which wine ministered; whence came also unlawful loves.

3. Harmony, however, was destroyed chiefly by a less ignoble vice, ambition, of which the symbol was the tower of Babel. Presently men divided off countries, and possessed them separately. Afterward, nevertheless, there remained among neighbours a common ownership, not of flocks to be sure, but of pasture lands, because the extent of the land was so great, in proportion to the small number of men, that it sufficed without any inconvenience for the use of many;

Genesis, x, xi.

[1] Josephus [*Antiquities of the Jews*, I. i. 4]: 'And this was the tree of keen mentality and understanding.' Telemachus, in Homer [*Odyssey*, XX. 309]:

All things I know
Both good and bad, nor am a child as heretofore.

To Zeno of Cittium wisdom was the knowledge of things good and evil and indifferent; the statement is in Diogenes Laertius [VII. 92]. Plutarch, *On Matters of Common Knowledge* [xvii=1067 A]: 'What will be the harm if evil shall be removed and there shall then be no prudence, but we shall have in the place of it another virtue, which is not the knowledge of good and evil, but of good alone?'

[2] Seneca, *Letters*, xc [xc. 25 ff.], explains this fully; read him, and also Dicaearchus in the writers already cited.

[3] Seneca, *Natural Questions*, III, at the end [III. xxx]: 'When wild beasts have been likewise destroyed, whose savage natures men have taken on.'

[4] Seneca, in the same connexion [*Natural Questions*, III. xxx]: 'They also will not continue in innocence, except while they are young.'

[5] Seneca, in the same work [Pliny, *Natural History*, XIV. xxii. 142]: 'A monstrous lust and forbidden pleasure are the chief fruits of drunkenness.'

> The field with bounds to mark, or limits set,
> Was not allowed.

Virgil, *Georgics*, I [line 126].

Finally, with increase in the number of men as well as of flocks, lands everywhere began to be divided, not as previously by peoples, but by families. Wells,[1] furthermore—a resource particularly necessary in a dry region, one well not sufficing for many— [114] were appropriated by those who had obtained possession of them. This is what we are taught in sacred history; and it is quite in accord with what philosophers and poets, whose testimony we have presented elsewhere, have said concerning the first state of ownership in common, and the distribution of property which afterward followed.

Genesis, xiii. *Genesis*, xxi. *Mare Liberum*, xv.

4. From these sources we learn what was the cause on account of which the primitive common ownership, first of movable objects, later also of immovable property, was abandoned. The reason was that men were not content to feed on the spontaneous products of the earth,[2] to dwell in caves, to have the body either naked or clothed with the bark of trees or skins of wild animals, but chose a more refined mode of life; this gave rise to industry, which some applied to one thing, others to another.

Moreover, the gathering of the products of the soil into a common store was hindered first by the remoteness of the places to which men had made their way, then by the lack of justice and kindness; in consequence of such a lack the proper fairness in making division was not observed, either in respect to labour or in the consumption of the fruits.

5. At the same time we learn how things became subject to private ownership. This happened not by a mere act of will, for one could not know what things another wished to have, in order to abstain from them—and besides several might desire the same thing—but rather by a kind of agreement, either expressed, as by a division, or implied, as by occupation.[3] In fact, as soon as community ownership was abandoned, and as yet no division had been made, it is to be supposed [4] that all agreed, that whatever each one

[1] On the wells near Oasis, which were the common property of many, see Olympiodorus in Photius [*Lexicon*, lxxx. 192].

[2] Procopius, *Gothic War*, II [II. xv], accurately describes for us the manner of life of the Scrithiphini, which was of this kind. Add Pliny [*Natural History*], XII. i [XII, proem.]; Vitruvius, II. i.

[3] See the passages from the Talmud and the Koran which Selden, the glory of England, has quoted on this subject in his work on the empire of the sea [*Mare Clausum*, I. iv].

[4] Cicero [*On Duties*, I. vii. 21]: 'And because from this there has begun to be private ownership of things that by nature had been common property, each man should keep possession of what has fallen to him.' He illustrates the same point by a comparison from Chrysippus drawn from the race-course [*On Duties*, III. x. 42], where it is lawful to vanquish the opponent by running, but not by pushing him from the course.

The Scholiast on Horace, *Art of Poetry* [line 128], says: 'As an ownerless house or field is common property, but when occupied it becomes private property.' Varro, *Age Modo* [cited by Servius

had taken possession of should be his property.[1] 'It has been granted,' says Cicero, 'that each may prefer to acquire for himself, rather than for another, whatever contributes to the advantage of life; and in this there is no conflict with nature.' To this should be added the sentence of Quintilian: 'If this is settled, that whatever has come into a man's possession is the property of the possessor, certainly what is rightfully possessed is not taken away without injustice.' And when the ancients called Ceres a 'lawgiver' and named her sacred rites the Thesmophoria they implied [2] that out of the division of lands a new law had arisen.

Cicero, *On Duties*, III [v. 22].

Declamations, xiii [xiii. 8].

Macrobius, *Saturnalia*, III. xii.

III.—*That certain things, such as the sea both as a whole and in its principal divisions, cannot become subject to private ownership, and why*

1. Having laid down these fundamental principles, we say that the sea, viewed either as a whole or in its principal divisions, cannot become subject to private ownership. Since, however, such ownership is conceded by some in the case of individuals but not in the case of nations, we bring forward proof, first on moral grounds.

The cause which led to the abandonment of common ownership here ceases to be operative. The extent of the ocean is in fact so great that it suffices for any possible use on the part of all peoples, for drawing water, for fishing, for sailing. The same thing would need to be said, too, about the air, if it were capable of any use for which the use of the land also is not required, as it is for the catching of birds.[3] Fowling, therefore, and similar pursuits, are subject to the law laid down by him who has control over the land.

2. The same conclusion must be reached in regard to the Syrtes. These are absolutely devoid of cultivable soil; they have no value except as depositories of sand, the supply of which is inexhaustible.

There is, furthermore, a natural reason which forbids that the sea, considered from the point of view mentioned, should become a private possession. The reason is that occupation takes place only

On the Georgics, II. 168], says: 'Formerly the earth was assigned to particular peoples for cultivation, as Etruria to the Tuscans and Samnium to the Sabellians.'

[1] Solon [Frag. XIII. 7–8]:

[124] Riches I wish to have, but those unjustly got
I do not want.

Cicero, *On Duties*, I [I. viii. 25]: 'Nor in truth should the increase of property be criticised, if harmful to no one; but injustice must always be avoided.'

[2] 'After laws had come into being, in consequence of the division of lands'; thus Servius, in commenting *On the Aeneid*, Book IV [line 58]: 'Ceres, giver of laws.'

[3] And the right of habitation. 'It is necessary to measure the sky as well as the ground,' says Pomponius, *Digest*, XLIII. xxiv. 21 [§ 2]; add also *Digest*, XVII. ii. 83.

in the case of a thing which has definite limits.[1] For this reason Thucydides calls unoccupied land 'devoid of boundaries', and I [cxxxix]. Isocrates characterized the land taken over by the Athenians as *Panegyric* [ix. 36]. 'having boundaries fixed by us'. Liquids, on the contrary, have *On Generation,* II. ii. no limits in themselves. 'Water', says Aristotle, 'is not bounded by a boundary of its own substance.' Liquids therefore cannot be taken possession of unless they are contained in something else; as being thus contained, lakes and ponds have been taken possession of, and likewise rivers, because they are restrained by banks. But the sea is not contained by the land, since it is equal to the land, or VII. xii larger;[2] for this reason the ancients said that the land is bounded [*Life of Apollonius of Tyana,* VIII. xxvi]. by the sea. 'The ocean has been thrown about the land as a fetter' are the words of Apollonius as quoted by Philostratus.

In Gellius, Sulpicius Apollinaris asks, 'What can be said to be II. xiii [XII. xiii. 20]. on this side of the Ocean, surrounding [115] and encircling, as it does, all lands from all sides?' Later he adds: 'Since in fact the Ocean flows about all lands on all sides, nothing is on this side of it; but since all lands are enclosed by the circuit of its waters, all things which are confined within its shores are in the midst of it.' Marcus Acilius, the consul, in his speech to his soldiers, which is found in Livy, refers to 'the Ocean, which with its embrace fixes the boundary [XXXVI. xvii. 15.] of the world'. In Seneca's *Suasoriae* the ocean is said to be the bond [I. ii.] of the whole world and the bulwark of the earth, while Lucan speaks [V. 619.] of it as 'the earth-encircling wave'.

A division of the sea, further, is not to be imagined; for when the lands were first divided the sea was still for the greater part unknown. In consequence, no system can be conceived by which races so widely separated could have come to an agreement regarding such a division.

3. Those things, therefore, which were common to all men, and were not divided in the first division, no longer pass into private ownership through division, but through occupation. And they are not divided until after they have become subject to private ownership.

IV.—*That unoccupied lands become the property of the individuals who become occupants of them, unless they have been taken over as a whole by a people*

Let us proceed to the things which can be made subject of private ownership, but have not yet become private property. Of

[1] So Horace [*Odes*, III. xxiv. 12] calls the acres which have no possessor 'unmeasured'.

[2] This was perceived, in regard to the Ocean, by Iarchas, cited by Philostratus, III. xi [*Life of Apollonius of Tyana*, III. xxxvii].

such sort are many places hitherto uncultivated,[1] islands in the sea,[2] wild animals, fish, and birds.

In this connexion two points must be noted. Possession may be taken in two ways, either of an undivided whole, or by means of individual allotments. The first method is ordinarily employed by a people, or by the ruler of a people; the second, by individuals. Possession by individual allotments, nevertheless, is more often taken in consequence of a grant than by free occupation.

If, however, anything which has been occupied as a whole has not yet been assigned to individual owners, it ought not on that account to be considered as unoccupied property; for it remains subject to the ownership of the first occupant, whether a people or a king. To this class ordinarily rivers, lakes, ponds, forests, and rugged mountains belong.

V.—*That wild animals, fish, and birds belong to the man who has caught them, unless a law forbids*

Covarruvias, *On Sext*, V. ult. 4, pt. ii, § 8.

Doctors, *On Code*, I. i. 1. Innocent and Panormitanus, *On Decretals*, V. xxxix. 1.

Covarruvias, passage cited above.

In regard to wild animals, fish, and birds, this observation needs to be made, that whoever has control over the lands and waters can by his order prohibit any person from taking wild animals, fish or birds, and thereby acquiring them. Such an order is binding even upon foreigners, the reason being that for the government of a people it is morally necessary that foreigners who mingle with them even temporarily—as happens when foreigners enter a country—should conform to the institutions of that people.

The principle stated is not at variance with what we often read in the Roman law, that according to the law of nature, or the law of nations, a man is free to hunt such animals. This holds true, in fact, so long as municipal law does not intervene; thus the Roman law left in their primitive condition matters concerning which different nations have established different usages. When, however, municipal law has laid down a different rule, the law of nature itself prescribes that this must be obeyed. For although municipal law cannot enjoin anything which the law of nature forbids, or forbid what the law of nature enjoins, it can nevertheless set limits to natural liberty, and forbid what by nature was permitted; thus, through exercise of the power which belongs to it, municipal law can by anticipation prevent an acquisition of ownership which by the law of nature might have been permitted.

[1] See Bembo, *History*, Book VI [near the beginning].

[2] As the Echinades, which Alcmaeon took possession of and made his own; Thucydides, II, at the end [II. cii].

VI.—*That in case of necessity men have the right to use things which have become the property of another, and whence this right comes*

1. Now let us see whether men in general possess any right over things which have already become the property of another.

Some perchance may think it strange that this question should be raised, since the right of private ownership seems completely to have absorbed the right which had its origin in a state of community of property. Such, however, is not the case. We must, in fact, consider what the intention was of those who first introduced individual ownership; and we are forced to believe that it was their intention to depart as little as possible from natural equity. For as in this sense even written laws are to be interpreted, much more should such a point of view prevail in the interpretation of usages which are not held to exact statement by the limitations of a written form.

2. Hence it follows, first, that in [116] direst need the primitive right of user revives, as if community of ownership had remained, since in respect to all human laws—the law of ownership included—supreme necessity seems to have been excepted.

3. Hence it follows, again, that on a voyage, if provisions fail, whatever each person has ought to be contributed to the common stock. Thus, again, if fire has broken out, in order to protect a building belonging to me I can destroy a building of my neighbour. I can, furthermore, cut the ropes or nets in which my ship has been caught,[1] if it cannot otherwise be freed. None of these rules was introduced by the civil law, but they have all come into existence through interpretations of it.

Dig. XIV. ii. 2. § 2. *Digest,* XLVII. ix. 3. § 7. *Dig.* IX. ii. 29. § 3.

4. Even among the theologians the principle has been accepted that, if a man under stress of such necessity takes from the property of another what is necessary to preserve his own life, he does not commit a theft.

Thomas Aquinas, II. ii. 66. 7. Covarruvias, *On Sext,* V. ult. 4, pt. ii, § 1. Soto, V, qu. iii, art. 4.

The reason which lies back of this principle is not, as some allege, that the owner of a thing is bound by the rule of love to give to him who lacks; it is, rather, that all things seem to have been distributed to individual owners with a benign reservation in favour of the primitive right. For if those who made the original distribution had been asked what they thought about this matter they would have given the same answer that we do. 'Necessity,' says Seneca the father, 'the great resource of human weakness, breaks every

[1] Such acts are not to be committed except in connexion with matters of great importance, when the need is pressing, as Ulpian says, *Digest,* XLIII. xxiv. 7 [§ 3–4], where he adds the illustration of destroying a house for the sake of stopping a fire.

P 2

law,'[1] meaning, of course, human law, or law constituted after the [xii. 28.] fashion of human law. Cicero in his eleventh *Philippic* averred: 'Cassius has set out for Syria, a province belonging to another, if men observed written laws; but since these have been suppressed, [VI. iv. 11.] it becomes his province by the law of nature.' In Curtius we read: 'In a common disaster each man has whatever falls to his lot.'

VII.—*That the right, in case of necessity, to use things belonging to others, holds when the necessity is in no way avoidable*

Admonitions, however, must be kept in mind, that this permission to use property belonging to another may not be carried beyond proper limits.

Lessius, Book II, xii, dub. 12, no. 70. The first is, that every effort should be made to see whether the necessity can be avoided in any other way, as, for example, by appealing to a magistrate, or even by trying through entreaties to [*Laws*, VIII = 344B.] obtain the use of the thing from the owner. Plato authorizes the taking of water from a neighbour's well only in case one in search of water has dug on his own land clear to the underlying stratum of chalk. Solon gives such authorization only in case one has dug on his own [*Solon*, xxiii = 91C.] land to a depth of forty cubits; in regard to Solon's rule Plutarch adds: 'He thought to minister to need, not to show indulgence to laziness.' In his answer to the people of Sinope Xenophon said: *Anabasis*, V [v. 16]. 'Wherever the right to purchase is not granted to us, whether on Greek or on barbarian soil, we take what we have need of, not from lawlessness but from necessity.'

VIII.—*That the right, in case of necessity, to use things belonging to another, holds except when the possessor has equal need*

In the second place, this right cannot be conceded if the owner himself is under an equal necessity; for in like circumstances the V. xvi [*Divine Institutes*, V. xvii. 27 ff.]. position of the owner gives him the preference. 'He is not foolish', says Lactantius, 'who has not, even for his own safety, pushed a shipwrecked man from his plank, or a wounded man from his horse; for he has kept himself from the inflicting of an injury, which would be a sin; and to avoid such a sin is wisdom.' Cicero had said, in his

[1] 'It defends whatever it has compelled one to do.' Thus Seneca in *Controversies*, IV. xxvii [IX. iv. 5]. He gives examples illustrating this in excerpts from the fourth controversy [IV. iv]: 'It is necessity which lightens ships by throwing over cargo; it is necessity which stops fires by destroying houses; necessity is the law of the moment.'

Theodore Priscian, an ancient physician, says [*Gynaecia*, VI. xxiii]: 'It is expedient for pregnant women, when their lives are in danger, to obtain sure safety often with the loss of a foetus, just as the cutting off of growing boughs is helpful for trees; and when overloaded ships are tossed about by a violent tempest they find their safety only in loss of cargo.' The first part of this passage implies the use of the 'obstetrical forceps', an instrument described by Galen and Celsus [VII. xxix]; and so the name of the same instrument must be restored in Tertullian, *On the Soul* [xxv].

third book *On Duties*: 'Should not the wise man, therefore, if he is exhausted with hunger, take food away from another man who is of no account? By no means. For my life is no more precious to me than the possession of such a spirit that I would not harm any one for the sake of my own advantage.' In Curtius we read: 'The man who will not part with his own has a better case than the man who demands what belongs to another.' [III. vi. 29.] [VII. i. 33.]

IX.—*That there is, further, an obligation to restore the things of another used in case of necessity, whenever restoration shall be possible*

In the third place, restitution of another's property which has been used in case of necessity must be made whenever this can be done. Adrian, [*Quaestiones*] *Quodlibeticae*, I, art. 2, col. 3.

There are some who hold a different opinion. Their plea is, that the man who has availed himself of his own right is not bound to make restitution. But it is nearer the truth to say, that the right here was not absolute, but was restricted by the burden of making restitution, where necessity allowed. [117] Such a right is adequate to maintain natural equity against any hardship occasioned by private ownership. Covarruvias, as cited [*On Sext*, V. ult. 4, pt.ii, § 8.]

X.—*Application of this right in the case of wars*

From what has been said we can understand how it is permissible for one who is waging a just war to take possession of a place situated in a country free from hostilities. Such procedure, of course, implies these conditions, that there is not an imaginary but a real danger that the enemy will seize the place and cause irreparable damage; further, that nothing be taken except what is necessary for protection, such as the mere guarding of the place, the legal jurisdiction and revenues being left to the rightful owner; and, finally, that possession be had with the intention of restoring the place as soon as the necessity has ceased.

'Henna was retained by an act either culpable, or justified by necessity,' says Livy; for whatever departs in the least degree from necessity is culpable. When the Greeks who were with Xenophon were in pressing need of ships, on the advice of Xenophon himself they seized the vessels that were passing by, yet took possession in such a way that they kept the cargoes unharmed for the owners, furnished provisions also to the sailors, and paid passage money. XXIV [xxxix. 7]. *Anabasis*, V [i. 11 ff.].

The first right then that, since the establishment of private ownership, still remains over from the old community of property, is that which we have called the right of necessity.

XI.—*That men possess the right to use things which have become the property of another, for a purpose which involves no detriment to the owner*

A second right is that of innocent use.

On Duties, I [xvi. 51 f.]. 'Why,' says Cicero, 'when a man can do so without loss to himself, should he not share with another things that are useful to the recipient and can be spared without annoyance to the giver?' *On Benefits*, IV [xxix]. Thus Seneca declares that opportunity to get a light for a fire is not to be considered a favour. [=703 B.] In Plutarch we read the following, in the seventh book of his *Symposiacs*: 'It is not right for us to destroy food, when we ourselves have more than enough; or to stop up or conceal a spring, when we have drunk all we wanted; or to obliterate the signs which mark the route for ships, or signs on land which have been useful to us.'

XII.—*Hence the right to the use of running water*

Thus a river, viewed as a stream, is the property of the people through whose territory it flows, or of the ruler under whose sway that people is. It is permissible for the people or king to run a pier out into it, and to them all things produced in the river belong. *Dig.* I. viii. 2. But the same river, viewed as running water, has remained common property, so that any one may drink or draw water from it.

[*Art of Love*, III, line 93 f.]

> Who would forbid from lighted torch a light
> To take, and guarded hold in hollow sea
> The waters vast?

says Ovid. In the same author Latona thus addresses the Lycians:

[*Metamorphoses*, VI. 349.]

> Why water me deny? Common to all
> The use of water is.

There also he calls the waves a public blessing, that is a blessing common to mankind, using a less appropriate meaning of the word 'public'. In that sense certain things are said to be public by the [*Aeneid*, VII. 230.] law of nations; and with this meaning Virgil referred to the wave as open to all men.

XIII.—*Hence, also, the right of passage over land and rivers, with explanation*

1. Similarly also lands, rivers, and any part of the sea that has become subject to the ownership of a people, ought to be open to those who, for legitimate reasons, have need to cross over them;

as, for instance, if a people has been forced to leave its own territories and is seeking unoccupied lands, or desires to carry on commerce with a distant people, or is even seeking to recover by just war what belongs to it. In such cases the reason is the same as that stated above; it is altogether possible that ownership was introduced with the reservation of such a use,[1] which is of advantage to the one people, and involves no detriment to the other. Consequently it must be held that the originators of private ownership had such a reservation in view.

Baldus, *Consilia*, III. 293.

2. A noteworthy example we find in the history of Moses. When he found it necessary to pass through the territories of others, he offered first to the Idumaeans, then [118] to the Amorites, these stipulations, that he would follow the king's highway and would not turn aside into private possessions; that if he should have need of anything belonging to them he would pay them a fair price. When these terms were refused, for that reason he waged a just[2] war against the Amorites. 'A passage void of wrong,' says Augustine, 'which according to the most equitable law of human society ought to have been freely granted, was refused.'

Numbers, xx, xxi.

On Numbers, IV, qu. xx [*On Heptateuch*, IV. xliv].

3. The Greeks with Clearchus said: 'We shall return home, if no one interferes with us; but if any one does us injury we shall endeavour, with the help of the gods, to defend ourselves.'

[*Anab.*, II. iii. 23.]

With much the same point of view Agesilaus,[3] when on his return from Asia he had reached the Troad, asked whether they wished him to pass through as a friend or as an enemy. Lysander,[4] too, put the question to the Boeotians, whether they wished him to pass through with spears raised, or lowered. According to Tacitus the Batavians announced to the inhabitants of Bonna, that 'their march would be void of harm if no one should resist them, but if arms should be taken up against them they would make a way with the sword.'

Plutarch, *Apothegms* [= 211 C].

Histories, IV. [xx].

When Cimon was bringing help to the Lacedaemonians, he led his forces through the Corinthian territory. He was criticized by the Corinthians for not having first obtained permission of the state; they declared that one who knocks at the door of another does not enter without the owner's permission. 'But', he replied, 'you did not knock at the doors of the Cleonians and Megarians, but

Plutarch, *Cimon* [xvii = 489 C].

1 Servius, *On the Aeneid*, VII [VII, line 229], the words 'we seek a harmless shore': 'A shore', he says, 'the defence of which could harm no one.'

2 'Just wars were waged by the sons of Israel against the Amorites,' says Augustine in the passage cited. Thus Hercules killed Amyntor, king of Orchomenos, for refusing him passage, as Apollodorus notes [*Library*, II. vii. 7]. The Scholiast on Horace's verses *Against Canidia* [*Epodes*, xvii. 8] notes: 'The Greeks made war on Josephus [Telephus] because he did not allow them to pass through his territory.' See also the *Law of the Lombards*, Book II, liv. 2.

3 See also Plutarch in his life [*Agesilaus*, xvi = 604 C, D; *Apothegms*, 211 C] on this subject.

4 Plutarch, in the life of this same man [*Apothegms, Lysander*, vii = 229 C; *Lysander*, xxii = 445 D].

you broke them down, thinking that all places ought to be open to the stronger.'

The correct view is that which lies between extremes. It holds that permission to pass ought first [1] to be demanded; but, if it is refused, passage can be made by force. So when Agesilaus [2] on his return from Asia demanded from the king of Macedonia permission to pass, and the latter had said that he would take the matter under advisement, Agesilaus replied: 'Let him take it under advisement; in the meantime we shall go across.'

4. Furthermore no one will be justified in raising the objection that he fears the numbers of those passing through. My right is not extinguished by your fear; all the less in this case, for the reason that there are precautions which can be taken, as, for example, by arranging that troops be sent across in separate detachments; or, as the people of Colonia Agrippina proposed to the Germans, without their arms,[3] a practice in vogue in ancient times, also in the country of the Eleans, as Strabo observed. Another precaution is, for the one who grants the passage to hire suitable garrisons for his own protection, at the expense of him who makes the passage; or to see that hostages are given,[4] following the example of Seleucus, who demanded hostages of Demetrius in return for the permission to remain within the limits of his empire.

Tacitus, *Histories*, IV [lxv].

VIII [iii. 33].

[Plutarch, *Demetrius*, xlviii = 912E.]

Thus, again, fear of the ruler, against whom the one requesting passage is waging a lawful war, cannot be urged as a valid excuse for refusing passage. Equally inadmissible is it to say that passage could be had by another route; for any one might say the same thing, and in that way the right of passage would be altogether done away with. But it is enough if passage is demanded without evil intent, by the route which is nearest and most convenient.

[1] Aristophanes, *Birds* [lines 188 f.]:

> As when to Delphi journey must be made
> The Boeotians for passage first we ask.

Here the Scholiast says: 'Only then a right of passage is demanded when an army is being led through.'

The Venetians gave passage to both Germans and French in the struggle for Marano; Paruta, [*History of Venice*,] Book XI. Likewise when the Germans [125] complained about the granting of passage to their enemies the Venetians showed that such passage could not have been hindered except by force of arms, and arms they were not accustomed to use except against open enemies; [Paruta] in the same book.

The Pope also offered a like excuse, according to the same author, Book XII [at the end].

[2] On this matter also see Plutarch, in his life [*Agesilaus*, xvi = 604 E].

[3] An example is found in the *Selections on Embassies*, xii, and in Bembo, *History of Italy*, Book VII [*History of Venice* (Venice, 1551), p. 104]. See also the notable treaties between Frederick Barbarossa and Isaac Angelus concerning a passage; Nicetas, *Isaac Angelus*, Book II, *passim* [II. iv. 7].

In the German Empire one demanding passage gives bond to make good the damage. See also Krantz, *History of Saxony*, Book X, and Mendoza, *Belgica* [*Commentaries*, I. x–xiv].

Caesar was unwilling to grant to the Helvetians a right of way through a province because he thought that men disposed to evil would not restrain themselves from wrongdoing and depredations; *Gallic War*, I [I. vii].

[4] You will find an example in Procopius, *Persian War*, II [II. xxi. 26].

If he who wishes to pass is obviously commencing an unlawful war, or if he is bringing enemies of mine with him,[1] I can refuse the passage; it would be right to meet him on his own ground, and hinder his passage.

5. Such passage, furthermore, ought to be conceded not only for persons but also for merchandise. No one, in fact, has the right to hinder any nation from carrying on commerce with any other nation at a distance. That such permission be accorded is in the interest of human society and does not involve loss to any one; if one fails to realize an anticipated gain, to which he is not entitled, that ought not to be accounted a real loss. To the evidence which we have elsewhere cited upon this point, we shall add an excerpt from Philo:[2] [*Mare Liberum*, viii and xii.]

> The sea in every part is traversed without danger by merchant vessels, carrying the commerce which [119] has grown up between nations out of a natural desire to maintain a social relationship, while the abundance of some ministers to the need of others.[3] For envy has never gained the ascendancy either over the whole world, or over any large part of it.

Another bit of testimony comes from Plutarch, who speaks of the sea in the following words: 'This element has united and has rounded out our life, which without it had been savage and without commercial intercourse; supplying, as it does, through mutual help what was lacking, and through the interchange of commodities fostering a social relationship and friendliness.' [*Whether Water or Fire is More Useful*, p. 957A.]

In harmony with this is the statement of Libanius: 'God did not bestow all products upon all parts of the earth, but distributed His gifts over different regions, to the end that men might cultivate a social relationship because one would have need of the help of

[1] This was said by the Franks, who were in Venetia, to Narses, who was bringing Lombards with him; *Gothic War*, IV [IV. xxvi]. Other examples of denial of the right to pass you find in Bembo, *History of Italy*, Book VII [*History of Venice* as cited, p. 104]; Paruta, *History of Venice*, V and VI.

[2] In his *Embassy to Gaius* [vii].

[3] In Florus, Book III [III. vi]: 'If you destroy commerce, you sunder the alliance which binds together the human race.' Servius, *On the Eclogues*, IV [line 38]: 'Navigation arises from consideration for merchandise.' The same commentator, *On the Georgics*, I [line 137]: 'He means that men acquired skill in sailing, and fondness for it, through the necessity of seeking interchange of goods.' 'It was a common good that the commerce of the sea was unhampered' [cf. Seneca, *On Benefits*, I. viii].

Ambrose, in his work on creation [*Hexaemeron*, III. v. 22]: 'The good sea is as it were the lodging-place of the rivers; the bearer of commerce, by which distant peoples are bound together.' The thought was borrowed from Basil, *Hexaemeron*, iv. Theodoret, *On Providence*, II [II. 509], elegantly says: 'The sea is the open market-place of the world; the islands are stations in the sea.'

I shall add the words of Chrysostom *To Stelechius* [*On Compunction*, v]: 'But how may one worthily set forth the facility given us for mutual commerce? For that the length of the journey might not cause hindrance to visits to one another, everywhere in the world God has arranged a shorter way, the sea, in order that, inhabiting the world as a common home, so to say, we might make frequent visits to one another, and that every one, sharing his own goods with others, might profitably receive their surplus in exchange; and that so, possessing only a small part of the earth, each might enjoy its fruits from every quarter, as if he possessed it all. In fact now, just as at a common table, each of the guests may pass the food in front of him to one sitting farther away, and receive the things in front of the others by merely extending his hand.'

another. And so He called commerce into being, that all men might be able to have common enjoyment of the fruits of earth, no matter where produced.' Euripides also in the *Suppliants*, where he represents Theseus as speaking, reckons navigation among the things which human reason has devised for the common good, using these words:

[Ll. 209–210.]

> The sea we traverse, that by interchange
> The lack of our own land we may supply.

III [vi]. In Florus are the words: 'If you destroy commerce, you sunder the alliance which binds together the human race.'

XIV.—*Whether a tax may be imposed upon merchandise passing through a country*

1. But the question is raised, whether merchandise in transit through a country, transported across the land, or by river, or over a part of the sea which may be considered as belonging with the land, can be made subject to taxes by him who holds the sovereign power in the country.

Surely equity does not permit the imposition of any burdens that have no relation to the merchandise actually in transit. Similarly, a capitation tax levied on citizens to help carry the expenses of the state cannot be collected from foreigners who pass through.

2. If, however, expenses are incurred in furnishing protection for the merchandise, or other burdens also are increased on account of it, then a tax may be levied upon the merchandise in order to make reimbursement, provided that in determining the tax the amount actually required shall not be exceeded;[1] for upon this depends the justice of a tax as well as of tribute.

I Kings, x. 28. In accordance with this principle King Solomon received a tax on horses and on linen thread which passed across the Isthmus of Suez. Of frankincense Pliny says: 'It cannot be exported except through the territory of the Gebanites,[2] and so a tax is paid to their king.' Thus the people of Marseilles were enriched from the canal which Marius had dug from the Rhone to the sea, 'collecting a tax[3] from those who went up or down the river by ship,' as Strabo says in his fourth book. In the eighth book the same author tells us that the people of Corinth even from the most ancient times

[*Natural History*,] XII. xiv.

[IV. i. 8; VIII. vi. 20.]

[126] [1] See the *Law of the Lombards*, xxxi. 33 [III. i. 31–2]; likewise the letter of the bishops to King Louis, which is found in the *Capitularies* of Charles the Bald, chap. xiv [*Mon. Germ. Hist., Leges*, II, vol. II, p. 438].

[2] A similar statement is found in Leo of Africa [*Description of Africa*, Book I], near the beginning.

[3] Aristophanes, alluding to this subject in the *Birds* [lines 190 ff.], wishes that the passage through the air may be obstructed, that the gods may be compelled to pay a tax on the fumes of the burnt-offerings.

collected a tax on merchandise which, in order to avoid the circuitous voyage around Cape Malea, was carried across the land from sea to sea. In the same way the Romans received toll for the crossing of the Rhine. 'Toll is paid even for crossing on bridges', says Seneca. In respect to the passage of rivers, the books of the jurists are full.

Tac., *Hist.*, IV [lxv. 6]. [*De Const. Sap.*, xiv.]

3. However, it frequently happens that the tax imposed is unfair. The emirs of the Arabs were charged with this abuse by Strabo, who adds: 'It is, in fact, difficult, among peoples that are powerful and wild, to obtain the fixing of a tax that will not be burdensome to the trader.'

Choppin, *De Domanio*, I. ix. Pereg., *De Jure Fisci*, I. i. 22. Angelus, *Cons.*, 190. Zabarella, *Cons.*, 38. Firmanus, in his *De Gabellis*. XVI [i. 27].

[120] XV.—*The right of temporary sojourn*

1. To those who pass through a country, by water or by land, it ought to be permissible to sojourn for a time, for the sake of health, or for any other good reason; for this also finds place among the advantages which involve no detriment. So in Virgil,[1] when the Trojans were forbidden to sojourn in Africa, Ilioneus dared to appeal to the gods as judges. The Greeks viewed as well founded the complaint of the people of Megara against the Athenians, who forbade the Megarians to enter their harbours, 'contrary to common right,' as Plutarch says. To the Lacedaemonians no cause for war seemed more just.

Victoria, *Relect. de Indis*, II. no. 1. [*Aeneid*, I. 543.] *Pericles* [xxix = 168 B]. Diodorus Sic., XII [xxxix]. Thucydides, I [lxvii].

2. A natural consequence of this is that it is permissible to build a temporary hut, for example on the seashore, even if we admit that possession of the coast has been taken by a people. For when Pomponius said that an order of the praetor must be obtained before one would be allowed to erect any building on a public shore or in the sea reference was made to permanent structures. To such the lines of the poet refer:

[*Digest*, XLI. i. 50.]

[Horace, *Odes*, III. i. 33.]

> The fish are conscious that a narrower bound
> Is drawn the seas around
> By masses huge hurl'd down into the deep.

XVI.—*Those who have been driven from their homes have the right to acquire a permanent residence in another country, in submission to the government there in authority*

Furthermore a permanent residence ought not to be denied to foreigners who, expelled from their homes, are seeking a refuge, provided that they submit themselves to the established government

[1] Servius comments on this passage [*On the Aeneid*, I, lines 540 ff.]: 'The possession of the shore belongs to the occupant. Hence they are shown to be cruel who try to keep others from the enjoyment of the common right.' According to the statement of the same author [*On the Aeneid*, I, line 619], Laomedon was killed by Hercules because he forced Hercules to leave the harbour of Troy.

and observe any regulations which are necessary in order to avoid strifes. This fair distinction the divine poet observes when he represents Aeneas as offering the following terms :

[Virgil, *Aeneid*, XII. 192f.]

> Latinus, as my sire, his arms shall keep,
> And as my sire his sovereign sway shall hold
> Inviolate.

[Dionysius Hal.,] I [lviii].

In the work of the Halicarnassian, Latinus himself says that the cause of Aeneas is just, if Aeneas had been forced to come to his country by the lack of an abiding-place.

XVII [i. 19]. *On Duties*, III. vii.

'It is characteristic of barbarians to drive away strangers,' says Strabo, following Eratosthenes ; and in this respect the Spartans failed to gain approval. In the opinion of Ambrose, also, those who keep foreigners out of their city are by no means worthy of approval.

Herod., I. [cl] and IV [cxlv]. Pausan., VII [ii. 2]. Orosius, VII ; Diodorus, V [lviii]. IV. vi [ext. 3].

In conformity with the principle stated the Aeolians received the people of Colophon ; the Rhodians, Phorbas and his companions ; the Carians, the people of Melos ; the Lacedaemonians, the Minyae ; and the Cumaeans, others who came to them. But in regard to the Minyae, when, after being admitted, they demanded a share in the government, Herodotus justly says : 'They were insolent and did what it was not right to do' ; Valerius Maximus declared that they returned a kindness by an injury.

XVII.—*The right of possession over desert places in respect to foreigners, and how this must be understood*

Again, if within the territory of a people there is any deserted and unproductive soil, this also ought to be granted to foreigners if they ask for it. Or it is right for foreigners even to take possession of such ground, for the reason that uncultivated land ought not to be considered as occupied except in respect to sovereignty, which remains unimpaired in favour of the original people.

On the Aeneid, XI [316]. [=p. 105 c.]

To the Trojans seven hundred [1] acres of hard, rough land were given, as Servius notes, by the Latin aborigines. In the seventh *Oration* of Dio of Prusa we read : 'They who bring under cultivation an untilled portion of the earth commit no wrong.'

Tacitus, *Annals*, XIII [lv].

Once the Ansibarii cried out : 'As the heavens were granted to the gods, so the lands of earth were granted to the race of mortals, and all lands that are unoccupied are public property. Nay more, the barbarians raised their eyes to the sun and the stars and asked these, as if speaking face to face, whether they wished to look upon soil unoccupied ; rather might they pour the sea over it against the monopolisers of the earth !' However, the Ansibarii made an

[1] The statement is derived from Cato, Sisenna, and others of the ancients [Servius, *On the Aeneid*, XI, line 316].

unfortunate application of these general principles to the case in hand, for the lands requested were not vacant, but furnished pasturage for the flocks and herds of the soldiers; and this consideration gave the Romans a just cause for refusal. With no less justice the Romans formerly asked the Senonian Gauls, 'What right they had to demand land from the rightful owners, or threaten these with war?' Livy, V [xxxvi. 5].

XVIII.—*The right to such acts as human life requires*

After the common right which relates to things follows the common right which relates to [121] acts.

The common right relating to acts is conceded either directly or by supposition. It is conceded directly in respect to acts indispensable for the obtaining of the things without which life cannot be comfortably lived. Here in fact the same degree of necessity is not required as for taking another's property; for it is not now a question of what may be done against the will of an owner, but rather of the mode of acquiring things with the consent of those to whom they belong; provided only that no obstacle be interposed by the passing of a law or by conspiracy. Such a hindrance, in fact, is at variance with the nature of society in relation to those matters of which I have spoken. This is what Ambrose [1] calls 'to separate men from relation with their common parent, to refuse fruits freely produced for all, and to do away with the community of life.' For we are here dealing not with things which are superfluous and ministrant to pleasures only, but with things which life requires, as food, clothing, and medicines. *On Duties*, III. vii [45].

XIX.—*The right to such acts as human life requires includes the right to buy the things that are necessary*

We affirm, therefore, that all men have the right to buy such things at a fair price, unless they are needed by the person from whom they are sought; thus in times of extreme scarcity [2] the sale of grain is forbidden. Covarruvias, *Var. Res.*, III. xiv. 3.

Not even in circumstances of so great need, however, can foreigners, who have once been admitted to a country, be expelled;

[1] Plutarch, in his *Pericles* [xxix = 168 B], says of the Megarians: 'They complained that, contrary to the laws of nations, they were hindered from all trading, and expelled from every port which the Athenians held.' On the line of Virgil [*Georgics*, I. 53]: 'And what each land may bear, and what it fails to yield,' Seneca, *Letters*, lxxxvii [20 f.], comments thus: 'Those products were assigned to different regions in order that commerce might be necessary for mortals, if they wished to get things from one another.' In another passage, *Natural Questions*, V. xviii, he says: 'What of the fact that he has given to all peoples commerce with one another, and has mingled races separated far from each other?'

See the complaints of the English against the Spaniards in De Thou, Book LXXI [LXXI. i], dealing with the history of the year 1580.

[2] Cassiodorus, I, letter xxxiv [*Var.*, I. xviii]: 'A supply of grain ought first to advantage the province where it grows.'

but Ambrose shows, in the passage already cited, that a common misfortune must be endured in common.

Molina, disp. 105. Aegidius Regius, *De Actibus Supernaturalibus*, disp. 31, dub. 2, no. 52. Caesar, *Gallic War*, I [II. xv]. Strabo, XVI [iv. 26].

XX.—*The right to such acts as human life requires does not oblige a man to sell what belongs to him*

But there is not an equally valid right obliging a man to sell what belongs to him; for every one is free to decide what he will or will not acquire.

Thus the Belgians formerly did not permit the importation of wine and other foreign wares. Of the Nabataean Arabs Strabo says: 'Some goods it is permissible to import,[1] but not others.'

XXI.—*The right to such acts as human life requires includes the right to seek marriages in foreign countries; explanation*

1. In this right, of which we have spoken, we think there is included also liberty to seek and contract marriages among neighbouring peoples; as, for example, in case a large number of men has been expelled from one place and has come to another. Although, to be sure, it is not entirely repugnant to human nature for a man to live without a woman, nevertheless this is repugnant to the nature of most men. Celibacy is suited only to those who possess superior endowments.

Livy, I [ix. 4]. Livy, IV [iii. 4]. *City of God*, II. xvii.

Men ought not, therefore, to be cut off from the opportunity to secure wives. In Livy Romulus urges his neighbours 'that as men they should not be reluctant to mingle their blood and race with men'. In the same author, Canuleius says: 'We ask the right of marriage, which is customarily granted to neighbours and to foreigners.' In the opinion of Augustine, 'The victor might by right of war justly secure marriages which had been unjustly denied.'

2. The civil laws of some peoples, which deny the right of marriage to foreigners, either support their contention by this consideration, that at the time when the laws were passed there were no peoples without an abundance of women, or else they do not treat of marriages of all kinds but only of those which are regular, that is, marriages which produce certain special effects in civil law.

XXII.—*The right to do those things which are permitted without distinction to foreigners*

Victoria, *Relectiones* [*de Indis*], II, no. 2, 3.

A common right by supposition relates to the acts which any people permits without distinction to foreigners; for if under such circumstances a single people is excluded, a wrong is done to it.

[1] See Krantz, *History of Saxony*, Book XI [XI. iii].

Thus if foreigners are anywhere permitted to hunt, fish, snare birds, or gather pearls, to inherit by will, to sell property, and even to contract marriages in case there is no scarcity of women, such rights cannot be denied to one people alone, except on account of previous wrong-doing.

It was for this reason that the rest of the Jews took away the right of intermarriage from members of the tribe of Benjamin. *Judges*, xx.

XXIII.—*Such a right must be understood as applying only to things permitted as it were by the law of nature, not granted as a favour*

What we have said about permissible acts must be understood as applying to acts which have been permitted as deriving from the force of natural liberty, which have not been annulled by any statute law; not as applying to acts which have been permitted by favour, as an exception to the law. In the refusal of a favour there is no injustice.

In this way, we believe, it is possible to reconcile [122] what Molina said, after Franciscus de Victoria, and as if in opposition to him. Disp. 105.

XXIV.—*Whether a contract is permissible with a people that it should sell its crops to those with whom it has made the contract, and not to others*

I recall that the question has been raised, whether it is permissible for a people to make an agreement with another people to sell to it alone products of a certain kind, which do not grow elsewhere.

I think that this is allowable, if the people which buys is prepared to sell to others at a fair price. It makes no difference, in fact, to other nations, from whom they buy what satisfies the demands of nature. It is lawful, however, for one people to anticipate another in obtaining a pecuniary advantage, especially if there is a reason; as, for instance, if the people which has obtained the concession has taken the other under its protection and on that account is incurring expense.

Such an arrangement to purchase, made with the intent of which I have spoken, is not at variance with the law of nature, although in practice it is sometimes forbidden by municipal law in the public interest.

CHAPTER III

OF ORIGINAL ACQUISITION OF THINGS, WITH SPECIAL REFERENCE TO THE SEA AND RIVERS

I.—*That original acquisition is accomplished through division or through occupation*

[127] FROM the view-point of individual right a thing becomes our own through acquisition, either original or derivative.

Formerly, when the human race could assemble, primary acquisition could take place also through division, as we have said; now it takes place through occupation only.

II.—*In this connexion other modes of acquisition, as the granting of an incorporeal right, are excluded from consideration*

Some one may perchance say that a kind of primary right is acquired through the granting of a servitude, or the giving of a pledge. To him who carefully weighs the matter, however, it will become apparent that under such conditions there is no new right except in form; for in essence the right was present in the proprietary right of the owner

III.—*The forming of a new property from existing materials is also excluded from consideration*

To the means through which acquisition may be accomplished
Dig. XLI. ii. 3. § 21. Paul the jurist adds also this—which seems altogether consistent with nature—'that we have caused something to come into existence'.

In nature, however, nothing is produced except from matter which previously existed. If, then, the material belonged to us, the ownership of that which is produced will continue, even though a new form is presented. If the material belonged to no one, in that case acquisition will be classed under the head of acquisition by occupation. On the other hand, if the material used was the property of another, the thing produced naturally does not belong to us alone, as will become apparent later.

IV.—*Occupation is twofold, having relation to sovereignty and to ownership; this distinction is explained*

1. It is, then, occupation—which since those primitive times has been, and remains, the only natural and primary mode of acquisition—with which we are concerned.

Now in respect to that which, in a proper sense, belongs to no one, there are two possible types of possession, sovereignty and ownership, in so far as ownership is distinguished from sovereignty. The difference between the two types is thus brought out by Seneca: 'To kings [1] belongs the power over all things; to individuals, proprietorship.' Dio of Prusa makes the distinction clear in this way: 'The territory belongs to the state, but none the less on that account does each person in it have his own property.' *Orations*, xxxi [= 324].

Sovereignty is customarily extended over two kinds of subject matter. The one, primary, consists of persons; this alone is sometimes in itself sufficient, as in the case of an army of men, women, and children seeking new places of habitation. The other, secondary, is extended over the place, which is called territory.

2. Although sovereignty and ownership are generally acquired by a single act, they are nevertheless distinct.[2] Consequently ownership passes not only to citizens but also to foreigners, while the sovereignty remains in the hands of him who previously held it. Siculus, in his work *On the Condition of the Fields*, says: 'When the lands assigned to colonies proved to be insufficient, those who were in charge of the allotment and division assigned to future citizens lands which they had taken from neighbouring territories. The jurisdiction over the lands which were assigned nevertheless remained under the control of those from whose territory they were taken.'

Demosthenes in his speech *On Halonnesus* calls the lands owned by residents of a territory 'properties', and those in a foreign territory 'non-resident properties'. [vii. 42 = 87.]

V.—*That the taking possession of movable things can be prevented by law*

We said above that in a place over which sovereignty has already been asserted the right to acquire movable things through occupation can be prevented by the municipal law.

This right exists, in fact, by permission of the law of nature, not by a positive provision that such permission should always be

[1] *On Benefits*, VII. iv [VII. iv. 2]. There follows also, v [VII. v. 1]: 'The king possesses all things by sovereignty, individuals by ownership'; again, vi [VII. vi. 3]: 'The emperor possesses all things; the imperial treasury is his private property only.' Symmachus, *Letters*, X. liv [lxi = 592 D, Migne], 'You rule all things, but you guard for each man his own.'

Philo, *On Noah's Planting* [xiii]: 'Although kings are masters of all things which are under their sway, even of those things which are the property of individuals, nevertheless they seem actually to have only that money the expenditure of which they commit to their governors and treasury officials, from whom they receive their annual income.' Pliny the Younger, *Panegyric* [l. 2]: 'Nevertheless the sovereignty of the emperor is greater than his inherited estate.'

[2] So you may see in Apollodorus [*Library*, III. ix. 1; xv. 1] that the lands, now of Arcadia, now of Attica, were divided, while 'all sovereign power' remained in the hands of one.

granted; for no such provision is demanded by the requirements of human society.

If some one says that there seems to be a law of nations implying such permission, I shall answer that, although in some parts of the world this is, or has been, the common usage, nevertheless such usage does not have the force of an agreement between nations, but is the expression of a law received by several countries individually, which can be abrogated by each of them. There are also many other practices which jurists, when they are dealing with the division of property and the acquisition of ownership, consider as belonging to the law of nations.

VI.—*On what right the ownership of property by infants and by insane persons rests*

It must be noted, further, that if we have in view the law of nature alone, ownership [128] is restricted to those who are possessed of reason. But in the common interest the law of nations introduced the provision, that both infants and insane persons should be able to acquire and retain ownership—the human race, as it were, meanwhile representing them.

Human laws indisputably have it in their province to go further than nature in regard to many points, but never to go contrary to nature. Hence this type of ownership, which by common acceptation of civilized nations has been introduced in favour of infants and those of similar condition, is limited to the first act, as the Schools say, and cannot extend to the second act; that is, it covers the right of proprietorship, but not the right of the owner himself to use what he owns. For alienation, and other acts similar thereto, by their very nature presuppose the action of a will controlled by reason, and in such persons a will subject to reason cannot exist. At this point you might not inappropriately refer to the statement of the Apostle Paul, that an heir, although the owner of an ancestral estate, while he is under age, differs in no respect from the bond-servants, of course as regards the exercise of the right of ownership.

Galatians, iv. 1.

We commenced above to say something about the sea; this ought now to be completed.

VII.—*That rivers can be acquired by occupation*

By occupation rivers can be acquired even though neither their upper nor their lower course is included in the same territory, but they are connected with water at the upper and the lower end, or with the sea. It is sufficient that the greater part, that is that the sides, shall be enclosed by banks, and that the river by itself shall be small in extent in comparison with the land.

VIII.—*That a part of the sea can likewise be acquired*

In the light of the example just given it would appear that the sea also can be acquired by him who holds the lands on both sides, even though it may extend above as a bay, or above and below as a strait, provided that the part of the sea in question is not so large that, when compared with the lands on both sides, it does not seem a part of them.

The same right, further, which is conceded to a single people or king, appears to be conceded also to two or three, if they have wished to occupy jointly a sea situated between them; in this way, in fact, rivers which flow between two peoples have been jointly occupied, and then divided.

IX.—*That formerly in the countries constituting the Roman Empire such ownership of a part of the sea was not conceded*

1. It must be admitted that, in the parts of the world that were known in connexion with the Roman Empire, from the earliest times even down to Justinian, it was not permitted by the law of nations that the sea be acquired by states through occupation, even in respect to the right to fish. Heed should not be paid to those who think that when, in the Roman law, the sea is spoken of as common to all, the meaning is that the sea is the common possession of all Romans. For in the first place the expressions are so general that they do not admit of such restriction. The expression in Latin meaning 'the sea is common to all' is interpreted by Theophilus in Greek, 'is common to all men'. Ulpian said that by nature the sea lies open to all, and so belongs to all just as the air does. Celsus declared that the use of the sea is common to all men. *Dig.* I. viii. 2. *Institutes,* II. i. 1. *Dig.* VIII. iv. 13. *Digest,* XLIII. viii. 3.

The jurists, furthermore, clearly distinguish the public possessions of a people, in which rivers, too, are included, from things that are common. Thus we read in the *Institutes*, 'By the law of nature some things are common[1] to all, some things are public property. ... Common to all by the law of nature are the following: air, running water, the sea, and, in consequence, the shores of the sea. All rivers and harbours, however, are public property.' The statement by Theophilus is: 'Therefore by the law of nature these things are common to all men, the air, ever-flowing water, the sea'; presently II. i. 1.

[1] Michael Attaliates [*Synopsis*, ii]: 'Certain things belong to all people, as the air, running water, the sea, and the shore of the sea.'

he adds, 'But all rivers and harbours are public possessions, and these now belong to the Roman people.'

Dig. XLI. i. 14.

2. Of the shores of the sea[1] Neratius said that they are not public possessions in the sense that those things are which have become the possession of a people by inheritance, but as those things which were at first the gift of nature and have not yet become subject to the ownership of any one, that is, not even of a people. This opinion is clearly at variance with what Celsus wrote: 'I think that the seashores, over which the Roman people possesses sovereign power, [129] are the property of the Roman people, but that the use of the sea is common to all men.'

Digest, XLIII. viii. 3.

These opposing views can evidently be reconciled if we say that Neratius is speaking of the seashore in so far as its use is necessary for those sailing the sea, or passing by, while Celsus is speaking of it with reference to possession for a use unlimited in time, as for a permanent structure. In the latter case, Pomponius tells us a permit was wont to be obtained from the praetor, just as a permit was required for the construction of a building in the sea, that is, in the part nearest the shore, which is reckoned as belonging to the shore.

Dig. XLI. i. 50.

X.—*That nevertheless the law of nature does not present any obstacle to such acquisition in respect to a part of the sea which is, as it were, shut in by lands*

1. Although what was just said is true, nevertheless it has resulted from established practice[2] rather than from natural reason that the sea was not occupied, or could not lawfully be occupied, in the sense in which we have spoken. A river also is public property, as we know, and yet the right to fish in a branch of a river can be acquired by an individual by occupation. But even concerning the sea Paul said: 'If a man does have a right of property in it, he is entitled to a decree of court protecting him in his possession'; the reason is that the case affects a private and not a public interest, since the question at issue concerns a right of user, which is inherent in a private, not a public matter. Paul's statement without doubt refers to a small portion of the sea[3] which is admitted into a private estate; we have

Digest, XLIV. iii. 7.

Digest, XLVII. x. 14.

[1] In *Selections from the Basilica,* I. i. 13: 'The shores are under the power of all.' See also LIII. vi.

[2] Such an established practice the English also utilized against the Danes. See the excellent Camden, *Elizabeth,* year 1600.

[3] Sallust [*Catiline,* xiii]: 'Mountains have been overthrown, seas have been built up by many private persons.' Horace, *Odes,* II. xviii [II. xviii. 20]:

> The shores of the sea against Baiae resounding
> You are extending;

and again, *Odes,* III. i [III. i. 33]:

> The fishes feel the seas are smaller made
> By mighty structures built out in the deep.

read that such use of the sea was made by Lucullus [1] and others. Of Gaius Sergius Orata, Valerius Maximus says: 'He made seas his individual possessions by shutting up waters in the inlets.' IX. i.

Afterward, in opposition to the opinions of the earlier jurists, Leo the Emperor extended the same law to the πρόθυρα, that is, the waters in front of villas, on the Thracian Bosporus,[2] so that these waters also could be shut in by certain barriers, which they called ἐποχάς (bars), and could thus be claimed as private property. *Digest*, XLVII. x. 13. § 7.

2. Now if a part of the sea can be added to estates of individuals, provided, of course, that it is enclosed and is so small that it can be considered a portion of an estate, and if the law of nature presents no obstacle to such procedure, why, also, may not a part of the sea enclosed by shores belong to that people, or to those peoples, to which the shores belong, provided that part of the sea, when compared in extent with the land of the country, is not larger than an enclosed inlet of the sea compared with the size of the private estate? That no objection can be raised on the score that the sea is not enclosed on all sides, can be understood from the example of the river and the admission of the sea into a villa.

3. But many things, which were permitted by nature, universal customary law, by a kind of common understanding, has been able to prohibit. Consequently, wherever such a law is in force, and has not, by common consent, been abrogated, a portion of the sea, however small and almost enclosed by shores, cannot become subject to the ownership of any people.

Velleius Paterculus [II. xxxiii] speaks of 'huge masses cast into the sea, and the sea received within hollowed mountains'. Seneca, *Controversies*, V. v, has this: 'The seas are pushed back by the mighty foundations hurled in.' Pliny says of the land, [*Natural History*,] II. xxxiii [II. lxiii. 157]: 'A way is washed out by waters that we may cause the sea to enter.'

Lampridius in his life of Severus [*Alexander Severus*, xxvi. 10] mentions huge fish-ponds made by admitting the sea; Cassiodorus [*Variae*], IX. vi: 'With how great masses of rock there have the bounds of the sea been fittingly entered? How far has the earth been pushed forward into the heart of the sea?' Tibullus [II. iii. 45 f.].

> And moles shut in the untamed sea, that sluggish fish
> Within the threats of winter's storms may disregard.

Pliny, [*Natural History*,] Book XXXI, vi, treats of such sea fish-ponds; also Columella, [134] *On Farming*, Book VIII, xvi and xvii, where, among other remarks, this is found: 'The luxury of the rich has shut in the very seas and Neptune.' Ambrose, *Hexaemeron*, V. x [V. x. 27], and *On Naboth*, iii [11–12], have similar remarks; also Martial, in several passages [as X. xxx. 19 ff.].

[1] Varro [*On Farming*, III. xvii. 9] says concerning him: 'After Lucius Lucullus had cut a channel through a mountain near Naples and had let the water of the sea into his fish-ponds, so that they would ebb and flow; he would not yield to Neptune in the matter of fishing.'

Plutarch in his life [*Lucullus*, xxxix = 518 c] says that 'he placed around his villas ponds of sea-water and straits full of fish, and built dining-rooms over the sea itself.'

Pliny, IX. liv [*Natural History*, IX. liv. 170]: 'By cutting a channel through a mountain near Naples Lucullus made a strait and brought in the sea at greater expense than it had cost to build the villa. And for this reason Pompey the Great used to call him the Xerxes of peace.'

[2] See the *Novellae* of Leo, lvii, cii, ciii, civ; Attaliates, *Pragmatica*, xcv; Harmenopulus, Book II, i, sec. περὶ προθύρων. See also that very able man, Jacques de Cujas, *Observations*, XIV. i.

XI.—*In what way such possession may be taken, and how long it will last*

It must also be noted that if in any place this universal customary law in regard to the sea has not been accepted, or has been abrogated, from the mere fact that a people has taken possession of the land, the inference would nevertheless not be warranted that it has obtained possession of the sea also; that, further, an act of the mind is not sufficient, but that there must be an outward act from which the taking of possession may be understood.

But if, on the other hand, possession resulting from occupation is abandoned, the sea again comes under the law of nature, that is, it is restored to common use. This opinion Papinian gave regarding the right to build on a shore and to fish in a branch of a river. *Digest*, XLI. iii. 45.

XII.—*That such possession does not give the right to impede innocent passage*

It is certain that one who has occupied a part of the sea cannot hinder navigation which is without weapons and of innocent intent, when such a passage cannot be prevented by land, where it is generally less necessary and more productive of damage.

XIII.—*That sovereignty can be acquired over a part of the sea, and in what way*

1. It has, however, been a fairly easy matter to extend sovereignty only [1] over a part of the sea without [130] involving the

[1] Philo, speaking of kings [*On Noah's Planting*, xvi], says: 'They have added to the lands also the seas, unlimited in number and immense in size.' Lycophron [*Alexandra*, line 1229] mentions

Sceptres over land and sea, and power of kings.

Virgil [*Georgics*, I, line 31]:

And thee as son-in-law would Tethys buy
With all her waves.

Julius Firmicus [*Mathesis*, VI. 1]: 'Possessing the sovereignty of sea and land.' Nonnus [*Dionysiaca*, XLII, line 474]:

And in her power Beroe held the sea.

John Magnus, *History of the Archbishops of Upsala*, xv, says that the boundary of the kingdom of Sweden was in the middle of the strait of Öresund. Curtius [IV. iv. 19] says of Tyre: 'It brought under its sway not only the neighbouring sea, but all the seas where her ships sailed.' Hence arose the proverbial expression 'Tyrian seas', found in Festus [under the word *Tyria*, p. 355, Mueller].

Isocrates [*Panathenaic Oration*, xviii = p. 243 C] says of the Lacedaemonians and Athenians: 'It came to pass that each state became the mistress of that land which was adjacent to the sea possessed by it and held the most of the cities in subjection.' Demosthenes, in his second *Philippic* [ix. 47 = 123], says of the Lacedaemonians: 'They were holding all the sea and the land.' The writer of the life of Timotheus [Nepos, *Timotheus*, ii]: 'And because of this act the Lacedaemonians abandoned their long contest and of their own will yielded the supremacy in sea power to the Athenians.'

The writer of the oration in regard to Halonnesus, which is included among the works of Demosthenes [*On Halonnesus*, vii. 14 = 80], speaking of Philip of Macedon, says: 'He seeks nothing else than to be established by us in the possession of the sea and to force a confession from us that without him we cannot retain even the guardianship of the sea.'

Julian the Emperor said of Alexander [*Orations*, III. 107 C] that he planned war with this intent, 'that he might become the lord of all land and sea'. His successor, Antiochus Epiphanes, according

right of ownership; and I do not think that any hindrance is put in the way of this by the universal customary law of which I have spoken. In ancient times the Argives complained to the Athenians because the Athenians had permitted the Spartans, enemies of the Argives, to pass through their sea; the Argives alleged a violation of the treaty, in which it had been provided that neither of the two peoples should permit the enemies of the other to pass 'through places under its jurisdiction'.

Bossius, tit. *De Aquis*, no. 36, citing Baldus, Caepolla et al. See *Code*, XI. xiii. 1.

Thucydides, Book VII [V. lvi].

During the year's truce in the Peloponnesian war, furthermore, permission was granted to the people of Megara to sail on 'the sea belonging to their own land and that of their allies'. Similarly,

Thucydides, Book IV [cxviii].

to Gorionides [Josippon, or Joseph ben Gorion; cf. Josephus, *Antiquities of the Jews*, III. xii], asks: 'Are not the land and the sea mine?' Concerning Ptolemy, another of Alexander's successors, Theocritus [*Idyls*, xvii. 76] says:

And over many lands and over many seas he rules.

[135] Also [*Idyls*, xvii. 91 f.]:

And all the land and sea,
Deep-sounding rivers, too, are ruled by Ptolemy the king.

But it is time to come to the Romans. According to Livy [XXX. xxx. 26], Hannibal said to the Elder Scipio: 'We Carthaginians, shut in by the shores of Africa, see that you, since the Gods have so willed, are ruling over the realms outside on land and sea.' Claudian [*On the Consulship of Stilicho*, III, Preface, lines 7–8] says of the Younger Scipio:

When first avenger of his country's slain
He forced the Spanish ocean under laws.

So the Romans generally call the Inner Sea their own; thus Sallust [*Jugurthine War*, xvii. 4]; Florus [I. xli. 9]; Pomponius Mela [I. v. 25], and others. But Dionysius of Halicarnassus [I. iii. 3] adds still more: 'The Roman people rules the whole sea, not only that within the Pillars of Hercules but also the outside ocean, so far as it is sailed upon.' Dio Cassius [Themistius, *Orations*, xix = 227 B] says of the same people: 'They rule over almost all the land and sea.' Appian in his Preface [ii], describing the greatness of the Roman Empire, enumerates under its dominion the Black Sea, the Sea of Marmora, the Hellespont, and the Aegean, Pamphylian, and Egyptian seas. To Pompey was given the military command over all the sea that lies within the Pillars of Hercules; thus Plutarch [*Pompey*, xxv = 631] and Appian [*Mithridatic Wars*, xiv. 94].

Philo, *Against Flaccus* [xii]: 'And from this the house of the Caesars acquired empire over land and sea.'

Of Augustus, Ovid [*Metamorphoses*, XV, line 831] says: 'The sea also shall serve him.'

Suetonius [*Augustus*, xxii] records an inscription in his honour: 'After subduing the earth and the sea Augustus closed the gate of Janus Quirinus, since peace had been thrice won on land and sea.' Speaking of the same Augustus he adds [xlix]: 'He stationed a fleet at Misenum, and another at Ravenna, for the defence of the Upper and Lower Sea.'

Valerius Maximus says to Tiberius [I, Preface]: 'The agreement of men and gods has willed that the rule over sea and land should belong to you.' Of the same emperor, Philo [*On the Embassy to Gaius*, xxi] says: 'He embraced in his rule both land and sea'; and he states [ii] concerning Gaius, the successor of Tiberius, that 'after the death of Tiberius, Gaius received the sovereignty of all land and sea.'

Josephus [*Jewish War*, III. viii. 9] calls Vespasian 'lord of land and sea.' Likewise in several passages Aristides assigns the same right to Antoninus [*Orations*, ix. 66 = 119]. Procopius [*On the Buildings of Justinian*, I. ii. = 398] relates that there were statues of the emperor represented as holding the earth in his hand, 'because land and sea were subject to him'.

In the letters of Louis II the patrician Nicetas is protector of the Adriatic shore [Goldast, *Constitut. Imperial.*, I. 118]. Constantine Monomachus is called in history 'emperor and lord of land and sea' [Joannes Episcopus Euchaitensis, *Versus Iambici*, 1224]. The Aegean Sea is reckoned among the provinces of the Roman Empire [Constantine Porphyrogenitus, *On the Provinces*, I. xvii]. Procopius, *Gothic War*, III [III. xxxiii], relates that the Franks ruled the sea about Marseilles. Concerning the rights of the Republic of Venice, see Paruta, Book VII, and his special history of the Uscochi.

To these authorities may be added the modern jurists *On Sext*, I. vi. 3; Bartolus, Angelus, Felinus, *On Decretals*, V. vi. 17; Baldus, *On Digest*, I. viii, col. 2; Afflictis, *On Feuds*, II. lvi; Cacheranus, [136] *Decisiones Pedemontanae*, clv, no. 4, where following Baldus he says that all the world uses this law; Alberico Gentili, *Advocatio Hispanica*, I. viii.

[XLII. v.] Dio Cassius, in his forty-second book, spoke of 'all the sea which belongs to the Roman Empire'. Themistius refers to the Roman Emperor as 'holding the land and the sea as subject to himself'. [*Halieut.* III. 4.] Oppian thus addresses the Emperor:

For subject to thy law sea's waters roll.

[xxxiv = 415D.] Dio of Prusa, again, in his second speech to the people of Tarsus, said that many favours had been bestowed on that state by Augustus, among them 'the jurisdiction over the river Cydnus and the nearest [*Aeneid*, I. 236.] part of the sea.' In Virgil we read:

That they in uncontested sway the sea,
The lands, should hold.

[*Attic Nights*, X. vii.] Gellius writes of the 'rivers that flow into the sea, which is subject to the power of Rome'. Strabo notes that the people of IV [i. 5]. Marseilles had taken much booty, having conquered in naval battles XII 'those who unjustly contended for control of the sea'. The same [iii. 11]. author says that Sinope asserted sovereignty over the sea as far as the Symplegades.

2. It seems clear, moreover, that sovereignty over a part of the sea is acquired in the same way as sovereignty elsewhere, that is, as we have said above, through the instrumentality of persons and of territory. It is gained through the instrumentality of persons if, for example, a fleet, which is an army afloat, is stationed at some point of the sea; by means of territory, in so far as those who sail over the part of the sea along the coast may be constrained from the land no less than if they should be upon the land itself.

XIV.—*That for certain reasons a tax can be laid upon those who sail upon the sea*

It will not, therefore, be contrary to the law of nature or of nations if he who has taken upon himself the burden of protecting navigation and of making it safe by night-flares and marks indicating shoals [1] shall impose a fair tax on those who sail.

[1] The Rhodians formerly collected port duties from the islands, also from Pharos near Alexandria, as Ammianus Marcellinus, Book XXII [XXII. xvi. 10], testifies. Caesar [*Gallic War*, III. viii. 1] says of the Veneti in Gaul: 'They collected tribute of almost all who were accustomed to sail in the same sea, since it was very rough and open and there were few ports, which they themselves held.'

Florus [II. vi. 2] says of the Romans [Carthaginians]: 'This famous people, after control of the sea had been taken away and their islands captured, was ashamed to pay the tribute which they had been accustomed to levy.'

Pliny, VI. xxii [*Natural History*, VI. xxii. 84], makes mention of Annius Plocamus, who had bought from the Imperial Treasury the customs duties for the Red Sea; and in the following chapter, treating of the sea on which one sails to India, he reports: 'Every year ships with cohorts of bowmen sailed over it; for pirates were especially troublesome.'

As to the due amount of the tax, see also the excellent discussion in Camden's *Elizabeth*, years 1582 and 1602.

Such was the toll collected by the Romans for the navigation of the Red Sea, in order to defray the costs of the maritime force maintained against the expeditions of pirates. Such, too, was the 'transit tax' which the people of Byzantium collected for the navigation of the Black Sea,[1] which, in earlier times, the Athenians, obtaining possession of Chrysopolis, had collected for the use of the same sea; to both facts Polybius bears witness. That the same Athenians formerly collected such a tax for the passage of the Hellespont Demosthenes shows in his speech *Against Leptines*[2]; and Procopius in his *Secret History* relates that the Roman Emperors levied such a tax also in his time.

Pliny, [*Natural History*,] XIX. iv. Strabo, XVII [i. 13]. [IV. xliv.] [xx. 60 = 475A.] [xxv.]

XV.—*Of the agreements which forbid a people to sail beyond certain bounds*

1. Examples of treaties are to be met with in which one people binds itself to another not to sail beyond a certain limit. Thus in ancient times an agreement was made between the kings who were in power about the Indian Ocean and the Egyptians, that the latter should not come into the Indian Ocean with a war-ship, or with more than one merchant ship. Thus in the time of Cimon[3] it was agreed between the Athenians and the Persians that no armed Persian ship should sail between the Symplegades and the Swallow Islands; after the battle of Salamis, the agreement defined the limits as between the Symplegades and Phaselis. In the year's truce of the [131] Peloponnesian war it was agreed that the Lacedaemonians should not go to sea with war-ships, and not with other ships of more than five hundred talents burden.

In the first treaty which, immediately after the expulsion of the kings,[4] the Romans made with the Carthaginians, they agreed

Philostratus, *Life of Apollonius of Tyana*, III. xi [35]. Plutarch, *Cimon* [xiii = 486 f.]. Diodorus, XI [lxi]. Arist., *Panath.* [= 294B]. Thuc., IV [cxviii]. Polybius [III. xxii. 4].

[1] Herodian in his life of Severus [III. i. 5] mentions the tax levied by Byzantium; Procopius in both his public and *Secret History* [xxv] mentions the ancient tax at the Hellespont, and also the new tax at the entrance to the Black Sea and at the Strait of Byzantium. Theophanes informs us that the tax of Byzantium was collected at the Blachernian temple, and the tax of the Hellespont at Abydos. Agathias, V [V. xii] calls the Abydos tax a 'tithe', that is, a tax of one tenth. Irene diminished it. The Emperor Immanuel Comnenus granted to some monasteries 'revenues from the sea', as Balsamon states on the Council of Chalcedon, can. iv, and Synod VII, can. xii.

[2] In the same chapter [*Against Leptines*, xx. 60 = 475A] he says that after taking Byzantium the Athenians became the masters of the sea. The Scholiast Ulpian [vol. II (Basle, 1572), p. 134 C] says that a tax of a tenth was paid there.

[3] This is 'a very notable treaty of peace', as Plutarch calls it [*Cimon*, xiii = 487A]. In it this also was stipulated, that the Persians should keep away from the sea the length of a race-course for horses, that is, forty stadia; Isocrates also mentions it in the *Panathenaic Oration* [xx = 244 E].

[4] Servius, *On the Aeneid*, IV [IV, line 628], 'Shores opposed to shores', says: 'Because it had been provided in the treaty that neither should the Romans approach the shores of the Carthaginians, nor the Carthaginians the shores of the Romans.' Similar was the Roman treaty with Tarentum, 'that the Romans should not sail beyond the Lacinian promontory'. This is found in the *Selections on Embassies* from Appian [=*Samnite History*, vii. 1]. Strabo, Book XVII [XVII. i. 19], relates that foreign ships which sailed to Sardinia or beyond the Pillars of Hercules were sunk by the Carthaginians.

that neither the Romans nor their allies should sail beyond Cape Bone, except when driven by storm or by the force of an enemy; further, that any who might have been forced to pass that limit should take nothing except necessaries and should leave within five days. In the second treaty,[1] the agreement was that the Romans should not go for plunder or for trade beyond Cape Bone, Massia, and Tarseia. In the treaty of peace with the Illyrians it was determined that the Illyrians were not to sail beyond Lissus with more than two boats, such boats to be unarmed. In the terms of peace with Antiochus, it was stipulated that he should not sail this side of the promontories of Calycadnus and Sarpedon, excepting with ships which carried tribute, ambassadors, or hostages.

Appian, *Illyrian Wars* [ii. 7]. Livy, XXXVIII [xxxviii. 9].

2. Such examples, nevertheless, do not show that occupation is had of the sea or possession of the right of navigation. Peoples, just as individuals, can in fact by agreements grant in favour of one concerned not only a right which they possess in their own name but also a right which they hold in common with all men. When this is done, the principle must hold which Ulpian stated in a case of this kind, in which an estate had been sold on the condition that tunny-fishing should not be carried on to the detriment of the seller; Ulpian declared that a servitude could not be imposed upon the sea, but that good faith in the contract demanded that the stipulation of sale be lived up to; that in consequence the persons of the possessors, and of those succeeding to their right, were bound by the agreement.

Digest, VIII. iv. 13.

XVI.—*Whether or not a change in the course of a river involves a change of territory is set forth, with a distinction*

1. When a river has changed its course frequently strifes arise between neighbouring states over the question whether at the same time the limits of jurisdiction are changed, and whether any additions made by the river belong to those to whose territories they have been added.

Disputes of this sort should be settled according to the nature and mode of acquisition. The surveyors tell us that there are three kinds of lands: the first, divided and allotted land, which the jurist

Julius Frontinus, [*De Agrorum Qualitate*, p. 38].

[1] In this was also the stipulation that the Romans should not land in Africa or Sardinia, except for the purpose of getting provisions or refitting their ships. After [by error instead of Before] the third Punic War the Carthaginian senate was complained of, because contrary to the treaty it was maintaining an army and had naval equipment. The reference is Livy, [*Epitome*,] xlviii and lix [xlix].

Similar is the grant obtained by the Sultan of Egypt in a treaty made with the Greeks, that he should be allowed once a year to send two ships through the Bosporus, as we find in Gregoras, Book IV [IV. vii. 60 c].

Among earlier examples, the peace with Antiochus contained this provision, that he should not have more than twelve armed ships; Appian, *Syrian Wars* [vii. 39]. Armed ships are forbidden by the Venetians [137] to enter the Adriatic Sea, on ground of treaties; see De Thou, Book LXXX [LXXX. x], dealing with the year 1584.

Florentinus calls delimited, because it has limits set off by artificial boundaries; the second, land allotted as a whole, or designated by measure,[1] as by hundred-acre parcels and by acres; and land having natural frontiers, which is so called, as Varro says, because it has boundaries suitable for keeping off enemies, that is, natural boundaries, as rivers and mountains.[2] These last are called by Aggenus Urbicus 'lands under occupation', since in most cases they are lands occupied either because they are vacant, or by right of war.

Dig. XLI. i. 16.

[p. 45, edit. Goes.]

In the case of the first two kinds of lands, even though a river changes its course no change of territory is occasioned; and if anything is added by alluvial deposits this will fall under the jurisdiction of the previous occupants.

2. In the case of lands having natural frontiers, a river by gradually changing its course [3] changes the boundary also, and whatever the stream adds to either side becomes subject to the jurisdiction of the state to whose territory it is added; it is in fact believed that [4] both states originally took possession of their territories with the intention that the river lying between should separate them as a natural boundary. Tacitus said: 'From this point the Rhine has a well-defined channel, which is suitable to serve as a boundary.' [5] In his account of the dispute between the peoples of Segesta and Selinus Diodorus Siculus remarks: 'A river serves as boundary between their territories.' Xenophon calls such a river simply 'the marker of limits', that is a boundary stream.

On the Customs of the Germans [xxxii]. XII [lxxxii]. *Anabasis*, IV [viii. 1].

3. The ancients relate that the Achelous river was of uncertain course, now dividing up into channels, now winding about in circuitous detour (whence it is said to have assumed the form of a bull and a serpent); and that for a long time it furnished a cause of war to the Aetolians and Acarnanians regarding the lands bordering upon it, [132] until Hercules restrained it by dikes. In recognition of this service Hercules obtained in marriage the daughter of Oeneus, king of the Aetolians.

Strabo, X [ii. 19].

XVII.—*What conclusion is to be reached if the bed of a river has been completely changed*

1. What has been said will be applicable only in case the river has not changed its bed. For a river, even where it serves as a boun-

[1] See an example in Servius, *On the Eclogues*, IX [IX, lines 7 and 28].

[2] Tacitus, *On the Customs of the Germans* [i]: 'It is separated from the Sarmatians and Dacians by mutual fear, or by mountains.' Pliny, Book XXXVI [*Natural History*, XXXVI. i. 2], speaking of the Alps: 'We are carrying away what was set up as boundaries to separate nations.'

[3] See Joannes Andrea and others cited by Reinkingk, I. v. i. [I. v. i. 85].

[4] An example is the river Vedasus [Bidassoa], in Mariana, Book XXIX [*History of Spain*, XXIX. xxiii].

[5] Spartianus, *Hadrian* [xii. 6]: 'In very many places where the barbarians are separated not by rivers but by boundary lines.' Constantine Porphyrogenitus, [*On the Government of the Empire*,] xlv, calls the river Phasis σύνορον, that is, forming a boundary.

dary between countries, is not considered to be merely where the water is, but where the water flows in a certain channel, and is confined by certain banks. Wherefore the addition or removal of particles, or Dig. V. i. 76. such a change as leaves the former appearance of the stream substantially unchanged, permits the river to seem the same.

If, however, the appearance of the river as a whole be at the same time changed, the case will be different. As a river which has been blocked by a dam in the upper part of its course ceases to exist, and a new river is formed in the excavated channel into which its water is conducted, so if a river, abandoning its old course, has burst through in a different channel,[1] it will not be the same as it was before, but a new river, the former river having ceased to be. In such a case the boundary of a country would remain in the middle of the channel which had last existed, just as if the river had dried up. For it must be held that the purpose of the peoples was to accept the river as a natural boundary between them. If, then, the river had ceased to exist, in that case each would retain what he had Digest, XLIII. xx. 3. § 2. previously possessed. In like manner, when the channel changes, the same rule ought to be observed.

2. In cases of doubt, however, sovereign states which border on a river must be considered as having a boundary set off by a natural frontier; nothing, in fact, is more suitable for separating such states than a boundary which is not easily crossed. It less often happens that states have boundaries set off by an artificial line of demarcation, or designated in terms of extent; but such cases arise less frequently from primary acquisition than from a grant made by another.

XVIII.—*That sometimes an entire river belongs to a territory*

Although, as we have said, in case of doubt the jurisdiction of two states bordering on the same river extends to the middle of the stream, nevertheless it might happen, and we see that in some places it has happened, that the river as a whole belongs to the one state; the reason being, of course, that jurisdiction over the opposite bank began to be exercised at a later time, after the river had already been occupied, or that the matter had been settled in such a way by agreement.

XIX.—*That things which have been abandoned become the property of him who takes possession of them, unless a state has acquired a general right of ownership over them*

1. It is not out of place to remark also that primary acquisition must be conceded as possible in the case of those things which have

[1] As the river Bardanus [Vardar], mentioned by Anna Comnena, Book I I. vii].

had an owner, but have ceased to have one, either because they have been abandoned, or because there are no longer persons having the right of ownership over them. Such things have returned to the condition in which they originally were.

2. The following point, however, must at the same time be noted, that sometimes primary acquisitions by a state or by the head of a state have been so made that not only the sovereignty—in which is included the right of eminent domain, of which I have treated elsewhere—but also full private ownership was first acquired in common for the state or its head; and that then a distribution was made individually to private persons, in such a way, nevertheless, that their ownership was dependent on that earlier ownership—if not in the way that the right of a vassal is dependent on the right of his lord, or the right of the permanent tenant on that of the landowner, yet in some other way that is less binding; for there are many forms of right over property, among which also is the right of one who administers a bequest for the benefit of some one else.

Says Seneca:[1] 'It is no proof that a thing is not yours, because you cannot sell it, or use it up, or injure or improve it. For that also belongs to you which is yours under a definite stipulation.' Dio of Prusa in his *Speech to the Rhodians* said: 'There are many [xxxi = and very different ways in which a thing may be said to belong to 325 D.] one; sometimes it is not permitted to sell, or to use according to one's own desire.' In Strabo I find the statement: 'He was owner [XII. except for the right to sell.' iii. 34.]

Tacitus presents among the Germans an example of what we *On the* have been saying: 'Lands proportionate to the number of culti- *Customs of the* vators are taken possession of in common, and these they forth- *Germans* with divide up among [133] themselves according to individual [xxvi]. standing.'

3. When, therefore, private properties distributed in the manner just described are dependent on common ownership, if any property is found to lack an individual owner, it does not belong to the occupant, but reverts to the community[2] or to the higher lord. Even without such a cause a right similar to this right of the law of nature could be conferred by a municipal statute, as we have already noted. [II. ii. 5.]

[1] This passage is found *On Benefits*, VII. xii; also in the eighth book, chap. xii [the same chap., VII. xii]: 'Certain things belong to certain persons under certain conditions.'

[2] Thus you may infer from the second book of the *Odyssey* near the end [lines 335–6], that the possessions of the man who died without children reverted to the people; and so Eustathius explains the verse of the fifth book of Homer's *Iliad* [V. 158]:

The rulers of the city divided up his wealth.

For he says the term used indicates the magistrate who administered the property of those who died without issue.

The histories teach us that a somewhat similar custom was in vogue formerly in the kingdom of Mexico.

CHAPTER IV

ON ASSUMED ABANDONMENT OF OWNERSHIP AND OCCUPATION CONSEQUENT THEREON; AND WHEREIN THIS DIFFERS FROM OWNERSHIP BY USUCAPTION AND BY PRESCRIPTION

[138] I.—*Why ownership by usucaption or by prescription properly so called does not occur between states or their rulers*

A SERIOUS difficulty arises at this point in regard to the right of usucaption. For since this right was introduced by municipal law (time, in fact, in its own nature has no effective force; nothing is done by time, though everything is done in time) it has no place, as Vázquez holds, in the relations between two independent states or kings, or between an independent state and a king; nor yet between a king and an individual not subject to him, nor between two subjects of different kings or states.[1]

Book II, li, no. 28.

This seems to be true except in so far as a thing or an act is governed by the laws of the land. But if we admit this, a very serious inconvenience clearly follows, in that contests about kingdoms and the boundaries of kingdoms never come to an end with lapse of time. Such a condition, again, not only tends to disturb the minds of many and to occasion wars, but is also contrary to the common sense of nations.

II.—*That nevertheless possession of long standing is wont to be urged as a right even between states or rulers*

Judges, xi. 26.]

For in the Scriptures, when the king of the Ammonites laid claim to the lands between the Arnon and the Jabbok, reaching from the Arabian deserts to the Jordan, Jephtha alleged possession for three hundred years, and asked him why, during so long a time, he himself and his ancestors had entered no claim. According to Isocrates the Lacedaemonians laid it down as a most sure maxim, accepted among all peoples,[2] that public, no less than private, possessions are so confirmed by long standing that they cannot be recovered; on the basis of this right they sent away those who demanded the return of Messene. The Greek words may be translated: 'All people consider that both public and private possessions are legally

Archidamus [ix].

[1] In the laws of the Twelve Tables was this provision [Cicero, *On Duties*, I. xii. 37]: 'A judgment is permanent against an enemy,' that is, against a foreigner.

[2] The Duke of Nevers reasoned thus on behalf of France, according to De Thou, Book LIX [LIX. iv], year 1574.

valid and inheritable if a long period of possession has intervened.'

The same Isocrates used these words to Philip: 'Since, the long lapse of time had rendered the possession fixed and irrevocable.' Relying on this right the later Philip said to Titus Quinctius that 'he would set free the cities which he had captured, but he would not withdraw from those which had been received by him from his ancestors by lawful and inherited possession.'[1] Sulpicius, arguing against Antiochus, showed that he was unjust in claiming the right, after several centuries, of reducing the Greek peoples in Asia to slavery because they had formerly been enslaved.

[See Dion. Hal., *On Isocrates*, ix = 155.] Livy, XXXII [x. 4]. Livy, XXXV [xvi. 7 ff.].

The historians[2] call the revival of old claims empty talk; Diodorus characterizes such claims as legendary and ancient tales. Cicero in the second book *On Duties* says: 'But how is it just for the owner to lose a field that has previously been held for many years, or even centuries?'

Tacitus, *Annals*, VI [xxxvii]. [XV. lxxviii.] [II. xxii. 79.]

III.—*The question is decided according to presumptions of human intent; and these presumptions are not based on words alone*

What shall we say? Actions at law, which are dependent on intent, cannot indeed be inferred from a mental act alone, unless that act has been indicated by certain outward signs. For to assign a legal effect to mere acts of the mind was not consistent with human nature, which is able to recognize such acts only from outward signs. And for this reason purely mental acts are not subject to human laws.

Outward signs, however, do not indicate mental acts with mathematical certainty, but only with probability. For men can say something different from what they desire and feel, and can disguise their intentions by their actions. Nevertheless the nature of human society does not allow that no effect be given to mental acts which are sufficiently indicated. And so whatever has been sufficiently indicated is considered as true in respect to him who has indicated it. Thus, as regards words, at any rate, the difficulty is solved.

IV.—*But such presumptions are based also on acts*

1. A thing which is thrown away is understood by the act to be abandoned, unless [139] the circumstances of the case are such

Dig. XLI. i. 9. § 8.

[1] [144] Florus, III, xiii: 'Nevertheless by reason of age, as it were by hereditary right, they held possession of habitations left by their ancestors.'

[2] This is what the Greeks, in allusion to Attic history, call 'the times before Euclid'. Among other authors, Nicetas in the first book of the life of Alexis, brother of Isaac, used this when treating of Henry, son of the Emperor Frederick: 'He was not ashamed to search out things which happened as it were before Euclid.'

Dig. XIV. ii. 8. *Digest,* XLVII. ii. 43. § 11. *Dig.* II. xiv. 2. *Digest,* XXIX. ii. 95.

that we ought to think it was thrown aside for the moment and with the intention of recovering it later. Thus a debt is considered discharged by the return of the note.[1]

'An inheritance', says Paul, 'can be refused not only by words, but also by act and any expression of intent.' Thus if any one is the owner of a thing and knowingly treats with another who has it in possession, as if with its owner, he is deservedly considered to have abandoned his right. And there is no reason why this should not be the case also between kings and independent states.

Digest, XLII. i. 57. *Dig.* I. xiv. 3.

2. Similarly, a higher officer who permits an inferior to do, or commands him to do, that which he cannot lawfully do unless he is freed by law, is understood to have freed him from the law.

The principle under consideration in fact has its origin not in municipal law but in the law of nature, according to which every man has the right to abandon his own; and further, in a natural presumption, in accordance with which one is believed to have wished that of which he has given sufficient indications. In this sense we can properly accept the statement of Ulpian, that verbal release of obligation belongs to the law of nations.

Digest, XLVI. iv. 8.

V.—*Such presumptions are based also on things not done*

1. Under acts, moreover, consistently with moral standards, failures to act are included, considered with relation to the circumstances which ought to be taken into account. Thus he who keeps silence, when present and cognizant of the facts, seems to give consent. This principle the Hebraic law also recognizes (*Numbers*, xxx. 5 and 12) unless circumstances show that the person was hindered from speaking by fear, or by some other condition. Thus a thing is considered lost if the hope of its recovery[2] is abandoned. For example, Ulpian says that hogs carried off by a wolf, and what we lose in a shipwreck, cease to be ours, not immediately, but when recovery seems impossible; that is, in cases in which there is no reason why any one should be expected to retain the thought of ownership, when no indications of such an intent exist. If persons had been sent to look for the property, or 'a reward' had been offered, we should have had to judge otherwise.

Digest, XLI. i. 44.

Thus a person who knows that his property is in the possession of another, and during a long period makes no claim against the possessor, unless some other reason is manifest, seems to have pursued this course with no other thought than because he no longer wished

[1] See *Digest,* II. xiv. 2.

[2] The Hebrew jurists call this 'despairing of the recovery of a lost object'.

that object to be considered among his possessions. Ulpian has elsewhere said this, that after long silence a house seems to be considered as abandoned by the owner. 'Unjustly', writes the Emperor Pius in a rescript, 'do you demand overdue interest, which the length of time intervening indicates that you had abandoned, because you did not think that this ought to be demanded of your debtor—evidently in order that you might be in greater favour with him.'

Digest, XXXIX. ii. 15, § 21.

Digest, XXII. i. 17. § 1.

2. Very similar to this is what appears in the establishment of a custom. For a custom also, without regard to the laws of a state which fix a certain time and manner for its introduction, can be introduced by a subject people in consequence of the fact that it is tolerated by the one who holds the sovereignty. But the time within which a custom receives the effect of law is not definitely fixed, but arbitrary, to wit, whatever length of time is sufficient to accord with the implied consent.

Thomas Aquinas, I. ii, qu. 97, art. 3. Suarez, *De Legibus*, VII. xv.

3. However, in order that silence may establish the presumption of abandonment of ownership, two conditions are requisite, that the silence be that of one who acts with knowledge and of his own free will. For the failure to act on the part of one who does not know is without legal effect;[1] and when another apparent cause for the action appears the inference of an act of will ceases to be in point.

VI.—*How length of time together with non-possession and silence amounts to an abandonment of right*

That these two conditions, then, may be considered to be present, is established by other indications, but, in the case of both, length of time is a paramount consideration.

In the first place it can hardly happen that, with length of time, property belonging to a man should not come to his notice, since lapse of time offers many opportunities for such cognizance. Nevertheless in the case of those who are at hand a shorter space of time suffices to establish this inference than in the case of parties who are absent, aside from the stipulations of municipal law. Again, fear, once inspired, is believed to endure for a time, [140] but not indefinitely, since length of time furnishes many opportunities for taking counsel against the fear, either by oneself or with the help of others, and even by leaving the territory of the one feared; in consequence, at length a complaint may be made concerning infringement of a right, or, what is better, an appeal may be made to judges or arbitrators.

[1] See II. xxii. 2 [II. xxi. 2]; add, if you have leisure, Bartholomaeus Socinus, *Consilia*, 187, col. 8; Meischner, *Decisiones Camerales*, IX, no. 113, vol. III.

VII.—*Time exceeding the memory of man ordinarily suffices for such a presumption; of what sort such time is*

Because a length of time exceeding the memory of man [1] is in its essential character practically infinite, a silence for that length of time will always seem sufficient to imply abandonment of ownership, unless there are very strong reasons to the contrary.[2] It has also been well remarked by the better jurists that time exceeding the memory of man is not the same as a century,[3] although these two limits often are not far apart, for the reason that a hundred years ordinarily constitute the limit of human life.[4] This period, again, generally equals three ages, or 'generations', of men.[5]

Digest, XLIII. xx. 3. § 4.

Eustathius, *On the Iliad*, I [line 250].

Livy, XXXIV [lviii. 10].

This fact was in point in the criticism of Antiochus by the Romans, when they showed that he was demanding the return of cities which he himself, his father, and his grandfather had never occupied.

VIII.—*Answer to the objection, that no one ought to be assumed to abandon his right*

1. The objection may be raised that, since men love themselves and their possessions, it ought not to be believed that they would abandon their own property; and that, in consequence, negative acts, even through a long space of time, are not sufficient to warrant the inference which I have mentioned. But again we ought to think that good should be expected of men; and for that reason it ought not to be supposed that they have such a disposition that, out of consideration for a mere perishable thing, they would wish a fellow man to live in a continual state of sin. Without such abandonment of ownership, such a result often cannot be avoided.

2. In regard to the exercise of sovereign power, although generally it is greatly esteemed, we ought to know that the burdens

[1] Andreas Knich in his treatise, *De Jure Territorii*; Reinkingk, Book I, class v, chap. ii, no. 5; Oldendorp, class III, art. 2.

[2] Menochio, *Consilia*, I, 90.

[3] Balbus, *De Praescriptionibus*, noted this; also Covarruvias on the same subject; Reinkingk, Book I, class v, chap. ii, no. 40. On the question of time exceeding memory, see the very learned Favre, *Consilium pro Ducatu Montisferratensi* [p. 155].

[4] This was called 'Time more than time' by Justinian in his fifth edict, published in the notes to the *Secret History* of Procopius [Nicolaus Alemannus, in *Procopii Hist. Arcana*, p. 155, 9 = *Corp. Script. Hist. Byzant.*, Procopius, III, p. 464].

[5] For a 'generation' is a 'period of thirty years', as Porphyry notes in his *Homeric Questions* [p. 99]. Herodian explained to Severus [III. viii. 10] that an age covers three 'generations'.

Philo, *On the Embassy to Gaius* [xx], remarks that there had been ten kings of Egypt in three hundred years. Plutarch, *Lycurgus* [xxix = 58 A], says that there were fourteen kings of Sparta in five hundred years.

Justinian, *Novels*, clix [clix. 2], forbids that a case be brought into court because four 'generations' have already elapsed.

are great, and that failure to administer them well renders a man subject to divine wrath. Just as it would be a wrong thing for two persons, who claim to be guardians, to go to law at the expense of the ward in order to determine which of the two should have the right of guardianship; or—to use the illustration which Plato has in connexion with this subject—for the sailors with danger to the ship to struggle in order to determine which of them would best do the steering, so those are not always worthy of praise who with the greatest loss, and often with the bloodshed of innocent people, desire to decide who is to control the government of that people. I [*Republic* VI. iv].

The ancients praise the words of Antiochus, who gave thanks to the Roman people because, 'freed from excessive cares of government,[1] he enjoyed modest boundaries'. Among many wise sayings of Lucan the following is not least: Cicero, *For Deiotarus* [xiii. 36]. Val. Max., XIV. i [IV. i. 9].

> With such an onset of new crimes
> Seek they to know which one shall rule the city? [II. 60 ff.]
> It scarce were worth so great a price that either should.

3. It is, then, to the interest of human society that governments be established on a sure basis and beyond the hazard of dispute; and all implications which point in that direction ought to be looked upon with favour. For if Aratus of Sicyon [2] thought it a hard thing that private possessions of fifty years' standing be taken away, how much more ought that saying of Augustus to be held in mind, that 'He is a good man and a good citizen who does not wish the present condition of the state changed'; and who, as Alcibiades says in Thucydides, 'will preserve the form of government which he received'. [Cicero, *On Duties*, II. xxiii. 81.] [Macrobius, II. iv. 18.] [VI. lxxxix.]

The expression 'to maintain the present form of government', Isocrates used in the oration *Against Callimachus*. Thus also Cicero, in a speech to the people *Against Rullus*: 'It is becoming for an advocate of quiet and harmony to defend the existing condition of the state'; and Livy says: 'All the best citizens rejoice in the present state of government.' [xxiii = 383E] [III. ii. 4.] XXXV [xxxiv. 3].

4. Now if those indications, [141] which I have mentioned, should not be present, nevertheless against the presumption, according to which it is believed that each man wishes to keep his own, the other presumption has greater weight, because it is not credible that anyone in a long time should give no clear indication of what he wishes.[3] Angelus de Clavasio, *Summa*, word *Inventa*.

[1] Jonathan, son of Saul, seems to have been of this mind [*1 Samuel*, xxiii. 17].

[2] Thus Thrasybulus, when peace had been restored at Athens, left all private possessions as they had been [Nepos, *Thrasybulus*, iii].

[3] Krantz, *History of Saxony*, XI, nos. 10 and 13.

IX.—*Without such presumption it seems that by universal customary law ownership is transferred by possession exceeding the memory of man*

Perhaps without improbability it can be said that this adjustment is not based on presumption alone, but that, in accordance with the volitional law of nations,[1] the provision was introduced that possession beyond the limits of memory, not interrupted nor called in question by appeal to the courts, should absolutely transfer ownership. It is in fact credible that the nations agreed in this, since it was of the greatest importance for the preservation of the common peace.

Moreover, with justification I used the expression 'uninterrupted possession', that is, as Sulpicius says in Livy: 'According to a single lasting tenure of right constantly enjoyed and never interrupted'; the same writer elsewhere spoke of 'a lasting possession never called in question'. For intermittent possession has no effect. This is illustrated by the reply of the Numidians to the Carthaginians: 'According to circumstances, now the Carthaginians, now the kings of Numidia, enjoyed the right, and possession was always in the hands of the one who was most powerful in arms.'

XXXV [xvi. 8 and 9].

[Livy] XXXIV [lxii. 13].

X.—*Whether unborn children can in like manner be deprived of a right*

1. At this point another and indeed an exceedingly difficult question arises, whether those not yet born can tacitly lose their right by such an abandonment. If we say that they cannot, the explanation just given has contributed nothing to the tranquillity of empires and estates, since most of these are held under such conditions that they ought to pass to the descendants. If we affirm that they can, it will seem strange that silence can harm those not able to speak, since in fact they do not exist; or that the act of one party should entail loss for another.

2. In order to solve this problem, the fact must be recognized that a person who is not yet born has no rights, just as a thing which does not exist has no attributes. If then the people, from whose will the right to rule arises, changes its will, it does no injustice to those yet unborn, since they have not yet acquired any right. Moreover as a people can change its will openly, so it can be believed to have changed its will tacitly. If, therefore, the people has changed

[1] Gregoras [XI. i. 5 = p. 239, Geneva, 1616] relates that when Phocaea had been given to the elders of Catana by the Greek emperors the provision was added that the individual successors should sign a written acknowledgement that they held the property under the right of administrators, 'lest the unobserved lapse of time should extinguish the right of the emperor'.

its will, while the right of those who may be expected to come is not yet in existence[1]—and besides that very right has been abandoned by the parents from whom those may be born who were to possess the right in their own time—there is nothing to hinder another from occupying property under these conditions as ownerless.

3. We are treating of the law of nature. For as other fictions have been introduced by the civil law, so this provision may be introduced also, that meanwhile the law should defend the persons of those who do not yet exist,[2] and should thus hinder anything from being seized to their disadvantage. Nevertheless we should not hastily judge that such is the intent of the laws, because in such cases private advantage is strongly opposed to public advantage.

Hence also, according to the more generally accepted opinion, those fiefs, which are not derived from the right of the last possessor but from the force of the original investiture, can be acquired in a sufficiently long time. Covarruvias, a jurist of excellent judgement, has with good reason extended this principle to the rights of the first-born and to property bequeathed in trust.

4. Nothing in fact makes it impossible that such a provision should be introduced into the law of a state that a thing, which cannot be lawfully alienated by a single act, can nevertheless, in order to avoid uncertainty of ownership, be lost by neglect for a fixed period of time; and even under such a provision those born later will have the right of personal action against those guilty of neglect, or against their heirs.

On Sext, V. ult. 2, pt. III, § 3. *Speculum,* tit. de feu., § *Quoniam*, vers. 3, *quaeritur.* Chassaneus, *De Consuetudine Burgundiae, De Mainsmortes,* § 6, vers. *Par an et jour,* no. 2. Cravetta, *De Antiquitatibus Temporum,* pt. IV, § *Materia,* no. 90.

XI.—*Even the right of sovereignty is gained by a people or king by long-standing possession*

From what we have said, it is plain that a king can acquire a right as against a king, and an independent state [142] as against an independent state, not only by express agreement, but also by abandonment of ownership and the occupation which follows it or assumes a new force from it. For the common saying, that 'what is not valid from the beginning cannot become valid from a subsequent act', is subject to the exception, 'unless a new cause has intervened capable in itself of producing a right'.

Similarly also the true king of a people may lose his sovereignty and become subject to the people; and he who in reality is not a king, but only the foremost citizen, can be made king with absolute

[1] There are many examples of such renunciations in history. See in Mariana, Book XIII. xviii, a notable instance in the case of Louis the Ninth, king of France, renouncing for himself and his children the right which he could have through his mother Blanche to the kingdom of Castile.

[2] This the civil law does in the case of an inheritance for which no heir appears [*Digest,* XLI. i. 34; XLIII. xxiv. 13. § 5].

power,[1] and the supreme authority, which was wholly in the power of either king or people, can be divided between them.

XII.—*Whether the civil statutes concerning ownership by usucaption and by prescription bind the one who holds sovereign power; explanation, with distinctions*

1. It is also worth while to investigate this question, whether a law dealing with ownership by usucaption or by prescription, and established by one who has sovereign power, can apply also to the right of sovereignty itself, and to the necessary parts of it which [I. iii. 6]. I have explained elsewhere.

Bartolus, *On Dig.* XLIX. xv. 24, and XXXIX. iii. 1. Jason, *Consilia,* III. 70. Aimone [Cravetta], *De Antiq. Temp.*, pt. iv, vers. *Materia ista,* no. 62. Antonio Corsetti, *De Excellentia Regia,* qu. 104. Balbus, *De Praescr.*, ii, pt. 5, pr., q. 2. Castaldus, *De Imperatore,* qu. liii. Covarruvias, *On Sext,* V. ult. 4, pt. II, § 9, end.

Not a few jurists, who treat of sovereignty in accordance with Roman municipal law, think that such a law does apply. But I think otherwise.[2] For in order that any one may be bound by a law, both power and intent, at least presumed, are requisite in the maker of the law. No one can bind himself after the manner of a law, that is after the manner of a superior. Hence it is that the makers of laws have the right to change their own laws. Still, one can be bound by his own law, not directly, but by implication; inasmuch as he is a member of the community,[3] he is under an obligation imposed by natural fairness, which desires that the parts be adjusted in relation to the whole. Sacred history notes that such an observance was characteristic of Saul in the beginning of his reign (*1 Samuel*, xiv. 40). But here this is not in point, because we are considering the maker of laws not as a part of the community but as the one in whom the power of the entire body resides. We are in fact treating of sovereignty as such.

Again, the intent is not presumed to have been present, because the makers of laws are not considered as intending to include themselves, except in cases where both the subject-matter and the reason for the law are universal, as in fixing prices. But sovereignty is not of like character with other things; rather, in its exalted rank it far exceeds other things. I have not seen any civil statute treating of prescription which included sovereignty, or could be considered with probability to have intended to include it.

2. From these considerations it follows that the time defined by such a statute is not sufficient for acquiring sovereignty or a neces-

[1] See Vázquez, *Controversiae Illustres,* Book I, xxiii. 3. Add in the same work Book II, lxxxii. 8–9 ff. [145] See also Panormitanus, *Consilia,* I. 82, and Peregrinus, *De Jure Fisci,* VI. viii. 10.

[2] Compare Don Garzia Mastrillus, *De Magistratu,* Book III, ii. 26; Johann Oldendorp, *Consilia Marpurgensia,* I. 5, no. 47.

[3] See below, II. xx. 22 [II. xx. 24]; Seneca, *Letters,* lxxxv [lxxxv. 35]: 'The pilot possesses a double character; the one he has in common with all those who embarked on the same ship in which he himself is the pilot; the other, the character of pilot, is peculiar to himself.' This subject is treated by Claude Seyssel, *De Republica Gallica,* I; Chassaneus, *Catalogus Gloriae Mundi,* V. v; Gail, *Observationes,* Book II, obs. 55, no. 7; Bodin, *De Republica,* I. viii; Reinkingk, I. xii [I. v. ix].

sary part of it, if the natural implications which we mentioned above are lacking; that so great a length of time is not required if such implications are present within the time to a sufficient degree; and, lastly, a civil statute, which forbids that property be acquired within a fixed time, does not have anything to do with matters of sovereignty.

Nevertheless, in a transfer of sovereignty, the people could express its will as to the manner and time in which the sovereignty might be lost by failure to exercise it. This expressed will would undoubtedly have to be followed, and could not be infringed upon even by a king possessed of sovereign power, because it applies not to the sovereignty itself but to the manner of holding it. But of this distinction I have spoken elsewhere. [I. iii. 11.]

XIII.—*Those rights of sovereignty which can be separated from it, or shared with others, are gained and lost by right of ownership based on usucaption or on prescription*

Those powers which do not belong to the nature of sovereignty, and do not have relation to it as essential parts, but can be naturally separated from it or at least shared with others, are entirely subject to such statutes of each people as have been passed concerning ownership by usucaption and by prescription. Thus we see that there are subjects who have acquired by prescription the right [143] to judge without appeal; yet in such a way that there is always some sort of appeal from them, as by petition, or by some other means. For that any one should be beyond the right of appeal is inconsistent with the character of a subject, and therefore this right belongs to sovereignty or to a part of it, and can be acquired in no other way than by the law of nature, to which sovereignties are subject. [Covarruvias, *On Sext*, V. ult. 2, pt. II, § 2, nos. 12 and 13.]

XIV.—*Refutation of the opinion alleging that subjects are always allowed to assert their liberty*

1. From this it is apparent to what extent we can accept the assertion of some,[1] that it is always permissible for subjects to regain their liberty, that is, the independence of the people, if they can. The reason given is that a sovereignty won by force can be overthrown by force, while a sovereignty which has arisen from the will of the people may be repented of, and the will may change.

In truth sovereignties which were at first won by force may receive lawful confirmation by tacit acceptance; and the will of the people, either at the very establishment of the sovereignty, or in

[1] As Vázquez, in the work already mentioned, Book II, lxxxii. 3.

connexion with a later act, may be such as to confer a right which for the future is not dependent on such will.

[*Jewish War*, II. xvi. 4.] According to Josephus, King Agrippa in an address to the Jews, who were called Zealots from their untimely zeal for the recovery of liberty, spoke thus :

> It is not now the proper time to strive for liberty. Formerly you ought to have fought not to lose it. For it is a hard thing to run the risk of slavery, and the strife to avoid it is honourable. But he who revolts, after having been once subdued, must be called not a lover of liberty but a disobedient slave.

[*Jewish War*, V. ix. 3.] Josephus himself also says to the same Jews :[1] 'It is indeed honourable to fight for liberty, but that ought to have been done formerly. But if those who have once been conquered and have obeyed for a long time shake off the yoke, they act like desperadoes and not like lovers of liberty.' This very remark Cyrus once made to the Armenian king, who, as the excuse for his rebellion, alleged the desire to recover his lost liberty.

Xenophon, *On the Training of Cyrus*, III [i. 10].

2. For the rest, I think it not in the least open to doubt that long indifference, such as I have described above, on the part of a king may suffice to warrant a people in recovering their freedom, on the ground of presumed abandonment of sovereign rights.

XV.—*Whatever belongs to faculty pure and simple is not lost by lapse of time ; explanation*

There are rights which do not involve daily exercise, but an adjustment once for all when it shall be convenient, as the redeeming of a pledge by payment.[2] Also there are rights of free action, to which the act engaged in is not directly opposed, but is included therein as a part in the whole ; an illustration would be if any one has had an alliance with one neighbour only during a hundred years, while nevertheless it was in his power to have alliances with others also.

These rights are not lost, except in consequence of a prohibition or restraint, and when obedience has been rendered thereto, with a sufficient indication of consent. Since this is in accord not only with municipal law but also with natural reason, it will properly apply also in the case of men of the highest rank.

[1] You will find almost the same words in the Count de Blanderat's speech to the Milanese ; Radevicus, I. xl.

[2] See Paruta, *History of Venice*, VII.

CHAPTER V

ON THE ORIGINAL ACQUISITION OF RIGHTS OVER PERSONS. HEREIN ARE TREATED THE RIGHTS OF PARENTS, MARRIAGE, ASSOCIATIONS, AND THE RIGHTS OVER SUBJECTS AND SLAVES

I.—*Concerning the rights of parents over children*

A RIGHT is acquired not only over things but also over persons. Such rights have their origin primarily in generation, consent, or crime.

[146] By generation parents acquire a right over children—both parents, I mean, the father and the mother. But if there is variance in the exercise of these rights the right of the father is given preference[1] on account of the superiority of sex.

II.—*Distinction in respect to the period of infancy, and concerning the ownership of property by infants*

1. Moreover in dealing with children three periods must be distinguished. The first is that 'of imperfect judgement', as Aristotle calls it, while there is lack of 'discretion', as the same author elsewhere says. The second is the period of mature judgement, but while the son still remains a part of the family of the parents, that is 'so long as he has not separated from it', as Aristotle says. The third is the period after the son has withdrawn from the family.[2]

Politics, I, last chap. *Nicomachean Ethics,* IV. iii [III. iv]. *Ethics,* V. x.

In the first period all the actions of children are under the control of the parents; for it is fair that he who is not able to rule himself be ruled by another. Such is the saying of Aeschylus:

[*Choephorae,* 753 f.]

> The age of infancy, like the dumb brutes,
> Requires another's mind to bring it up.

[1] Seneca, *Controversies,* III. xix [VII. iv. 4]: 'The first place belongs to the father, the second to the mother.' Chrysostom, *On First Corinthians,* xi. 3 [Homily XXVI. ii]: 'Deservedly the woman is made subject to the man, for equality in rank produces strife'; and *On Ephesians,* iv [v. 33 = Homily XX, iv]: 'The second power is the woman, but she should not for that reason claim equal rights for herself (for she is subject to the head); nor should her husband despise her because she is subject to him, for she is the body.' Later he says [Homily XX, vi]: [161] 'Hers is the second power, also possessing rule and much honoured by her consort; but nevertheless the husband has somewhat more power.'

Augustine, *Letters,* cxci [cclxii. 11]: 'A legitimate son is more under the power of the father than of the mother.' Gregoras in Book VII [VII. v. 7], where he treats of Andronicus Palaeologus and Irene: 'He added that the father had more power than the mother, and there was no reason why the wishes of the father concerning the son should not prevail even in preference to the mother's.'

On the respect due to the mother see the *Code,* VIII. xlvi (xlvii). 4.

[2] In this period they belong to their parents just as other things which the parents possess, says Maimonides, *Canones Poenitentiales,* vi. 2.

But naturally no one except the parents can be found to whom such control may be committed.

2. Nevertheless in this period also a son or a daughter, according to universal customary law, is capable of ownership of property, though the exercise of the right is hindered on account of the imperfection of judgement which I have mentioned. As Plutarch says of children, they have the right 'to possess' but not 'to use'. Wherefore it is not due to natural right that all the possessions of children are acquired by their parents, but to the laws of certain peoples, which also in this matter distinguish the father from the mother, sons not of age from those that are of age, and illegitimate children from legitimate. But nature ignores these distinctions, except as regards that supremacy of sex which I have mentioned, in case of conflict of the parents regarding the exercise of parental rights.

Above, [II.] iii. 6. *On the Fortune of Alexander*, II [v = 337 D].

III.—*Of the period of life in the family beyond infancy*

In the second period, when judgement has now matured with age, no other actions are subject to the rule of parents except those which in some way are important for the position of the family in relation to the father or the mother.[1] It is in fact fair that the part should conform to the interest of the whole.

In other actions, then, children in that period have 'power', that is, a moral faculty of action; but nevertheless in those acts they are bound to desire always to please their parents. However, since this obligation does not arise from the moral faculty, as in the previous case, but from filial affection, respect, and gratitude, it does not make void anything done contrary to it, just as the donation of anything which has been made by the owner contrary to the rules of economy is not void.

IV.—*Concerning the right of restraining children*

In both these periods the right to govern embraces also the right to chastise, in so far as children must be forced to do their duty, or must be corrected.

[II. xx. 7.] There will elsewhere be an opportunity of discussing what ought to be thought in regard to severer punishments.

V.—*Concerning the right of selling children*

Although the paternal authority is so attached to the person and 'character' of the father that it cannot be taken away and transferred to another, nevertheless by natural right a father can pledge

[1] Thus Maimonides explains the law, which is found in *Numbers*, xxx. 10 [xxx. 6].

his son as security, if the civil law does not prevent, and can even sell him[1] if it is necessary and there is available no other means of supporting him.

This legal provision, which arose from an ancient law of the Thebans (this Aelian quotes in his second book), seems to have passed to other peoples also. Further, the Theban law itself seems to have come from the Phoenicians, and before that from the Jews. Apollonius in his letter to Domitian relates that the same right prevailed among the Phrygians. Indeed nature herself is deemed to give the right to everything without which that cannot be obtained which she demands. [*Var. Hist.*, II. vii.] [*Exodus*, xxi. 7.] [Philostratus, *Life of Apollonius of Tyana*, VIII. vii. 12.]

VI.—*Of the period of life beyond infancy and outside of the family*

In the third period, [147] though filial affection and respect are always due, since the cause remains, yet the son is in all things 'independent' and his own master.

From this it follows that the acts of kings cannot be said to be void on this account, because they have parents.

VII.—*Distinction between the power of parents by the law of nature and that by the municipal law*

Whatever powers there are beyond those mentioned arise from volitional law, which is different in different countries.[2] Thus by the law which God gave to the Jews the father's power over a son or a daughter to annul vows was not perpetual, but lasted only so long as the children were members of the father's household.[3] Again, Roman citizens possessed a special power of the father even over sons who were the heads of families of their own, so long as they had not been emancipated. The Romans themselves in fact claimed that other peoples did not have such power over their children. *Numbers*, xxx. 2, 3, 4, 5. [Kotzi,] *On the Precepts of the Law, Precepts Forbidding*, 242. *Institutes*, I. ix. 2.

In the third book of his *Pyrrhoneia*, Sextus Empiricus says: [*Pyr.*, III. xxiv. 211.]

> The Roman lawgivers[4] have ordained that children should be in the power of their fathers as if slaves, and that the children should not have control of their own property, but that this should remain in the hands of their parents until the children should be manumitted, in the same manner as slaves. But such authority other peoples reject as tyrannical.

[1] Jordanes, *History of the Goths* [xxvi. 135]: 'Parents in fact do not act otherwise in providing for the safety of their children; they think it better to lose freedom than life, while the one who is sold, to be brought up with compassion rather than to die, is saved.'

I find that such a law was also in force among the Mexicans.

[2] Seneca, *On Benefits*, III. xi: 'Because it is useful for youth to be governed, we have placed it as it were under family magistrates.'

[3] Otherwise at the age of thirteen the son was capable of incurring obligations, according to the Hebraic customs; thus they explain the passage cited in *Numbers*.

[4] Philo, *On the Embassy to Gaius* [v]: 'For according to the law of the Romans power of every kind over the son belongs to the father.'

[xxxvii = p. 199.] Simplicius in the commentary on the *Manual* of Epictetus says:

> The ancient laws of the Romans, having regard not only to that superiority which arises from nature, but also to the labours which parents sustain for their children, and wishing besides that children be without exception subject to their parents, and, as I believe, trusting also in the natural love of parents, have given to parents the right of selling their children, if they wish, and of killing them without punishment.

Nicomachean Ethics, VIII. xii [VIII. x]. A similar right of the father among the Persians Aristotle indicts as tyrannical. These laws we report for this reason that we may distinguish accurately between municipal law and the law of nature.

VIII.—*Concerning the right of the husband over the wife*

1. Rights which arise over persons from consent come either from association or from subjection.

The most natural association appears in marriage. However, on account of the difference in sex the authority is not held in common, but 'the husband is the head of the wife', of course in matters relating to marriage and in matters relating to the family. The wife, in fact, becomes a member of the husband's family, and so the husband has the right to determine matters of domicile. *Ephesians,* v. 23.

If any right beyond these is conceded to husbands, as in Hebraic law the right to annul vows of the wife, and among some peoples the right of selling the wife's property, such a right does not come from nature but from enactment. This subject requires us to see what the nature of marriage is.

2. Marriage, then, according to the law of nature we consider such a cohabitation of a man with a woman that it places the woman under the eye of the man and under his guardianship. Such a union it is in fact possible to see even in some kinds of dumb animals. But in the case of man, as an animate being endowed with reason, there is added to this the vow by which the woman binds herself to the man.

IX.—*Whether denial of divorce and restriction to one woman are necessary to marriage according to the law of nature or only according to the law of the Gospel*

1. Nature does not seem to require anything more in order to constitute a marriage, nor indeed does the divine law seem to have demanded anything further before the spread of the Gospel. For both men who were holy before the law [1] had more than one wife,

[1] Chrysostom, speaking of Sarah [*On First Corinthians,* xi. 16 = Homily XXVI. vi]: 'She again desired to afford to him some consolation for her barrenness, from her maidservant; for at that time such acts had not been forbidden.' See the same author, *On First Timothy,* iii [= Homily X].

Augustine, *On Christian Doctrine,* III. xii [III. xii. 20]: 'The custom of having several wives at the same time was blameless.' A similar statement is found in III. xviii [III. xviii. 26]; also in III.

and in the law [1] certain precepts are given to those who have more than one wife; and the king is enjoined not to have too great a number of wives nor horses. The Jewish interpreters of the passage last referred to note that eighteen [148] wives or concubines had been allowed the king. Also God reminds David that He had given him many and noble wives.[2]

Deuteronomy, xxi. 15. *Deuteronomy,* xvii. 16, 17. *2 Samuel,* xii. 8.

2. Furthermore, the method is prescribed for one who wishes to divorce a wife, and no one is hindered from marrying a divorced woman except the one who divorced her, and the priest.[3] Nevertheless this liberty of passing to another husband ought to be so restricted by the law of nature that confusion of offspring may not arise. Hence arises that question of pontifical law in Tacitus, 'whether a woman after conception, but before the birth of the child, might lawfully marry'. Among the Jews it is ordered that three months intervene between the two marriages.

Deuteronomy, xxiv. 4. [*Annals,* I. x. 7.]

But the law of Christ has brought marriage between Christians, as it has other matters, to a higher norm of perfection, in that both the one who divorces a woman that is not an adulteress, and the one who marries a divorced woman, are pronounced guilty of adultery. Further, Paul, the apostle and interpreter of the law, gives not only to the husband as much right over the person of the wife as was found also in the state of nature (says Artemidorus: 'The one joined to a woman by the laws of marriage has complete mastery of her person'), but also equal right to the wife in turn over the person of the husband. Lactantius says: [4]

Matthew, v. 32, xix. 9. *1 Corinthians,* vii. 4. [*Oneirocritica.*]

Not in fact, as the system of public law says, is the woman alone an adulteress who takes another husband, and the husband free from the charge of adultery though

xxii [III. xxii. 32]: 'There are in fact many things which in that time were done in accordance with duty, which now cannot be done except lustfully.' Further, *On the City of God,* XVI. xxxviii: 'Since, for the sake of increasing offspring, no law prohibited having several wives.'

[1] Josephus, *Antiquities of the Jews,* Book XVII. i [XVII, i. 2]: 'It is an ancestral custom for us to have several wives at the same time.'

[2] Josephus in the same place in his history [*Antiquities of the Jews,* VII. vii. 3]: 'Since God had given to him wives, whom he could justly and lawfully possess.' The author of the *Pesichta,* on *Leviticus,* xviii [fol. xxiv. 1] says: 'It is very well known that he who says that it is forbidden to have more than one wife does not know what the law is.'

[3] *Leviticus,* xxi. 7. In the same chapter, verse 14, the widow is added to the divorced woman. Philo [*On Priests,* ix] and most modern interpreters have understood this of the High Priest on account of what precedes (verses 10 ff.); but [162] that it ought to be understood of any priest is shown by Ezekiel (*Ezekiel,* xliv. 22), and Josephus, both in the explanation of this law, as well as *Against Apion,* I [I. vii]. This law, then, must be connected with the beginning of the chapter, so that what is said of the High Priest was inserted parenthetically.

[4] *Divine Institutes,* VI. xxiii [VI. xxiii. 24–9], where also is the following: 'The wife ought to be taught by an example of continence that she should live chastely. For it is unfair to demand that which you cannot yourself furnish.' The same thought occurs in Gregory Nazianzen [*Orations,* XXXI. 500 C]: 'How do you ask, and not give in return?'

Jerome, *To Oceanus* [*Letters,* lxxvii. 3]: 'Different are the laws of the Caesars and the laws of Christ, and different are the teachings of Papinian and of our Paul. Among the former free rein is given to unchastity on the part of the men; and, while violation of freeborn women and adultery alone are condemned, licence is everywhere permitted with prostitutes and slave girls, as if the rank of the person, and not the will, constituted the crime. Among us what is not permitted to women is equally unpermissible to men, and the same subjection to the laws is assigned on equal terms.'

he has several wives; but the divine law joins the two in marriage into a single body with such equal right that whichever one has broken this union of the body by union with another is considered guilty of adultery.

3. I know that in regard to both these points the view is held by many that Christ did not establish a new law, but restored the law which God the Father had established in the beginning. They seem to have been brought to this opinion by the words of Christ Himself, where He recalls that beginning to us. But the reply can be made that from that first condition, in which God assigned only one woman to one man, that is sufficiently apparent which is best and most pleasing to God. It follows that this has always been excellent and praiseworthy. Yet it was not wrong to do otherwise, because where there is no law there is no transgression of law. There was in fact no law on that question in those times.

Thus when God said through Adam, or through Moses, that so strong was the bond of marriage that the husband ought to leave the family of his parent in order to establish a new family with his wife, he said almost the same as is said to the daughter of Pharaoh in the eleventh verse of the forty-fifth Psalm: 'Forget also thine own people and thy father's house.' And from the establishment of this so close friendship it is quite apparent that it is most pleasing to God[1] that that union should be perpetual. But it is not thereby

[1] This custom was preferred formerly by many of the wise also. Thus Euripides, *Andromache* [lines 177 ff.], in the character of Hermione:

> For fitting it is not
> That one as husband bear rule o'er two wives.
> Let him remain content with couch of but one spouse
> Who shall desire a house well managed.

Also in a chorus [*Andromache*, lines 464 ff.]:

> Never the stock from rival mothers born,
> Nor double marriage couches shall I praise,
> [163] For these are seeds of hate and bitter strife.
> One partner only of his trusted couch
> The husband ought to know as his alone.
> Two rulers do not better govern lands
> And cities, than one hand the sceptre holding.
> Nay thus is burden upon burden piled
> And raging discord rouses citizens
> To arms, and sundered now the bonds of union are.
> Unhappy contests even the Muses join
> Between two poets, rivals now in song.
> And when upon the sea a favouring breeze
> Swells all the canvas of the moving craft
> The right hand of one steersman at the helm
> Is far more worth than strength of twain distraught,
> Or goodly company e'en of the wise.
> One single power the city should control,
> One power should rule the home, if this be true
> That in our hearts we long for tranquil peace.

Again, Plautus, *Mercator* [lines 824–5]:

> For with one husband a good wife contented is;
> Why, then, should not the man with one wife be content?

proved that God had then commanded [1] that this bond should not be broken for any cause whatever. But what God had by the institution joined, Christ forbade man to sunder, taking most worthy matter for a new law from that which is best and most acceptable to God.

4. It is certain that in antiquity most peoples permitted freedom of divorce, and marriage with more than one woman. Tacitus relates that in his time the Germans, almost alone among barbarians, were content with a single wife for each; and to a similar custom the histories both of Persia and of India [2] in various places bear witness. Among the Egyptians [3] the priests alone ordinarily had but a single wife. Also among the Greeks, on the testimony of Athenaeus, Cecrops was the first who 'assigned one wife only to each husband'. Nevertheless we learn from the example of Socrates, and of others, that this rule was not long observed even at Athens. *On the Customs of the Germans* [xviii]. Diodorus [Siculus], I [lxxx]. [XIII. i.] Gellius, XV. xx.

If, then, any peoples have lived with greater continence, as the Romans did, who always refrained from plural [149] marriages and for a long time from divorce, truly they have drawn near to the state which is best. Hence among the same Romans the marriage of the wife of the priest of Jupiter was not annulled except by death. Nevertheless from what has been said it does not follow that all sinned [4] who did otherwise before the preaching of the Gospel.

X.—*That according to the law of nature alone marriages are not void by reason of lack of consent of the parents*

1. Now let us see what marriages are valid by the law of nature. In reaching a decision on this matter we ought to remember that not all acts which are contrary to the law of nature are rendered invalid by it, as is apparent from the example of the extravagant gift; but only those are invalid in which the essential point is lacking to give validity to the act, or in which the fault continues in the result of the action. The essential principle, both here and in other human acts, out of which right arises, is that right which we have explained as a moral capacity for action, joined with a will sufficiently free. But what freedom of will is sufficient to produce validity of action will be more conveniently discussed below, where we shall treat of promises in general.

[1] So also in a case of polygamy, Ambrose, *On Abraham*, Book I, iv [I. iv. 23], distinguishes between what God had praised in paradise and his condemnation of the opposite. This passage is cited by Gratian, *Decretum*, II. xxxii. 4 [II. xxxii. 4. 3].

[2] Also the Thracians, concerning whom there are some verses of Menander [Strabo, VII. iii. 4], and of Euripides in the *Andromache* [lines 215 ff.].

[3] See Herodian, Book II [cf. Herodotus, II. xcii].

[4] Augustine, *Against Faustus*, Book XXII, xlvii: 'So long as it was an established custom it was not a crime.' Gratian [*Decretum*, II. xxxii. 4. 7] cites this also, but under the name of Ambrose.

Under the moral right of action, the question here arises concerning the consent of the parents, which certain writers require as if by the law of nature for the validity of marriage. But in this they are wrong. For the arguments they offer prove nothing else than that it is in accord with the duty of children to obtain the consent of their parents. This I plainly grant, with the proviso that the wish of the parents be not manifestly unfair. For if children owe respect to their parents in all things, certainly they owe it especially in a matter which concerns the whole family, as marriage does. But from this it does not follow that the son lacks that right which is characterized as faculty or power to act. For a man who takes a wife ought to be of mature age, and since he withdraws from the family, he is not subject to family rule in this matter. Moreover, the duty of proper respect alone has not the effect of rendering of no effect an act opposed to it.

2. Moreover, the rule established by the Romans, and some other peoples, that certain marriages are void because the consent of the father is lacking, is not derived from the law of nature, but from the will of the lawgivers. For in the same law the mother, who is nevertheless naturally entitled to respect from the children,[1] does not make the marriage void by withholding consent; and not

Digest, XXIII. ii. 25. even the father of a son freed from parental control has that power. Besides, if the father himself is under the power of his father, both

Digest, XXIII. ii. 16. § 1. the grandfather and the father should give consent to the marriage of the son. For a daughter the authority of the grandfather suffices. These distinctions, unknown to the law of nature, show clearly enough that the practices in question have arisen from the civil law.

3. In the Scriptures, to be sure, we see that holy men, and in even more cases women, have followed parental authority in con-

Code, V. iv. 20. tracting marriage (to women indeed, on account of modesty, it is especially fitting to act on another's authority in this matter,[2] wherefore also that is in point which we read concerning the marriage of

vii. 36. a maiden in the *First Epistle to the Corinthians*); nevertheless the

[1] The will of the grandfather also, if he is a free man, has more weight than that of the father who is a slave (*Decretum*, II. xxxii. 3).

[2] Ambrose, *On Abraham*, Book I, last chap. [I. ix. 91], says: 'It is, in fact, not consistent with maidenly modesty to choose a husband.' In a manuscript of Gratian this is inserted in the *Decretum*, II. xxxii. 2 [II. xxxii. 2. 13].

Donatus, *On the Andria* [line 742], says: 'Absolute control over the marriage of the daughter rests with the father.'

In Euripides [*Andromache*, lines 987–8], Hermione says:

> I grant my father full control of marriage,
> For that decision is not in my power.

In Musaeus [lines 179–180] Hero says:

> [164] The law of wedlock cannot join us twain,
> Since mother, father both unwilling are.

marriage of Esau is not declared void, nor the children illegitimate, because he had contracted marriage without such authority. Quintilian, having in mind the law of nature in a strict sense, says: 'But if a son is ever allowed against the will of the father to do anything which in other respects shall not deserve blame, nowhere indeed is that freedom so necessary as in respect to marriage.'[1] *Genesis*, xxxvi. *Declamations*, cclvii.

XI.—*That according to the law of the Gospel marriages with the husband or wife of another are void*

Marriage with a woman who is married to another is undoubtedly void according to the law of nature, unless the former husband has divorced her; for up to the time of divorce his right over her continues; according to the law of Christ, his right continues until death has severed the bond. The marriage is void for this reason, that the moral faculty [150] is lacking; this was taken away by the former marriage, and all the results are faulty. The individual acts in fact involve an unlawful appropriation of that which belongs to another.

On the other hand, according to the law of Christ a marriage with a man already married to another woman is void on account of the right which Christ gave to a virtuous woman over her husband.

XII.—*That according to the law of nature marriages of parents with children are unlawful and void*

1. The marriage of those who are united by blood or by relationships of marriage presents a difficult question, which not infrequently gives rise to heated discussions. For if one tries to assign definite natural causes why such marriages are unlawful—just as they are forbidden by laws or customs—he will learn from experience how difficult, if not impossible, the task is.

For the reason suggested by Plutarch in his *Roman Questions*,[2] and accepted by Augustine in the *City of God* (Book XV, chapter xvi), that friendships are extended more widely by contracting marriage alliances in many places, is not of so great weight that anything cvii [cviii = 289 D].

[1] Eugraphius, *On the Andria*, Act I, scene v [line 238]: 'This point also is touched upon, whether children ought to obey the commands of their parents. It is, in fact, agreed that sons have free choice in respect to marriage.' Cassiodorus, VII. iv [*Variae*, VII. xl]: 'It is hard not to have entire freedom in respect to marriage, from which children are born.'

[2] Philo, *On Special Laws* [III. iv–v] says: 'What need have men to forbid relationships and bonds of union with one another, and to restrict to the narrow limits of a single home so great and excellent a work, which can extend itself and spread to countries, and islands, and even to the whole world? For alliances of marriage with strangers create new bonds of union between men, not of less moment than those which come from blood. This Moses had in view when he forbade many other marriages between relatives.'

Chrysostom, *On First Corinthians*, xiii. 13 [Homily XXXIV. iv]: 'Why do you restrict to narrow limits the breadth of love? Why do you needlessly destroy the cause of friendship, through which you could obtain another opportunity for winning friendship by marrying a woman from abroad?'

contrary to it would have to be considered void and unlawful. That which is less advantageous is not in fact thereby also illegal.

Add a situation which may arise. This lesser advantage may be offset by another greater advantage, not merely in the case of which

[*Deut.*, xxv. 5.] God made an exception in the law given to the Jews, where a man has died without offspring; or in the similar provision, which was

[*Numbers*, xxxvi. 8.] established by the Hebraic and the Attic law [1] with reference to maidens who are sole heiresses, which they call ἐπίκληροι, for the purpose of keeping ancestral estates in the family; but also in many other cases, which are commonly observed, or can be imagined.

2. From this general principle I except the marriage of parents of any degree with their descendants, the reason for the unlawfulness of which is, unless I am mistaken, quite apparent. In such a case the husband, who by the law of marriage is the superior, cannot show such respect to his mother as nature demands, nor the daughter to her father; for although the daughter in the marriage relation is inferior, nevertheless marriage itself introduces such an association that it excludes the respect belonging to the former relationship

Digest, XXIII. ii. 14. § 2. When Paul the jurist had said that in contracting marriages regard should be had for the law of nature and modesty,[2] he well added that it was contrary to modesty to marry one's own daughter. Therefore we must not doubt that such marriages are both unlawful and void, because the fault inheres permanently in the effect.

3. Neither ought we to be disturbed by the argument of Diogenes and Chrysippus drawn from poultry and other dumb creatures, by which they tried to prove that such unions were not

[Prolegomena, 9.] contrary to the law of nature. For, as I have said at the beginning of this work, it is sufficient for a thing to be considered unlawful if it is opposed to human nature; and in this category is incest, which,

Digest, XXIII. ii. 68. as Paul [3] the jurist has written, is by universal customary law a crime committed between parents and descendants. Such is that law

Socr., IV [*Memorabilia*, IV. iv. 19 ff.]. which Xenophon said was not less a law because it was held in contempt by the Persians.[4]

[1] See Demosthenes, *To Leochares* [xliv. 3]; the rhetorician Fortunatianus [*Art of Rhetoric*, I, p. 49]; Donatus, *On the Phormio*, Act I, scene ii [line 125], and *On the Adelphi*, IV. v [line 651].

[2] Philo, *On Special Laws* [III. iii], develops this subject excellently, where he says 'It is an unspeakable crime to defile the bed of a dead father, which ought to be left untouched as sacred; and not to show respect for the age and name of mother, and to be at the same time son and husband of the same woman, to have the same woman as mother and wife.'

[3] Thus also Papinian expresses himself in the law, *Digest*, XLVIII. v. 39 (38). § 2.

[4] Philo [*On Special Laws*, III. iii] notes that God punished their crimes in this matter with continuous wars and the slaughter of brothers. Jerome, *Against Jovinianus*, Book II [II. vii. 335], adds to the Persians also the Medes, Indians, and Ethiopians. Concerning barbarians generally, Hermione in the *Andromache* of Euripides [lines 173 ff.] says:

> And of such sort is every race barbaric,
> The father weds with daughter, the mother with the son,
> The brother with the sister; and to murder come
> The next-of-kin; no law prevents such awful deeds.

According to the commentary of Michael of Ephesus *On Nicomachean Ethics*, [V. iv.] that in fact is rightly said to be in accord with nature 'which is the practice of most peoples that are uncorrupted and live according to nature'. Hippodamus the Pythagoraean [=Hipparchus, *De Animi Tranquilitate*, cited by Stobaeus, cviii. 81.] speaks of 'unrestrained and unnatural desires, mad impulses, abominable pleasures'. Lucan says of the Parthians: [VIII. 401 ff.]

> With feastings mad, and wine,
> The royal house shrinks not from lawless matings.

[151] And later he adds: [VIII. 409 f.]

> For one who shares a mother's bed,
> What should I think a crime?

Dio of Prusa in his twentieth *Oration* wisely assigns a faulty education [xxi = p. 270 c.] as the particular cause of this Persian custom.

4. In this connexion we may well be surprised at the comment of Socrates. According to Xenophon, he found nothing blameworthy [*Memorabilia*, IV. iv. 23.] in such marriages except the disparity of age; for from that cause, he says, either sterility or deformity of offspring results. If this in fact were the only reason opposed to such a marriage, the marriage would surely not be void or unlawful, any more than a marriage between other persons, one of whom is as much older than the other as parents ordinarily are older than children.

5. This point ought rather to be discussed, whether, in addition to that which, as we have already said, can be attained to by reason, there does not exist, implanted in men who have not been corrupted by evil education, a kind of revulsion against unions with parents or with children, especially since such unions are naturally avoided by certain dumb animals. So in fact others have thought, and so Arnobius says in his fifth book *Against the Heathen*: [V. ix.]

> Did Jupiter even conceive an unspeakable lust for his mother, and could not be turned from the burning passion of such a desire by the horror which nature herself has implanted not in men alone but also in some animals, and by that universal inborn feeling?

On this topic in the ninth book of Aristotle's *History of Animals* [=IX. xlvii.] (chapter xlvi) there is a noteworthy story about a camel and a Scythian horse.[1] A similar report appears in Oppian, *On Hunting* (Book I). [I. 239 ff.] Seneca says in his *Hippolytus*: [913–4.]

> And likewise beasts themselves avoid the crimes of lust,
> And shame unwilling keeps the laws of blood.

[1] Pliny, *Natural History*, VIII. xlii [VIII. xlii. 156], treating of horses says: [165] 'Another horse, when it had discovered, through the removal of the cloth covering, that it had mated with its own mother, rushed to a precipice and was killed. And in the district of Reate we find that the attendant holding the mare was wounded for the same cause. For in horses also there is a recognition of relationships.' Similar instances you find in Varro, *On Farming*, II. vii [II. vii. 9], and in Antigonus Carystius, *Marvelous Stories* [lix]; also in Aristotle's treatise with the same title [ii].

XIII.—*That marriages of brothers with sisters, mothers-in-law with sons-in-law, fathers-in-law with daughters-in-law, and other similar marriages are unlawful and void by volitional divine law*

1. Next comes the question concerning all the different degrees of marriage and of blood relationship in collateral lines, particularly those which are expressly mentioned in the eighteenth chapter of *Leviticus.* For even granted that those prohibitions do not come from the pure law of nature, nevertheless they may seem, by a command of the divine will, to have passed over into that which is forbidden. In truth this command is such that it binds not only the Jews, but rather all men, as seems to be inferred from the following words of God to Moses: 'Defile not ye yourselves in any of these things; for in all these the nations are defiled which I cast out from before you.' Later come the words: 'And ye shall not do any of these abominations; for all these have the men of the land done, that were before you, and the land is defiled.'

Leviticus, xviii. 24, 25, 27.

2. For if the Canaanites and their neighbours sinned in committing such acts, it follows that some law had preceded. And since such a law is not purely natural, the alternative is that it was given by God, either to those people in particular, which is not probable nor sufficiently supported by the words, or to the human race, either at the creation, or at the restoration after the flood.

Now those laws which were given to the whole human race do not seem to have been annulled by Christ, but merely those laws which separated the Jews from other nations as if by an interposed wall. An additional point is that Paul severely reproves the marriage of a step-son with a step-mother, although no particular teaching of Christ on that question exists; and he does not use any other argument than this, that such union seems impure even to heathen peoples.[1]

Ephesians, ii. 14. *1 Corinthians,* vii. 25 [v. 1].

The truth of the last statement is shown by other facts and also by the laws of Charondas, which brand such a marriage with disgrace. There is also this statement in an oration of Lysias: [152] 'That most impure of all men was husband of mother and daughter.' Consistent with this, in a not dissimilar case, is the statement of Cicero in the speech *For Aulus Cluentius*; for having stated that a mother-in-law had married her son-in-law, he adds: 'O incredible crime of a woman, unheard of in all the life of man except in the case of this one woman!' When King Seleucus gave his wife Stratonice

[=Andocides, i. 124.] [vi. 15.]

[1] Tertullian, *Against Marcion,* V [V. vii]: 'I do not maintain that according to the law of the Creator the man has sinned who has married the wife of his father. Let him follow the rule of the common public religion.'

in marriage to his son Antiochus, according to Plutarch,[1] he feared that she might be offended 'at the unlawful act'. There is also the verse of Virgil: [*Aeneid*, X. 389.]

Daring to pollute his own stepmother's bed!

If this common opinion did not have its origin in a necessary dictate of nature, the conclusion is warranted that it comes from an ancient tradition which was derived from some divine command.

3. In respect to this part of the divine law the ancient Jews are interpreters not to be despised; and Moses Maimonides, who read and with great judgement explained all their writings, says that there are two causes for the laws about marriage which have been handed down in the eighteenth chapter of *Leviticus*. The first cause is a kind of natural modesty, which does not permit parents to have intercourse with their own offspring, either directly or through persons closely connected by blood relationship or by marriage[2]; and the second is, that too close association daily and unobserved of certain persons might pave the way to unchastity and adultery, if such loves could be cemented in marriage.

If we wish to adapt these two causes judiciously to those divine laws cited from *Leviticus*, it will easily appear that in the case of relatives by marriage who are in the direct line (not to mention parents and children now, since, as I think, the union of these is sufficiently forbidden by natural reason without a formulated law), and likewise in blood-relationship of the first degree in collateral lines,[3] which is usually called the second degree because of origin from a common stock, the first cause has weight on account of the very recent likeness of the parents in the children; and such avoidance comes from the fact that, if nature does not order it, she certainly calls it more honourable. Many things of this kind furnish subject-matter for divine and human laws.

4. Consequently the Jews wish to include in the direct line the degrees not mentioned in the law, on account of the apparent identity of reason. The following are the designations of degrees among them: the mother's mother, the mother of the mother's father, the father's mother, the mother of the father's father, the wife of the father's father, the wife of the mother's father, the son's daughter-in-law, the daughter-in-law of the son's son, the daughter's daughter-in-law, the daughter of the son's daughter, the daughter of the son's son,

[1] In the life of *Demetrius* [xxxviii=907 E]; also reported by Appian in his *Syrian Wars* [x. 59], who calls such passion 'impious love'.

[2] Philo [*On Special Laws*, III. v]: 'Although in fact the parties have been separated, they retain the right of fraternal affection and are bound by blood relationship as by a natural bond.'

[3] Both Peruvians and Mexicans refrained from marriage with relatives of this degree [Jean de Léry, *Itinerary*, chap. xvii, near the beginning].

the daughter of the daughter's daughter, the daughter of the daughter's son, the daughter of the wife's son's daughter, the daughter of the wife's daughter's daughter, the mother of the wife's father's mother, the mother of the wife's mother's father, that is, to use the Roman terms, all grandmothers and great-grandmothers, stepmothers' mothers, great-granddaughters, stepdaughters' daughters, daughter-in-laws' daughters, and mother-in-laws' mothers; because, of course, under the title of relationship on the father's side is included similar blood relationship, and under relationship in the first degree relationship in the second degree; and under relationship in the second degree the third degree, beyond which it is scarcely possible that controversy should arise, since if it could the same reckoning might go on to infinity.

5. Now these laws, and also the law that brothers and sisters should not marry, the Jews think were given to Adam at the same time with the laws to worship God, to administer justice, not to shed blood, not to worship false gods, not to take what is another's; but with the condition that the laws regulating marriage should not have effect until after the human race had multiplied sufficiently, [153] because in the very beginning this could not take place without the marriage of brothers and sisters.

And the Jews do not think that the fact that this provision was not mentioned by Moses in the proper place makes any difference.[1] Moses considered it sufficient to have tacitly indicated it in the law itself, when he condemns foreign nations on that account. There are, in fact, many such provisions in the law, which are not given in the proper order of time, but as circumstances suggest. Hence the widely accepted opinion among the Jews, that in the law there is no first or last; that is, many things are presented in inverse order.

See Cajetan, *On Matthew*, xix. [V. vii.]

6. In regard to the marriage of brothers and sisters, these are the words of Michael of Ephesus *On Nicomachean Ethics*, Book V: 'For a brother to marry a sister was in the beginning a matter of indifference; but since a law has been established against such unions, it makes a great deal of difference whether the law is observed or not.' Diodorus Siculus calls it a common custom of mankind that brothers should not marry sisters, but excepts the Egyptians from the custom. Dio of Prusa makes barbarians the exception. Seneca has written: 'We join the gods in marriage, and that too not reverently, as brothers forsooth with sisters.' Plato in the eighth book of the *Laws* calls such marriages 'least holy, and hated of deity'.

I [xxvii].

[In Augustine, *City of God*, VI. x.]

[VIII. vi = p. 838B.]

[1] For neither was that law related according to which Judah wished Thamar burned [*Genesis*, xxxviii. 24]. Thus Judith, [*Judith*,] ix. 2, says that the Sichemites were justly killed because they had violated a maiden, and Reuben is cursed by his father on account of incest [*Genesis*, xlix. 4].

7. All these statements show that there was an ancient tradition concerning a divine law against marriages of this kind, and for that reason also we see that the word 'impious' is used about such marriages. Moreover, the law itself indicates [1] that all brothers and sisters are meant, by including both relatives on the father's side and blood relatives of that degree in general, whether born and brought up within or without the home.

XIV.—*That the same objection does not seem to hold in case of marriages with relatives of a degree farther removed*

1. This plain statement seems to indicate the distinction between these and other more distant relatives. For it is forbidden to marry an aunt on the father's side; it is not, however, forbidden to marry a brother's daughter,[2] where the degree of relationship is the same, and there are to be found examples of such a marriage among the Jews. Tacitus says: 'New among us is the marriage with a brother's daughter, but it is customary among other peoples and not forbidden by any law.' Isaeus shows that such marriages were permitted at Athens, and likewise Plutarch, in the life of *Lysias*. The reason given by the Jews is that young men constantly visit the homes of grandfathers and grandmothers, or even live in them along with their aunts; but their access to the homes of brothers is less frequent, and in these they do not have the same rights.

Annals, XII [vi].

[=Demosthenes, *Against Leochares,* xliv. 10.]

[=p.836B.]

If we accept this explanation, which seems quite consistent with reason, we shall acknowledge that, from the time when the human race began to be numerous, the law against the marriage of relatives in the direct line and with sisters has been permanently valid, and common to mankind, since it rests on a natural sense of honour. In consequence, whatever is done contrary to this law becomes void, since the defect is permanent. The other laws nevertheless are not on the same basis, since they contain a mode of prevention rather, which can be exercised in other ways.

2. Surely in the earliest canons, which are called Apostolic, the man who had married two sisters, one after the other, or 'a niece', that is, the daughter of a brother or a sister, was merely excluded from the clerical office.

Canon xix.

[1] On this compare the Chaldaean paraphrase. The Spartans and Athenians distinguished these faultily, and indeed in a different way.

[2] Josephus thinks that Sarah bore this relationship to Abraham [*Antiquities of the Jews,* I. xii. 1]. The same author gives us an example, after the promulgation of the law, in the person of Herod, who had married his brother's daughter and had betrothed his own daughter to his brother Pherotas. See *Antiquities of the Jews,* XII and XVI [XVI. i. and XVII. i].

According to Ovid, *Metamorphoses* V [V, lines 1 ff.], Andromeda had been betrothed to her uncle Phineus. Though such a marriage was forbidden among the Romans, Claudius permitted it. Nerva forbade it, and Heraclius again permitted it.

Further, it is not difficult to reply to what we have said concerning the sin charged against the Canaanites and the neighbouring peoples. The general expression can in fact be restricted to the special points of the chapter [of *Leviticus*], as intercourse of males with males, intercourse with animals, with parents, with sisters, and with the wives of others; other laws were added as 'an outpost', as the Greeks say, or as an advanced line of fortifications, as the Jews say, for the defence of these main positions.

The proof that the general expression cannot be understood of the individual parts may be found in the prohibition of having two sisters in marriage at the same time. For the righteousness of [154] Jacob, who broke that law, does not permit us to believe that this prohibition had previously been made general for the human race. The act of Amram, the father of Moses, can be added as an example; for before the times of the law he married his aunt on his father's side. Similarly among the Greeks Diomedes and Iphidamas married maternal aunts.[1] Alcinous married Arete, his brother's daughter.

Eustathius, *On the Iliad*, XII [line 224], and *On the Odyssey*, VII [line 63].

3. Nevertheless the early Christians acted rightly in observing, of their own accord, not only those laws which were given to all men in common but also the other laws which were written particularly for the Jewish people. They also extended the bounds of natural modesty to some degrees of relationship which were farther removed, that in this virtue, not less than in others, they might surpass the Jews.

From the canons it appears that this was done by common consent. Speaking of the marriage of first cousins[2] among the Christians, Augustine says: 'By custom this, which was permitted by law, rarely took place; the divine law did not forbid it, and human law had not yet forbidden it. Nevertheless, even the lawful act was avoided because of its nearness to an unlawful act.' This extension of the bounds of natural modesty was afterward sanctioned by laws of kings and states. Thus the *Code*[3] of Theodosius forbade

City of God, XV. xvi.

[1] We learn from the *Electra* of Euripides [line 311] that Electra was betrothed to her uncle Castor.

[2] Aeschylus [*Suppliants*, 37] speaks of the marriages arranged for the Danaids as 'marriages which the law forbids', and says [225] that thus 'the race is defiled'. But the Scholiast adds that those marriages were unlawful because the father of the maidens was still alive, as, after his death, they would have been lawful, according to the law 'of sole heiresses'.

Livy [XLII. xxxiv. 3] represents Spurius Ligustinus, a Roman citizen, as saying: 'My father gave to me the daughter of his brother as wife.' See also Plautus, *Poenulus* [line 1156 ff.].

[3] Aurelius Victor [*Epitome*, xlviii. 10] says of him: 'He laid such stress on modesty and continence, that he forbade marriages with first cousins as if with sisters.' Also Libanius mentions this in the oration *De Angariis*.

In the *Theodosian Code* (III. xii. 3) there is a law of Arcadius and Honorius with like import. Another law of Honorius and the Younger Theodosius in the same *Code*, III. x [III. x. 1], shows that such marriages were nevertheless allowed by special dispensation of the Emperors. The Gothic kings followed the practice.

Cassiodorus, VII. xlvi [*Variae*, VII. xlvii. 123]: 'Wise men, following this example, have passed on to posterity this observance of natural modesty, reserving to the Emperor alone the privilege of uniting first cousins in marriage.' There also is found the formula for such a dispensation.

the marriage of first cousins, and Ambrose praised the decree as righteous. *Letters*, lxvi.

4. But it must at the same time be understood that what is forbidden by human law, if done, is not also void,[1] unless the law has added a provision to this effect, or indicated that it will be. The sixtieth Elberic canon has this provision: 'If anyone after the death of his wife has married her sister [2] and she be of the faith, he is denied communion for five years.' The provision itself indicates that the marriage bond remains. And as we have already said, according to the Apostolic canons the man who has married two sisters or a brother's daughter is merely excluded from the clerical office.

XV.—*That certain marriages, which are classed by the laws as concubinage, can take place and are lawful*

1. To proceed to other topics, this observation should be made, that a certain form of concubinage is in reality a valid marriage, although it is deprived of certain effects peculiar to municipal law, or even loses certain natural effects by the hindrance of the municipal law. For example, by Roman law [3] cohabitation and not marriage is said to exist between a male and a female slave. Nevertheless, in such a union nothing essential to the nature of marriage is lacking; for this reason it was called 'marriage' in the early canons.

Similarly, concubinage and not marriage is said to exist between a free man and a slave girl. Hence this term by a kind of analogy has been extended to other unions between persons of unequal rank, as at Athens the union of a citizen and a woman of foreign birth. Hence in commenting on the verse of Virgil, [*Aeneid*, VII. 283.]

Substituted bastard foals begot from stolen mother,

Servius explains 'bastard' as ignoble and obscure on the mother's side. In the *Birds* of Aristophanes one who had said, 'You are a [Lines 1650 ff.]

[1] [166] In the Council of Agde, after enumerating prohibited marriages, and among them that with a brother's widow, there is added: 'We forbid such marriages at the present time, but in such a way that we do not annul those which have been contracted up to this time.' Gratian placed this in the *Decretum*, II. xxxv. 2 and 3. 8.

This is similar to what Paul has reported among his *Sententiae*, Book II, title xx [II. xix. 2], 'that marriages contracted without the consent of the parents are unlawful, yet so that they are not annulled', unless, perchance, the last clause was added by Arrianus. Tertullian treating of a marriage with a non-Christian says, *To His Wife*, II [II. ii]: 'The Lord has rather decreed that such marriages be not contracted than that they be altogether annulled.' See below, xvi.

[2] *Law of the Lombards*, II. viii. 13 [II. viii. 3]: 'Because the canons decide the same concerning two sisters as concerning two brothers.'

[3] But the unions of slaves were called marriages in Greece, Carthage, and Apulia; see prologue to the *Casina* of Plautus [line 68]. So also in the *Law of the Lombards*, II. xii. 10 and xiii. 3; and in the *Salic Law*, title xiv. 11. But among the Jews such marriages were not valid without the consent of the masters, as is observed by the Rabbis on *Exodus*, xxi, where mention is made of such marriages. That the same rule held among the Greek Christians is noted by Basil in his canons [*To Amphiloch.* xlii = *Epist. Class.*, II. 199].

We see in Cassiodorus, *Variae*, VII. xl, that it was customary to ask the Emperor for a dispensation to marry a woman of lower rank

bastard and not of noble birth,' proves his statement by adding, ' since you were born of a foreign woman.' And in Aelian the word meaning ' lawfully begotten ' is defined as ' one whose parents are both citizens '.

[*Var.Hist.*, VI. x.]

2. Under these conditions in the state of nature there could be a true marriage between such persons as I have mentioned if the woman was under the husband's protective care and had promised him fidelity. Also under the Christian law [1] that will be a true marriage between a male and a female slave, or between a free man and a slave woman; and much the more between a citizen and a foreign woman, or a senator and a freedwoman, if the necessary conditions according to the divine law of Christianity are present, to wit: an indissoluble union of one man with one woman, even if certain effects of the municipal law do not follow, or if effects which would otherwise naturally follow are hindered by the law.

[*Decretum*, I. xxxiv. 4.]

It is in this sense that the words of the first Council [155] of Toledo must be taken: ' For the rest, one who has not a wife, but has a concubine in the place of a wife,[2] should not be refused communion; provided, however, that he shall be content with the union with one woman, either wife or concubine, as he has preferred.' On this topic add also the passage in the *Constitutions* of Clement (Book VIII, chapter xxxii). Pertinent in this connexion is the fact that Theodosius and Valentinian call a certain kind of concubinage an unequal marriage, and, further, that it is said that from such a marriage the charge of adultery may arise.

Code, V. xxvii. 3. *Digest*, XLVIII v. 14 (13).

XVI.—*That certain marriages can be unlawfully contracted and nevertheless be valid*

1. Again, if a human law forbids that marriage be contracted between certain persons, it does not therefore follow that the marriage, if in fact contracted, will be invalid. To prohibit and to annul are in fact two different things. For a prohibition can exert its force through a penalty, whether express or arbitrary; and Ulpian [3]

Institutes, I [i].

[1] See the collection of Gratian [Gregory], *Decretals*, IV. ix. 1.

[2] Concerning such a concubine Augustine, *On Faith and Works* [xix. 35], says: ' Also if a concubine has promised that she will have intercourse with no other man, even if she is sent away by the man to whom she has been subject, there is no proper ground for doubt whether or not she ought to be permitted to receive baptism.' The same author, *De Bono Conjugali*, v, adds: ' When a man and a woman, he unmarried and she not the wife of another, cohabit, not for the sake of having children but to satisfy passion, yet with such fidelity that neither he does this with another woman nor she with another man, the question is raised whether such a relation ought to be called marriage. And perhaps it can be called marriage without absurdity if they have decided to live thus until the death of one of them, and if, although the having of children was not the cause of their union, they have nevertheless not so avoided offspring that they were unwilling to have children, or even took unlawful means to prevent children.' Likewise in the *Capitulary* of the Kings of France, VII. cclv. it is said: ' A man who has a wife cannot at the same time have a concubine, lest the affection for the concubine should take him away from his wife.'

[3] Livy, Book X [X. ix. 5-6]: ' Although the Valerian Law had forbidden the whipping or execution

applies the word 'imperfect' to laws which forbid anything to be done, but do not annul it when done. Such was the Cincian Law, which forbade gifts above a certain limit but did not make them void when given.

2. We know that among the Romans the rule was afterward introduced by a law of Theodosius that, if a law merely prohibited some act without specifically saying that whatever was done contrary to the law ought to be without effect, nevertheless the act itself was void, without effect, and as if it had never been done—of course in case the matter should come into court. *Code*, I. xiv. 5.

Such extension, however, does not arise from the force of the prohibition alone, but from the effect of the new law, which other peoples do not find it necessary to follow. Often, in fact, there is greater impropriety in the act than in its results; often, again, the inconveniences which result from annulment are greater than the improprieties themselves,[1] or than the disadvantage of the act itself.

XVII.—*The right of the majority in associations of any kind*

Besides the most natural association of marriage there are other associations, both private and public. Public associations are formed either by a people or by peoples. All associations have this in common, however, that in those matters on account of which the association was formed the entire membership, or the majority in the name of the entire membership, may bind the individual members. In general it must be believed that it was the wish of those who united in an association that there should be some method of conducting business. But it is manifestly unfair that the majority should be ruled by the minority. Therefore, naturally, the majority has the same right as the entire body, if due exception is made of agreements and laws[2] which prescribe the form of conducting business. Victoria, *De Potestate Civili*, no. 14.

Thucydides says: 'Whatever the majority votes has full power.' Also Appian: 'The majority controls both in the elections and in V [xxx]. [*Civil Wars*, III. viii. 52.]

of the one who had appealed, it added nothing beyond the illegality of the act against those who had done so. Such was the modesty of men at that time, I believe, that the bond of the law seemed sufficiently strong, but now one would scarcely so threaten a slave.'

Ulpian [*Institutes*, i. 2 = *Jurisprudentiae Ante-Justinianae*, I. ii] states that the Furian Law on wills forbade any one, outside the list of persons excepted, to take a legacy or donation on account of death exceeding a thousand asses, and decreed a fine of four times the amount received against any one who accepted more.'

Macrobius, near the end of what he wrote *On the Dream of Scipio* [II. xvii. 13], says: 'Among laws, that one is accounted imperfect in which no penalty is decreed against the violators.' See above in this chapter, at the end of xiv. Of this character [167] is a rescript of the Emperor Marcus Aurelius [*Digest*, XI. vii. 14. § 14]: 'The heir, who prevents the funeral from being conducted by the one chosen by the deceased, acts not rightly, yet no punishment has been decreed against him.'

[1] Thus King Alcinous decided that Medea should be returned to her father, if she was still a virgin, as Apollonius Rhodius, *Argonautic Expedition* [IV, lines 1106 ff.], and his Scholiast note, and also Apollodorus, *Library* [I. ix. 25].

[2] As those laws which require a two-thirds vote, such as *Decretals*, I. vi. 6.

[Dion. Halic., II. xiv ;] VII [xxxvi and xxxix]. *Politics*, IV. viii ; VI. ii. [X. vi. 15.] [*Against Symmachus*, I. 598 f.] [I. 606 f.]

the courts.' Dionysius of Halicarnassus likewise: 'Whatever has seemed best to the majority prevails'[1]; in another passage: 'Whatever the majority of the votes repeals, we must conform to'; and similarly: 'Whatever the majority votes to rescind, that controls.' Says Aristotle: 'The decision of the majority [...] rules.' Also Curtius in the tenth book: 'Let that be valid which the majority has decided.' Prudentius writes:

> Among the few, as numbers now were waning,
> Existed in reality nor fatherland nor senate;

and again:

> Let the weak voice of the minority
> Give way, and in its lesser part
> Be still.

[*Anabasis*, VI. i. 18.] In Xenophon are the words: 'To do all things in accordance with the opinion that prevails.'

XVIII.—*Which opinion should prevail in case of a tie vote*

If the votes are equal, no action will be taken, because [156] there is not sufficient weight to carry a change. For this reason, where the votes for and against are equal, the accused is considered acquitted.[2] This right of acquittal the Greeks called the vote of Minerva, in remembrance of the story of Orestes; the subject is [470 ff.] dealt with in tragedy by Aeschylus in the *Furies*, and by Euripides in the *Orestes* and the *Electra*.[3]

Further, under such a condition the possessor of a thing retains it, as was not badly noted by the author of the *Problems* ascribed to Aristotle (chapter xxix). In one of the *Controversies* of Seneca is the statement: 'One judge condemns, another acquits; in differences of opinion let the milder prevail.'[4] Thus also in dialectic the conclusion supports the side which presents the less difficulty.

XIX.—*What opinions should be divided and what joined*

At this point question is usually raised in regard to the combining or separating of votes. According to the pure law of nature,

[1] The Chaldaean paraphrase and the rabbis attribute this meaning to the statement in *Exodus*, xxiii. 3.
Add *Digest*, XLII. i. 39 and 36, and what I give below, in III. xxx. 24 [III. xx. 4]; also what Ambrose [*Letters*, xviii] says, in accord with Prudentius, *Against Symmachus* [I. v. 599 f., 607 f.].

[2] *Digest*, XLII. i. 38 [beginning]. See Julian, *On Eusebia* [*Orations*, III=p. 115 A, ed. Spanh.].

[3] Also in the *Iphigenia among the Taurians* [line 1470]. In the *Electra* [lines 1268 f.] the verses are:

> And for the future this shall be the law for all,
> A tie of jurors sets free the accused.

[4] Seneca in his *Controversies* [I. v. 3] declares: 'Power which wins by pity is not hated.' Further among the Jews condemnation by a majority of one is considered void; so the Chaldaean paraphrase

that is, if no other rules have been laid down by agreement or by statute, clearly a distinction should be made between opinions that are entirely different and those of which one contains a part of the other, so that the latter ought to be combined in whatever they agree,[1] but the former cannot be combined.

Thus when some favour a fine of 20, others of 10, they will unite on 10 against the vote for acquittal. If, however, some vote for the death penalty, and some for banishment of the accused, these votes will not be combined, because they are different, and banishment is not included in the death penalty. But neither will those who vote for acquittal be combined with those who vote for exile, because, although they agree in not favouring the death of the accused, nevertheless this is not what the vote itself declares, and the matter is one of inference; for he who votes for banishment does not vote for acquittal.

Pliny, then, rightly said, when something of this kind happened in the senate, that the difference in the motions was so great that no count could be made except for each motion separately; and that it made little difference that senators agreed in opposing the same motion, since there was no motion on which they did agree. Polybius,[2] again, notes that the praetor Postumius acted illegally in taking the votes, since he combined those voting for condemnation of the captive Greeks with those voting for temporary detention, as against those who voted for acquittal.

Letters to Aristo, VIII [xiv. 24].

Selections on Embassies.

There is a question of this kind in the ninth book of Gellius, and in the work of Curius Fortunatianus, *De Quantitatum Comparatione*; also in the *Controversies* of Quintilian the Father (ccclxv), where are the following words: 'Now united you plainly have the more, now that very number, which, united, might do harm, you destroy the effect of by making a division in it. Two vote for exile, two for degradation. Do you desire that I unite those who separate themselves?'

[IX. xv. 7.]

to the passage in *Exodus*, xxiii [verses 2–3]; and Moses de Kotzi gives the same explanation, *Precepts Bidding*, 98, and [*Precepts*] *Forbidding*, 195.

[1] So, when a motion contained several parts, the Roman senators were ordered to vote the parts separately, as Asconius testifies in his commentary *On* [*Cicero's*] *For Milo* [xliv].

Cicero, *Letters*, I. ii [I. ii. 1], says: 'And so when Bibulus had first made a motion, that three delegates should restore the king, and secondly Hortensius, that you should restore him without an army, and in the third place Volcacius, that Pompey should restore him, the demand was made that the motion of Bibulus be divided. The part of the motion referring to the religious aspect of the case, to which opposition could no longer be made, was passed. On the question of the three delegates, the majority voted for everything else but that.'

Seneca, *Letters*, xxi [II. ix. 9]: 'What is the usual custom in the senate I think ought to be made the custom in philosophy also. When some one has proposed what pleases me in part I bid him divide his statement, and I follow the part I approve.' He says also, *On the Happy Life*, iii [iii. 2]: 'The right of decision rests with me; and so in one case I shall follow a man, in another I shall bid him divide his proposition.'

Pliny, *Letters*, VIII. xiv [VIII. xiv. 13 ff.], mentions the same practice.

[2] [*Selections on Embassies*, cxxix, p. 1331, edit. Amster. = Polybius, XXXIII. i]. See also the notes of Fulvius on this passage.

XX.—*That the right of those who are absent accrues to those present*

This point must also be added. If any members cannot avail themselves of their right by reason of absence or some other hindrance, their right in the meantime accrues to those present. This, too, Seneca expresses in his *Controversies*[1]: 'Suppose you are the slave of more than one master; you will serve the one who is present.'[2]

XXI.—*What rank is to be observed among equals, even kings*

Dig. L. iii. 1. The natural order[3] of rank among members of an association is the order in which they entered it. So this order is preserved among brothers, since the first born takes precedence, and so on in succession, with disregard of all other qualities. As Aristotle says, 'Brothers in fact are equal, except as age distinguishes them.' [*Nicom. Ethics*, VIII. xii.]

Code, XII. iii. 1. Theodosius and Valens in a *Constitution* prescribe the order of rank to be observed as between the consuls: 'Of those holding the same official rank, who in fact ought to have precedence except the one who first attained to the rank?'[4] In ancient times this custom prevailed in the association of Christian kings and peoples, that in councils[5] concerned with Christian matters those who had first accepted Christianity took precedence of the rest.

XXII.—*In associations which are based upon property, the votes must be counted according to the shares which each has in the property*

Yet the following must be added. In the case of an association [157] having its foundation based on property in which all do not share equally, as in an inheritance or an estate, in case one has a half, another a third, another a quarter, then not only must the order according to the amount of participation be followed, but also the votes must be counted in proportion to the shares, that is, to use a technical expression, *pro rata*. This is in accord with natural justice and was approved by the laws of the Romans also. *Dig.* II. xiv. 8; XVI. iii. 14; XLII. v. 16.

[1] *Controversies*, Book III, xix [VII. iv. 4].

[2] So that even the power over the whole may fall to one person, *Digest*, III. iv. 7; see Wesenbeck on this provision. See also *Digest*, II. xiv. 10; Zasius, *Paratitla Dig. De Pactis* [II. xiv]; Bartolus, *On Digest*, L. iii. 1; Bohier, *Decisions*, i, no. 4; Antoine Favre, *Codex Sabaudicus*, I. ii. 40; Reinkingk, Book I, class v, chap. viii.

Nevertheless often also in this case, as in that rule concerning the majority, the laws make exceptions, as that two thirds should be present; *Digest*, III. iv. 3; *Code*, X. xxxii. 45; again, that those absent should be able [168] to give their proxies to those present or to give their vote through an attorney; *Sext*, I. vi. 46.

[3] On the right of precedence, if you wish, examine M. Antonius Natta, *Consilia*, 600, no. 22, and *Consilia*, 678, no. 31; Martin Wacher, *Consilia Caesarea*, in *Controversia Saxonica*.

[4] Add *Code*, XII. viii. 2; *Digest*, L. vi. 6; *Code*, XII. xliii. 3.

[5] John Fiçe., *Consilia Latina*, 77, no. 16; Afflictis, *Decisiones Neapolitanae*, i, no. 8; Bartolus, *On Digest*, L. iii. 1; Innocent, *On Decretals*, I. xxxiii. 7; Anthony Tessaurus, *Quaestiones Forenses*, I, qu. xlviii, no. 5; Tiberius Decianus, *Responsa*, xix, nos. 183 ff.; Innocent, Butrio, Felinus, *On Decretals*, I. xxxiii. 15; Baldus, *On Code*, I. ii. 16, 2. But, above all, see Aeneas Sylvius in his *History of the Council of Basel*.

Thus Strabo relates that when Libyca and three neighbouring cities had united into one body politic it was agreed that the others should have one vote each, but Libyca two, because it contributed much more to the common interest than the others. The same author reports that in Lycia there were twenty-three cities, of which some had three votes each,[1] some two, and some only one, and that they distributed the burdens in the same proportion. But Aristotle rightly notes that such a division would be fair only in case 'the association was entered into on account of property'.

XIII [iv. 17].

XIV [iii. 3].

Politics, III. ix.

XXIII.—*The right of a state over its subjects*

An association in which many fathers of families unite into a single people and state gives the greatest right to the corporate body over its members. This in fact is the most perfect society. There is no lawful act of men which does not have relation to this association either of itself or by reason of the circumstances. And this is what Aristotle expressed in saying that 'the laws prescribe concerning matters of every kind'.

Morals [*Nicom. Ethics*], V. iii.

XXIV.—*Whether it is permissible for nationals to withdraw from a state; explanation, with a distinction*

1. Here the question is commonly raised, whether it is permissible for nationals to withdraw from their state without permission.[2]

We know that there are peoples among whom such withdrawal is not permissible, as the Muscovites; and I do not deny that a civil society can be formed on such terms, and that such a custom may receive the force of agreement. By the Roman laws, at least the later laws, a man could at any rate change his place of habitation, but none the less the person who had done so was subject to the burdens of his native town. This applied, however, only to those who remained within the limits of the Roman Empire, and the regulation itself had special reference to the payment of taxes.

Dig. L. i. 22.

2. But we are inquiring what would naturally be the rule if nothing else were agreed upon; and not regarding a part of a state, but a whole state, or even the limits of a single empire. And surely, that the nationals of a state cannot depart in large bodies[3] is quite

[1] Thus in the treaty of Smalkald the Elector of Saxony had two votes.

[2] On this question see the Swiss treaties in Simler [*De Republica Helvetiorum*, I = p. 203] and in other authors. Servius, in the Fuldensian excerpts, says [*On the Aeneid*, II, line 156]: 'It had been an ancient custom, that the man who was passing over into a family or nation first withdrew from the one in which he had been, and under such a condition was received by the other.' See in Mariana's *History* some examples of renouncing fidelity to kings, especially the last notable one in XXVIII. xiii.

[3] Zonaras [XIV. v. 25], speaking of the king of the Lazes, who had revolted from the Persians to the Romans, says: 'This was the beginning of the war between the Romans and the Persians, because the Roman Emperor enticed away the subjects of the Persians.'

clear from the necessity underlying its purpose, which in moral matters takes the place of law. For if such migration were permissible the civil society could not exist.

The withdrawal of individuals, on the contrary, seems a different matter, just as it is one thing to draw water from a river and another to conduct the stream into a canal. Tryphoninus says: 'Each has the unrestricted right to choose his own state.' Cicero in the speech *For Balbus* praises the law that 'no one is forced to remain in a state against his will', and calls 'each man's power to retain or to abandon his right the foundation of liberty'.

Digest, XLIX. xv. 12. § 9. [xiii. 31.]

Yet here also we must observe the rule of natural justice which the Romans followed in putting an end to private associations, that a thing should not be permitted if it is contrary to the interests of society. 'Always, in fact,' as Proculus rightly says, 'it is the custom to observe, not what is to the interest of an individual associate, but what is to the interest of the association.'[1] Moreover, it will be to the interest of the civil society that the national do not withdraw if a heavy debt has been contracted, unless the national is prepared to pay his share at once; likewise if war has been undertaken because of confidence in numbers, and especially if a siege threatens, unless the national is prepared to furnish an equally capable substitute to defend the state.

Digest, XVII. ii. 65. § 5.

3. With the exception of these cases, it is to be believed that peoples consent to the free withdrawal of their nationals, [158] because from granting such liberty they may experience not less advantage than other countries.

XXV.—*The state has no legal claim against exiles*

Thus the state has no legal claim against exiles.[2] According to Euripides the descendants of Hercules, expelled from Argos by Eurystheus, through their defender Iolaus speak as follows:

[*Heraclidae,* 187 ff.]

> By what right does he now claim us as of Mycenae,
> Whom, there abiding, he from that city drove?
> Citizens, therefore, we no longer are.

In an oration of Isocrates the son of Alcibiades, discussing the period of his father's exile, says: 'When our state had no relation with him.'[3]

[*De Bigis,* xvi. 14 = 349 D.]

The association of several peoples, either of themselves or through their heads, is a league; regarding the nature and effect of such association there will be an opportunity to speak when I come to the question of obligation arising out of a compact.

[1] Bembo, Book VII.

[2] See below, III. xx. 41.

[3] Nicetas, *Isaac Angelus*, Book I [I. ix]: 'It is no wonder that any one who has perceived that his own people are hostile to him courts an enemy and makes a friend of him.'

XXVI.—*The right, arising from consent, over an adopted child*

Subjection by consent is either private or public.

Private voluntary subjection can be of many kinds, as there are many kinds of authority. The noblest form is adult adoption, by which a person so gives himself to another family that he is subject to it in the same way in which a son of mature age is subject to his father. A father, however, cannot give his son to another in such a way that the full right of the father passes to the other, and that he himself is released from the duty of a father; for nature does not permit this. But the father can entrust his son to another, and allow him to be brought up by the other as in his place.

XXVII.—*The right over slaves*

1. The basest form of voluntary subjection is that by which a man gives himself into complete slavery, as those among the Germans who staked their liberty on the last throw of the dice; 'The one who lost', says Tacitus, 'went into voluntary slavery.' Such slavery prevailed even among the Greeks, as Dio of Prusa relates in his fifteenth *Oration*: 'Innumerable persons, though free, give themselves into slavery to serve according to contract.'[1] *On the Customs of the Germans* [xxiv]. [= 241B.]

2. That is complete slavery which owes lifelong service in return for nourishment and other necessaries of life; and if the condition is thus accepted within natural limits it contains no element of undue severity.[2] For the lasting obligation to labour is repaid with a lasting certainty of support, which often those do not have who work for hire by the day. Consequently that often comes to pass which Eubulus said: [Athenaeus, VI. l.]

> He fain would stay with them and without pay,
> With food alone content.

The same writer of comedy elsewhere said: [Stobaeus, lxii. 32.]

> To his own manger many a slave returns,[3]
> Who once had run away and lived as free.

So Posidonius the Stoic noted in his *Histories*, that formerly there were many who, conscious of their weakness, of their own [Athenaeus, VI. lxxxiv.]

[1] This was formerly forbidden to the Egyptians [Diodorus Siculus, I. lxxix. 1]. It was permitted at Athens up to the time of Solon, who established that the body should not be security for debt; so Plutarch, *Solon* [xv = 86]. The Petilian law established the same principle at Rome [Varro, *Latin Language*, VII. cv; Livy, VIII. xxviii].

[2] On this subject see the excellent dissertation of Busbecq, in the third of his foreign letters [*Letters of the Turkish Embassy*, iii].

[3] In Plautus [*Casina*, 293] some one says:

> If I were free I'd live at my own risk,
> But now I live at yours.

Melissus Spoletinus, the grammarian, did not wish to be set free [Suetonius, *Grammarians*, xxi].

accord gave themselves into slavery to others, 'so that the masters would provide them with the necessaries of life, and they themselves in turn would do what work they could'. [159] Others add the example of the Mariandyni, who for the same reason made themselves the slaves of the Heracleots.

[Athenaeus, VI. lxxxiv; Strabo, XII.iii. 4.]

XXVIII.—*To what extent the right of life and death may be said to exist in the right over slaves*

Masters do not have the right of life and death (I am speaking of complete moral justice) over their slaves. No man can rightly kill a man unless the latter has committed a capital crime. But according to the laws of some peoples the master who has killed a slave for any reason whatsoever goes unpunished. This is the case also with kings everywhere who have the most unrestrained power.

On Benefits, III. xviii.

Seneca had already made this comparison: 'If necessity and fear of suffering the worst prevents a slave from acquiring merit, the same obstacle will hinder one who has over him a king or a general, since to them equal powers are granted, though under a different title.' Nevertheless, although a slave may without doubt receive injury at the hands of his master, as the same Seneca rightly affirms, yet impunity in action is not properly called a right.

On Benefits, III. xxii.

Sextus Empiricus, *Pyrrhoneia*, III [=211C.]

Such a right over children both Solon and the ancient laws of the Romans assigned to parents. Sopater says: 'Since he was a father, he was permitted to kill his children, of course in case they had committed a crime; for the law granted this permission to him, because it was believed that he would be a fair judge.' Dio says in his fifteenth *Oration* that among many peoples famed for their laws the same right prevails.

[=240C.]

XXIX.—*What according to the law of nature should be decided concerning those who are born of slaves?*

1. The question is more difficult in regard to the children of slaves.

[III. vii. 2.]

By the Roman law and by the universal customary law relating to captives, as we shall state elsewhere, in the case of persons of servile rank, as in the case of animals, the offspring follows the mother. Nevertheless this is not in satisfactory agreement with the law of nature, in case the father can be recognized with sufficient certainty. For since in the case of dumb animals the fathers no less than the mothers care for the offspring,[1] this fact shows that the offspring is

[1] See below, II. viii. 18; Pliny, [*Natural History*,] X. xxxiv, says concerning doves: 'Love of offspring is equal in both parents.'

common to both. If, then, municipal law had been silent on the subject, the children would not be less likely to follow the condition of the father than that of the mother.[1]

Let us suppose, to make the difficulty less, that both parents are in servitude, and let us see whether the children will naturally be of servile condition. Surely, if there were no other method of bringing up the children, the parents could adjudge to slavery, along with themselves, the offspring liable to be born to them, since under such conditions parents are allowed to sell children born free.

2. But since this right derives its origin from necessity only, without such necessity the parents do not have the right to enslave their offspring to any one.[2] Consequently in this case the right of masters over the children of slaves will arise from the furnishing of nourishment and other necessaries of life ; [3] and so, since the children of slaves have to be supported for a long time before their work can be useful to their masters, and since the services which follow are in return for support in that period, it will not be permissible for those who are born under such an obligation to flee from slavery unless they return adequate compensation for their support.

Surely the generally approved opinion is that, if the cruelty of the master is excessive, even those slaves who have voluntarily given themselves into slavery can take counsel for their welfare by flight. For the prohibition by which the Apostles and the early canons forbid slaves to leave their masters [4] is a general prohibition, which

Lessius, V [II]. v, dub. 5.
1 Cor., vii. 21 ; *Gal.* [*Ephes.*], vi. 5 ; *Coloss.* iii. 22.

[1] Seneca, *On Benefits*, VII. xii [VII. xii. 1] says : 'In what manner are the children common to father and mother ?'

In the *Visigothic Law*, X. i. 17, we find : 'If the son is begotten and created by both parents, why should he belong to the rank of the mother only—he who could not [169] have been conceived without the father ?' Then this is added : 'By this law consistently with nature we are compelled to divide equally between the two masters the offspring of a female slave who had been united with a slave belonging to another.'

The offspring of a male and female slave followed the father, according to the *Speculum Saxonicum*, iii. 73. The same custom existed in some places in Italy ; *Decretals*, IV. ix. 3.

Among the Lombards and Saxons the children take the status of the parent having inferior rank ; *Speculum Saxonicum*, i. 16. The same rule held among the Visigoths in Spain during the time of Isidore, as you may learn from the *Decretum*, II. xxxii. 4. 15.

The child born of a slave and a free woman becomes a slave by the same *Visigothic Law*, III. ii. 3 ; IV. v. 7 ; IX. i. 16. The children born of a slave and a slave woman are divided between masters. If there is only one son, the owner of the father has him and pays half the value to the owner of the slave woman [X. i. 17]. In the case of children of serfs bound to the soil the owner of the father receives two thirds, the owner of the mother one third, according to the edict of Theodoric in Cassiodorus, [*Variae*,] lxvii.

In England one is free or bond-servant according to the condition of the father, and the same rule is observed in other distinctions of rank ; Littleton, *On Tenures*, and [Fortescue,] *On the Praises of the Laws of England*.

Thomas Aquinas [Suppl., qu. lii, art. 4, concl.] recognizes that these laws, though opposed to the Roman civil law, are not at variance with the law of nature. Furthermore by the Mensian Law, when either of the parents was of foreign birth, the child was considered a foreigner, as Ulpian explains in the *Institutes*, V. viii.

[2] So Charles the Bald also decreed, *Edictum Pistense*, xxxiv [*Monumenta Germaniae Historica, Leges*, II, vol. II, pp. 325 ff.].

[3] See Leo of Africa, Book VI, concerning Barca [ed. of 1632, p. 598].

[4] See below, III. vii. 6.

Titus, ii. 9; *1 Peter*, ii. 16. *Decr.*, II. xvii. 4. 37. is opposed to the error of those that denied all subjection, either private or public, as inconsistent with Christian liberty.

XXX.—*Different kinds of slavery*

Besides the complete slavery, which we have already treated, there are also [160] varieties of incomplete slavery, such as that which is temporary, or under a condition, or for certain purposes. Such is the state of freedmen, of those who have been promised freedom conditionally, of debtor bondsmen both voluntary and from court decree, of serfs bound to the land, of the seven year servitude among the Jews and of the other kind which lasts till the year of Jubilee, of the Penestae among the Thessalians, of tenants of land held under the law of mortmain, and finally of men hired for pay.[1]

These distinctions are dependent either on laws or on agreements. Also, for reasons mentioned above, seemingly by the law of nature, incomplete slavery exists in the case of those that are born of one parent who is free while the other is a slave.

XXXI.—*The right gained by consent over a people which submits*

Public subjection is that condition in which a people is that surrenders itself to some man, or to several men, or even to another [I. iii. 8.] people. The formula of such a subjection we have given above in [Livy, I. xxxviii.2.] the example of Capua. Similar is that of the people of Collatia:

> Do you surrender the people of Collatia, the city, the fields, the water, the boundaries, the shrines, and all appliances divine and human, into my power and that of the Roman people?
>
> We do.
>
> And I accept them.

[Lines 258 f.] Alluding to this formula, Plautus in the *Amphitruo* says:

> They yield themselves, and all things human and divine,
> Their state and children, to the Theban people's rule and will.

The Persians called this the giving of earth and water. This, then, is complete subjection.

There are also other degrees of subjection which are less complete, either in the manner of holding sovereign power or in the plenitude of it; the different degrees can be derived from the dis- I. iii. cussion previously given by us.

[1] Among these, they who in England are called apprentices approach very close to the condition of slaves during the time of their training.

XXXII.—*The right over a person resulting from a crime*

Subjection as a result of crime arises also without consent, whenever a person who has deserved to lose his liberty [1] is by force brought under the power of him who has the right to exact the penalty. We shall see below who has the right to inflict punishment. [II. xx. 3.]

In this way individuals can be brought under private subjection, as at Rome those were who did not respond to conscription,[2] those who did not correctly report their property to the censors, and afterward also women who cohabited with another's slave; and also peoples can be brought into public subjection for a public crime. But there is a difference in this respect, that the servitude of a people is naturally lasting, since the succession of the parts does not prevent it from remaining one people. On the other hand the penal servitude of individuals does not pass beyond the persons themselves, because the crime attaches to the person of the criminal. Cicero, *For Caecina* [xxxiv. 99].

Moreover, both kinds of penal servitude, private as well as public, can be either complete or incomplete, according to the degree of the crime and punishment inflicted. Below, when we come to the results of war, there will be an opportunity to speak of slavery, both private and public, which arises from the volitional law of nations. [III. vii.]

[1] As those companions of Ulysses who plundered the Egyptians; Homer, *Odyssey*, XIV [XIV, lines 271–2]:

> Part of our men they with sharp weapons slew,
> And part they dragged away alive, to work as slaves.

So when Jupiter wished to hurl Apollo into Tartarus he was persuaded by Latona to sentence him to slavery; see Apollodorus, Book III [III. x. 4].

[2] So thieves among the Lycians; see Nicholas of Damascus [frag. 20, p. 148, edit. Dindorf]; and among the Visigoths many condemned for other crimes, as appears from their laws.

CHAPTER VI

ON SECONDARY ACQUISITION OF PROPERTY BY THE ACT OF MAN; ALSO, ALIENATION OF SOVEREIGNTY AND OF THE ATTRIBUTES OF SOVEREIGNTY

I.—*What is necessary, on the part of the giver, that the alienation of a right should be valid*

1. A THING becomes ours by secondary acquisition either through the act of man or by operation of law.

After the introduction of ownership it is of the law of nature that men, who are the owners of property, should have the right to transfer the ownership, either in whole or in part. For this right is present in the nature of ownership, at least of full ownership. Thus Aristotle says: 'The definition of ownership [. . .] is to have within one's power the right of alienation.'

Rhetoric, I. v.

Two matters only are to be noted, the one affecting the giver, the other the receiver. In the case of the giver a mental act of will is not sufficient, but together with it either words or other external signs are required, because a mere mental act, as I have said elsewhere, does not meet the requirements of human society.

Soto, IV, qu. v, art. 1.

[II. iv. 3.]

2. The requirement that delivery of the property take place arises from municipal law. But because this has been received by many nations it is improperly called a principle of universal law. Thus we see that in some places it is the custom to require a declaration in the presence of the people, or before a magistrate, and insertion in the public records; and it is quite certain that all these formalities arise from municipal law. But the act of will, which is expressed by a sign, must always be understood to be the act of a rational will.[1]

Lessius, II. iii, dub. 3.

II.—*What is necessary on the part of the receiver*

In the case of the receiver, in turn, if we disregard the municipal law, the requirement by the law of nature is willingness to receive, accompanied by its natural sign. This willingness ordinarily follows the giving, but it can also precede, as, for instance, if any one has asked that a thing be given or granted to him. It is in fact believed that the willingness continues unless a change becomes apparent.

The other conditions, which are required both for the transfer of a right and for its acceptance, and the question how both can take place, will be treated below in the chapter on promises. For

[1] Cassiodorus, [*Variae*,] II. ii: 'Alienation of property demands absolute freedom of decision.'

in these matters the method of alienation and that of promising are alike,[1] at least by the law of nature.

III.—*That sovereignty can be alienated, sometimes by the king, sometimes by the people*

Moreover, as other things, so also sovereignty can be alienated by the one under whose control it in reality is; that is, as we have shown above, by the king, if he holds the sovereignty by inheritance, [I. iii. 12.] otherwise by the people,[2] but with the consent of the king, because he also has a certain right as possessor of a kind of life interest which ought not to be taken away against his will. These considerations apply to sovereignty in its entirety.

IV.—*That sovereignty over a part of a people cannot be alienated by the people against the will of the part*

In the alienation of a part of a people there is the additional requirement that the part whose alienation is under consideration also give consent.[3] For those who unite to form a state form a kind of perpetual and lasting association by reason of the character [171] of those parts which are called integral.

From this it follows that these parts are not so dependent on their body as are the parts of a natural body, which cannot live without the life of the body, and, therefore, may rightly be cut off for the advantage of the body. This body of which we are treating is in fact of a different kind, since it was formed from voluntary compact. For this reason, again, the right of the whole over its parts must be measured from the original intent, which we ought not to believe was such that the body should have the right to cut off parts from itself and give them into the power of another.

V.—*That a part cannot alienate the sovereignty over itself except in case of extreme necessity*

Likewise in turn it is not right for a part to withdraw from the body unless it is evident that it cannot save itself in any other way.[4]

[1] So also gifts can be sent by messenger to those who are absent, as Servius remarks *On the Aeneid*, Book IX [IX. 361], 'when absent he was joining'.

[2] See Baldus and Oldradus, *On Decretals*, II. xxiv. 33.

Also, Baldus, *Consilia*, 327, no. 7; Cardinal Toschi, *Practicae Conclusiones*, 40, no. 1, and 694. Examples are given in Haraeus, [*Annales Ducum Brabantiae et utriusque Belgii*,] vol. II, year 1526, and in Guicciardini, Book XVI.

[3] Gail, *De Pace Publica*, II. xv. 14; see De Serres in the life of Charles the Wise [*Inventaire de l'Histoire de France*, 1627, p. 194], and the same historian on the life of Francis the First, where he speaks of Burgundy [p. 565].

[4] Compare what is said below, II. xxiv. 6. For this reason the Spartans acquitted Anaxilaus, who had surrendered Byzantium, when compelled by hunger; Xenophon, *Greek History*, Book I [I. iii. 19].

[II. ii. 6.] For, as I have said above, in the case of all rules of human devising, absolute necessity seems to make an exception, and this reduces the matter to the strict law of nature. In the eighteenth book of the
[XVIII.] ii. *City of God*, Augustine says: 'Among almost all nations this utterance of nature has in some way been heard, that they should prefer to yield themselves to the conquerors rather than to be exterminated
Herodotus, VII. [cxxxii]. with every kind of war's destruction.' And so in the oath of the Greeks, in which those who should have yielded to the Persians were devoted to death, there was added the exception, 'unless they should be actually forced'.[1]

VI.—*The reason for the difference indicated*

Hence it can be clearly enough understood why, in this respect, the right which the part has to protect itself is greater than the right of the body over the part. The part, in fact, employs the right which it had before entering the association, but not so the body.

Furthermore no one should say that sovereignty exists in a body as in a subject, and so can be alienated by it, just as ownership can. Just as the soul, in fact, exists in bodies that are suited to it, so sovereignty resides in the corporate body as in a subject which is entirely filled, and not divisible into several bodies. But necessity, which restores a thing to the law of nature, cannot exert its force here, because in the law of nature use indeed is included, as eating, and as keeping, which are natural acts, but not the right of alienating, because that was introduced by act of man, and so by that fact the extent of its validity is measured.

VII.—*That sovereignty over a place can be alienated*

Nevertheless, I see nothing to hinder a people, or even a king with the consent of the people, from alienating sovereignty over a place, that is, a part of its territory, for example, a part that is uninhabited or deserted. For because a part of the people possesses freedom of choice, so also it possesses the right of refusal; but both the whole territory and its parts are the undivided common property of the people, and therefore subject to the will of the people.

If, on the other hand, the people is not allowed to alienate the sovereignty over a part of the people, as we have just said, still less

[1] The Emperor Anastasius even thanked the commanders, who had surrendered Martyropolis to the Persians, because it could not be defended; Procopius [*On the Buildings of Justinian*, III. ii]. The same Procopius, *Gothic War*, IV [IV. 23]: 'Valor refuses to dwell with hunger, and nature does not suffer the same persons to be famished and to fight bravely.'

In Anna Comnena, Book VI [V. v], there is a letter of Cephales from the besieged Larissa to the Emperor Alexis: 'Slaves to necessity (for what can be done against the force of nature ?), we have decided to surrender the town to those who are not only besieging us but are most plainly strangling us.'

can a king do so, though possessed of absolute authority, since this power is not without restrictions, as I have shown above.

VIII.—*Refutation of the opinion that a king can lawfully alienate portions of his dominion for reasons of advantage or necessity*

I cannot agree, therefore, with the jurists who add two exceptions, public advantage and necessity, to the rule concerning the inalienability of parts of a state, except with this understanding, that when the common advantage is the same, both for the corporate body and for its parts, the consent of the people and of its parts seems easily established from a silence of no long duration, but more easily still if the necessity is apparent. But when an opposing desire is manifest, either on the part of the whole state or of a part, the act must be understood to be null and void, except, as I have said, where a part has been compelled to withdraw from the corporate body.

Belluga, *Speculum Principis*, viii.3 and 4. Rochus de Curte, *De Consuetudine*, vol. I, qu. 5, col. 6, and others quoted by Vázquez, I. ix.

IX.—*That infeudation and pledging are contained in alienation*

Under the head of alienation is properly included infeudation with liability of forfeiture in case of felony or lack of issue; for this is a conditional alienation. Therefore we see that infeudations of kingdoms, as well as alienations, which [172] kings have made without consulting the people, have been held void by most peoples.[1] But we are to understand that the people has given its approval, whether it has assembled as a whole, as was formerly the custom among the Germans and Gauls, or has expressed its will through satisfactorily instructed delegates of integral parts. For we do also that which we do through the agency of another.[2]

Furthermore, a part of a state cannot be given in pawn except with similar consent, and not merely for the reason that alienation customarily results from giving in pawn, but also for the reason that both the king is under obligation to the people to exercise his sovereign authority in person, and the whole people is likewise bound to its parts to preserve in entirety this exercise of that authority for the sake of which they united in civil society.

Smith, *De Republica Anglorum*, ix. Buchanan, life of Baliol [*History of Scotland*, VIII. xvii]. Froissart, [*Chronicles*,] I. ccxiv and ccxlvi. Monstrelet, *Chroniques*, xxii. 5. Guicciardini, XVI.

X.—*That for alienating inferior powers also the consent of the people is required, either express or inferred from custom*

Nothing, however, hinders the people from being able by hereditary right to bestow the inferior offices of government, since

[1] Also remissions of homage; see Kromer, *Poland*, Book XXV.

[2] [174] Thus in the Empire in the case of alienations the consent of the Electors, according to custom and agreements, takes the place of the consent of the constituent states.

Cravetta, *Consilia*, 894, no. 2. Zoanettus, *De Imperio Romano*, no. 162.

those do not at all diminish the integrity of the state as a whole, or of its sovereignty. But the king cannot do this without consulting the people, if we are to remain within the bounds of the law of nature; because a temporary right, such as that possessed by elected kings, or those succeeding to sovereignty by the law of nature, can produce no effects except those which are equally temporary. Nevertheless silence introduced by custom, as well as the express consent of the people, could have assigned this right to kings, and this we see is now the rule generally. And so we read in history, that formerly the kings of the Medes and Persians exercised this right of granting towns or whole provinces as permanent possessions.[1]

XI.—*That the public domain cannot be alienated by kings*

Alberico de Rosate, *On Decretals*, II. xxiv. 33; Bart., *On Digest*, XLIII. xxiv. 3. § 4; Corsetti, *De Excellentia Regia*, qu. 4. Loazes cited by Vázquez, v; Natta, *Consilia*, 367; Bonifacius Rugerius, *Consilia*, 49, no. 43.

Also the public domain, the fruits of which have been assigned to support the burdens of government or of royal rank,[2] cannot be alienated by kings,[3] either in whole or in part; for in this they have no greater right than of usufruct. And I do not admit an exception if the thing is of little value; for I have no right to alienate even a small part of that which is not my own. But the consent of the people is more easily inferred from knowledge and silence in the case of small than of great matters.

With this in mind we can apply to the public domain what we have said above [I. iii. 12] concerning the necessity and public advantage in alienating parts of the state, and with even more cogency, because here a matter of less moment is at stake. The public domain was, in fact, established for the sake of the state.

XII.—*That it is necessary to distinguish the income arising out of public domains from the domains themselves*

But many are deceived on this point, because they confuse the income from the public domains with the domains themselves. Thus the right of acquiring alluvial additions ordinarily belongs to the domain, but the alluvial lands added belong to the income. The right of collecting taxes belongs to the domains, the money coming from the taxes to the income. The right of confiscation concerns the domains, the estates confiscated belong to income.

[1] As the city and island of Samos was given to Syloson by Darius [Herodotus, III. cxl–cxlix].

[2] The ancient Greeks called the portion of public land assigned to a king τεμένη. Examples you find in Homer: in regard to Bellerophon among the Lycians, *Iliad*, VI [VI. 194]; in regard to Meleager, *Iliad*, IX [IX. 578]; and concerning Glaucus the Lycian, *Iliad*, XII [XII. 313]. See the Scholiasts on these passages.

[3] Without the consent of the constituent bodies of the state. An example is found in De Thou, Book LXIII [LXIII. xx], year 1577.

XIII.—*To what extent parts of the public domain can be pledged by kings, and why*

Parts of the public domain can for good and sufficient reasons be pledged by kings possessed of absolute power, that is, by those who have the right to levy new taxes for good and sufficient reasons. For as the people is bound to pay taxes justly levied, so also it is bound to redeem property pledged for good reason. Such redemption is, in fact, a kind of tax.

The public domain, moreover, is pledged to the king as a security for the obligations due from the people; and what has been pledged to me can be pledged in turn. However, what I have said thus far is valid only on the condition that no law has been enacted for the state which either has increased or diminished the power of king or people. *Dig.* XX. i. 13. § 2.

XIV.—*That a will is a form of alienation and formed upon the law of nature*

1. While we are treating of alienation, the fact should be recognized that wills also are included in this class. Though in fact a will, as other acts, can take a definite form in accordance with [173] municipal law, nevertheless in its essential character it is related to ownership, and, if we grant that, it belongs to the law of nature. I can, in fact, alienate my property, not only absolutely but also under conditions, and not only irrevocably but also with right of recovery, even meanwhile retaining possession with unrestricted right of user. Aristotle, *Politics*, II. vii.

A will, however, becomes an alienation only in the event of death. Up to that time it is recoverable, and the right of possession and enjoyment is meanwhile retained. Plutarch rightly observed this, for having said that the right to make wills was granted to the citizens by Solon, he added: 'He made every man the master of his own property with full ownership.' Quintilian the father says in a declamation: 'Even an inherited estate can seem a burden if the possession is not absolute; and although absolute power over it is entrusted to us while living, it may be taken away at death.' In accordance with this right, if Abraham had died without children he would have left his possessions to Eliezer, as is indicated in *Genesis*, xv. 2.[1] [*Life of Solon*, xxi = 90A.] [*Declamations*, cccviii.]

[1] You find in Sophocles, *Trachiniae* [lines 1191 ff.], the will of Heracles; in Euripides [*Alcestis*, lines 280 ff.], that of Alcestis; and in Homer, *Odyssey*, XVII [lines 79 ff.], a donation by Telemachus in case of death, and this is itself a sort of will.

2. The fact that the right to make a will is not everywhere granted to foreigners is not due to a universal principle of law but to a special statute of a particular state; and, unless I am mistaken, the restriction goes back to the time when foreigners were considered almost as enemies. In consequence, among the more civilized nations, this restriction has deservedly fallen into disuse.

There are also in Homer last wishes in respect to deeds to be done, as Plutarch [*On the Life and Poetry of Homer*, II. clxxxviii] shows from the words of Penelope and Andromache.

Other examples of ancient wills I have presented above, I. iv [iii]. 12, in the text and notes. It appears from *Deuteronomy*, xxi. 16, that wills were in use among the Jews. See the *Son of Sirach* [=*Ecclesiasticus*], xxxiii. 25 [xxxiii. 24].

CHAPTER VII

ON DERIVATIVE ACQUISITION OF PROPERTY WHICH TAKES PLACE IN ACCORDANCE WITH LAW; AND HEREIN, INTESTATE SUCCESSION

I.—*That certain laws of states are unjust and therefore do not transfer ownership; such as those which confiscate the goods of shipwrecked persons in favour of the state treasury*

[175] DERIVATIVE acquisition, or alienation, which takes place in accordance with law, is based either on the law of nature or on volitional universal law, or on a statute.

It is not our purpose to treat of the statutes of states, for that would be an endless task, and the particular disputes arising from wars are not decided in accordance with municipal law. However, attention should be called to the fact that certain laws of states are plainly unjust,[1] such as those which confiscate in favour of the state treasury the goods of shipwrecked persons. It is, in fact, pure injustice to take away from any one his ownership of property when no adequate cause precedes. Euripides has well said in the *Helena*: *Authent.*, after *Code*, VI. ii. 18.

I come a shipwrecked stranger whom 'tis impious to rob.[2] [Line 449.]

In the words of Constantine [Antoninus], 'What right has the imperial treasury in another's disaster, that it should try to find profit in so grievous a condition?' Dio of Prusa in his seventh *Oration* says of a shipwreck: 'Far be it from us, O Jupiter, to seek such gain from men's misfortune!' *Code*, XI. vi. 1. [=p. 109B.]

II.—*That according to the law of nature property is justly acquired by a man who has received another's property to satisfy a debt; when this may take place*

1. According to a law of nature, which has its origin in the very character and essence of ownership, alienation takes place in two ways, by legal compensation and by succession.

[1] As formerly in England, Brittany, and Sicily. An ancient law of this sort in Greece is mentioned by Sopater, and by Syrianus, *On Hermogenes*.

Christian, king of Denmark, said that he lost a hundred thousand pieces of gold a year by the repeal of the law confiscating the goods of shipwrecked persons. Bridget, [*Revelationes Brigittae*,] VIII. vi, mentions this evil custom, as does the *Speculum Saxonicum*, II. xxix, in speaking of the Danes.

See also the canon, *Decretals*, V. xvii. 3. Also Krantz, *Vandalica*, XIII. xl; XIV. i; Kromer, *Poland*, XXI.

[2] Add the law, *Digest*, XLVII. ix. 7. Nicetas of Chonae on the reign of Andronicus [II. iii] calls this 'a most unreasonable custom'. See also Cassiodorus, IV. vii.

How did it occur to Bodin [I. x. 267] to defend such practices? However, the same writer [III. iv. 458–59] criticized Papinian, because he preferred to die rather than to violate his conscience.

Alienation by legal compensation takes place when, from one who retains my property or is in debt to me, I receive, as of equal value,[1] something which is not yet mine but which ought to be given to me in the place of a thing belonging to me or due to me, and I am unable to obtain the thing itself. For whenever expletive justice cannot acquire the same thing it tries to obtain something of equal value which, morally, is considered the same. Moreover, the transfer of ownership in this manner is proved by the result, which is morally the best proof. In fact I shall not be able to acquire the fulfilment of my right unless I become owner; for possession of the property will be fruitless if I cannot use it as I wish.

Sylvester, word *bellum*, II, qu. 13.

There is an ancient example of this matter in the *History* of Diodorus, when Hesioneus receives the horses of Ixion in satisfaction for the non-fulfilment of Ixion's promises to his daughter.

[Diodorus Siculus], IV [lxix].

2. We know that it is forbidden by the civil statutes, at any rate, to take the law into one's own hands, so that it is called violence if any one recovers by force what is due to him; and in many places the one who has done this loses his right to the debt. Further, even if the civil law should not directly forbid such violence, the illegality of it would nevertheless be inferred from the establishment of the courts.

Dig. XLI. ii. 5; XLVII. viii. 2. § 18; IV. ii. 13; XLVIII. vii. 7 and 8. Thomas Aquinas, II. ii. 66, art. 50 [art. 5].

The right which I have mentioned will, therefore, be in force when the courts cease to act, for a continuous period. How this may take place I have explained above. When the closing of the courts is of short duration, the seizing of property will in fact be lawful in the circumstances that you cannot otherwise recover your own, if perchance the debtor is absconding; but actual ownership will have to wait for the decree of the judge. This usually happens in the case of reprisals, a subject which will be treated later. However, if the right is certain, but at the same time it is morally certain that enforcement of the right cannot be obtained from a judge, for the reason, for instance, that proof is lacking, the truer opinion is that in these circumstances [176] the law of the courts ceases to apply and one has recourse to primitive right.

[I. iii. 2]. *Code*, X. xxxii. 54; I. iii. 12. Doctors *On Dig.* IX. ii. 39. § 1, end. Bartolus, *On Reprisals*, qu. lix.

[1] See what is said below, III. vii. 6.

Thus by the law of nature Irenaeus defends the Jews because they took property of the Egyptians in compensation for their work. He says [*Against Heretics*, IV. xxx. 1]: 'The Egyptians in fact were indebted to the people not only for property but also for their lives.'

Tertullian, treating of the same subject in the second book *Against Marcion* [II. xx], says: 'The Egyptians demand of the Jews their vessels of gold and silver. In reply the Jews put forward like claims, alleging that [189] pay ought to be given to them for their toil in servitude.' He shows, further, that much less was demanded than was due.

In Diodorus Siculus, Book IV [IV. lxix], the story is told that Hesioneus received the horses of Ixion in return for the things which Ixion had promised to his daughter but which were not furnished. With this agrees what is said below, III. ii.

III.—*How intestate succession has its origin in nature*

Aside from all positive law, intestate succession, as it is called, after ownership has been established, has its origin in natural inference as to the wishes of the deceased.[1] Since the force of ownership was such that it could be transferred to another at the will of the owner, so also in case of retention of ownership at the time of death, as I have said above, if any one had given no indication of his wishes, nevertheless, since it was not credible that his intention was to yield his property after his death to the first who would take it over, the inference is that his property is to belong to the person to whom it is especially probable that the dead man had wished that it should belong. Pliny the Younger says: 'To know the wishes of the dead takes the place of law.' In case of doubt, moreover, it is credible that each man wished what was most just and honourable. But among things of this kind the first class includes what is actually due; and the next class, that which, though not actually due, is consistent with duty.

Soto, *De Iustitia*, iii, art. 2. Cajetan, [*On II. ii.*,] 66.

IV. x [3]; II. xvi [2]; V. vii [2].

IV.—*Whether any of the property of parents is due to children according to the law of nature; explanation, with a distinction*

1. The jurists discuss the question whether parents are under obligation to support their children. Some indeed think that it is sufficiently in accord with natural reason that parents should support their children, yet that there is no legal duty.

I think that we ought to distinguish accurately the meanings of the word duty. This word sometimes is taken strictly for that obligation which is imposed by expletive justice; and sometimes, more freely, to indicate what cannot be neglected with honour, although in this case honour does not have its origin in expletive justice but in another source. We are concerned with duty in its larger sense, except when a human law intervenes.

Consequently I accept what Valerius said: 'Parents by bringing us up have imposed upon us the duty of bringing up their grandchildren.' Plutarch in his admirable treatise *On the Love of Offspring* says: 'Children expect the inheritance as their due.'[2] There is a saying of Aristotle: 'Who gives the form gives what is necessary

Franciscus Pisci, *De Statu Excellentium Feminarum*, no. 133. Menochio, *On Authent.*, after *Code*, III. xxviii. 6, no. 296. Tell. Fernandes, *Taurinenses Quaestiones*, X. qu. iv.

[II. ix. 1.]

[=497B.]

[1] Paul says (*Digest*, XXIX. vii. 8. § 1): 'Therefore bequests in trust can be given to the successors of a person dying without a will, because the head of a family is supposed of his own accord to leave to such succeeding heirs their lawful inheritance.'

[2] Julian says in *The Caesars* [334 D]: 'It is right that an inheritance be left to children.' Also the history of Job near the end [*Job*, xlii. 15] bears witness that according to the most ancient law daughters were next in order after the sons as heirs of their parents.

Having in mind this principle of fairness Augustine desired that the Church should not accept the property of those who disinherited their children. The passages are found in the *De Vita Clericorum*,

to the form.' Therefore the one who brings a human being into existence is under a duty to look out for it as much as he can, and as much as is necessary, in those things which are essential to human life, that is, for the natural social existence for which man was born.

2. For this reason, of course by natural instinct, the other living creatures also provide necessary nourishment for their offspring. On account of this fact the saying of Euripides,

[*Andromache*, 418 f.]

> To all men
> Children are as life itself,

was corrected by Apollonius of Tyana to read:

[Philostratus, *Life of Apollonius of Tyana*, II. xiv. and xv.]

> To all animate beings
> Offspring is as life itself;

and he adds a great number of arguments by which he proves that this affection is inborn[1]; these may be seen in Philostratus, VII. vii and viii. With this opinion that expressed by Oppian, *On Hunting*, Book III [III. 107], and *On Fishing*, Book I [I. 646], is in perfect agreement. Also in the tragedy *Dictys* the same Euripides says that 'there is this one law for all, which is common to men both among themselves and along with other animals'.

[Stobaeus, lxxxiii. 17 = 702.]

In consequence the ancient jurists ascribe the bringing up of children to the law of nature, that is, to that law which reason herself enjoins upon us, while natural instinct commends it to other animals also. As Justinian says: 'A natural impulse, that is, affection, impels parents to bring up their children'; and [177] in another place he has this: 'The father is obliged by nature herself to support a son or a daughter.'

[*Institutes*, I. ii. pr. *Dig.* I. i. 1. § 3. *Code*, V. xiii. 1. § 5 c. *Code*, VI. lxi. 8. § 4 D.]

Diodorus Siculus states the case thus: 'Nature is the best teacher of all animate beings as regards the preservation not only of themselves but also of their offspring, to the end that as a result of this affection for kin the stock by uninterrupted succession may complete the circle of eternity.' In Quintilian a son says: 'I claim my part by universal law.' Sallust said that a will was impious which disinherited a son.

[II. 1. 7.]

[*Institutes of Oratory*, VII. i. 46.] [*Letter to Mith.*, viii]

Because this duty is according to nature, a mother ought to nourish her children that were begotten indiscriminately.

[*Digest*, XXV. iii. 5. § 4.]

3. Although it was the intent of the Roman laws that nothing should be left to children born of an illegal union, just as also the

II [I. iii = *Sermones de Diversis*, ccclv. 4], and *Sermones ad Fratres in Eremo*, lii [*Sermones de Diversis*, ccclv. 5], if indeed this work is the work of Augustine. Gratian placed these passages in the *Decretum*, II. xiii. 2 [II. xiii. 2. 8], and II. xvii. 4. 43.

Procopius, *Persian War*, I [I. xi], says: 'Laws, which for the rest among men are opposed to one another by the greatest differences, on this one point agree as completely among barbarians as among the Romans, that they declare the children owners of the property left by the father.'

[1] Pliny, X. xxxiii [*Natural History*, X. xxxiii. 66–67, 92], says of swallows: 'With the greatest fairness they feed their young in turn.'

law of Solon had provided that it should not be necessary to leave anything to bastards, the canons of the Christian Church have ameliorated this severe restriction. They teach that that which is necessary for support is rightly left to all children whatsoever, or rather, ought to be left in case there is need. In this way we are to understand the common saying, that the lawful portion cannot be taken away by human laws, with the restriction, to be sure, that in that lawful portion only the necessaries of life are included. For what is over and above the necessaries of life can be taken away without transgressing the law of nature. [Cf. Plutarch, *Solon*, xxii = 90E.] [*Decretals*, IV. vii. 5.]

4. Furthermore our descendants not only of the first degree, but also of the second, ought to be provided for, if there is need, and even beyond that. This Justinian shows when he declares that naturally we ought to provide not only for children but also for those who come after them; and this rule is even extended to those who are descended from us through the female line, if they cannot otherwise be supported. [*Code*, VI. lxi. 8. § 4 D. *Digest*, XXV. iii. 5. §§ 1 and 5, and iii. 8.]

V.—*That in a succession children are preferred to the father and mother of the deceased, and why*

1. Support is due likewise to parents. This duty has been fixed not only by laws, but also by the common proverb which bids 'to cherish in return'.[1] For this reason, in fact, Solon is praised, because he branded with disgrace those who did not provide for parents. [Diogenes Laertius, *Life of Solon* [I. ii. 55].]

Nevertheless this practice is not so universal as that which we have indicated with respect to children. For when children are born they bring nothing with them upon which to live. Another consideration is that they have a longer time to live than their parents; consequently, just as honour and obedience are due to the parents, not to the children, so support is due to children rather than to parents.

With this meaning I accept the statement of Lucian, that 'nature bids that children be loved by parents more than parents by children.' Similar is this of Aristotle: 'The producing cause feels more affection for that which is produced than that which is produced feels for the producing cause; for what any one has brought into being is, as it were, his own.' [[*Abdicat.*, 175.]] [*Nicomachaean Ethics*, VIII [xiv].]

2. Hence it happens that, even without the help of municipal law, the first right of succession to property falls to the children; the parents are believed to have wished to provide for them, as parts of their own body, most abundantly, not only the necessaries of life but also those resources which make it possible to spend life more

[1] See Leo of Africa, Book IX [p. 388], concerning the vulture [ed. 1632, p. 768].

pleasantly and honourably, especially after the time when the parents can no longer enjoy their property themselves. Paul the jurist says: 'Natural reason, as a sort of silent law, allots to children the inheritance from their parents by calling them to a succession that is, so to speak, their due.'

Digest, XLVIII. xx. 7.

Further, Papinian says:[1] 'The inheritance from children is not due to the parents in the same way that the inheritance from parents is due to the children. Parents are admitted to the estates of their children out of compassion, children to the property of parents by the common will of nature and of the parents.' That is, the inheritance falls to children partly in consequence of an express natural obligation and partly in accordance with a natural presumption, which warrants the belief that the parents desire to provide for their children as well as possible. [178] 'He left it as an honour to the ties of blood', says Valerius Maximus of Quintus Hortensius, who had willed his property to a daughter of whom he did not approve. And this is the force of that saying of the Apostle Paul: 'For the children ought not to lay up for the parents, but the parents for the children.'

[*Digest,* XXXVIII vi. 7. § 1.] V. ix [2]. *2 Corinthians,* xii. 14.

VI.—*The origin of vicarious succession, which is called representation, or succession in the place of and with the rights of another*

Because it is ordinarily the case that the father and mother provide for their children while they are alive, it is understood that grandfathers and grandmothers are not bound to furnish support. But when the parents, or either one of them, has died, it is fair that the grandfather and grandmother undertake the care of the grandsons and granddaughters, in the place of the deceased son or daughter. This, again, is extended in like manner to degrees of parentage farther removed.

Dig. I. vi. 7. *Digest,* XXVII. i. 2. § 7. *Novels,* cxxvii. pr. [*Orat.,* vi. 41.]

From such an origin comes the law that the grandson succeeds in the place of the son,[2] as Ulpian states. Says Modestinus: 'The son fills the place of the dead father.' Justinian says: 'He assumes the position of the father.' In the speech on the inheritance of Philoctemon Isaeus calls this 'to enter again upon'. Philo Judaeus

[1] Philo, *On the Life of Moses,* III [III. xxxii], says: 'As it is a law of nature that children inherit the property of their parents and not the parents the property of their children, Moses covered with a veil of silence that which was contrary to the wishes of the parents and of evil omen.'

Xenophon, *Sayings of Socrates,* Book II [*Memorabilia,* II. ii. 5], reports a saying of Socrates: 'For the children that he expects to have a man prepares everything which he thinks will be of advantage for their livelihood, and indeed in as great abundance as possible.'

[2] The Jews say: 'The son inherits even in the tomb'; and likewise: 'The sons of sons are as sons.' Iacchiades [Joseph bar Chijah ?], *On Daniel,* v. 2, mentions this as a natural right.

Justinian [*Institutes,* III. i. 6] says: 'It seems perfectly fair that grandsons and granddaughters inherit in the place of their father.' Eginhard in the life of Charlemagne [ix] refers this to loyalty to kin. Michael Attaliates [*Synopsis,* xli] says that 'descendants in each case take the place of parents'.

says: 'When the parents are dead, grandchildren hold the place of children with their grandparents.' This vicarious succession, which takes place *per stirpes*,[1] by modern jurists is preferably called representation. *On the Embassy to Gaius* [v].

The same kind of succession was valid also among the Jews, as is quite clearly shown by the division of the promised land among the sons of Jacob. As the son and the daughter are each man's nearest relatives, so also are the children of a son or a daughter, as Demosthenes says in his speech *Against Macartatus*. [xliii. 25.]

VII.—*On abdication and disinheritance*

What we have thus far said about the presumption of intent is valid in case there are manifest no indications to the contrary.

Among such indications the first to be mentioned is disowning,[2] which was common among the Greeks, and disinheritance, to which the Romans frequently resorted. Yet this cutting off of a child that had not deserved death because of crimes is subject to the condition that support be provided for him, for the reason stated above.

VIII.—*Concerning the rights of illegitimate children*

1. To the rule just stated an exception must be admitted, in case there is not satisfactory agreement as to who the father of the child is.

It is true that absolute certainty is not to be found in an induction from facts. But whatever is wont to happen in the sight of people derives its own degree of certainty from evidence. And in this sense it is said that there is certainty in regard to the mother, because both men and women are available who were present at the birth and witnessed the bringing up. The same degree of certainty, however, cannot be had concerning the father, as Homer indicates by saying: [*Odyssey*, I. 216.]

> No man himself is sure from whom he is descended.

This was imitated by Menander: [In Eustathius, *On Odyssey*, i. 221.]

> No man himself knows from whom he is sprung.

Elsewhere Menander says: [In Stobaeus, lxxvi. 7.]

> The mother loves her children more than does the sire;
> The mother knows that they are hers, the father thinks they are.

[1] Thus in allotting the cities among the Heraclidae Procles and Eurysthenes, since they were descended from Aristodemus, together drew but one lot as against Temenus and Cresphontes. So Apollodorus, Book II [*Library*, II. viii. 4]; Pausanias, *On Corinth* [*On Messene*, IV. iii. 5]; and Strabo, VIII [VIII. v. 4].

[2] See the treatise *Baba Kama*, ix. 10, and later in this chapter, sect. 25.

It was necessary, therefore, to devise some method by which it might be established with probability who the father of each child was. That method is marriage, taken in its natural limits; that is, the union in which the woman is placed under the guardianship of the man. [179] But if in a given case it is established in any other way who the father was, or if the father himself has considered it established, then by the law of nature the child concerned will have right of succession not less than any other child; and why not? For even a person of admitted foreign birth,[1] if accepted as an adopted child, has right of succession from the presumption of the desire of the adoptive parent.

2. But illegitimate children also have a right even after the distinction between them and the legitimate children has been introduced by law. Euripides has said: [*Frag.* 141.]

> In nothing is the bastard less than lawful son;
> By law he is held down.

Nevertheless such children can be adopted, unless the law prevents. Formerly a Roman law of Anastasius permitted such adoption. *Code*, V. xxvii. 6. Afterwards, in order to favour lawful marriage, a rather more difficult system of putting illegitimate on a par with legitimate children was devised, through nomination of the son to the municipal senate, or by subsequent marriage.

An example of an ancient adoption of illegitimate children is found among the sons of Jacob, who were placed on an equality with the sons of free mothers and shared the inheritance equally.

3. On the other hand it can happen, not only in accordance with law but also by agreement, that such children, just as may be the case with those born in wedlock,[2] shall have support only, or shall be excluded, at any rate, from the principal share of the inheritance. The Jews give the name of concubinage to a marriage based on such an agreement, even if it be with a free woman. Such was the marriage of Abraham with Keturah, whose children, therefore, *Genesis*, xxv. 6. just as Ishmael, son of the handmaid Hagar, received gifts, that is, certain legacies, but did not share the inheritance. Such marriages now are called morganatic.

Not far different, in effect, are second marriages among the people of Brabant.[3] For the real estate, which was held when the end of the first marriage came, passes to the first wife's children.

[1] [190] Or a grandson adopted as a son, as in the case of the grandsons Ephraim and Manasseh, adopted by Jacob [*Genesis*, xlviii. 5].

[2] As formerly all the sons except the eldest, in the country of Mexico [López de Gomara, *Historia Generalis Indiae Occidentalis*, II. lxxvi].

[3] See a similar law of the ancient Burgundians [*Lex Romana*], I. i. 2.

IX.—*When there is neither a will nor a precise law covering the matter, if there are no children the ancestral property should be returned to those from whom it came, or to their children*

1. When there are no children to whom the succession would naturally come, the case is less clear, and in no other matter is there greater divergence among the laws. Nevertheless the entire range of variation can be traced to two sources. In the one case regard is had to nearness of relationship; in the other, the aim is to return the property to those from whom it came, according to the regular formula: 'The father's property to the relatives of the father, the mother's property to the relatives of the mother.'

It is clear that we ought to distinguish accurately between paternal or ancestral property,[1] such as is ordinarily expressed in the formula which cuts a spendthrift off from property, and recent acquisitions.[2] In the case of the former this statement of Plato should be binding: 'As lawgiver I decree that you are not your own masters, and that your patrimonies are not yours, but that all belongs to your family, not only that which was, but also that which is to come.' On this ground Plato proposes that the 'paternal estate' be preserved for the family from which it came. [*Laws*, XI. vi = p. 923 A.]

I should not wish to have this principle accepted with the implication that by the law of nature it would not be permissible to dispose of paternal and ancestral estates by will (often, in fact, the poverty of a friend makes such a device not only praiseworthy but even necessary [3]); but rather as making clear, in case of doubt, the presumption of the desire of one who died intestate.

We grant, in fact, that full ownership belongs to him with whose wishes we are concerned.

2. But since he cannot retain his ownership after death, and it ought to be considered altogether certain that he would not be willing to lose an opportunity of conferring a favour, we should ascertain what above all is the natural order in the conferring of favours. Aristotle well says: 'It is better to make return to one who has done a kindness to us than [180] to confer a favour on a friend.' Also Cicero says: 'No duty is more necessary than the [*Nic. Ethics*, IX. ii.] [*On Duties*, I. xv. 47.]

[1] In Hebrew, moraschah, 'estate'.

[2] In Hebrew, nahalah, 'property'. See this distinction in the *Burgundian Law*, I. i. 1.

[3] Seneca, *On Benefits*, Book IV. ii [IV. xi. 4]: 'What, then, when we have reached the end of life and are making our wills? Do we not distribute favours which will be of no advantage to us? How much time do we spend, how long do we ponder in secret as to how much and to whom we shall give? What difference, in fact, does it make to whom we give, since we shall receive return from no one? And yet, never do we give with greater pains, never do we more carefully exercise our judgement than when, having laid aside all thought of advantage, we fix our gaze only on that which is honourable.'

[*On Duties*, I. xv. 48.] return of favours'; in another passage: 'Inasmuch as there are two kinds of generosity, one of conferring favours, the other of requiting them, it lies within our power whether we shall confer favours or not; but for a good man it is not permissible not to return favours, provided only he can do this without injustice.' Ambrose declares: [*On Duties*, I. xxxi.] 'It is noble to have a more kindly consideration of him who has conferred some favour upon you or has done you a service'; later he adds: 'For what is so contrary to duty as not to make a return for what you have received?'

Now a favour is returned either to the living or the dead.[1] As [XX.] Lysias has shown in his *Funeral Oration*, 'A favour is returned to the dead in the persons of their children, who are by nature a part of their parents, and upon whom the parents, if living, would especially wish favours conferred.'

[*Code*, VI. lxi. 3; VI. lviii. 13. § 2; VI. lix. 11; *Novels*, lxxxiv. [*Nicom. Ethics*, VIII. xiv.] V. v.] 3. The framers of the body of civil law, compiled under Justinian, being most zealous for absolute fairness, have followed this principle of natural equity in deciding between full brothers, brothers on the father's side, brothers on the mother's side, and in the cases of certain other relatives. Aristotle says: 'Brothers mutually love each other, because they are born from the same parents. For common origin makes them as it were the same.' Valerius Maximus says: 'As the receiving of very many and very great favours is considered the first bond of affection, so the receiving of favours at the same time ought to be considered the second bond.' [X [Curtius, X. vii. 2.]] In Justin it is said to be a principle of universal law that brother should succeed to brother.

4. Now if the one from whom the property has directly come is not to be found, nor his children, then it remains to return the property to those to whom it is due less directly, but nevertheless in the next degree after the first recipient; that is, to the parent of the degree above, and to his children, especially since in that way it remains among the nearest relatives, both of him whose inheritance is under consideration, and of him from whom the property [[*Nicom. Ethics*, VIII. xiv.]] directly came. Aristotle says the same: 'First cousins on the father's side and other cognates are united through their parents in so far as they have their origin from the same persons; and in such a way that some are more closely, others less closely united in respect to origin.'

[1] Thus in Procopius, *Persian War*, I [I. iv. 4], a man who is about to die says: 'On me you will confer the favours which you will bestow on my children.' See an example in the act of Theodosius, who bestowed favours on Valentinian the Younger, in return for obligations due to the father of Valentinian; Zosimus, Book IV [IV. xlvii].

By the law of Moses, *Numbers*, xxvii. 11 [xxvii. 10], the uncle on the father's side stood next in the succession after the brothers, as being nearer to the first possessor than the brother's sons.

X.—*Possessions recently acquired go to the nearest relatives*

1. In the case of newly acquired possessions, which Plato called 'that over and above the inheritance', the duty of requiting favours ceases; it remains, then, that succession should be conferred on the person who is believed to have been most dear to the deceased. That person, moreover, is the one who is most nearly related to the deceased.[1] This Isaeus says was the rule among the Greeks: 'The property of the deceased falls to the most nearly related member of the family'; and he adds, 'What is more just than that the property of a relative should pass to relatives?' The same opinion is found in Aristotle, in the *Rhetoric to Alexander*, chapter ii. [*Laws*, XI. vii = p. 923 D.] [IV. xv; IV. xxiii.]

Cicero says: 'The social relationship and union of men will be best preserved if each shall bestow the largest measure of kindness on those who shall be most closely related to him.' Elsewhere likewise he places especially intimate relatives next after the children.[2] So also does Tacitus: 'Nature has willed that each man's children and kin should be most dear to him.' In still another passage Cicero, speaking of relatives, says: 'To these especially the necessary support of life is due.' *On Duties*, I [xvi. 50]. [*Agricola*, xxxi. 1.] [*On Duties*, I. xvii. 58.]

This duty to relatives, however, does not have its origin in expletive justice, but in 'natural fitness'. Cicero, again, after treating the affection for relatives, adds: 'From these feelings of affection arise wills as well as remembrances on the part of the dying.' The same author declares that it is more just that our property be given and bequeathed to relatives than to strangers. Ambrose says: 'This also is generosity worthy of approval, that you do not neglect your next of kin.'[3] [*On Ends*, III. xx. 65.] [*On Duties*, I. xiv. 44.] *On Duties*, I. xxx [150].

2. Further, the intestate succession with which we are dealing is nothing else than a tacit will [181] derived from inference as to wishes. Quintilian the father says in a declamation: [cccviii. 1.]

The relatives hold the next place after the legatees of the will; and the case is similar if a person has died intestate and without children. This principle holds not because

[1] See *Deuteronomy*, xv. 11; xxiii. 7; *Proverbs*, xi. 17. This point Servius treats, *On the Aeneid*, VI [VI. 611], on the words

And to their own a part they did not give.

Hierocles [*On the Golden Verses of Pythagoras*, line 4] says: 'Affection for relatives will receive its due measure from natural relationship, so that after the parents as much will be conferred upon each of the relatives as his nearness of relationship to the parents demands.'

Possidius says of Augustine [chap. xxiv]: 'He saw that it was just and fair that either the children, or parents, or relatives of the dead preferably should possess them,' that is, the inheritances of which he was treating.

[2] These two passages of Cicero, cited later, are from the same first book *On Duties* [I. xvi. 50; xvii. 58].

[3] Taken from *Isaiah*, lviii. 7. You find similar statements in Chrysostom, *On First Corinthians*, iv. 7 [*On First Timothy*, v. 8 = Homily XIV, i], and in Augustine, *On Christian Doctrine*, II. xii.

it is assuredly just that the property of the deceased should fall to these, but because property abandoned and, as it were, left out of ownership, seems to fall to no one else by preference.

What we have said of property recently acquired, that it is naturally bestowed on the nearest relatives, will also take place in the case of paternal and ancestral estates if neither the persons from whom they have come, nor their children, are alive. Under such circumstances requital of gratitude finds no opportunity for expression.

XI.—*Diversity of laws about succession*

1. Although what I have said is particularly in accord with natural presumption, nevertheless according to the law of nature it is not of the things established by necessity. Hence in consequence of the diversity of causes influencing human choice there arises a great variation in pacts, laws, and customs. Those who admit succession through the right of another within certain degrees of relationship do not admit it in other degrees.[1] Some consider the origin of the possessions, others do not take this into consideration. There are countries where the first-born receive more than the younger children, as is the case among the Jews; there are others where the children are placed on an equality.

In some countries, again, account is taken only of relatives on the father's side, in others all blood relatives receive the same as the relatives on the father's side. Also in some places sex has influence, in others not; and in some places consideration of blood relationship is confined to the nearer degrees, elsewhere it has a wider range. To enumerate these diversities would be tedious, and this is not a part of my plan.

2. Nevertheless this principle should be kept in mind, that whenever there are no quite definite indications of intent it is to be believed that each person in regard to his succession had in mind that which the law or custom of his people approves. Such belief is based not only on the power of government, but also on presumption regarding the wishes of the deceased, which has weight even with those who possess sovereign power. For also those who possess sovereign power are believed to have rendered a perfectly fair judge-

[1] The ancient customs of the Germans did not recognize such substitution or representation even among children. Childebert first introduced this law into France by an edict. It was introduced into the regions across the Rhine by Otho, son of Henry, as Wittekind testifies in Book II. See the *Law of the Lombards*, II. xiv. 18.

Likewise the ancient Scottish law regarded only the nearness of the degree of relationship. See Pontanus, *Danish History*, VII [year 1291], where he relates that such relationship was decreed by the king of England, who had been appointed umpire.

ment in matters affecting themselves, which they have either themselves sanctioned by laws, or approved in custom; I mean in those matters where there is no question of any loss to themselves.

XII.—*What is the manner of succession in hereditary kingdoms*

In the matter of succession to kingdoms we ought to distinguish those kingdoms which are held with unrestricted right of possession, and are patrimonial, from those which derive the form of possession from the consent of the people. This is a distinction we have treated above.

Kingdoms of the first class can be divided between male[1] and female offspring,[2] as we see was formerly done in Egypt and Britain. [I. iii. 11.] Lucan says: [X. 91–2.]

> Not hindered by her sex
> A queen can rule o'er Pharos.

Of the Britons Tacitus writes: 'In fact they make no distinction of sex in governing.' [*Agricola*, xvi. 1.]

Further, because of assumed intent in the matter of succession, adopted children are not at a disadvantage in comparison with true children. Thus Hyllus, son of Hercules, succeeded by adoption to the kingdom of Aepalius, king of the Locrians. Molossus, a bastard,[3] by the will of his father Pyrrhus, who had no legitimate children, succeeded to the throne of Epirus. King Atheas considered adopting Strabo, IX [iv. 10]. Pausanias, I [xi]. Justin, IX [ii].

[1] In Asia brothers ruled at the same time, but in such a way that the right to the crown was the special privilege of one; Polybius, *Selections on Embassies*, xciii [= XXX. ii].

[191] You will find in Livy [XLIV. xix; XLV. xi] and in the same Polybius [lxxxix = XXIX. xxiii. 3] that Egypt was divided between the Ptolemies, who were brothers. The sons of Attila demanded that the different peoples be divided between them in equal shares; Jordanes, *History of the Goths* [l].

Gregoras in Book VII [VII. v] says of Irene, wife of Andronicus Paleologus: 'What was especially astonishing, instead of one being made Emperor according to the ancient custom of the Empire of Constantinople, she desired that after the fashion of the rulers of the West the cities and countries should be divided among the individual sons, in order that the kingdoms, as each one's inheritance, might pass from father to son, just as ordinarily happens in the inheritances of common men; and that they should continue thus to descend to each one's children and heirs. She was, in fact, planning to introduce there without precedent a custom which had originated in the Western Empire and which she had borrowed from that source.'

[2] Concerning Alexander and Laodice see Polybius, *Selections on Embassies*, cxl [= XXXIII. xviii]; concerning the daughter of Auletas, see Strabo, XVII [XVII. i. 11].

Arrian in his *Anabasis* [I. xxiii. 7] relates that in Asia after Semiramis many women ruled. Such are Nitocris at Babylon, Artemisia at Halicarnassus, and Tomyris in Scythia. Servius, *On the Aeneid*, I [I. 654], says: 'Because formerly women also ruled'. The same commentator, *On the Aeneid*, IX [IX. 596], shows that this custom prevailed among the Rutulians.

[3] Among the Tartars illegitimate and legitimate sons were on equal footing; but of the Persians Herodotus [III. ii] says: 'It is not their custom that an illegitimate son shall rule if a legitimate son is available.'

In Spain two Vandals ruled, Gontharis, the legitimate son, and Genseric, the illegitimate son, of Godigisclus, as Procopius [*Vandalic War*, I. iii] reports. Adam of Bremen, *Historia Ecclesiastica*, cvi, and Helmold, *Slavica*, Book I, li and lii, are witnesses to a similar ancient custom of the northern nations.

Michael, ruler of Thessaly, was succeeded by Michael, his illegitimate son, since legitimate heirs were lacking; Gregoras, Book II [II. viii]. To the second Michael in like manner an illegitimate son succeeded; the same Gregoras, Book IV [IV. ix].

On Molossus, natural son of Pyrrhus, see Servius, *On the Aeneid*, III [III. 297].

Sallust, *Jugurtha* [x] Cassiodorus; Paulus Diaconus, *History of the Lombards*, VI.

Philip to succeed him in Scythia. Jugurtha, a bastard, but adopted, succeeded to the throne in Numidia; just as also in the kingdoms which the Goths and Lombards gained by force of arms we read that adoption gave a similar right.

Furthermore, the throne will pass to those relatives of the last king who are not connected by blood with the first king, if such a method of succession has been adopted in those places. So in Justin Mithridates says that 'Paphlagonia had come by inheritance to his father on the extinction of the line of native kings'

XXXVIII [v. 4].

XIII.—*That if hereditary kingdoms are indivisible the eldest child is given preference*

If it is expressly stated that the kingdom shall not be divided, but no direction has been given as to the person to whom it ought to go, the child that is the oldest,[1] whether male or female, [182] will have the kingdom. In the chapter of the Talmud on kings we read: 'The one who has the principal right to the inheritance has it to the possession of the kingdom.' Thus an older son is preferred to a younger. 'It is the custom among all peoples that the eldest should receive the throne,' says Herodotus. Elsewhere the same author often calls this the 'law' or custom of kingdoms. Speaking of two brothers who were striving for the kingship of the Allobroges, Livy says that the younger was inferior in right but superior in force. In Pompeius Trogus is the statement: 'Artabazanes the eldest claimed the kingdom by privilege of age; a right which order of birth and nature itself have granted among nations.' Elsewhere the same author calls this a universal principle of law; and so likewise Livy, who calls it succession according to age and nature.

VII [ii]. XXXI [XXI. xxxi. 6]. Justin, II [x. 2]. [XXXIV. iii. 7.] XL [xi. 7].

This principle of succession is to be understood as applicable unless the father has otherwise ordered, as Ptolemy did, according to the same Trogus. But the one who has succeeded to a kingdom under such conditions will be bound to pay to the coheirs according to the valuation of their shares, if that is within the bounds of possibility.

XVI [ii. 7] and XXXIV [iii. 7].

[1] Concerning the Swedes see Bridget, IV. iii; concerning the Danes see Saxo, XII and XIII. Appian in his *Mithridatic Wars* [ii. 13] says: 'He judged it right that the kingdom should belong to the eldest.'

Nicetas of Chonae in *Joannes Comnenus* [xii] says: 'Nature, following her own order, honours the first-born. But in conferring the greatest privileges God does not always insist on that order.' The same author in *Manuel* [I. i.], speaking of Isaac, says: 'He was called to the succession to the throne on account of order of birth.'

In Josephus [*Jewish War*, I. vi. 2] Antipater said: 'The kingdom belonged to Hyrcanus by order of birth.'

See also Leunclavius, *Turkish History*, XVI.

XIV.—*That in case of doubt a kingdom which is hereditary only with the consent of the people is indivisible*

But those kingdoms which have been made hereditary by the voluntary consent of the people are handed down in succession according to the presumed will of the people. But it is presumed that the people desired what is most to its advantage. From this is derived the first principle, that the kingdom is indivisible; for that is of the utmost importance for protecting the kingdom and maintaining the harmony of the people.

An exception is made, however, if there is law or custom to the contrary.[1] Thus it is apparent from the story of Zethus and Amphion,[2] and from that about the sons of Oedipus, that the royal power of Thebes in Boeotia was divisible between the sons. Similarly, ancient Attica was divided among the sons of Pandion ; the district of Rhodes, among the brothers Camirus, Ialysus, and Lindus ; and the Argive kingdom among the four sons of Perseus.

Justin in Book XXI says : 'They thought that the kingdom would be stronger if it should remain under the power of one, than if it should be divided into parts among the sons.' [XXI.i.2.]

XV.—*That the right to such kingdoms does not continue beyond the last descendants of the first king*

A second principle is that the succession is limited to those who are descended from the first king. That family, in fact, seems to have been chosen on account of its nobility ; and so, when it has become extinct, the royal power reverts to the people. Curtius in Book X said that ' the strength of sovereign power would remain in the same house and family ; that the royal line would defend its hereditary sovereign authority ; and that the subjects were accus- [X.vii.15.]

[1] Dardanus and Lasius ruled together in Troy, as Servius says, *On the Aeneid*, II [III, line 15], in explanation of ' allied households '. In Crete, Minos and Rhadamanthus ruled together ; Julian, *Against the Christians* [*Orations*, II. lxxxii= 190 D].

At Alba, Numitor [192] and Amulius were joint rulers, as says the author, *On Famous Men* [Aurelius Victor, i]. Others say that the money fell to Numitor, the kingship to Amulius, as Plutarch declares [*Romulus*, iii = 19 A]. So also some have related that the Theban kingdom fell to Eteocles and the necklace of Hermione to Polynices in lieu thereof [Scholiast on Euripides, *Phoenician Maidens*, line 71].

In like manner in Norway one son had the crown and the other the ships and the profit from expeditions at sea.

[2] Euripides in the *Mad Hercules* [lines 29, 30] says :

> Before the kingdom came to the two sons of Zeus,
> To Zethus and Amphion, for white horses famed.

tomed to respect and honour the very name of Philip; and no one else assumed that name, unless born to rule.'

XVI.—*That in such kingdoms illegitimate children have no right of succession*

The third principle is that only children who are legitimate according to the laws of the country shall be entitled to the succession. Not only are illegitimate children excluded because they are subject to scorn, since their father did not deem the mother worthy of a true marriage, and moreover because their paternity is considered less certain, whereas in kingdoms it is to the advantage of the people to have the greatest certainty possible, in order to avoid contests. And this is the reason why the Macedonians thought that the kingdom belonged to Demetrius, the younger son, rather than to Perseus, the older; for Demetrius was born in lawful wedlock. In Ovid we read:

Livy, XXXIX [liii. 3].

[*Heroides*, iv. 121–2.]

> But she was neither bride nor with the marriage torches wed;
> And why, except that you, a bastard, should not have your father's realms?

But adopted children also are excluded from succession, because the nobility of a truly royal family causes the kings to be more reverenced and greater expectations to be entertained concerning them.

[Horace, *Odes*, IV. iv. 30.]

> There is in cattle, and in horses too,
> The merit of their sires.

XVII.—*That in such a kingdom male descendants are preferred to female descendants of the same degree of relationship*

The fourth principle is that among those who are admitted equally to the succession, either because they are of the same degree of relationship, or because [183] they succeed to the degree of their parents, males are given preference over females.[1] The reason is that males are thought to be better suited than females, not only for war, but also for the other functions of government.

XVIII.—*That among the male descendants the eldest is given preference*

1. The fifth principle is that of the male descendants the eldest is given preference,[2] or of the female descendants in case male descendants are lacking. It is, in fact, believed that the oldest is already,

[1] See Nicetas of Chonae, *Manuel*, IV [IV. iv].
[2] Homer, *Iliad*, XIII [lines 354–55], speaking of the throne of Crete, says:

> We both are of one family and of one native land,
> But Jupiter the elder and more skilful is.

or sooner will be, of more mature judgement. In Xenophon Cyrus says: 'I leave my kingdom to the older son as naturally having had the larger experience.' [*Training of Cyrus.* VIII. vii. 9.]

Further, because this preference of age is purely temporary, while that of sex is permanent, the prerogative of sex takes precedence over that of age. So when Herodotus had said that Perses, son of Andromeda, succeeded to the kingdom of Cepheus, he adds the reason: 'For Cepheus had no male children.' According to the version of Diodorus, Teuthras left the kingdom of Mysia to his daughter Argiope, 'for the reason that he had no male children'. Trogus said that the empire of the Medes belonged to the daughter, because Astyages had no male descendant. Similarly in Xenophon Cyaxares declared that Media belonged to his daughter, adding, 'For I have no legitimate son.' Of King Latinus Virgil says: VII [lxi]. IV [xxxiii. 12]. [Justin, I. iv. 7.] [*Training of Cyrus,* VIII. v. 19.]

> By the gods' destiny no son nor offspring male
> Had he; a son was born, but died in early youth.
> The line and so great power an only daughter kept.

[*Aeneid,* VII. 50–2.]

In like manner before the rule of the descendants of Hercules over the Spartans, Eurotas was succeeded by Sparte, his daughter, or by her children, as the children of Helen also succeeded Tyndarus, because there were no male descendants living. Eurystheus, again, was succeeded in the rule of Mycenae by his uncle Atreus, as Thucydides states. In accordance with the same law it is noted that the royal power of Athens fell to Creusa,[1] and of Thebes to Antigone, because there were no sons. Also the Argive kingdom came to Argus, the son of Phoroneus's daughter.[2] Pausanias, III [i. 3]. II [I. ix].

2. From this it is to be understood that, although children in some degree take the place of the parents who die before them, yet it is to be understood also that they are capable of succession only along with the others; and that among those who are capable of succession the prerogative first of sex, and then of age, is maintained. For the quality of sex, and that of age, in so far as they are considered in this matter by the people, are so united with the person that no separation is possible.

Here Homer, as he usually does, has wisely given the reason why the older sons have received the preference in the succession to royal power. For the most part this reason holds good, and that is all that is necessary in such matters. Zosimus in his second book [II. xxvii] says of the Persian law: 'Since the law gave the supreme power to the eldest of the king's sons.'

Periander succeeded his father on the throne of Corinth, 'because he was the eldest child', as Nicholas of Damascus says in the *Excerpta* [= frag. 57, p. 44, edit. Dindorf], which we owe to the kindness of that excellent scholar, Nicholas Peiresc.

[1] See Euripides, *Ion* [72, 73, 578].

[2] And if Orestes had died without offspring, Electra would have succeeded him in the same kingdom of Argos, as we learn from the *Iphigenia among the Taurians* of Euripides [lines 681 f., 695 ff.].

Thus the kingdom of Calydon came to Andraemon, son-in-law of Oeneus [Apollodorus, *Library*, I. viii. 6], and the kingdom of Asterius to his son-in-law Minos [*Library*, III. i. 3], as Apollodorus in both cases notes; and he assigns as the reason the fact that there were no male children.

XIX.—*Whether such a kingdom is a part of an inheritance*

The question is raised whether a kingdom subject to such rules of succession is a part of an inheritance.

It is nearer the truth to say that it is a kind of inheritance,[1] but separated from the inheritance to the other possessions in the same manner as the special form of inheritance seen in certain fiefs, in subinfeudations, in rights of patronage, and in rights of special legacies requiring predelivery before the general distribution of the estate. In consequence the kingdom may belong to the person who can be also an heir to property, if he wishes, but in such a way that the kingdom can be inherited without the estates and their burden.

The reason is that the people is believed to have wished the succession to the kingdom to take place on the best terms possible. In fact it makes no difference to the people whether estates are inherited by the king or not, since it did not choose the order of hereditary succession with that in view; the desire of the people was that there might be something certain about the succession, that respect might be gained by prestige of family, that at the same time there might be expectation of noble qualities from birth and nurture, and that the possessor of the kingdom might care for it more deeply, and defend it more bravely, if he should expect to leave it to those whom he held in the highest regard, either on account of favours received or from affection.

XX.—*That the presumption is that such a form of succession was established in the kingship as was customary in other things at the time of the founding of the kingdom. First, if the royal power is free from rights of tenure*

When, however, the custom of succession was different in fiefs and in land held allodially, if [184] the kingdom is not a fief, or certainly was not originally a fief, even if afterward homage was done on behalf of it, then the succession takes place according to the law which was applicable in allodial estates at the time of its foundation.

XXI.—*Secondly, if the royal power is held as a fief*

In the case of those kingdoms which were originally given as fiefs by one who had absolute authority, the feudal law of succession will need to be followed. This will not always be the Lombard law, which we have in the form of a code, but the law which was received by each people at the time of the first investiture. For the

[1] Innocent III thought that the succession to such a kingdom was forfeited by an heir who should not have carried out the last instructions of the deceased; *Decretals*, III. xxxiv. 6.

Goths, Vandals, Alemans, Franks, Burgundians, Angles, and Saxons, all the Germanic tribes which by right of war seized upon the best parts of the Roman Empire, had their particular laws and customs in regard to fiefs no less than the Lombards.

XXII.—*What cognate lineal succession is; and of what character the transmission of right in it is*

1. Again, frequently in kingdoms there is a different kind of succession, which is not hereditary but is called lineal.[1] In this kind it is not the custom to observe the right of substitution in the place of another which is called representation, but, instead, to hold the right of transmitting the future succession as if already conferred, since the law founds a sort of true right upon the expectation, which, of course, of itself produces nothing. Of such a kind, in fact, is the right to property which is due under a conditional agreement.[2] *Institutes,* III. xv. 4.

Now this succession is of such a sort that the unimpaired right necessarily passes to the descendants of the first king and in a fixed order, so that the last possessor's descendants of the first degree are first called, both those living and those dead; and the distinction first of sex, and then of age, is made in the case of both the living and the dead. If the right of those who are dead proves to be the stronger, it passes to their descendants, again with like preference in respect to sex and age among those of equal degree; and the right of the dead is always transmitted unimpaired to the living, and that of the living to the dead. If the last possessor has no children, the succession passes to the others who are most nearly related, or would be if they were alive, while the same rule of transmission, and distinction of sex and age among equals of the same line, is preserved, so that they never pass from one line to another on account of sex or age.

[1] See Cardinal Toschi, *Practicae Conclusiones,* 88, words *regni successio*; William of Montferrat, *De Successionibus Regum,* in the work *Oceanus Juris* [vol. XVI]; Peregrinus, *De Jure Fisci,* I. ii. 44 and V. i. 109.

See examples of such succession to the throne of Norway in the *Danish History* of that very learned and industrious scholar, John Pontanus, Book IX [year 1388]; for the customs of Normandy regarding the nearer relationship of heirs, see John de Serres in the *Life of Louis the Fat,* concerning the Bolognese [Bourbon] dispute [1627 ed., p. 107].

D'Argentré, *Histoire de Bretagne,* VI. iv, says: 'In successions the children of the first-born, whether male or female, and similarly the children of the second-born, if the first-born have died without offspring, by right of primogeniture, represent the persons of their fathers in the succession to fiefs, and exercise such rights of successions and of primogeniture just as if their fathers were living, to the exclusion of uncles on both father's and mother's sides; this is in accordance with a general and well-known custom in successions both in [193] the direct line and in the collateral lines. In accordance with the above-mentioned usage and custom the daughter succeeds in fiefs, whether they are duchies, earldoms, peerages, or baronies, no matter how great and noble; and such was the practice in Artois, Champagne, Toulouse, and Brittany.'

Such an order of succession was prescribed for the Marquisate of Mantua by the Emperor Sigismund in the year 1432; and by the Emperor Charles V and Philip II, king of Spain, in their kingdoms and principalities, in the years 1554 and 1594.

[2] Likewise in the case of legacies, of which the ownership has passed to the heir, but the time of payment has not arrived [*Digest,* XXXVI. ii. 5].

The consequence of this is that a son's daughter is preferred to a daughter's son, and a brother's daughter to a sister's son, and in like manner the son of an older brother to the son of a younger brother, and so on among the rest. This is the order of succession in the kingdom of Castile, and in that kingdom the same rule holds in regard to the rights of primogeniture.

Covarruvias, *Practicae Quaestiones*, II. xxxviii. no. 5. Molina, *De Hispanorum Primogenitorum Origine et Natura*, viii.

2. If law and precedents are lacking, an evidence of lineal succession can be drawn from the order which is observed in public assemblies. For if in that case consideration is had of lineal descent it will be a sign that expectation has by law been strengthened into a right, so that it can pass from the dead to the living. This, moreover, is cognate succession, in which females and their children are not excluded, but receive a secondary place in the same line, so that the succession returns to them if males have been lacking, or descendants of males of a nearer or equal degree.

The foundation of this type of succession, in so far as it differs from hereditary succession, is the hope, on the part of peoples, that the best training will be had by those who have the best-founded expectation of possessing royal power. Such are those whose parents would have had succession if they had lived.

XXIII.—*What agnate lineal succession is*

There is also another kind of lineal succession called agnate, which passes from male to male; this is commonly called the succession according to Frankish law,[1] from the example of a very famous kingdom. In so far as agnate differs from cognate succession, it was introduced especially with the aim in view that sovereignty might not pass to foreign blood through the marriages of daughters.

In both kinds of lineal succession, however, those who are related
[185] in even the most remote degree to the last possessor are admitted, provided that they are descended from the first king. There are also cases where the cognate succession is substituted in case the agnate succession fails.[2]

XXIV.—*The succession in which nearness of relationship to the first king is always considered*

Other types of succession also can be introduced, either by the will of the people or by that of a ruler who holds his kingdom as

[1] Ancient testimony to this French custom is found in Agathias, Book II [II. xiv, end].
There was the same order of succession in the line of David after Solomon; see 2 *Chronicles*, xx. 3 [xxiii. 3].

[2] As in the province of Narbonne; see De Serres on Charles VIII [*History of France*, p. 322, Paris ed., 1627]. In accordance with such a law, I suppose, Theodoric, dying without issue, was succeeded by his sister's son, Athalaric [Procopius, *Gothic War*, I. ii]. The custom seems formerly to have prevailed in Aragon also.

a patrimonial estate, in such a way that he can alienate it.[1] He may, for example, determine that in every case those who shall be in the nearest degree related to himself shall succeed to the throne; [2] just as formerly among the Numidians, from some such cause, I suppose, the brothers of the last possessor were given precedence over the children. The same custom was formerly in vogue in Arabia Felix, as I infer from Strabo. Modern writers have reported a similar arrangement in the Crimea. It is not so long a time since in Africa [3] the kings of Morocco and Fez followed the same practice.

Livy, XXIX [xxix. 6].

XVI [iv. 25].

The truer opinion is that in case of doubt this rule is to be followed also in the disposition of a property left to a family in trust. The rule is in fact in agreement with the Roman law, though some scholars have a different interpretation.

Digest, XXXI. xxxii. 6. Covarruvias, *Practicae Quaestiones*, II. xxxviii. Molina, as above, vi. no. 47.

If the systems discussed are thoroughly understood, it will be easy to settle disputes concerning the right to kingdoms which, on account of the conflicting opinions of jurists, are considered most difficult.

[1] Among the Ethiopians formerly kings were succeeded by their sisters' sons, as Nicholas of Damascus testifies [frag. 22, p. 148, edit. Dindorf]. The same custom was in vogue among the Picts, and the relatives from female lines always had the succession, as Bede notes [*Ecclesiastical History*, I. i].

Tacitus [*On the Customs of the Germans*, xx] says of the Germans: 'The sons of sisters, who stand in honour with the father. Some think that this bond of relationship is closer and more sacred.' Osorius and others inform us that the same custom was in vogue among some of the Hindoos.

[2] This custom prevailed in Africa, according to Genseric's will. Procopius in the first book of the *Vandalic War* [I. vii] says: 'After some time Genseric died. He was advanced in years, and had made a will in which he not only had given many other instructions to the Vandals, but also had directed that the Vandalic throne should always pass to that descendant who should be most nearly related to Genseric himself through the male line; and among these, the one who should be oldest.'

Jordanes [chap. xxxiii] says: 'After reigning a long time, Genseric before his death summoned all his descendants and ordered that there should be no strife among them out of rivalry for the throne, but that each should succeed the others in his turn and degree, that is, that his eldest son should be succeeded by the second, and he in turn by the one next younger.'

Victor of Utica [Vitensis] in his second book [II. v] says: 'To whom among the grandsons, because he was the eldest, the kingdom belonged above all others by the constitution of King Genseric.'

Here not the last possessor but the founder of the kingdom is always considered. Whether Genseric took this form of succession from Africa, where we have shown in the text that it prevailed, or, in fact, from some of our northern peoples, remains a matter of doubt. For also among the Lombards, though King Vaces left sons, no one of these was entitled to succeed him, but Risiulfus of the same family, as Procopius bears witness in the third book of his *Gothic War* [III. xxxv].

Also Nicetas of Chonae, on the reign of Manuel, Book IV [IV. i], relates that when Iatra had died not his children but his brother had the right to the crown of Hungary. Probably in the same class should be placed the kind of succession in vogue among the Patzinacitae and rather indefinitely referred to by Constantine Porphyrogenitus in his *De Administrando Imperio*, xxxvii.

The same type of succession was in vogue in Denmark, [194] as Krantz in his *Danish History*, IV [IV. xxxiv], and *Swedish History*, V [V. xiv], reports. Also at Alba not Iulus born of Ascanius, the eldest son of Aeneas, succeeded to the throne, but Silvius, the second son of Aeneas [Dionysius of Halicarnassus, *Roman Antiquities*, I. lxx. 3; Aurelius Victor, *Origo Gentis Romanae*, xvii. 4].

[3] Livy [XXIX. xxix. 6] says of Masinissa: 'While he was serving with the Carthaginians in Spain his father died. The father's name was Galba. And the kingdom passed to Desalces, the king's brother, for such was the custom among the Numidians.' In regard to Mauretania as a whole, see Mariana, Book XXIX [XXIX. xxii].

In imitation of this practice also among the Saracens, who had come from Africa into Spain, brothers had the preference over sons down to the time of Abderamen; Roderick of Toledo, *Historia Arabum*, vi. De Thou, *History*, Book LXV [LXV. 16], year 1578, says of Hamet: 'By the will of his father he was called to the throne next after the brothers, to the exclusion of their sons.'

The same form of succession prevailed in the kingdoms of Mexico and of Peru, as I learn from the histories of those countries.

XXV.—*Whether a son can be disinherited in respect to succession to the throne*

The first question is, whether a son can be so disinherited by his father that he shall not succeed to the throne.

In this inquiry we must distinguish alienable kingdoms, that is, kingdoms which are patrimonial from those that are inalienable. For there is no doubt that disinheritance can take place in alienable kingdoms, since they differ in no respect from other possessions. Consequently, whatever laws or customs in respect to disinheritance [1] are binding will be operative in this matter also. If, on the other hand, there should be no laws or customs in effect, nevertheless by the law of nature disinheritance will be permitted, except for bare support, or even without this exception, if the son has committed a crime deserving of death, or has otherwise grievously sinned, and, besides, has means of support. Thus because of an offence Reuben was deprived of the right of primogeniture by Jacob, and Adonijah was deprived of the throne by David.[2] Even more, the son will be considered as tacitly disinherited who has committed a serious crime against his father, if there are no indications that the offence has been pardoned.

Digest, XXXI. lxxxviii. 11; XXXIV. iv. 31. § 2. Hostiensis and others, *On Decretals*, III. xxxiv. 6.

In inalienable kingdoms, however, even though they are hereditary, the same rule will not hold; for while the people has indeed chosen the hereditary method of succession, it is hereditary in the sense that it is not subject to a will.[3] Still less will disinheritance hold good in lineal succession, where the throne passes on to individuals in prescribed order from the gift of the people, and without any semblance of ordinary inheritance.

XXVI.—*Whether any one can abdicate the throne for himself and his children*

A similar question is, whether the throne, or the right of succession to the throne, can be abdicated.

There is no doubt that a ruler can abdicate for himself; whether he can abdicate for his children is a subject of controversy. However, the matter ought to be settled by the extension of the distinction just made. For he who abdicates his right to inheritances can transfer nothing to his children. On the other hand, in lineal succession the act of the father cannot harm children already born, because they

[1] What Baldus says on the introduction to the *Decretals* of Gregory is to be understood of such a kingdom, that the king could choose, as a successor, the son whom he wished. An example is found in Mexican history also.

[2] The kingdom of David was, in fact, an absolute possession, not indeed by right of war, but by the gift of God himself.

[3] Not by will nor by adoption; on the kingdom of Naples, see Mariana, Book XX [XXIX. iv].

have by law gained their own right as soon as they have begun to exist; and it cannot work harm to those yet to be born, because it cannot hinder the right from falling to them also at the proper time, as the gift of the people.

This point of view, moreover, is not inconsistent with what I have said about transmission. The power of transmission which the parents possess is, in fact, of necessity, not voluntary. Between existing children and those who are yet to come there is this difference: those who are to come do not yet have any right, and so a right can be taken away from them by the will of the people, if it has also been yielded by the parents, whose interest it is to transmit it to their children. Here also is applicable that which we said above about abandonment of ownership. [II. iv. 10.]

XXVII.—*Absolute decision regarding the succession belongs neither to the king nor the people*

1. This question, furthermore, is often raised, whether [186] the king who is now ruling, or the people by themselves or through appointed judges, can decide concerning the succession to the throne.

Both alternatives must be rejected so far as the decision is concerned, on grounds of jurisdiction. For jurisdiction belongs only to a superior, since it includes not merely the bare consideration of the person but also of the cause, and this must be examined with its attendant circumstances. But a cause of succession is not subject to the reigning king; [1] this is apparent from the fact that the king who is now reigning cannot bind his successor by any law. Succession to sovereign power is not, in fact, included in sovereign power, and in consequence has remained in the state of nature, in which there was no jurisdiction.

2. Nevertheless, if the right of succession is disputed, those who claim the right will act in a correct and high-minded way if they will agree upon arbitrators, a subject which will be treated later. The people, in truth, has transferred all its right of jurisdiction to the king and royal family, and it has no remnants of that power so long as the former are in existence; I am speaking of a true kingdom and not of the mere possession of supreme authority.

Nevertheless, if question should arise concerning the original intention of the people, it will not be out of place for the people [2] which now exists, and is considered identical with that which formerly existed, to express its opinion on the matter. In that case the judge-

[1] In regard to the kingdom of France, see De Thou, Book CV [CV. xi], year 1593; see also Guicciardini.

[2] Either in the general assembly of the orders, as was done in England and Scotland, as Camden shows, years 1571 and 1572; or by delegates chosen for this task, as was done in Aragon, as Mariana shows in Book XX [XX. iii and iv].

ment of the people will have to be followed, unless it is quite certainly established that formerly the desire of the people was different, and that the right in question was derived from that desire. Thus King Euphaes allowed the Messenians to decide which one of the royal family of the Aepitidae ought to rule; and the people decided in the contest between Xerxes and Artabazanes.

Pausanias, IV [x. 5]. Justin, II [x. 9]. Plutarch, *On the Love of Brothers* [xviii = 488 D, E].

XXVIII.—*That a son born before the father came to the throne should have preference over one born afterward*

To proceed now to other questions, it holds true of every kind of succession that in an indivisible kingdom a son who was born before his father's accession to the throne should have the preference over a son born in the royal state. For in a divisible kingdom such a son will undoubtedly receive a part, as in the case of other possessions in regard to which no distinction is ever made on account of the time in which they were acquired. The son, then, who in a divisible kingdom would receive a share in an indivisible kingdom, received the preference by reason of age. For this reason the fief goes to the son who was born before the first investiture.

Hotman, *Quaestiones Illustres*, 2; Tiraqueau, *De Primogenitorum Jure*, qu. 31.

Also, again, in lineal succession, as soon as a throne has been acquired, some expectation has been acquired by the children already born. If, in fact, it is assumed that other children are not born later, no one will say that those born previously ought to be excluded. In this kind of succession, a hope once established gives a right, and this right does not cease in consequence of a later act, except that in cognate succession it is suspended in consequence of the privilege of sex.

The opinion which I have stated was held valid in Persia in the contest between Cyrus and Arsica;[1] in Judaea, between Antipater, son of Herod the Great, and his brothers; in Hungary when Geissa obtained the throne; and in Germany in the contest between Otto the First and Henry, though not without resort to arms.[2]

[Josephus, *Antiquities of the Jews*, XVI. iii. 3; iv. 6.]

XXIX.—*The rule stated holds unless it appears that the kingship was conferred under a different condition*

We read that a rule contrary to that just stated was followed in Sparta, in accordance with a special law of that state which gave the preference to children born during the reign because greater

[1] To whom the name of Artaxerxes Mnemon was given; see Plutarch, *Artaxerxes* [i = 1011 F].

[2] See on this subject Sigebert [*Chronographia*] and the notes [Meibom's] to Wittekind, III.

Bayezid and Gemes contended with each other for the succession to the throne of Turkey. Bayezid was the older, but Gemes was born during the reign of the father. Bayezid won the throne. Mariana, Book XXIV [XXIV. xxi].

Constantine Ducas left the empire to his sons, two of whom were born while he was in a private station, the third 'after he had put on the imperial purple'; Zonaras [XVIII. ix. 19–20]. See Corsetti, *De Prole Regali*, III, qu. xxvi.

pains were taken with their education. It will be possible for the same thing to occur in accordance with a special law of the original investiture, if the power of governing is given in fief to a vassal and to his descendants.

Ludovico [Sforza] seems to have relied on this argument as against his brother Galeazzo, in the contest for the duchy of Milan. However, in Persia Xerxes,[1] who obtained the throne in opposition to his brother Artabazanes, as Herodotus states, prevailed rather by the influence of his mother Atossa than by right. In the same Persia again, when afterward a dispute of the same kind arose, as we have already noted, between Artaxerxes Mnemon and Cyrus, the sons of Darius and Parisardis, Artaxerxes as the elder, though born in private station, was declared king. [VII. iii.]

XXX.—*The question whether the son of an older son is to be given preference to a younger son; explanation, with a distinction*

1. No less bitter is the contest, even with wars and single combats, [187] over the question whether the son of an older son should be given the preference over a younger son.[2]

In lineal succession this question presents no difficulty. For in lineal succession the dead are considered as if living in this respect, that they may transmit their right to their children. In such a succession, therefore, the son of the first-born son will have preference without any regard to age; and in kingdoms having succession not restricted to male issue even the daughter of the first-born will have preference, for in such kingdoms neither age nor sex will furnish a reason for departing from the line.

Hotman, *Quaestiones Illustres*, qu. 3. Tiraqueau, *De Primogen. Jure*, qu. 40. Molina, *De Hisp. Primigen. Origine*, III. vi.

In divisible hereditary kingdoms, however, such grandchildren will share in the division except in those regions where substitution in the place of another is not allowed, as was formerly the case among many peoples in Germany;[3] for grandchildren were admitted late to share the inheritance with the children. In case of doubt we ought rather to believe that the succession by substitution may take place, because it is favoured by nature, as we have stated above.

2. If substitution in the place of the deceased parent has been

Wittekind, *History of Saxony*, II. Molina, *De Primig. Origine*, III. viii.

[1] Further, Artaxerxes was made joint ruler with Xerxes, but not Darius and Hystaspes, though they were older; for they were born before their father received the royal power. But perhaps it is true that the kingship of Persia was dependent on popular election, though choice was restricted to the royal family; for Ammianus Marcellinus in his twenty-third book [XXIII. vi. 6] relates this of the Arsacidae, the Parthians who ruled the Persians; and Zonaras in his account of Justinus [XIV. v = 59 c] says this of the Persian kings, who followed the Parthians.

[2] See Choppin, *De Domanio*, Book II; Thomas Grammaticus, *Decisiones Neapolitanae*, I; Johannes le Cirier, *De Primogenitura*, which is inserted in the *Oceanus Juris* [vol. x]; Mariana, Book XX [XX. iii] and Book XXVI [XXVI. xi]; Kromer, Book XXX.

[3] See what I have noted above on sec. 10 [11].

For this [195] reason in the Palatinate formerly Rupert, a younger brother, was given the preference over another Rupert descended from the eldest son. See Reinkingk, Book I, class IV, xvii, no. 35.

openly introduced by the civil law of the country, it will take place even if mention is made of the nearest relative in some statute. The reasons, which are adduced from the Roman laws for this procedure, are not strong; this will become apparent to the person who examines the laws themselves. But this is the best reason that, when the subject-matter admits of it, the signification of words ought to be extended to the fullest possible meaning, to include not only the general but also the figurative use, in such a way that under the term children adopted children should be comprised, and, under that of death, civil death, for the reason that the law is accustomed to use terms in this fashion. Therefore that one will rightly be included under the term next of kin whom the law advances to the nearest degree of relationship.

In indivisible hereditary kingdoms, where substitution in the place of another has not been excluded, neither always the grandson nor always the second son will be given the preference; but the elder son will be given preference as among equals, at any rate, by the effect of the law as to the equalizing of the degrees of relationship; for we have shown above that in hereditary kingdoms preference due to age is not transferred by inheritance.

Among the Corinthians the eldest of the children of the deceased king always obtained the succession, as George the Monk has shown from the sixth book of Diodorus Siculus. So also among the Vandals, by the provision that the heir should be next of kin and eldest, an older second son was given preference over the first son's son.[1] Thus in Sicily Robert was given preference over the son of his older brother Martel, not specially for the reason which Bartolus accepted, because Sicily was a fief, but because the kingdom was hereditary.

Procopius, *Vandalic War*, III [I. vii, viii]. Conrad Vicerius, *Life of Henry VII.*

3. There is an example of a similar succession in the kingdom of the Franks, in the person of Guntram; but this came rather through election by the people, which at that time had not completely ceased. But after agnate succession has been introduced the matter is free from contest; this was the case at Sparta, where, after the throne was given to the descendants of Hercules, a similar male lineal succession existed. Thus it happened that Areus, the son of an older brother, was given preference over his uncle Cleonymus.

Aimoin, III. lxii.

But also in the cognate succession a grandson will be given preference, as in England Richard II, the grandson of Edward [III] by his first-born son,[2] was preferred to Hermon and Thomas, sons

Plutarch, *Lycurgus* [*Pyrrhus*, xxvi = 400 E]. Justin, *Histories*, III [ii. 5]. Pausanias, III. [vi. 2].

[1] Henry [Honoric], son of Genzon, took precedence of Gondemond. On this order of succession see above, sec. 24, text and notes.

[2] See De Serres [*Invent. de l'Hist. de France*, p. 196, edit. 1627] on Charles the Wise; also Mariana, Book XVIII [XVIII. i], who says that no contest was made by the sons of Edward. When the same Mariana, Book XIV [XIV. viii], treated of the contest between the son of Alfonso and his grandson, born of a son, he says that in the assembly the decision was in favour of the son, Sanchez, but it is uncertain whether rightly or wrongly.

of the same Edward. This provision is also established by law in the kingdom of Castile.

XXXI.—*Likewise, whether a surviving younger brother of the king ought to be given preference over the son of an older brother*

It is with the help of the same distinction that answer should be made to the question of succession between the surviving brother of the last king and the son of an older brother; excepting that in many countries succession to the place of the deceased is admitted among the children when it is not allowed in the collateral line.

But in cases in which the right is not clear we ought rather to incline to the view which puts the children in the place of their father,[1] because natural justice points to this point of view, [188] that is, in respect to ancestral possessions. And no obstacle is presented by the fact that Justinian calls this right among the sons of brothers a privilege; for he does this out of regard not for natural justice, but for the ancient law of the Romans. *Novels*, cxviii [3].

Let us now briefly mention the other questions which Manuel de Costa proposes. [*De Rebus Dubiis.*]

XXXII.—*Whether the son of a brother should be preferred to an uncle of the king*

Costa rightly says that the son, or even the daughter, of a deceased brother is given preference over the uncle of a king, not in lineal succession only, but also in hereditary succession, in realms where substitution in the place of the deceased is observed. This is not the case in kingdoms which in explicit words follow the natural order of relationship; for in these the person will have the preference who shall have the advantage in the matter of sex or age. *Digest*, XXVI. iv. 3. § 5.

XXXIII.—*Whether the son of a son should have preference over the daughter of a king*

He adds that a grandson, born of a son, takes precedence of a daughter. This is correct, and by reason of sex; but exception must be made if the question arises in a country which among the children takes account of nearness of relationship alone.

XXXIV.—*Whether a younger grandson, born of a son, has preference over an older grandson, born of a daughter*

He adds that a younger grandson, issue of a son, is given pre-

[1] See De Serres, in his account of Philip Augustus [p. 118], on the contest between John and Arthur [in England]. The same author tells of a decision in favour of the lineal succession in the duchy of Brittany in his account of Philip of Valois and of Charles VIII [pp. 165, 166, 422].

ference over an older grandson who is born of a daughter. This is true in cognate succession,[1] but not equally so in hereditary succession, unless supported by a special law. Moreover the reason alleged, that the father of the one would have excluded the mother of the other from succession, is not sufficient; for the result would have come about from purely personal superiority, which is not capable of transmission.

XXXV.—*Whether a granddaughter born of an older son should be preferred to a younger son*

He adds that it seems to him probable that a granddaughter, born of the eldest son, would exclude a younger son from succession.

This cannot be accepted for hereditary kingdoms, even if succession by substitution in the place of the deceased is admitted; that, in fact, merely makes one eligible to the succession, but among those who are eligible the prerogative of sex ought to have weight.

XXXVI.—*Whether the son of a sister ought to be preferred to the daughter of a brother*

Illescas, *Historia Pontifical*, VI. xix. Afflictis, *De Natura Succedendi*, i, col. 5, no. 20. Aguirre, *Apologia*, no. 82.

In accordance with this rule, in the kingdom of Aragon[2] the son of a sister has been given preference over the daughter of a brother.

XXXVII.—*Whether the daughter of an older brother takes precedence over a younger brother*

In like manner in hereditary kingdoms the daughter of the eldest brother should be placed in the succession after the king's younger brother.

[1] Mariana, Book XXVI [XXVI. xi], approves of the order of succession in Portugal. Yet he says that, contrary to it, Emmanuel, by the favour of the people, was preferred to the Emperor Maximilian. The same author, Book XII [XII. vii], says that in the kingdom of Castile Ferdinand, son of Berengaria, younger sister of the deceased king Henry, was preferred over Blanche, the elder sister of the same king; this preference grew out of hatred of France, into the royal family of which Blanche had married.

[2] Mariana says that it was formerly believed that the brother of the king, not the daughters, ought to succeed. Afterward, however, they accepted the lineal succession so completely that the son of a sister was given preference over the descendants of a brother, who were a degree farther removed; Books XV. xiii; XIX. xxi; XX. ii and viii.

The same author, Book XXIV [XXIV. xviii], treating of Alfonso, says: 'He decreed that for the inheritance of the crown of Aragon his grandsons should be preferred to the sons of Ferdinand, and even the sons of a daughter, if male offspring were lacking, rather than Ferdinand's daughters.' And he adds: 'Thus the right of succession to the crown is often changed at the will of kings.'

See Mariana again, Book XXVII. iii.

CHAPTER VIII

ON ACQUISITIONS COMMONLY SAID TO BE BY THE LAW OF NATIONS

I.—*That many rights are said to have their origin in the law of nations, of which, if we speak accurately, this is not true*

1. [196] The order of our subject has brought us to the acquisition of property which takes place by that law of nations that we previously called the volitional law of nations, distinct from the law of nature. Such is the acquisition made by right of war, but we shall treat of this more properly below, when the effects of war will be explained.

When the Roman jurists treat of acquiring ownership of property, they enumerate many methods, which they say are according to the law of nations. If, however, any one will examine these closely, he will find that with the exception of the right of war none of them have anything to do with that law of nations with which we are concerned; but that they must be referred, either to the law of nature—not, to be sure, in its original state, but in the state which followed the introduction of property ownership and preceded all civil law—or they must be referred to the civil law itself, not alone of the Roman people but of many surrounding nations.[1] I believe that this is the case, because the origin of such law or custom had come from the Greeks, whose institutions, as Dionysius of Halicarnassus and others note, were followed by the peoples of Italy and their neighbours.

2. This law of nations is not international law, strictly speaking, for it does not affect the mutual society of nations in relation to one another; it affects only each particular people in a state of peace. For this reason a single people can change its determination without consulting others; and even this happens, that in different times and places a far different common custom, and therefore a different law of nations (improperly so called), might be introduced. This, we see, did actually happen when the Germanic peoples invaded almost all Europe. For as formerly the Greek laws, so then the

[1] Pliny [*Natural History*] notes a similar agreement, for causes that are not certain, on the part of nations in other customs also that have nothing to do with law; such are, that the bodies of children whose first teeth have not appeared are not cremated, VII. xvi [VII. xvi. 72], that the Ionian characters are used in writing, VII. lvii [VII. lvii. 210], that barbers are employed, VII. lix [VII. lix. 211], that time is noted by hours, VII. lx [VII. lx. 212], that a certain religious veneration is accorded to the knees, XI. xlv [XI. xlv. 250], and that lightning flashes are adored by clucking with the tongue, XXVIII. ii [XXVIII. ii. 25].

Germanic customs were everywhere accepted, and these are even now in force.

Now the first method of acquiring property, which by the Romans was ascribed to the law of nations, is the taking possession of that which belongs to no one. This method is without doubt in accord with the law of nature, in the state to which I referred, after the establishment of property ownership, and so long as no statute established any provision to the contrary. For property ownership can be brought about also by the civil law.

II.—*That fish in ponds and wild animals confined in parks are private property according to the law of nature, contrary to the ruling of the Roman law*

First under this head the capture of wild beasts, birds, and fish comes up for discussion. The question is by no means settled, how long these may be said to belong to no one. Nerva the son said that the fish which are in our fish-ponds belong to us, but not those in a lake; also that wild beasts which are confined in a park are our property, but not those which wander at large in forests that are fenced in. But fish in a private lake are no less shut in than in a fish-pond, and well-fenced forests detain wild beasts no less effectively than parks, which the Greeks called 'places for raising wild beasts'; and these differ in no other respect than that one is a narrower, the other a less restricted confinement. Therefore in our time with greater justice the opposite opinion has prevailed, so that it is understood that we have right of ownership over wild beasts in private forests, and fish in private lakes, just as we have possession of them.

Dig. XLI. ii. 3. § 14.

III.—*That wild beasts, even if they have escaped, are none the less the property of those who captured them, if they can be properly identified*

Dig. XLI. i. 3. § 1.

The Roman jurists affirm that wild animals cease to be our property as soon as they regain their natural liberty. But in all other things [197] ownership, which begins with possession, is not lost when possession is lost; rather, ownership gives us the right to recover possession. Besides it makes no great difference whether another takes away our possessions from us, or they themselves escape, as a runaway slave. The truth, then, is rather that ownership is not actually lost because the wild beasts have escaped, but because of the natural inference that we have abandoned ownership on account of the difficulty of pursuit,[1] especially since the wild creatures which belonged to us cannot be distinguished from others.

Dig. XLI. ii. 13.

[1] We have noted above, on II. iv. 5, that this was called by the Jews 'despairing of the recovery of a lost object'.

This inference, however, can be made invalid by other inferences, such as would be warranted, for example, if 'identification marks',[1] or bells,[2] were placed on the wild creature; this, we know, has been done in the case of deer and hawks, which, when identified thereby, have been restored to their owners.[3] Moreover an actual physical possession is requisite in order to acquire ownership. It is, then, not sufficient to have wounded an animal, a view that is rightly held in opposition to Trebatius. Hence came the proverb, 'You started the hare, but others caught it.'[4] Again, in the fifth book of Ovid's *Metamorphoses*, we read that it is one thing to know where a thing is, and another to find it. *Dig.* XLI. i. 5. § 1. [V. 519–20.]

IV.—*Whether possession may be acquired with the help of appliances, and how?*

Now this physical possession of wild creatures can be acquired not only by the hands, but also by appliances, such as traps, nets, and snares, provided that two conditions are observed: first, that the appliances are in our possession; then, that the wild creature has been caught in such a way that it cannot escape. On this basis the question of the boar caught in a snare should be decided. *Dig.* XLI. i. 55.

V.—*That it is not contrary to the law of nations that wild creatures should be the property of kings*

The principles stated will therefore be applicable if no statute has prevented. Modern jurists, in fact, are greatly mistaken who think that these rules are so bound up with the law of nature that they cannot be changed. They are not a part of the law of nature absolutely, but are such only under a certain condition, that is, if no provision has otherwise been made. Thus the peoples of Germany, since properties had to be assigned to their kings and princes for the maintenance of the proper rank, wisely considered that a beginning ought to be made with those things which could be so assigned without loss to any one.[5] To this class belong all things which have not become the property of any one. Hostiensis and others, *On Decretals*, III. xxx. 22. Jason, *Consilia*, 119.

I see that the Egyptians availed themselves of this right. For in Egypt also the revenue collector of the king, whom they called Strabo, XVII [i. 12].

[1] See Donatus *On Terence's Eunuch*, IV. vi [IV. vi. 15]. These are signs which the Greeks call 'recognition marks' or 'identification marks'.

[2] Apuleius, *Apologia* [lx], uses the word in this sense.

[3] Harmenopulus, II. i [II. i. 21]: 'He who has wounded a wild beast does not become owner of it unless he also has taken it.'

[4] Petronius [cxxxi]. Ovid [*Art of Love*, III, lines 661–2] says:

> And so the hare you started will belong to others.

By the *Law of the Lombards* [I. xxii. 4 and 6], the one who kills a wild animal, or finds a wild animal wounded by another, takes away a shoulder and seven ribs. The one who wounded the animal has a right to the rest, but only within the space of twenty-four hours.

[5] But on the abuse of this law see John of Salisbury, *Policraticus* [I. iv].

by a title meaning his personal representative, took possession of property of that kind. A statute law could transfer the ownership of such things before occupation, since a law alone is sufficient to produce ownership.

Covarruvias, *On Sext*, V. ult. 4, ii. 8.

VI.—*How the possession of other things lacking an owner may be acquired*

In the same manner as wild animals, other 'things without a master', as the Greeks say, that is other ownerless objects,[1] are acquired. For, if we follow the law of nature alone, these also belong to the one who finds and takes possession of them. Thus the deserted island of Acanthus was adjudged to the Chalcidians, who had first entered it, and not to the Andrians, who had first thrown a javelin upon it. The reason is that the beginning of possession is the connexion of body with body; such connexion, in the case of movable things, is made with the hands; and, in the case of land, with the feet. To know where a thing is, is not the same as to find it, as we read in the fifth book of Ovid's *Metamorphoses*.

Plutarch, *Greek Questions*, xxix [xxx=298 A].

[V. 519-20.]

VII.—*To whom a treasure-trove naturally falls; the diversity of the laws on this subject*

Among 'ownerless objects' is also treasure-trove, that is, money the owner of which is unknown. Now that which is not known is reckoned as if it did not exist. Therefore treasure-trove also naturally becomes the property of the finder, that is of the one who has removed it from its place of concealment and taken possession of it.

Dig. XLI. ii. 3.

Nevertheless this natural presumption does not hinder the possibility of establishing a different rule by laws or customs.[2] In such cases Plato wished that information should be given to the magistrates, and that an oracle should be consulted. Apollonius would assign a treasure, as if a gift from God, to the person who seemed to him the best. [198] From the parable of Christ found in *Matthew*, chapter xiii, the inference seems to be warranted that according to the accepted rule among the Jews a treasure that had been found belonged to the owner of the land.[3] From the story in Philostratus, Book VI, chapter xvi, I infer that the same law held good in Syria.

[*Laws*, XI. i=913 f.]

Philostratus, [*Life of Apollonius of Tyana*,] II. xv [II. xxxix]. [II.xxxix.]

[1] [204] In Portugal whales cast ashore belong to the king; Jorge Cabedo, *Decisiones Lusitanae*, pt. II, xlviii.

[2] There is a law of the people of Byblos, 'that you should not carry away anything found, unless you had originally placed it there.' Apollonius approved of this maxim, according to Philostratus [*Life of Apollonius of Tyana*, II. xxxix].

[3] It seems that this was the law also at Rome in the time of Plautus; for Callicles says [*Trinummus*, line 178]:

> Would not that wealth belong to him who bought the house?

And again [line 1146 f.]:

> And then by common law the buyer of the house
> That treasure would demand from me for his estate.

The laws of the Roman Emperors on this subject vary greatly. This is apparent partly in their constitutions, partly in the Histories[1] of Lampridius,[2] Zonaras, and Cedrenus. The German peoples assigned treasure-trove, as other 'ownerless objects', to their rulers. That is, in fact, now a common law, and in a sense a law of nations; for it is observed in Germany,[3] France, England, Spain, and Denmark. Why the charge of injustice cannot be brought against this law, I have already sufficiently explained.

Thomas Aquinas, II. ii. 66. 5, and Cajetan thereon. Covarruvias, *On Sext*, V. ult. 4, iii. 2.

VIII.—*That the regulations of the Roman law regarding islands and alluvial deposits belong neither to the law of nature nor to the law of nations*

Let us now come to the fluvial additions of land, to which the ancient jurists devoted many rescripts, and modern jurists even entire commentaries.[4]

Bartolus, *Tyberiad*; Baptista Aymus, *De Alluvionum Iure*; Connan, *Commentaria Juris Civilis*, III. v.

The principles which they have laid down regarding this subject, however, are for the most part drawn from the established custom of certain nations, and by no means from the law of nature, though often commended through reference to that source. For most of their definitions rest on this basic principle, that not only the river banks belong to the possessors of the nearest estates, but also the river beds, as soon as these have been left dry by the river. The resulting inference is that islands which are formed in the stream belong to the same owners.

Dig. XLI. i. 7.

In the case of an overflow by a river, to be sure, the jurists do make the distinction that a slight overflow does not take away ownership, but a greater one does; with this condition, nevertheless, that if the river should recede all at once the estate which had been submerged would revert to its original owner by postliminy; but, if the river should recede gradually, ownership would not in like manner revert, but rather would fall to the nearest landowners.

Dig. XLI. i. 7. § 5. *Dig.* XLI. i. 30 and 38.

Now I do not deny that all these regulations might have been introduced by law, and defended on account of a certain advantage

[1] See Tacitus on the treasures in Africa, which Nero had already devoured in anticipation; *Annals*, XVI [XVI. 1].
See Philostratus on the life of Atticus [*Lives of the Sophists*, II. i. 2], a passage which Zonaras has copied in his account of Nerva [XI. xix = p. 582].

[2] [Spartianus,] *Hadrian* [xviii]; and [Lampridius,] *Severus* [xlvi].

[3] See *Speculum Saxonicum*, xxxv; *Constitutiones in Sicilia Friderici*, I. lviii and ciii [*Monumenta Germaniae Historica, Leges*, II].
The Goths had the same custom. According to Cassiodorus, [*Variae*,] IV. xxxiv, King Theodoric says: 'It is not greed to take away what no owner bemoans losing.' In the same work, VI. viii, he says: 'Also let deposits of money, which through lapse of time have lost their legal owners, by your diligent search be brought into our treasury; for all ought to offer us freely the possessions of others, since we allow them to possess their own. The man who does not lose his own property suffers no loss in giving up things that he has found.'

[4] John Boreo; Antonius Marsa; John Gryphiander [*De insulis*, xviii], besides those whose names are given in the marginal note.

in protecting the banks;[1] but I do not for a moment concede that they belong to the law of nature, as the jurists seem to think.

IX.—*That by the law of nature an island in a river and a dried out bed belong to the one who owned the river or the part of the river, that is, to the people*

See above, II. iii, end. 1. For if we take into consideration that which generally happens, peoples have taken possession of lands[2] not only with sovereignty, but also with property ownership, before the fields have been assigned to individuals. Seneca says: 'We designate as territories of the Athenians, or of the Campanians, those lands which afterward neighbours divide among themselves by private boundaries.' So also Cicero: 'By nature, moreover, there is no private ownership, but such arises either from ancient occupation, as in the case of those who formerly entered unoccupied territory; or from victory, as in the case of those who have gained possession by war; or from some law, agreement, condition, or lot. The result is that the land of Arpinum is said to belong to the people of Arpinum, and the land of Tusculum to the Tusculans; and the characterization of the properties of individuals is similar.'

On Benefits, VII. iv [3].

On Duties, I [vii. 21].

[=p. 325 c.] Dio of Prusa says in his *Rhodian Oration*: 'Many things can be found which, as a whole, the state considers its own, but which have been divided among individual owners.' Of the Germans Tacitus says: 'Lands are taken possession of in common by villages' ('alternately' is a bad reading), 'in proportion to the number of cultivators; and they presently divide the lands among themselves according to rank.'

[*Germany*, xxvi.]

Consequently, whatever was originally occupied by the people, and has not since been distributed, must be considered the property of the people. As an island formed in a privately owned river, or the bed of such a river that has dried out, is the property of individuals, so in the case of a public stream both belong to the people, or to him to whom the people has granted it.

2. What I have said about the bed of the river should in like manner be held in regard to the bank,[3] which is the extreme edge of the bed, that is of that in which the river usually flows. And such we see is now the usual custom. In Holland and the neighbouring regions, where in ancient times there were very frequent controversies in regard to these matters on account of the lowness of the land, the size of the rivers and the nearness of the sea, [199] which

[1] See a passage of Cassius [Longinus] in [Aggenus] Urbicus [*Commentary on Frontinus*, viii= *Schriften der römischen Feldmesser*, vol. 1, p. 17], and Boethius [*On Geometry*, ii= *op. cit.*, p. 399].

[2] See above, II. iii. 19, both text and notes.

[3] Such is the law in France, *Sanction des Eaux et Forêts*, II. i.

takes up mud in one place and, by tidal changes, carries it away to another, it has always been the established rule that islands, which were really islands, belonged to the public domain; and likewise, abandoned beds of the Rhine and Meuse, a position often confirmed by court decisions, and supported by the best of reasons.

3. For the Roman jurists themselves concede that an island which floats in a river,[1] supported, let us say, by bushes, is public property; in fact an island formed in a river ought to belong to the person who has a title to the river. But the legal status of the river and of the bed are the same, not only from that point of view which the Roman jurists took into consideration, because the bed is covered by the river, but also from the other point of view which we mentioned above, because the river and its bed were taken possession of by the people at the same time and have not passed into private ownership. *Dig.* XLI. i. 65. §§ 1, 4; XLIII. xii. 1. § 7.

In consequence I do not accept, as in accord with the law of nature, the principle which they maintain, that if the fields have received definite boundaries the island belongs to the first occupant. Such an acquisition of ownership would take place only in case the river itself, and its bed along with it, had not been taken possession of by the people,[2] and there should remain a possibility of occupation just as in the case of an island formed in the sea, which becomes the property of the first occupant. *Digest,* XLIII. xii. 1. § 6.

X.—*That by the law of nature in an inundation the ownership of the land is not lost*

1. Again, if we follow natural reason only, loss of ownership ought not to be admitted any more in the case of a greater than of a smaller flood. For though the surface of the land may be completely turned into sand, nevertheless the lower part of the ground remains solid; and though it changes its quality somewhat, it does not change its essential character any more than the part of a field which is swallowed up by a lake, the right to which, as the Roman jurists correctly perceived, is not changed. Their assertion is not in accordance with nature, that rivers perform the function of treasury *Dig.* XLI. i. 12; XXXIX. iii. 24. § 3; XVIII. i. 69.

[1] There is a description of floating islands in Seneca, *Natural Questions,* III. xxv [III. xxv. 7 ff.]; Pliny, the Elder, [*Natural History,*] II. xcvii [II. xcv]; Macrobius, *Saturnalia,* I. vii [I. vii. 28].

A charming description of such islands in Lake Vadimon is found in Pliny the Younger, [*Letters,*] VIII. xx; and of such islands in Flanders, in a book by Chifflet, which is worth reading.

[2] Siculus Flaccus, in his book *De Conditionibus Agrorum* [=*Schriften der römischen Feldmesser,* vol. 1, p. 157], says: 'In some regions the measure of the river formed a part of the territory assigned, and in some regions it was merely left in the undivided portion. In others, however, it was made an exception, and there was an assignment of the river only.'

On the undivided portions see the remarks of Salmasius *On Solinus,* which are excellent, as are all of his comments. On this whole subject of rivers and alluvial additions, if you have leisure, examine Rosenthal, *De Jure Feudorum,* v, corol. 23; Sixtinus, *De Regalibus,* II. iii; and Caepolla, *De Servitutibus Rusticorum Praediorum,* xxxi.

officials,[1] and take from public ownership to transfer to an individual, and from the individual to transfer to the public treasury.

[XVII. i. 3.] The Egyptians handled these matters rather well, and in regard to them we find the following in Strabo:

> There was need of an accurate and minute division of fields for the reason that the Nile, adding and taking away by its overflows, changes the appearance of the surface and the landmarks, and confuses the boundaries by which the land of one is distinguished from that of another. On this account the surveying of the land had often to be done over.

2. This opinion is not contrary to the principle which the [*Digest*, L. xvii. 11.] Roman writers themselves have handed down, that what is ours does not cease to be ours except by our own act, or, again, by law. But we have noted above that under acts are included also failures to act, in so far as they warrant an inference as to intention. Wherefore we grant this, that if there is a very great inundation, and there are no other indications which suggest an intention of retaining ownership, it is easily assumed that the land has been abandoned. Such an assumption from the nature of the case is indefinite, on account of the variety of circumstances, and such cases should be committed to the decision of an honest man; consequently they are ordinarily decided by municipal law. Thus in Holland land is considered abandoned which has been submerged more than ten years, if no indications of continued ownership exist. And in this case, not without adequate reason, we have accepted a principle which *Dig.* VII. iv. 23. the Romans rejected, that possession may be considered as retained even by fishing, if not otherwise possible.

But princes were accustomed to set a limit of time within which the original possessors of the lands were obliged to drain their lands. If they did not do this, then those who held mortgages on the lands were warned; and then again, those who held civil jurisdiction merely, or both civil and criminal jurisdiction over the lands. If all these delayed action, then their entire right fell to the prince, and he either himself drained the lands and made them a part of his patrimony, or he assigned them to others to drain, while retaining a part for himself.

[200] XI.—*That in cases of doubt alluvial deposits also belong to the people*

Dig. XII. i. 4; XLI. i. 30. § 2; XLI. i. 7. § 1. As regards alluvial deposits, that is, the addition of soil particle by particle, these can be claimed by no one because the place of

[1] Compare Cassiodorus on the land surveyor [*Variae*, III. lii]: 'After the fashion of a great river, he takes away territory from some and grants rights to others.'

origin is unknown; otherwise, according to the law of nature, they would not change ownership.

It ought to be considered certain that such deposits also belong to the people, if the people owned the river, as must be believed in case of doubt; otherwise such accretion would belong to the first occupant.

XII.—*But that such alluvial deposits seem to be conceded to those whose lands have no other boundary than the river*

1. But as the people can grant to others the right to such lands, so also it can grant the same right to the possessors of the nearest estates. The people seems indeed without doubt to have so granted this right in case the lands have no boundary on that side except the natural boundary, that is, the river itself. On this point, then, we ought not to view with contempt the painstaking of the Roman jurists, who distinguished fields limited by natural bounds from other fields, if only we remember that in this respect a measured field has equal rights with a field so bounded. For what we said above of states, when we were treating of their acquisition, likewise holds good of private lands, but with this distinction, that when in doubt it is to be believed that states have natural boundaries, since this is most in accord with the nature of a country; private lands, on the contrary, are not supposed to have natural boundaries, but are either measured or bounded by a certain measure, because this is more consistent with the nature of private possessions.

Dig. XLI. i. 16; XLIII. xii. 1. § 6. Baldus, *On Feuds*, I. iv. 5 (*si quis de manso*), § 1 (*si de iure feud. contr. fuerit*).

2. Yet we do not deny that a people can assign its lands with the same right with which it has itself held them, that is, up to the stream itself; and if this is apparent, then it can assign the right over the alluvial deposits. This, in fact, was so decided in Holland some centuries ago in regard to the fields bordering on the Meuse and Issel, the reason being that both in the deeds and in the tax lists they had always been described as bordering on the river. Further, if such lands are sold, they retain their special character and the right over alluvial deposits, even though some measurement has been mentioned in the terms of sale, provided nevertheless they are not sold according to measure, but as a whole. This practice has come down to us in the Roman laws also, and is now general.

Digest, XIX. i. 13. § 14.

XIII.—*That the same opinion is to be held in regard to a bank abandoned by a river, and a part of the bed that has dried out*

What I have said about alluvial deposits ought also to be held in regard to a bank abandoned by a river and a part of a river bed that has dried out; to wit, that in the case of rivers having no owners such parts belong to the first occupant, but to the people in the case of rivers owned by the people.

Moreover, such parts belong to individuals in case these have received from the people, or from some one acting for the people, the land bordering on the river as so bounded.

XIV.—*What is to be considered alluvial deposit and what an island*

Since, as we have said, the ownership of islands is subject to one law and of alluvial deposits to another, disputes frequently arise in regard to the title under which that land ought to be held which, though somewhat raised, is so joined to the nearest estates that the level ground between is under water. We see that this condition is common enough in our country on account of the inequality of the ground.

In this matter customs vary. In Gelderland all such ground that can be reached with a loaded cart is assigned to the nearest estates, if also there is ownership by right of possession. In the region of Putten such ground is similarly assigned, if a man on foot with a drawn sword can make his way to it.[1] But it is especially in accord with the law of nature that decision in such matters be governed by the consideration whether the passage is ordinarily made by boat during the greater part of the time.

XV.—*When alluvial deposits belong to vassals*

1. No less hackneyed is the question regarding ownership of alluvial deposits arising between a prince, who enjoys sovereign authority over his people, and his vassals, who have received a power inferior to his.

In the mere grant of the right to govern, it is quite clear that the right to alluvial additions is not included. But we should note that along with this limited authority some of the vassals at the same time received the full ownership of the land, with the exception of that which was in private possession, either because such land formerly belonged to the people or to the prince, or because it had been drained by the prince. In such cases there is no doubt [201] that the vassals possess the right which belonged either to the people or to the prince. Thus we see that in Zeeland even the vassals, who appoint the judges only for civil cases, pay the land tax for the whole

[1] This agrees with the most ancient [205] custom of the Germanic peoples. Paulus Diaconus [III. xxxi] says of Autharis, king of the Lombards: 'On horseback Autharis advanced as far as that (column in the sea), and touched it with the point of his spear, saying: "Up to this point the territory of the Lombards shall extend."'

A similar story you find concerning the lance which the Emperor Otto hurled into the sea, saying that he marked the limit of his empire in the Baltic Sea; Saxo, X [p. 165], and others.

district, collecting a part from the individual owners according to their individual possessions; and with these vassals no contest is raised on the score of alluvial additions.

There are some to whom the river itself has been granted, who therefore rightly claim as their own the islands, whether formed by mud deposits or from a part of the river bed which the water has surrounded.

2. There are others in whose grants neither of the rights specified has been included, and they have a poor case against the public treasury unless the custom of the district favours them, or a sufficiently long and uninterrupted possession, reinforced by the requisite conditions, has given a right to them.

But if the land has been granted as a fief without any right of governing, the nature of the land must be considered, as we have said above. For if the land has natural boundaries alluvial additions will be considered as included in the fief, not from any special right belonging to the prince, but from the character of the land. For *Dig.* VII. i. 9. § 4. in such a case the alluvial addition would be of value only to the one who had the right of user.

XVI.—*Answer to the arguments by which the Roman jurists defend their law as the law of nature*

In order to prove that the law regarding alluvial additions adopted by them is according to nature, the Roman jurists are accustomed to quote this maxim: 'It is in accord with nature that a man should acquire the advantages of anything to the disadvantages of which he is subject. Therefore since the river often washes away a part of my land, it is fair that I should enjoy a favour granted by it.' This rule, however, is not in point, except where the advantages acquired arise from our own property. But in the case under consideration the advantages arise from the river, which belongs to another. Again, it is in accord with nature that whatever loss there is should fall upon the owner. And finally, the fact that the jurists make an exception of measured lands shows that their proposition is not universal. I may pass over the fact that it generally happens that the river enriches some and impoverishes others. Lucan says: [VI. 277–8.]

> The land escapes its owners there, but here new fields are won
> By farmers through the bounty of the Po.

XVII.—*Naturally a road prevents gain by alluvial addition*

Also the assertion, that a public highway does not prevent gain [*Digest*, XLI. i. 38.] by alluvial addition, has no foundation in nature, unless the land is private property that has to furnish thoroughfare.

XVIII.—*That it is not according to nature that the ownership of the offspring should be determined from the mother alone*

Another method of acquiring property, which is said to be based on universal legal principles, is through the breeding of animals. In this matter the rule established by the Romans [1] and some other peoples, that the ownership of the offspring is determined from the mother, is not according to nature, as I have said above, except in so far as the sire is in most cases unknown. But if the sire should be determined on satisfactory grounds no reason can be assigned why the offspring should not in some measure belong to him. For it is certain that the offspring is a part of the father also; but whether more comes from the father or from the mother is a subject of dispute among the natural philosophers. Plutarch discusses the matter thus: 'Nature so mingles the persons of the two sexes that it blends the elements taken from each and makes the offspring the common result of the two [2] to such a degree that neither parent can distinguish what is his own and what is the other's.' And this rule the ancient laws of the Franks and the Lombards followed.

[*Conjugal Precepts*, xx=140 E. F.]

XIX.—*That according to nature a thing fashioned out of another's material becomes common property in the same manner as in the intermingling of properties*

[*Institutes*, II. i. 25.]

1. If any one had fashioned a thing out of material belonging to another, the school of Sabinus maintained that it belonged to the one who had been the owner of the material. Proculus assigned the thing to the one who had made it, because through the maker that which before had no existence had come into being. At length an intermediate position was adopted, that if the material could be restored to its previous [202] form the owner of the material should be the possessor of the thing; but if it could not, then he who had fashioned the thing should have it.

III. vi.

Connan disapproves of this view and wishes only one point considered, whether there was greater value in the work or in the material; whichever, then, had the greater value should by its superior force draw to itself that which was of less value. His proof is obtained from what the Roman jurists have handed down on the subject of accession.

[1] With this agrees the *Edictum Pistense* of Charles the Bald, chap. xxxi [*Monumenta Germaniae Historica, Leges*, II, vol. II, p. 324]. On the laws of others on this subject see above, text and notes of II. v. 29.

[2] See in Galen's *De Semine*, II, an apt passage on this subject; and also what he has cited from Athenaeus. Chrysostom, *On Ephesians*, v [v. 31=Hom. XX, iv], says: 'The child originates in the mixture of the two seeds.'

2. If, however, we consider the truth of nature just as the Roman jurists also have concluded that in the case of mingling of materials common ownership is introduced in proportion to what each has furnished, because an adjustment could be made naturally in no other way, so when things consist of material and form, as if of parts, if the material belongs to one and the form to another, it naturally follows that the ownership becomes common in proportion to the value that each has. The form in fact is a part of the substance, not the whole substance; and this was perceived by Ulpian, when he said that the substance was almost destroyed by changing the form. *Dig.* X. iv. 9. § 3.

XX.—*The principle stated holds true even if the material has been intentionally injured*

It is not an unjust rule that those who, with fraudulent intent, expend labour on material belonging to another, should lose their labour. That nevertheless is a penal enactment, and so does not come under the law of nature. Nature, in fact, does not fix penalties, nor take away ownership, on account of an offence in and of itself, although those who do wrong naturally deserve punishment. *Dig.* X. iv. 12. § 3.

XXI.—*That it is not natural that a thing of less value should be absorbed by one of greater worth on account of superiority in value. Here also errors of the Roman jurists are noted*

However, that a thing of less value should be taken over by one of greater value, which is the basis of Connan's argument, is naturally consistent with the facts but not with right. He in fact who is the owner of one twentieth of an estate remains a part owner as well as the one who has the nineteen twentieths. Therefore what the Roman law has decreed in some cases, or what may be decreed in others, concerning accession on account of superiority in respect to worth, is not law of nature but civil law, and has in view the transacting of business more easily. Nevertheless the law of nature is not opposed, because statute law has the right of conferring ownership.

Yet there is scarcely any legal question regarding which there are so many divergent opinions and errors of the jurists. For who would allow that, if copper and gold have been mixed, the one cannot be separated from the other, as Ulpian has written; or that by soldering a blending of materials is produced, as Paul says; or that there is one rule for writing and another for painting, so that the panel belongs with the painting, the writing with the tablet? *Dig.* VI. i. 5. § 1. *Dig.* VI. i. 23. § 5. [*Digest*, XLI. i. 9. § 2.]

XXII.—*That by planting, sowing, or building on another's ground a community of ownership naturally is produced*

Institutes, II. i. 33, 34. In like manner it is an established rule of law that what is planted and sown goes with the soil, and the reason for this is that such things are supported by the soil. Thus a distinction is made in regard to a tree, according to whether it has put out roots. Yet the nourishment forms only a part of the thing, which was already in existence. So just as the owner of the ground acquires a certain right over the produce from the nourishment of it, so the owner of the seed, plant, or tree does not on that account naturally lose his right. Consequently in such cases also a common ownership is produced.

The same principle is not less applicable to a house, of which the component parts are the ground and the structure. For if the house is movable the owner of the ground has no right over it, as *Dig.* XLI. i. 60. Scaevola also decided.

XXIII.—*That in community of ownership a person who merely has possession of a thing is not entitled to the income of it, but can charge for expenses incurred*

Dig. V. iii. 25. § 11. [*Institutes*, I. i. 35.] In such cases of community of ownership it is likewise not in accord with nature that one, who has in good faith become the possessor of a thing, should consider as his own all the income he has received from it; but he should merely have the right of charging for expenses incurred and useful labour expended, and on this account to deduct from the income received. Such a possessor may even retain the growing crops, if he is not otherwise repaid.[1]

XXIV.—*The same right holds even if possession has been obtained fraudulently*

Also it seems that the same rule should be applied to one who has gained possession fraudulently, in case the penal law does not prevent. *Dig.* V. iii. 38. The jurist Paul says: 'It is more considerate [203] that an account of expenses incurred should be allowed, even in the case of a thief. The plaintiff, in fact, ought not to acquire gain from another's loss.'

XXV.—*That actual delivery is not required naturally in order to establish transfer of ownership*

The last way of acquiring property that is classed under the II. vi. 1. volitional law of nations is by actual delivery. But we have said above that such delivery is by nature not necessary for transfer of

[1] On this subject see the *Speculum Saxonicum*, II. xlvi, in which there are many very just rules.

ownership.[1] This the Roman jurists themselves also recognize in certain cases, as in donations subject to the former owner's right of use; or in the transfer of ownership to one who already has possession, or to one who keeps property loaned to him; and in the case of things thrown out for distribution. Further, in some cases ownership passes even before acquiring possession, as in inheritances and legacies, and in gifts made to churches, holy places, or states, or for the support of the poor; and in the case of property over which a common partnership has been established.

Code, VIII. liii. 28. *Dig.* XLI. i. 21. *Institutes,* II. i. 44. *Dig.* XLI. ii. 23. *Digest,* XLVII. ii. 65 (64). *Code,* I. ii. 23. *Code,* VIII. liv (lv). 1. *Digest,* XVII. ii. 1. § 1, and 2.

XXVI.—*The application of what has thus far been said*

These observations I have written down in order that he who finds the expression 'law of nations' in the Roman legal writers may not at once take as meant that right which cannot be changed, but may carefully distinguish precepts according to nature from those which are according to nature only under certain circumstances; and may distinguish, further, the laws common to many peoples separately from those which contain the bond of human society.

For the rest, this should be understood, that if by this law of nations, improperly so called, or even by a statute of a people, a single method of acquiring property has been introduced without distinction of citizen or foreigner, immediately thereupon foreigners acquire a right; and if the enjoyment of that right is hindered the injury is such that it may furnish a just cause of war.

[1] It is certainly not necessary. See the *Laws of the Visigoths,* V. ii. 6: 'True delivery seems then to have taken place when the deed of gift is in the hands of the legatee.'

Among the ancient Romans property transferable only by formal purchase was acquired by the formula of the bronze coin and the balances; see Varro, *Latin Language,* IV [VII. cv]; Pompeius Festus, word *Rodus* [p. 265]; Ulpian, *Institutes,* tit. xix [xix. 3]; Boethius, *On Cicero's Topics* [III].

CHAPTER IX

WHEN SOVEREIGNTY OR OWNERSHIP CEASES

I.—*Ownership and sovereignty cease when he who possessed the right is taken away and leaves no successor*

I HAVE already sufficiently explained in what manner not only private properties but also sovereign powers are originally acquired, and how they are transferred; let us now see how they are terminated.

We have already shown above, in passing, that such rights are extinguished by abandonment, for the reason that, when the desire ceases, ownership does not continue. There is also another mode of extinguishment, when the subject, in whom the sovereignty or the ownership resides, is taken away before there is any transfer of ownership, either expressed or implied; such a case arises in succession to one who dies intestate. If, therefore, a person dies without having given any indication of his will and without leaving any blood relative, all the rights which he possessed are extinguished. In consequence, unless some human law prevents, his slaves will be free, and peoples that had been subject to his sway will become independent, because from their very nature such things cannot be acquired by possession unless they voluntarily yield their liberty. Other possessions of the deceased, however, will become the property of the first one who takes possession.

II.—*Similarly the rights of a family are extinguished when the family dies out*

The same rule is to be applied in case a family, which possessed certain rights, has become extinct.[1]

III.—*So also the rights of a people are extinguished if the people ceases to exist*

On Peace [cxx = 183 D]. [*Letter to Argives*, p. 411 B, Span. ed.]

1. The result is the same if a people has ceased to exist. Isocrates, and after him the Emperor Julian, said [206] that states are immortal; that is, they can continue to exist because a people

[1] As in former times the Danish family. Krantz, *Vandalica*, VIII. xxiii. Similar examples are the House of Rügen, *op. cit.*, VIII. xii; that of the Pelasgi and Thessalians, Gregoras, VII [VII. xiii. 3]; that of the Usanchanids in Persia, Leunclavius, XVI.

Add Leo of Africa, Book II [p. 252, in edition of the Hakluyt Society], concerning Tarodent, and if you wish, also Ernest Cothmann, *Consilia*, xli, no. 1 and following.

belongs to the class of bodies that are made up of separate members,[1] but are comprehended under a single name, for the reason that they have 'a single essential character', as Plutarch says, or a single spirit, as Paul the jurist says. Now that spirit or 'essential character'[2] in a people is the full and perfect union of civic life, the first product of which is sovereign power; that is the bond which binds the state together, that is the breath of life which so many thousands breathe, as Seneca says. These artificial bodies, moreover, are clearly similar to a natural body; and a natural body, though its particles little by little are changed,[3] does not cease to be the same if the form remains unchanged, as Alfenus argues after the philosophers.

Dig. XLI. iii. 30; [*De Animae Procreatione*, xxv =p.1025C; *Dig.* VI. i. 23. § 5;] Achilles Tatius, *On Aratus*. Seneca, *On Clemency*, I. iv. *Dig.* V. i. 76. *Letters*, lviii [22].

2. And so the statement of Seneca, that no one of us is the same in old age as he was in youth, ought properly to be so interpreted as to be understood only of that which is material. Similarly

[1] Seneca, *Letters*, cii [cii. 6], says: 'Some bodies are of like substance throughout, as man; some are composite, as a ship, a house; and finally all bodies which have been made by joining different parts into a single whole; and other bodies consist of ununited members whose parts are still separate individuals, as an army, a people, or a senate.'

This distinction was borrowed from Achilles Statius [Tatius], *On Aratus* [xiv, Petav. ed.], and his words were taken from Conon, the discoverer of the constellation Coma Berenices:

'The mathematician Conon has observed that things are said to be bodies which consist of a single substance of like essential character. Moreover, this essential element is the spirit, which holds together the body. But composite bodies are those which are not made up of a single element, as a ship or a house, for the one is constructed of many planks and the other of many stones; and there are bodies made up of different elements, as a chorus. But even the latter are of two kinds, differing from each other; for some are made up of particular bodies, whose number it is easy to know, and others consist of unlimited numbers, as the people.'

It is apparent that this is the source of what Pomponius said in a law quoted in the *Digest*, XLI. iii. 30, and of the statement of Paul that a statue is united by a single spirit, *Digest*, VI. i. 23. § 5, where he likewise distinguishes between bodies formed of cohering particles and those made up of separate and distinct particles. Others also have used this distinction, as Philo Judaeus, *On the World* [= *That God is Immutable*, vii]: 'The essential element is a spirit circulating within itself'; and again [=*On the Indestructibility of the World*, xxiv]: 'The essential element is the spiritual bond of union, a tie not incapable of being sundered, but difficult to break.'

See also Boethius, *Arithmetic*, I [I. i], and observe that when we speak of the 'constituting principle' or spirit of a people we do not use the word in its strict sense, as Conon did, but 'analogically', by a sort of comparison such as we use when we call the people a body. Alfenus in the *Digest*, V. i. 76, calls this spirit the form of the thing.

[2] Aristotle in his *Politics*, IV. xi [IV. xi. 3], says: 'Government is the life of the city.'

[3] Alfenus, cited [211] above, gives an example in the case of a ship. Also Ulpian in a law of the *Digest*, VII. iv. 10, remarks: 'They say that the ship is the same if it has been renewed part by part, but that it is a different thing if it has been entirely broken up and rebuilt.' See also *Digest*, XLVI. iii. 98. § 8.

Plutarch in his *Theseus* [xxiii= 10 C] says: 'The ship, equipped with thirty oars, in which Theseus sailed with the chosen youth and returned in safety, was preserved by the Athenians down to the time of Demetrius Phalereus. They removed timbers that were decayed with age and put in others, so that the craft held together. In consequence the ship became a stock illustration for philosophers, engaged in discussing the question of growth, some affirming that the ship was the same up to the end, and others denying it.'

In this case discussed by the philosophers jurists have wisely preferred the affirmative side. Also Tertullian, who was well acquainted with the law, says in his book *On the Resurrection of the Flesh* [lx]: 'We have often observed that a ship, that has been shattered by storm or ruined by decay, is the same after all of its parts have been repaired and restored, even though it boasts of its restoration.' It must be understood that the keel remains, just as the word *resoluta* [error for *dissoluta*, that is, 'entirely broken up'] must be understood in the expression of Paul in the *Digest*, XLV. i. 83. § 5; this is also proved by what precedes in Tertullian and what follows in Paul's statement.

Philo Judaeus, *On the World* [= *On the Indestructibility of the World*, xxvii] says: 'That is not destructible of which the parts gradually perish, but that of which all the parts perish together and at the same time.'

[xix = p. 402 A.] Heraclitus, as cited by Plato in the *Cratylus* and by Seneca in the passage just quoted, said [1] that we do not twice descend the same river. This saying Seneca rightly corrects thus: 'The name of the river remains the same, but the water has been borne along.' Likewise also, in comparing a river to a people, Aristotle said that rivers bear the same name, though different water is always replacing that which is flowing on. Again, it is not an empty name merely that remains, but 'the essential character', which Conon defines as an 'inherent bodily character', Philo as a 'spiritual bond', and the Latins as a spirit.

Politics, III. ii [III. iii].

[Achilles Tatius, *loc. cit.*] [*On the Indestructibility of the World,* xxiv.]. [xv = p. 559 A.]

In this sense, then, as Alfenus, and Plutarch *On the Delayed Vengeance of the Deity*, say, a people is considered the same at this time as it was one hundred years ago, although not one of the men of that time is now alive. A people survives 'so long as that common union, which makes a people and binds it together with mutual bonds, preserves its unity'; such are the words of the same Plutarch in this connexion. Hence arose the custom of speech, that in addressing a people which now is we ascribe to it what happened to the same people many ages ago. This it is possible to observe not only in the historians but also in the Scriptures,[2] as in *Mark* (x. 3), *John* (vi. 32; vii. 19, 22), *Acts* (vii. 38). Thus in Tacitus Antonius Primus serving under Vespasian reminds the soldiers of the third legion of their former exploits, how 'under Marc Antony they had defeated the Parthians, under Corbulo, the Armenians.'

Histories, III [xxiv].

3. As a result of hatred, then, and not in accordance with truth, in the writings of the same Tacitus, Piso says that the Athenians of his time are not Athenians,[3] since these had been destroyed by so many slaughterings, but are the offscouring of the nations. That influx from abroad had perhaps lessened their prestige somewhat, but it had not made them a different people. Piso, in fact, was not unaware of this, since he reproached those very Athenians of his own time with their ancient defeats by the Macedonians and their cruelty to their fellow citizens. But while the change in the individual members does not cause a people to cease to be what it was even for a thousand years or more, yet it cannot be denied that a people may cease to exist. The extinction of a people, moreover, may be brought about in two ways: either by the destruction of the body, or by the destruction of that form or spirit which I have mentioned.

[*Annals,* II. lv.]

IV.—*Such extinction takes place if the essential parts have been destroyed*

A body perishes if the parts without which the body cannot

[1] Also Epicharmus, quoted by Diogenes Laertius [III. xi].

[2] Add *Matthew,* xxiii. 35; *Acts,* iii. 22.

[3] Julian in his *Misopogon* [p. 348 B] speaks to the contrary concerning the same Athenians.

exist have at the same time been destroyed, or if the corporate bond of union has been destroyed.[1]

Under the first type of destruction we must class the engulfing of peoples by the sea, as the peoples of Atlantis mentioned by Plato, and others [2] by Tertullian; likewise the destruction of peoples that an earthquake or a chasm in the earth has swallowed up, of which there are examples in Seneca, Ammianus Marcellinus, and elsewhere; and also of those who have voluntarily destroyed themselves, as the Sidonians and Saguntines. Pliny says that fifty-three [207] peoples of ancient Latium had perished without leaving a trace.

[*Critias*, iii = p. 108 E.] *On the Pallium* [ii = p. 39]. *Letters*, xcii [xci. 9]. *History*, XVII [vii. 13]. Diodorus, *Library*, XVI [xlv. 4 ff.]. [*Nat. Hist.*, III. v. 70.]

What if there are so few survivors of such a people that they cannot constitute a people? It will be possible for the ownership of the property, which the people possessed as private citizens, still to remain in their hands; but not what belonged to the people as a people. The same principle holds true also in regard to a corporation.

Dig. III. iv. 7. § 2; XLIX. xv. 12. § 13.

V.—*The rights of a people are extinguished when the body of the people as a whole is broken up*

The body politic of a people is broken up if by reason of pestilence or rebellion the citizens withdraw from the association of their own accord, or if they are so scattered by force [3] that they cannot unite together again, as sometimes happens in wars.

VI.—*The rights of a people are extinguished when the form of organization, under which the people exists, is destroyed*

A people's form of organization is lost when its entire or full enjoyment of common rights has been taken away. In such cases the individual citizens may also become subject to personal slavery; thus, the people of Mycenae were sold by the Argives, the Olynthians by Philip, the inhabitants of Thebes by Alexander, and the Bruttians were made public slaves by the Romans. Citizens, again, may be deprived of the right of government, though personal liberty is left to them. So Livy tells us that in regard to Capua the Romans decided that it should be inhabited as a city, but that there should be no body politic, no senate, no council of the common people, and no magistrates, but that the population should be without a public assembly and without authority, and that a prefect sent from Rome

Aristotle, *Politics*, III. ii [III. iii]. [Diodorus Siculus, XI. lxv. 5; XVI. liii. 3; XVII. xiv; Aulus Gellius, X. iii. 19.] XXVI [xvi. 9–10].

[1] Servius in the *Fuldensian Excerpts, On the Aeneid*, Book I [I. 70], says: 'An army is destroyed in two ways, either by slaughter or by dispersion.'

[2] Myus, mentioned by Vitruvius [IV. i]; Helice and Buris, by Pausanias [VII. xxv], Strabo [I. iii. 18], Seneca, *Natural Questions*, V. xxiii and xxxii [VI. xxiii and xxxii], and in the *Anthology*.

[3] Philo, in his book *On the World* already quoted [*On the Indestructibility of the World*, xvi], says: 'Bodies, which are made up of separate units, as flocks, herds, choruses, armies, perish by separation and dispersion, just as truly as bodies which are formed of members firmly knit together.' Add what was said above [p. 311, note 3] concerning a ship.

Cicero, *Against Rullus*, I [vi. 19]. Theodoret, *Ecclesiastical History*, V. ix [xx]; Zonaras, *On Valentinian and Theodosius* [XIII. xviii]; Herodian, *Hist.*, V [III. vi. 9]. Florus, II. xv.

should administer justice.[1] And so Cicero in his first speech before the people *Against Rullus* says that not even the shadow of statehood [2] had been left to Capua. The same thing should be said of peoples that have been reduced to the form of a province, and likewise of those that have been subjected to the sway of another people. Thus Byzantium was made subject to Perinthus by Severus,[3] and Antioch to Laodicea [4] by Theodosius.

VII.—*The rights of a people are not extinguished by reason of migration*

If, however, a people has migrated, either of its own accord, because of famine or other misfortunes, or under compulsion, as the people of Carthage did in the third Punic war, the people does not cease to exist,[5] provided the outward form, which I have mentioned, remains; and surely a people does not cease to exist if only the walls of its city have been levelled. And so when the Spartans refused to allow the Messenians to take oath to maintain the peace of Greece, because the walls of their city had been destroyed, the case was decided against them by the common assembly of the allies.

Plutarch, *Agesilaus* [xxxv = 616 A].

VIII.—*Such rights are not extinguished by a change of government; and herein also the question of what is due to a new king or to a liberated people is treated*

1. Furthermore, it makes no difference in what way a people is governed, whether by royal power, or by an aristocracy, or by popular government. The Roman people, in fact, is the same under kings, consuls, and emperors. Nay more, though the king rules with absolute power, the people will be the same as it was before, when it was its own master, provided that the king governs it as the head of that people and not of another. For the sovereign power, which resides in the king as the head, remains in the people as the whole body, of which the head is a part; and so when the king, if elective, has died, or the family of the king has become extinct, the sovereign power reverts to the people, as I have shown above.

Politics, II. iii [III. iii = p. 341].

There is no reason why any one at this point should cite Aristotle against me. Aristotle declares that the state does not remain the same

[1] See Festus, under the word *praefectura* [p. 233 M]; Velleius, II [II. xliv. 4]: 'Their rights were restored to them about 152 years after Capua had been reduced by the Romans to the form of a prefecture in the course of the Punic war.'

Add the illustrations, which are given in the text and notes above, I. iii. 8.

[2] The right to have a senate Severus gave to the Alexandrians, who had lived under the administration of a judge without a public council.

[3] See Xiphilinus, in the life of *Severus* [Dio Cassius, LXXIV. xiv]; Herodian, III [III. vi. 9]. Add what is said below in this book, II. xxi. 7.

[4] [212] See Zonaras [XIII. xviii = II, p. 36 A].

[5] As the inhabitants of Gela were transported to Phintias; Diodorus Siculus, in the *Excerpta Peiresciana* [= XXII. ii. 2].

when the form of government is changed; just as a melody, he says, does not remain the same when it is transposed from the Dorian to the Phrygian mode.

2. We must, in fact, recognize that there may be several forms of a single artificial thing, as in a legion there is one form of organization through which it is governed, and another by means of which it fights. Thus one form of the state is the association of law and government, another the relation to each other of those parts which rule and are ruled. The political scientist has under consideration the latter, the jurist the former. And this did not escape the notice of Aristotle, when he added: 'But whether, after a change in the form of government, the debts ought to be paid or not, is another question.' That is, the question of payment of debts belongs to a different science, which Aristotle does not confuse with political science, lest he should himself commit the fault which he censures in others, 'of jumping from one subject of discussion to another.' [*Politics*, III. iii.]

3. A people by making itself subject to a king does not [208] cease to owe the money which it owed when free. For it is the same people, and it retains its ownership of all public property; it even retains its sovereignty over itself, although this must now be exercised not by the body, but by the head.

From this principle is derived the answer to the question sometimes actually raised as to the place which ought to be occupied in assemblies by one who has acquired the sovereignty over a people previously free. Of course he is entitled to the same place which the people itself had occupied. Thus in the Amphictyonic Council Philip of Macedon received the place of the Phoceans. In like manner a free people will take the place which had belonged to their king.

IX.—*What becomes of such rights if peoples are joined together?*

Whenever two peoples are united,[1] their rights will not be lost but will be shared in common. Thus the rights first of the Sabines, and then of the Albans, were taken over by the Romans, and the peoples were made into a single state, as Livy says. The same principle should be applied in the case of kingdoms which are united not by treaty or by the fact merely that they have a king in common, but in a true union. I [xiii. 5 ff.; xxviii. 7; xxx. 1 f.]

X.—*What becomes of such rights if a people is divided?*

On the contrary, it may happen that what had been a single state may be divided, either by mutual consent or by the violence

[1] As the Celtiberians were formed from the Celts and the Iberians, according to Diodorus Siculus [V. xxxiii. 2]. If you have leisure, on this subject, see Reinkingk, I, class IV, xvii, no. 95, and the citations there made.

of war, as the Persian Empire was divided among the successors of Alexander. When such a division takes place several sovereignties exist in the place of one, with their respective rights over the individual parts. In such cases, whatever common property there was will have to be either administered in common, or divided *pro rata*.

The same reasoning must apply also in the separation of a people which occurs by mutual consent in sending out colonies. For thus also a new people arises, possessed of its own rights. The colonists, in fact, are not sent out as slaves, but possessed of equal rights,[1] as
I [xxxiv; xxvii]. Thucydides says. The same author relates that the Corinthians sent a second colony to Epidamnus with equal rights. According to
III [xi. 1]. Dionysius of Halicarnassus, king Tullus said: 'We think it neither true nor just that mother cities should rule their colonies as if by the law of nature.'

XI.—*Who is now possessor of the rights which once belonged to the Roman Empire, in so far as they do not appear to have been alienated?*

1. Among historians and jurists there is also the notable question, who is now the possessor of those rights which once belonged to the Roman Empire. Many hold that these now belong to the kingdom of Germany as it was formerly called, or the Empire (it makes no difference by what name you call it); and they imagine some sort of a substitution of the latter empire in the place of the former, although it is nevertheless well known that Great Germany, or Germany beyond the Rhine, was outside the territory of the Roman Empire during the most of its existence.

It seems to me that a changing over or transfer ought not to be assumed, unless it is supported by sure proofs. I say, therefore, that the Roman people is the same that it formerly was, although mingled with an increment of foreigners, and that the empire has remained within it as if in the body in which it once existed and lived. For whatever the Roman people in former times could rightfully do, before the emperors ruled, it had the same right to do after each emperor had died, and so long as there was not yet a successor. Besides, the election of the emperor belonged to the people, and was sometimes made by the people in person, or through the senate.[2]

[1] Nevertheless the respect due to the parent city, of which I have treated in I. iii. 21, should be preserved. Cf. Curtius, IV [IV. ii. 10]: 'The Tyrians founded Carthage and were always cherished as parents.'

[2] Examples are commonly found of elections made or ratified by the senate, as of Hadrian, Pertinax, Julian, Severus, Macrinus, Maximinus, Balbinus, Aurelian, Tacitus, Florian, Probus, mentioned by Dio Cassius, Spartianus, Capitolinus, Lampridius, and Vopiscus.

Before Aurelian the Empire was without a head for six months and the soldiers urged the senate again and again to make a choice. In Capitolinus [Scriptores Historiae Augustae, *Albinus*, xiii] there

Moreover, the elections, which were made by different groups of legions, were not rendered valid by the right of the legions (for there could not be any sure right in an empty name) but by [209] the approval of the people.

2. The fact that all the inhabitants of the Roman Empire were made Roman citizens by the constitution of Antoninus is not inconsistent with this view. By that constitution the subjects of the Roman Empire, in fact, obtained the rights which formerly the Roman colonies, municipal towns, and provinces had possessed, so that they both shared the honours and enjoyed the rights of Roman citizens. But the source of sovereign power [1] did not reside in the other peoples in the same way as in the people of the city of Rome. This it was not in the power of the emperors to confer; they were, in fact, unable to change the mode and basis of holding the sovereign power.

The right of the Roman people was in no degree diminished by the fact that afterward the emperors preferred to reside in Constantinople rather than in Rome. But even then the whole people had to ratify the election made by the part which lived in Constantinople; and for this reason Claudian called the Byzantines Roman citizens. [*Against Eutropius*, II. 136]. The Roman people furthermore kept a far from unimportant survival of its right in the pre-eminence of the city,[2] the distinction of the consulship,[3] and other privileges. Therefore

is a noteworthy letter [speech] of Albinus on the rights of the senate, and a letter of the senate in behalf of the Gordiani [*Maximini*, xv]. Macrinus [*Macrinus*, vi. 5 f.] says in a speech: 'They have conferred the imperial power upon me. I accept the defence of it for the time being, conscript fathers, and I shall retain the sovereignty, if you also shall ratify what the soldiers have voted.'

Tacitus, the Emperor, says in Vopiscus' life of Probus [Scriptores Historiae Augustae, *Probus*, vii]: 'The senate, in fact, has made me emperor in accordance with the wise choice of the army.' According to the same Vopiscus [*ibid.*, xi] Probus says: 'The action taken last year, Senators, was lawful and in due form, with the result that your kindly choice gave to the world an emperor, and indeed from among you, who are and always have been the rulers of the world, and so will be to your latest descendants.' Majorinus [Majorianus] says to the senate in the *Novels* [IV. iii]: 'Senators, know that I have been made emperor by the choice of your election and by the proclamation of the invincible army.'

[1] According to Herodian [VII. vii. 5] the senate urges the provinces in behalf of Gordian 'to obey the Romans, who have possessed the sovereignty from ancient times, to whom by ancient right the other nations manifest love and obedience.'

In the same author [VIII. vii. 5] Maximus says in an address to the soldiers: 'For this Empire is not the property of a single person but from ancient times the common possession of the Roman people. In this city the fortune of the principate has been placed; but I have been chosen along with you, soldiers, that we may care for and protect whatsoever belongs to the Empire.' Claudian says of Rome [*On the Consulship of Stilicho*, III. 136 f.]:

Parent of arms and laws, that over all
Her sway extends.

[2] Zonaras says [XIII. iii] that 'pre-eminence' was preserved at Rome, because from that place the Empire had extended. Ammianus in his fourteenth book [XIV. vi. 6] says of Rome: 'Nevertheless by all the parts of the Empire, however many in number, she is looked upon as mistress and queen.' Claudian [*On the Sixth Consulship of Honorius*, 407–8] says of Honorius, residing at Ravenna:

How long, I pray, shall power from home be exiled,
And sovereignty from its own borders wander?

[3] For one of the consuls was from the city of Rome, and he took precedence of the other; Procopius, *Secret History* [xxvi].

whatever right the inhabitants of Constantinople could have had in choosing a Roman emperor was dependent on the will of the Roman people. To pass by other considerations when, contrary to the will and custom of the Roman people [1], the inhabitants of Constantinople had submitted to the rule of a woman, Irene,[2] the Roman people very properly revoked its expressed or implied acceptance and independently chose an emperor and proclaimed his election by the utterance of the first citizen, that is, the bishop. Such was the procedure also in the Jewish state; when there was no king, the person of the high priest ranked first.

3. This election, moreover, was personal in the case of Charlemagne and certain of his successors, who carefully distinguished the right of sovereignty which they had over the Franks and also over the Lombards from the right of sovereignty which they had over the Romans, as if this had been acquired on new grounds.[3] Later, to be sure, the Franks were divided into the western Franks, who now possess France, and the eastern, who hold Germany or Alemania [4]; for they were called the two kingdoms of the Franks by Otto of Freising. When now the eastern Franks had begun to choose their kings by election (for up to this time the succession of the Frankish kings, though implying agnate succession, had not depended so much on fixed rights as on the choice by the people),[5] the Roman people decided not to choose its own king, but to accept the king whom the Germans had elected, in order that it might have a more dependable assurance of protection. Nevertheless it did reserve for itself a measure of right to approve or disapprove of the election, in so far as this affected the Roman people.[6]

4. Such approval, furthermore, was customarily proclaimed by the bishop and solemnly attested by a special coronation. In con-

[1] [213] Nero in the fourteenth book of the *Annals* of Tacitus [XIV. xi] brings charges against his mother, 'because she had hoped for a share in the government, and that the pretorian cohorts would take the oath of allegiance to a woman, which would be a disgrace to senate and people'. Priscus says in the *Selections on Embassies* [*Byz. Corpus*, vol. XIV, p. 151]: 'The principate of the Roman Empire belongs not to women but to men.'

Lampridius says after the death of Elagabalus [Scriptores Historiae Augustae, *Heliogabalus*, xviii. 3]: 'Every precaution was taken that a woman should never enter the senate and that the life of the man who should accomplish such an act should be consecrated and devoted to the gods of the underworld.' Trebellius Pollio [*idem, Thirty Tyrants*, xxvii] says to Herennianus [Herennius]: 'Zenobia, having usurped the sovereign power, held control of the state longer than was fitting for a woman.'

[2] They took oath to her, as Zonaras says [XV. xi= II, 117 B].

[3] See the Council of Pont-Yon in the *Capitularies* of Charles the Bald [*Monumenta Germaniae Historica, Leges*, I, 532]. Also Paolo Emilio, Book III, on Charlemagne.

[4] See Wittekind, Book I, and the notes of Meibom, as also the treaty between Charles and Henry according to the *Capitularies* of Charles the Bald, with the notes of the very wise and learned man, Jacques Sirmond. Wipo calls the western part of the kingdom of the Franks the Latin kingdom, because a romance tongue was in use there, as it is to-day also, while the nations across the Rhine used the German language.

[5] This was noted by Priscus in the *Selections on Embassies* (=*Byz. Corp.*, vol. XIV, p. 152) and by Regino on the year 816. See the will of Charlemagne: 'Now if any one of these three sons should have a son.'

[6] This is an absolute fact, openly attested by Wipo in the life of Conrad Salicus.

sequence the one that has been chosen as king by the seven electors who represent the whole of Germany has the right to rule the Germans in accordance with their customs; but it is by the approval of the Roman people that the same king becomes the Roman king or Roman emperor, or, as historians often style him, king of the kingdom of Italy.[1] Under that title he holds subject to his sway all possessions that belonged to the Roman people, in so far as these have not passed under the rule of other peoples by treaties, or by occupation of abandoned territory, or by right of conquest.

From this it can easily be understood also by what right, in the case of a vacancy in the Empire, the Bishop of Rome assigns investitures of fiefs of the Roman Empire.[2] The reason is that he holds the primacy among the Roman people who are at such a time free. The business of a corporate body is ordinarily administered in the name of that body by its leading person,[3] as I have said elsewhere. In fact [210] the principle laid down by Cynus and Rayner that, if the Roman Emperor is prevented from discharging the duties of his office by disease or captivity, a substitute can be appointed for him by the Roman people itself, is by no means unsound.

XII.—*Concerning the rights of heirs*

It is a clear legal principle that the person of the heir is considered the same as the person of the deceased in all that concerns the continuation of ownership of both public and private property.

XIII.—*Concerning the rights of the conqueror*

In what degree the conqueror succeeds to the rights of the conquered will be discussed below, in treating the effects of war.

[1] Thus the Pope in the excommunication of Henry expressly names the kingdom of the Germans and of Italy. See Otto's privilegium granted by Alderamus as published by Meibom after the *Saxonica* of Wittekind. See also Krantz, *Saxonica*, V [V. xiii], on the oath of Otto, which Gratian cites, *Decretum*, I. lxiii [I. lxiii. 33]: 'I will make no decree or order in Rome about all the matters which belong to you (the Pope) and to the Roman people, without your advice.'

[2] Just as in the German Empire the Elector Palatine and the Elector of Saxony are substitutes for the Emperor in separate parts of the realm. See De Serres, *Life of Louis XII* [p. 505, ed. 1627].

[3] Also in Poland during an interregnum 'the Archbishop of Gnesen takes the place of the king' and 'sits on the royal seat', as if first among the orders; Philip Honorius in the dissertation *On the Kingdom of Poland* [of Horatius Spanorchius, in Honorius' *Thesaurus Politicus*, 1617 ed., p. 430].

[214] CHAPTER X

ON THE OBLIGATION WHICH ARISES FROM OWNERSHIP

I.—*The origin and nature of the obligation to restore the property of another to its owner*

1. Having explained, so far as our purpose requires, the right which belongs to us over persons or over things, we must see also what obligation in consequence rests upon us. Such obligation, moreover, arises either from things which exist or from things which do not exist. Under the term things I shall now include persons, so far as may be convenient for us.

2. From things which exist there arises the obligation by which a person, who has property of mine in his possession, is bound to do what he can to restore it to my control.[1] He is bound, I say, to do what he can; for there is no obligation to do what is impossible, or even to return the property at his own expense. The possessor is, however, under obligation to make the possession known, in order that the other may recover his own. Just as, in the state of community ownership, a certain equality had to be observed, that one might have the use of the common property as well as another, so after the introduction of property ownership a kind of mutual arrangement was entered into between owners, that one who had another's pro-

[1] Among the positive commands of the law given to the Jews is this, that a thing which has been found should be restored to its owner. *Precepts Bidding*, 74. This is based not only on natural justice [218] but also on *Deuteronomy*, xxii. 1. Chrysostom, *On First Corinthians*, v. 8 [Homily XV, v], says: 'Even the laws of this world, which constitute right for all except the plunderer and the thief, approve of our demanding our possessions from those who have them, no matter of what sort they are.' Jerome [Origen], *On Leviticus* [vi, Homily IV], says: 'Many think that they are free from sin if they retain property of another which they have found; and they say, "God gave it to me; to whom do I have to return it?" They should know that this sin is similar to robbery, if one does not return a thing found.'

Augustine, in his *On the Words of the Apostle*, XIX [=*Sermones de Scripturis*, clxxviii. 9], says: 'If you have found anything and have not returned it, you have stolen it.' Later he adds: 'The one who refuses to return another's property would also steal it, if he could.' Gratian has cited both these passages in *Decretum*, II. xiv. 5 [II. xiv. 5. 6]. Augustine, *On Faith and Works* [vii], likewise says: 'Just as by the law of real property a man is very properly called the rightful possessor so long as he is in ignorance that he is in possession of another's estate, but when he has found this out and has not withdrawn from the other's property, then he will be accounted a possessor in bad faith, then will he justly be called an unjust possessor.' This point is covered also in the *Law of the Visigoths*, IX. i. 9. Sometimes for grave reasons municipal law expands and increases this obligation, as the *Law of the Burgundians* (I. vi) in the case of a runaway slave.

Property which Domitian had unjustly taken from the owners, Nerva ordered to be restored; this is recorded by Xiphilinus [*Nerva*, 227=Dio Cassius, LXVIII. ii]. According to Procopius, *Gothic War*, II [II. vi], Belisarius says: 'I at any rate think that the person who willingly retains another's property and does not restore it is in the same class with the thief.'

perty in his possession should restore it to the owner. If, in fact, the force of ownership had been limited to this, that property should be restored to the owner only on demand, the right of ownership would have been too weak, and the protection of property too expensive.

3. No consideration is here given to the question, whether a person has obtained possession of the property honestly or dishonestly; for the obligation arising from a wrong is one thing, and that from possession of property another. The Lacedaemonians cleared themselves from the crime of Phoebidas, who contrary to the treaty had captured the Cadmeia, the citadel of Thebes, by condemning him; but they were themselves accused of injustice[1] because they nevertheless kept possession of the citadel. Xenophon remarks that this outstanding act of injustice was punished by a special divine providence. So Cicero accused Marcus Crassus and Quintus Hortensius because they had retained their shares of an inheritance in accordance with a will which had been forged, though they were not to blame for the forgery.

Diodorus, XV [xx.2] Plutarch, *Pelopidas* [v=280 B]. *On the Training of Cyrus*, V [*Greek History*, V. iv. 1]. *On Duties*, III [xviii. 73].

4. Now inasmuch as this obligation is binding upon all men, as if by a universal agreement, and creates a certain right for the owner of property, the result follows that individual agreements, as being later in point of time, are thereby restricted. This throws light on the passage of Tryphoninus:

Digest, XVI. iii. 31. § 1.

> Property stolen from me was deposited by a robber with Seius, who was ignorant of the crime of the depositor. Ought Seius to restore the property to the robber, or to me? If we take into account only the depositor and the recipient, good faith requires that the depositor receive the property which he has deposited. If we consider the equity of the whole matter, which includes all the persons having an interest in the transaction, [215] the property must be restored to me, from whom it was most wrongfully stolen.

He rightly adds:

> And I agree that that is justice which gives to each man his own in such a way that it is not taken away from him in response to a more just demand of any other person.

Beyond doubt the demand of the owner is more just according to that right which we have said is as old as ownership itself. And from this is derived the following rule, which is found in the same Tryphoninus, that a person, who in ignorance has accepted his own property on deposit, is not bound to return it. Furthermore the question raised by the same author a little previously in regard to goods deposited by a person whose property has been confiscated must be decided in accordance with the principle stated rather

[1] So Diodorus judges, Book XV [XV. xx] Plutarch in his *Agesilaus* [xxiii=609 B] says: 'He persuaded the state to transfer the blame to itself by retaining the Cadmean citadel.' Similar was the deed of Bayezid in regard to Nicopolis, recorded by Leunclavius, Book VI.

than according to what Tryphoninus says about the utility of punishments.

5. As regards the nature of ownership, it makes no difference whether ownership arises from the universal principles of law or from the law of a particular country. Ownership, in fact, always carries with it its natural implications, and among these is the obligation on the part of every possessor to restore property to its owner. This is affirmed by Marcianus when he says 'that by universal principles of law suit can be entered for property against those who possess it wrongfully.' From this source arises the rule laid down by Ulpian, that the finder of another's property is under such obligation to return it to the owner that he is not even to ask 'a reward' for finding it. Moreover, the income of the property also should be restored, after deducting expenses.

Digest, XXV. ii. 25.

Digest, XLVII. ii. 43. § 9.

II.—*The obligation to restore any gain that a person has made from another's property; this is illustrated by many examples*

Cajetan, *On II. ii.*, 62, art. 6; *Dig.* V. iii. 20. § 6.

1. As regards property no longer in existence, mankind has adopted this rule, that if you have been made richer through possession of my property, while I did not have possession of it, you are under obligation to the extent that you have been enriched. The reason is that in the degree that you have been enriched from my property you have more while I have less. Now property ownership was introduced for the purpose of preserving equality to this end, in fact, that each should have his own. 'It is contrary to nature', says Cicero, 'that a man should increase his own advantage to the disadvantage of another man.'[1] In another passage he adds: 'Nature does not suffer this, that we should increase our means, riches, and resources from the spoils of others.'

On Duties, III [v. 21 and 22].

Dig. L. xvii. 206, and the commentators thereon.

2. So great is the justice of this maxim, that in accordance with it jurists decide many cases outside the narrow purview of the laws, always appealing to it as most obviously fair. A man who has placed a servant in charge of business is bound by the act of the servant, unless he has given warning that the servant should not be trusted; but even though such a warning has been given, in case the servant has made personal gain under an agreement, or it has been turned to the profit of the master, action for fraud will be admissible. 'The man who seeks gain from another's loss', says Proculus, 'seems to act with fraudulent intent,' and in this connexion the word fraudulent includes everything which is contrary to natural law and equity.

Digest, XIV. iii. 17. § 4.

[1] Cassiodorus, [*Variae*,] X. xvi, says: 'In our times we consider it a hostile act for one to rejoice in the misfortune of another.'

If at the mother's request a person has given bail for the defender of her son, he has no right of action against the defender under the agreement, nor has he, properly speaking, acted on behalf of the defender, because he furnished bail out of consideration for the mother. Nevertheless, according to the view of Papinian, such a person will *Digest,* have right of action (in equity, unless I am mistaken) against the XVI. i. 7. defender for services rendered, because the defender was freed by the money of the bondsman.

Similarly a wife, who has given to her husband money, which she could collect by law, is entitled to a civil action for restitution, or an action in equity for the thing purchased with the money; for, says Ulpian, it cannot be denied that the husband is richer in con- *Digest,* sequence, and the question is what of his wife's property he has in XXIV. i. 55. his possession.

If you have spent money, which my slave stole from me, thinking that it was his, I am entitled to an action for recovery against you on that account, just as if my property had come into your possession without a legal title. *Digest,* XIX. i. 30. pr.

According to the Roman law wards are not bound to repay loans; nevertheless an action in equity will lie if the ward has thereby *Digest,* become richer. Again, if a debtor has pawned another's property XIII. vi. 3. and the creditor has sold it, the debtor is released, as regards his debt to the creditor, to the amount of the price received. The reason is, Tryphoninus says, that no matter what [216] the obliga- *Digest,* tion is, it is more just that the price received through the instru- XX. v. 12. § 1. mentality of the debtor should profit him than bring gain to the creditor. The debtor, however, will be liable to the purchaser, that he may not seek gain for himself from another's loss. For even if the creditor had received from the possessor income in excess of interest, he would be under obligation to place all the excess income to the debtor's credit.

Similarly, if you have had dealings with my debtor, thinking that he was in debt to another and not to me, and have borrowed money from him, this you are bound to pay to me, not because I have loaned the money to you (for such a transaction could not be consummated except between parties to an agreement), but because it is fair and right that my money, which has come into *Dig.* XII. your possession, should be restored to me. i. 32.

3. The later jurists rightly extend these principles to analogous cases. For example, a man, whose goods have been sold on his non- Accursius, appearance, is entitled to the money received from his property, on *On Dig.,* XX. v. 12. properly filing an exception to the action. Another case is that Jason, *On* a person who has loaned money to a father for the purpose of sup- *Dig.,* XII. porting a son, in case the father had become insolvent, would have i. 32.

the right of action against the son, when the son should have possession of his mother's property.

If the two rules stated have been rightly understood, it will not be difficult to reply to the questions which are commonly raised by jurists and by theologians who lay down rules for the tribunal of conscience.

Soto, IV. vii, art. 2; Covarruvias, *On Sext*, V. ult. 4, pt. ii, § 1; Sylvester, word *restitutio*, no. 3, qu. 6; Medina, *De Contractibus*, qu. 10; Lessius, II. xiv; Navarrus, xvii, no. 7.

III.—*That a person who has honestly come into possession of another's property is not bound to make restitution, if the property has perished*

In the first place it is clear that a person who is honestly in possession of a thing does not have to make restitution if the thing has perished. In such a case the thing itself is not in his possession, and he has not received gain from it. The dishonest possessor will be liable for his own wrongdoing in addition to accounting for the property.

IV.—*That such a possessor of another's property is bound to restore the income that still remains*

Secondly, a possessor in good faith is bound to restore any income of the property that still remains. I speak of income from the property; for the income from the possessor's industry is not due to the property, even if it could not be obtained without the property. The reason for this obligation arises from ownership. For the person who is the owner of a thing is likewise naturally the owner of the income derived from it.

V.—*That such a possessor is likewise bound to make good the income which has been used up, if under other circumstances he would have used an equivalent*

Thirdly, the possessor in good faith is bound to make restitution for the property and its income that have been used up, provided that he would have used just as much under other conditions. For in that degree he is judged to be richer. Thus in the beginning of his reign Gaius Caesar Caligula receives praise because to those to whom he restored their kingdoms he paid the income of the intervening period.

Suetonius, [*Caligula*,] xvi.

VI.—*That such a possessor is not bound to restore income which he neglected to collect*

Fourthly, a person in possession of such property is not liable for income from it which he has neglected to collect; for he owns neither the property nor anything in place of it.

VII.—*That such a possessor is not bound to make restitution of the property which he has given to another; herewith a distinction*

Fifthly, if such a possessor has given to another a thing which was given to himself, he is not liable for it, unless he would have given the same amount in any case, if he had not had this; for in that case the sparing of his own property will be considered as a gain.

VIII.—*That such a possessor, again, is not under obligation if he has sold a thing which he has bought; likewise herewith a distinction*

Sixthly, if such a possessor has sold property which he bought, he is not bound to make restitution except in so far as he may have sold it at a higher price. If he has sold property which was given to him, he is bound to restore the value, unless he has squandered the amount which he would not otherwise have wasted.

Digest, XLVII. ii. 48. § 7. *Dig.* V. iii. 22 and 25. *Dig.* XII. i. 23.

IX.—*When a person, who in good faith has bought property of another, can reserve the cost, or a part thereof*

1. Seventhly, another man's property, though bought in good faith, must be restored, and the price which it cost cannot be demanded back. This rule, it seems to me, ought to be qualified with the proviso, 'except in so far as the owner in all probability could not have recovered possession of his property without some expenditure,' as, for example, if the property was in the hands of pirates.[1] In such a case, then, whatever amount the owner would willingly have expended can be deducted. Actual possession, in fact, especially of an object difficult to recover, can be reckoned in terms of value. In this respect, therefore, the owner is considered to have been made richer than he was after the loss of the thing.

Code, III. xxxii. 3 and 23; *Digest*, XVIII. i. 16; XXI. ii. 1; XIV. ii. 2. § 3; Aegidius Regius, disp. 31, dub. 7, no. 126; Hostiensis, *On Decretals*, V. xxxviii, verse *Quid de praedam ementibus*.

Consequently, although in ordinary legal usage the purchase of one's own property [217] is not valid, yet Paul the jurist says that it is valid if from the beginning the agreement is that the actual possession, which is lodged with a second party, is being bought. I do not here make the requirement that the thing should have been

Digest, XVIII. i. 34.

[1] The following stands in Terence, *Self-tormentor*, Act IV, sc. v [IV. v. 42 ff.]:

> But what I said to you
> About the money which she owes to Bacchis,
> This must be paid to her at once. Nor will you shirk
> Indeed with this excuse, 'What matters it to me?
> Then was it paid to me? Did I command? Or could
> She pawn my daughter 'gainst my will?' That which they say
> Is true, Chremes: 'The strictest law is oft the deepest wrong.'

On this see also Eugraphius. Such justice is also approved by the Jewish Rabbis and by the *Law of the Visigoths*, I. ix. 9 and 15. Alciati, *Praetermissa*, III. xxix; Menochio, *De Praesumptionibus*, V. xxix, no. 26; Straccha, pt. II, no. 18.

bought with the intention of restoring it to the owner,[1] for some say that in such a case there arises a right of action for services rendered, though this is denied by others. The right of action for services rendered, in fact, arises from the civil law; it contains none of those basic elements by virtue of which nature imposes an obligation. But we are here trying to find out what the law of nature is.

Baldus and Castrensis, *On Dig.*, XXXV. v. 1.

2. Similar is what Ulpian wrote about funeral expenses, that in this matter a just judge does not merely have in view the action for services rendered, but rather freely follows equity, since such a course is permitted to him by the nature of the action. Similar, likewise, is the statement made elsewhere by the same authority, that if any one has carried on my business without regard for my interest, but for the sake of his own gain, and has incurred some expense in transacting my business, he has a right of action, not indeed for what he has expended, but for the amount by which I am made richer. Thus also, in fact, the owners of goods, which have been thrown overboard to lighten a ship, recover a part of the value from the others whose property was saved by the lightening. The reason is that the person who has saved property that otherwise was about to perish seems in this respect to be made richer.

Dig. XI. vii. 14. § 12; Balsamom, on canon x of Gregory Thaumaturgus. *Digest*, III. v. 6. § 3. Cajetan, *On II. ii.*, 62. 6; Soto, IV. vii, art. 2; Covarruvias, *On Sext*, V. ult. 4, pt. II; *Digest*, XIV. ii. 1.

X.—*That purchased goods, if they belong to another, cannot rightfully be returned to the seller*

Eighthly, the person who from one man has bought property belonging to another cannot return it to the seller, in order to save the purchase price; for the obligation of restoring it to the owner commenced at the moment when the object came into his possession.

XI.—*That a person who has in his possession property of which the owner is unknown is not bound to turn it over to any one*

Ninthly, the man who has in his possession property of unknown ownership is not obliged by the law of nature to give it to the poor, although this is a very noble act,[2] and such procedure is rightly established as a law in many places. The reason for this is that according to the principle of ownership no one except the owner has any right to the property. But non-existence of an owner, and not knowing who the owner is, amount to the same thing, so far as the man who does not know the owner is concerned.

[1] *Speculum Saxonicum*, II. xxxvii; *Landrecht*, tit. xv.
[2] Chrysostom, passage cited [*On First Corinthians*, v. 8=Homily XV, v].

XII.—*That according to the law of nature money received for a shameful cause, or under other circumstances for an act which one is under obligation to perform, does not have to be restored*

Tenthly, by the law of nature whatever a person has received for a shameful cause, or for an honourable service which it was his duty to perform, does not have to be restored. Yet such a rule has been introduced, not undeservedly, by certain laws. The reason is that no one is bound to render account for property unless it belongs to another. But in the case under consideration the ownership passed with the consent of the former owner.

Thomas, II. ii. 62, art. 5, ad 2; Cajetan thereon. Covarruvias, *On Sext*, V. ult. 4, pt. II, § 2. *I Samuel*, xii. 5, 6.

The case will be different if there was illegality in the method of receiving the money, as, for example, by extortion.[1] That, in fact, involves a different principle of obligation, with which I am not here concerned.

XIII.—*Refutation of the opinion that ownership of goods which are weighed, counted, or measured, changes without the consent of the owner*

Let us add also this, which has been incorrectly asserted by Medina, that the ownership of another's property can pass to us without the consent of the owner if the things are such as are ordinarily reckoned by weight, number, and measure. For it is said that things of this kind admit of substitution, that is, that they can be replaced by that which is of the same kind. Even in this case, however, such use can be made only if consent has preceded, or may be presumed from law or custom to have preceded, as in the case of a loan; or if the thing cannot be given back because it has been consumed. But such a substitution of an equivalent does not take place without consent, expressed or implied, or in the case of necessity.

De Restitutione, qu. 10.

Dig. XII. i. 11. § 2.

[1] Augustine, *Letters*, liv [cliii. 21 ff., ed. Benedict.], has well made this distinction.

[219]

CHAPTER XI

ON PROMISES

I.—*Refutation of the opinion that by the law of nature a right does not arise from promises*

1. The order of our work has brought us to the obligation which arises from promises. Here we find ourselves at once opposed to François de Connan, a man of exceptional learning. For he main-
I. vi ; V. i. tains the opinion that according to the law of nature, as well as the law of nations, no obligation is created by those agreements which do not contain an exchange of considerations ; that nevertheless such agreements are honourably carried out if only the matter is of such a nature that it would have been honourable and consistent with some other virtue to fulfil them even without the promise.

2. Furthermore in support of his opinion he brings forward not only the statements of jurists but also these reasons, that the individual, who rashly believes a person that makes a promise without any reason for it, is not less at fault than the person who has made a worthless promise ; then, that the fortunes of all would be greatly imperilled if men should be bound by a mere promise, which proceeds often from the love of display rather than from a purpose, or from a purpose, indeed, but a trivial and ill-considered purpose ; finally, that it is just to leave something to the honesty of each person and not to exact fulfilment according to the necessity of an obligation ; that it is disgraceful not to fulfil promises, not because the act is unjust, but because it reveals the worthlessness of the promise.
[*On Duties*, I. x. 32.] He cites also the testimony of Cicero, who said that promises ought not to be kept if they are of no advantage to those to whom you have made the promise, or if they are more harmful to you than they are advantageous to him to whom you made the promise.

If, however, freedom of action is no longer possible, Connan thinks that there is due to a man not the thing which was promised, but only what is to his interest ; that, for the rest, the force which agreements have they do not derive from themselves but from the contracts in which they are contained or to which they are added, or from the delivery of the property ; and that under such conditions on the one side actions lie and on the other exceptions are filed and recovery forbidden. Those agreements, in truth, which have the force of an obligation according to the laws, such as those containing stipulations, and certain others, derive [220] their force from the beneficence of the laws, which have the effect of rendering obligatory that which in itself is only honourable.

3. Now this opinion, in the general terms in which it is stated by Connan, cannot stand. For, first, it follows therefrom that agreements between kings and different peoples have no force so long as no part of such agreements has been carried out, especially in the regions where no set form of treaties or guaranteed engagements exists. Again, no reason can, in fact, be found why laws, which are a sort of common agreement of the people and are so characterized by Aristotle and Demosthenes, should be able to add the force of an obligation to agreements, while the desire of each individual striving in every way to bind himself is unable to add such force, especially in cases where the civil law offers no impediment. *Rhetoric,* I. xv. [*Against Aristogeiton,* XXV. 16 = p. 774.]

There is the further fact that ownership of property can be transferred by an act of will which is sufficiently manifest, as we have said above. *Digest,* I. iii. 2. [II. vi. 1.] Why then, since we have equal right over our actions and over our property, may there not be transferred to a person also the right to transfer ownership (this right is less than ownership itself) or the right to do something?

4. To these considerations we must add the accordant opinion of wise men.[1] For just as the jurists say, that nothing is so in accord with the law of nature as that the wish of the owner should be held valid when he desires to transfer his property to another, *Institutes,* II. i. § 40. in like manner it is said that nothing is so in harmony with the good faith of mankind as that persons should keep the agreements which they have made with one another. *Dig.* II. xiv. i. Thus the edict concerning a promised payment of money, when on the part of the person who made the promise no cause for the debt except the agreement had preceded, is said to agree with natural justice. *Digest,* XIII. v. 1. Paul the jurist also says that 'the man who according to the law of nations ought to pay, and on whose good faith we have relied'—and here the word 'ought' implies a kind of moral necessity—'is indebted by the law of nature'. *Dig.* L. xvii. 84. § 1.

Furthermore, that is not to be admitted which Connan says, that we are considered to have relied on one's good faith only when action according to the agreement has commenced. For in that passage Paul was treating of an action to recover money wrongfully paid, which is void if the money was paid in accordance with any agreement whatsoever, for the reason that both according to the law of nature and according to the law of nations the obligation to pay existed before any payment was made, though the civil law, in order to remove occasions for lawsuits, did not furnish support.

[1] The Hebrew jurists go as far as to say that in a matter not admitting of delay silence has the force of an agreement (*Baba Kama,* x. 4).

On Duties, I [vii. 23]. [*Odes*, I. xxiv. 6 f.] *On Plato* [II. vii]. Plato, *Republic*, I [v = p. 331 C, D].

5. Cicero, moreover, in his treatise *On Duties*, attributed to promises such force that he calls good faith the foundation of justice. Horace calls her the sister of justice, while the Platonists often designate justice by the Greek word meaning 'truth', which Apuleius has translated 'fidelity'. Simonides, in fact, explained that justice consists not only in returning what had been received but also in speaking the truth.

6. Now in order that the matter may be properly understood, we ought carefully to distinguish the three ways of speaking concerning things yet to come, which either are under our control, or, according to our expectation, soon will be.

II.—*That bare assertion does not create a binding obligation*

The first of these three modes of speech is an assertion, setting forth a present intention concerning something in the future. That this assertion may be free from fault, the true expression of the opinion held at present is required, but not the continuance of that opinion. The human mind, in fact, has not only a natural power, but also a right, to change its opinion. If there is anything wrong in the change of opinion, as at times happens, this is not inherent in the change, but comes from the subject-matter, as, for example, because the first opinion was better.

III.—*That by the law of nature a promise is binding, but that no legal right is thereby gained by another*

In the second mode of speech the intention shapes itself in respect to future time with a sufficient manifestation to show the necessity of continuance. This also may be called a sort of promise, which, without regard to the civil law, is binding either absolutely or under conditions, but [221] gives no right, properly speaking, to the second party. In many cases it happens that a moral obligation rests upon us, but no legal right is acquired by another, just as becomes apparent in the duty of having mercy and showing gratitude; similar to these is the duty of constancy or of good faith. So in the face of such a promise the property of the one promising can be retained, and the promisor cannot be compelled by the law of nature to keep faith.

IV.—*What the kind of promise is by which a second party acquires a legal right*

1. In the third way of making a promise, such a purpose as that just mentioned is manifested by an outward sign of the intent

to confer the due right upon the other party. This is a perfect promise, and has an effect similar to alienation of ownership. It is, in fact, an introduction either to the alienation of a thing or to the alienation of some portion of our freedom of action. To the former category belong promises to give; to the latter, promises to perform.

A noteworthy proof of what I am saying is furnished by the Scriptures, which teach us that God Himself, who cannot be bound by any established law, would act contrary to His nature if He did not make good His promises (*Nehemiah*, ix. 8; *Hebrews*, vi. 18, x. 23; *First Corinthians*, i. 19 [i. 9], x. 13; *First Thessalonians*, v. 24; *Second Thessalonians*, iii. 3; *Second Timothy*, ii. 13).[1] From this it follows that the obligation to perform promises arises from the nature of immutable justice, which in its own fashion is common to God and to all beings possessed of reason. In addition to this there is the judgement of Solomon: *Proverbs*, v. 1 [vi. 1–2].

> My son, if thou art become surety for thy neighbour,
> If thou hast stricken thy hand with a stranger,
> Thou art snared with the words of thy mouth,
> Thou art taken with the words of thy mouth.

Hence a promise is called by the Jews 'a bond', and is compared to a vow (*Numbers*, xxx. 4, 5, 6).[2]

Similar is the origin of the word for promise in Greek, as is noted by Eustathius on the second book of the *Iliad*: 'The one to whom a promise is made in some way captures and binds the promisor.'[3] The thought is also well expressed by Ovid in the second book of the *Metamorphoses*, where the promisor says to the one to whom he has given his promise, 'My word has become yours.' [II. 349.] [II. 51.]

2. With these considerations in mind we shall have no difficulty in replying to the arguments of Connan. For the sayings of the jurists about mere promises have in view the custom introduced by Roman law,[4] which required a formality as the indispensable sign of a deliberate intent. And we do not deny that there are similar laws among other peoples. Seneca, when speaking of human law and a promise not made in proper form,[5] says: 'What law obliges us to perform what we have promised to any one?' *On Benefits*, V. x [V. xxi

[1] So Baldus, *On Digest*, II. xiv. 1.

[2] In offering their vows men bargain, so to speak, with the gods; Scholiast on Horace [*Odes*, III. xxix. 59].

[3] From this they are called the bonds of good faith; Donatus *On the Eunuch* [of Terence, I. ii. 22].

[4] Paul, in his *Sententiae*, Book II. xiv [II. xiv. 1], cautiously says: 'If a bare agreement has been entered into in regard to the interest to be paid, it is of no importance; for among Roman citizens no action arises from a bare agreement.'

[5] That is to say, not by a legally ratified pledge. Thus he distinguishes in his *Letters*, xix [xix. 1]: 'No longer are they promising in regard to you, but they are giving a pledge.' A stipulation and a pledge are called 'solemn verbal expressions' by Paul, in Book V of his *Sententiae* [V. vii. 1], and by Gaius under the title *Concerning obligations which arise from consent* [II. ix. 4].

3. Naturally there can be other signs of a deliberate intent besides the formality, or whatsoever it is, that the civil law requires in order to fix the rights of the parties. What is done without deliberate intent does not, as we also believe, attain to the force of [Stobaeus, xliv. 22.] an obligation, a fact which Theophrastus noted in his book on *Laws*. As to that which is done deliberately, but without an intent to grant a corresponding right to another, we declare that a right of enforcement is not thereby naturally given to any one, although we admit that there arises not only a question of honour, but also a kind of [*On Duties*, I. x. 32.] moral necessity.

The passage taken from Cicero we shall treat below, when we [II. xvi. 27.] speak of the explanation of agreements; but let us now see what is required to constitute a perfect promise.

V.—*That for a perfect promise the possession of reason on the part of the promisor is requisite; herein the law of nature is distinguished from the civil statutes in regard to minors*

1. The first requisite is the use of reason; consequently the promises of madmen, idiots, and children are null and void. A different opinion should be held in regard to minors. Although it is in fact believed that minors possess a rather weak judgement, as also women, nevertheless this is not a lasting condition, and in itself it is not sufficient to destroy the force of an action.

2. Now the time when a boy begins to employ reason cannot be absolutely [222] fixed, but must be assumed from his daily acts, or even from what commonly happens in any region. And so among the Jews a promise was valid which was made by a youth who had completed his thirteenth year, or by a girl who had completed her twelfth. Elsewhere, not only among the Romans but also among [lxxiv = 638 D.] the Greeks, as Dio Chrysostom states in his seventy-fifth *Oration*, the civil laws with good reason declare certain promises of wards and minors void; and against certain other promises they provide the favour of restitution.

These, however, are the special effects of municipal law, and they therefore have nothing in common with the law of nature or the law of nations, except that it is natural that they should be observed in the places where they are in force. In consequence, if a foreigner makes an agreement with a citizen, he will be bound by the laws of the latter's country, for the reason that a person who makes a contract in any place is under the law of that place as a temporary subject.

3. The case will be clearly different if the agreement is made on the sea, or on a desert island, or by means of letters between

those who are at a distance. For such agreements are governed by the law of nature alone, as are also the agreements of those who hold sovereign power, in so far as this affects their sovereign right. For in the promises which they make in their private capacity even those laws have effect which make the act void where this is to their own advantage, but not when the act is to their loss.

VI.—*Whether a promise given under a misapprehension is by the law of nature binding, and to what extent*

1. The treatment of agreements based on a misapprehension is perplexing enough. It is, in fact, customary to distinguish between errors which affect the substance of the matter and those which do not; to consider whether a contract was based on fraud or not, whether the person with whom the contract was made was a party to the fraud, and whether the act was one of strict justice or only of good faith. For in view of the diversity of these cases the writers declare some acts void and others binding, but in such a way that they may be annulled or changed at the choice of the one injured. The majority of these distinctions come from the Roman law, not only the old civil law, but also the edicts and decisions of the praetors; and some of them are not entirely true or accurate.

Antoninus, II.i.xvii.6. Doctors, *On Dig.* L. xvii. 23. Covarruvias, *De Contractibus*, qu. 57; Medina, *De Restitutione*, qu. 33.

2. Now a method of ascertaining the truth according to nature is furnished to us by the fact that as regards the force and effect of laws nearly every one agrees that, if [the application of] a law rests upon the presumption of a certain fact[1] which does not actually obtain, then that law does not apply; for the whole foundation for the [application of the] law is overthrown when the truth of the [alleged] fact fails. The decision when a law has been based on such a presumption must be inferred from the substance, words, and circumstances of the law.

In like manner, then, we shall say that, if a promise has been based on a certain presumption of fact which does not so obtain,[2] by the law of nature it has no force. For the promisor did not consent to the promise except under a certain condition which, in fact, did not exist. To this principle should be referred the question in the first book of Cicero's *On the Orator*, concerning the man who, falsely believing that his son was dead, had named another as heir.

Felinus, *On Decretals*, I. ii. 1, qu. 40; Baldus, *On Code*, I. xviii. 10; Covarruvias, *On Sext*, V. ult. 2, pt. II. § 6, no. 8; Navarrus, chap. xii, no. 13.

[xxxviii. 175.]

3. If, however, the promisor was careless in investigating the matter, or in expressing his thought, and another has suffered loss therefrom, the promisor will be bound to make this loss good, not

[1] See the example in the *Code* of Justinian, VI. i. 5; in Gail, *Observations*, I. ii. 7; in Dumoulin, *Ad Consuetudines Parisienses*, I. xiii, gl. 3.

[2] Seneca, *On Benefits*, IV. xxxvi [IV. xxxvi. 3]: 'He is a madman who keeps a promise that is based on error.'

from the force of the promise, but by reason of the loss suffered through his fault, a subject which we shall treat below.

On the other hand, if there was an error present indeed, but the promise was not based thereon, the action will be valid, since true consent was not lacking. But in this case also, if the person to whom the promise is made has by fraud caused the error, according to that other principle of obligation he will have to make good whatever loss the promisor has suffered in consequence of the error. If the promise only in part was based on error, it will be valid as to the remainder.

[223] VII.—*That a promise made under the influence of fear is binding, but that the person who caused the fear is under obligation to secure the release of the promisor*

1. No less involved is the discussion of that which is done under the influence of fear. For in this case also a distinction is ordinarily made between a fear that is very great, either in its own nature or with reference to the person fearing, and a fear that is slight; between a fear that is justly and one that is unjustly occasioned; again, whether the fear was caused by the one to whom the promise is made, or by another; and also a distinction is recognized between acts that are generous and those that are burdensome. In accordance with these distinctions some acts are said to be void, others revocable at the will of the promisor, and others entitling to entire restitution. In regard to all these cases there is a great variety of opinions.

Sylvester, word *metus*, qu. 8.

2. On the whole I accept the opinion of those who think that the person that makes a promise under the influence of fear is bound by it, if the municipal law, which can annul or diminish an obligation, is not taken into consideration. For in such a case there is a consent, not conditional, as we just now said in regard to the person in error, but absolute. As Aristotle, in fact, has rightly stated, the man who throws his property overboard because of the fear of shipwreck would wish to save it conditionally, if there was no danger of a shipwreck. But, considering the circumstances of the place and time, he is willing to lose his property absolutely.

Nicomachean Ethics, III [i].

Sylvester, word *restitutio*, 2, dict. 7; Navarrus, chap. xvii, no. 15, and xxii, no. 51, § 7. Covarruvias, *On Sext*, V. ult. 4, pt. ii, § 3, no. 7.

At the same time, this, I think, is indubitably true, that if the person to whom the promise is made has inspired a fear, not just but unjust, even though slight, and the promise has resulted therefrom, he is bound to release the promisor, if the latter so wishes, not because the promise was without force, but on account of the damage wrongfully caused. The exception to this, which is allowed by the law of nations, I shall explain below in its proper connexion.[1]

[1] In this Book, xvii. 19, and III. xix. 1 [III. xix. 11].

3. The rule, that some acts are made void on account of fear inspired by a different person[1] from the one with whom the agreement is made, belongs to municipal law, which often makes void or revocable acts that were freely performed, but performed by a person possessed of weak judgement. Here I wish to assume also the repetition of what I said above about the force and effect of municipal law. What effect an oath has in strengthening promises we shall discuss below. *Dig.* IV. ii. 14. § 3.

VIII.—*That, in order that a promise may be valid, that which is promised ought to be within the power of the promisor*

1. In order that a promise may be valid, the subject of it ought to be either actually or potentially under the control of the promisor.

In the first place, then, promises to perform an act which is in itself illegal are not valid; for no one has, and no one can have, a right to do anything that is unlawful. A promise, as I said above, takes its force from the power of the promisor, and does not extend beyond. When Agesilaus was asked about a promise, he replied: 'If it is just, well and good; but if not, I only said it, I did not make a promise.' [Plutarch, *Apothegms*, *Agesilaus*, iv=p. 208 C, D.]

2. Again, if the thing is not at present within the power of the promisor, but may be at some future time, the validity of the promise will be in suspense; under such circumstances the promise ought to be thought of as made on the condition that the thing should come into the power of the promisor. But if the condition under which the thing can come into the power of the promisor implies his power to obtain it, the promisor will be bound to do whatever is morally right, in order to fulfil the promise.

3. In this class also ordinarily the civil law makes many promises void which would naturally be binding. Such is the promise of future marriage by a man or woman who is now married; such also are not a few promises made by minors, or by children subject to parental control.

IX.—*Whether by the law of nature a promise to do an illegal act is binding; explanation, with a distinction*

At this point the question is customarily raised, whether the promise to perform an act which by nature is morally wrong is by

[1] Seneca, *Controversies*, IV. xxvi [=IX. iii. 9], following nature, says: 'Engagements made under the pressure of violence or necessity are rescinded on this condition, if the violence and necessity arose from the party making the engagement. For', he says, 'it is not in my interest that you are compelled, if you are not compelled by me. The fault should be mine, in order that the punishment become mine.'

Cf. what is said below, III. xix. 4.

the law of nature valid; as if, for instance, something should be promised to a man for committing a murder.

In such a case it is clear that the promise itself is criminal; for it is made to this end, that another may be induced to commit a crime. However, not everything which is done wrongfully loses the effect of a right, as is apparent in the case of an extravagant gift. But there is this difference, that when such a gift has been made the wrongful act comes to an end; [224] for the property is left in the hands of the recipient, without further harm. In promises made for a wrongful cause, however, the fault continues as long as the crime has not been committed; for during so long a time the fulfilment of the promise as an allurement to crime carries a moral blemish within itself, and this comes to an end only after the crime has been committed. Hence it follows that up to this time the effectiveness of such a promise is in suspense, just as we said above in regard to the promising of a thing which is not in our power. But when the crime has been committed the force of the obligation, which from the beginning was not intrinsically lacking but was restrained by the accompanying wrong, is revealed. An example of this can be adduced in the case of Judah, the son of Jacob, who paid the promised hire to Tamar, whom he thought a courtesan, as if it were due.[1]

Cajetan, *On II. ii* qu. 32, art. 7.

Genesis, xxxviii.

Now if the injustice of the one to whom the promise was given has furnished the occasion for it, or if there is unfairness in the contract, the proper remedy is a different question, which we shall treat presently.[2]

X.—*What should be thought of a promise made to obtain a thing which was already due before the promise*

If we look to the law of nature, what is promised for a cause already due is not on that account the less obligatory, in the light of the principles which we stated above in regard to the accepting of another's property. For a promise, even if made without a cause, by the law of nature would be binding. But in this case also loss through extortion, and unfairness in the contract, will have to be made good according to the rules which are to be laid down later.

[II. x. 11 and 12.]

XI.—*The method of making a firm and binding promise in person*

As regards the mode of making a promise, that also, as we said about the transfer of ownership, requires an external act, that is, an

[1] According to nature indeed, under the laws of which people then lived. Gaius Aquilius judged otherwise according to civil law, as Valerius Maximus testifies, VIII. ii. 2.

[2] In the next chapter, secs. 9, 10, and 11.

adequate indication of intent, for which sometimes a nod may suffice, but more often the spoken word or writing is employed.

XII.—*The method of making a binding promise through the agency of others ; also concerning ambassadors who exceed their powers*

But we may be obligated also by another, if there is no doubt concerning the intent with which we chose him as our agent,[1] whether specifically for the business in hand, or under a general appointment. In the case of a general authorization it can happen that our agent may obligate us by acting contrary to our desires as expressed to him alone. In such a case two acts of will must be distinguished, one by which we bind ourselves to ratify whatever our agent does in business of such a nature, and the other by which we bind him not to act except according to our directions, which are known to him but not to others.

This distinction is to be noted with respect to those promises which are made on behalf of kings by ambassadors, by virtue of the power contained in their credentials, but which exceed their secret instructions.[2]

XIII.—*To what extent obligations incurred through the agency of ship-captains and through business agents arise from the law of nature ; wherein also an error of the Roman law is pointed out*

From this we can understand also that actions associated with the transactions of ship-captains and business agents, which, strictly speaking, are elements of actions rather than actions, come within the purview of the law of nature.

In this connexion it should be added that by the Roman law the provision was wrongfully introduced that shipowners should individually be wholly responsible for the acts of the captain. This provision, in fact, is neither in accord with natural justice, which considers it sufficient if individuals are responsible according to their proportionate shares, nor is it advantageous for the public good. Men are deterred from engaging in commerce if they are afraid that they will be held accountable for the acts of the captain as if to any limit.

For such reasons among the Dutch, whose commerce has greatly flourished for a long time, that law of the Romans was not formerly, and is not now, observed. On the contrary the principle has been

[1] Servius, *On the Aeneid*, IX [IX. 361], commenting on the words, 'When plighting friendship though absent', says: 'through the agency of messengers.'
See what is said above, chap. vi. 2.
[2] See an example in Mariana, XXVII. xviii [XXVII. xix]; another in Guicciardini, vol. I.

established that, in respect to responsibility for the acts of the captain, all the owners together are liable for no more than the value of the ship and the cargo.

XIV.—*That the acceptance of a promise is necessary to make it binding*

In order that a promise may transfer a right, the acceptance of it is no less necessary than when a transfer of ownership [1] is made; yet in this case also it is understood that a preceding request continues, and has the force of an acceptance. [225] And no obstacle is presented to this view by the rule of the civil law concerning promises made to the state. Nevertheless this consideration has led some to judge that the act of promising is alone sufficient. However, the Roman law does not say that the promise has full binding force before the acceptance, but forbids the revocation of the promise, in order that the acceptance [2] may be possible at any time.

Digest, XLI. ii. 38. Gomez, vol. II, ix, no. I.

Molina, disp. 263.

This effect does not follow from the law of nature but merely from the civil law. Not unlike it is the effect of the custom which the law of nations has introduced on behalf of infants and idiots. For in the interest of such persons, just as the law supplies the intent to possess the things which are sought, so it supplies also the intent to accept them.

Cf. II. ii, iii. 6 [II. iii. 6] and II. iv. 10.

XV.—*Whether an acceptance ought to be made known to the promisor; explanation, with a distinction*

This question is also commonly raised, whether it is sufficient that the acceptance be signified, or whether, in fact, the acceptance ought also to be made known to the promisor before the promise attains its full effect.

It is certain that a promise can be made in both ways, either thus: 'I desire that this be valid, if it be accepted'; or thus: 'I desire that this shall be valid if I shall have understood that it has been accepted'. In promises which deal with mutual obligations the latter meaning is assumed, but in merely generous promises it is better that the former meaning should be believed to be present, unless something else should appear.

XVI.—*That a promise can be revoked if the one to whom it was made died before accepting it*

Hence it follows that before acceptance a promise can be revoked without injustice, since the right has not yet been transferred; and

Code, IV. l. 6; *Digest*, XL. ii. 4.

[1] Tertullian, speaking as one having a knowledge of law, says in his book, *On Fastings*, xi: 'When a vow has been accepted by God, it constitutes a law for the future.'

[2] [228] See a similar provision in the *Law of the Visigoths*, V. ii. 6.

such a revocation will even be without inconsistency if in truth the promise was made with the intent that it should begin to be binding only after acceptance.

Furthermore a promise can be revoked if the person to whom it was made dies before accepting it, for the reason that the acceptance seems to have been submitted to his decision and not to that of his heirs. It is, in fact, one thing to wish to give to a man a right which will pass to his heirs, and another to wish to give directly to the heirs;[1] for it makes a great difference upon whom the favour is conferred. This is in accord with the response of Neratius, 'that it did not seem to him that the prince would have granted to a dead man what he had granted to the person who he thought was living.' *Dig.* L. xvii. 191.

XVII.—*Whether a promise is revoked on the death of an intermediary; explanation, with distinctions*

1. A promise can be revoked also on the death of the person who has been chosen to convey orally the promisor's intent, for the reason that the obligation had been based on his words. The situation is different in the case of a messenger who has not an instrumental part in the obligation, but is merely the bearer of the obligatory instrument. Similarly letters, which indicate consent, can be carried by any one. *Digest,* XVII. i. 57; Clarus, Book IV, § *donatio,* qu. xii.

Further, we must distinguish between the servant who has been chosen to report the promise and the agent authorized to make the promise himself. In the former case the revocation will be fully binding, even if it be not known to the servant; but in the second case a revocation will not be valid, because the right of promising was dependent on the will of the representative himself, and this will was without fault in promising, because lacking knowledge of the revocation. So, again, in the former case a donation can be accepted after the death of the giver,[2] as being completed on the one side, though it had been subject to revocation; and this is easier to perceive in the case of embassies. In the second case the gift cannot be accepted, because it was not made but merely ordered to be made. *Digest,* XVII. i. 15. *Code,* VIII. liii. 6.

2. In case of doubt the conclusion is that it was the intent of the person who directed the making of the promise that it be fulfilled, unless some great change has occurred, such as the death of that person. Nevertheless there may be presumptions which suggest a different decision, and which ought to be easily admitted, so that Covarruvias, *Var. Res.,* xiv, no. 16; *Dig.* XL. ii. 4.

[1] So in order to avoid ambiguity it was customary to say: 'to him and to his children'; Servius, *On the Aeneid,* IX [IX. 299]. See also the *Law of the Visigoths,* V. ii. 6.

[2] See the book [Littleton's] *De Tenuris Angliae,* vii.

a gift which was to be given for a worthy cause may be made. In a similar manner the question formerly discussed, as to whether a right of action on the order to make a promise exists against the heir, can be settled; on this matter the author of the *Ad Herennium* reports that the praetor Marcus Drusus gave a decision on one side, and Sextus Julius on the other. [II. xiii. 19.]

XVIII.—*Whether a promise is revocable after acceptance by a proxy; explanation, with distinctions*

1. Disputes are wont to arise also in regard to an acceptance given by proxy. In such cases we must distinguish between a promise made to me [226] about giving something to another and a promise conveyed in the name of the person to whom the thing is to be given. If the promise has been made to me without regard to the question whether I am personally interested—a distinction which was introduced by the Roman law—it seems that in accepting by the law of nature I am given the right of effecting the transfer of the right to the other party, if he also accepts, and in such a way that in the meantime the promise cannot be revoked by the promisor. On the other hand I who have received the promise may remit it. For this opinion is not inconsistent with the law of nature, and it is particularly in harmony with the wording of such a promise. And to me it is not a matter of indifference whether another person receives a favour through me.

Covarruvias, *On Decretals*, V. xli. 10, pt. II, § 4, 13.

Alexander, *Consilia*, I. 204, and Charles Dumoulin thereon.

2. Now if the promise has been conveyed in the name of the person to whom the thing is to be given the distinction must be made whether the one who accepts it has a special authorization to accept it, or an authorization so general that such an acceptance ought to be considered as included therein, or whether he has no authorization whatever. Where such an authorization has preceded I do not think that we should insist on the further inquiry whether the person is his own master or not, as the Roman law provides; we should rather consider that by such an acceptance the promise is fully completed, because consent can be transmitted and indicated even by the agency of a servant. I am in fact considered to wish what I have entrusted to the will of another, if he also wishes it.

When, however, there is no authorization, if another to whom the promise was not made should with the permission of the promisor accept it, the result will be that the promisor is not permitted to revoke his promise until the person whom it concerns has accepted or refused. Yet in the meantime the one who has accepted cannot remit the promise, for in this case he was not employed to accept a right, but merely to bind the good faith of the promisor in fulfilling the favour. And yet the situation is such that, if the promisor should revoke his promise, he would be acting contrary to good faith and not against the individual right of any one.

XIX.—*At what time a burdensome condition can be added to a promise*

From what has been said we can understand also what ought to be thought about the addition of a burdensome condition to a promise. This can, in fact, take place so long as the promise has not been completed by acceptance, nor made irrevocable by giving a pledge. Moreover a burdensome condition to the advantage of a third party can be revoked so long as it has not been accepted by that party.

Code, VIII. liv. 4. Bartolus, *On Dig.*, XLV. i. 122. § 2.

There are, nevertheless, some who think differently in regard to this matter, as well as on other questions. But the natural equity is so easily apparent to one who examines the matter rightly that it does not need many proofs.

XX.—*How an invalid promise can be made binding*

The question is also commonly discussed, how a promise, which was based on a misunderstanding, can be made valid if, after the error has been found out, the promisor wishes to keep his promise. The same question can be raised also in regard to promises which the civil law makes void because of fear, or for any other cause, if the cause has afterwards ceased to have effect.

Navarrus, III. xxii. 51 and 80. Sanchez, *De Sancti Matrimonii Sacramento Disputationes*, II. xxxii, no. 8.

To confirm such promises some require merely a mental act which, joined with the previous external act, they consider sufficient to produce a binding obligation. Others, who are dissatisfied with this requirement, because an external act cannot be the sign of a mental resolve which comes later, require a new verbal promise and acceptance.

The truth rather lies between these two views. An external act is indeed required, but it is not necessarily expressed in words; for the retention of the thing promised by the person to whom the promise was made, and the abandonment of it on the part of the promisor, or some similar act, may suffice to indicate consent.

XXI.—*That promises without cause are not void by the law of nature*

In order that the civil law may not be confused with the law of nature, this statement also must not be omitted, that promises, which have no cause expressed, [227] are not by the law of nature void, any more than material gifts.

XXII.—*To what degree a person who has promised an act of another is bound by the law of nature*

Covarruvias, *On Decretals*, V. xli. 10, pt. II, § 5. II [xxxi. 11].

A person who has promised the act of another is not held accountable for the material interest involved, provided he has not omitted to do what he could on his own part to secure the action, unless the words of the promise or the nature of the business add a more strict obligation. 'As if he had fulfilled his pledge', says Livy,[1] 'because he had not been to blame for its non-performance.'

[1] Cf. what is said below, III. xx 30 [III. xxi. 30].

CHAPTER XII

ON CONTRACTS

I.—*The division of men's acts which are advantageous to other men; first, into simple acts and acts of a mixed character*

Of the acts of men which are advantageous to other men, some are simple, others of a mixed character.

II.—*The division of simple acts into those that are merely acts of kindness and those that involve a mutual obligation—*

Some simple acts are merely kind, others are reciprocal.[1] The kindnesses either are unmixed or involve a kind of mutual obligation. Unmixed kindnesses are either fulfilled in the present, or are directed to the future. A useful deed is accomplished in the present, and in regard to this it is not necessary to speak; while it is advantageous, to be sure, it has no legal effect. Of the same character is a donation by which ownership of property is transferred, and that topic we treated above, when the matter of acquiring ownership was under consideration. Not only promises to give but also promises to perform are directed toward the future; these also we have already treated.

Advantageous acts which involve a mutual obligation are those which dispose of property without alienation, or accomplish a deed in such a way that some effect remains. Such in regard to things is the permission to use, which is called a gratuitous bailment; and in regard to deeds the undertaking of a costly service, or one implying obligations, which is called a mandate; one form of the mandate is the deposit in trust, which involves the expenditure of labour in guarding and keeping a thing. Similar to such acts, again, are
[229] promises to act, except that, as we have said, the latter are directed toward the future; and this we wish to have understood also concerning the acts which are now to be discussed.

III.—*Also into reciprocal acts, which sometimes separate the parties*

1. Reciprocal acts either separate the parties or produce a community of interests. Those acts which are separative the Roman jurists rightly divide into these classes: I give that you may give;

[1] Aristotle [*Rhetoric*, I. v] includes all acts of the former class under the term 'of gift', of the latter under the term 'of sale'.

I do that you may do; I do that you may give. On these classes see the jurist Paul in the *Digest*, XIX. v. 5.

2. But from this classification the Romans omitted certain contracts, which they themselves called specified contracts, not so much for the reason that they have a special name (for reciprocation, which they exclude from the specified contracts, has this characteristic) as for the reason that such contracts had received a certain force and character from their more frequent use,[1] so that that could be understood from their name alone, even if nothing had been specified in particular. For this reason also certain formulas of action had been established in relation to such contracts, while in the other and less usual contracts only that was included which had been stated; in consequence no common and customary formula was given to them, but one appropriate to the act, which was therefore called a formula in prescribed words.

By reason of more frequent use in specified agreements, if certain required conditions were present (as in a sale, if the price had been agreed upon),[2] the necessity of carrying out the agreement was imposed, even if the matter was still fresh, that is, before anything had been done by either of the parties. But in those less common contracts, while the matter was still fresh there was granted liberty to withdraw, that is exemption from penalty, because the civil law withdrew its compelling force from such agreements, so that they were based on the good faith of the contracting parties alone.

3. But the law of nature ignores these distinctions; and indeed the contracts, which are called unspecified by the jurists, are neither less natural nor less ancient. In fact the exchanging of commodities, which is reckoned among the unspecified contracts, is both simpler and more ancient than purchase.[3] And Eustathius in his comment on

[1] See Vázquez, *Controversies*, chap. x, at the end.

[2] Among the Jews a sale was not considered complete until after delivery, either real or imagined.

[3] This is apparent from the verses of Homer [*Iliad*, VII. 472 ff.; VI. 234 ff.] quoted in the *Digest*, XVIII. i. 1. Of the Germans Tacitus [*Germany*, v] says: 'The tribes farther from the border use the simpler and older custom of barter.'

Servius, *On the Eclogues*, IV [IV. 39], explains the expression 'They will exchange merchandise' thus: 'For the reason that the ancients were accustomed to barter for goods.' Again, *On the Georgics*, III [III. 306], on the words 'Fleeces may be exchanged', he says: 'They may be bought at a great price. For among the ancients all trading was by barter, and this fact Gaius established by an example from Homer.'

Pliny, XXXIII. ii [*Natural History*, XXXIII. i. 6], says: 'In an age how much happier, when goods were bartered for goods, just as it is agreed that Homer thought was the case in Trojan times.' Again, in regard to the Chinese, in Book VI, xxii: 'Their goods, displayed on the farther bank near the objects for sale, are taken away by the traders, if they are pleased with the exchange.' Mela [III. vii. 10] says of the same people: 'The Chinese dwell between, a race absolutely just in trade, which they carry on while absent by leaving their goods in a desert place.'

Of the same folk Ammianus, in Book XXIII [XXIII. vi. 68], says: 'When strangers have crossed the river to buy thread or some other things, without any interchange of words the prices of the things offered are determined by the eyes alone.' Mela [II. i. 95] says of the Sarmatians: 'They practise commerce by barter.' Concerning the Colchians, see Busbecq, *Epistolae Exoticae*, Book III [p. 205], and Olaus Magnus, Book IV, v, about the Laplanders.

Homer's *Iliad* (Book X), in treating of a public contest for which a prize had been offered, explains the Greek word for 'seek to gain' in Homer as 'take in exchange', adding that 'this and other such matters are a sort of contract'; and in fact it is of the class 'I do that you may give'. Therefore, in accordance with nature we shall refer all those separative contracts to the three classes which we have mentioned, without making any distinction of the specified and unspecified. [XXII. 160.]

4. We shall say, then, that in the agreement to give that there may be giving in return a person gives a thing directly for a thing, as in that form which is particularly called exchange of commodities, and is, without doubt, the most ancient form of commerce; or money is given for money,[1] which merchants in ancient Greece called money-changing and we to-day call exchange; or a thing is given for money, as in buying and selling; or the use of one thing for another thing, or the use of one thing for the use of another, or the use of a thing for money; this last is called letting and hiring. But under the term 'use' we here understand not only the bare use but the use which is joined with the enjoyment of the income, whether this is temporary, or restricted to a person, or hereditary, or restricted in any other manner whatsoever; an example among the Jews is the contract which lasted till the year of jubilee. Aristotle, [*Nicomachean*] *Ethics*, V. viii; *Politics*, I. ix; *Digest*, XVIII. i. 1.

One gives as a loan, however, in order that, after an intervening time, the same amount, and that of the same kind, may be given back; and this is applicable to those things which are reckoned by weight, number, or measure, to other things as well as to money.

5. The exchanging of an act for an act may have innumerable forms, according to the diversity of the acts. But I do that you may give. In the one case, I do that you may give money; this in acts of daily service is called letting and hiring, and in the act of guaranteeing indemnity [230] against chance losses it is called a guarding against risk, or, in everyday speech, insurance, a form of contract which was formerly scarcely known, but is now very common. In other cases [I do] that you may give a thing or the use of a thing.

IV.—*Reciprocal acts that sometimes contribute to a community of interests*

Acts which contribute to a community of interests bring about a sharing in activities or in things, and turn these to the common advantage; all such acts come under the head of joint undertakings. In this class is included also an association for purposes of war, as among us the frequent union of privately owned vessels against pirates

[1] On this, see Procopius, *Secret History* [xxv]. Coined money was formerly brought from Illyricum into Italy in the place of goods. Pliny, [*Natural History*,] XXXIII. iii.

or other assailants, which is now commonly called an admiral's force, and by the Greeks was named 'a sailing together' or 'a joint sailing'.

V.—*That acts of mixed character may be mixed in respect to their main elements*

Acts are of a mixed character, either in their essential elements or through the association of another act. Thus if I knowingly buy a thing at a price higher than it is worth, and give the excess in price to the seller, the act will be partly gift, partly purchase. If I promise money to a jeweller for making rings for me out of his own gold, the transaction will be partly purchase, partly hiring. So in a partnership it happens that one party contributes services and money, the other money only.

In a feudal contract the granting of the fief is a kindness, but the agreement to render military service in return for protection is a contract, of the form 'I do that you may do'. If, furthermore, the burden of a yearly payment is added, the transaction to that extent is blended with leasing. Also a loan on things at sea is a mixed contract, which consists of a contract for a loan and an insurance against loss.

VI.—*Or such acts may be of mixed character only by reason of an additional act*

An act becomes of mixed character by the addition of another act, as in giving security, or in putting up a pledge. For the giving of security, if you look at the transaction as between the surety and the principal debtor, is in the main a mandate; as between the creditor and the surety, who receives nothing, it seems merely an act of generosity, but because the giving of security is added to burdensome contracts it is customarily judged a part of the same act. So the giving of a pledge seems in itself an act of generosity, by which the retention of a thing is granted; but this also derives its nature from the contract, for which it furnishes security.

VII.—*What acts are called contracts*

Dig. L. xvi. 19. Now all acts of benefit to others, except mere acts of kindness, are called contracts.

VIII.—*That equality is required in contracts; and first, equality as regards preceding acts*

The law of nature enjoins that there be equality in contracts, and in such a way that the party who receives less acquires a right of action from the inequality.

This equality is required both in the acts and in the matter with which the transaction is concerned; and in respect to the acts it covers the preceding as well as the principal acts.

IX.—*That equality is required in contracts as regards knowledge of the facts*

1. To the preceding acts consideration pertains that the person who is making a contract with any one ought to point out to him the faults of the thing concerned in the transaction which are known to himself.[1] This is not only prevailingly established by the civil laws but is also consistent with the nature of the act. For between the contracting parties there is a closer union than ordinarily obtains in human society. In this way an answer is made to what Diogenes of Babylon said in treating of this question, that all things which are not mentioned are not concealed, and that it is not necessary for me to say everything which it is useful for you to know, as in the case of the heavenly bodies.

Digest, XIX. i. 1.

Cicero, *On Duties*, III [xii. 52].

The nature of a contract which was devised for the sake of mutual advantage in fact demands something more intimately related.[2] Ambrose well said:

On Duties, II. x [III. x. 66].

> In contracts it is ordered that the faults in things which are sold be made known; and if the seller has not declared these the contracts are held void by action for fraud, even if the property has passed into the possession of the purchaser.

Lactantius had said:

[*Divine Institutes*, V [xvii. 32].

> The man who, having in view only his own gain and advantage, has not called attention to the mistake of the seller, in order that he may buy a piece of gold at a cheap price, or does not declare the truth about a runaway slave or a fever-infected house that he is selling, is not a wise man, as Carneades would have him seem, [231] but a shrewd and clever rogue.

2. The same thing, however, should not be said in regard to circumstances which have no direct connexion with the thing contracted for; as if any one should know that many ships were in route bringing grain. The giving of such information is, in fact, a part of one's duty, and praiseworthy, so that often it cannot be omitted without violating the rule of love. Yet such omission is not unjust,

Thomas Aquinas, II. ii. 78, art. 3; Baldus, *On Dig.*, XXI. i. 1; Covarruvias, *On Sext*, V. ult. 4, pt. 11, § 4, no. 6.

[1] [239] See the Scholiast on Horace, on the verse [*Satires*, II. iii. 285 f.]:

> For mind the owner would not vouch,
> Unless he wished a suit.

[2] Valerius Maximus, Book VIII, ii. 1, says: 'One who sells in good faith ought neither to exaggerate the hope of advantages nor to hide the knowledge of disadvantages.' In that passage he is treating of a house ordered to be destroyed by the augurs, a fact which the seller had concealed from the purchaser.

that is, it is not inconsistent with the right of the one with whom the contract is made. That, then, is in point here, which the same Diogenes, as quoted by Cicero, aptly said: 'I have brought my goods, I have displayed them for sale; I am selling my own at no higher price than others, perhaps even at a lower price, since I have a greater amount. Whom do I injure?'

Loc. cit. [*On Duties*, III. xii. 51].

In general, therefore, it is not necessary to follow the statement of the same Cicero, that you practise concealment when, for the sake of your own gain, you wish that those, whose interest it is to know, shall be in ignorance of what you know. This is applicable only when those facts are considered which are intimately connected with the subject of the transaction, as in the case of a house which is infected with pestilence, or which the magistrates have ordered to be pulled down; examples which you may find in the same passage of Cicero.

Digest, XIX. i. 1.

[Cicero, *On Duties*, III. xvi. 67.] [*Epistles*, II. ii. 17 f.]

3. But it is not necessary that faults known to the person with whom you are dealing should be mentioned, as the servitude attached to the house which Marcus Marius Gratidianus sold to Gaius Sergius Orata, after having previously bought it of him. Equal knowledge on both sides, in fact, puts the contracting parties on an equal footing.[1] Horace says:

> Scot free the man will take his price, I think;
> Forewarned you bought a faulty thing.

[XI. ii = p. 916.]

This point was noted also by Plato in the eleventh book of the *Laws*.

X.—*That equality is required in contracts as regards freedom of choice*

Not only in the knowledge of facts but also in the freedom of choice there ought to be a kind of equality between the contracting parties. Not indeed that any preceding fear, if justly inspired, ought to be removed, for that is outside of the contract; but that no fear should be unjustly inspired for the sake of making the contract, or, if such fear has been inspired, that it should be removed.

Greek History, III [ii. 31].

With this point in view the Lacedaemonians annulled the purchase of land which the Eleans had forced the owners to sell by reason of fear, 'thinking that it was no more just to extort property from weaker persons under the semblance of purchase than through fear alone,' as Xenophon says. Yet, in the proper place, we shall see what exception there is to this rule, according to the law of nations.

[1] *Edict of Theodoric*, chap. cxli.

XI.—*Secondly, that equality is required in the act of making a contract, if it be a contract requiring an exchange*

1. The equality demanded in the principal act of a contract is, that no more be exacted than is just. This is hardly applicable in the case of contracts involving beneficence. For if any one should make a bargain for something as a slight reward in return for a loan, or for service rendered in executing a commission, or in looking after a deposit in trust, he will not act wrongfully, but he will be mixing the contract, that is, he will make it in part a contract of exchange instead of being wholly beneficent. *Institutes,* III. xxvi. § 13; *Dig.* XVI. iii. 1. § 9.

In all contracts with exchange of considerations, however, the rule should be carefully observed. And there is no reason why one should say that whatever either party has promised in excess should be considered a donation. Such is not ordinarily the intention of persons making contracts of this kind, and such an intention ought not to be assumed unless it is apparent. Whatever, in fact, the parties promise or give, they should be believed to promise or give as on an equality with the thing which is about to be received, and due by reason of that equality.

2. John Chrysostom says: 'In making contracts, and in buying or selling anything, whenever we strive and toil in every way to pay less than a fair price, is there not a kind of thievery in the act?' The author of the life of Isidore in Photius relates [232] that when Hermias wished to buy anything which was offered at less than a fair price he added whatever was lacking so as to pay the proper price, because he thought that to act otherwise was a form of injustice, and injustice of a sort to escape the notice of most persons. Also the Jewish scholars in this way interpret the law found in *Leviticus*,[1] xxv. 4 and 7 [xxv. 14 and 17]. [*Commentary on John*, Homily LX, vi.] [= p. 1044.]

XII.—*Thirdly, there should be equality in the subject of the contract; explanation thereof*

1. There remains equality in the subject of the contract, consisting in this, that although nothing has been concealed which ought to have been said, and no more has been exacted than was considered due, nevertheless if an inequality has been detected in the transaction, although without the fault of either party—because, for example, the fault was hidden, or because there was a mistake in the price—this inequality should be made good, and something should be taken

[1] See Moses de Kotzi, *Precepts Bidding*, 82.

from the one who has more and given to the one who has less; for in the contract it was proposed, or ought to have been proposed, on both sides, that each should receive the same amount.

2. The Roman law did not establish this rule to apply to every inequality, for it does not follow up trivial differences, since it judged that a multitude of lawsuits would result; but the rule is applicable in sufficiently important differences, as those which exceed one-half of the just price. Beyond doubt, as Cicero says, the laws deal with injustices so far as these can be laid hold of, but the philosophers deal with injustices so far as they can be distinguished by reason and intelligence. Those persons, in fact, who are not subject to the civil laws ought to follow the same rule, which right reason tells them is fair. Furthermore, this rule should be observed even by those who are subject to laws whenever the transaction involves what is morally right and blameless, even if the laws do not grant or take away a right, but merely for certain reasons refuse to lend their aid to what is right.

Loc. cit. [*On Duties*, III. xvii. 68].

XIII.—*What equality ought to obtain in acts that are wholly acts of kindness, or partly acts of kindness*

1. But it is to be noted that a kind of equality is to be maintained also in contracts of beneficence, not indeed of the same degree as in contracts requiring an exchange but in accordance with the supportive character of the transaction, in order that a person may not suffer loss from his own generosity. Therefore a mandatary ought to be indemnified for expenses incurred and for loss which he has suffered in consequence of the mandate. A bailee, too, is bound to make good a thing lost, because he is under obligation to the owner not merely on account of the thing, that is, by reason of the force of ownership, by which, as we stated above, a temporary possessor would be bound, but also by reason of the acceptance of a favour. This rule holds good except in case the thing would have completely perished also in the possession of the owner;[1] for in such a case the owner would have lost nothing through the bailment. The acceptor of a gratuitous deposit, on the contrary, receives nothing beyond confidence in his good faith, and so, if the thing is lost, he will not be held liable, either in respect to the thing, because it does not exist and he is not made richer by it, or by reason of the acceptance of the thing, since in accepting he did not receive a favour but conferred it.

Sylvester, word *bellum*, pt. 1, no. 7; Thomas Aquinas, II. ii. 62, art. 6.

In the case of a pledge, as also of a thing that has been hired, an intermediate course ought to be followed, in order that the receiver may not be made liable for any and every mishap, as a borrower is.

[1] *Laws of the Visigoths*, V. v. 1–3.

And yet he ought to exhibit more diligent care than one who accepts a deposit; for the acceptance of a pledge is usually without profit, but is ordinarily associated with a burdensome contract.

2. Now all these rules are in truth in conformity with Roman law. Yet they did not have their origin in the Roman law, but in natural justice, and therefore the same legal provisions will be found among other nations also. Thus among other writers they are found in the *Guide of the Perplexed* (Book III, chapter xliii) by the Jew Moses Maimonides.[1] Seneca had reference to this rule when he said that some are under obligation to exhibit fidelity, others to furnish protection. In accordance with this rule judgement must be passed on other contracts also. *On Benefits,* VII. xix [2].

Having now discussed the general subject at sufficient length for our purposes, let us run over some special questions in regard to contracts.

XIV.—*In what way the price of an object ought to be estimated in a sale, and for what reasons it may justly increase or decrease*

1. The most natural measure of the value of each thing [233] is the need of it, as Aristotle has rightly shown. This becomes the paramount consideration in the exchange of objects among barbarous peoples. Nevertheless this is not the only measure. For the desire of men, which controls the price of things, covets many things more than their need requires. 'Luxury', says Pliny, 'set the price for pearls.'[2] In his argument *Against Verres*, Cicero says of statues: 'The limit of value in these things is the same as the limit of our desire for them.' *Nicomachean Ethics,* V. viii. [*Natural History,*] IX. xxxv [124]. [IV. vii. 14.]

On the contrary, it happens that the most necessary things are of less value because of their abundance. Seneca has made this plain by many examples in his *On Benefits*, Book VI, chapter xv, where he adds also the statement: 'The price of everything depends upon circumstances. Though you have praised those things highly, they are worth only as much as they can be sold for.' Paul the jurist *Digest,* XXXV. ii. 63.

[1] This agrees with the passage in *Exodus*, xxii. 6. 10–13 [xxii. 7. 10–13]; Moses de Kotzi, *Precepts Bidding*, 88 and 89.

[2] Likewise in Book XXXVII [XXXVII. vi. 85] he says about gems: 'The passionate desire of individuals, and especially of kings, sets the price in each case'; also in Book XXXII [XXXII. ii. 21]: 'The value of coral is as great among the people of India as of Indian pearls among us. For these objects derive their value from the fancy of the peoples.'

Augustine, in his *City of God*, XI. xvi, says: 'But why is it strange, since in consequence of the fixing of value by men themselves (whose nature is certainly of the highest dignity) often a horse is bought at a higher price than a slave, and a gem than a slave girl? And so, with such freedom in passing judgement, the estimate of the one who weighs the matter differs greatly from that prompted by the necessity of one in need, or the pleasure of the one who eagerly desires, since reason considers what an object is worth in itself in the scale of things, but need considers its worth according to what it seeks. Reason, again, makes search for that which may appear true to an intelligent mind, but pleasure seeks that which in an agreeable manner may gratify the bodily senses.'

says: 'The prices of things are not fixed by the desire or the use of individuals, but by common estimation';[1] that is, as he elsewhere explains, the value which all put upon them. Hence it comes about that a thing is valued at the price commonly offered or given for it; and that price is not so limited that it may not have a range of variation within which more or less may be given or asked, except in cases in which the law has established a definite price 'at a fixed point', as Aristotle says.

Dig. IX. ii. 33.

2. Moreover, with respect to the current price, account is ordinarily taken of the labours and expenditure[2] of the dealers. The price, again, is wont to change suddenly according to the abundance or scarcity of buyers, of money, and of commodities. Also circumstances may by accident arise, on account of which a commodity may lawfully be bought or sold above or below its normal price; such, for example, as an expected loss, absence of profit, personal fancy, or sale or purchase, as a favour to another, of that which would not otherwise have been bought or sold. Such exceptional circumstances should be made known to the person with whom we are dealing. Also, we can take into account the loss or absence of gain which arises from deferred or anticipated payments.

XV.—*When according to the law of nature a sale is completed, and when ownership is transferred*

1. It must also be noted that in selling and purchasing the ownership may be transferred without delivery from the very moment of the contract, and that this is the most simple form. So in the opinion of Seneca[3] a sale 'is an alienation and a transfer to another both of one's property and of one's right'; for that is also the method used in an exchange of commodities. But if it has been agreed that ownership shall not pass immediately the seller will be under obligation to give possession according to contract, and in the meantime both gain and loss in the commodity will fall to the seller.

These, then, are fictions of the civil law not universally recognized, that sale and purchase consist in guaranteeing that one may have the property and right of recovery if dispossessed; also that the property shall be at the risk of the purchaser and that the income from it shall belong to him even before ownership passes. On the contrary many lawgivers have enacted that up to the time of delivery

[1] Pliny, XVIII. xxxi [*Natural History*, XVIII. xxxi. 320]: 'It is the proper course for a proprietor to use the price of grain of each year.'

[2] And Augustine does not disapprove of this, *On Psalm LXX* [lxx. 17]: 'But the dealer himself says: "I bring my goods from a great distance . . .; I seek pay for my labour in order to make a living." . . . "The labourer is in fact worthy of his hire"; but the matter in question is the lying and perjury, not the business transaction.'

[3] *On Benefits*, V. x.

the seller should have the profit of the commodity, as well as the risk, as Theophrastus noted in a passage found in Stobaeus;[1] in the same passage you may find also many other rules concerning the formalities of sale, of payment to bind the bargain, and of retraction, all very different from the Roman law. Thus also among the people of Rhodes, as Dio of Prusa noted in his *Rhodian Oration*, a sale and some other contracts were commonly completed by entry in the public records. [*Orations*, xxxi = p. 326.]

2. This rule also should be known, that if an object has been sold twice, of the two sales that will be effective which has included in itself immediate transfer of ownership, either by delivery or in some other way. For by this act the essential control over the object passes from the seller, a result which is not brought about by a promise alone.

XVI.—*What monopolies are contrary to the law of nature or the law of love*

Not all monopolies are contrary to the law of nature.[2] [234] Sometimes, in fact, monopolies may be permitted by the sovereign power for a just cause and with a fixed price. The history of Joseph, when he ruled Egypt as royal governor, furnishes us a notable example of such a case. So also under the Romans the Alexandrians had a 'monopoly' of Indian and Ethiopic wares, as Strabo relates.[3] [Aristotle, *Politics*, I. vii [I. xi].]

A monopoly can also be established by private persons, if only with a fair price. But those who make a compact, as did the oil merchants in the Velabrum,[4] that goods may be sold at a higher price than the current range of prices, or by violence or fraud hinder a larger supply from being imported, or buy up all the goods in such a way that they sell at a price which is unfair at the time of sale, are committing a wrong, and are bound to make good the loss. If in any other way they hinder the importation of merchandise, or so buy it up that they may sell it at a price which is higher, but under the circumstances not unfair, they are violating the rule of love, as Ambrose shows by many proofs in his third book *On Duties*; but, properly speaking, they do not violate the rights of another. [Chap. vi.]

[1] *On Laws* [XLIV. xxii].

[2] The history of Thales in respect to the olive harvest is known [Diogenes Laertius, I. xxvi]. The plan of Pythocles in regard to the buying of Tyrian lead, by which the people of Athens made a profit, is found in Aristotle, *Economics*, II [II. ii. 36]. On the monopoly of hedgehog skins, by which cloth is carded, see Pliny, VIII. xxxvii [*Natural History*, VIII. xxxvii. 135]. On the silk monopoly, see Procopius, *Secret History* [xxv].

[3] Book XVII [XVII. i. 13]. See also Cassiodorus, [*Variae*,] II. iv and xxvi.

[4] There is a fair and wise law in the *Code*, IV. lix; also a notable passage in Lysias [*Orations*, xxii. 5] directed against the grain merchants, who were advancing the price with false reports. Add Cassiodorus, *Variae*, IX. v, and *Decretum*, II. xiv. 4. 9.

XVII.—*How money serves as the medium of exchange*

As regards money, we should know that it acquires its function naturally, not by reason of its material alone, nor by reason of a special name or form, but because it has a more general character [1] by which it is compared either with all things, or with the things that are most necessary. Its value, if not otherwise agreed upon, must be fixed according to the time and place of payment. Michael of Ephesus, in his commentary *On the Nicomachean Ethics*, Book V, says:

[*On Nicomachean Ethics*, V. viii.]

> It is possible in the case of coined money to see the same thing which happens as a result of need. For as our need is not always the same, and what others have is not always equally necessary for us, so coined money does not always have the same value but varies; while formerly it had a greater value, later it has had less or none. Nevertheless, in general, the value of coined money is more stable,[2] and on that account we are accustomed to use it as a measure of other things, which are compared with it.

The meaning of the passage is, that whatever is employed as a measure of value for other things ought to be of such a character that in itself it shall vary as little as possible. Such, moreover, in the class of things possessed of value, are gold, silver, and copper. For in themselves these metals have almost the same value everywhere, and always. But just as other things of which men are in need are plentiful or rare, so likewise money made of the same material and of the same weight has now a greater value, now a less.

XVIII.—*By the law of nature nothing should be deducted from the price of rent on account of unfruitfulness or similar misfortunes; also what rule holds if the first renter is hindered from using a thing and it has been rented by another*

Digest, XIX. ii. 2.

'Renting and hiring', as Gaius rightly said, 'is very near to selling and buying, and is subject to the same rules.' The price, in fact, corresponds to the rent or hire, and the ownership of the thing to the right of user. Therefore, as the loss of the property itself falls upon the owner, so by the law of nature, in the case of unfruitfulness and other misfortunes which hinder the use, the loss is borne by the renter; and the person letting the property will not on that account have less right to the promised rental, for the reason that he himself transferred the right to use, which had that value at the time.

[1] Not so much from the material as from the quantity; *Digest*, XVIII. i. 1. Here the bodies are not considered but the quantity; *Digest*, XLVI. iii. 94. § 1.

[2] [240] The value is fixed by public authority and is lasting; *Digest*, XVIII. i. 1.

This rule, however, can be changed both by laws and by agreement. Nevertheless if the landlord has rented the land to another tenant while the first renter was hindered from working it, whatever he has thereby gained he will repay to the first renter, in order that he may not become richer at another's expense.

XIX.—*How a just payment for services may be increased or diminished*

In regard to a sale I said that a thing can be sold at a higher price [235] or bought at a lower one if it is sold or bought as a favour to the other party, when it would not otherwise have been sold or bought. The same rule should be understood in regard to the renting or hiring of property or service. If one service can be useful to more than one person, as for the undertaking of a journey, and if the contractor has bound himself firmly to several individuals, in case the law interposes no hindrance, he will be able to demand from each the payment which he would have exacted from the one. The fact that the service will be useful to a second person also is outside the contract which was entered into with the first party, and it does not in any degree diminish the value of the service in respect to the first party.

XX.—*By what right interest is forbidden*

1. In connexion with a mutuum the question is commonly raised, by what right is interest forbidden?

Although it is the more generally accepted opinion that interest is forbidden by the law of nature, yet Abulensis holds the opposite view. And the arguments advanced on the other side do not seem to be such as to require assent. For what is said of a mutuum, namely, that it is without charge, may be said also of a commodate.[1] And yet, although it is not unlawful to demand a price for the use of a thing, such a demand may cause the contract to pass under another name.

[Tostado,] *On Matthew*, xxv, qu. 171 and 172.

The argument is not more convincing, that money is by its own nature unproductive. For houses and other things naturally unfruitful[2] are rendered productive by the industry of men. This is

[1] [A mutuum is a contract by which a thing consumable by first use is given to another with the obligation of returning at a stated time a similar thing and in the same species and goodness. A commodate is a contract by which a thing not consumable by first use is given to another with the obligation of returning at a stated time the same thing unimpaired.] For the commodate and the mutuum, as the letting of property and lending of money, are in fact very similar. See the *Code of Theodosius*, II. xxxi. 1, *pecuniam commodat* (he loans money). Justinian [*Code*, IV. xxvi. 13] has used the expression *mutuam dat* (he gives a loan). Horace, in his *Satires*, I. ii [I. ii. 9], said: 'Coins let out at interest'; and hereon the Scholiast explains that interest is the gain, the pay, for the use.

[2] Money in fact ought not to be unproductive; *Digest*, XXVII. iv. 3. § 4; XXII. i. 7.

more plausible, that in the case under consideration the thing is returned for the thing; that the use of the thing cannot be distinguished from the thing when the use of the thing consists in using it up; and that, therefore, nothing ought to be demanded for such use.

2. But it is to be noted that although the usufruct of things which perish in use, or are transferred to the ownership of another, is said to have been introduced by a decree of the Senate, nevertheless it was not thereby brought about that there should be a usufruct
Dig. VII. v. 2. properly speaking; but the word usufruct was dealt with, and certainly according to its proper interpretation this word does not accord with such a law. Yet from this it does not follow that there
Digest, XXXV. ii. 1. § 9. is no such right, or that it is not capable of evaluation, since on the contrary it is certain that if any one should yield such a right to the owner money could be demanded on that account. So also the right of repaying money or wine only after a certain time is something capable of being evaluated; for he pays less who pays later. And so 'in reciprocal usage'[1] the use of money is compensated for by the fruits of an estate. What is said against interest by Cato, Cicero, Plutarch, and others,[2] has in view not so much its intrinsic nature as its usual accompaniments and results.

3. Whatever may be thought of this matter, for us the law given by God to the Jews, which forbids Jews to loan money on interest to Jews, ought to suffice. For the substance of this law, if not necessary, is at any rate honourable[3] from the point of view of morals; and for this reason it is added to other specially moral
[xiv. 5.] precepts in the Psalm which is numbered fifteenth in the Jewish
[xviii. 8.] Bible and fourteenth in the Latin,[4] and also in the eighteenth chapter of *Ezekiel*.

Moreover, precepts of this kind are binding also upon Christians, since they are called upon to give loftier examples of the virtues; and the duties, which at that time the Jews and other circumcised persons, being of equal condition, were ordered to perform, ought now to be performed by every person, since the Gospel has removed all distinctions between peoples,[5] and a broader meaning has been
Luke, x. 29. given to the word neighbour. Besides other passages, this is shown by the noteworthy parable of Christ concerning the Samaritan.

[1] *Digest*, XX. ii. 8; *Code*, IV. xxxii. 14.

[2] As in Appian, *Civil Wars* [I. vi. 54].

[3] The Jewish scholars think that the word *neschek* means interest on loaned money, but *tarbith*, interest on anything. Jerome, *On Ezekiel*, xvii [xviii = VI. xviii. 210], says: 'Some persons think that interest is taken for money only; but the Divine Scriptures, foreseeing this interpretation, take away all excess, that you may not receive more than you have given.'

[4] Also *Psalms*, cii [cxii. 5]: 'Good is the man that dealeth graciously and lendeth.'

[5] Arnobius in Book IV [IV. xxxvi] says that Christians 'share their possessions with all men whom union joins in the bond of brotherhood'. Elsewhere he adds: 'They love all men as brothers.'

And so Lactantius, treating of the duties of a Christian, says: 'He will not lend money on interest, for this is to seek gain from another's misfortunes.' Says Ambrose: 'To assist the one in need is an act of humanity, but it is harshness to extort more than you have given.' [1] Augustus Caesar himself branded with disgrace certain persons because they had borrowed money [236] at a low rate of interest and lent it at a higher rate.

Epit. of Div. Inst., ii [lix]. *On Duties*, III. ii [III. iii. 20]. Suetonius, [*Augustus*,] xxxix.

XXI.—*What advantages do not come under the head of interest*

Nevertheless the observation should be made that there are certain advantages which approach the character of interest,[2] and commonly seem to be interest, although they are agreements of another kind; such are agreements for making good the loss which one who lends money suffers because he misses the use of the money for a long time; and likewise for the loss of gain on account of a loan, with a deduction, of course, in view of the uncertainty of expectations and of the effort which it would have been necessary to put forth. So again, it is not, in fact, usury if something is demanded for the expenses of the man who lends to many and keeps cash on hand for this purpose, as well as for the danger of losing the principal, in case proper security is not taken.

In his oration *Against Pantaenetus*, Demosthenes declares that it is not right to burden with the name of usurer a man who lends at a moderate interest [3] money which he has made by trade or honourable labour, partly in order that he may preserve his property, and partly that he may do a favour to another.

[xxxvii. 54 =p. 982.]

[1] Cyprian, *On the Lapsed* [vi], enumerating the graver faults, adds: 'To add to one's gain by interest which multiplies debts.' Chrysostom, *On Fasting*, V, says: 'If you fast, see to it that you do not place your money at interest. Do you fast? Cancel the written bonds of your unjust contracts.' Likewise *On First Corinthians*, dealing with the last chapter [=Homily XLIII, iv, end] he says that money gained by interest if given in alms is no more acceptable to God than if given from gains of harlotry.

Augustine, *Letters*, liv [cliii. 25], says: 'What shall I say of interest, which even the law and the judges order paid? Then is he more cruel who robs or steals some thing from a rich man than one who murders a poor man with usury?' Maximus in his third homily, *De Quadragesima* [xliv. 136], says: 'Rightly you will attend the church, brother, if that greedy interest does not entangle your feet in its deadly snares.'

Add to these Basil's homily *On the Sermon of Our Lord on the Mount* [*On Psalms*, xiv, *Against Usurers*],and what Gratian has collected from the councils and sacred writers in *Decretum*, II. xiv. 3 and 4.

[2] And if we wish to speak in the manner of the Roman jurists, the name of usury is hateful, but not in like manner interest. 'Interest is charged not for the gain of those who demand it, but because of the delay of those who pay it'; *Digest*, XXII. i. 17. § 3. Cujas, *Paratitla on Code*, IV. xxxiii (*De Nautico Fenore*), says: 'Extortion is what is added above the principal for the sake of gain; interest, what is added that the creditor may not suffer loss.' Because many have misused the word usury, it has now begun to be taken in a worse sense, and the word interest is substituted for it in the good sense.

[3] Procopius, *Gothic War*, III [III. xl], says in praise of Germanus, a relative of Justinian: [241] 'He loaned great sums of money to all who had need, but he never took from them interest deserving of the name.'

XXII.—*What the force of the civil laws is in this matter*

There are, in fact, human laws which allow that a return may be agreed on for the use of money, or of anything else. Thus in Holland it has long been lawful for other persons to collect 8 per cent.[1] per annum, but for merchants to exact 12 per cent. If such laws truly keep within the natural limit of compensation for that which is, or can be, out of one's possession, they are not inconsistent with natural or divine law; but if they exceed that limit they may grant impunity,[2] but they cannot give a right.

XXIII.—*What valuation ought to be put on a contract for securing against loss or insuring*

A contract for securing against risk, which is called insurance,[3] will be null and void if either of the contracting parties knew that the property in question had either arrived at its destination in safety, or had been lost. This rule is valid not only by reason of that fairness which the nature of contracts for exchange requires, but also because the particular substance of the contract is the uncertainty of the loss. Moreover, the price of such insurance against risk ought to be fixed in accordance with common estimation.

XXIV.—*What rule applies in the case of a partnership; wherein many kinds of partnerships are explained*

1. In a business partnership,[4] where the capital is made up from payments of funds, if the investments are equal then the partners ought to have equal shares in the loss and gain; but if the investments are unequal the division should be made proportionately. The principle was set forth by Aristotle at the end of the eighth
[VIII. xvi.] book of the *Nicomachean Ethics* in these words: 'In an association with capital those receive more who contributed more.'

The same will hold true if equal or unequal shares of work were contributed. But also money can be associated with work, or with money and work, as in the common saying:

[Plautus, *Asinaria*, 172.] Like to like gives recompense, when work and funds are joined.

[1] The same rate is legalized in the Empire [of Austria].

[2] Thus Justinian considered it his duty to reduce to a fairer rate the interest permitted before his time; *Novels*, xxxii, xxxiii, xxxiv.

[3] Suetonius in his *Claudius* [xviii] said that he took the loss on himself. Thus Cicero took security for the public money, that the people might be guarded against the risk of transportation; *Letters*, XII. xvii [*To Friends*, II. xvii. 4].

[4] According to Pliny you have an illustration of a partnership among dolphins, IX. viii [*Natural History*, IX. viii. 33]; and in the case of the mussel and the mussel-crab IX. xl [IX. xlii. 142]. Cicero, too, speaks of that matter in his *On Ends* [III. xix. 63].

2. But this joint contribution is not made merely in one way; for either the work is united with the bare use of the money, in which case the loss of capital falls upon the owner, and the capital, if saved, belongs to the owner; or the work is associated with the ownership of the money, in which case the one who contributes his work becomes a sharer in the capital.

Navarrus, xvii, no. 250; Covarruvias, *Variae*, III. ii; Lessius, II. ii. 25 [II. xxv.], dub. 3.

In the first case there is joined with the capital, not the work, but the danger of loss of the capital and of the gain which might reasonably be expected from it. In the second case the value of the work is considered as if added to the capital; and according to the value of it the one who furnishes work has a share in the capital. What we have said about work ought to be understood as applicable to the work and peril of voyages and similar undertakings.

3. Moreover, it is contrary to the nature of a partnership that one of the partners should share in the gain, when he has immunity from loss. Nevertheless, an agreement with this end in view can be made without injustice. Under such conditions the agreement will become a mixed contract of partnership and insurance against loss, [237] in which equality will be preserved if the one who has taken upon himself the risk of loss shall receive an equivalent increase in profit over what he would otherwise have received. In such a case, however, the risk of loss without the chance of gain ought not to be permitted, because the sharing in advantages is so essential to partnerships that a partnership cannot exist without it.

Angelus, word *societas*, i. § 7; Sylvester, word *societas*, i, qu. 2; Navarrus, xvii, no. 255; Covarruvias and Lessius, as cited above. *Digest*, XVII. ii. 29.

The statement of the jurist, that when the shares in a partnership are not designated they are understood to be equal, must be considered as true only in case the amounts contributed to the capital are equal. In a partnership covering all the possessions of the partners it will be necessary to compare not the profit which has arisen from this or that share, but that which could reasonably have been expected.

XXV.—*Concerning joint undertakings for maritime operations*

In a joint undertaking of ships the common advantage is defence against pirates; sometimes also booty. Ordinarily a valuation is placed on the ships and on their cargoes, and from this the total is reckoned, so that the losses which occur, in which the care of the wounded is included, may be borne by the owners of the ships and cargoes in proportion to the shares of the whole which they possess.[1]

Livy, XXXIX [XXIII. xlix]; Aristotle, *Politics*, III. vi.

What we have said up to this point is in accordance with the law of nature.

[1] See a similar provision in the *Laws of the Visigoths*, V. v. 5.

XXVI.—*According to the law of nations, so far as external acts are concerned, no consideration is given to an inequality in terms which has been agreed to; in what sense this may be said to be consistent with the law of nature*

1. In these matters no change seems to have been made by the volitional law of nations, with the one exception that, when there has been no falsehood or concealment of what ought to have been said, an inequality in terms is considered an equality as regards external acts; consequently, as no action at law was allowed against such an inequality by the civil law before the constitution of Diocletian, so among those who base their association on the law of nations alone no demand or collection on that account is allowed.

Dig. IV. iv. 16 [§ 4]; XIX. ii. 22 [§ 3]. This, in fact, is the same point that Pomponius maintains, that by the law of nature it is permissible for men to cheat one another in the price of sale and purchase; but here 'permissible' is used not in the sense of morally right, but with the meaning that no remedy exists against the man who in such a case chooses to defend himself on the basis of the agreement.

2. In this passage, and elsewhere at times, the law of nature has been used to designate that which is everywhere the accepted custom.[1] So in the writings of the Apostle Paul nature herself is said to teach that it is disgraceful for a man to wear long hair, though nevertheless this is not repugnant to nature, and has been customary among many nations. So the writer of the *Book of Wisdom* calls all men, meaning only the worshippers of idols, 'vain by nature', and the Apostle Paul alluded to those who are 'by nature the children of wrath', although he spoke not so much in his own person as in that of the Romans, with whom he was then living. Evenus, the ancient poet, says:

I Corinthians, xi. 14. [*Book of Wisdom*,] xiii. 1. *Ephesians*, ii. 3. [Gnomici, p. 131.]

> That which you long think o'er will lasting be, O friend,
> And this I think is nature's law for mortal men.

An ancient saying with the same meaning is found in Galen: 'Habit is a second and acquired nature.' With similar meaning Thucydides says: 'Human nature is superior to laws.' So the Greeks call both virtues and vices 'naturalized' after they have become firmly rooted. In Diodorus Siculus we read: 'Since necessity, that is, strength of mind, conquered nature.' Thus when the jurist Pomponius had said that the Roman law did not allow a civilian to die both testate and intestate, he added that these things were by nature opposed to each other, though that rule is dependent on

III [lxxxiv. 2]. [XVI. xviii. 2.] *Dig.* L. xvii. 7.

[1] Thus Gellius, IX. x [IX. x. 1], says of the conjugal act: 'It is a thing to be done in private by the law of nature.'

Roman customs alone and has no place among other peoples; [238] and even among the Romans themselves it does not apply in the case of soldiers' wills.[1]

3. However, the advantage of introducing the rules which I have mentioned is manifest for the termination of disputes which would be without number; which, furthermore, would be interminable on account of the uncertain price of things among persons who have no common judge, and which would be unavoidable if men were allowed to withdraw from agreements on account of inequality of terms. 'This is the substance of purchase and sale,' say the emperors—meaning by the word 'substance' the lasting custom—'that since the buyer desires to purchase at a cheaper price and the seller to sell at a higher price, they reach this agreement; and with difficulty after much bargaining,[2] while the seller gradually lowers the sum which he had asked, and the buyer adds to his offer, they finally agree on a definite price.' *Code*, IV. xliv. 8.

In accordance with this principle Seneca says: 'What difference does it make how much they are worth, after the price has been agreed upon between the buyer and the seller? He who has gotten a good bargain owes nothing to the seller.' *On Benefits*, VI. xv [4]. Andronicus of Rhodes says, to the same effect: 'A gain, which is made with the consent of the contracting parties, is neither unjust nor subject to suit. In fact, the law has granted permission for such transactions.' *On Nicomachean [Ethics]*, V. v [end].

4. The writer of the life of Isidore, whom I mentioned further back, says that buying at less than a fair price or selling at more than a fair price is an injustice, which is permitted indeed by law, but which in fact destroys justice. [In Photius, *Bibliotheca*, cod. 242 = p. 1044.]

[1] On the contrary, often in the wills of civilians, when complaint is entered of a will contrary to duty; *Digest*, V. ii. 19, 15, 24; *Code*, III. xxviii. 13.

[2] Festus says [word *Coctiones*]: 'Brokers seem to be so named from their delaying, because in buying and selling goods they arrive slowly at the limit of a just price. Consequently, among the ancients the first syllable of their name, *cocio*, was written with the letter V.' Quintilian in his declamation *For the Citizens* [xii. 21] says: 'He haggled for a long time.'

CHAPTER XIII

ON OATHS

I.—*How great the force of an oath is, even in the opinion of heathen peoples*

1. [242] AMONG all peoples, and in every age, the force of an oath regarding promises, agreements, and contracts has always been very great. For as Sophocles says in the *Hippodamia* :

[In Stobaeus, *Sermones*, xxvii. 6.]

> The mind is wont by oath to be aroused
> With earnest care to shun these evils twain,
> That friends should blame, and gods should take offence.

On Duties, I [III. xxxi. 111].

'Our ancestors', says Cicero, 'provided that there should be no stronger bond for guaranteeing good faith than an oath.'

2. Hence at no time has it failed to be believed that a severe punishment awaits perjurers. So Hesiod said in regard to an oath :

[*Theogony*, 231 f.]

> From such a source to mortal man disasters come,
> Whenever they take oath with lying heart.

In their view even posterity might pay the penalty for the sins of ancestors,[1] an opinion that was held only with regard to the worst crimes ; and the wish also, without the act, might bring punishment on itself. Both of these statements are substantiated by Herodotus in the story of Glaucus, son of Epicydes, who had merely deliberated whether he should falsify his sworn pledge in regard to a deposit in trust ; and in the same passage Herodotus records these verses of the Pythian prophetess :

II [VI. lxxxvi.].

> But from an oath is born a nameless child ;
> No hands, no feet, yet with great power he comes,
> And all the house and stock annihilates.[2]

[xiii. 208 f.]

Juvenal, recalling the same story, thus concludes :

> Such punishments the mere desire to sin
> Suffers.

On Duties, III [xxix. 104].

3. Cicero well said : 'An oath is a religious affirmation. That moreover which you have firmly promised, as if with God as your

[1] [252] See Servius in the Fuldensian excerpts, *On the Aeneid*, Book I [*On the Georgics*, I, line 502].

[2] See *Zachariah*, v. 1–3, and Chrysostom as interpreter of this passage in *On the Statues*, XV [XV. v].

witness, must be maintained.' He adds also this: 'Now, in fact, the matter belongs not to the anger of the gods, which has no existence, but to justice and good faith.' If under the term anger Cicero means mental disturbance, the statement ought to be believed; but if he means some sort of a feeling or a wish to harm he should by no means be followed, as Lactantius rightly shows.

[*On Duties*, III. xxix. 104.]

On the Anger of God.

Let us now see whence the force of an oath arises, and to what point it extends.

II.—*That a deliberate intention is required, that is, that a person has willed to take oath*

First, the statement which we made about promises and contracts, that a mind possessed of reason and a deliberate intention are requisite, is in place here. If, then, a person has uttered the words of an oath without thinking that he is swearing, as is related of Cydippe,[1] the same remark applies which is assigned to her by Ovid: [II. xi. 5.] [*Heroides*, xxi. 135.]

> The mind it is that swears; therewith have I not sworn.[2]

This is taken from Euripides, who had said in the *Hippolytus*: [Line 612.]

> The tongue has sworn; I swore not with the mind.[3]

If any one has been willing to swear but unwilling to bind himself, he is none the less bound, because the obligation is inseparable from the oath and is a necessary result of it.

Soto, VIII. i, art. 7. Covarruvias, *On Decretals*, V. xli. 10, pt. i, § 5.

III.—*That the words of an oath are binding in the sense in which it is believed that they were understood by the one to whom the oath was sworn*

1. But if any one has deliberately uttered the words of an oath, yet without the intention of swearing, some writers state that he is not bound, but yet that he sins by swearing rashly. It is, however, nearer the truth to say that he is bound to make true the words

[1] A similar story is found in the *Metamorphoses* of Antonius [Antoninus] Liberalis concerning Ctesylla and Hermochares [chap. i].

[2] *Ibid.* [Ovid, *Heroides*, xxi, lines 137 ff.]:

> Good counsel and forethoughtful mind take oath;
> No bonds have strength except as judgement binds.

Then he adds,

> But if without the heart we senseless speech
> Have uttered, all in vain the words, of strength
> Deprived. I have not taken oath; merely
> The words of one who swears I read.

See also the verses which follow.

[3] Because Hippolytus had understood the words of the nurse concerning the concealment of an honourable act, not of adultery and incest.

which he has called God to witness. For that act, which is binding in itself, proceeded from a deliberate intention.

From this it naturally follows that in the main the statement of Cicero is true, that 'It is perjury not to do that which [243] you have sworn to "on your conscience"'. Akin to this is what Calypso, according to Homer, says in making oath to Ulysses:

[*On Duties*, III. xxix. 108.]

[*Odyssey*, V. 188.]

But I shall say the same my mind has thought.

2. Nevertheless there may be an exception in this, that the person taking oath should know, or should reasonably believe, that the words are understood differently by the one with whom he is dealing; for in calling to God to witness his words he ought to make them true as he thinks they are understood.[1] And this is what the same Cicero said: 'An oath sworn with the clear understanding, in the mind of him who swears, that it ought to be performed, should be kept.' We read in Tacitus: 'Those who were troubled by a guilty conscience became fearful, and by every kind of expedient tried to alter the words of the oath.'

[*On Duties*, III. xxix. 107.]

Histories, IV [xli].

Augustine says: 'Men who, keeping the letter of the oath, have deceived the expectation of those to whom they have sworn, are perjurers.' Also Isidore:[2] 'No matter how artful the words with which a person takes oath, nevertheless God, Who is the witness of the conscience, accepts it just as the man to whom the oath is made has understood it.' This is what is called to take oath clearly.[3] And so Metellus rightly refused to swear obedience to the Apuleian law, although there were some who said that the law was not valid on

Letters, ccxxiv [cxxv. 4].

Appian, *Civil Wars*, I [iv. 31].

[1] Augustine, *Letters*, ccxxiv [cxxv. 3], speaking of the one who, after leaving the Carthaginian camp, had returned to the camp and had then come to Rome, says: 'Thus those who removed him from the senate considered not what he had thought when taking oath, but what those, to whom he had sworn, expected from him.' See also the rest of the passage.

Cf. also what was well said on this matter in the Council of Trosly in Sirmond's edition of *Concilia*, vol. III, and by Hincmar in the treatise, *De Divortio Lotharii et Tetbergae*, interrogation vi [p. 603], where he rightly speaks to this purport concerning God:

Who heard the oath not as you swore, but as he thought
You swore who took your oath; so are you bound to both.

In the oath sworn by the Jews throughout Spain is this provision: 'If you shall not have done it with the same understanding as I declare it was heard and understood by us.'

[2] *De Summo Bono*, Book II, xxxi. 1, cited in the *Decretum*, II. xxii. 5. 9.

[3] On that see Donatus, *On* [*Terence's*] *Andria* [lines 729 f.]:

For if, perchance, I must to my master swear
I did not place it there, with conscience clear I may.

'With clear conscience' means openly and plainly.

Nicetas in the life of *Alexis* [I. iii], censuring the deceit of Andronicus Comnenus, says: 'We ought not to twist the meaning of our words with an unusual expression, but utter them as they have been regularly understood.' Also in another passage he says of Alexius, taking words in a sense contrary to their natural meaning: 'He clung fast to those words as flies to a cut made by a whip.'

The court of Arcadius sinned grievously against this rule; it caused a man to be killed at Chalcedon who had come to Constantinople under promise of safe-conduct affirmed on oath. Zozomen, Book V [Zosimus, V. xviii].

Add also what is said in chap. xvi, 2.

account of the illegality of its passage, and that the oath to support the law ought to be understood as binding only in case the law had been proposed and passed in due form.

Panormitanus, *On Decretals*, II. xxviii. 35. Sylvester, word *iuramentum*, 4, qu. 23; [*Hebrews*,] vi. 17; Thomas Aquinas, thereon.

3. Although in the case of other promises a tacit condition, which absolves the promisor, is easily understood, nevertheless this ought not to be admitted in the case of an oath. Here the notable statement of the Apostle in the *Epistle to the Hebrews* applies: 'Wherein God, willing more abundantly to show unto the heirs of promise the immutability of His counsel, confirmed it by an oath; that by two immutable things, in which it is impossible for God to deceive'—for so I think it right to translate ψεύδεσθαι, as plain speaking is called the truth (*Daniel*, vii. 16; viii. 26; x. 1)—'we may have a strong encouragement.' In order to understand these words, we ought to know that the sacred writers often speak of God 'as having human feelings', and rather as He seems to us than as He is.

Jonah, iv. 2.

4. For in reality God does not change His decrees. Nevertheless He is said to change them and to be influenced by repentance [1] as often as He acts otherwise than His words seemed to mean; and this may happen on account of a condition tacitly understood,[2] which has ceased to exist; *Jeremiah*, xviii. 8. It is possible to find examples in *Genesis*, xx. 3, *Exodus*, xxxii. 14, *1 Kings*, xxi. 29, *2 Kings*, xx. 1, *Isaiah*, xxxviii. 1, *Jonah*, iii. 5 and 11 [10]. In this sense God cannot properly be said even to deceive us, and the word 'to deceive', which appears in the passage of the *Epistle to the Hebrews*, quoted above, ordinarily refers to an event which disappoints expectation. This can be seen both in other passages and in *Leviticus*, vi. 2, *Joshua*, xxiv. 27, *Isaiah*, lviii. 11 [lvii. 11], *Hosea*, i. 2 [ix. 2], and *Habakkuk* [3] (iii. 17). But this apparent deception occurs most easily in threats, because these confer right upon no one. It appears at times also in promises, when indeed there is a tacit condition secretly present.

5. For this reason, then, the Apostle names two things which denote unchangeability: the promise, because it confers a right; and the oath, because it admits of no tacit conditions or conditions in any way concealed, as we may see in the *Psalms* (lxxxix. 30–6). For it is a different thing if the nature of the transaction itself openly indicates certain conditions. To such a case some refer the promise found in *Numbers*, xiv. 30. But it is more true to say that the land was said to have been promised on oath to them not as individuals but as a people, to the descendants, undoubtedly, of

[1] Cf. *Council of Toledo*, VIII. ii: 'For God to swear is not to overthrow anything whatever that has been ordained by Himself; to repent, however, is to change what He has ordained, when He will.' This was cited by Gratian in the *Decretum*, II. xxii. 4 [II. xxii. 4. 9]. Explain as in our text.

[2] [253] See Seneca, *Natural Questions*, II. xxxvii.

[3] Add *Job*, xli. 6 [xl. 28]; *Hosea*, ix. 2.

those to whom God had sworn in verse 23. Such a promise, moreover, can be fulfilled at any time, and is not restricted to particular individuals.

IV.—*When an oath procured by means of fraud is binding*

1. From what I have said it can be understood what ought to be thought of an oath procured by means of fraud. If it is certain that the person [244] who took an oath believed to be true some fact which is not true,[1] and would not have sworn if he had not believed this, the oath will not be binding. If, however, it shall be doubtful whether he would not have taken the same oath even without the erroneous supposition, he will have to stand by his words, because in an oath the greatest possible simplicity is required.

Navarrus, xii, no. 13.

2. And under this head I class the oath which Joshua and the leaders of Israel took to the Gibeonites. These had, in fact, been deceived by the Gibeonites, who pretended that they had come from a distant region. But it did not follow therefrom that Joshua and the leaders would not have spared them if they had known that they were a neighbouring people. For they had said this to the Gibeonites: 'Peradventure you dwell among us. And how shall we make a covenant with you?' These words are open to the interpretation that the Gibeonites were asked what sort of a treaty they desired, one of alliance or of surrender, or even that the Jews thereby indicated that they were not allowed to make a treaty of alliance with certain peoples; but the words do not also indicate that life would not be granted to them if they should surrender. For the divine law, which devoted those peoples to destruction, from comparison with the other law,[2] was to be so understood that it would hold good unless the peoples concerned should obey the commands immediately on being summoned. This contention is proved by the story of Rahab[3]—among others—who was spared on account of her good offices,

Joshua, ix [15].

Deuteronomy, xx. 10.

[*Joshua*, ii.]

[1] As Hippolytus, of whom we have just made mention. On the passage of Sophocles in the *Oedipus at Colonus* [lines 230 ff.],

> Deception on deception heaped will be repaid
> With due destruction, not with kindnesses,

[the Scholiast] says: 'The Thebans think that on receiving Oedipus they promised him immunity as regards the cause stated by him, for they had not learned that he was held guilty of a crime in his family. Similar also is the well-known verse,

> My tongue has sworn; I swore not with my mind.

For also Hippolytus had sworn in consequence of having been deceived.'

[2] And also for the reason added to the law concerning their destruction; *Exodus*, xxiv. 33 [xxiii. 33]; *Deuteronomy*, vii. 4. For that reason, in fact, it loses its effect in the case of those who accept the commands of the sons of Noah and pay tribute. Thus Maimonides and Samson Micosi; also Moses de Kotzi, in his *Precepts Bidding*, 15 and 118.

[3] So also the inhabitants of Gazer in *Joshua*, xvi. 10. The Gergesenes continued to exist up to the times of Christ, as appears from the Gospel, *Matthew*, viii. 28. For they had surrendered in the very beginning, and so are omitted in the enumeration of enemies; *Deuteronomy*, xx. 17; *Joshua*, ix. 1.

and that of Solomon, who received the remnant of the Canaanites as subjects and payers of tribute. *1 Kings, ix. 21.*

3. This view is supported also by the statement in the book of *Joshua*, that there was no state of those seven peoples that made peace; they had, in fact, been hardened that they might not find favour. Since, then, it was credible that if the Gibeonites had declared the truth, which they did not do on account of fear, they would nevertheless have obtained the preservation of their lives on the condition of surrendering, the oath was valid, and valid in such a degree that by the authority of God most severe punishments were inflicted for the violation of it. *xi. 19, 20.* *2 Samuel, xxi. 6.*

In his discussion of this narrative, Ambrose says [1]: 'Nevertheless Joshua thought that he ought not to annul the peace, which he had granted, because it had been confirmed by a religious oath, lest, while censuring the faithlessness of others, he should himself break faith.' However, the Gibeonites did suffer some punishment for their fraud, since by their surrender they were made subjects of the Jews. For they were assigned to a kind of personal slavery,[2] although if they had acted openly they might have been received as tributaries.

V.—*That the words of an oath should not be stretched beyond the meaning supported by ordinary use*

Yet the meaning of an oath ought not to be stretched beyond the usage of ordinary speech. So when the other Jews had taken oath that they would not give their daughters in marriage to the Benjamites they did not perjure themselves even though they permitted the girls, who had been carried off, to live with the men who had taken them. It is, in fact, one thing to give, another not to demand the return of something that has been lost.[3] Ambrose says in regard to this matter: 'And that kindness seems not to have been without a punishment meet for the lawlessness of the men, since they were permitted to enter wedlock only by stealing wives and not through the sacrament of marriage.' *On Duties, II. xiv [III. xix. 110].*

Not unlike is the case of the Achaeans. For when the Romans disapproved of some things which they had done and confirmed by oath they asked that the Romans themselves should make such *Livy, XXXIX [xxxvii. 21].*

[1] *On Duties*, III. x [III. x. 69].

[2] As the Bruttians formerly by the Romans; Gellius, X. iii [X. iii. 19]; Festus, under the word *Bruttiani*.

[3] Josephus [*Antiquities of the Jews*, V. ii. 12] says in regard to this story: 'The Israelites neither urged them to do it nor forbade them.' Seneca in the *Excerpts* [*Controversies*], VI. ii, says: 'That man is subject to the law who aids an exile, not he who allows an exile to be aided.' Symmachus [*Letters*, X. liv] says: 'He who asserts that you are guilty in the sight of those who grant, unless you are odious to those who remove, is trying to instil an empty fear into your divine mind.'

changes as should seem best, and not place the Achaeans under the necessity of annulling what they had ratified by oath.

VI.—*That an oath to perform an unlawful act is not binding*

In order that an oath may be valid, the obligation taken ought to be lawful.[1] Therefore a sworn promise relating to an illegal act will have no force either by the law of nature, or by divine interdict, or even by human law, which we shall discuss later. Philo the Jew [2] well said:

> [245] Let every one, who undertakes to perform an unjust act because of an oath, know that he will not be keeping but breaking an oath, which is worthy of great care and scruple, and by which honourable and upright acts are wont to be confirmed. He in fact adds fault to fault who joins an unlawful act to an oath wrongfully made, from which it would have been better to refrain. Let him abstain, then, from the unlawful act and let him pray to God to grant to him the mercy which is suitable for him. For to choose two evils, when you have it in your power to be relieved of one, is an evidence of an incurable frenzy and lack of sense.

I Samuel, xxv. [*On Duties,* III. xxv. 95.] II [XI. xi]. [*Hercules Oetaeus,* 480 f.]

An example may be given in the case of David, who spared Nabal, whom he had sworn to kill. Cicero gives a similar example in the vow of Agamemnon; Dionysius of Halicarnassus offers still another in the conspiracy of the decemvirs to seize the government. Seneca says:

> I do confess that I can keep my silent pledge,
> If it is free from crime; sometimes good faith is crime,

where the Latin text has 'meanwhile' with the meaning 'sometimes'.

On Duties, I, last chapter.

Ambrose says: 'It is in fact sometimes contrary to duty to fulfil a promise, to keep an oath.' Says Augustine:[3] 'If good faith is shown in committing a sin, marvellous it is that it is called good faith.' In his second letter *To Amphilochius*, Basil has the same teaching.

VII.—*That an oath is not binding which hinders a greater moral good*

1. Furthermore, even if the thing which is promised is not unlawful, but only hinders a greater moral good,[4] under such a con-

[1] Ambrose deals well with this subject in the treatise *On Duties*, I [I. l. 254], and likewise other authors cited in the *Decretum*, II. xxii. 4. Canon vii of the Council of Ilerda applies to this, cited in volume III of the *Councils of France*. There are also many examples in the works of Hincmar.

[2] *On Special Laws* [II. iv].

[3] *De Bono Conjugali*, iv. This passage is quoted in the *Decretum* just cited [II. xxii. 4. 20].
See also Gail, *De Pace Publica*, Book I, iv. 16; and the story about Albinus, in Paulus Diaconus, Book II, xxvi [II. xxvii].

[4] Such as the oath of Honorius never to make peace [254] with Alaric, as Zosimus relates [V. xlix]. See *Decretum*, II. xxii. 4. 22, and the Council of Ilerda in the *Councils of France*, vol. III, canon vii. Also Hincmar in the work cited above, *Liber de Divortio*, Interrogation xiv [p. 651], and Interrogation vi [pp. 602 ff.] and xiv.

dition also the oath will not be valid; in truth we are under obligation to God to advance in goodness in such a way that we have not the power to cut off from ourselves the opportunity of growth in grace. It will not be out of place to quote a noteworthy passage of Philo the Jew, whom I cited above, as bearing on this point: 'There are some people so controlled by a hard and unsociable nature, or by hatred of the human race, or by a harsh overmastering wrath, that they strengthen their savageness of character with an oath that they will not sit at table or stay in the same house with a certain man, that they will never do him a favour, that they will not receive anything from him even until death.' But the kind of oath, which he said certain persons swore, never to do a favour to this or that man,[1] the Jews called 'an oath of beneficence', 'an oath to do good', *Leviticus*, v. 6 [v. 4]. According to the Jewish rabbis the formula of this was, 'Let all the advantage you might receive from me be consecrated to God'; and with this the Syriac, in the old version of *Matthew*, xv. 5, agrees: 'If you have ever received any good from me, let it be a gift consecrated to God'; for that is the meaning of the expression 'given to God'.

[*On Special Laws*, II. iv.]

2. The Jewish rabbis, who are the worst interpreters of this portion of the divine law, thought that a vow was perfectly valid in case the penalty of consecration had been added, even if the vow had been made against parents. That opinion is refuted by Christ in the passage cited; for according to his words 'to honour' is 'to do good to', as is apparent from the parallel passage of Mark and also from the words of Paul in *1 Timothy*, v. 3 and 17; also from *Numbers*, xxiii. 11. But even if an oath has been taken against other persons we shall rightly say that it is not binding, because, as we have said, it is a barrier to our growth in goodness.

Thomas Aquinas, II. ii. 89, art. 7; and Cajetan thereon. Gratian, *Decretum*, II. xxii. 4. 23. § 6. Soto, VII. i, art. 3, circa 2.

VIII.—*That an oath is not binding to perform an act which is impossible*

It is not necessary to speak of impossibilities. It is, in fact, sufficiently evident that no one is bound to do that which is quite impossible.

[246] IX.—*What if an act, for which an oath has been taken, is impossible for the time being?*

As regards what is impossible for the time being, or in the opinion of the one who took the oath, the obligation is in suspense. Consequently, a person who has taken oath under such a supposition ought to do what he can to render his oath possible.

[1] See *Baba Kama*, ix. 10, and the observations of the learned Constantine thereon.

X.—*That an oath is sworn in the name of God, and in what sense*

In regard to form, oaths differ in words, but agree in substance. An oath ought to contain this element, that God is invoked, as, for example, in this way: 'God be my witness', or 'God be my judge', two expressions which amount to the same thing. For when a superior having the right to punish is called as a witness[1] punishment of faithlessness is at the same time asked from him. And He who knows all things is the avenger, because He is a witness. Plutarch says: 'Every oath comes to an end in curses in case one has committed perjury.'

Roman Questions [xliv = 275 D].

To the same category belong the ancient formulas for treaties, for which it was the custom to use sacrificial victims, as appears from *Genesis*, xv. 9 ff. Similar are the Roman formulas in Livy: 'Do thou, Jupiter, so smite that people as I smite this pig.' In another passage of the same author: 'He prayed to the gods that they should so slay him as he himself had slain the lamb.' See also the example in Polybius and Festus: 'If I knowingly deceive, so may Jupiter cast me away as I cast away this stone.'

I [xxiv.8]. XXI [xlv. 8]. [III. xxv. 8.] [Under the words *lapidem silicem*.]

XI.—*But that an oath is sworn also in the name of other things with respect to God*

1. But it was also an ancient custom to swear in the name of other things or persons, either because they were invoking such things or persons to become harmful to themselves, as the sun, the earth, heaven, their ruler, or because they were demanding that they be punished in respect to such things as their heads, their children, their country, their ruler. And this was not a custom of the heathen nations only, but also of the Jews, as the same Philo teaches us.[2] For he says that those who are about to take oath ought not for any and every thing and at once 'to have recourse to the author and parent of all things', but should swear by their parents, heaven, earth, and the universe.

Similar to this is the point noted by the commentators on Homer, that the ancient Greeks were not accustomed 'to swear easily by the gods but by other things at hand',[3] as by the sceptre; and Porphyry and the commentator on Aristophanes report that that oath was introduced by Rhadamanthus, a most just king. So Joseph

[Eustathius, *On the Iliad*, I. 234.] [*On Abstaining*, III. xvi = p. 285.] [*Birds*, 521.]

[1] Ambrose writes to the Emperor Valentinian [*Letters*, xvii. 9]: 'What is the taking of an oath except to confess the Divine power of Him whom you call upon as witness to your good faith?' See the excellent formula of the Chagan of the Avars in Menander, *Selections on Embassies* [= frag. 63, p. 123, edit. Dindorf].

[2] *On Special Laws* [II. ii].

[3] See Apollonius concerning Socrates in Philostratus, VI [VI. xix]: 'He swore by those things not as by the gods, but that he might not swear by the gods.'

is said to have sworn by the life of Pharaoh, in accordance with the *Genesis*, xlii. 15. accepted custom of the Egyptians, as Ebenesdras notes in the commentary on the passage; so Elisha swore by the life of Elijah.[1] *2 Kings*, ii. 2.

And in the fifth chapter of *Matthew* Christ does not, as some think, mean that such oaths shall be less lawful than those sworn explicitly in the name of God. But since the Jews had less regard for them, in accord with an opinion not unlike that of the man who [Ovid, *Remedy for Love*, 784.] said 'He does not believe the sceptre to be the gods,' Christ shows that these also are true oaths. Ulpian, too, most excellently said: 'He who swears by his own safety seems to swear by God, for he swears with respect to the divine power.'[2] *Dig.* XII. ii. 33. So Christ shows that the man that swears by the Temple swears by God, who presides over the Temple, and the man that swears by heaven swears by God, *Matthew*, xxiii. 21. whose throne is, as it were, in heaven.

2. But the Jewish teachers of those times were of opinion that men were not bound by oaths sworn by created things unless a penalty was added, as if the thing by which they swore were consecrated to God. This, then, is the oath called κορβᾶν, or 'by way of gift', of which there is mention not only in the passage of *Matthew* cited, but also in the laws of the Tyrians, as we learn from the discussion of [I. xxii. 167.] Josephus, *Against Apion*. And not for any other reason should I think that the Oriental peoples were called κάρβανοι (barbarous) by the Greeks, a word found in Aeschylus and Euripides; note also [*Agamemnon*, 1061; *Suppliants*, 118.] καρβάνα δ' αὐδάς, of 'barbaric speech', in the same Aeschylus.

This error Christ opposes in the passage cited. Tertullian says: [*Apology*, xxxii.] 'The ancient Christians took oath by the safety of the ruler, which [247] was more revered than all the Geniuses.' In Vegetius [II. v.] there is a formula, of which we made mention above, according to which Christian soldiers swore not only by God but also by the majesty of the Emperor, which by the human race ought to be loved and cherished next after God.

XII.—*That an oath is binding even if one swears by false gods*

But also if any one has sworn by false gods the oath will be binding.[3] For although possessed of false notions, he nevertheless has a respect for divinity under a general aspect; and so, if perjury has been committed, the true God interprets it as done to His harm. We see that holy men never proposed an oath in such a form, and still less swore in that way (I wonder that Duaren considered such

[1] Add *2 Kings*, iv. 30; *Song of Songs*, ii. 7.

[2] So also Gratian, *Decretum*, II. xxii. 1.

[3] *Book of Wisdom*, xiv [xiv. 31], thus given in the Latin version: 'It is not the uprightness of those by whom one swears, but the punishment of the guilty, which ever attends upon the falsehoods of the unjust.'

a form allowable); but nevertheless, if those with whom they had dealings could not be induced to take oath in any other way, they made contracts with them, and they themselves would swear as their duty required, but they would accept from the others such an oath as could be procured.

Augustine, *Letters*, cliv [xlvii. 2], *To Publicola*, cited in *Decretum*, II. xxii. 1. 16.

An example of this kind is found in the case of Jacob and Laban (*Genesis*, xxxi. 53). This is what Augustine says:[1] 'Whoever swears by a stone, if he swears falsely, is perjured'; and further: 'The stone does not hear you speaking, but God punishes if you deceive.'

XIII.—*The effects of an oath; hence from an oath a twofold obligation arises, one at the moment of the oath, another afterward; this is clearly explained*

1. The chief effect of an oath is to put an end to disputes. 'In every dispute the oath is final for confirmation,' says the inspired writer of *To the Hebrews*. Similar to this is the statement of Philo: 'An oath is the witnessing of God in a matter under dispute.' Not unlike it is the statement of Dionysius of Halicarnassus: 'The strongest pledge of good faith[2] among men, both Greeks and barbarians, which no time will destroy, is that which makes the gods sponsors by means of sworn agreements.' Thus among the Egyptians an oath was 'the strongest pledge of men to one another'.

[vi. 16.] [*Lex Allegoriarum*, III. lxxiii.] [VI. lxxxiv. 3.] Diodorus Siculus [I. lxxvii].

2. Therefore the person who takes an oath is bound in two ways: first, that his words should agree with his intent, which Chrysippus calls 'to swear truly'; and secondly, that his action should be consistent with his words, which the same writer calls 'swearing faithfully'. The person who does wrong in regard to the first requirement is said by the same Chrysippus 'to swear falsely';[3] in the second, 'to perjure himself', a distinction which is clear enough, though these matters are at times wont to be confused.

[In Stobaeus, *Florilegium*, xxviii. 15.]

XIV.—*When, as a result of an oath, a right is acquired for a man and for God; when for God alone*

If the matter should be such, and the words of an oath so phrased that they may be referred not only to God but also to a man, without doubt a right will be acquired for the man from the oath itself, as if from a promise or contract, which ought to be understood in the simplest way. But if either the words do not have a man in view

[1] *On the Words of the Apostle*, XXVIII [= *Sermones de Scripturis*, clxxx. 13], cited in *Decretum*, II. xxii. 5. 10.

[2] Procopius, *Persian War*, II [II. x. 10] says: 'An oath, which by all men is considered the last and strongest pledge of good faith and truthfulness.'

[3] To swear falsely is forbidden in *Exodus*, xx [xx. 7 and 16]; to perjure oneself, in *Leviticus*, xix [xix. 12]; as the Jewish commentators explain, *Precepts Bidding*, 240.

for the conferring of a right upon him, or if they do have him in view, but if there is something which can present an obstacle to his claim, then the force of the oath will be such that the man will indeed acquire no right, but nevertheless he who has sworn will be under obligation to God to keep his oath.

An example of this occurs in the case of one who by means of an unjust fear furnished the cause of a sworn promise.[1] For he acquires no right, or a right which he is obliged to relinquish, because he caused the loss. Thus we see that the Jewish kings were both rebuked by the prophets [2] and punished by God, because they had not kept their sworn pledge to the Babylonian kings. Cicero praises the tribune Pomponius, who kept the oath which he had sworn under the compulsion of fear; 'so great', he says, 'was the power of an oath in those times.' For such reasons not only Regulus was obliged to return to imprisonment, most unjust though it was, but also those ten, whom Cicero mentions, had to return to Hannibal; for an oath had been taken.

Ezekiel, xvii. 12, 13, 15. *On Duties*, III [xxxi. 112]. Toledo, IV. xxii.

On Duties, III [xxxii. 113].

[248] XV.—*Refutation of the opinion that one who has given his oath to a pirate or a tyrant is not obligated to God*

1. The principles stated are applicable not merely with respect to public enemies, but to any persons whatsoever. For not only the person to whom the oath is given is taken into consideration, but also God, by whom one swears,[3] and the reference to God is sufficient to create an obligation. Therefore we must thrust Cicero aside when he says that there is no perjury if the ransom for life, which had been agreed upon even under oath, is not paid to pirates, for the reason that a pirate is not entitled to the rights of war, but is the common enemy of mankind, with whom neither good faith nor a common oath should be kept. Elsewhere he said the same thing about a tyrant, as Brutus also did, according to Appian: 'With a tyrant the Romans keep no faith, have no scruple regarding an oath.'

Thomas, II. ii. 89, art. 7, and Cajetan thereon. Alexander of Im., *On Decretals*, II. xxiv. 15. Soto, VIII. i, art. 7. [*On Duties*, III. xxix. 107.]

Civil Wars, II [xix. 139].

2. Although it is true that according to the established law of nations there is a difference between a public enemy and a pirate—that will be pointed out by us below—yet the difference cannot be in point here where, even if the right of the person fails,[4] we have to reckon with God; and for this reason an oath is called a vow. Again, that is not true which Cicero assumes, that there is no common

[III. iii. 1.]

[1] Augustine in his *Letters*, ccxxiv and ccxxv [cxxv and cxxvi], teaches that even an oath extorted by force must be kept, on account of reverence for God.

[2] See also *Jeremiah*, xxix. 7 [xxxix. 5].

[3] Gregoras [X. v = 307 c]: 'Perjury charges God with the fault of negligence.'

[4] Plutarch in his *Lysander* [viii = 437 c] says: 'He that has cheated an enemy by an oath shows that the enemy is feared, and God despised, by him.'

Digest, XVI. iii. 31. ground of right with a robber. For Tryphoninus was right in giving the opinion that, according to the law of nations, if the true owner does not appear a deposit must be returned to a robber.[1]

3. Consequently I am not able to approve of the view held by certain persons, that one who has promised anything to a robber can discharge the promise with a momentary payment, so that it may be permissible for him to recover what he has paid. For in an oath the words relating to God ought to be understood in the simplest manner possible and so as to have effect. And so the man who secretly returned to the enemy and went away a second time did not satisfy the oath in regard to his return, as was rightly judged by the Roman senate.

XVI.—*Whether one who has given his oath to a faithless person ought to keep his oath; explanation, with a distinction*

[Cicero, *On Duties*, III. xxviii. 102.] 1. There is this in Accius:

> T. Your good faith you have broken.
> A. Faith which I neither gave, nor do I give,
> To one who faithless is.

The rule here implied can be approved if the sworn promise clearly was related to the promise of him to whom the oath was given, and *Dig.* XII. ii. 39. that had been blended with it,[2] forming as it were a condition; but it cannot be approved if the promises are of a different kind and without mutual relation. For in the latter case each must absolutely [VI. 63 f.] make good what he has sworn, and on this account Silius in praising Regulus thus addresses him:

> You who through ages long with fame increasing still
> Will be recalled as he who kept his faith
> With faithless Carthage.

2. We said above that inequality in contracts gives naturally an opportunity for annulling or correcting them. And although the law of nations has changed this somewhat, nevertheless by municipal law, which is valid between the different parts of the same people, a return is often made to that which was lawful by nature, as we [II.ii.6.1.] likewise showed above. But in this case also, if an oath has been *Authent.*, after *Code*, II. xxviii. 1. added, even if nothing, or a little, is due to the person, faith will have to be kept with God. And so the writer of the *Psalms*, when *Psalms*, xv [4]. enumerating the virtues of a good man, adds this also: 'He that sweareth to his own detriment, and changeth not.'

[1] And to the one who has invaded a kingdom unlawfully, as the deposit was returned to Orofernes by the Prienians; Polybius [*Excerpta de Virtute et Vitiis*, p. 1470 = XXXIII. xii], and Diodorus Siculus in the *Excerpta Peiresciana* [p. 334 = XXXI. xxxii].

[2] *Decretals*, II. xxiv. 3. Add the law in the *Digest*, XVIII. iii. 5.

XVII.—*That when a person has given his oath to God alone his heir is in no degree obligated*

This, again, must be noted, that when in consequence of some such defect as I have mentioned no right is created for a person but good faith is pledged to God, no binding obligation rests upon the heir of the man who took the oath. For as the property passes to the heir, that is, things bought or sold among men, so also the burdens on the property; but not in like manner other obligations, to which a person has been subject by reason of a duty imposed by religious feeling, gratitude, or good faith. These obligations do not, in fact, belong to what is in a strict sense called among men a right, as we remember having explained elsewhere also.

XVIII.—*That he is not guilty of perjury who does not keep his oath to a person that does not wish to have it kept, or in case the special character of the person, to whom the oath was sworn because of that character, has been laid aside*

But also where no right is created for a person, if nevertheless [249] the oath has in view the advantage of some other person, and the other person does not wish to have that advantage,[1] the one who took the oath will not be bound. So also he will not be bound if the condition under which he swore to some one has ceased,[2] as if a magistrate should cease to be a magistrate. In the second book of Caesar's *Civil War* Curio speaks to those who had been the soldiers of Domitius as follows: 'How could he hold you bound by your oath when he has thrown aside the insignia of office, laid down his command, and as a private citizen and a captive has come under the power of another?' Presently he says that the oath was annulled by the loss of civic rights. [II. xxxii.]

XIX.—*When anything which is done contrary to an oath becomes void*

The question is raised, whether anything done contrary to an oath is merely unlawful, or also void. *Decretals*, III. v. 25.

In this matter I think that a distinction ought to be made. If good faith alone has been pledged, the act done contrary to the oath will be valid, as, for example, the making of a will, or a sale; but such an act will not be valid if the oath was so phrased that it contained at the same time full abdication of the right of action. Covarruvias, *On Decretals*, V. xli. 10, pt. ii, § 2, no. 10.

[1] Plautus, *Rudens* [line 1414]: 'Excuse the man, I beg you, from his oath.'

[2] Similar laws in the *Digest*, XXVII. i. 6. § 14; in Gail, *Observationes*, II, obs. 144, no. 8, and *De Arrestis*, X. ix; and in Azor, *Moral Institutes*, V. xxii, qu. 6, pt. 1.

These distinctions, at any rate, naturally accompany an oath. In accordance therewith judgement should be passed on the oaths of kings, and the oaths which foreigners take to one another, since in such cases the act is not subject to the law of the place.

XX.—*What power the act of superiors has with respect to that which a subject has sworn, or with respect to an oath given to a subject, is set forth, with distinctions*

1. Let us now see what powers are possessed by superiors, that is, by kings, fathers and masters, and also by husbands, so far as conjugal rights[1] are concerned. The act of superiors cannot indeed bring it to pass that an oath does not have to be fulfilled, in so far as the oath was truly binding; for such fulfilment is required by both the law of nature and divine law. However, because our acts are not fully within our own power, but are related in such a way that they are dependent also on our superiors, there may be a twofold action by superiors concerning whatever is sworn, the one action directed against the person who takes the oath, the other against the person to whom the oath is given.

Thomas Aquinas, II. ii, qu. 89, art. 9.

2. The person who takes the oath can be directed, either by making the oath void before it is sworn, in the degree that the right of the inferior is subject to the power of the superior, or by forbidding that the oath be fulfilled after it has been taken. For the inferior, in so far as he was inferior, could not have put himself under obligation except in so far as his act should meet the approval of his superior; for he would have no power beyond that. On such grounds, according to the Hebraic law, husbands could annul the oaths of their wives, and fathers the oaths of their children so long as these were subject to parental authority. This question is proposed by Seneca: 'What if a law should be passed that no one should do what I had promised that I would do for a friend?' He answers thus: 'The same law which forbids me also defends me.'

Decretals, II. xxiv. 19. *Feuds*, II. lv. *On Benefits*, IV. xxxv [1].

But an act may also result from the mingling of the rights of both parties, as if a superior should order that what an inferior has sworn in this or that case, as, for example, in consequence of fear, or from weakness of judgement, shall be valid only on the condition that it be approved by himself. Under such a condition absolutions from oaths can be defended. Such absolutions were formerly granted by princes,[2] but now, with the permission of the princes, by the

Dig. L. i. 38. Molina, disp. 149.

[1] [255] Augustine, *Letters*, ccxl and ccxli [lxii and lxiii].

[2] Suetonius, *Tiberius*, xxxv. Also Fernando Vázquez (*De Successionum Creatione*, II. xviii) notes that such was the custom for a long time in Spain.

dignitaries of the Church, in order that greater regard may be had for religious scruple. *Decretals*, II. xxiv. 8.

3. Furthermore, the act of the superior can be directed against the person to whom the oath is sworn by taking from him the right which he has acquired, or, if there is no right, by forbidding that he should receive anything in accordance with such an oath. This, again, by virtue of the power of sovereignty, may be done in two ways, either for a punishment or for the public advantage. In case the one who takes the oath is not under the same governmental authority as the one to whom the oath is sworn, it can be understood from this what power the rulers of the two parties have in respect to the oath.

However, a person who has promised something on oath to a guilty person as such, as, for example, a pirate, for this very reason cannot take away from him the promised right under the name of penalty; for then his words would be of no effect, a result which ought in every way to be avoided. And for a similar reason what has been promised cannot be given as a compensation for a right which was in controversy before, [250] if the agreement was entered into after the controversy began.

4. Again, a human law can remove an impediment, which it had placed on acts of a certain kind, if an oath either in general terms, or in a special form, has been added. This the Roman law did in the case of those impediments which did not have directly in view the public good, but the private advantage of the one taking the oath. If such a case arises, the sworn act will be valid in the same way that it would naturally have been valid without human law, either by binding good faith only, or also by giving a legal right to another, according to the diverse nature of acts, which has been set forth by us elsewhere.

XXI.—*To what kind of oath the teachings of Christ in regard to not taking an oath are properly applicable*

1. The fact ought here incidentally to be noted, that what is said in the teachings of Christ and by St. James against the taking of oaths does not, properly speaking, apply to an oath of assertion, of which there are some examples extant in the writings of the Apostle Paul,[1] but to the promise of a future uncertainty. This is plainly shown by the opposition in the words of Christ: 'Again ye have heard that it was said to them of old time, thou shalt not forswear thyself, but shalt perform unto the Lord thine oath. But I say unto [*Matthew*, v. 33.]

[1] *Romans*, i. 9, ix. 1; *2 Corinthians*, i. 23, xi. 31; *Philippians*, i. 8; *1 Thessalonians*, ii. 9 [ii. 5]; *1 Timothy*, ii. 7.

[*Epistle*, v. 12.] you, swear not at all.' A second point is the reason, which James adds: 'that ye be not found deceptive'; for ὑποκρίσεως has that force among the later Greek writers, as appears from *Job*, xxxiv. 30, *Matthew*, xxiv. 51, and elsewhere.

2. The same thing is convincingly shown by the words of Christ, 'But let your speech be Yea, yea, Nay, nay,' which James explains thus: 'But let your yea be yea; and your nay, nay.' Here the figure is clearly what the rhetoricians call 'interlocking', as in the [Virgil, *Eclogues*, VII. 70.] verse:

From that time on is Corydon for us the only Corydon.

[Aquila Romanus, in *Ant. Rhet. Lat.*, p. 19.] Also in another similar passage: 'Up to that day Memmius was Memmius indeed.' For the former 'yea' and 'nay' indicate a promise, the latter its fulfilment. 'Yea', in fact, is a word of promising, and so is explained as 'amen' in *Revelation*, i. 7; it has the same meaning as the Syriac word for 'so be it' in this passage. The corresponding words of Rabbinical Hebrew and Arabic have [*Digest*, XXXII. iii. 39. § 1; XLV. i. 1. § 2.] a like force, just as among the Roman jurists 'yes indeed' and 'why not' are the expressions for one replying to an agreement. Paul, in *2 Corinthians*, i. 20, takes it as the medium of a promise when he says that all the promises of God in Christ are 'yea and amen'. Hence comes the ancient expression of the Jews, 'that of a just man the yea is yea, and the nay is nay.'

3. On the other hand, those whose deeds differ from their words are said by those teachers to be 'yea and nay' (*2 Corinthians*, i. 18–19); that is, their 'yea' is 'nay' and their 'nay' is 'yea'. So the Apostle Paul himself explains. For having declared that he did not 'show fickleness', he added that his word was not 'yea and nay'. Festus, reporting many opinions concerning the meaning of the word *naucum*, thus writes: 'Some say that it is from the Greek words meaning "yes and no",[1] and signifies an unreliable person.' If 'yes and no' indicates unreliability, it follows that 'yea, yea, and nay, nay' will signify constancy.

4. Christ, then, says the same thing as Philo:[2] 'It is best, most useful, and most in harmony with a rational nature to abstain from oaths and so to accustom oneself to veracity that the bare words may be accepted in place of an oath.' Also in another passage:[3] 'Let the speech of a good man be as an oath which is firm, unchangeable, and incapable of deception.' Josephus says this about the [*Jewish War*, II. viii. 6.] Essenes: 'Whatever they have said is stronger than an oath; [251] and it is considered by them a superfluity to take an oath.'

[1] The word for 'No' should properly be written οὐκί in this passage of Festus [p. 166 M], as often in Homer; for it approaches nearer to the word *naucum*.

[2] *On the Ten Commandments* [xvii].

[3] *On Special Laws* [II. i].

5. From the Essenes, or from those of the Jews whom the Essenes imitated, Pythagoras [1] seems to have borrowed the doctrine expressed in the maxim: 'An oath ought not to be taken by the gods; for every man ought to take care that he should be believed without an oath.' [2] On the authority of Curtius the Scythians say of themselves to Alexander: 'Do not think that the Scythians make their friendship firm by an oath; they take oath by keeping faith.' Cicero, in the speech *For Roscius the Comic Actor*, says: 'The same punishment has been appointed by the immortal gods for the deceitful man as for the perjurer. For the gods are wont to be angry, and incensed, not on account of the formula of words which contains an oath, but by reason of the faithlessness and wickedness by which snares are set for another.'

[Diogenes Laertius, VIII.xxii.] [VII. viii. 29.] [xvi. 46.]

Well known is the saying of Solon: 'Let him be of such uprightness that he will be believed rather than his oath.' Clement of Alexandria, too, said that it was the duty of a good man to show faith in his promises by the firmness and steadfastness of his words and life. Alexis the comic actor says:

[Diogenes Laertius, I. lx.] [*Stromata*, VII. viii. 50.] [Stobaeus, *Sermones*, xxvii. 3.]

My nod is just as valid as an oath.

In the oration *For Cornelius Balbus* Cicero says that at Athens when a certain man, who had lived among them with uprightness and dignity, had given his testimony publicly and was approaching the altar to take oath, with one accord all the judges cried out that he should not take oath; for they did not wish his faith to seem bound by religious scruple rather than regard for the truth.

[v. 12.]

6. The comment of Hierocles on the *Golden Verses* does not differ from the teaching of Christ: 'He, who in the beginning had told us to reverence an oath, by that very injunction had bidden us to abstain from swearing concerning those matters which can either happen or not happen,[3] and which are subject to the uncertain

[=p. 164.]

[1] For also the Pythagorean Hermippus said that the philosophy of Pythagoras was derived from the Jews, as Origen testifies, *Against Celsus* [I. xv = p. 334]. It is likewise stated by Josephus, a Jew [*Against Apion*, I. xxii. 162], and by Iamblichus, a Pythagorean.

[2] Philo [*On the Ten Commandments*, xvii]: 'The person from whom an oath is exacted is already suspected of bad faith.' In the *Oedipus at Colonus* of Sophocles Oedipus had said [lines 650 f.]:

I would not force an oath from you as a base man,

and Theseus replies:

For you would have no more than sound of voice.

Marcus Antoninus in his description of a good man [Marcus Aurelius, III. v] says: 'Nor having need of an oath.' Chrysostom, *On the Statues*, XV [XV. v], says: 'If you believe that he, with whom you are dealing, is truthful, do not impose upon him the necessity of an oath; if you know that he will lie, do not oblige him to perjure himself.'

[3] Chrysostom has well noted, *On the Statues*, XII [XIV. i]: 'Even if it should not fall to your lot to take oath when carried away by an impulse or under compulsion or without thought, yet the very nature of the matter at times will bring it to pass that you will be found to have sworn falsely with full knowledge and consent.' Later he adds [XIV. ii]: 'Therefore it is dangerous to take oath

outcome of chance. Such things in fact ought to be considered of slight moment, and they are changeable, whence it is neither worth while, nor safe, to swear concerning them.' Among the praises of a Christian emperor, Libanius has this, ' that he is so averse to perjury that he fears even to swear to the truth.' In commenting on the
[XIV.171.] words of the Odyssey,

> But yet an oath we surely shall allow,

Eustathius says : ' In matters that are uncertain an oath should not be used for confirmation, but prayers for a possible outcome.'

XXII.—*What unsworn pledge of good faith has by custom the force of an oath*

Decretals, II. xxiv. 10. Diodorus, XVI [xliii]. Panormitanus, *On Decretals*, I. xl. 3. Jason, *On Dig.*, XII. ii. 3. § 4. Mynsinger, *Observ.*, I. xvii. [Sueton., *Augustus*, xlii.] [Plut., *Eumenes*, v = p. 585 F.] [iii. 8.] *Politics*, III. xiv.

In many places instead of an oath it is found that good faith is pledged by joining the right hands,[1] which was ' the strongest bond of faith among the Persians ' ; or by some other sign having such force that, if the promise should not be fulfilled, the promisor is considered no less detestable than if he had committed perjury. Especially regarding kings and princes it was a very common saying that their pledge of faith was as good as an oath. In fact they ought to be such that they can say with Augustus, ' I am a man of good faith ' ; [2] and with Eumenes, that they would rather lose their lives than break faith. Also the verses of Gunther, in the *Ligurinus* [III. 511 f.], bear on this point :

> In his bare word the king is wont to show
> Right and respect greater than any oath.

Cicero, in his oration *For Deiotarus*, praises the right hand of Gaius Caesar, ' as not stronger in wars and battles than in promises and good faith '. Aristotle, too, noted that in heroic times the holding of the sceptre upright counted as the oath of kings.

even regarding one's own act ; for the very nature of affairs takes out of our power many things which are subject to chance.'

[1] Mentioned by Eustathius, *On the Odyssey*, xxiv [for *Iliad* xxiv, line 669] ; Scholiast on Aristophanes, *Clouds* [line 81, and *Acharnians*, line 307] ; Diodorus Siculus, Book VIII [XVI. xliii. 4] ; Krantz, *Saxonica*, XI. xxvii. In *Decretals*, I. xl. 3, an oath and pledged good faith are put on an equality.

[2] Isocrates says of Evagoras, King of Salamis [*Evagoras*, xix = 197 E] : ' Guarding his verbal agreements in like manner as his oaths.' Symmachus, X. xix, says : ' Nowhere is there greater hope of dependability than in the promises of good princes.' Nicetas says of Alexis, the brother of Isaac, Book III [III. iv] : ' Kings must place the good faith of an oath above everything else.'

Cicero, *For Cornelius Balbus* [v. 12] : ' Men say that at Athens, where a certain man who had sworn [lived] among them with uprightness and dignity had given his testimony in public, and, in accordance with the custom of the Greeks, was approaching the altars to take oath, all the judges with one voice cried out that he should not take oath.'

[256]

CHAPTER XIV

ON PROMISES, CONTRACTS, AND OATHS OF THOSE WHO HOLD SOVEREIGN POWER

I.—*The opinion that restitution in full, which arises from municipal law, pertains to the acts of kings as such, is refuted; also, that a king is not bound by an oath*

1. THE promises, contracts, and oaths of kings, and of others who like them hold the chief power in the state, present peculiar questions in regard to what is permitted to them as regards their own acts; also, what is permitted to them in relation to their subjects and in regard to their successors.

As regards the first point, the question is whether a king can restore to himself his rights in full, as he can restore those of his subjects, or can make a contract void, or can absolve himself from an oath. Bodin is of the opinion that a king who has been over- I. viii
reached by the fraud or deceit of another, or induced by error or [135].
fear, can be restored to his original rights for the same reasons that a subject would be restored, not only in matters which pertain to the rights of sovereignty, but also in matters which relate to his private affairs. He adds that a king is not even bound by an oath if the agreements are of a kind from which the law permits withdrawal, even though they are consistent with honour; he is not, in fact, bound because he has taken oath, but because every one is bound by just agreements, in so far as another has an interest therein.

2. Here also we think that a distinction ought to be made, just as elsewhere, between the acts of a king which belong to the kingly office and those which are private. For whatever the king does in acts belonging to his kingly office should be considered in the same way as if the state did them. But as the laws made by the state itself would have no power over such acts, because the state is not superior to itself, so laws emanating from the king would not. Wherefore, restitution will not take place against such contracts, for restitution arises from municipal law. No exception, then, ought to be admitted against contracts of kings which they have made in their minority.

II.—*To what acts of kings the laws apply is set forth, with distinctions*

1. Evidently if a people has placed a king in power without absolute authority, but subject to certain laws, his acts contrary to

those laws can be rendered void by them, either wholly or in part, because to that extent the people has preserved its own right. The acts of kings who rule with absolute power but do not hold their kingdoms as proprietary owners, acts by which the kingdom, or a part of the kingdom, or its revenues are alienated, we have treated [II. vi. 4.] above; and we have shown that by the very law of nature such acts are null and void, just as if they had been performed in respect to the property of another.

2. The private acts of a king, on the contrary, ought to be considered as acts not of the state, but of a part of the state, and therefore done with the intention [257] that they should follow the common rule of the laws. In consequence the laws which render some acts either void, or voidable by the injured party, will apply here also, just as if the contract had been made with that as a condition. Thus we see that certain kings have availed themselves of the aid of the laws against extortionate interest charges. Nevertheless a king will be able to exempt from the operation of such laws his own acts, as well as the acts of others; whether he intended so to do must be judged from the circumstances. If he has done so, the case will have to be judged by the bare law of nature.

This should be added, that if any law renders an act null and void, not in the interest of the doer, but for his punishment, this will have no force in regard to the acts of kings; so also other penal laws, and whatever has the force of compulsion, will not apply. For punishment and coercion can proceed only from different wills; and so, to compel, and to be compelled, require separate persons, and separate aspects of the same person do not meet the requirement.

III.—*When a king is bound by his oath, and when not*

A king can render an oath null in advance, just as a private person may, if by a former oath he has plainly deprived himself of the power to swear to any such thing. But after an oath has been taken he cannot render it void, because here also separate persons are required. For whatever is rendered void after an oath has been taken already in advance contained in itself this exception, 'unless his superior should be unwilling'. But to swear so that you would be bound only if you should yourself be willing is altogether ridiculous, and contrary to the nature of an oath. Although from an oath of this character no right may be gained for the other party, because of some fault in himself, yet, as we have shown above, the person who took oath is under obligation to God. This applies no less to [I. viii. 135.] kings than to others, although Bodin, in the passage cited, maintains the opposite view.

IV.—*How far a king is bound with reference to things which he promised without cause*

It has also been shown above that promises which are complete and unconditional, and have been accepted, naturally confer a right. This in like manner applies to kings no less than to others, so that in this sense at least the opinion of those who deny that a king is ever bound by promises which he has made without cause must be disapproved. Nevertheless, we shall presently see in what sense even this may be true.

Angelus, *On Dig.* XXI. ii. 11. Curtius Junior, *Consilia*, cxxxviii, no. 4.

V.—*Application of what has been said about the force of law as regards the contracts of kings*

As for the rest, what we said above, that the municipal law of a kingdom has no force in the agreements and contracts of kings, was correctly seen by Vázquez also. But his inference ought not to be conceded, that buying and selling without fixed price, letting and hiring without stated amount, and permanent right of land tenure without a written document, are valid if they are the acts of kings. The reason is that such acts are not ordinarily performed by a king as king, but by him just as by any person.

Controversiae Illustres, II. li. 34. Suarez, III. xxxv. 14.

So far is it from being true that the laws of the realm have no force in respect to acts of this kind, that we believe that the king is subject even to the law of the town in which he lives; for the king maintains himself there in a special manner as a member of that society. Yet the matter stands, as we have said, only in case circumstances do not show that the king has been pleased to free his own act from the operation of that law. Another illustration which Vázquez presents, in regard to a promise made in any way whatsoever, is quite in point, and can be explained in the light of that which we have said above.

VI.—*In what sense a king may rightly be said to be under obligation to his subjects by the law of nature only, and also by municipal law*

1. Almost all jurists believe that the contracts, which a king enters into with his subjects, are binding upon him by the law of nature only, and not by municipal law.

This is a very obscure way of speaking. For legal writers sometimes improperly speak of a natural obligation as referring to that of which the fulfilment is by nature honourable, although not in reality due, as the payment of legacies in full [258] without the deduction allowed by the Falcidian Law, the payment of a debt

Baldus, *On Dig.* II. xiv. 1. *Dig.* I. iii. 31. *Code*, II. iv. 43; III. xxxiv. 2. Doctors, *On Decretals*, I. ii. 1.

Baldus, *On Code*, IV. vi. 10; *On Dig.* VI. xxiii. 3. *Dig.* XII. vi. 19. *Code*, VI. l. 1. *Dig.* V. iii. 25. § 11.

from which one had been freed by a criminal penalty inflicted on the creditor, or the requiting of a favour with its like, acts of which none permits of an action to recover anything unjustly paid. But sometimes the words are more properly used with reference to that which does in truth bind us, whether the other party has acquired a right therefrom, as in contracts, or has not acquired it, as in a full and firm promise.

The Jew Maimonides, in his *Guide of the Perplexed*, Book III, chapter liv, appropriately distinguishes the three cases just mentioned, and says that what is not due falls under the head of 'bounty', which other interpreters of *Proverbs* (xx. 28) explain as 'overflowing of goodness'.[1] In the Hebrew language what is due according to the strict sense of the law is called 'a judgement'; and what is due in accordance with honour is defined by the Hebrew word meaning justice, that is, equity. So the interpreter of *Matthew* (xxiii. 23) has used ἔλεος (mercy), κρίσις (justice), and πίστις (faith), where by πίστις he expresses the idea for which δικαιοσύνη (justice) is generally used by the Hellenists. For in *First Maccabees* (vii. 18 and 32) you may find κρίσις used for that which is strictly due.

2. According to civil law also a person can be said to be bound by his own act, either in this sense, that an obligation results not from the law of nature alone but from the municipal law, or from both together, or in the sense that the obligation gives a right to action in a court of law. Therefore we say that a true and proper obligation arises from a promise and contract of a king, which he has entered into with his subjects, and that this obligation confers a right upon his subjects; such is the nature of promises and contracts as we have shown above; and this holds even between God and man.

Jason, *On Digest*, XII. iv. Bk. v. Castaldus, *De Imperatore*, qu. iii, 81. Vázquez, *Controversiae Illustres*, I. iii. 1. Bodin, I. viii.

Now if the acts are such as may be done by a king, but also by any one else, municipal law will be binding in his case also; but if they are the acts of the king as king, municipal law does not apply to him. This distinction has not been observed with sufficient care by Vázquez. Nevertheless, from both these acts a legal action may arise, at least so far that the right of the creditor may be declared; but compulsion cannot follow on account of the position of the parties with whom the business is conducted. For it is not permissible for subjects to compel the one to whom they are subject; equals, however, by the law of nature, have this right against equals, and superiors against inferiors even by municipal law.

[1] To this class belong those acts which are performed with no other motive than generosity and bountifulness, as this is expressed in the *Digest*, XXXIX. v. 1. Plutarch, *Cato the Elder* [v = 339 A]: 'Generosity flows from the bounteous spring of a kindly disposition.'

VII.—*In what way a right lawfully obtained by subjects may be taken away*

This also ought to be known, that through the agency of the king even a right gained by subjects can be taken from them in two ways, either as a penalty, or by the force of eminent domain. But in order that this may be done by the power of eminent domain the first requisite is public advantage; then, that compensation from the public funds be made, if possible, to the one who has lost his right. Just as such a result is accomplished in other things, then, so also in respect to the right which is created by a promise or contract.

Vázquez, *Controversiae Illustres*, I. v. pr., and I, *passim*, and Castrensis, *Consilia*, I. ccxxix.

VIII.—*Here the distinction between rights gained by the law of nature and by municipal law is rejected*

Herein by no means should the distinction be conceded which some persons make, between a right gained through the force of the law of nature and a right which arises from municipal law. The right of the king is, in fact, the same over both kinds of rights, nor can the one any more than the other be taken away without cause. For when ownership or any other right has been acquired by any one in a legitimate manner it is a provision of the law of nature that this may not be taken away from him without cause. If a king should act to the contrary he is without doubt bound to make good the damage inflicted, because he is acting against a true right of the subject.

The right of subjects, then, differs from the right of foreigners in this, that over the right of foreigners, that is, over those who are in no way subject, the power of eminent domain has no control. In regard to penalties we shall see below. But the right of subjects is subordinate to that of eminent domain so far as the public interest may require.

IX.—*Whether the contracts of kings are laws, and when*

From what we have said it becomes apparent how false is the opinion which some advocate, that the contracts of kings are laws. For no one acquires a right against a king from the laws; if therefore he revokes them, he does a legal [259] injury to no one. Nevertheless he commits a moral wrong if he pursues such a course without just cause. Right, however, does arise from promises and contracts. Only the contracting parties are bound by the contracts, while all are subject to the laws. Nevertheless, some mixtures of contracts and laws are possible, as treaties made with a neighbouring king, or a contract with a farmer of the revenues which is at the

Baldus, *On Dig.* XXXIX. iv. 15. Bartolus, *On Dig.* III. iv. 7. Jason, *Consilia*, vol. I, i. 4, and others cited by Vázquez, *Controversiae Illustres*, I. iii. 5.

same time published as a law, in so far as there are provisions in it which have to be observed by the subjects.

X.—*In what way the contracts of kings are binding on the heirs of all their possessions*

Let us come now to the successors.[1] In regard to these a distinction must be made, whether they are the heirs at the same time of all the possessions as those who inherit an hereditary kingship by will, or in default of a will; or are successors to the kingship only, as for example in consequence of a new election, or in accordance with a prescribed rule; or by a sort of imitation of ordinary inheritance, or otherwise; or whether, finally, they succeed by a mixed right. For there must be no doubt that those who are heirs of all the possessions, as well as of the kingship, are bound by the promises and contracts. The rule that the property of the deceased is subject to his personal debts also is as old as property ownership itself.

XI.—*In what way those who succeed to the kingship only may be bound by the same contracts*

1. But there are those who succeed to the royal power only,[2] or to the property in part and to the royal power in its entirety. The question to what extent they are obligated is one which is all the more worthy of investigation, for the reason that previously it has been confusedly handled. Now it is sufficiently clear that such successors to a kingship are not in that capacity directly, that is to say immediately, bound; [3] they do not receive their right from the one who has last died, but from the people, whether that succession approaches more nearly to the right of ordinary inheritance, or is farther removed from it. This distinction has been treated above.

2. Such successors may be bound through an intermediary, that is through the interposition of the state.[4] This will be understood as follows. An association, as well as an individual, has the right to bind itself by its own act, or by the act of a majority of its members. This right it can transfer, not only explicitly, but also as a natural consequence, as for example in transferring the sovereign authority. For in morals he, who grants the end, grants the means which lead to the end.

[1] See the authors cited by Reinkingk, Book I, class III, x.

[2] See Aimoin, edited by Freher, p. 373.

[3] Thus Solomon was not obliged to keep the promise which David had made to Shimei [*I Kings*, ii. 9].

[4] See similar cases in *Decretals*, III. xxiii. 1; *Sext*, II. xiv. 3, is more in point, where these words should be noted: 'When both the donation of the above-mentioned grandfather and the acquisition of the stipulated lands were made in the name of the kingdom.' See also Treutler, I. vi. 7; Syring, *De Pace Religionis*, concl. 19.

XII.—*To what extent those who succeed to the kingship only may be bound by the same contracts*

1. Nevertheless this transfer of obligations cannot go on to an unlimited extent. The unlimited power of imposing obligations is, in fact, not essential to the proper exercise of sovereignty, just as it is likewise not necessary for guardianship or trusteeship; it is necessary only in so far as the nature of the power demands. 'A guardian is considered as holding the place of the master,' says Julian, 'as long as he manages the estate well, not when he is robbing his ward.' [1] In this sense the statement of Ulpian, that the agreement made by the master of a society not only may help it but may also injure it, is to be understood.

Digest, XLI. iv. 7. § 3; XXVII. x. 12; *Code*, II. iii. 22; *Dig.* II. xiv. 28. § 1. *Dig.* II. xiv. 14. *Code*, II. iv. 12.

Nevertheless, this matter [a contract by a king] does not, as certain persons think, have to be handled according to the nature of business undertaken for others, so that the act should then be considered to be ratified, if it has turned out advantageously. For it is dangerous for the state itself to reduce the ruler of the state to such straits. Therefore it is not to be believed that the people held such an opinion when it conferred the sovereign power. But the decision rendered by the Roman emperors in the case of a city, that action taken by the magistrates in a doubtful matter was valid, but not if that was undoubtedly given away which could be collected, ought and can be made to apply to our question concerning the whole people, if due proportion has been preserved.

Alphonsus de Castro, *De Potestate Legis Poenalis*, I. v; Victoria, *Relectio de Potestate Papae et Concilii*, no. 18. Thomas, I. ii, qu. 95, art. 3. Panormitanus, *On Decretals*, I. ii. 7, no. 14. Felinus, no. 60. Torquemada, *On Decr.*, II. xi. 3. 1 concl. 6 and 7, nos. 8 and 9. Others, *On Decr.*, II. iii. 34. 6.

2. Consequently, just as not all laws bind the subjects—for even in addition to laws which command something illegal there can be laws that are plainly foolish and ridiculous [2]—so also the contracts of rulers are binding upon subjects if they have a reasonable motive; and in case of doubt such a motive ought to be presumed by reason of the authority of those who rule.[3] This distinction is much [260] better than the one commonly suggested by many writers, which is based on the slight or great injury of the outcome.

[1] The statements of Camden (*History of Elizabeth*, pt. IV, Year 1595) apply on this point; also, what Kromer in Book XXVII [p. 593] has concerning the debts of George, king of Bohemia, unwisely assumed by Wladislaus.

[2] As the law of Cabades, king of Persia, in Procopius [*Persian War*, I. v. 1], and Agathias [IV. xxvii–xxviii].

Peter, ambassador of Justin II to Chosroes, when discussing the promises which Justinian seemed to have made to the Saracens, applies this principle of law to alienations: 'No state, in fact, will ever be condemned by reason of the practice of one man, nor even a bad law, though it should be the emperor who has established such a practice, or has confirmed it by law' [Menander Protector, frag. 15, p. 39, edit. Dindorf].

[3] Sidonius, Book V, letter xvii [V. xvi. 2]: 'The state ruled by a prince will always make good what the prince has promised.' See Ambrose, on the praises of Theodosius [*De Obitu Theodosii*, v]; Symmachus, IV. vii and xix, and V. xxxvii; *Council of Toledo*, V. vi, and *Decretals*, III. xxiv. 3. Corippus in Book II [II, line 389] relates that the debts of Justinian, which were very great, were paid by Justin, his successor in the Empire.

Aguirre, *Apologia*, pt. 1, no. 70.

In this matter, in fact, not the outcome, but the reasonable motive, ought to be kept in view. If a reasonable motive is present, both the people itself will be bound, if by any chance it has commenced to be independent, and also the king's successors, as being the rulers of the people. For also in case a free people should have made a contract the obligation would be binding upon the one who should afterward accept the sovereignty, even with the most unlimited powers.

3. Titus Caesar is praised on this account,[1] because he did not allow petitions to be made to himself for the favours granted by his predecessors, although Tiberius and the emperors who followed him had not considered the benefactions of their predecessors valid, unless these had been expressly confirmed by themselves. Following the example of Titus, the most excellent emperor Nerva, in an edict preserved in Pliny,[2] says: 'I am unwilling that any one should think that what he obtained from another emperor, either privately or publicly, is annulled by me in order that he may be under obligation to me if I ratify and confirm it; and the congratulations of any one do not need to be accompanied by petitions for renewal.' But

Histories, III [lv].

also Tacitus, having related of Vitellius that without regard for posterity he had torn the Empire to pieces while the common crowd were thronging to secure his extravagant gifts, and some people were even buying them with money, adds, 'Among wise men those gifts were considered void which could neither be given nor accepted without the ruin of the state.'[3]

[1] The story is in Suetonius, [*Titus*,] viii; Xiphilinus from Dio [Dio Cassius, LXVI. xix. 3]; [Aurelius] Victor [*On the Caesars*, x. 2]. There is a similar thing in the *Decretum*, II. xxv. 1. 15; Gail, *Observationes*, II. lx. 15. See also the history of Radevic. Gunther, *Ligurinus*, V [lines 569 ff.]:

And kings who follow cannot overthrow,
Nor yet revoke, a deed that has been done.
The proofs made safe with royal seal he left,
And also, for the Duke, sure documents.

[262] In Book VIII [lines 579 ff.]:

So great this famous king's indulgence was,
That whosoever had possessed the grants
Of former kings with faith unto this time,
And this could prove or show by documents,
Rejoices in the king's assent, and still
Retains possession.

[2] Pliny, *Letters*, Book X, lxvi [X. lviii. 9].

[3] Mariana, XXIV. xvi, cites this and applies it to the boundless munificence of Frederick, king of Naples. Galba recalled the gifts of Nero from the purchasers with the exception of a tenth; Tacitus, *Histories*, I [I. xx], and Plutarch [*Galba*, xvi = p. 1060 A]. Pertinax even exacted from the freedmen what they had appropriated under the pretence of sale when Commodus was emperor [Capitolinus, *Pertinax*, viii. 1].

Basil the Macedonian as emperor revoked what the Emperor Michael had given away. Zonaras [XVI. viii] says of him: 'It was decided with unanimous consent that those who had received money for no good cause should make a refund, some of the entire amount, some of a half.'

See the same author on Isaac Comnenus [XVIII. iv]. See de Serres, *Charles VIII* [p. 413], on the donations of Louis XI. See Philippe de Comines, Book IX, on grants of the same king which, though made to churches, were revoked.

4. Here also this should be added, that if by any chance a contract should begin to lead not merely to some loss, but to the ruin of the state, so that the contract, if carried to conclusion, would have to be considered as unjust and illegal from the beginning, then it is possible not exactly to revoke it, but rather to declare that it has no further binding force,[1] as if made under a condition without which it could not have been made justly.

5. What we have said about contracts is also to be understood in regard to the alienation of the public funds,[2] or of anything else which, according to law, the king can alienate for the public good. Here also a similar distinction must be maintained, whether there was a reasonable motive for giving, or otherwise alienating.

6. But if the contracts have to do with the alienation of the kingdom, or of a part of it, or of the royal patrimony, in so far as this has not been placed in the king's hands, they will not be valid, for the reason that they have been made in regard to the property of another. The same will hold in limited monarchies, if the people has reserved any matter, or kind of act, from the royal power. For in order that such acts may be valid the consent of the people is required, such consent being given either in person or through those who lawfully represent it, as can be understood from what I have said above about alienation. [Chap. vi.]

With the help of these distinctions it will be easy to judge whether the pleas made by those kings that have refused to pay the debts of their predecessors, whose heirs they have not been, were just or unjust. It is possible to find examples of such pleas in Bodin. I. viii. 163.

XIII.—*What grants of kings are revocable, and what are not, is set forth, with a distinction*

This, again, which has been affirmed by many,[3] that the grants of rulers made from generosity can always be recalled, ought not to be allowed to pass without a distinction. There are, in fact, certain gifts which a king makes at his own expense, and which have the force of an absolute grant, unless there is inserted a clause implying termination at will. Such grants cannot be revoked,[4] except in relation to subjects for the purpose of punishment, or in the public interest—in the latter case, with compensation if possible.

Curtius Junior, *Consilia*, cxxxviii. 4, and clvii. 18. Cravetta, *De Antiquitatibus Temporum*, II, pt. 1, no. 38.

See Mariana concerning the revocation of the grants which Ramirus, king of Aragon, had made (X. xvi), and concerning the revocation of the grants of Isabella by herself (XXVII. xi).

See Kromer, XII [XIII, pp. 322–3] on the will of Casimir, king of Poland, which was partly accepted, partly annulled.

[1] *Decretals*, III. xxx. 9. There is an example in the Acts of Alphonso and Sanchez given by Mariana in Book XII, last chapter, and in Camden for the years 1595 and 1597 in the Hanseatic controversy.

[2] There are matters related to this in the *Councils of France*, vol. III.

[3] See those cited by Reinkingk, II. ii. 8, nos. 26 ff.

[4] See Afflictis, *Decisiones*, cxxviii, no. 10.

Belluga, *Speculum Principis,* xxvi. Anton. Gabrieli, *Conclusiones,* I, tit. *De jure quaestionis non tollendo,* vi. 20 and vii.

There are other grants which take away the binding force merely of a law without any contract, and these are revocable. The reason is that, as a law which has been annulled in regard to all people can always be re-enacted for all, so also, when a law in respect to a particular person has been annulled, it can be restored in regard to that person. Here, in fact, no right was acquired against the author of the law.

XIV.—*Whether the rightful possessor of the throne is bound by the contracts of usurpers*

Neither peoples nor rightful kings will be bound by the contracts of those who have unlawfully [261] seized the sovereign authority. For these do not have the right to place a binding obligation on the people. Nevertheless they will be bound for what has been spent for their advantage, that is, in so far as they have been made richer.

CHAPTER XV

ON TREATIES AND SPONSIONS

I.—*What public conventions are*

[263] Ulpian divided conventions into public and private. Public conventions he explained, not, as some think, by definition, but by giving examples. His first example is the convention 'which is arranged in time of peace'; and the second, 'When the generals in command in a war conclude certain agreements with each other.' Ulpian, then, understands that public conventions are such as can be made only by the right of a higher or lower authority of government; and in this respect they differ not only from the contracts of private persons, but also from the contracts of kings which are concerned with private affairs. *Dig.* II. xiv. 5.

However, from such private contracts also causes of war are wont to arise, although more frequently from public contracts. Having, therefore, sufficiently treated of compacts in general, we ought to add some details which relate to this more excellent kind of agreement.

II.—*Conventions are divided into treaties, sponsions, and other agreements*

We can divide these public conventions, which the Greeks call συνθήκας (articles of agreement), into treaties, sponsions, and other agreements.

III.—*The difference between treaties and sponsions; to what extent sponsions are binding*

1. For the distinction between treaties and sponsions, Livy may be cited, in Book IX, where he correctly shows us that treaties [IX. v.] are made by order of the highest authority, and that in respect to such treaties the people itself is liable to divine wrath if it does not keep its agreements. Such treaties, according to custom, were made among the Romans by the fetials together with the ratifying priest. A sponsion is made when those who do not have from the supreme authority a commission for such an act promise something which essentially affects that authority.

[*Jugurtha*, xxxix. 3.] In Sallust we read: 'As was proper, the senate decreed that no treaty could have been made without its authorization and that of the people.' Hieronymus, king of Syracuse, had made an agreement XXIV [vi. 3]. of alliance with Hannibal, as Livy relates; but afterward he sent to Carthage in order to make the agreement of alliance into a treaty of alliance. Hence the statement in Seneca the father:[1] 'The commanding general made a treaty; the Roman people seems to have made it and is bound by the treaty.' This refers to those commanders of ancient times who had received a special commission for such an act.

In kingdoms, however, the kings have the right to make treaties.[2] [1188 ff.] Says Euripides in the *Suppliants*:

> This treaty oath Adrastus needs to swear;
> For having royal power, the right he has
> To bind the state with treaty made by him.

In this passage, in fact, the verb at the end is to be read as an infinitive, as we have given it, not in the indicative.

2. Moreover, just as the magistrates do not bind the people by their acts, so a minority of the people does not. This principle [Livy, V. xlix. 2.] favours the Romans as against the Senonian Gauls; for the majority of the people were with the dictator Camillus. It is not possible, as [XIII. xvi. 1.] we find in Gellius, to treat with a people in two divisions.

3. But let us see wherein those are obligated who, without the authority of a people, have promised something which is within the power of the people. Some one may perhaps think that in this case the promisors have fulfilled their pledge if they have done their utmost to have their promise carried out in accordance with the principles which we have previously stated[3] in regard to a promise made by a third party. But in this matter, [264] in which a contract is involved, nature desires a much stricter obligation. For whoever in making a contract gives or promises something of his own wishes in turn that something in fact be furnished to him; hence, according to the civil law, which rejects the promise of another's act, the promise to have an act ratified is nevertheless binding, so far as the promisor is concerned.

[1] *Controversies*, IV. xxix [=IX. ii. 15].

[2] See below, Book III, xx. 2, and following. Servius, *On the Aeneid*, Book II [II, lines 160 f.], on the words

> And mayest thou, Troy, be saved,
> And keep thy pledge of faith,

says: [273] 'Because the state seems to promise what the king promises.' And when Aeneas makes a treaty with Latinus before fighting in single combat Servius adds [*On the Aeneid*, XII, line 212]: '[The poet] does not introduce Turnus as taking the oath, for the reason that in the presence of the king he did not have the power.'

[3] II. xi. 22.

IV.—*Rejection of the classification of treaties which Menippus made*

According to Livy,[1] Menippus, ambassador of King Antiochus to the Romans, made a classification of treaties rather for his own purpose than according to the rules of his craft. He said that there are three kinds of treaties which kings and states make with each other. One kind is consummated when terms are dictated to those who have been conquered in war; in this class of treaties the victor has the decision as to what he wishes the conquered to have and to be deprived of. The second kind of treaty is made when those who are equal in war come into relations of peace and friendship by an equal alliance; in such cases restitution is asked and granted by the agreement, and if the possession of anything has been disturbed by the war a readjustment is made either in accordance with the terms of the ancient right or to the mutual advantage of both parties. The third kind is consummated when those, who have never been enemies, unite in a league of friendship with each other through a treaty of alliance; in such cases the signatories neither impose terms nor accept terms. XXXIV [lvii. 7].

V.—*The classification of treaties: first, treaties which establish the same rights as the law of nature; whence this arises*

1. But it is necessary for us to make a classification with greater painstaking. First, then, we shall say that some treaties establish the same rights as the law of nature, while others add something thereto. Treaties of the first class not only are wont to be made between enemies who cease from war, but formerly also they were often made, and were in some degree necessary, as between those who previously had made no compacts with each other.

Hence arose the rule of the law of nature, that by nature there is a kind of relationship between men, and therefore it is an impious crime that one should be injured by another. Though this rule was in force in the olden time before the Flood, yet some time after the Flood it was effaced again by evil customs, so that it was considered lawful to rob and to plunder strangers without declaration of war.[2] This Epiphanius calls 'the Scythian fashion'. [*Against Heresy*, pr. and I=p. 4.]

[1] Add Diodorus Siculus, *Selections on Embassies*, iv [= XXVIII. xv. 2].

[2] Caesar says of the Germans [*Gallic War*, VI. xxiii. 6]: 'Acts of brigandage committed outside of the boundaries of any state involve no disgrace.' Tacitus is an additional witness, *On the Customs of the Germans* [xiv and xxvi]; also Saxo, Book XIV [pp. 259–60] and elsewhere.

The same thing was written about the Etruscans by Servius, *On the Aeneid*, VIII [VIII. 479] and X [X. 184]; and about other peoples, *On the Aeneid*, I [I. 317]. Diodorus Siculus [V. xxxiv. 6] says the same of the Lusitanians. And with him Plutarch agrees, *Marius* [vi = 408]: 'Up to that time brigandage was considered by the Spaniards among the most noble occupations.'

Similar is the fact that the Jews maintain that a loss that has been occasioned to one who is neither a Jew, nor allied to the Jews, ought not to be made good [*Baba Kama*, I. 2, p. 13].

2. In consequence the question in Homer,[1] 'Are you plunderers?' is a friendly inquiry, of which Thucydides [2] also makes mention. In the ancient law of Solon there are companies 'of those who go out for booty'. Indeed, as Justin says, up to the times of Tarquin piracy was considered an honour. In the Roman law this principle is stated, that if it is considered that neither friendship nor hospitality nor any treaty for the sake of friendship has been made with any peoples these are not indeed public enemies; yet whatever has come to them from the Romans should belong to them, and a free Roman captured by them would be a slave. The same thing, again, would happen if any one came from them to the Romans; and in this case also postliminy should be granted.

Digest, XLVII. xxii. 4. XLIII [iii. 5].

Thus formerly, before the period of the Peloponnesian War, the Corcyraeans were not public enemies of the Athenians, but they had neither peace nor treaties with them, as is apparent from the speech of the Corinthians in Thucydides. Of Bocchus Sallust says: 'Known to us neither in peace nor in war.' Hence the taking of plunder from barbarians was commended by Aristotle, and in ancient Latium the word *hostis* means only a stranger.

[I. xl.] [*Jugurtha*, xix. 7.] [*Politics*, I. viii.]

3. In this class I include also treaties in which provision is made that there shall be rights of hospitality and commerce on both sides, in so far as such rights come under the law of nature, a subject which we have treated elsewhere. According to Livy Arco uses this distinction in his speech to the Achaeans, in which he said that the question at issue is not regarding an alliance but regarding a stipulation for granting and obtaining a right of commercial intercourse, in order that, to be specific, the slaves of the Macedonians might not find a refuge among them. The entire class of conventions the Greeks call in a strict sense 'peace', and they contrast it with 'treaties', as may be seen both elsewhere and in the oration of Andocides *On the Peace* with the Lacedaemonians.

Livy, XLI [xxiv. 15 ff.]. [*Orations*, iii. 11.]

[265] VI.—*Treaties which add something beyond the rights of the law of nature; what treaties are on equal terms*

1. Conventions which add something beyond the rights based on the law of nature are either on equal or on unequal terms. Those are on equal terms [3] which are of the same character on both sides,

[1] *Odyssey*, III [III. 71], where the Scholiast says: 'Among the ancients, brigandage was not only free from disgrace, but in addition was considered full of glory.'

[2] Book I [I. v]; and he adds: 'This kind of life did not yet involve disgrace, but rather was considered praiseworthy.'

[3] Thus Pliny [*Natural History*, VI. xxv. 112] says that the Parthians lived on terms of equality with the Scythians. In Lucan [VIII. 231–2] Pompey says of the same people, the Parthians:

The Parthian alone approaches me on equal terms.

'which are equal and common on both sides', as Isocrates says in the *Panegyric*. To such a convention the verses of Virgil apply: [iv. 176 = p. 77 E.] [*Aeneid*, XII, lines 190–1.]

> Nor seek I kingdoms for myself; on equal terms
> Unvanquished let the nations both alliance form
> That shall endure for ever.

The Greeks call conventions of the first type sometimes simply 'covenants', sometimes 'covenants on like and equal terms', as may be seen in Appian and Xenophon. The second type they call more properly 'treaties'; and in so far as these are concerned with inferiors they call them 'arrangements imposed by command'. In his speech *On the Freedom of the Rhodians*, Demosthenes says that such treaties ought to be avoided by those who love liberty, because they approach very near to servitude. [*Maced. Aff.*, xi. 5 f.; *Greek History*, VII. i. 1 f.] [= Isocrates, *Archidamus*, li = 126 c.]

2. Treaties of both types are made for the sake either of peace or of some alliance.

Equal treaties of peace are those, for example, which are commonly arranged for the restoration of captives and of captured property, and for safety; these will be discussed below in connexion with the effects and consequences of war.

Equal treaties of alliance have to do either with commerce, with joint action in war, or with other matters. Equal agreements in regard to commercial relations may have various ends in view, as, for example, that no import duties should be paid on either side, an article of agreement in the ancient treaty between Rome and Carthage, containing an exception to cover that which was regularly given to the clerk and the public crier; or that no greater duties should be levied than at present; or that duties should be levied only up to a certain amount.

3. So also in an alliance for war the agreement may be that equal auxiliary forces of cavalry, infantry, and ships shall be furnished, either for every war, which the Greeks call 'an offensive and defensive alliance',[1] and Thucydides explains as 'having the same enemies and friends'—this you may often find in Livy also—or for protecting the boundaries only, which the Greeks call 'a defensive alliance'; or for a particular war; or against particular enemies; or against all enemies, to be sure, but with the exception of allies, as in the treaty between the Carthaginians and Macedonians, which is found in Polybius. Likewise the Rhodians by treaty promised aid to Antigonus and Demetrius against all enemies whatsoever except Ptolemy. [III. lxxv.] [XXIII. xxxv. 3.] [VII. ix. 9.] Plutarch, *Demetrius* [xxii = p. 899 A].

An equal treaty, as we have said, may apply also to other matters, with provisions such as these, that neither signatory shall have fort-

[1] The ancient Greeks called it 'a union for battle'; Zosimus, Book V [V. xlii].

resses in the territory of the other,[1] or defend the subjects of the other, or furnish a passage to the enemy of the other.

VII.—*What treaties on unequal terms are; such treaties, again, are subdivided*

1. From the discussion of treaties on equal terms it may easily be understood what unequal treaties are. Unequal terms, moreover, are promised either by the party of higher rank or by the party of lower rank. Such terms are unequal on the part of the superior if he promises aid, but does not require it, or promises greater aid. Unequal terms on the part of the inferior, or, in accordance with what Isocrates says in the *Panegyric* just cited, 'those who oppress the other party more than is just', are those which, as we have said, were called 'arrangements imposed by command'.

Such treaties, again, are either accompanied by impairment of sovereignty, or are without such impairment.

2. Such treaties may be accompanied by impairment of sovereign power, as the second treaty of the Carthaginians with the Romans, [Livy, XXX. xxxvii. 4.] which contained the provision that the Carthaginians should not make war on any one without the sanction of the Romans. From that time, as Appian says, 'the Carthaginians, by treaty, were subject to the Romans.'

To this kind of treaty there may be added a conditional surrender, excepting that such a surrender involves not an impairment but a transfer of the whole sovereign power; on this subject we have spoken elsewhere. Such an agreement Livy designates as a treaty [IX. xx. 7.] both elsewhere and in Book IX: 'The Teates in Apulia begged that a treaty should be granted to them, and yet that they should not be on equal terms, but under the sway of the Roman people.'

3. In treaties without impairment [266] of sovereign power the burdens are either temporary or permanent.

The temporary burdens are concerned with the payment of an indemnity, the destruction of fortifications, the withdrawal from certain places; or the giving of hostages, of elephants, of ships.

The permanent obligations are, for example, to recognize the sovereignty and respect the majesty of the other signatory; what the force of such a stipulation is we have said elsewhere. Closely related to this is the provision that the one signatory should have as enemies and friends those whom the other signatory desires; and that a passage through his territory, or supplies, should not be given to any army with which the other is at war. Then there are the other matters of less moment, that it should not be permissible to

[1] See an example in Procopius, *Persian War*, I [I. ii. 15].

build fortresses in certain places, or to lead an army thither, or to have ships beyond a certain number, or to build a city, or to engage in navigation, or to enlist soldiers in certain places; that they should not attack the allies, nor aid enemies with provisions, nor receive persons coming from another place; and that treaties previously made with other peoples should be annulled. Examples of all these provisions may be found in Polybius, Livy, and other historians.

4. Unequal treaties, moreover, are wont to be made not only between victors and vanquished, as Menippus thought, but also between more powerful and less powerful peoples that have not even engaged in war with each other. [Livy, XXXIV. lvii. 6 ff.]

VIII.—*That treaties with those who are strangers to the true religion are permissible by the law of nature*

A question frequently raised concerning treaties is whether they are lawfully entered into with those who are strangers to the true religion.

According to the law of nature this is in no degree a matter of doubt. For the right to enter into treaties is so common to all men that it does not admit of a distinction arising from religion. There is, however, a question in regard to the teaching of the divine law, and in consequence not only the theologians[1] but also some jurists treat the question; among these are Oldradus and Decianus. Thomas, II. ii, qu. 10, art. 10. Oldradus, *Consilia*, lxxi; Decianus, *Consilia*, III. xx.

IX.—*That treaties with those who are strangers to the true religion are not, generally speaking, prohibited by the Hebraic law*

1. Let us first consider the divine law as set forth in the Old Testament, and afterward discuss the teaching of the New.

Before the law of Moses it was permissible to make with strangers to the religion a treaty not to inflict injury. An example is the treaty between Jacob and Laban—not to speak now of Abimelech, since it is not sufficiently established that he was an idolater. And no change in this respect was made by the law of Moses. Let the Egyptians serve as an example. They without doubt were at that time idolaters; yet the Jews are forbidden to hold aloof from them. An exception must be made of the seven peoples condemned by a divine sentence, which the Jews were chosen to execute; for Israelites are forbidden to spare them, because they are obstinate in their idolatry and refuse to submit to overlordship. To these the Amalekites likewise were joined by divine decree. *Genesis*, xxxi. 44. [*Genesis*, xxi. 28.] *Deuteronomy*, xxiii. 7. *Deuteronomy*, vii. 1. *Deuteronomy*, xxv. 17.

2. Treaties of commerce also, and other similar conventions, which are to the common advantage, or to the advantage of either

[1] As Antoninus, Cajetan, Toledo, Molina, Valdes, Malderen.

party, may be entered into with pagans according to the law. Nothing, in fact, is found which is opposed to this view. Further, we have examples of the treaties which David and Solomon made with Hiram, king of Tyre; and the point is to be noted that in the Scriptures it is stated that this treaty was made by Solomon according to the wisdom which God had given him.

2 Samuel, v. 11. *1 Kings*, v. 12.

3. The law of Moses does indeed specially command Jews to do good to their own people, 'to love their neighbour'. Further, the peculiar food and system of morals prescribed for the Jews scarcely admitted of familiar intercourse with other men. But from this it does not follow either that they were not permitted to do good to strangers, or even that such doing of good was not praiseworthy, though this inference has been erroneously drawn by the faulty interpretation of later teachers. From such a source comes the statement of Juvenal about the Jews:

Leviticus, xix. 8 [xix. 18]. *Deuteronomy*, xxii. 1.

[*Satires*, xiv. 103.]

> The way he does not show except to one
> Who shares with him his sacred rites.

In this passage the example of pointing out the way stands for the forces which are least troublesome and costly, which Cicero and Seneca say ought to be granted even to strangers. Of like import is the statement of Tacitus concerning the same people: 'In their relations with one another, inflexible good faith, ready compassion; against all others, hostility and hatred.'

On Duties, I [xvi. 51]. *On Benefits*, VI. ix [IV. xxix]. *Histories*, V [v].

Similarly in the New [267] Testament we read that the Jews were not accustomed to live, 'to have dealings', 'to eat', 'to join', or 'to associate', with those of foreign origin. Also Apollonius Molo said, in reproach of the Jews, that 'those who had different views about God were not received by them, and that they did not have anything in common with those who differed from them in mode of life'. According to Diodorus friends of Antiochus bring against the Jews the charge that 'they alone of all peoples are unsociable with foreigners to such a degree that they consider all other men as enemies'. There follows this about the same people: 'With no other race do they eat in common, nor do they wish well to others.'

[*John*, iv. 9; *Acts*, x. 28.] [Josephus *Against Apion*, II. xxxvi. 258.] [XXXIV. i.]

Presently 'hatred of the human race' is alleged against them. In Philostratus Apollonius of Tyana speaks thus of the Jews: 'They have found a kind of life so withdrawn from human intercourse that they do not even eat in common with others.' Likewise also in Josephus 'the unsociable mode of life' of the Jews is in many passages objected to.

[*Life of Apollonius*, v. 33.]

4. That such is not the meaning of the law Christ taught us by His example, when He did not refuse to accept water from the Samaritan woman, though He is everywhere most observant of the

[*John*, iv. 7.]

law. But also formerly David had sought refuge among peoples not of the faith, and he is nowhere criticized on that account. In Josephus this utterance is assigned to Solomon, when dedicating the Temple and praying that God might there hear even the prayers of foreigners: 'We are not of unhuman disposition, nor ill-disposed towards strangers.' [*1 Samuel*, xxvii.] *Antiquities of the Jews*, VIII. ii [VIII. iv. 3].

5. Not only are the peoples who were mentioned above to be excepted from this rule, but also the Ammonites and Moabites, who are spoken of in *Deuteronomy* (xxiii. 6): 'Thou shalt not seek their prosperity'—this is here a better interpretation of the Hebraic word than 'their peace'—'nor their good all thy days for ever'. By these words beneficent treaties with the peoples mentioned are forbidden, though the right to make war is not also granted; or at any rate, according to the opinion of some of the Jews, it was forbidden to seek peace from them, or even to accept it when offered. Surely the right to make war on the Ammonites is denied to the Jews in *Deuteronomy* (ii. 19); and Jephthah did not commence war against them until the ways of a fair peace had been tried, nor did David, except when provoked by cruel injuries. *Judges*, xi. 16. *2 Samuel*, x.

6. There remains the question of an alliance for purposes of war.

Before the giving of the law such an alliance with heathen peoples was permissible, as is apparent from the example of Abraham,[1] who helped the impious Sodomites in war. In general no change in the law of Moses in regard to this matter is read of. Consistent with the position stated was the view of the Asmonaeans, as we see, a people both skilled in the law and very religious,[2] as is apparent from their careful observance of the Sabbath, the defence only of themselves, and their use of weapons for no other purpose. Nevertheless, with the approval of their priests and people, they made treaties with the Lacedaemonians and the Romans; even more, they performed public sacrifices in behalf of the safety of those peoples. The cases which are cited to prove the contrary have special reasons. [*1 Maccabees*, viii. 20; xii. 6 ff.]

7. If, in fact, God had indicated through the prophets that

[1] He likewise made an alliance with Eshcol and Aner [*Genesis*, xiv. 13]. So also David made an alliance with Achish and Nahash, Solomon with the Egyptians, Asa with Ben-hadad [*1 Samuel*, xxvii; *2 Samuel*, x. 2; *1 Kings*, iii. 1 and xv. 19].

[2] Praise of them is found in the Chaldaean *Targum*, in the Books of the *Maccabees*, and in the *Epistle to the Hebrews*. Following their example, the Christian emperors and kings have made treaties either with non-Christians or with those who were not truly Christian, as Constantine with the Goths and Vandals; Justinian with the Lombards; Theodosius, Honorius, Leo, Heraclius, Basil, Isaac Angelus, and Palaeologus with the Saracens, Alani, Gepidae, Franks, Suevi, and Vandals.

With the Moors treaties were made by the kings of Spain, Alfonso of Seville, Ramiro, Alfonso the Chaste, Sanchez of Castile, and Ferdinand called Saint, as well as Peter, king of Leon, and Alfonso of Castile, a very wise king. Rudolf of Hapsburg made a treaty with the Tartars. Consult Joannes de Carthagena, *De Jure Belli Romani Pontificis*, Book III, i.

Pope Julius II employed the Turks.

any kings or peoples, besides those that had been mentioned in the law, were hateful to Him and condemned to misfortune, without doubt it would have been an impiety to undertake their defence or to make an alliance with them. With this harmonizes the statement of the prophet to Jehoshaphat[1] in regard to the king of Israel: [268] 'Shouldst thou help the wicked, and love them that hate God?[2] For this thing wrath is upon thee from before God.' The prophet Micah had already, in fact, foretold the unhappy outcome of the war. Then there are the words of the other prophet to Amaziah: 'Let not the army of the Israelites go with thee; for the Lord is not with Israel, *to wit*, with all the children of Ephraim.'

2 Chronicles, xix. 2.

2 Chronicles, xxv. 7.

That this attitude was not determined by the nature of the treaty, but by some peculiar quality of the person, is shown even by the fact that Jehoshaphat was severely reproved, with threats also, because he had entered into an alliance with Ahaziah, king of the Israelites, for the sake of commerce, similar to the alliance which David and Solomon had made with Hiram; and they, as we have said, in part were not criticized, in part were praised, on that account. For the additional statement that Ahaziah had acted very wickedly ought to be referred to his whole life; and on that account God was hostile to him and all his undertakings. In this way the narrative is explained in the work which is entitled the *Constitutions of Clement* (Book VI, xviii).

2 Chronicles, xx. 37.

8. This also should be noted, that the case of those descendants of Jacob that had deserted God, Who was well known to them, was worse than that of foreign peoples. For the rest of the people took up arms against those deserters in accordance with the law, which is found in *Deuteronomy*, xiii. 13.[3]

9. There are cases also where treaties are censured by reason of a fault in the intent with which they were made. Thus Asa was reproved by the prophet for the reason that he had made an alliance with the Syrian because he distrusted God. This distrust he had shown when he sent to the Syrian things that were consecrated to God. But the same king was further censured because he had put his hope in doctors, and not in God. Consequently, it no more follows from this narrative that it is inherently and universally wrong to make an alliance with such peoples as the Syrians than it is to consult doctors. The intent, in fact, vitiates many acts which are not unpermissible, such as the numbering of the people in the case of David, the display of treasures in the case of Hezekiah. Similarly in another passage confidence placed in the Egyptians is censured,

2 Chronicles, xvi. 2, 7; *Isaiah*, viii. 6. *2 Chronicles*, xvi. 12. Ambrose, *On Romans*, iii. Auctor Imperfectus, *On Matthew*, xvi. *2 Samuel*, xxiv. *2 Kings*, xx. 13. *Isaiah*, xxxi. 1.

[1] Josephus [*Antiquities of the Jews*, IX. i. 1] says: 'He accused him of making an alliance with Achab, an impious and wicked man.'

[274] [2] Gratian wrote to his uncle Valens asking aid against the Scythians: 'It is not right to join arms in alliance with one who is an enemy of God'; Zonaras [XIII. xvii].

[3] Add the example in *Joshua*, xxii.

although it was permissible for Solomon to make an alliance with them.

1 Kings, iii. 1. *Deuteronomy*, xxviii. 7. *Proverbs*, i. 15; xiii. 20; xxii. 24; xxiv. 1.

10. To the considerations already presented this also should be added, that under the ancient law the Jews had clearly expressed promises of victory if only they observed the law, so that they were less under the necessity of having recourse to human help. In Solomon, again, there are not a few maxims about avoiding association with the wicked. These, however, are the admonitions of prudence, not precepts of the law; and those very admonitions, as moral precepts in most cases, have a great many exceptions.

X.—*That treaties with those who are strangers to the true religion are not prohibited by the Christian law*

Victoria, *De Indis Relectiones*, I, nos. 15 and 17. Franciscus Arias, *De Bello*, no. 192. Cajetan, *On II. ii*, qu. 40, art. 1. Molina, ii. 112. *Matthew*, v. 45. [*Against Marcion*, iv. 16.]

1. Moreover, the law of the Gospel made no change in this matter. Rather it extends even greater favour to treaties by which those who are strangers to the true religion receive help in a just cause; for the doing of good to all men, whenever there is opportunity, has not only been left free and praiseworthy, but has even been enjoined by precept. By the example of God, who maketh His sun to rise on the good and on the evil, and sendeth rain for both, we are bidden to exclude no class of men from our deeds of kindness. Tertullian well said:

> So long as the covenant was confined to Israel, He properly commanded that compassion should be shown only to brethren. But when He had given to Christ 'the gentiles as His inheritance and the ends of the earth for His possession', then began to be fulfilled that which was spoken by Hosea: 'Ye are not my people, who were my people; ye have not obtained mercy, who once obtained mercy'—that is, the nation. Thenceforth Christ extended to all the law of brotherly kindness, excepting no one from His compassion, just as He had excepted no one from His invitation.

Galatians, vi. 10.

VII. iii [VII. i, end].

On Duties, I. iii [I. xxx. 148].

Nicomachean Ethics, IV [xii].

2. Now this law ought to be received with due regard to difference in degree, so that we should be doers of good to all, but particularly to those who share the same religion. In the *Constitutions of Clement* we read: [269] 'Service ought to be rendered to all, but in such a way that greater consideration should be shown to those that are holy.' Says Ambrose: 'Perfect generosity is commended by reason of faith, cause, place, and time, so that you labour first on behalf of the servants of the faith.' The statement of Aristotle is similar: 'It is not, in fact, fair that equal care should be taken for strangers and for friends.'

3. Furthermore, familiar association with men who are strangers to the true religion is not prohibited; and not all intercourse, but only that which is unnecessarily intimate, is forbidden even with

those whose case is worse, who have fallen away from the rule of
2 Thessalonians, i. 15 [iii. 15]. Christian teaching; and not even that is forbidden if it furnishes the hope of their correction.

2 Corinthians, vi. 14. This is the force of the passage in the writings of Paul: 'Be ye not unequally yoked with unbelievers; for what fellowship have righteousness and iniquity? or what communion hath light with darkness? And what concord hath Christ with Belial? or what portion hath a believer with an unbeliever?' The passage refers to those who joined in the feasts at the temples of idols, and thus either were guilty of idolatry, or at any rate presented the appearance of being guilty. This is shown by the words which follow: 'What agreement hath a temple of God with idols?' Statements similar
1 Corinthians, x. 21. to these appear in the *First Epistle* to the same Corinthians: 'Ye cannot partake of the table of the Lord and of the table of demons.'

4. Proof again will by no means naturally follow from this fact, that we ought not of our own will to submit to the rule of the heathen, or contract marriages with them. For in both these cases it is apparent that there is greater danger, or at any rate greater difficulty is thrown in the way of practising the true religion. Add also the consideration that such ties are more lasting, and in marriage the choice is freer, while treaties have to be made to satisfy the exigencies of the time
Sylvester, word *bellum,* pt. 1, no. 9, concl. 3. and place. Moreover, as it is not wrong to do good to the heathen, so it is not wrong to implore their aid, as Paul invoked the aid of Caesar and the tribune.

Panormitanus, *On Decretals,* III. xxxiv. 8.

XI.—*Cautions in regard to such treaties*

1. In such alliances, therefore, wrongfulness is not inherent nor universal, but is subject to judgement according to the circumstances.[1] Pains must, in fact, be taken that too great intimacy may not bring contamination to the weak. With this end in view it will be advantageous that the homes be kept separate, as the Israelites dwelt apart from the Egyptians. Not without reason are those
[Athenaeus, VII. lv.] verses of Alexandrides [Anaxandrides]:

> I cannot as your fellow-soldier fight;
> For neither our laws nor customs harmonize,
> But differ by great intervals.

I. ii [9. 3]. Here also the remarks apply which I have elsewhere made concerning the religious scruples of the Jews and Christians in respect to joint military service with the heathen.

[1] See the oration of Phartaza to the Lazi in Agathias, III [III. xi]. Saxo, in Book IX [p. 158], says in the words of Louis, king of France, to Hurald: 'No harmony of spirit can exist between those who have embraced different religious faiths. Wherefore the seeker for aid has need first to be united in the bond of the same religion, and those cannot be partners in great undertakings whom the creed of divine worship has separated.'

2. But also if, as a result of such an alliance, the power of the heathen is going to be greatly increased, it should be refrained from except in direst need. Applicable here is what Thucydides said in a similar case: 'Those who are treacherously attacked, as we are by the Athenians, ought not to be looked upon with disfavour if they seek safety not only in the aid of the Greeks but also in that of the barbarians.' No right whatsoever is sufficient to warrant committing what will probably be harmful to religion, indirectly, if not directly. For as a matter of first importance the kingdom of heaven is to be sought, that is, the spread of the Gospel.

Sylvester, word *bellum*, pt. 1, no. 9, 3. I [lxxxii]. *Matthew*, vi. 33.

3. It were greatly to be desired that to-day many princes and peoples should take to heart the generous [270] and noble utterance of Fulk, formerly Archbishop of Reims, who thus admonished Charles the Simple: 'Who would not be greatly alarmed that you desire the friendship of the enemies of God,[1] and are receiving heathen armies in detestable alliance, to the destruction and downfall of the Christian name? For it makes no difference whether any one allies himself with the heathen or denies God and worships idols.' There is a saying of Alexander found in Arrian: 'They do a grievous wrong against the rights of Greeks who serve with the barbarians in war against the Greeks.'[2]

Flodoard, *Historia Ecclesiae Remensis*, IV. vi. [I. xvi.]

XII.—*That all Christians are under obligation to enter a league against the enemies of Christianity*

At this point I shall add that, since all Christians are members of one body, and are bidden to share one another's sufferings and misfortunes, just as this principle applies to individuals, so also it is applicable to peoples as such, and to kings as such. For every man ought to serve Christ not only personally, but also with the power that has been entrusted to him. This, however, kings and peoples cannot do while an impious enemy is raging in arms, unless they furnish aid to one another.[3] Such aid, again, cannot be rendered effectively unless an alliance is made for that purpose. Such a league was formerly made, and the emperor of the Holy Roman Empire was unanimously chosen as its head. To this common cause, therefore, all Christians ought to contribute men or money, according to their strength. How they can be excused from making such a contribution, I do not see, unless they are kept at home by an unavoidable war or some other equally grievous misfortune.

I Corinthians, xii. 18, 26.

[1] Mancafa furnishes an example in Nicetas, *On Isaac Angelus*, II [II. iii]. The religiousness of Emmanuel, Duke of Savoy, is praised, for the reason that, though he might have done so, he was unwilling to recover Cyprus with the help of the Turks.

[2] [The Greek words quoted by Grotius are a paraphrase of Arrian.]

[3] On this subject see Mariana, XXX [XXX. xxiii]; Paruta, Book IV; Bizarri, VII and XII.

XIII.—*To which ally help should by preference be given when several are at war, is explained, with distinctions*

1. This question also frequently arises. If several are at war, to which of two parties ought aid preferably to be given by one who is in alliance with both?

First, then, that is to be recalled which we previously said, that there is no obligation to undertake unjust wars. Therefore that one of the allies who has a just cause for war ought to have the preference[1] if the contest is with one who is not in alliance. The same will likewise hold if the contest is with another ally. Thus in his speech
[xvi. 9–10 = p. 204.] in regard to Megalopolis Demosthenes showed that the Athenians ought to give aid to their allies the Messenians against the Lacedaemonians, who were also allies, if the latter were the aggressors.

The principle stated holds true only if there is no clause in the agreement forbidding that aid be sent to an ally. In the agree-
Polybius, VI [VII. ix. 9]. ment of Hannibal with the Macedonians there was the clause: 'We shall be the enemies of your enemies, with the exception of the kings, states, and ports with which we have treaties of friendship.'

2. Now if allies are engaged in war with each other for unjust causes on both sides—and this can happen—it will be necessary to
[= p. 220] refrain from aiding either party. Thus Aristides says, in his fifth speech *On Leuctra*: 'If indeed they were asking for aid against others, it would be an easy matter; but if each of the allies was requesting aid against the other they did not wish to mix in the affair.'

3. If, on the contrary, two allies are waging war against others, and each for a just cause, aid in men and money will have to be sent to both, if this can be done, just as happens in the case of personal creditors. But if the undivided co-operation of the one who has promised is required, reason demands that preference be shown to the ally with whom the treaty is of longer standing.[2] This, accord-
IX [xxxii]. ing to Polybius, is what the Acarnanians said to the Spartans. And the answer given by the Roman consul to the Campanians has the
[Livy, VII. xxxi. 2.] same effect: 'It is right that friendships be so established that the more ancient friendship and alliance shall not be violated.'[3]

Sylvester, word *bellum*, pt. 1, no. 7. 4. But an exception needs to be made if the later treaty has something beyond the promise which, so to speak, contains in itself

[1] See below, III. xxv. 4 [II. xxv. 4]. In the feudal oath of fidelity are the words (*Feuds*, II. vii): 'And if I know that you wish to attack some one justly, and if in consequence I have been summoned either by a general or by a special summons, I will furnish aid to you as I shall be able.'

[2] See *Feuds*, IV. xxxi [II. xxviii. 4].

[3] According to Appian, in the *Selections on Embassies* [= *Of Sicily and the Other Islands*, I] Ptolemy says to the Athenians [Carthaginians]: 'Help should be furnished by friends against enemies, not against friends.'

the transfer of ownership;[1] that is, some form of subjection. For so also in a sale[2] we say that the earlier promise receives the preference, unless a later promise has transferred ownership. So in Livy the Nepisini held the pledge of surrender [271] more sacred than that of alliance. VI [x. 4].

Others draw these distinctions more subtly, but what I have said, as more simple, is, I think, nearer the truth.

XIV.—*Whether an alliance may be considered as tacitly renewed*

An alliance ought not to be considered as renewed tacitly on the expiration of the time, except in consequence of acts which admit of no other interpretation. A new obligation, in fact, is not easily presumed. Decio, *Consilia*, ccccvii.

XV.—*Whether the one party may be freed by the perfidy of the other*

If one party has violated a treaty of alliance, the other will be able to withdraw from it; for the individual terms of an alliance have the force of conditions. This instance in Thucydides may serve as an example: 'Those do not bear the blame of breaking a treaty of alliance who, abandoned, turn to others for help, but those who do not in fact furnish the aid which on oath they had promised.' There is another example in the same author: 'If either of the parties should deviate from the terms ever so little, the alliance would be broken.' This, however, is true only in case there has been no agreement to the contrary; for sometimes such an agreement is made in order that withdrawal from the league may not be permissible for a slight offence. Decio, *Consilia*, cclxv. Caepolla, *Consilia*, ccccli, ccccIv, ccccIxi. I [Ixxi]. [IV. xxiii.]

XVI.—*To what the signers are bound if a sponsion signed by them is rejected; also concerning the sponsion of the Caudine Forks*

1. Sponsions can have as many kinds of subject-matter as treaties. Sponsions and treaties, in fact, differ only in the power of the persons who make them. But in regard to sponsions there are two questions that are commonly raised.

The first question is, in case a sponsion is disapproved by the king or state, to what are the signers bound; whether they are to make good the loss, or to restore matters to the state in which they were in before the sponsion, or to be surrendered in person. The first alternative seems to be in harmony with Roman civil law; the second, with equity—and this was urged by the tribunes Lucius

[1] See Radevicus, II. vii.

[2] *Edict of Theodoric*, chap. cxxxviii.

Livius and Quintus Maelius in the Caudine controversy; while the third opinion has been approved in practice, as is apparent from the examples of the two famous sponsions of the Caudine Forks and
[Florus, I. xi. 9; I. xxxiv. 7.] Numantia.

Now the point which ought to be maintained above all others is that the one who holds the sovereign power is under no obligation
[Livy, IX. ix. 16.] whatsoever. Postumius well said to the Romans: 'You have made no compact with the enemy; you have not commanded any citizen to make one for you. Therefore you have no dispute with us, to whom you gave no commission, nor with the Samnites, with whom
[Livy, IX. ix. 4.] you have made no engagement.' Equally well did he say this: 'I declare that nothing can be so sanctioned as to bind the people
[Livy, IX. ix. 7.] without the order of the people.' This again is not less to the point: 'If there is anything to which the people can be obligated, it can be obligated to all things.'

2. Therefore the people was not bound either to give compensation or to make restitution. For if the Samnites had wished to have dealings with the people, they ought to have kept the army at the Caudine Forks and to have sent envoys to Rome, to treat with the senate and the people concerning a treaty of peace, in order that the people itself might judge of how great value the safety of the army was to it. Then, if at length the treaty had not been kept, they could have said, what Velleius says was maintained by both the Samnites and the Numantines, that the violation of the public faith ought not to be expiated with the blood of a single individual.

3. With greater plausibility it can be said that all the soldiers were bound by the obligation.[1] And this would certainly be fair if the sponsion had been made by the signers on their order and in their name, as we see was done in the case of the treaty which Hannibal made with the Macedonians. If now the Samnites were satisfied with the good faith of the signers,[2] and of the six hundred hostages whom they had levied,[3] they had only themselves to blame.

Again, if the signers claimed the power to execute agreements in the name of the state, they were bound to make restitution for the loss suffered by reason of their deceit. If deceit was not apparent,

[1] Thus the Numantines thought that the army, freed from the sponsion, ought to be surrendered to them, in case the sponsion should not be ratified [Orosius, V. v. 3].

[2] These were the two consuls, two quaestors, four prefects, twelve tribunes, according to Appian [*Selections on Embassies*, iii = *Samnite History*, iv. 6]. All these were surrendered in accordance with the Caudine agreement. According to the Numantine agreement only the consul was surrendered; the others were spared on account of Tiberius Gracchus, as Plutarch relates in the lives of the Gracchi [*Tiberius Gracchus*, vii = 827 A].

[3] Pontius, the son, according to Appian said [*Samnite History*, iv. 4]: 'I shall choose the noblest of the knights to be hostages until the people confirms the convention.' In a similar case the Portuguese thought it was sufficient to leave the hostages at the will of him who held them; Mariana, XXI. xii. They who accept those who have been surrendered are held to remit the penalty; Polybius, *Selections*, cxxii [=XXXII. vii. 11–12].

they were bound to have that ratified which was called for by the force of the negotiations. And in this case not only the bodies but also the property of the signers would be under obligation to the Samnites, unless they had imposed a penalty in the place of their loss. [272] For there had been an agreement in regard to the hostages, that their lives were forfeited if the compact was not adhered to. Whether the same penalty was agreed upon in regard to the signers, is not clear; but the stipulation of a penalty affects what is done in such a way that there is no other obligation if the deed cannot be performed. For a certain advantage has succeeded to the place of an uncertain one. Moreover, it was the current opinion of those times that even a life could be lawfully pledged as security.

4. Among us who hold a different opinion, I think that in such a sponsion first the property is liable up to the amount of the loss; and if that is not sufficient, then the person is subject to slavery. Formerly Fabius Maximus, when the senate had rejected an agreement which he had made with the enemy, sold his estate for 200,000 sesterces and made good his promise.[1] Besides, the Samnites rightly thought that Papius Brutulus,[2] who broke a truce, ought to be surrendered together with his property.

The writer [Aurelius Victor,] *On Famous Men,* xliii; Plutarch, *Fabius Maximus* [vii = 178 F]. Livy, VIII and IX [VIII. xxxix. 15].

XVII.—*Whether a sponsion that has not been rejected is made binding through knowledge of it and through silence is set forth, with distinctions; likewise concerning the sponsion of Luctatius*

1. A second question is whether a sponsion is binding upon the sovereign authority in consequence of the knowledge of it, and of silence.

Here the distinction should be made, first, whether the sponsion was made unconditionally, or on the condition that it should be considered as valid by the supreme authority. For this condition, if unfulfilled, makes the sponsion null and void, for the reason that conditions ought to be carried out exactly. And this applies perfectly to the sponsion of Luctatius with the Carthaginians; there was the further fact that the people had declared that it was not bound by that sponsion, because it had been made without its order. And so another entirely new treaty was made with the public sanction.

Livy, XXI [xix. 3]. Polybius, III [xxix].

2. Then the point should be investigated whether, in addition to silence, there is anything else having a bearing on the matter. For silence, unless reinforced by some thing or act, does not supply a sufficiently probable basis for determining intent, as may be under-

[1] Diodorus Siculus, *Excerpta Peiresciana* [Dio Cassius, *Excerpta Valesiana,* p. 597 = XIV. xv]; Valerius Maximus, IV. viii.

[2] Dio Cassius, *Selections on Embassies,* v [= VII. viii].

stood from what we have said above regarding the abandonment of ownership. But if in addition there shall have been certain acts which cannot with probability be referred to any other cause, then the agreement will be understood to have been ratified. Cicero notes, in the speech *For Balbus*, that in this way the treaty which had been made with the people of Gades was approved.

[xv. 34–6.]

Polybius and Livy as cited above.

3. Against the Carthaginians the Romans pleaded their silence as regards the treaty compact with Hasdrubal. But since that compact had been expressed negatively, that the Carthaginians should not cross the Ebro river, it was hardly a case where silence alone should have the power to imply ratification of another's act, since no act of their own would have followed except when some Carthaginian who wished to cross the Ebro had been hindered by the Romans, and the Carthaginian had obeyed their order. Such action, in fact, has the force of a positive act, and does not remain within purely negative limits. But if the compact signed by Luctatius had had more provisions, and it was apparent that the others, which were at variance with common rights, had always been observed by the Romans, there would then have been a sufficiently strong implication of the approval of the compact.

4. It remains to say something here about the agreements which leaders or soldiers make, not concerning what belongs to the sovereign authority, but concerning their personal affairs, or matters entrusted to them. But there will be a better opportunity to treat of these matters when we come to the incidental occurrences of war.

[275] CHAPTER XVI

ON INTERPRETATION

I.—*How promises are outwardly binding*

1. If we consider only the one who has promised, he is under obligation to perform, of his own free will, that to which he wished to bind himself. 'In good faith what you meant, not what you said, is to be considered,' says Cicero. But because internal acts are not of themselves perceivable, and some degree of certainty must be established, lest there should fail to be any binding obligation, in case every one could free himself by inventing whatever meaning he might wish, natural reason itself demands that the one to whom the promise has been made should have the right to compel the promisor to do what the correct interpretation suggests. For otherwise the matter would have no outcome, a condition which in morals is held to be impossible. *On Duties*, I [xiii. 40]

It was, perhaps, with this thought in mind that Isocrates, treating of agreements in his speech *Against Callimachus*, said: 'We men constantly apply this universal rule in our relations with one another,' as the passage was correctly emended by Peter Faber, a man of most eminent learning; for not only Greeks but also barbarians were meant, as the author had said a little before. [xii. 28 = p. 376 D.]

2. Applicable here also is the ancient treaty formula given by Livy: 'Without wicked deceit, and as these words here to-day have been most rightly understood.' [1] The measure of correct interpretation is the inference of intent from the most probable indications. These indications are of two kinds, words and implications; and these are considered either separately or together. I [xxiv. 7].

II.—*If other implications are lacking, words are to be understood in their ordinary sense*

[276] If there is no implication which suggests a different conclusion, words are to be understood in their natural sense, not according to the grammatical sense which comes from derivation,[2] but according to current usage, [Horace, *Art of Poetry*, 72.]

> To whose behest belong the law and rule of speech.

[1] The Jewish scholars note, on *Numbers*, xxx, that vows ought to be interpreted as they are commonly understood.

[2] Procopius, *Vandalic War*, I [I. xi. 4], treating of the word 'confederates', well says: [286] 'Length of time is not wont to preserve words in the sense originally given to them. Things themselves, in fact, are changed as men wish, and men care not at all for the names at first assigned to things.'

The Locrians,[1] then, availed themselves of a stupid evasion in their perfidy; for they took oath that they would keep the agreement as long as they should stand on that ground and should bear heads on their shoulders; then they threw away the earth which they had placed in their shoes, and the heads of garlic which they had laid on their shoulders, as if in that manner they could free themselves from the religious obligation. This story is found in Polybius; and in Polyaenus there are several instances of similar perfidy which it is not necessary to repeat, since there is no doubt concerning them. Cicero has rightly said that by deception of this kind perjury is made worse, not lessened.

[II. vi; VII. xxxiv.] *On Duties*, III [xxxii. 113].

III.—*Technical terms are to be explained according to their technical use*

In the case of technical terms,[2] which the people scarcely understand, the explanation of those who are expert in the particular art will need to be utilized, just as the teachers of rhetoric refer the question, what *majestas* is, or parricide, to a definition. Cicero, in fact, said truly in the first book of the *Academics*: 'The words of the logicians do not belong to common speech. They use their own technical terms; and indeed this practice is common to almost all the arts.' Thus, if an army has been spoken of in a compact, we shall explain that an army is a body of soldiers, which has dared openly to invade the territory of the enemy.

[I. vii. 25.]

The historians, in fact, everywhere distinguish what is done secretly, or in the manner of brigands, from what is done by a regularly constituted army. Wherefore the forces which constitute an army ought to be estimated in proportion to the strength of the enemy. Cicero calls six legions with their auxiliary forces an army. Polybius says that a Roman army generally consisted of 16,000 Romans and 20,000 allies. But even a smaller number can satisfy the interpretation of the word; for Ulpian says that a man is in command of an army who has only one legion with the auxiliary forces; according to Vegetius such an army consists of 10,000 infantry and 2,000 cavalry. Livy reckons a true army at 8,000 men. In like manner one must judge in regard to a fleet. Similarly a fortress is a place which for a time can resist a hostile army.[3]

Paradoxes, vi [45]. [III. lxxii. 11.] *Dig.*, III. ii. 2. III. i. [XXV. vi. 14.]

[1] Polybius, Book XII [XII. vi. 3]. Similar is the fact that the Boeotians, having promised to restore a city, restored it not unharmed, but destroyed; Thucydides, V [V. xlii]. Likewise the Sultan Mahomet, after capturing Euboea, cut in two the man whose head he had promised should be safe [J. Cuspinian, *De Turcarum Origine*, p. 132, on Mahomet II].

[2] Augustine in his *Principles of Rhetoric* [ix] says: 'As many new things are named, as well by technical writers and mathematicians as by philosophers, we ought to accept such terms not so much on the ground of current usage as in accordance with the technical character of the meaning.'

[3] Servius, *On the Aeneid*, I [I, line 20]: 'Citadels (*arces*) are so named from the verb *arceo* (keep away), because the enemy are kept away from that spot, that is, are prohibited.'

IV.—*Resort is to be had to conjectures in the case of ambiguous and contradictory expressions, or if conjectures naturally suggest themselves*

1. It is necessary to resort to conjectures when the words or sentences are 'interpreted in different ways', that is, admit of several meanings. The rhetoricians call this topic 'ambiguity', but the dialecticians make a finer distinction, calling it 'homonymy' if a single word, and 'ambiguity' if a sentence, has more than one meaning. Similarly there is need of conjectures whenever in compacts there is 'an appearance of contradiction'. For then interpretations are to be sought which will reconcile the different parts with one another, if this is possible.

In case the contradiction is real, a later agreement between the contracting parties will annul earlier agreements, since no one could at the same time have had contradictory desires. Such is in truth the nature of acts dependent on the will that they can be relinquished through a new act of volition, either 'on the one part', as in a law or a will, or conjointly, as in the case of contracts and compacts. The rhetoricians call this topic 'antinomy'. In such cases, in fact, the evident obscurity of the words compels us to have recourse to conjectures.

2. But at times the conjectures themselves are so evident that they naturally suggest themselves, even against the more commonly accepted interpretation of the words. The Greek rhetoricians call this topic 'concerning the word and the meaning'; and the Latins call it 'of the written word and the meaning of the word'. The elements from which are derived [277] conjectures as to meaning are especially the subject-matter, the effect, and the connexion.

V.—*Conjectures from the subject-matter*

Of the subject-matter[1] is the word day, in case a thirty days' truce has been made; and this ought to be understood as meaning not natural days, but civil days, for that meaning is consistent with the subject-matter. So the word 'to bestow' is assumed to mean 'to complete a transaction', according to the nature of the business. Similarly the word 'arms', which sometimes means instruments of war and sometimes armed soldiers, will have to be interpreted now with the former, now with the latter meaning, according to the subject-matter.

Everard, on the subject *A Subjecta Materia.*

Digest, XIX. ii. 15. § 4.

Again, he who has promised to deliver up men ought to deliver them living, not dead, contrary to the quibble of the Plataeans;

[Thucydides, II. vi, vii.]

[1] Tertullian, *On Modesty* [viii]: 'Speech ought to be explained according to the nature of the matter spoken of.' The same is found in his work *On the Resurrection of Christ* [*On the Resurrection of the Flesh*, xxxvii].

and those who were commanded to deliver up their iron fulfilled the command by giving up their swords, not also their buckles, as Pericles craftily maintained. Thus the free withdrawal from a city ought so to be understood that the journey also shall be safe, contrary to what Alexander did. Finally, in a division one-half of the ships ought to be understood of whole ships, and not as one-half of each ship cut in two, as the Romans maintained in taking advantage of Antiochus. In similar cases let the same decision be reached.

[Frontinus, IV. vii. 17.] [Plut., *Alex.*, lix =698 c.] [Valerius Maximus, VII.iii,iv.]

VI.—*Conjectures from the effect*

Everard, on the subject *Ab Absurdo.* *Dig.*, I. iii. 19. Thucydides, IV [xcviii].

As regards the effect, especially important is the case when a word taken in its more common meaning produces an effect contrary to reason. For in the case of an ambiguous word that meaning ought preferably to be accepted which is free from fault. In consequence we ought not to admit the quibble of Brasidas, who, having promised that he would withdraw from the Boeotian country, denied that the land which he occupied with his army was Boeotian, as if that word ought to be understood of warlike possession and not of ancient boundaries; for in the former sense the compact would have been meaningless.

VII.—*Conjectures from elements that are connected, either in origin or also in place*

Everard, on the subject *A Conjunctione Duarum Legum.* [*Iliad*, III. 92, 281, 309.] Plutarch, *Symposiacs*, IX. xiii. [=743 A].

Statements are connected either in origin[1] or also in place. Those are connected in origin which proceed from the same will, although uttered in different places and on different occasions; hence arises the need of conjecture, because in doubtful cases the will is believed to have been consistent. Thus in Homer the agreement between Paris and Menelaus, that Helen should belong to the victor, must so be understood from what follows that he who had killed the other should finally be recognized as the victor. Plutarch gives this reason: 'Judges incline to that which is less ambiguous, passing by that which is more obscure.'

VIII.—*To what the conjecture drawn from reasonable motive applies; and when, and how, it is in point*

Among the elements which are connected in respect to place, the chief force is given to the reason for a law,[2] which many confuse

[1] Augustine, *Against Adimantus*, iv [xiv. 2], well says: 'They choose out certain portions of the Scriptures in order to deceive the ignorant, without connecting these with the context which precedes and follows, from which the will and intent of the author can be understood.'

[2] Cicero, *For Caecina* [xx. 57], says: 'From the point of view of law, as regards this kind of act, it makes no difference whether I have been ejected by your agent, who is said to be the legal representative in charge of all the possessions of one who is not in Italy or is away on public business, who

with the intent, although it is only one of the indications from which we trace the intent.

Nevertheless among conjectures this is the strongest, if it is established with certainty that the will has been influenced by some reason as the only cause. Often, in fact, there are several reasons, and sometimes the will without reason determines itself from the power of its own freedom; and this is sufficient to produce a binding obligation. Thus a present made by reason of a wedding will not be valid if the wedding does not take place.

IX.—*The distinction between broad and narrow meanings*

Furthermore, the fact should be recognized that many words have several meanings, the one narrower, the other broader. This is the case for many reasons. One is that the name of the genus may be applied to a species, as in words of relationship and adoption; likewise also in masculine nouns, which are ordinarily used as common nouns when words of common gender are wanting. Another is that the technical use of a term may give a broader meaning than the everyday use, just as the word for death is extended by the civil law to cover banishment,[1] though it does not have this meaning in ordinary speech.

X.—*Division of promises into favourable, odious, mixed, and median*

At the same time it should be noted that of promises which are made some are favourable, [278] some odious, some mixed, and some median. Alciati, *Responsa*, V. xvii.

Those promises are favourable which are made on a basis of equality and promote the common advantage. The greater and more extended this advantage is, the greater the favourableness of the promise; this, then, is greater in promises that contribute to peace than in those that contribute to war, greater also in promises for defence in a war that has been begun than for other causes.

Odious promises are those which impose burden on one party only, or on one party more than the other; which contain penalties in themselves which render acts null and void, and which bring about some change in previous agreements. If, again, a promise is of a mixed character, as changing former agreements, to be sure, but with a view to peace, this will be considered now favourable and now odious, as the amount of good or of change predominates,

is almost as the owner himself, that is, represents the rights of another; or whether it be your farmer, or neighbour, or client, or freedman, or any one whatsoever, who has done the deed of violence, or has accomplished the ejection, at your request or in your name.'

[1] See Guicciardini, Book XVI [p. 341], where the compacts of Charles V relating to the duchy of Milan are related.

but in such a way that, other things being equal, it should preferably be considered favourable.

XI.—*The rejection of the distinction between contracts of good faith and those of strict legal right in relation to the acts of peoples and kings*

Gl., *On Dig.*, I. iii. 12.

The distinction between acts of good faith and those granting a strict legal right, in so far as it is drawn from the Roman law, does not belong to the law of nations. In a certain sense, however, the distinction can be applied here; thus, for example, if in any countries some acts have a certain common form, in so far as that form is unchanged, the distinction may be understood to be present in the act. But in other acts, which are in themselves indefinite in respect to form, such as a donation and a generous promise, more attention should be paid to the words.

XII.—*In accordance with the distinctions of meanings and promises stated, rules are formulated in regard to interpretations*

1. In the light of the principles stated the following rules should be observed:

In agreements that are not odious the words should be taken with their full meaning according to current usage; and, if there are several meanings, that which is broadest should be chosen, just as the masculine gender is taken for the common gender, and an indefinite expression for a universal. Thus the words, 'from which one has been ejected', will have reference even to the restoration of one who has been hindered by force from entering into possession of what belongs to him; the expression, taken more loosely, has that force, as Cicero rightly maintained in his oration *For Aulus Caecina.*

Bartolus, *On Dig.*, XLI. iii. 15. Covarruvias, *Variae*, III. iii. 5. Tiraqueau, *De Legibus Connubialibus*, gl. v, no. 115.

2. In more favourable agreements, if the speaker knows the law or avails himself of the advice of lawyers, the words should be taken rather broadly, so as to include even a technical meaning, or a meaning imposed by law. But we should not have recourse to meanings that are plainly unsuitable [1] unless otherwise some absurdity or the uselessness of the agreement would result. On the other hand words are to be taken even more strictly than the proper meaning demands if such an interpretation shall be necessary in order to avoid injustice or absurdity. And even if there be no such necessity, but there is manifest fairness or advantage in the restriction, we ought to confine ourselves to the narrowest limits of the proper meaning unless circumstances persuade to the contrary.

3. In odious agreements even figurative speech is sometimes

[1] See an example in the *Code*, VI. xlii. 16.

admitted, in order to lighten the burden. Consequently in the case of a donation, and in the surrender of one's right, no matter how general the words are, they are ordinarily restricted to the matters which were in all probability thought of. In such cases that will sometimes be understood to have been taken possession of which there may be hope of being able to retain. Thus the promise of auxiliary forces by one party only will be understood to be an obligation at the expense of the one who asks for them. Barbatia, *Consilia*, IV. lxii

XIII.—*Whether under the term 'allies' future allies are included, and in what degree; also, concerning the treaty of the Romans with Hasdrubal, and similar controversies*

1. A notable question is, whether under the term 'allies' only those are included who were allies at the time of a treaty, or also future allies, as in the treaty between the Romans and the Carthaginians after the war in regard to Sicily: 'The allies of each people shall be safe at the hands of the other people.' From this the Romans inferred that, although the treaty with Hasdrubal about not crossing the Ebro brought no advantage to them, since the Carthaginians had not ratified it, war could nevertheless be declared on the ground of treaty violation if the Carthaginians should approve of the action of Hannibal in attacking the Saguntines, whom the Romans had accepted as allies after the treaty. Livy sets forth the reasons as follows: XXI [xix. 4 ff.].

[279] Sufficient provision had been made for the Saguntines when exception was made of the allies of both parties. For no proviso had been added 'to those, who were then allies'; nor was there a proviso 'that no allies should thereafter be taken'.[1] Since, then, it was permissible to take new allies, who would think it right to receive any one into a relation of friendship without services rendered, or not to defend those who had been so received, provided only that the allies of the Carthaginians should not be incited to revolt, or should not be received when revolting of their own accord?

This appears to have been taken almost word for word from Polybius. *Histories*, III [xxix. 4].

What shall we say? Indeed there can be no doubt that, with due regard for correctness of speech, the word 'allies' can be accepted in the narrower sense of those who were allies at the time of the treaty, and in a second and broader meaning, which is extended also to future allies. Which of the two interpretations, then, ought to have the preference will need to be inferred from the rules given above. In accordance with those rules we say that future allies are not included, because the breaking of a treaty, which is an odious matter,

[1] This was added in the Peloponnesian treaty of peace between the Lacedaemonians and the Athenians; Thucydides, Book V [V. xviii].

is involved, also the taking away from the Carthaginians of unrestricted freedom to restrain by force of arms those who were believed to have done injury to them. Such freedom is, in fact, natural, and is not to be considered as given up without good reason.[1]

2. Was it not permissible to the Romans, then, to admit the Saguntines to an alliance, or to defend them after they had been admitted? Certainly it was permissible, not indeed by virtue of the treaty, but according to the law of nature, which had not been renounced in making the treaty. Consequently in their relation to both parties the Saguntines were placed in the position in which they would have been if no agreement had been made in regard to allies; and under these conditions neither the Carthaginians would be acting contrary to the treaty if they commenced a war which they thought just against the Saguntines; nor the Romans, if they defended the Saguntines.

Polybius, *Histories*, III [xxv. 3].

Just so in the time of Pyrrhus an agreement had been reached between the Carthaginians and the Romans, that if either of these peoples should make a treaty with Pyrrhus it should be made with the reservation of the right to send aid to the one whom Pyrrhus might attack in war. I do not say that the war could have been just on both sides, but I declare that it had nothing to do with the violation of the treaty.[2] In like manner, as regards the question of aid sent to the Mamertines by the Romans, Polybius makes the distinction whether that act was just, and whether it was permitted by the treaty.

[III. xxvi. 6 f.]

I [xxxv].

3. This, again, is the very thing which, according to Thucydides, the people of Corcyra said to the Athenians, that it was permissible for the Athenians to send them aid, and that the fact that the Athenians had a treaty with the Lacedaemonians presented no obstacle, since according to that treaty they were permitted to acquire new allies. And the Athenians followed that opinion afterward; for in order not to break the treaty they ordered their men not to fight against the Corinthians except when these should be preparing to make a hostile landing on Corcyra. Moreover, it was not inconsistent with the treaty, that those whom the one party was attacking should be defended by the other, while in other respects [3] peace was still maintained.

Same reference [Thucydides, I xlv].

[1] When the Samnites wished to make war on the Sidicini and asked the Romans to permit them to do this, the Romans made answer that 'nothing hindered the Samnite people from making a free decision in regard to peace and war'; Livy, Book VIII [VIII. ii. 3]. In the treaty of Antiochus are the words: 'If any of the allies of the Roman people should of their own initiative make war on Antiochus, he shall have the right to repel their attack, provided that he neither hold any city by right of war, nor receive any city into an alliance of friendship'; Livy, XXXVIII [XXXVIII. xxxviii. 16]; Polybius, *Selections on Embassies*, xxxv [=XXII. xxiii. 24].

[2] Procopius, *Persian War*, II [II. i]: 'Alamundarus, king of the Saracens, used to say that he was not violating the treaty between the Persians and Romans, since he had not been included by either party in the agreement.'

[3] [287] Thus after the times mentioned the people of Corcyra decreed 'that they would

In discussing those times, Justin says: 'The truce which they had made in their own name they broke in the person of their allies, just as if they were less guilty of perjury in bearing aid to their allies than if they had fought in open warfare.' So also in the speech *On Halonnesus*, which has a place among the orations of Demosthenes, it appears that in a certain treaty of peace between the Athenians and Philip there was a provision that the states of Greece which were not included in the treaty should be free; that it should be permissible for those who were included in the peace treaty to defend them, in case any one should make an attack upon them. This is, in fact, an example in an equal alliance. III [vii. 14]. [vii. 30 = p. 84.]

XIV.—*In what way the clause, that one people may not make war without the consent of the other, ought to be interpreted*

As applicable to an unequal alliance we shall present a second possibility; that is, if it has been agreed that one of the allies shall not be able to wage war without the consent of the other.

We have mentioned above that such a provision was made a part of the treaty between the Romans and the Carthaginians after the Second Punic War. A similar provision was contained in the treaty [280] of the Macedonians with the Romans before the time of King Perseus. The expression 'to wage war' can apply to every war, both offensive and defensive; in case of doubt we shall in this connexion take it in the narrower sense, that liberty may not be too greatly restricted. Livy, XLII. [xxv. 4].

XV.—*Concerning the words 'Carthage shall be free'*

In the same class is the promise which the Romans had made, that Carthage should be free.[1] Although from the nature of the act this promise could not be understood as implying absolute power (the Carthaginians had, in fact, already lost the right of undertaking war, and some other rights), nevertheless it left to them a degree of liberty, at any rate so great a degree that they were not bound to move their city from its location at the command of another. In vain, therefore, the Romans laid stress on the word 'Carthage', alleging that the citizens were meant, and not the city. The distinction, while not applicable, may be conceded by reason of the word 'free', which is more in harmony with citizens than city.

observe the alliance of arms with the Athenians in accordance with the agreements, and preserve the rights of friendship with the Lacedaemonians [Peloponnesians]' [Thucydides, III. lxx. 2].

[1] Diodorus Siculus, *Selections on Embassies*, xxvii, reports the matter thus: 'that their laws, territory, sacred places, tombs, liberty, should remain to them'.

For there was a manifest quibble in the expression, ' to be left free ', [*Punic Wars*, VIII. xii. 83.] or 'autonomous', as Appian says.

XVI.—*What compacts are to be considered personal, and what real, is set forth, with distinctions*

1. To this topic is to be referred the question that frequently arises in regard to personal and real compacts. If indeed an agreement has been made with a free people, there is no doubt that what is promised is in its nature real, because the subject is a permanent thing. Further, even if the condition of the state shall be changed into a kingdom, the treaty will continue, for the reason that, although the head has been changed, the body remains the same; and, as we [II. ix. 8.] have said above, the sovereignty, which is exercised through a king, does not cease to be the sovereignty of the people. An exception will have to be made if it is apparent that the cause of the treaty resided in the free condition of the state; such would be the case if free states had made a treaty for the purpose of protecting their freedom.

2. But if a compact has been made with a king the treaty will [*Dig.*, II. xiv. 7. § 8.] not immediately have to be considered personal; for, as Pedius and Ulpian have rightly said, the name of the person is for the most part inserted in a compact, not in order that the compact may become personal, but in order to show with whom it was made. Now if the addition is made to the treaty, that it shall be lasting, or that it was made for the good of the realm, or with the king himself and his successors (and this addition shall be accompanied by the phrase, ' and to his descendants ', which is commonly added in treaties, as Libanius says in his defence of Demosthenes), or if the treaty was made for a definite time, the fact that it is real will be sufficiently apparent.

The treaty of the Romans with Philip, king of Macedonia,[1] seems to have been of this sort; for when Philip's son, Perseus, denied that it was applicable to him on that account a war arose. But other words also, and at times the subject-matter itself, will warrant a not improbable conjecture.

3. Again, if the indications are evenly balanced on both sides, the result will be that favourable treaties are to be believed real, and odious treaties personal. Treaties made for the sake of peace or commerce are favourable. Treaties made for the sake of war are not all odious, as some persons think; but ' alliances for defence ', that is, treaties for the sake of protecting each party, incline rather toward favourableness, and ' offensive alliances ' incline more toward burdensomeness. There is the further point, that in the case of a treaty

[1] Livy, XLII [XLII. xxv. 1]. It is assumed that consideration is had of the prudence and scrupulousness of the man with whom one deals. See Paruta, Books V and VII.

which contemplates any war whatsoever the presumption is that consideration has been had of the prudence and loyalty of the party with whom the engagement is made, as being one who clearly not only would not undertake a war unjustly, but not even rashly.

4. To the commonly accepted statement, that associations are terminated by death, I give no place here; for this pertains to private associations and belongs to civil law. Therefore, we cannot rightly decide whether the Fidenates,[1] Latins,[2] Etruscans, and Sabines justly or unjustly renounced their treaties on the death of Romulus, Tullus, Ancus, Priscus, and Servius, for the reason that the words of the treaties are not preserved. A not dissimilar controversy is found in Justin, the question being whether the states which had been tributary to the Medes had changed [281] their condition when the sovereignty was changed. The point to be considered is, in fact, whether in the agreement they had chosen the faith of the Medes.

Decio. *Consilia*, I. xxii.

[I. vii. 2.]

Least of all should the argument of Bodin be admitted, that treaties do not pass to the successors of kings, for the reason that the force of an oath does not go beyond the person. It is true enough that the obligation of the oath can bind the person only, while the promise itself can bind the heir.

Book V, last chapter.

5. Furthermore the assumption on which Bodin proceeds, that treaties are based on an oath as a kind of foundation, is not valid. The fact is that in most cases there is sufficient binding force in the promise itself, and that the oath is added thereto in order to secure the reinforcement of greater religious scruple. Under Publius Valerius as consul the Roman plebeians had taken oath that they would assemble at the command of the consul. When Valerius died, Lucius Quinctius Cincinnatus succeeded him. Some of the tribunes dealt captiously with the obligation, as if the people were not bound by religious scruple. The opinion of Livy follows:

III [xx. 5].

> The disregard of the gods, which characterizes the present generation, had not yet come. In those days men would not universally through interpretation make their oaths and the laws adapted to their own desires, but rather they were accustomed to fit their practices to their obligations.

[1] See Dionysius of Halicarnassus, Book III [III. vi].

[2] Concerning the Appuli [Apiolae] and Latins, see the same author, Book III [Dionysius of Halicarnassus, III. xlix]; on Turnus, Herdonius and the Latins, the same author, Book IV [IV. xlvi]. Ammianus in Book XXVI [XXVI. iv. 6] says:

> The king of Persia threw himself upon the Armenians, hastening by an over-violent attack to bring them again under his sway, but unjustly; for he made it as his excuse that after the death of Jovian, with whom he had made a treaty of peace, nothing ought to hinder him from recovering those places which as he showed had previously belonged to his ancestors.

See similar statements about Justinian's treaties with the Saracens in Menander Protector [frag. 11, p. 21, edit. Dindorf].

Add what the Swiss alleged after the death of Henry the Third, according to De Thou, Book XCVII, on the Year 1589. See also the notable passage in Camden, on the Year 1572, where he speaks of an ancient treaty between the French and the Scotch.

XVII.—*That a treaty entered into with a king is continued with him though he may have been expelled from his kingdom*

A treaty entered into with a king surely continues, although the king himself or his successor has been expelled by his subjects from the kingdom. The right to the kingdom, in fact, still belongs to him, although he has lost possession. In this connexion the words of Lucan about the Roman senate are pertinent:

[*Pharsalia*, V. 29 f.]

> Its rights the order never lost
> By change of place.

XVIII.—*That such a treaty does not apply to the usurper of a kingdom*

On the contrary there is no violation of the treaty if a usurper of another's kingdom is attacked in war at the wish of the true king, or if the oppressor of a free people is attacked before an adequate approval on the part of the people is secured for the treaty. The reason is that, while such persons may have possession, they have no legal right.[1] And this is what Titus Quinctius said to Nabis: 'Relations of friendship and common interest were by us entered into not with you, but with Pelops, the just and lawful king of Sparta.' Such elements in the treaties of a king and his successor, and similar elements, betoken a right, properly speaking; and the cause of the usurper is odious.

Livy, XXXIV [xxxii. 1].

XIX.—*To whom a promise is due if it was made to the one who should do something first, and several have done the thing at the same time*

[Plutarch, *On the Contradiction of the Stoics*, xxiii = 1045 D.]

Chrysippus in ancient times discussed the question whether a promise which had been made to the one who should first arrive at the goal would be due to each if two arrived together, or to neither.

The truth is that the word 'first' is ambiguous;[2] for it designates either the one who surpassed all or the one whom no one surpassed. But because awards for virtues are to be viewed with favour the more just opinion is that they will together share the

[1] Thus Valens did not accept the excuse of the king of the Goths, who said that he had sent aid to Procopius, the usurper of the throne. Ammianus, Book XXVII [XXVII. v. 2], calls this an utterly groundless excuse. The same story is found in the Greek writers, but under the name of Scythians, for by that name they called the Goths.

Thus Justinian declared that he would not be breaking the treaty which he had made with Genseric if he should begin war against Gelimer, who had deprived the rightful king Ilderich of his crown and liberty [Procopius, *Vandalic War*, I. ix. 19].

See Cardinal Toschi, on the word *tyrannus*, in *Practicae Conclusiones*, 309. 6, and Cacheranus, *Decisiones*, lxxix. 35.

[2] See Alberico de Rosate, *De Statutis*, qu. cvi and cvii.

prize, although Scipio,[1] Caesar, and Julian more generously assigned individual prizes to those who had mounted the walls at the same time.

Let what has been said suffice in regard to the interpretation which is adapted to the proper or improper meaning of words.

XX.—*A conjecture which presents itself in the one case broadens the meaning; when this occurs*

1. There is also another kind of interpretation from conjectures outside of the meaning of the words in which the promise is contained. This, again, is of two sorts, either broadening the meaning or narrowing it.

Everard, on the subjects *A Ratione Legis ad Restrictionem* and *A Ratione Legis ad Extensionem.*

Now the interpretation which broadens the meaning proceeds with greater difficulty; that which narrows the meaning proceeds more easily. For as in all other things the absence of a single one of the causes is sufficient to prevent the result, and all causes need to concur that the effect may be produced, so also in the case of an obligation a conjecture which extends the obligation ought not rashly to be admitted. The difficulty here is much greater than in the case of which we were speaking above, where the words admit of a rather broad interpretation, though one less generally accepted; for here we are in search of a conjecture outside of the words of the promise. Such a conjecture ought to be very certain in order to create an obligation; and a similar reason is not sufficient, but [282] an identical reason is required. Again, it is not always sufficient for us to affirm that the extension ought to be made in accordance with reason; for, as we were just saying, reason often moves in such a way that the will nevertheless may be a sufficient cause in itself, even without reason.

2. That such an extension, then, may be rightly made, it must be agreed that the reason, under which comes the case that we wish to include, is the sole effective cause which influenced the promisor, and that the reason was considered by him in its general sense, because otherwise the promise would have been unfair and useless. This topic also is ordinarily dealt with by the Greek rhetoricians under the heading *Concerning the word and the meaning*; and a form of this they posit as often as we are constantly uttering the same thought. But also the other title, *By means of reasoning*, belongs here; for assuredly here we derive what was not written from what was written, as Quintilian says. And we include also whatever is taught by the jurist concerning matters done fraudulently.[2]

[*Institutes of Oratory*, VII. viii.]

[1] When New Carthage was captured in Spain [Livy, XXVI. xlviii. 13].

[2] Seneca in the excerpts from the *Controversies*, VI. iii, well said: 'A documentary fraud always hides the crime under the appearance of law; what is apparent in it is lawful; what is hidden is deceptive.' Says Quintilian in the *Controversies* [*Declamations*], cccxliii: 'And, in fact, we never

3. As an example, suppose that there is an agreement that a certain place shall not be surrounded with walls, and that this agreement was made at a time when there was no other kind of fortification.[1] It will not be permissible to surround that place even with an earthwork, if it is fully established that the sole reason why walls were prohibited lay in the intent that the place should not be fortified.

Ordinarily an illustration is taken from the condition that a posthumous child has died, if such a child is included in the will of one who fully expected a posthumous child. Under such conditions the intent of the will is extended to cover the alternative, if no posthumous child has been born, because it is agreed that the will of the speaker was determined by consideration of the non-existence of offspring. It is, in fact, possible to find this very example in the writings not only of the jurists but also of Cicero [2] and Valerius Maximus.

On the Orator, I [xxxix. 180] and II [xxxii. 141]; *Brutus* [lii. 195 and liii. 197]; and *For Caecina* [xviii. 53, 59, 63]. [Val. Max., VII. vii. 1.]

4. Cicero presents this reason in his speech *For Caecina*: 'What then? Had sufficient provision been made for this in the words? Not at all. What is it then that is valid? The intent; and if this could be understood by us without speech we should not use words at all. Because it cannot be so understood, words were invented, not to hinder, but to express the intent.' A little later in the same speech he says that the rule of law is the same when 'the cause of the equity appears to be one and the same',[3] that is, of the reason, which was the only motive; so the form of the interdict, 'from which you have expelled me by violence with a force of armed men', is in point against every form of violence which affects the person and life.

[*For Caecina,* xxii. 63.]

'Such violence', says Cicero, 'is generally committed through the agency of a force of armed men; if it has been committed on a different plan, but with the same peril, they wished the right to be the same.'

[*Declamations,* cccl.]

In a declamation of Quintilian the Father this example is found:

Murder seems to connote blood and steel; but if a man has been killed by any other kind of murder we shall have recourse to the same law. If he has fallen among robbers, or has

have recourse to this law', that is, the law concerning documentary fraud, 'unless a just right is excluded by wickedness.'

You find an example in Pliny, *Natural History*, Book XVIII [XVIII. iii. 17]: 'Also a limit of five hundred acres had been set by the law of Licinius Stolo; and he himself was condemned under his own law, because he held more than that by substituting the person of his son.' The same story appears in Valerius Maximus, VIII. vi. 3.

See another example in Tacitus, *Annals*, XV [XV. xix], concerning fictitious adoptions. There is another in a *Novella* of Manuel Comnenus found in the Graeco-Roman law [*Greek Books on Roman Law*, chap. vi; edit. v, Labb.].

[1] Fuscus Arellius in Seneca, *Controversies*, II. x [II. ii. 5], says: 'This was without doubt the intention of those who took the oath, [288] that they should not be separated by force, since they made provision to safeguard also this point, that they should not be separated by death.'

[2] Also [Cicero,] *On Invention*, II [II. xlii. 122].

[3] Thus Philo, *On Special Laws* [III. xii], maintains that adultery is committed against the betrothed of another, and gives as a reason: 'Betrothals have the same force as marriage.' So in the law of Moses all domestic animals are understood under the term 'ox', and any ditch whatsoever under the term 'pit'; *Exodus*, xxi. 28 and 35. Chassaneus, *Catalogus Gloriae Mundi*, V. xlix.

been thrown into water, or has been cast down some immense height, he will be avenged by the same law as the person who has been stabbed with a sword.

Similar is the argument of Isaeus in the oration *On the Inheritance of Pyrrhus*, when from the fact that by the Attic law the making of a will without the consent of the daughter was forbidden he infers that against the will of a daughter not even an adoption was allowed. [III. 68 ff.]

XXI.—*Herein also concerning the execution of a mandate in a different way*

From the principles stated comes the solution of the famous question found in Gellius, whether the obligation of a mandate may be satisfied, not with the identical thing, but with something else equally useful, or more useful than was that which the giver of the mandate had prescribed. I. xiii.

Such an adjustment is, in fact, permissible in case it is determined that what had been prescribed was not prescribed in a special form, but in a more general way,[1] which made possible a different fulfilment of the conditions. So it was held by Scaevola that one who had been ordered to give security to a creditor could direct him to pay the money to a third party. For the rest, when the matter is not sufficiently determined, the rule found in the passage in Gellius is to be retained, [283] that obligation to the one who gives the order is disregarded if, in response to what he has been ordered to do, a person makes answer, not with due obedience, but with advice, which was not desired. *Digest*, XVII. i. 62.

XXII.—*In the other case the conjecture restricts the meaning; and this may happen by reason of an original defect in the intent, which is inferred from its absurdity*

A restrictive interpretation, outside of the natural meaning of the words containing the promise, is derived either from an original defect in the intent, or from the incompatibility with the intent of a case occurring. A defect inherent in the intent is recognized from the absurdity which evidently would otherwise result, or from the cessation of the reason which alone furnished the full and effective motive for the intent,[2] or from a defect in the subject-matter.

The first case has its foundation in this principle, that no one ought to be believed to wish absurdities.

[1] Quintilian, *Controversies*, clvii [*Declamations*, cclvii]: 'Slaves do some things more freely from good intentions, and sometimes bond-servants that have been purchased think it a mark of loyalty not to obey.' You have an example in the *Selections on Embassies*, in that part in which the manner of engaging in and receiving embassies is dealt with; also in the things that John, one of the generals of Justinian, did against the orders of Belisarius [Justinian]; [Procopius,] *Gothic War*, II [II. x] and IV [IV. xxiii].

[2] An example is to be found in the *Digest*, XXXVII. xiv. 6. § 2.

XXIII.—*Conjecture may restrict the meaning by reason of the cessation of the only reason*

The second case is founded on the principle that, when such a reason is added, or there is agreement concerning it, the content of the promise is considered not simply by itself, but only in so far as it comes under that reason.

XXIV.—*Conjecture may restrict the meaning by reason of a defect in the subject-matter*

The third case is based on the consideration that it is always to be understood that the subject-matter is viewed from the point of view of the speaker, even if the words have a broader meaning. This phase of interpretation also is treated by the Greek rhetoricians under the heading *Concerning the word and the meaning*, and bears the title, ‘ When the same thought is not always expressed.’

XXV.—*An observation concerning the conjectures last mentioned*

1. In regard to the reason, it is to be noted that under it certain things are often included, not from the point of view of existence, but in relation to their force from the point of view of morals. When such a case arises, no restriction ought to be made. Thus if provision has been made that an army or a fleet should not be conducted to some place it will not be possible to conduct it to that place, even without the intent of doing harm. The reason is that in the agreement not a certain loss but danger of any possible kind was in contemplation.

2. The question also is commonly raised, whether promises contain in themselves the tacit condition, ‘ if matters remain in their present state ’.

To this question a negative answer must be given, unless it is perfectly clear that the present state of affairs was included in that sole reason of which we made mention. Thus constantly in the histories we read that ambassadors gave up their mission and returned home from the journey on which they had set out, alleging as the reason that matters had been so changed that the entire matter or cause of the mission was at an end.

Paschal, *Legatus*, xlix [lvii].

XXVI.—*Or conjecture may restrict the meaning when a case which arises is incompatible with the intent; and this is assumed in regard to what is unlawful*

1. The incompatibility of an actually occurring case with the intent is also ordinarily referred by the Greek teachers of rhetoric to

the topic *Concerning the word and the meaning*, which I have mentioned. Such incompatibility is twofold; for the desire is inferred either from natural reason or from some other sign of intent. For the judging of intent from natural reason Aristotle, who treated this subject very carefully, attributed to the intellect a special quality, the 'judgement', or 'good sense', that is, 'the perception of what is fair'; but to the will he assigned 'the quality of fairness', that is, 'justice', and this he wisely defined as the correction of that in which the law, by reason of its general character, is at fault.[1] [*Magna Moralia*, II. ii.]

Now the use of these qualities, within proper limits, ought to be made applicable to wills also, and compacts. For since all contingencies can neither be foreseen nor set forth, a degree of freedom is needed in order to make exceptions of cases which the person who has spoken would make an exception of, if he were present. Yet recourse to such a restriction of meaning should not be had rashly—that, in fact, would be to make oneself master of another's act—but only on sufficient implications.

2. The most certain implication is if the literal meaning would in any case involve something unlawful, that is, at variance with the precepts of the law of nature, or of divine law. Of necessity an exception must be made of such cases, since they are not capable of imposing a legal obligation. 'Certain things,' says Quintilian the Father, 'although they are not included in any expression of the law, are nevertheless by nature excepted.' Thus a person who has promised to return a sword which he received in trust will not return it to a madman, lest he bring danger either to himself or to other innocent persons. [284] Similarly an object received in trust will not be returned to the person who deposited it if the rightful owner demands it. Tryphoninus says, 'I am satisfied that this is justice, which so assigns his own to each that it is not withdrawn by reason of a more just demand of any other person.' The reason, as I have noted elsewhere, is that the force of ownership, when once introduced, is such that it is in every way unjust not to restore property to the owner, when he is known. [*Declamations*, cccxv.] *Dig.* XVI. iii. 31. [II. x. 1, 2.]

Molina, disp. 294. Sylvester, on the word *commodatum*, 4. Lessius, II. xxvii. 5.

XXVII.—*Conjecture may restrict the meaning when the condition is too burdensome as regards the act*

1. A second implication will become manifest if, while the literal interpretation may not in itself involve something unlawful, the obligation, in the view of one who judges the matter fairly, shall

[1] Seneca, *Controversies*, IV. xxvii [IX. iv. 9]: 'In the law, you say, there is no exception. But there are many things which, though not considered exceptions, are understood, and the written form of the law is restricted, the interpretation broad. Some things, however, are so manifest that they have no need of provision.'

appear to be burdensome and unbearable, whether the condition of human nature is considered in the abstract, or the person and matter under consideration are brought into comparison with the result of the act itself. Thus a man who has lent a thing for some days will be able to demand its return within those days, if he himself is greatly in need of it; for the nature of a generous act is such that it is not to be believed that any one has wished to obligate himself to his own great disadvantage. Thus, again, one who has promised aid to an ally will be entitled to excuse in so far as he himself needs his troops as long as he is in danger at home. Also the exemption from taxes [1] and tribute is to be understood as covering the usual daily and yearly requirements, not requirements imposed by extreme necessity, which a state cannot do without.

Angelus, *On Dig.*, XIV. ii. 7. Vázquez, *Controversiae Illustres*, xxxi. [Cicero, *On Duties*, I. x. 32.]

2. From this it is clear that the statement of Cicero was made too loosely, that promises without advantage to those to whom you have made them ought not to be kept, nor if they are more harmful to you than they are advantageous to the one to whom you made them. For the promisor ought not to judge whether a thing will be useful to the promisee, except perhaps in the case of madness, of which we have spoken above.

Furthermore, a certain harm to the promisor is insufficient to prevent the promise from being binding, but the harm should be such as to require that it be considered an exception in view of the nature of the act.[2] Thus one who has promised to work for a neighbour for some days will not be bound if the dangerous illness of his father or his son should detain him. Rightly Cicero in the first book *On Duties* says: 'If you have agreed that you will appear in person in court as advocate for some one, and in the meantime your son has begun to be seriously ill, it would not be contrary to duty not to do what you have promised.'

[*On Duties*, I. x. 32.]

3. We ought, further, to accept in the same sense, and not to press too far, what we read in Seneca: [3]

On Benefits, V, xxxv 2].

Then I shall break faith, then I shall hear the reproach of inconstancy, if, when all things are the same as they were when I promised, I do not fulfil my promise. Whatever

[1] See Rosenthal, *De Feudis*, V. lxxviii. 2; Heigh, *Quaestiones Illustres*, XVIII. xvi. 1; Cothmann, *Consilia*, xi, no. 32; Clarus, sec. *Feudum*, xxix. 2; Andrew Knich, *De Vestitis Pactis*, II. v. 20; Henry Bocer, *De Collectis*, iv. 12.

[2] See Charles Dumoulin, *Ad Consuetudines Parisienses*, I. ii, gl. 4, no. 3; Fernando Vázquez, *De Successionum Creatione*, II. xviii. 80; Antoine Favre, *De la Jurisprudence de Savoie*, IV. xxx; Zasius, *On Digest*, XLV. i. 61; add *Decretals*, II. xxiv. 25, and Alciati, *On Decretals*, II. xxiv. 28.

[3] The following passage is in the same author, *On Benefits*, IV. xxxix: 'I shall go out to dinner because I have promised, even if it shall be cold. I shall leave the table to assist at a betrothal because I have promised, even though my dinner is not digested; but not if I have a fever. I shall give bond for you because I have promised, but not if you shall bid me to give bond for an unlimited amount, or if the obligation is to the treasury. There is, I say, a tacit exception present—if I shall be able, if it shall be my duty, if matters shall be thus and so. Cause that the condition be the same, when the demand is made, as it was when I promised.

'It will not be a mark of fickleness to fail in a promise, if something new has intervened. Why

is in any way changed gives me the opportunity to reconsider, and releases my pledge. I have promised to be an advocate ; afterwards it has become apparent that by means of that case an injury to my father is contemplated. I have promised to go abroad with some one, but it is reported that the route is infested with brigands. I was about to appear in person in a lawsuit, but I am detained because my son is sick, or my wife is in labour. All things ought to be the same as they were when I made the promise, if you would hold me to it.

In this passage understand ' all things ' according to the nature of the act in question, as I have just now shown.

XXVIII.—*Conjecture may be restricted in view of other indications, as when the parts of a document are in conflict*

We have said that there may be also other indications of the intent, which show that an exception ought to be made. Among such indications none is stronger than words found in another place, not words directly opposed in meaning, for that is ' antinomy ', which is mentioned above, but words which come into conflict in consequence of some unexpected turn of affairs ; and this the Greek rhetoricians call ' a conflict arising from circumstances '.

XXIX.—*What rules ought to be observed in such cases*

1. Of the ancient authors Cicero [1] laid down certain rules for the settlement of such a question, as to which part of the document ought to prevail when the conflict arises from chance. Although these ought by no means to be disregarded, yet it seems to me that they were not arranged in their proper order. Accordingly I shall arrange them in this way :

[285] That which permits should yield to that which orders.[2] The reason is that he who permits something seems to grant permission on the condition that nothing else hinders than that which is under consideration ; in consequence, as the author of the *Ad* XIII
Herennium says, ' A command prevails over a permission.' [II. x. 15].

That which is to be done at a definite time should have preference over that which can be done at any time. From this it follows that generally a clause in an agreement which forbids

do you wonder that my purpose has been changed now that the condition, in which I was when I promised, has changed ? Make everything else the same in relation to me, and I am the same. We give bond for appearance in court, yet fail to appear. But action is not allowed against all, for a stronger reason excuses the failure to appear.'

The English have often made use of such an evasion. See Camden, on the Year 1595, not only for the dispute with the Dutch, but also for that with the Hanseatic cities.

[1] In the second book *On Invention* [II. xlix. 144], and thereto Marius Victorinus.

[2] Quintilian, *Declamations*, ccclxxiv : ' The law which forbids is always stronger than that which permits.' Donatus, *On* [*Terence's*] *Phormio*, I. ii [I. ii. 76] : ' Rightly it commands ; for [289] the law which permits anything has less force than that which commands.'

See Cicero, *Against Verres*, II [II. li. 127], and what Connan has in Book I. ix.

outweighs a clause which orders, because an agreement of prohibition is binding at any and every time, but an agreement of command is not binding to the same extent, unless the time has been stated, or the command contains an implied prohibition. Among agreements which are equal in respect to the qualities mentioned, that should be given preference which is most specific and approaches most nearly to the subject in hand; for special provisions are ordinarily more effective than those that are general. Also in prohibitions that which adds a penalty should be given preference over that which lacks a penalty, and that which threatens a greater penalty should have the preference over that which threatens a lesser penalty.

Then, that provision should prevail which has either the more honourable or the more expedient reasons.

Finally, that which was last said should prevail.

2. Here this should be repeated from the previous discussion, that the force of sworn agreements is such that they ought to be understood according to their most generally accepted meaning; and so all restrictions that are implied, and not absolutely necessary from the nature of the case, should be rejected. If, then, a sworn compact is at variance in some particular with one which has not been sworn to, preference ought to be given to the compact which has the sanctity of an oath.[1]

XXX.—*That in a doubtful case a written document is not required for the validity of a contract*

This question also is commonly raised, whether in a doubtful case a contract ought to be considered perfect before the written form has been completed and delivered.

Appian, *Mithridatic Wars* [ix. 64].

This, in fact, was the point which Murena argued against the treaty that had been arranged between Sulla and Mithridates. To me it seems clear that, unless it has been otherwise agreed, we ought to believe that writing has been employed as evidence of the contract, not as a part of its content.[2] Otherwise the form of expression is customary which is found in the truce with Nabis: 'From the day on which the terms should be copied out and delivered to Nabis.'

Livy, XXXIV [xxxv. 3].

[1] Acontius in Ovid [*Heroides*, xx. 159–62] says:

> Her father promised her, and she to her lover swore.
> He called men to witness, she the goddess called.
> He feared to be a liar, she to be forsworn.
> Then do you doubt which was the greater fear?

[2] *Digest*, XXII. iv. 4 and 5; *Code*, II. iii. 17. So Bartolus, Jean Faber, and Saliceto interpreted the law in the *Code*, IV. xxi. 17, and their opinion has prevailed in the courts against that of Baldus and Castrensis; Mynsinger, Decade X, cons. 91; Neostad, *De Pactis Antenuptialibus*, obs. 18. Therefore there is not sufficient probability in what Ligniacus derives from Guicciardini (*History of Italy*, II) concerning a document signed by a king but lacking the seal and signature of the secretary.

XXXI.—*The contracts of kings are not to be interpreted according to Roman law*

I shall not, however, admit the rule, which has been adopted by some writers, that the contracts of kings and peoples ought to be interpreted according to Roman law so far as possible, unless it is apparent that among certain peoples the body of civil law has been received as the law of nations in respect to the matters which concern the law of nations. Such a presumption ought not rashly to be admitted.

Alciati, *Consilia*, V. xvii.

XXXII.—*Whether the words of the one who accepts the condition, or the words of the one who offers it, ought to carry greater weight, is set forth, with a distinction*

As regards the point which interests Plutarch in his *Symposiacs*, whether more weight ought to be given to the words of the one who offers or of the one who accepts a condition, it seems to me that when the one who accepts is the promisor his words determine the form of the matter, if they are complete and perfect in themselves. For if by affirmation they look to the words of the one who offers the condition, then, from the very nature of relative words, they will seem to be repeated in the promise. But it is certain that before the condition is accepted the one who made the offer is not at all bound. For no legal right has been gained up to that time, as is apparent from what I have said concerning a promise; and the offering of a condition is still less than a promise.

Symposiacs, ix. 13 [=742 B].

CHAPTER XVII

ON DAMAGE CAUSED THROUGH INJURY, AND THE OBLIGATION ARISING THEREFROM

I.—*That fault creates the obligation to make good the loss*

[II. i. 2.] WE have said above that there are three sources of our legal claims, pact, wrong, and statute. Enough has been said about contracts. Let us come now to what is due by the law of nature in consequence of a wrong.

By a wrong we here mean every fault, whether of commission or of omission, which is in conflict with what men ought to do, either from their common interest or by reason of a special quality. From such a fault, if damage has been caused, by the law of nature [1] an obligation arises, namely, that the damage should be made good.

II.—*That damage is understood to be that which conflicts with one's right taken in a strict sense*

1. Damage, the Latin word for which, *damnum*, was perhaps derived from the word meaning to take away,[2] *demere*, in Greek is 'the being less'; that is, when any one has less than belongs to him, whether by a right that accrues to him from the law of nature alone, or is reinforced by the addition of a human act, as by ownership, contract, or legal enactment.

By nature [290] a man's life is his own, not indeed to destroy, but to safeguard; also his own are his body, limbs, reputation, honour, and the acts of his will. The previous part of our treatise has shown how each man by property right and by agreements possesses his own not only with respect to property but also with respect to the acts of others. In a similar manner every one acquires his particular rights from the law, because the law has the same power, or greater power than individuals have over themselves or their property. Thus a ward has the right to demand a certain degree of diligence and care from his guardian, and likewise the

[1] Called 'action for neglect' by the Greeks [Hesychius]. See *Decretals*, V. xxxvi, and *Digest*, XI. ii, and adjoining rubrics.

[2] So Varro, Book V [*Latin Language*, V. clxxvi]: '*Damnum* (damage) is derived from *demptio* (a taking away), when the recognized value has been made less by the act.'

Others prefer the derivation from the Greek δαπάνη (expense), so that the word should be first *dapnum* and then *damnum*, as ὕπνος gives *sopnus* and *somnus*. And it would not be absurd for you to derive the word from the Greek δάμνω (I subdue), which has a force similar to that of βιάζω (I overpower); or from ζημία (damage) through *damia* to *damnum*, as *regia* (palace) and *regnum* (kingdom).

state from an official; and not the state only, but also individual citizens, as often as the law indicates such a requirement explicitly, or by a sufficiently clear implication.

2. But true ownership and the consequent necessity for restitution do not arise from aptitude alone, which is not properly called a right and which belongs to distributive justice; for one does not have ownership of that to which one has merely a moral claim. 'The man who out of stinginess does not assist another with his money commits no crime against justice properly speaking,' says Aristotle. Cicero in the oration *For Gnaeus Plancius* says: 'This is the condition of a free people [...] that, in the case of every person, it is able by means of votes either to give or to take away what it wishes.' Yet presently he adds that it happens that a people may do what it wishes to do, and not what it ought to do, using the word 'ought' in its broader sense.

Nicomachean Ethics, V. iv.

[iv. 11.]

III.—*That aptitude must be carefully distinguished from legal right in a strict sense, when they coexist*

At this point care must be taken not to confuse things which are of different kinds. For one who has been entrusted with the duty of appointing magistrates is under obligation to the state to choose a man who is worthy, and the state has a special right to demand this. If, therefore, the state has suffered damage from the choice of an unworthy person, the man having the responsibility of choice will be bound to make the loss good.

So also any citizen who is not unworthy, although he has no special right to any office, nevertheless has a true right to be a candidate for an office along with others; and if he is hindered in the exercise of this right by force or fraud he will be able to collect the estimated value, not of the entire thing sought, but of that uncertain damage. The case will be similar if a testator has been hindered by force or fraud from willing anything to a man. For the capacity to receive a legacy is a kind of right, and in consequence it is an injury to interfere with the liberty of the testator in such a matter.

Thomas Aquinas, II. ii. 62, art. 2, and Cajetan thereon. Soto, IV. vi. Lessius, Book II, xii. 18. Covarruvias, *On Sext*, V. ult. 4, pt. 2, § 7.

IV.—*That damage extends also to income*

Moreover, a person will be understood to have less, and therefore to have suffered loss, not only in the property itself, but also in the products which strictly belong to it, whether these have actually been gathered or not, if he might have gathered them; but expenditures for the improvement of the property will need to be deducted, or expenditures necessary for gathering the fruits, in

Soto, IV. vii; Lessius, II. xii, 16, no. 3.

accordance with the rule which forbids us to become richer at the expense of another.

V.—*How the principle stated applies to the cessation of income*

Digest, XXXV. ii. 73. § 1.

Also the expectation of gain from our property will be estimated, not at its full amount, but in proportion to its nearness to completion, as the expectation of the harvest at the sowing.

VI.—*Those who by their act cause damage primarily*

Thomas Aquinas, II. ii. 62, art. 4. Soto, Book IV, vi. 5.

Besides the one who causes damage in person and 'directly', others also are liable, by reason of their act or their failure to act. By an act some are liable primarily, others secondarily. He is liable primarily who orders the act, or gives the necessary consent, or aids, or receives stolen goods, or in some other manner shares in the crime itself.

VII.—*Those who by their act cause damage secondarily*

Those are liable secondarily who give advice, praise,[1] or approval to the act. 'What difference is there', says Cicero in the second *Philippic*, 'between one who advises an act and one who approves of the act?'[2]

[xii. 29.]

VIII.—*Likewise those who by not doing what they ought cause damage primarily*

Likewise an obligation is created by failure to act, either primarily or secondarily; primarily, when one, who is in strict legal duty bound to forbid the act by a command, or to render aid [291] to one who has been injured, does not do so.[3] Such a person by the Chaldean paraphraser, *On Leviticus*, xx. 5, is called 'a strengthener of wrong-doing'.

IX.—*Those who by not doing as they ought cause damage secondarily*

Lessius, Book II, xiii. 10.

A person is liable secondarily who does not dissuade when he ought, or who keeps to himself a fact which he ought to make known.

[1] Totila in his speech to the Goths in Procopius, *Gothic War*, III [III. xxv], says: 'For he who praises one who is doing anything must himself be considered as responsible for the deed.' Ulpian, *Digest*, XI. iii. 1. § 4, says: 'Even if the slave were going to run away or commit the theft in any case, if this man has praised his purpose, he will be held liable. An evil deed, in fact, ought not to be increased by praise.'

[2] [294] Ammianus in Book XXVII [XXVII. xi. 5] makes application of this saying to Probus, the prefect. In the *Law of the Lombards*, Book IV, title iv [I. iv. 1, 4], even the one who gives advice is summoned to the settlement. See *Romans*, i, at the end [verse 32], and the ancient commentaries thereon.

[3] Nicetas of Chonae in the life of *Michael Comnenus* [*Manuel Comnenus*, I. iii] says: 'A fire is not only to be charged against the one who applied the torch, but also against the person who would not put it out when he could.'

But in all these cases we refer the word 'ought' to that true legal right which is the object of expletive justice, whether it arises from statute law or from a special quality. For if one is under obligation according to the rule of love, by omission he will sin indeed, but he will not be held to make reparation; for the source of the obligation to make good is the true right, properly speaking, as we have previously said.

X.—*What kind of effective participation in the act is requisite to create such obligation*

It should also be understood that all those whom we have mentioned are under obligation to make good if they have really been the cause of damage; that is, if they have contributed to the damage either in whole or in part. For in the case of those in the second class who act or fail to act, and sometimes even in the case of some in the first class, it often happens that the one who has caused the damage would have been sure to cause it even without the act or neglect of the others. In such cases the others, whom I have mentioned, will not be liable.

Thomas Aquinas, II. ii. 62, art. 6. Soto, Book IV, vii. 3.

Yet this must not be understood in such a way that, if there were no lack of others to advise or aid, those who did advise and aid should not be liable in case the one who caused the damage would not have caused it without their aid or advice. For even the others would have been liable if they had advised or aided.

Cajetan, *On II. ii*, 62, art. 6. Medina, qu. 7.

XI.—*In what order such persons are held liable*

Now those are liable in the first instance who by command or otherwise have impelled any one to a harmful act. When such are lacking, the perpetrator of the crime is so held. After him the others, who have caused the act, are individually liable for the whole loss, if the whole act has proceeded from them, though not from them alone.[1]

Lessius, Book II, xiii. 5 and 4.

XII.—*That the liability is extended even to resulting damage*

Again, the one who is liable for an act is at the same time liable for the consequences resulting from the force of the act.[2] In one of the *Controversies* of Seneca [3] this is illustrated by the burning of a plane tree, from which a house caught fire and burned. In this connexion he states an opinion thus: 'Although there was a part of the damage which you did not wish to cause, you are liable for it all, just as if you had caused it intentionally. In fact, the person who

[1] *Laws of the Lombards*, I. ix. 5.
[2] See Thomas, II. i. 20, art. 5, and *Digest*, IX. ii. 27. § 8.
[3] *Excerpta Controversiarum*, V. v.

defends himself on the ground of not intending wrong ought not to have willed any part of the wrong.'

Strabo, XII [ii. 8]. [Halys.] Because Ariarathes, king of Cappadocia, had wantonly blocked the outlet of the river Melanus, when it broke through its dam the Euphrates was flooded and devastated a part of Cappadocia and did great damage to Galatia and Phrygia. The decision of the issue was left to the Romans, and the king paid damages in the sum of three hundred talents.

XIII.—*An example in homicide*

Let the following serve as examples.

Lessius, Book II, ix. 19. One who unjustly takes human life is bound to pay the expenses, if any have been incurred, for doctors. He is, furthermore, bound to give to those whom the dead man was accustomed to support from a sense of duty, as parents, wife, and children, so much as that expectation of support was worth in view of the age of the person killed. Diodorus Siculus, IV [xxxi. 5]. Thus Hercules is reported to have paid a fine to the children of Iphitus, whom he had slain, in order that he might more easily obtain expiation for his crime. Michael of Ephesus, *On Aristotle's Nicomachean Ethics*, Book V, [V. ii.] says: 'But also in a way the one who has been killed receives recompense. He, in fact, in a certain sense receives what his wife, children, and relatives receive.'

We are speaking of unjustifiable homicide, that is, of homicide by one who has not the right to do that from which death results. Lessius, II. ix. 21. Navarrus, xv, no. 22. Therefore if any one has had the right, but has sinned against the law of love, as one who has been unwilling to flee from an attack, he will not be liable. Moreover, in the case of a freeman no valuation is put on the life. It is otherwise in the case of a slave, who could have been sold.

XIV.—*An example of one who has used violence in a different way*

One who has maimed another will in like manner be liable for the expenses, and for [292] the estimated value of the decrease in earning power of the one who has been maimed.[1] But, as in the instance mentioned above, the life, so here the scars, are not susceptible *Dig.* IX. iii. 7. of valuation in the case of a freeman. The same should be said of false imprisonment.

XV.—*Of the adulterer and seducer*

Lessius, II. x. 6. So also an adulterer and adulteress are bound not only to indemnify the husband for the support of the offspring, but also to

[1] The same rule was observed among the Jews, *Baba Kama*, viii. 1. Also among the English and the Danes; see a treaty of these peoples in the learned Pontanus's treatise on the sea [*Discussiones Historicae*, I. xxi].

repay to the legitimate children whatever loss they may suffer from the sharing of such a child in the inheritance.

He who has debauched a virgin by violence or fraud is bound to pay to her the value of her diminished expectation of marriage. Furthermore, he is bound even to marry her, if by so promising he obtained the enjoyment of her person. Lessius, II. x. 2, 3.

XVI.—*Of a thief, robber, and others*

The thief and the robber are bound to restore the thing taken together with its natural increase, and make good the resulting loss or failure to secure gain. If, again, the thing has been destroyed, they should repay not the highest, nor the lowest, but a fair valuation. Lessius, II. xii. 17.

In this class also those should be placed who by fraud avoid the payment of their legitimate taxes. Those are similarly liable who have caused loss by an unjust sentence, or by false accusation, or by perjured testimony. Lessius, II. xxxiii. 8. Covarruvias, *On Sext*, V. ult. 4, pt. ii.

XVII.—*Of one, who has procured a promise through deceit or an unjust fear*

Furthermore, one who has caused a contract or promise to be made by means of deceit or violence, or an unjust fear, is bound to free absolutely the person thus dealt with. The reason is that such persons had the right not to be deceived, not to be constrained; this right in the former case arose from the nature of the contract, in the latter case from natural liberty also.

In the class with those mentioned ought to be included those who have not been willing, except for pay, to do what they were bound to do from duty. Covarruvias, *On Sext*, V. ult. 4, pt. ii, §§ 3 and 5.

XVIII.—*What if the promise has been motived by a just fear according to the law of nature?*

But one who has given cause why he ought to suffer violence, or ought to be constrained by fear, has himself to blame for it. For an involuntary act, which has its origin in a voluntary act, is morally considered a voluntary act. Lessius, II. xvii. 6.

XIX.—*What of the fear, which is considered just by the law of nations?*

But by the consent of nations the rule has been introduced that all wars declared and waged by the authority of the sovereigns on both sides should be considered lawful as regards their external effects, of which we shall speak below; and so also it follows that the fear of such a war is considered as just up to the point that what has been obtained by it cannot be demanded back. In this sense

On Duties, III [xxix.108]. Bodin, *De Republica*, Book V, vi.

the distinction of Cicero can be admitted, between public enemies, on the one side, with whom by the agreement of nations we have, as he says, many rights in common, and on the other side pirates and robbers. For if pirates and robbers have extorted anything by fear its return can be demanded, unless an oath prevents; but such a demand cannot be made on public enemies.

[III. xiii.] The opinion of Polybius, therefore, that the Carthaginians had a just cause for the Second Punic War, because the Romans by threatening war had forced from them the island of Sardinia, and also money, when they were occupied with the revolt of their mercenaries, has a certain appearance of natural justice; it is, however, at variance with the law of nations, as will be explained elsewhere.

XX.—*To what extent civil authorities are liable for loss caused by their subjects; wherein is the question of captures made at sea from allies contrary to public command*

1. Kings and public officials are liable for neglect if they do not employ the remedies which they can and ought to employ for the prevention of robbery and piracy. On this account the inhabitants of Scyros were in ancient times condemned by the Amphictyonic League.

Plutarch [*Cimon*, viii = 483 c.]

At a time when the rulers of our country had given to very many persons letters of marque and reprisal as against the enemy at sea, and some of these had seized the property of friends, had abandoned their native land and were wandering about at sea without returning even when recalled, I remember that I was asked whether the authorities were liable on that account, either because they had utilized the services of wicked men, or because they had not required a bond. I replied that they were under no obligation except to punish the offenders as guilty, in case they could be found, or surrender them; that in addition they should see to it that the property of the freebooters should be rendered liable. For I maintained that they themselves had not been [293] the cause of the wrongful freebootery, and that they had not had any share in it; that they had also forbidden by laws that friends should be harmed; that they had not been bound by any law to require a bond, since even without a letter of marque they could give to all their subjects the right of plundering the enemy, as had formerly been done; that such a permission was not the cause of loss inflicted on allies, since even without such a permission private persons could fit out vessels and go to sea; I said that in truth it could not have been foreseen, whether the men were going to be wicked men; and that in truth we could not avoid utilizing the services of wicked men, that otherwise an army cannot be collected.

2. Kings, again, are not liable if their soldiers or sailors have injured friends contrary to orders; and this rule has been approved by witness of France [1] and England. The liability of one for the acts of his servants without fault of his own does not belong to the law of nations, according to which this question has to be settled, but to municipal law; and that not a universal rule, but one introduced as against sailors and some other persons for particular reasons. A decision was rendered to that effect by the judges of the supreme court against certain Pomeranians; and this decision was in accordance with a precedent established two centuries earlier in a similar case.

Constitutions of France, III. iii, year 1583, chap. xliv.

XXI.—*That according to the law of nature no one is liable for damage done by his animal or his vessel without his fault*

This also is to be noted, that it is likewise a principle of municipal law that a slave or animal, which has caused damage or loss, is to be delivered up for punishment. For by the law of nature the owner who is not in fault is not in any degree liable.

Furthermore, he is not liable whose ship without fault on his part has caused damage to the ship of another. Yet by the laws of many peoples, as also by our laws, it is customary that such a loss be divided, on account of the difficulty of fixing the blame.

XXII.—*That damage may be caused to reputation and honour, and how it may be repaired*

But, as we have said, damage is also done to honour and reputation, as by blows, insults, abuse, calumny, derision, and other similar means. In these acts, no less than in theft and other crimes, the criminality of the act must be distinguished from its effects. For to the former punishment corresponds, and reparation for the loss to the latter; and reparation is made by confession of the fault, by manifestation of honour, by witness of innocence,[2] and through the other means which are similar to these. Nevertheless, such a damage may be made good with money, if the injured party so desires, because money is the common measure of useful things.

Lessius, Book II, ii. 19, 25, 27. Soto, Book IV, vi. 3.

[1] See also *Constitutions of France,* Vol. III, title ii, in the constitution of the year 1543, chap. xliv.
[2] See Cassiodorus, IV. xli, for the example of Vivian, who was led by penitence in consequence of an unjust accusation.

CHAPTER XVIII

ON THE RIGHT OF LEGATION

I.—*That certain obligations, such as the right of legation, have their origin in the law of nations*

THUS far we have treated of rights for which we are indebted to the law of nature; we have added thereto only a few from the volitional law of nations, in so far as any addition had been made to the law of nature from that source.

It remains for us to discuss the obligations that the law of nations, which we call volitional, has itself introduced. In this class the subject of prime importance is the right of legation. Everywhere, in fact, we find mention of the sacred affairs of embassies, the inviolability of ambassadors,[1] the law of nations which is to be observed with reference to ambassadors, divine and human law, the right of

[1] Pomponius, *Digest*, L. vii. 18: 'If any one has struck an ambassador of the enemy, he is thought to have thereby violated the law of nations, because ambassadors are considered sacred; therefore if, while ambassadors of some nation are in our country, war should be declared against it, the ambassadors will remain free. For this is in accordance with the law of nations. And so Quintus Mucius used to give it as his opinion that one who had struck an ambassador ought to be surrendered to the enemy, to whom the ambassador belonged.' According to the response of Ulpian (*Digest*, XLVIII. vi. 7), 'if any one is accused of having struck or injured ambassadors, having written or oral communications, or their suite', he is liable under the Julian Law concerning public violence.

Josephus, *Antiquities of the Jews*, Book XV [XV. v. 3], vaunts the sanctity of ambassadors, who, he says, have a name in common with the angels, the messengers of God. Varro in his third book *On the Latin Language* [Nonius Marcellus, XII, p. 529] says: 'The persons of ambassadors are sacred.' Cicero in his third pleading *Against Verres* [I. xxxiii. 85, and *On the Response of the Soothsayers*, xvi. 34] says: 'The rights of ambassadors are protected by divine and human safeguarding,' and their title ought to be so sacred and venerated 'that it should remain unharmed not only under the laws of allies, but also among the weapons of enemies.'

The writer of the life of Epaminondas [Nepos, *Pelopidas*, v. 1] says: 'Since he thought he was protected by the right of legation, which is ordinarily held sacred among all nations.' Diodorus Siculus in the *Excerpta Petresciana*, no. 248 [= XXXIII. v. 4], speaks of 'the security arising from the inviolability of ambassadors'. In Papinius Statius, II [*Thebaid*, II. 373 f.], we read:

> And for ambassadors return is safe.

And likewise [*Thebaid*, II. 486 f.]:

> And sacred to the nations through all time the name
> Ambassador.

[301] Chrysostom says: 'They did not even show respect for the common right of men, which makes ambassadors safe from every wrong.' Servius, *On the Aeneid*, X [XI, line 101], says: 'To those protected from every injury by the law of nations.'

Not to make note of all passages, add Livy, Book I [I. xiv], concerning the Laurentes; Dio Chrysostom, *On Law and Custom* [*Orations*, lxxv and lxxvi]; Velleius Paterculus, Book II, beginning; Menander Protector [frag. 9, pp. 7–8, edit. Dindorf], and the letter of Felix to Zeno in the appendix to the *Theodosian Code* given by Sirmond.

In Procopius, *Gothic War*, III [III. xvi], Totila says: 'To speak generally, it is the custom of all barbarians to reverence ambassadors.' The same is said about barbarians by von Aschaffenburg. To King Clovis Aimoin has assigned these words: 'Finally it is in accord at the same time with divine and with human laws, which ordain that those who become mediators in the midst of hostile arms ought to be free from injuries. For in the midst of arms an embassy alone is the mediator of peace. He who undertakes an embassy puts off the character of enemy.'

See also Radevicus, in the Appendix; for the Poles, Kromer, Book XX; for the Turks, Leunclavius, Books VIII and XVII; for the Moors, Mariana, Book XII [XII. xiv].

legation sacred among nations, treaties sacred with reference to nations, the alliance of the human race, and the sacredness of the persons of ambassadors. Thus in Papinius [Statius] we read: [*Thebaid*, II. 486.]

> Sacred to the nations through all time the name.

Cicero in his speech *On the Response of the Soothsayers* says: 'For [xvi. 34.] so I think that the rights of ambassadors have not only been fortified by the protection of men, but also guarded by divine law.' [295] To violate this law, therefore, is by the acknowledgement of all not only unjust but also impious,[1] as Philip says in his *Letter to the* [Demosthenes, xii. 4 = p. 159.] *Athenians*.

II.—*Among whom the right of legation is in force*

1. First, then, it should be understood that this law of nations, whatever it is, which we are going to treat, pertains to those representatives whom rulers with sovereign powers send to one another. For in addition to these there are representatives of provinces, municipalities, and others, who are not governed by the law between different nations, but by municipal law. In Livy an ambassador calls I [xxxii. 6]. himself the public messenger of the Roman people. Elsewhere in VI [xvii. 8]. the same Livy the Roman senate says that the right of embassy is granted to a foreigner, not to a citizen. In showing that ambassadors ought not to be sent to Antony, Cicero says: 'For we do not have [*Philippics*, V. x. 27.] to deal with Hannibal, a public enemy, but with a citizen.' Moreover, Virgil, as clearly as any jurist, has indicated who are to be considered foreigners: [*Aeneid*, VII. 369 f.]

> Every land which free is, and not subject to our rule,
> I hold as foreign.

2. Consequently, peoples who are united in an unequal alliance[2] will possess the right of legation so long as they do not cease to be their own masters; likewise also those that are in part subject, and in part not, will have the right of legation for that part in respect to which they are not subject. Nevertheless, kings who have been conquered in a formal war, and have been expelled from their kingdoms, along with their other royal possessions, have lost also the right of legation. On such grounds Publius Aemilius kept as prisoners the heralds of Perseus, whom he had conquered.

3. In civil wars, however, necessity sometimes opens the way for the exercise of this right, though in an irregular fashion. Such

[1] 'An impious act', says Plutarch in the life of Aemilius [*Aemilius Paulus*, xiii = 261 D], relating the deed of Gentius. Josephus in the fifteenth book of his *Antiquities of the Jews* [XV. v. 3] says: 'This title has the power to reconcile enemies with enemies; what, then, can be more impious than to kill ambassadors pleading in behalf of justice?'

[2] Kromer, XXX.

a case will arise when a people has been divided [1] into parts so nearly equal that it is doubtful which of the two sides possesses sovereignty; and again, when two persons with practically equal rights are contending for the succession to the throne. Under such circumstances a single people is considered for the time being as two peoples. Tacitus censures the followers of Vespasian [2] for the reason that in their relations with the followers of Vitellius in the frenzy of civil strife they had violated the rights of ambassadors, which even among foreign nations were sacred.

Histories, III [lxxx. 4].

Pirates and brigands, who do not constitute a state, cannot avail themselves of the law of nations. According to the statement of Tacitus, Tiberius was indignant when Tacfarinas had sent ambassadors to him, because a deserter and bandit was treating with him in the manner of an enemy. Sometimes, nevertheless, persons of such a character obtain the right of legation on the strength of a pledge of good faith, as in ancient times fugitives in the passes of the Pyrenees.

Annals, III [73].

Caesar, *Civil War*, III. [xix. 2].

III.—*Whether an embassy ought always to be admitted*

1. Now there are two rights of ambassadors which we see are everywhere referred to the law of nations. The first is that they be admitted; [3] the second, that they be free from violence.

On the first point there is a passage of Livy in which Hanno, a senator of Carthage, thus inveighs against Hannibal: 'Our excellent commander has not admitted to his camp ambassadors coming from allies, and in behalf of allies. He has broken the law of nations.' Nevertheless, this ought not to be taken so literally. The law of nations, in fact, does not enjoin that all be admitted,[4] but it does forbid the rejection of ambassadors without cause. The cause, again, may arise in the case of the one who sends the ambassador, or in the case of the one who is sent, or in the reason for the sending.

XI [XXI. x. 6].

2. Melesippus, a Spartan ambassador, was dismissed from Attic territory by the advice of Pericles, because he was coming from an enemy in arms. So the Roman senate declared that it could not admit a Carthaginian embassy, because a Carthaginian army was in Italy.[5] The Achaeans did not admit the ambassadors of Perseus, since he was planning war against the Romans. So Justinian refused

Thucydides, II [xii]. Zonaras [IX. xiii]. Livy, XLI [xxiv. 20].

[1] Concerning the ambassadors of the city of Toledo to King John, see Mariana, XXII. viii; for the people of Flanders, see Krantz, *Saxonica*, XII. xxxiii.

[2] And Zosimus, in Book II [II. xlvii], accuses Magnentius: 'Magnentius was debating in his mind whether he should dismiss Philip unanswered or violate the right of legation and detain him.' Philip had come from Constantius.

[3] Donatus, *On* [*Terence's*] *Hecyra*, Prologue [Second Prologue], says: 'It is the law of nations that an ambassador ought to be heard.'

[4] See Camden, under the year 1571, on the fourth of the questions there suggested.

[5] On this custom of the Romans see Servius, *On the Aeneid*, VII [VII. 168].

to receive the embassy of Totila, and the Goths at Urbino the representatives of Belisarius. Also Polybius relates that the ambassadors of the Cynethensians were everywhere expelled because they were a wicked nation. Procopius, *Gothic War*, [II. xix] and III [xxxvii]. IV [xxi].

The second cause is illustrated in the case of Theodorus, who was called 'the atheist', whom Lysimachus was unwilling to hear, though Theodorus [296] had been sent to him by Ptolemy. The same thing has happened to other ambassadors by reason of personal hatred. [Diogenes Laertius, II. cii.]

The third cause which we mentioned becomes operative either when the cause of the sending is suspected,[1] just as the embassy of the Assyrian Rabshaketh was by Hezekiah deservedly suspected of stirring up the people; or when the embassy is not of proper rank, or when it comes at an inopportune time. So the Romans forbade the Aetolians to send any embassy without permission of the Roman commander, and ordered that Perseus should send his embassy not to Rome but to Licinius. Further, the ambassadors of Jugurtha were ordered to depart from Italy within ten days,[2] unless they had come to surrender their kingdom and their king. But permanent legations, such as are now customary, can be rejected with the best of right; for ancient custom, to which they were unknown, teaches how unnecessary they are. *2 Kings*, xviii [36]. Livy, XXVII [XXXVII. xlix. 8]. Livy, XXXII [XLII. xxxvi. 5 ff.]. Sallust, *Jugurtha* [xxviii. 2].

IV.—*Against ambassadors, who are undertaking dangerous missions, defence is permissible, but not the exaction of a penalty*

1. The question regarding the inviolability of ambassadors[3] is more difficult, and has been handled in varied fashion by the distinguished minds of this generation. We need to speak of the persons of ambassadors, then of their suite and property.

As regards their persons, some think that by the law of nations the persons of ambassadors are protected from unjust violence only; for their view is that the privileges of ambassadors are to be explained according to common law. Others hold that violence may be done to an ambassador not on all grounds, but merely if the law of nations has been violated by him; and this is sufficiently comprehensive, for in the law of nations the law of nature is included, so that an ambassador can be punished for all crimes excepting only those which are committed against municipal law. Others restrict this right to

[1] Thus Andreas Burgus, ambassador of the Caesars, was not allowed to enter Spain; Mariana, Book XXIX [XXIX. xv]. There is a similar case in Kromer, Book XX.

[2] The Emperor Charles V gave orders that the ambassadors of France, Venice, and Florence, who had been sent to declare war, should be conducted to a place which was thirty miles from his court; Guicciardini, Book XVIII [XVIII, p. 472]; Bellay, Book III [III, fol. 103, ed. of 1573].

[3] Menander Protector [frag. 26, p. 59, edit. Dindorf] says of the Emperor Justinus II [Baianus]: 'He held the ambassadors of the Avars in chains, contrary to the right of legation.' See Ernest [302] Cothmann, vol. v, respons. xxxii, no. 29 ff.

crimes which are committed against the security of the state, or the dignity of the official to whom the ambassador is sent. There are also those who think that even this right is fraught with danger; that complaints ought to be made to the one who has sent the ambassador, and the decision entrusted to him. Some, again, think that kings and peoples that have no interest in the case ought to be brought in as advisers. This may be an evidence of prudence, but it is not required by law.

2. The reasons which the advocates of these views severally allege lead to no definite conclusion; for this law does not certainly arise from definite reasons, as the law of nature does, but takes its form according to the will of nations. Now the nations could have made provision for ambassadors either covering all cases or with certain exceptions. For on the one side lies the advantageousness of punishment of grave offenders; on the other is the usefulness of embassies, and the ease in sending embassies is best promoted by making their safety as secure as possible. The question, then, ought to be considered to what extent have nations reached an agreement? This question cannot be answered on the basis of precedents alone; for there is a sufficient number of precedents on both sides. We must, therefore, have recourse not only to the opinions of wise men, but also to the implications.

3. I have two particularly notable opinions. The one is of Livy, the other of Sallust.

[II. iv. 7.] The opinion of Livy relates to the ambassadors of Tarquin, who had incited a revolt at Rome: 'Although they seemed to have committed so great an offence that they might be treated as enemies, yet the law of nations prevailed.' Here we see that the law of nations is extended even to those who commit hostile acts.

The statement of Sallust applies to the suite of an embassy, of which I shall speak presently, not to the ambassadors themselves; but the argument will proceed naturally from the greater, that is,
Jugurtha the less credible, to the less, that is, the more credible. Sallust speaks
[xxxv. 7]. thus: 'Bomilcar, his companion, who had come to Rome under a pledge of good faith on the part of the state, was brought to trial, rather in accordance with equity and justice than according to the law of nations.' Equity and justice, that is, the pure law of nature, allow that punishment shall be inflicted when he who has committed wrong is found. But the law of nations makes an exception of ambassadors and of those who, like them, come under a pledge of public faith. Wherefore it is contrary to the law of nations that ambassadors should be brought to trial; and on that account many things, which the law of nature permits, are commonly forbidden.

4. The implications, furthermore, favour this side, [297] for

it is nearer the truth to understand special privileges in such a way that they may add something to a common right. If, now, ambassadors were protected only from unjust violence, there would be nothing great, nothing outstanding in that provision. There is the further consideration that the security of ambassadors outweighs any advantage which accrues from a punishment. For punishment can be inflicted through the one who sent the ambassador, if he so wills. If, on the contrary, he is unwilling, punishment by means of war can be exacted from him as having approved the crime. Some raise the objection that it is better that one should be punished than that many should be involved in war. Yet, if the one who sent the ambassador approves of his act, the punishment of the ambassador will not exempt us from war.

On the other hand, the safety of ambassadors is placed on an extremely precarious footing if they are under obligation to render account of their acts to any other than the one by whom they are sent. For since the views of those who send the ambassadors are generally different from the views of those who receive them, and often directly opposed, it is scarcely possible that in every case something may not be said against an ambassador which shall present the appearance of a crime. And although some things are so obvious that they do not admit of doubt, yet the universal peril is sufficient to establish the justice and advantage of the universal law.

5. My unqualified conclusion, therefore, is that the rule has been accepted by the nations that the common custom, which makes a person who lives in foreign territory subject to that country, admits of an exception in the case of ambassadors. Ambassadors as if by a kind of fiction are considered to represent those who sent them; thus of a certain ambassador Cicero says: 'He had borne with him the majesty of the senate and the authority of the state.' In consequence, by a similar fiction, ambassadors were held to be outside of the limits of the country to which they were accredited. For this reason they are not subject to the municipal law of the state within which they are living. If, therefore, the crime should be such that according to all appearances it can be treated lightly, it will either need to be overlooked, or the ambassador should be ordered to leave the country,[1] as was the ambassador who, according to Polybius,[2] had furnished the means of escape to hostages at Rome. In this connexion it should be understood that, though at another time an ambassador of Tarentum, who had committed the same offence, was

Philippics, VIII [viii. 23].

[1] Stephen, king of Poland, did this to the Muscovites; De Thou, Book LXXIII [LXXIII. ix], on the Year 1581. Elizabeth did the same to a Scotch and a Spanish ambassador; both examples you find in Camden, under the years 1571 and 1584.

[2] [Barbeyrac notes that Grotius erroneously attributes this to Polybius, following Gentili, *On Embassies*, II. xxi.]

scourged, that was in consequence of the fact that the Tarentines had been conquered and had begun to be subject to Rome.[1]

If the crime should be particularly atrocious and bid fair to bring harm to the state, the ambassador should be sent back to the one who sent him,[2] with the demand that he be punished or surrendered. [Livy, V. xxxvi. 8.] Thus we read that the Gauls demanded that the Fabii be surrendered to them.

6. But, as we have several times remarked, all human laws have been so adjusted that in case of dire necessity they are not binding; and so the same rule will hold in regard to the law of the inviolability of ambassadors. Nevertheless, this extreme necessity does not warrant the infliction of punishment, which in other cases also is removed by the law of nations, as will appear below, when we treat of the effects of regular warfare. Such extreme necessity will be concerned still less with the place, time, and manner of inflicting punishment, but rather with guarding against serious hurt, especially to the state. Therefore that an immediately threatening peril may be met, if there is no other proper recourse, ambassadors can be detained and questioned. So the Roman consuls arrested the ambassadors[3] of [II. iv. 7.] Tarquin, taking special care, as Livy says,[4] that none of the letters should be lost.

7. But if an ambassador should attempt armed force he can indeed be killed, not by way of penalty, but in natural defence. So [V. xxxvi. 7.] the Gauls could have killed the Fabii, whom Livy calls violators of human right. And so in the *Children of Hercules*, by Euripides, Demophon restrained by force the herald who had been sent by Eurystheus and was trying to drag away the suppliants by force; and when the herald said:

[*Children of Hercules*, lines 271–2.]

> Do you thus dare to slay a herald hither sent?

Demophon replied:

> Unless the herald now withholds his hand from force.

[*Lives of Sophists*, II. v.] [298] Philostratus in his *Life of Herod* relates that the herald's name was Copreus,[5] and that he was killed by the Athenian people because he employed force.[6]

[1] So Charles V commanded the ambassador of the Duke of Milan, as his subject, not to leave his court; Guicciardini, in the work already referred to [XVIII, p. 337, n. 3].

[2] Dio, in the *Selections on Embassies* [frag. 61], says: 'When certain young men, ambassadors of Carthage, had come to Rome and had conducted themselves insultingly there, they were sent to Carthage, and were surrendered to the Carthaginians; they suffered no harm at the hands of the Romans, and were dismissed unscathed.'

[3] Pelopidas was put in chains by Alexander of Pherae for the reason that, though an ambassador, he was inciting the Thessalians to freedom; Plutarch [*Pelopidas*, xxvii = 292 E], and the Latin author of the life of Pelopidas [Nepos, *Pelopidas*, v. 1].

[4] See De Serres, on Henry IV [Monliard, *Supplement* to De Serres, p. 844].

[5] See *Iliad*, XV [XV, line 639].

[6] So that must be interpreted which, according to Procopius, *Gothic War*, I [I. vii], Theodatus the Goth says to the ambassadors of Justinian: 'Sacred among men and full of honour is the title

By a not unlike distinction Cicero solves this question, whether a son ought to bring accusation against his father as a traitor to the country. Cicero thinks that he should, in order to avert imminent peril, but not in order to punish the deed after the peril has been averted. *On Duties,* III [xxiii. 90].

V.—*That the person to whom the ambassador was not sent is not bound by the right of legation*

1. Now the law which I have mentioned concerning the inviolability of ambassadors is to be understood as binding on the one to whom the embassy was sent, and especially in case he has received it, just as if from that moment, in fact, a tacit agreement had been entered into. But warning can be given, and in such cases commonly is given, that ambassadors should not be sent; and that, if they are sent, they will be treated as enemies. Thus warning was given to the Aetolians by the Romans; previously the Romans had given warning to the ambassadors of Veii, that if they did not leave the city the Romans would do as Lars Tolumnius had done; and the Romans were warned by the Samnites that they would not go away unharmed if they visited any assembly in Samnium. Livy, XXVII [XXXVII. xlix. 8]. Livy, IV [lviii. 7]. Livy, X [xii. 2].

This law, then, does not apply to those through whose territory ambassadors pass without receiving a safeguard. For, if they are going to, or coming from, the enemies of this people,[1] or are planning any hostile measure, they can even be killed; such was the fate allotted by the Athenians to the ambassadors between Persia and Sparta, and by the Illyrians to the ambassadors between the Issii and the Romans. And much the more can they be thrown into chains; such was the decision of Xenophon against certain ambassadors; of Alexander against those sent from Thebes and Lacedaemon Thucydides, II [lxvii]. Appian, *Illyrian Wars*[ii. 7]. *Anabasis,* VI [iii. 11]. Arrian, [*Anabasis of Alexander,*] II [xv. 3].

of ambassador. But ambassadors safeguard this right for themselves only so long as they maintain the dignity of embassy by their proper demeanour. For men think that it is right even to kill an ambassador if he acts wrongfully toward the ruler to whom he is sent, or violates another's marriage rights.'

When now the ambassadors had shown that they were entirely free from the suspicion of adultery, since they never went out without a guard, they prudently added: 'If an ambassador has spoken what he has heard from the ruler who sent him, and his words are not welcome, he himself should not bear the blame, but the one who sent him. For nothing else was allowed to him except to discharge the mission entrusted to him.'

See also Camden in the passage cited for the year 1571 [p. 338, n. 3].

[1] The Sicilians, who were allies of the Athenians, captured ambassadors of Syracuse who had been sent to other states; Thucydides, Book VII [VII. xxxii]. So also the Argives captured and conducted to Argos ambassadors sent from Athens by a small faction; Thucydides, Book VII [VIII. lxxxvi]. The people of Epirus intercepted the ambassadors of the Aetolians to the Romans and forced them to pay ransom. One of them was set free on the written request of the Romans; Polybius, *Selections on Embassies,* xxvii [=XXII. ix].

On the French ambassadors to Turkey, whom the Spaniards captured on the Po and killed, see the opinion of Paruta (Book XI) and Bizarri (Book XXI). See Krantz, *Saxonica,* XII. xxxiii, regarding the Flemish ambassadors to [303] France who were captured by Maximilian.

The clemency of Belisarius is praised because he spared the ambassadors of Gelimer. These had been sent into Spain and had returned from Spain to Carthage, which had then become subject to the Romans; Procopius, *Vandalic War,* I [I. xxiv].

Livy, XXIII [xxxiii ff.]. XXIX [iv. 2 ff.].

to Darius; of the Romans against the ambassadors of Philip to Hannibal,[1] and of the Latins against the ambassadors of the Volsci.

2. If there is no such reason, and ambassadors are mistreated, it is to be understood that not the law of nations, which we are discussing, has been violated, but the friendship and dignity either of the one who sent or of the one who received the embassy.[2] Justin says of the later Philip, king of Macedonia:

> After that he sent an ambassador to Hannibal in order to make an alliance with him by letter. The ambassador was captured and was brought before the (Roman) senate; he was dismissed unharmed, not out of honour to the king, but from fear that one who was still wavering might be made an undoubted enemy.

VI.—*That the enemy to whom an ambassador has been sent is bound by the law*

For the rest, when an embassy has been admitted it is under the protection of the law of nations even among public enemies,[3] and

[V. lxxv. 1.]

still more among those who are merely unfriendly. Diodorus Siculus said that for heralds peace exists in the midst of war. The Lacedaemonians, who had killed the fetials of the Persians, are said on that account 'to have violated the rights of all mankind'. Pomponius says: 'If any one has struck the ambassador of an enemy, it is thought that a crime has been committed against the law of nations, because ambassadors are considered sacred.' Tacitus calls this right which we are treating 'the right of enemies and sanctity of embassy and divine law of nations'.

Herodotus, VII [cxxxvi]. *Dig.* L. vii. 18. *Annals*, I [xlii].

[I. xxxiii. 85.] III. ii [5].

Cicero in his first pleading *Against Verres* says: 'Ought not ambassadors to be unharmed among enemies?' Seneca says in *On Anger*: 'He violated embassies, breaking the law of nations.' In his account of the ambassadors whom the people of Fidenae had slain, Livy says that it was a slaughter which violated the law of nations, a crime, an unspeakable act, an impious slaughter. Elsewhere he says: 'The ambassadors had been brought into peril and not even the laws of war had been left to them.' Curtius says: 'The heralds whom he sent to induce them to make peace, the Tyrians, in violation of the law of nations, killed and threw into the sea.'

Livy, IV [xvii and xxxii]. XXIV [xxxiii. 3]. IV [ii. 15].

Such expressions of opinion are justified; for not only do very many matters come up in war which cannot be handled except through ambassadors, but also peace itself is hardly to be made by any other means.

[1] See Appian, *Selections on Embassies*, xix [=*Macedonian Affairs*, i].

[2] It would be a different matter if any one should lay an ambuscade for another's ambassador outside of his own territories; in that case the law of nations would, in fact, be violated. This is contained in the plea of the Thessalians against Philip, as given by Livy [XXXIX. xxv. 10].

[3] See the passages just cited II. xviii. 1 [n. 1]. Donatus, *On Terence's Eunuch* [III. ii. 14=line 467] on the words 'To meet and to converse', says: 'This is to be understood as if he should say, May that be permitted by you, soldier, which is permitted even among enemies and in war.'

VII.—*That the right of retaliation cannot be claimed against ambassadors*

The question is also commonly raised, whether an ambassador can be killed or mistreated by right of retaliation, if he comes from one who has committed some such act.

There are, to be sure, sufficiently many examples of such vengeance in history; but, of course, the histories relate both just deeds and also unjust, wrathful, and violent deeds. The law of nations safeguards not only the dignity of the one who sends, [299] but also the safety of the one who is sent; therefore there is a tacit agreement with the latter also. Accordingly a wrong is done to the one who is sent, even if no wrong is done to the one who sent him.

Consistently with the principle stated, then, when Carthaginian ambassadors had been brought before Scipio after Roman ambassadors had been ill-treated by the Carthaginians, and he was asked what ought to be done to them, he replied, not only nobly, but also in accordance with the law of nations, that no such treatment should be accorded to them as had been inflicted by the Carthaginians.[1] Livy adds that 'he said that he would do nothing unworthy of the established customs of the Roman people'. Valerius Maximus, in a similar but more ancient case, puts this utterance into the mouths of the Roman consuls: 'The good faith of our state, Hanno, frees you from that fear.' For at that time also Cornelius Asina had been put in chains by the Carthaginians, contrary to the right of legation.

Appian, *Punic Wars* [vi. 35].

XXX [xxv. 10].

VI.vii [VI. vi. 2].

VIII.—*The right of ambassadors is also extended to the suite of an ambassador, if the ambassador has desired it*

1. The suite also, and the effects of ambassadors, in their own way are inviolate. Hence arose the expression in the ancient formula of the fetials: 'King, do you appoint me the royal messenger of the Roman people the Quirites, and do you designate my suite and effects?' By the Julian Law on public violence, those who have done an injury not merely to ambassadors, but also to their suites, are declared to be held guilty. But these rights are sacred as accessories and, therefore, only so far as seems good to the ambassador.[2]

[Livy, I. xxiv. 5.]

Digest, XLVIII. vi. 7.

[1] Diodorus Siculus in the *Excerpta Peiresciana* [=XXVII. xii. 1] says: 'Scipio said that they ought not to do that which they blamed in the Carthaginians.' The Romans themselves dismissed the ambassadors after they learned of the deed of the Carthaginians. See Appian. Constantius dismissed Titian, who had been sent to him by Magnentius, though the latter was detaining Philip, who had been sent to him by Constantius; Zosimus, Book II [II. xlix].

See also the narratives in Kromer, Books XIX and XXI; and Paruta, Book VII, concerning the Venetian ambassadors who were detained on their way into France.

[2] See the *Letters* of Du Fresne de la Canaye, pp. 75 and 279.

If, now, members of the suite have committed a great crime, the demand can be made on the ambassador to surrender them; for they ought not to be taken away by force.[1] When force was employed by the Achaeans in the case of certain Lacedaemonians, who were with the Roman ambassadors, the Romans cried out that the law of nations was being violated. Also the judgement of Sallust concerning Bomilcar, which we have cited above, can be referred to on this point. If, however, the ambassador is unwilling to surrender such members of his suite, the same course will need to be pursued as we just now mentioned in the case of an ambassador.

Pausanias, VII [xiv].

[II. xviii. 4. 3.]

2. The question whether an ambassador has jurisdiction over his own household, and whether any one who takes refuge with him has a right of asylum in his residence,[2] depends on the concession of him in whose domain the ambassador resides; for that right does not belong to the law of nations.

IX.—*The right of ambassadors is extended likewise to their movable goods*

Again, it is the better established opinion that the movable goods of an ambassador, which in consequence are considered as attached to his person, cannot be seized as security, or in payment of debt or by order of the court, or, as some claim, by the hand of the king. For an ambassador ought to be free from all compulsion—such compulsion as affects things of which he has need as well as that which touches his person—in order that he may have full security. If, then, he has contracted a debt and, as ordinarily happens, possesses no landed property in the country, payment should be demanded in a friendly way from him personally; and if he refuses, then payment should be requested from the one who sent him, so that finally those methods may be employed which are customarily used in the case of debtors outside the country.

X.—*Examples of an obligation without the right of compulsion*

1. There is no reason for fearing that, as some think, no one can be found who would be willing to make contracts with an ambassador, if such is the ambassadorial right. For kings, who are not subject to compulsion, do not fail to have creditors; and Nicholas of Damascus informs us that among some nations it was the custom that action at law should not be granted in relation to contracts based on credit, any more than against ungrateful persons, with

[frag. 34, p. 150, edit. Dindorf.]

[1] De Serres [*Supplement* to De Serres] on Henry IV.

[2] Generally in such cases a distinction is made as regards the crimes. See Paruta Book X; where the king of France, though angered for this cause, is appeased. See Book IX of the same author.

the result that men were compelled to carry out their contracts at the same time, or to be contented with the bare promise of the debtor.

This is the state of affairs that Seneca desires:[1] 'Would that we could persuade men to give credit only to men who wish to pay; would that no contract bound the buyer to the seller, and that compacts and agreements were not guarded by the attachment of seals; would that they might be kept rather by good faith and a mind that cherishes a sense of fairness!' Appian says that the Persians also objected to 'taking money on loan, [300] since that was a transaction exposed to fraud and deceit.'[2] *Civil Wars,* I [vi. 54].

2. Aelian says the same of the Indians; and Strabo supports him in the following words: 'There are no courts except for murder or injury; for these a man cannot hinder from happening to him. Contracts, however, are within the power of every person; and so, if any one violates his pledge, this must be endured. Each one ought in advance to consider whom he should trust, and not to fill the state with lawsuits.' Also Charondas established the rule, that one who had taken a promise in place of payment should not have the right to prosecute. This was approved by Plato.[3] [*Various History,*] IV [i]. XV [i. 34]. Stobaeus, *On Laws* [xliv. 40].

The fact was noted also by Aristotle: 'Among some peoples there is no right of action in these matters; for they think that men ought to be content with the pledge of good faith which they have accepted.' Elsewhere he adds: 'There are countries where the laws forbid action at law on account of debt, as if one ought to deal only privately with a man with whom he has made a contract, and whose good faith he has trusted.' Opinions opposed to this view, which are derived from the Roman law, do not apply to ambassadors, but to the representatives of provinces or municipalities. *Nicomachean Ethics,* VIII. xv. *Nicomachean Ethics,* IX. i.

XI.—*Of how great importance this right of legation is*

Profane histories are full of wars undertaken on account of the ill-treatment of ambassadors.[4] Also in the Scriptures[5] there is mention of a war which David waged against the Ammonites on that account. Cicero thinks that no other cause was more just for the war against Mithridates. *2 Samuel,* x. [*For the Manilian Law,* v. 11.]

[1] *On Benefits,* III. xv.

[2] Herodotus, I [I. cxxxviii] calls this 'owing a debt'.

[3] *On Laws,* VIII [VIII. xiv].

[4] On this account the Romans began war against the Senones, Appian, *Selections on Embassies,* iv and x [=*Gallic History,* xi]; against the Illyrians and Ligurians, Polybius, *Selections on Embassies,* cxxv and cxxxiv [=II. viii. 134]; against the inhabitants of Issa, Dio, *Selections on Embassies,* ii [*Leg. Rom.,* vi]; against the Corinthians, Livy, Book II [*Epitome,* lii]; against the Tarentines, Dionysius of Halicarnassus, *Selections on Embassies,* iv [=XIX. 5]. Of the French and the Germans you find examples in Aimoin, III. lxi and lxxxviii, and in Wittekind, II.

[5] See Chrysostom, *To Stagirius,* Book III [III. viii].

CHAPTER XIX

ON THE RIGHT OF SEPULCHRE

I.—*The right of burial of the dead has its origin in the same law of nations*

[Cf. Book I, xiv. 1.]

1. The burial of the dead also is an obligation which has its origin in the law of nations; and this, in turn, has its origin in the will.

On Custom [*Orations*, lxxvi = p. 649]. *Controversies*, I. i [14]. [*Jewish War*, IV. vi. 3.] *Letters*, last ed., 491. [*Various History*,] XII [lxiv]; XIII [xxx]. [line 378.] [*Panathenaic* = p. 202 B.] [*Pharsalia*, VII. 801.] [*Thebaid*, XII. 642.] *Annals*, VI [xxv]. [*Orations*, ii. 9.] *War with Gildo* [397 ff.]. *Novels*, liii.

Among usages or 'customs' which Dio Chrysostom [304] contrasts with 'the written laws', after the rights of ambassadors he declares that 'the burial of the dead should not be prevented'. Also Seneca the father includes the committing of a dead body to earth among the laws which are unwritten but more sure than all written laws. The Jews Philo and Josephus call this a law of nature, and Isidore of Pelusium, 'an established ordinance of nature'; we have said elsewhere that common customs which are in accord with natural reason are customarily included under the term nature.

In Aelian are the words: 'Since common nature herself enjoins that the dead be buried.' Elsewhere the same author speaks of 'the earth and burial as common, and equally due to all men'. Euripides in the *Suppliants* called burial 'laws of mankind';[1] Aristides, 'a common law'; Lucan, 'the customary rites of men'; Papinius [Statius], 'the laws of earth and a compact of the world'. Tacitus speaks of 'sympathy for the common lot of mankind'; the orator Lysias, of 'the common hope'. Whoever hinders burial is said by Claudian 'to put off the nature of man'; by the Emperor Leo, 'to bring disgrace upon nature', and by Isidore of Pelusium, 'to violate sacred right'.

Loc. cit. [line 563.] [*Antigone*, 450 ff.]

2. Because the ancients were accustomed to refer to the gods as authors the rights which are common to civilized men, in order that these might seem more sacred, we see that this right, as well as that of legation, is generally ascribed to the gods. And so in the tragedy just mentioned, the *Suppliants*, you will find it called 'the law of the gods';[2] and in Sophocles Antigone thus makes answer to Creon, who had forbidden the burial of Polynices:

> For this decree not Jupiter supreme
> Nor holy law of dead now deified,
> From whom the human race derived its other rights,

[1] Eusebius, *History*, VIII. xix [*On the Martyrs of Palestine*, ix], speaks of 'the laws of nature'.

[2] Sophocles, *Ajax* [line 1130]. The same author speaks of 'laws of the gods' in the *Antigone* [line 454].

Proclaimed. And I have not believed that your commands
So potent are that you of mortal birth
Could violate the laws unwrit but by the will
Of gods ordained, and everlasting. Not of late
Are they in force, but from all time,
And hid their origin. Then should I not
Obedience render to the mighty gods,
And with stout heart the fear of mortal wrath disdain?

3. Isocrates treating of the war of Theseus against Creon speaks thus: *Pan-athenaic Oration* [clxviii f.]

Who does not know, who has not learned, even in the Dionysiac festivals from the writers of tragedies, what evils befell Adrastus before Thebes, when, wishing to reinstate the son of Oedipus, his son-in-law, he lost the most of his Argive troops and saw the leaders themselves lying slain; when he himself, disgracefully surviving, could not obtain a truce to bury the dead, he came as a suppliant to Athens, which Theseus then was ruling, and besought Theseus not to count it a trivial matter that such men lay unburied, and not to allow the contemptuous disregard of the ancient custom and ancestral right, which all men have in common, not as if established by man, but ordered by a divine power; and Theseus, when he heard this, without delay sent an embassy to Thebes.

[*Panegyric*, xv; *Praise of Helen*, xv; *Plataic*, xx.] [IX.xxvii.] [IV. lxv.] [VI. v. 46.] [II. 7.] [= p. 204 A.] Cic., *For Quintius*. Lact., *Div. Inst.*, VI. xi and xxii. Val. Max., V. i. Quintilian, *Inst. Orat.*, XII. ult. Sen., *On Ben.*, V. xx [5]. [Philo, *On Joseph*, v.] [Tac., *Ann.* VI. xxv.] *Dig.* XI. vii. 14. § 7; XXVIII. vii. 27. Cap., *Marc. Ant.* [xiii]. [Eur., *Sup.*, 379 et al.] [Lact., *Div. Inst.*, VI. xii. 31.] [Prud., *Hymn*, X. 63.] Opt., VI [vii]. [*Thebaid*, XII. 165 f.]

Later the same author censured the Thebans [1] because they had put the decrees of their own state above the divine laws. He mentions the same story also elsewhere, in the *Panegyric*, in the *Praise of Helen*, and in the *Plataic Oration*. Herodotus, too, mentions it in his ninth book, Diodorus Siculus in his *Histories*, Book IV, Xenophon in his *Greek History*, Book VI, and Lysias in the oration in honour of the dead; finally, Aristides has the story in his *Panathenaic Oration*, and he says that this war was undertaken [305] on behalf of the common nature of men.

4. Here and there among the authors cited we see that the names of the noble virtues are assigned to this discharge of duty. For Cicero and Lactantius [2] call this a manifestation of humaneness; Valerius Maximus, of 'humaneness and kindliness'; Quintilian, of 'compassion and religious scruple'; Seneca, of 'compassion and humaneness'; Philo, of 'compassion for the common nature of mankind'; Tacitus, of 'sympathy for the common lot of mankind'; Ulpian, of 'compassion and devotion'; Modestinus, of the 'memory of the lot of man'; Capitolinus, of 'mercy'; Euripides and Lactantius, 'justice'; and Prudentius, of 'the work of kindness'. The Donatists, who forbade the burial of the bodies of the Catholics, are accused of impiety by Optatus of Milevis. In Papinius [Statius] one reads:

And Creon must be forced by war and arms
To heed the customs of mankind.

[1] Plutarch in his *Theseus* [xxix = 14] maintains that the right of burial was obtained from the Thebans by agreement, not by battle. Pausanias in the *Attica* [I. xxxix] says by battle.

[2] Also this in his [*Divine Institutes*,] VI. xii [VI. xii. 25]: 'That is the last and greatest duty of respect, the burial of strangers and of the poor.'

Spart., *Carac.*, [iv. 2]. VIII [xxiv. 15]. [*Ibid.*, XXII. 395.] VI [xii. 27]. *Thebaid*, III [98].

Spartianus says that such men are 'without reverence for humanity'; Livy calls the refusal of burial an act of cruelty 'evincing human rage beyond belief'. Homer has styled such acts 'shameful deeds'.[1] Lactantius calls 'impious' 'the wisdom of those who hold burial superfluous'; for the same reason Eteocles was called impious by Papinius [Statius].

II.—*Whence the right arose*

Genesis, l. 2; Tacitus, *Histories*, V [v]. [*Laws*, II. xxii. 56.] [Stobaeus, *Eclogues*, I. viii. 38.]

1. All do not seem to hold the same opinion regarding the cause of the introduction of the custom that bodies should be covered with earth, whether first embalmed, as among the Egyptians, or cremated, as among most of the Greeks, or buried as they are now; the last-mentioned, Cicero, and after him Pliny,[2] noted as representing the most ancient custom. Moschion thinks that the occasion was given by the savagery of the giants in devouring men, and that burial marked its abandonment. He, in fact, speaks as follows:

> By laws then 'twas ordained to give to earth
> The bodies of the dead, or sprinkle with the dust
> Those not yet buried, lest the dreadful signs
> Of former feastings should be left to view.

[*Tusculan Disputations*, III. xxv. 59.]

2. Others think that in this way men as it were of their own will paid a debt which otherwise nature demands of them even against their will. For not only did God make known to Adam, but also Greek and Latin writers generally acknowledge, that the body of man arose from earth and to earth must be returned.[3] Cicero quotes from the *Hypsipyle* of Euripides:

> Earth must be to earth restored.

Ecclesiastes, xii. 7. [lines 531 ff.]

Also in the words of Solomon we read that 'the dust returneth to earth, as it was, and the spirit returneth unto God, who gave it'. Euripides in the *Suppliants*, touching upon this very subject in the person of Theseus, thus speaks:

[1] The same poet in the *Iliad*, XXIV [XXIV. 113 ff.], says that Jupiter and the gods were angry at Achilles on account of the ill-treatment of the body of Hector.

[2] *Natural History*, VII. liv [VII. liv. 187], where also this is found: '"Interred" (*sepultus*) means laid away in some fashion, but "buried" (*humatus*) means covered with earth.'

[3] *Job*, x. 9. Philo, *Against Flaccus* [xxi]: 'Nature has assigned the earth as the proper place for men, not only when living but also after death, that the same earth which received them at their birth may receive them also on their departure from this life.'

Nevertheless as there is nothing praiseworthy in man, of which God has not placed a trace in some other kind of animate being, so it has come about in this matter also. Pliny, [*Natural History*,] Book XI, xxx [XI. xxx. 110], says of ants: 'They alone of living creatures, except man, practise burial.' But he himself says of the dolphins in Book IX, viii [IX. viii. 33]: 'And they have been seen carrying away one that was dead, that it might not be torn to pieces by sea monsters.' Also Virgil [*Georgics*, IV. 255-6] says of bees:

> Then bodies of the dead
> From hives they carry forth, and make sad funeral trains.

This Servius explains: 'Naturally with a funeral procession.'

Now let the dead be covered in the lap of earth;
Whence everything its origin received,
Thereto it is restored. The spirit to heaven returns,
The body to the earth. For not by right of sale,
But as a loan and for brief time 'twas given.
Soon earth asks back what it has nourished.

Lucretius similarly says of earth: [V. 259.]

Mother of all she is, and common tomb of things.

In his second book *On Laws*, Cicero quotes from Xenophon: 'The body is restored to earth; thus placed and buried it is, so to speak, covered with the veil of its mother.' Pliny also wrote [306] that the earth receives us at birth, nourishes us after birth, and always supports us when we have reached maturity; finally, when we have been abandoned by the rest of nature, as a mother she takes us to her bosom and hides us. [II. xxii. 56.] [*Natural History*, II. lxiii. 154.]

3. There are some who think that by burial as a kind of memorial the hope of resurrection was handed down by the first parents of the human race to their descendants. For by the witness of Pliny, Book VII, chapter 55, Democritus taught that bodies ought to be preserved on account of the promise of living again. Moreover, the Christians often refer the custom of honourable burial to such a hope. Prudentius says: [*Hymn*, X. 53 ff.]

What mean, I pray, the hollowed rocks,
Or what tomb structures beautiful,
Unless there is to them entrusted
A thing not dead, but by sleep overcome?

4. A simpler explanation is that, since man surpasses the other animate beings, it has seemed an unworthy fate that other animals should feed on his body; wherefore, that this might be so far as possible avoided, burial was invented. Quintilian said that because of the compassion of men dead bodies were guarded against the attacks of birds and beasts.[1] Cicero says in his first book *On Invention*: *Declamations*, vi [vi. 3]. [I. lv. 108.]

[1] See the prophecy about the children of Jeroboam in punishment of his sins *I Kings*, xiv. 11. Also Tertullian, *On the Resurrection*.

Homer, *Odyssey*, III [III. 258–9], says of Aegisthus:

[311] On him slain, then, no earth they lightly cast,
That dogs and birds his bones might lacerate.

As an adulterer and usurper of the kingdom, the Argives had left him unburied. Nevertheless with greater humanity Orestes, as will be told later [line 310], committed his remains to earth.

According to Sophocles, Menelaus says of Ajax [*Ajax*, lines 1064–5]:

But he, stretched out upon the pale sea-sand,
A welcome feast for sea-birds will provide.

But this also Ulysses, a model of prudence, forbids.

In praise of Antigone herself, Sophocles, in his *Antigone* [lines 696–8], says:

She would not suffer that her gore-stained brother
Unburied lie, to furnish food for ruthless birds and savage dogs.

'Torn by wild beasts in death he lacked the common honour of burial.' Also in Virgil we read:

[*Aeneid*, X. 557 ff.]

> No loving mother shall bury thee in earth,
> Nor lay thy weight in the ancestral tomb.
> A prey to ruthless birds shalt thou be left.

Jeremiah, xxii [19]. In the prophets God threatens the kings that are hated by Him, that they shall have the burial of an ass, that dogs will lick their blood. VI [xii. 30]. Lactantius has no other thought in mind regarding burial when he says: 'For we shall not suffer the form and image of God to be left a prey to beasts and birds.' So also Ambrose, whose words are: *On Tobias* [i. 5]. 'There is no nobler duty than this, to confer a favour on one who can no longer requite it; to deliver from birds, to deliver from beasts, one who shares your nature.'

5. Even the dead should not be exposed to such injuries, nevertheless with good reason it seems foreign to the dignity of man's nature that a human body should be trodden under foot and torn to pieces. Not inconsistent with this point of view is the statement in the *Controversies* of Sopater:

> It is a noble act to bury the dead; and by nature herself this boon was granted as it were to corpses, that they might not be exposed to shame after death by rotting away in nakedness. Whether the gods or the demigods granted this honour to bodies that are done with life, such disposition of the dead is agreeable to all men. In fact, since it is at variance with reason that the secrets of human nature should be exposed to the view of all after death, we have accepted from antiquity the custom of burying human bodies in order that, concealed in a tomb, they might waste away in secrecy, far removed from sight.

Of similar purport are the words of Gregory of Nyssa in his *Letter to Letoius*: 'In order that that which is a blemish upon human nature may not be exposed to the sun.'[1]

6. Hence is it that the office of burial is said to be performed not so much for the man, that is, for the person, as for mankind, *On Ben.*, V. xx [5]. Quint., *Decl.*, vi [3]. [*Satires*, cxiv.] that is for human nature.[2] Therein is the reason why Seneca and Quintilian called burial a humane public act, and Petronius characterized it as prescribed by custom. A natural consequence of this is that [307] burial ought not to be denied either to private or to public enemies.

Appian, in the *Civil Wars*, I [I. viii. 73], says of those who were slain at the command of Marius: 'It was not permissible for any one to bury any of the slain, but birds and dogs tore in pieces such excellent men.' Ammianus Marcellinus at the beginning of Book XVII [XVII. i. 1] says of Julian: 'Anxious lest birds of prey should consume the bodies of those that had been slain, he gave orders that all without distinction should be buried.'

[1] In a similar manner Agathias [V. xiii] says that it was the custom to conceal the afterbirth. So it is apparent how, according to nature, we are nothing at birth and at death. To make this plain the Hebrew sages forbade that those of the highest or of the lowest rank should be wrapped differently in any way either at birth or at death.

[2] Servius, *On the Aeneid*, XI [XI, line 106], says: 'The favour of burial is universally due to all mankind.'

As regards private enemies there is in Sophocles a fine disquisition by Ulysses governing the burial of Ajax, in which, among other sentiments, these lines appear: [*Ajax*, 1091–2.]

> O Menelaus, when so much is wisely said,
> Beware of doing injury to a man who is dead.

Euripides in the *Antigone* gives this reason: [Stobaeus, *Florilegium*, cxxv. 6.]

> Death is for mortal man the end of strifes;
> Then what else greater can to death be added?

The same dramatist also in the *Suppliants*: [lines 528–9.]

> If Argives have done ill to you in aught,
> Fallen they are; against a foe such vengeance is enough.

And Virgil says: [*Aeneid*, XI. 104.]

> No strife is there with vanquished men, and those
> Bereft of heaven's air.

Citing this thought the author of the *Ad Herennium*[1] adds: 'For that which is the last of evils has already happened to them.' Papinius [Statius] says: [*Thebaid*, XII. 573 ff.]

> We fought, 'tis true;
> But hate has ceased, and gloomy wrath
> By death is quenched.

Optatus of Milevis, too, assigns the same reason: 'If the contest was between those living, then let the death of the other appease your hatred. He with whom you strove before is now silent.' [VI. vii.]

III.—*That burial is due also to public enemies*

1. Consequently, all agree that even public enemies are entitled to burial.[2] Appian calls this 'a common right of wars'; Philo, 'the common interchange in war'. Says Tacitus: 'Not even enemies begrudge burial.' Dio Chrysostom says that this right is observed even 'among enemies'; he adds, 'even though hatred has reached the utmost limit'. [Appian, *Punic Wars*, xv. 104.] [*Annals*, I. xxii.] [= p. 649 c.]

In treating of the same matter, Lucan says that the laws and customs of humanity must be observed in the case of an enemy. The same Sopater, who was cited above, asks: 'What war has deprived the human race of this last honour? What enmity has [VII. 801.]

[1] [Barbeyrac notes that this passage is not found in the *Ad Herennium*, but that Grotius is following here Alberico Gentili, *De Iure Belli*, II. xxiv.]

[2] Philo, *Against Flaccus* [ix], says: 'Men who possess a larger measure of goodness and humaneness usually bury at their own expense those that have fallen in war; others, however, who extend their hatred even to the dead, give up the bodies under agreements, that they may not lack what custom imposes as a last honour.'

extended the memory of evil deeds to such a point that it would [=p. 647 D.] dare to violate this law?' And Dio Chrysostom, whom I have just cited, in his oration *On the Law*, says: 'For this reason no one judges enemies after death, and wrath and insult are not extended to their bodies.'

Aelian, *Var. Hist.*, XII [xxvii]. Diodorus, XVII [xl]. [Livy, XXII. vii. 5; lii. 6; XXV. xvii. 4 ff.; Sil. Ital., *Pun.*, 389 f.; Val. Max., V. i. 2; Appian, *Mith.*, xvi. 113; Plutarch, *Demetr.*, xvii = 896 A; *Ant.*, iii = 917 B; Diodorus, XI. xxix.]

2. Examples are found[1] everywhere. So Hercules buried his enemies, Alexander, those who fell at Issus. Hannibal sought out for burial the Romans, Gaius Flaminius, Publius Aemilius, Tiberius Gracchus, and Marcellus.[2] 'You might believe', says Silius Italicus, 'that a Carthaginian leader had fallen.' The same duty was discharged to Hanno by the Romans, to Mithridates by Pompey, to many by Demetrius, and to King Archelaus by Antony. In the oath of the Greeks, when they were making war on the Persians, there was this: 'I will bury all allies; as victor in war, even the barbarians.'

Quite generally in the histories you may read that an armistice was granted 'for the removal of the dead'.[3] There is an instance in the *Attica* of Pausanias: 'The Athenians say that the Medes were buried by them, for the reason that it is right that all dead bodies be committed to earth.'

[I. xxxii.] [*Leviticus*, xxi. 1 ff.] Ambrose, *On Duties*, II. xxviii [142].

3. For such reasons, according to the explanation of the Jews of the olden time, the high priest, though otherwise forbidden to be present at a funeral, nevertheless was even enjoined to bury a human body found unburied.[4] The Christians esteemed burial so highly that they thought it permissible to melt down [308] or sell even the consecrated vessels of the Church for this purpose, as well as for the support of the poor or the ransom of captives.

4. There are, to be sure, some examples to the contrary, but they are universally condemned. In Virgil are the words:[5]

> Ward off this rage, I pray;

[*War with Gildo*, 397 f.] and in Claudian,

> Blood-thirsty he put off the nature of a man,
> And to the slain begrudged the scanty gift of sand.

V [xxix]. Diodorus Siculus says: 'It is the part of a beast to wage war against the dead who were of the same nature.'

[1] Josephus [*Antiquities of the Jews*, IV. viii. 24] says about the laws: 'Let dead enemies also be buried.' Agamemnon buried the Trojans; *Iliad*, VII [VII. 395 ff.].
According to Plutarch [*Pyrrhus*, xxxiv = 406 A], Antigonus buried Pyrrhus. See the same author in the life of *Theseus* [xxix = 14 A].

[2] Plutarch, *Marcellus* [xxx = 316 A].

[3] See below, III. xx. 45.

[4] Servius notes the same from the Roman pontifical law [*On the Aeneid*, VI, line 176].

[5] [*Aeneid*, X, line 905.] Servius thus explains: 'The wrath of his enemies desiring to exercise cruelty even after death.'

IV.—*Whether the right of burial is obligatory in the case of notorious criminals*

1. Nevertheless I see that there are reasons for doubt in regard to notorious malefactors. The divine law given to the Jews, which is the teacher of all virtue as well as of humaneness, commands that even those who had been hanged on the gallows should be buried on the same day. The gallows was considered the most disgraceful punishment (*Numbers*, xxv. 4; *Deuteronomy*, xxi. 23; *2 Samuel*, xxi. 26 [xxi. 6]). Hence Josephus says that the Jews have so great regard for burial that before sunset they take down and bury in the earth even those whose bodies have been condemned to public execution. Other Jewish scholars add that such reverence was manifested for the divine image, after which man was fashioned. [*Jewish War*, IV. v. 2.]

In the third book of the *Odyssey*, Homer relates that Aegisthus, who to the murder of the king had added adultery, was buried by Orestes, the son of the king who was murdered. But Ulpian says that also among the Romans the bodies of those who are condemned to death ought not to be refused to their relatives; still further, Paul the jurist gave it as his opinion that they should be given to any one who might ask for them. The Emperors Diocletian and Maximinian rendered this decision: 'We do not forbid that criminals be allowed burial after they have suffered the fitting penalty.' [1] [III. 309.] *Digest*, XLVIII. xxiv. 1. *Digest*, XLVIII. xxiv. 3. *Code*, III. xliv. 11.

2. We read in the histories, to be sure, that examples of those left unburied [2] are more frequent in civil than in foreign wars; and to-day we see that the bodies of some condemned criminals are left for a long time in the sight of the people. Nevertheless, not only statesmen but also theologians are discussing the question whether or not this custom is praiseworthy. Rochus, *De Consuetudine*, fol. 12. Abbas, *On Decretals*, III. xxviii. 5. Sylvester, word *sepultura*, qu. 13.

3. On the contrary we see that praise has been given to commanders who ordered the burial of the bodies of those that had not allowed this privilege to others; such is the case of Pausanias, the Spartan king, who, though urged by the Aeginetans to avenge in like manner the action of the Persians against Leonidas, rejected the proposal as unworthy of himself and of the Grecian race. According to Papinius [Statius], Theseus thus addresses Creon: [Herodotus, IX. lxxvi.] [*Thebaid*, XII. 780 f.]

> Go forth and offer utmost punishment,
> Yet at the end be sure of burial.

The Pharisees buried King Alexander Jannaeus, who had treated most shamefully the dead of their people. If God at times punished Josephus, *Antiquities of the Jews*, XIII. xiii [XIII. xvi. 1] and Gorionides.

[1] [312] Mention is made of this Roman custom in Philo, *Against Flaccus* [x].
[2] Josephus [*Antiquities of the Jews*, XIII. xv. 5] on the death of Alexander, king of the Jews, said: 'To insult the dead by non-interment.' Add Quintilian, *Declamations*, iv [iv. 9].

certain persons with loss of burial, He did this by His own right as being above the laws. And the act of David in keeping the head of Goliath for show was done, in fact, against a foreigner, who was a despiser of God, and under that law which limited the characterization of neighbour to the Jews alone.

V.—*Whether the right of burial is obligatory in the case of those who kill themselves*

Jewish War, III. xxv [III. viii. 5]. Hegesipp., III. xvii. Gellius, XV. x. Plutarch, *On the Noble Traits of Women* [xi = 249 BCD]. Pliny, [*Natural Hist.*,] XXXVI. xv [107]. [Plutarch, *Cleom.*, xxxviii = 823 B.] *Nic. Eth.*, V. xv. *Orations*, lxiv [= p. 592]. Stobaeus, cxxvi [cxxv. 14], and Sophocles, *Ajax* [1266].

1. Nevertheless, the fact is not unworthy of notice that even among the Jews the rule concerning the burial of the dead had an exception in the case of those who had committed suicide; this, in fact, we learn from Josephus. And this is not strange, since no other punishment can be devised against those who are beyond the reach of the death penalty. Thus the maidens of Miletus were kept from suicide by fear, and likewise formerly the plebeians at Rome,[1] though this is denied by Pliny. [309] So also Ptolemy ordered that the body of Cleomenes, who had committed suicide, should be hanged.

Aristotle says that it is everywhere the accepted custom [2] that those who have committed suicide should be punished with some disgrace; and in explaining this passage Andronicus of Rhodes says that their bodies were denied burial. A provision of this kind Dio Chrysostom praises among other wise laws of Demonassa, queen of Cyprus. It is no objection to this custom that Homer, Aeschylus, Sophocles, Moschion, and others say that the dead are without feeling; in consequence they are not affected by injury or shame. It is, in fact, sufficient that what happens to the dead is feared by the living, that so they may be restrained from sinning in this way.

2. Most excellently, in opposition to the Stoics and all the rest who considered the avoidance of slavery and disease, and even the hope of glory, as a just cause for suicide, the Platonists think that the soul ought to be kept in the custody of the body, and that migration from this life ought not to be undertaken without the order of Him by whom the soul was given to us. Many statements on this point it is possible to find in the writings of Plotinus, and Olympiodorus, and of Macrobius *On the Dream of Scipio*.

[1] Servius, *On the Aeneid*, XII [XII. 603], says: 'Truly we should know that provision had been made in the pontifical books, that whoever had hanged himself should be thrown out unburied. For that reason he deservedly names it "a hideous death", as if of a most disgraceful death. Since, then, nothing is more hideous than such a death, we should consider that the poet spoke also in view of the rank of the queen. Cassius Hemina says that when Tarquinius Superbus had compelled the people to dig sewers and many had hanged themselves on account of this injustice the king gave orders that their bodies should be nailed to crosses. Then for the first time it was considered disgraceful to commit suicide.'

[2] At Athens in the time of Aeschines the hand of a man who had killed himself was buried apart from his body; Aeschines, *Against Ctesiphon* [ccxliv]. Add Hegesippus, III. xvii.

Following this opinion, Brutus had at one time condemned[1] the deed of Cato, which he afterwards imitated, 'maintaining that it was neither loyal nor manly to yield to fortune and to try to escape from impending misfortunes, which ought to be borne bravely.' Also Megasthenes noted that the deed of Calanus was condemned by the wise men of India, and that such an end for men dissatisfied with life[2] was not approved by their teachings. Not otherwise, as it seems, was the opinion of the Persians, whose king Darius, according to Curtius, says: 'I prefer to die by another's crime rather than by my own.' [Plutarch, *Brutus*, xl = p. 1002 E.] Strabo, XV [i. 68]. V [xii. 11].

3. And so 'to die' the Jews expressed as 'to be set free', that is 'to be dismissed'; this it is possible to see not only in *Luke* (ii. 29), but also in the Septuagint text of *Genesis* (xv. 2) and *Numbers* (xx. end).

This form of expression is usual for the Greeks also. Themistius, *On the Soul*, remarks: 'They say that one who dies is dismissed, and they call death dismissal.' In Plutarch's *Consolation* are words to this effect: 'Until the deity himself dismisses us.' [xiii = 108 CD.]

4. Some of the Jews,[3] however, make one exception to the law against killing oneself, considering it a 'commendable exit', as it were, if any one should see that thereafter he would be living as a reproach of God Himself. For because they assign the right over our lives not to ourselves, but to God, as Josephus rightly teaches his countrymen, they think that the presumption of the will of God alone justifies the determination to hasten death. [*Jewish War*, III. viii. 5.]

To this justification they refer the case of Samson, who saw that the true religion was an object of derision in his own person; also that of Saul, who fell on his sword that he might not be made sport of by the enemies of God and of himself. For they make out that Saul returned to his senses after the shade of Samuel had predicted his death; and after he knew that his death was at hand if he should fight he did not decline battle for his native land and the law of *1 Samuel*, xxxi. 4.

[1] Also not a few of the philosophers besides the Stoics. Seneca, *Letters*, lxx [lxx. 14], says: 'You will find also men who profess to be wise, who declare that violence ought not to be offered to one's own life, and judge it an impious crime to commit suicide, that the end, which nature decreed, should be awaited.'

Procopius, *Gothic War*, IV [IV. xii], says: 'To depart from life by violence is a useless, foolish, impulsive act; and the boldness, which leads one to death, since it lacks prudence, is judged by the wise undeservedly to have assumed the name of bravery. Then, too, this ought to be considered, that you should not be ungrateful toward God.'

[2] The same view was held by the Arabs no less than by the Indians and Persians, as you can learn from *Job*, iii. 21.

[3] On this question the opinions of the Jews varied, as you may learn from Josephus [*Jewish War*, I. xiii. 10], where he treats of the death of Phasael, and from the passage dealing with Herod's deliberation [*Antiquities of the Jews*, XVII. vi. 5]. According to Philo [*On the Embassy to Gaius*, xxxii], the Jews said to Petronius: 'We shall shed our blood together, voluntarily taking our lives. Then your commands may be laid upon the dead. Not even God would blame us, intent upon two purposes, to reverence the Emperor and to keep our sacred laws. So at length it will be permitted to accomplish this, if we depart hence, despising life as of least account.'

God, thence meriting eternal glory, according to the witness of David; those who had buried Saul with honour received from David the acknowledgement of a deed rightly done. A third case is that of Razis, a senator of Jerusalem, in the history of the Maccabees.

2 Maccabees, xiv. 37.

Furthermore, in the history of Christianity we find similar examples of those who committed suicide in order that, when put to torture, they might not forswear the religion of Christ;[1] also of virgins, who threw themselves into a river that they might not lose their chastity;[2] the virgins the Church enrolled in the list of martyrs. But nevertheless it is worth while to see what Augustine[3] thinks of such cases.

City of God, I. xxvi; *Letters*, lxi, [cciv], *To Dulcitius*; and *Against Gaudentius*, II. xxiii [I. xxiii]. Diodorus, XVI [xxv. 2]. [=318.] [=834A.]

5. I see that a second exception to the law of burial was in force among the Greeks; [310] and this the Locrians maintained against the Phocaeans, 'that it was a custom common to all Greeks that those who were guilty of sacrilege should be left unburied'. So also Dio of Prusa says in his *Rhodian Oration*, that 'the sacrilegious and impious' are deprived of burial. Plutarch in his *Antiphon* says that the same rule was established at Athens against traitors.[4]

But to return to my subject, with great unanimity the ancients agreed that war is lawfully undertaken on account of the denial of burial. This is apparent from the story of Theseus, which Euripides

[1] See Eusebius [*Ecclesiastical History*, VIII. xii].

[2] Cicero in his speech *On the Consular Provinces* [iii. 6] relates that 'the noblest maidens threw themselves into wells and avoided unspeakable disgrace by a voluntary death'. Such is the story that Jerome, *Against Jovinianus* [I. xli= p. 48], tells of the Milesian maidens, and there is an ancient epigram of the *Anthology*, Book III [VII. 492], with the title *On Youths*, which begins with the words 'We leave thee, O Milesian.'

Also the Jews relate that a woman on board ship, who was being importuned to commit adultery, asked her husband whether bodies submerged in the sea would rise again; and when he had affirmed that they would she threw herself into the sea.

[313] Moreover, of Christian women we have many examples, as the women of Antioch under Diocletian, Sophronia under Maxentius, found in the Martyrologies [Eusebius, *Ecclesiastical History*, VIII. xii and xiv]; in Zonaras [XII. xxxiii], and in Sextus Aurelius [Pomponius Laetus, published with Eutropius, Victor, and others in the Lyons edition of 1592]. Procopius, *Persian Wars*, II [II. viii], adds other women of Antioch under Chosroes.

Ambrose [*On Virgins*, III. vii] praises the maidens who had guarded their chastity by death. Jerome in the *Commentary on Jonah*, end of the first chapter [i. 12], says: 'And for this reason also in persecutions it is not permitted to perish by my own hand, excepting only when chastity is endangered.'

[3] To these we may add Chrysostom, *On Galatians*, i. 4, and the *Third Council of Orleans*: 'We think that oblations on behalf of the dead, who have perished in some crime, ought to be accepted, unless they are proved to have committed suicide.' And nevertheless Augustine himself in the first book of his *City of God*, chap. xvi [I. xvii], says: 'What human heart would be unwilling to pardon these women, who killed themselves for this reason, that they might not suffer any indignity of that kind?'

Moreover, the *Capitulary* of the Franks, Book VI, lxx, has this: 'It has been resolved concerning the one who has killed himself or hung himself, that if any one out of pity wishes to give alms he may do so and may say prayers in the chanting of the *Psalms*. But the suicides themselves should be deprived of oblations and masses, because the judgements of God are inscrutable, and the depth of His wisdom no man can find out.'

See also the same reference, VII. ccccxliii.

[4] But Nicetas in the third book of the life of *Alexis*, brother of Isaac [III. vi], after relating the death of John Comnenus Crassus, who had sought the sovereign power through sedition, makes this statement: 'After the body was carried out, it was exposed as a prey for dogs and birds. But this seemed to all people foreign to human feeling, and almost brutish.'

treats in the tragedy of the *Suppliants* already mentioned, and Isocrates in the passage which we cited.

VI.—*What other rights impose obligation by virtue of the law of nations*

There are also some other rights, which impose obligation by virtue of the volitional law of nations. Such are the right to things possessed for a long time, the right of succession to one who dies intestate, and the rights which are created by a contract, no matter how unfair. For although all these rights are in some degree derived from the law of nature, yet from human law they acquire a kind of support, either against the uncertainties of conjecture, or against certain exceptions which otherwise natural reason seems to suggest; and this was shown by us above in treating the law of nature.

CHAPTER XX

ON PUNISHMENTS

I.—*Definition and origin of punishment*

[II. i. 2.] [314] 1. Above, when we began to speak of the reasons for which wars are undertaken, we said that acts must be considered in two categories, according as they can be repaired or punished. The former class we have already discussed. There remains the latter, which concerns punishments. This we must consider all the more carefully because the lack of a clear understanding as to the origin and nature of punishment has given rise to many mistaken opinions.

Now punishment in general means an evil of suffering which is inflicted because of an evil of action. For although it is customary to assign certain tasks to persons as a punishment, yet these tasks are regarded from the point of view of their burdensomeness, and so are to be classed with sufferings. However, the inconveniences, such as exclusion from public meetings or offices, which are anywhere suffered on account of a contagious disease, or a bodily deformity, or other manifestations of uncleanness (many of these are mentioned in the Hebraic law), are not, strictly speaking, punishments, although they are called by this name on account of a certain resemblance and through a misuse of the term.

2. Moreover, among those things which nature itself declares are permissible and not sinful is this, that he who does evil shall suffer evil; this the philosophers call the most ancient law, and law of Rhadamanthus, as we have said elsewhere.

[v=p. 601 B.] A sentence of Plutarch in his book *On Exile* contains the same idea: 'Justice walks with God, as an avenger upon those who sin against divine law: to whom all men naturally have recourse against [*Euthyphro*, ix.] all men in so far as they are citizens.' Plato[1] said: 'No god or man will dare to say this, that he who does wrong is not obliged to pay the [Stobaeus, ix. 55.] [=p. 124 Needh.] penalty.' Hierax, furthermore, from this most noble viewpoint defined justice as 'the exacting of punishment from those who have first done wrong', and Hierocles [315] as 'a curative for wickedness'. [*On the Anger of God*, xvii [6].] There is a saying of Lactantius:[2] 'Those are deceived by

[1] So the interpreter of Irenaeus, Book III, chap. xiv [III. xxv], uses his words. 'And God indeed, according to an old saying, having the beginning and the middle of all things which are, acts rightly, proceeding according to nature. Moreover Justice always attends Him as an avenger against those who sin against divine law.'

[2] With this accords the well-known saying of Belisarius in Procopius, *Vandalic War*, I [I. xii]: 'The first proof of justice would be the exaction of a penalty from those who have slain unjustly.' See also Agathias, V [V. iii], on Anatolius.

no small error who defame censure, either human or divine, by calling it bitterness and maliciousness, thinking that he must be called a worker of injury who afflicts with punishment them that do injury.'

3. What we have said of punishment properly so called is summed up in this, that it is a return for a crime. This was noted also by Augustine, who said: 'Every punishment, if it is just, is a punishment for a sin.' This applies even to punishments which are inflicted by God, although sometimes in these, owing to human ignorance, as the same writer says, 'The fault is concealed, while the punishment is apparent.' [*Retractions*, I. ix. 5.]

II.—*That punishment is related to expletive justice, and in what way*

1. But opinions differ as to whether punishment falls within the sphere of attributive or of expletive justice. For, on the ground that he who has committed the greater sin is punished more heavily, and he who has committed the lesser is punished more lightly, and that the penalty is given as it were by the whole to a part, punishments are assigned by some to the sphere of attributive justice.

However, this first principle which they lay down, that attributive justice comes into play whenever an equality is established between more than two terms, we have shown to be untrue at the beginning of this work; then, as regards the fact that those who have [I. i. 8.] done greater injury are punished more severely, and those who have done less injury are punished more lightly, that happens only as a consequence, not because it is aimed at first and for its own sake. For first and for its own sake a balance is aimed at between the guilt and the penalty;[1] on this point Horace says: *Satires*, I. iii [77–9].

> Why does not Reason her own weights and measures use,
> And each crime check by fitting penalties?

And elsewhere, [*Satires*, I. iii. 117–19.]

> We need a rule to fit just punishment to sins,
> Nor ply him with the scourge who but the whip has earned.

[1] Seneca, *On Anger*, II. vi: 'A man is unjust who is equally angry in like measure with persons who are not equally guilty.' Tacitus, *Annals*, Book III [III. l]: 'But even if crimes and wrongs have no limit in their checks and punishments, yet the moderation of the prince [348] and the examples of your ancestors and of you yourselves distinguish foolish things from criminal, and words from criminal acts. Here is an opportunity to use judgement, so that this man's crime will not go unpunished and we shall not regret either our leniency or our severity.'

Ammianus, Book XXVIII [XXVIII. i. 24]: 'Ready to pray that the punishments might not be greater than the crimes.' The Scholiast on Horace [*Satires*, I. iii. init.]: 'If the heaviest penalties are used for the slightest sins, the result is that the greatest sins will go unpunished or new punishments must be sought out.'

Law of the Visigoths, XII. iii. 1: 'For although some laws recognize differences in guilt, yet they do not distinguish penalties in the same way, but confusedly the crimes of transgressors are entrusted to the penal judgement of a single law. Neither is the measure of punishment adapted to the measure of guilt, although the greater and the lesser transgression ought not to be condemned to the penalty of a single chastisement. Especially since the Lord ordains in His law that the number of the stripes shall be in proportion to the measure of the crime.' See below, II. xx. 28 and 32, and III. xi. 1 [III. xi. 1. 2].

5 [*Deut.*, xxv. 2–3]. [cv.] The tenor of a divine law in *Deuteronomy*, xxv, and of a novel of Leo, is the same.

2. Neither is the second principle which they lay down more true, that all punishments come from the whole to the part; this will appear from what we have to say. We have, in fact, shown above that the true nature of attributive justice properly consists neither in such a balance nor in the transference from the whole to
[I. ii. 8.] a part, but in taking account of the aptitude, which does not contain in itself right strictly so called, but furnishes an opportunity for it. Although, to be sure, he who is punished ought to be fit or worthy to be punished, this does not mean that something should befall him which attributive justice demands.

Nor yet do those give a better explanation who claim that expletive justice, which they commonly call commutative, is exercised in punishments. For in so doing they consider this a business transaction, as if something were paid to the wrongdoer, in accordance with the usage of contracts. They are deceived by current speech, whereby we say that punishment is due to him who sins. This is plainly 'misleading'. For he to whom something is properly owed has a right against another. But when we say that punishment is due to some person we mean nothing more than that it is proper for him to be punished.

3. Nevertheless, it is true that expletive justice is exercised in penalties primarily and for its own sake, because he who punishes, that he may punish rightly, must have the right to punish; and this right arises from the crime of the guilty. In this matter, therefore, there is something that approaches the nature of contracts.[1] For just as he who sells, even if he says nothing specifically, is considered to have obligated himself to all the things [316] which are naturally involved in a sale, so he who does wrong seems by his own will to have

[1] Servius mentions this often, *On the Aeneid*, IV [IV. 696]: 'For those who exceed the measure of crime justify punishment upon themselves'; and in the same book [699]: 'To condemn is to free from debt, whence the phrase you also will condemn by vows.' *On the Aeneid*, X [X. 32], 'They wash away their sins': '"They wash" means "they pay off". We have also said "I wash away punishment", but here it is better to use "crime", for crime is absolved by punishment. For punishment frees from former obligation him who is in bondage to crime. On the contrary, one cannot say "I wash away punishment", as though the punishment were paid off. Nevertheless authority confuses these things wilfully, in the way in which a subsequent is often confused with a precedent and vice versa.'

The words of the Holy Scripture frequently indicate the same. For, as Tertullian says, *De Oratione* [vii]: 'Debt in the Scriptures is a figure for crime, since that is owed to judgement and is exacted by it.' Chrysostom, in his address *On the Earthquake*, which is in vol. v [*On Lazarus*, VI. ix], dealing with that rich man who is contrasted with Lazarus, and explaining the word ἀπέλαβε, which is in that place in the Gospel [*Luke*, xvi. 25], says: 'Punishments were owed to him . . . and pains were owed to him.' Also in his *On Penitence*, II [VII. iii]: 'Crimes are considered as debts.'

Augustine, *De Libero Arbitrio*, III [III. xv. 44]: 'And so, if one does not pay by doing justice, he shall pay by suffering pain, because in either thing that word "due" enters. This may be expressed also in the following manner: if he does not pay by doing what he ought, he will pay by suffering what he ought.'

obligated himself to a penalty, because a serious crime cannot be unpunishable; hence, whoever directly wills to sin, by consequence has willed also to deserve a penalty. In this sense the Emperors say to a person, 'You yourself have subjected yourself to this punishment,'[1] and those who take evil counsel are already punished at that time, that is they are said of their own will to have contracted for the recompense of punishment. In Tacitus a woman who had married a slave is said to have agreed to subject herself to slavery, because that penalty had been ordained for such persons.

Digest, XLIX. xiv. 34. *Code*, IX. viii. 6.

Annals, XII [liii].

4. Michael of Ephesus, *On Aristotle's Nicomachean Ethics*, Book V, says: 'There is here a kind of giving and receiving, which constitutes the essence of contracts; for whoever has taken property or stolen anything else pays the penalty for it.' Later, again, 'The ancients termed contracts not merely what men have willingly agreed to perform toward one another but also the things that are forbidden by the laws.'

[*On Nic. Eth.*, V. ii.]

III.—*That nature does not determine to whom punishment is due, but that according to the law of nature those free from like offences may exact punishment*

1. But the subject of this right, that is the agent to whom the right is given, has not been definitely fixed by nature itself. For reason declares that the criminal may be punished. It does not, however, declare who ought to inflict the punishment, excepting so far as this, that nature makes it clear enough that it is most suitable that punishment be inflicted by one who is superior; yet not to the degree that this is shown to be altogether necessary, unless the word superior is understood to imply that he who has done wrong by that very act may be considered to have made himself inferior to some one else and as it were to have demoted himself from the class of men into the class of beasts[2] which are subject to man.

This view has been advanced by certain theologians. Says Democritus: 'It is in harmony with nature that the better should rule.' Aristotle, too, says that baser things have been prepared for the use of the better, alike in the case of things that have their origin in nature and those that are of artificial origin.

Thomas, II. ii. 64. 1, and Cajetan thereon. [Stobaeus, xlvii. 19.] *Politics*, VII. xiv.

2. Wherefore it follows that in any case a guilty person ought not to be punished by one equally guilty. This is the meaning of Christ's saying (*John*, viii. 7): 'Whoever of you is without sin'—that is, clearly, sin of the same sort—'let him cast the first stone.'

[1] Philo, at the end of the first book, *On the Life of Moses* [lix]: 'Hastening to commit sin, you hasten to pay the penalty.'

[2] So also Moses Maimonides, *On Deuteronomy*, xxxiii.

He said this for the reason that at that time the morals of the Jews were most corrupt, so corrupt that those who wished to appear most holy were involved in adulteries and like wickednesses, as one may see from *Romans*, ii. 22.

In consequence the Apostle also said what Christ had said before: 'Wherefore thou art without excuse, O man, whosoever thou art that judgest; for wherein thou judgest another, thou condemnest thyself; for thou that judgest dost practise the same things.' Here [*On Chance Remedies*, vii. 1.] a familiar saying of Seneca is in point: 'A judgement can have no authority where he who condemns is himself worthy of condemnation.' [*On Anger*, II. xxviii. 8.] Also his remark in another passage: 'Consideration for ourselves will make us more moderate if we ask ourselves whether we ourselves have not committed any such crime.'[1] Ambrose [II. ii.] in his *Defence of David* says: 'Let each one who is to judge of another first judge of himself, and let him not condemn lesser shortcomings in another when he himself has committed more grievous sins.'

IV. *That punishment having in view some advantage must among men be inflicted differently than by God; and why*

1. Another question is concerned with the purpose aimed at in punishments. What we have said thus far does at least show this, that injustice is not done to the guilty if they are punished. Nevertheless, it does not follow that they are in every case to be punished. This in fact is not true; for God and men pardon many things in many guilty persons, and for this cause they are wont to be praised.

Laws, IX [ii=854 D] and XI [xii=934 A]. The saying of Plato is famous: 'For no punishment is designed for evil'; in another passage, 'It is not because a wrong has been done that punishment is exacted (for what has been can never be undone), but to prevent recurrence.' This is [317] translated by *On Clemency*, I. xvi [*On Anger*, I. xix]. Seneca thus: 'No wise man punishes because a sin has been committed, but that sin may not be committed. For what has passed cannot be recalled, but what is to come may be prevented.' In [II. xxxi.] another passage he says: 'We are not to do harm to a man because he has sinned, but that he may not sin. Punishment will never have reference to the past, but to the future; for it is not inflicted in [III. xliv.] anger, but is a measure of precaution.' In Thucydides, Diodotus in addressing the Athenians with regard to the Mitylenaeans said: 'Even if I should show that they have acted with the greatest injustice I shall not vote that they are to be killed, unless that is expedient.'

2. Now these things are true in the case of men who inflict

[1] Here applies also Ambrose on the Psalm, *Blessed are the undefiled*, and the verse, *Let thy mercies, O Lord* [*Psalms*, cxviii, verse 156], in the discourse [*On Psalm CXVIII*, sermo xx, nos. 31, 36, 37, 39] cited in the *Decretum*, II. iii. 7 [II. iii. 7. 4]; also Cassiodorus, [*Variae*,] VI. xxi.

punishment, for one man is so bound to another by ties of common blood that he ought not to do harm to another save for the sake of attaining some good.[1] With God the case is otherwise, although Plato wrongly extends to Him the principles that have been stated. For the actions of God can be based upon the right of the Supreme Power, particularly where a man's special desert is concerned, even if they have in view no end outside themselves. In this sense, in fact, some of the Jews explain the saying of Solomon which has reference to this matter, so that it will mean 'God creates each thing singly, for its own sake, even the wicked man for the day of evil.' That is, even then when He punishes a wicked man, He does so with no other purpose than of punishing him.

Gorgias [lxxxi].

Moses Maimonides, *Guide of the Perplexed*, III. xiii, and Rab. Immanuel, *On Proverbs*, xvi. 4.

Nevertheless, even if we follow the more generally accepted interpretation it comes to the same thing, so that God is said to have made all things for His own sake, that is by right of the highest freedom, not seeking or regarding any perfection outside Himself; just as God is said to be 'self-existent' because He is not born of any one. Assuredly, Holy Writ bears witness that the punishments of those that are irretrievably lost are not exacted by God for any other purpose, when it says that He derives pleasure from their woe, and that the impious are derided and mocked by God. Then in truth both the Last Judgement, after which no mending of ways is looked for, and indeed certain inconspicuous punishments in this life, such as hardening of heart, demonstrate that what we maintain against Plato is true.

Deuteronomy, xxviii. 63; *Isaiah*, i. 24; *Proverbs*, i. 26.

3. But when man punishes a man who is his equal by nature he ought to have a definite purpose in view. And this is what the schoolmen say, that the mind of the avenger ought not to rest content with the woe of a man. Even before their time, Plato in the *Gorgias* said that those who punish any one with death or exile or a fine ought not 'to desire this simply', but to desire it 'for some good'. Seneca,[2] too, said that we must come to vengeance 'not as though it were sweet to take vengeance, but as though it were useful'. Aristotle, also, in his *Politics*, VII. xiii, says that certain things are honourable *per se*, certain others by virtue of some necessity; and as an example of the latter he mentions the inflicting of punishment.

Thomas, II. ii. 108. Sylvester, word *vindicta*. [Plato, *Gorgias*, xxiii.] *On Anger*, II. xxxii [II.xxxiii.]

V.—*In what sense vengeance may be forbidden by nature*

[Publ. Syr., *Sent.*, 294.] [*For Caecina*, xii. 35.]

1. As for the saying of comedy: 'An enemy's pain soothes the injured one's woe'; and Cicero's dictum that pain is assuaged by

[1] Cassiodorus [Peter of Blois], *On Friendship*: 'But if by some chance the one hand injures the other, that which is injured does not strike back nor raise itself to take vengeance.'

[2] Also, *On Anger*, II. xii [I. xii]: 'I shall take vengeance because it is necessary, not because it causes pain.'

[*Aratus*, xlv = 1048 E.] punishment, and Plutarch's quotation from Simonides: 'A sweet thing and far from grievous is it to apply as a remedy to a spirit distressed and enflamed the means of obtaining satisfaction'—these befit that natural instinct which man has in common with animals.[1] For anger in men as in animals is 'a warmth of the blood at the heart [*On Nic. Eth.*, VI. I.] from the desire to avenge pain',[2] as Eustratius rightly defines it. But this mere desire is so lacking in reason that it often acts against things that have done no injury, as the young of a dangerous animal, or against inanimate objects,[3] as the stone with which a dog is struck.

But a desire of this sort, taken by itself, is incompatible with the faculty of reason, whose function is to govern the desires.[4] It is, furthermore, incompatible with the law of nature, [318] because that is the dictate of nature in so far as it is governed by reason and takes account of society; and reason forbids a man to do anything whereby another may be harmed, unless this action has some good end in view. In the bare spectacle of the suffering even of an enemy, there is only a false and imaginary good, as in superfluous riches and many other things of the same sort.

2. Accordingly, in this sense, vengeance among men is censured not only by Christian men of learning, but also by philosophers,[5] *On Anger*, II. xxxii. like Seneca, when he said: 'Vengeance is an inhuman term, although accepted as just, and only differs from insult in degree. He who avenges his grief, sins, although with more excuse.' In truth, if we [*Dissertations*, xviii. 9.] are to believe Maximus of Tyre, 'He who takes vengeance is more wicked than he who did the wrong.' Musonius says: [In Stobaeus, xix. 16.] 'To meditate how one may bite the one who bit him and harm the one who has done harm is the mark of a beast and not of a man.' In Plutarch Dion, [*Dion*, xlvii = p. 979 A.] who applied the Platonic philosophy to public acts, says: 'In the judgement of law the revenge is considered more just than the wrong committed; but by nature it arises from the same spiritual defect.'

3. Therefore, it conflicts with nature for a man who acts against another to be sated with the other's pain, merely as pain. And so the less each man employs his reason, the more apt he is to [*Satires*, xiii. 180 ff.] seek vengeance. Witness Juvenal:

> But vengeance is a good, sweeter than life itself.
> So forsooth think unlearned men,[6] whose passions you do see

[1] Hence the saying of Homer [*Iliad*, IV. 23]: 'And fierce anger had seized him [her]'; [349] also [IX. 629]: 'He has stirred his proud spirit to fury in his breast'; and [IX. 496]: 'But Achilles, tame thy proud spirit.'

[2] Hence in Homer: 'To quench one's wrath' [*Iliad*, IX. 678].

[3] Seneca, *On Anger*, II. xxvi: 'How absurd it is to be angry with these things which have neither deserved our wrath nor are conscious of it.' The savages of Brazil take vengeance upon iron as upon a man.

[4] See what Seneca has to say on this point, *On Anger*, I. v.

[5] Plato, *Gorgias*. See also Theodoret, *Curatio*, Book XX.

[6] Seneca, *On Anger*, I. xiii: 'And those most prone to anger are infants, old men, and sick persons; while everything that is weak is by nature peevish.'

Enflamed, for slight, or even for no cause;
However trivial the occasion is, enough to stir their wrath.
Not thus would speak Chrysippus, nor the gentle heart
Of Thales, nor the sage of sweet Hymettus,
Who, in bondage cruel, wished not to share with his accuser
The hemlock he must drink. The happy man
All faults and errors step by step puts off,
Him wisdom first the right way teaches. A mind
Small, weak and mean, will ever pleasure take
In vengeance. Mark this at once, that in revenge
A woman does rejoice above all others.[1]

With this Lactantius agrees in saying: 'Ignorant men and fools, whenever they receive an injury, are seized with blind and unreasoning madness, and attempt to pay back those who harm them.' VI [xviii. 22].

4. From this it is clear that man cannot rightly be punished by man merely for the sake of punishing. Let us, therefore, try to see what useful ends render punishment just.

VI.—*The threefold advantage of punishment*

1. Here, furthermore, applies the classification of punishments which is found in Plato's *Gorgias* and in Taurus the philosopher, who is quoted by Gellius, V. xiv. For these classifications are made in accordance with the end in view. However, while Plato recognized two ends, namely correction and example, Taurus adds a third, 'vengeance',[2] which Clement of Alexandria defines as 'a retribution for evil which contributes to the advantage of him who exacts it'. Aristotle, who omits punishment for the sake of an example, accepts only this third form, and that applied for correction, and says that this is employed 'for the satisfaction of him who exacts it'. [*Gorgias*, lxxx.] [*Paedagogus*, I. viii. 70.] *Rhetoric*, I. x.

This was sanctioned also by Plutarch when he said: [319] 'The punishments which immediately follow the crime not only restrain boldness in sinning for the future but also give the greatest comfort to those affected by the wrong.' This is properly the sort of punishment that Aristotle also attributes to the 'justice' which he himself calls 'commutative'. [*On the Delayed Vengeance of the Deity*, ii=548 E.] [*Nic. Eth.*, V. vii.]

[1] Terence, *Hecyra* [III. i. 30 ff.]:

Children are with each other wroth, for causes slight.
And why? For weak within them is the mind that governs.
And women, too, like them are weak of judgement.

Ammianus Marcellinus, XXVII [XXVII. vii. 4], speaks of anger thus: 'Wise men define it as a lingering and sometimes perpetual ulcer of the spirit, accustomed to arise from mental weakness, and they support this view with the plausible argument that sick persons are readier to anger than well persons, women than men, old men than youths, and the unfortunate than the fortunate.'

[2] These three: Correction, Vengeance, Example, are recognized also by Chrysostom, *On First Corinthians*, xi. 32 [Homily XXVIII, ii].

2. We must, however, examine this question in greater detail. We shall say then that in the case of punishment we must consider the advantage either of the person who does wrong, or of the person against whose interest the wrong was committed, or of other persons in general.

To the first of these three ends belongs the punishment which by the philosophers is called now 'admonition', now 'correction', and now 'exhortation'; by Paul the jurist, punishment applied for correction; by Plato, 'for wisdom'; and by Plutarch, 'surgery of the soul', which has the object of making better the man who has sinned, like medical treatment which operates by remedies the opposite of the disease. Since every action, especially one that is deliberate and repeated, produces a certain inclination towards itself, which, when developed, is called habit, for this reason the enticement must be removed as soon as possible from vices. This cannot be accomplished more successfully than by causing them to lose the flavour of sweetness by some subsequent pain.[1] The Platonic philosophers, quoted by Apuleius, teach that 'It is a more serious and unpleasant matter than any punishment if impunity is extended to the guilty and he is not in the meantime harassed by the censure of his fellow men.' In Tacitus we find the saying: 'A mind that is diseased and feverish, being at the same time corrupt and an agent of corruption, must be held in check by remedies as severe as the vices from which it suffers.'

[*Digest*, XLVIII. xix. 20.] [Plato, *On Laws*, XI. 12.] [Plutarch, *On the Delayed Vengeance of the Deity*, iv, xvi = 550 A, 559 F.] [*On Plato*, II. xvii.] *Annals*, III [liv].

VII.—*Proof that punishment for the good of the wrong-doer may be exacted by any one at all according to the law of nature*

Thomas, II. ii, qu. 33, art. 3.

1. The punishment which serves this end is by nature permitted to any one of sound judgement who is not subject to vices of the same kind or of equal seriousness, as is apparent from reproof that is administered verbally.

Plautus, *Trinummus* [23 ff.].

> To chide a friend for guilt deserving blame
> Is a thankless task, but at times useful.

However, in the case of corporal chastisement and other punishments that contain an element of compulsion, the distinction between those who may or who may not apply them[2] is not made by nature (for this could not be the case, except in so far as reason entrusts to

[1] Seneca, *On Anger*, I. v [I. vi]: 'Just as we heat some twisted spear-points to straighten them, and laying them on the anvil hammer them, not to break them, but to perfect them, so we correct serious depravities by bodily and mental pain;' and *On Anger*, II. xxvii: 'Among these will be good magistrates, parents, and judges, whose chastisements are received like a surgeon's knife, abstinence, and other things that cause pain for our good.'

[2] See Augustine, *Enchiridion*, lxxii.

parents in a special sense the exercise of this right over their children on account of the tie of relationship) but by the laws which have limited that common connexion of the human race to the nearest relationships for the sake of obviating quarrels. This one may see from the section of Justinian's *Code* on the right of correction of relatives, and elsewhere. [IX. xv.]

Here also applies the saying of Xenophon to his soldiers: 'If I have beaten any one for his own good, I admit that I owe him a penalty such as parents owe to their children and teachers to their pupils. Physicians in fact even burn and cut a sick man for his own good.' Lactantius, in Book VI, says: 'God commands us to hold our hands continually over minors, that is, in order that we may correct them when they err by diligent chastisements and not train them for evil and rear them for vices through useless love and excessive indulgence.' [*Anabasis*, V. viii. 18.] [xix. 8.]

2. This form of punishment, nevertheless, cannot be made to include the death penalty, unless by the process of reduction whereby negatives are reduced to their opposing positives. For, as Christ said that it would have been better, that is not so bad, for certain ones, if they had never been born, so it is better, that is it is a lesser evil, for men of incurable natures to die than to live, when it is certain that by living they will grow worse. It is about such persons that Seneca speaks when he says that sometimes it is to their own advantage that men should die. [320] Further, Iamblichus declares: 'Just as in the case of gangrene it is better for a man to be cauterized than to have no treatment, so it is better for a wicked man to die than to live.' *Mark*, xiv. 21. *On Anger*, [I] vi. [*Protrepticon*, ii.]

Such a person Plutarch calls: 'of a truth harmful to others, but most of all to himself'. And when Galen said that men are punished with death, first that they may not live to do harm, and secondly that others may be deterred by fear of the punishment, he adds: 'And thirdly it is to their own advantage to die, since they are so diseased in mind that they cannot be brought back to health.' [*On the Delayed Vengeance of the Deity*, vi = 551 E.]

3. There are some who think that these are the very ones of whom the Apostle John says that they sin unto death.[1] But because the proofs of this are deceptive, charity bids us hold no man for lost without clear proof. Punishment for this purpose may in consequence only be applied upon rare occasions. *I John*, v. 16.

[1] Chrysostom calls them 'persons held by an incurable disease', *On Second Corinthians*, xiii. 9 [xiii. 7 = Homily XXIX, iv]. Julian in the second book *On Constantius* [*Orations*, ii = 89 B] says: 'Since there are two sorts of sin, the one sort showing hope of improvement and not utterly refusing to be cured, and the other sort committed by incurable sinners, for the latter the laws have devised death as a means of escaping evils, not so much for their advantage, as for the advantage of others.'

VIII.—*Likewise for the good of him who has been wronged, where it concerns vengeance permitted by universal common law*

1. The advantage of him to whose disadvantage the wrong was committed[1] consists in this, that subsequently he may not [VII. xiv. 9.] suffer any such thing from the same man or from others. Gellius quotes from Taurus the following description of this type of good: 'When the dignity or authority of him who has been wronged must be protected so that the neglect to inflict punishment may not make him despised and disgraced.' What is said there with regard to injured authority must be understood to apply to the liberty of a person, or any other of his rights that has been transgressed. In [*Annals*, XIV. lxi.] Tacitus we read: 'Let him take counsel for his safety by a just revenge.'

To secure a man who has been wronged from suffering harm at the hands of the same person is possible in three ways: first, by the removal of the wrong-doer; second, by depriving him of the power to do harm; finally, by teaching him to cease from his evil ways, which is closely allied with the reformation that we have already discussed. He who has been wronged may be secured from harm by others, not by an ordinary punishment, but by one that is public and conspicuous in the nature of an example.

2. Accordingly, vengeance, even if it is exacted by private individuals, is not unlawful according to the bare law of nature, that is apart from divine and human laws and from chance circumstances, provided that it is employed for these objects and within the bounds of right. It is all the same whether vengeance is exacted by one who was injured himself or by another, since it is in harmony with nature that man should be helped by man.

On Invention, II [xxii. 65]. In this sense we may agree with Cicero, who, while saying that the law of nature is not what opinion but what innate force supplies to us, among his examples thereof places vengeance, which he contrasts with pardon. And that no one might be in doubt as to how much he wished to include under this term he defines vengeance as 'that through which by defending ourselves and taking vengeance we deliver ourselves and those who should be dear to us from violence and insult, and through which we punish crimes'. Mithradates, XXXVIII [iv. 2]. in a speech which Justin has excerpted from Trogus, says: 'Even if men are unwilling to take the sword against a robber to save themselves, yet for vengeance sake they all wish to gird it on.' This very [xlv = 1048 D.] thing Plutarch, in his life of Aratus, calls the 'law of self-defence'.

[1] Even among animals there is some trace of this. 'A lion gets up to punish an adulteress'; Pliny, *Natural History*, VIII. xvi.

3. Samson, defending himself by this law of nature [1] against the Philistines, claims that he will be guiltless if he in turn brings harm to the Philistines who had first wronged him ; and after having taken [*Judges*, xv. 3.] his revenge he justifies himself by the same argument, saying that he had done to them what they had first done to him. The Plataeans, in Thucydides, say : 'We have justly taken vengeance on them accord- [III. lvi.] ing to the law recognized by all, that it is permissible to ward off him who comes as a foe.' Demosthenes, in his speech *Against Aristocrates*, [xxiii. 61 = p. 639.] says that it is a law common among men that we have the right to take vengeance on him who violently despoils us. And Jugurtha,
[321] according to Sallust, when he said that Adherbal had plotted [*Jugurtha*, xxii. 4.] against his life, added that the Roman people 'would act neither well nor justifiably if they should exclude him from this right allowed by universal common law', that is, from taking vengeance.

Aristides, the orator, declares that poets, legislators, proverbs, *For the Four* [*Platonic*, ii=p. 259]. and orators, in short all approve this, 'that vengeance should be taken upon those who have first assailed us'. Ambrose praises the Maccabees [2] because even on the Sabbath they avenged the death of *On Duties*, I. xl [196]. their innocent brethren.[3] Also, arguing against the Jews who complained bitterly that a synagogue had been burned by the Christians, he speaks thus : 'And assuredly, if I should act according to the *Letters*, xxix [xl. 15]. universal common law, I should state how many churches the Jews burned in the time of the reign of Julian.' Here he calls it the universal common law to repay like with like.[4] And from the same point of view Civilis, in Tacitus, says : 'As a noble reward for my *Histories*, IV [xxxii]. labour I received the death of my brother, my own bonds, and the most cruel demands of this army, calling for my execution ; from whom I demand punishment by the universal common law.'

4. But since in our private affairs and those of our kinsmen we are liable to partiality, as soon as numerous families were united at a common point judges were appointed, and to them alone was given the power to avenge the injured, while others are deprived of the freedom of action wherewith nature endowed them. Says Lucretius : [V. 1148–50.]

> For that each one in wrath prepared his own revenge,
> More bitter than our equal laws allow,
> The present age of men full weary is of force.

[350] [1] 'Murder has been atoned for by murder,' said Romulus on the slaughter of Tatius by the Laurentines, in Plutarch [*Romulus*, xxiii=32]. See also Plutarch on the ill-treatment of the Mantineans by the Achaians [*Aratus*, xlv=1048 D] : 'And these very actions contained in themselves the justification of vengeance.'

Belisarius in Procopius, *Vandalic War*, I [I. xvi. 5] : 'For the hostility of an injured man against him who has attacked him is a natural thing.'

[2] See also the same writer in his oration against Symmachus [*Letters*, xviii. 19 f.].

[3] See Josephus, *Antiquities of the Jews*, XIII. i, on the avenging of the death of John.

[4] So also Livy, I [I. xiv. 1] : 'Since the Laurentines acted in accordance with the law of nations.'

[liv. 19.] Likewise Demosthenes, in his oration *Against Conon*, declares: 'It has been agreed that justice for each of these wrongs should be found in the law, but not that they should be judged in accordance with [*Declamations*, xiii. 11.] individual anger and caprice.'[1] And Quintilian says: 'Personal requital of a wrong is not only hostile to law but also to peace; for there are laws, courts, judges, unless any one is ashamed to vindicate *Code*, I. ix. 14. himself by legal means.' The Emperors Honorius and Theodosius decided that 'the power of the courts and the guardianship of the public law is established for this purpose, that no one may be able Cassiodorus, *Letters*, IV. x. to grant himself the right of vengeance'. And King Theodoric wrote: 'To this end the sacred respect for the laws arose, that nothing might be done by violence, nothing by private passion.'

5. Nevertheless, the old natural liberty remains, especially in places where there are no courts, as, for example, on the sea. An example of this is perhaps the conduct of Julius Caesar. He, while yet a private citizen, with a hastily levied fleet pursued the pirates by whom he had been captured, sank some of their ships, and put the rest to flight. When the proconsul failed to punish the pirates who had been taken, he himself set out to sea and crucified them. Vel. Pat., II [xlii] and Plut., *Caes.* [ii= p. 708]. The same right will exist in desert places, or where men lead a nomadic life. Thus Nicholas of Damascus narrates that among the

[1] Tyndareus thus declaims against Orestes in Euripides, *Orestes* [lines 491–511]:

With this man here what question could there be of wisdom?
If to all apparent are both just and unjust ways,
What man was there more dull of wit than he,
Who saw not what was just,
Nor had recourse to Hellas' common law?
When Agamemnon forth did breathe his life
With cloven skull, beneath my daughter's hand—
A shameful deed, one I shall ne'er approve—
Then ought he to have taken the penalty of blood
In lawful vengeance, and from the house his mother
To have cast. So had he won a name for wisdom in his grief,
Held to the law, and pious still remained.
But now he shares his mother's plight,
For justly judging her to be unjust,
[351] By slaying her himself more wicked still was made.
And, Menelaus, thee I'll question thus:
If this man by his wedded wife be slain,
Who in her turn at his son's hand shall fall,
And next his child shall pay for death with death,
Where then shall be the end of all these woes?

These concluding words, full of wisdom, have afforded material for argument both to philosophers and to orators.

Maximus of Tyre, in his dissertation on retaliation [*Dissertations*, XVIII. vi], writes: 'For if the one who has been wronged avenges himself, the injustice will, as it were, pass with a bound from the one to the other, and injustice will follow upon injustice. If, granting this right, you permit him who has suffered ill to avenge himself on him who inflicted it, it follows that the right of vengeance will pass again from the former to the latter. For it is just that each should have an equal right. If this is so, O Zeus, what is this that thou hast done, that justice should consist in unjust acts? And whither will the evil lead, and where will it end?'

Aristides in his speech, *On Peace* [ii=p. 78]: 'For what Greek will survive if, for the sake of those who are already dead, others in turn shall continually meet the same end?' Aristides expresses a similar idea also in his second speech *On Leuctra*.

Umbrici[1] each man was his own avenger. This is true to-day among the Moschians, when a certain time has elapsed after the appeal to a judge. In Stobaeus, *On Laws* [X. lxx =frag. 7, p. 146, edit. Dindorf].

Herein is the origin of the duels which the Germanic tribes[2] employed before the Christian era and which they have not yet entirely given up. And so, according to Velleius Paterculus, the Germans marvelled when they saw the Roman form of administration of justice, because justice put an end to injuries, and what they were accustomed to decide by force was terminated by legal procedure. II [cxviii].

6. The Hebrew law permits a relative of a slain man to kill the slayer outside of places of asylum. [*Numbers*, xxxv. 19.] And Hebrew interpreters rightly note that retaliation may be made for a dead man by force; that, however, a man can only avenge himself, for a wound for example, through a judge, clearly because moderation is more difficult to observe where one's own suffering is concerned. Sen., *On Clemency*, I. cciii [I. xx].

From the words of Theoclymenus in [322] Homer, *Odyssey*, XV, [XV. 271 f.] it is clear that a similar custom of avenging death through private persons existed among the Greeks of very early times. But examples of this custom occur with especial frequency among those who have no common judicial authority. Hence, on the testimony of Augustine, 'just wars are customarily defined as those which avenge injuries'. *On Joshua*, VI, qu. x [*Heptat.*, VI. x]. Plato sanctions warlike measures 'until the guilty shall have been compelled to pay the penalty by those who have suffered innocently.' *Rep.*, XIV [V. xvi].

IX.—*Likewise for the good of the whole*

1. The good of mankind in general, which was the third object of punishment, involves the same problems as those presented by the good of one who has been wronged. For in this case the punishment may be inflicted to prevent the man who has injured one person from injuring others, which is accomplished by removing him or weakening him or restraining him so that he cannot do harm, or by reforming him. Or the punishment may be inflicted to prevent others from being induced by a feeling of security to annoy any persons whatsoever.[3] This is attained by the infliction of outstanding penalties, which the Greeks call *παραδείγματα*, the Romans *exempla*, 'examples'. These exemplary punishments are employed so that the punishment of one may cause many to fear, and that others may be frightened by

[1] Did he mean the Umbrians in Italy? Leo the African, Book II, in the chapter on the Tefechi, Teiguta, and elsewhere, testifies that the same custom prevailed among many peoples of Africa.

[2] King Theodoric, rebuking his Goths, said: 'Put off customs that are abominably outworn. Let a dispute be settled by words and not by arms,' in Cassiodorus, [*Variae*,] III. xxiii; and [III. xxiv] 'Why do you rush to the duel? What need has man of his tongue if his armed hand pleads his cause?' In Trachonitis in the East it is customary to avenge the death of kinsmen by every possible means [Josephus, *Antiquities of the Jews*, XVI. ix. 1].

[3] 'Polybius saw lions crucified for an attack on a man, so that others might be deterred from the same crime by fear of a like penalty'; Pliny, [*Natural History*,] Book VIII, chap. xvi.

Code, IX. xx. 7; IX. xxvii. 1. the nature of the punishment, as the laws say, or, according to Demosthenes, 'that others may learn wisdom and be afraid'. [*Orations*, lix. 77.]

2. And the possession of the right to punish for this purpose also, according to nature, may rest with any person whatever. Thus Plutarch[1] says that a good man is appointed by nature to be a magistrate and indeed a perpetual one; for by the very law of nature leadership is conferred on him who acts justly. Thus Cicero proves by the example of Nasica that no wise man can ever be a mere private citizen, and Horace calls Lollius 'a consul not limited to a single year'. Euripides in his *Iphigenia in Aulis* says:

Political Precepts [xxiii = p. 817 DE]. [*Tusc. Disp.*, IV. xxiii. 51.] [*Odes*, IV. ix. 39.] [Line 374.]

> He whose mind is strong in wisdom holds a magistracy.

Nevertheless, within the state these things must be interpreted with reference to its laws.

[In Stobaeus, xliv. 16–17.] 3. Concerning this law of nature Democritus, whose words I shall quote because they are important, speaks as follows: First, the question of the right to kill wild beasts presents itself to him in this way: 'In the matter of killing or not killing animals the situation is this: whoever has killed animals which actually do or desire to do harm is innocent, so much so indeed that to have done this is more justifiable than to have failed to do it.' And shortly after: 'It is absolutely necessary to kill all those things which unjustly do us harm.' And surely it is not improbable that good men lived in this fashion prior to the flood,[2] before God revealed His will to adapt to human nourishment other sorts of animals. Again he says: 'What we have written concerning foxes and poisonous reptiles, the same it seems should be done in the case of men also.' Then he continues: 'One is innocent who kills a robber or a thief in any way at all, either by his hand, or by his order, or by his vote.'

It seems to me that Seneca had these sayings in mind when he

[1] Likewise in his *Pelopidas* [xxiv = p. 290 C]: 'The first and as it seems most valid law designates as a natural magistrate him who is able to preserve those who have need to be saved'; and his *Philopoemen* [xii = p. 363 A]: 'He delivered his fellow citizens who did not wait for the time for legislation and election, but followed him on the ground that the stronger naturally rules the weaker.' We find the same idea at the close of his *Life of Titus Flamininus* [*Comp. of Philop. and Titus*, iii = p. 382 EF].

A writer on the causes of the decline of eloquence, [Tacitus,] *On Orators* [xxxvi. 5], says: 'Not even as private citizens did these men lack power, since they ruled both the people and the senate through their counsel and influence.'

Chrysostom, *On Second Corinthians*, vii. 13 [vii. 12 = Homily XV, iii], writes of Moses: [352] 'Even before he led out the people under his hand, he was their leader by virtue of his deeds themselves. So it was extremely foolish when the Jew asked him "Who appointed thee as a ruler and a judge over us?" What sayest thou? Thou seest the deeds and thou dost dispute about the name, as if some one seeing a physician skilfully operating and thus benefiting a diseased limb of the body should say to him, "Who appointed thee a physician, who bade thee to operate?" "My art, my good man, and thy disease." In like manner the skill of Moses gave him such power. For ruling is not merely a dignity, but also an art, and indeed the most exalted of all arts.'

Chrysostom also employs this same argument, *On Ephesians*, iii, end [Homily VII, iv]: 'Thy injustice,' he says, 'and thy savagery have made me thy ruler and thy judge.'

[2] And others afterward who remembered the primaeval custom; according to Dicaearchus and others cited in testimony by Jerome, *Against Jovinianus* [II. xiii].

said: 'When I order the neck of a guilty man to be severed, I am of the same countenance and mind as when I transfix reptiles and poisonous animals.'[1] And elsewhere: 'We would not slay even vipers and adders and other creatures which harm by bite or sting, if only we could tame them for the future, or render them innocuous to ourselves and others. Therefore, we will not harm a man because he has sinned, but to prevent him from sinning.'

On Anger, II [I. xvi. 5]. [II. xxxi. 8.]

4. But since both the inquiry into the fact often demands great care and the evaluation of the punishment requires much prudence and fairness, to prevent strife arising from each man claiming too much for himself, while others refuse to yield, in communities animated by a sense of right men have agreed [323] to select as arbiters those who they think are the best and wisest, or hope will prove to be such. So Democritus: 'The laws would not have prevented each man from living according to his own judgement, had not one been wont to abuse another. For envy marks the beginning of civil strife.'

[In Stobaeus, xxxviii. 57.]

5. But as we just now remarked in the case of vengeance, so too in the matter of this punishment, as an example, traces and survivals of primitive right persist in those places and among those persons who are subject to no fixed tribunals, and in some other exceptional cases. For instance, according to Jewish customs the Jew who fell away from God and the law of God, and made himself a leader in false worships, could be killed at once by any person whatsoever.[2]

Deut., xiii. 9.

The Jews call this the judgement of zeal,[3] which they say was first exercised by Phineas and thence became a custom. Likewise Mathatias slew a certain Jew for defiling himself with Greek rites. Similarly, three hundred other Jews are said to have been killed by

Numbers, [xxv. 7 ff.].

2 Macc. [*I Maccabees*, ii. 25].

[1] 'Therefore just as we kill vipers and scorpions and other poisonous creatures, at once, without delay, before they bite or wound us or make any attempt against us, anticipating our suffering any harm from the evil that is in them; in the same way it is right to punish men also, who, although they are endowed with a kindly disposition through reason which is the basis of society, in their habits have assumed the cruelty of wild beasts, and take pleasure and profit from injuring as many as they can.' Thus Philo, *On Special Laws*, II [III. xviii].

Claudius of Naples, in Porphyry, *On Abstaining from Animal Food*, I [I. xiv], said; 'There is no one who does not kill, if he can, a serpent he has seen, to prevent it wounding either himself or another.' See also, if at leisure, the following, a little further on [I. xx]: 'We kill a snake and a scorpion, even if they do not set upon us, to prevent them from injuring another, and thus we defend the common interests of mankind.'

Porphyry himself says in Book II [II. xxii]: 'For just as, although we have a certain community with evil men who are driven by a certain innate spirit of wickedness, as if by a violent wind, to injure anyone at all, we believe that it is right for us to punish all such, so, consequently, it is not without reason to kill those dumb animals which are naturally unjust and dangerous, and which are impelled by their nature to rush upon whomever they meet [353] to do them harm.' This is also the view of Pythagoras, according to Ovid, *Metamorphoses*, XV [XV. 108–9]:

Bodies that seek our harm
Are sent to death, we grant, full righteously.

[2] See also the passage in Josephus, XII. 8 [XII. vi. 2]; also Moses Maimonides, *On the XIII Articles*, and *Guide of the Perplexed*, III. xli.

[3] See *I Maccabees*, ii. 24, 26.

their fellow countrymen, in the book which is commonly called *Third Maccabees.* Upon the same ground occurred the stoning of Stephen and the conspiracy against Paul; and numerous examples of this custom are to be found in Philo[1] and in Josephus.

Acts, vii. 57; xxiii. 13.

6. Furthermore, among many peoples the full right of punishment, even unto death, continued to be exercised by masters over their slaves and parents over their children. Thus at Sparta the Ephors could kill a man without trial.

From this discussion one may understand the character of the law of nature in regard to punishments and the extent to which it still persists.

X.—*What the law of the Gospel has established in this matter*

1. Now we must see whether the law of the Gospel has more narrowly restricted freedom of action in this regard. Surely, as we have said elsewhere, it is not strange that some things which are permissible according to nature and by municipal law are forbidden by divine law, since this is most perfect and sets forth a reward greater than human nature; to obtain this reward there are justly demanded virtues which surpass the bare precepts of nature.

[II. I. 10. I.]

From the very nature of the case it is sufficiently clear that punishments[2] which leave neither loss of reputation nor permanent injury, and which are necessary by reason of the age or another characteristic of the person punished, provided that they are inflicted by those who have the right to inflict them according to the laws of men, as by parents, guardians, masters or teachers, are in no way contrary to the teachings of the Gospel. For these are remedies of the mind which are as harmless as unpalatable drugs.

2. With vengeance the situation is far different. For we have shown above that in so far as it merely gratifies the spirit of the sufferer it is unlawful even according to nature, and in so far does it fail to harmonize with the Gospel. Moreover, the Hebraic law not only forbids hatred to be cherished against a neighbour, that is a fellow countryman (*Leviticus*, xix. 17), but also provides that certain common kindnesses be shown to enemies of this sort (*Exodus*, xxiii. 4, 5). Therefore, since the Gospel has extended the conception of neighbour to include all men, it is obviously required of us not only

[II. xx. 5.]

[1] He speaks thus in *On Those Who Offer Sacrifices* [xi]: 'Such a one is to be punished as a public and common enemy; little heed must be taken of kinship with him, his beliefs must be published abroad by all who love piety, so that men may run from all sides without delay to exact punishment from the impious man, firmly believing that this desire to slay him is a holy thing.' There is another equally noteworthy passage near the end of his *On Monarchy* [vii].

[2] 'It is sinful not to check the sins of slaves and children', says Lactantius, *On the Anger of God*, xviii, where there is more on this topic.

not to injure our enemies but even to do them good, as is plainly enjoined in the Gospel of *Matthew* (v. 44).

Nevertheless, the law allowed the Jews to avenge the more serious injuries, although not by force but by recourse to a judge. However, Christ does not allow us this privilege, as is clear from the contrast presented in the passage commencing 'You have heard that it has been said an eye for an eye', and what follows, 'But I say unto you.' For although His words that follow properly deal with the prevention of injury and [324] somewhat restrict freedom in this respect also, yet they are still more to be taken as censuring revenge, because they reject the old permission as befitting a less perfect age; [1] 'not because vengeance that is justly taken is unjust but because patience is preferable to it', as the reason is stated in the *Constitutions* of Clement, Book VII, chap. xxiii [VI. xxiii].

3. On this point Tertullian expresses himself thus: [2]

> Christ clearly teaches a new kind of patience, since He even prohibits the return for injury that was permitted by the Creator in requiring an eye for an eye and a tooth for a tooth, while He himself on the contrary commands rather to offer the other cheek and to give the coat in addition to the cloak. Clearly Christ has added these injunctions as supplementary, in harmony with the teaching of the Creator. Therefore we must immediately determine whether the discipline of patience is enjoined by the Creator. Verily through Zacharias He taught that no one should remember his brother's wrong or that of his neighbour. And further: 'Let no one', He says, 'brood over his neighbour's malice.' Much more then has He ordained us to be patient under wrong, who ordained us to forgetfulness of it. And when He said, 'Vengeance is mine and I will repay,' He thereby teaches the patience that waits for the infliction of vengeance.
>
> Therefore, inasmuch as it is impossible that the same one should seem to exact a tooth for a tooth, an eye for an eye in return for injury, and at the same time forbid not only vengeance but even the remembrance and recollection of injury, it is made plain to us in what sense He required an eye for an eye, and a tooth for a tooth; that is, in order not to allow a second injury as retaliation, which He had prohibited by forbidding vengeance, but to check the first wrong which He had prohibited by the appointment of a penalty, so that each one out of regard to the freedom of the second injury would restrain himself from committing the first. For He knows that violence is more easily restrained by making clear the immediate prospect of retaliation than by a general promise of vengeance. Now, in consideration of the nature and faith of men,

[1] 'An eye for an eye [. . .], which, if one may say so, is the justice of the unjust', says Augustine, in the exposition of Psalm cviii, cited in the *Decretum*, II. xxiii. 3. 1.

[2] *Against Marcion*, IV [IV. xvi]. He says also in *On Patience* [vi]: 'Christ while adding grace to enlarge the law appointed His patience as an aid in fulfilling the law, because this alone had previously been lacking in the doctrine of justice.'

Chrysostom, *On Ephesians*, iv. 13 [iv. 31 = Homily XVI, iii]: 'For this reason He said "an eye for an eye, a tooth for a tooth," to bind the hand of the aggressor, not to raise your hands against him; not only to secure your eyes from harm but also to preserve his in safety. But what I was asking was this, why, if vengeance is permitted, are they held guilty who have recourse to it?' And shortly after: 'God pardons those, whom perchance a feeling of insult has carried away and anger has led to take revenge. For this He said, "an eye for an eye"; but elsewhere, "the ways of the wrathful [lead] unto death". But if the penalty for the wrathful is so great when it was permitted to pluck out an eye for an eye, how much greater will it be for those who, having suffered evils, are bidden to offer themselves to further injuries.'

each provision had to be established, so that he who believed in God would await vengeance from God, while he who had less faith would fear the laws prescribing retaliation.

4. This purpose of the law, which was hard to understand, was revealed and made intelligible by Christ as the Lord of the Sabbath and of the law and of all His Father's dispensations, when He bade us to offer the other cheek also, to the end that the more effectually He might extinguish the return for an injury, which the law had wished to check by retaliation and which prophecy had openly restrained both by prohibiting us to remember wrong and by reclaiming vengeance for God. And so whatever teaching Christ introduced, not in opposition to the law but supplementary to it, did not destroy the rules of conduct laid down by the Creator. Finally, if we look to the very reason for ordaining patience, and especially such full and perfect patience, it will not hold good if it does not come from the Creator, who promises vengeance, who holds the position of judge.

Otherwise, if He is not going to defend me, who has placed upon me so great a burden of patience not only in not returning blow for blow but also in offering the other cheek, and not only in not answering abuse with abuse but even with blessing, and not only in not retaining my coat but further of yielding my cloak also, He has ordained patience in vain; for He has not revealed to me the reward of obedience to His command, I mean the fruit of such patience; for there is vengeance, which He ought to have permitted to me if He himself did not guarantee it, or He himself should guarantee it if He did not entrust it to me, since it is to the interest of discipline also that injury should be avenged. By fear of vengeance, in fact, every iniquity is held in check. But vengeance will gain complete control if licence is accorded to it—it will pluck out both eyes and knock out every tooth as a result of immunity from punishment.

5. As we see, Tertullian thinks not only that Christians are forbidden to demand retaliation but that not even the Jews are allowed it, even although it contains nothing vicious, that a greater evil may be avoided. That this view is right in the case of such a demand arising from hatred is not to be doubted, as the foregoing proves. For that was disapproved of even [325] by those of outstanding wisdom among the Jews, who regarded not merely the letter of the law but its spirit also. This appears in Philo, who makes the Jews of Alexandria on the occasion of the fall of Flaccus, the persecutor of the Jews, speak thus: 'We do not rejoice, Sir, in taking revenge upon an enemy, for we have been taught by our holy laws to have compassion upon men.'[1]

[*Against Flaccus*, xiv.]

This is the force of what Christ demands from us all without exception, that we forgive all who have sinned against us (*Matthew*, vi. 14, 15). That is, we ought not to procure or wish for evil to others because we feel that we have suffered evil. For he who does this, to speak with Claudian, 'is a cruel man and seems to claim for himself the vengeance of the laws.' Therefore, Lactantius, recalling the statement of Cicero: 'It is the first task of justice to see that no one injures another unless he has been provoked by a wrong,' says that this simple and true statement is spoiled by the addition of two words.

[*On the Cons. of Manlius Theod.*, 224 f.] [*Div. Inst.*,] VI. xviii. [*On Duties*, I. vii. 20.]

[1] See Origen, *Against Celsus* [VII. xxv].

Ambrose declares that this sentence of Cicero's lacks the sanction of the Gospel. *On Duties*, xxviii [I. xxviii. 131].

6. What then shall we say of revenge, not as a retaliation for the past, but as a preventive for the future? Clearly Christ wishes us to forgo this also; first, if he who has wronged us shows acceptable proofs of repentance,[1] as in *Luke*, xvii. 3, where there is question of an even fuller pardon, that is, one which would restore the sinner to the right of his former friendship, whence it follows that nothing is to be demanded of him by way of punishment; and second, even if signs of such repentance are lacking, by His doctrine of the surrender of the coat Christ teaches that we must not consider the wrong to be excessively serious. *Ephesians*, iv. 32. *Colossians*, iii. 13.

Plato too said that wrong must not be repaid 'even if we have to suffer worse things than before'. The same is the opinion of Maximus of Tyre. Musonius declared that he would not institute, or advise any one to institute, an 'action for insult', that is an action for the sake of some insult that had been received, such as Christ refers to in mentioning a blow on the cheek; for such things are more rightly pardoned. [*Crito*, x.]

7. But if self-restraint involves great danger we ought to be satisfied with the precaution that does the least possible harm. For not even among the Jews was revenge customary, according to Josephus and other learned Jews, but the man who had been wronged was accustomed to accept monetary payment[2] in the place of retaliation, in addition to such expenses as he had been forced to incur, with regard to which there is a law in *Exodus*, xxi. 19. The payment is a simple restitution without penalty;[3] there was also a Roman custom, as Favorinus says in Gellius. [*Antiquities of the Jews*, IV. viii. 35.] [*Attic Nights*,] XX. i.

Accordingly, Joseph, guardian of our Lord Jesus, when he believed that his wife was guilty of adultery, preferred to divorce her[4] rather than to prosecute her. And he is said to have done this because he was a just man, that is, upright and merciful. On this point Ambrose says that 'the nature of a just man is foreign not only to the cruelty of vengeance but also to the harshness of accusation'.[5] Before him, again, Lactantius had said: 'Neither will a just man be allowed to accuse anyone for a capital crime.' Justin,[6] dealing with the accusers of the Christians, says: 'We do not wish to punish those [*On Psalm CXVIII*, sermo vii, no. 24.] [*Div.Inst.*,] VI. x [VI. xx. 16].

[1] See Moses Maimonides cited by the learned [Emperor] Constantine, *De Damno Dato*, viii. 7.

[2] *Law of the Visigoths*, VI. 13 [VI. iv. 3].

[354] [3] See Constantine, cited above, [*De Damno Dato*,] viii. 1.

[4] [*Matthew*, i. 19.] Augustine in Book II of his *De Adulterinis Conjugiis* [II. xv]: 'If indeed, as is said with greater truth, a Christian may not kill his adulterous wife, but only put her away.'

[5] See Hincmar, *De Divortio*, v. fin., *Decretum*, II. ii. 7. 5, and Panormitanus thereon. Gail, *De Pace Publica*, viii. 3. Also see *Decretals*, V. i. 8, as it is in Burchard.

[6] [*Apology*, I. vii.] He also says [*Dialogue with Trypho*, xviii=516 B]: 'Having no desire to requite even a slight injury upon anyone, as our new Lawgiver has ordained.' See also II. xx. 15, below.

who speak evil of us. Their own baseness and ignorance of what is good is punishment enough.'

8. Finally, we have to consider punishments inflicted, not for the good of an individual, but for the public good; partly by removing the wrong-doer or by restraining him from doing harm, partly by deterring others through the severity of punishment as an example.

Elsewhere we have proved beyond question that Christ did not abolish these punishments, because while laying down His own instructions [326] He testified that He did not cancel anything in the law. Moreover, the law of Moses, which in these matters was to last as long as the state itself, strictly ordered the magistrates to punish homicide and certain other crimes (*Exodus*, xxi. 14; *Numbers*, xxxiii. 14, 37 [xxxv. 16–34]; *Deuteronomy*, xxix. 13 [xix. 13]). But if the teachings of Christ could accord with the law of Moses in so far as the latter demanded even capital punishment [1] they can also be in accord with human laws which imitate the divine law in this respect.[2]

XI.—*The answer to the argument drawn from the mercy of God revealed in the Gospel*

1. In order to defend the opposite point of view some cite the exceeding great mildness of God in the New Covenant, which men are thereby obliged to imitate, even when magistrates, as being vicars of God.

Although we do not deny that there is truth in this to a certain extent, it does not apply so widely as they claim. For the great mercy of God revealed in the New Covenant concerns especially sins against the primeval law, or even against the law of Moses committed before men had knowledge of the Gospel (*Acts*, xvii. 36 [xvii. 30]; *Romans*, ii. 25; *Acts*, xiii. 38; *Hebrews*, ix. 15). For the sins committed subsequently, especially if in a spirit of contempt, are threatened with a judgement much more severe than that which was prescribed by Moses (*Hebrews*, ii. 23; iv–x. 29 [ii. 2, 3; x. 29]; *Matthew*, v. 21, 22, 28).[3] Nor is it only in the other life, but in this life also that God often punishes such offences (*1 Corinthians*, xi. 30). And pardon for such sins is not usually obtained, unless a man should in a sense exact punishment from himself (*1 Corinthians*, xi. 3) [4] through deep sorrow of heart (*2 Corinthians*, ii. 27 [ii. 7]).

[1] Josephus [*Antiquities of the Jews*, XIII. x. 6] praises the 'moderation' of the Pharisees with regard to punishments. Hence come so many exceptions to the laws concerning punishments for public offences, and the rule that when death is actually to be inflicted this must be done as humanely as possible; this as is stated in the Talmud, title *Ketuboth*.

[2] Augustine, *Evangelical Questions*, Book I, qu. x.

[3] The same view is found in Chrysostom, in the oration *To the Believing Father* [chap. iii], and the second homily *On Fasting* [*On Penitence*, VI. v].

[4] 'The sinner must weep for himself before he obtains pardon,' Tertullian, *On Penitence* [vi].

2. The same persons urge that freedom from punishment must be accorded at least to those who have been induced to repent. But passing over the fact that it is scarcely possible for men to agree on the matter of true repentance, and that there is no one who would not obtain immunity for his crimes if it were enough for him merely to profess repentance in any chance fashion, God Himself does not always remit the full punishment to those who have been brought to penitence. This is clear from the example of David. Therefore, just as God was able to remit the punishment of the law, that is a violent or otherwise untimely death, so that He might afflict him who had sinned with evils by no means easy to bear, in like manner now He is able to remit the penalty of eternal death and at the same time Himself to punish the sinner by an untimely death,[1] or even to permit him to be punished in this way by a magistrate. Synesius, *Letters*, xliv.

XII.—*Answer to the argument drawn from the exclusion of repentance*

1. Again, others attack punishment on this ground, that with the taking away of life the opportunity for repentance is likewise removed. But they know that upright magistrates take serious account of this matter, and that no one is hurried to execution without having time to acknowledge his sins and seriously abhor them. The example of the thief crucified with Christ proves that repentance of this kind, even if it cannot be followed by good works which are precluded by death,[2] may be accepted by God.

But if it should be said that a longer life would have been advantageous to a more serious reformation one may reply that sometimes there are found those to whom may be applied fittingly the saying of Seneca[3]: 'We shall bestow on you death, the only good thing that still awaits you,' as also this other remark of his, 'that they may cease to be bad men, in the only way in which this is possible for them'. This Eusebius the philosopher had expressed thus: 'Since they can do so in no other way, let them then set themselves free in this manner from the present bondage of evil and procure for themselves a means of escape.' *On Anger*, I. xvi. [*On Anger*, I.] xv. [In Stobaeus, xlvi. 41.]

2. Therefore let these things, in addition to what we have said at the opening of our work, be an answer to those who claim that punishments, whether of all kinds, or merely capital punishments, are without exception prohibited for Christians. The Apostle teaches [I. ii. 9. 4 and iii. 3. 2.]

Ambrose, *On Psalm XXXVII*; Chrysostom, *On First Corinthians*, Homily XXVIII [XXVIII. ii], and *On Matthew*, Homily XLII [XLII. iii]. Cf. *2 Corinthians*, vii. 9 and 10.

[1] Jerome, *On Nahum*, chap. i, a passage cited in *Decretum*, II. xxiii. 5. Agathias, V [V. iv], quoting Plato.

[2] Jerome, *To Damasus*, cited in the *Decretum*, II. xxxiii. 3. 1. 58.

[3] He says also, *On Benefits*, VII. x [VII. xx]: 'The end of life is the cure for such natures, and it is the best thing for him to meet who will never return to his senses'; and 'with the same hand I shall bestow a favour upon all; I shall bestow it even upon him, since the end of life is a cure for such natures.'

us the contrary, by including the use of the sword in the royal office [327] as a symbol of divine vengeance, and elsewhere saying that we are to pray that kings may become Christians and by virtue of their office be a protection to the innocent. Owing to the wickedness of a great part of mankind even after the Gospel has been spread abroad, this result can only be obtained if the boldness of the rest is checked by the death of some offenders, especially since the innocent are scarcely safe even when there are so many capital punishments inflicted.

3. Nevertheless, it will be profitable for Christian rulers, at least in some measure, to set before themselves for imitation the example of Sabaco, king of Egypt [1], most famous for his uprightness, who, according to Diodorus, changed capital punishments into condemnations to hard labour, with most fortunate results.

I [lxv].

Strabo says that even among some of the peoples of the Caucasus 'they put no one to death even for the most severe crimes'. Nor should we scorn the saying of Quintilian: 'No one will doubt that, if guilty men can be reformed in any way, as is agreed may sometimes occur, it is of more advantage to the state to save them than to punish them.' Balsamon notes that the Roman laws which formerly proclaimed the punishment of death were in many cases altered by later Christian Emperors [2] so as to prescribe other penalties,[3] so that in this way repentance might be forced upon the condemned more sharply and the longer punishment might better serve as an example.

XI [xi. 8]. [*Inst. Orat.*] XII. i. [42]. [*On Photius, Nomocanon,* xvi. 5.]

XIII.—*A rejection of incomplete classifications of punishments*

1. In the enumeration which we have made of the purposes of punishment something seems to have been overlooked by Taurus the philosopher, whom Gellius quotes as follows:

[VII. xiv. 4.]

> And so whenever there is either great hope that he who has sinned will voluntarily correct himself without punishment; or whenever, on the contrary, there is no hope of his being better and corrected; or whenever there is no need to fear a diminution of the dignity which has been sinned against; or whenever no sin has been committed which must be remedied by fear as a necessary example, then whatever sin has been committed does not seem worthy of the effort to impose a penalty upon it.

Here he speaks as if punishment is done away with when one purpose of punishment is removed, although on the contrary all the

[1] And in great measure that of the Romans also, none of whom after the Porcian Law could be executed or scourged except for treason or when condemned by the people themselves.

[2] See below, II. xxiv. 2. See the oath of Isaac Angelus in Nicetas, [*On Isaac Angelus,*] I [I. iv]. Nicetas says also that in the reign of John Comnenus no one was executed [*On John Comnenus,* xii]. Cf. Malchus, *On Zeno* [*Selections on Embassies,* iv], and Augustine, *Letters,* clviii and clix [cxxxix and cxxxiii], *To Count Marcellinus,* cited in the *Decretum,* II. xxiii. 5. 1 ff.; also Chrysostom, oration *Against the Jews,* V [VIII. ii], on the punishment of Cain.

[3] Especially labour. Augustine, *Letters,* clx [cxxxiv. 4]: [355] 'Let their sound limbs serve some useful task.' See also the letter of Nectarius to Augustine, which is cci [xc].

purposes should be removed, so that there be no occasion for punishment. Then he omits the purpose effected by the removal of a man whose manner of life is incurable, to prevent his committing other or more serious crimes. What he says with regard to loss of dignity, moreover, must be extended to other losses which are to be feared.

2. With more justice Seneca said: 'In punishing injuries the law has aimed at these three things, which the Prince ought also to aim at; they are either to reform him whom it punishes, or to make others better by his punishment,[1] or by removing evil men to permit the rest to live in greater safety.' For here, if you understand by 'the rest' both those who have already been wronged and those who may be wronged hereafter, you have a complete division of the matter, except that to 'remove' you must add 'or restrain'. For either imprisonment or any other means of limiting their power has the same result. *On Clemency*, I. xxi [I. xxii].

The following division which Seneca himself makes in another place is less complete: 'This he will keep in view always in inflicting punishments of every sort, that one kind of punishment is applied to reform the bad, another kind to remove them.' Somewhat more incomplete still is the saying of Quintilian: 'Every punishment has reference not so much to the crime as to the example.' *On Anger*, I. ult. [I. xix. 7]. [*Declamations*, cclxxiv. end.]

XIV.—*It is not safe for Christians, as private citizens, to exact punishment, even when universal common law allows it*

From what we have said up to this point one may gather how unsafe it is for a Christian in a private capacity to exact punishment, especially capital punishment, from any wicked person whatsoever,[2] either for his own or for the public good, although we have said that this is sometimes allowed by universal common law.[3] It is, therefore, a praiseworthy custom on the part of those peoples among whom those who are about to set sail receive warrants, by the public authority, to destroy whatever pirates [328] they discover on the sea; so that if the occasion offers they may be able to act as public servants and not upon their own initiative.

XV.—*Neither should Christians of their own accord be too zealous in making accusations*

In harmony with the foregoing is the widely current opinion, that not any and every person should be allowed to bring accusations

[1] These two objects are also stated by Philo, *On the Embassy*, [i]: 'Because punishment frequently reforms and corrects even the one who has sinned; and even if it fails in this, at any rate it affects others, to whose attention it comes.; For the punishments of others make many better through fear of a similar penalty.' [2] See above, I. iii. 3. [3] II. xx. 8.

for crimes,[1] but that there should be certain persons upon whom this task is laid by the public authorities. The purpose is that no one may do anything toward shedding another's blood except by the necessity of his office.

Can. 73.] This is the object of the canon of the Synod of Seville, which ordains: 'If any of the faithful appears as an informer, and through his deposition any one is proscribed or put to death, he is forbidden to receive the communion even when dying.'

XVI.—*Nor should Christians seek the office of criminal judge*

Likewise, it may be perceived from the preceding that it is by no means advisable, and not even becoming, for a man who is truly a Christian to enter of his own accord upon a public office which may have to decide upon the shedding of blood,[2] and to think and profess that it is right that the power of life and death over his fellow citizens be conferred upon himself, as if he were the most exalted of them all and a sort of god among men. For surely here applies absolutely the warning of Christ that it is a dangerous thing to pass judgement upon others, because in like cases we must ourselves expect from God the judgement we have meted out to others.

Matthew, vii. 1.

XVII.—*The distinction between human laws which confer the right to kill as a punishment and those which merely give impunity for such action*

1. It is no unimportant question whether the laws of men which permit the execution of certain persons confer upon the executioners a true right even in the eyes of God, or merely freedom from retribution among men. The latter point of view is supported by Covarruvias and Fortunius, whose opinion, however, is so displeasing to Fernando Vázquez that he calls it accursed. There is no doubt, as we have said also elsewhere, that in certain cases the law can confer either power. And which one it does confer must be gathered partly from the substance. For if the law gives play to resentment it gives immunity from human punishment, but not from sin, as in the case of a husband who kills an adulterous wife or an adulterer.[3]

Covar., *De Matrim.*, II. vii, no. 8. Fortunius, *De Ultima Fine Legum*, illat. ii. Vázquez, *Controversiae Illustres*, IV. viii. [II. i. 14; iii. 3. 2.]

2. But if the law regards the danger of subsequent harm arising from deferring the punishment, it must be considered as conferring

[1] Chrysostom, *On Penitence*, VIII [VIII. ii, ed. Migne, vol. VIII, p. 759]: 'Therefore it is a good thing, as I have said, to anticipate private suits by friendly settlements, so that you may guide your friend to this goal of the action. However, as to public accusations, I shall not advocate breaking them off by reaching a settlement, but never commencing them.'

[2] As to whether a wise man should enter public life, see Seneca, *On the Leisure of the Wise Man*.

[3] See Augustine, *City of God* [rather, partly Jerome, *On Ezekiel*, ix, and partly an unknown writer], cited in the *Decretum*, II. xxiii. 8. 33. Cf. also the *Decretum*, II. xxxiii. 2. 6 and 7.

upon a private individual both right and public authority, so that he is no longer in a mere private capacity.

Such a law is the one in Justinian's *Code*, under the rubric 'When it is lawful for any one without recourse to a judge to execute judgement for himself or for the public service', where permission is given to any one at all to repress by punishment soldiers engaged in plundering. The following reason is given: 'For it is better to intervene in time than to seek justice after the damage has been inflicted. Therefore we allow you to take vengeance for yourselves, and because it is a serious thing to punish even by virtue of a judicial decision we have subjoined in the edict, that no one shall spare a soldier whom he ought to oppose with arms as a robber.' [*Code*, III. xxvii. 1.]

A similar law, again, is the one which follows, dealing with the suppression of deserters, which says: 'Let all men know that against public robbers and deserters from military service they have been granted the right to exercise public vengeance for the common peace.' The remark of Tertullian is here in point: 'Against traitors and public enemies every man is a soldier.' [1] [*Apology*, ii.]

3. But the right of killing exiles, whom we call outlaws, differs from laws of this type, because in that case we have to do with a particular sentence, but here with a general edict which, when evidence of the fact appears,[2] gains the force of a judicial sentence.

XVIII.—*Internal acts are not punishable by men*

Now let us consider this, whether all vicious actions are such as to be punishable by men.

We must consider it as definitely established that they are not all of such a kind. For, in the first place, purely internal acts, even if they should come to the attention of others by some chance, as by subsequent confession, cannot be punished by men, because, as we have said before, [329] it is not in accord with human nature that a right or an obligation should arise among men from purely internal acts. And in this sense we must take the teaching of the Roman laws, that 'No one deserves to be punished for his thoughts'. However, this does not prevent internal acts, in so far as they influence external ones,[3] from being taken into consideration, not on their own account, but in the light of the external actions which receive from them the quality of their desert. [II. iv. 3.]

[1] Agathias, IV [IV. x]: 'For not only should the aim of well-doing be born and dwell in generals and other persons of influence, but it is possible and fitting for every one who wishes to be stirred by the evils of that state to which he belongs, and to promote the public advantage to the limit of his ability.' See also II. xx. 9, above.

[2] Quintilian, *Declamations*, cclx: 'There are certain wrongs done to the state for the recognition of which the evidence of our eyes is sufficient.'

[3] So Sayrus, *Thesaurus*, III. vi.

XIX.—*Extrinsic acts which human frailty cannot avoid are not punishable by men*

[Hier., in *Golden Verse*, = p. 192 Needh.] [Sen., *Cont.*, II. iv. 4.] [Thuc., III. xlv.] *On Anger*, II. xxxi. [Stobaeus, xlvi. 59.] XIII [xxi]. XVII [xxxviii].

1. In the second place, actions inevitable to human nature cannot be punished by men. For although one cannot sin except one does so of one's own will, nevertheless the total and perpetual abstinence from all sin is a condition that is more than human. Therefore, the belief that it is natural for man to sin has been expressed by the philosophers Sopater, Hierocles, Seneca, and Philo among Jewish writers,[1] the historian Thucydides, and very many Christian writers.

'If', said Seneca,[2] 'every one must be punished who has a base and malicious nature, no one will avoid punishment.' Moreover, Sopater said: 'If any one should punish men on the basis of complete freedom from sin, he oversteps the natural limits of correction.' This Diodorus the Sicilian[3] calls 'to sin against the common weakness of mankind', and, in another place, 'to forget the infirmity that is human and common to all'. Sopater, whom I have mentioned above, says that we must overlook 'the small and habitual sins'.

2. Indeed, one may doubt whether such things are rightly and properly called sins, since they lack, when considered in general, the freedom of action which they seem to have in particular instances. Plutarch in his *Solon* says: 'The law should be drawn up with a view to what is possible, if it aims to punish a few advantageously, and not punish many without advantage.' [xxi = p. 90 A.]

There are also certain actions which are not inevitable to human nature itself, but to a particular person at a particular time, because of a bodily condition which influences his mind,[4] or because of a mature habit. Such actions are wont to be punished not so much

[1] *On the Life of Moses*, III [III. xvii]. One may add Aben = Ezra, *On Job*, v. 7; and Rabbi Israel, viii.

[2] He says also, in chap. xiv of the same book, *On Anger* [I. xiv]: 'There is found none who could acquit himself.' In chap. ix [II. x] he says: 'Among the other disadvantages of mortality there is also this mental blindness, which is not so much the necessity of erring as a love of error.' Later, chap. xxvii [II. xxviii]: 'Who is he who claims that he is innocent before all laws?'; and in Book III, chap. xx [III. xxvi]: 'We are all evil.'

Again [Seneca], *On Clemency*, I. viii [I. vi]: 'We all have sinned; some more seriously, some more lightly, some with premeditation, some through impulse, or influenced by the wickedness of others; some of us have failed to abide boldly by our good counsels, and [356] against our will and endeavour have lost our innocence. We have not only sinned but we shall sin to the end of time. Even if any one has so cleansed his mind that nothing further can disturb him or deceive him, nevertheless it is through sin that he has arrived at innocence.'

Procopius, in the speech of Belisarius, *Gothic War*, III [III. xi], says: 'Complete freedom from sin is not a human characteristic nor in accord with the order of nature.' Compare the Emperor Basil, [*Paraeneticon ad Leonem Filium*,] chap. l.

[3] Also in the fragments [*Selections*, XXVI. i]: 'One must not defame the weakness of human nature.'

[4] Seneca, *On Anger*, II. xviii [II. xix]: 'A mixture of elements produces varieties of character, and men's natures incline to different characters according to the predominance of this or that element.' In another place he says that these things are due to the condition of birth and bodily temperament; *Letters*, xi [xi. 6].

for their own sake as on account of the guilt that precedes them,[1] because either the remedies therefor have been neglected, or corrupt thoughts have willingly been received into the mind.

XX.—*Acts by which human society is not injured, directly or indirectly, are not punishable by men. The explanation thereof*

1. In the third place we are not to punish sins which neither directly nor indirectly affect human society or a fellow man. The reason is that there is no cause for not leaving such sins to be punished by God, who is most wise in perceiving them, most just in judging them, and most able to requite them. For men, therefore, to institute punishment for such acts would be clearly futile, and consequently inadequate.

From this broad statement we must except corrective punishments, the purpose of which is to improve the sinner, even although perhaps this does not concern others. And further, we are not to punish actions which are contrary to the virtues in regard to which nature rejects all compulsion, such as mercy, liberality, and gratitude.

2. Seneca discusses this problem, whether the fault of an ungrateful man ought to go unpunished; and he advances many arguments why it ought not to be punished. His chief argument, which may be extended to other similar problems, is this: 'Since it is a most honourable thing to show gratitude, it ceases to be honourable if it is compulsory,' that is, it loses its high degree of honour, as is shown by the following words: 'For no one will praise the grateful man any more than him who has restored a deposit, [330] or one who has paid what he owed without being sued.' Further: 'To show gratitude is not a glorious thing, unless it is safe to remain ungrateful.'[2] *On Benefits*, III. vi and vii.

To faults of this sort we may apply the saying of Seneca the Father, in his *Controversies*: 'I do not desire the accused to be praised, but to be acquitted.'[3]

XXI.—*A refutation of the view that pardon is never permissible*

We must next consider whether it is permissible at times to forgive or to excuse.

[1] See *Decretum*, II. xv. 1. 9.

[2] Also, *On Benefits*, I. i: 'And so surely it is shameful not to repay (kindnesses) even if one does not have to.' Seneca the Father says, *Controversies*, V. xxxiv [= X. v. 15]: 'You tell me it is not necessary to do this; but a high evaluation is set upon this thing, and so there is no punishment for not doing it.'

Augustine, *Against Petilianus*, II. lxxxiii [II. lxxxiii. 184]: 'And so for this purpose laws have been established against you; you are not thereby compelled to act rightly, but you are prevented from doing wrong.'

[3] This is in *Controversies*, IV. xxiii [X. iv. 11]. A similar idea is found in IV. xxiv [=IX. ii. 19]: 'We do not hope that he will approve, but that he will pardon.' Also in *Excerpts*, vi. 8: 'There is a great difference between censure and punishment.' For, as Plutarch says in his *Cimon* [ii = p. 480 A], there are certain things which are 'omissions of virtue rather than crimes arising from a vice'.

[Stobaeus, xlvi. 50.] [xxx. 62.] [II. vii.] The Stoics deny that it is,[1] as one may see in a fragment of Stobaeus under the title *On Magistracy*, in Cicero's speech *For Murena*, and at the conclusion of Seneca's work *On Clemency*; but their argument is a trivial one. 'Pardon', they say, 'is the remission of a punishment that is deserved'; 'the wise man, moreover, does what he ought to do.' Here the fallacy lies in the word 'deserved'. For if you understand that he who has sinned deserves punishment, that is, can be punished without injustice, it will not thereby follow that one who fails to punish him does what he ought not to do. However, if you take the view that the punishment is deserved at the hands of the wise man, that is, ought by all means to be exacted, we shall say that this does not always happen, and therefore from this point of view punishment cannot be deserved but merely permitted. This, furthermore, may be true both prior to the laying down of penal law and subsequent to it.

XXII.—*Proof that pardon is permissible prior to the penal law*

1. Even before the establishment of the penal law beyond doubt there may be room for punishment, because the wrong-doer is naturally in the state where punishment may be permitted. But it does not follow from this that the punishment ought to be exacted,[2] for this depends upon the connexion between the purposes for which the punishment is instituted and the punishment itself. Consequently if these purposes of themselves are not necessary on moral grounds, or if they are opposed by other purposes not less useful or necessary, or if the purposes set for punishment can be attained in another way, it is clear that there is nothing which strictly compels the exaction of the punishment.

Take as an example of the first case a crime known to very few persons, the bringing of which to public notice is therefore unnecessary, or even harmful. Here is applicable what Cicero said of a certain Zeuxis: 'Since he has been brought to trial, perhaps he ought not to be acquitted, [. . .] but it was unnecessary to have prosecuted him.' An example of the second case is one who pleads either his own deserts or those of his parents, which are worthy of reward, to counterbalance his guilt; for, as Seneca says: 'The surpassing benefit does not suffer the injury to appear.' An example of the third case is one who is corrected by reproof, or who has made verbal satisfaction to the injured person, so that there is now no need of punishment to attain the desired ends.

Letters to his Brother Quintus, I. xxi [I. ii. 2. 5].

[*On Benefits*, VI. vi. 3.]

[1] They are ably controverted by Diodorus Siculus [*Selections*, XXI. viii]: 'Pardon is more desirable than vengeance.' The Christian view is given by Cyprian, *Letters*, lii [lii. 16]: 'The teaching of the Stoic philosophers is different; for they say that all sins are equal, and that a serious man ought not to be easily influenced. But there is a wide gap between Christians and philosophers.'

[2] Julian, *On Eusebia* [*Orations*, III = 115 B]: 'For even if some persons are deserving of ill-treatment and punishment, it is not of certainty necessary that they should perish.'

2. This is one aspect of clemency, that it frees from punishment. With respect to this the Hebrew Wise Man said: 'The just man must love his fellow men.' For because every punishment, especially if of a more serious kind, contains something which viewed in itself is opposed, not indeed to justice, but to regard for others, reason readily permits us to refrain from punishment, unless a greater and more just regard for others almost irresistibly restrains us. The remark of Sopater is to the point here: [*Wisdom*,] xii. 19. [Stobaeus, xlvi. 60.]

The corrective element of justice in the matter of contracts altogether spurns the family of the Graces. But the element that is concerned with punishments does not shun their mild and kindly countenance.

The first part of the thought Cicero expressed thus: 'In certain things the way of right is such that regard for others has no place.' The latter part is thus phrased by Dio of Prusa in his oration *To the Alexandrians*: 'It is the part of a good governor to pardon.' As Favorinus says: 'What men call clemency is a relaxation of strict justice at the opportune time.' *Letters to Quintus*, I ii [3. 10]. [xxxii = p. 366.] [Gellius, I. iii. 27.]

[331] XXIII.—*But pardon is not permissible in all cases*

There are these three possibilities. Either the penalty is to be exacted absolutely, as in crimes of the worst type;[1] or it is not to be exacted at all, as when the public good requires its omission; or either alternative may be possible, in which case, as Seneca says, clemency has freedom of judgement. In this last case, say the Stoics, the wise man spares, but does not pardon. As if, indeed, following the common people who determine the use of language, we could not call 'to pardon' what the Stoics call 'to spare'. In truth both here and elsewhere, as Cicero, Galen, and others point out, a great part of the Stoic arguments is taken up with discussions about terms,[2] which a philosopher ought especially to avoid. For as the writer of the *Ad Herennium* said with the greatest truth: 'It is a bad thing to raise a dispute over a change of terms', or, as Aristotle had put it: 'One must avoid [. . .] disputing over the name.' [*On Clemency*, II. vii. 3.] II [xxviii. 45]. *Topics*, I. xxiv [I. xviii. 4].

XXIV.—*Proof that pardon is permissible even after the establishment of the penal law*

1. There seems to be a greater difficulty with regard to pardon after the establishment of the penal law, because the lawmaker is in some way bound by his own laws. But this we have said is true in so far as the lawmaker is regarded as a member of the state,[3] not in so

[1] Josephus says [*Antiquities of the Jews*, XVII. v. 5]: 'Parricide is a crime both against nature and against human life, and he who fails to punish it sins himself against nature.'

[2] To no purpose, as the Scholiast on Horace says. Augustine, *Against the Academics* [II. xi]: 'It is disgraceful for persons in a discussion to linger over a question of words when no difference on questions of fact remains.'

[3] See above, II. iv. 12, in text and notes.

far as he sustains the person and authority of the state itself. For in so far as he does this he can even suspend the whole law because it is the nature of a human law to depend upon a human will, not merely in its origin but also in its duration. However, the lawmaker should not suspend the law except for a worthy reason, otherwise he will sin against the principles of governmental justice.

2. But just as the lawmaker can suspend the whole law, so he can suspend its obligation in respect to a particular person or fact, while in other respects the law remains in force. According to Lactantius, God Himself furnishes an example; for 'When He established the law, He did not thereby take from Himself all power, but retained this right to pardon freely.' 'The Emperor', says Augustine, 'may repeal a sentence,[1] and acquit a defendant on a capital charge and pardon him,' giving as the reason 'that he who has it in his power to create laws is not bound by the laws'. And Seneca wishes Nero to reflect on this: 'No one can put to death against the law; nobody can save except me.'

[*On the Anger of God*, xix.]

[*Questions on the Old and New Testaments*, cxv.]

On Clemency, I. v. 4.

3. But this step also is not to be taken except for a worthy reason. Although we cannot define with exactness what are worthy reasons, nevertheless we must hold that they ought to be more cogent after the institution of the law than those which were accepted before the law, because to the reasons for punishing there is added the authority of the law which it is expedient to preserve.

XXV.—*What intrinsic causes are sufficient to cause the suspension of the law*

Now the causes for freeing any one from the punishment of the law are internal or external.

An intrinsic cause occurs when the punishment, although not unlawful, is severe in comparison with the act.

XXVI.—*What extrinsic causes are sufficient*

An extrinsic cause for freeing any one from the punishment of the law arises from some merit, or from some other commendatory thing, or even from a strong hope entertained for the future. This type of cause is especially effective if the reason for the law, at least in the particular instance, should cease with respect to the act in question. For although the general reason, when not opposed by a contrary reason, is sufficient ground for maintaining the efficacy of

[1] Symmachus writes, *Letters*, III. lxiii: 'For the condition of the magistrates, whose judgements appear to be corrupt if they are milder than the laws authorize, is one thing; something different is the power of the emperors, who ought to soften the asperity [357] of a harsh law.' The same distinction between king and judge is found in Themistius, *Orations*, v [xix = pp. 227–28].

the law, nevertheless an absence of the reason, even in a particular instance, renders it possible to suspend the law more easily and with less loss of authority.[1]

This occurs especially in the case of crimes which are committed through ignorance, even if it is not altogether excusable, or through some mental infirmity that is conquerable indeed, but only with difficulty. These things ought to be taken into especial consideration by a Christian ruler, that he may imitate God, who even in the Old Covenant desired that many crimes of this sort should be expiated by the offering of certain victims; *Leviticus*, [332] iv and v. And in the New Covenant by word and by examples He has shown that He is ready to pardon such things to those who repent (*Luke*, xxiii. 34; *Hebrews*, iv. 15; v. 2; *1 Timothy*, i. 13). John Chrysostom in fact notes that Theodosius the Great[2] was led to pardon the men of Antioch by these words of Christ in the Gospel of St. Luke, 'Father, forgive them, for they know not what they do.' [*On the Statues*, Homily XXI, iv.]

XXVII.—*Rejection of the view that there is no just cause to suspend the law, unless it is one that is contained in the law as an implied exception*

Now from this it is clear how far wrong Fernando Vázquez was in saying that the only just cause of suspending the law, that is of freeing from the operation of the law, is that with regard to which the lawmaker, if consulted, would say that it was not his intention that the law should be observed. For he has not distinguished between 'equity', which serves to interpret the law, and relaxation. Upon this ground in another place he censures Thomas Aquinas and Soto for saying that the law continues to be binding even if the cause should cease in a particular case, as though they thought that the law consisted merely in what was written; an idea that never occurred to them. I. xlvi. I. xxvi and xlvi.

However, we are so far from having to attribute every relaxation of the law, which may often be given freely or omitted, to what is properly called equity, that not even the relaxation due either to regard for others or to ruling justice can be referred thereto. For it is one thing to annul the law for a worthy or even a pressing cause, and another to declare that an act from the beginning was not embraced in the intent of the law.

Now that we have discussed exemptions from punishments, let us consider their measure.

[1] Gratian has assembled much useful information on this point, *Decretum*, II. i. 7.
[2] See the account in Zonaras [XIII. xviii. 30–2].

XXVIII.—*The measure of punishment according to what is deserved*

From what has been previously said it appears that in applying punishments we must have regard to two things: that for which, and that for the sake of which. That for which is what is deserved; that for the sake of which is the advantage to come from the punishment.

[II. xx. 2. 2.] *Letters to Brutus*, xv [I. xv. 3]. *Digest*, XLVIII. xix. 41. [*On Leuctra*, i = p. 94 c.] [*Letters*, iii. 4.]

No one is to be punished beyond what he has deserved.[1] This view is supported by what we have previously quoted from Horace, and by the saying of Cicero: 'In punishment as in other things there is a measure and a sort of moderation.' Thus Papinian calls punishment by the name of evaluation. Aristides in his second speech *On Leuctra* says that it accords with human nature to find in each crime some point beyond which vengeance ought not to proceed. Moreover, Demosthenes in his letter on behalf of the children of Lycurgus says that in the matter of punishment we must not regard the bare balance, as in the case of weights and measures, but we must weigh the purpose and the wish of him who has committed the wrong. Within the limits of their desert, sins are punished more or less severely with an eye to the advantage to be attained.

XXIX.—*A consideration, in this connexion, of the causes which lead to crime, and a comparison of these with one another*

1. In estimating what is deserved we must take into consideration the compelling cause,[2] the cause which ought to have restrained, and the disposition of the person toward each. Scarcely any one is bad for no purpose, while if any one delights in wickedness for its own sake he is beyond the pale of humanity. Most people are led to sin by their

James, i. 15.

desires; 'The lust when it hath conceived beareth sin.'

Now under the name of desire I include also the impulse to avoid evil, which is very natural and consequently the most honourable of desires. Hence, unjust actions committed for the sake of avoiding death, imprisonment, pain, or extreme poverty, usually seem in great measure excusable.

[xlv. 67.]

2. Here applies the saying of Demosthenes:

> It is right to be more angry with those who are bad when they are rich than with those who are so under the pressure of poverty. For with judges of a humane disposition necessity has some value as an excuse, while those who are unjust while enjoying wealth have no worthy pretext.

IV [xxx. 2 ff.].

On this ground Polybius excuses the Acarnanians for not fulfilling the terms of the treaty concluded with the Greeks against the

[1] On this question the Milanese discoursed ably in the speech contained in Guicciardini, XVII [pp. 387 ff.]. Compare what we have said in II. xx. 2, and what we shall have to say in III. xi. 1.

[2] Chrysostom says, *On the Statues*, X [X. vi]: 'For not all sins deserve the same punishment but those which are easy to correct bring upon us the heavier penalty.' In his second homily dealing with the obscurity of the Old Testament [*On the Obscurity of the Prophecies*, II. viii] he proves on this ground that a calumniator is worse than a libertine, a thief, or a homicide.

Aetolians, in view of the danger which threatened them. Aristotle also declares: [333] 'Incontinence is more voluntary than cowardice; for the former arises from hope of pleasure, but the latter from fear of pain. Pain, moreover, as it were, carries a man out of himself,[1] corrupting his nature; but pleasure does no such thing, and so is the more voluntary.'[2] Of the same sense is a significant passage in Porphyry,[3] *On the Abstaining from Animal Food*, Book III. [*Nicom. Ethics*, III. xv.] [III. xviii.]

3. But the other desires aim at some good, whether true or imaginary. True goods, apart from virtues and their actions, which do not lead to sin (for virtues harmonize with one another) are either pleasing things or the cause of pleasant things, which are called advantageous, as abundance of possessions. Imaginary but not true goods[4] are superiority over others, apart from virtue and advantage, and revenge. And the further these depart from nature, the more shameful they become.

Now these three desires John expresses in the following words: 'the lust of the flesh, the lust of the eyes, and the vain glory of life.' For the first member includes the desires for pleasures, the second the greed of possessing, and the third anger and the pursuit of vain glory. Philo, in his explanation of the *Ten Commandments*, says that 'All things are evil that arise from the desire either for money or for glory or for pleasure'; and Lactantius, in his sixth book, that 'Virtue consists in restraining anger, abating greed, and bridling lust. For almost all unjust and wicked acts arise from these desires.' This idea he expresses in another place also. [*I John*, ii. 16.] [xxviii.] [VI. v. 13.] [VI. xix. 4 ff.]

XXX.—*Also a consideration of the causes that should have restrained from sin; with a discussion of the order of the commandments of the decalogue that apply to one's neighbour, and some other things*

1. The general cause, which ought to restrain from wrong-doing, is injustice. For here we are not dealing with sins of all kinds, but only with such as carry their effect beyond the criminal himself. The injustice is the greater the heavier the loss that is brought upon another. Therefore, in order of seriousness, the first place is assigned to crimes actually carried out, and the next place to those which have proceeded to certain actions but not to the final act.

[1] See the excellent comparison between the thief and the adulterer in *Proverbs*, vi. 30.

[2] Philo, *On the Ten Commandments* [xxviii], says: 'For all affections of the mind are severe, and influence and disturb it in an unnatural manner, and do not permit it to be healthy. But the most severe is desire; for each of the other affections attacks and falls upon the mind from without, and seems to be involuntary, but desire alone has its beginning in ourselves and is voluntary.'

[3] There is a like passage in Marcus Aurelius, *Meditations*, II [II. x], where he contrasts anger and lust. Plutarch in his *Romulus* [*Comparison of Theseus and Romulus*, iii = 38A]: 'The cause which awakes anger rather excuses him who has been influenced by a stronger cause, as though by a heavier blow.'

[4] Seneca, *Letters*, xvi: 'Natural desires are limited; but those that arise from a false opinion have no bounds.' See Chrysostom, in his moral discussions *On Romans*, vi [Homily X ff.]; *On Second Corinthians*, xi. 12 [Homily XXIII, v]; *On Ephesians*, i. 14 [Homily II].

Among the latter each is more serious the farther it has proceeded. In either sort of crimes that form of injustice is prominent which disturbs the public order and therefore harms the greatest number.

Next in importance comes the injustice which affects individuals. Here the greatest injustice is that which affects human life; the next that affecting the family, the basis of which is marriage; and the last that affecting desirable things severally, either by directly taking them away or through evil intent giving rise to loss.

2. These things may be analysed with greater precision, but we have indicated the order that God has followed in the Decalogue. For under the name of parents, who are magistrates by nature, it is right for us to understand other rulers whose authority extends over human society. There follows the forbidding of homicide; then the sanction of matrimony by the prohibition of adultery; then thefts and the bearing of false witness; and, finally, unconsummated crime.

However, among the reasons that should deter from crime we ought to include not only the character of the crime that is actually committed, but also the character of what is likely to follow, for in the case of arson and the destruction of a dike most serious injuries and even death in the case of many persons are to be looked for.

3. In addition to injustice, which we have stated as the general reason for abstaining from wrong, there is sometimes added another vice,[1] as impiety toward one's parents, cruelty toward neighbours, and ingratitude toward benefactors, which add to the seriousness of the offence. Also the depravity appears to be greater if one sins frequently,[2] because evil habits are worse than evil acts.

From this we may see how far the Persian custom is by nature right, which takes into consideration a man's former life along with [334] his crime.[3] This ought, to be sure, to have a place in the case of those who, while not otherwise prone to evil, have suddenly been carried away by some charm felt in sinning; but not in the case of those who have changed the whole character of their life. Regarding them God Himself, according to Ezekiel, says that no
[*Ezekiel,*] account must be taken of their previous life. We may also apply to
xviii [24]. them the words of Thucydides: 'They are worthy of a twofold
I [lxxxvi]. penalty, because from good men they have become bad'; and also

[1] See the notable passage in the words of Luke, in the excerpts of Xiphilinus from Dio Cassius [LXXI. xxiv ff.].

[2] [Diodorus Siculus, *Selections,* XXI. xv]: 'It is a human trait to have been at times ignorant of what life requires; but to err frequently in the same matters is the mark of one who has lost the power of reason, for the more frequently we fall into sin the more worthy we become to receive a greater punishment.'

[3] Asinius Pollio [in Seneca, *Suasoriae,* VI. xxiv]: 'Judgement should be passed on a man according to the general state of his life and character.' Cicero, *For Sulla* [xxv. 69]: 'In all things, judges, which are serious and important, we must consider what any one has desired, planned, and done, not from the crime itself, [358] but from the character of him who is accused.'

what he has said in another place: 'Because it least of all became them to sin.' III [lxvii].

4. Consequently, the early Christian writers, in adjusting punishments according to the Canons, very rightly desired that the crime should not be considered by itself alone,[1] but with it the preceding and subsequent life; as one may see from the Council of Ancyra and other Councils.

But the enactment of a law against a particular crime also adds a sort of special wickedness thereto. So Augustine teaches: 'The law by its prohibition [. . .] renders all crimes doubly guilty;[2] for it is not a simple crime to do what is not only wrong but is also forbidden.' According to Tacitus: 'If you desire what is not yet forbidden, you may fear that it will be forbidden; but if you transgress with impunity what is prohibited there is no fear or sense of restraint remaining.'

Romans, vii. 13. *On the True Religion*, vi [xxvi. 48]. *Annals*, III [liv].

XXXI.—*Also the inclination of the sinner toward incentives to and deterrents from sinning, which is considered from various points of view*

1. The fitness of the person, either to take into consideration deterrent causes, or to receive incentive desires, is usually considered to be the result of his bodily constitution, age, sex, education, and the immediate circumstances of the act. For alike children, women, and men of dull intellect and bad education, are not well able to appreciate the distinction between just and unjust, lawful and unlawful. Those too who suffer from an excess of bile are prone to anger, and those who have an excess of blood are prone to lust; moreover, youth leads to the latter, while old age tends to the former. Says Andronicus of Rhodes: 'It appears that a natural inclination toward what is bad provides a sort of defence for these acts, and renders the crime more tolerable.'

On Nicomachean Ethics, VII. x.

Reflection upon a threatening evil increases fear, and pain that is fresh and not yet assuaged fires one's anger, so that they scarcely permit reason to be heard. And the crimes that arise from such impulses are deservedly less hateful than those which spring from a desire for pleasure, both because this affects one less powerfully and because it can be more easily deferred and can find for itself another object without suffering harm.[3] As Aristotle says in his *Nicomachean*

[1] Canon of the Council of Ancyra, XXV. Chrysostom, *On Second Corinthians*, ii [ii. 7 = Homily IV, iv]: 'Whence we learn, that in defining the limits of repentance we must have regard not only to the nature of the sins but also to the intent and the character of the sinners.' The same author, in the third book *On the Priesthood* [II. iv]: 'For we must not inflict the punishment solely with regard to the measure of the sins. But we must also try to discover the intention of the one who has sinned.'

[2] Chrysostom well says [*On Romans*, Homily V, iv]: 'Here [. . .] he not only shows the equal right and worth of the Jew and of the Greek, but also that the Jew is heavily burdened by the gift of the law.' Then [Homily V, iii]: 'For he who has received the fuller instruction deserves the greater penalty if he transgresses the law.'

[3] Chrysostom, *On Galatians* [v. 12]: 'Lust seeks mere sexual gratification, but not with any special person.' Tertullian, *To his Wife*, Book II [II. i]: 'For in proportion as continence, which ministers to

[VII. vii.] *Ethics*, Book VII: 'Anger and severity are more natural than the desires for excessive and unnecessary things.'

2. We must in fact absolutely adopt this point of view, that the more the judgement of a mind that can choose is restricted, and the more this restriction is due to natural causes, the less the offence
[VII] vi. that is committed. According to Aristotle in the book cited: 'Rather should we call intemperate the man who, without suffering from desire, or suffering but slightly, pursues excesses and shuns moderate pains, than he who does so under the influence of strong passion. For what are we to think the former would do if he should be influenced by youthful desires or severe pain along with the lack of
[Stobaeus, ii. 3.] necessities?' With this agree the words of Antiphanes:

> He who when rich yet does act wickedly,[1]
> What think you he would fail to do, were he but poor,

[335] and what we read everywhere in comedy about the loves of old men.

Accordingly, for these reasons we must estimate the desert which punishment ought not to exceed.

XXXII.—*The desert of punishment may be extended to include a greater harm than the sinner has actually inflicted. The reasons therefor*

1. Further, we must hold that the teaching of the Pythagoreans that justice is 'suffering in return for suffering'[2]—that is, the suffering of the punishment equalling the suffering of the wrongs—ought not to be taken in the sense that he who has injured another with intent and without reasons that sensibly diminish his guilt ought only to suffer the equivalent of the harm he has wrought and nothing more.
[*Exodus*, xxii. 1.] That this is not so is shown in fact by that law which is the most perfect example of all laws, when it provides that thefts are to be atoned for by fourfold or fivefold restitution. In Attic law, again, a thief, besides the condemnation to double damages,[3] was kept in
[xxiv. 105.] prison for some days, as Demosthenes informs us in his speech *Against Timocrates*.

widowhood, is difficult, so it may seem pardonable if it is not maintained; for pardon is readily granted in difficult things. However, in proportion as it is easy to wed in the Lord, seeing that it is within our power, the more blameworthy it is not to observe what you are able.' And soon after [II. iii]: 'The more it was within one's power to avoid sin, the more is he burdened with the crime of obstinacy.'

See also Marcus Aurelius, in the passage just cited [*Meditations*, II. x], where he names Theophrastus as his authority.

[1] Chrysostom, *On Providence*, IV [Oration V, end]: 'Whenever you see a rich man who is unjust, grasping and rapacious, pity him especially for this, since he does these things because he is rich. For by reason of this he will pay a greater penalty.'

[2] 'Suffering the same thing,' as Harmenopulus says [*Promptuarium*, I. ii. 34].

[3] There is an allusion to this in *Revelation*, xviii. 6: 'Restore twofold.' Hercules compelled the Minyans, who had unjustly exacted tribute from the Thebans, to restore to the latter double the tribute; Apollodorus, Book II [II. iv. 11].

'The laws', says Ambrose, 'order that those things which have been taken away from anyone with injury to the person or the thing itself shall be restored with interest, so that either they may deter the thief from taking them by the punishment provided, or recover the loss by the fine.' According to Aristides in his second speech *On Leuctra*: 'Those who follow up their wrongs in court are allowed by the law to inflict upon those who have wronged them, in the way of punishment, more than they have suffered.' Seneca, speaking of the judgement after this life, says:

On Duties, III. iii [21]. [= p. 133 C.] [*Hercules Raging*, 746 f.]

> Our [your] sins are weighed
> With heavier measure.

2. Among the peoples of India,[1] as Strabo notes, he who had maimed another, in addition to suffering retaliation, was punished by the loss of a hand. And in the *Magna Moralia* attributed to Aristotle we read: 'It is not just that one, who has struck out another's eye, should only have his struck out in turn, but he should suffer something more.' The reason is that it is not fair that the danger to the innocent and the guilty should be equal, as Philo[2] rightly proves in discussing the punishment of homicide.

XV [i. 54]. I. xxxiv [14].

This we can judge also from the fact that certain unaccomplished crimes, which are accordingly less heinous than those which have been accomplished,[3] cause an injury equal to the intent, as is shown in the Hebraic law of false witness,[4] and in the Roman law concerning one who goes about armed for the purpose of killing a man. Thereupon it follows that a heavier punishment answers to crimes that have been executed; but since there is no punishment heavier than death, and this can be inflicted only once, as Philo notes in the passage referred to above, punishment necessarily stops with this, nevertheless with the occasional addition of torture, as the crime may deserve.

Deut., xix. 19.

XXXIII.—*Rejection of the idea of a harmonic proportion in punishments*

However, we must take into consideration the extent of the punishment, not only by itself but in relation to the one who suffers it. For the fine that will burden a poor man will not burden one who is rich; and to a man of no repute ignominy will be a trifling harm, while for a man of consequence it will be serious.

[1] Nicholas of Damascus has noted that among other Indian peoples a thief was punished by death [frag. 34, p. 150, edit. Dindorf].

[2] *On Special Laws*, Book II [II. xv].

[3] Pliny [*Natural History*, VIII. xvi] writes of the lion: 'When he has been wounded he recognizes with wonderful keenness the one who has struck him, and seeks him out, no matter how many surround him. However he seizes and strikes down, but does not wound, one who has hurled a spear but failed to strike him.'

[4] Also concerning one who has falsely accused his wife of adultery in order to secure her dowry; *Deuteronomy*, xxii. 19. And concerning one who has unjustly brought any one into court on other grounds, claiming another's property for himself; *Exodus*, xxii. 9.

The Roman law often makes use of this kind of difference. From
On the Republic, VI. ult. that Bodin built up his harmonic proportion; although in reality we have here a simple proportion like a numerical equation, between the desert and the punishment, just as in contracts which set goods over against money, although the same goods have now more value, now less, in the same way as money. But we must admit that in the Roman law this is not done 'without regard to persons', that is not without too much regard to persons and qualities extraneous to the fact. This fault is always completely absent from the Law of Moses. Such, as we have said, is the intrinsic measure of punishment.

XXXIV.—*Punishment may be mitigated on the ground of regard for others, unless a greater regard for others opposes*

But within the conceded limits [336] regard for him who is punished tends to exact the minimum penalty, unless a more just regard for the greater number urges a contrary course for an extrinsic reason. This reason is sometimes the great danger from him who has sinned, but more often the need of an example. This need, moreover, usually has its origin in the general inducements to sin, which cannot be checked without sharp remedies. Of these inducements the strongest are habit and opportunity.

XXXV.—*How the opportunity to commit sin may urge to its punishment; also how the habit of sinning may urge to the punishment of the sin or dissuade from it*

Because of the opportunity, the divine law given to the Jews punished more severely a theft committed in the field than one in
[II. ii. 6.] the house [1] (*Exodus*, xxii. 1 and 9). Justin, writing of the Scythians, says: 'Among them no crime is considered more serious than theft, for, if stealing were permitted, what could they hold safe, seeing that they keep their flocks and herds without the protection of roof and
[xxix. 14.] walls?' In Aristotle's *Problems*, section xxix, we find this similar statement: 'The lawgiver, considering that the owners were not able to protect their property in these places,[2] established the law as a guard.'

Although the habitual performance of an act detracts somewhat
[*Letters,* IV. ix.] from its guilt ('Not without reason', says Pliny, 'did he pardon an act that was forbidden indeed, but yet habitual'), still from one point

[359] [1] See Maimonides, *Guide of the Perplexed,* iii. 41. Cicero, *For Sextus Roscius Amerinus* [xl. 116]: 'And cognizance must be taken especially of those crimes which it is most difficult to guard against.'

[2] The reference is to the public baths. At Athens those committing theft in the baths were punished with death if the damage was greater than ten drachmas; Demosthenes, *Against Timocrates* [cxiv]. See also *Digest,* XLVII. xvii. 1.

of view it requires severity in the punishment. For, as Saturninus says, 'When very many disturb the peace we must make an example'. Now in passing judgements we must aim at leniency, but in framing laws at severity, taking due account of the time when the statutes or the judgements are made known; because the advantage derived from punishment is considered more in the generality with which the statutes deal, while the guilt varies in individual cases. *Digest*, XLVIII. xix. 16 [§ 10].

XXXVI.—*The use of clemency in mitigating punishments*

1. A second aspect of clemency, moreover, is to be found in what we have said, that, where great and pressing grounds for punishment are lacking, we should be the more ready to mitigate the punishment; its first aspect we have held to consist in the complete suspension of punishment. 'Since an exact balance is difficult,' said Seneca, 'whatever is in excess should weigh on the side of humanity.' And in another passage: 'Let him execute the punishment, if he can with safety, but if not, let him moderate it.' *On Clemency*, I. 1 [I. ii. 2]. [*On Clemency*, I] xx.

Diodorus Siculus, too, praises an Egyptian king because he imposed 'penalties less than the deserts'.[1] Capitolinus says of Marcus Aurelius: 'This was a habit of the Emperor, to visit all crimes with a lighter punishment than that provided by the laws.' Isaeus the orator also said that it was necessary that the laws be drawn up with severity, but that punishments milder than the laws should be exacted.[2] And we have the advice of Isocrates: 'Punishments should be made less than the crimes deserve.' [I. lxx.] [xxiv.] [Stobaeus, xlviii. 25.] [*To Nicocles*, vii = p. 19 D.]

2. Augustine[3] thus admonishes the Count Marcellinus of his duty:

> I feel the greatest anxiety, lest perchance your Exalted Highness should think that these men are to be punished with such a strict application of the laws that they should suffer punishments the equivalent of their crimes. And so in these two letters I beseech you by the faith which you have in Christ, through the mercy of our Lord himself, not to do this nor to permit it to be done at all.

In another passage he says: [*Letters*, cliii. 8.]

> Divine reproof has terrified even the very avengers of crime, although in this duty they are not prompted by their own anger but are servants of the laws, and avengers not of their own wrongs but of the wrongs of others, after examination, as befits good judges.

[1] [The Emperor] Justin II, writing to the Huns, says: 'It is a custom among the Romans not to demand punishment of equal severity with the injuries' [Menander Protector, frag. 28, p. 64, edit. Dindorf].

[2] The Emperor Henry wished to signify this by assuming the device of a peach, with the motto: *Subacre*. The king [Theodoric], in Cassiodorus, [*Variae*,] XI. xl, says: 'If sometimes we are just at a risk to ourselves, it is always with security that we pardon.'

[3] *Letters*, clix [cxxxiii. 1], which is cited in the *Decretum*, II. xxiii. 5. 1. See, if you wish, the letter of Macedonius to Augustine and the latter's reply; *Letters*, liii and liv [clii and cliii]. Also what is said of the Emperor Theodosius the Younger in the excerpts of John of Antioch, *Excerpta Peiresciana* [p. 850]. Macedonius writes to Augustine: 'It is the duty of a priest to intercede for the accused' [Augustine, *Letters*, clii. 2].

Therefore they reflect on the mercy of God necessary to pardon their own sin, and do not think that it is a guilty neglect of their duty if in some degree they act mercifully toward those over whom they have the power of life and death which the laws confer.

XXXVII.—*What the Jews and the Romans thought should be taken into consideration in punishments is brought into relation with the foregoing discussion*

We hope that we have omitted nothing that would greatly contribute to the understanding of this problem, which is sufficiently difficult and obscure. For we have discussed in their proper place the four things which Maimonides [1] says we should take into chief consideration in punishments: the greatness of the crime, that is of the harm done, the frequency of such [337] crimes, the strength of illicit desire, and the opportunity for the act.

Digest, XLVIII. xix. 16. We have also discussed the seven points which Saturninus treats in a rather confused fashion in his consideration of punishments. For the person of him who has done the wrong is of the greatest importance in fitly judging the penalty, and the person of him who suffers the wrong sometimes is of weight in estimating the greatness of the guilt. The place of the wrongdoing usually contributes a particular degree of guilt to the injustice,[2] or has a bearing also upon the opportunity for the deed. According as the time was long or short it increases or restricts freedom of judgement, at times also reveals the depravity of the mind. The quality of the crime has to do partly with the kinds of desires, and partly with the reasons which should have deterred from sinning. The degree also must be taken into consideration in relation with the desire. The outcome must be viewed in relation to the deterrent reasons.

XXXVIII.—*On war waged to inflict punishment*

We have previously shown, and histories everywhere teach, that wars are usually begun for the purpose of exacting punishment. But very often this cause is joined with a second, the desire to make good a loss, when the same act was both wicked and involved loss; and from these two characteristics two separate obligations arise.

However, it is quite clear that war should not be undertaken for every sort of crime. For even the vengeance of the laws, which is

[1] *Guide of the Perplexed,* III. xli. Compare the *Decretals,* V. xii. 6.

[2] Philo, *On Special Laws,* I [I. xxxiii]: 'For it is not the same thing to strike one's father and a stranger, or to abuse a magistrate and a private person, or to perform a prohibited act in profane and in sacred localities, at festivals, public gatherings, or public religious celebrations.'

With this agrees Ulpian's citation from Labeo, *Digest,* XLVII. x. 7, § 8: 'The wrong becomes more wicked through the person, as when it is done to a magistrate, to a parent, or to a patron; through the time, if at the games and in public view, for he says that there is the greatest difference whether an injury has been done in the sight of the Roman people or in seclusion.'

exercised in safety and only harms the guilty, does not follow upon every wrong. As we have just now said, Sopater justly declares that crimes which are of little importance and common should be passed over and not avenged. [II. xx. 19.]

XXXIX.—*By distinguishing various cases, it is explained whether a war waged to punish wrongs that have been merely attempted is just*

1. The saying of Cato in his speech for the Rhodians, that it is not just that any one should be punished for a thing which he is accused merely of having wrongly desired to do, was not badly urged in this connexion; for no decree of the people of Rhodes could in fact be adduced, but only conjectures of changing intent. The principle, however, cannot be accepted as a universal proposition. For the will which proceeds to external acts (we have said above that internal acts are not punished by men) is usually liable to punishment. According to Seneca the Father, in his *Controversies*:[1] 'Crimes are punished even although they have not been carried to completion.' 'He who is about to commit a wrong has already committed it,' says the younger Seneca.[2] Cicero in his speech *For Milo* said that not the outcome of deeds but the purposes were punished by the laws.[3] There was also a saying of Periander: 'Punish not only those who sin but also those who intend to sin.' [Gellius, VII. iii [38].] [II. xx. 18.] [*On Anger*, III [I. iii. 1].] [vii. 19.] [Diog. Laer., I. xcviii.]

On these grounds the Romans thought that they ought to wage war with King Perseus, unless he should make amends in respect to the plans which he had formed for waging war against the Roman people, seeing that he had already gathered arms, troops, and a fleet. This very point is rightly emphasized in the speech of the Rhodians recorded in Livy, that neither in the customs nor in the laws of any state is it provided that he who wishes his enemy to perish, assuming that he has done nothing to bring this about, is condemned to capital punishment. [Livy, XLII [xxx].] [XLV. xxiv.]

2. But, on the other hand, not every wicked intention, which has been revealed by some fact, gives an occasion for punishment. For if all crimes that have been committed are not punished, much less are all those which have been planned and initiated. In many cases we may apply the saying of Cicero: 'I do not know whether or not it is enough for him who has done harm to repent of his wrong- [*On Duties*, I [xi. 34].]

[1] *Excerpts*, IV. vii.

[2] Also *On Benefits*, V. xiv: 'A brigand is one even before he has soiled his hands, for the reason that he is already armed to kill and has the intention of robbing and killing.'

Philo, *On Special Laws*, I [III. xv]: 'We ought to class as homicides not merely those who actually kill, but also those who do everything for the purpose of killing, either openly or secretly, even if they have not yet committed their crime.'

[3] Valerius Maximus [VI. i. 8], speaking of Gnaeus Sergius Silus who had been condemned for promising money to a married woman: 'Not the action but the intent was taken into consideration, and it was more to his disadvantage to have wished to sin than to his advantage not to have sinned.'

doing.' The law given to the Jews made no special provision against many crimes begun against piety, or even against human life, without premeditation; because it is easy to err in divine things which are not clear to us, and the impulse of anger is not undeserving of pardon.

3. However, in the midst of so many opportunities for marriage, to disturb the marriages of others, or in the case of a fair division of property [338] to devise fraud whereby one might enrich himself through the loss of another, was by no means tolerable. For although the command 'Thou shalt not covet', contained in the Decalogue, is of wide meaning if you look at the object of the law, that is 'the spiritual object' (for the law desires all to be most pure even in mind),[1] nevertheless the external command, 'the carnal injunction', so far as it extends, refers to the movements of the mind which are revealed by
x. 19. action. This is abundantly clear from the evangelist Mark who has given that same command, 'Do not defraud', and that too after he had previously enjoined, 'Do not steal.' In this sense, in fact, the Hebrew word and its Greek equivalent are found in *Micah* (ii. 2) and elsewhere.

4. Crimes that have only been begun are therefore not to be punished by armed force, unless the matter is serious, and has reached a point where a certain damage has already followed from such action, even if it is not yet that which was aimed at; or at least great danger has ensued, so that the punishment is joined either with a precaution against future harm (about which we spoke above in the chapter on Defence), or protects injured dignity, or checks a dangerous example.

XL.—*A discussion whether kings and peoples may rightly wage war on account of things done contrary to the law of nature, although not against them or their subjects; with a refutation of the view that the law of nature requires right of jurisdiction for the exaction of punishment*

1. The fact must also be recognized that kings, and those who possess rights equal to those kings, have the right of demanding punishments not only on account of injuries committed against themselves or their subjects, but also on account of injuries which do not directly affect them but excessively violate the law of nature or of nations in regard to any persons whatsoever. For liberty to serve the interests of human society through punishments, which originally, as we have said, rested with individuals, now after the

[1] Chrysostom, *On Romans*, iii. 13, and vii, says much on this point [Homily VII and XII f.].

organization of states and courts of law is in the hands of the highest authorities, not, properly speaking, in so far as they rule over others but in so far as they are themselves subject to no one. For subjection has taken this right away from others.

Truly it is more honourable to avenge the wrongs of others rather than one's own, in the degree that in the case of one's own wrongs it is more to be feared that through a sense of personal suffering one may exceed the proper limit or at least prejudice his mind.

2. And for this cause Hercules was famed by the ancients
because he freed from Antaeus, Busiris, Diomedes and like tyrants *On Benefits*, I. xiv
the lands [1] which, as Seneca says, he traversed, not from a desire to [I. xiii].
acquire but to protect, becoming, as Lysias points out, the bestower Isocrates,
of the greatest benefits upon men through his punishment of the *Praise of Helen*,
unjust. Diodorus Siculus speaks of him thus: 'By slaying lawless [xiii].
men and arrogant despots he made the cities happy.' In another [*Orations*, ii. 16.]
passage Diodorus said: 'He traversed the world chastising the [IV. xvii.]
unjust.' Of the same hero Dio of Prusa said: 'He punished wicked [V. lxxvi.]
men and overthrew the power of the haughty or transferred it to [i. end.]
others.' Aristides in his *Panathenaic Oration* declares that Hercules [=p. 187–8.]
deserved to be elevated among the gods because of his espousal of the common interest of the human race.

In like manner Theseus is praised because he removed the robbers Sciron, Sinis, and Procrustes. Euripides in the *Suppliants* [lines 340–2.] represents him as speaking thus about himself:

> Already throughout Greece my deeds to me
> This name have given; scourge of the wicked I am called.[2]

Of him Valerius Maximus wrote: 'All that was anywhere monstrous V. iii
or criminal, he suppressed by the courage of his heart and the strength [Ext. 3].
of his right hand.'

3. So we do not doubt that wars are justly waged against those who act with impiety towards their parents, like the Sogdianians before Alexander taught them to abandon this form of barbarity; Plutarch, *On the Fortune of Alexander* [I. v=328 c].
against those who feed on human flesh,[3] from which custom, according

[1] And seas. Philo, *On the Embassy to Gaius* [xi]: [360] 'Hercules cleansed land and sea, undertaking contests most necessary and most beneficial to all men, for the purpose of doing away with injurious or harmful beings, among men and among animals.'

[2] And there to the herald who says [line 574]:

> Did thy father then beget thee as a match for all?

Theseus replies:

> For the insolent at least; good deeds we do not punish.

Plutarch, in his *Life of Theseus* [*Comparison of Theseus and Romulus*, i= 37]: 'He freed Greece of cruel tyrants,' and 'Although having suffered no wrong himself he assailed wicked men on behalf of others.'

[3] Alexander taught the Scythians to give up this custom also [Plutarch, *loc. cit.*].

to Diodorus, Hercules compelled the ancient Gauls to abstain ;[1] and against those who practise piracy. [339] Says Seneca: 'If a man does not attack my country, but yet is a heavy burden to his own, and although separated from my people he afflicts his own, such debasement of mind nevertheless cuts him off from us.' Augustine says: 'They think that they should decree the commission of crimes of such sort that if any state upon earth should decree them, or had decreed them, it would deserve to be overthrown by a decree of the human race.'

On Benefits, VII [xix. 9].

City of God, V [i].

Regarding such barbarians, wild beasts rather than men, one may rightly say what Aristotle wrongly said of the Persians, who were in no way worse than the Greeks, that war against them was sanctioned by nature; and what Isocrates said, in his *Panathenaic Oration*, that the most just war is against savage beasts, the next against men who are like beasts.

[*Politics*, I. viii.]

[66.]

4. Thus far we follow the opinion of Innocent, and others who say that war may be waged upon those who sin against nature.[2]

Innocent, *On Decr.*, III. xxxiv. 8.

The contrary view is held by Victoria, Vázquez, Azor, Molina, and others, who in justification of war seem to demand that he who undertakes it should have suffered injury either in his person or his state, or that he should have jurisdiction over him who is attacked. For they claim that the power of punishing is the proper effect of civil jurisdiction, while we hold that it also is derived from the law of nature; this point we discussed at the beginning of the first book. And in truth, if we accept the view of those from whom we differ, no enemy will have the right to punish another, even after a war that has been undertaken for another reason than that of inflicting punishment. Nevertheless many persons admit this right, which is confirmed also by the usage of all nations, not only after the conclusion of a war but also while the war is still going on; and not on the basis of any civil jurisdiction, but of that law of nature which existed before states were organized, and is even now enforced, in places where men live in family groups and not in states.

Arch. Flor., III. xxii. § 5; Sylvester, word *Papa*, § 7.

Victoria, *Relectiones de Indis*, I, no. 40.

Vázquez, *Cont. Ill.*, I. xxv [I. xxiv].

[1] See the statement of Dionysius of Halicarnassus [I. xxxviii] that Hercules abolished this and many other customs, making no distinction in his benefits between Greeks and barbarians. The equally great benefits of the Romans towards mankind are lauded by Pliny, [*Natural History*,] XXX. i: 'One cannot adequately compute what a debt is owed to the Romans, who have done away with those monstrous practices in which the slaughter of a man was considered a most sacred act, and to devour him most healthful' Add also what will be said in section 47 of this chapter.

Thus Justinian forbade the rulers of the Abasgi to castrate the male children of their subjects, as Procopius, *Gothic War*, IV [IV. iii], and Zonaras, in the history of Leo, the Isaurian [XV. i], record. The Incas, kings of Peru, forcibly compelled the neighbouring peoples, who did not listen to a warning, to abstain from incest, from the intercourse of male persons, from the eating of human flesh, and from other crimes of that kind. And in this way they won for themselves an empire, the most just of all that we have read of, except in its religion.

[2] See Joseph Acosta, *De Procuranda Indorum Salute*, II. iv.

XLI.—*The law of nature must be distinguished from widely current national customs*

But at this point certain precautions need to be stated.

First, national customs are not to be taken for the law of nature, although they have been received on reasonable grounds among many peoples. Of this type chiefly were the things which distinguished the Persians from the Greeks, to which you may rightly apply the saying of Plutarch: 'To wish to impose civilization upon uncivilized peoples is a pretext which may serve to conceal greed for what is another's.' [*Pompey*, lxx = p. 656 E.]

XLII.—*The law of nature must be distinguished also from the Divine law that is not voluntarily recognized by all*

Second, we should not hastily class with the things forbidden by nature those with regard to which this point is not sufficiently clear, and which are rather prohibited by the law of the Divine Will. In this class we may perhaps place unions not classed as marriages [1] and those which are called incestuous, as well as usury.

XLIII.—*In the law of nature we must distinguish between what is evident and what is not evident*

1. Third, we should carefully distinguish between general principles, as, for example, that one must live honourably, that is according to reason, and certain principles akin to these, but so evident that they do not admit of doubt, as that one must not seize what belongs to another, and inferences; such inferences in some cases easily gain recognition, as that, for example, accepting marriage we cannot admit adultery,[2] but in other cases are not so easily accepted, as the inference that vengeance which is satisfied with the pain of another is wicked. Here we have almost the same thing as in mathematics, where there are certain primary notions, or notions akin to those that are primary, certain proofs which are at once recognized and admitted, and certain others which are true indeed but not evident to all. *Digest*, XLVIII. v. 39. § 4.

2. Therefore, just as in the case of municipal laws we excuse those who lack knowledge or understanding of the laws, so also with regard to the laws of nature it is right to pardon those who are ham-

[1] Asterius, Bishop of Amasea: 'Those who heed only the lawmakers of this world leave unrestricted freedom to lust.' See the passage of Jerome, *To Oceanus*, cited in note to II. v. 9.

[2] Philo, *On Joseph* [ix], testifies that adultery is punished everywhere; Ulpian, that it is by nature base, *Digest*, L. xvi. 42.

Lactantius, *Epitome of the Divine Institutes* [lxiv]: 'To ruin the married life of others is condemned even by the common law of nations.'

Matthew, x. 15; *Luke*, xii. 47, 48. pered by weakness of their powers of reasoning or deficient education.[1] For as ignorance of the law, if it is unavoidable, cancels the sin, so also, when it is combined with a certain degree of negligence, it lessens the offence. [340] And for this reason Aristotle compared barbarians, who err through want of training in such things, to men having desires corrupted by disease. Plutarch says that there are certain 'diseases and sufferings of the mind which cause a man to lose his natural character'.

Nicom. Ethics, VII [vi].

3. Finally, to avoid repeating often what I have said, we must add this word of warning, that wars which are undertaken to inflict punishment are under suspicion of being unjust, unless the crimes are very atrocious and very evident, or there is some other coincident reason. Perhaps Mithridates was not far wrong in saying of the Romans: 'They assail not the faults of kings but the power and authority of kings.'

Justin, XXXVIII [vi. 1].

XLIV.—*Whether war may be waged on account of crimes against God*

1. Our order of treatment has brought us to the discussion of crimes which are committed against God; for there is a dispute whether war may be undertaken to avenge these. This question has been treated at sufficient length by Covarruvias. But he, accepting the position of others, thinks that the power to punish does not exist apart from jurisdiction, properly so called. This view we have already rejected. Consequently, just as in the affairs of the Church the bishops are said in some way to have been 'entrusted with the care of the Universal Church',[2] so kings, in addition to the particular care of their own state, are also burdened with a general responsibility for human society.

On Sext, V. ult. 4, pt. ii, § 10.

A stronger argument for the view which denies that such wars are just is this, that God is able to punish offences committed against Himself, whence the sayings, 'The injuries of the gods are the care of the gods,' and 'perjury has a sufficient avenger in God'.

[Tacitus, *Annals*, I. lxxiii.] [*Code*, IV. i. 2.]

2. We must, however, recognize the fact that this same thing may be said about other crimes as well. For without doubt God is able to punish these also, and yet no one disputes that they are rightly punished by men. But some will insist and say that other crimes are punished by men in so far as other men are injured or endangered

[1] Jerome, *Against Jovinianus*, II [II. vii]: 'Every people thinks that that which it has been taught is the law of nature.'

[2] This is found in the *Constitutions*, which bear the name of Clement [VI. xiv]. Cyprian, *Letters*, xxx, says: 'For it becomes us all to keep watch for the body of the whole Church, whose limbs are [361] scattered through each separate province.' And, *On the Unity of the Church* [chap. v]: 'There is one bishopric, of which each individual holds an integral part.

Instances of this universal care are found in many passages of Cyprian; an especially notable instance is in *Letters*, lxvii. See in addition, Chrysostom, in the *Praise of St. Eustathius* [iii].

thereby. But it must be noted, on the other hand, that men do not only punish the sins which directly harm others but also those which harm by their consequences, such as suicide, intercourse with animals, and some other things.

3. Moreover religion, although it is in itself effective in winning the favour of God, nevertheless has also in addition important effects on human society. For not undeservedly does Plato call religion the bulwark of authority and the laws and the bond of right training. Plutarch in like manner calls it 'the cement of all society and the basis of legislation'. In the view of Philo 'the worship of one God[1] is an unfailing means of inspiring love and an indissoluble bond of kindly good will'. Everything opposite flows from impiety: [*Against Colotes*, xxxi = 1125 E.] [*On Monarchy*, vii.]

> Alas, the first cause of crime for weak men
> Is ignorance of the nature of God.[2]

Silius Italicus [IV.792f.].

Plutarch says that every false belief in regard to divine matters is harmful, and, if coupled with a disturbance of the soul, very harmful. Iamblichus preserves a Pythagorean dictum: 'The knowledge of the gods is virtue and wisdom and complete happiness.' For these reasons Chrysippus said that law is the queen of things divine and human; Aristotle[3] held that among public obligations the chief was that concerning divine things; and to the Romans jurisprudence was the knowledge of things divine and human. Philo thought that the art of ruling consisted in 'the care of private, public, and sacred matters'. [*On Superstition*, i = 164 E.] [*Protrepticon*, iii.] [*Digest*, I. iii. 2.] *Politics*, VII [viii]. [*Dig.*, I. i. 10. § 2.] *De Creatione Principum* [i].

4. All these things are to be taken into account not merely in any one state, as when, in [341] Xenophon, Cyrus says that his subjects will be more devoted to him the more they fear the gods, but also in human society generally. 'If piety is removed', said Cicero, 'with it go good faith and the friendly association of mankind, and the one most excellent virtue, justice.' In another place he says: 'Justice arises when we fully understand what the godhead of our supreme ruler and lord is, what his purpose, what his will.' *On the Training of Cyrus*, VIII [i. 28]. *On the Nature of the Gods*, I [ii. 4]. *On Ends*, IV [v. 11].

A clear proof of all this is that Epicurus, after having abolished divine providence, left nothing of justice except the empty name,[4]

[1] The same writer, *On Courage* [vii], says: 'The highest and greatest cause of harmony is the belief in one God, from which, as from a spring, there comes an indissoluble friendliness that binds souls together.' Moreover, Josephus, in the book *Against Apion* [II. xix], says: 'For to hold one and the same belief about God, and to have no differences in manner of life and customs, causes the fairest concord in the minds of men.'

[2] So also Josephus, in the second book *Against Apion* [II. xxxv], gives these reasons why many states have been badly organized: 'Their lawgivers did not know from the beginning the true nature of God, and, not reaching a clear knowledge of what they were able to comprehend, did not, in the light of this, give another form to their constitution.' See also the excellent passage that follows.

[3] Justin Martyr, calling upon the Emperors to take cognizance of these things, adds: 'And this would be a truly royal task' [*Apology*, II. iii].
Add what Covarruvias says, *On Sext*, V. ult. 2 [V. ult. 4, pt. II], § 10.

[4] Seneca, *Letters*, xcvii [xcvii. 15]: 'Therein we differ from Epicurus, when he says that nothing is just by nature, and that crimes are to be avoided because fear cannot be avoided.'

so that he could say it arose from agreement only and endured no longer than the common advantage therefrom endured; that one must then abstain from the things which are likely to injure another solely through fear of punishment. His own remarkable words on
[X. cl. f.] this point are found in Diogenes Laertius.

5. Aristotle also perceived this relation, and in his *Politics*, Book V, chapter xi, speaks thus of the king: 'For the people will be less afraid of suffering anything unlawful from their prince if they believe that he fears the gods.' Galen, too, in the ninth book, speaking of the precepts of Hippocrates and Plato, after saying that many inquiries are conducted with regard to the earth and the nature of the gods without any advantage to morality, recognizes that the inquiry concerning the nature of providence is of the greatest advantage alike to private and to public virtues. Homer also saw this, and
[VI. 120; VIII. 576.] in the sixth and ninth books of the *Odyssey* contrasts with men who are 'insolent and fierce' those whose 'mind is god-fearing'.

[XXXVI. ii. 16.] [XVI. ii. 37.] [*Divine*] *Institutes*, V [xiv. 12]. [Lactantius,] *On the Anger of God* [vii. 13].

In like manner Justin, following Trogus, praises the justice of the ancient Jews that was bound up with their religion;[1] just as Strabo calls the same Jews 'truly pious and righteous'. Lactantius says: 'If then piety is a knowledge of God, and the sum of this knowledge is His worship, then he who does not accept the religion of God is ignorant of justice. For how can he know it who knows not whence it comes?' In another place, again: 'Justice is peculiar to religion.'

6. Religion is of even greater use in that greater society than in that of a single state. For in the latter the place of religion is taken by the laws and the easy execution of the laws; while on the contrary in that larger community the enforcement of law is very difficult, seeing that it can only be carried out by armed force, and the laws are very few. Besides, these laws themselves receive their validity chiefly from fear of the divine power; and for this reason those who sin against the law of nations are everywhere said to transgress divine
Code, I. v. 4. law. Therefore, the Emperors have well said that religious corruption affects all to their hurt.

XLV.—*What ideas of God are most generally accepted; and how these are indicated in the first commandments of the Decalogue*

1. To penetrate more deeply into the whole matter, we must observe that true religion, which is common to all ages, rests mainly upon four principles. Of these the first is, that God is, and is One; the second, that God is none of the things which are seen, but is

[1] Philo, *On Abraham* [xxxvii]: 'Piety and humanity are characteristics of the same nature, and in the same person one observes both filial respect toward God and justice toward man.'

something more exalted than these; the third, that God has a care for human affairs, and judges them with the most righteous judgements; and the fourth, that the same God is the creator of all things besides Himself. These four principles are likewise set forth in the commandments of the Decalogue.

2. For in the first commandment the oneness of God is openly revealed; in the second his invisible nature, for on this account it is forbidden to make a likeness of him (*Deuteronomy*, iv. 12). As also Antisthenes [1] said: 'He is not seen with the eyes, he is not like unto anything, therefore no one can learn to know him from an image.' Moreover, Philo said: [2] 'It is impious to depict the Invisible One' in painting or sculpture. Diodorus the Sicilian says of Moses: 'He *Selections* [from XL].
[342] set up no image [3] because he did not believe that God was of the likeness of men.' According to Tacitus: 'The Jews recognize [*Histories*, V. v.] but one divinity and that with the mind only. They treat as impious those who fashion images of the gods out of perishable materials in the likeness of men.' Plutarch, indeed, gives this reason for Numa's [*Numa*, 65 c.] removal of images from the temples [4]: 'That it is not possible to reach a conception of God except in thought.'

In the third commandment we perceive God's knowledge and care of human things, even of thoughts; for this is the basis of oaths. Since God is a witness even of the heart, He is invoked as an avenger if any one should swear falsely, which very fact reveals both the justice and the power of God. In the fourth commandment we see the origin of the whole world with God as its creator, in memory of which there was formerly instituted the Sabbath,[5] and this with a certain peculiar sanctity above other rites. For if any one should transgress other religious rites the punishment of the law was discretionary, as in the case of forbidden foods; but if against the Sabbath, the punishment was death. The reason is that the violation of the Sabbath, owing to the nature of its establishment, implied a denial that the world was created by God. However, the creation of the world by God declares both His goodness and wisdom, and His eternity and power.

[1] Cited by Clement of Alexandria [*Protrepticum*, VI. 71]. From Antisthenes, Seneca in his *Natural Questions*, VII. xxx, seems to have borrowed this: 'He who arranges these things, who has created, who has established all this, and placed it about himself, and is the greater and better part of his own work, escapes the sight of our eyes, and must be seen with the mind alone.'

[2] King Agrippa says this in Philo [*On the Embassy to Gaius*, xxxvi].

[3] Dio Cassius, XXXVI [XXXVII. xvii]: 'Neither had they any image in Jerusalem itself; for they believed that God could not be seen nor defined in words.' See also Strabo, XVI [XVI. ii. 35].

[4] On this ordinance of Numa see also Dionysius of Halicarnassus [cf. Cyril, *Against Julian*, VI. 193].

[5] The author of the *Responsa ad Orthodoxos*, qu. lxix [in Justin Martyr, *Opera Spuria*], says: 'Accordingly, to preserve among men the remembrance of the creation of the world, God ordained to this end that the number seven in the Holy Scripture should be regarded as more honourable than the rest.' See also what precedes.

3. Now from these speculative ideas arise opinions leading to action, that God is to be honoured, to be loved, to be worshipped, and also to be obeyed. Thus Aristotle has said that he who denies that we must honour the deity or love our parents must be subdued not by arguments but by punishment; in another passage, that some things are considered honourable in one place, others in another, but that everywhere it is held honourable to worship the deity. Moreover, the truth of the ideas which we have called speculative can doubtless be shown also by arguments drawn from the nature of things.

Topics, I. ix [I. xi. 9].

Topics, II. iv [II. xi].

Among such arguments this is the strongest, that our senses show that some things are made, but the things which are made lead us absolutely to something that is not made. But because all persons do not grasp this reason and others of a like nature it is enough to say that in every age throughout all lands, with very few exceptions, men have accepted these ideas; both those men who were too dull to wish to deceive, and others who were too wise to be deceived. This agreement [1] in so great a variety of laws and diversity in expressions of opinions regarding other matters sufficiently reveals the tradition that has been handed down to us from the beginning of the human race and has never been conclusively refuted; and that fact of itself is sufficient to cause belief.

4. These points which we have recalled concerning God were brought together by Dio of Prusa when he said that we have one 'conception', that is belief concerning God that is born with us and brought out by reasoning, and another 'acquired' by tradition. The same is called by Plutarch 'an ancient belief, than which we can name or discover no clearer proof, the common foundation established for piety'. Said Aristotle: 'All men have a belief about the gods.' And with this Plato in his *Laws*, Book X [chapter iii], agrees.

[*Orations*, xii = p. 204.]

[*Amatorius*, xiii = p. 756 B.]

De Caelo, III [I. iii].

[1] Tertullian, *Against Marcion* [I. x], says: [362] 'A consciousness of God is a dowry of the mind, from the beginning.' Diodorus Siculus in the fragments [*Selections*, XXIII. xi] speaks of 'a piety that is from nature'.

Philo, *On the Rule of One* [*On Monarchy*, iv], writes: 'Nothing that is a work of art arises by chance. But the world is a work of the highest art, and bears witness that it has been made by one most skilful in his craft and of the highest perfection. In this way arises the knowledge from which we believe in the existence of God.'

Again Tertullian, *Against Marcion*, I [I. xviii]: 'We hold that God must first be known from nature, then reapprehended by teaching. By nature, that is, by His works; by teaching, that is, from prophecy.'

Said Cyprian, *On the Vanity of Idols* [ix]: 'This is the height of wickedness, to refuse to recognize Him of whom you could not be ignorant.' Julian, *To Heraclitus* [*Against Heraclius*; *Orations*, VII. 209 C], declares: 'We all without teaching are convinced that there is some divinity, and that we must look to this and strive toward it; and I believe that our minds so look toward God, as things that see toward the light.'

XLVI.—*Those who first do violence to these common ideas may be punished*

1. Wherefore those are not free from blame who repudiate these ideas, even if they are too dull-witted to be able to discover or understand positive proofs thereof, since they have guides to the right path, and the contrary view rests upon no good reasons.

Since, however, we are dealing with punishments, and indeed punishments inflicted by men, we must introduce distinctions among the ideas themselves and in the manner of departing from them. These ideas, that there is a divinity (I exclude the question of there being more than one) and that he has a care for the affairs of men, are in the highest degree universal, and are [343] absolutely necessary to the establishment of religion, whether it be true or false. 'He that cometh to God (that is, he who has religion; for the Jews called religion an approach unto God) must believe that He is, and that He is the rewarder of them that seek after Him.' *Hebrews*, xi. 6.

2. In like manner Cicero said: *On the Nature of the Gods*, I [ii. 3].

> There are, and have been, philosophers who think that the gods take no care for the affairs of men. But if their view is correct, what piety can there be, what holiness, what religion? For all these things are to be rendered to the divinity of the gods with purity and freedom from sin if they are perceived by them, and if there is something contributed by the immortal gods to the human race.

So also Epictetus: 'In piety toward the gods, know that this is the essential thing, to hold right conceptions about them, as existing and as directing the universe well and righteously.' [*Manual*, xxxi.] Aelian says that none of the barbarians fell into atheism, but that they all declare that there is a divinity and that he has care for us.[1] [*Various History*,] II. xxxi.

Plutarch, in his *On Matters of Common Knowledge*, declares that if we take away providence we also take away the idea of God, 'for God must be conceived and thought of not only as immortal and blessed, but as loving man and caring for him and benefiting him'. [xxxii = p. 1075 E.] Said Lactantius: 'Neither can any respect be owed to God if He in no way aids him who worships Him, nor any fear if He is not angry with him who does not worship.' [*On the Anger of God*, vi.] And in very truth to deny that God exists, or to deny that He takes notice of human actions, if we look to the moral effect, amounts to the same thing.

3. Wherefore, as though under the influence of necessity itself, these two ideas have been preserved through so many ages, among almost all the peoples of whom we have knowledge.[2] For this reason

[1] Seneca, *Letters*, xcv [50]: 'The first thing in the worship of the gods is to believe in the gods; the next, to attribute to them their majesty, to attribute to them their goodness, without which there is no majesty.'

[2] Seneca, *Letters*, cxvii [6]: 'Among other reasons, we have this for believing that the gods

Digest, I. i. 2. [*Memorabilia*, IV. iv. 19.] [I. xvi. 43.] [II. xxii. 65.] [= p. 201.] Pomponius incorporates the worship of God in the universal common law; and, according to Xenophon, Socrates said that 'to reverence the gods' is a law which has authority among all men. So Cicero also affirms both in his first book *On the Nature of the Gods* and in his second book *On Invention.* Dio of Prusa in his twelfth *Oration* calls it 'a belief held by the whole human race in common, alike by the Greeks and by the barbarians, necessary and implanted by nature in every reasoning being'. A little further on he adds: 'A belief exceedingly strong and perpetual, beginning and remaining from all [IV. xlvii.] time and among all peoples.' Xenophon in the *Symposium* says that both Greeks and barbarians believe this, that both the present and the future are known to the gods.

4. I think, therefore, that those who first begin to abolish these ideas may be restrained in the name of human society, to which they do violence without a defensible reason; just as they are regularly restrained in well-organized states, as happened, we read, to Diagoras Aelian, IX [xii]. of Melos and to the Epicureans,[1] who were banished from cities that [Photius, *Library*, cod. 243.] maintained good morals. Himerius the Sophist in the suit against Epicurus said: 'Do you then demand punishment for a belief? No, but for impiety. For it is allowable indeed to preach one's beliefs, but not to assail piety.'

XLVII.—*But we may not punish others in like manner, as is shown by an argument from the Hebraic law*

1. Other ideas are not equally evident, as, for example, that there are not more gods than one; that none of the things which we see is God, neither the earth, nor the sky, nor the sun, nor the air; that the earth is not from all eternity nor even its matter, but that they were made by God. Consequently [344] we see that the knowledge of these things has disappeared among many peoples through lapse of time, and is as it were extinct; and the more easily so because the laws gave less attention to these ideas, seeing that some religion at any rate could exist without them.

2. The law of God itself was given to that people which the Prophets, and also prodigies, in part seen and in part brought to them

exist, that in all men there is an innate opinion with regard to the gods; and there is no people anywhere so far outcast from law and morality that they do not believe in some gods.' Also, *On Benefits*, IV. iv: 'All mankind would not have united in this madness of addressing divinities that are deaf and gods that are helpless,' etc.

See also Plato, *Protagoras* [xii = p. 322], and *Laws*, X [X. iii = p. 887 DE]; also the excellent remarks of Iamblichus, *On the Mysteries of the Egyptians*, after the introduction, where he says that it is as natural for a man to know there is a God as it is for a horse to neigh.

[1] Moxus, the Lydian, drowned all the inhabitants of the city of Crambus whom he had taken by siege, 'as atheists', seeing that they neither recognized nor worshipped any god; Nicholas of Damascus, *Excerpta Peiresciana* [= frag. 18, pp. 19–20, edit. Dindorf].

by the report of indubitable authority, had imbued with a knowledge of these things neither obscure nor uncertain; and although this law most strongly censures the worship of false gods, nevertheless it does not punish with death all who are convicted of guilt in this matter, but merely those whose cases present a peculiar circumstance. Such is he who has first led others astray, *Deuteronomy*, xiii. 16; or the city which begins to worship gods previously unknown, *Deuteronomy*, xii. 23; or he who worships the stars so that he abandons the whole law and therefore the worship of the true God, *Deuteronomy*, xvii. 2, which Paul calls 'to serve the creature rather than the Creator',[1] λατρεύειν τῇ κτίσει παρὰ τὸν κτίσαντα; for the Greek word παρὰ here and elsewhere often has an exclusive force. Even among the descendants of Esau this was at one time liable to punishment, as we may see in *Job*, xxxi. 26, 27. Such also is he who sacrificed his children to Moloch, that is to Saturn (*Leviticus*, xx. 2). [xiii. 1 and 6.] [xiii. 12 and 13.] [*Romans*, i. 25.]

3. Moreover, God did not judge that the Canaanites and the neighbouring peoples which had formerly fallen into base superstitions should be immediately punished, but only when they had increased this iniquity by heinous crimes (*Genesis*, xv. 16). So also among other peoples he excused the times of ignorance about the worship of false deities (*Acts*, xvii. 38). Beyond doubt it was rightly said by Philo that to each one his religion seems the best, since this is most often judged not by reason but by affection. Not very dissimilar is the saying of Cicero, that no one approves any philosophic system except that which he himself follows. He adds that most men are held in bondage before they are able to judge what is the best. [xvii. 30.] *On the Embassy to Gaius* [xxxvi]. *Acad.*, IV [*Acad. prior.*, II. iii. 8].

4. Just as those are worthy to be excused, and certainly not to be punished by men, who, not having received any law revealed by God, worship the powers of the stars or of other natural objects, or spirits, either in images or in animals or in other things, or even worship the souls of those who have been pre-eminent for their virtue and their benefactions to the human race, or certain intelligences without bodily form, especially if they themselves have not invented such cults, nor deserted for them the worship of the supreme God,[2] so we must class with the impious rather than with the erring those who establish with divine honours the worship of evil spirits, whom they know to be such, or of personified vices, or of men whose lives were filled with crimes.

[1] Philo *On the Ten Commandments* [xiii], speaks of such persons thus: 'There are some who go exceedingly far in impiety, not attributing any equal honour to God and to His works; for upon the latter they bestow all honour that can be devised, but, not deeming that most universal good worthy of any remembrance, they pass over the only thing that they ought to have remembered, wilfully wretched, bringing down upon themselves the oblivion they have sought.' Maimonides, *Guide of the Perplexed*, III. xli, also interprets thus the passage of *Deuteronomy*.

[2] Thus the Jews allowed in the Temple victims offered by the kings of Egypt, by Augustus, and by Tiberius. This is vouched for by Josephus and by Philo [*On the Embassy to Gaius*, xl].

Justin, XIX [i. 10]. Plutarch, *Apothegms* [p. 175 A], and *On the Delayed Vengeance of the Deity* [vi = p. 552 A]. Plutarch, *Roman Questions,* xii [lxxxiii = p. 283 F].

5. To be classed as impious also are those who worship gods with the shedding of innocent blood. For compelling the Carthaginians to abstain from this practice both Darius,[1] king of the Persians, and Gelon, tyrant of Syracuse, have won renown. Plutarch also records that the Romans once intended to punish some barbarians, who sacrificed human victims to their gods, but did no harm to them when they defended themselves on the ground of the antiquity of this custom; and only forbade them to do the like in future.

XLVIII.—*Wars cannot justly be waged against those who are unwilling to accept the Christian religion*

1. What shall we say of those wars that are waged against certain peoples for the reason that they have refused to embrace the Christian religion when proffered to them? I shall not discuss here whether the religion proffered was such as it ought to be, or whether it was proffered in the manner in which it ought. Let us grant that it was; then we say that two things must be taken into account.

The first is that the truth of the Christian religion, in so far as it makes a considerable addition to natural and primitive religion, cannot be proven by purely [345] natural arguments, but rests upon the history both of the resurrection of Christ and of the miracles performed by Him and by His Apostles. This is a question of fact, proven long ago by irrefutable testimonies, and of fact already very ancient. Whence it results that this doctrine cannot be deeply received in the mind of those who hear it now for the first time, unless God secretly lends His aid. This aid, when given to any persons, is not given as a reward of any work; so that, if it is denied or granted less generously to any, this occurs for reasons that are not unjust indeed but are frequently unknown to us, and hence not punishable by the judgement of man.

Decretum, I. xlv. 5.

Here applies the canon of the Council of Toledo: 'The holy synod ordains that no one should be constrained to believe by force.[2] For God takes pity upon whom he wishes, and hardens whom he wishes.' For it is the usage of the Sacred Writings to assign the divine will as a cause for those things whose causes escape our notice.[3]

2. The second point to be considered is this, that Christ as the author of the new law desired that absolutely no one should be induced to receive His law by punishments in this life, or by fear

[1] The son of Hystaspes, and father of Xerxes. Cf. II. xx. 11 [II. xx. 40], above.

[2] So Josephus [*Life,* xxiii] thinks that 'each man should worship God from his own choice, but not from compulsion'.

[3] [363] Servius, *On the Aeneid,* III [III, line 2], says: 'As often as the reason or the basis of judgement is not clear, then there is introduced "It seemed good to the Gods".' Similarly, Donatus, [*On Terence's*] *Eunuch,* V. ii. 36=875. Abrabanel observes that the Hebrew word חפץ is used in this sense.

thereof[1] (*Romans*, viii. 15; *Hebrews*, ii. 15; *John*, vi. 67; *Luke*, ix. 54; *Matthew*, xiii. 24). In this sense the saying of Tertullian is most true: 'The new law does not avenge itself with the avenging sword.' In the ancient book called the *Constitutions* of Clement, it is said of Christ: 'He has set free man's power of judgement, not sentencing him to death that is temporal, but calling him to account for this in another existence.' Said Athanasius:[2] 'The Lord, not applying compulsion, but leaving to the will its freedom, to said indeed all publicly, "If any one wishes to come after me"; to the Apostles however, "Do ye wish to depart also?"'[3] Chrysostom, commenting on this same passage of John, says: 'He asks, "Do ye wish to depart also", which is the saying of one who has removed all constraint and obligation.' [V. xxii.] [Homily XLVII. iii.]

3. This view is not inconsistent with the fact that in the parable of the wedding it is ordered that some be compelled to come in, *Luke*, xiv. 23. For just as in the parable itself the word 'compel' indicates the perseverance of the summoner,[4] so it does in the application also, and in this sense a word of like meaning is employed in *Luke*, xxiv. 29, as well as in *Matthew*, xiv. 22; *Mark*, vi. 45; and *Galatians*, ii. 14. Procopius, in a passage of his *Secret History*, informs us that the plan of Justinian,[5] which led to the conversion of the Samaritans to Christianity by force and threats, was criticized by men of wisdom. He recounts also the disadvantages which ensued from this course, as you may read in his work. [xi.]

XLIX.—*Wars are justly waged against those who treat Christians with cruelty for the sake of their religion alone*

1. Those who subject them that teach or profess Christianity to punishment for this cause certainly act against the dictates of reason itself. For there is nothing in the Christian teaching (here I am

[1] Gregory Nazianzen discusses this in the discourse *Cum assumptus est a patre*; also Bede, [*Ecclesiastical History*,] I. xxvi.

Isidore says of King Sisebut: 'Who at the beginning of his reign by influencing the Jews toward Christianity showed a zeal for God indeed, but not according to knowledge; for he compelled by his power those whom he should have called to the faith by reason.' Roderic has copied this into his *History*, II. xiii. On the same charge Osorius and Mariana accuse subsequent kings in Spain; see Mariana, XXVI. xiv [XXVI. xiii] and XXVII. v.

[2] *Letter to the Monks* [I = p. 855 A].

[3] Cyprian, *Letters*, lv [lv. 7]: 'Turning to His Apostles He said: "Do ye wish to go also?" Clearly respecting the law, by which a man who is left to his own freedom, and resting upon his own judgement, of his own accord seeks for himself death or salvation.'

[4] Cyprian, *On the Vanity of Idols* [xiv], having this passage in mind, says: 'The disciples scattered throughout the world, at the bidding of their Master and God, gave forth the precepts of God for salvation, led men from their wandering in darkness to the way of light, and gave eyes to the blind and ignorant for the recognition of the truth. And that the proving might not lack seriousness, and that their confession of Christ be not a matter of pleasure, they are tried by tortures, by crucifixions, by many kinds of punishments.'

[5] See the letter of Theodahad to the same Justinian in Cassiodorus, [*Variae*,] X. xxvi.

dealing with this by itself, and not with any impurities mingled therewith) which is injurious to human society, or rather, nothing which is not beneficial to it. The facts speak for themselves, and those not of the faith are obliged to recognize them. Pliny says that the Christians were bound by a mutual oath not to commit theft or robbery, and not to break faith. Ammianus [1] says that this religion teaches nothing but what is mild and just. And it was a common saying, 'Gaius Sejus is a good man, excepting that he is a Christian'.

[*Letters*, X. xcvi.]

Tertullian, *Apology*, iii, and *Against the Nations*, I. iv.

Nor can we accept as an excuse for persecution that all new things are to be distrusted, especially gatherings of men. For we ought not to fear doctrines however new, provided that they lead to all honourable things and to an exhibition of obedience to those in authority; nor should we mistrust meetings of good men, and [346] of those who do not seek concealment unless they are forced to. Here I may fitly apply what Philo [2] records that Augustus said of the meetings of the Jews, that they were not drunken revels or gatherings to disturb the peace, but schools of virtue.

2. Those who show cruelty to such persons are themselves in the condition where they may be punished with justice, as Thomas Aquinas also thinks. And for this reason Constantine waged war on Licinius,[3] and other emperors on the Persians; [4] although these wars were directed rather to the defence of the innocent, which we shall discuss below, than to the exaction of punishment.

Thomas [Aquinas], II. ii. 108.

L.—*Wars may not be justly waged against those who err in the interpretation of the Divine law; as is proven by authorities and examples*

1. Likewise those who oppress with punishment persons that accept the law of Christ as true, but who are in doubt or error on some points which are either outside the law or appear to have an

[1] [Ammianus, XXII. xi. 5.] The same author, indeed, calls the Christian religion pure and simple [XXI. xvi. 18]. Zosimus [II. xxix], himself a pagan, said: 'The promise of the Christian faith is a release from every sin and impiety.' Pagan writers everywhere called the Christians a sect which annoyed no one, as we learn from Tertullian, *Scorpiace* [i].

Justin Martyr in his *Second Apology* [I. xii] says: 'We are your supporters and allies for the peace of the whole world, because we teach that the wicked, or the avaricious, or the treacherous, or the upright cannot escape the notice of God; and that each one proceeds to eternal punishment or salvation according to the merit of his works.'

Arnobius, Book II [*Against the Heathen*, IV. xxxvi], speaking of the gatherings of the Christians, says: 'In them they hear nothing but what makes them compassionate, gentle, reverent, modest, chaste, and ready to share their goods with all who are bound together by the tie of brotherhood.'

[2] *On the Embassy to Gaius* [xl]. Likewise in the book *On Those Who Offer Sacrifice* [xii] he eloquently shows the great difference between the synagogues and pagan mysteries. Both passages are worth reading. Josephus says something similar in his *Against Apion*, Book II.

[3] See Zonaras [XV. i]. A similar case occurs in Augustine, *Letters*, l [clxxxv. 7. 28]: '(Maximian, Bishop of Bagai,) sought aid from a Christian emperor against the enemies of the Church, not so much to avenge himself as to protect the Church entrusted to his care.' This is cited in the *Decretum*, II. xxiii. 3 [II. xxiii. 3. 2].

[4] [364] See Menander Protector [frag. 32 and 41, pp. 68 and 79, edit. Dindorf].

ambiguous statement in the law and are variously explained by the early Christians, act most wickedly. This is proven both by our previous discussion and by the ancient conduct of the Jews. For although they had a law which was supported by the punishments of this life, they never subjected to punishment the Sadducees, who rejected the doctrine of the Resurrection; a doctrine most true indeed, but in that law revealed only obscurely and in involved phraseology and metaphors.

2. What now shall we say if the error be more serious, and one which may be easily refuted before impartial judges by sacred authority, or by the agreement of ancient writers? Here we must take into account also the great power of habitual opinion, and the degree to which freedom of judgement is hampered by zeal for one's own sect; an evil, as Galen says, more incurable than any leprosy. On this point Origen fitly says: 'It is easier for a man to change his habits in other things, even if he should be most strongly attached to them, than in matters of doctrine.' [1] Remember also that the degree of guilt in this matter depends upon the method of enlightenment and other mental conditions, which it is not given to men fully to know. [*Against Celsus*, I. lii.]

3. In the view of Augustine [2] a heretic is one who either creates or follows new and false opinions for the sake of some temporal advantage and especially for his own glory and pre-eminence.[3] Let us listen to Salvianus on the Arians: [*On the Government of God*, V. ii.]

They are heretics, but not knowingly; in short they are heretics in our eyes, but not in their own; for they consider themselves so thoroughly catholic, that they insult us ourselves with the name of a base heresy. What therefore they are to us, this we are to them. We are confident that they do wrong to the Divine generation, because they say that the Son is less than the Father. They think that we do wrong to the Father, because we believe that Father and Son are equal. The truth is on our side, but they claim it is on theirs. The honour of God is with us, but they think that what they believe in is the honour of the Divinity. They are undutiful, but to them this is the supreme duty of religion. They are impious, but they think that this is true piety.

They err therefore, but they err with good intent,[4] not through hatred but through love of God, believing that they honour and love the Lord. Although they have not the true faith, yet they believe that this is the perfect love of God; and how they are to be punished for this error of false belief on the Day of Judgement no one can know but

[1] This is followed by Chrysostom, *On First Corinthians*, ii [Homily VII, vii]: 'Whenever a habit arises in matters of belief, it becomes much more firmly established. For one could change everything else more easily than the things which pertain to religion.'

[2] *On the Utility of Belief* [i]. The passage is cited in the *Decretum*, II. xxiv. 3 [II. xxiv. 3. 28]. Augustine adds that he does not consider a heretic and a believer in heretical doctrines to be identical. See also his *Letters*, clxii [xliii. 1]. Heresy is 'the madness of too obstinate a mind'; *Code*, I. i. 2.

[3] The writer of *Responsa ad Orthodoxos*, qu. iv [in Justin Martyr, *Opera Spuria*], says: 'It is evident that all the sects have arisen from the love of fame or from the rivalry which animated their founders.' Chrysostom, *On Galatians*, v [V. 13], calls 'the desire for primacy the mother of heresies'.

[4] Agathias, *Histories*, I [I. vii], having discussed the foolish superstitions of the Alemanni, says: 'All who miss the truth deserve to be pitied rather than to be censured and should obtain the widest pardon. For in truth they do not intentionally wander and go astray, but in their search for the good; but then, erring in their judgement, for the future they hold doggedly to the views once formed, of whatever character these may be.'

the Judge.[1] Therefore in the meantime, in my opinion, God shows patience towards them because He sees that even if they do not believe aright they err through a devotion to a pious belief.

4. Regarding the Manicheans, let us listen to him who for a long time was involved in their dull follies, Augustine :

[*Contra Epistolam Manichaei*, ii and iii.]

Those rage against you, who know not with what labour the truth is found, and with what difficulty errors are guarded against. Those rage against you, who know not how rare and difficult a thing it is to conquer by the calmness of a pious mind the vain imaginings of the flesh. Those rage against you, who know not with what difficulty [347] the eye of the inner man is healed, so that he may be able to gaze upon his own sun. [. . .] Those rage against you, who know not what groans and sighs it costs to be able to know God in the smallest degree. Finally, those rage against you, who have been deceived by no such error as they see deceives you. [. . .] But I cannot rage against you at all, you whom now I should bear with just as with myself at that time, and in dealing with whom I should manifest such patience as those nearest me showed to me when, mad and blind, I went astray in your doctrine.

5. Athanasius, in his *Letter to the Monks*, bitterly assails the Arian heresy[2] because the Arians first used the power of the courts against their adversaries, and strove to draw to themselves by violence, scourging, and imprisonment those whom they could not persuade by argument. 'And in this way', he says, 'they reveal themselves as being neither pious nor worshippers of God,' referring, unless I am mistaken, to what we read in *Galatians*, iv. 29.[3]

Hilarius, in his address to Constantius, expresses similar views. Long ago in Gaul[4] the judgement of the Church condemned the bishops who had seen to it that the Priscillians should be punished with the sword; and in the East the Synod, which had sanctioned

[1] Chrysostom says, Homily [IV], *Against Those Who Anathematize*: 'That which is hidden the Judge of the ages alone shall judge without peril, who alone knows both the measure of knowledge and the amount of faith. For tell me, I beseech you, whence do we know with what words each will accuse or defend himself on that day when God shall judge the hidden things of men? Verily His judgements are inscrutable, and His ways past finding out.'

[2] Not undeservedly do we detest those who introduced such a bad precedent among the Christians. See their cruel deeds in Eusebius, *On the Life of Constantine*, I. v. 38, and Socrates, IV. xxix; Procopius, on Hunerich, *Vandalic War*, I [I. viii], and on Amalarich, *Gothic War*, I [I. xiii]; and Victor Utunensis [Victor Vitensis, *Persecution of the Vandals*, II. ii].

Epiphanius says of the Semi-Arians: 'They persecute those who teach the truth, and they do not confute them by arguments, but subject the true believers to hatreds, to wars, and to slaughter. For not in one city and one country only have they wrought this destruction, but in many.' Of such occurrences Gregory, Bishop of Rome [Gregory the Great, *Letters*, III. xi. 56], wrote to the Bishop of Constantinople: [365] 'This is a new and unheard-of preaching, which exacts beliefs by blows.'

[3] On this passage see Jerome, cited in the *Decretum*, II. xxiii. 4. 13.

[4] Sulpicius Severus [II. xlvii] says: 'Then, however, Idacius and Ithacius pressed on more sharply, thinking that the evil could be checked at its outset; but unwisely they approached the secular judges, in order that the heretics might be driven from the cities by edicts and executions.' Then: 'There followed as accusers the bishops Idacius and Ithacius, whose zeal in crushing the heretics I would not censure had they not striven with an unbecoming desire to conquer. But in my opinion at any rate both defendants and accusers alike are censurable' [II. l]. Afterwards: 'Martin, appointed at Trèves, ceased not to urge Ithacius to desist from his accusations; to beseech Maximus to abstain from shedding the blood of the unfortunate, on the ground that it was enough and more than enough to banish from the churches the heretics who were condemned by the decree of the bishops.' See also what follows.

the burning of Bogomil, was condemned. Plato wisely said that the punishment of the erring is: to be taught.[1] [*Republic*, I. xi.]

LI.—*But war may justly be waged against those who show impiety toward the gods they believe in*

1. More justly are those punished who are irreverent and irreligious toward the gods in whom they believe.[2] This cause in fact among others was alleged for the Peloponnesian War between the Athenians and the Lacedaemonians, and by Philip of Macedon against the Phocians, concerning whose sacrilege Justin said: 'This had to be expiated by the forces of the whole world.' Jerome wrote: 'As long as the vessels (of the Jews) were in the temple of the idol of Babylon, God was not angry (for they seemed to have dedicated the property of God according to a base superstition indeed, but yet to divine worship), but after they desecrated divine things for the use of men punishment followed immediately upon the sacrilege.' Thuc., I [cxxvi]. Diod., XVI [lx]. VIII [ii. 6]. [*On Daniel*, v. 4, chap. vi.]

Beyond doubt Augustine thought that the Empire of the Romans was increased by God because they had at heart a religion, although a false one; and, as Lactantius says, they sought after the supreme duty of man, in intent if not in fact. [*City of God*, V. xii.] [*Divine Institutes*, II. iii. 14.]

2. We have said also above that, whatever the divinities which are so considered may be, perjury against them is avenged by the true Divinity. Says Seneca: 'He is punished because he acted as towards God; his belief subjects him to the punishment.' Thus I understand also that other saying of Seneca: 'The punishment for the desecration of religion varies in different places; but everywhere there is some punishment.' In fact Plato appoints the death penalty for those who violate religion. [II. xiii. 12.] *On Benefits*, VII. vii. *On Benefits*, III. vi. *Laws*, X [xv].

[1] Seneca says in a tragedy [*Hercules Raging*, 1237]:

Who has ever given to error the name of guilt?

The same author, *On Anger*, I. xiv: 'A wise man does not hate those who err; otherwise he will hate himself.' Says Marcus Aurelius, IX [IX. xi]: 'Correct me, if you can. But if not, remember that gentleness was given you for this purpose; and even the gods are gentle with such persons.'

Chrysostom, *On Ephesians*, iv. 17 [Homily XIII, i], says: 'He who is ignorant should not be abused or accused, but it is right that he should learn what he is ignorant of.' Ammianus Marcellinus, Book XXX [XXX. ix. 5], praises Valentinian in these words: 'He disturbed no one, neither ordered that this or that should be worshipped; he did not, through threatening prohibitions, bend the neck of his subjects to adore what he himself worshipped, but left these matters undisturbed as he found them.'

[2] See on this point the excellent remarks of Cyril, in his book *Against Julian*, v and vi. According to Plutarch, *Solon* [xi = p. 83 F], on the advice of Solon, the Delphic Amphictyony attacked the people of Cirrha, because they had done violence to the temple at Delphi. So also those who falsely assume the name of prophet are justly punished; see Agathias, V [V. v].

CHAPTER XXI

ON THE SHARING OF PUNISHMENTS

I.—*How punishment may pass to those who have shared in the crime*

[366] 1. WHENEVER question arises in regard to the sharing of punishment, the question concerns either those who are accessories in the wrong,[1] or other persons.

Those who are accessories in the wrong are punished not so much for another's as for their own misdeed. Who these are may be seen [II. xvii. 6.] from our previous discussion of damage unjustly inflicted. In fact one comes to participation in a wrong in almost the same way as to participation in the infliction of injury. Yet where a liability for damages arises there is not always a wrong, but only when a more notable evidence of evil intent is at hand; for any sort of fault may frequently be sufficient to give rise to a liability for damages inflicted.

2. Therefore, those who order a wicked act, or who grant to it the necessary consent,[2] or who aid it,[3] or who furnish asylum,[4] or those who in any other way share in the crime itself; those who give advice,[5] who praise, or approve;[6] those who do not forbid such an act although bound by law properly so called to forbid it,[7] or who do not bring aid to the injured although bound to do so by the same law; those who do not dissuade when they ought to dissuade; those

[1] Tertullian says, *On the Resurrection of the Flesh* [chap. xvi]: 'For they will say that servants and associates have the choice of serving and allying themselves, and have the power to exercise their will either with regard to other men or with regard to themselves. Therefore they deserve to share the deserts of the authors of crime, whom they have aided of their own accord.'

[2] 'Saul stoned with the hands of all,' Augustine, *Sermones de Sanctis*, V. iv [I. iv=Appendix, ccxv. 4]. Something similar occurs in I. iii [=Appendix ccxv. 3] on the same subject, and in XIV [=Appendix, clxxxix].

[3] Actively. See *Institutes*, IV. i. 11, and the *Edict of Theodoric*, chap. cxx.

[4] Jerome, *On the Parables* [xxix], says: 'Not the thief alone is guilty, but he also who, although cognizant of the theft, does not reveal it to the owner who seeks his goods.'

Chrysostom, *On the Statues*, XIV [XIV. iii]: 'For not only perjurers, but also those who know of the perjury and conceal it, share in the crime.'

[5] See the citations from the *Institutes* and the *Edict of Theodoric* already given. Androcides [Andocides], speaking of the Attic law [*On the Mysteries*, xciv], says: 'He who formed the plan is not less responsible than he whose hand did the thing.' Aristotle, in the *Poetics*, chapter xvii [*Rhetoric*, I. vii]: 'For it would not have been done without previous counsel.'

[6] Said Chrysostom, *On Romans*, i, end [Homily V, i]: 'For he who praises a sin is worse than he who has sinned.' He who is present and encourages a wrong-doer is treated as a wrong-doer himself by the *Lombardic Law*, I. ix. 25. See our citations from Philo and Josephus on II. xxi. 17, below [p. 544].

[7] Chrysostom, *Against the Jews*, I [IV. vii], says: 'Just as both those who steal and those who are able to prevent them, but fail to do so, pay the same penalty.' The same author, *On Second Corinthians*, vii [vii. 7=Homily XIV, iii], declares that he who prevents a sick man from being healed is considered as responsible as if he had wounded him.

who conceal the fact which they are bound by some law to make known—all these may be punished, if there is in them evil intent sufficient to deserve punishment, according to the discussion which immediately precedes.

II.—*A community, or its rulers, may be held responsible for the crime of a subject if they know of it and do not prevent it when they could and should prevent it*

1. The matter will become clearer from illustrations. A civil community, just as any other community, is not bound by the acts of individuals, apart from some act or neglect of its own. For Augustine well says: 'The particular sin committed by the individual in a state is one thing, and differs from a common sin, which is done with one mind and one will, when the multitude has been united for some purpose.' Hence we find in the formula for treaties the clause, 'If he has violated this by public agreement'.[1] [*Questions on Heptateuch*, III. xxvi.]

According to Livy, the Locrians showed the Roman Senate that the blame for their defection did not rest on the public will. The same author relates that Zeno, who interceded for the Magnesians with tears, besought Titus Quintius and the delegates who accompanied him 'not to blame the state for the madness of one man; each man's folly should be a peril to himself.' And the Rhodians, in the presence of the Senate, separated the public cause from the cause of individuals, saying: 'There is no state which does not have wicked citizens sometimes, and an ignorant populace all the time.' So the father is not bound by the wrong-doing of his children, nor the master by that of his slave, nor any others of superior station [by crimes of inferiors], unless they themselves make manifest something blame-worthy in themselves. [XXIX. xvii.] [XXV. xxxi.] Livy, XLV [xxiii. 8].

2. Now of the ways in which those who have control over others come to participate in a crime, there are two which are especially common, and which require careful consideration, toleration, and refuge.

With respect to toleration we must accept the principle that he who knows of a crime, and is able and bound to prevent it but fails to do so, himself commits a crime. Cicero, in his speech *Against Piso*, declares: 'There is not much difference, especially in the case of a consul, whether he himself troubles the state by dangerous [v. 10.]

[1] [379] Said Chrysostom, *On the Statues*, III [III. i]: 'The crime was not one common to the city, but committed by some foreigners and strangers, who in everything exhibit boldness and ignorance of the laws rather than prudence. It would not be right, then, that such a city should be despoiled, and that those who had done no wrong should be punished, on account of the lack of discipline in a few.'

Ammianus said of the Quadi, Book XXX [XXX. vi. 2]: 'They asserted that no wrong had been done us by a common plan of the chiefs of their nation.'

laws or wicked harangues, or permits others to do so.' Brutus wrote to Cicero: 'Will you then, you will say, hold me responsible for another's fault? Certainly for another's, if it could have been foreseen and prevented.' Agapetus, commenting on Justinian, says: 'Not to restrain wrong-doers is the same as the committing of wrong.' 'Whoever suffers a sinner to sin,' says Arnobius, 'lends strength to his boldness.' [367] Says Salvianus: 'He who has it in his power to prevent an action orders its accomplishment if he does not check it.' With truth Augustine adds: 'Whoever fails to oppose an act, when he can, gives his consent to it.'

[*Letters to Brutus*, I. iv. 3(5).] [*Parainetica*, xxviii.] *Against the Heathen*, IV [xxxii]. [*On the Government of God*, VII. xix.] [Cited in *Decr.* II. xxiii. 3. 11.] *Dig.* XL. viii. 7. *Dig.* IX. iv. 2. Paul, *Sententiae*, V [xxx. 2].

3. Thus he who suffers a slave to be prostituted, when he could save her from such abuse, is held by the Roman laws to have prostituted her. If a slave has killed a man with the knowledge of his master, the latter is liable for full damages, for it is as if he himself had done the killing. The Fabian Law punished the master whose slave with his knowledge had enticed away a slave belonging to another.

4. But, as we have said, to participate in a crime a person must not only have knowledge of it but also have the opportunity to prevent it. This is what the laws mean when they say that knowledge, when its punishment is ordained, is taken in the sense of toleration,[1] so that he may be held responsible who was able to prevent a crime but did not do so; and that the knowledge to be considered here is that associated with the will, that is, knowledge is to be taken in connexion with intent.

Dig. IX. ii. 45. *Digest*, XLVII. vi. 1. § 1.

Consequently, the master is not to be held responsible in case the slave has formally claimed his freedom, or if he has treated his master with contempt; for surely he is blameless who knows of an intended crime, but is unable to prevent it. Thus parents are responsible for the misdeeds of their children, but only the misdeeds of those who are still under their parental authority. On the other hand, even if parents have children under their authority and otherwise could have restrained them, they will not be held responsible unless they also had knowledge. For that one person may be held responsible for the act of another, these two elements, knowledge and the failure to prevent, should be present in like degree.

Dig. IX. iv. 4. *Dig.* L. xvii. 50, 109. *Dig.* III. ii. 1, 13. § 1, 19. *Digest*, XLVII. vii. 7. § 5.

All that has been said of those in authority is with equal justice to be applied to those under authority; for these obligations spring from natural equity.

[*Works and Days*, 240.]

5. To the line of Hesiod—

> Full oft the state pays penalty
> For the wickedness of one

[1] Cf. *Law of the Visigoths*, VIII. iv. 11, 26, and elsewhere, and IX. i. 1.

Proclus adds the excellent comment: 'Since, when it could, it did not prevent the evil conduct of that one man.' So in the army of the Greeks, when Agamemnon himself and other chiefs acted in accordance with a common plan, not undeservedly—

> For all the madness of their kings
> Do the Achaeans suffer; [Horace, *Epistles*, I. ii. 14.]

it was, in fact, in their power to compel Agamemnon [1] to restore to the priest his daughter.

Likewise afterwards their fleet is said to have been burned—

> For the guilt and frenzy of Ajax alone,
> The son of Oileus.[2]

Of this deed Ovid in the *Metamorphoses*, Book XIV, says: [XIV. 468 ff.]

> By the rape of the maid
> He brought on all the punishment
> Which he alone deserved,

because the others had not hindered the seizing of the maiden priestess.

In Livy we find the following:

> The relatives of King Tatius maltreated the envoys of the Laurentians, and when the Laurentians sought redress under the law of nations partiality for his relations and their entreaties had the greater influence with him. In consequence he brought upon himself the punishment that was theirs. Livy, I [xiv. 1].

Here properly applies what Salvianus says about kings: 'A power great and most influential, since it can prevent the greatest crime,[3] approves, as it were, the doing of a thing if, having knowledge thereof, it suffers the thing to be done.' [*On the Government of God*, VII. xix.]

1 So Cyril interprets this incident, *Against Julian*, V [= 175].

2 [Virgil, *Aeneid*, I. 41.] Euripides, *Trojan Women* [lines 70–1] makes Neptune speak thus:

> When Ajax' hand with violence dragged off Cassandra

and Minerva answer him:

> And yet naught heard he from the Greeks, nor suffered punishment.

With equal right Chrysostom involves all the men of Antioch in the crime of the statues in the first homily on this theme [*On the Statues*, II. iii], saying: 'Lo, the sin was that of a few, but the accusation is brought against all. Lo, on account of these we are now all in fear, and for what they have dared to do we ourselves await the punishment. But if we had anticipated them, by driving them from the city, and had treated the diseased part as we ought to have done, we should not now be thus afraid.'

The same homily [II. iv]: 'On account of this very thing, he says, suffer punishment, and pay the extreme penalty, because you were not present, because you did not prevent it, because you did not restrain the disorderly, because you took no risk for the honour of the Emperor. But you did not share in the audacious deeds? That I praise and account it good. But neither did you hinder what was going on; and this is ground for an accusation.'

3 Philo says, *Against Flaccus* [v]: 'For he who could have punished, or at least restrained if he did not prevent, must be held to have permitted, or even to have encouraged, what was done.'

Dio Cassius [LXIII. ii] remarks of Galba: 'For private citizens, it is enough if they do no wrong themselves; but those who hold authority must see to it that no one else is an evil-doer.'

In Canon IV, of the Synod of Pistes, which is found in the *Capitularies* of Charles the Bald, we read: 'He who fails to correct what he is able to correct is not free from complicity; wherefore, without doubt, he makes himself a participator in the crime.' [*Monumenta Germaniae Historica, Leges*, II, vol. II, p. 308.]

See also Nicetas of Chonae, II [II. iii], on Andronicus.

I [lxix]. In Thucydides the principle is stated: 'He who is able to prevent [a crime and does not] in very truth commits it.' Thus,
I [xxx] according to Livy, the Veientes and the Latins excused themselves
and VI [x]. before the Romans on the ground that it was without their knowledge that their subjects had aided the enemies of the Romans. But on
Polybius, the other hand, the plea of Teuta, queen of the Illyrians, was not
II [viii]. accepted when she alleged that piracy was not practised by herself but by her subjects, for the reason that she had not restrained them. In ancient times the people of Scyros were condemned by the Delphic Amphictyony[1] because they had permitted some of their number to practise piracy.

6. Moreover we may presume that acts which are conspicuous, or frequent, are easily known, for 'none can be ignorant of what is
[Polybius, done by many', as Dio of Prusa says in his Rhodian speech. Polybius
IV. xxvii.] severely censures the Aetolians because, although they did not wish to appear as enemies of King Philip, they secretly permitted their citizens to commit [368] acts of hostility against him, and rewarded with offices the leaders in such enterprises.

III.—*Likewise a community, or its rulers, may be held responsible for refuge afforded to those who have done wrong elsewhere*

1. Let us now come to the second question, which concerns
[II. xx. 7.] the affording a refuge against punishment. As we have said above, any one who cannot be charged with a like crime has a natural right to exact punishment. But, since the organization of states, it is agreed that the crimes of individuals, in so far as they properly concern the community to which they belong, should be left to the states themselves and their rulers, to be punished or condoned at their discretion.

2. But so comprehensive a right has not been granted to states and their rulers in the case of crimes which in some way affect human society, and which it is the right of other states and their rulers to follow up, just as in each state it is possible for any citizen to initiate a prosecution for certain offences. Much less do states and their rulers possess this full authority in the case of crimes by which another state or its ruler is in a special sense injured, and on account of which that ruler or state, for the sake of dignity or security, has the right to exact punishment, in accordance with our previous conclusions. Therefore the state in which the guilty person dwells, or its ruler, ought not to interfere with this right.

[1] [380] Plutarch, *Cimon* [viii = p. 483 C].

IV.—*Such responsibility rests upon a community or its rulers unless they either punish or surrender the guilty parties, as is shown by examples*

1. Since as a matter of fact states are not accustomed to permit other states to cross their borders with an armed force for the purpose of exacting punishment, and since such a course is inexpedient, it follows that the state in which he who has been found guilty [1] dwells ought to do one of two things. When appealed to it should either punish the guilty person as he deserves, or it should entrust him to the discretion of the party making the appeal. This latter course is rendition, a procedure most frequently mentioned in historical narratives.[2]

2. For example, the other Israelites demanded of the Benjamites that they give up certain guilty persons (*Judges*, xx). The Philistines asked the Jews to give up Samson to them, as if he were a criminal (*Judges*, xv). So the Lacedaemonians made war on the Messenians because the latter did not surrender a man who had slain Lacedaemonians, and at another time for the failure to give up those who had assaulted maidens sent on a sacred mission. Pausanias, XIV [IV. 4]. Strabo, VIII [iv. 9].

Cato desired that Caesar be handed over to the Germans for having attacked them unjustly. So the Gauls demanded that the Fabii be given up to them,[3] because they had fought against them. The Romans required the Hernici to surrender to them those who had ravaged their land, and the Carthaginians to give up Hamilcar, not the famous general, but another one of that name, who was urging the Gauls to hostility; and afterward they demanded Hannibal.[4] According to Sallust, the Romans demanded the surrender of Jugurtha by Bocchus with these words: 'That you may at one and the same time relieve us from the bitter necessity of punishing alike you who are making a mistake and him who is a consummate villain.' [Cf. I. iii. 5. 4.] [Dion. Halic., VIII. lxiv.] [Livy, XXXI. xi. 6.] [*Jugurtha*, cii. 5.]

The Romans themselves gave up the men who had attacked the ambassadors of the Carthaginians, and also of the Apolloniates. The Livy, XXVIII [XXXVIII. xlii. 7].

[1] For the judicial investigation should precede the surrender; it is not fitting 'to give up those who have not been tried,' says Plutarch, *Romulus* [vii = 21 C].

According to Camden, on the year 1585, the king of Scotland said to Queen Elizabeth that he would send to England Fernihurst, and also his chancellor, if they could be convicted by clear and legitimate proofs of having with premeditation violated the promised security and joined in a plot to murder.

[2] Lucullus demanded from Tigranes the surrender of Mithridates and, when he refused, made war on him; Appian, *Mithridatic Wars* [lxxxiii], and Plutarch, *Lucullus* [xxi = 505 D]. The Romans required the surrender of the Salyi by the Allobroges; Appian, *Selections on Embassies*, xi [= *Gallic History*, xii].

Regarding the bishop whom the Romans wished to surrender to the Scythians, see Priscus, *Selections on Embassies*, xxi. The Duke of Beneventum was given up to Ferdinand, ruler of Castile, by the king of Gascony; Mariana, XX. i.

[3] Plutarch, *Camillus* [xvi–xvii = pp. 136–7]; Appian, *Selections on Embassies*, ix [= *Gallic History*, ii].

[4] Diodorus Siculus, fragments [XXV. v]; Livy, [XXI. vi. 8].

[Livy, XXXVIII [xxxi. 2].] Achaeans required the Lacedaemonians to surrender those who had besieged the village of Las, adding that, unless these should be given up, they would consider the league violated. [Diod., XVI [xcii].] So the Athenians proclaimed by a herald that if any one fomented a conspiracy against Philip, and fled to Athens, 'he would be liable to surrender'. [Plutarch, *Narr. Amat.* [iv = p. 774].] The Boeotians required from the Hippotians the surrender of those who had slain Phocus. [Val. Max., VI. vi.]

3. All these examples nevertheless must be interpreted in the sense that a people or king is not absolutely bound to surrender a culprit, but, as we have said, either to surrender or to punish him. [[Pausanias, VI. ii.]] Thus we read that the Eleans made war upon the Lacedaemonians because the latter did not punish those who had wronged them; that is, the Lacedaemonians neither punished nor surrendered the guilty. There is in fact an alternative in the liability.

4. Sometimes the choice is given to those who demand the guilty,[1] in order that they may receive more ample satisfaction. [Livy, VII [xx. 6 and 7].] According to Livy the people of Caere informed the Romans that 'The men of Tarquinii, passing through their territory in hostile array, although they had sought nothing but the right to march through, had drawn along with them some [369] of the rural population, who had shared in the ravages with which the Caeretans were charged; that they were ready to surrender these, if the Romans so desired, or, if the Romans desired their punishment, to inflict the penalty.'

5. In the second treaty between the Carthaginians and the [[III. xxiv. 10.]] Romans, which is found in Polybius, there is a passage which generally is badly punctuated and interpreted: 'But if this is not done (what 'this' is, remains uncertain, for what precedes is mutilated), let each privately prosecute his claim; but if any one has done this (unless justice is done him) let the state be held responsible for the crime.' Aeschines, in his reply to the accusation of Demosthenes, *Concerning* [[cxvii.]] *the Badly Conducted Embassy*, records that when he was negotiating with Philip of Macedon about peace for the Greeks he said, among other things, that it was not just that the states should atone for the wrongs that had been done, but that those who had committed the wrongs should pay the penalty, and that no harm should be done to the states which made such persons appear for trial. Quintilian, in his *Declamations*, cclv, declared: 'I think that those who receive deserters are almost as bad as the deserters themselves.[2]

[1] See the treaty between the kings of England and Denmark referred to in Pontanus, *De Mari* [*Discussiones Historicae*, I. xxi].

[2] Zonaras [XVII. v. 50] says that the Emperor Basil Porphyrogenitus 'sent to Khosroo to ask him not to receive the rebel who had attacked his proper lord, in order that Khosroo might not establish a precedent dangerous to himself'.

On the pirates wrongly received at Lesbos see Chalcocondylas, Book IX [X. beginning].

6. In his address to the men of Nicomedia, Dio Chrysostom enumerates among the evils that arise from differences between states the fact that 'It is possible for those who have done wrong to one state to flee for refuge to another'. [*Oration*, xxxviii = p. 480.]

7. Here the question arises whether those who have been surrendered by their own state, and not received by others, continue to be citizens. Publius Mucius Scaevola thought that they did not remain citizens, because the people seemed to banish from their state one whom they had surrendered, just as they would do if they forbade him water and fire. *Dig.* L. vii. 18.

The contrary opinion is upheld by Brutus, and after him by Cicero. And this is the more correct view. The reason is not, however, that adduced by Cicero, who holds that, as with giving, so with surrendering, the act cannot be understood without an acceptance. For the act of giving cannot be completed unless by the agreement of two persons. But the surrendering with which we here have to do is nothing more than the entrusting of a citizen to the power of another state, for it to decide about him as it may wish. This entrusting neither confers nor takes away any right; it merely removes an impediment to the exaction of punishment. If therefore the other state does not make use of the right that is granted to it, the condition of him who has been surrendered will be such that he may either be punished by his own people (as happened to Clodius, who was given up to the Corsicans and not received by them) or not punished by them, since there are many crimes which may be acted upon in either way. *On the Orator*, I and II [I. xl. 181; II. xxxii. 137]; *Topics* [viii. 37]; *For Caecina* [xxxiv. 98]. Valerius [Max.], VI. iii.

Further, the right of citizenship, just as other rights and properties, is not lost on account of a mere fact but through some decree or judicial sentence, unless some law requires the fact to be considered as equivalent to a judicial decision; and that cannot be said in this case. Likewise also goods, if they have been given but not received, will remain the property of their former owner. If, however, the surrender has been accepted, and afterward, by some chance, he who had been surrendered is restored, he will not be a citizen unless by a new grant. In this sense the opinion of Modestinus on the status of a person who has been surrendered is correct. *Digest*, XLIX. xv. 4.

8. What we have said with regard to the surrender or punishment of guilty parties applies not merely to those who have always been subjects of the state in which they are at the time found, but also to those who after having committed a crime have fled to another state for refuge.

V.—*The rights of suppliants belong to the unfortunate, and not to the guilty, with exceptions*

1. The view just stated is not inconsistent with the much discussed rights of suppliants [1] and cases of asylum. These are in fact for the benefit of those who suffer from undeserved enmity, not those who have done something that is injurious to human society or to other men. The Spartan Gylippus, in Diodorus Siculus dealing with the right of suppliants, speaks thus: 'Those who first established such rights desired that the unfortunate indeed should look for mercy, but that those who had done wrong with evil intent should look for punishment.' Later: 'Let these not blame their ill-fortune, or give themselves the name of suppliants, if [370] they have fallen upon these ills through evil purpose or in consequence of an unjust desire for what belongs to another. For the name of suppliant is rightly due to those men whose mind is innocent, but with whom fortune is angry.[2] Those whose life is full of wicked acts have no way left through which they may find pity or asylum.'

Library, XIII [xxix].

Menander made an excellent distinction between these two things—misfortune and wrong:

[Stobaeus, *Exc. de Mor.*, vii.]

> A mishap and a wrong have this distinction:[3]
> Chance brings the one, the other comes from choice.

With this agrees the saying of Demosthenes: 'It is right to pity, not unjust men, but those who are undeservedly unfortunate,' which in his second book *On Invention* Cicero translates thus: 'We ought to pity those who suffer through ill-fortune, not through wickedness.' There is also the statement of Antiphanes [Antiphon]: 'What happens not of one's own will is the work of fortune; what happens in accordance with will is an act of judgement.' Lysias, too, says: 'What he has willed comes to no one as ill-fortune.'

Against Aphobus, I [lxviii]. [II. xxxv 109.] [Antiphon, *Orations,* xiv.] [*Orations,* xxxi. 10.]

Accordingly in that most wise law places of asylum were available for those from whose hands a chance missile had slain a man, and a refuge was provided also for slaves; but those who had deliberately slain an innocent man, or who had disturbed the peace of the state,

Deut., xix. 1; xxiii. 15. *Exodus,* xxi. 14; *1 Kings,* ii. 29; 2 *Kings,* xi. 13 ff.

[1] 'The common laws of supplication', according to Polybius, and Malchus, in the *Selections on Embassies.*

[2] An ancient oracle [Aelian, *Various History,* III. xliv] says:

> While your friend you defended, you slew him, but yet
> You stained not yourself with crime; for your hand
> More pure is than before.

[3] According to Philo, *On the Judge* [v]: 'Mercy is due to the unfortunate; but he who does wrong by voluntary choice is not unfortunate but unjust.'

Thus Marcus Aurelius [*Meditations,* IX. xxii] wishes us to examine the mind, 'so that you may perceive what is due to ignorance and what to intention, and at the same time consider that which is natural'. So Totila in Procopius, *Gothic War,* III [III. ix], distinguishes 'what is due to ignorance or forgetfulness', and 'what is intentional'.

were not protected even by the most holy altar of God Himself. In interpreting this law Philo says: 'The temple does not offer an asylum to the unholy.' Such, furthermore, was the view of the ancient Greeks. It is related that the Chalcidians refused to surrender Nauplius to the Achaeans,[1] and the reason given is that he had adequately cleared himself from the charges brought by the Achaeans.

On Special Laws [III. xv]. Plutarch, *Greek Questions*, xxxii [xxxiii = 298 D].

2. At Athens there was an altar of Mercy, mentioned by Cicero, Pausanias, and Servius,[2] by Theophilus, too, in his *Institutes*; it is described at length by Statius in the *Thebaid*, Book XII. But who were entitled to its protection? Listen to what the poet says:

[Paus., I. xvii.] [*Inst.*, I. xxi.] [XII. 483.]

> And the unfortunate have hallowed it.

Further on he says that there came to it— [XII. 507 f.]

> Those who were vanquished in war, exiles from home and from country,
> And rulers bereft of realms.

Aristides declares that it was a glory peculiar to the Athenians[3] 'to receive and console the ill-fated from all lands'; in another passage, 'For all the unfortunate among every people there is a common good fortune, the kindness of the city of Athens, by which they are assured of safety.' In Xenophon Patrocles of Phlius, speaking at Athens, said: 'I was enamoured of this city, because I had heard that all who were wronged and were in fear, if they had fled thither, were assured of help.' The same thought occurs in the letter of Demosthenes on behalf of the children of Lycurgus.

Panathenaic [= 187 B]. *On Peace*, ii [*On Leuctra*, i = p. 89A]. [*Greek Hist.*, VI. v. 45.] [*Letters*, III. ii.]

Hence Oedipus, fleeing for refuge at Colonus, in Sophocles' tragedy of that name[4] thus bears witness: [521 ff.]

> Alas, ye sons of Cecrops, ills many have I borne;
> But God my witness is, no ills I suffered
> From deeds in malice done.

To this Theseus replies:

> A stranger, such as I see you are, Oedipus,
> [371] I never scrupled at all times to aid.
> I know myself a mortal.

[1] King Pepin received and refused to surrender those who fled to him from Neustria to escape the tyranny; this is according to Fredegarius' chronicle of Pepin, for the year 688. The Emperor Louis the Pious even received those who fled from the Church of Rome, as appears from his decree of the year 817, in *Concilia Galliae*, vol. ii. Charles the Bald received those who fled to him from the territory of his brother Louis; Aimoin, Book V, chap. xxxiv.

Regarding Cegenas Patzinacas, who was not given up [381] to Tyrachus who demanded him, see Zonaras' account of Constantine Monomachus [XVII. xxvi]. So also the governor Inunginus did not surrender Osmanes to Eskisar; Leunclavius, *Turkish History*, II. As Mariana records, XVI. xviii, the Portuguese did not surrender D'Alberquerque.

[2] *On the Aeneid*, VIII [VIII. 342].

[3] Mariana, XX. xiii, gives the same praise to the people of Aragon. The Gepidae preferred to perish, one and all, rather than give up Ildichis to the Romans or Lombards; Procopius, *Gothic War*, IV [IV. xxvii].

[4] See the whole passage, for it merits reading.

In like manner, Demophon, son of Theseus, when the descendants of Hercules had fled to Athens, speaks thus :

[Euripides, *Children of Hercules*, 329–32.]

> Ever of old she chooseth, this our land,
> To help the helpless ones in justice' cause.
> So hath she borne for friends unnumbered toils.
> Now see I this new struggle looming nigh.

And in this way the Athenians did that for which Callisthenes especially praised them, saying that 'on behalf of the children of Hercules[1] they took up arms against Eurystheus, who was at that time the oppressor of Greece'.

3. On the other hand, you find that this is said of an evil-doer in the same tragedy :

[Euripides, fragm. 1036, in Stobaeus, xlvi. 3.]

> Who conscious of his crimes, and trusting not in laws,
> A suppliant, falls at altars of the gods,
> I scruple not to drag before the court ;
> For always should he suffer ills who evil does.

[1315 ff.] The same poet in the *Ion* :

> Unmeet it is
> With guilty hand to touch the gods ; but just it was
> That shrines become a refuge for the good
> Against injustices.

Against Leocrates [xciii].

The orator Lycurgus tells of a certain Callistratus who had committed a capital offence, and who, when he had consulted an oracle, received the response that, if he went to Athens, 'he would meet with justice'.[2] Accordingly, he fled to the most sacred altar at Athens,[3] relying upon its sanctity ; but nevertheless he was put to death by that city, which was most scrupulous in the observance of its religious duties, and thus the promise of the oracle was fulfilled. *Annals*, III [lx]. Tacitus censures the custom, which in his day was prevalent among the Greek cities, of protecting the crimes of men as one would the rites of the gods. [III. xxxvi.] He says also : 'The emperors indeed are like the gods : but even the gods do not hear the prayers of suppliants unless they are just.'

4. Such persons, then, are to be punished, or surrendered, or I [clx]. at least removed from the country. Thus, according to Herodotus, when the people of Cyme did not wish to surrender Pactys the Lydian, and did not dare to keep him, they allowed him to depart to Mitylene. Livy, XXII [xxxiii. 3]. From King Philip of Macedon the Romans demanded Demetrius of

[1] See the *Children of Hercules* by Euripides [329–32] and Apollodorus [*Library*, II. viii. 1].

[2] 'Only just prayers of suppliants are heard by the gods', says Tacitus, *Annals*, Book III [III. xxxvi].

[3] Mariana, Book XXI, records that in Portugal Ferdinand, the chief chamberlain, was dragged from the shrine in which he had sought refuge and burned to death, for the wrong done to a maiden of the nobility. On asylums see also the book of the great Paul of Venice, of the order called Servites.

Pharos, who had fled to Philip after he had been vanquished. Perseus, king of Macedon,[1] in his defence before Marcius, dealing with those who were reported to have plotted against Eumenes, said: 'As soon as I learned, upon information from you, that they were in Macedon, I had them sought out and ordered them to leave the kingdom, and closed my frontiers to them for all time.' The Samothracians informed Evander, who had plotted against Eumenes, that he must free the temple from the profanation of his presence. Livy, XXXVII [XLII. xli. 8]. [Livy, XLV. v.]

5. In the present and in recent generations, and in the majority of European countries, this right, which we have discussed, of demanding for punishment those who have fled beyond the frontier, has been exercised only with respect to crimes that affect the public weal or that manifest extraordinary wickedness. It has become customary mutually to ignore lesser crimes, unless some more definite agreement has been made by the terms of a treaty.[2] We must, however, recognize this, that robbers and pirates who have become so strong that they have made themselves formidable may justly be received and defended, so far as their punishment is concerned, because it is to the advantage of mankind that they should be brought back from their wicked ways through confidence in their freedom from punishment, if such reform is in no other way possible; [372] and any people or ruler may undertake to accomplish this.

VI.—*Nevertheless suppliants are to be protected pending the hearing of their case; under what law the hearing is to be conducted*

1. This, furthermore, must not be forgotten, that, during the time when the justice of their case is being investigated, suppliants are to be protected. Thus Demophon says to the ambassador of Eurystheus: [Euripides, *Children of Hercules*, 251 ff.]

> If crime you prove against these guests, justice
> You will obtain; by force you shall not drag them hence.

[1] Appian has this also in the *Selections on Embassies*, xx [=*Macedonian Affairs*, xi.]. Something similar appears in the Latin life of Themistocles [Cornelius Nepos, *Themistocles*, viii]: 'When he [Themistocles] was publicly demanded by the Athenians and Lacedaemonians, Admetus (king of the Molossians) did not betray his suppliant, but advised him to take thought for his safety. So he gave orders that Themistocles be conducted to Pydna, and gave him an adequate escort.' And in like manner, according to Procopius, *Gothic War*, III [III. xxxv], the Gepidae sent away the Lombard Ildichis.

See also the letter of Theodoric to Thrasamund, king of the Vandals, on the reception of Giselic, [Cassiodorus, *Variae*,] V. xliii, xliv; and also what is found in the life of King Louis. In this way the Emperor Rudolph II got rid of Christopher Sborowski, as is recorded by De Thou, Book LXXXIII, on the year 1585.

Elizabeth replied to the Scots that she would either give up Bothwell to them or drive him from England; so Camden, on the year 1593. On Alphonso, Count of Gegion, condemned by the king of France and refused admission into Spain, see Mariana, XIX. vi.

[2] As Simler quotes in the treaty between the Swiss and the Milanese. The treaties of the English with the French require the surrender of rebels and deserters; those with the Burgundians, their expulsion; Camden on the year 1600.

[Sophocles, *Oedipus at Colonus*, 911 ff.] In another tragedy Theseus addresses Creon:

> Creon, thou hast dared a deed unworthy of thee
> And of thy Thebes and of thy ancestors.
> Entering a city that respects what holy is and pious,
> And all things executes in law's due form,
> Forgetful of our habits, what pleases thee
> Thou dost attempt, thinking thou canst carry all by force.
> Dost thou believe the city so bereft of men,
> So obedient to a yoke, and me of no account?
> Amphion's city did not teach thee this,
> A state not wont to rear unfeeling men,
> And it will not approve when it has heard that thou
> Against rights of the gods and my rights trespassest,
> Dragging from place of refuge wretched suppliants.
> Had I set foot in the city of Labdacus,
> Even though my cause were just beyond dispute,
> On no man had I sought to lay my hand
> Save by consent of him who ruled the land,
> Mindful of what befits a stranger in a foreign town.
> An undeserving land thou coverest
> With shame and with disgrace—old of a truth
> In years, but not in wisdom.

2. If the crime of which the suppliants are accused is not forbidden by the law of nature or of nations, the case must be judged according to the municipal law of their own country. This is well [387 ff.] put in the *Suppliants* of Aeschylus, where the king of Argos thus addresses the daughters of Danaus coming from Egypt:

> If the sons of Aegyptus should lay hands upon thee
> And say that by law of their state 'tis the right
> Of the nearest of kin, who would dare to oppose them?
> Wherefore thy task is to plead that by law of thy homeland
> Right over thee they have none.

VII.—*How subjects share in the crimes of their rulers, and members of a community in those of the community; and how the punishment of a community differs from that of individuals*

1. We have seen how guilt passes to rulers from subjects, whether these are subjects of long standing, or recent. Conversely, guilt will pass from the highest authority to those subject to it, if those subject to it have consented to crime, or if they have done anything by order or advice of the highest authority which they could avoid doing without committing wrong. But it will be better to discuss this point later on, when we shall be investigating the duties of subjects.

[*Questions on Heptateuch*, III. xxvi.] A wrong may also be shared by both a community and individuals, [373] because, as Augustine says in a passage previously cited, 'where there are communities, there are individuals also. Communities cannot exist save as made up of individuals; for individuals assembled in some place, or taken as a whole, form communities.'

2. Guilt, however, attaches to the individuals who have agreed to the crime, not to those who have been overmastered by the votes of others. For the punishments of individuals and of a community are different. Just as death is at times the punishment for individuals, so 'the death of a state is its dissolution', and such dissolution takes place when the civil body is dissolved; this question we have discussed elsewhere.

Lycurgus [*Against Leocrates*, lx]. Above, II. ix. 4.

If now a state in this way ceases to exist, the right of enjoyment therein, as Modestinus rightly says, is terminated as though by death. As a punishment, individuals are reduced to slavery, as the Thebans by Alexander of Macedon, those being exempted from this fate who had opposed the decree for breaking off the alliance with him. Similarly, too, a state suffers political slavery in being reduced to a province. Individuals lose their property by confiscation. In like manner it is customary to take from a state also what belongs to it as a whole, its fortifications, naval arsenals, ships of war, arms, elephants, public treasure, and public lands.

Dig. VII. iv. 21. Plutarch, *Alexander* [xi = 670 E].

3. On the other hand, it is unjust for individuals to lose their private property because of a wrong done by the community without their consent, as Libanius rightly shows in his speech on the sedition at Antioch. He approves the act of Theodosius,[1] who had punished the crime of the community by forbidding the use of the theatre, of the public baths, and of the name Metropolis.

VIII.—*How long the right of inflicting punishment upon a community continues*

1. At this point the important question arises, whether punishment may be exacted always for the crime of a community. It seems that such punishment may be exacted so long as the community exists, because the same body remains, although composed of changing elements, as we have shown elsewhere. But on the contrary it must be remembered that in the case of a community certain things are said to belong to it primarily and necessarily, as a public treasury, laws, and the like; while certain things belong to it only through its individual members. Thus we say that a community is wise and brave which has a great number of wise and brave members.

[II.ix.3.1.] Aristotle, *Politics*, VII. xiii.

[1] Chrysostom, *On the Statues*, XVII [XVII. ii], says the same as Libanius about this affair. Capitolinus affirms that Marcus Aurelius, the philosopher, had previously punished the men of Antioch in a similar way [*Marcus Antoninus*, xxv]; so Severus punished the Byzantines, taking away their theatre, baths, honours, and all ornaments, and making the city itself subject to Perinthus; see Herodian, II [III. vi. 9], Zonaras [XII. viii], and what we have said above.

Into this class of things falls whatever a community deserves; for primarily this concerns individuals, as having an intelligence which the community in and of itself lacks. When, therefore, those individuals are dead through whom the community derived its desert, the desert itself lapses also; and likewise the debt of punishment which we have said cannot exist without the desert. As Libanius says in the oration cited: 'For it seems to me you should be content with the thought that none of those who have done this wrong survives.'

[*Anabasis of Alexander*, II. xiv.] 2. We must, then, approve the view of Arrian, who condemns Alexander's punishment of the Persians,[1] for the reason that those Persians who had wronged the Greeks had perished long before. On the slaughter of the Branchidae by the order of the same Alexander [VII. v. 35.] the judgement of Curtius is: 'If this had been planned against the true authors of the treachery, it would seem to be a just vengeance, not an act of cruelty. But as the case stands, the guilt of ancestors was atoned for by their descendants, who had not even seen Miletus, and consequently had not been able to betray it to Xerxes.'

[*Anabasis of Alexander*, III. xviii f.] In another place Arrian expresses a similar opinion regarding the burning of Persepolis in revenge for what the Persians had done at Athens. 'But', he says, 'Alexander in doing this does not seem to me to have acted wisely, nor does this seem to have been in truth a punishment of those Persians who long ago had ceased to exist.'

[Plutarch, *Apothegms*, = 176 F.] 3. No one can help laughing at the excuse of Agathocles, who replied to the complaints of the people of Ithaca regarding injuries inflicted upon them, that in former times the Sicilians had suffered greater harm at the hands of Ulysses. Plutarch, in his criticism of [*On the Malice of Herodotus*, xxii = 860 A.] Herodotus, says that it is far from true that the Corinthians wished to avenge an injury received from the Samnians 'after the lapse of three generations'. Nor can we accept the defence of this and similar [374] actions which may be read in Plutarch's work *On the Delayed Vengeance of the Deity*; [xii = 557 B.] for the right of God is one thing, and the right of men is another, as will soon be shown more plainly.

One cannot argue that, if it is right for descendants to receive honours and rewards for the deserts of their ancestors, it is also right that they should be punished for their ancestors' sins. The character of a benefit permits its being conferred upon any one at all without injury; that is not the case with a punishment.

[1] Wherefore Julian, in his eulogy of Constantius [*Second Oration, Heroic Deeds of Constantius*, 95 B], assigns another cause for this war, saying: 'It is plain even to a child that no former war, that was considered to have been just, [382] ever had so good an excuse, not that waged by the Greeks against Troy, nor that by the Macedonians against the Persians. For they did not seek a tardy vengeance for ancient wrongs upon the grandchildren or upon the children of the wrong-doers, but they made war on those who were doing violence to the children of well-deserving men, who were taking away their kingdoms.'

IX.—*Whether punishment may be shared without sharing the crime*

We have spoken of the ways in which a participation in punishment arises from a participation in guilt. It remains for us to consider whether there may still be a participation in the punishment when there is none in the guilt. To understand this matter aright, and to avoid confusing, through similarity of name, things which in reality are different, there are certain points which must be kept in mind.

X.—*The distinction between that which is inflicted directly and that which comes as a consequence*

1. In the first place, there is a difference between a loss directly inflicted and one that comes as a consequence.

By a loss directly inflicted I mean when a person loses something to which he had a special right; by a loss that comes as a consequence, when one does not have what he would otherwise have had, since the condition has ceased without which he did not have the right. Ulpian gives an illustration: 'If I have opened a well on my land, from which it results that streams that would flow through to your land are cut off', he declares that in this case damage has not been inflicted by a wrongful act on my part, since I have merely exercised my own right. *Digest,* XXXIX. ii. 24. § 12.

In another place Ulpian says that there is a great difference between suffering loss and being prevented from enjoying an advantage which one had hitherto made use of. Paul the jurist also says: 'It is absurd for us to be called possessors before we have acquired something.' *Digest,* XXXIX. ii. 26. *Digest,* XXXV. ii. 63.

2. Consequently, when the property of their parents has been confiscated children experience some inconvenience indeed, but strictly speaking this is not a punishment, because the property that was to be theirs would not become theirs actually unless it had been preserved by their parents to the end of life. Alfenus has rightly pointed this out, saying that by the punishment of their father children lose that which would have come to them from him, but that those things remain intact which are due to them not from the father but from natural conditions or from some other source. With similar thought Cicero writes that the children of Themistocles suffered want, and he does not think it unfair that the children of Lepidus should suffer the same misfortune; this, he says, was in accordance with an ancient custom, recognized in all countries. However, the custom experienced considerable modification through later Roman laws. *Digest,* XLVIII. xxii. 3. *Letters,* II. xi and xix [*Letters to Brutus,* I. xv. 11 and xii. 2]. *Digest,* XLVIII. xx. 7.

Now, when the community is at fault through the crime of the majority, who, as we have said elsewhere, represents the personality [II. v. 17.]

of the community, and when, for this cause, it loses the things that we have mentioned—political liberty, fortifications, and other profitable things—the loss is felt also by the individuals who are innocent, but only in respect to such things as belonged to them not directly but through the community.

XI.—*The distinction between what is done owing to the occasion of a crime and what is done owing to the cause of the crime*

1. Furthermore, we must bear in mind that harm is sometimes done to a person, or some good taken away from a person, because of a fault committed by another, yet not in such a way that that fault is the proximate cause of the act, if the right behind the act is considered. Thus he who has promised something because of another's debt suffers loss, according to the ancient proverb, 'Go surety, and expect loss'; but the immediate cause of the obligation is the promise itself. For as he who has gone surety for a purchaser is not, strictly speaking, bound by the purchase but by his promise, so he who gives security for a wrong-doer is bound not by the wrong but by his surety. Hence it comes about that the harm inflicted upon him who goes security is not measured by the other's wrong, but by the power which he has of fulfilling his promise.

[Stobaeus, iii. 79.]

2. In consequence, it follows that, according to the view which we believe to be the more correct, no one may be put to death by reason of suretyship, because we hold that no one has such a right over his life [375] as to be able to take it away from himself or to bind himself to have it taken away. Nevertheless, the ancient Romans and Greeks thought differently on this point, and so they believed that sureties were liable to a capital sentence,[1] as we see from a line of Ausonius and from the well-known story of Damon and Pythias. Often, too, they put hostages to death, as we shall recall later on.[2]

[*Technopaegnion*, xii. 1.]

What we have said regarding a man's life must be understood to apply to his limbs also; for the right has not been given to a man to deprive himself of these except in order to save the body.

3. If the promise covers exile, or pecuniary loss, and the condition thereof is fulfilled by the other's wrong, the guarantor will

[1] This is clearly seen in the words of Reuben to his father, Jacob (*Genesis*, xlii. 37), and in Josephus, *Antiquities of the Jews*, Book II, chap. iii [II. vi. 5]. These sureties Eutropius in his *Caligula* [rather Dio Cassius, LIX. viii] calls 'substitutes for a life', and Diodorus Siculus, *Excerpta Peiresciana*, 'sureties for death'.

Says Chrysostom, *On Galatians*, ii [iii. 13]: 'Just as, when a man has been condemned to death, another who is guiltless rescues him from punishment by choosing to die in his behalf.' Augustine, *Letters*, liv [cliii. 17], *To Macedonius*, says: 'And sometimes he who was the cause of a death is more to blame than he who slew another: as if someone should deceive his surety, and the latter should pay the legal penalty for him.'

[2] III. iv. 14.

suffer the loss; yet this, if we speak with exactness, will not be a punishment upon him.

A similar case arises in connexion with a right that one possesses in such a way that it is dependent upon the will of another. Such a right is one terminable at the pleasure of the grantor, where account is taken of ownership of the thing concerned; or the right of private possession, in relation to the right of eminent domain, which the state enjoys for the public good. If something held by such a right be taken from any one by reason of another's wrong, there is in this not properly a punishment, but the execution of an antecedent right that was vested in the person who takes the thing away. Thus, since, strictly speaking, no wrong can be attributed to animals, when an animal is killed, as the law of Moses provides [1] in case of sexual intercourse with a man, this is not in fact a punishment, but an exercise of man's proprietary right over the animal.

XII.—*That, properly speaking, no one may be justly punished for another's wrong, and why*

Having drawn these distinctions, we shall say that no one who is innocent of wrong may be punished for the wrong done by another.

The true reason for this is not the one advanced by Paul the jurist, that punishments are established for the correction of mankind; for it is clear that an example may be made apart from the person of the wrong-doer, but yet of a person whose punishment affects him, as we shall soon point out. But the true reason is that an obligation to punishment arises from desert; and desert is something personal, since it has its origin in the will, than which nothing is more peculiarly ours; hence the expression 'in one's own power'. [*Digest*, XLVIII. xix. 20.]

XIII.—*That children may not be punished for the sins of their parents*

1. 'Neither the virtues nor the vices of parents', says Jerome, 'are attributed to their children.' Augustine declares that God Himself would be unjust if He should condemn an innocent man. Dio Chrysostom, after saying that by the sanction which the Athenians appended to the laws of Solon descendants of the guilty were doomed to punishment, adds the following words regarding the law of God: 'It does not, like the former, punish the children and the house of those who sin; but, under it, each one is responsible for his own ill-fortune.' *Letters*, III, *On the Death of Nepotianus* [lx. 8]. *Letters*, cv [cxciv]. [*Orations*, lxxx = 667.]

Here applies the common saying, 'Guilt is personal'. 'We ordain', say the Christian Emperors, 'that punishment shall fall [*Dig.* IX. iv. 43.] *Code*, IX. xlvii. 22.

[1] On this see Moses Maimonides, *Guide of the Perplexed*, III. xl.

where the guilt is.' Then, 'Therefore, let those responsible for crimes be held for them; and let not the fear of punishment extend beyond those in whom an offence may be found.'

On Special Laws, II [III. xxx]. [VIII. lxxx.] 2. It is just that those should suffer the punishments who have committed the sins, Philo declares,[1] censuring the custom of some peoples who punished with death the guiltless children of tyrants and traitors. This practice is condemned also by Dionysius of Halicarnassus, who shows that the excuse accepted for such action, that it is considered that the children will become like their parents, is wicked, since this is doubtful and since fear of something that is uncertain should not be enough to cause any one to be put to death.

Code, IX. viii. 5. § 1. Some one dared to advise the Christian Emperor Arcadius that those who, it might be feared, would imitate their father's crime, should

XXVIII [ii. 1]. like him be punished with death. Ammianus recounts that certain children, although still very young, were put to death 'to prevent their growing up to follow the example of their parents'.

Fear, again, does not constitute a more just reason for taking

Victoria, *De Iure Belli*, no. 38. vengeance, although the belief that it does gave rise to the Greek proverb:

> Mad is he who kills the father but the children spares.

On Anger, II. iv [II. xxxiv]. Herodotus, I [lxxxviii]. 3. [376] Seneca says: 'There is nothing more unjust than to make an heir subject to the enmity against his father.' Pausanias, the Greek commander, inflicted no harm upon the children of Attagines, who was responsible for the desertion of the Thebans to the Medes, 'saying that they in no way shared in the guilt of Medism'. Marcus Aurelius Antoninus, in a letter to the Senate, wrote: 'Wherefore you will grant pardon to the sons, to the son-in-law, and to the wife of Avidius Cassius[2] (the one who had conspired against him). And, yet, why do I speak of pardon, since they have committed no wrong?'

[1] Philo also says in his book *On Piety* [*On Nobility*, vii]: 'I do not know whether there could be a more pernicious doctrine, if punishment will not pursue the wicked children of good parents, or if honour shall not be given to good sons born of wicked parents; the law, which judges each man according to his own actions, does not commend him for the virtues of his relations or punish him for their vices.' Josephus [*Antiquities of the Jews*, XIII. xiv. 2] calls the opposite conduct in Alexander, king of the Jews, 'a method of punishing not becoming to man'.

Says Ovid [*Metamorphoses*, IV. 670 f.]:

> Unjustly had Ammon ordained that Andromeda, though she was guiltless,
> Punishment there should suffer for words that her mother had spoken.

[2] See also Vulcacius, *Life of Avidius* [xii].

Julian [*Second Oration*, 101–2] praises similar humanity in Constantius, and shows that often good children come from wicked parents, as bees fly out of rocks, figs spring from bitter wood, and the pomegranate rises from thorns. The following are the words of the same writer [*First Oration*, 49 A]: 'But in no way did you permit the infant son of the dead man to share in his father's punishment. Thus your conduct, always tending toward leniency, becomes the proof of perfect virtues.'

XIV.—*Answer is made concerning the acts of God with regard to the children of the wicked*

1. It is true that in the law given to the Jews God threatens to avenge upon descendants the iniquity of the parents; but He Himself possesses the most complete right of ownership, both over our property and over our life, as it is His gift, which He can take away from any one when He pleases, without any reason and at any time. Consequently, if He carried off by a violent and untimely death the children of Achan, of Saul, of Jeroboam and of Ahab, He exercised His right of ownership over them,[1] not of punishment, but thereby He punished their parents all the more heavily. [*Exodus*, xx. 5.] [*Joshua*, vii. 24.] *2 Sam.*, xxi. *1 Kings*, xiv. *2 Kings*, viii. 9, 10 [*1 Kings*, xviii. 9, 10].

For if the parents survive, a contingency which the divine law has in view above all else (it is with this in view that the law does not extend these threats beyond great-grandchildren,[2] *Exodus*, xxv, since it is possible for men to live long enough to behold these), they are certainly punished by the sight of such a loss, which is harder for them to bear than their own suffering, as Chrysostom, with whom Plutarch agrees, rightly says: 'No other punishment causes greater suffering than the sight of our descendants suffering for our sake.' But if the parents do not live long enough to see this, it is nevertheless a heavy punishment for them to be put to death while fearing it. 'The obstinacy of mankind', says Tertullian, 'had compelled a resort to such remedies, in order that out of a regard for their posterity at any rate men might obey the divine law.'[3] [*Exodus*, xx. 5.] Homily XXIX [vi], *On Genesis*, ix. [Plutarch, *On the Delayed Vengeance of the Deity*, xviii = 561 A.] [*Against Marcion*, II. xv.]

2. At the same time the fact must be recognized that God does not make use of this more severe punishment except to punish crimes committed as a direct insult to Himself, such as false worship, perjury, and sacrilege. This was the view of the Greeks also; for the crimes which were believed to implicate posterity, and which they called 'pollutions',[4] are all of this nature. Plutarch has discoursed ably on this subject in his book *On the Delayed Vengeance of the Deity*. In Aelian[5] is found the following Delphic oracle:

> But divine justice pursues the authors of crime;
> Avoid it they cannot, not even if children of Zeus.
> The life of such men, and their offspring, it threatens,
> While woe follows woe in their house.

[1] This is the view of Rabbi Simeon Barsema, by far the most correct.
[2] You have examples in Zimri and Jehu.
[3] Alexander says in Curtius, Book VII [VIII. viii. 18]: 'You ought not to know what I had decided with regard to these, that you might perish in greater grief.'
[4] See Plutarch, *Pericles* [xxxiii = 170 A], and what has been said above, II. xiii. 1.
[5] [*Various History*,] III. xliii.

In this case it was a question of sacrilege,[1] and the view thus expressed is supported by the story of the gold of Toulouse, recounted in Strabo and Gellius. With regard to perjury, we have cited similar opinions already. However, even if God has threatened to inflict such punishment, He does not always make use of this right, especially if some remarkable virtue [2] appears in the children of the guilty, as we may see from *Ezekiel*, xviii, and as Plutarch proves by certain examples in the book just mentioned.

[IV. i. 13.] [III. ix.] [II. xiii. 1.]

3. Although the punishments that await the impious after this life are set forth in the New Covenant more openly than they were in the older time, yet in this Covenant there is no threat extending beyond the persons of the sinners.[3] This is particularly indicated also in the prophecy of Ezekiel referred to, although, after the manner of prophets, less openly.

Nevertheless, it is not permissible for men to imitate the action of God in this matter. They have not the same justification, because, as we have said before, God has a right over men's lives without regard to their guilt, but men only in consequence of deep guilt, and that too when the guilt is distinctly individual.

4. Wherefore [377] that same divine law forbids not only that parents be made subject to the penalty of death for the deeds of their children, but also that children should be put to death for the deeds of their parents.

Deut., xxiv. 16.

This ordinance, we read, was observed by God-fearing kings,[4] even in cases of treason. It is warmly praised by Josephus and Philo; a similar Egyptian law is praised by Isocrates, and a Roman enactment by Dionysius of Halicarnassus.[5] There is a saying of Plato that 'The disgrace and the punishments of the father follow none of his children.' This was expressed in Latin by Callistratus the jurist as follows: 'A father's crime or punishment can put no blemish upon the son'; he added the reason, 'for each is subject to the fate resulting from his deeds, and no one can be appointed to succeed to the crime of another.'

Josephus, II [*Ant. of Jews*, IV. viii. 39]. Philo, *On Special Laws*, II [III. xxix]. Isocrates, *Busiris*[x]. Dionysius, VIII [lxxx]. [Plato, *on Laws* IX. iii.] *Digest*, XLVIII. xix. 26.

'Would any state', says Cicero, 'suffer one to propose a law of this kind, that a son or grandson should be condemned if his father

[1] [383] As Libanius also says: 'For these things some have already paid the penalty; others not yet, but there is no one who shall deliver them. I say not only them but also their children, and those who shall be descended from these.' Similar views Libanius expresses in the oration published by Godefroy [in 1631].

[2] And a public denouncement of his father's crime, such as was made by the Emperor Andronicus Palaeologus, in Gregoras, Book V, chap. lxxxi [VI. i].

[3] Tertullian says, *On Monogamy* [vii]: 'The sour grapes eaten by the fathers have ceased to set on edge the teeth of the children; for each one will die in his own crime.'

[4] As Amasias [*2 Kings*, xiv. 6].

[5] Who speaks thus: 'This is a custom peculiar to the Romans, to exempt the children from any punishment for the wrongs their fathers have done.' The provision is found in the *Law of the Visigoths*, VI. i. 8.

or grandfather should have done wrong?' Hence it comes about that to punish with death a pregnant woman was considered criminal[1] by the laws of the Egyptians, Greeks, and Romans.[2] *On the Nature of the Gods,* IV [III. xxxviii. 90]. [Diod. Sic., I. lxxvii; Plut., *On Delayed Vengeance,* vi = 552 D.]

XV.—*Much the less are other relatives to be punished*

If, then, the human laws which prescribe the death of children for the crimes of their parents are unjust, more unjust still is the law of the Persians and Macedonians which decreed the death of their relatives also,[3] that those who had committed wrong against the king might meet a more grievous end, as Curtius says. Ammianus Marcellinus[4] wrote that all other laws were surpassed in cruelty by this law. *Daniel,* vii. 22 [vi. 25]; Justin, X [ii]. [VIII. viii. 18.] [Amm.,] XXIII [vi. 81].

XVI.—*Nevertheless to children and relatives of the guilty something may be denied which they otherwise could have had; instances thereof*

At this point it must be noted that if the children of traitors have possession of, or may look forward to possession of, something the direct right over which belongs not to them but to the people or the king, this may be taken away from them by a kind of right of ownership; the exercise of such right, however, at the same time may turn into a punishment of those who have done the wrong. As an illustration we may recall that the children of Antiphanes [Antiphon], on the ground that he was a traitor, 'were declared disqualified for honours,' as Plutarch recounts; that is, they were excluded from public offices,[5] as were the children of those proscribed by Sulla in Rome. Likewise in the law of Arcadius already mentioned there is this reasonable restraint upon the children, 'that they may attain to no civil and no military offices'. [*Lives of Ten Orators,* 833 A.] [*Code,* IX. xlvii. 22.]

With regard to slavery, in what manner and to what degree it may without injustice be transmitted to children, we have explained elsewhere. [II. v. 29.]

XVII.—*Subjects may not properly be punished for a wrong committed by their king*

1. What we have said with regard to the inflicting of evil upon children because of the wrong-doings of their parents may be applied

[1] This attitude is praised by Philo, in his *On Humanity* [xviii]

[2] *Digest,* I. v. 18, and XLVIII. xix. 3.

[3] Philo [*On Special Laws,* III. xxx] said that it was the custom of tyrants to execute with the condemned the five families most closely related to them. See Herodian, Book III [Herodotus, III. cxix]. An instance from Milan, upon the death of Galeazzo, occurs in Bizarri, Book XIV [p. 334, ed. of 1579].

[4] He calls them abhorrent laws. See also the Council of Toledo, IV.

[5] You will find a like provision in the *Decretals,* V. xxxvii. 12.

also in the case of a people that is truly subject (for a people that is not subject may be punished because of its own guilt, that is for its negligence, as we have said), if the question is raised whether such a people may suffer for the crimes of its king or its rulers. At present we are not inquiring whether the consent of the people itself is involved,[1] or whether there has been any other act on the part of the people deserving of punishment; we are concerned merely with the relation which arises from the nature of the body whose head is the king, and whose members are the other citizens.

2. It is true that because of David's sin God consumed the people with a pestilence, although they were innocent, as David thought, but God had the supreme right over their lives. In reality, it was not the people but David who was thus punished; for, as a Christian writer says, 'the most grievous punishment of kings who have sinned is the punishment inflicted upon their people'. As the same writer remarks, this is as if some one who had sinned with his hand should be scourged on his back. In a similar discussion Plutarch says that this must be regarded as the cauterizing of a thumb by a physician in order to heal the thigh. Why it is not permissible for men to inflict such punishments we have already shown.

Quaestiones ad Orthodoxos, cxxxviii. [*On the Delayed Vengeance*, xvi = 559 F.]

XVIII.—*Individuals, who have not consented thereto, cannot be punished for the wrong-doing of the community*

The same principle must be applied with respect to the infliction of harm upon individuals who have not given their consent, in the case of a wrong done by the community, that is so far as their interest as individuals is concerned.

XIX.—*Heirs are not subject to punishment as such; reasons therefor*

The heir is bound to discharge other obligations, but not to undergo punishment,[2] as Paul the jurist wrote: 'If anyone has been condemned to punishment, [378] it is agreed by the interpreters of the law that this does not pass to his heirs.' The true reason is that the heir represents the person of the deceased, not in what he deserved, which is purely personal, but in his property,[3] to which, according to

Digest, XLVIII. xix. 20.

[1] Philo, speaking of the subjects of the king of Egypt in the time of Abraham, says [*On Abraham*, xix]: 'The whole household suffered punishment together with him, for the reason that no one had censured the breach of the law, but all, by their praise of it, had made themselves participants in the crime.'

Josephus [*Antiquities of the Jews*, VIII. xi. 1] thus narrates the prophecy pronounced against Jeroboam: 'And the people also shall share in his punishment, shall be banished from the goodly land, and shall be scattered throughout the regions beyond the Euphrates, because they followed after the impieties of the king.'

[2] Maimonides, title גולה, vii. 6. Also Gemara, *Baba Kama*, ix. 11 [x. 1].

[3] See the Council of Toledo, VIII, in the case of Recceswinth; see also what [has been said] above, II. xiv. 10. 'There is no one who more properly takes the place of him who has departed this life' than his heir, as Cicero says in his *On Laws*, II [II. xix. 48].

a custom established in connexion with ownership, attach the debts owed to any one in consequence of unequal distribution of things.

Dio of Prusa says in his address to the Rhodians: 'They are responsible for all debts, those of their ancestors not less than their own, contracted with any persons from the founding of their race. For you will not say that the inheritance has been refused by them.' [*Orations*, xxxi = p. 329.]

XX.—*Nevertheless heirs may be subject to punishment if this has passed over into an obligation of another kind*

From what has been said, it follows that if, apart from what the deceased deserved, some new cause of liability has arisen, then that which was in the penalty may become an obligation of the heir, although not strictly as a penalty. Thus in one case, after a judicial sentence in another, after the settlement of a suit (these things give the force of a contract), a pecuniary penalty will become an obligation of the heir as well as those things which were introduced into the agreement. For now a new cause of liability has developed.

[384] # CHAPTER XXII

ON UNJUST CAUSES [OF WARS]

I.—*The distinction between justifiable and persuasive causes is explained*

II. i. 1. We said above, when we set out to treat the causes of wars, that some were justifiable, others persuasive. Polybius, who was the first to observe this distinction, calls the former 'pretexts', because
[XXXVII. liv. 13.] they are wont to be openly alleged (Livy sometimes employs the term 'claim'), and the latter by the name of the class, 'causes'.[1]

2. Thus in the war of Alexander against Darius the 'pretext' was the avenging of the injuries which the Persians had inflicted upon the Greeks, while the 'cause' was the desire for renown, empire, and riches, to which was added a great expectation of an easy victory arising from the expeditions of Xenophon and Agesilaus. The 'pretext' of the Second Punic War was the dispute over Saguntum, but the cause was the anger of the Carthaginians at the agreements which the Romans had extorted from them in times of adversity, and the encouragement
[III. vi ff.] which they derived from their successes in Spain, as was observed by
I [xxiii ff.; lvi ff.]. Polybius. Likewise Thucydides thinks that the true cause of the Peloponnesian War was the power of Athens, which was on the increase and was regarded with suspicion by the Lacedaemonians, but that the pretext was the dispute over Corcyra, that over Potidaea, and other points of difference; in this, however, he confuses the terms 'cause' and 'pretext'.[2]

[1] So they are distinguished by Plutarch in his *Life of Galba* [xxii = p. 1062 D], by Dio Cassius in his account of Caesar and Pompey [XLI. lxii], and by Polybius, where he discusses the war of the Romans against the Illyrians, *Selections on Embassies*, cxxvi [*Histories*, II. viii. 1]. With Suetonius [*Julius Caesar*, xxx] you would justly call the former 'pretexts', the latter 'causes'. For he speaks thus of Julius Caesar: 'And his pretext for civil war was this indeed; however, men think that the causes were different.'

Thucydides elsewhere distinguishes 'pretext' and 'the truth', saying that in the expedition of the Athenians against Sicily the pretext was to bring aid to the people of Egesta, but the fact was that they desired to seize Sicily for themselves. Hermocrates, in his oration, when speaking of the Athenians, calls the former their 'pretext', the latter their 'intention'. Both passages are in Thucydides, VI [VI. vi and xxxiii].

Appian also has adopted the word 'pretexts' in his *Mithridatic Wars* [viii. 57]. In his *Civil Wars*, V [V. ix. 77], where he discusses the rupture of the treaty between Octavius and Sextus Pompey, he says that some of the 'causes' were hidden, others openly avowed. What the others call 'pretext' is called by Agathias 'fiction and colour', with which he contrasts 'cause' in his account of the Hun Zabergan in Book V [V. xii].

Add what we have said above in II. i. 1.

Procopius in his *Persian War*, Book II [II. xv] says that it is foolish not to speak freely when justice is one's guide, and advantage one's companion.

[2] So also in Book V, [390] when discussing the action of the Argives against the Epidaurians [V. liii], he designates as 'cause' what he had previously termed 'pretext'. Similarly we have pointed out in II. i. 1 [page 169] that the Greek word ἀρχαί, the Latin *principia*, and others of this sort, are of ambiguous meaning. The historians of the Byzantine Empire often call 'patroclus' what others call 'pretext', clearly from the story of Achilles, who found in the death of Patroclus an argument for resuming hostilities.

The same distinction appears in the speech of the Campanians to the Romans, when they said that they fought against the Samnites nominally on behalf of the Sidicini, but in reality for themselves; because they saw that when the Sidicini had been consumed the conflagration would spread to them. Livy records also that Antiochus made war upon the Romans alleging as his reasons the execution of Barcillas and some other occurrences, but really because he had conceived great hopes of success from the decline in Roman discipline. In like manner Plutarch observes that Cicero incorrectly taunted Antony with being the cause of the civil war, since Caesar, having already decided upon war, merely found in Antony his pretext.[1]

Livy, VII [xxx]. XXXVI [vi].

II.—*Wars which lack causes of either sort are wars of savages*

There are some who rush into war without a cause of either sort, led, as Tacitus says, by the desire of incurring danger for its own sake.[2] But the offence of these men is more than human; Aristotle calls it 'the savagery of wild beasts'. Concerning such persons Seneca wrote: 'I can say that this is not cruelty, but ferocity,[3] which delights in savagery. We can call it madness; for there are various sorts of madness, and none is more unmistakable than that which turns to the slaughter and butchery of men.'

[*Histories*, III. xli; V. xix.] [*Nic. Eth.*, VII. i.] *On Clemency*, II. vii [II. iv].

Altogether similar to this expression of opinion is that of Aristotle, in the last book of the *Nicomachean Ethics*: [385] 'For anyone would seem to be absolutely murderous if he should make enemies of his friends in order that there might be fighting and bloodshed.' Said Dio of Prusa: 'To wage war and to fight without a pretext, what else is this than utter madness and a craving for evils arising therefrom?' The same idea is expressed by Seneca in his fourth *Letter*: 'No one proceeds to shed human blood for its own sake, or at any rate only few do so.'

[X. vii.] *Orations*, xxxvii [xxxviii = p. 473]. [*Letters*, XIV. 9.]

III.—*Wars which have persuasive but not justifying causes are wars of robbers*

1. In most cases those who go to war have persuasive causes, either with or without justifiable causes. There are some indeed who clearly ignore justifiable causes. To these we may apply the dictum

[1] 'These things furnished him with a form of pretext and a plausible excuse for war such as he had long sought.' The words are in Plutarch, *Life of Mark Antony* [vi = p. 918 D]. But Lucan [*Pharsalia*, I. 263 ff.] says:

All restraints of shame
By fate are broken. Fortune strives to make
The leader's acts seem just, and causes finds for war.

[2] Ammianus in Book XXXI [XXXI. ii. 22] says of the Alani: 'As men of a quiet and peaceful disposition desire tranquillity, so these delight in dangers and warfare.'

[3] The same author in his *On Anger*, Book II, chap. v, having spoken of Apollodorus and Phalaris, says: 'This is not anger; it is ferocity.'

uttered by the Roman jurists, that the man is a robber who, when asked the origin of his possession, adduces none other than the fact of possession.[1]

Rhetoric, I. iii. With regard to those who advocate war Aristotle says: 'Do they oftentimes give no thought to the injustice of enslaving neighbours and those who have done no wrong?'

[Livy, V. xxxvi. 5.] 2. Such a one was Brennus, who was wont to say that all things belonged to the stronger. [XI. 183 f.] Such, in the view of Silius Italicus, was Hannibal, for whom—

> The sword
> The place of treaties and of justice took.

[Seneca, *Hercules, Raging,* 407 f.] Such was Attila, and such were those whose lips are made to say:

> The issue of the war and not its cause
> We seek;

[Lucan, *Pharsalia,* VII. 260.] again:

> Guilt will be his who in this battle fails;

[Tacitus, *Annals,* XV. i.] and

> When fortune's at its height, strength is the same as right.

City of God, IV. vi. To these you may fitly apply the saying of Augustine: 'To make war upon our neighbours, and thence to advance against others, and from the mere lust of ruling to crush peoples who have not troubled us, what must we call this but wholesale robbery?' [II. iii. 3.] Of wars of this type Velleius says: 'They are wars entered upon for no good reasons, but for the gain they bring.' In the first book of Cicero, [I. xix. 62.] *On Duties*, we read: 'That exaltation of spirit seen in times of danger and toil, if it is devoid of justice [. . .], not only has in it no quality of virtue, but rather is a manifestation of a brutality that is hardened to all human feeling.'[2] [*On Nic. Ethics,* IV. ii. end.] Andronicus of Rhodes declared: 'Those who, for the sake of great gains, take things whence they should not, are called wicked, impious and unjust. In this class are tyrants,[3] and those who lay waste cities.'

[1] *Digest*, V. iii. 11. ult., ff.
Of this sort was the war of the Heruli against the Lombards, 'a war without pretext' [Procopius, *Gothic War*, II. xiv]. According to Livy, Book V [V. xxxvi. 5], the Gauls 'claimed that their right rested on their arms, and all things belonged to men of courage'.

[2] Agathias says in Book II [II. i]: 'They who for the sake of gain or unreasonable hatred, without any just pretext, invade the territories of others and harm those who have done no wrong, are both lawless and wicked.' Menander Protector gives us a famous example [frag. 63, p. 121, edit. Dindorf]: 'Baian, chagan of the Avars, without any cause or pretext, and not even deigning to bring a false charge against the Romans, [. . .] broke the treaty in a most shameful and barbarous manner.'

[3] Philo, *On the Ten Commandments* [xxvi], well says: 'Now men who have acquired the strength of robbers lay waste whole cities, taking no thought of punishments, because they appear to be stronger than the laws. These are men whose nature is unsuited to civil life, who seek after tyrannies and despotisms, who carry out plundering on a large scale, concealing under the respected names of government and authority what is more correctly called robbery.' These views are in excellent accord with the quotations from Curtius, Justin, Seneca, and Augustine, made in the afore-mentioned II. i. [page 170].

IV.—*There are certain causes which present a false appearance of justice*

Others allege causes which they claim to be justifiable, but which, when examined in the light of right reason, are found to be unjust. In such cases, as Livy says, it is clear that a decision based not on right [XXI. vi. 2.] but on violence is sought. Very many kings, says Plutarch, make use *Pyrrhus* of the two terms, peace and war, as if they were coins, to obtain not [xii=p. 389 E]. what is right but what is advantageous.

Now causes which are unjust may, up to a certain point, be recognized from the foregoing discussion of just causes. What is straight is in fact a guide to what is crooked. For the sake of clearness, however, we proceed to mention the principal kinds of unjust causes.

V.—*Such a cause is the fear of something uncertain*

1. We have said above that fear with respect to a neighbouring [II. i. 17.] power is not a sufficient cause. For in order that a self-defence may be lawful it must be necessary; and it is not necessary unless we are certain, not only regarding the power of our neighbour, but also regarding his intention; the degree of certainty required is that which is accepted in morals.

2. Wherefore we can in no wise approve the view of those who declare that it is a just cause of war when a neighbour who is restrained by no agreement builds a fortress on his own soil, [386] or some other fortification which may some day cause us harm. Against the fears which arise from such actions we must resort to counter-fortifications on our own land and other similar remedies, but not to force of arms. The wars of the Romans against Philip of Macedon, Zonaras [IX. xv]. and of Lysimachus against Demetrius, were, therefore, unjust, unless Pausanias I [x]. there was some other cause for them.

I am greatly pleased with what Tacitus says of the Chauci: [*Germany*, xxxv.] 'The noblest people of the Germans, who choose to defend their greatness by justice alone, without greed, without lawlessness. They are peaceful and retiring. They provoke no wars; they do not ravage with plunderings and brigandage. This is the outstanding evidence of their worth and power, that their position of superiority has not been attained by wrongful means. Yet all have arms in readiness, and, if the situation demands, they provide an army. They have great numbers of men and horses, and their reputation remains the same even though they are at peace.'

VI.—*Another such cause is advantage apart from necessity*

Advantage does not confer the same right as necessity.

VII.—*A cause of war presenting the appearance of justice is the refusal of marriage, when there is a great abundance of marriageable women*

So, when there is abundant opportunity for marriage, a refusal of marriage cannot furnish a cause for war; although in former times Hercules seized upon such a cause against Eurytus, and Darius[1] against the Scythians.

VIII.—*Such a cause, again, is the desire for richer land*

The desire to change abode, in order that by abandoning swamps and wildernesses a more fruitful soil may be acquired, does not afford a just cause for war. Tacitus says that this was a cause of warfare among the ancient Germans.

Histories, IV [lxxiii].

IX.—*Such a cause is also the discovery of things previously taken over by others*

Victoria, *Relectiones de Indis*, I, no. 31.

Equally shameless is it to claim for oneself by right of discovery what is held by another, even though the occupant may be wicked, may hold wrong views about God, or may be dull of wit. For discovery applies to those things which belong to no one.

X.—*What course is to be followed if the previous occupants are insane*

Victoria, *De Bello*, nos. 5, 6, 7, 8; *De Indis*, II, no. 18.

[II. iv. 10.]

1. For the exercise of ownership neither moral nor religious virtue, nor intellectual excellence, is a requirement; except that the view seems defensible that, if there exist any peoples wholly deprived of the use of reason, these cannot have ownership, but merely for charity's sake there is due to them what is necessary to maintain life. What we have said elsewhere regarding the maintenance of ownership, which universal common law guarantees on behalf of minors and insane persons, applies to those peoples with whom there exists an interchange of agreements; but such are not peoples absolutely deprived of reason, if any of this sort are to be found, which I very much doubt.

Plato, *Republic*, II. iii [V. xvi]; Euripides, *Hecuba* [*Iphigenia in Aulis*, 1400]; Livy, XXXI [xxix. 15]; Isocrates, *Panathenaic Oration* [lxvi].

II. xx. 40.

2. The Greeks were, therefore, wrong in saying that the barbarians were their enemies as it were by nature, because of their differences in customs, perhaps also because the barbarians seemed to be inferior to them in intellect. However, to what extent ownership may be taken away because of vicious crimes, which offend against both nature and human society, is another question, which we just now discussed when dealing with the right of punishments.

[1] Also Antonius [Antoninus] Caracalla against Artabanus, king of Parthia. See Xiphilinus [*Epitome of Dio*, LXXVIII. i].

XI.—*An unjust cause of war is the desire for freedom among a subject people*

Liberty, whether of individuals or of states, that is 'autonomy', cannot give the right to war, just as if by nature and at all times liberty was adapted to all persons.[1] For when liberty is said to be an attribute by nature of men and of peoples this must be understood of the law of nature which precedes all human conditions, and of liberty 'by exemption', not of that which is 'by opposition'; that is to say, that by nature no one is a slave, but not that man has the right never to enter slavery, for in that sense no one is free.

Here applies the saying of Albutius: 'No one is born free, no one a slave; it is after birth that fortune has imposed these distinctions upon individuals.' Also that of Aristotle: 'By law one man is a slave and another free.' Wherefore those who from a lawful cause have come into personal or political slavery ought to be satisfied with their state, as Paul the Apostle teaches in the words: 'Hast thou been called to be a slave? Be not concerned thereat.'

Seneca, *Controversies*, III. xxi [VII. vi. 18]. *Politics*, I [iii]. *I Corinthians*, vii. 21.

[387] XII.—*An unjust cause of war also is the desire to rule others against their will on the pretext that it is for their good*

Not less iniquitous is it to desire by arms to subdue other men, as if they deserved to be enslaved, and were such as the philosophers at times call slaves by nature. For even if something is advantageous for any one, the right is not forthwith conferred upon me to impose this upon him by force. For those who have the use of their reason ought to have the free choice of what is advantageous or not advantageous, unless another has acquired a certain right over them.

With infants the case is clearly different; for since they do not have the right of exercising 'independence of action' and of directing their own movements, nature confers the control over them upon persons who undertake it and are fitted therefor.

Victoria, *De Indis*, no. 24 [I. 24]. Ayala, *De Iure Belli*, I. ii. 29; Covarruvias, *On Sext*, V. ult. 4, pt. II, § ix, no. 5 ff.

XIII.—*An unjust cause of war is the title to universal empire which some give to the Emperor, and which is shown to be inapplicable*

1. I should hardly trouble to add that the title which certain persons give to the Roman Emperor is absurd, as if he had the right of ruling over even the most distant and hitherto unknown peoples, were it not that Bartolus, long considered first among jurists, had

On Dig., XLIX. xv. 24.

[1] [391] See the Council of Toledo, IV, and what we have said above in II. iv. 14 [page 229].

dared to pronounce him a heretic who denies to the Emperor this title. His ground, forsooth, is that the Emperor at times calls himself lord of the world,[1] and that in the sacred writings that empire, which later writers call Romania,[2] is designated as 'the inhabited world'.[3] Of like character is this expression:

Digest, XIV. ii. 9.

Now the whole earth the victorious Roman held,

[Petronius, cxix.]

as are many similar expressions used in a broad sense, or in hyperbole, or in high praise; as when, in the same Holy Writ, Judaea alone often appears under the designation of 'the inhabited world'.[4] It is in this sense that we are to take the ancient saying of the Jews that the city of Jerusalem is situate in the centre of the earth, that is in the centre of Judaea,[5] just as Delphi, in the middle of Greece, is likewise called the navel of the world.

Luke, ii. 1.

[*On Monarchy,* II.] Nor should any one be influenced by the arguments of Dante, by which he strives to prove that such a right belongs to the Emperor because that is advantageous for the human race. The advantages which it brings are in fact offset by its disadvantages. For as a ship may attain to such a size that it cannot be steered, so also the number of inhabitants and the distance between places may be so great as not to tolerate a single government.

Aristotle, *Politics,* VII. iv.

2. Again, even if we should grant that the ascription of such a right to the Emperor is advantageous, the right to rule by no means follows, since this cannot come into existence except by consent or by punishment. The Roman Emperor at present does not have this right even over all the former possessions of the Roman people; for as many of these were acquired by war, so by war they have been lost; while others by treaties, others still by abandonment, have passed under the authority of other nations or kings.[6] Some states, too, that were once completely subject, later began to be subject only in part, or merely federated on unequal terms. For all these ways either of losing or of modifying a right are not less valid against the Roman Emperor than against others.

Sylvester, word *bellum,* I, no. 21; Covarruvias, *loc. cit.,* no. 9.

1 As in the Council of Chalcedon, acts xi and xii.

2 As Athanasius, *Letter to the Monks* [I=p. 832]. This was scarcely the sixth part of the then known world.

3 Philo, *On the Embassy to Gaius* [ii]: 'I am speaking of the most extensive and significant parts of the world, which one might call the world in a special sense, bounded by the two rivers, the Euphrates and the Rhine.'

4 Jerome: 'The name "earth", even when there is added the adjective "whole", should be limited to that portion which is under discussion.'

5 This you may learn from Josephus, *Jewish War,* III [III. iii. 5].

6 Take an example from Spain, on which see Gomez, *On Institutes,* IV. vi. 29, no. 5; Panormitanus, *On Decretals,* I. vi. 34, col. 9; Jason, *On Code,* I. i. 1, col. 2; Menochio, *Consilia,* II, no. 102; Cardinal Toschi, *Practicae Conclusiones,* 345, § *rex Hispaniae*; Dumoulin, *Consuetudines Parisienses,* no. 20, pr.; Chassaneus, *Catalogus Gloriae Mundi,* V. 28; Azor, *Moral Institutes,* II. v. 2.

XIV.—*An unjust cause of war is the title to universal empire which others give to the Church, and which also is shown to be inapplicable*

1. There have also been some who claimed for the Church a right over the peoples even of the hitherto unknown parts of the earth, although the Apostle Paul himself clearly stated that he did not have the right to judge those who are outside the bounds of Christendom, saying: 'For what have I to do with judging them that are without?' (*1 Corinthians*, v. 12).

Victoria, *Relectiones de Indis*, 21 ff. Ayala, I, no. 29.

Yet the right of judging possessed by the Apostles, even although it extended in its own way to earthly things, was of a heavenly nature, so to say, and not of earthly quality; it was to be exercised indeed not by the sword and scourge but by the word of God enunciated in general terms and applied to particular conditions, through the revelation or denial of the signs of divine grace, according as each might deserve; in last resort even by a punishment not according to nature but from a higher source than nature, therefore emanating from God. [388] A punishment of this kind appeared in the cases of Ananias, Elymas, Hymenaeus, and others.

2. Christ Himself, the source of all ecclesiastical power, whose life is set as an example to the Church, in so far as it is His Church, declared that His kingdom was not of this world, that is, of the same character as other kingdoms; adding that otherwise He might make use of soldiers in the manner of other kings. As it was, if He had wished to call for legions, He would have called for legions not of men but of Angels (*Matthew*, xxvi. 53). Whatever He did by right of authority vested in Himself, He did not by human but by divine power, even when He cast the money-changers out of the Temple. For on that occasion also the scourge was a sign, not an instrument, of divine anger; as at other times the spittle and oil were a symbol of healing,[1] not a remedy.

John, xviii. 36; see Peter Damian, *Letters*, II. ix [IV. ix], and Bernard, *Letters*, ccxxi.

Augustine thus comments on the passage of John referred to:

[*On the Gospel of John*, cxv. 2.]

> Hear then, ye Jews and Gentiles; hear, O circumcision; hear, O uncircumcision; hear, all ye kingdoms of the earth! I do not interfere with your rule in this world[2]—'My kingdom is not of this world'. Fear ye not with the utterly empty fear with which the elder Herod trembled when the birth of Christ was announced, and slew so many children in order that death might reach that child; for he was rendered more cruel by his fear than by his anger.
>
> 'My kingdom', He said, 'is not of this world.' What more do ye seek? Come to the kingdom that is not of this world; come believing, and rage not through fear.

[1] This is well explained by Abulensis [Tostado], *On Matthew*, ix.

[2] Hilary of Arles: 'For Christ had not come to this end, that He might encroach upon another's glory, but that He might confer his own; not that He might seize an earthly kingdom, but that He might grant a heavenly one.'

3. Among other things Paul forbids the bishop to use force (*1 Timothy*, iii. 2). Chrysostom[1] said that 'to rule by compulsion', the compulsion, of course, which is derived from human power, 'is the right of kings, not of bishops'. Elsewhere he declares: 'Power has not been given to us to restrain men from crimes by the authority of our sentences,' sentences, that is, which involve the right of execution by royal or military power, or the deprivation of any human right whatsoever.[2] He says also that the bishop should perform his office 'not by compulsion but by persuasion'. From this it is abundantly clear that bishops, as such, have no right to rule over men in the manner of this world. In comparing the king and the bishop, Jerome[3] declares that 'the former is set over unwilling, the latter over willing subjects'.

On the Acts of the Apostles, Homily III [iv]. *On Titus*, Homily I [iv]; *On First Thessalonians*, Homily IV [II. ii]; *On the Priesthood*, II [iii].

4. The question whether even kings may use armed force as a means of punishment against those who reject the Christian religion we have previously discussed, so far as is necessary for our purpose, in the chapter 'On Punishments'.

[II. xx.]

[1] His words are, *On the Priesthood*, Book II [II. iii]: 'Above all things Christians are not permitted to punish by violence the crimes of the guilty. The secular judges, indeed, when they find criminals subject to the power of the law, exercise considerable authority and prevent them against their will from living as they desire. But among us this is to be done not by compulsion but by persuasion, in order that a man who is of that sort may turn out better. For the right to coerce sinners has not been given to us by laws, and even if it had been given to us we should have had no opportunity to exercise this right, since God crowns those who refrain from evil not of necessity, but of free will; wherefore we have need of much toil to persuade those who are sick to offer themselves of their own accord to the priestly healing.' And shortly after [II. iv]: 'For he who strays from the faith cannot be violently constrained, much less compelled by fear.'

Chrysostom says also, *On Ephesians*, iv [iv. 16=Homily XI, v]: [392] 'Moreover, we have been appointed for the teaching of men, not to authority, not to the exercise of power. We hold the place of advising counsellors. He who gives counsel speaks on his own authority; he does not compel his hearer, but leaves him free choice about that which is said.' 'The priest indeed reveals his office, but exercises no right of authority,' says Ambrose, *On Cain and Abel*, II. iv, as cited in the *Decretum*, II. xxxiii. 3 (De Penitencia), i. 51.

[2] For to kings and not to the Church does it pertain to judge in the matter of fiefs, *Decretals*, II. i. 13 and III. xx; and in the matter of possessions, *Decretals*, IV. xvii. 7. For in temporal things kings least of all recognize a superior, *Decretals*, IV. xvii. 13.

'Christ has willed that the Christian Emperors should depend upon the Popes for eternal life, and that the Popes should make use of the imperial laws for the movement of temporal interests, in order that the spiritual action might be kept free from connexion with worldly enterprises, and that he who serves God might involve himself very little in temporal affairs'; *Decretum*, I. x. 8 and I. xcvi. 6.

With this harmonizes what has been stated in I. ii. 9. 13, following the eighty-sixth [eighty-second] of the so-called Apostolic Canons, and what is further cited there on this subject in the text and notes [page 88].

[3] The same writer says in the *Epitaph of Nepotianus* [*Letters*, lx. 14]: 'The bishop has less power than the king. For the former is set over unwilling subjects, the latter over willing. The former subjects men to fear; the latter is appointed for service.' Cassiodorus, XI [*Variae*, XI. iii], in his letter to the bishops, writes: 'Let the bishop teach, that the judge may not be able to find anything to punish.'

The Emperor Frederick I in Gunther, *Ligurinus* [VI. 362 f.], says of the Pope:

Let him govern his Church and administer laws divine;
To us let him leave the Empire and symbols of power.

When Bishop William of Roskilde tried to exclude from entrance into a church Sweyn, the excommunicated king of Denmark, by presenting his crozier, and the royal servants laid hands upon their sword-hilts, he did as became a bishop, and offered them his neck. [See Saxo Grammaticus, xi = pp. 189–90.]

Add what we have above in I. 5 [I. iv. 5].

XV.—*An unjust cause of war is also the desire to fulfil prophecies, without the command of God*

Not without reason shall I give this warning, that the hope derived from an interpretation of divine prophecies [1] does not furnish a just cause of war. For from a comparison of modern with ancient events I foresee the danger of great evil from this source, unless we guard against it. Apart from the fact that without prophetic inspiration it is hardly possible to interpret with certainty prophecies that have not yet been fulfilled,[2] even the times set for the coming of things that are certain may be hidden from us. Finally a prediction, unless it is a definite command of God, confers no right, since the things which God foretells He often permits to be accomplished through the agency of wicked men or base deeds.

XVI.—*An unjust cause of war is also the desire to obtain something that is owed by an obligation not strictly legal but arising from some other source*

This principle, too, must be recognized. If a person owes a debt that is not an obligation from the point of view of strict justice, but arises from some other virtue, such as generosity, gratitude, pity or charity, this debt cannot be collected by armed force any more than in a court of law. For either procedure it is not enough that the demand which is made ought to be met for a moral reason, but in addition we must possess some right to enforce it.

This right is at times conferred by divine and human laws even in the case of obligations that arise from other virtues; and when this happens there arises a new [389] cause of indebtedness, which relates to justice. When this is lacking, a war undertaken on such

[1] On a certain Theodotus in the time of Gratian, see Zosimus [IV. xiii] and Ammianus Marcellinus [XXIX. i. 8 ff.]; on John of Cappadocia, see Procopius, *Persian War*, II [II. xxx], and Leunclavius, *Turkish History*, Book XVIII.

[2] The books of prophecy are closed and sealed even until the time appointed, so that they may not be understood (*Daniel*, xii. 4, 8 and 9). Jerome, *On Daniel* [xii. 8], says: 'If the prophet heard and did not understand, what shall they do who through presumption of mind have interpreted a book that is sealed and involved in many obscurities until the time of consummation?'

Procopius writes, *Gothic War*, II [I. xxiv]: 'I consider it beyond human power to discover the sense of the Sibylline oracles before the occurrence of the event.' The same author, shortly afterward: 'It is impossible for any man whatsoever to understand the Sibylline oracles before the event, but we must wait till the day itself, when the prophecy has been fulfilled and its words have been confirmed by the fact, [393] becomes the inerrant interpreter of the verses.'

Gregoras says, Book V [V. v.]: 'And just as other predictions are most difficult in regard to conjecture and interpretation because they contain much that is involved and receive many explanations, so too this oracle deceived everybody, including the emperor himself, so long as he lived. When, however, he had been taken away from human affairs, the oracle revealed itself to men.' Beware, ye overbold theologians! Be on your guard, ye politicians, against overbold theologians!

There is a passage worthy of inspection in De Thou, Book LXXIX, on the year 1583, concerning Jacob Brocard.

grounds is unjust, such as the Roman war against the King of Cyprus on the charge of ingratitude. He who confers a kindness has no right to demand gratitude; otherwise there would be an agreement, not an act of kindness.

XVII.—*The difference between a war the cause of which is unjust and a war in which there is a wrong of another kind; and the different effects of each*

Victoria, *De Iure Belli*, no. 2.

1. It is to be observed that this often happens, that a just cause for a war may in fact exist, but that in making war a wrong may arise from the intent of the party who engages in hostilities. This may come about either because some other thing, not in itself unlawful, in a greater degree and more effectively influences his purpose than the right itself, as, for example, an eager desire for honour,[1] or some advantage, whether private or public, which is expected from the war considered apart from its justifiable cause. Or there may be present a manifestly unlawful desire, such as the delight of him who has pleasure in another's ill, without regard to what is good. From this point of view Aristides in his oration *On the Alliance* says that the Phocians perished in accordance with their deserts, but that Philip did not act rightly when he overthrew them, seeing that he did not act out of zeal for religion, as he pretended, but in order to extend his empire.

[ii=p. 256–7.] [*Letter of Mithridates*, v.] [*Histories*, IV. lxxiv.] Seneca, *Hippolytus* [540 f.] *Against Faustus*, XXII. lxxiv. Covarruvias, d. § 1, no. 2; Cajetan, *On II. ii*, qu. 40, art. 1; Sylvester, word *bellum*, no. 2; *Summa Angelica*, word *bellum*, no. 5; Trovamala, *Summa*, word *bellum*, nos. 3 and 8. Thomas Aquinas, II. ii. 66. 8.

2. 'The sole cause of warfare, and that an ancient one,' says Sallust, 'is a deeply rooted desire for power and riches.' 'Gold and wealth, the chief causes of wars,' we find in Tacitus. In a tragedy we read:

> Impious lust of gain and wrath impetuous
> Have broken the alliance.

With these quotations you may rightly associate the passage of Augustine: 'The eager desire to injure, the cruelty of vengeance, the unappeased and unappeasable mind, the savagery of rebellion, the lust of ruling, and whatever else there is akin, these are the things which are justly censured in warfare.'

3. However, when a justifiable cause is not wanting, while these things do indeed convict of wrong the party that makes war, yet they do not render the war itself, properly speaking, unlawful. Hence no restitution is due as a result of a war undertaken under such conditions.

[1] A vice which entices us through a certain similitude of virtue. But Augustine rightly cautions us, *City of God*, III. xiv: 'It is better to suffer the penalties of lack of enterprise in any degree than to seek glory in these wars.'

Consult what we have quoted from Agathias on section 3, above [II. xxii. 3. 2, note].

CHAPTER XXIII

ON DOUBTFUL CAUSES OF WAR

I.—*On the source of the causes of doubt in moral questions*

What Aristotle wrote is perfectly true, that certainty is not to be found in moral questions in the same degree as in mathematical science. This comes from the fact that mathematical science completely separates forms from substance, and that the forms themselves are generally such that between two of them there is no intermediate form,[1] just as there is no mean between a straight and a curved line. In moral questions, on the contrary, even trifling circumstances alter the substance, and the forms, which are the subject of inquiry, are wont to have something intermediate,[2] which is of such scope that it approaches now more closely to this, now to that extreme. *Nicomachean Ethics,* I. i.

Thus it comes about that between what should be done and what it is wrong to do there is a mean, that which is permissible; and this is now closer to the former, now to the latter. Hence there often comes a moment of doubt, just as when day passes into night, or when cold water slowly becomes warm. This is what Aristotle means when he says: 'Oftentimes it is hard to decide what choice one should make.' Andronicus of Rhodes states the matter thus: 'It is hard to distinguish what is truly just from that which appears to be so.' *Nicomachean Ethics,* III [i]. [*On Nic. Ethics,* I. iii.]

[394] II.—*Nothing is to be done contrary to the dictates of one's mind, however erroneous they may be*

1. First of all we must hold to the principle that, even if something is in itself just, when it is done by one who, taking everything into consideration, considers it unjust, the act is vicious. This in fact is what the Apostle Paul meant by saying, 'Whatsoever is not of faith, is sin,' where 'faith' signifies the judgement of the mind on the matter.[3] For God has given the power of judgement as a guide for human actions, and if this is treated with contempt the mind becomes brutish. *Romans,* xiv. 23.

[1] In these the transition is made 'to the opposite'; in the former, 'to the mean'.

[2] [399] See Chrysostom, *On Ephesians,* iv [Homily XVI, ii]; *Morali.,* II [Aristotle, *Magna Moralia,* I. ix].

[3] Of like purport is the following from the same Epistle of Paul and the same chapter [*Romans,* xiv. 5]: 'Let each man be fully assured in his own mind'; also [*ibid.,* 22], 'Happy is he that judgeth not himself in that which he approveth.'

Ambrose says [*On Romans,* xiv. 23]: 'That is a sin which is done without one's approval.' Augustine follows the same teaching. Both are cited by Gratian after *Decretum,* II. xxviii. 1. 14.

Not very different is this statement of Plutarch in his *Timoleon* [vi = p. 238 C]: 'It is required not only that what is done should be honourable and just, but that there should also be a firm and stable conviction as the source of the action, that whatever is done may be so done because the mind has judged that it ought to be done.'

2. Nevertheless, it often happens that the judgement presents no certainty, but is undecided. If this indecision cannot be dissipated by careful consideration, we must follow the precept of Cicero: 'That is a good rule which they lay down who bid you not to do a thing when you are in doubt [1] whether it is right or wrong.' The Jewish teachers also say: 'Hold aloof from a doubtful matter.'

On Duties, I [ix. 30]. [Rabbi Gamaliel in *Pirke Aboth*, i. 16.]

This course, however, cannot be pursued where one really must do one of two things, and yet is in doubt whether either is right. In that case he will be allowed to choose that which appears to him to be less wrong. For always, when a choice cannot be avoided, the lesser evil assumes the aspect of the good. 'We must take the least among evils,' says Aristotle; and Cicero, 'Of evils one must choose the least.' Quintilian writes: 'In a comparison of evils, the lesser evil takes the place of the good.'

Covarruvias, vol. I, *De Matr.*, pt. II, vii, § 2, no. 9. *Nic. Eth.*, II. ix. *On Duties*, III [i. 3]. [*Inst. of Oratory*, VII. iv. 12.]

III.—*One's judgement may be influenced in either direction by arguments from facts*

Very often in a doubtful matter, however, after some investigation the mind does not remain neutral but is influenced to this side or that by arguments drawn from the facts, or by the opinion which it gathers from other men [2] who express their view of the matter. For here also is the saying of Hesiod [3] true, that the most excellent thing is to be wise of one's self; the next best, to be directed by the help of others.

Vázquez, *Disputations on II. i*, 62, i, no. 1; Medina, *On II. i*, qu. 14.

Arguments from the facts are drawn from causes, effects, and other collateral circumstances.

IV.—*One's judgement may be influenced in either direction by authority*

To consider aright the arguments to which we have made reference, one must have a certain degree of experience and skill. Those who do not have such skill and experience are bound to listen to the counsels of the wise, in order that they may rightly mould their

Victoria, *Relectiones de Indis*, I, no. 12; and *De Iure Belli*, 21 and 24.

[1] Pliny, *Letters*, I. xix [I. xviii]: 'Do not do that in regard to which you are in doubt.'

[2] Augustine, *On Order*, Book III [II. v. 16]: 'It is a twofold way which we follow when the obscurity of things affects us, we follow either reason or authority.' This is explained by Gabriel Vázquez, *Disputations*, 62. iii. 10.

[3] This thought of Hesiod is applied by Minutius after a lost battle, in Livy, XXII [XXII. xxix. 8]: 'The man stands first who forms a plan which is effective; next after him is the man who listens to one that gives advice; he who knows neither how to look out for himself, nor how to obey another, is of the lowest intelligence.' Cicero, *For Cluentius* [xxxi. 84], says: 'Men say that he is the wisest into whose mind the idea which is needed comes; next ranks the man who follows the able devices of another.'

The verses of Hesiod [*Works and Days*, 293 ff.] from which these views are derived run as follows:

Best is the man who sees what useful is, what not,
And even keeps in mind the distant goal,
Next is the man who well has learned wise plans to follow.
But he who has no power to plan, and hearkens not
To others' good advice, is void of usefulness.

practical judgement. For, on the testimony of Aristotle, 'things generally admitted', or probable things, 'are those which seem so to all, or to the majority, or at any rate to those who are wise; and again, of the wise, either to all, or to the majority, or to the more eminent'. This method of judging is especially employed by kings, who hardly have the time to learn or to weigh thoroughly the principles of the branches of knowledge. Aristotle, *Topics*, I. [7].

The throng of wise men makes the ruler wise. [Gellius, XIII. xviii.]

Aristides, addressing the Rhodians in his discourse *On Concord*, said that just as in questions of fact that is held to be true which is supported by the most and especially competent witnesses, so in matters of judgement we must follow the opinions which are supported by the more numerous and most eminent counsellors. Thus the ancient Romans used not to make war without consulting the college of the Fetials, organized for this purpose, and the Christian Emperors rarely did so without giving a hearing to the bishops, that they might be advised of anything which might give rise to religious scruples. [=p. 378 BC.]

V.—*If in a weighty matter there is doubt on both sides, and one of two courses must be chosen, that which is the safer is to be adopted*

1. In many controversies it may happen that strong arguments are forthcoming in support of both sides, whether drawn from the facts in the case or supported by the authority of others. When this occurs, if the matters which are in question are of slight moment the choice may evidently be free from harm, no matter on which side it may fall. But if the question is one of great importance, such as the infliction of capital punishment, in that case, because of the great difference between the courses to be chosen, the safer is to be preferred,[1] as is commonly said:

Nevertheless 'tis better on this side to err. [Terence, *Brothers*, II. i. 20.]

And so it is better to acquit one who is guilty than to condemn one who is innocent.

2. The author of the *Problems* which are attributed to Aristotle says: [395] 'Each of us would prefer to acquit a guilty man on the ground that he had not done wrong than to condemn an innocent man for having done wrong' (in this passage μὴ ἀδικοῦντος is commonly read for ἀδικοῦντος, and conversely). Shortly after he adds the xxix [13].

[1] Ammianus Marcellinus, Book XXVIII [XXVIII. i. 40]: 'If anger is unappeasable, it is a mark of the greatest harshness. If, on the other hand, it can be assuaged by entreaty, it shows the greatest lenity. Nevertheless leniency, even in the case of crimes, is to be preferred to harshness.' This is explained by Vázquez in the work cited [*Disputations*, 62], iv, no. 21.

reason, which we have already given: 'For, whenever anyone is in doubt, he must choose that in which there is less wrong.' Antiphon declares: 'If it is necessary to err in any way, it is more in accordance with right to set free without justification than wrongfully to condemn. For in the one case a mistake is made, but the condemnation of an innocent person is a crime.'

[*Orations*, xiv.]

VI.—*Whence it follows that in case of doubt we must refrain from war*

Now war is of the utmost importance, seeing that in consequence of war a great many sufferings usually fall upon even innocent persons. Therefore in the midst of divergent opinions we must lean towards peace. Silius Italicus praises Fabius, for—

I [679 f.].

> With cautious mind the future did he scan,
> Nor took delight
> To stir up war for causes
> Slight and doubtful.

There are, moreover, three methods by which disputes may be prevented from breaking out into wars.

VII.—*First, war may be obviated by a conference*

On Duties, I [xi. 34]. Victoria, *De Iure Belli*, no. 28.

1. The first method is by a conference. Says Cicero: 'Since there are two methods of settling a difference, the one by argument, the other by force, and since the former is characteristic of men, the latter of beasts, we should have recourse to the second only when it is not permitted to use the first.' And Terence has this:

[*Eunuch*, IV. vii. 19 f.]

> The wise man should try all things before arms;[1]
> How know you if my bidding she will do
> Without constraint?

[III. 185.] Apollonius Rhodius said,

> Not at once with force ere with words we try to win him;

[*Suppliants*, 347.] and Euripides:

> With words shall I try to win; if that fails, then with force.

[1] Dionysius of Halicarnassus in the *Selections on Embassies* [704, ed. Oxon.]: 'One must not resort to deeds before the way of words has been tried.' Menelaus in Libanius [*Orations*, i = p. 196 D]: 'It is more fitting for a man first to try argument rather than to rush at once to arms.'

In accord with this point of view are the words of the chorus in the *Helena* of Euripides [1150 ff.]:

[400]
> Fools in sooth are they who set
> A single test for virtue—steel;
> Who seek for human strife no pause
> Save by the ruthless sword;
> For if in blood alone can virtue be discerned
> Then raging discord never will desert
> The states once embattled.

The same author in his *Suppliants* thus rebukes the states which have failed to try this method: [748.]

> You too, O cities, that by slaughter prefer
> To decide what words might settle.

Again, in the *Iphigenia in Aulis*, Achilles says: [1017 ff.]

> If he obeys the right, no need have you of aid
> From me; in this alone is there enough of safety.
> At once a friend's good will shall I retain,
> And from my whole array less censure have,
> If this by reason, not by strife, I settle.

Also, in his *Phoenician Maidens*, we read this: [516 f.]

> For parley will accomplish all
> That foemen's steel would e'er effect.

The same thought is more fully expressed in Livy by Phaeneas:[1] [XXXV. xlv. 4.] 'To avoid the necessity of fighting, men voluntarily relinquish many things which they could not be compelled to give up by war and force.' In Book VII of Herodotus, Mardonius criticizes the Greeks [VII. ix.] in this regard: 'They ought, speaking the same tongue, to settle their controversies by the use of heralds and envoys rather than by battle.'

2. In Dionysius of Halicarnassus Coriolanus declares: 'Not to [VIII. viii.] desire the things of others, but to demand the things that are one's own and, if these are not obtained, [396] to fight for them, all would agree is fair.' In the same Dionysius King Tullus says: 'The [III. xi.] things that cannot be settled by words are decided by arms.' In Tacitus Vologeses uses these words: 'What my ancestors had won [*Annals*, xv. ii.] I should have preferred to retain by justice rather than blood, by reason rather than arms.' Says King Theodoric: 'Then only is it [Cassiodorus, *Variae*, III. i.] expedient to resort to arms when justice cannot find a place among our adversaries.'

VIII.—*Second, war may be obviated by arbitration; with a discussion of the duty of Christian kings in regard to warring parties*

1. The second method is by agreement to arbitrate.[2] This is applicable among those who have no common judicial authority.

[1] Donatus, *On [Terence's] Eunuch* [I. ii. 94]: 'For it is a well-known fact that the very thing that you would have defended to the limit of your strength if attempt had been made to wrest it from you, afterward you may abandon to him who does not try to seize it.'

[2] A way very often scorned by the more powerful. See Connestagio, *On the Union of the Kingdoms of Castile and Portugal*. It is a worthy way, however, which lovers of justice and peace should pursue. Great kings and peoples, who have been mentioned in the text, have done so. Let us add others.

Arbitrators were accepted between Magnus, king of Norway, and Canute, king of Denmark, who were rivals for both kingdoms; just as Julian, first of that name, wished by an interdict to come to terms with Severus who opposed him for the Roman principate [Spartianus, *Life of Pescennius Niger*,

[I. lxxxv.] [IV. lxv.] 'It is not lawful', says Thucydides, 'to proceed against one who offers arbitration, just as against a wrong-doer.' Thus, as Diodorus relates, Adrastus and Amphiaraus entrusted to Eriphyle the decision regarding the kingdom of Argos. Concerning Salamis three Lacedaemonians were chosen to judge between the Athenians and the [I. xxviii.] Megareans. In Thucydides, who was just now quoted, the Corcyreans notify the Corinthians that they are ready to adjust their disputes before cities of the Peloponnesus upon which they shall mutually [*Platonic*, ii=p. 248 B.] agree. Aristides praises Pericles because, to avoid war, he desired 'to reach an agreement before a tribunal regarding their differences'. [lxxxiii.] Isocrates [Aeschines], in his speech *Against Ctesiphon*, commends Philip of Macedon for being ready 'to entrust to some fair and impartial city' the settlement of the differences which he had with the Athenians.

Livy, VIII [III. lxxi]. [Cicero, *On Duties*, I. x. 33.] Xenophon. *Training of Cyrus*, II [iv. 8]. [Livy, XL. xvii.] 2. In like manner in former times the people of Ardea and Aricia, and afterwards the Neapolitans and the inhabitants of Nola, submitted their disputes to the judgement of the Roman people. The Samnites in a controversy with the Romans appealed to mutual friends. Cyrus brings in the king of India as an arbiter between himself and the king of Assyria. The Carthaginians in their quarrel with Masinissa appealed to legal tribunals in order to escape war.

VIII [xxiii]. XXXII [x. 5]. Plutarch, *Pompey* [xxxiii=p. 637 C]. [*Numa* xii =p. 68 A.] In Livy the Romans themselves in the case of a controversy with the Samnites appeal to common allies. Philip of Macedon in his dispute with the Greeks says that he will accept the decision of peoples with whom both parties may be at peace. At the request of the Parthians and Armenians Pompey appointed arbitrators to fix their boundaries. Plutarch says that this was the chief duty of the Roman Fetiales, 'not to permit military operations before all hope of a judicial settlement was cut off'. Regarding the Druids in

chap. ii]. Magnus, king of Sweden, was accepted as arbitrator between the two Erics, kings of Denmark and Norway.

Five Spartans, Critolaidas, Amompharetus, Hypsechidas, Anaxilas, and Cleomenes, were chosen to judge between the Athenians and the Megarians with regard to Salamis [Plutarch, *Solon*, x=p. 83 E]. In the treaty between the Lacedaemonians and Argives, in Thucydides, V, the provision is inserted: 'Who wish to submit to arbitrators according to ancestral custom.' Shortly after: 'If any of the allied states should have a controversy with another ally, let them refer the matter to a state which shall seem impartial to both.' Both citations are in Thucydides, Book V [V. lxxix].

Marcus Antoninus [Antoninus Pius] was chosen by many peoples outside the Roman Empire to arbitrate their differences, in order that they might avoid war; as [Aurelius] Victor [*Epitome*, xv. 3] and others record. In Procopius, *Gothic War*, III [III. xxxiv], the Gepidae say to the Lombards: 'We are ready to settle our differences by recourse to an arbitrator; it is wicked violently to assail those who are willing to abide by the decision of a tribunal.' In the same author, *Gothic War*, IV [IV. xxiv], Theudebald, king of the Franks, shows that he is ready to accept a judge to decide his disputes with the Romans.

See also the intimation given in olden times to Philip by the Romans in Polybius, *Selections on Embassies*, iv [=*Histories*, XVI. xxxiv], and what is in the treaty of Antiochus from Polybius, also in the same *Selections*, xxxv [=*Histories*, XVIII. xlviii and i].

The king of England was judge concerning the succession in Scotland; Count Holsatus between the king of Denmark and his brothers, as Pontanus [401] records in his *Danish History*, Book VII. Add the examples in Mariana, XXIV. xx and XXIX. xxiii; in Paruta, VII and XI; in Bizarri, XII [p. 260]; in Krantz, *Saxonica*, VI. xv; and our own, below, III. xx. 46.

Gaul Strabo says : 'Formerly they both served as arbitrators between those at war and often separated those who were about to engage in battle.' The same author bears witness that in Spain the priests discharged the same function. IV [iv. 4]. XI [iii. 6].

3. Especially, however, Christian kings and states are bound to pursue this method of avoiding wars.[1] For if certain arbiters were established both by Jews and by Christians in order that the sentences of strange judges might be avoided by those of the true faith, and this was prescribed by Paul, how much more should this be done to avoid a far greater disadvantage, that is, war? Thus Tertullian argues somewhere that the Christian must not serve as a soldier, seeing that he is not even permitted to go to law; but this argument, in accordance with what we have said in another place, is to be interpreted with a certain degree of moderation. Victoria, *De Iure Belli*, no. 28. [I. ii. 9. 4.]

4. Both for this and for other reasons it would be advantageous, indeed in a degree necessary, to hold certain conferences of Christian powers, where those who have no interest at stake may settle the disputes of others, and where, in fact, steps may be taken to compel parties to accept peace on fair terms.[2] Diodorus and Strabo relate that this was the function of the Druids among the Gauls.[3] We read also [397] that the kings of the Franks entrusted the decision on the division of their kingdom to their leading men. Molina, disp. 103, § *Quando inter*. Aegidius Regius, *De Actibus Supernat.*, disp. 31, dub. 4, no. 72. [Diodorus, V. xxxi.] [Strabo, IV. iv. 4.]

IX.—*Third, war may be obviated even by lot*

The third method is by lot.[4] The use of the lot for this purpose was recommended by Dio Chrysostom in his second speech *Against Fortune*, and much earlier by Solomon (*Proverbs*, xviii. 18). Thomas, II. ii, qu. 95, art. 8, and Cajetan thereon. [*Orations*, lxiv = p. 599.]

X.—*Whether single combat may be permitted as a means of avoiding war*

1. Something akin to the lot, furthermore, is single combat. Resort to single combat it does not seem necessary altogether to reject if two persons, whose disputes would otherwise afflict whole peoples with very serious evils,[5] are ready to settle their dispute by arms, as

[1] Gregoras, *On Alexander the Bulgar*, X [X. iv. 279]: 'It is unseemly for Christians to fight among themselves with such bitterness, when there are ways of agreeing upon peace, and of turning their common forces against the wicked.'

[2] See the example in Cassiodorus, [*Variae*,] III, 1, 2, 3, 4; and Gail, *De Pace Publica*, II, chap. xviii, no. 12.

[3] In this respect, and with better right, the bishops were the successors of the Druids. See the letter of the bishops to King Louis in the *Capitularies* of Charles the Bald; and, on the bishops of Spain, Roderic of Toledo, Book VII, chap. iii.

[4] See Augustine, *On Christian Doctrine*, I. xxviii.

[5] The author of the tragedy at Thebes [Euripides, *Phoenician Maidens*, 564] writes:

> Seek which of you shall be the king,
> But let the kingdom still remain.

Dio Cassius says of Otho [Xiphilinus, *Excerpta Dionis*, LXIV. xiii]: 'For it is more fitting and more just that one should die for all than many for the sake of one.'

Herodotus, VII [IX. xxvi]. Plutarch, *Greek Questions* [xiii = p. 294 B]. Strabo, VIII [iii. 33]. Livy, XXVIII [xxi. 6]. V [I. xxiii. 9]. loc. cit. [VIII. iii. 33].

in olden times Hyllus and Echemus for the Peloponnesus, Hyperochus and Phemius for the country adjacent to the Inachus, Pyraechma an Aetolian and Degmenus the Epean for Elis, and Corbis and Orsua for Iba. In fact it seems clear that, if the combatants should themselves not act aright, assuredly the decision might be accepted by their states as the lesser evil. According to Livy, Metius addressed Tullus as follows:

> Let us follow some course by which it may be decided which people shall rule the other, without a great disaster and without much bloodshed of either people.

Strabo says that this was the ancient custom of the Greeks; and in Virgil[1] Aeneas says that it was right that the dispute between himself and Turnus should be decided in this way.

[I. ii. end.]

2. This, among other customs of the ancient Franks,[2] is strongly commended by Agathias in his first book, and I shall cite his own words because they are notable:

> But if it should happen that any disputes arise between their kings, then all form in line of battle for the purpose of waging war and reaching a decision by force of arms, and they march to meet one another. But when the armies on either side behold each other, straightway they cast aside their anger and change to friendship, and they bid their kings to settle their disputes rather by arbitration. If these are unwilling to do this, they bid their kings to fight in single combat and incur danger in their own persons, on the ground that it is not just and right, nor in accord with the practices of their forefathers, that because of their private enmity they should weaken or destroy the common good.
>
> Immediately, therefore, they disband their armies; with the restoration of peace they enjoy intercourse with one another in safety, since the causes of the troubles have been removed. So great among their subjects is the zeal for justice and the love of country; and, on the other hand, the spirit of their rulers is mild and easily persuadable by their subjects.

XI.—*Where the doubt on either side is equal, he who is in possession has the more advantageous position*

Dig. L. xvii. 128. Victoria, *De Iure Belli*, nos. 27 and 30: Lessius, *De Iustitia*, xxix, dub. 10; [II. v. 18.] [xxix. 13.]

Although when the cause involves doubt each party is bound to try to find conditions under which war may be avoided, nevertheless the party who asserts claims is under greater obligation to do this than the party who is in possession.[3] For it is in accordance not only with the civil but also with the law of nature, that when each party has a cause equally just the case of the party having possession is the better. The reason for this we have adduced elsewhere from the *Problems* which are attributed to Aristotle.

[1] *Aeneid*, XI [XI. 115]:

> For Turnus had it been more just to meet this death.

For a like reason Antony challenged Octavius to single combat; Plutarch, *Antony* [lxii = p. 944 E].

[2] See the Capitulary of Charles the Bald in St. Arnulf, and the Treaty of Aix-la-Chapelle. The same equitable custom prevailed among the Lombards; see Paul Warnefrid [Paulus Diaconus], I. xii; IV. xvii; V. xl.

[3] See Herrera, vol. II.

At this point we must add that war cannot permissibly be waged by him who knows that he has a just cause but has not adequate proofs to convince the possessor of the injustice of his possession; the reason is that he does not have the right to compel the other to surrender possession.

Molina, disp. 103, § *in secundo vero*; Lorca, *On II. ii*, § 3, disp. 53, no. 4.

[398] XII.—*When the doubt on either side is equal, if neither party is in possession the thing under dispute should be divided*

In cases in which the right is in doubt, and neither party is in possession, or each holds possession in an equal measure, he is to be considered in the wrong who rejects a proposed division of the thing under dispute.

Lorca, *On II. ii*, qu. 40, disp. 53; Soto, *De Justitia et Jure*, V, xli, art. 7.

XIII.—*The question whether a war may be just from the view-point of both parties is discussed, with many qualifications*

1. From what we have said it is possible to reach a decision regarding the question, which has been discussed by many, whether, if we take into consideration the prime movers, a war may be considered just from the point of view of each of the opposing sides.

We must distinguish various interpretations of the word 'just'.[1] Now a thing is called just either from its cause, or because of its effects; and again, if from its cause, either in the particular sense of justice, or in the general sense in which all right conduct comes under this name. Further, the particular sense may cover either that which concerns the deed, or that which concerns the doer; for sometimes the doer himself is said to act justly so long as he does not act unjustly, even if that which he does is not just. This distinction between 'acting wrongly' (τὸ ἀδικεῖν) and 'doing that which is unjust' (τὸ ἄδικον πράττειν) is rightly made by Aristotle.

2. In the particular sense and with reference to the thing itself, a war cannot be just on both sides, just as a legal claim cannot; the reason is that by the very nature of the case a moral quality cannot be given to opposites as to doing and restraining. Yet it may actually happen that neither of the warring parties does wrong. No one acts unjustly without knowing that he is doing an unjust thing, but in this respect many are ignorant. Thus either party may justly, that is in good faith, plead his case. For both in law and in fact many things out of which a right arises ordinarily escape the notice of men.

3. In the general sense that is usually called just which is free from all blame on the part of the doer. However, many things are done without right and yet without guilt, because of unavoidable

Covarruvias, *On Sext*, V. ult. 4, § 10, no. 6; Alciati, *Paradoxa*, II. xxi; Fulgosius, *On Dig.*, I. i. 5; Piccolomini, *Civil.Phil.*, VI. xxi; Alberico Gentili, I. vi. *Ethics*, V. x, xi; *Rhetoric*, I. xiii. Aug., *City of God*, XV. v; XIX. xv; Covarruvias, *On Sext*, V. ult. 4, § 10, no. 2; Victoria, [*De Iure Belli*,] no. 32; Suarez, *De Legibus*, III. xviii; Alphonsus de Castro, *De Potestate Legis Poenalis*, I. i and iii.

[1] So Gratian, after *Decretum*, II. xi. 3. 65, distinguished a 'justice of cause, of sequence, of mind'.

ignorance. An example of this is the case of those who fail to observe a law of which they are ignorant through no fault of their own, after the law itself has been promulgated and a sufficient time has elapsed for them to know of it. So it may happen in the case of legal claims also, that each party is guiltless, not only of injustice, but also of any other fault; this is especially true where each party, or even one of the two, pleads not in his own name but in the name of another, for example because of his duty as a guardian, which cannot abandon a right even if it is uncertain.

Rhetoric, III. xvii. II. viii [*Institutes*, II. xvii. 31]. *Topics*, I. xiii [I. xv. 10]. *Nicom. Ethics*, V. xii.

In this sense Aristotle declares that in suits concerning a disputed right neither party is dishonourable or, as he says, 'wicked'. In agreement therewith Quintilian says that it may happen that an orator, that is a good man, may speak on either side. Furthermore Aristotle also says that a judge is said to judge justly in a twofold sense, for this means that he judges either 'as he ought', without any ignorance, or 'in accordance with his own judgement'. And in another place he says: 'If a judge has rendered judgement through ignorance, he is not unjust.'

4. In the case of war, however, it is scarcely possible that rashness and lack of kindly feeling should not play some part, because of the seriousness of the business. The seriousness of war is in all respects such that, not satisfied with merely acceptable causes, it demands causes that are perfectly evident.

5. If we interpret the word 'just' in relation to certain legal effects, in this sense surely it may be admitted that a war may be just from the point of view of either side; this will appear from what we shall have to say later regarding a formal public war. So, in fact, a judgement not rendered according to law, and possession without right, have certain legal effects.

CHAPTER XXIV

WARNINGS NOT TO UNDERTAKE WAR RASHLY, EVEN FOR JUST CAUSES

I.—*Often a right should be given up in order to avoid war*

[402] 1. Although it does not seem properly to be a part of this work, which is entitled *On the Law of War*, to inquire what other virtues enjoin or admonish with regard to war, nevertheless we must proceed to correct an error, in order to prevent any one from thinking that, where a right has been adequately established, either war should be waged forthwith, or even that war is permissible in all cases. On the contrary it frequently happens that it is more upright and just to abandon one's right.

That we may honourably neglect the care of our own lives in order that, to the best of our ability, we may safeguard the life and eternal salvation of another, has been stated above in its proper place. Such conduct is above all becoming for Christians. In this they imitate the most perfect example set by Christ, for He was willing to die for us who were as yet ungodly and hostile (*Romans*, v. 6). This fact of itself much the more urges us not to follow up our own interests, or what may be due to us, so far as to cause others the suffering that wars bring with them.

Victoria, *De Iure Belli*, no. 14 and 33.

2. That war is not to be undertaken for every just cause[1] is the advice of Aristotle and of Polybius. The ancients did not praise Hercules because he made war on Laomedon and Augeas on account of the failure to receive recompense for his toil. Dio of Prusa, in his oration *On War and Peace*, says that it is customary not only to inquire 'whether an injury has been done by those upon whom it is proposed to make war', but also 'how great is the estimate of the damage done'.

Polybius, IV [xxxi]. *Rhet. to Alex.*, iii. Pausanias, V [ii]. [*Orations*, xxxii= p. 275.]

[1] Seneca, *Suasoriae*, V [V. viii]: 'Gallio has said that war is to be undertaken in defence of liberty, of wives, of children; it is not to be undertaken for the sake of a superfluous thing which would cause no harm if it should be done.'

Something further was said by Apollonius to the king of Babylon, according to Philostratus, i. 23 [*Life of Apollonius of Tyana*, i. 38]: 'Moreover, he added that he should not dispute with the Romans over villages, smaller than those often possessed by individuals, and that he should not go to war even for great causes.'

Josephus, in his second book *Against Apion* [II. xxxvii. 272], says of his countrymen: [408] 'Our people do not develop their courage in order that they may increase their territory, but that they may preserve their laws. While therefore we endure other losses easily, when there are those who try to force us to abandon our laws, we even undertake wars that are beyond our strength, and hold out to the bitter end.'

II.—*Especially the right to inflict punishments ought to be given up in order to avoid war*

1. There are in truth many reasons which admonish us to forgo punishments. Let us observe how many things fathers pass over in
[XLIV. xxxii.] their sons; with regard to this there is a discourse of Cicero in Dio Cassius. As Seneca says:[1] 'Unless many great wrongs have overcome his patience, unless what he fears is more than what he condemns, a father will not take up the pen for condemnation.' This differs but little from the saying of Phineus, in the account of Diodorus
V [IV. xliv]. Siculus: 'No father willingly exacts punishment from his sons, unless by the enormity of their wicked deeds they overcome the natural love of parents for their children'; and from that of Andronicus of
[*On Nic. Ethics*, VIII. xviii.] Rhodes: 'No father cuts off his son unless he should be excessively wicked.'

2. Now whoever wishes to punish another assumes in some
[*Letters*, cxxxiii. 2.] measure the character of a ruler, that is of a father.[2] With this in mind, Augustine said to Count Marcellinus: 'Perform, O Christian
[*Orations*, ii=p. 50.] judge, the function of a dutiful father.' The Emperor Julian praises the saying of Pittacus, 'who sets pardon above vengeance'. Libanius, in his oration on the riot at Antioch, says, 'Let him', who desires to be like unto God, 'take delight rather in forgoing punishments than in exacting them.'

3. At times the circumstances of the case are such that to refrain from the exercise of one's right is not merely praiseworthy

[1] *On Clemency*, I. xiv. Augustus, acting as an adviser to a father with regard to his son, who had been caught in attempted parricide, said: 'That the son should be banished, to whatever place the father should approve. He did not sentence the son to the sack and the serpents, or to prison; he was mindful, not of him upon whom he was passing sentence, but of him whom he was assisting in counsel; he said that a father should be satisfied with the most lenient form of punishment.' The words are from Seneca in the same book, chap. xv.

Terence says in the *Andria* [V. iii. 32]:

For a great fault a little punishment may satisfy a father.

Philo says [*On Nobility*, ii]: 'Fathers pronounce the sad words of disinheritance, and cut off their sons from their home and all their relationship, only then when that love which, strong and exalted above all things, nature gave to parents, has been overcome by the wickedness of the sons.'

Cicero, *For Ligarius* [x. 30]: '"Pardon him, judges; he has done wrong; he has fallen; he did not stop to think; if ever again." In this way a plea is wont to be made to a father.'

[2] Seneca, *Letters*, lxxxvii [lxxxviii. 30]: 'Clemency spares the blood of another, as if it were one's own, and knows that it is not for a man to make wasteful use of his fellow man.' Diodorus Siculus in the fragments [XXI. xvii] says: 'Not absolutely all who have done wrong are to be punished, but those who feel no repentance for their sins.'

Chrysostom, *On the Statues*, VI [VI. iii]: 'Let all who are strangers to our faith know that the reverence which is shown to Christ is so great as to impose restraints upon any power. Honour thy master; pardon the sins of thy fellow bondmen, so that Christ Himself shall much the more honour thee, and in that day of judgement show thee a calm and kindly countenance, being mindful of this leniency of thine.'

Gratian, *Decretum*, II. xxiii. 4 [II. xxiii. 4. 35], cites from Augustine [rather Bede, *On Galatians*, chap. vi]: 'When we use these two terms, man and sinner, they are not spoken in vain; because he is a sinner, reprove him; because a man, pity him.' See also what follows, and what we have noted above on II. xx. 12, 26, and 36 [pages 483, 492–3, 501].

but even obligatory, by reason of the love which we owe even to men who are our enemies, whether this be viewed in itself or as the most sacred law of the Gospel demands. From that point of view we have said that there are some persons for whose safety we ought to desire to die, even if they should restrain us, because we know that they are necessary, or extremely useful, to mankind in general. If Christ desires that some things be overlooked in order to avoid engaging in lawsuits, then in proportion as a war is more harmful than a lawsuit the more earnestly must we believe that He desired us to pass over greater things in order to avoid going to war.

Molina, *De Iustitia*, ii, disp. 103; Lorca, disp. 153, no. 11; Aegidius Regius, *De Actibus Supernaturalibus*, disp. 31, dub. 7, no. 107.

4. 'For a good man to surrender a part of his [403] right is not only generous, but generally advantageous also,' is the saying of Ambrose. Aristides advises states to 'come to terms and to pass over whatever is of only moderate importance'. As a reason he adds: 'For among private persons also, you praise those who are complaisant and prefer to suffer some wrong rather than to dispute with any one.' Xenophon in the sixth book of his *Greek History* says: 'It is the duty of wise men not to undertake war, even if the differences are no mean matters.' And Apollonius in Philostratus advises: 'War ought not to be waged even for great things.'

On Duties, II. ii [II. xxi. 106].

[VI. iii. 5.]

[I. xxxviii.]

III.—*A right should be given up, especially by a king who has been wronged, in order to avoid war*

1. Regarding punishments it is first of all our duty, if not as men, assuredly as Christians,[1] readily and gladly to pardon the wrongs done to us, just as God pardons us in Christ (*Ephesians*, iv. 32). 'To be free from anger', says Josephus,[2] 'in respect to the things for which guilty men are liable to the penalty of death, approaches the nature of God.'

2. Seneca says of the prince:

On Clemency, I. xx.

Let him be far more ready in forgiving the wrongs done to himself, than those done to others. For, just as the generous man is not one who gives from what belongs to another but one who gives to another what he takes from himself, so I shall not call that prince gentle who is easy-going when another suffers, but him who, when goaded by personal injuries, does not lose self-mastery; who perceives that it is the mark of a great soul when a man possessing unlimited power endures wrongs, and that nothing is more glorious than a prince who has received a wrong without avenging it.[3]

[1] Theodosius was induced by the Bishop Flavian to pardon the citizens of Antioch for their crime against him, through these very words of Christ: 'Father, forgive them, for they know not what they do.' The incident is related by Chrysostom, *On the Statues*, XX [XXI. iv].

[2] *Antiquities of the Jews*, II. iii [II. vi. 8].

[3] Chrysostom, in praise of clemency [*On Gentleness*, near the end], says: 'Clemency can be a noble adornment for every man, but especially for those who [409] have been placed in authority. For although the royal power may permit everything, to hold itself in check and to hold before it the divine law as a guide for its actions constitutes an excellent claim to fame and glory.'

Augustine, in his *Letters*, civ [clxxxix. 8], *To Count Boniface*, says: 'Remember to pardon quickly, if any one has sinned against you and has sought pardon.'

[*Inst. of Oratory*, V. xiii. 6.] [*For Ligarius*, xii. 35.]

Quintilian says: 'We shall persuade the prince to desire the praise won by humanity rather than the pleasure derived from vengeance.' In his praises of Gaius Caesar, Cicero puts in the first place the fact that he was 'wont to forget nothing except the wrongs' done to himself.

[LV. xix.]

According to Dio, in addressing Augustus, Livia said: 'Most persons think that rulers should punish those who do harm to the common interest, but should bear with those who cherish some enmity against them.' Antoninus the philosopher,[1] in a speech to the senate, declared: 'For in the case of an Emperor the avenging of his own suffering is never pleasing; the more just it is, the more harsh it seems.' Ambrose in a letter to Theodosius wrote: 'You have made a gift of your injury to the men of Antioch.' In his eulogy of the same Theodosius to the senate Themistius said: 'The good king should show himself superior to those who have wronged him, not in repaying injury, but in conferring kindness.'

[*Letters*, xl. 32.] [*Orations*, xix = p. 227.]

[*Nic. Eth.* IV. viii.] *On Duties*, I [xxv. 88].

3. Aristotle declares that one who is magnanimous is not 'mindful of his wrongs'. This is expressed by Cicero in the words: 'Nothing is more worthy of a great and outstanding man than readiness to be appeased, and forbearance.' Signal examples of this exalted virtue are presented to us in Holy Writ, in the case of Moses (*Numbers*, xi. 12) and of David (*2 Samuel*, xvi. 7).

Driedo, *De Libertate Christiana*, II. vi. [*On Duties*, I. xi. 33.] [*On Clemency*, II. vii. 4.]

This obligation to pardon rests upon us with greatest weight when either we too are conscious to ourselves of some sin, or when the sin committed against us is the result of some human and pardonable weakness, or when it is sufficiently clear that he who has wronged us is repentant. 'There is a limit of avenging and punishing', said Cicero, 'and I do not know but that it is sufficient that he who has wronged us should repent of his wrong-doing.'[2] 'The wise man', said Seneca, 'will remit many penalties; he will save many persons whose character is not sound but is curable.'

These reasons for refraining from war have their origin in the love which we either owe to our enemies or rightly manifest toward them.

IV.—*Even for the sake of one's self and one's dependants a ruler must often refrain from war*

1. Often indeed we find an obligation resting on ourselves and ours[3] to prevent [404] a recourse to arms. Plutarch, in his *Life of*

[1] In Vulcacius Gallicanus, *Life of Avidius Cassius* [xii].

[2] Procopius, *Vandalic War*, II [II. xvi]: 'Seasonable repentance manifesting itself in those who have sinned usually induces the injured to grant pardon.'

[3] Procopius, *Gothic War*, II. [II. vi], says that the Goths thus addressed Belisarius: 'Since these things are so, it will be the duty of the rulers of both peoples not to subordinate the safety of their subjects to zeal for their own glory, but to prefer what is just and useful, not for themselves only but also for their enemies.'

Numa, says that, after the Fetiales had declared that war could justly be undertaken, the senate debated whether it would be advantageous to undertake the war.[1] In one of Christ's parables it is said that, if a king has to strive in war with another king, he will first sit down, as is the custom of those who take counsel seriously, and will weigh within himself whether he who has ten thousand soldiers can be a match for an enemy who leads twice that number. If he sees that he will not be a match for his adversary, before the foe comes within his borders he will send an embassy with instructions to arrange a peace. [xii= p. 68 B.] [*Luke*, xiv. 31.]

2. In this way the people of Tusculum,[2] by yielding everything and refusing nothing,[3] gained peace from the Romans. In Tacitus we find: 'In vain was a cause of war sought against the Aedui. When ordered to surrender money and weapons, of their own accord they offered supplies in addition.' Likewise Queen Amalasuntha informed the envoys of Justinian[4] that she would not resist with armed force. Livy, VI [xxvi]. [*Histories*, I. lxiv.]

3. A limit in yielding may also be manifested, as Strabo records of Syrmus, king of the Triballi, who forbade Alexander of Macedon to enter the island of Peuce, and at the same time honoured him with presents in order to show that he did what he did from a just cause of fear, and not from hatred or contempt of Alexander. VII [iii. 8].

What Euripides said concerning the states of Greece, you may apply to any others you may wish: [*Suppliants*, 481 ff.]

> Whenever men proceed to vote on war
> No one reflects that death hangs over him,
> But each destruction for the other plans;
> Had we, when casting votes, with our own eyes
> The funerals beheld, the funerals as we voted,
> Would not have perished war-frenzied Greece.

In Livy we read: 'Place before your mind not only your resources, but also the power of fortune, and War's uncertainty.' Also in Thucydides: 'Reflect on the unexpected element in warfare before you engage in it.' [XXX. xxx. 20.] [I. lxxviii.]

V.—*Rules dictated by prudence regarding the choice between things that are good*

1. When men weigh such matters as those mentioned, they deliberate in part regarding ends, not indeed intermediate but ulti-

[1] Diodotus, in Thucydides, III [III. xliv], says: 'For even if I declare that they have done wrong in the utmost degree I shall in any case not give orders that they be killed unless this is advantageous.'

[2] See Plutarch, *Camillus* [xxxviii = p. 149].

[3] The king of Armenia did the same in the time of Severus, as Herodian records in Book III [III. ix. 2].

[4] See Procopius, *Vandalic War*, II [II. v], and *Gothic War*, I [I. iii].

mate ends; and in part regarding the means which lead thereto. The end is always something good, or at least an avoidance of evil, which may take the place of a good. Moreover, the means which lead to this or that end are not sought for their own sake but only in so far as they lead to the ends in view. Wherefore, in deliberations the ends must be compared with one another; and also the means which may be employed, the effective power of each for contributing to the end, must be considered. For, as Aristotle rightly said, *On the*
[vii.] *Movement of Animals*: 'The purposes which produce actions are of two kinds, those arising from that which is good and those arising from that which can be accomplished.'

For this sort of comparison there are three rules.

2. The first of the rules is this. If, from the moral point of view at any rate, the matter under consideration seems to have an equal effectiveness for good and for evil, it is to be chosen only if the good has somewhat more of good than the evil has of evil. That is what
[*On Peace*, i = p. 63B.] Aristides states thus: 'When the good is less than the evil, it is better to give up the good.' In his description of a large-souled
[*On Nic. Eth.*, IV. iv.] man Andronicus of Rhodes says that he will not incur dangers for any and every cause, but only for causes that are of the highest importance.

3. The second rule is: if the good and evil, which may proceed from the matter under consideration, seem to be equal, it is only to be chosen if its effectiveness for good be greater than for evil.

The third is: if the good and the evil seem to be unequal, and the effectiveness for these things not less unequal, then the thing is to be chosen only if its effectiveness for good is greater when [405] compared with its effectiveness for evil than the evil itself compared with the good;[1] or if the good is greater in comparison with the evil than the effectiveness for evil compared with that for good.

4. These ideas we have presented in rather studied terms;
On Duties, I [xxiv. 83]. but Cicero moves toward the same goal by a more direct path when he says that we must avoid offering ourselves to dangers without cause, for nothing could be more foolish than that; consequently in approaching dangers we should imitate the practice of physicians, who cure by light treatments those who are not seriously ill, but are compelled to apply dangerous and doubtful remedies to more serious diseases. Wherefore he says that it is the part of a wise man, when a storm arises, to withstand it with all possible means, 'especially if you gain more good from a successful issue than evil from the risk incurred'.

[1] This rule is used with prudence by Narses, according to Procopius, *Gothic War*, II [II. xviii].

5. In another place Cicero says: 'When no great advantage can be won, and even a slight failure may do harm, what need is there to incur danger?' Dio of Prusa in his *Second Tarsus* oration has this: 'Granted that that which is to be borne may be hard and unjust. Yet, if something unjust happens, we ought not on that account to expose ourselves to misfortunes by striving against it.' The same writer, further on: 'Just as, if such burdens press so heavily upon us that we are unable to sustain them, we seek to cast them off; yet, if we are weighed down only moderately and with such burdens that we see that either these or others more grievous must be borne, we adjust ourselves so as to follow with our load as light as possible.' Aristides, in his *Second Sicilian Oration*, says: 'Whenever fear is greater than hope, why is it not right to take precautions?'

Letters to Atticus, XIII. xxvii.

[*Orations*, xxxiv = p. 416.]

[= p. 52D.]

VI.—*An example in a deliberation between devotion to freedom and devotion to peace; whereby the slaughter of a people may be avoided*

1. Let us draw an illustration from the question which, as Tacitus relates, was once debated by the Gallic states: 'Whether they desired freedom or peace.'

[*Histories*, IV. lxvii.]

By freedom, understand civil liberty, that is, the right of a state to be governed by itself. This right is complete in a democratic state, but limited in an aristocratic state; it is especially complete in a state where no citizen is excluded from office.

By peace, again, understand such a peace as will obviate a war of annihilation, that is, as Cicero somewhere says in explaining this problem in the Greek tongue: 'If the city should be likely for this cause to endanger the lives of all.' An example is where a correct forecast of the future seems to augur almost no alternative but the destruction of a whole people. Such was the condition of the people of Jerusalem when besieged by Titus. Everybody knows what Cato, who preferred to die rather than obey a sole ruler, would have said in this case. Here also apply the lines:

Letters to Atticus, IX. cxii [IX. iv].

> How easy is the virtuous act
> By one's own hand to flee from slavery;

[Lucan, *Pharsalia*, IV. 576 f.

and many other things of this sort.

2. But right reason teaches otherwise. Life, to be sure, which affords the basis for all temporal and the occasion for eternal blessings, is of greater value than liberty. This holds true whether you consider each aspect in the case of an individual or of a whole people. And so God Himself reckons it as a benefit that He does not destroy men but casts them into slavery. And again, through the prophet He advises

2 Chronicles, xii. 7–8.
Jeremiah, xxvii. 13.

the Jews to yield themselves as slaves to the Babylonians that they may not perish of hunger and disease.[1] Wherefore, although praised by the ancients,

Lucan, *Pharsalia*, III. 350.]

> The ills Saguntum hath, by Punic soldiery besieged,

should not be approved, nor the considerations leading thereto.

Augustine, *City of God*, XXII. vi.

3. The slaughter of a people in a case of this kind ought to be considered as the greatest possible evil. Cicero in the second book *On Invention* gives an example of necessity. He says that it was necessary for [406] the people of Casilinum to surrender to Hannibal, although the necessity had this qualification, 'unless they preferred to perish by famine'.[2] On the Thebans who lived in the time of Alexander of Macedon there is preserved this judgement of Diodorus Siculus: 'They brought complete destruction upon their country, in a spirit of courage rather than of prudence.'[3]

[II. lvii. 171.]

XVIII [XVII. x].

4. On Cato, whom we have mentioned, and on Scipio, both of whom declined to yield to Caesar after his victory at Pharsalus, we find the following judgement in Plutarch: 'They are to be blamed for the needless destruction of many good men in Libya.'

[*Otho*, xiii = p. 1072 D.]

5. What I have said regarding liberty I wish to apply also to other desirable things, if the expectation of a greater evil from the opposite side is warranted in a greater, or even in an equal, degree. As Aristides rightly says, it is the custom to save the ship by casting out the cargo, not the passengers.

[*Platonic*, ii = p. 283 B.]

VII.—*He who is not much the stronger ought to refrain from exacting penalties*

In exacting penalties, moreover, this must be observed particularly, that war is not to be waged on such a pretext against him whose forces are equal to our own. For, as in the case of a civil judge, he who wishes to avenge crimes by armed force ought to be much more powerful than the other party.

[1] In Gunther [VIII. 155 ff.] Guido of Blanes speaks as follows in an address to the Milanese:

> To keep our liberty secure we shall endure
> All things. But no man of sound mind loves liberty
> At risk of life. Destruction certain to provoke,
> Which can be shunned, and without other hope,
> Vain glory must be called, not love of liberty.

[2] The defence of Anaxilas, who had surrendered Byzantium on account of famine, was this, that men should fight against men, not against natural conditions. Such is the account of Xenophon [*Greek History*, I. iii. 19].

Procopius says, *Gothic War*, IV [IV. xii]: 'Men do not praise a voluntary death, as long as hope is greater than the danger.'

[3] The same writer [XVIII. x], after explaining the reasons for the war which the Sithonienses [Athenians] undertook after the death of Alexander the Great, says that in the opinion of the men of deeper insight 'they had indeed chosen the right course for glory, but had strayed from the path of advantage', seeing that they had hastened 'to rush into danger under no irresistible compulsion', without even permitting themselves to be warned by the noble ruin of the Thebans.

Not merely prudence, in truth, or love of one's own people, ordinarily demands that we refrain from a dangerous war, but oftentimes justice also requires it; that is, rectorial justice, which from the very nature of government binds the superior to care for his inferiors no less than it binds the inferiors to obedience. From this follows the view rightly handed down by the theologians, that the king who undertakes a war for trivial reasons, or to exact unnecessary penalties, is responsible to his subjects for making good the losses which arise therefrom. For he perpetrates a crime, if not against the foe, yet against his own people, by involving them in so serious an evil on such grounds. According to Livy: 'War is just for those for whom it is necessary, and arms are blameless for those who have no hope left save in arms.' Such a condition Ovid, in the first book of the *Fasti*, hopes for:

Cajetan, *On II. ii*, qu. 95, art. 8; Molina, *De Iustitia*, i, disp. 102. X [IV. i. 10]. [I. 715.]

> Arms let the soldier bear, that arms
> He may restrain.

VIII.—*It results that war is not to be undertaken, unless of necessity*

Therefore a cause for engaging in war which either may not be passed over, or ought not to be, is exceptional;[1] as for example when, as Florus says, rights are more cruel than arms. Seneca says: 'It is right to rush into dangers when we fear like evils if we remain quiet.' This idea is expressed by Aristides in the following way: 'Then must one choose to take the path of danger, even if the future is unknown, whenever it is evidently worse to follow a peaceful course.'

[IV. xii. [*On Clemency*, I. xii. 5.] [*On Peace*, i = p. 67 B.]

'A miserable peace is well exchanged for war', says Tacitus, certainly when, as he says, 'either liberty will follow those who dare, or if conquered their condition will be the same'; or 'when', as Livy declares, 'peace is more burdensome to those who are in servitude than war to freemen'. The last statement does not hold if the outcome appears to be such that, as Cicero has it, if you are beaten you will be proscribed; and if you gain the victory you will still be a slave.

[*Annals*, III. xliv.] [*Histories*, IV. xxxii.] X [xvi. 5]. *Letters to Atticus*, VII. vii [7].

IX.—*Again, war is not to be undertaken save from a most weighty cause at a most opportune time*

A second occasion to engage in war is when, after inquiring into the matter as one ought, the war is found to be in accordance with right, and at the same time—which is of the highest importance—the necessary resources are available. This is what Augustus used to

Suetonius, xxiv [*Augustus*, xxv].

[1] [410] Servius, commenting *On the Aeneid*, X [X. 758 f.]:

> [The gods] pity the vain wrath of both,
> And so great sufferings of mortal men,

gives as the reason: 'Because no cause is so just that war should be waged on account of it.'

say, that war ought not to be undertaken save when the hope of gain was shown to be greater than the fear of loss. What Scipio Africanus and Lucius Aemilius Paulus were wont to say about risking a battle may be fittingly applied here: 'One should not fight unless a supreme necessity [1] or a most favourable opportunity should be presented.'

Gellius, XIII. iii; Valerius Maximus, VII. ii [2].

Such an opportunity will be found particularly when there is hope that the matter may be settled by inspiring fear and on the strength of reputation,[2] with little or no risk, as Dio advised for liberating [407] Syracuse. In Pliny's *Letters* occurs the statement: 'He subdued by fear, which is the most excellent kind of victory.'

Diodorus, XVI [xvii]. [II. vii.]

X.—*The evils of war placed before our eyes*

1. War is a cruel thing, says Plutarch, and it drags in its train a mass of wrongs and insults. Augustine stated the case wisely:

Camillus [x= p. 134 B]. *City of God*, XIX. vii.

If I should wish worthily to portray the many and manifold disasters, the bitter and hard necessities resulting from these evils [he is speaking of those that arise from war], although I am by no means equal to the task, what would be the limit of my discourse, extended though it might be? But, they say, the wise man will wage wars that are just. As if, provided he remembers that he is a man, he will not much rather grieve that the necessity of just wars has arisen; for if they were not just he would not have to wage them, and in that case there would be no wars for the wise man. It is the wrong-doing of the opposing party which forces the wise man to wage just, and indeed necessary, wars.

This wrong-doing is to be deplored by a man, because it is human,[3] even if no need of waging war should arise from it. Everyone, then, who with pain thinks on these evils, so great, so terrible, so ruthless, must acknowledge that this is misery. If, again, anyone endures or reflects upon these things without anguish of soul, his plight is all the more wretched, because he considers himself happy, while in fact he has lost his feeling for humanity.

[1] Plutarch says, in his *Life of the Gracchi* [*Comparison of Cleomenes and the Gracchi*, iv = p. 845 A]: 'To resort to the steel, when not absolutely necessary, is characteristic neither of a good physician nor of a good ruler.'

There is a saying of Marcian in Zonaras [XII. xxv. 32]: 'A king ought not to engage in war so long as he is permitted to enjoy peace.'

Augustine, *Letters*, l [clxxxix. 6], *To Boniface*, writes: 'We should will to preserve peace; war should be the result of necessity only, that God may free us from the necessity and keep us at peace.'

[2] 'The lion, despising missiles, defends himself for a long time by the mere terror he inspires, and, as it were, bears witness that he is compelled to fight.' This is in Pliny, *Natural History*, VIII. xvi.

[3] The Lacedaemonians, in the address which is found in Diodorus Siculus, Book XIII [XIII. lii], say: 'Since we see that enmities in vast number, and atrocities in vast number, arise from war, we thought it our duty to bear witness to all gods and men that the responsibility for these things does not rest upon us.'

Plutarch in his *Numa* [*Comparison of Lycurgus and Numa*, iv = p. 78 B], says: 'Hereupon if anyone should say to me, "Has not Rome made the greatest progress through her wars?" he will present a question that requires an extended answer, particularly for men who estimate progress in terms of wealth, luxury, and military authority, and not in the safety of the people, in gentleness, and in justice that is satisfied with what is its own.'

Stephen, the physician of Khosroo, king of the Persians, says in Procopius, *Persian War*, II [II. xxvi]: 'For you, most mighty king, who have been occupied with massacres and battles and the taking of cities, other titles may perhaps be fitting, but it cannot come to pass that you should be thereby believed to be good.'

Add the excellent passage in Guicciardini, XVI.

The same author in another passage says: 'To carry on war seems to bad men felicity, to good men a necessity.' Maximus of Tyre declares: 'Even if you remove the element of injustice from war, the necessity of it is in itself pitiable.' The same Maximus, again: 'War seems not to be undertaken by the just except of necessity, by the unjust of their own initiative.' *City of God*, IV. xv. [*Dissertations*, XXX. i and ii.]

2. To this we must add the saying of Seneca, that it is not for a man to put his fellow man to wasteful use. Philiscus advised Alexander to pursue renown indeed, but upon this condition, that he should not make himself a plague or a violent disease. He meant that the slaughter of peoples and the wasting of cities are the work of a pestilence, but that nothing is more befitting a king than to have regard for the safety of all; and this is accomplished by peace. [*Letters*, lxxxviii. 30.] Aelian, XIV. xi.

If by the Hebraic law even he who involuntarily slew a man was obliged to flee; if God forbade David, who is said to have waged blameless wars, to build His Temple, because he had shed much blood;[1] if among the ancient Greeks even those had need of expiation who had innocently stained their hands with bloodshed, who does not see, especially if he be a Christian, how unfortunate and ill-omened the matter is, and with what effort a war, even if not unjust, is to be avoided? At any rate the Greeks who professed Christianity long observed the canon by which those who had killed an enemy in a war of any sort whatever were for a time[2] excluded from the sacraments. [*Numbers*, xxxv; *Deut.*, xix.] [*I Chronicles*, xxviii. 3.] Basil, *To Amphil.*, X. 13. [*Letters*, clxxxviii. 13.]

[1] 'God did not permit him to construct the Temple because he had waged many wars and had been polluted with blood—that of enemies, it is true, but yet blood.' The words are from Josephus [*Antiquities of the Jews*], Book VII, chap. iv [VII. iv. 4], where there is more to the same effect.

Pliny [*Natural History*], Book VII, chap. xxv, after summarizing the battles of the Dictator Caesar, says: 'I at any rate should not count as glory the infliction of so much suffering on the human race, even though accomplished under compulsion.'

Philo writes, *On the Life of Moses* [I. lvii]: 'For although it is permitted by the laws to kill enemies, still he who has killed a man, no matter how justly, even in self-defence and because he has been attacked, still appears to have polluted himself in some degree on account of the common relationship derived from the Supreme Cause. Wherefore those who had slain enemies had need of some purification, to wash away the pollution which seemed to have been acquired.'

[2] For three years: Zonaras, *Nicephorus Phocas* [XVI. xxv. 23].

[411] CHAPTER XXV

ON THE CAUSES OF UNDERTAKING WAR ON BEHALF OF OTHERS

I.—*War may rightfully be undertaken on behalf of subjects*

I. v. 1. In the earlier part of this work, when we dealt with those who wage war, we asserted and showed that by the law of nature each individual was justified in enforcing not merely his own right but also that of another. The causes, therefore, which are just in relation to the person whose interest is at stake are just also in relation to those who give assistance to others.

Navarrus, xxiv, no. 18. 2. Now the first and particularly necessary concern is for subjects,[1] either those who are subject to authority in a family, or those who are subject to a political authority. They are, in fact, as it were a part of the ruler, as we said in the same connexion. For this reason, under the leadership of Joshua, the Jewish people took arms on behalf of the Gibeonites, who had submitted to them. (*Joshua*, x. 6.) 'Our ancestors', said Cicero, addressing the Romans, 'often waged wars because their traders and sailors had been wrongfully treated.' [*For the Manilian Law*, v. 11.] In another speech he said: 'How many wars did our ancestors [...] wage, because it was said that Roman citizens had been wronged, sailors detained, and traders robbed!' (*Against Verres*, act. II [V. lviii, 149].)

The same Romans considered it necessary to take up arms on behalf of peoples who had surrendered (that is, had been made subjects), for whom they had refused to take up arms as allies. The Campanians declared to the Romans: 'Even if you will not protect our interests with justifiable force against violence and wrong, you will surely defend your own.' [Livy, VII. xxxi. 3.] Florus says that the alliance formerly made by the Campanians was rendered more sacred by the surrender of all that was theirs. [I. xvi.] 'Good faith', said Livy, 'seemed to require that those who had surrendered should not be betrayed.' (VII [xxxi].)

II.—*Yet war is not always to be undertaken on behalf of subjects*

Nevertheless, wars are not always to be waged on behalf of subjects even though the just cause of some subject places the ruler under obligation to undertake them. Such wars are to be undertaken only when this can be done without loss to all the subjects, or to the majority of them. The duty of the ruler concerns the whole rather than parts; and the greater a part is, the more nearly it approaches the character of the whole.

[1] Procopius, *Persian War*, II [II. xv], says: 'He who does wrong to no one is not completely just unless also he has the determination to protect those entrusted to him against the wrongs of others.'

III.—*Whether an innocent subject may be surrendered to an enemy, in order that danger may be avoided*

1. Thus if one citizen, although innocent, is demanded by an enemy, to be made away with, there is no doubt that he may be abandoned to them[1] if it appears that the state is by no means a match for the power of the enemy. Soto, *De Iustitia et Iure*, V, qu. i, art. 7.

This view is opposed by Fernando Vázquez; but, if you consider his purpose rather than his words, he seems to be making this point, that such a citizen is not to be hastily abandoned, where there is hope that he may be defended. For he also cites the story of the Italian infantry who deserted Pompey when his cause was not yet clearly desperate, but when they had been assured of their safety by Caesar. This conduct he deservedly censures. *Controversiae Illustres*, I. xiii.

2. Still the learned do discuss the question whether an innocent citizen may be delivered into the hands of the enemy, in order to prevent the ruin otherwise threatening the state; and the same question was debated long ago, as when Demosthenes brought forward the notable fable of the dogs, which the wolves demanded should be surrendered to them by the sheep for the sake of peace. That such a surrender may be made is denied not merely by Vázquez but also by Soto, whose opinion is attacked by Vázquez as bordering on treachery. Nevertheless, [412] Soto holds that such a citizen is bound to surrender himself to the enemy; but this also is denied by Vázquez, on the ground that the nature of political society, which each enters for his own advantage, does not require it.

3. But from this nothing more follows than that a citizen is not bound to surrender himself by law properly so called; it does not follow also that love permits him to do otherwise. For there are many duties which are not in the domain of justice properly speaking, but in that of affection, which are not only discharged amid praise (this Vázquez does not recognize) but cannot even be omitted without blame.

Such a duty seems quite clearly to be this, that a person should value the lives of a very large number of innocent persons above his own life. Praxithea in the *Erechtheus* of Euripides says: [Frag 362, 19–21.]

> For if I numbers know and from the less
> The greater can distinguish, then the ill
> That but one house afflicts is less by far
> Than that of a whole city, nor with this compares.[2]

[1] See the advice of the Patriarch Nicephorus given to Michael Rhangabe in regard to the return of deserters to the leader of the Bulgars so as to secure peace, where we find in Zonaras [XV. xvii. 20] these words: 'We should consider it better that a few should suffer ills than a vast multitude.'

[2] 'It is unfair that the whole should be considered an adjunct of a part.' The passage is in Philo, *On the Life of Moses*, at the end of Book II [I. lix], where there is more that is well worth reading.

Diodorus, XVII [xv]. Thus Phocion used to urge Demosthenes and others, after the example of the daughters of Leos and Hyacinthus,[1] to die themselves rather than to permit an incurable evil to be inflicted on their country.

[xx. 45.] In his speech *For Publius Sestius* Cicero said:

> If it had befallen me, when sailing with my friends on board some vessel, that from many directions many pirates threatened to attack the ship with their fleets unless my friends should have surrendered me alone to them, and if the voyagers refused to do this, and preferred to perish with me, rather than surrender me to my enemies, I would rather have cast myself into the deep, in order to save the rest, than bring to certain death, or even into great risk of their lives, those who loved me so well.

[III. xix. 64.] The same author in the third book *On Ends* says: 'A man who is good and wise and obedient to the laws, and who understands the duty of a citizen, consults the interest of all rather than of any single XLV [xxvi. 8]. individual or of himself.' In Livy we read in regard to certain Molossians: 'I have often heard tales of those who sought death for their country's sake; but these are the first yet found who thought it right that their country should perish for them.'

4. But on the supposition that a citizen demanded by the enemy ought to surrender himself to them there remains the question whether he may be compelled to do that to which he is morally bound. Soto declares that he cannot, and by way of illustration cites the case of the rich man who by the precepts of mercy is bound to give alms to the poor man, but who nevertheless cannot be forced to do so. We must observe, however, that the relation of parts among themselves is one thing, and that of superiors, when they are contrasted with those subject to them, is quite another. For an equal cannot be compelled by an equal, except to perform what is owed in accordance with a right properly so called. But a superior can compel an inferior to do other things also, which some virtue demands,[2] because this is Lessius, II. ix, dub. 7. embraced in the proper right of the superior as such. Thus during a grain famine citizens may be compelled to contribute what they have to the common store.

Hence in this argument of ours it seems even more true that a citizen may be constrained to do that which regard for others Plutarch, *Life of Phocion* [xvii = p. 749 C]. requires. Thus Phocion, whom I have just mentioned, pointing out a certain man, Nicocles by name, who was a very great friend of his, said that such a climax of evils had been reached that, if Alexander should demand Nicocles, he himself should vote that Nicocles should be surrendered.

[1] See Apollodorus, *Library* [III. xv. 8].

[2] Thus among the Lucanians punishment was appointed for wasteful persons; among the Macedonians for ingrates; among the same [416] Lucanians, and the Athenians, for idlers. Add the notes to I. i. 9.

IV.—*Wars may rightfully be undertaken also on behalf of allies of equal or unequal standing*

Next to subjects, and indeed on an equal footing with them in this respect, that they ought to be defended, are allies, in whose treaty of alliance this obligation is embraced, whether they have surrendered themselves to the guardianship and good faith of others, or have agreed to give and receive mutual assistance. 'He who does not protect an ally from wrong, when he can do so, is at fault, just as he who does the wrong,' says Ambrose. *On Duties,* I. xxxvi.

We have said elsewhere, however, that such agreements cannot be stretched to include wars for which no just cause exists.[1] This in truth is the reason why the Lacedaemonians, before they made war upon the Athenians, permitted all their allies to pass judgement upon [413] the justice of the cause; and it was for that reason that the Romans allowed the Greeks to pass judgement on the war against Nabis. We may now add this principle, that not even under such conditions is an ally bound to render aid if there is no hope of a successful issue. The reason is that an alliance is formed for the sake of good, and not of ill. However, an ally is to be protected even against another ally that is in alliance on the same terms, unless in the previous treaty there is some particular provision to the contrary. Thus the Athenians were able to defend the Corcyreans, provided that the cause of the latter was just, even against the Corinthians, who had been their allies for a longer time. [Thucydides, I. cxix and cxxv.] Livy, XXXIV [xxii].

V.—*Wars may rightfully be undertaken on behalf of friends*

The third cause for undertaking wars on behalf of others is obligation to friends,[2] to whom aid has not been promised, to be sure, but yet is owed under a certain principle of friendship, if it can be rendered easily and without loss. For such a reason Abraham took up arms in behalf of his kinsman Lot; on such grounds the Romans forbade the people of Antium to practise piracy upon the Greeks, alleging that the Greeks were related to the Italians. The Romans also frequently waged wars, or threatened to wage war, not only on behalf of their allies, to whom they owed this obligation in accordance with a treaty, but also on behalf of their friends. Victoria, *Relectiones de Indis,* pt. II, no. 17; Cajetan, *On II. ii,* qu. 4, art. 1.

[1] See Simler, *De Republica Helvetiorum* [p. 160].
'Whenever a lord makes war upon anyone, if it is known that this is justly done, or in case it shall be a matter of doubt, his vassal is bound to aid him. But when it is evident that the lord is making war without cause the vassal shall aid him in defence, but not aid him to attack another', *De Feudis,* II. xxviii, at the end.

[2] An ancient oracle [Aelian, *Various History,* III. xliv] runs thus:

Though present thou didst not assist thy dying friend,
Naught will I answer thee save 'Forth from the temple go'.

VI.—*Wars, finally, may rightfully be undertaken on behalf of any persons whatsoever*

Cicero, *On Ends*, III [xix. 64]; *On Duties*, II [v. 16]; *Dig.* I. i. 3. *On Anger*, I. vii [I. v]. *On Clemency*, II. v [II. vi]. [267 ff.]

The final and most wide-reaching cause for undertaking wars on behalf of others is the mutual tie of kinship among men, which of itself affords sufficient ground for rendering assistance. 'Men have been born to aid one another,' says Seneca. From the same author come the words: 'The wise man, whenever he shall be able, will interpose between fortune and fortune's victims.' In his *Suppliants* Euripides says:

> The rocks afford a refuge for wild beasts,
> And altars protect slaves, but cities crushed with ills
> In other towns their bulwark find.

On Duties, I [xxvii. 129]. I. v [2].

In the view of Ambrose: 'Courage [. . .] which defends the weak [. . .] is perfect justice.' This point also we have previously discussed.

VII.—*Nevertheless the obligation to undertake war may be disregarded without wrong, if one fears for himself, or even for the life of an innocent person*

Laws, IV [IX. xvii]. Diodorus, I [lxxvii]. [*On Duties*, I. vii. 23.] [In Ammianus Marcellinus, XXX. iv. 7.] [*Letter to Mithridates*, i.]

1. At this point the question arises, whether a man is bound to defend a man, or one people another people, from wrong. Plato thinks that he who does not defend another from violence should be punished;[1] and this was provided for even in the laws of the Egyptians. But first, if danger is evident, it is certain that a man is not so bound, for he may prefer his own life and interests to those of others. In this sense I think we must interpret the words of Cicero: 'He who does not prevent or oppose a wrong, if he can, is as much at fault as if he should desert his parents, or country, or associates.' The word 'can' we may understand as 'with advantage to himself'; for the same author says also in another place: 'Perhaps men cannot be defended without incurring censure.'

In the histories of Sallust we find the following: 'All men who, when their affairs are prosperous, are besought to join an alliance for war, ought to reflect whether they may at that time maintain peace; then whether what is asked of them is sufficiently blameless, safe, glorious, or dishonourable.'

2. This statement of Seneca[2] also should not be scorned: 'I shall come to the aid of the perishing, but in such a way that

[1] And the Jews; Moses de Kotzi, *Precepts Bidding*, lxxvii, lxxx; *Forbidding*, clxiv, clxv.

[2] The passage is in *On Benefits*, II. xv. Another of not unlike purport is in Book I, chap. x: 'I shall defend one who deserves it, even at the cost of my blood, and shall assume a part of the danger; but if by raising a shout I shall be able to deliver an unworthy man from robbers I shall not trouble to utter the cry which would bring safety to the man.'

See above, II. i. 8 [page 176].

I myself may not perish, unless I am to be the price of a great man or a great cause.' But not even in the latter case will a man be obliged to render aid if the person oppressed cannot be delivered save by the death of the oppressor. (Lessius, II. iv, dub. 15.) For if the person who is attacked can put the life of the aggressor above his own, as we have said elsewhere, he will [II. i. 9.] not do wrong who either believes or desires that the person attacked may prefer this also; especially when in the case of the aggressor there is the greater danger of irremedial and eternal loss.

VIII.—*The question whether a war for the defence of subjects of another power is rightful is explained by a distinction*

1. This too is a matter of controversy, whether there may be a just cause for undertaking war on behalf of the subjects of another ruler, in order to protect them from wrong at his hands. Now it is certain that, from the time when political associations were formed, each of their rulers has sought to assert some particular right over his own subjects. As we see in the *Children of Hercules*, by Euripides: [143 f.]

> [414] Just are we who within our city dwell,
> And judgment we may render with full power.

Here too applies the following: [*Phoenician Maidens*, frag.]

> Sparta, which is thy lot, adorn;
> We for Mycenae shall have care.

Among the signs of supreme power Thucydides reckoned 'having [V. xviii.] their own courts of justice' no less than 'the right to make their own laws and levy taxes'. Akin is the thought of the poet: Virgil, *Aeneid*, I [138 f.].

> Not to him but to me by lot was given
> The rule of the sea and the trident's realm.

Quite similar is the following: Ovid, *Metamorphoses*, XIV [784 f.].

> To the gods is it never permitted
> The acts of the gods to revoke.[1]

In Euripides we find this: *Hippolytus* [1328 f.].

> Among the gods the usage fixed is this:
> 'Tis wrong for one to thwart the other's will.

The purpose no doubt is, as Ambrose correctly explains, 'to prevent men from provoking wars by usurping the care for things under the control of others'. *On Duties*, I [xiii].

[1] From the same author, *Metamorphoses*, III [III. 336 f.], is the following:

> For neither may a god annul
> What another god has done.

V [I. xliii]. In Thucydides the Corinthians find it just that 'each party should punish its own subjects'.[1] Perseus, in his speech to Marcius, refused to present a defence of his conduct toward the Dolopes, saying: 'I have acted by virtue of my right, since they belonged to my kingdom and were subject to my authority.' But all these rights have force in cases where subjects are actually in the wrong, and also, you may add, where the cause is doubtful. For such purposes in fact this division of authorities was established.

Livy, XLII [xli. 13].

Victoria, *Relectiones de Indis* [Pt. II], no. 15.

2. If, however, the wrong is obvious, in case some Busiris, Phalaris, or Thracian Diomede should inflict upon his subjects such treatment as no one is warranted in inflicting, the exercise of the right vested in human society is not precluded. In conformity with this principle Constantine took up arms against Maxentius and Licinius, and other Roman emperors either took up arms against the Persians,[2] or threatened to do so, unless these should check their persecutions of the Christians on account of religion.

Victoria, *Relectiones de Indis*, pt. II, no. 13.

3. If, further, it should be granted that even in extreme need subjects cannot justifiably take up arms (on this point we have seen that those very persons whose purpose was to defend the royal power are in doubt), nevertheless it will not follow that others may not take up arms on their behalf. For whenever the check imposed upon some action arises from the person concerned and not the action itself, then what is refused to one may be permitted to another on his behalf, provided that the matter is such that the one may therein be of service to the other.

[I. iv. 8.]

Thus a guardian, or some other person, goes to law on behalf of a pupil, who is personally incapable of legal action; and counsel may appear for one who is absent, even without authority. The restriction, in fact, which prevents a subject from resisting, does not arise from a cause which is identical in the case of a subject and of one who is not a subject, but from the personal condition which is not transferred to others.

[*On Benefits*, VII. xix. 9.]

4. Hence, Seneca thinks that I may make war upon one who is not one of my people but oppresses his own, as we said when dealing with the infliction of punishment; a procedure which is often connected with the protection of innocent persons. We know, it is true, from both ancient and modern history, that the desire for what is another's seeks such pretexts as this for its own ends; but a right does not at once cease to exist in case it is to some extent abused by evil men. Pirates, also, sail the sea; arms are carried also by brigands.

[1] Augustine, *On Free Will*, II [II. i. 2]: 'To show kindnesses to strangers is a mark of goodness on the part of any one, but to punish strangers is not in the same way a mark of justice.' Procopius, *Vandalic War*, I [I. ix], says: 'It befits an honourable man to wield the authority which falls to his lot, and not to assume authority over others.'

[2] You have a similar example in the history of Pepin in Fredegarius, at the end.

IX.—*Military alliances and mercenary service without dissemination regarding the causes of war are unjust*

1. Again, just as military alliances, which were entered into with the intention that aid should be rendered for any sort of war without distinction of cause,[1] are not permissible, as [415] we have said, so no manner of life is more wicked than that of those who serve as soldiers for hire without regard to the cause of hostilities, and for whom Sylvester, word *bellum*, I, § 10, near end.

> Where greatest profit is, there too is right.

This Plato shows from the example of Tyrtaeus. [*On Laws*, I. v.]

Such conduct, we read, was censured in the Aetolians by Philip; and in the case of the Arcadians by Dionysius of Miletus, with these words: 'The market for soldiery is open, and the ills of the Greeks nourish the land of the Arcadians, while men under arms go hither and thither without giving any consideration to the cause.' Truly a wretched thing, as Antiphanes says, is Livy, XXXII [xxxiv]. [Philostratus, *Lives of the Sophists*, I. xxii.]

> The soldier who, to maintain life, hires himself to death.[2] [Stobaeus, liii. 9.]

Dio of Prusa says: 'What is more necessary for us than life, or what is accounted of greater value? Yet even this not a few lose through quest of gain.' [*Orations*, xvii = p. 29.]

2. It would in truth matter little that mercenaries sell their own lives, if they did not sell also the lives of others, who are often innocent. In this respect they are much more abominable than an executioner, in the degree that it is worse to slay without cause than with cause.[3] So Antisthenes used to say that executioners are more free from guilt than tyrants, because they execute criminals, while tyrants slay those who are innocent. Philip the Elder of Macedon said that to men of this type, 'whose livelihood comes solely from mercenary service', war was peace and peace was war. Belli, *De Re Militari*, pt. II, tit. ii, no. 4. [Stobaeus, xlix. 47.] Diodorus, XVIII [x]

3. Warfare has no place among the useful arts. Nay, rather,

[1] On this point consult Simler again [see page 581, note 1].

[2] 'That at the cost of life the things are amassed wherewith life is worn out,' said Seneca, *Natural Questions*, V. xviii.

Plautus in the *Two Bacchises* [frag. 7] has:

> Who sell their lives for gold.

Gunther [*Ligurinus*, VII. 511 ff.] refers to

> Troops hired by cash, and soldiery in quest
> Of largesses, accustomed for a price
> To change allegiance, choosing war for gain,
> And their employers' enemy to count their own.

[3] Seneca, *Natural Questions*, V. xviii, says: 'What else than madness would any one call this? To carry dangers all about, and to rush against persons whom you never saw, to be angry without being wronged, to lay waste all in one's path, and after the manner of wild beasts to kill him whom you do not hate?'

On the Words of he Lord according to Matthew, cited in *Decretum*, II. xxiii. 1 [5].

it is so horrible that only the utmost necessity, or true affection, can render it honourable. How this is possible may be gathered from what we have said in the last of the preceding chapters. In the opinion of Augustine, ' to serve as a soldier is no crime : but to do so for the sake of plunder is a sin.'

X.—*It is also particularly wrong to take service merely for the sake of plunder or pay*

The same principle applies in the case of military service for pay, if this is the sole or chief aim in view.

1 Corinthians, x. 7 [ix. 7].

On other grounds it is altogether permissible to receive pay. ' What soldier ever serveth at his own charges ? ' says the Apostle Paul.

[417]

CHAPTER XXVI

ON JUST CAUSES FOR WAR WAGED BY THOSE WHO ARE UNDER THE RULE OF ANOTHER

I.—*Who may be said to be under the rule of another*

We have dealt with those who are independent of any control. There are others in a condition which requires them to render obedience, as sons in a household, slaves, subjects, also individual citizens considered in relation to the body politic of their state.

II.—*What those under the rule of another should do if they are summoned to share in deliberation, or have a free choice of action*

If those under the rule of another are admitted to a deliberation, or there is given to them a free choice of going to war or remaining at peace, they should be governed by the same rules as those who, at their own discretion, take up arms for themselves or on behalf of others.

Aegidius Regius, *De Actibus Supernaturalibus*, disp. 31, no. 80.

III.—*If those under the rule of another should be ordered to go to war, and should believe the cause of the war to be unjust, they ought not to serve*

1. If those under the rule of another are ordered to take the field, as often occurs, they should altogether refrain from so doing if it is clear to them that the cause of the war is unjust. That God must be obeyed, rather than men, was said not only by the Apostles, but also by Socrates;[1] and among the learned men of the Jews[2] is found an opinion indicating that one must no longer obey a king who issues commands contrary to the law of God. There has been preserved this saying of Polycarp at the point of death: 'To authorities and powers ordained of God we have learned to render the honour which is fitting and which in no way harms us.'

Victoria, *De Iure Belli*, no. 22.
Acts, v. 9 [v. 29].
[Eusebius, *Ecclesiastical History*, IV. xv. 22.]

Paul the Apostle said: 'Children, obey your parents in the Lord;[3] for this is right.' On this Jerome comments thus: 'It is

Ephesians, vi. 1.
[*On Ephesians*, vi. 4.]

[1] Plato tells us this in the *Apology* [xvii]; Apollonius, too, who met the edict of Nero with this line of Sophocles [Philostratus, *Life of Apollonius of Tyana*, IV. xxxviii]:

It was not Jupiter who gave me these commands.

[2] This also Josephus, *Antiquities of the Jews*, XVII [XVII. vi. 3], attributes to them in the words: 'It is not strange indeed if those things which were written down at the behest and under the guidance of God, and which Moses left us, we believe more worthy to be observed than your commands.'

Add Rabbi Tanchuma, as cited by van den Driesche on the passage of the *Acts* [v. 29].

[3] Chrysostom [*On Ephesians*, vi. 1 = Homily XXI, i] explains the words 'in the Lord' as follows: 'That is, in things in which you will not offend God.' He says also, *To the Unbelieving Father* [chap. ix]: 'For no small reward is set before us if we show honour to our parents; but we are bidden to

a sin on the part of children not to obey their parents; and since parents may order something wicked, he has added "in the Lord".' In regard to slaves [1] he adds: 'When the Lord of the flesh commands other than the Lord of the Spirit, he is not to be obeyed.' In another passage the same author says: 'Men should be subject to masters and parents only in those things that are not contrary to the ordinances of God.' The same Apostle also had said that each one, whether bond or free, would receive the recompense of his own work.

Ephesians, vi. 8.

[On Idolatry, xv.]

Moreover, Tertullian says: 'We have it sufficiently ordained, that it behooves us to be in all obedience, according to the precept of the Apostle, being subject to magistrates,[2] princes and powers, but within the limits of discipline.' In the Martyrology Sylvan the Martyr declares: 'We hold in contempt the laws of Rome, that we may obey the commands of God.'

Phoenician Maidens [1648–9].

In Euripides, when Creon asks,

> Does not right itself command his orders to obey?

Antigone replies:

> What right does not command, it is not right to do.

Stobaeus, tit. *liberos parent. honorand.* [lxxix. 51].

Musonius speaks thus: 'If any one does not obey a father or a magistrate [3] or a master who orders him to do what is base or wicked to perform, he is not disobedient, he does no wrong, and he commits no sin.'

[Attic Nights,] II. vii.

2. Gellius declares that it is right to hold that not everything a father orders must be obeyed. 'For what', he says, 'if a father shall order his son to betray his country, to kill his mother, or to do some other base and unholy act? The middle view therefore seems the best and safest, that some commands are to be obeyed, and some other commands not.' Says Seneca the father: [4] 'Not all commands are to be obeyed.'

consider them as masters, and to render them obedience both in words and in deeds, except to the injury of piety.' And so understand the saying of Jerome, 'Go on, trampling upon thy father' [*Letters*, xiv. 2], as oratorical phraseology, borrowed from the orator Latro in Seneca [*Controversies*, I. viii. 15]; and likewise what is in Ambrose, *On Virginity*; in Augustine, *Letters*, xxxviii [ccxliii], *To Laetus*, and Canon IV of the First Council of Nice, in the Arabic translation.

[1] Chrysostom, *On First Corinthians*, vii. 24 [Homily XIX, iv], says: [422] 'Slaves too have their limits of action prescribed by God; to what degree they ought to serve is also ordained, and it is not permitted them to exceed this. Where the master orders none of the things of which God disapproves, they should follow and obey, but no further.' Clement of Alexandria [*Stromata*, IV. xix. 125], in speaking of the mistress of the household, says: 'She will obey her husband in all things, and will do nothing against his will, except what she believes to concern her virtue and salvation.'

[2] As notable examples both of punishment and of praise see *1 Samuel*, xxii. 18 and 19; *1 Kings*, xviii. 4 and 13; *2 Kings*, i. 10, 12, and 14. Among Christians, Manuel and Georgius refused their services in killing the empress; Nicetas, *Alexis, Son of Manuel* [chap. xvii].

[3] Among the pagans there are two noble examples of men who refused to obey princes in committing dishonourable deeds. That of Papinian is sufficiently well known; the other is that of Helpidius in Ammianus, XXI [XXI. vi. 9]. Severus wished to inflict punishment even upon those who had followed the Emperor in accomplishing the death of a senator. See Xiphilinus [*Excerpta Dionis*, LXXIV, beginning].

[4] *Controversies*, I. i [I. i. 8].

Quintilian [1] presents the thought thus: *Declamations,* cclxxi.

[418] It is not necessary for children to do everything that their parents command. There are many things which may not be done. If you should order your son to give an opinion contrary to what he may think, if you should command him to give testimony concerning a thing of which he is ignorant, or to express an opinion in the senate; if you bid him to set fire to the Capitol, or seize the citadel, he has a right to say: 'These are things which should not be done.'

Seneca says: 'We are not able to give all orders, nor are slaves compelled to render obedience to all commands. They will not carry out orders against the state: they will not set their hands to a crime.' Sopater writes: '"One must", he says, "obey one's father." If his commands are lawful, that is right. But if they are inconsistent with honour it is improper.' *On Benefits,* III. xx.

In former times men laughed at Stratocles,[2] who had proposed a law at Athens that whatever pleased King Demetrius should be held to be reverent toward the gods and just among men. Pliny somewhere says that he had striven to show that to render a service to a criminal is a crime.[3] [Plutarch, *Demetrius,* xxiv = p. 900 A.] *Letters,* III [ix. 14], *To Minucius.*

3. The civil law, which readily grants pardon to excusable crimes, is lenient to those who are under obligation to obey, but not so in respect to all things. It makes an exception in the case of those acts which display heinousness of deed or crime, which, as Cicero says, are 'of themselves atrocious and abominable'; or, as this is interpreted by Asconius, deeds of evil which ought to be shunned instinctively, not in consequence of the discussions of jurists, but by a natural reaction. *Dig.* L. xvii. 157 *Against Verres,* III [I. xlii. 108]. [Thereon.]

4. Josephus relates, on the authority of Hecataeus, that the Jews who served under Alexander of Macedon could not be forced by blows or other indignities to heap up earth in company with the rest of the soldiers for the restoration of the temple of Baal, which was at Babylon. But an instance more suited to our argument we have in the Theban legion, of which we have previously spoken. Another is the case of the soldiers under Julian, of whom Ambrose speaks thus: [*Against Apion,* I. xxii. 192.] [I. ii. 9. 15, and iv. 7. 10 ff.]

The Emperor Julian, although an apostate, nevertheless had Christian soldiers under him. When he said to them, 'Go into battle in defence of the state,' they were obedient [*Decretum,* II. xi. 3. 94 = Augustine, *Letters,* cv.]

[1] Also in another place [*Declamations,* cccxxxiii]: 'Even parents are not to be obeyed in all things. Otherwise nothing is more dangerous than to accept favours, if they bind us to every form of service.'

[2] Similar is the bond that was exacted from Basil Camaterus by Andronicus Comnenus, 'that in the patriarchate he would do what was agreeable to Andronicus, even though it should be obviously wicked; on the other hand he would avoid doing what did not meet with the approval of Andronicus' [Nicetas, *Alexis,* xv].

[3] Tertullian, *On the Soul* [xl]: 'He who gives the order is more severely punished, although he who obeys is not excused'; also, *On the Resurrection of the Flesh* [xv]: 'Since human correction is considered the more perfect in the degree that it searches out even the agents who had a part in each deed, neither sparing them nor being prejudiced against them, in order that these may share with their principals the infliction of punishment or the reward of favour.' See Gail, *De Pace Publica,* I. iv. 14.

to him; but when he would say to them, 'Bear arms against Christians,'[1] then they recognized only the ruler of Heaven.

So also we read that military executioners who had been converted to Christ chose rather to die than to lend their hands to the carrying out of the edicts and decisions against the Christians.

Victoria, *De Iure Belli*, no. 23. [II. xxiii. 2.]

5. The case will amount to the same thing if any one is convinced that what is ordered is unjust. For the thing is not permissible for him so long as he is unable to get rid of that view. This is clear from the previous discussion.

IV.—*What they who are under the rule of another, and are ordered to go to war, should do if they are in doubt*

1. Now if one who is under the rule of another is in doubt whether a thing is permissible or not, is he to remain inactive, or obey? Very many think that he should obey; and further, that he is not hindered by the famous maxim, 'What you question, do not do,' because he who doubts as a matter of reflection does not doubt in a decision involving action, for he can believe that in a matter of doubt he must obey his superior.

Dig. L. xvii. 169. *Dig.* IX. ii. 37. *Dig.* L. xvii. 167. § 1.

It cannot in truth be denied that this distinction of a double judgement applies in many actions. The municipal law, not only of Rome but of other nations as well, under such circumstances not only grants immunity to those who obey,[2] but also refuses to admit a civil action against them. He does the injury, they say, who orders

[1] For Julian did not abstain from all violence against the Christians, especially when he thought that he had found some pretext for it. 'Julian, the strangler of a Christian army,' is a phrase found in Jerome's *Epitaph of Nepotianus* [*Letters*, lx. 15 = p. 26 c]; Augustine, *City of God*, I. lii [XVIII. lii], recounts that under Julian's rule a persecution was begun at Antioch, and a certain young man was tortured.

In the martyrologies is celebrated the memory of St. Eliphius, a Scot, and his thirty-three companions, whom Julian caused to be beheaded between Toul and Grand.

See also John of Antioch in the *Excerpta Peiresciana* [*Excerpta de Virtutibus et Vitiis*, I = p. 199].

Augustine, *Letters*, l [clxxxv], *To Boniface*, cited by Gratian, *Decretum*, II. xi. 3 [II. xi. 3. 98], says: 'Julian arose as an unbelieving emperor. Did he not stand forth as a wicked apostate and idolater? Christian soldiers served an infidel emperor, but when it came to a question of Christ they recognized none but Him who was in heaven; when he wished them to worship idols and offer them incense they set God before him.'

[2] Chrysostom, *On Providence*, III, says: [423] 'Oftentimes many magistrates have been accused of unjust executions and punished. But no one has haled to court the executioners, who performed the service of killing, who furnished the aid of their hands; indeed, no one has even started inquiry regarding them. They are excused by the necessity which arises from the authority of him who gives the order and the fear of him who obeys.'

Ulpian, citing Celsus, says that 'a slave who has obeyed his master's order has done no wrong', *Digest*, IX. iv. 2; and 'He who obeys the authority of a father, or of a master, is not believed to have willed the deed', *Digest*, L. xvii. 4, and the commentary of Cujas.

Seneca [*Letters*, lxi. 3] declares: 'There is no compulsion in the case of him who acts willingly.' Add the *Lombard Law*, I. iv. 2.

Mithridates dismissed unpunished the freedmen of Atilius who were party to the plot for his assassination, and also the sons of him who had rebelled; Appian, *Mithridatic Wars* [xv. 102]. Tiberius Gracchus was freed from responsibility for the treaty of Numantia, since he had done wrong on the order of another [Plutarch, *Tiberius Gracchus*, vi, vii = pp. 826, 827 A].

that it be done; there is then no guilt on the part of him who has to obey. The constraint of authority excuses; and like arguments.

Paul, *Sententiae*, V. xxii. 1 [2].

2. Aristotle himself in his *Nicomachean Ethics*, Book V [V. xii], counts the slave of a master, who issues the order to do wrong, among those who do something wrong, but not wrongfully. Moreover, Aristotle says that he acts wrongfully with whom the action originates, assuredly because there is not full deliberative power in a slave; this is indicated by the proverb,

Law of the Lombards, tit. 96, *de termino effosso*; *Law of the Visigoths*, II. ii. 2; VIII. i. 1 [3, 4]; VII. iv. 2 [1].

[419] One forced to enter slavery
One-half his virtue lacks;

[Longinus, *On the Sublime*, xliii.]

and the similar proverb,

From those for whom a life of servitude
Is willed by Jupiter he takes away
One-half their reason;

[Homer, *Odyssey*, XVII. 322–3.]

also that which Philo quotes:

Your lot is that of a slave, in reason you have no share.[1]

[*That Every Virtuous Man Is Free*, vii.]

Pertinent is the saying of Tacitus: 'To the prince the gods have given the supreme right of decision; for his subjects there remains the glory of obedience.' The same writer relates that the son of Piso was acquitted by Tiberius of the charge of rebellion, on the ground that 'the commands were in fact his father's, and the son could not refuse'. Says Seneca:[2] 'The slave is not the censorer, but the servant, of his master's order.'

[*Annals*, VI. xiv.] [*Annals*, III [xvii].

3. With regard to military service in particular Augustine is in agreement with the view stated. He speaks as follows:

Against Faustus, XXII. lxxiv [lxxv].

Therefore a just man, who happens to serve under an impious king, may justly fight at the latter's command, either if he is certain that the command given him, preserving the order of the public peace, is not contrary to the law of God, or if he is uncertain whether it is so; so that an unjust order may perhaps render the king responsible, while the duty of obedience preserves the innocence of the soldier.

Augustine elsewhere says:

City of God, I. xxvi.

When a soldier, in obedience to the authority under which he is lawfully placed, slays a man, no law of his state will hold him guilty of homicide.[3] Rather, he is guilty of neglect, and contempt of command, if he does not do so. But if he had done this of his own accord and authority, he would have incurred the charge of shedding blood. And so where he is punished, if he acts without orders, there he would be punished if he did not act when ordered.

[1] Themistius in *Orations*, ix [vii. 88], says that princes resemble reason, soldiers anger.

[2] *On Controversies*, III. ix.

[3] Augustine also in his treatise *On Free Will*, I [I. iv], says: 'If it is homicide to kill a man, it may sometimes occur without sin, for it does not seem to me that the soldier who kills an enemy, and a judge or his minister who executes a guilty person, and he from whose hand a missile has escaped against his will or without his knowledge, commit sin when they kill a man; but such are ordinarily not even called homicides.' This is cited by Gratian, in *Decretum*, II. xxiii. 5 [II. xxiii. 5. 41].

Syl., word *bellum*, I, no. 9, concl. 4; Castr., *On Dig.* I. i. 5; Soto, V. i. 7, and iii. 3; Vict., *De Iure Belli*, no. 32; Covarr., *On Sext*, V. ult. 4, pt. ii, § 10. [Lucan, *Pharsalia*, I. 126 f.] Adrian, *Quaest. Quodl.*, II. [*Jewish War*, II. viii. 7.] [*Life of Pythagoras*, clxxxvi.]

Hence the view is widely accepted that, so far as subjects are concerned, a war may arise that is just, that is to say free from injustice on either side. To such a war applies the verse—

> Which one more justly takes up arms
> 'Tis wrong to know.

4. This view, however, is not free from inherent difficulty. Our countryman Adrian, who was the last Pope of Rome from north of the Alps, supports the contrary opinion,[1] and this may be established, not exactly by the reason which he adduces, but by the more pressing one that whoever hesitates, when reflecting, in his decision to act ought to choose the safer course. The safer course, however, is to refrain from war. The Essenes are praised because they swore among other things 'not to injure any one, even if ordered to'; also their imitators the Pythagoreans, who, on the testimony of Iamblichus, refrained from war, giving as their reason that 'war organizes and ordains slaughter'.

Baldus, *Consilia*, II. 385; Soto, *De Ratione Detegendi Secretum*, membr. iii, qu. ii, reply to obj. 1.

5. It is no objection that on the other side there is danger of disobedience. For when either course is uncertain that which is the lesser of two evils is free from sin; for if a war is unjust there is no disobedience in avoiding it. Moreover, disobedience in things of this kind, by its very nature, is a lesser evil than manslaughter, especially than the slaughter of many innocent men. The ancients relate that when Mercury, who had been accused of the slaying of Argos, rested his defence on the command of Jupiter, the gods even then did not dare to acquit him. Nor did Martial acquit Pothinus, the hanger-on of Ptolemy, when he wrote:

[*Epigrams*, III. lxvi. 5 f.]

> But yet is the case of Antonius worse than that of Pothinus.

The latter did wrong for his master, the former for himself.

Victoria, *De Iure Belli*, no. 25.

[420] That is not of great weight which some adduce, that if this principle should be admitted the state would in many cases perish, the reason being that oftentimes it is not expedient that the reasons for policies should be made public. Although this may be true of persuasive causes, it is not true of justifiable causes, which ought to be clear and open and, further, should be such as may and ought to be openly set forth.

Apology, iv; *Against the Heathen*, I. vi.

6. What Tertullian has said in perhaps too indefinite a manner with regard to laws refers with perfect justice to those laws or edicts which concern the waging of war: 'A citizen does not faithfully observe a law if he does not know what sort of thing it is that the law

[1] Examples of those who adhere to this view are found in Lambert von Aschaffenburg.

avenges. No law must keep to itself alone the understanding of its uprightness, but must impart such knowledge also to those from whom it expects obedience. A law, however, which does not wish itself to be approved becomes an object of suspicion; such a law, moreover, is wicked if it should enforce itself without having been approved.' In Statius Achilles says to Ulysses, who is inciting him to war: [*Achilleid*, II. 47 f.]

> Proclaim what causes the Greeks have for so great a war;
> From these just anger may at once arise.

In the same author Theseus cries: [*Thebaid*, XII. 648.]

> Go swiftly and, I pray, have confidence in such a cause.

Propertius had said: [*Elegies*, IV. vi. 51 f.]

> The soldier's cause increases or weakens his strength;
> If it be not just, shame causes his weapons to fall.

On a level with this is the saying of the Panegyrist: 'In war a good conscience assumes so much importance that now victory has begun to be not more a matter of valour than of rightness.' Thus some scholars interpret the Hebrew word 'jarek', which is read in *Genesis*, xiv, 14,[1] in the sense that before the battle the servants of Abraham were by him made fully aware of the justness of their warfare. [Nazarius, *Panegyric of Constantine*, vii.]

7. Declarations of war in fact, as we shall shortly be saying, were wont to be made publicly, with a statement of the cause, in order that the whole human race as it were might judge of the justness of it. Of a truth wisdom is the virtue characteristic of the ruler, as it seemed to Aristotle also; but justice is the virtue characteristic of a man, in so far as he is a man. [*Politics*, III. iv.]

8. It seems then that the view which we said was that of Adrian is absolutely to be followed, if a subject not only hesitates, but, led by more convincing arguments, leans rather to the view that the war is unjust; especially if it is a question of attacking others, not of defending one's own. Aegidius Regius, *De Actibus Supernaturalibus*, disp. 31, dub. 5, no. 85; Báñez, *On II. ii*, qu. 40, art. 1; Molina, ii, disp. 113.

9. Further, it is probable that even the executioner, who is going to put a condemned man to death, should know the merits of the case, either through assisting at the inquiry and the trial or from a confession of the crime, in such a degree that it is sufficiently clear to him that the criminal deserves death.[2] This practice is

[1] Some attribute the same sense to the word 'ḥanîkhâw' and interpret it as 'instructed by him'. Herod in his address to the Jews after the defeat in Arabia said: 'Moreover, I wish to show you with what justness we have undertaken this war, driven to it by the insults of our enemies. For if you understand this it will prove a great incentive to your daring', in Josephus [*Antiquities of the Jews*, XV. v. 3].

[2] Thus the servants of Saul, more worthy than Doeg, did not wish to kill the priests who dwelt

Deut., xvii [7]. observed in some places, and such is the intent of the Hebraic law, when it ordains that the witnesses shall take the lead of the people in stoning him who has been condemned.

V.—*Sense of duty requires that subjects who doubt in regard to the justness of a war should be spared, but the burden of an extraordinary tax may be imposed upon them*

1. Now if the minds of subjects cannot be satisfied by an explanation of the cause of a war it will by all means be the duty of a good magistrate to impose upon them extraordinary taxes rather than military service; particularly where there will be no lack of others who will serve. For an upright king may make use not only of his subjects' good will but also of their evil purposes, just as God uses the means of the Devil and impious persons that are at hand; just as, again, he is free from blame who, under stress of poverty, takes money from a wicked usurer.

Sylvester, word *bellum*, I, no. 7, near end.

2. Furthermore, even if there can be no doubt respecting the cause of war, still it does not seem at all right that Christians should be compelled to serve against their will; the reason is that to refrain from military service, even when it is permissible to serve, is the mark of a somewhat greater holiness, which was long demanded from ecclesiastics and penitents, and recommended in many ways to all other persons. To Celsus, who rebuked the Christians for shirking military service, Origen [421] replies as follows:

[*Against Celsus*, VIII. lxxiii.]

> To those who, being strangers to our faith, bid us serve in defence of the state and slay men, we shall thus make answer:
>
> 'Those who are the priests of your idols, whom you consider the special priests of the gods, keep their right hands pure on account of the sacrifices, that with hands free from blood and unstained with any slaughter they may offer sacrifices to those who are believed to be gods; and if any war arises priests will not be enrolled in the ranks. If then that is not without reason, with how much more reason, while others bear arms, are these also to be considered as rendering military service after their own fashion, as priests and worshippers of God, who keep their hands pure indeed, but strive before God with prayers for those who serve as soldiers justly, and for him who with justice rules?'

In this passage he calls all Christians priests, following the example of the holy writers (*Revelation*, i. 6; *1 Peter*, ii. 5).

at Nob, without a hearing; *1 Samuel*, xxii. 17. And the third officer of Achab was unwilling to harm Elijah; *2 Kings*, i. 13 ff. Sometimes even executioners, after having been converted to Christ, for the future renounced this office as being dangerous. See the *Martyrology*, and Bede, [*Ecclesiastical History*,] I. vii.

VI.—*When it may be just for subjects to bear arms in a war that is unjust*

1. However, I think that the case may arise in which there may be a just defence of subjects who engage in a war that is not merely doubtful but obviously unjust. For since an enemy, although waging a just war, does not have the true and perfect right of killing innocent subjects, who are not responsible for the war, unless either as a necessary defensive measure or as a result and apart from his purpose (for these are not liable to punishment), it follows that, if it is certain that the enemy comes with such a spirit that he absolutely refuses to spare the lives of hostile subjects when he can, these subjects may defend themselves by the law of nature, of which they are not deprived by the law of nations.

2. But even then we shall not say that the war is just on both sides; for it is not a question of the war, but of a certain and definite act. This act, moreover, although done by him who in other respects has a right to make war, is unjust, and hence is justly resisted.

[424]

HUGO GROTIUS

ON

THE LAW OF WAR AND PEACE

BOOK III

CHAPTER I

GENERAL RULES FROM THE LAW OF NATURE REGARDING WHAT IS PERMISSIBLE IN WAR; WITH A CONSIDERATION OF RUSES AND FALSEHOOD

I.—*The order of treatment in the discussion which follows*

We have considered both those who wage war and on what grounds war may be waged. It follows that we should determine what is permissible in war,[1] also to what extent, and in what ways, it is permissible.

What is permissible in war is viewed either absolutely or in relation to a previous promise. It is viewed absolutely, first from the standpoint of the law of nature, and then from that of the law of nations. Let us see, then, what is permissible by nature.

II.—*The first rule: In war things which are necessary to attain the end in view are permissible. This is explained*

1. First, as we have previously said on several occasions, in a moral question things which lead to an end receive their intrinsic value from the end itself. In consequence we are understood to have a right to those things which are necessary for the purpose of securing a right, when the necessity is understood not in terms of physical exactitude but in a moral sense. By right I mean that which is strictly so called, denoting the power of acting in respect to society only.

Victoria, *De Iure Belli*, no. 15.

Hence, if otherwise I cannot save my life, I may use any degree of violence to ward off him who assails it, even if he should happen to be free from wrong, as we have pointed out elsewhere. The reason is that this right does not properly arise from another's wrong, but from the right which nature grants me on my own behalf. [II. i. 3.]

2. Furthermore, [425] I can also take possession of another's property from which an imminent danger threatens me, without

Victoria, *De Iure Belli*, nos. 18, 39, and 55.

[1] It has been well said by Augustine, *Letters*, lxx [ccxx. 12], *To Count Boniface*: 'May you, in war itself, if it is still necessary for you to engage in war, cleave to the faith, and seek peace.' Again in *Letters*, ccv [clxxxix. 6]: 'Be therefore a man of peace, even when engaged in war.'

Regarding the maintenance of justice in waging war, [437] there is an excellent discourse of Belisarius to his soldiers in Procopius, *Vandalic War*, I [I. xvi]. Orosius, Book VII [VII. xxi], says: 'Behold in what fashion civil wars are waged by Christian kings in Christian ages, when they cannot be avoided.' The same author [VII. xxiii] refers thus to Theodosius: 'Let them mention some one war, from the time of the founding of the city, which was undertaken by reason of so righteous a necessity, and concluded with so divine a felicity, that battle did not exact great slaughter or victory a bloody vengeance.'

taking account of the other's guilt; yet not in such a way as to become its owner (for this procedure is not adapted to that end), but in order to guard it until adequate security has been given for
II. ii. 10. my safety. This point also we have treated elsewhere.

Thus I have by nature a right to seize property of mine which another is holding; and if such seizure is too difficult I have the right to seize something else of equal value, as in the case of recovering a debt. From these causes ownership also arises, because the equality
Sylvester, word *bellum*, I, no. 10, v. *prima*. which has been disturbed can in no other way be restored.

3. Where therefore the punishment is just, all use of force necessary for the infliction of the penalty is likewise just; and everything which is a part of the penalty, as the destruction of property by fire or by other means, is certainly within the limit of that which is just and befits the crime.

III.—*The second rule: A right is to be viewed as arising not only from the origin of the war but also from causes which subsequently develop*

In the second place the fact must be recognized that our right to wage war is to be regarded as arising not merely from the origin of the war but also from causes which subsequently develop; just as in lawsuits a new right is often acquired by one party after suit has been brought. Thus those who associate themselves with him who assails me, either as allies or subjects, confer upon me the right to protect myself against them also.

In like manner those who join in a war that is unjust, especially if they can or ought to know that it is unjust, obligate themselves to make good the expenses and losses incurred, because through their guilt they cause the loss. Similarly, those who join in a war that has been undertaken without a cause worthy of approval draw upon themselves the desert of punishment, in a degree proportionate to the
[*Republic*, V. xvi = 471 B.] injustice which lies in their action. For this reason Plato approves of war 'until the guilty are compelled, by the guiltless who have suffered, to pay the penalty'.

IV.—*The third rule: Some things, which are not permissible according to the purpose of a war, may follow therefrom without wrong; a precaution is added*

1. In the third place, it must be observed that in addition to
Victoria, *op. cit.*, no. 37. [II. i. 4.] the right of action many things follow indirectly, and beyond the purpose of the doer,[1] for which in and of themselves a right would not exist. We have explained elsewhere how this may occur in a case

[1] See on this point Thomas Aquinas, II. i, qu. 73, art. 8; Molina, tract. ii, disp. 121.

of self-defence. Thus in order to obtain what is ours, if we cannot get that by itself, we have the right to accept more, subject to the obligation, nevertheless, of restoring the value of the excess. Similarly we may bombard a ship full of pirates, or a house full of brigands, even if there are within the same ship or house a few infants, women, or other innocent persons who are thereby endangered. Says Augustine: 'A man is not guilty of homicide if he has built a wall about his property and another is killed by the fall of it when trying to make use of it.' *Letters,* cliv [xlvii. 5], *To Publicola.*

2. But, as we have admonished upon many occasions previously, what accords with a strict interpretation of right is not always, or in all respects, permitted. Often, in fact, love for our neighbour prevents us from pressing our right to the utmost limit.

Wherefore we must also beware of what happens, and what we foresee may happen, beyond our purpose, unless the good which our action has in view is much greater than the evil which is feared, or, unless the good and the evil balance, the hope of the good is much greater than the fear of the evil. The decision in such matters must be left to a prudent judgement, but in such a way that when in doubt we should favour that course, as the more safe, which has regard for the interest of another rather than our own. 'Let the tares grow', said the best Teacher, 'lest haply while ye gather up the tares ye root up the wheat with them.' Said Seneca: 'To kill many persons indiscriminately is the work of fire and desolation.' History teaches us with how deep repentance Theodosius, on the admonition of Ambrose, expiated such an unrestrained vengeance. *Matthew,* xiii. 29; Thomas Aquinas, II. ii, qu. 64, art. 2. Seneca, *On Clemency,* II, end [I. xxvi. 5].

3. Further, if at times God does something of this kind, it is not for us to take that as an example, in view of the most perfect [426] right of dominion which He has over us, but which He has not granted to us over one another, as we have noted elsewhere. [II. xxi. 14.] And yet God Himself, lord of men in His own right, is wont to spare a community of evil men, however large, for the sake of a very few good men; in this He makes manifest His fairness as a judge, as the conference of Abraham with God regarding Sodom clearly teaches us. *Genesis,* xvii [xviii] 23 ff.

From these general rules we may learn how much is by nature permissible against an enemy.

V.—*What is permissible against those who furnish supplies to our enemies is explained through distinctions*

1. But there often arises the question, What is permissible against those who are not enemies, or do not want to be called enemies, but who furnish our enemies with supplies? For we know that this subject has been keenly debated in both ancient and modern

times, since some champion the relentlessness of warfare and others the freedom of commercial relations.

2. First, we must make distinctions with reference to the things supplied. There are some things, such as weapons, which are useful only in war; other things which are of no use in war, as those which minister to pleasure; and others still which are of use both in time of war and at other times, as money, provisions, ships, and naval equipment.[1]

Procopius, *Gothic War*, I [iii]. Regarding the first class of things, the saying of Amalasuntha to Justinian holds true, that he who supplies an enemy with things necessary for warfare is on the side of the enemy.

[*On Benefits*, VII. xx.] Things of the second sort give rise to no complaint. Thus Seneca says that he will do a favour to a tyrant, if the kindness will not give to the tyrant greater powers for the ruin of all[2] nor strengthen the powers which he has; that is, a kindness which may be done to him without harm to the state. In explaining this Seneca adds:

> Money, by means of which a satellite may be kept in service, I shall not supply. If he shall desire marbles and robes, that which his luxurious taste amasses will harm no one; soldiery and arms I shall not furnish. If, as a great favour, he seeks craftsmen of the stage and things which may soften his savagery, I shall gladly proffer them. To him to whom I would not send triremes or ships with bronze rams, I shall send pleasure craft, and sleeping-barges, and other follies of kings who revel on the sea.

On Duties, I. xxx [144]. In the judgement of Ambrose, to be generous toward him who conspires against his country is not approvable liberality.

3. Regarding things of the third sort, useful in both war and peace, we must take into account the conditions of the war. For, if I am unable to protect myself without intercepting the goods which [II. ii. 6.] are being sent to the enemy, necessity, as we have elsewhere said, *Decretals*, V. vi. 6 and 17. will give me a right to intercept such goods, but with the obligation to make restitution, unless another cause arises.

If, now, the enforcement of my right shall be hindered by the supplying of these things, and if he who supplied them has been in a position to know this (for example, in case I should be holding a town under siege or keeping ports under blockade, and a surrender or the conclusion of peace should already be in anticipation), then he will be liable to me for injury culpably inflicted, just as one who releases a debtor from prison or secures his escape, to my detriment. As in the case of the infliction of an injury, his goods may be seized, and ownership over them may be sought, for the purpose of recovering damages.

[1] Designated by the Athenians ἀπόρρητα; that is, 'things of which the export is forbidden', rope, water-skins, timber, wax, and pitch. See the Scholiast on Aristophanes' *Clouds* [rather *Frogs*, line 365], and *Knights* [line 282].

[2] See Paruta, Book VII.

If he who furnishes supplies has not yet caused me injury, but has wished to do so, I shall have the right, through the retention of his goods, to oblige him to give security for the future, by means of hostages, by pledges, or in some other way. Sylvester, word *restitutio*, pt. III, § 12.

If, moreover, the injustice of my enemy toward me is palpably evident and the one who furnishes supplies to him strengthens him in a very wicked war, in that case the latter will be responsible for the injury, not only by civil law but also by criminal law, just as one would be who should deliver an obviously guilty party from a judge who is about to inflict punishment. On this ground it will be permissible to pass upon the furnisher of supplies a sentence which suits his crime, in accordance with what we have said regarding punishments; within the limits there indicated he may even be despoiled.

4. For the reasons which have been stated, those who engage in war usually address public proclamations[1] to other peoples, with

[1] See the examples in the joint war against the Egyptians, Saracens, and others; *Decretals*, I. xxxvi. 11; V. vi. 11; *Extravagantes*, viii. un.; *Extravagantes Communes*, V. ii. 1.

There has been published in Italian a book called *Consolato del Mare*, in which have been collected the edicts of the emperors of Greece and Germany, and of the kings of France, Spain, Syria, and Cyprus; also those of the Balearic Isles, the Venetians, and the Genoese. In title cclxxiv of that book questions of the kind under consideration are discussed, and the following principles are stated:

If both the ship and the cargo belong to the enemy, the case is clear that they become the property of those who take them; if, however, the ship belongs to those who are at peace, but the cargo to the enemy, the belligerents may force the ship to convey the cargo to some port belonging to them, upon condition, however, of paying the cost of the voyage to the owner of the vessel. On the other hand, if the ship belongs to the enemy, but the cargo to others, the latter must bargain for the price of the vessel; or, if the shippers do not wish to bargain, they must be compelled to go with the ship to some port belonging to the side of the captor, and to pay to the captor the price due for the use of the vessel.

In Holland, in the year 1438, when the Dutch were at war with Lübeck and other cities on the Baltic and the Elbe, in a full meeting of the Senate it was decided that merchandise clearly belonging to others, even if it were found in vessels of enemies, did not form part of the booty; and since then this has been recognized as the law there. This was also the view of the king of Denmark, when, in 1597, he sent an embassy to the Dutch and their allies to claim for his subjects freedom of navigation and of carrying merchandise to Spain, with which the Dutch were waging a very bitter war.

In France there has always been granted to those at peace freedom to carry on commerce, even with those who were enemies of the French. So indiscriminately has such freedom been taken advantage of that the enemy have often concealed their property under the names of others, as appears from an edict of the year 1543, chap. xlii, which has been carried over into an edict of the year 1584, and subsequent edicts. In these edicts it is expressly provided that it is permissible for those on friendly terms with the French to carry on commerce in time of war, provided that this is done in their own ships, and by their own people, ships, and cargoes; it is permissible to carry their goods wherever they may wish, provided that these goods shall not be material serviceable in war, by means of which they wished to help the cause of the enemy; in case material serviceable for war should be transported, the French are permitted to take such material for themselves, paying a fair price for it. Here we must note two things; by these [438] laws material of war did not become legitimate spoil, and innocent merchandise was much farther removed from the same danger.

I should not deny that the northern nations have at times made use of another right, but in different ways, and having in view rather a temporary advantage than the maintenance of permanent justice. For when, making a pretext of their own wars, the English interfered with the commerce of the Danes, for this cause war arose between the peoples with the result that the Danes imposed tribute upon the English. Although the cause of the payment was changed, the name of it, *Danegeld*, remained until the time of William [the Conqueror], who founded the dynasty now ruling in England; this is recorded by the very reliable De Thou, in his history of the year 1589 [XCVI. xv].

Again, Elizabeth, the wisest queen of England, in the year 1575, sent Sir William Winter and Robert Beal, Secretary of the Royal Council, to Holland in order to make it plain that the English could not suffer the Dutch, in the very midst of Holland's war with Spain, to detain English ships which had

the object of making clear both the justice of their cause and the probable hope of enforcing their right.

5. In this inquiry we have referred back to the law of nature for the reason [427] that in historical narratives we have been

sailed for Spanish ports. This is reported by Van Reyd for the year 1575 in his *Dutch History*, and by the Englishman Camden for the following year. However, when the English had themselves become enemies of the Spaniards and were interfering with the exercise of the right of navigation to Spain on the part of German cities, from the controversial writings of both peoples, which deserve to be read for an understanding of this controversy, it appears that the English had availed themselves of such interference without any clear right. It is to be noted that the English themselves in their writings admit this, when they adduce as the two chief points in support of their case that the things which were being carried by the Germans to Spain were material for war, and that previous treaties had forbidden such transportation.

Such treaties were afterward made by the Dutch and their allies with Lübeck and its allies in 1613, providing that neither the one party nor the other should permit subjects of the enemy to trade within their territory, or aid the enemy with money, soldiers, ships, or provisions. Later, in 1627, it was agreed between the kings of Sweden and Denmark that the king of Denmark should prevent all commerce with the people of Danzig, who were enemies of Sweden, and should not permit any merchandise to pass through the Cimbrian Strait [Baltic Sound] to the other enemies of Sweden; for these services the king of Denmark stipulated certain advantages for himself.

These, however, are special agreements, from which no inference can be drawn which would be binding upon all. This was in fact said also by the Germans in their writings, that not all merchandise was excluded by the treaties in question but only such merchandise as had been imported into England or manufactured there. The Germans, nevertheless, were not the only ones who opposed the English when the latter forbade commerce with their enemy. Even Poland sent an embassy and complained that the law of nations was being infringed upon when, because of the war between England and Spain, the Poles were deprived of the freedom of commercial relations with the Spaniards; this is related under the year 1597 by Camden and Van Reyd, whom we have cited already.

Moreover, after the Treaty of Vervins had been made with Spain, while Elizabeth, queen of England, remained at war, the French refused to accede to the request of the English that the English should be allowed to search French ships that were sailing to Spain, in order that munitions of war might not be secretly conveyed therein; the reason alleged was that this was seeking a pretext for plundering and disturbing commerce. In the treaty which the English made with the Dutch and their allies in 1625, an agreement was reached that other nations, to whose interest it was that the greatness of Spain should be diminished, should be invited voluntarily to forbid commerce with the Spaniards; if, nevertheless, the nations should not do this of their own accord, it was decided that vessels should be searched to see [439] if they carried any war material, but that otherwise neither the ships nor their cargoes should be detained, and that damage should not be done on this pretext to those who remained at peace.

In the same year it happened that certain men sailed from Hamburg for Spain in a ship laden chiefly with military stores; these stores were seized by the English, but the value of the rest of the merchandise was paid. The French, however, when French ships sailing for Spain were confiscated by the English, made it plain that they would not permit such procedure.

We have, therefore, well stated the case in saying that public proclamations are required. The English themselves came to hold the same opinion. An example of such a proclamation made by them is given by Camden under the years 1591 and 1598. However, such proclamations have not always been obeyed, and distinctions have been made between times, causes, and places. In 1458, in fact, the city of Lübeck decided that it would not obey the proclamation made by the city of Danzig, forbidding them to carry on trade with Malmö and Memel, then at war with Danzig. Similarly the Dutch in 1551 refused to obey when Lübeck notified them that they should refrain from commerce with the Danes, who were then their enemies.

In 1522, when there was war between the Swedes and the Danes, the king of Denmark requested the Hanseatic cities not to carry on commerce with the Swedes. Some of the cities, being in need of his friendship, complied, but the others did not. When war was raging between Sweden and the king of Poland, the Dutch never suffered themselves to be prohibited from commerce with one or the other nation. The Dutch, moreover, always restored to France the French ships which on their way to or from Spain were intercepted by Dutch vessels, Holland and Spain being at war. See the speech of Louis Servin, one time royal advocate, delivered in 1592 in the case of citizens of Hamburg.

But the same Dutch did not permit merchandise to be brought by the English into Dunkirk, off which they kept a fleet: just so the city of Danzig, in 1455, notified the Dutch not to carry anything into the city of Koenigsberg, as Gaspar Schütz narrates in his *Prussian History*. Add Cabedo, *Decisiones*, xlvii. 2, and Seraphinus de Freitas in his book *On the Just Asiatic Empire of the Portuguese*, where he cites various others.

unable to find anything established by the volitional law of nations [1] to cover such cases. The Carthaginians sometimes captured Romans who had brought supplies to their enemies; and they surrendered such persons to the Romans who demanded them. When Demetrius was occupying Attica with an army, and had already taken the near-by towns of Eleusis and Rhamnus and was intending to starve Athens into surrender, he hanged both the master and the pilot [2] of a ship that attempted to carry in grain; having in this way deterred others he made himself master of the city.

Polybius, I [lxxxiii].

Plutarch, *Demetrius* [xxxiii = p. 904 E].

VI.—*Whether it is permissible to use a ruse in war*

1. So far as the manner of conducting operations is concerned, violence and frightfulness are particularly suited to wars. The question is often raised, however, whether one may resort to ruses also. Homer, at any rate, said that one must harm his foe—

> By ruse or violence, by open ways or hidden.

[Cf. Homer, *Odyssey*, I. 296; Stobaeus, liv. 46.]

In Pindar we find:

> And every means must be employed
> To bring the foeman low.

[*Isthmaean Hymns*, iii. 69.]

In Virgil there is also this:

> Whether craft or valour, who would ask in war?

[*Aeneid*, II. 390.]

Soon there follows,

[II. 426 f.]

> Ripheus, who among the Trojans was the one most just,
> And most observant of the right.

We read that Solon, who had a famous reputation for wisdom, sought to follow this type. Silius [Italicus], narrating the exploits of Fabius Maximus, says:

[Plutarch, *Solon*, viii = p. 82.]

XV [327].

> Deceit henceforth on valour's side is placed.

2. In Homer Ulysses, the typical man of wisdom, is at all times full of wiles against the enemy; whence Lucian deduced the rule that those who deceive the foe deserve praise. Xenophon asserted that in war nothing is more useful than deceptions. In Thucydides Brasidas says that the renown won by the stratagems of war [3] is

Lucian, *Philopseudes* [beginning].

Xen., *Training of Cyrus*, I [vi. 29 f.]; and *On Horsemanship* [*The Cavalry Commander*, v. 9].

[1] The learned Jan de Mers has much on this topic in his *History of Denmark*, I and II. There you will see that Lübeck and the Emperor are for commercial intercourse, and the Danes against it. See also Krantz, *Vandalica*, XIV [XIV. xxix]; De Thou, on the aforementioned year 1589, *Histories*, XCVI [XCVI. xv]; and Camden, besides the places previously cited, on the years 1589 and 1595, where the dispute between the English and the Germans, who are called Hanseatics, is discussed.

[2] Not very different is the incident related of Pompey by Plutarch in his *History of the Mithridatic War* [*Life of Pompey*, xxxix = p. 639 E]: 'He placed guards at the Bosphorus to watch for any traders who might sail in; for those who were caught the penalty was death.'

[3] So says Virgil also, *Aeneid*, XI [XI. 515], and Sallust, who is cited by Servius.

Thuc., V [ix]. Plutarch, *Apoth.* [=p. 209 B]. Polybius, IX [xii]. V [100]. Plutarch, *Marcellus* [xxii=p. 311 B]. [*Lysander*, vii=p. 437 A.] [*Philopoemen*, xiii=p. 363 E.]

particularly conspicuous; and in Plutarch Agesilaus declares that to deceive an enemy is both just and permissible.

Polybius thinks that what is accomplished by main force in war is to be considered of less importance than what is done by taking advantage of opportunities and by the use of deception. Hence Silius represents Corvinus as saying:

> War must be waged with guile;[1] force brings less fame to the leader.

Similar, according to Plutarch, was the view even of the stern Spartans: he observes that a larger victim was sacrificed by the one who had gained a victory through a ruse than by him who had won by open fighting. The same writer thinks highly of Lysander[2] for 'varying with ruses most of the operations of war'. Plutarch counts it among the merits of Philopoemen that, having been trained in the Cretan system, he combined the straightforward and honourable method of fighting with craft and ruses. It is a saying of Ammianus that 'All successful issues of war are to be praised without distinction of valour or guile'.

[XVII. v. 6.]

Dig. IV. iii. 1. § 3. *Digest*, XLIX. xv. 26.

3. The Roman jurists call it a good ruse 'whenever any one lays a plot against the enemy'; and again, they say that it makes no difference whether any one escapes from the power of the enemy by force or by trickery. This is 'deception which cannot be censured, such as that of a general', as Eustathius notes in his commentary on the fifteenth book of the *Iliad*. Among the theologians, Augustine declares: 'When one undertakes a righteous war, it makes no difference, [428] in respect to justness, whether he fights openly or by ambuscades.' Chrysostom says that generals who have won a victory by a ruse receive the highest praise.

On Joshua, qu. x [*On Heptateuch*, VI. x]. *On the Priesthood*, I [viii].

4. However, there is no lack of opinions which seem to advocate the opposite view, and some of these we shall present below. The final conclusion will depend upon the answer to the question whether deceit belongs to the class of things that are always evil, in regard to which the saying is true that one must not do evil that good may come; or whether it is in the category of things which from their very nature are not at all times vicious but which may even happen to be good.

[1] There is a similar saying of Mohammed, 'el-ḥarbu ḥud'atun', [440] that is, 'battles require deceit'. According to Virgil [*Aeneid*, XII. 336], in the following of Mars are:

> Wrath and ambuscades.

Thereon Servius comments: 'He shows that he is accompanied not only by valour, but also by stratagems.'

[2] Plutarch compares him to Sulla, in whose soul Carbo used to say there were a lion and a fox [*Sulla*, xxviii=p. 469 E].

VII.—*In a negative action, deceit is not in itself unpermissible*

It must be observed, then, that deceit is of one sort in a negative action, of another sort in a positive action. The word deceit I extend, on the authority of Labeo, even to those things which occur in a negative action; he classes it as deceit, but not harmful deceit, when any one 'protects his own or another's possessions through dissimulation'. It cannot be doubted that Cicero spoke too sweepingly when he said: 'Pretence and dissimulation must be removed from every phase of life.' For since you are not required to reveal to others all that you know or desire, it follows that it is right to dissimulate, that is to conceal and hide some things from some persons. 'One may', said Augustine,[1] 'conceal the truth wisely, by the use of dissimulation in some degree'. Cicero himself in more than one place admits that such dissimulation is absolutely necessary and unavoidable,[2] especially for those to whom the care of the state is entrusted.

Dig. IV. iii. 1. § 2.

On Duties, III [xv. 61].

Against Lying, x; Thomas, II. ii, qu. 40, art. 3, ans. to obj., and qu. 71, art. 7; Sylvester, word *bellum*, pt. 1, no. 9. Cicero, *For Milo* [xxiv. 65]; *Letters*, VII. ix [X. viii. 4]; *For Gn. Plancius* [vi. 16].

The narrative of Jeremiah (*Jeremiah*, chap. xxxviii) offers a notable example touching this point. The prophet had been questioned by the king as to the outcome of the siege, but in the presence of the princes, at the king's request, he wisely concealed that fact, assigning another and yet not untrue reason for the conference. With this, again, we may class the action of Abraham[3] in concealing his marriage and calling Sarah his sister, that is, according to the usage of the time, a near relative.

Genesis, xx; Thomas, II. ii, qu. 110, art. 3, ans. to obj.

VIII.—*Deceit in a positive action falls under two heads: deceit exhibited in actions not limited in significance, and that exhibited in actions the significance of which is, as it were, fixed by agreement; it is shown that deceit of the former sort is permissible*

1. Deceit which consists in a positive action, if it is exhibited in acts, is called pretence; if in words, falsehood. Some persons establish this distinction between the two terms, because they say that words are naturally the signs of thoughts, while acts are not. But the contrary is true, that words by their very nature and apart from the human will have no significance, unless perchance a word is confused and 'inarticulate', such as is uttered by a person in grief, when it comes rather under the term act than speech.

If now the assertion is made that the nature of man possesses

[1] Also on Psalm v, verse 'Thou wilt destroy all': 'It is one thing to lie, and another to conceal the truth.' This is cited in the *Decretum*, II. xxiii. 2 [II. xxii. 2. 14].

[2] See Chrysostom, *On the Priesthood*, I [I. viii. end].

[3] 'He wished the truth to be concealed, but not to utter a lie': Augustine, *On Genesis*, qu. xx [*On Heptateuch*, I. xxvi], quoted by Gratian, in the aforementioned *Decretum*, II. xxii. 3 [II. xxii. 2. 22].

superiority over that of other living creatures in this, that it can convey to others the ideas of the mind and that words were invented for this purpose, that is true. But it must be added that such conveying of thought is accomplished not by means of words alone but also by *Digest,* XXXIII. x. 7. § 2. signs,[1] as among dumb persons, whether these signs naturally have something in common with the thing signified or whether they possess significance merely by agreement.

Digest, XLIV. vii. 38. Similar to these signs are those characters which, as Paul the jurist says,[2] do not express words formed by the tongue but objects themselves, either from some resemblance, as in the case of hieroglyphic signs, or by mere arbitrary convention, as among the Chinese.

2. At this point then we must introduce another distinction, such as we employed to remove the ambiguity in the term law of nations. For we said that the term law of nations includes both what is approved by separate nations without mutual obligation and what contains a mutual obligation in itself. Words, then, and signs, and the written characters we have mentioned, were invented as a means *On Interpretation,* iv. of expression under a mutual obligation; as Aristotle called it, 'by convention'. This is not the case with other things. Hence it comes about that we may avail ourselves of other things, even if we foresee that another person will derive therefrom a false impression.[3] [429] I am speaking of what is intrinsic, not of what is incidental. And so we must give an example, in which no harm follows as a consequence,[4] or in which the harm itself, without consideration of the deceit, is permissible.

Luke, xxiv. 28. 3. An example of the former case is found in Christ, who in the presence of His companions on the way to Emmaus 'made as though He would' go further, that is, gave the impression of intending to go further; unless we prefer truly to believe that He wished to go further, on condition, nevertheless, that He should not be detained by a great effort. Thus God is said to will many things which do *Mark,* vi. 48. not come to pass, and in another place Christ is said to have intended to pass by the Apostles who were in a ship, that is had He not been *Acts,* xvi. 3. urgently entreated to embark.

Another example may be found in Paul's circumcision of Timothy, when he was well aware that the Jews would interpret this as though the injunction of circumcision, which had in fact already

[1] Pliny, on the nation of the Ethiopians, [*Natural History,*] VI. xxx, says: 'Some of them use noddings of the head and movements of the limbs instead of speech.' See *Decretals,* IV. i. 25.

[2] 'We are not', he says, 'bound by the form of the letters, but by the speech which the letters express, in so far as it is agreed that what is indicated by the writing has not less force than what is indicated by words formed by the tongue.' In a truly philosophic spirit has he said 'it is agreed', in order to show that these things have force 'by convention' (ἐκ συνθήκης).

[3] See Augustine, *On Christian Doctrine,* II. xxiv [II. xxxiv].

[4] As in the deed of Michal, *I Samuel,* xix. 16.

been done away with, was still binding upon the children of Israel, and as though Paul and Timothy themselves thought so. However, Paul did not have this in view, but merely sought to obtain for himself and Timothy the opportunity of associating with the Jews on more intimate terms. After the removal of the divine law circumcision no longer implied such an obligation by agreement; and the evil arising from the error, which followed for the time being, and was later to be corrected, was not of so great importance as the good which Paul sought, that is the introduction of the truth of the Gospel.

This sort of pretence the Greek fathers often call 'management'.[1] In regard to it there is a notable opinion of Clement of Alexandria, who in a discussion of the good man speaks thus: 'For the benefit of his neighbour he will do things which otherwise he would not do of his own accord and original purpose.' Of this nature was the act of the Romans who threw bread from the Capitol into the posts of the enemy that they might not be believed to be distressed by famine. [*Stromata*, VII. ix.] Livy, V [xlviii. 4].

4. An example illustrating the latter case is found in a pretended flight, such as Joshua ordered his men to make so as to take Ai by storm, and such as other commanders have frequently ordered. For in this instance we regard the injury which follows as legitimate according to the justice of war. Moreover, flight itself has no significance by agreement, although an enemy may interpret it as a sign of fear; such interpretation the other party is not obliged to guard against in his use of his freedom to go hither and thither, more or less rapidly, and with this or that gesture or outward appearance. In the same category we may class the actions of those of whom we read that they made use of the weapons, standards, uniforms, and tents of their enemies. *Joshua*, viii; Sylvester, word *bellum*, pt. 1, no. 9.

5. All these things are in fact of such a sort that they may be employed by any one at his discretion, even contrary to custom; for the custom itself was introduced by the choice of individuals, not as it were by universal consent, and such a custom constrains no one.

IX.—*The difficulty of the inquiry in respect to the second sort of deceit is indicated*

1. Of greater difficulty is the discussion with respect to those types of deceit which, if I may so say, are in common use among men in commerce and in which falsehood in the true sense is found.

[1] For so this is to be called, and not ἀπάτη, that is, 'deceit', according to Chrysostom in the work previously cited, *On the Priesthood*, I [I. ix].

The same author comments as follows *On First Corinthians*, iv. 6 [Homily XII, i]: 'Here there was no deceit, but a sort of obedience and management.' Also, in his comment on ix. 20 [Homily XXII, iii]: 'For that he might correct those who were in truth such, he himself became such, not in truth being other than what he was, but pretending to be, doing such things as they did, but not with the same purpose.' With this we may associate the pretended madness of David.

There are many injunctions against falsehood in Holy Writ. 'A righteous man', that is the good man, 'hateth lying' (*Proverbs*, xiii. 5); 'Remove far from me falsehood and lies' (*Proverbs*, xxx. 8); 'Thou wilt destroy them that speak lies' (*Psalms*, v. 6); 'Lie not one to another' (*Colossians*, iii. 9).

This point of view is rigidly maintained by Augustine; and even among the philosophers and poets there are those who are seen to be in sympathy with it. Well known is this saying of Homer: [*Iliad*, IX, 312 f.]

> To me as hateful as the jaws of Hell is he
> Whose mind thinks other than his tongue reveals.

[Fr. of *Creusa*, in Stobaeus, xii. 4.] [430] Sophocles says:

> What is foreign to truth it is never fitting to utter.
> Yet, if the telling of truth will bring sure doom to another,
> Pardon to him must be granted who does that which is not fitting.

[Menander, in Stobaeus, xii. 16 a.] Cleobulus has this line:

> Falsehood is hateful to him who in his heart is wise.

[*Nicom. Ethics*, IV. xiii.] Aristotle said: 'Falsehood in itself is base and worthy of censure, but truth is noble and deserving of praise.'

2. Nevertheless authority is not lacking in support of the opposite view also. In the first place in Holy Writ there are examples of men cited without a mark of censure;[1] and, in the second place, there are the declarations of the early Christians, Origen, Clement, Tertullian, Lactantius, Chrysostom, Jerome, and Cassian, indeed of nearly all, as Augustine himself acknowledges. Although disagreeing with them, he nevertheless recognizes that it is 'a great problem', 'a discussion full of dark places', 'a dispute in which the learned are at variance', to use words that are all his own. [*On Lying*, i. 1 and xviii. 38.]

3. Among the philosophers there stand openly on this side Socrates and his pupils Plato and Xenophon; at times, Cicero; if we may trust Plutarch and Quintilian, also the Stoics, who among the endowments of the wise man include ability to lie in the proper place and manner. In some places Aristotle too seems to agree with them, for his phrase 'in itself', which we have quoted, may be interpreted generally, that is, considering the thing without regard to attendant circumstances. The commentator upon Aristotle, Andronicus of Rhodes, thus speaks of the physician who lies to a sick man: 'He deceives indeed, but he is not a deceiver,' adding the reason: 'for his aim is not the deception of the sick man, but his cure'. [Plato, *Republic*, I, II and V. Xen., *Socrates*, IV [*Memorab.*, IV. ii. 16 ff.] Plutarch, *Contrad. of Stoics* [xlvii = p. 1055, 1056]. Quintilian, [*Inst.*,] XII. i [38]. *Nic. Eth.*, VII. iii; IV. viii [II. vii; IV. xiii]. [*On Nic. Ethics*, V. viii.]

[1] Irenaeus learned from the instruction of an ancient presbyter, and taught that: 'We should not become accusers in things which the Scriptures simply state, but do not censure.' The passage is in Book IV, chap. l [IV. xxxi].

4. Quintilian, whom I have mentioned, in defending this same view says that there are many things which are made honourable or base, not so much by the nature of the facts as by their causes. Says Diphilus : [*Inst. Or.*, XII. i. 36.] [Stobaeus, xii. 12.]

> The falsehood told for safety's sake,
> If I may judge, can cause no detriment.

In Sophocles, when Neoptolemus asks : [*Philoctetes*, 108 f.]

> Do you not think a lie is base ?

Ulysses answers :

> If safety from the lie arise, I do not.

Similar views may be cited from Pisander and Euripides. In Quintilian, again, I read : 'For to tell a lie is sometimes permissible even for the wise man.' Eustathius, Metropolitan of Thessalonica, commenting *On the Odyssey*, II, writes : 'The wise man will lie when occasion demands' ;[1] and on this point he adduces evidence from Herodotus and Isocrates. [Euripides, *Hecuba*, 247 f.] [*Inst. Or.*, II. xvii. 27.]

X.—*Not every use of an expression, which is known to be taken in another sense, is unpermissible*

1. Perhaps we may find some way of reconciling such divergent views in a wider or more strict interpretation of the meaning of falsehood. Thomas Aquinas, II. ii, qu. 110, art. 1. ans. to obj.

Adopting the point of view of Gellius when he distinguishes between telling an untruth and lying, we do not understand as a falsehood what an ignorant person happens to say ;[2] but we are concerned with that which is consciously uttered with a meaning that is at variance with the idea in the mind, whether in understanding or in an act of will. For ideas of the mind are what are primarily 'and immediately' indicated by words and similar signs; so he does not lie who says something untrue which he believes to be true, but he lies who says that which is indeed true but which he believes to be false. [431] Falsity of meaning, therefore, is that which we need to exemplify the general nature of falsehood. Gellius, XI. xi.

From this it follows that, when any term or phrase has 'several meanings', that is, may be understood in more than one way, either

[1] On occasion, as Donatus says, *On* [*Terence's*] *Brothers*, IV. iii. [IV. iii. 18]: 'And some writers on moral obligations think that it is right for one to deceive on occasion.' Cicero, *For Quintus Ligarius* [v. 16], calls such a falsehood 'an honourable and merciful lie'.

[2] 'Nothing except a guilty mind makes a guilty tongue', and 'No one is to be considered a liar who has said something false which he thinks to be true, because, so far as it is in his power, he himself does not deceive, but is deceived'. These are the words of Augustine, in his *On the Words of the Apostle*, XXVIII [=*Sermones de Scripturis*, clxxx. 2], and *Enchiridium*, xxii [xviii], cited by Gratian, in the *Decretum*, II. xxii. 1 [II. xxii. 2. 3 and 4].

from common usage, or the practice of an art, or some figure of speech easily understood, then, if the idea in mind fits one of these meanings, it is not held to be a lie, even if it is thought that he who hears it will understand it in another way.[1]

2. It is indeed true that the rash employment of such a mode of speech is not to be approved. It may nevertheless be justified by incidental causes, as, for instance, if thereby aid is rendered in the instruction of one who has been entrusted to our care, or in avoiding an unfair question.

John, xi. 11. Christ Himself gave an example of the former sort, when He said: 'Lazarus our friend is fallen asleep', which the Apostles understood as though it were said of the sleep of the living. Again, *John*, ii. 20–1. what He had said about rebuilding the Temple, meaning it in regard to His own body, He knew the Jews took with reference to the actual *Luke*, xxii. 30. Temple. Similarly when He promised to the Apostles twelve exalted seats next to the King, like judges of the tribes among the *Matthew*, xxvi. 25 [xxvi. 29]. Jews, and elsewhere that they should drink of a new wine in His Father's kingdom, He seems to have been fully aware that they took this to refer to none other than some kingdom in this life, with *Acts*, i. 6. the expectation of which they were filled until the very moment when Christ was about to ascend up into heaven. On another occa- [*Matthew*, xiii. 13.] sion also He spoke to the people through the indirectness of parables, that those who heard Him might not understand, unless, that is, they should bring thereto such earnestness of mind and readiness to be taught as were required.

Tacitus, *Annals*, VI [XI. xxxiv]. An example of the latter use may be given from profane history in the case of Lucius Vitellius, whom Narcissus pressed to explain his ambiguities and reveal the truth fully, but whom he could not force to refrain from giving replies that were dubious and capable of varied interpretation.[2] Here applies a saying of the Jews:[3] 'If any one knows how to use ambiguous language, it is well: but if not, let him remain silent.'

3. On the other hand, a case may arise when it is not only not praiseworthy but even wicked to employ such a mode of speech; as

[1] Just as [441] Abraham spoke deceptively to his servants; on this incident Ambrose [*On Abraham*, I. viii. 71] passes judgement with approval. He is followed by Gratian, after the afore-mentioned *Decretum*, II. xxii. 2. 20.

[2] The same Tacitus, *Histories*, III [III. iii], says: 'He spoke obscurely, with the intention of interpreting his words in such a way as might be advantageous.' Also [III. lii]: 'Having so phrased his statements that, according to the outcome, he might repudiate connexion with what was unfavourable, or assume credit for what was successful.'

[3] To the Jews belongs the following also: 'It is permissible to speak ambiguously for the sake of a good thing.' This is cited by the erudite Manasses Ben-Israel in his *Conciliator*, qu. xxxvii.

Chrysostom, *On the Priesthood*, I [I. ix. end], says: 'He is rightly called a deceiver who avails himself of such a means unjustly, but not he who does so for a beneficial purpose.'

when the glory of God,[1] or the love due to our neighbour,[2] or reverence toward a superior, or the nature of the thing in question requires that everything which is thought in the mind shall be completely
revealed. Just so in the case of contracts, we said that that must [II. xii. 9.
be made known which the nature of the contract is understood to
demand; and in this sense we may not inaptly interpret the rule [*On
of Cicero, 'All falsehood must be removed from matters of contract', *Duties*,
which is taken from the ancient Athenian law prohibiting 'the III. xv.
uttering of falsehoods in the market-place'. In these passages 61.]
apparently the word falsehood receives so broad a meaning that it Demosthenes,
covers even an obscure statement. But this, strictly speaking, we *Against Leptines*
have already excluded from the idea of a falsehood. [xx. 9 = 459.]

XI.—*The character of falsehood, in so far as it is unpermissible, consists in its conflict with the right of another; this is explained*

1. In order to exemplify the general idea of falsehood, it is necessary that what is spoken, or written, or indicated by signs or gestures, cannot be understood otherwise than in a sense which differs from the thought of him who uses the means of expression.

Upon this broader signification, however, a stricter meaning of falsehood must be imposed, carrying some characteristic distinction. This distinction, if we regard the matter aright, at least according to the common view of nations, can be described, we think, as nothing else than a conflict with the existing and continuing right of him to whom the speech or sign is addressed; for it is sufficiently clear that no one lies to himself, however false his statement may be.

By right in this connexion I do not mean every right without relation to the matter in question, but that which is peculiar [432] to it and connected with it. Now that right is nothing else than the liberty of judgement[3] which, as if by some tacit agreement, men who speak are understood to owe to those with whom they converse. For this is merely that mutual obligation which men had willed to introduce at the time when they determined to make use of speech

[1] Philo, *On the Life of Moses* [III. xxi]: 'I am speaking of things which concern the glory of God, in regard to which even one who is otherwise of a lying disposition must speak the truth. For truth is the companion of God.' Augustine, *Letters*, viii [xxviii. 3]: 'It is one question, whether a good man should ever lie; and another question, whether a writer of the Holy Scriptures should lie.' See what follows below in III. i. 15.

[2] Aeschylus, *Prometheus Bound* [lines 609 ff.]:

> Openly shall I say what you seek to hear,
> In simple speech, and not in dubious phrase,
> But as is right to hold discourse with friends.

[3] Hence the Hebrews say that he who takes away the means of knowing 'steals the heart'; *Genesis*, xxxi. 20, 26–7, with the commentary of Onkelos thereon, and the *Septuagint*. Also Rabbi David in his *Book of Roots*, Rabbi Salomon in his commentary, and Aben-Ezra.

and similar signs; for without such an obligation the invention of speech would have been void of result.

2. We require, moreover, that this right be valid and continuing at the time the statement is made; for it may happen that the right has indeed existed, but has been taken away, or will be annulled by another right which supervenes, just as a debt is cancelled by an acceptance or by the cessation of the condition. Then, further, it is required that the right which is infringed belong to him with whom we converse, and not to another, just as in the case of contracts also injustice arises only from the infringement of a right of the contracting parties.

Republic, I [v. end = 331 D]. Perhaps you would do well to recall here that Plato, following Simonides, refers truth-speaking to justice; that falsehood, at least the type of falsehood which is forbidden, is often described in Holy Writ as bearing false witness or speaking against one's neighbour; [*Enchiridium*, xxii.] and that Augustine himself in determining the nature of falsehood regards the will to deceive[1] as essential. *On Duties*, I [x. 31]. Cicero, too, wishes that inquiry in regard to speaking the truth be referred to the fundamental principles of justice.

3. Moreover, the right of which we have spoken may be abrogated by the express consent of him with whom we are dealing, as when one says that he will speak falsely and the other permits it. In like manner it may be cancelled by tacit consent, or consent assumed on reasonable grounds, or by the opposition of another right which, in the common judgement of all men, is much more cogent.

The right understanding of these points will supply to us many inferences, which will be of no small help in reconciling the differences in the views which have been cited above.

XII.—*The view is maintained that it is permissible to say what is false before infants and insane persons*

The first inference is that even if something which has a false significance is said to an infant or insane person no blame for falsehood attaches thereto. For it seems to be permitted by the common opinion of mankind that

Lucretius [I. 939]. The unsuspecting age of childhood may be mocked.

[*Institutes of Oratory*, XII. i. 38.] Quintilian, speaking of boys, said: 'For their profit we employ many fictions.' The reason is by no means far to seek; since infants and insane persons do not have liberty of judgement, it is impossible for wrong to be done them in respect to such liberty.

[1] Lactantius, *Institutes*, VI. xviii: 'Let him never lie in order to deceive or do harm.'

XIII.—*It is permissible to say what is false when he to whom the conversation is not addressed is deceived, and when it would be permissible to deceive him if not sharing in it*

1. The second inference is that, so long as the person to whom the talk is addressed is not deceived, if a third party draws a false impression therefrom there is no falsehood.

There is no falsehood in relation to him to whom the utterance is directed because his liberty remains unimpaired. His case is like that of persons to whom a fable is told when they are aware of its character, or those to whom figurative language is used in 'irony', or in 'hyperbole', a figure which, as Seneca says, reaches the truth by means of falsehood,[1] while Quintilian calls it a lying exaggeration. There is no falsehood, again, in respect to him who chances to hear what is said; the conversation is not being held with him, consequently there is no obligation toward him. Indeed if he forms for himself an opinion from what is said not to him, but to another, he has something which he can credit to himself, not to another. In fine, if, so far as he is concerned, we wish to form a correct judgement, the conversation is not a conversation, but something that may mean anything at all.

On Benefits, VII. xxiii. [*Inst. Or.*, VIII. vi. 67.]

2. Cato the censor therefore committed no wrong in falsely promising aid to his allies, nor did Flaccus, who said to others that a city of the enemy had been stormed by Aemilius, although in both cases the enemy was deceived. A similar ruse is told of Agesilaus by Plutarch. Nothing in fact was said to the enemy; the harm, moreover, which [433] followed was something foreign to the statement, and of itself not unpermissible to desire or to accomplish.

To this category Chrysostom and Jerome[2] refer Paul's speech, in which at Antioch he rebuked Peter for being too zealous a Jew. They think that Peter was well aware that this was not done in earnest; at the same time the weakness of those present was humoured.

Livy, XXXIV [xii]. Appian, *Spanish Wars* [xiii. 81]. [*Agesilaus*, xvii = p. 605 c.] [Chrysost. *On Gal.*, ii. 7–8; Jerome, *Letters*, cxvi. 10.] [*Galatians*, ii. 14.]

XIV.—*It is permissible to say what is false when the conversation is directed to him who wishes to be deceived in this way*

1. The third inference is that, whenever it is certain that he to whom the conversation is addressed will not be annoyed at the infringement of his liberty in judging, or rather will be grateful therefor, because of some advantage which will follow, in this case

[1] 'He makes unbelievable assertions, in order to arrive at what is believable.' Seneca, in the same passage.

[2] Also Cyril, *Against Julian*, IX, near the end. Not very differently also Tertullian, *Against Marcion*, Books I and III [I. xx; IV. iii].

also a falsehood in the strict sense, that is a harmful falsehood, is not perpetrated; just so a man does not commit theft who with the presumed consent of the owner uses up some trifling thing in order that he may thereby secure for the owner a great advantage.

In these matters which are so certain, a presumed wish is taken as one that is expressed. Besides, in such cases it is evident that no wrong is done to one who desires it. It seems, therefore, that he does not do wrong who comforts a sick friend by persuading him of what is not true, as Arria did by saying what was not true to Paetus after the death of their son; the story is told in the *Letters* of Pliny.[1] Similar is the case of the man who brings courage by a false report to one who is wavering in battle, so that, encouraged thereby, he wins victory and safety for himself, and is thus 'beguiled but not betrayed', as Lucretius says. [I. 941.]

[Stobaeus, xii. 13.] [*Training of Cyrus*, I. vi. 31.] [*Stromata*, VII. ix. 53.] [*Dissertations*, xix. 3.]

2. Democritus says: 'We must speak the truth, wherever that is the better course.' Xenophon writes: 'It is right to deceive our friends, if it is for their good.' Clement of Alexandria concedes 'the use of lying as a curative measure'. Maximus of Tyre says: 'A physician deceives a sick man, a general deceives his army, and a pilot the sailors; and in such deception there is no wrong.' The reason is given by Proclus in commenting on Plato: 'For that which is good is better than the truth.'

Socrates, IV [*Memorabilia*, IV. ii. 17]. Livy, XXXIV [I. xxvii. 8]. [Livy, II lxiv. 6.]

To this class of untruths belong the statement reported by Xenophon,[2] that the allies would presently arrive; that of Tullus Hostilius, that the army from Alba was making a flank movement by his order; what histories term the 'salutary lie' of the consul Quinctius, that the enemy were in flight on the other wing; and similar incidents found in abundance in the writings of the historians. However, it is to be observed that in this sort of falsehood the infringement upon the judgement is of less account because it is usually confined to the moment, and the truth is revealed a little later.

XV.—*It is permissible to say what is false when the speaker makes use of a superior right over one subject to himself*

1. A fourth inference, akin to the foregoing, applies to the case when one who has a right that is superior to all the rights of another[3] makes use of this right either for his own or for the public

[1] III. xvi.

[2] 'And when Agesilaus had come into Boeotia and had learned that Pisander had been beaten in a naval battle by Pharnabazus and Conon he gave orders that the opposite should be told to his troops; and he came forth wearing a wreath, and he offered sacrifice as if in gratitude for a victory.' Plutarch, *Agesilaus* [xvii = p. 605 c].

[3] In the *Iliad*, II [II. 73 f.], Agamemnon the leader of the Greeks says:

> But first I shall prove the Greeks with words, as my right is,
> And bid them swiftly to flee with their brazen ships.

good. This especially Plato seems to have had in mind when he conceded the right of saying what is false to those having authority. Since the same author seems now to grant this privilege to physicians,[1] and again to deny it to them, apparently we ought to make the distinction that in the former passage he means physicians publicly appointed to this responsibility, and in the latter those who privately claim it for themselves. Yet Plato also rightly recognizes that falsehood is not becoming to deity, although deity has a supreme right over men, because it is a mark of weakness to take refuge in such devices.

Republic, III [iii = 389 D].

[*Republic,* II = 382 D E.]

2. An instance of blameless mendacity, of which even Philo approves, may perhaps be found in Joseph,[2] who, when ruling in the king's stead, accused his brothers first of being spies, and then of being thieves, pretending, but not really believing, that they were such. Another instance is that of Solomon, who gave an example of wisdom inspired by God, when to the women who were disputing over the child he uttered the words which indicated his purpose to slay it, although his real intent was the furthest possible from such a course, and his desire was to assign to the true mother her own offspring. [434] There is a saying of Quintilian: 'Sometimes the common good requires that even falsehoods should be upheld.'

[*On Joseph,* xxviii.]

[*1 Kings,* iii. 25.]

II. xviii [*Inst. Or.,* II. xvii. 36].

XVI.—*It is perhaps permissible to say what is false when we are unable in any other way to save the life of an innocent person, or something else of equal importance*

A fifth inference may be applicable to cases where the life of an innocent person, or something else of equal importance, cannot be saved without falsehood, and another person can in no other way be diverted from the accomplishment of a wicked crime.[3] Such was the deed of Hypermnestra, who is often lauded for this reason:

> Nobly false[4] and for all time
> A maiden famed.

Horace, *Odes,* III. xi [35].

[1] [442] Chrysostom, in the aforementioned *On the Priesthood,* I [I. ix], adduces examples of physicians.

[2] 'When with pretended severity he accuses his brothers of espionage', says Cassiodorus [Peter of Blois] in his *On Friendship.*

[3] Augustine, *On Psalm V* [§ 7], cited by Gratian, in *Decretum,* II. xxii. 2. 14, says: 'There are, however, two sorts of lies in which there is no great fault, yet which are not entirely free from fault. The one sort is told when we are joking, the other when we lie for the benefit of our neighbour. Now the first sort, which consists in a joke, is not so dangerous, because it does not deceive. For he to whom it is told knows that it has been told in jest. But the second sort of lie is still less dangerous, because it contains some element of kindness.'

Tertullian, *On Modesty* [chap. xix], classes among the sins of daily occurrence, to which we are all subject, the necessity of lying.

[4] On this the Scholiast comments: 'Fittingly. For it is noble to lie for the sake of justice.' Of like tenor is what Chrysostom [*On Penitence,* VII. v] says of Rahab: 'O fair falsehood, O praiseworthy deception, not of one who breaks divine commands, but of one who is a guardian of the truth', or, as other manuscripts have it, 'guardian of true piety'.

Republic, II [xxi = 382 c]; *Training of Cyrus*, II [I. vi. 28], and *Socrates*, V [*Memorabilia*, IV. ii. 16]; Philo, *On the Migr. of Abr.* [*On the Cherubim*, v]; Chrysostom, *On the Priesthood*, I [viii]; *1 Samuel*, xi [10]; *1* [*2*] *Kings*, vi. 18 ff. [Frontinus, *Stratagems*, II. iv. 9]. [*Inst. Or.*, XII. i. 39]. Thomas, II. ii, qu. 110, art. 1 and 3; Covarruvias, *On Sext.*, I. xviii. 2, pt. 1, § 5, no. 15; Soto, *De Iustitia*, V, qu. 6, art. 2; Toledo, IV. xxi; V. lviii; Lessius, *De Iustitia*, II. xlii, dub. 9.

XVII.—*The authors who have judged that falsehood spoken in the presence of enemies is permissible*

1. The principle which the learned generally lay down, that it is permissible to speak falsely to an enemy, goes beyond what we have just said. Accordingly, to the rule forbidding a lie the exception, unless against enemies, is added by Plato and Xenophon; also by Philo among the Jews, and by Chrysostom among the Christians.[1] To this exception you would perhaps refer the lie of the men of Jabesh when under siege, as recorded in Holy Writ, and the similar deception on the part of the prophet Elisha;[2] also that of Valerius Laevinus, who boasted that he had slain Pyrrhus.

2. To the third, fourth, and fifth of the conclusions which we have stated, applies the passage of Eustratius, Metropolitan of Nicaea, *On Nicomachean Ethics*, Book VI [VI. ix]:

> He who gives good counsel does not necessarily speak the truth. It can in fact happen that he who plans aright makes falsehood itself a part of his plan, that he may lie intentionally, either to an enemy, in order to deceive him, or to a friend, to deliver the friend from evil; historical narratives are full of instances of this sort.

Quintilian says that, if a footpad must be deterred from killing a man, or if an enemy must be deceived to save the country, we shall find it necessary to praise in the wise man himself conduct that otherwise we should have to censure in slaves.

3. These doctrines do not meet with the approval of the school of writers of recent times, since in almost all matters they have chosen to follow Augustine[3] alone of the teachers of antiquity. But the same school admits of unspoken interpretations, which are so repugnant to all practice that one may question whether it would not be more satisfactory to admit to certain persons the use of falsehoods in the cases we have mentioned, or in some of them (for I assume that nothing has been settled here), than so indiscriminately to exempt such interpretations from the definition of falsehood. Thus when they say 'I do not know', it may be understood as 'I do

In regard to the Egyptian midwives, Augustine [*On Heptateuch*, II, beginning] says: 'O great instinct of humanity, O pious lie uttered to save life!' Jerome, *On Ezekiel*, xxvii [xxxviii] and *On Isaiah*, lvi [lxv], praises these same midwives and believes that rewards, even eternal rewards, have been given to them. Also Ambrose, *Letters*, VI [V. 10], *To Syagrius*, and Augustine himself, *Against Lying*, *To Consentius*, chap. xv, varying, as often.

Tostado denies that there is sin in this. Augustine, *On Exodus*, II [*On Heptateuch*, II. i], and Thomas Aquinas, II. ii, qu. 110, art. 55, ans. to obj. 4, and Cajetan thereon, are doubtful. See, if you have the time, Erasmus, in his *Praise of Folly*, and the erudite Maes, *On Joshua*, ii. 5.

[1] He speaks thus: 'If you should call to account the most eminent generals, you would find that most of their victories have been won through deception; and yet such generals receive more praise than those who have won by open warfare.'

[2] A similar act of the same Elisha is recorded in *2 Kings*, viii. 10, according to the reading of the Masorites, which is followed by the Latin Vulgate version.

[3] Augustine's later view in this matter has been opposed by the Abbot Rupert.

not know so as to tell you'; and when they say 'I have not' it may be understood as 'so as to give you'; and other things of this sort which the common sense of mankind repudiates, and which, if admitted, will offer no obstacle to our saying that whoever affirms anything denies it himself, and whoever denies affirms.

4. It is assuredly quite true that in general there is no word which may not have a doubtful meaning;[1] for all words, in addition to the significance which is called that of the first notion, have another of a second notion,[2] and this significance varies in the different arts;[3] moreover, words have different meanings also in metaphor and other figures of speech.

Again, I do not approve of the view of those who apply the term jokes to falsehoods which are uttered with a particularly serious expression and tone, as if they shrank from the word rather than the thing.

XVIII.—*The use of falsehood is not to be extended to statements containing a promise*

We must, however, bear in mind that what we have said regarding falsehood is to be applied to assertions, and such indeed as injure no one but a public enemy, but not to promises.[4] For by a promise, as we have just begun to say, a new and particular right is conferred upon him to whom the promise is made.

This holds true even among enemies, without any [435] exception arising from the hostility existing at the time. It holds true not only in the case of promises actually expressed, but also in the case of those that are implied, as we shall show in discussing the demand for a parley when we come to the part that deals with the observing of good faith in warfare.

XIX.—*The use of falsehood is not to be extended to oaths*

This also must be repeated from the portion of our foregoing discussion which dealt with the subject of oaths, that whether the oath is assertive or promissory it has the force to exclude all exceptions which might be sought in the person of him with whom we are dealing. The reason is that an oath establishes a relation not only [II. xiii.]

[1] This view is supported by Chrysippus in Gellius, [*Attic Nights*,] XI. xii. It is championed also by Seneca, *On Benefits*, II. xxxiv: 'There is a vast number of things without name which we do not designate by characteristic terms, but by convenient borrowed names.'

[2] Augustine, *De Magistro* [vii. 20]: 'We have learned of no symbol which, among the things that it signifies, does not signify itself also.'

[3] See what we have noted above, on III. i. 10.

[4] Agesilaus, and with him Plutarch [*Agesilaus*, ix = p. 600 D], make this distinction: [443] 'To violate sworn agreements is to despise the gods. Otherwise, to deceive the enemy with words is not only just but glorious, and brings glory and satisfaction together with gain.'

with a man, but also with God, to whom we are bound by the oath, even if no right arises for the man.

In the same place we have furthermore stated that in an oath we do not, as we do in other speech, admit that interpretations not wholly without warrant may be put upon words, in order to absolve us from falsehood; but we do require that the truth be spoken with the meaning which a man listening is supposed to understand in perfect good faith. Obviously, then, we must abhor the impiety of those who did not hesitate to assert that it is proper to deceive men by oaths just as boys do by means of dice.

XX.—*Nevertheless it is more noble, and more becoming to Christian simplicity, to refrain from falsehood even toward an enemy; this view is illustrated by comparisons*

1. We know, too, that certain types of fraud, which we have said were naturally permitted, have been rejected by some peoples and persons. But this does not happen because they view such means of deception as unjust, but because of a remarkable loftiness of mind, and, in some cases, because of confidence in their strength. There is in Aelian a saying of Pythagoras, that in two things man comes very close to God, in speaking the truth at all times and in doing good to others; and in Iamblichus veracity is called a guide to all good things, divine and human. For Aristotle 'the magnanimous man is a lover of free speech and of the truth'. For Plutarch 'to lie is worthy of a slave'.[1]

[*Various History*, XII. lix.] [*Protrepticon*, xx.] *Nic. Eth.*, IV. viii. [*On Ed. of Children*, = p. 11 c.]

Arrian says of Ptolemy: 'And for him, who was a king, it was more disgraceful to lie than for another.' In the same author, Alexander declares: 'The king must speak nothing but the truth to his subjects.' Mamertinus says of Julian: 'In our emperor there is a marvellous agreement between mind and tongue. He knows that lying is not only a mark of a low and mean spirit, but also a slavish vice; and in truth, since want or fear makes men liars, the emperor who lies is ignorant of the greatness of his fortune.' In Plutarch, praise is given to Aristides' 'character rooted in firm morality and tenacious of justice, not even resorting to falsehood in any kind of sport'. Of Epaminondas Probus says that he was 'so devoted to truth that he did not lie even in jest'.

[*Anabasis of Alexander*], I [preface]. VII [v]. [*Panegyric of Julian*, xx.] [*Aristides*, ii = p. 319 D.] [Nepos, *Epaminondas*, iii.]

2. This point of view assuredly is all the more to be insisted on by Christians; for not only is simplicity enjoined upon them (*Matthew*, x. 16), but vain speaking is forbidden (*Matthew*, xii. 36);

[1] Philo, in the book *That Every Virtuous Man is Free* [xxi], says: 'Whence men are accustomed to style illiberal, and of a servile mind, those who are two-faced and deceptive.'

and He is set for their example in whose mouth no guile was found. Lactantius says: 'And so the true and upright traveller will not quote that saying of Lucilius: [*Divine Institutes*, VI. xviii.]

I lie not to a man who is my friend and intimate.

But he will think that he should not lie even to an enemy and a stranger; nor will he ever consent that his tongue, the interpreter of his mind, shall disagree with his meaning and thought.'

Of like opinion is Neoptolemus in the *Philoctetus* of Sophocles 'excelling in simplicity and nobleness', as Dio of Prusa rightly observes, for to Ulysses, who urges him to practise deception, he thus replies: [*Orations*, lii = p. 552.] [Sophocles, *Philoctetes*, 86 ff.]

Child of Laertes, what plans with grief I hear
With far more loathing would I carry out;
For to devise deceits I was not born, [436] nor he
Of by-gone days, my sire, as men relate;[1]
But by main force, not wiles, the captive to bear off,
Prepared am I.

Euripides in the *Rhesus* says: [510 f.]

Upon the foe a noble soul cannot inflict
A guileful death.

3. Thus Alexander declared that he would not steal a victory. Polybius relates that the Achaeans shrank from all deceit against the enemy, because they considered that the only sure victory which, if I may express his meaning in the words of Claudian, [Plutarch, *Alex.*, xxxi = p. 683 D.] IX [XIII. iii.]

Conquers foes whose minds have been subdued. [*On the Sixth Consulship of Honorius*, 249.]

Such was the attitude of the Romans almost to the close of the second Punic War. Aelian records that 'The Romans know that they are brave, and that they have not overcome their foes by artifice . . . and trickery'. Hence when Perseus, king of Macedon, was deceived by hopes of peace, the elder senators declared that they did not recognize the methods of the Romans, that the ancestors of these never boasted that they had waged war more by craft than by courage; that it had been the Roman method to wage war not by the ruses of the Carthaginians, nor by the subtlety of the Greeks, who would esteem it [*Various History*, XII. xxxiii.] [Livy, XLII. xlvii. 4–8.]

[1] Achilles, of whom Horace says, *Odes*, IV. vi [lines 13 ff.]:

He did not hide in the horse which feigned to be
An offering to Minerva, to deceive the Trojans
In untimely festivals, and the court of Priam
Gay with choral dances;
But openly he fought, and harsh was he to the captives.

See also what follows, upon which the Scholiast remarks: 'Achilles never fought by underhand means, but always openly, in reliance upon his valour.' Note the phrase 'In reliance upon his valour', which fits excellently with what we have said in the text at the beginning of this paragraph.

more glorious to outwit an enemy than to overcome him by force. Then they added the following:

> In some cases, for the moment, more is accomplished by deceit than by valour, but only his mind is forever conquered from whom the confession has been extorted that he has been conquered not by artifice, nor by chance, but after joining forces in battle in a just and righteous war.

Annals, II [lxxxviii]. Scholiast on Apollonius, II [1010]. [VII. ix.]

Later we read also in Tacitus: 'The Roman people takes vengeance on its enemies, not by fraud, nor in secret, but openly with arms in hand.' Such men were the Tibareans also, who even agreed upon the place and time of battle. In Herodotus Mardonius makes a similar assertion regarding the Greeks of his time.

XXI.—*It is not permissible for us to force any one to do what is right for us but not for him*

To the conduct of operations this principle also applies, that it is not permissible to force or to entice any one to anything which may not be permissible for him to do.[1] The following may serve as examples. It is not permissible for a subject to slay his king, nor to surrender towns without public consent, nor to despoil his fellow-citizens. Therefore it is not permissible to influence a subject, who remains such, to do these things. For he who gives to another cause to sin always sins himself as well.

[*On the Customs of the Catholic Church*, II. xvii. 57.]

It is not enough to urge in reply that for him who forces such a man to a crime an act of this kind, as the killing of an enemy, is legitimate. The deed it is in fact permissible for him to compass, but not in this way. Augustine well says: 'It makes no difference whether you yourself commit the crime, or whether you wish another to commit it for you.'

XXII.—*Nevertheless we may make use of assistance voluntarily offered*

Dig. XLI. i. 51.

The case is different when for a thing which is permissible for him a person avails himself of the help of one who does wrong voluntarily and not at his instigation. That this is not wicked we have proved elsewhere by the example of God Himself.[2] 'We receive a deserter by the law of war', says Celsus; that is, it is not contrary to the law of war for us to receive him who abandons the side of the enemy and chooses our own.[3]

[1] This is also the teaching of Maimonides in *Halakot Toubal*, v. 10.

[2] In II. xxvi. 5.

[3] And such persons are not to be surrendered, unless this has been agreed upon in the terms of peace, as in the peace with Philip, the Aetolians, and Antiochus. See Polybius, *Selections on Embassies*, ix, xxviii and xxxv [=*Histories*, XVIII. xliv; XXI. xxx; XXI. xlv]. Menander Protector also supports this view [frag. 11, p. 22, edit. Dindorf].

CHAPTER II

HOW BY THE LAW OF NATIONS THE GOODS OF SUBJECTS MAY BE HELD FOR THE DEBT OF THEIR RULERS; AND THEREIN, ON REPRISALS

I.—*By natural law no one except an heir is bound by the act of another*

1. Let us proceed to principles derived from the law of nations. These principles relate in part to war in general, and in part to a particular aspect of war. Let us begin with the general considerations.

By the strict law of nature no one is bound by another's act, except one who inherits his property; for the principle that property should be transferred with its obligations dates from the establishment of proprietary rights.[1] The Emperor Zeno says that it is contrary to natural justice for persons to be harassed for the debts of strangers. [*Code*, XI. lvii. 1.] Hence the titles in the Roman Law; the wife is not to be sued for her husband, nor the husband for his wife, the son for his father, nor the father or mother for their son. [*Code*, IV. xii, xiii.]

2. The debt of the corporation, moreover, is not a debt of the individuals, [444] as Ulpian well declares, especially if the corporation has property; [*Dig.* III. iv. 7. § 1.] for the rest the members of a corporation are bound not as individuals, but as a part of the corporate body. Seneca says: 'If any one lends money to my country, I shall not say that I am his debtor, nor will I admit this is my loan; yet I shall give my share towards paying it off'.[2] [*On Benefits*, VI. xx] He had previously said: 'As one of the people I shall not pay as though for myself, but I shall contribute as for my country'; [VI. xix.] also, 'Individuals will be indebted not as if for their personal debt, but for a share of the public debt.' [[VI] xix.]

Hence in the Roman Law it was specifically provided that no member of a village should be held for the debts of other villagers; [*Code*, XI. lvii. 1.] and elsewhere it is ordered that no property of one person is to be sued for the debts of others even if public debts. [*Code*, XII. lx. 4.] In a novel of Justinian, 'pledge-taking',[3] that is, the taking of sureties for others, is forbidden, and the reason given is that it is not reasonable for one person to be the debtor and another to be made to pay. [*Novels*, lii and cxxxiv [7].] Here also exactions of this sort are called hateful. King Theodoric, in Cassiodorus, calls it disgraceful to permit one person to give sureties for another. [*Variae*, IV [x].]

1 See above, II. xxi. 19. Add *Decretals*, V. xvii. 5; *Decretals*, V. xix. 9.

2 See the *Law of Sicily*, Book I [title c].

3 *Sext*, V. viii. 1: 'Sureties which current speech commonly calls reprisals (*repressalias*).' It would be more correct to write, as certain books do, *reprensalias*, for this corresponds exactly to the Saxon word 'withernam', but usage has accepted the other.

II.—*Nevertheless it has been established by the law of nations that both the possessions and the acts of subjects are liable for the debt of a ruler*

1. Although what has just been stated is true, nevertheless by the volitional law of nations there could be introduced, and appears to have been introduced, the principle that for what any civil society, or its head, ought to furnish, whether for itself directly, or because it has bound itself for the debt of another by not fulfilling the law, for all this there are held and made liable all the corporeal or incorporeal possessions of those who are subject to such a society or its head.

This principle, furthermore, is the outgrowth of a certain necessity, because otherwise a great licence to cause injury would arise; the reason is that in many cases the goods of rulers cannot so easily be seized as those of private persons, who are more numerous. This then finds place among those rights which, as Justinian says, have been established by civilized nations in response to the demands of usage and human needs.

Institutes, I. ii. 2.

2. This principle, however, is not so in conflict with nature that it could not have been introduced by custom and tacit consent, since sureties are bound without any cause, merely by their consent. It was hoped that members of the same society would be able through mutual relations to obtain justice from one another, and provide for their indemnification, more easily than foreigners, to whom in many places slight consideration is given. Hence the advantage derived from this obligation was common to all peoples, so that he who might now be burdened by it at another time might in turn be relieved.

Thomas Aquinas, II. ii, qu. 40, art. 1; Molina, disp. 120 and 121; Valentia, *Disputations*, iii, qu. 16, no. 3; Navarrus, xxvii, no. 136.

3. That this usage has been accepted, appears from the perfect wars[1] which peoples wage against peoples. The practice observed in such wars is in fact revealed by the formulas of declaration, as: 'I declare and make war upon the peoples of the ancient Latins and the men of the ancient Latins,' and in the question 'whether they wished and ordered that war be declared upon King Philip and the Macedonians who were under his rule'. It is evidenced also by the decree itself, as, 'The Roman People orders that war be waged upon the people of the Hermunduri and upon men of the Hermunduri', which is cited from Cincius on military affairs; and elsewhere, as, 'Let him be an enemy, and also those who are within his defences.'

Livy, I [xxxii. 13]. Livy, XXXI [vi. 1]. Gellius, XVI. iv. Livy, XXXVIII [xlviii. 9], and elsewhere.

[1] The wise Nicholas of Damascus distinguishes wars from seizures of this sort, in showing that Herod, who had no right to make war upon the Arabs, could 'take reprisals' (ῥύσια λαμβάνειν) to use as a pledge for what was due to him in accordance with a contract. The words are those of Josephus, *Antiquities of the Jews*, VI [XVI. x. 8], where we find also this: [448] 'After relating that five hundred talents were owed to Herod, and that the written bond regarding these stipulated that when the day appointed had passed Herod could seize sureties from all the territory of the Arabs, he [Nicholas] declared that this invasion was not an invasion, but the just collection of a debt.'

We see that the same right is invoked also where a state of perfect war has not yet been reached, but where nevertheless there is need of an enforcement of a right by violent means, that is, by means of an imperfect war. Long ago Agesilaus said to Pharnabazus, who was a subject of the king of Persia: 'Formerly, Pharnabazus, when we were friends of the king, we treated his possessions as became friends; now that we have become enemies, we treat them as belonging to a foe. Since, therefore, we see that even you desire to be classed among the king's possessions, we do right to strike at him through you.' Plutarch, *Agesilaus* [xii = p. 602 D E], and Xenophon, *Greek History*, IV [*Hellenica*, IV. i. 34 ff.].

[445] III.—*An example in the seizure of persons*

1. One form of the enforcement of right regarding which I am speaking was what the Athenians called 'seizure of men'. Of this a law of Attica said: 'If any one die by a violent death, for his sake it shall be right for his relatives and next of kin to proceed to apprehend men, until either the penalty has been paid for the murder, or the murderers are given up. Such seizure may extend to three persons, and no more.' [Demosthenes, *Against Aristocrates*, xxiii. 82 = p. 647.] Here we see that for the debt of the state, which is bound to punish its subjects who have injured others, there is put under obligation a certain incorporeal right of its subjects, that is, their liberty of remaining where they wish and of doing what they wish; in consequence such subjects are temporarily in servitude, until the state does that which it is bound to do, that is, until it punishes the one who is guilty.

Although the Egyptians, as we learn from Diodorus Siculus, [I. lxxix.] used to maintain that neither a person nor his liberty should be bound for a debt, nevertheless there is nothing in this that is repugnant to nature, and the practice not only of the Greeks, but of other nations also, has prevailed to the contrary.

2. Aristocrates, the contemporary of Demosthenes, had proposed a decree to permit the apprehension anywhere of any one who should slay Charidemus, and to number among the public enemies any who should resist such seizure. In this proposal Demosthenes criticizes many points: first, that Aristocrates did not distinguish between killing justly and killing unjustly, although sometimes it may be just to kill; secondly, that he did not require that a trial be previously demanded; and, further, that he wished those who received the homicide to be held responsible and not those among whom the killing was done. The words of Demosthenes are: [*Against Aristocrates*, xxiii. 84–5 = p. 648.]

For the law ordains that if those, among whom the wrong is suffered, do not pay the penalty nor surrender the culprits, these shall be apprehended to the number of three. But he lets these indeed go unpunished, and makes no mention of them; while he proposes that those shall be outlawed who have received the murderer when he has taken refuge with them if they do not freely surrender him; I shall state the case in accordance with the custom common to mankind, which bids us receive the fugitive.

The fourth point of criticism is that Aristocrates at once brings the matter to a state of perfect war, when the law would have been satisfied with an arrest.

3. Of these criticisms the first, second, and fourth are not without reason. But the third objection, unless it is restricted to the single case of killing by accident or in self-defence, can only have been offered rhetorically, and more for the sake of argument than according to truth and right. For the law of nations that suppliants
II. xxi. 7 [5]. shall be received and protected applies, as we have previously said, only to those who are endangered by ill fortune and not by crime.

4. In other respects the law is the same for those among whom the crime has been committed and for those who refuse to punish or surrender the guilty person. Therefore either that very law, on which Demosthenes relies, received from practice the interpretation that I give, or afterward it was more explicitly formulated against such quibbles. That one of these alternatives is true will not be denied by any one who has given attention to the following definition
[*Onomasticon,*] VIII. vi [VIII. 1.] of Julius Pollux: 'Seizure of men takes place when any one upon demand does not receive murderers who have fled to some persons for refuge, for in that case he has the right [446] to carry off as many as three persons of those who have not surrendered the culprits.'
[under word ἀνδρο-ληψία.] In the same sense Harpocration says: 'Seizure of men is the right to carry off men from some city. For they used to take sureties from a city which held a murderer and would not give him up for punishment.'

5. Similar to this right of seizure is the right of detention of citizens of another state in which a manifest wrong has been done to a national, in order to secure his recovery. Accordingly at Carthage certain persons prevented the seizure of Ariston of Tyre, giving it
Livy, XXXIV [lxi. 13]. as their reason that 'The same thing will happen to Carthaginians both at Tyre and in the other commercial centres to which they go in large numbers'.

IV.—*An example in the seizure of goods*

Baldus, *Consilia,* III. 58; Bartolus, *On Reprisals,* qu. v, ans. to obj. 3, no. 9. Another form of the enforcement of right by violence is 'seizure of goods' or 'the taking of pledges between different peoples'.[1] This is called by the more modern jurists the right of reprisals; by the Saxons and Angles 'withernam', and by the French, among whom such seizure is ordinarily authorized by the king, 'letters of

[1] This is called σύλας by Demosthenes in his oration *For the Crown* [*For the Crown of the Trierarchy,* li. 13 = p. 1232]; also by Aristotle, *Economics,* II [II. ii. 10].

marque'. This enforcement of right occurs, as the jurists say, where a right is denied.

V.—*Seizure is warranted after a right has been denied, and when it may properly be considered as settled that this has been done; wherein it is shown that a judicial decision does not properly give or take away a right*

1. Seizure by violence may be understood to be warranted not only in case a judgement cannot be obtained against a criminal or a debtor within a reasonable time, but also if in a very clear case (for in a doubtful case the presumption is in favour of those who have been chosen by the state to render judgement) judgement has been rendered in a way manifestly contrary to law; for the authority of the judge has not the same force over foreigners as over subjects.

Even among subjects such a decision does not cancel a true obligation. 'A true debtor, even though he is absolved, still remains a debtor by the law of nature,'[1] says Paul the jurist. 'And when *Dig.* XII. vi. 60.
by a wrongful decision of a judge a creditor had taken away from its owner, as if it had been bound over to him, property which did not belong to the debtor, and the question was raised whether, after the payment of the debt, this should be restored to the debtor, Scaevola *Dig.* XX. v. 12. § 1.
approved of its restitution.' There is this difference, that subjects cannot legally hinder by force the execution of a judgement even if it is unjust, or assert their rights by force against it, because of the effectiveness of the authority over them; but foreigners have the right of compulsion, which they may not use, however, so long as they can obtain what is theirs by a judgement. Innocent and Panormitanus, *On Decretals*, III. xlix. 8; Soto, III, qu. iv, art. 5.

2. The principle, therefore, was not introduced by nature, but has been widely accepted in practice, that for such a cause the persons,[2] or movable property, of the subjects of him who does not render justice, may be seized. The most ancient instance is given by Homer, in the *Iliad* [XI. 674]. Here it is recounted that Nestor seized the flocks and herds of the men of Elis in revenge for the horses stolen from his father, 'taking reprisals',[3] as the Poet Jac. de Can., Ancharano, Domin., Franciscus, *On Sext*, V. viii. 1; Fulgosius and Salic., *On Auth., Code*, IV. x; Jac. de Belvisio, *On Auth., Ut non fiant pignora*;

[1] Here applies what is said by Gail, *De Pace Publica*, II. viii. 7, and Vázquez, *Controversiae illustres*, IV. x. 41.

[2] See the example in Ammianus, Book XVII [XVIII. ii], where Julian detains certain of the Franks until the prisoners should be set free according to the agreement. Add what Leo of Africa has on the subject of Mt. Beni Gualid, Book III [= p. 435].

[3] You will find *ῥύσια* in this sense in the *Selections on Embassies*, from Polybius, no. xxxviii [=p. 276], where he speaks of the Achaeans acting against the Boeotians; and in no. cxxiii [= p. 352] *ῥυσιάζειν* is found in the *Excerpta Peiresciana* [*Excerpta de Virtutibus et Vitiis*, I = p. 214] from Diodorus Siculus. Elsewhere, however, the phrase *ῥύσια καταγγέλλειν* is employed in speaking of war, as we shall say shortly in III. iii. 7; for these things are closely connected.

Syl., word *repressalia*; Bartolus, *On Reprisals*; Guy de la Pape, qu. xxxii; Gail, *De Pigno.*, i no. 5; Victoria, *De Iure Belli*, no. 41; Covarruvias, *On Sext*, V. ult. 4, pt. ii, § 9. [Homer, *Iliad*, XI. 705.] Livy, II [xxxiv. 4]. Halicar., VII [xii].

says; in this passage Eustathius explains 'reprisals' as 'what is confiscated in return for something, that is, dragged off and seized in return for what has been previously taken'. The narrative goes on to say that all those to whom anything was owed by the Eleans were summoned by proclamation to secure their rights, surely,

Lest any one of his just due should be deprived.

Another instance is in Roman history, in the case of the Roman ships which Aristodemus, the heir of the Tarquins, held at Cumae as compensation for the property of the Tarquins. Dionysius of Halicarnassus states that slaves, cattle, and money were held. Still another instance is given by Aristotle, in the second book of the *Economics*, on the law of the Carthaginians relating to seizure of the ships of foreigners, 'if any one has a right of seizure', as the condition is there expressed.

VI.—*Such seizure does not warrant the taking of human life*

That for such a cause the lives of innocent subjects are liable, has perhaps been believed among some peoples, because [447] they supposed that every man has in himself a full right over his life, and that it was possible to transfer this to the state. That supposition, as we have elsewhere said, is by no means capable of proof, nor is it in harmony with a more sound theology.

[II. xv. 16; xxi. 11.]

Nevertheless it may happen that those who wish by force to hinder the enforcement of a right may be killed, not intentionally but accidentally. But if this can be foreseen, we have shown elsewhere that we ought rather to surrender the furthering of the right, in accordance with the law of love. According to this law, particularly for Christians, the life of a man ought to be of greater value than our property, as has been proved in another connexion.

I [II]. i. 12 and 13.

VII.—*The distinction between what there is relating to this matter in municipal law and in the law of nations*

1. In this matter, no less than in others, we must take care not to confuse the things which properly belong to the law of nations and those which are established by municipal law or treaties between peoples.

2. By the law of nations all subjects of him who does the injury are liable to the furnishing of sureties, provided they are subjects from a permanent cause, whether native or immigrant, and not persons who are present anywhere for the purpose of travel or for a brief residence. The furnishing of pledges is treated after the manner of burdens which are imposed in order to pay the public debts, and from which those are immune who are only temporarily

Decio, *Consilia*, ccclii; Baldus, *On Digest*, I. xxii. 3.

subject to the laws of the place. However, ambassadors are excepted by the law of nations from the number of subjects, provided that they have not been sent to our enemies; and their goods also are excepted.

3. By the municipal law of states, however, the persons of women and children are often excepted; and in fact even the property of those who are engaged in literary pursuits or come to carry on trade. By the law of nations individuals possess the right of taking sureties, as at Athens, in the seizure of men. By the municipal law of many countries this right is ordinarily sought in some cases from the supreme authority, in other cases from judges.

By the law of nations ownership is acquired over seized goods by the mere act of seizure, up to the limit of the debt and expenditure, in such a way that the residue shall be restored.[1] By the municipal law the parties concerned are usually summoned, and afterwards by public authority the property is sold or assigned to those who are affected. But for these and other topics reference should be made to those who discuss the municipal codes; on this subject particularly Bartolus, who has written on reprisals.

4. A further statement I shall add, because it concerns the mollification of this law, which is in itself sufficiently rigorous. Those who, by not paying what they owe or by not furnishing satisfaction, have given occasion for the taking of sureties, by natural and divine law are bound to make good the damages [2] to others, who for that reason have incurred a loss.

Aegidius Regius, *De Actibus Supernaturalibus*, disp. 13, dub. 7, no. 117.

[1] Gregoras, Book IX [IX. v], records that the Venetians followed this principle of justice, upon the capture of the Genoese ships at Galata: 'But they did not destroy any of the cargo of the ships they had taken, which cargo consisted of wheat and barley, and in addition salt fish from the Copaic and Maeotic Marshes and the river Don. These they preserved with care, in their full measure, until they should restore them intact upon the receipt of what was owed them.'

[2] Plutarch, in his *Cimon* [viii = p. 483 C], says of the Scyrians: 'The majority did not wish to make a monetary contribution, but they gave orders that those who possessed or had seized the property of others should make good the loss.'

CHAPTER III

ON WAR THAT IS LAWFUL OR PUBLIC ACCORDING TO THE LAW OF NATIONS; AND THEREIN, ON THE DECLARATION OF WAR

I.—*A public war according to the law of nations is a war between different peoples*

[449] 1. In a previous passage[1] we began to say that by authors of repute a war is often called lawful not from the cause from which it arises, nor, as is done in other cases, from the importance of its exploits, but because of certain peculiar legal consequences. Of what sort a lawful war is, however, will best be perceived from the definition of enemies given by the Roman jurists.

Dig. L. xvi. 118. *Digest,* XLIX. xv. 24.

'Enemies are those who in the name of the state declare war upon us, or upon whom we in the name of the state declare war; others are brigands and robbers', says Pomponius. Similarly Ulpian:

> Enemies are those upon whom the Roman people have publicly declared war, or who have themselves declared war upon the Roman people; others are called thieves and brigands. And so he who has been captured by robbers is not their slave,[2] and has no need of the right of postliminy. But he who has been captured by enemies, as by the Germans or Parthians, is a slave of the enemy, and recovers his former status by postliminy.

Digest, XLIX. xv. 19. § 2. *Digest,* XLIX. xv. 21. § 1.

Paul says: 'Those who are captured by pirates[3] and brigands remain free.' There is a further statement by Ulpian:

> In civil contentions, although the state is thereby often injured, nevertheless the destruction of the state is not aimed at; the citizens who support either side after the manner of enemies are not in the position of those who possess rights of captivity or postliminy. In consequence it has been decided that for those who have been captured, sold, and later set free, it would be superfluous to attempt to recover from the emperor their free status, which they had not lost by captivity.

Philippics, IV [vi. 14].

2. It needs only to be noted further that we may understand that any one who has the supreme authority in a state may take the place of the Roman people in our illustration. 'An enemy', says Cicero, 'is the one that has a state, a senate, a treasury, the agreement and concord of the citizens, and the power, if the course of events leads thereto, to conclude peace and an alliance.'

[1] I. iii. 4.

[2] Hence the plot of the *Poenulus* of Plautus, and the *Eunuch* of Terence. Such a one was also Eumaeus, *Odyssey,* XV [lines 402 ff.].

[3] Pompey pronounced those free who had been captured by the pirates; Appian, *Mithridatic Wars* [xiv. 96]. See also Herrera, vol. II.

II.—*The distinction between a people, although acting unjustly, and pirates or brigands*

1. Moreover, a commonwealth or state does not immediately cease to be such if it commits an injustice, even as a body; and a gathering of pirates and brigands is not a state, even if they do perhaps mutually maintain a sort of equality, without which no association can exist. The reason is that pirates and brigands are banded together for wrongdoing;[1] the members of a state, even if at times they are not free from crime, nevertheless have been united for the enjoyment of rights, and they do render justice to foreigners. If the treatment of members of other states is not in all respects according to the law of nature, which, as we have showed elsewhere, [II. xv. 5. 1.] has become partly obscured among many peoples, it is at least according to agreements entered into with each state or in accordance with customs.

Accordingly the scholiast on Thucydides notes that, at the time [I [v].] when it was considered legitimate to plunder at sea, the Greeks refrained from murder and raids by night, and from the seizure of the cattle of ploughmen. Strabo relates that other peoples also, who [XI [ii. 12].] lived in like manner by plunder, upon returning home after being at sea, sent word to the owners in order that these might, if they wished, recover their stolen property at a fair price.[2] To such persons applies the passage in Homer's *Odyssey*, XIV: [XIV. 85 ff.].

> Themselves eager for loot, who to the land
> Of strangers fare; if gods above grant booty,
> With laden ships they leave and homeward go,
> And dread fear falls on those they leave behind.

[450] 2. In moral questions, furthermore, the principal element is considered as determining the essential character. As Cicero has rightly said in the fifth book *On Ends*: 'The whole of [V. xxx. 92.] an object takes its name from that constituent of it which comprises the most important elements and has the most far-reaching effect.' With this accords the saying of Galen: 'Names are taken from the most potent element in the compound.' The same author often designates such things as 'named after the chief element'.

Cicero, then, spoke too sweepingly when he said, *On the Commonwealth*, Book III, that where an unjust man is king, or where the [In August., *City of God*, II. xxi.] aristocracy or the people itself is unjust, there is not a wicked state, but

[1] 'A mob not in lawful association, but brought together in order to commit wrong'; Procopius, *Vandalic War*, II [II. xv].

[2] Such were those who are mentioned by Saxo, XIV [p. 234]. To such a degree, as Plutarch [*Cimon*, viii = p. 483 C] notes, the Scyrians had deteriorated in course of time: 'Although from antiquity they had practised piracy at sea, finally they did not refrain from committing injury upon those who were sailing to them to carry on trade.'

On the City of God, XIX.xxiv. none at all. In correction of this view Augustine says: 'Nevertheless, I should not go so far as to assert that the people as such does not exist, or that its organization is not a state, so long as there remains some sort of union in a reasoning populace, associated through harmonious participation in the things which it chooses.' A body that is sick is nevertheless a body still; and a state, although seriously diseased, is a state so long as there remain tribunals and the other agencies that are necessary in order that foreigners, no less than private citizens, in their relations one with the other may there obtain their rights. *Borysthenitica* [*Orations,* xxxvi = p. 443], and *On the Law* [*Orations,* lxxv. end]. [*On Concord* = p. 385 A B.] Dio Chrysostom offers a more correct judgement in saying that the law (especially that which goes to make up the universal common law) exists in a state just as the mind in the human body; for when this is taken away the state ceases to exist.[1] In the speech in which he urges the Rhodians to harmony, Aristides shows that many good laws may exist even under a tyranny. Aristotle in his *Republic* [*Politics*], Book V, chapter ix, says that if any one presses the violence of the few, or of the people, too far, the state first becomes full of faults, and finally ceases to be.

Let us illustrate this subject by examples.

3. We heard Ulpian saying above that captives taken by brigands do not belong to those who capture them. [*Digest,* XLIX. xv. 24.] He says further that captives taken by the Germans lose their freedom. And yet among the Germans marauding expeditions which are sent beyond the borders of a state 'involve no disgrace', as Caesar states. [*Gallic War*], VI [xxiii]. Of the Venedi, Tacitus says: 'With their marauding expeditions they overrun the forests and mountains that lie between the Peucini and the Fenni.' *On the Customs of the Germans* [xlvi]. In another place he says that the Chatti, a famous people of Germany, engaged in marauding expeditions. *Annals,* XII [xxvii]. In the same author the Garamates are a nation fertile in marauding expeditions, but still a nation. *Histories,* IV [l].

The Illyrians without distinction were accustomed to plunder on the sea, yet a triumph was celebrated over them; Appian, *Illyrian Wars* [ii. 9]. Pompey celebrated no triumph over the pirates. So great is the distinction between a people, however wicked it may be, and those who, although not forming a people, associate together for the sake of crime.

III.—*Sometimes a transformation is effected*

Nevertheless a transformation may take place, not merely in the case of individuals, as when Jephthes, Arsaces, and Viriathus instead of being leaders of brigands became lawful chiefs, [*Judges,* xi. 3 ff.] [Justin, XLI. iv; XLIV. ii.] but also in

[1] Cicero, *Letters,* X. i [X. i. 1]: 'There are neither laws, nor courts, nor any semblance and trace of a state.'

the case of groups, so that those who have only been robbers upon embracing another mode of life[1] become a state. In discussing brigandage Augustine says: 'If by accessions of desperate men this evil grows to such proportions that it holds lands, establishes fixed settlements, seizes upon states and subjugates peoples, it assumes the name of a kingdom.' *On the City of God*, IV. iv.

IV.—*It is essential to the nature of a public war that it should have the support of the sovereign power; in what way this is to be understood*

What persons have the sovereign power, we have already stated. Hence it may be understood that, if any possess the sovereign power in part, they may to that extent wage a lawful war.

This principle applies with even greater force to those who are not subjects, but are allied on an unequal footing.[2] So we learn from history that all formalities of lawful war were observed between the Romans and their allies, the Volsci, Latins, Spaniards, and Carthaginians, although these had an inferior status in the alliance. Cajetan, *On II. ii*, qu. 40, art. 1.

V.—*A declaration of war is also requisite*

That a war may be lawful in the sense indicated, it is not enough that it be waged by sovereign powers on each side. It is also necessary, as we have said, that it should be publicly declared, and in fact proclaimed so publicly that the notification of this declaration be made by one of the parties to the other;[3] whence [451] Ennius spoke of battles proclaimed in advance. [Cf. Gellius, xx. 10.] In the first book *On Duties* Cicero says: 'But the right usage of war has indeed been most scrupulously prescribed by the fetial law of the Roman people. [I. xi. 36.] According to this we are given to understand that no war is lawful unless it is waged for the recovery of property, or has been previously threatened and proclaimed.'

More concisely speaks an ancient writer in Isidore: 'A lawful war is one that is waged by declaration, for the recovery of property or to repel enemies.' [*Etymologies*, XVIII. i.] Thus Livy, in his description of a lawful war, says that the war is waged openly and in accordance with public I [xxvii. 3].

[1] An example is found in the case of the Mamertini; Diodorus Siculus, fragments [XXI. x and XXII].

[2] Like the Duke of Lorraine, in Krantz, *Saxonica*, XII. xiii. The city of Stralsund declared war upon its Pomeranian rulers; Krantz, *Vandalica*, XIV. xxxv.

[3] Josephus, *Antiquities* [455] *of the Jews*, XV [XV. v. 3], says: 'It is not lawful to wage a war that has not been previously declared.'

For examples of this practice among the nations see Krantz, *Saxonica*, XI [XI. v], and Oderborn in his *Life of Basilides*, III. The opposite conduct of the Turk Olizasthlan [Chlizasthlan], and the Serb Neemon, are censured by Nicetas, [*On Manuel Comnenus*,] III [III. vi] and IV [V. iv].

XXXI [xiv. 10]. decree. Also, after relating that the Acarnanians had laid waste Attic territory, he adds: 'This was the first manifestation of hostile feeling; afterward a lawful war was declared by decrees and voluntary proclamations of the states.'

VI.—*What element in the declaration of war is in accordance with the law of nature, and what is peculiar to the law of nations, is set forth with distinctions*

1. To understand the foregoing passages, and others dealing with the declaration of war, we must carefully distinguish what is due according to the law of nature, what is not due by nature but is honourable, what is required by the law of nations to secure the effects peculiar to this law, and what, in addition, is derived from the particular institutions of certain peoples.

In a case where either an attack is being warded off, or a penalty is demanded from the very person who has done wrong, no declaration is required by the law of nature. This is what Sthenelaidas,
I [lxxxvi]. the ephor, says in Thucydides:[1] 'We who have been wronged in more than words are not to seek satisfaction in words or judicial
[*Rom. Ant.*,] I [lviii]. proceedings.' Latinus in Dionysius of Halicarnassus declares: 'Every one who is attacked repels him who begins the war.' Aelianus,
[*Tactica*, i.] quoting from Plato, says that a war which is undertaken to repel force is proclaimed, not by a herald, but by nature. Hence Dio
[*Orations*, xxxviii = p. 473.] Chrysostom, in his address *To the Nicomedians*, says: 'Most wars begin without declaration.'

[XXXV. li. 2.] For no other reason Livy criticizes Menippus, an officer of Antiochus, because he had slain certain Romans when war had not yet been declared, and when no hostilities had been engaged in, so that they could have heard that swords had been drawn or even that blood had been shed; by this he shows that either of these two steps could have sufficed to justify the action. Not more necessary, by the law of nature, is a declaration of war in case an owner wishes to seize what belongs to him.

2. But whenever one thing is seized in place of another, or the property of a debtor is taken for his debt, and all the more if one wishes to take possession of the property of those who are subject to the debt, then a demand for settlement is required, to establish the fact that it is impossible in any other way to obtain what is ours

[1] See also Thucydides, Book III [III. lvi], in the speech of the Plataeans: 'According to the law that is in vogue among all peoples, it is right to defend ourselves against him by whom we are assailed in a hostile manner.'

In Diodorus Siculus, *Excerpta Peiresciana* [i = p. 272], Flaminius 'called all the gods and men to witness that the war had been begun by the king'. See also what is in Mariana, XIX. xiii. On war that has not been declared see Dexippus, *Selections on Embassies* [= frag. 22, p. 195, edit. Dindorf].

or what is owed to us. For this is not a primary right, but a secondary and vicarious right, as we have elsewhere explained. Thus, even before the possessor of sovereign power is attacked for the debt or crime of a subject, a demand for settlement should be made, which may place him in the wrong, and in consequence of which he may be held either to be causing us loss or to be himself committing a crime, according to the principles which have previously been discussed.

3. But even in case the law of nature does not require that such a demand be made, still it is honourable and praiseworthy to make it,[1] in order that, for instance, we may avoid giving offence, or that the wrong may be atoned for by repentance and compensation, according to what we have said regarding the means to be tried to avoid war.[2] Here applies this verse also: [Seneca, *Agamemnon*, 153.]

At first no one has sought to try extremes.

Here, too, applies the command which God gave to the Jews,[3] that they should first invite to peace the city which was to be attacked. This command, although given to that people for a particular case, has been wrongly confused by some with the law of nations. For the peace there referred to is not peace in general, but one dependent upon a condition of subjection and tribute. [452] When Cyrus came into the territory of the Armenians, before doing harm to any one he sent to the king those who represented him in order to demand the tribute and soldiery due according to the treaty, 'thinking that this was a more friendly procedure than to advance without a previous declaration', as Xenophon says in his *History*. But by the law of nations a proclamation is required in all cases in order to secure these particular effects, not, however, from both parties but from either one. [*Deuteronomy*, xx. 11 [xx. 10].] [*History*, II [*Training of Cyrus*, II. iv. 32].]

VII.—*A declaration of war is sometimes conditional, sometimes absolute*

1. Now the declaration of war is either conditional or absolute.

It is conditional when it is joined with a demand for restitution. Moreover, under the title of things sought in recovery,[4] the fetial law included not merely a claim by right of ownership, but also the effort to obtain that which is owed on a civil or criminal charge,

[1] See Mariana, XXVII. xiii.

[2] II. xxiii. 7.

[3] Josephus, *Antiquities of the Jews*, V. ii [V. ii. 9]: 'But the council of the elders restrained them, showing them that they should not suddenly wage war on their fellow citizens, before the causes of complaint had been argued in words, since the law did not permit them to lead an army even against foreigners when they had suffered wrong, unless they had first sent an embassy and tried means by which the wrongdoers might be brought back to a more reasonable frame of mind.'

[4] See Paruta, *On the War in Cyprus*, Book I; Bizarri, Book XXIII, with regard to the Turks; Reinkingk, II. iii. 4.

as Servius [1] rightly explains. Hence arises this phase in the formulas,
[II. i. 2. 2; xxi. 4.] 'to be restored, satisfied, surrendered', where, as we have elsewhere said, 'surrendered' must be understood with a reservation, to wit: unless those on whom the demand is made prefer to punish the guilty party themselves. Pliny [2] bears witness that this demand for restitution was called a 'verbal demand'.

VIII [xxiii. 7]. A conditional declaration is recorded by Livy: 'That they would themselves use every means to free themselves from this injury unless it were removed by those who had inflicted it.' Another *Annals*, I [xlviii]. is given by Tacitus: 'unless they should inflict punishment upon the guilty, he would carry out a general massacre.' There is also an [385 ff.] ancient example in the *Suppliants* of Euripides, when Theseus gives to the herald these instructions for his mission to Creon the Theban:

> Theseus, who holds the neighbouring kingdom's soil,[3]
> The dead demands for burial; granted that,
> Erechtheus' people will become your friend.
> If this with favour meet, retrace thy steps;
> But if no heed is given, these other words employ:
> Let them soon look to see my youth in arms.

[*Thebaid*, XII. 598.] Papinius in his description of the same event has:

> Proclaim either funeral pyres for the Danai
> Or for Thebes, battles.

[IV. liii.] Polybius calls this 'to give notice of reprisals', and the ancient Romans 'to give formal notice'.

An absolute declaration is what is called in particular a proclamation or edict. This is made when one party either has begun hostilities [*Etymologies*, XVIII. i.] (and this is what in Isidore is said to be a war for the repulse of enemies), or has himself committed crimes that call for punishment.[4]

2. Sometimes, indeed, an absolute declaration follows one that is conditional, although this is not necessary but superfluous. Hence [Livy, I. xxxii. 10.] arises the formula:

> I bear witness that this people is unjust, and does not give satisfaction.

There is also a second formula:

> Whatever things, disputes, causes of complaint,[5] of which the *pater patratus* of the Roman people of the Quirites has formally notified the *pater patratus* of the people of the

[1] *On the Aeneid*, X [line 14].

[2] [*Natural History*,] XXII. xii [XXII. xii. 2]: 'And when ambassadors were sent to the enemy to make verbal declaration, that is, audibly to demand back the things that had been carried off, one of them was called the Verbenarius.' Again, in speaking of the plant verbena, the same author says, XXV. ix: 'This it is which, as we have pointed out, the ambassadors carried to the enemy.' See Servius, *On the Aeneid*, IX [line 53], and X [line 14].

[3] A similar formal declaration is in the *Battle of the Frogs and Mice* [line 135 ff.], and at the beginning of the *Amphitruo* of Plautus [203 ff.]. See also Kromer, XXI.

[4] See the example in Bembo, Book VII.

[5] Compare the Greek of Dionysius of Halicarnassus, *Selections on Embassies*, ii [= p. 9].

Ancient Latins, which things the men of the Ancient Latins ought to have surrendered, done, paid, which things they have not paid nor surrendered nor done, these things I hold ought to be sought in just and righteous warfare ; and I agree and approve.

The third formula is :

Whereas the tribes of the Ancient Latins have acted and committed offences against the Roman people of the Quirites, whereas the Roman people of the Quirites has ordered that there be war with the Ancient Latins, and the Senate of the Roman people of the Quirites has decreed, consented, agreed that war should be waged with the Ancient Latins, for this cause I and the Roman people declare and make war upon the tribes of the Ancient Latins.

That in this case, as I have said, a proclamation is not strictly necessary, becomes apparent from the fact that it was formally made at the nearest garrison point. So the fetials declared when consulted in the case of Philip of Macedon, and afterward in the case of Antiochus, since the first proclamation had to be made to the person who was attacked in the war. The declaration against Pyrrhus [453] was in fact made to one of his soldiers, and that too in the Circus Flaminius, where this soldier was ordered to purchase a bit of ground for form's sake, as Servius narrates in his commentary on the ninth book of the *Aeneid*. [IX. 52.]

Livy, XXXI [viii. 3] and XXXVI [iii. 7].

3. Further proof of the superfluity of this formality is found in the fact that war is often declared by both parties. Thus the Peloponnesian War was declared by the Corcyreans and by the Corinthians, although it is sufficient that such a declaration be made by either one party or the other. [Thucydides, I. xxix.]

VIII.—*What elements in declarations of war pertain to municipal law and not to the law of nations*

To the customs and institutions of certain peoples, moreover, and not to the law of nations, belong the use of the herald's staff among the Greeks ;[1] the sacred herbs and bloody spear used first by the Aequicolae, then by the Romans, who followed their example ; the renunciation of any existing friendship or alliance ; the period of thirty days set after the demand for restitution ; the hurling of the spear[2] the second time ; and other formalities of this sort which should not be confused with those that properly belong to the law of nations.

Arnobius informs us that in his time a great part of these formalities had ceased to be observed ; and, indeed, some were

Arnobius, *Against the Heathen*, II [lxvii].

[1] The origin of the herald's staff you will learn from Pliny, [*Natural History*,] XXIX. iii, and Servius, *On the Aeneid*, IV [IV. 242] and VIII.

[2] See Servius, *On the Aeneid*, IX [IX. 53] ; Ammianus, XIX [XIX. ii. 6], with the notes of the erudite Lindenbrog.

Varro, *On the Latin Language*, IV. [LII. xv.] already neglected in the time of Varro. The third Punic War was begun at the same time with the declaration. In Dio, Maecenas holds that certain of these formalities are peculiar to a democratic state.

IX.—*A war declared against any one is at the same time declared against his subjects and allies, in so far as they take his side*

Furthermore, a war declared against him who holds the sovereign authority in a state is held to be declared at the same time not only upon all his subjects, but also upon all who will join him as allies in such a way as to become an accession to him. This is what the more modern jurists mean when they say that defiance of the prince is defiance of his supporters; for to declare war they call to send forth defiance. (Baldus, *On Code*, VII. ix. 2, no. 70.)

This principle is to be understood as applicable to the type of war waged against him upon whom it has been declared in the manner illustrated in the war against Antiochus. It was decided not to declare war against the Aetolians separately, because they had openly associated themselves with Antiochus. 'The Aetolians have voluntarily declared war against themselves', was the response of the fetials. (Livy, XXXVI [iii. 11].)

X.—*A war declared against any one is not held to be at the same time declared against his subjects and allies in so far as they are considered by themselves; illustration by examples*

If, on the conclusion of a war declared against one who holds the sovereign power, another people or king is to be attacked, because of the aid that they have furnished, a new declaration of war will have to be made in order to meet the requirements of the law of nations. For in such a case the people or king is now not regarded as an accessory, but as a principal. It was therefore rightly said that the war of Manilius against the Gallo-Grecians and that of Caesar against Ariovistus were not lawful wars according to the law of nations.[1] The Gallo-Grecians and Ariovistus were in fact attacked not as accessories to another war, but principals; and for such a procedure by the Roman law a new authorization of the Roman people was required, just as a new declaration was required by the law of nations.

What was said in putting the question in regard to the war against Antiochus: 'Did they desire, and did they direct, that war be begun with King Antiochus and with any who had espoused his (Livy, XXXVI [i. 5].)

[1] Unlawful also was that of the companions of Ulysses against the Ciconians, who were at one time allies of Priam, and who are mentioned by Homer, *Odyssey*, I [rather ι = IX. 39 ff.], and Didymus thereon.

cause,' also what was provided in the decree against King Perseus, should, as it seems, be understood as meaning, so long as there should be a war with Antiochus or Perseus, and as referring to those who actually had a part in this war. [Livy,] XLII [xxxi. 1].

XI.—*The reason why a declaration is required in order to secure certain effects*

Furthermore the reason why nations required a declaration for the kind of war which we have called lawful according to the law of nations was not that which some adduce, with the purpose that nothing should be done secretly or deceitfully, for this pertains to an exhibition of courage rather than to law, just as certain nations are said to have even appointed the date and place of battle.[1] The purpose was, rather, that the fact might be established with certainty that war was being waged not by private initiative but by the will of each of the two peoples or of their heads. Alberico Gentili, I. ii [II. i].

From this consideration arise the peculiar effects which do not develop in a war against brigands, nor in a war which a king wages against his subjects. Thus Seneca distinguishes 'wars declared upon neighbours, or waged with citizens'. *On Anger*, III. ii.

XII.—*The effects referred to are not found in other wars*

What certain writers point out and teach by citing examples, to the effect that even in [454] such wars what is seized belongs to those who take it, is indeed true, but only from one standpoint, that of the law of nature. It is not true by the customary law of nations, since this concerns nations only, not persons who have no existence as a nation or form a part of a nation. Ayala, I. v.

The writers in question err in this also, that they think that a war undertaken for the defence of one's person or property does not require a declaration. Such a war does require a declaration, not indeed of itself, but for the sake of those effects of which we have begun to speak, and which we shall shortly explain. Alberico Gentili, II. ii [II. i], just cited.

XIII.—*Whether war may be waged simultaneously with its declaration*

This also is not true, that war cannot be waged at once upon being declared. That was the procedure of Cyrus against the Armenians, and of the Romans against the Carthaginians, as we

[1] Just as the Romans did to Porsena, as is recorded by Plutarch in his *Publicola* [xvi = p. 105 c]. The Turks kindle a great number of fires two days before a battle; Chalcocondylas, VII [= p. 344, edit. Bekker].

have stated above. By the law of nations, in fact, no interval of time is required after the declaration. Nevertheless, it may happen that, from the character of the affair, by the law of nature some time may be required, as when restitution or punishment for a guilty person has been sought, and this has not been refused. In such a case time must be granted in order that that which has been sought may be properly performed.

XIV.—*Whether war must be declared against him who has violated the right of embassy*

Even if the right of embassy has been violated, there will not cease to be need of a declaration of war, for the sake of the effects of which I speak. However, it will be sufficient that this be made in a way in which it may be done with safety, as by means of writing, for example; for custom sanctions the use of writing for both summonses and other notices to be served in unsafe places.

[456] CHAPTER IV

ON THE RIGHT OF KILLING ENEMIES IN A PUBLIC WAR, AND ON OTHER VIOLENCE AGAINST THE PERSON

I.—*The effects of a public war are explained in general terms*

1. On the verse of Virgil, [*On Aeneid*, X. 14.]

> Then to strive in hatred, then to plunder,
> Will become permissible,

Servius Honoratus, after tracing the fetial law from Ancus Martius, and more remotely from the Aequicoli, makes this comment:

> If at any time it happened that either men or cattle had been carried off from the territory of the Roman people by any nation, the *pater patratus*, with the fetials, that is, the priests who preside over the conclusion of treaties, would set out, and standing before the frontier would state the cause of war in a loud voice; if they refused to restore the things that had been carried off, or to surrender the wrongdoers, he would hurl a spear toward them. This constituted the beginning of hostilities, and then it was permissible to pillage in accordance with the usage of war.

Servius, moreover, had previously said: 'The ancients were accustomed to use the words " to inflict injury (*laedere res*) " where we say " to pillage (*rapere*) ", even if no crime of pillaging had been committed; in like manner they used to say " to make restitution (*res reddere*) " where we say " to give satisfaction (*satisfacere*) ".' [*On Aeneid*, X. 14.]

From these facts we learn that a war declared between two peoples, or the heads of two peoples, has certain particular effects [1] which do not arise from the nature of war itself. This conclusion, again, agrees excellently with what we have just now cited from the Roman jurists.

II.—*A distinction is made between the word 'permissible' as referring to that which is done with impunity, although not without moral wrong, and to that which is free from moral wrong even if virtue would enjoin not to do it; with examples*

1. But let us see the import of the 'will become permissible' in Virgil's line. For sometimes that is said to be permissible which is right from every point of view and is free from reproach, even if there is something else which might more honourably be done, as indicated in that statement of Paul the Apostle: 'All things (that [*1 Corinthians*, vi. 17 [vi. 12].]

[1] Krantz, *Saxonica*, XI. v.

is of the sort which he had touched upon and was going to discuss) are lawful for me, but not all things are expedient.'

[*To Pollentius*,] I. xviii. Thus it is lawful to contract marriage, but for a holy purpose the chastity of celibacy is more worthy of praise,[1] as Augustine, following the same apostle, wrote to Pollentius. Also to marry a second time is lawful, but it is more honourable to be content with one marriage; this is according to the correct elucidation of that question by Clement of Alexandria.[2] A Christian husband may lawfully leave his pagan wife, as Augustine thinks[3] (this is not the place to discuss in what circumstances this is true), but he may also keep her, and so Augustine adds: 'Either course is indeed equally permissible according to the justice which waits upon the Lord; and so [457] the Lord forbids neither of them, but each one is not expedient.' Ulpian says of the seller who is permitted to empty out wine after the appointed day: 'Nevertheless it is more praiseworthy if he does not empty it, when he might do so.'

To Pollentius, I. xv [I. xiii, xix].

Digest, XVIII. vi. 1. § 3.

2. In another sense, however, something is said to be permissible, not because it can be done without violence to right conduct and rules of duty, but because among men it is not liable to punishment.[4] In this sense fornication is permitted among many peoples; among the Lacedaemonians and Egyptians even thieving was permissible. In Quintilian we find: 'There are certain things which are not praiseworthy according to nature, but which are legally

[*Institutes*,] III. viii [III. vi. 84].

[1] Tertullian, *Against Marcion*, I [I. xxix], says: 'The proof of abstinence is wanting if permission to act is taken away.' See on this point, and on the question of flight in time of persecution, the same author, *To his Wife*, Book I [I. iii]. Jerome, *Against Helvidius* [*On Perpetual Virginity*, xxi], says: 'A virgin is worthy of greater praise, because she despises that which she could do without sin.' [465] Also *Against Jovinianus* [I. xii]: 'Christ loves the virgins the more for this, that of their own accord they offer what was not demanded from them.' Again, *To Pammachius* [*Letters*, lxvi. 8]: 'Great things are always left to the judgment of those who dare. Constraint is not laid upon you, to the end that your will may attain the reward.'

Chrysostom, *On First Corinthians*, vii [Homily XIX, ii, on verse 9], declares: 'He [Paul] shows that chastity is preferable.' *On Romans*, vii. 6 [Homily XII. iv], he says: 'He has threatened us with Gehenna, unless we obey his commands, and he shows that the things which he demands are not among those which men may offer in zealous emulation, such as virginity and the renunciation of possessions, but those which absolutely must be fulfilled.' In his second discourse *On Fasting*, II [*On Penitence*, VI. iii], he says: 'He has left virginal chastity outside of the course, outside of the rules of the contest, that those who offer it may show the greatness of their spirits, and those who do not offer it may enjoy the mercy of God.' The same thought he shortly after applies to 'the renunciation of possessions'.

Add also what Gratian has cited from Augustine and other writers in *Decretum*, II. xiv. 1.

[2] *Stromata*, IV [III. xii. 82], where, among other things, he says of the man who contracts a second marriage: 'He does not indeed sin against the covenant, for there is no law to prevent him, but he does not accomplish the most excellent perfection of the life according to the Gospel.'

[3] In *De Conjugiis Adulterinis ad Pollentium*, I. xiii and xix; from these passages Gratian has cited at length in *Decretum*, II. xxviii. 1.

[4] Tertullian, in his *Exhortation to Chastity* [chap. viii], says: 'Permission is oftentimes the trial of teaching.' In the same passage: 'All things are permissible, but all things are not for salvation.' Chrysostom, *On Penitence*, VIII [VIII. iii, ed. Migne, vol. VIII, p. 762], says: 'He who lived upon herbs and wild honey said with authority to him who was accustomed to have set before him a splendid and regal table, "This is not permissible for you." Nevertheless all things appear permissible for a king.'

Columella, in the preface to Book VII [*On Farming*, I. vii. 2], declares: 'We must not assert our right to whatever is permissible, for the ancients held that the extreme enforcement of right is extreme cruelty.' Jerome, *To Jovinianus* [*To Innocentius*, *Letters*, i. 14], says: 'The extreme insistence on right is the extreme of wickedness.'

permissible; thus according to the Twelve Tables it was permitted to divide the body of the debtor among his creditors.'

This, however, is hardly a proper meaning of the word 'permitted' in the strict sense, as Cicero rightly observes in his *Tusculan Disputations*, Book V. Here, speaking of Cinna, he says: 'To me, on the contrary, he seems wretched not only because he did this, but also because he so conducted himself that it would be permissible for him to do it. Although it is not permissible for any one to do wrong, still we are misled by an error of speech; for we say that that is permitted which each one is allowed to do.' This is, nevertheless, an accepted meaning, as shown by Cicero's address to the judges in his plea *For Rabirius Postumus*: 'You should have regard to what becomes you, not merely what is permissible for you; for if you seek only what is permitted you may remove from the state whomsoever you wish.' [V. xix. 55.] [v. 11.]

Similarly it is said that for kings all things are permitted because they are 'not liable to be held accountable', that is, they are beyond the reach of human punishments, as we have said elsewhere. But for the instruction of a king, or an emperor, Claudian rightly says: [*On the Fourth Consulship of Honorius*, 267 f.]

> Consider not what you may do, but that of which the doing will honour bring.

Musonius rebukes those kings 'who are in the habit of saying, "This is permissible for me", not "This is right for me".' [In Stobaeus, xlviii. 14.]

3. In this sense we often see what is permitted contrasted with what is right. Such a contrast is presented by Seneca the Father[1] more than once in his *Controversies*. Ammianus Marcellinus says: 'There are some things which it is not right to do, even if it is permitted.' With this accords what Pliny says in his *Letters*: 'It is right to avoid what is dishonourable, not as being not permissible, but as being shameful.' Ammianus, XXX [viii. 8]. Pliny, V [xiii].

Cicero, again, in the speech *For Balbus*, has this: 'For there is something which is not right, even if it is permitted.' In the speech *For Milo* he refers the standard of right (*fas esse*) to nature, and the standard of what is permissible (*licere*) to the laws. In a declamation of Quintilian the Father there is a saying that it is one thing to have regard to rights, and another to have regard to justice. [iii. 8.] [xvi. 43.] *Declamations*, ccli.

III.—*The effects of a public war in general are concerned with permission that grants impunity*

With this restriction, therefore, it is permitted to harm an enemy, both in his person and in his property; that is, it is per-

[1] In his *Controversies*, IV. xxiv [=VII. viii. 1], and elsewhere.

missible not merely for him who wages war for a just cause, and who injures within that limit, a permission which we said at the beginning of this book was granted by the law of nature, but for either side indiscriminately.

As a consequence, he who happens to be caught in another's territory cannot for that reason be punished as a murderer or a thief, and war cannot be waged upon him by another on the pretext of such an act. With this meaning we read in Sallust: 'To whom in the hour of victory all things were permitted by the law of war.'

[*On Public Administration*, addressed to Caesar, II. iv. 1.]

IV.—*Why such effects have been introduced*

The reason why such effects met with the approval of nations was this. To undertake to decide regarding the justice of a war between two peoples had been dangerous for other peoples, who were on this account involved in a foreign war; just so the Massilians said, in relation to the struggle between Caesar and Pompey, that it was not within the province of their judgement or their power to determine which party had the juster cause. Furthermore, even in a lawful war, from external indications it can hardly be adequately known what is the just limit of self-defence, of recovering what is one's own, or of inflicting punishments; in consequence it has seemed altogether preferable to leave decisions in regard to such matters to the scruples of the belligerents rather than to have recourse to the judgements of others. The Achaeans in their speech to the Senate, as recorded by Livy, said: 'In what way do those things which have been done in accordance with the law of war [458] come under discussion?'

[*Civil War*, I. xxxv.]

XXXIX [xxxvi. 12].

In addition to this effect of permissibility, that is of impunity, there is another, that of ownership, which we shall discuss later.

V.—*Testimony regarding these effects*

1. Moreover that licence to injure, which we have now begun to consider, extends in the first place to persons; in regard to it there are many evidences in writers of authority. There is a Greek proverb from a tragedy of Euripides: [1]

> Pure are all they who shed the blood of foes.

According to an ancient custom of the Greeks it was not lawful to bathe, to eat or drink, and much less to perform sacred rites, in company with those who had slain a man in time of peace; but to do so with those who had killed in war was right.

[1] *Ion* [line 1334].

In general, killing is called a right of war. Says Marcellus in Livy: 'Whatever I have done to the enemy is defended by the law of war.' In the same writer Alco says to the men of Saguntum: 'But I think that you ought rather to endure these things than to suffer your bodies to be butchered, your wives and children to be seized and dragged off before your faces in accordance with the law of war.' Again, in another passage, after telling of the slaughter of the Astapenses, Livy adds that this was accomplished in accordance with the law of war.

XXVI [xxxi. 2]. XXI [xiii. 9]. XXVIII [xxiii. 1].

In his speech *For Deiotarus*, Cicero says: 'Why should he be your enemy, when he remembered that he and his son had been made kings by you, who would have been justified by the law of war in killing him?' Also, in the speech *For Marcus Marcellus*: 'For although by the terms of victory itself you might lawfully have slain us all, we were preserved by the mercifulness of your judgement.' Caesar informed the Aeduans 'That those through his kindness had been preserved whom according to the law of war he could have put to death'. Josephus says in his *Jewish War*: 'It is a noble thing to die in war, but by the law of war, that is, at the hands of the victors.' Papinius [Statius] has this:

[ix. 25.] [iv. 12.] *Comm.* [*on Gallic War*], VII [xli]. [III. viii. 5.] [*Thebaid*, XII. 552 f.]

> And we mourn not the fallen; such are the rights of war [1]
> And hazards of arms.

2. However, it is clear from other passages that when these writers say 'by the law of war' we must not understand such a law as would free what is done from all blame, but such immunity from punishment as I have mentioned. Tacitus says: 'In peace we consider causes and deserts; when war breaks out, innocent and guilty fall together.' The same author elsewhere has this: 'Human justice would not permit them to approve such slaughter, nor the principles of warfare to avenge it.'

Annals, I [xlviii]. *Histories*, III [li].

In no other sense should we understand the right of war which, according to Livy, the Achaeans refrained from availing themselves of against Aeneas and Antenor because these had always been advocates of peace. Seneca, in his tragedy the *Trojan Women*, says:

[I. i. 1.] [335.]

> Whate'er he will, 'tis permitted the victor to do.

In his *Letters*, also: 'Deeds which they would atone for with their lives if committed in peace, we praise them for having done under arms.' [2]

Letters, xcvi [xcv. 31].

Cyprian declares: 'Murder committed by individuals is a crime;

Letters, ii [i. 6].

[1] Servius, *On the Aeneid*, II [II. 538], in the Fuldensian excerpts: 'In accordance with the law of war Pyrrhus had slain Polites; but why before his father's eyes?' Spartianus, in his *Life of Septimius Severus* [chap. xiv], writes: 'In addition to those whom the law of battle destroyed.'

[2] Cf. II. i. 1, above.

when accomplished by public authority it is called a virtue. Wicked deeds acquire immunity not on the plea that they are void of guilt but because their ruthlessness is on a grand scale.' Later he adds: 'The laws have come to terms with crimes; whatever is public
Div. Inst., IV. ix [VI. ix. 4]. begins to be permissible.' Similarly Lactantius says that the Romans in accordance with law inflicted injuries. And in the same sense
Pharsalia, I [2]. Lucan speaks of 'right given over to crime'.

VI.—*Out of this right arises the right to kill and injure all who are in the territory of the enemy*

Furthermore, this right of doing what is permissible has a wide application. In the first place it extends not only to those who actually bear arms, or are subjects of him that stirs up the war, but in addition to all persons who are in the enemy's territory. This is
XXXVII [XXXVIII. xlviii. 9] and numerous other passages. made plain by that very formula in Livy: 'Let him be accounted an enemy, and those who are within his defences.' The reason is that injury may be feared from such persons also; and this is sufficient, in a prolonged and general war, to give rise to the right which we are discussing.

The situation is different from that which arises from the taking
[III. ii. 7.] of guarantees, which, as we have said, originated in the manner of the impositions levied for the payment of the debts of a state.
On Dig., I. i. 5. Therefore, as Baldus notes, it is no wonder that much [459] more is permissible in war than in the exacting guarantees.

At any rate what I have said is beyond all dispute true of foreigners who enter hostile territory after a war has commenced and they are aware of it.

VII.—*What is the situation in case foreigners have entered a country before the outbreak of war?*

But foreigners who have gone to a country in a period prior to the war, after the lapse of a moderate time,[1] in which they could have departed, are apparently to be regarded as enemies according to the law of nations. Accordingly the Corcyreans, who were going
Thucydides, I [xxvi]. to blockade Epidamnus, first gave to the foreigners an opportunity of leaving the city, telling them that if they should remain they would be regarded as enemies.

[1] Bembo, *History*, Book VII. Cicero makes use of this principle in his speech *For Ligarius* [ii. 4]. You have an example in Livy, Book XXV [XXV. xxii. 11], with regard to the citizens of Campania. Others in Thucydides, Books I and V [IV. cv].

VIII.—*The right to inflict injury extends to subjects of enemies anywhere, unless the law of the foreign territory prevents it*

1. Now those who are truly subjects of the enemy, that is to say from a permanent cause, may in respect to their persons be lawfully injured in any place whatsoever, according to the law of nations. For when war is declared upon any one it is at the same time declared upon the men of his people, as we showed before in the formula of declaration; so also in the proposal for voting: 'Did they wish, did they command, that war be declared upon King Philip and the Macedonians who were under his rule?' Livy, XXXI [vi. 1].

Moreover, according to the law of nations, any one who is an enemy may be attacked anywhere. As Euripides says: [frag. 1076.]

> The laws permit to harm a foe where'er he may be found.

Marcianus the jurist says: 'It is permissible to slay deserters, just the same as enemies, wherever they may be found.' *Digest*, XLVIII. viii. 3. § 6.

2. Such persons therefore may be slain with impunity in their own land, in the land of an enemy, on land under the jurisdiction of no one, or on the sea. The fact that it is not permissible to slay or injure such persons in territory which is in a state of peace is based on a right derived not from their persons but from the right of him who exercises sovereignty there.[1] For political societies were able to agree that no violent measures should be taken against persons who are in territory at peace except by recourse to legal proceedings; of such purport is the passage from Euripides which we have already quoted: [*Children of Hercules*, 251 ff., cited above in II. xxi. 6. 1.]

> If some charge against these guests you prove,
> Justice you shall obtain; by violence
> You shall not drag them hence.

Where tribunals exist regard is had to the deserts of individuals, and that promiscuous right of inflicting injury, which we say arises as between enemies, there ceases. Livy[2] records that seven Carthaginian ships of war were in a harbour that fell under the authority of Syphax, who at that time was at peace with the Carthaginians and the Romans. Scipio came to the harbour with three ships of war, which might have been sunk by the Carthaginians before they entered the harbour; but a strong wind brought them into port XXVIII [xvii. 12].

[1] Compare what we have to say below, III. vi. [466] 26, and Alberico Gentili, *Hispanica Advocatio*, I. vi; Wechner, *Consilia Franconica*, xcii.

[2] For a similar act of the Venetians, who prevented the Greeks from injuring Turks in a port under Venetian jurisdiction, see Chalcocondylas, IX [IX=p. 478]; with regard to the Venetians and Turks at Tunis, Bembo, IV; with regard to the Pisans and Genoese in Sicily, Bizarri, *On the Pisan War*; and with regard to Rostock and Greifswald, Paulinus of Gotha.

before the Carthaginians weighed anchor. Then, in fact, the Carthaginians did not dare to make any attack in the port since it belonged to the king.

IX.—*The right to inflict injury extends even over infants and women*

1. But to return to the point under consideration: How far this right to inflict injury extends may be perceived from the fact that the slaughter even of infants and of women is made with impunity, and that this is included in the law of war.

Deuteronomy, ii. 34. *Deuteronomy*, xx. 16.

I shall not urge, in support of this statement, that the Jews killed the women and children of the Hesbonites, and that they were commanded to execute a like vengeance upon the Canaanites and those who were allied with the Canaanites [1]; for these are the works of God, whose right over men is greater than that of men over brutes, as we have explained elsewhere. Of greater pertinence, as evidencing the common practice of nations, is the fact that in the *Psalms* it is said that he will be happy who dashes the infants of the Babylonians against a rock. This is paralleled by the saying of Homer: [2]

Psalms, cxxxvi [cxxxvii. 9]. [*Iliad*, XXII. 63 f.]

> Bodies of infants dashed upon the ground,
> While ruthless war all things affrights.

I [VII. xxix]. [*Anabasis of Alexander*, I. viii.] [*Spanish Wars*, vi. 32.] *Annals*, I [li].

[460] 2. In ancient times, as Thucydides relates, upon capturing Mycalessus the Thracians slew both women and children. Arrian records the same of the Macedonians when they had taken Thebes. After Ilurgia, a city in Spain, had been captured,[3] the Romans 'slew alike both children and women', to use the words of Appian.

Tacitus records that Germanicus Caesar laid waste the villages of the Marsi, a people of Germany, with fire and sword, and adds: 'Neither sex nor age found mercy.' Titus even exposed Jewish children and women to be slaughtered by wild beasts in a public spectacle. And yet these two men are believed to have been by no means cruel in disposition—to such an extent had cruelty of this

[1] Like the Amalekites, of whom Josephus, in relating the history of Saul, VI. viii [*Antiquities of the Jews*, VI. vii. 2] writes: 'He proceeded to slay even women and children, considering that in this he was doing nothing cruel or contrary to human nature, first because those to whom he did it were enemies,' &c.

[2] Severus, threatening the Britons, cited [in Xiphilinus, LXXVI. xv] these words from the same Homer [*Iliad*, VI. 58]:

> Nor will he cruel fate escape,
> Who still lies hidden in his mother's womb

[3] Scipio, after the capture of Numantia; the soldiers of Julian, who slew the women that had been left at Dacira, Zosimus, III [III. xv]. Ammianus in Book XIV [XXIV. iv. 25] says that after this same Julian had taken Majozamaltha 'the violence of the enraged soldiery slew whatever they met in their onset without distinction of age or sex'.

sort become a custom. It is, then, less surprising if old men too are killed, as Priam by Pyrrhus. *Aeneid*, II [550 ff.].

X.—*The right to inflict injury extends even over captives, and without limitation of time*

1. Not even captives are exempt from this right to inflict injury.[1] In Seneca Pyrrhus says, in accordance with the accepted custom of the time, *Trojan Women* [333].

> No law the captive spares or punishment restrains.

In the *Ciris*, attributed to Virgil, such is said to be the law of war, even against captive women; Scylla there speaks thus: [447.]

> But by the law of war a captive you had slain.

Also in the passage cited from Seneca the killing of a woman, Polyxena in fact, was under discussion. This practice gave rise to that saying of Horace: [*Epistles*, I. xvi. 69.]

> When you can sell a prisoner, slay him not;

for the words imply the postulate that it is permissible to kill a captive.

Donatus says that those were called slaves (*servi*) who had been saved (*servati*), 'when by the law of war they could have been killed'. [*On Terence's*] *Adelphi*, II. i [128]. Thus the captives from Epidamnus were slain by the Corcyreans, as Thucydides relates. I [xxx]. Thus five thousand prisoners were put to death by Hannibal. Appian, *Hann. Wars* [iii. 14]. In the *African War* of Hirtius a centurion of Caesar thus addresses Scipio: 'I thank you for having promised life and safety to me, although a captive by the law of war.' Dio Cass., XLVII [xlviii]. [Hirtius, *African War*, xlv.]

2. So far as the law of nations is concerned, the right of killing such slaves, that is, captives taken in war, is not precluded at any time, although it is restricted, now more, now less, by the laws of states.

XI.—*The right to inflict injury extends even over those who wish to surrender, but whose surrender is not accepted*

Furthermore we meet with frequent examples of the slaughter of suppliants, as by Achilles in Homer, and in Virgil the cases of Mago and Turnus. These instances of the killing of suppliants, we see, are related in such a way that they are defended by the law of [Homer, *Iliad*, XX. 463; XXI. 74; Virgil, *Aeneid*, X. 524; XII. 930.]

[1] In Josephus [*Antiquities of the Jews*, IX. iv. 3] Elisaeus 'said that it was right to slay those who had been made prisoners by the law of war'. And so Virgil [*Aeneid*, X. 524 f.] introduces a prisoner who utters the prayer:

> By the shades of thy sires, by thy hope in the youthful Iulus,
> Preserve, I beseech thee, this life to my son and my sire.

Wittekind, Book II [III, p. 34], relates that Otho put to death 70,000 [700 in Wittekind's text] Slavs who had been made prisoners.

City of God, I. ii [I. i]. war of which I have spoken. In fact, Augustine also, when praising the Goths, who had spared suppliants and those that had taken refuge in temples, says: 'What would have been permissible by the law of war they judged was not permissible for them.'

Again, the surrender of those who give themselves up is not always accepted. Such was the case of the Greeks who fought in the service of the Persians at Granicus; in Tacitus is another instance, *Annals*, XII [xvii]. that of the Uspenses, who sought pardon for their freemen: 'Their plea the victors rejected', he says, 'that they might rather perish by the law of war.' Note here also the expression 'the law of war'.

XII.—*The right to inflict injury extends even over those who have surrendered unconditionally*

Livy, II [xvii. 6]. Dion., XLV [XLIII. ix]. [Dio Cassius, XL. xli.] But you may read also that captives, whose unconditional surrender was accepted, have been put to death,[1] as the rulers of Pometia by the Romans; Samnites, by Sulla; Numidians, and Vercingetorix himself, by Caesar.

There was indeed almost a permanent custom among the Romans with respect to the commanders of the enemy, whether captured or received by surrender, that they should be put to death on the day [V. xxx. 77.] of the Roman triumph.[2] So Cicero informs us in his fifth oration [XXVI. xiii. 15.] *Against Verres*, Livy both in Book XXVIII and elsewhere, Tacitus in his *Annals*, Book XII, and many other authors. As Tacitus [XII. xix.] also relates, Galba ordered the decimation of those whom he had *Histories*, I [xxxvii]. received under his protection as suppliants; and Cecinna, after receiving the surrender of Aventicum, punished Julius Alpinus, one [*Histories*, I. lxviii.] of the foremost men, as the instigator of the war, and left the rest to the mercy, or savagery, of Vitellius.

[461] XIII.—*It is incorrect to refer this right to other causes, as retaliation, or obstinacy of defence*

1. Sometimes historians assign the reason for the slaughter of enemies, particularly of captives or suppliants, either to retaliation, or to obstinacy in resisting;[3] but these causes, as we have indicated elsewhere, are plausible rather than justificatory. In fact, retaliation that is lawful, and properly so called, must be inflicted upon the very person who has done wrong, as may be seen from what has previously been said on the sharing of punishment.

In war, on the contrary, what is called retaliation very frequently brings harm to those who are in no way to blame for that on which

[1] See De Thou, Book LXX [LXX. xvii], on the year 1580, with regard to events in Ireland.
[2] There is a similar occurrence in the *Chronicle* of Regino for the year 905.
[3] As Chalcocondylas, Book VIII.

the issue is joined. The point of view is thus set forth by Diodorus Siculus: 'Having learned from actual experience, since the hazard of war is the same for all belligerents, they were not unaware that either side if defeated must expect to receive the treatment which it would have accorded to the vanquished.' In the same author Philomelus, leader of the Phocians, 'made the enemy cease from their insolent and cruel punishment by inflicting an equivalent penalty'.[1] [XIV. xlvi.] [XVI. xxxi.]

2. In truth there is no one who holds that an obstinate devotion to one's party is worthy of punishment; this is illustrated by the reply of the Neapolitans to Belisarius, in Procopius. The statement holds particularly true when the party to which allegiance is maintained has been assigned by nature, or chosen for an honourable reason. *Gothic War*, I [viii].

In fact, so far from there being any crime involved in such allegiance, it is accounted a criminal act to desert one's post. This was insisted on especially in the military law of ancient Rome, which in such cases hardly admitted any excuse of fear or danger. 'Among the Romans to leave one's post is a capital crime', says Livy. For his own advantage, therefore, each one resorts to so extreme severity in cases in which it seems expedient; moreover, such severity is defended among men by the law of nations, of which we are now treating. Polybius, I [xvii] and VI [xxxvii]. XXIV [xxxvii. 9].

XIV.—*The right to inflict injury extends over hostages also*

This right to inflict injury has also been exercised against hostages, not merely against those who had bound themselves, as by an agreement, but also against those who have been surrendered by others. In ancient times two hundred and fifty hostages were put to death by the Thessalians; and hostages of the Volsci Aurunci, to the number of three hundred, by the Romans. Plutarch, *On Noble Traits of Women* [= p. 244 B]. Dionysius, [*Roman Antiquities*,] XVI [VI. xxx].

Furthermore we must remember that even boys were commonly given as hostages; we read that this was done by the Parthians and by Simon, one of the Maccabees. Women also were given as hostages by the Romans in the time of Porsena, and by the Germans, according to Tacitus. Tacitus, *Annals*, XII [x]. *I Maccabees*, xiii. 17 [xiii. 16]. *Histories*, IV [*Germany* viii].

XV.—*By the law of nations it is forbidden to kill any one by means of poison*

1. However, just as the law of nations, through that form of permission which we have now explained, permits many things which

[1] See the same Diodorus on Spondius and Hamilcar Barca in the *Excerpta Peiresciana* [*Excerpta de Virtutibus et Vitiis*, i = p. 262].

are forbidden by the law of nature, so it forbids certain things which are permissible by the law of nature. If you take account only of the law of nature, in case it is permissible to kill a person, it makes no difference whether you kill him by the sword or by poison. By the law of nature, I repeat, for it is indeed more noble to kill in such a way that he who is killed may have a chance to defend himself; but this is not an obligation due to one who has deserved to die. Nevertheless from old times the law of nations—if not of all nations, certainly of those of the better sort—has been that it is not permissible to kill an enemy by poison.

Agreement upon this matter arose from a consideration of the common advantage, in order that the dangers of war, which had begun to be frequent, might not be too widely extended. And it is easy to believe that this agreement originated with kings, whose lives are better defended by arms than those of other men, but are less safe from poison, unless they are protected by some respect for law and by fear of disgrace.[1]

Livy, XLII [xviii. 1]. *War with Gildo* [274]. *On Duties,* III [xxii. 86]. [*Attic Nights,*] III. viii. V. v [VI. v. 1]. *Annals,* III [II. lxxxviii.]

2. In speaking of Perseus Livy calls the poisoning of enemies secret crimes. Claudian, in discussing the plot against Pyrrhus which was rejected by Fabricius, characterizes it as impious, and Cicero, touching on the same story, refers to it as an atrocity. From the point of view of an example for all, it is important that no such deed be done, say the Roman consuls [462] in the letter to Pyrrhus which Gellius quotes from Claudius Quadrigarius. In Valerius Maximus is the saying, 'Wars ought to be waged with weapons, not with poisons.'

Tacitus records that, when the leader of the Chatti offered to bring about the death of Arminius by poison, Tiberius refused the offer, by this glorious act placing himself on a level with the generals of olden days. Wherefore those who argue that it is permissible to kill an enemy by poison,[2] as does Baldus, following Vegetius, have regard to the law of nature only; they quite overlook that which takes its rise in the will of the nations.

Consilia, II. 188.

XVI.—*By the law of nations it is forbidden to poison weapons or waters*

1. Different in a degree from poisoning of this sort, and more closely allied with the use of force, is the poisoning of javelins. This is a doubling of the causes of death which Ovid relates of the Getae,[3]

[Ovid, *From the Pontus,* I. ii. 15 ff.]

[1] The senators [the Consuls, rather] wrote to Pyrrhus: 'that if anything should befall you it may not bring infamy upon us' [Plutarch, *Pyrrhus,* xxi = p. 396 C].

[2] On the Venetians, see Bembo, Book III, end.

[3] Of the Scythians Pliny, [*Natural History,*] XI. liii, observes: 'The Scythians foul their arrows with the poison of vipers and human blood; this wickedness, for which no remedy can be found, produces death at once by a light touch.' On the Serbians see Helmold, *Supplement,* chap. iv.

Lucan of the Parthians, Silius of certain of the Africans, and Claudianus of the Ethiopians in particular. But this also is contrary to the law of nations,[1] not indeed of all nations, but of European nations, and of such others as attain to the higher standard of Europe.

[Lucan, VIII. 304 Silius, III. 273; Claud., *On Consulship of Stilicho*, I. 351.]

John of Salisbury has rightly stated the principle in these words: 'I do not read that it is permissible under any law to use poison, although I see that poisoning is sometimes resorted to by unbelievers.' Of like implication are the words of Silius, 'To disgrace iron with poison.'

John of Salisbury, [*Policraticus*,] viii. 20. [III. 273.]

2. The poisoning of springs also, though the act either is not secret or does not long remain so, is said by Florus to be not only contrary to ancestral custom but also contrary to the law of the gods; just as we have pointed out elsewhere, writers frequently ascribe the laws of nations to the gods. It should not indeed seem remarkable if there exist some such tacit agreements among belligerents to lessen the risks of war, when in olden times the Chalcidians and Eretrians, while at war, covenanted 'not to make use of missile weapons'.

II [xx]. [II. xix. 1. 2.] Strabo, X [i. 12].

XVII.—*It is not forbidden by the law of nations to pollute waters in another way*

Pausanias, ult. [X. xxxvii] Frontinus, [*Strata-gems*,] III [vii. 6]: Aeschines, *On the Badly Conducted Embassy* [cxv]. [*Halieutica*, IV. 687 f.]

The rule just stated has not been established in regard to the pollution of waters without the use of poison,[2] in such a way that one cannot drink from them. Such pollution, we read, Solon and the Amphictyons considered lawful against barbarians; and according to Oppian, in his *On Fishing*, Book IV, it was customary in his time. This is considered to be like the diverting of a river, or cutting off the veins of a spring,[3] which is permissible by nature and by convention.

XVIII.—*Whether or not the use of assassins is contrary to the law of nations*

1. The question is frequently discussed whether, according to the law of nations, it is permissible to kill an enemy by sending an assassin against him.

In general a distinction must be made between assassins who violate an express or tacit obligation of good faith, as subjects resorting to violence against a king, vassals against a lord, soldiers against him

[1] And so Ilus, the son of Mermerus, refuses Ulysses poison for his spears, *Odyssey*, I [I. 263]:
[467] Fearing the wrath of the immortal gods.

[2] With corpses, or with asbestos, which Belisarius used in the siege of Auximium, Procopius, *Gothic War*, II [II. xxvii]; or with lime, as the Turks at Dibra, Nicetas, *On Alexis*, I [I. vii], brother of Isaac [Comnenus]. Similar acts are related by Otto of Freising, and Gunther, *Ligurinus*.

[3] See Priscus, *Selections on Embassies* [p. 29].

whom they serve, those also who have been received as suppliants or strangers or deserters, against those who have received them; and such as are held by no bond of good faith. In the latter class is Pepin,[1] the father of Charlemagne, who, accompanied by one attendant, is said to have crossed the Rhine and to have slain an enemy in his bedchamber; a similar deed was attempted upon
[V. lxxxi.] Ptolemy of Egypt, and Polybius, attributing it to Theodotus the Aetolian, calls it 'a manly deed of daring'.

Of such a character was also the attempt of Quintus [Gaius]
Livy, II [xii. 9]. Mucius Scaevola,[2] celebrated by historians, which he himself defended thus: 'As an enemy I wished to slay an enemy.' Porsena himself
III. iii [II. iii. 1]. saw nothing but bravery in this deed. Valerius Maximus calls it an attempt free from reproach and brave; and Cicero also praises it
[xxi. 48.] in his speech *For Publius Sestius.*

2. Not merely by the law of nature but also by the law of nations, as we have said above, it is in fact permissible to kill an enemy in any place whatsoever; and it does not matter how many there are who do the deed, or who suffer. Six hundred Spartans
Justin, II [xi. 15]. with Leonidas entered the hostile camp of the enemy and made straight for the tent of the king. The same venture would have
Livy, XXVII [xxvii]. been permissible for a smaller number.[3] Those were few in number who from an ambuscade surrounded and slew the consul Marcellus;
Tacitus, *Histories,* V [xxii]. and few likewise were those who all but stabbed Petilius Cerialis in his bed. [463] Ambrose praises Eleazer [4] for attacking an elephant
On Duties, I. xl [197]. which towered above the rest, in the belief that the king was seated thereon.

According to the law of nations not only those who do such deeds, but also those who instigate others to do them, are to be
Livy, II [xii. 14]. considered free from blame. Scaevola was incited to his daring deed by those Roman senators of old, who were so scrupulous in warfare.

3. No one ought to be influenced by the fact that when persons who have made such attempts are caught they are usually subjected to refined tortures. This result does not follow because they have
Digest, XLVIII. viii. 3. § 6. violated the law of nations, but because, by that same law of nations, anything is permissible as against an enemy. In such cases, however, each decides upon a more severe or more lenient punishment from the point of view of his personal advantage.

[1] See Paul Warnefrid [Paulus Diaconus], VI [VI. xxxvii].

[2] Who is, in Plutarch [*Publicola,* xvii = p. 106 B], 'a man pre-eminent in all virtue'.

[3] Valens promised a monetary reward to any one who should have brought in the head of a Scythian. Thus peace was secured; Zosimus, IV [IV. xxii].

[4] Also Josephus, *Antiquities of the Jews,* XV. xiv [XII. ix. 4]. A similar act of Theodosius against Eugenius is mentioned by Zosimus, IV [IV. lviii]; of the Gauls against the Persian king, in Agathias; of ten Persians against Julian, in Ammianus, XXIV [XXIV. iv. 4], and Zosimus, III [III. xx]; of Alexius Comnenus against Toruses, in Nicetas of Chonae, *On Manuel,* IV [IV. iv]; and of the Bulgars against the Emperor Nicephorus, in Zonaras [XV. xv].

Under these conditions spies, whose sending is beyond doubt permitted by the law of nations—such as the spies whom Moses sent out, or Joshua himself—if caught are usually treated most severely. 'It is customary', says Appian, 'to kill spies.' Sometimes they are treated with justice by those who clearly have a just care for carrying on war; by others, however, they are dealt with in accordance with that impunity which the law of war accords. If any are to be found who refuse to make use of the help of spies, when it is offered to them,[1] their refusal must be attributed to their loftiness of mind and confidence in their power to act openly, not to their view of what is just or unjust. *Punic Wars* [xxxix].

4. But a different point of view must be adopted in regard to those assassins who act treacherously. Not only do they themselves act in a manner inconsistent with the law of nations, but this holds true also of those who employ their services. And yet, in other things those who avail themselves of the aid of bad men against an enemy are thought to sin before God, but not before men; that is, they are thought not to commit wrong against the law of nations, because in such cases— [Plautus, *Trinummus*, 1037.]

Custom has brought law beneath its sway;

and 'to deceive', as Pliny says, 'in the light of the practices of the age, is prudence'. *Letters*, VIII [xviii. 3], *To Rufinus*

Nevertheless the warrant of custom in such cases does not extend to the right of killing; for he who makes use of another's treachery in causing death is believed to have violated both the law of nature and the law of nations. This is apparent from the words of Alexander to Darius: 'You are waging an unrighteous war; and, although you have arms, you set a price on the heads of your enemies.' Later he says: 'You who have not even observed the laws of war towards me.' In still another passage: 'I must pursue him to the death, not as a just foe, but as an assassin and a poisoner.' Curtius, IV [i. 12–13]. XIV [IV. xi. 18].

Of similar purport is the statement concerning Perseus: 'He was not undertaking a just war with the spirit of a king, but was making his attacks by means of all the secret crimes of robbers and poisoners.' In treating these same deeds of Perseus, Marcius Philippus said: 'In the ruin of his fortunes he will perceive how hateful all his acts are to the gods also.' Here, again, the statement of Valerius Maximus applies: 'The slaying of Viriathus[2] produced a twofold Livy, XLII [xviii. 1]. Livy, XLIV [i. 10]. IX. vii [IX. vi. 4].

[1] See Kromer, [Book V,] p. 113.

[2] The author of *De Viris Illustribus* [Aurelius Victor, lxxi] says: 'This victory, because it had been purchased, was not approved of by the Senate.' Eutropius [IV. xvi] says: 'When his murderers sought the reward from the consul Caepio, they received the reply that the Romans never approved of a general being killed by his own troops'; perhaps one should read 'the reward promised by the consul Caepio'. Similarly the assassination of Sertorius is condemned by Ammianus, XXX [XXX. i. 23].

charge of treachery: against his friends, because he was killed by their hands; against Quintus Servilius Caepio, the consul, because he was the instigator of the crime by his promise of immunity, and did not earn his victory, but purchased it.'

5. The reason why in this matter men have reached a conclusion different from that adopted in other cases is the same that we advanced above with regard to the use of poison. It has in view the purpose to prevent the dangers to persons of particular eminence

Justin, XIV [i. 12]. from becoming excessive. According to Justin, Eumenes declared that 'he did not believe that any general wished to conquer by such means that he would set a very bad example against himself'.

XII [v. 10 ff.]. In Justin, again, the murder of Darius by Bessus is said to be an example and a cause common to all kings; and, in Sophocles, Oedipus, when about to avenge the death of King Laius, says:

[*Oedipus the King*, 141.]

> Then in avenging him I serve myself.

Likewise in Seneca's tragedy on the same theme:

[*Oedipus*, 242.]

> Kings, above all, king's safety must protect.

[Gellius, III. viii.] The Roman consuls wrote in a letter to Pyrrhus: 'It seemed an example of good faith for all that we should desire your safety.'

6. In a public war, therefore, or among those who [464] have the right to declare a public war, the practice under consideration is not permissible; however, apart from a public war, by the same law of

Annals, XI [xix]. nations it is held to be permissible. Accordingly, Tacitus does not admit that a plot of this sort laid against the renegade Gannascus

VII [v. 20]. was degrading.[1] Curtius says that the treachery of Spitamenes could seem less hateful, since no one thought anything wicked that was done against Bessus, who slew his king. So, too, treachery towards robbers and pirates is not indeed blameless, but goes unpunished among nations by reason of hatred of those against whom it is practised.

XIX.—*Whether rape is contrary to the law of nations*

1. You may read in many places that the raping of women in time of war is permissible, and in many others that it is not permissible. Those who sanction rape have taken into account only the injury done to the person of another, and have judged that it is not

[1] Thus Ammianus [XXVI. ix. 10] says of Florentius and Barchalba, who handed over the rebel Procopius: 'If they had betrayed a legitimate prince, justice itself would have declared that they could have been rightly killed; but if they had betrayed a rebel and an opponent of peace within the state, as it was said, they should have received a rich reward for the memorable deed.' So Artabanes is praised for the death of Gontharides, in the historian Procopius, *Vandalic War*, at the end of Book II [II. xxviii]. Compare Kromer, Book XXVIII [p. 604], on the killing of Sechodolius.

inconsistent with the law of war that everything which belongs to the enemy should be at the disposition of the victor. A better conclusion has been reached by others, who have taken into consideration not only the injury but the unrestrained lust of the act; also, the fact that such acts do not contribute to safety or to punishment, and should consequently not go unpunished in war any more than in peace.

The latter view is the law not of all nations, but of the better ones. Thus Marcellus, before capturing Syracuse, is said to have taken pains for the protection of chastity,[1] even in the case of the enemy. In Livy, Scipio says that it is a matter of concern for himself and for the Roman people 'that they should not violate what is anywhere held sacred'. 'Anywhere', that is to say, among the more advanced peoples. Diodorus Siculus says of the soldiers of Agathocles: 'They did not abstain from insults and lawlessness[2] towards women.' Aelian, having related that the chastity of the women and girls of Pellene was violated by the victorious Sicyonians, exclaims: 'These are most brutal acts, ye gods of Greece, and not held honourable even among barbarians, so far as my memory serves.'

Augustine, *City of God*, II [I. vi].

XXVI [xlix. 14].

[XIX. viii.]

Various History, VI [i].

2. Among Christians[3] it is right that the view just presented shall be enforced, not only as a part of military discipline, but also as a part of the law of nations; that is, whoever forcibly violates chastity, even in war, should everywhere be subject to punishment. No one could have committed such an act with impunity under the Hebraic law, as may be perceived from that part which deals with the taking of a woman[4] captive and not subsequently selling her. On this passage the Jewish rabbi Bacchai comments: 'God wished that the camp of the Israelites should be holy, not abandoned to fornication and other abominations like the camps of the Gentiles.'

Deuteronomy, xxi. 10.

Arrian, after relating that Alexander, captivated by the love for Roxane, 'did not desire to misuse her as a captive, but thought it proper to marry her', adds his approval of the act. Of the same act Plutarch says: 'He did not misuse her, but took her to wife, as was becoming for a philosopher.' Plutarch relates also that a certain Torquatus was banished to Corsica[5] by a decree of the Romans, because he had violated a maiden of the enemy.

[*Anabasis of Alexander*, IV. xix. 9.]

[*On the Bravery of Alexander*, xi = p. 332 E.]

Parallels [xiii = p. 308 F].

[1] Also Lucullus, according to Xiphilinus [Dio Cassius, XXXVI. iv]. See the proclamation of the Moor Cabaon in Procopius, *Vandalic War*, I [I. viii].

[2] Appian, *Mithridatic Wars* [xlvii], says of the captured Chians: 'The women and children were barbarously violated by those who carried them off.'

[3] Belisarius everywhere observed this, as did Totila at the capture of Cumae and Rome. This is recorded by Procopius, *Gothic War*, III [III. i, viii and xx].

[4] As Philo eloquently explains in his book, *On Humanity* [xiv]. Says Josephus, *Against Apion*, II [II. xxix. 212]: 'The law also cared for prisoners of war, that they might be protected, especially the women, from insult.'

[5] But Chosroes, the Persian king, crucified a man who had assaulted a girl of Apamea; Procopius, *Persian War*, II [II. xi].

[468] CHAPTER V

ON DEVASTATION AND PILLAGE

I.—*Enemy property may be destroyed and pillaged*

On Duties, III [vi. 32]. THAT it is not contrary to nature to despoil him whom it is honourable to kill,[1] was said by Cicero. Therefore it is not strange that the law of nations has permitted the destruction and plunder of the property of enemies, the slaughter of whom it has permitted. [V. xi.] Consistently with this, Polybius in the fifth book of his *Histories* says that the plunder or destruction of enemy fortifications, harbours, cities, men, ships, crops, and anything else of the kind, is included XXXI [xxx. 2–3]. in the law of war. We read in Livy that 'there are certain rules of warfare which it is proper for us both to enforce and to endure: the burning of crops, the destruction of buildings, and the driving off of men and cattle as spoil.'

On almost every page of historical writings you may find accounts of the destruction of whole cities, or the levelling of walls to the ground, the devastation of fields, and conflagrations. It must be noted furthermore that such acts are permissible also against those *Annals*, XIII [xli]. who have surrendered. 'The townsmen', says Tacitus, 'voluntarily opened the gates and placed themselves and their belongings in the hands of the Romans, and this secured safety for themselves; but Artaxata was set on fire.'

II.—*Even enemy property that is sacred may be destroyed and pillaged; how this is to be understood*

1. Now the law of nations in itself, apart from the consideration of other obligations of which we shall speak below, does not exempt things that are sacred, that is, things dedicated to God or to the *Dig.* XI. vii. 36. gods. 'When places are taken by the enemy, all things cease to be sacred',[2] says Pomponius the jurist. 'Victory had made profane the sacred things of Syracuse', says Cicero in his fourth oration [IV. lv. 122.] *Against Verres*.

[1] Suetonius, *Nero*, xl: 'As though by the law of war an occasion had arisen for plundering the wealthiest provinces'. Cyprian, *On Mortality* [chap. viii]: 'So when possession has been taken of a state through an invasion of enemies, captivity falls upon all alike.'

[2] Tertullian, *Apology* [xxv]: 'Furthermore wars and victories consist very often in the capture and destruction of cities. Such procedure is not without injury to the gods. There is the same destruction of fortifications and of temples, a like slaughtering of citizens and of priests, a like plundering of treasures sacred and profane. Thus the sacrileges of the Romans are as numerous as their trophies, their triumphs over gods as numerous as those over peoples; and their spoils of war are numbered by the images of captured gods which remain unto this day.' Soon after [xl]: 'And rightly so, for if any reverse has overtaken the cities their temples have suffered the same ruin as their walls.'

The reason is that the things, which are called sacred, are in fact not withdrawn from human use, but are public [1]; however, they are called sacred from the purpose to which they are devoted. The proof of what I say is that when any people surrenders itself to another people, or to a king, there are also at the same time surrendered the things which are called divine. This is clear from I. iii. 8 the formula which we have cited elsewhere from Livy; [Livy, VII. xxxi. 4]. and with that the verse in the *Amphitruo* of Plautus agrees,

> Their city, lands, their altars, hearths, and persons [226.]
> Let them give up;

and then:

> They yield themselves and all possessions, human and divine. [258.]

2. In consequence Ulpian says that even sacred things are [*Digest*, I. i. 1. § 2.] included under public law. In his description of Arcadia Pausanias [VIII. xlvi.] says that it was a custom common to both Greeks and barbarians, that sacred things should be at the disposal of those who had captured cities. Thus he relates that when Troy was taken the image of Hercaean Jupiter was granted to Sthenelus; and he gives many other examples of the same custom. Thucydides, in Book IV, [IV. xcviii.] says: 'It was the custom among the Greeks, that those who had power over a country, whether large or small, should also possess its shrines.' [2] With this agrees the statement in Tacitus: 'In the *Annals*, XII [III. lxxi]. Italian towns, all ceremonies, and temples, and statues of the gods, are subject to the Roman law and authority.'

3. Hence, furthermore, a people, having changed its mind, *Digest*, XLV. i. 83. § 5, and 137. § 6. may make profane what has been sacred, as is clearly indicated by the jurists Paul and Venuleius. We see that, under the necessity of the times, sacred things have been converted to the uses of war [3] by those who had consecrated them. This, we read, was done by Pericles, though with a promise of restitution, by Mago in Spain,

[1] Marsilius of Padua in the *Defensor Pacis*, chap. v, pt. 2; Nicolas de Bohier, *Decisions*, lxix, no. 1; Bossius, *Practica Criminalia*, *De Foro Competente*, no. 101; Cothmann, *Consilia*, c, no. 30.

[2] This custom is also revealed by a passage from Polybius cited below, III. viii. 4.

[3] As by the Syracusans in the time of Timoleon, in whose life Plutarch records this [*Timoleon*, xxiii = p. 247 E]. The Chians made up even from the sacred vessels the fine which Mithridates laid upon them; Appian, *Mithridatic Wars* [vii. 47]. Pliny, Book VII, last chapter [*Natural History*, XVII. xxviii. end], in speaking of Marcus Porcius Cato, says: 'He sanctioned the cutting down of sacred trees [471] and groves, after the offering of sacrifice; and he has handed down the reason for this in the same volume.'

In the Mithridatic War, Sulla removed the votive offerings from Olympia, Epidaurus, and Delphi, as is related by Plutarch [*Sulla*, xii = p. 459 B] and Appian [*Mithridatic Wars*, viii. 54]; and he also restored their value; Diodorus Siculus in the *Excerpta Peiresciana* [*Excerpta de Virtutibus et Vitiis*, i = p. 322]. Augustus borrowed treasures from the temples, as we learn from Appian, *Civil Wars*, V [V. ii. 13]. Cassiodorus relates that Agapetus gave sacred vessels in pledge, [*Variae*,] XII. xx.

In time of grave need Heraclius coined money from the vessels of the Church, but afterwards restored their value, as Theophanes relates. See also Anna Comnena, V [V. ii] and VI [VI. iii]; Kromer, XXIII; and the speech of Laurentianus in Bembo, Book VI. Add what is to be said below in III. xxi. 23.

by the Romans in the Mithridatic War, [469] by Sulla, Pompey, Caesar, and others. In Plutarch Tiberius Gracchus says: 'There is nothing so sacred and holy as offerings to the gods. Nevertheless no one has hindered the people from using, moving, or transferring these.'

[*Tiberius Gracchus*, xv = p. 832 A.]

In the *Controversies* of Seneca[1] the Father we read: 'Oftentimes the temples are stripped for the sake of the state, and we melt down offerings to serve as pay.' Trebatius, a jurist of the time of Caesar, says: 'That is profane, which, from being religious or sacred, has been transferred to the use and ownership of men.'[2] Of this law of nations, therefore, Germanicus made use against the Marsi, when, as Tacitus relates: 'Profane and sacred structures alike, even the temple most famed among these peoples, which they called the shrine of Tanfana, were levelled to the ground.' Here apply the lines of Virgil:

Macrobius, *Saturnalia*, III [iv].

Annals, I [li].

[*Aeneid*, XII. 778 f.]

> If I your altars always have revered,
> Which the Trojans have profaned in war.

Pausanias has recorded that gifts to the gods are as a rule seized by the victors[3]; and Cicero, speaking of Publius Servilius, calls this the law of war. 'He removed statues and ornaments', Cicero says, 'from the city of the enemy which had been taken by force and valour, in accordance with the law of war and the right of a commander.' Thus Livy says that the adornments of the temple, which Marcellus brought to Rome from Syracuse, 'were acquired by the law of war'. Gaius Flaminius, in speaking for Marcus Fulvius, says: 'Statues were carried off and other things done which are usually done when cities are captured.' Fulvius[4] also in a speech calls this very thing the law of war. Cato [Caesar] in a speech reported by Sallust, in recalling what usually happens to the vanquished, mentions likewise the pillaging of shrines.[5]

VIII [xlvi]. *Against Verres*, III [I. xxi. 57].

XXV [xl. 2].

[Livy, XXXVIII. xliii. 10.]

[Livy,] XXXIX [iv. 12].

[*Catiline*, li. 9.]

4. Nevertheless this is true, that if a divinity is believed to

[1] In the *Excerpta*, IV. iv.

[2] Servius, *On the Aeneid*, II [II. 713], says of the temple of Ceres: 'Aeneas knew that it had previously been profaned.' He says the same *On the Aeneid*, III, IX, and XII. Moreover, *On the Eclogues*, VII [VII. 31], he remarks: 'Gifts offered to deities are sacred, and may be called offerings, only so long as they have not been profaned.'

[3] Virgil, *Aeneid*, V [line 360]:

> By Greeks ta'en down from Neptune's sacred door.

Plutarch, in his *Fabius* [xxii = p. 187 C, D], relates that he captured a statue of Hercules at Tarentum and sent it to the Capitol; he left to the Tarentines the rest of their gods, because they were hostile. In harmony with this is the quotation we have just made from Tertullian, and also the following from the same author, *Against the Nations*, II [II. xvii]: 'Hence as many triumphs over gods as over peoples. Still remaining among them are their captive idols, and if these perceive their conquerors they do not love them.'

[4] See Polybius, *Selections on Embassies*, xxvii [= *Histories*, XXI. xxx].

[5] See Kromer, Book XVII [p. 402]. With regard to the property of the Church at Antioch captured by Chosroes, see Procopius, *Persian War*, II [II. ix].

reside in an image it is unlawful that the image shall be defiled or destroyed by those who share such belief. On the assumption that such a belief is held, those who have committed acts of this character are sometimes accused of impiety or of contravention of the law of nations. The case is different if the enemy do not hold the same view; so the Jews were not only permitted but even enjoined to destroy the idols of the Gentiles. *Deuteronomy*, vii. 5.

The reason why the Jews were forbidden to take the idols of their enemies was, that they might the more abominate the superstitions of the Gentiles, having been warned against contamination by the very prohibition of contact. The purpose was not to spare what was sacred to others, as Josephus[1] explains, doubtless from flattery to the Romans, just as in his explanation of the other command, about not naming the gods of the Gentiles; for he explains this as though the Jews were forbidden to speak evil of the gods of the Gentiles, when in fact the law would not permit them to be named for the sake of honouring them, or without execration. The Jews in fact knew, through the most certain admonition of God, that in these idols there dwelt, not the spirit of God, nor good angels, nor the power of the stars, as the misguided Gentiles thought, but base demons, hostile to the human race. As Tacitus rightly said in describing the institutions of the Jews: 'In their view all things are profane which among us are sacred.' Hence it is not strange if we read that the Maccabees more than once set fire to temples of a profane cult. *Histories*, V [iv]. *I Maccabees*, v [44] and x [84].

When, therefore, Xerxes destroyed the images belonging to the Greeks, he did nothing contrary to the law of nations, although Greek writers exaggerate this greatly in order to arouse enmity. For the Persians did not believe that there were any divinities in idols,[2] but thought that God was the sun, and any fire was a part of him. By the Hebraic law, as Tacitus also rightly says: 'None but the priests were permitted to cross the threshold of the Temple.' Asconius Pedianus, *On* [*Cicero's*] *Against Verres*, III [I. xviii. 48]. [*Histories*, V. viii, ix.]

5. Nevertheless Pompey, according to the same author, 'entered the Temple by right of conquest'; or, as Augustine, referring to the same incident, says, 'not with the devotion [470] of a suppliant, but by the right of a conqueror'. He did well to spare the Temple and its furnishings, although, as Cicero expressly says, he did so from shame and fear of his critics, not from respect; but he did wrong to enter, seeing that he despised the true God, an attitude which the Prophets censured in the Chaldaeans also. For this reason some persons even believe that the wonderful providence of God caused *City of God*, XVIII. xlv. *For Flaccus* [xxviii. 68]. *Daniel*, v. 23.

[1] Josephus, *Antiquities of the Jews*, IV. viii [IV. viii. 10], and *Against Apion*, II [II. xxxiii. 237].
[2] Diogenes Laertius at the beginning [procem., vi] says: 'Idols are condemned by the magi.'

the Pompey whom I mentioned to be slain as it were in the sight of Judaea, at Cassius, a promontory of Egypt.

Still, if you consider the point of view of the Romans, nothing in relation to the Temple in Jerusalem was done contrary to the law of nations. Thus Josephus relates that the Temple was destroyed by Titus, and adds that it was destroyed 'in accordance with the law of war'.

Jewish War, VI. xxiv and xxxiv [VI. iv. § 3 and v. § 2].

III.—*Enemy property that is consecrated may be destroyed or pillaged ; a caution is added*

What we have said of sacred things should be understood of consecrated things as well; for these, also, do not belong to the dead but to the living, being the possession of a people or of a family. Therefore Pomponius in the passage cited above wrote that, just as sacred places, so consecrated places ceased, when taken by enemies, to be such; and Paul the jurist said: 'The burial-places of the enemy are not consecrated for us, and so we can use for any purpose stones that have been removed from them.'

[*Dig.* XI. vii. 36.]

Digest, XLVII. xii. 4.

Nevertheless the principle laid down must be so interpreted that the bodies of the dead are not to be mistreated, because that is contrary to the law of burials; and the law of burials, as we have shown elsewhere, was introduced by the law of nations.

[II. xix. I. I.]

IV.—*How far deceit is permissible in these matters*

At this point I shall briefly repeat, that enemy property may be seized not alone by force, but that ruses which do not involve breach of faith are held to be permissible; permissible, again, is even the inciting of another to treachery. In truth the law of nations begins to wink at these frequent minor wrongs, just as municipal laws at harlotry and usury.

CHAPTER VI

ON THE RIGHT OF ACQUIRING THINGS TAKEN IN WAR

I.—*What the law of nature is regarding the acquisition of things taken in war*

[472] 1. Besides the impunity among men in relation to certain actions, which we have discussed up to this point, there is also another effect characteristic of public war according to the law of nations.

According to the law of nature, by a lawful war we acquire things which are either equal to that which, although it was owed to us, we could not otherwise obtain,[1] or we inflict upon the guilty a loss that does not exceed an equitable measure of punishment,[2] as has been said elsewhere. By this law Abraham gave to God a tithe [3] of the spoils which he had taken from the five kings, as the inspired writer of the *Epistle to the Hebrews* (vii. 4) explains the story which is found in *Genesis*, xiv. In like manner the Greeks also, the Carthaginians, and the Romans consecrated to their gods, such as Apollo, Hercules, and Jupiter Feretrius, a tenth of their booty.

Jacob, too, in leaving to Joseph a special legacy in preference to his brothers, said: 'I give thee a portion above thy brethren, which I took out of the hand of the Amorite with my sword and with my bow' (*Genesis*, xlviii. 22). In this passage the words 'I took' [4] apparently are to be understood, in the prophetic manner of speech, as 'I shall assuredly take', and there is attributed to Jacob that which his descendants called by his name were to do, as if the persons of the progenitor and his children were the same. It is in fact more correct to take the meaning thus than to refer these words, as the Jews do, to the pillaging of Shechem, which had already been accomplished by the sons of Jacob; for Jacob, as became his uprightness, always condemned this act as having been associated with treachery, as one may see in *Genesis*, xxxiv. 30, and xlix. 6.

2. Moreover it is clear from other passages also that God approves of this right of spoil within the natural limits which I have mentioned. In His own law, when speaking of the city that has

[1] II. vii. 2.

[2] II. xx [II. xx. 28 ff.].

[3] And victuals to his servants, and a part of the spoil to his allies. See Josephus on this story [*Antiquities of the Jews*, I. x. 2], and what follows below, III. xvi. 3.

[4] The Chaldaean commentator interprets this as accomplished through prayers to God, who by a certain exceptional benevolence had preserved Shechem for Jacob and his posterity.

Deut., xx. 14. been stoned after the rejection of peace, God speaks thus: 'Even all the spoil thereof thou shalt take for a prey unto thyself: and thou shalt eat the spoil of thine enemies, which Jehovah thy God hath given thee.' The men of the tribe of Reuben, of Gad, and part of the tribe of Manasseh are said to have conquered the Ituraeans and their neighbours, and to have taken much spoil from them; and the reason is given, that they had called upon God in the war, and He had listened to them with favour. It is likewise recorded that the pious king Asa, after calling upon God, won both a victory and spoil from the Ethiopians, who were harassing him in an unjust war. The result is all the more noteworthy, because in these cases force was resorted to, not by a special warrant, but by a right common to all.

I Chron., v. 20, 21, 22.

2 Chron., xiv. 13.

Joshua, xxii. 8. 3. Joshua, again, when following with his blessing the very men of the tribes of Reuben, Gad, and a part of the tribe of Manasseh, whom I have mentioned, said: 'Divide the spoil of your enemies with your brethren.' And David, when he sent to the Jewish elders spoils won from the Amalekites, gave value to the gift in saying: 'Behold, a present for you of the spoil of the enemies of Jehovah.'

[*I Samuel*, xxx. 26.]

On Benefits, III. xxxvii [III. xxxiii]. In fact, as Seneca said, for soldiers it is perfectly fair to enrich some one with spoils taken from the enemy. Divine laws also regarding the division of booty are to be found in *Numbers*, xxxi. 27. Philo says that it is among the curses of the law that the land should be harvested by the enemy, whence follows 'famine for friends, but abundance for the foe'.

On Curses [i].

II.—*What the law of nations is; evidences are cited*

1. By the law of nations not merely he who wages war for a just cause, but in a public war also any one at all becomes owner, without limit or restriction, [473] of what he has taken from the enemy. That is true in this sense, at any rate, that both the possessor of such booty, and those who hold their title from him, are to be protected in their possession by all nations; and such a condition one may call ownership so far as its external effects are concerned.

Xenophon, *On the Training of Cyrus*, V [VII. v. 73]. In Xenophon Cyrus says: 'It is an eternal law among men that, whenever a city of the enemy is taken, their property and money belong to the captors.' Plato said: 'All goods of the conquered become the property of the conqueror.' Elsewhere, among the quasi-natural modes of acquisition, he places that 'by warfare', which he also calls 'by pillage', 'by combat', and 'by strength of hand'. In this matter Plato has the approval of Xenophon, whom I have mentioned. In Xenophon's work Socrates, by means of questions, leads Euthydemus to the admission that it is not always

Laws [I. ii = 626 B]. *Sophist* [= 219 ff.]. *Comm.* IV [*Memorabilia*, IV. ii. 15].

unjust to plunder, as when plundering is done to the detriment of an enemy.

2. On the authority of Aristotle also we read: 'The law is a sort of agreement, according to which things taken in war belong to those who take them.' Of the same purport is the saying of Antiphanes [Antisthenes]: 'One ought to pray that the enemy have possessions without courage; for in that case their possessions become the property, not of those who have them, but of those who seize them.' In Plutarch's *Life of Alexander* [1] we read: 'The possessions of the vanquished should be, and should be called, those of the victor.'

Politics, I [vi].

[In Stobaeus, liv. 41.]

[xx = p. 676 A.]

The same author elsewhere says: 'The goods of those who are conquered in battles lie as prizes for those who conquer.' The passage is taken from the second book of Xenophon, *On the Training of Cyrus*. King Philip in his *Letter to the Athenians* said: 'All these cities we hold either because they were left to us by our ancestors or because we have obtained possession of them by war.' Aeschines says: 'If indeed, after making war upon us, you took the city by force of arms, you are in rightful possession of it, since you have it by the law of war.'

[II. iii. 2.]

[Demosthenes, *Orations*, xii. 22 = p. 164.]

On the Badly Conducted Embassy [xxxiii].

3. In Livy Marcellus says that what he took from the Syracusans he took by the law of war.[2] The Roman envoys said to Philip with regard to the cities of Thrace and other cities that, if he had taken them in war, by the law of war he would hold them as the reward of victory; and Masinissa declared that he held by the law of nations the territory that his father had taken in war from the Carthaginians. Likewise, in Justin, Mithridates said: 'He had not withdrawn his son from Cappadocia, of which, as victor, he had taken possession by the law of nations.'

[XXVI. xxxi. 9.]

Livy, XXXIX [xxix. 2].

XXXIX [XL. xvii. 4].

XXXVIII [v. 6].

Cicero states that Mitylene had come into the possession of the Roman people 'by the law of war and the right of victory'. He says also that some things began to be private property either by taking possession of that which was without an owner, or by war; that is, in the latter case things became the property of those who obtained them by victory. Dio Cassius affirms: 'The possessions of the conquered fall to the victors.' Even Clement of Alexandria says that the property of enemies may be carried off and acquired by the law of war.

Against Rullus, II [xvi. 40].

On Duties, I [vii. 21].

[XLI. lvi.]

Stromata, I [xxiii. 157].

4. 'What is taken from the enemy, by the law of nations becomes at once the property of those who take it,' says Gaius the

Dig. XLI. i. 5. § 7.

[1] In the same work [xxxii = p. 684 A]: 'Conquerors acquire also for themselves the things which belong to their enemies.'

[2] [487] Diodorus Siculus, *Excerpta Peiresciana*, no. 467 [*Excerpta de Virtutibus et Vitiis*, i = p. 323], says: 'What is acquired by arms and won by the law of war is not to be given up.' In Agathias, Book II [I. v], the Goths said of Theodoric, after he had conquered Odoacer: 'He held by the law of war all that had belonged to Odoacer.'

Institutes, II. i [17]. Aristotle, *Politics,* I. viii.

jurist. Theophilus, in the Greek *Institutes*, calls this a 'natural acquisition', in the sense in which Aristotle said 'acquisition by war is a method according to nature'. The reason doubtless is that the bare fact, not the cause, is held in view, and in the fact the right has its origin.

Dig. XLI. ii. 1. § 1.

With precisely similar meaning Nerva the Son, as the jurist Paul relates, used to say that the ownership of things arose from natural possession, and that a trace of this remains in relation to those things which are taken on land, in the sea, or in the air; likewise in respect to the things taken in war, all of which become at once the property of those who were the first to take possession of them.

Greek History, III [*Hellenica,* III. i. 26 ff.].

5. Furthermore, what is taken from the subjects of an enemy is also considered as taken from the enemy. Thus Dercyllides argues in Xenophon, [474] that since Pharnabazus was an enemy of the Lacedaemonians, and Mania was a subject of Pharnabazus, the property of Mania stood in such a relation that it could rightfully be seized, according to the law of war.

III.—*When a thing capable of being moved may be held to have been captured, according to the law of nations*

Dig. XLI. i. 44.

1. In this inquiry in regard to war, however, the nations have agreed that he is to be understood as having captured a thing who retains it in such a way that the original possessor has lost probable expectation of regaining it, or so that the thing has escaped pursuit, as Pomponius says in a similar inquiry. In the case of things that are movable, this principle is so extended that such things are said to have been captured when they have been brought within the borders, that is to say, the defences, of the enemy.

Digest, XLIX. xv. 19. § 3; 30. *Digest,* XLIX. xv. 5. § 1; *Institutes,* II. i. § 17. [*Digest,* XLIX. xv. 5. § 1.]

A thing in fact is lost in the same manner by which it returns, by postliminy; it returns when it begins to be within the borders of the state, and that is elsewhere explained as within the defences. Paul says clearly, with regard to a man, that he is lost when he has gone outside of our frontiers; and Pomponius explains that a captive in war is he whom the enemy have taken from among our men and brought within their own defences. Such a man, before he is brought within the defences of the enemy, remains a citizen.

Institutes, loc. cit.; *Dig.* XLI. i. 5. § 7.

2. Now as regards this aspect of the law of nations, the same reasoning was applied to a man and to a thing. Whence it is easy to understand that the statement elsewhere made, that captured things immediately become the property of those who capture them, should be understood as implying the condition that possession continue up to this point.

Hence it seems to follow that on the sea ships and other things may be considered as captured only when they have been brought into dockyards or harbours, or to the place where a whole fleet is stationed; for then recovery begins to appear hopeless. But in the more recent law of nations we see the doctrine introduced among European peoples that such things may be considered as captured when they have been for twenty-four hours [1] in the power of the enemy.

Consolato del Mare, cclxxxiii. and cclxxxvii; *Constitutions of France,* XX. xiii. 24.

IV.—*When territory may be held to have been captured, according to the law of nations*

1. Nevertheless territory is not considered as captured at the moment it is occupied. While it is true that that part of a territory which an army has invaded in great force is temporarily possessed by it, as Celsus has noted, still such possession is not sufficient for that effect which we are discussing, for which secure possession is required. The Romans were so far from considering as lost the land outside the gate which Hannibal was occupying with his camp, that at that very time it sold at a price no lower than before. Therefore only that territory will be regarded as captured which is so surrounded by permanent fortifications that the other party will have no access to it openly unless these have first been taken.

Cornelius a Lapide, *On Genesis,* xiv; Molina, disp. 118. *Dig.* XLI. ii. 18. Livy, XXVI [xi. 6].

2. The origin of the word 'territory' as given by Siculus Flaccus from 'terrifying the enemy' (*terrendis hostibus*) seems not less probable than that of Varro from the word for ploughing (*terendo*), or of Frontinus from the word for land (*terra*),[2] or of Pomponius the jurist from 'the right of terrifying' (*terrendi iure*), which is enjoyed by the magistrates. So Xenophon, in his book *On Taxes*, says that the possession of territory in time of war is retained by means of fortifications, which he calls 'walls and entrenchments'.

[p. 3, edit. Goes.] [*On the Latin Language,* V. xxi.] [*Dig.* L. xvi. 239, § 8.] [IV. xliii f.]

V.—*Property which does not belong to the enemy is not acquired by war*

This also is clear: In order that something may become ours by the law of war, it must belong to the enemy. Those things which are in the enemy's possession, to be sure, in their towns, for example, or within their fortifications, but of which the owners are neither subjects of the enemy nor hostilely inclined, cannot be acquired by war. It has been shown, among other things, in a passage of Aeschines

[*On the Badly Conducted Embassy,* xxxiii.]

[1] That this custom is observed on land also may be learned from De Thou, Book CXIII, on the year 1595. The rule is derived from the Germanic laws, and follows the precedent which these people, not without reason, had established for themselves in regard to a wounded wild animal, as in the *Law of the Lombards,* I. xxii. 6. Alberico Gentili, *Hispanica Advocatio,* I. iii, says that the same rule is observed in England and in the kingdom of Castile.

[2] [Grotius seems to have misread a passage of Godefroy's note on *Digest,* L. xvi. 239, which states that Frontinus derived it from *terrendis hostibus,* Cujas from *terra.*]

previously cited, that Amphipolis, which was a city of the Athenians, could not have become the property of Philip as a result of Philip's war against the citizens of Amphipolis. For this would be unreasonable, and the right of changing ownership by means of force is too offensive to merit wider application.

VI.—*What of goods found in ships of the enemy?*

Consequently the current statement that goods, which are found in ships of the enemy, are to be considered as belonging to the enemy,[1] should not be accepted as if it were a fixed provision of the law of nations, [475] but as indicating a certain presumption. This presumption, however, may be overthrown by valid proofs to the contrary.

Consolato del Mare, cclxxiii.

In our native country of Holland formerly, in the year 1438, when war was raging with the Hanseatic towns, a decision to that effect was reached at a full session of the Senate, as I have found, and from that decision the provision passed into a law.

VII.—*Things which our enemies have taken from others by war become ours according to the law of nations; this is attested by evidence*

1. The principle, however, is beyond dispute—if we have reference to the law of nations—that what has been taken by us from the enemy cannot be claimed by those who had possessed it before it came into the possession of our enemy, and had lost it in war. The reason is that the law of nations, through external ownership, first made our enemy the owner, and then us.

Judges, xi. 23, 24, 27.

By this right, among others, Jephtha defends himself against the Ammonites, because that territory, which the Ammonites claimed, had by the law of war passed from the Ammonites; just so another part also had passed from the Moabites to the Amorites, and from the Amorites to the Jews. Likewise David[2] regarded as his own,

1 Sam., xxx. 20.

[1] But the ships of friends do not become prizes because they are carrying goods of the enemy, unless this happens with the consent of the owners of the ship, *Digest*, XXXIX. iv. 11; Rodericus Suarez, *De Usu Maris*, consilium ii, no. 6.

In this sense I think we must interpret the laws of France, which render vessels liable to seizure because of their goods, and goods because of the ships which carry them. Such are the laws of Francis I issued in 1543, chap. xlii; of Henry III, issued in March, 1584, chap. lxix; and the Portuguese Law, Book I, tit. xviii.

Elsewhere the goods themselves are alone liable to seizure; Meurs, *Danish History*, II. Thus in the war between the Venetians and the Genoese Greek ships were searched and any enemies who were concealed in them were removed; Gregoras, IX [IX. v]. See also Krantz, *Saxonica*, II, and Alberico Gentili, *Hispanica Advocatio*, I. xx

[2] And so Rezin, king of Syria, gave the city Eloth, which had belonged to the Idumaeans, not to the Idumaeans but to the Syrians, for them to dwell there, according to the reading of the Masorites, *2 Kings*, xvi. 6.

and distributed, what he himself had taken from the Amalekites, and the Amalekites had taken from the Philistines.

2. According to Dionysius of Halicarnassus, when the Volscians[1] demanded their former possessions, Titus Largius in the Roman Senate expressed his opinion thus: [*Roman Antiquities*,] VI [xxxvi].

We Romans consider as our fairest and most lawful possessions those which we have taken and hold by the law of war; and we would not foolishly suffer valour to be forgotten by surrendering these possessions to those who have lost them. Such possessions we think are not only to be shared in by our citizens who are living, but are also to be left for posterity. If we allow ourselves to be deprived of what we now have, we shall injure ourselves in the same manner in which we injured the enemy.

Similar was the answer given by the Romans to the Aurunci: 'We Romans think that with perfect right one may hand down, as his own, to his descendants, whatever he has acquired by courageously wresting it from the enemy.' Elsewhere, in reply to the Volscians, the Romans speak as follows: [Dion. Hal., VI. xxxii.] VII [VIII. x].

But we consider as our best possessions those which we have taken by conquest in war. We were not the first to establish this right, nor do we think that it is a law of men rather than of the gods; but we know that all, both Greeks and barbarians, make use of it, and we would not yield to you anything in cowardice, nor abandon what we have won in war. For it would be the utmost disgrace if any one through cowardice and folly should be deprived of what had been won by courage and bravery.

There is a similar thought in the reply of the Samnites: 'Since we have acquired these things in war, which is a perfectly fair law of acquisition.' *Selections on Embassies* [p. 10].

3. After relating that the land near Luna was divided by the Romans, Livy speaks of it thus: 'This land had been taken from the Ligurians; it had belonged to the Etruscans before the Ligurians.' By such a right Appian notes that the Romans retained Syria, and did not restore it to Antiochus Pius, from whom Tigranes, an enemy of the Romans, had taken it.[2] Justin, quoting from Trogus, represents Pompey as replying thus to the same Antiochus: 'Since Pompey had not taken the kingdom from Antiochus when Antiochus held it, inasmuch as Antiochus had yielded it to Tigranes, Pompey XLI [xiii. 5]. *Mithridatic Wars* [xv. 106]. XL [ii. 4].

[1] Plutarch, *Romulus* [xxv = p. 33], tells the same story with regard to Veii: 'The people of Veii began the war with the demand that Fidenae should be restored to them, just as if it belonged to them. This was not only unjust but also ridiculous, seeing that they had not aided Fidenae when in distress and engaged in war, but had permitted the population to perish, and now laid claim to the houses and fields from those who held possession of these as the result of war.'

[2] Appian [*Syrian Wars*, viii. 49] speaks as follows: 'It was not right that the Seleucidae, who had been dispossessed by Tigranes, should occupy Syria, rather than the Romans who had conquered Tigranes.' And elsewhere [*Mithridatic Wars*, xv. 106]: 'He believed that since he had driven the conqueror of Antiochus from this land he had thereby acquired it for the Romans.' Antiochus himself, in Polybius, *Selections on Embassies*, lxxii [= p. 307], 'thought that the possession acquired in war was the surest and most honourable'.

would not give to him what [476] he did not know how to defend.' Likewise the Romans held as their own those parts of Gaul [1] which the Cimbri had wrested from the Gauls.

[Appian,] *Civil Wars*, I [iv. 29].

VIII.—*The opinion, which holds that things taken from the enemy become the property of the individuals who capture them, is refuted*

It is a more serious question, Who acquires the goods of the enemy in a public and formal war: the people itself or the individuals who are of it or within it?

Bartolus, *On Dig.*, XLIX. xv. 28; Alexander and Jason, *On Dig.*, XLI. ii. 1; Angelus, *On Inst.*, II. i. § 17; Panormitanus, *On Decretals*, II. xxiv. 13, no. 7; Thomas Grammaticus, *Decisiones Neapolitanae*, lxxi, no. 17; Martinus Laudensis, *De Bello*, qu. 4.

On this point the more recent interpreters of the law hold very diverse opinions. The majority of them, having read in the Roman law that captured things become the property of those who take them, but in the collection of canons that booty is divided according to the will of the people, have declared—one following the other, as is usually the case—that in the first place and by the law itself things captured belong to the individuals who lay hands on them, but that they are to be assigned to the commander for distribution among the soldiers. Since this view is as widely current as it is false, we must refute it with so much the greater pains, that it may serve as an example of how little trust, in controversies of this sort, is to be placed in such authorities.

However, it is not to be doubted that by agreement of the nations either practice may be established; that is, that the ownership of captured goods may fall to the people which wages the war, or to any one who lays hands upon them. But we are inquiring what their will has been; and we say that the nations have decided that the property of enemies should stand to enemies in the same relation as ownerless property, as we have already indicated from the saying of Nerva the Son.

[III. vi. 2. 4.]

IX.—*By the law of nature both possession and ownership may be acquired through another*

1. Things which are ownerless, to be sure, become the property of those who take them, but they become just as much the property of those who obtain possession of them through others as of those who take them for themselves. Consequently not only slaves and children, but also free men, who in fishing, fowling, hunting, or gathering pearls, have given their assistance to others, at once acquire

[1] The Franks did not restore to the Romans the lands of Italy which they had received from the Goths; Procopius, *Gothic War*, IV [IV. xxiv]. See what the king of Sweden says, in De Thou, Book LXXVI, on the year 1582.

what they have taken for those persons whom they serve. Modestinus the jurist was right in saying: 'What is acquired naturally, as a possession, we acquire through any person at all, if we wish to possess it.' *Dig.* XLI. i. 53.

In his collected *Sententiae* Paul says: 'We acquire possession by means of the will and of the body; by our own will, that is, but by either our own body or that of another.' The same writer thus comments on the *Edict*: 'We acquire possession through an agent, a guardian, or an executor'; and he explains that this happens when they act with the intention of rendering us such service. Thus among the Greeks, those who competed in the Olympic games acquired prizes for those by whom they were sent. The reason is that naturally one man by his own volition becomes the instrument of another's will, as we have also said elsewhere. V. ii [§ 1]. *Dig.* XLI. ii. 1. § 20. [I. v. 3.]

2. Therefore the distinction in regard to acquisitions, which is handed down as between free and unfree persons, belongs to the civil law, and properly applies only to acquisitions under the civil law, as appears from the passage cited from Modestinus. Nevertheless the Emperor Severus afterward made such acquisitions approach more closely to the type of natural acquisitions, not in the interest of utility only, as he himself claims, but in that of jurisprudence also. If, then, we disregard the civil law, the principle holds good that one may do through another what he can do himself, and that the effect is the same whether any one acts for himself or through another. *Digest,* XLIV. vii. 56. *Dig.* XLV. i. 38. § 17. *Code,* VII. xxxii. 1. *Sext,* V. xii. 68 and 72.

X.—*The distinction between hostile acts as public or private*

In our investigation, therefore, we must distinguish between acts of war that are truly of a public character, and private acts which are committed on the occasion of a public war. By private acts a thing is sought primarily and directly for private persons; by public acts, for the people.

It was, then, in accordance with the law of nations that Scipio, as Livy relates, treated thus with Masinissa: 'Syphax has been beaten and captured under the auspices of the Roman people. In consequence he himself, his wife, his kingdom, land, towns, the men who inhabit them, in short whatever belonged to Syphax, are the spoil of the Roman people.' In the same manner Antiochus the Great argued that Coele Syria had been acquired by Seleucus and not by Ptolemy, on the ground that the war was the war of Seleucus, to whom assistance had been rendered by Ptolemy. The account is in Polybius, Book V. Livy, XXX [xiv. 9–10]. [V. lxvii.]

[477] XI.—*Territory is acquired for a people, or for him whose war it is*

1. Landed property is not usually taken except by a public act, upon the entry of an army and the establishment of garrisons. Thus, [*Digest*, XLIX. xv. 20.] in the opinion of Pomponius, 'Land that has been taken from the enemy is public property', that is, as he explains in the same passage, 'it is not classed as booty', if we take the word booty in its strict sense. In Procopius,[1] Solomon the praetorian prefect said: 'It is not unreasonable that captives and other things should go to the soldiers as booty'—on the understanding that this is done by public consent, as we shall explain below—'but that the land itself should belong to the Emperor and the Roman state.'

2. Thus among the Jews[2] and the Lacedaemonians land taken *Dig.* XXI. ii. 11. *Dig.* VI. ii. 15. § 1. by force was divided by lot. So the Romans either kept captured territory in order to lease it, in some cases leaving a small portion to the original possessor as a mark of honour; or they sold it in parcels, or assigned it to colonists, or made it subject to taxes. For such disposition of conquered territory there is abundant evidence in the laws and histories, and in the treatises of the land-surveyors.

[I. i. 7.] In the first book of his *Civil Wars* Appian writes: 'In conquering Italy by war, the Romans confiscated a part of the land.' In the [II. xix. 140.] second book he says further: 'Whenever they conquered an enemy, they did not take away all his land, but seized a part of it.' Cicero, [xlix. 128.] in his speech *For* [*On*] *his House* addressed to the pontiffs, notes that territory taken from the enemy was in some cases consecrated by the victorious commander, but at the command of the people.

XII.—*Movables, or things capable of motion, when captured by a private act, become the property of the individuals who take them*

1. But things which are movable, or are themselves capable of motion, if captured are taken either in the public service or outside of it. If they are taken outside of the public service, they become the property of the individuals who take them. To this principle *Dig.* XLI. i. 51. § 1. should be referred the statement of Celsus: 'Goods of the enemy which are in our midst are not public property but belong to those who have seized them.' By the words 'which are in our midst' we are to understand 'which are found in our midst after war has begun'.

[1] *Vandalic War*, II [II. xiv]. See also what follows there. Even Severus granted to the generals and soldiers on the frontiers lands taken from the enemy, [488] as Lampridius notes [*Alexander Severus*, lviii]. In the Swiss constitution it is provided that towns and fortresses that have been captured fall to the cantons in common, according to many passages of Simler.

[2] Among the same people the king merely received as much of the captured territory as each tribe; this is indicated in the *Digest of the Talmud*, title *On the King*.

The same practice was observed with regard to men also, at the time when, in respect to the principle stated, captive men were classed with captured property. On this point a passage of Tryphoninus is noteworthy: 'But those who, in time of peace, have arrived among other peoples, if war suddenly breaks out, become the slaves of those among whom, now their enemies, it is their fate to be caught'; for we must here read 'fate', and not 'act' or 'agreement' as the texts have it. This result is ascribed by the jurist to fate because they fall into slavery through no desert of their own.[1] To attribute such things to fate is common. An example is the line of Naevius: 'At Rome by fate the Metelli are made consuls,' that is, without merit of their own.

Digest, XLIX. xv. 12.

[Asconius Pedianus, *On Cicero's Against Verres*, II. i. 29.]

2. From the same principle it follows that if soldiers capture anything when they are not in formation or engaged in executing an order, but when they are acting under a general right or by mere permission, this they at once acquire for themselves; for they do not make the capture in the capacity of servants. Such are the spoils which are torn from an enemy in single combat; such also are spoils seized by soldiers in free and unauthorized raids at a distance from the army—beyond ten miles the Romans used to say, as we shall see shortly. This sort of booty the Italians at the present day call 'raid-spoil' (*correria*), and distinguish from 'sack' (*bottino*).

Saliceto, *On Code*, VIII. l. 2; Thomas Grammaticus, *Decisiones Neapolitanae*, lxxi, no. 18.

XIII.—*Movables, or things capable of motion, when captured by a private act, do not become the property of individuals if the municipal law determines otherwise*

But our statement, that by the law of nations things movable or capable of motion are directly acquired by individuals, must be understood as applicable to the law of nations as unmodified by any municipal law covering the matter. Each people may in fact establish other rules valid over its citizens, and may thus forestall individual ownership; as we see is done in many places with regard to wild animals and birds. In like manner it may also be provided by a law that goods of enemies which are discovered in our midst should become public property.

XIV.—*Things captured by a public act become the property of the people or of him whose war it is*

1. With regard to those things, however, which are captured by an act of war, the situation is different. In this case [478]

[1] So Servius, *On the Aeneid*, I [I. 32], 'Driven on by fate', also contrasts these two ideas: 'Virgil seeks to ascribe nothing to the deserts of the Trojans, but everything to the fates.'

individuals represent the person of the state, and act in its stead; hence through them, unless a statute otherwise decrees, the people obtains both possession and ownership, and transfers this to whomever it wishes. Because this view is in direct conflict with common opinion, I feel that I must cite proofs more fully than usual from the examples of outstanding peoples.

2. I shall begin with the Greeks, whose practice Homer describes in more than one passage:

[*Iliad*, I. 125.]

> But the spoil which we took from the cities now has been divided.

In the same poet Achilles, speaking of the cities which he had stormed, says:

[*Iliad*, IX. 330 ff.]

> From all of these much rich spoil did I ravish,
> And all I brought and gave to Atreus' son;
> But he by the swift ships remained behind,
> And, taking it, shared some with others, but kept much.

Here Agamemnon is to be regarded, on the one hand, as at that time ruler of all Greece, and so taking the place of the people, and by that right dividing the booty, with the approval of his council; and on the other as filling the post of general, hence obtaining a greater share than the rest from the common store. The same Achilles addresses Agamemnon himself as follows:

[*Iliad*, I. 163 f.]

> Never have I with you of spoil an equal share,
> When Grecian valour has o'erthrown a Trojan town.

[*Iliad*, IX. 279 ff.] [*Aeneid*, II [762 ff.].]

Elsewhere Agamemnon offers to Achilles, by public agreement, a ship full of bronze and gold, and twenty women, to fall to his lot from the spoil. Upon the capture of Troy, as Virgil narrates:

> Phoenix and hard Ulysses chosen guards
> Watched o'er the booty: hither from all sides
> The spoil of Troy snatched from the blazing shrines,
> With tables of the gods and mixing bowls
> Heavy with gold, and captured raiment, high
> Is heaped.

[Plutarch, *Aristides* [v = p. 321 D]. Herodotus, IX [lxxx ff.]. Plutarch, *Lysander* [xvi = p. 442 A].]

In like manner at a later time Aristides guarded the booty from Marathon. After the battle at Plataea it was strictly forbidden that any one should remove anything from the spoil on his own authority; later the spoil was distributed on the basis of the deserts of the several peoples. When Athens afterward was conquered, the booty was transferred by Lysander to the public treasure. Among the Spartans [1] the name of a public office is 'sellers of booty'.

[1] While Agesilaus was operating in Asia, Spithridates had abstracted booty from the camp of Pharnabazus, which had been captured; but when an inquiry was set on foot by the Lacedaemonian Erispides he took flight [Plutarch, *Agesilaus*, xi = p. 601 F].

3. If we come to Asia, the Trojans, as Virgil teaches us, were accustomed 'to draw lots for booty', as is usually done in dividing things held in common. At other times the decision to divide booty rests with the commander; and by this right Hector, upon the express stipulation of Dolon, promises him the horses of Achilles, so that you may perceive that the right of acquiring ownership was not in the mere act of seizure.

[*Aeneid*, IX. 268.]

Homer, *Iliad*, X [321]; Euripides, *Rhesus* [182].

Spoil was brought to Cyrus, the conqueror of Asia; and likewise, at a later date, to Alexander. If we look to Africa, the same custom is found. Thus what was captured at Agrigentum, [479] and in the battle of Cannae, and elsewhere, was sent to Carthage. Among the ancient Franks, as we see from the *History* by Gregory of Tours, things which had been captured were divided by lot[1]; and the king himself had nothing else from the spoil than what the lot assigned to him.

Pliny, [*Nat.His.*,] XXIII. iii [XXXIII. iii]. Plutarch, *Alexander* [xxxiv=p. 685 B ff.]; Curtius [VIII. iv]; Diodorus, XVII [lxvi and lxxi]; Strabo, XV [iii. 6]. Diodorus, XIII [xc]. Livy, XXIII [xii]. Gregory of Tours, II. xvii [II. xxvii].

4. But the Romans are more worthy of our consideration in respect to their examples in a degree commensurate with their superiority to the other nations in the art of war. Dionysius of Halicarnassus, a most careful observer of Roman customs, informs us on this point as follows: 'The law ordains that whatever has been captured from the enemy in battle becomes public property, in such a way that not only no private person may become owner of it, but not even the commander of the army himself. The quaestor takes possession of the things captured and auctions them off, and deposits the money in the public treasury.' These are the words of those who accuse Coriolanus, and they are to some extent framed to arouse ill-will towards him.

[Dion. Hal., VII. lxiii.]

XV.—*Nevertheless in such things some right of decision is usually granted to commanders*

While it was true that the people were the owners of the spoil,[2] it was not less true that, in the time of the free republic, the commanders were entrusted with the decision in regard to its disposal.[3] In Livy, Lucius Aemilius says: 'Cities that have been captured, not surrendered, are sacked, and nevertheless the decision in regard to them belongs to the commander, not to the soldiers.'

XXXVII [xxxii. 12].

[1] This you find in Gregory of Tours, II. xxvii; in Aimoin, I. xii, and in the *Epitome*, edited by Freher, chap. ix. The same custom is an old one among other peoples also. Servius, *On the Aeneid*, III [III. 323], 'She did not endure any casting of lots', says: 'Because captives and spoil were divided by lot among the victors; as: "to draw a lot for spoil".'

With respect to the collecting of the spoil for the common use, and the justification by oath among the Swedes and Goths, see Johan Magnus, XI. xi [Barbeyrac believes this a misquotation].

[2] See also on this point Simler, in the *Helvetica*.

[3] Polybius, in the *Excerpta Peiresciana* [p. 1454], says of Lucius Aemilius Paulus: 'Although he had become master of the entire kingdom, and could dispose of everything at his pleasure, he sought nothing for himself.'

This right of decision, which custom vested in the generals, they themselves at times referred to the Senate, as Camillus did, in order that they might be the more free from all suspicion. The commanders who retained the right are found to have made varied use of it, according as they were influenced by scrupulousness, regard for their reputation, and ambition.

Livy, V [xxii. 1].

XVI.—*Commanders may turn booty over to the public treasury*

1. Generals who wished to be, or wished to be believed to be, most scrupulous, did not touch the booty at all.[1] If there was money in the booty, they ordered that it should be taken over by the quaestor of the Roman people; if there were other things, they ordered that these be auctioned off by the quaestor; and Favorinus, in Gellius, thinks that the money procured by such means was called 'proceeds of spoils' (*manubiae*). Such money was placed by the quaestor in the treasury, after having been first publicly exhibited if the victory had warranted a triumph.

XIII. xxiii [XIII. xxv].

In the fourth book of Livy it is said of the consul Gaius Valerius: 'There was considerable booty from the constant raids, because all the loot had been brought together in a safe place. The consul ordered the quaestors to sell this booty at auction, and deposit the proceeds in the treasury.' The same thing was done by Pompey, with regard to whom the words of Velleius are: 'The treasure of Tigranes, in accordance with Pompey's usual practice,[2] was placed in the hands of the quaestor and entered in the public accounts.' Marcus Cicero pursued the same course, and in his letters to Sallust he writes thus of himself: 'Of the spoil I have taken, no one except the city quaestors, that is, the Roman people, has touched or will touch a quarter of a penny.' This was the practice especially in the ancient and better days, and Plautus has this in mind when he speaks thus:

[IV. liii. 10.]

II [xxxvii].

Letters, II. vii [II. xvii. 4].

[*The Two Bacchises*, 1075.]

> Now all this booty to the quaestor I shall take.

In like manner, of captives he says:

[*Captives*, 111.]

> Whom I bought from the quaestors, out of the spoil.

2. But others sold the booty themselves, without the aid of the

[1] 'Manius Curius swore that he had touched nothing from the booty except a vessel of beechwood with which to offer sacrifice' [Pliny, *Natural History*, XVI. xxxviii]. The author of the *De Viris Illustribus* [Aurelius Victor], in speaking of Mummius [chap. clx], says: 'He robbed Corinth of statues and paintings, but, although he filled all Italy with them, he collected nothing in his own house.'

Of the Aemilius Paulus just referred to, Plutarch [*Aemilius Paulus*, xxviii = p. 270 D] says: 'Men bestowed no less praise upon his generosity and his magnanimity, because he did not wish even to inspect the great quantity of gold and silver collected from the king's treasures, but gave it to the quaestors to transfer to the public treasury.'

[2] As on many occasions. See what is cited from Lucan in the following paragraph [III. vi. 17. 4].

quaestor, and deposited the proceeds in the treasury, as we may gather from Dionysius of Halicarnassus in the words which follow [in the passage just cited]. Thus we read that in early times, after the defeat of the Sabines, the spoil and the captives were sent to Rome by King Tarquin. Thus, again, it is related that the consuls Romulius and Veturius sold the booty because of the poverty of the treasury, although the army was annoyed thereat.

Livy, I [xxxvii. 5].

Livy, III [xxxi. 4].

Since in fact we frequently find statements showing how much each of the generals deposited in the treasury either through himself or through his quaestor, from Italian, African, Asiatic, Gallic, and Spanish triumphs, [480] there is no need to accumulate examples. Rather is this to be noted, that the booty, or part of it, was given at times to the gods, at times to the soldiers, and at times to others. To the gods either the articles themselves were given, such as the spoils which Romulus hung in the temple of Jupiter Feretrius, or the money derived from them, as when from the proceeds of the booty from Pometia [Tarquinius] Superbus built the temple of Jupiter on the Tarpeian mount.

Dionysius of Halicarnassus, II [xxxiv].

Livy, I [liii. 3].

XVII.—*Or commanders may divide the booty among the soldiers; in what way such a division may be made*

1. The early Romans regarded the granting of the spoil to the soldiers as a form of bribery. Thus Sextus, the son of Tarquinius Superbus, but an exile at Gabii, is said to have given booty to his soldiery with the object of securing power for himself in this way. In the Senate Appius Claudius attacked a largess of similar character as being new, prodigal, and ill-considered.

Livy, I [liv. 4].

Livy, V [xx. 5].

The booty granted to the soldiery is either divided or left for pillage. It may be divided on the basis of pay or of merit.[1] Appius Claudius desired that the booty be divided on the basis of pay, in case he should be unable to secure the transfer of the money derived from its sale to the treasury. Polybius carefully explains the whole system of distribution. For full days, or for watch periods, a half of the army, or a smaller portion, was regularly sent to collect booty. Each man was ordered to bring into camp what he had found, that it might be equally divided by the tribunes; and a share was given both to those who had guarded the camp (a practice which, we read, was sanctioned also by King David among the Jews, and which from that source passed into law) and to those who had been absent on account of ill-health or assignment to details.

Livy, V [xx. 5].

X [xvi].

I Sam., xxx. 24.

2. Sometimes the booty itself was not granted to the soldiers,

Livy, XLV [xxxiv. 6, xl, xliii. 6].

[1] From Josephus, *Antiquities of the Jews*, Book III [III. ii. 5], we learn that this was done among the Jews.

but the money derived from it was given to them in place of the booty; this was often done on the occasion of a triumph.

This is the proportionate distribution that I find. A single share was given to a foot-soldier, a double share to a centurion, and a threefold share to a cavalryman. Sometimes a single share was allotted to a foot-soldier, and a double share to a cavalryman. Again, a single share was given to a foot-soldier, a double share to a centurion, and a fourfold share to a tribune and a cavalryman.[1] In many cases account was taken also of merit, as when Marcius was granted a share from the booty of Corioli[2] by Postumius, because of his brave conduct.

Livy [XLV. xl. 5; xxxiv. 5]. Suetonius, *Caesar* [*Divus Julius*], xxxviii; and Appian, *Civil Wars*, II [xv. 102]. Livy [Dion. Hal., VI. xciv].

3. Without regard to the way in which the division was made, the commander was allowed his selection[3]; that is, he was permitted to take for himself, as first choice, as much as he chose, in other words, as much as he considered fair. This privilege was at times accorded to others also on account of their valour.[4] Euripides in his *Trojan Women*, speaking of the women of Troy of high birth, says:

[33 f.]

> Outstanding women, who had been given to the chiefs
> Of the Grecian host.

[*Trojan Women*, 274.] Of Andromache the same dramatist says:

> Pyrrhus received that noble woman for himself.

[*Aeneid*, IX. 269 f.] In Virgil, Ascanius says of a horse:

> Him, the shield, and the ruddy crest, from the lot
> I shall exempt.

[IX. lxxxi.] Herodotus relates that after the battle of Plataea, as choice things, women, horses, and camels, were given to Pausanias. In this way King Tullius received Ocrisia, the chief woman of Corniculum. In Dionysius of Halicarnassus, Fabricius[5] says in an address to Pyrrhus: 'Of these things seized in war it was lawful for me to take as much as I chose.'

[Dion. Hal.,] IV [i]. [*Selections on Embassies*, p. 18.]

[1] To a tribune and a prefect of horse, says Appian, *Civil Wars*, II [II. xv. 102].
[2] See Plutarch, *Coriolanus* [ix and x = p. 218 A, B].
[3] See Leunclavius, *Turkish History*.
[4] Thus Nestor acquired a woman—

> Exempted from the lot
> By the gift of the Greeks.

[489] That is in the *Iliad*, XI [XI. 626 f.]. But in the *Odyssey*, XIV [XIV. 232 f.], Ulysses says:

> Excellent Meneaeceus I received [Of this I'd choose what chanced to please my mind],
> But after, by the lot, I much obtained.

Euripides says of Cassandra [*Trojan Women*, line 249]:

> Her the elder son of Atreus made his special prize.

On what 'was chosen' from the spoil for the Athenian general Demosthenes, that is, was given him by right of pre-eminence, see Thucydides, Book II [III. cxiv].

[5] Whom Julian set as an example for himself and his soldiers; Ammianus, XXIV [XXIV. iii. 5].

With this in mind Isidore, in discussing military law, mentions 'The disposition of the booty, the just division in proportion to the rank [481] and services of individuals, and the portion of the prince'. Tarquinius Superbus, as Livy has it, wished both to enrich himself and to win over the affections of the people with spoil. Servilius in his speech for Lucius Paulus says that he could have made himself wealthy by a division of the booty. There are some writers, among whom is Asconius Pedianus, who take the view that the term *manubiae* more correctly designates this share of the commander.

[*Etymologies*, V. vii.]

[I. lvii. 1.]

Livy, XLV [xxxvii. 10].

[*On Cicero's*] *Against Verres*, III [I. lix. 154].

4. But those commanders have won greater renown who, giving up their right, took nothing for themselves from the booty. Such was the Fabricius whom I have mentioned, who 'despised wealth, even when acquired justly, in comparison with fame'; and this he declared that he did after the example of Valerius Publicola and some others.

These commanders were imitated also by Marcus Porcius Cato in his victory over the Spaniards, when he declared that none of the spoils of war would come into his hands, with the exception of those things which he had consumed in food and drink; and yet he added that he did not blame the commanders who had made use of the privileges conceded to them, but that he preferred to rival the best in point of virtue rather than the richest in point of wealth. Very nearly the same praise was merited by those who took of the spoil in moderation, as Pompey, who is praised by Cato in Lucan:

Plutarch, *Marcus Cato* [*the Elder*, x = p. 342 A].

[*Pharsalia*, IX. 197 f.]

> More than he withheld
> Did he contribute.

5. Sometimes in making the distribution account was taken of the absent also, as Fabius Ambustus decided at the capture of Auxur. Sometimes, too, for some reason in such a distribution no account was taken of certain persons even though they were present; this was the case with the army of Minucius, in the dictatorship of Cincinnatus.

Livy, IV [lix. 8].

Livy, III [xxix. 2].

6. Furthermore this right, which the commanders had enjoyed under the old republic, after the fall of the republic appears from Justinian's *Code* to have passed to the masters of the soldiers; for under the *Code* there are exempted from inclusion in the reports of military exploits the largesses of movable objects or those capable of locomotion. These the masters of the soldiers grant to their troops from the spoils of the enemy, whether in the actual conduct of wars or in places in which they are known to be stationed.

Code, VIII. liii. 36. § 1.

7. But this kind of division in olden times was often exposed to calumny, as though by this means leaders were seeking to win the goodwill of individuals. On such grounds charges were brought

Dion. Hal., VI [xxx], and VII [lxiii]. Livy, V [xxxii. 8]. Dionysius of Halicarnassus, VII [lxiv].

against Servilius, Coriolanus, and Camillus, that they had granted largesses to their friends and clients from the public funds. In reply they defended themselves on the ground of the public advantage, 'that those, who had shared in the undertaking, after having gathered the fruit of their labours, might be the more ready to enter upon other campaigns'—if we may cite the words of Dionysius of Halicarnassus on this matter.

XVIII.—*Or commanders may permit pillaging*

Dion. Hal., IV [l]. Livy, IV [xlvii. 4]. [Livy, V. xxi. 14.] Dionysius, IV; VI [xxix]; IX [lv]; X [xxi].

1. I now come to pillaging. This was conceded to the soldiers either in the devastation of a country, or after a battle, or after the storming of a town, with permission to scatter at a given signal. It was a practice rather unusual in early times, yet it did not lack examples. Tarquin gave over Suessa to his soldiers for pillage; Quintus Servilius, the dictator, the camp of the Aequians; Camillus, the city of Veii; the consul Servilius, the camp of the Volscians. Also Lucius Valerius permitted pillaging in the land of the Aequians, Quintus Fabius, after the rout of the Volscians, and after the capture of Ecetra. Such pillaging was afterward permitted by others on many occasions.

Livy, XLVI [XLIV. xlv. 4]. [Livy, XLV. xxxiv. 1.] Appian, Mithridatic Wars [xii. 85]. [I. xlv. 85.]

Upon the defeat of Perseus, the consul Paulus granted the spoil of the beaten army to the infantry, and the booty of the surrounding country to the cavalry. The same consul, in accordance with a decree of the Senate, gave over the cities of Epirus [1] to the soldiers to plunder. When Tigranes was conquered, Lucullus [2] for a considerable time restrained his troops from collecting spoils, but later, when victory was assured, he yielded the right to plunder the enemy. Cicero, in his first book *On Invention*, among the ways of acquiring ownership, includes the capture of anything from the enemy, when a public sale of this booty has not taken place.[3]

VI [V. xx. 6].

2. Those who condemn this practice [482] say that hands greedy for pillage 'will snatch away the rewards of brave warriors, since it usually happens that the more slothful man takes to plunder',[4] while all the bravest 'are wont to seek the chief share of toil and peril'—to quote the words of Appius in Livy. Not very different

[1] As Sulla did in the case of Athens; Appian, *Mithridatic Wars* [vi. 38].

[2] Plutarch [*Lucullus*, xxix = p. 511 E] relates that he turned over Tigranocerta for his soldiers to plunder, and besides gave to each man eight hundred drachmas from the spoil. Severus granted his troops the plunder of Ctesiphon; and likewise ordered the tribunes, officers, and soldiers to keep the loot from the villages, as Aelius Spartianus records [*Severus*, xvi; Aelius Lampridius, *Alexander Severus*, lv].

Mohammed II promised his soldiery the people of Constantinople with the booty and slaves.

[3] Varro [*On Farming*, II. x] enumerates six ways by which one may lawfully become a proprietor: through the acquisition of a lawful inheritance, through purchase, cession, usucaption, sale of booty at auction, and public auction, when a person's property is divided and sold.

[4] See what we shall cite from Procopius on III. vi. 24..

is the saying of Cyrus in Xenophon: 'I am well aware that in pillaging the worse element would get the greater amount.' [*Training of Cyrus*, VII. ii. 11.]

On the opposite side it is said that what each soldier had taken from the enemy with his own hand and had carried off home would prove to be more acceptable and afford greater pleasure than many times as much allotted to him by another's decision. Livy, V [xx. 8].

3. Sometimes, too, pillaging was permitted because it could not be prevented. In the storming of Cortuosa, an Etruscan town, as Livy relates: 'The tribunes decided to reserve the booty for the state, but the order was slower than the decision; for already the spoil was in the hands of the soldiers, and could not be taken away without causing ill-feeling.' So also we read that the camp of the Galatians was plundered by the army of Gaius Helvius against the will of the commander. VI [iv. 11]. Livy, XXXVIII [xxiii. 4].

XIX.—*Or commanders may grant the spoil to others*

The practice already mentioned, that in some cases the booty, or money derived from the sale of booty, might be assigned to others than the soldiers, usually had as its purpose to make an equivalent reimbursement to those who had contributed funds for the war. Dionysius of Halicarnassus, V [xlvii].

You may also note that public spectacles were at times produced with the money derived from the booty.

XX.—*Or commanders, having divided the booty into portions, may employ now one method of distribution and now another; in what way*

1. Not only in different wars are different methods employed in the disposition of booty, but in the same war booty is often diverted to different uses, after it has been divided into portions or the different kinds have been distinguished.

Thus Camillus gave a tenth of the spoil to the Pythian Apollo,[1] following a Greek precedent, which had previously come from the Jews; at this time the pontiffs decided that the dedicated tenth included not only movable things but also the city and its territory. When Camillus was again victor the greatest part of the spoil from the Faliscans was assigned to the quaestor; not so much was given to the soldiers. In like manner Lucius Manlius 'either sold the spoil, in so far as it had to be contributed to the public treasury, or divided it among the soldiers, taking care that it should be as fairly divided as possible'; the words are those of Livy. Livy, V [xxiii. 8]. Livy, V [xix. 8]. XXXVIII [xxiii. 10].

2. The classes into which booty may be divided are these: prisoners, herds, and flocks, which the Greeks when speaking with

[1] This is also recorded by Appian in the *Excerpta Peiresciana* [ii = *Concerning Italy*, viii. 1].

exactness call 'pillageable property'; money, and other movables, costly or cheap.

Dionysius, VIII [lxxxii]. Dionysius, X [xxi]. Quintus Fabius, after defeating the Volscians, gave orders that the pillageable property and spoils be sold by the quaestor; he himself brought back the money. The same general, after the conquest of the Volscians and the Aequians, gave the captives, with the exception of the Tusculans, to the soldiers, and permitted them to carry off the population and the herds in the land belonging to Ecetra. *Ibid.* When Antium was captured, Lucius Cornelius deposited in the treasury the gold, silver, and copper, sold the prisoners and booty through the agency of the quaestor, and allowed the troops to have articles of food and clothing. Livy, X [Dion. Halic., X. xxv]. Similar to this was the policy of Cincinnatus, who, after taking Corbio, a town of the Aequians, sent the more valuable objects in the booty to Rome, and divided the rest among the centuries.

Livy, V [xxii. 1]. After the capture of Veii Camillus contributed nothing to the public treasury except the money from the sale of the captives; and when the Etruscans were beaten and the captives sold, from the money thus obtained he paid back to the women the gold they had contributed, and set up three libation saucers of gold in the Capitoline temple. VI [iv. 2–3]. [Livy, VI. xiii. 6.] When Cossus was dictator, all the booty from the Volscians, except the persons of freemen, was granted to the soldiers.

Dionysius, *Fragments* [*Selections on Embassies*, p. 18]. 3. Fabricius, after conquering the Lucanians, Bruttians, and Samnites, enriched his troops, paid back the war taxes to the citizens, and contributed forty talents to the public treasury.[1] Livy, XXV [xiv. 12–13]. Quintus Fulvius and Appius Claudius, when the camp of Hanno was captured, sold the booty and made a division, giving largesses to those whose services had been exceptional. Appian, *Punic Wars* [xx. 133]. On the taking of Carthage, Scipio gave what was in the city to the troops to plunder, excepting the gold and silver [483] and the votive offerings. Livy, XXXVII [v. 3]. Acilius, on the capture of Lamia, in part divided and in part sold the spoil. Livy, XXXVIII [xxiii. 10]. When the Galatians had been beaten and the arms of the enemy burned in accordance with a Roman superstition, Gnaeus Manlius ordered all to bring together the rest of the spoil, and either sold it, in so far as it was to be brought to the public treasury, or divided it among the soldiers, taking care that the division should be as fair as possible.

XXI.—*The committing of peculation in the distribution of booty*

1. From what we have said it appears that among the Romans, not less than among most other nations, booty was the property of the Roman people, but that some right of decision as to its dis-

[1] Fabius did likewise with the money from the sale of the prisoners after the capture of Tarentum, although he distributed the rest of the spoil to the soldiers.

tribution was granted to commanders; nevertheless, as we have previously stated, under the condition that they owed to the people an accounting for their actions. This, among other things, we learn from the case of Lucius Scipio, who was condemned in a trial for peculation, because, as Valerius Maximus states, he had received 480,000 sesterces in silver more than he transferred to the treasury; and also from the cases of others to which we have previously referred. V. iii, and Livy, XLV [XXXVIII. lv. 6].

2. Marcus Cato, in the speech which he wrote on the subject of booty, according to Gellius, complained in passionate and noble language of the impunity and licence accorded to peculation. Of the speech there remains this fragment: 'Those who steal from private persons pass their days in bonds and fetters; those who steal from the state pass theirs in gold and purple.' II. xviii [XI. xviii].

On another occasion the same speaker had said that 'he wondered that any one dared to place as furniture in his house statues that had been captured in war'. Cicero also increases resentment at the peculation of Verres, by pointing out that he had carried off a statue which in fact had been taken from the spoil of the enemy. Priscian, [*Institut. Gramm.*,] VII [xix. 95]. *Against Verres*, IV [xli. 88].

3. Not commanders alone, but even soldiers, were held on the charge of misappropriation of booty if they had not brought it to the public treasury; for, as Polybius says, they were all bound by an oath 'that no one would appropriate anything from the booty, but would carry out his pledge in scrupulous regard for his oath'. [X. xvi.] To this we may perhaps refer the formula of the oath in Gellius, by which, within the lines of the army or within the range of about ten miles, the soldier was enjoined not to carry off anything which was of greater value than a silver sestertius; or in case he had taken anything of the sort, to bring it to the consul, or to confess the fact within the next three days. XVI. iv. Hence we may understand what Modestinus meant by the statement: 'He who has secreted booty captured from the enemy is guilty of peculation.' *Digest*, XLVIII. xiii. 15 (13). This statement of itself should be sufficient to warn interpreters of the law against believing that things captured from the enemy are acquired by individuals, since it is clear that peculation can only occur in connexion with property that is public, sacred, or religious. *Digest*, XLVIII. xiii. 1.

All these considerations clearly lead to the view which we have expressed above, that, apart from the civil law, and primarily, what is captured in acts of war becomes the property of the people or of the king who wages the war.

XXII.—*Some change may be made with respect to this common right of booty by a legal enactment or by another's act of will*

1. In the statement just made we said, 'apart from the civil

law', and 'primarily', or directly. The former restriction is added because with regard to things that have not yet been actually acquired a law may ordain in the public interest, whether that legislative act is a law of the people, as among the Romans, or the law of a king, as among the Jews and elsewhere. Besides, under the name of law we wish to include also custom when rightly introduced.

The second qualification leads to this, that we may know that booty, just as other things, may be conceded by a people to others not only after acquisition, but also prior to acquisition, in such a way that, when the capture has ensued, the claims thereby arising are immediately united in title, as the jurists say. And this concession can be made not only to specific persons, but also to classes, as in the times of the Maccabees part of the spoil was given to widows, old men, and needy wards; or even to chance persons, after the fashion of the things thrown to the mob, which the Roman consuls made the property of those who caught them.

2 Maccabees, viii. 28, 30.

2. Furthermore, this transference of a right, which is brought about by a law or grant, is not [484] always a mere gift. It sometimes represents the fulfilment of a contract; sometimes either a payment of what is owed, or a reimbursement for losses which some one has suffered, or compensation for a personal contribution to the war in money, or in service, as when allies and subjects serve either without any pay or for such pay as does not correspond with their service. It is for these reasons, as we see, that an assignment of the whole booty, or a part of it, has usually been made.

Calderinus, *Consilia*, 85; Joh. Lupus, *De Bello*, § *si bene advertas*; Jason, *On Dig.*, XXX. i. 9; Franciscus à Ripa, *On Dig.*, XLI. ii. 1, no. 5; Covarruvias, *On Sext*, V. ult. 4, pt. 2, § 11; Bonfini, Decade V, Book IV.

XXIII.—*Thus booty may be granted to allies*

Our jurists, in fact, note that almost everywhere the custom has been tacitly followed, that either allies or subjects, who wage war without pay, at their own expense and danger,[1] appropriate what they capture. In the case of allies [2] the reason is evident, for naturally one ally is bound to make good to another the losses which ensue from a joint or public enterprise.

There is also the further consideration that it is hardly customary for service to be rendered gratis. 'Thus physicians', says Seneca, 'are paid the price of service, which they earn, because they are called from their own affairs and are at our disposal.' Quintilian judges the same thing fair in the case of orators, because the very giving of their service and time to the business of others deprives them of the opportunity of earning in other ways. This is what Tacitus called 'Neglecting the affairs of one's house in order that

On Benefits, IV. xv [VI. xv. 2]. [*Inst. Or.*, XII. vii. 10.] *Annals*, IX [XI. vii].

[1] See Kromer, *Poland*, XIX [=p. 430].

[2] Amalasuntha makes use of it in a letter to Justinian; [Procopius,] *Gothic War*, I [I. iii].

one may apply himself to the business of others'. Therefore it is credible that, unless some other cause should appear, as for instance pure kindness, or a preceding agreement, the hope of enriching oneself from the enemy was regarded as recompense for loss and service.[1]

XXIV.—*Booty is often granted to subjects; with illustration by means of various examples on land and sea*

1. In the case of subjects the right to booty does not follow with equal clearness, because subjects owe their service to their state. But this reason is offset by the fact that where not all subjects but only a part are in service the latter are entitled to compensation from the body of the state for having contributed more service and expense than the others, and they are much more entitled to compensation for losses. In place of this clearly defined compensation the expectation of the whole or a part of an uncertain booty is readily, and not without reason, conceded. And so the poet writes: Propertius [*Elegies*, III. iv. 21].

> Let the booty fall to those whose labours earned it.

2. With respect to allies, there is an example [2] in the Roman treaty by which the Latins were admitted to an equal share of the booty in the wars which were waged under the auspices of the Roman people. So in the war which the Aetolians waged with the Romans as their helpers, the cities indeed, and the territory, fell to the Aetolians, but the captives and movable property to the Romans. After the victory over King Ptolemy, Demetrius gave a part of the booty to the Athenians. Ambrose, in discussing the story of Abraham, shows the fairness of this custom: 'He wisely asserted that a part of the gain, as recompense for their toil, should be allotted to those who had been with him, perhaps as allies to give him aid.'

Livy, IV and XXIV [II. xxxiii]; Dion. Hal., VI [xcv]. Polybius, XI [X. xvi–xvii]; Livy, XXXIII [xiii. 10]. Plutarch, *Demetrius*, [xvii = p. 896 A]. *On Abraham*, I. iii [17].

3. With respect to subjects there is an example in the case of the Jewish people; half of the spoil fell to those who had been under arms.[3] The soldier of Alexander made his own the booty which he had seized from private persons, excepting that he was accustomed to bring certain things of special value to the king; hence we see that those who were said to have conspired at Arbela

Numbers, xxii [xxxi], 27, 47; *1 Sam.*, xxx. 22, and later; *2 Maccabees*, viii. 28, 30. Plutarch, *Apothegms* [= p. 180 c].

[1] See Plutarch, *Marcellus* [viii = p. 302].

[2] The Roman people furnished the ancient Latins with the third part of the spoil; Pliny, Book XXXIX, v [*Natural History*, XXXIV. v]. The Swiss cantons divide the spoil according to the proportion of the soldiers furnished, as Simler attests. In the war against the Turk, the Pope, the Emperor, and the Venetians made the division on the basis of expenditures; Paruta, VIII. Pompey granted Lesser Armenia to Deiotarus, king of Galatia, because he had been an ally in the Mithridatic War [Eutropius, VI. xiv].

[3] The Pisans gave a part of the booty to those who had guarded the houses; Chalcocondylas, Book V [V = p. 244].

were accused of claiming for themselves all the booty, so that they would bring nothing into the treasury.

4. But in the case of Alexander's army what had been the public property of the enemy, or royal property, was exempt from this licence. In consequence we read that, when the Macedonians had broken into the camp of Darius at the river Pyramus, they carried off a huge amount of gold and silver, and left nothing untouched except the king's tent,[1] 'in order that', says Curtius, 'following the traditional custom, they might receive the victor in the tent of the vanquished king.' Similar to this was the custom of the Jews, who placed the crown of the conquered ruler upon the victorious king and [485], as we read in the *Digest of the Talmud*, allotted to him the royal furniture taken in the war.

[III. xi. 23.] *2 Sam.*, xii. 30. Title *On the King*.

In the same category is that which we read in the exploits of Charlemagne; when he had conquered the Hungarians, the riches of private individuals fell to the soldiers, the riches of the king to the public treasury. But among the Greeks the 'booty' was public property, as we have shown above, and the 'spoils seized while fighting' were the property of individuals. They call 'spoils seized while fighting' (σκῦλα) what is taken from the enemy in the course of the battle, and 'booty' (λάφυρα) what is taken afterwards. This distinction is observed also by some other peoples.

5. However, from what we have said before it is quite clear that among the Romans, at least in the period of the early republic, not so much was granted to the soldiers. In the civil wars they began to receive somewhat greater indulgence. Thus you may read that Aeculanum was sacked by the soldiers of Sulla. After the battle of Pharsalus Caesar turned the camp of Pompey's forces over to his soldiers to plunder, according to Lucan, with these words:

Arias, *De Bello*, no. 162; Bellini, pt. II, tit. xviii, no. 3; Doneau, *Commentaries*, IV. xxi; Sylvester, word *bellum*, I. pr., from Trovamala. Wesenbeck, *On Institutes*, II. i. § 17. Appian, *Civil Wars*, I [vi. 51]. [*Pharsalia*,] VII [738 ff.].

> Your reward for bloodshed remains.
> This it is my part to point out; for I shall not call a donation
> What each to himself shall give.

The troops of Octavian and Anthony pillaged the camp of Brutus and Cassius. In another civil war, when the Flavians had been led to Cremona, although night was at hand, they hastened to take the rich colony by assault. They feared that otherwise the riches of Cremona would come into the possession of the prefects and legates; for they knew that in fact, as Tacitus says, 'the spoil of a city that has been stormed belongs to the soldiers; that of one which has been surrendered, to the general'.

Appian, *Civil Wars*, IV [xvii. 135]. Tacitus, *Histories*, III [xix].

[1] See also Diodorus, Book VI [XVII. xxxv], and Plutarch, *Alexander* [xx = p. 676]. See similar accounts in Xenophon, *On the Training of Cyrus*, II [IV. vi. 11], and Book IV of his war [*Anabasis*, IV. iv. 21] and VII.

6. As discipline declined such looting was the more willingly conceded to the troops, that they might not neglect the enemy and burden their hands with spoil while there was still danger. Disregard of such precaution has made very many victories fruitless.

When Corbulo had stormed the fort Volandum in Armenia, 'the mob unfit for war', as Tacitus relates, 'was sold at auction, and the rest of the booty fell to the victors'. According to the same writer, in a battle in Britain Suetonius urges his men to continue the slaughter without thinking of the booty, adding that when the victory should be won everything would fall to their lot. Similar accounts you may find among other authors generally. Add also what we have just cited from Procopius.[1] Tacitus, *Annals*, XIII [xxxix]. *Annals*, XIV [xxxvi].

7. There are, however, certain things of so slight value that they are not worth making public property. These things everywhere by consent of the people belong to those who take them. Such under the early Roman republic were spears, javelins, firewood, fodder, water-skins, leathern money-bags, torches, and money smaller than a silver sestertius; for we read in Gellius that these exceptions were added to the military oath. XVI. iv.

Very like this concession is that which is made to sailors even when they are paid for their service. The French call this spoliation or pillage, and therein include clothing, and gold and silver under ten crowns. Elsewhere a certain part of the booty is given to the soldiers, as in Spain, where now a fifth,[2] now a third, and again a half remains with the king, and a seventh, or at times a tenth, with the commander of the army; the rest belongs to the individual captors, with the exception of ships of war,[3] which fall wholly to the king. *Constitutions of France*, XX. xiii. 10 and 16. *Law of Spain*, IV. xxvi. 2.

8. It may happen also that the division of the booty is made after account has been taken of services, dangers, and expenses, as among the Italians, where a third of a captured ship falls to the master of the victorious vessel, an equal part to those whose goods were in the ship, and the same to those who engaged in the fighting. *Consolato del Mare*, cclxxxv.

Sometimes, again, this occurs, that those who conduct a war at their own risk and expense do not receive all the spoil, but owe a part to the public authority, or to him who derives his right from the public authority. Thus among the Spaniards, when in a war

[1] He records, *Vandalic War*, II [II. xxi], that when Solomon was carrying on war against the Levathae his soldiers were angry with him because he held back the spoil. He said [490] that he did this in order that, when the war was ended, he might distribute it according to each man's deserts. Procopius says also, *Gothic War*, II [II. vii], that all the spoil from Picenum was brought to Belisarius, who divided it on the basis of merit, and adds the reason: 'It was not fair that some, at the cost of much effort, should kill the bees, while others, at their ease, should feed upon the honey.'

[2] This custom is attributed to the Turks also by Leunclavius, [*Turkish History*,] III and V.

[3] So among the Goths an exception was made of engines of war for the kings; Johan Magnus, *Historia Suedica*, XI. xi [Barbeyrac believes this a misquotation].

[*Law of Spain,*] XIX. xxvi. 2. 14. *Constitutions of France,* XX. xiv. 1. *Instructiones Rei Maritimae,* xxii.

ships are fitted out at private expense, part of the spoil is due to the king, and part to the highest naval authority. According to the French practice the latter receives a tenth, and the same [486] is customary among the Dutch, but with them a fifth part of the booty is first deducted by the state. On land, however, it is now the general custom that in the sack of towns, or in battle, each should have as his own what he has taken; but what is taken in raids should be the common property of those in the detachment, to be divided among themselves according to their rank.

XXV.—*The application of what has been said*

As a result of these considerations we are to know that, if within the jurisdiction of a nation that is not involved in war a dispute arises with respect to something that has been captured in war, the thing is to be adjudged to him whose case is supported by the laws or customs of the people on whose side capture has been effected; if this is impracticable, then by the common law of nations the thing is to be adjudged to the people itself, provided only that it has been taken in an act of war.

From what we have previously said, it is abundantly clear that what Quintilian adduces in favour of the Thebans is in general not true, that in a matter which can be brought into court the right of war does not hold good, and that what is taken by armed force can only be retained by armed force.

[*Institutes of Oratory,*] V. iv [V. x. 114].

XXVI.—*Whether things which have been taken outside the territory of either belligerent may be acquired by the law of war*

1. Things which do not belong to the enemy, even if found among the enemy,[1] do not become the property of the captors; for this, as we have said already, is not in accordance with the law of nature and has not been introduced by the law of nations. Thus the Romans say to Prusias: 'If this territory had not belonged to Antiochus, clearly it would not have been made territory of the Roman people.'[2] Nevertheless if in such things the enemy enjoys any right which is connected with possession, as a right of pledge, restraint, or servitude, there is nothing to prevent this right being acquired by the captors.

III. vi. 5.

Livy, LV [XLV. xliv. 11].

2. The question is also often raised whether things captured outside the territory of either belligerent may become the property

[1] See above, III. iv. 7.

[2] Thus, after Jugurtha was conquered, Bocchus did not acquire the land which had not belonged to Jugurtha, but to the children of Bocchus [or rather Massinissa]; Appian, *Selections on Embassies,* xxviii [= *Numidian Affairs,* iv]. See a similar instance in Krantz, *Saxonica,* XII [XII. vii].

of the captors; and this is debated with regard both to things and to persons.

If we take into account the law of nations only, I think that this subject need not be considered, since we have said that an enemy may be justly slain in any place. But he who holds authority in a place may by a law of his own prohibit any such action; and if such an act is committed contrary to his law he can demand satisfaction for it as for a crime. Similar to this is the ruling that a wild animal caught on the land of another belongs to the captors, but access to it may be prohibited by the owner of the land. *Dig.* XLI. i. 3. *Dig.* VIII. iii. 16.

XXVII.—*In what way the right of which we have spoken is peculiar to a public war*

Now this external right of acquiring things taken in war is so peculiar to a war that is public according to the law of nations that in other wars it finds no place. For in other wars with foreigners property is not acquired by the violence of war but as compensation for a debt which cannot otherwise be obtained. Sylvester, word *bellum*, I, §§ 3 and II, verse 8.

In wars between citizens, whether these be great or small, no change of ownership is made except by the authority of a judge.

CHAPTER VII

ON THE RIGHT OVER PRISONERS OF WAR

I.—*According to the law of nations all persons captured in a war that is public become slaves*

1. By nature at any rate, that is, apart from a human act, or in the primitive condition of nature, no human beings are slaves, as we have said elsewhere.[1] In this sense it is correct to accept what
Dig. I. v. 4. § 1. was said by the jurists, that slavery is contrary to nature. Nevertheless, as we have shown also in another connexion,[2] it is not in conflict with natural justice that slavery should have its origin in a human act, that is, should arise from a convention or a crime.

2. But in the law of nations, which we are now discussing, slavery has a somewhat larger place, both as regards persons and as regards effects. For if we consider persons, not only those who surrender themselves, or promise to become slaves, are regarded as slaves, but all without exception who have been captured in a formal public war become slaves from the time when they are brought within
Digest, XLIX. xv. 5. § 1. *Digest,* XLIX. xv. 12. the lines, as Pomponius says. And no crime is requisite, but the fate of all is the same, even of those who by their ill-fortune, as we have said, are caught in the enemy's territory when war has suddenly broken out.

[II. lviii.] 3. Polybius says in the second book of his *Histories*: 'What should these persons suffer so as to pay a fitting penalty? Perhaps, one would say, being sold as slaves with wives and children, after they have been conquered in war. But this is also appointed by the law of war[3] for those to endure who have done no impious deed.'
That Every Virtuous Man is Free [iii]. Hence comes what Philo notes in these words: 'Often at unforeseen times many good men have lost their inherited freedom.'

Orations, xv [=p. 242]. 4. Dio of Prusa, after enumerating the ways of acquiring [491] ownership, says: 'And a third form of possession is whenever one has taken a prisoner in war and in this way holds him as

[1] II. xxii. 11. [2] II. v. 27.

[3] Servius, *On the Aeneid,* I [I. 619], says of Hercules: 'When Laomedon tried to ward him from this gate, he was killed, and his daughter, Hesione, was carried off in accordance with the law of war, and delivered to Telamon, Hercules's comrade, who had first scaled the wall; of this union Teucer was the issue.' Again, *On the Aeneid,* X [X. 91], in telling the same story: 'The Greeks refused to restore Hesione to the Trojans, saying that they held her by the law of war.'

Josephus, in Book XIV [*Antiquities of the Jews,* XIV. xii. 2], says: 'Since they had not been captured in accordance with the law of war.' 'By the law of captives' and elsewhere, 'By the law established for prisoners of war', says Menander Protector [frag. 29, p. 66, edit. Dindorf].

In the preceding chapter you find much that is applicable also here, for the reason that writers either combine, or treat identically, captured things and captive men.

a slave.' So Oppian in his second book *On Fishery* calls it a law of war to carry off into slavery boys that have been captured in war. [*Halieutica*, II. 316.]

II.—*Also the descendants of persons captured in war become slaves*

Not only do the prisoners of war themselves become slaves, but also their descendants for ever, that is to say those who are born of a slave mother after her enslavement. This is what Marcianus said, that by the law of nations those become our slaves who are born of our slave women. In speaking of the wife of a German chief, Tacitus said that her womb was subject to slavery. *Dig.* I. v. 5. § 1. *Annals*, I [lix].

III.—*What may be done to prisoners of war with impunity*

1. Moreover the effects of this law are unlimited, just as Seneca the Father said that there is nothing which a master is not permitted to do to his slave. There is no suffering which may not be inflicted with impunity upon such slaves, no action which they may not be ordered, or forced by torture, to do, in any way whatsoever; even brutality on the part of masters towards persons of servile status is unpunishable except in so far as municipal law sets a limit and a penalty for brutality. 'Among all nations alike', says Gaius, 'we may see that masters have had the power of life and death over slaves.' Then he adds that limits have been set to this power by the Roman law, that is on Roman soil. Here applies the note of Donatus on Terence, 'What is it not lawful for a master to do to his slave?' *Controversies*, I. v [X. v]. *Dig.* I. vi. 1. § 1. *Institutes*, I. viii. § 1. [*On*] *Andria*, Act I, scene i [36].

2. Also everything that has been captured is acquired, along with the person, for the master. The slave who is himself under the power of another, says Justinian, can have nothing of his own. *Inst.* II. ix. § 3.

IV.—*The property of captives, even if incorporeal, belongs to their master*

On these grounds the view of those who say that incorporeal rights are not acquired by the law of war [1] is refuted, or at any rate restricted. It is true that such rights are not acquired primarily and directly, but through the medium of the person to whom they had belonged.

Nevertheless, we have to make exception of those rights which have their source in a peculiar capacity of the person and are hence inalienable, as the right of the father. For if these rights can remain, they remain with the person; if not, they are extinguished.

[1] Valerius Maximus, VI. ix. 11, says of Gnaeus Cornelius Asina: 'As consul he was captured by the Carthaginians at the Lipara Islands, after he had lost everything by the law of war.' 'The slave has lost the right of ownership over other things not less than over himself,' says Philo, *That Every Virtuous Man is Free* [vii].

V.—*The reason why the law has thus been established*

1. All these rights have been introduced by the law of nations, with which we are dealing, for no other reason than this: that the captors, mollified by so many advantages, might willingly refrain from recourse to the utmost degree of severity, in accordance with which they could have slain the captives, either immediately or after a delay, as we have said before. 'The name of slaves (*servi*)', says
Dig. L. xvi. 239. § 1. Pomponius, 'comes from the fact[1] that commanders are accustomed to sell prisoners and thereby to save them (*servare*) and not to kill them.' I have said 'that they might willingly refrain'; for there is no suggestion of an agreement whereby they may be compelled to refrain, if you are considering this law of nations, but a method of persuading them by indicating the more advantageous course.

2. For the same reason this right is transferred to others, just as the ownership of things. Further, it has been agreed that ownership should be extended to children; the reason is that otherwise, if the captors had used their full right, the children would not have been born. Whence it follows that children who were born before the catastrophe do not become slaves, unless they are themselves captured.

Moreover, it has been acceptable to the nations that children should follow the status of the mother, for the reason that the unions of slaves were regulated neither by law nor by definite oversight, and consequently the father was indicated by no adequate presumption. In this sense we are to understand the statement of
Dig. I. v. 24. Ulpian: 'It is a law of nature, that he who is born outside of lawful matrimony follows the status of his mother'; that is, the law represents a general custom which has grown up from a natural reason,
II. xiii. 26. just as we have elsewhere shown that the term 'law of nature' is at times employed with some inexactness.

3. The rights under consideration, moreover, have not been introduced by the nations in vain. This we may perceive from what happens in civil wars, in which we find that on many occasions captives [492] have been killed because they could not be reduced
[xiv=p. 1073 c.] [II. xliv.] to slavery. The fact is noted by Plutarch in his *Otho*, and by Tacitus in the second book of his *Histories*.[2]

4. Whether those who have been captured become the property of the people, or of individuals, must be decided by what we have said in regard to booty; for in this case the law of nations has

[1] See also Servius, *On the Aeneid*, Book V [IV. 327], where he explains the origin of the word *saltem*.

[2] Also in Book III [III. xxxiv], regarding the captured inhabitants of Cremona, whom 'the united opinion of Italy had caused to be a prey useless to the soldiers'.

put men in the same category as things. Gaius the jurist said in his *Daily Questions*, Book II: 'Also what is captured from the enemy becomes at once, by the law of nations, the property of the captors, to the extent indeed that even free men are led off into slavery.' *Dig.* XLI. i. 5 and 7.

VI.—*Whether it is permissible for those who have been captured to flee*

1. Nevertheless, as regards the belief of some theologians, that it is unlawful for those to flee who have been captured in an unlawful war, or are born of captives, unless they flee to their own people, I have myself no doubt that the view is erroneous. There is indeed this difference, that if captives make their escape to their own people while the war is still in progress they attain their freedom by right of postliminy;[1] if they flee to others, or to their own people, after peace has been made, they must be given up to the master who claims them. But it does not follow as a consequence that a bond of conscience is laid also upon the captives; there are many rights which look only to an external judgement, and such are the rights of war which we are now explaining. Lessius, I. v, dub. 5.

There is, further, no reason for any one to raise the objection that from the nature of ownership such an obligation becomes binding on the mind. For I shall reply that, since there are many forms of ownership, it is possible that one may exist which is valid only in a judgement that is human and at the same time continues a condition which arises also in other kinds of rights.

2. Such in fact, to some extent, is also the right of nullifying wills, on account of the lack of some formality which the civil laws prescribe. The more acceptable view is, that what has been left by such a will may be retained with a clear conscience, at least as long as the will is not contested. Soto, *De Iustitia et Iure*, IV, qu. iv, art. 3; Lessius, II, xiv, dub. 3.

Not very different is the ownership of one who in accordance with the civil laws has exercised prescription in bad faith; for his ownership also is protected by the civil courts. By making the distinction, we easily loosen the knot which Aristotle ties in his *Sophistical Refutations*, Book II, chapter v: 'Is it not right for each one to have what is his own? But what any judge may decide according to his opinion, even if this be false, is valid according to the law. Therefore the same thing is both right and wrong.' [*Sophistical Refutations*, xxv. 9.]

3. In the question before us no reason can be imagined why the nations should have had in view anything else than that external restraint. For the opportunity of claiming a slave and restraining

[1] See below, III. ix. 5. Pliny, *Natural History*, VII. xxviii, says of Marcus Sergius: 'Twice captured by Hannibal, he twice escaped from his chains.'

him, and further, of putting him in bonds and retaining his property, was enough to induce captors to spare captives. If the captors were so ferocious as not to be influenced by these advantages, certainly they would not have been affected by the imposition of any moral restraint. Yet, if they believed such a restraint at all necessary for themselves, they could have exacted an assurance or an oath.[1]

4. However, in a law which has been established not according to natural equity, but to avoid a greater evil, we should not rashly adopt an interpretation which would make criminal an act otherwise permitted. Florentinus the jurist says: 'It makes no difference how a captive has returned; whether he has been set free, or has escaped from the power of the enemy by force or by guile.' (*Digest*, XLIX. xv. 26.) This is so because the right of captivity is of such a sort, that in another sense it is often also a wrong, a characterization which is applied to it by the jurist Paul. It is a right in respect to certain effects; a wrong, if we regard its intrinsic nature. (*Digest*, XLIX. xv. 19. pr.)

Hence this also is apparent. If any one who has been captured in an unlawful war has come into the power of the enemy, his conscience is not tainted by the crime of theft if he secretly takes away his own property, or a recompense for his toil,[2] in case it is right that any should be furnished him over and above his keep, provided that he neither in his own name, nor in that of his state, is in any way [493] indebted to his master, or to him whose right his master has received. And it does not matter that such flight and abstraction when detected are usually punished with severity. (Báñez, *On II. ii*, qu. 40.) For these things and many others are done by the more powerful, not because they are just, but because it is to the advantage of the more powerful to do them.

5. Certain canons[3] forbid any one to persuade a slave to desert his master's service. (*Decretum*, II. xvii. 4. 37 f.) If you refer this to slaves who are undergoing a just punishment, or have bound themselves by a voluntary agreement, it is a just injunction. But if you refer it to those who have

[1] Bembo, *History*, X, holds that the soul is not tainted by the crime of theft, if one removes his own property.

[2] Here applies what we have quoted above from Irenaeus and Tertullian, in the notes to II. vii. 2, where there is a discussion regarding the Jews after their exodus from Egypt.

To these the following relates, from Philo's *On the Life of Moses* [I. xxv]: 'Moreover when they were being driven out and pursued, being mindful of their noble race, they began a work worthy of freeborn men, who had not forgotten what they had suffered through injustice and deceit. [495] For they carried forth much spoil, in part on their persons and in part on beasts of burden. Their motive was not avarice, nor, as some calumniator has said, greed of another's property—for whence could this have occurred to them?—but they desired, first, to have the pay which was necessary for so long a period of service; and in the second place, they sought in recompense for servitude forcibly imposed upon them a penalty, not commensurate with it, but far less.' And more that follows in the same author.

There is a similar story of St. Malchus given by Jerome in his *Letters*, and of the Lombard Leupges, which his great-grandson Paul Warnefrid [Paulus Diaconus] tells us in Book IV [IV. xxxix]. Add also, if you please, the *Confession* published under the name Lanicius Patricius.

[3] From the Synod of Gangres. See above II. v. end.

been captured in an unlawful war, or have been born of captives, it teaches that Christians should encourage Christians to be patient rather than to engage in an action which, although permissible, might yet offend minds alien to Christianity or otherwise weak.

In a similar way we may understand the admonitions of the Apostles to slaves, except that these are seen rather to demand obedience from slaves while in servitude. This is in accord with natural justice; for food and service have a reciprocal connexion.

VII.—*Whether it is permissible for those who have been captured to resist their master*

But I think that it was correctly said by the theologians to whom I have just referred, that a slave cannot resist a master who is exercising that external right without violating the duty of justice.

Between this case and that which we have just discussed there is a manifest difference. The external right, which consists not only in impunity of acting but also in the protection of the courts, will be of no effect if a right to offer resistance remains on the other side. For if it is permissible forcibly to resist a master, it will also be permissible forcibly to resist a magistrate who protects the master, when, nevertheless, according to the law of nations, the magistrate should defend the master in such ownership and the enjoyment thereof. This right therefore is like that which we have elsewhere attributed to the highest authorities in each state, in saying that it is not legally nor morally permissible forcibly to resist them. Thus Augustine also joined the two rights when he said: 'Princes are to be endured by the commons, and masters by their slaves, in such a way that temporal things may be borne in the exercise of long-suffering, and things eternal may be hoped for.'

VIII.—*The law under consideration has not always existed among all nations*

But the fact must further be recognized that this law of nations with regard to captives has not always been accepted, nor accepted among all nations, although the Roman jurists speak of it as universal, designating the more prominent part by the name of the whole. Thus among the Jews,[1] who by their special institutions were separated from the common practice of other peoples, there was an asylum for slaves; at least, as the commentators rightly note, for slaves who had come into this unhappy condition through no fault of their own. *Deut.*, xxiii. 15.

From such a source it seems that there may have arisen the

[1] See [Moses de Kotzi,] *Precepts Forbidding*, 180.

Bodin, *De Republica*, I. v.

right of claiming their freedom which is given to slaves in the country of the Franks; although we see that this is now granted not only to those captured in war, but also to other slaves of any sort.

IX.—*The law under consideration does not now exist among Christians; what has been substituted for it*

Bartolus, *On Digest*, XLIX. xv. 24; Covarruvias, *On Sext*, V. ult. 4, pt. II, § ii, no. 6; Victoria, *De Iure Belli*, no. 42; Bohier, *Decisions*, clxxviii; Sylvester, word *bellum*, I, no. I. [Gregoras,] IV [ix].

Plato, *Republic*, V [xv = 469 c].

Bartolus, *On Digest*, III. v. 20; Bohier, *Decisions*, clxxviii; *Constitutiones Regni Hispaniae*, VIII. xxvi. 2.

1. Christians [1] furthermore have as a whole agreed that those who are captured in a war which has arisen among themselves do not become slaves so as to be liable to be sold, constrained to labour, and suffer the fate of slaves in other respects. In this they are surely right, because they have been, or should have been, better instructed in the teachings of Him who has sanctioned all charity than to be unable to be restrained from the slaughter of unfortunate men in any other way than by the concession of a lesser cruelty.

Gregoras [2] writes that this treatment of captives in former times was handed down from ancestors to descendants among those who professed the same religious belief, and that it was not peculiar to those who lived under Roman rule but was also common to Thessalians, Illyrians, Triballians, and Bulgars. And so this degree of progress at any rate, small though it is, has been accomplished by reverence for the law of Christ; a degree of progress which Socrates [494] failed to secure, although he had recommended such treatment of captives by the Greeks among themselves.

2. Moreover, the practice of Christians in this matter is followed also by Mohammedans among themselves.[3] Nevertheless, even among Christians the custom still prevails of keeping prisoners under guard until a ransom is paid, the amount of which is decided by the victor, unless some definite agreement has been made.

Furthermore the right of guarding captives is usually granted to the individuals who have taken them, except in the case of persons of high rank; for the customs of most nations give the right over these to the state or its head.

[1] And also the Essenes, from whom the first Christians originated. See Josephus [*Antiquities of the Jews*, XVIII. i. 5].

[2] Gregoras, Book IV [IV. ix], where these words are found: 'This is a custom which has descended from antiquity to posterity, and has never been corrupted, not only among the Greco-Romans and Thessalians, but also among the Illyrians, Triballians, and Bulgars, because of a belief common to all, that it is permissible to collect plunder, but not to make men prisoners nor to kill them after the time of battle.'

Adam of Bremen says of Saint Ansgar: 'Thence he returned to Hammaburg and reproved the peoples north of the Elbe for the sale of Christians.' Bohier also mentions this custom, *Decisions*, clxxviii, and adds that it is a practice in France, England, and Spain, that if the prisoner is a duke, count, or baron, he does not belong to the soldiers but to the ruler who is waging the war.

[3] Chalcocondylas, Book III; Leunclavius, Books III and XVII; Busbecq, *Epistolae Exoticae*, iii.

CHAPTER VIII

ON THE RIGHT TO RULE OVER THE CONQUERED

I.—*By war also civil authority is acquired, sometimes as vested in a king, sometimes as vested in a people ; the effects of such acquisition*

1. It is not at all strange if he, who can subject individuals to himself in personal servitude, is able to subject to himself an aggregation of men—whether they formed a state, or a part of a state—in a subjection which may be purely civil, or purely personal, or mixed.

Some one in Seneca's *Controversy* about a native of Olynthus uses the following argument : ' He, whom I purchased in accordance with the law of war, is my slave. This, men of Athens, is advantageous for you ; otherwise your empire, in so far as it has been acquired by war, is reduced to its ancient limits.' With similar purport Tertullian said that empires are sought by arms and expanded by victories. Quintilian declares that kingdoms, peoples, and the territories of nations and cities, depend upon the law of war. In Curtius, Alexander says that laws are laid down by the victors and accepted by the vanquished. [*Controversies*, X. v. 15.] *Apology* [xxv]. [*Inst. Or.*, V. x. 113.] [IV. v. 7.]

In his speech to the Romans Minio asks : [496] ' Why do you send a praetor every year with authority and rods and axes to Syracuse and the other Greek cities of Sicily ? Clearly, you would say, for no other reason than this, that you have imposed these laws upon those who have been conquered in war.' In Caesar Ariovistus says : ' It is the law of war that those who have conquered should rule those whom they have conquered, just as they please ' ; also : ' The Roman people has been accustomed to rule the conquered, not according to another's dictation but according to its own judgement.' Livy, XXXV [xvi. 4]. *Gallic War* [I. xxxvi].

2. Justin, quoting from Trogus, relates that up to the time of Ninus those who waged war had sought for themselves not sovereignty but glory, and, being content with victory, had abstained from empire ; that Ninus was the first who extended the borders of his empire, and subjugated other peoples in war ; and that from him this had passed into a general custom. Bocchus, in Sallust, declares ' that he had taken up arms to protect his kingdom ; for the part of Numidia, from which he had expelled Jugurtha, had become his by the law of war.' [I. i. 7.] *Jugurthine War* [cii. 13].

3. Sovereignty, furthermore, may be acquired for the victor ; either such sovereignty merely as is vested in a king [1] or other ruler,

[1] After the battle at Gaugamela Alexander was hailed as king of Asia [Plutarch, *Alexander*, xxxiv = p. 685 B]. The Romans asserted that what had belonged to Syphax was theirs ' according to the law

and in that case the victor succeeds to the right of the ruler only, and nothing beyond; or such as is vested in a people,[1] in which case the victor holds sovereignty in such a way that he can even alienate

I. iii. 11. it, just as the people could. We have elsewhere said that thus it has come about that certain kingdoms were held as a patrimony.

II.—*The right of a master may be acquired over a people, which then ceases to be a state*

1. Even a more fundamental change may be accomplished, so that, for instance, what was a state may cease to be a state. In such cases the state that was may become an accession of another state, as the Roman provinces did; or it may not be attached to a state, as when a king waging war at his own expense so subjects a people to himself that he wishes it to be governed not for the good of the people but above all else for that of the ruler, and this is the rule of a master, not of civil authority.

[VII. xiv.] In his *Politics*, Book VII, Aristotle says: 'There is government... for the good of the ruler, and government for the good of the ruled. The former is the government of masters and slaves; the latter, the government of free men.' A people, then, which is subject to a power of this kind, will for the future be no state, but a great

[*Excerpta ex Trag. et Com. Gr.*, edit. Grotius, p. 639.] domestic establishment. It has been well said by Anaxandrides:

A state of slaves, good sir, nowhere exists.

Annals, XII [xi]. 2. The two types of authority are thus contrasted by Tacitus: 'To conceive himself as a governor among freemen, not as a despot

[*Agesilaus*, i. 22.] among slaves.' Of Agesilaus Xenophon says: 'The states which he brought under his authority he relieved of all the obligations which

of war'; Appian, *Selections on Embassies*, X. xxviii. In Agathias, Book I [I. v], the ambassadors of the Goths said of Theodoric: 'Since he had conquered Odoacer, the stranger from Scyros, he held by the law of war all that had been his.' But when the Huns claimed that the Gepidae were their subjects, because they had captured the king of the Gepidae, the Romans denied this claim on the ground that the Gepidae had a chief rather than a king, and that they did not form a part of his patrimony. This is recorded by Menander Protector [frag. 28, pp. 63–5, edit. Dindorf].

[1] In the same writer Menander [frag. 46, p. 92], the Persians say with regard to the territory of the city of Daras: 'Since the city itself had been conquered by them according to the law of war, it was reasonable that what had been subject to it should belong to them.' After the conquest of the Vandals, Belisarius claimed that even Lilybaeum in Sicily should yield to the Roman authority, on the ground that the Goths had given it to the Vandals. But the Goths denied that they had so given it; Procopius, *Vandalic War*, II [II. v].

Henry, son of Frederick Barbarossa, after having captured Sicily, laid claim to Epidamnus, Saloniki, and other places held by the Sicilians; Nicetas, *On Alexis*, brother of Isaac [Comnenus], Book I [I. vii]. Baianus, Chagan of the Avars, said to the emperor with regard to Sirmium: [498] 'That that city belonged to him, seeing that it had belonged to the Gepidae, who had been conquered by the Avars' [Menander, frag. 64, p 127, edit. Dindorf].

Peter, the ambassador of Justinian, said in a speech to Chosroes: 'For how shall he who is lord of the principal not be lord of the accessory also? For neither the Lazi nor the Suani ever raised a dispute on this point, that Suania has not from antiquity belonged to the Lazi' [Menander, frag. 11, p. 26, edit. Dindorf]. Each of these citations is from Menander Protector. Add what is in III. viii. 4.

slaves render to their masters, and he exacted from them only the things in which freemen obey their rulers.'

III.—*Sometimes the two types of authority are mixed*

Hence we may understand the nature of that mixed authority, which I have said is in part civil and in part that of a master, that is to say, an authority in which servitude is mixed with a degree of personal liberty. Thus we read that arms have been taken from peoples; that peoples have been forbidden to have any iron except for agricultural purposes; and that other peoples have been compelled to change their language and manner of life.

IV.—*The possessions of a people, even such as are incorporeal, are also acquired; herewith is discussed the question of the written bond of the Thessalians*

1. Moreover, just as the possessions which belonged to individuals are, in accordance with the law of war, acquired by those who place the owners in subjection to themselves, so also the possessions of the aggregation of individuals as a whole become the property of those who subject the aggregation to themselves, if they so wish. Livy says in regard to those who have capitulated: 'In case all [XXXIV. lvii. 7.] possessions have been surrendered to him who is superior in arms,[1] the victor has the absolute right to decide what he wishes the vanquished to keep, and of what he wishes to deprive them'; and this statement holds true of those who are conquered in a public war. Surrender in fact voluntarily permits what force would otherwise take.

In Livy Scaptius says that 'the land under [497] dispute III [lxxi. 7]. had been a part of the territory of the Coriolani; and when Corioli was captured, by the law of war it became public land of the Roman people.' Hannibal, in a speech to his soldiers, recorded by the same author, declared: 'All the possessions of the Romans, won and XXI [xliii. 6]. amassed in so many triumphs, will become ours along with the masters themselves.' The same author makes Antiochus say: 'Since, when XLIII [XXXIII. xl. 4]. Lysimachus was conquered, all his possessions were transferred to Seleucus in accordance with the law of war, he thought that they

[1] See above, I. iv. 8 [I. iii. 8]; II. v. 31; and III. v. 2, and below, III. xx. 49. Add also the following from Polybius, *Selections on Embassies*, cxlii:

'Those who surrender themselves to the Roman authority, first give up the territory which was theirs, and the cities within that territory, then all men and women who are in this territory or these cities; finally, all rivers, harbours, everything sacred and hallowed in its entirety, so that the Romans are masters of all, but those who have surrendered themselves are masters of nothing at all.'

See what has just been said, III. vii. 4. Justin, in Book XXXV [XXXVI. iii. 8], speaking of the Jews, says: 'Afterwards along with the Persians themselves they passed under the sway of Alexander the Great.'

Strabo, XII [iii. 1]. were now under his rule.' Similarly Pompey acquired for the Roman people what Mithridates had captured in war and had annexed to his empire.

2. Consequently, the incorporeal rights also, which had belonged to the aggregation as a whole, will become the property of the victor, in so far as he wishes. Thus when Alba was conquered the Romans claimed for themselves the rights which the Albans had exercised. (Dionysius of Halicarnassus, III [xxxi].)

Hence it follows that the Thessalians were entirely acquitted of their debt of one hundred talents. Although they owed this sum to the Thebans, upon becoming master of Thebes, Alexander the Great, by right of victory, made the Thessalians a present of it. Nor is that true which is adduced on behalf of the Thebans in Quintilian, [*Inst. Or.*, V. x. 116.] that only what the victor himself holds is his, but a right that is incorporeal cannot be seized by force; and that the position of an heir and that of a conqueror are fundamentally different, because a right passes to the former, but only property to the latter. In fact he who is master of persons is also master of their possessions and of every right which pertains to the persons. He who is the possession of another does not possess for himself, and he who is not his own master does not have anything in his own power. (*Dig.* L. xvii. 118. *Digest*, XLVIII. v. 22.)

3. Furthermore, if any one should leave to a conquered people the right to form a state, he might still take for himself certain things which had belonged to the state. It rests with him to decide what he wishes the measure of his beneficence to be. Caesar imitated the act of Alexander by making to the people of Dyrrachium a present of the debt which they owed to some one of the opposite party. In this case, however, the objection might have been raised that the war of Caesar was not of the kind in respect to which this law of nations has been established.[1] (Cicero, *Letters to Brutus*, vi [I. vi].)

[1] Anthony ordered the Tyrians to restore the territories of the Jews which had not been granted them by the Roman senate and which had not been held prior to the war of Cassius. This is recorded by Josephus [*Antiquities of the Jews*, XIV. xii. 4]. See also Bizarri, *History of Genoa*, X.

CHAPTER IX

ON POSTLIMINY

I.—*The origin of the word postliminy*

1. Just as in regard to those things which are captured from the enemy, so also in regard to the right of postliminy (*postliminium*) no very sound view has been advanced by those who in more recent times have laid claim to a knowledge of the law. The subject was treated with greater painstaking by the ancient Romans, but often rather confusedly, so that the reader could not distinguish what they ascribed to the law of nations and what to the Roman civil law.

2. With regard to [499] the word *postliminium* we must reject the view of Servius [Servius Sulpicius], who thinks that the latter part is a lengthening of the word without significance; we must rather follow Scaevola, who taught that the word was a compound of *post*, which indicates a return, and *limen*.[1] For *limen* (threshold) and *limes* (boundary) differ in ending and manner of declension, although for the rest they are identical in origin—for they come from the ancient word *limo*,[2] which signified *transversum* (across)—and in original idea, just as *materia* and *materies*, *pavus* and *pavo*, *contagio* and *contages*,[3] *cucumis* and *cucumer*; although in later usage it developed that *limen* referred rather to private, *limes* to public things. So the ancient word which meant 'to eject from a country' was *eliminare*, and the Romans called exile *eliminium*.[4]

Cicero, *Topics* [viii. 36], and Boethius thereon.

II.—*Where postliminy may occur*

1. Postliminy, therefore, is a right which arises from a return to the threshold,[5] that is, to the public boundaries. Thus Pomponius says that he who has begun to be within our fortified lines has returned

Digest, XLIX. xv. 5. § 1.

[1] Whence the name *Postvorta Dea* [Aulus Gellius, *Attic Nights*, XVI. xvii].

[2] Servius, *On the Aeneid*, XII [XII. 120], and Donatus, *On* [*Terence's*] *Eunuch*, on the phrase *limis oculis* [III. v. 63]. Festus: '*Limus*, "oblique", that is, "transverse", whence also *limina*.'

Isidore [*Etymologies*], XV. xiv: '*Limites* are called from the ancient word for "across", for everything that was "across" the ancients called *lima*, from which comes the *limina ostiorum*, through which one goes out and in; and *limites* because by them one goes out into the fields.' In the Glossary, *limes* is translated as πλάγια ὁδός [*Corpus Glossariorum Latinorum*, vol. II, p. 123].

[3] *Compages* and *compago*, a word which itself was formerly *compagen*, as we see from its genitive case, and the verb derived from it, just as *sanguis* was formerly *sanguen*.

[4] And *colliminium* in Solinus [chap. xv] is what is commonly called *collimitium*.

[5] Hence, Tertullian, *On Modesty* [xv], metaphorically speaking says: 'The postliminy of the peace of the Church.'

Digest, XLIX. xv. 19. § 3. by postliminy; Paul defines such a return when the captive has entered our frontier.

On similar grounds the agreement of nations has brought the matter to this point, that postliminy occurs also if a man, or a thing of the sort in regard to which it has been decided that postliminy is possible, has come to our friends, as Pomponius says in the passage cited; or, as Paul explains by offering an example, to a king who is our ally or friend. In these passages we are to understand as friends or allies not merely those with whom we are at peace,[1] but those who take the same side in a war. Those who come to such friends, as Paul says, begin to be protected in the name of the state. It makes no difference in fact whether a man or thing has come to them or to his own people.

2. Among those who are friends, it is true, but not on the same side, prisoners of war do not change their status unless by Polybius, III [xxiv]. a special arrangement. Thus in the second treaty drawn up between the Romans and the Carthaginians it was agreed that if any prisoners taken by the Carthaginians from peoples who were friends of Rome should reach ports subject to the Romans their freedom could be asserted, and that the friends of Carthage should enjoy an equal Plutarch, *Flaminius* [xiii = p. 376 F]. right. In consequence those Romans who were captured in the second Punic War and had come to Greece by way of sale did not have the right of postliminy there,[2] because in that war the Greeks had supported neither side, and hence it was necessary for the captives to be ransomed in order to be set free. In Homer, too, in more than one passage we see that those captured in war were sold in places that were at peace, as Lycaon, *Iliad*, XXI [lines 35 ff.], and Eurymedusa, Odyssey, VII [lines 8 ff.].

III.—*By postliminy some things return and some things are recovered*

The ancient Roman mode of speech had it that free men also were recovered by postliminy.

Pompeius Festus [on the word *postliminium*]. Aelius Gallus, in the *Terms Which Apply to the Law*, Book I, says that by postliminy there is recovered (for we must adopt this reading) the freeman who has gone from one state into another, and returns to the same state, according to the law established in regard to postliminy. The same is true of the slave who has gone from us into the power of the enemy, and afterwards returns to us and into the power of his former master, according to the law of postliminy. The same reasoning is applied to a horse, to a mule, and to a ship in recovery by postliminy (for so I think that with a slight change we may

[1] That this was the view of the king of Morocco and Fez, appears from De Thou, Book CXXX [CXXX. iii], on the year 1603.

[2] Valerius Maximus, V. xi. 6; Diodorus Siculus, *Selections on Embassies*, iii. So also the Rhodians as an act of generosity restored to Athens the Athenian citizens whom they had bought during the war of Athens with Philip; Polybius, *Selections on Embassies*, iii.

retain these three words which that incomparable student of the Roman law, Jacques Cujas, thinks should be deleted) as to a slave; and the same kinds of things, which return from the enemy to us by postliminy, may return from us to the enemy. [*Observations*, XI. xxiii.]

The later Roman jurists, however, with greater clarity have distinguished two forms of postliminy, according as we ourselves return, or something is recovered by us. *Digest*, XLIX. xv. 14.

IV.—*The right of postliminy exists in peace and in war. What is to be done if it has not been mentioned in time of peace?*

1. We must, further, maintain the view of Tryphoninus, who says that the right of postliminy [500] is effective both in war and in peace; the meaning is slightly different from that with which Pomponius had said the same thing. *Digest*, XLIX. xv. 12. *Digest*, XLIX. xv. 5, cited above.

In peace postliminy, unless it is otherwise agreed, exists for those who have not been conquered by armed force, but caught by their ill-fortune,[1] as those who are found in the land of the enemy when war has suddenly broken out. For other captives, however, there is not postliminy in time of peace, unless this was provided for in the terms of peace[2] (according to the excellent emendation of the passage of Tryphoninus by the learned Peter Faber, of which Cujas approves); for the reason which is added and the contrasted clause clearly decide this. *Semestria*, I. vii.

'He made peace, releasing the prisoners, for so it had been agreed,' says Zonaras. Pomponius says: 'If a prisoner, for whose return in time of peace a guarantee had been given, remains with the enemy of his own accord, for him there is subsequently no postliminy.' Paul states the matter thus: 'If a prisoner of war has fled to his home after peace has been made, by postliminy he returns Vol. III. *Digest*, XLIX. xv. 20. *Digest*, XLIX. xv. 28.

[1] See the example in Paruta, *On the War in Cyprus*, I.

[2] See Josephus, *Antiquities of the Jews*, XIII. ii [XIII. ii. 3]. Polybius mentions agreements providing for the restoration of captives in the peace with Philip, with the Aetolians, although in this case with an exception, and with Antiochus; *Selections on Embassies*, ix, xxviii and xxxv [= *Histories*, XVIII. xliv; XXI. xxx; XXI. xlv]. Livy [XXXIV. xxxv. 4] furnishes the same examples, and an additional example in the peace with Nabis.

Zosimus offers several similar instances, as, for example, the peace of Probus with the Burgundians and the Vandals, which began thus: 'Upon condition that they should restore all the booty and all the prisoners which they had,' Book I [I. lxviii]. He records a similar peace between Julian and the Germans [III. iv], and likewise with the Quadi, who were in Germany, Book III [III. vii].

Ammianus Marcellinus in Book XVII [XVII. x. 3–4] says of Suomarius, king of the Alemanni: 'On bended knees he sought peace, and obtained it, with forgiveness for the past, upon condition that he should restore our captives.' Shortly afterwards [XVII. xii. 11] he says of the Sarmatians: 'Upon being ordered to occupy without fear the lands they held, they restored our prisoners.' In another passage he says the same with regard to another part of the Sarmatians.

In Zonaras there are many such instances. Among others, in the history of Michael, son of Theophilus, speaking of the Bulgarian king this author says [XVI. vi. 3]: [507] 'He promised to release his prisoners of war.' Nicetas in Book II [*Manuel Comnenus*, II. viii] says that all the prisoners were set free, except the Corinthians and Thebans, men and women.

Sometimes it was agreed that prisoners who were held by the state should be restored, as in Thucydides, V [V. xviii].

to him who captured him in the late war, provided that it has not been agreed in the terms of peace that prisoners should be restored.'

2. As indicating the reason why the view just stated came to be held with reference to those who have been captured by valour in war, Tryphoninus quotes the following from Servius, 'that the Romans preferred that their citizens should place their hope of return in military prowess rather than in terms of peace', for from antiquity they were in truth, as Livy says, a state by no means merciful to prisoners. But this reason characteristic of the Romans could not have established the law of nations, though it might have been among the causes that led the Romans to embrace that law which had been developed by other nations.

[*Digest*, XLIX. xv. 12.]

[XXII. lix. 1.]

The truer explanation is this, that kings and peoples who undertake war wish that their reasons for so doing should be believed to be just, and that, on the other hand, those who bear arms against them are doing wrong. Now since each party wished this to be believed, and it was not safe for those who desired to preserve peace to intervene, peoples at peace were unable to do better than to accept the outcome as right,[1] and also to consider prisoners thus taken in the act of defending themselves as captured for a just reason.

3. But the same thing could not be said with regard to those who were caught [in hostile territory] after war had broken out; for in them no desire to injure could be imagined. Nevertheless it seemed not unfair that while the war lasted they should be detained, in order to lessen the strength of the enemy; but when the ending of the war had been arranged no reason could be offered for not releasing them. Consequently this was agreed upon, that with peace such prisoners should always obtain their liberty on the ground that they were innocent, by admission of the parties; but that over the others each should assert what he wished to be considered his right, except in so far as agreements should prescribe definite stipulations.

For the same reason neither slaves[2] nor things taken in war are restored with peace, unless this has been stipulated in agreements, since the victor wishes it to be believed that he had the right to seek these things. To controvert this principle would in truth be to make wars spring up from wars.

[1] See Priscus, *Excerpta Legationibus*, XXVIII, and Bizarri, on the War between Genoa and Venice [*On the Venetian War*], Book II.

[2] Totila declared to Pelagius, the deacon whom the Romans had sent to him, that he would not discuss the question of the restoration of the slaves of the Sicilians, saying that it would be unjust for the Romans [i.e., Goths] to give up their fellow soldiers to their old masters. The passage is in [Procopius,] *Gothic War*, III [III. xvi].

In the light of these considerations it is clear that the argument in Quintilian on behalf of the Thebans was ingeniously presented, [*Inst. Or.*, V. x. 115.] but not in accordance with the truth, that is, that prisoners are free if they have returned to their own country, because things won in war may only be held by the same use of force. We have said enough with regard to peace.

4. In war men who were free before being captured return by postliminy;[1] but slaves and certain other things are recovered.

V.—*When a free man may return by postliminy while war is in progress*

A free man returns by postliminy only when he has come to his own people with the purpose of sharing their fortunes, as the principle was stated by Tryphoninus. (*Digest*, XLIX. xv. 12. § 9, and 5. § 3, cited above.) The reason undoubtedly is that for a slave to become free he must, so to speak, acquire himself, which is not done unless he wishes it. But it makes no difference whether a man has been recovered from the enemy by force of arms,[2] or has escaped by a ruse, as Florentinus has pointed out. (*Digest*, XLIX. xv. 26. *Code*, VIII. l. 5.) It will even be sufficient if he has been voluntarily handed over by the enemy.

What happens if [501] a man comes to his own people after being sold in trade by the enemy,[3] as the custom is? This question is discussed by Seneca,[4] in the case of the Olynthian who was purchased by Parrhasius. Since a decree had been issued by the Athenians whereby it was ordered that the Olynthians should be free, he inquires whether it was provided in the decree that they should be made free or should be considered free; the latter of the two interpretations is more correct.

VI.—*What rights a free man returning by postliminy may recover, and what he may not recover*

1. A free man, moreover, after he has returned to his own people, not only acquires himself for himself, but also all the possessions, whether corporeal or incorporeal, which he had when the peoples were at peace. Peoples at peace accept the fact as indicating a right in the case of the man who has been set free just the same

[1] Julian, in his oration *Against the False Cynics* [*Orations*, vi = p. 195], says: 'In this way even the prisoners of war whom we set free would be slaves. But to such the laws grant freedom when they have returned to us.'

[2] As those, who had been captured by the Slavs and were set free by the Huns, likewise in Procopius, *Gothic War*, III [III. xiii].

[3] As in the same book of Procopius [III. xiv], the young Childubius said: 'Since he had returned to his own country, for the future he would be a free man in the eyes of the law.' But Leunclavius [*Turkish History*, XIV] notes that among the Turks there was formerly no right of postliminy for prisoners of war.

[4] *Controversies*, V. xxxiv [X. v].

as in the case of the prisoner, in order that they may show themselves fair to both sides. Therefore the proprietorship, which he who possessed the prisoner by the law of war had over the prisoner's possessions, was not free from all limitation; it could in fact cease against his will, if the prisoner should reach his own country. Consequently, the possessor of the prisoner loses these things just as he loses the man to whom they belonged.

2. But what if the possessor of the prisoner has alienated the prisoner's possessions? Will he, who has his title from the man that was at the time owner by the law of war, be protected by the law of nations, or will these things also be recovered? I am speaking of the things which were with a people that did not participate in the war.

It seems clear that we must distinguish between things which are of such a kind that they may return by postliminy, and those which are not of that kind. This distinction we shall shortly explain, so that the things of the former class will seem to have been alienated with a characteristic cause and under a condition, but the latter absolutely. By alienated things I understand also things which have been granted or acknowledged as received.

VII.—*Rights against a free man returning by postliminy also are restored*

Digest, XLIX. xv. 12. § 6; 6.

Again, just as rights are restored to him who has returned by postliminy, so also rights are revived against him; and, as Tryphoninus says, such are held just as if he had never been in the power of the enemy.

VIII.—*Why those who surrender do not have the right of postliminy*

Digest, XLIX. xv. 17.

To this rule in regard to free men Paul justly adds the following exception: 'Those who have been conquered in battle and have surrendered to the enemy do not possess the right of postliminy.' This is doubtless for the reason that agreements with the enemy are valid by the law of nations, as we shall say elsewhere, and against such agreements no right of postliminy holds.

[VI. xviii.]

Thus in Gellius those Romans who had been captured by the Carthaginians say that 'They did not have legal postliminy, since they were bound by their oath'. Wherefore, as Paul has properly pointed out, there is no postliminy during the period of an armistice. But Modestinus delivered the opinion that those who are given up to the enemy, that is without any agreement, return by postliminy.

Digest, XLIX. xv. 19. § 1.

Digest, XLIX. xv. 4.

IX.—*When a people may have the right of postliminy*

1. What we have said in regard to individual persons holds true, I think, in the case of peoples also; those who were free may recover their liberty in case the power of their allies delivers them from the rule of the enemy. But if the population, which formed the state, has been dispersed, I think it more correct not to consider the people as the same, nor to restore their property by postliminy in accordance with the law of nations, for the reason that a people, like a ship, obviously perishes by the dissolution of its parts, since its whole nature consists in perpetual union.

That was, then, not the same state of Saguntum which previously existed, when this site was restored, eight years later, to the former inhabitants. It was, again, not the same Thebes, after the Thebans had been sold into slavery by Alexander. Hence it is apparent that what the Thessalians had owed the Thebans was not restored to the Thebans by postliminy, and that for two reasons: first, because it was a new people; and, secondly, because Alexander, at the time when he was their master, was able to alienate this right and did so. There is a further reason, that a debt is not in the number of the things which return by postliminy.

2. With what we have said regarding a state [502] agrees closely the fact that according to the ancient Roman law, by which the dissolution of marriage was permitted, it was held that the marriage relation was not restored by postliminy,[1] but renewed by a new agreement. *Digest*, XLIX. xv. 8; 14. § 1.

X.—*What are the provisions of the municipal law in the case of those who return by postliminy*

1. From the preceding discussion the nature of postliminy may be understood according to the law of nations, as regards free men. But by municipal law that same right, in so far as it affects what is done within a state, may both be restricted by the addition of exceptions and conditions and extended to other interests. Thus, by the Roman civil law, deserters are excluded from the number of those who return by postliminy, even the sons of households over whom apparently the authority of the father, which was peculiar to the *Digest*, XLIX. xv. 19. §§ 4 and 7.

[1] Otherwise among Christian peoples. Pope Leo wrote to Nicetas, Bishop of Aquileia [Leo the Great, *Letters*, clix]: 'So that, just as postliminy is observed in the case of slaves or land, or even in the case of houses and other property, for those who have been led into captivity and have returned from captivity former marriages may be re-established, even if the parties have been united to others.' See Hincmar, *De Divortio Lotharii et Tetbergae*, Interrogation xiii, and the reply of Pope Stephen, chapter xix, in *Concilia Galliae*, II.

Quirites, should have been exercised. But Paul says that this was acceptable, because Roman parents valued the discipline of the camp above their affection for their children. This is consistent with what Cicero says of Manlius, that through his personal grief he sanctioned the discipline of military authority, in order that he might have regard for the safety of his fellow citizens, with which he perceived that his own safety was bound up, and that he set the right of public authority above nature herself and the affection of a father.

On Ends, I [x. 35].

The right of postliminy is also in a measure limited by this provision, which we read was first established by the Athenian laws, then by those of the Romans, that the person who should be ransomed from the enemy should serve the one who ransomed him until he paid back the price.[1] But this very provision appears to have been introduced in the interest of liberty, in order that many might not be left in the hands of the enemy because the hope of reimbursement in the sums paid as ransom had been cut off. This kind of servitude is in fact mitigated in many ways by the same Roman laws; and finally by the law of Justinian it is terminated with five years' service. On the death of the ransomed the right of recovering the money also is extinguished, just as it is held to be remitted by the contraction of marriage between the ransomer and the ransomed; and the right is lost by the prostitution of a ransomed woman. Many other provisions were established by the Roman law to favour those who pay ransom, and to punish the next of kin who do not redeem their relatives.

Demosthenes, *Against Nicostratus* [liii. 11 =p. 1249].

Code, VIII. l. 20. *Digest*, XLIX. xv. 15. *Code*, VIII. l. 13. *Code*, VIII. l. 7.

2. On the other hand, the right of postliminy has been expanded by the civil law in this, that not only those things which are included in postliminy by the law of nations, but all things, and all rights, are treated just as if he who has returned had never been in the power of the enemy; and this was also the practice in Attic law. For, as we read in the fifteenth *Oration* of Dio of Prusa, a certain person declared that he was the son of Callias, that he had been taken prisoner in the defeat at Acanthus, and had been in slavery in Thrace; after his return to Athens by postliminy, he claimed the inheritance of Callias from its possessors, and the only question investigated in the trial was whether he was really the son of Callias. The same writer records that, although the Messenians had been in slavery for a long time, they at length recovered both their liberty and their land.

[=p. 239.] [=p. 242.]

Further, the things which were deducted from a property by usurpation or by liberation, or which seemed to have become extinct

Code, VIII. l. 18.

[1] The same provision occurs in Charles the Bald, *Edictum Pistense*, chap. xxxiv [*Monumenta Germanica Historica, Leges*, II. vol. II, p. 325].

by non-use, are restored by an action for annulment; for in the edict concerning the complete reinstatement of persons of age there is included the man who is in the power of the enemy. This at any rate comes from the ancient Roman law. *Dig.* IV. vi. 1. § 1.

3. The Cornelian Law even consulted the interest of the heirs of those who had died as prisoners among the enemy, by conserving their property just as if the captive who did not return was already dead at the time when he was captured. If you should annul these civil laws, there is no doubt that as soon as any one had been captured by the enemy his property would have fallen to those who should seize it,[1] because he who is in the enemy's possession is held to be non-existent. If he who had been captured returned, he would recover nothing except those things which have postliminy by the law of nations. However, the assignment of the goods of prisoners to the treasury, if there should be no heir, is the effect of a special Roman law. *Digest,* XLIX. xiv. 31; xv. 22. § 1.

[503] We have considered the persons who return; let us now consider the things which are recovered.

XI.—*How slaves are recovered by postliminy, even those who have run away; how those who have been ransomed are recovered*

1. Among recoverable possessions are, first, male and female slaves, even when having been often alienated,[2] or after manumission by the enemy.[3] The reason is that it is not possible for one of our citizens, who is the owner of a slave, to be affected by a manumission in accordance with the law of the enemy, as Tryphoninus well observes. *Digest,* XLIX. xv. 12. § 9. But for the recovery of a slave, it is necessary that he be actually held by his former master, or that he should be easily obtainable. Therefore, although in the case of other things it is enough for them to have been brought within the frontier, in the case of a slave this will not suffice for the right of postliminy, unless the fact is also known; for it is the view of Paul that such a slave who is in Rome, but is hidden, is not yet recovered. *Digest,* XLIX. xv. 30.

Just as a slave differs in the respect suggested from inanimate things, so in turn the slave differs from a free man in this, that for

[1] See the *Visigothic Law,* V. iv. 15.

[2] But in the *Edict* of Theodoric [chap. cxlviii] the rule was laid down thus: 'Let slaves or *coloni* who have been captured by the enemy, and have returned, be restored to their masters, unless they have been previously acquired by another by purchase from the enemy.' See also Cassiodorus, [*Variae,*] III. xliii.

By the *Visigothic Law,* however, a slave recovered in war is restored to his master, and he who recovered him receives a third of a fair price for him. If he has been recovered after being sold by the enemy, he is restored to his master after return of the purchase price and the cost of improvements in his condition (V. iv. 21).

[3] As those set free by Mithridates, who were brought back into slavery; Appian, *Mithridatic Wars* [ix. 61].

his recovery by postliminy it is not required that he should come with the intention of adopting our cause. This in fact is required in the case of the man who is going to recover himself, not in the case of him who is to be recovered by another; and, as Sabinus wrote, 'Every one has a full freedom of choice with regard to his own state, but not in relation to the right of his master.'

Digest, XLIX. xv. 12. § 9.

2. The Roman law furthermore does not exempt runaway slaves from the operation of this law of nations. The master recovers his former right over these also, as Paul teaches us, the intent being that the exercise of a contrary right should not be so injurious to him, who always remains a slave, as fraught with damage for his master. In regard to the general treatment of slaves who are recovered by the valour of the soldiers, the emperors have stated a principle which some persons mistakenly apply to all possessions, that 'We should regard those who have been recovered as not having been captured, and our soldiers ought to be their defenders, not their masters'.

Digest, XLIX. xv. 19. § 5.

Code, VIII. l. 12.

3. By the Roman law slaves who have been ransomed from the enemy become forthwith the property of the person who ransoms them; but when the price has been paid back they are held to have been recovered.

To explain these things in greater detail is the business of the interpreters of the civil law. For some points were changed by later laws; and, to induce captured slaves to return, freedom was offered immediately to those who had broken a limb, and to others after the lapse of five years, as may be seen in the military laws collected by Rufus.

XII.—*Whether subjects may be recovered by postliminy*

We are more concerned with this question, whether peoples who were subject to a foreign rule also relapse into their former relation.

This may be considered in the case that not he to whom the chief command belonged, but some one of his allies, had delivered the people from the enemy. In this case I think we must give the same answer as in the case of slaves, unless it has been otherwise agreed in the treaty of alliance.

XIII.—*Territory is recovered by postliminy*

Digest, XLIX. xv. 20. § 1.

1. Among things recoverable we have first to do with territory which falls under the right of postliminy. 'It is true', says Pom-

ponius, 'that when the enemy have been expelled from the territory which they have taken the ownership of it returns to the former proprietors'.

Furthermore, the enemy ought to be considered as expelled from the time when they are no longer able to approach openly, as we have explained elsewhere. Thus the Lacedaemonians restored to the early proprietors [1] the island of Aegina, which had been wrested from the Athenians. Justinian and other emperors restored to the heirs of the old possessors the lands which had been recovered from the Goths and Vandals, and did not admit against the proprietors those prescriptive rights [2] which the Roman laws had introduced.

Strabo, VIII [vi. 16]. *Novels*, xxxvi. Valentinian, *Novels*, *De Episcopali Iudicio*; Procopius, *Vandalic War*, I [iii]; Cujas, *Observations*, X [xii].

2. The law regarding every right which is connected with the soil I consider to be the same as that regarding territory. Pomponius has written that consecrated and holy places, which have been captured by the enemy, if they have been freed from this misfortune, are restored to their original condition as though returned by a sort of postliminy. With this agrees what Cicero, in the passage on the statues in his speech *Against Verres*, says of the Diana of Segesta: 'Through the valour of Publius Africanus it recovered its veneration together with its seat of worship.' With the right of postliminy Marcianus compares [504] the right by which the ground occupied by a building is restored to the shore, upon the fall of the building.

Dig. XI. vii. 36. [IV. xxxv. 78.] *Dig.* I. viii. 6.

Wherefore we shall be obliged to say that the usufruct of land that has been recovered is restored, following the precedent set by the response of Pomponius with regard to inundated land. By the law of Spain, provision has been made that the holdings of counts and other hereditary jurisdictions return by postliminy. The larger holdings return without limitation; the smaller, if they are claimed within four years after their recovery, with the exception that the king has the right of retaining a castle lost in war and recovered in any way at all.

Digest, VII. iv. 26. *Constitutions of France*, X. xxix. 2.

[1] That is, those who were of the Lacedaemonian faction. Cf. what has been said above, III. vi. 7.

[2] And this in accordance with a law of Honorius, who, although he relinquished Spain to the Vandals, would not [508] permit a prescription of thirty years to prejudice the proprietors, while the Vandals were in occupation of it; as is recorded by Procopius, *Vandalic War*, I [I. iii]. Valentinian, in his Novel *De Episcopali Iudicio*, says: 'We have ordained that the rights which were preserved in perpetuity or for an unlimited number of ages shall be terminated by a limit of thirty years; with the exception of the affairs of Africans, who shall prove that they have been subject to the constraint of the Vandals; so that in their cases there may be deducted from the allotted thirty years such time as shall be proven to have been passed under hostile domination.'

In the Council of Seville, cited in *Decretum*, II. xvi. 4 [II. xvi. 3. 13], we read: 'Just as by the law of the state their former possessions are restored to those who have returned by postliminy, after suffering the cruelty of the barbarians in an enforced captivity.' With this agrees the canon, *Decretals*, II. xxvi. 10. See also Cujas, *Paratitla on Code*, VII. xxxix.

XIV.—*The distinction that was formerly observed with regard to movable things*

1. With regard to movable things there is a general rule to the contrary, that they do not return by postliminy but belong with the spoil; thus Labeo contrasts such things. Therefore, also, what has been acquired in trade, wherever it is found, remains the property of him who bought it, and the former owner has not the right to reclaim it if it is found among those who are at peace, or brought within the frontier.

In ancient times we see that things which were of use in war were excepted from this rule, which the nations seemed to have sanctioned, in order that the hope of recovery might render men more zealous in procuring them. In those times the institutions of very many states were organized for warfare; wherefore an agreement was easily reached in this matter.

Moreover those things are considered to be of use in war which we lately cited from Aelius Gallus, but which are more specifically designated both in Cicero's *Topics* and in Modestinus. They are warships and transports, but not yachts and fast boats acquired for pleasure; mules, but only such as are pack animals; horses and mares, which have been broken to the bit. And these are possessions which the Romans held were legally disposed of in wills, and entered into claims for the division of an inheritance.

[*Topics*, viii. 37.] *Digest*, XLIX. xv. 2 and 4.

Digest, XXX. i. 9.

Dig. X. ii. 22 and 23.

2. Arms and clothing are indeed of use in war, but they do not return by postliminy because those who lose arms or clothing in war are by no means deserving of favour; in fact such loss was accounted a disgrace, as is abundantly clear in the historical writings. But in this respect, it is noted, arms differ from a horse, because a horse may dash away without fault of his rider. We see, further, that this distinction of movables was in force in the west, even under the Goths, down to the time of Boethius. For he, in explaining Cicero's *Topics*, seems to speak of this right as one which retained its force to his own time.

XV.—*What is the current law with regard to movable things?*

But in recent times, if not previously, the distinction noted seems to have been done away with. For those who are familiar with customs generally record that movable things do not return by postliminy; and we see in many places that this has been made a rule with regard to ships.[1]

Bartolus, *On Dig.*, XLIX. xv. 28; Angelus and Saliceto, *On Code*, VIII. li. 2; *Constitutiones Gallicae*, XX. xiii. 24; *Consolato del Mare*, cclxxxvii.

[1] *Decisiones Genuenses*, ci.

XVI.—*What things may be recovered in such a way as not to need postliminy*

Things which, although seized by the enemy, have not yet been brought within his fortifications, have no need of postliminy, because by the law of nations they have not yet changed ownership. Also things which pirates or brigands have taken from us have no need of postliminy, as Ulpian and Javolenus decided; the reason is that the law of nations does not concede to pirates or brigands the power to change the right of ownership. *Digest,* XLIX. xv. 24 and 27; 19. § 2.

Relying upon this principle the Athenians wished to receive Halonnesus as restored, not as given by Philip, because the pirates had taken it from them, and Philip had taken it from the pirates.[1] Demosthenes, *On Halonnesus* [vii. 2=p. 77]. So things which have been captured by freebooters may be claimed wherever they are found, excepting that, as we have elsewhere held, on the basis of the law of nature, he who has obtained possession of a thing at his own expense should be reimbursed in the sum which the owner himself would have been glad to pay for its recovery. II. x. 9, above.

XVII.—*Charges introduced by municipal law as affecting those subject to it*

Nevertheless a different rule may be established by municipal law. Thus by [505] the Law of Spain ships captured from pirates become the property of those who take them from the pirates.[2] It is in fact not unjust that private interests should yield to the public advantage, especially when the difficulty of recovery is so great. But such a law will not hinder foreigners from claiming their property. XXXI. xxix. 2; Covarruvias, *On Sext,* V. ult. 4, pt. II. § 2, no. 8.

XVIII.—*How postliminy has been observed among those who were not enemies*

1. That is more surprising, to which the Roman laws bear witness, that the right of postliminy was effective not only among enemies, but also between the Romans and foreign peoples. But we have said elsewhere that such laws were relics of the nomadic age, II. xv. 5. in which the usages had dulled the natural social sense which exists among men. In consequence even among nations which were not waging a public war there was a certain licence of war among individuals, proclaimed as it were by the usages themselves. To prevent this licence from extending to the killing of men, it was acceptable that the rights of captivity should be introduced among

[1] See Philip's very letter in the works of Demosthenes [xii].

[2] The Venetians had the same law, as appears from the *Letters* of Du Fresne de la Canaye, vol. I.

them, and from this it resulted that there was also a place for postliminy, on a different basis than with brigands and pirates, because this use of force led to fair agreements which are usually held in contempt by brigands and pirates.

2. Formerly it seems to have been a disputed right whether those from an allied people, who are in servitude among us, return by postliminy, in case they have made their way home. Thus Cicero presents the problem, *On the Orator*, Book I. Aelius Gallus indeed speaks as follows: 'With peoples that are free, and with peoples in alliance, and with kings, we have postliminy just as with enemies.' On the other hand Proculus declares: 'I have no doubt that allied and free peoples are foreign to us; there is no postliminy between us and them.'

[I. xl. 182.] [Festus, on the word *postliminium*.] *Digest*, XLIX. xv. 7.

3. I think that a distinction should be made between treaties, in order that, if there were any which were entered into for the sake of settling or avoiding a public war, these should not for the future stand in the way of captivity or of postliminy. If, on the contrary, there were treaties containing this provision, that whoever should come from one side to the other should be protected in the name of the state, then with the abolition of captivity postliminy also should cease. It seems to me that Pomponius indicates this, when he says:

Digest, XLIX. xv. 5. § 2.

> If with any people we do not have relations of friendship or hospitality, nor a treaty made for the sake of friendship, they are not indeed enemies; but whatever of our belongings goes to them becomes theirs, and a free man of our people captured by them becomes also their slave. It is the same if anything comes to us from them; and so in this case also postliminy is recognized.

When Pomponius said a 'treaty for the sake of friendship', he showed that there could be other treaties also, in which there is no right of hospitality or friendship. That by peoples in alliance with one another are to be understood those who have promised friendship or secure hospitality, is also made abundantly clear by Proculus, when he adds: 'For what need then is there of postliminy between us and them, when they in our country retain both their liberty and the proprietorship of their own possessions as fully as among themselves, and we have the same privileges in their country?' Therefore what follows in Aelius Gallus, that 'There is no postliminy with the nations which are under our sway', as Cujas correctly reads it, must be supplied with the addition, 'nor with those with whom we have a treaty establishing friendship'.

Observations, IX. xxiii.

XIX.—*When the right of postliminy may be enforced at the present day*

Bodin, *De Republica*, I. vii.

1. In our times, however, not only among Christians but also among most Mohammedans, both the right of captivity apart from

war, and likewise that of postliminy, have disappeared, since the necessity for either was removed by the restoration of the force of the relationship which nature has wished to prevail among men.

2. Nevertheless that ancient law of nations could be applied if there should be an affair with a people so barbarous that without declaration or cause it should consider it lawful to treat in a hostile manner all foreigners and their possessions.

While I was writing these words, a judgement to that effect was rendered in the highest chamber at Paris, under the presidency [506] of Nicholas of Verdun. The decision held that goods which had belonged to French citizens, and had been captured by the Algerians, a people accustomed in their maritime depredations to attack all others, had changed ownership by the law of war, and therefore, when recaptured by others, became the property of those who had recovered them. In the same suit this decision was recorded, to which we just now referred, that to-day ships are not among the things which are recovered by postliminy.

CHAPTER X

CAUTIONS IN REGARD TO THINGS WHICH ARE DONE IN AN UNLAWFUL WAR

I.—*With what meaning a sense of honour may be said to forbid what the law permits*

1. I must retrace my steps, and must deprive those who wage war of nearly all the privileges which I seemed to grant, yet did not
III. iv. grant to them. For when I first set out to explain this part of the law of nations I bore witness that many things are said to be 'lawful' or 'permissible' for the reason that they are done with impunity, in part also because coactive tribunals lend to them their authority; things which, nevertheless, either deviate from the rule of right (whether this has its basis in law strictly so called, or in the admonitions of other virtues), or at any rate may be omitted on higher grounds and with greater praise among good men.

[333 f.] 2. In the *Trojan Women* of Seneca, when Pyrrhus says:

> No law the captive spares, nor punishment restrains,

Agamemnon makes answer:

> What law permits, this sense of shame forbids to do.

In this passage the sense of shame signifies not so much a regard for men and reputation as a regard for what is just and good, or at any rate for that which is more just and better.

[*Inst.* II. xxiii. § 1.] So in the *Institutes* of Justinian we read: 'Bequests in trust (*fideicommissa*) were so called, because they rested not upon a legal obligation, but only upon the sense of honour in those who were [*Declamations*, cclxxiii.] asked to take charge of them.' In Quintilian the Father, again: 'The creditor goes to the surety, without violating his sense of honour, only in case he is unable to recover from the debtor.' With this meaning you may often see justice associated with the sense of honour.
[*Fasti*, I. 249 ff.] [Thus Ovid]:

> Not yet had justice fled before men's guilt;
> Last of divinities she left the earth,
> And sense of honour in the place of fear
> [509] Ruled o'er the people without force.

Works [*Works and Days*, 192 ff.]. Hesiod sang:

> Nowhere a sense of honour, nowhere golden Justice;
> The base assail the better wantonly.

The sentence of Plato, in the twelfth book of his *Laws*, 'For Justice is called, and truly called, the virgin daughter of Honour' (παρθένος γὰρ αἰδοῦς Δίκη λέγεταί τε καὶ ὄντως εἴρηται), I would emend by πάρεδρος, so that the sense would be: 'Justice is called the councillor of honour, and this has been said with truth.' For in another place Plato also speaks thus: 'The deity, fearing for the human race, lest it should utterly perish, endowed men with a sense of honour and justice, in order that there might be adornments of cities and bonds of friendship.'

[*Laws*, xii. 2=p. 943 E.]

Protagoras [xii=p. 322 C].

In like manner Plutarch calls 'justice' a 'house-companion of the sense of honour,' and elsewhere he connects 'sense of honour' and 'justice'. In Dionysius of Halicarnassus, 'sense of honour and justice' are mentioned together. Likewise Josephus also links 'sense of honour and equity'. Paul the jurist, too, associates the law of nature and the sense of honour. Moreover Cicero draws the boundary line between justice and a sense of reverence (*verecundia*) in this way, that it is the function of justice not to do violence to men, that of the sense of reverence not to offend them.

To an Unlettered Prince [iv=p. 781 B C]. *Theseus* [vi=p. 3]. VI [xxxvi]. *Antiquities of the Jews*, XIII. xix [XIII. xi. 3]. *Digest*, XXIII. ii. [14. § 2]. *On Duties*, I [xxviii. 99].

3. The verse which we quoted from Seneca is in complete agreement with a statement in his philosophical works: 'How limited the innocence to be innocent merely according to the letter of the law?[1] How much more widely extend the rules of duty than the rules of law? How many things are demanded by devotion to gods, country and kin, by kindness, generosity, justice, and good faith? Yet all these requirements are outside the statutes of the law.' Here you see 'law' distinguished from 'justice', because he considers as law that which is in force in external judgements.

On Anger, I. xxvii [II. xxviii].

The same writer elsewhere well illustrates this by taking as an example the right of the master over slaves: 'In the case of a slave you must consider, not how much he may be made to suffer with impunity, but how far such treatment is permitted by the nature of justice and goodness, which bids us to spare even captives and those bought for a price.' Then: 'Although all things are permissible against a slave, yet there is something which the common law of living things forbids to be permissible against a human being.' In this passage we must again note the different interpretations of the term 'to be permissible', the one external, the other internal.

On Clemency, I. xviii.

[1] Seneca, *On Benefits*, V. xxi, says also: 'Many good things are not covered by any law, and find no form of procedure in court, but yet they are protected by the practice of human society, which is more potent than any law.'

Quintilian, *Institutes of Oratory*, III. viii [III. vi. 84], declares: 'For there are certain things which are not naturally praiseworthy, but are permitted by law, as the provision in the Twelve Tables that the body of a debtor could be divided among his creditors, a law which public practice repudiates.'

Cicero, *On Duties*, III [III. xvii. 68], writes: 'For the laws dispose of sharp practices in one way, and philosophers in another; the laws in so far as they can apply physical force, but philosophers in so far as they can apply reason and intelligence.'

II.—*The principle stated is applied to the things which we said were permitted by the law of nations*

Livy, XXVI [xxxi. 2].

1. Of the same effect is the distinction which was drawn by Marcellus in the Roman Senate: 'What I have done does not enter into the discussion, for the law of war defends me in whatever I did to the enemy, but what they deserved to suffer'; that is, according to the standard of that which is just and good.

Politics, I. vi.

III [lxvi].

Aristotle approves the same distinction when he is discussing whether the slavery which originates in war ought to be called just: 'Certain people, regarding only a part of what is just (for a law is something just),[1] declare that slavery arising through war is just. But they do not say absolutely just; for it may happen that the cause of war was not just.' Similar is the saying of Thucydides in the speech of the Thebans: 'We do not thus complain regarding those whom you slew in battle; for that fate befell them in accordance with a kind of law.'

Digest, XLIX. xv. 19. pr. *Letters*, xxxii [xxxi. 11]. XXVIII [XXIX. i. 16–17]. *Orations*, xv [= p. 242].

2. Thus the Roman jurists themselves at times characterize as a wrong what they often define as the right of captivity; and they contrast it with natural right. Seneca, having in mind what often occurs, says that the name of slave has sprung from a wrong. In Livy also the Italians, who retained the things which they had taken in war from the Syracusans, are called stubborn in retaining their wrongful gains. Dio of Prusa, having said that those captured in war recovered their liberty if they returned to their own people, [510] adds, 'just as those who were wrongfully in servitude'.

[*Divine Institutes*, VI. vi].

Lactantius,[2] in speaking of philosophers, says: 'When they are discussing the duties that belong to the military life their whole argument is adapted not to justice, nor to true virtue, but to this life and to the practice of states.' Shortly after, he says that wrongs have been legally inflicted by the Romans.

III.—*What is done by reason of an unjust war is unjust from the point of view of moral injustice*

In the first place, then, we say that if the cause of a war should be unjust, even if the war should have been undertaken in a lawful

[1] Seneca, *To Helvia*, vi [*On Consolation*, vii], says: 'Some have acquired for themselves by force of arms a right over territory belonging to others.' There seems to be a conflict between 'right' and 'belonging to others'. But they may be reconciled, as the text here shows. Consult what is above in III. iv. 2.

[2] However, Augustine in his fourth letter, which is addressed to Marcellinus [*Letters*, cxxxviii. 14], writes: 'And therefore, if this earthly commonwealth should observe the teachings of Christ, even wars would not be waged without kindness.' In dealing with the diverse practices of the Church the same writer says [cf. *Decretum*, II. xxiii. 1. 6]: 'Among the true worshippers of God even wars are brought to a state of peace.'

way, all acts which arise therefrom are unjust from the point of view of moral injustice (*interna iniustitia*). In consequence the persons who knowingly perform such acts, or co-operate in them, are to be considered of the number of those who cannot reach the Kingdom of Heaven without repentance. True repentance, again, if time and means are adequate, absolutely requires that he who inflicted the wrong, whether by killing, by destroying property, or by taking booty, should make good the wrong done.[1]

1 Cor., vi. 10.

Thus God says He is not pleased with the fasting of those who held prisoners that had been wrongfully captured[2]; and the king of Nineveh, in proclaiming a public mourning, ordered that men should cleanse their hands of plunder, being led by nature to recognize the fact that, without such restitution, repentance would be false and in vain. We see that this is the opinion not merely of Jews[3] and Christians, but also of Mohammedans.[4]

Jonah, ii. 10 [iii. 8].

Precepts of the Law, Precepts Bidding, 16.

IV.—*Who are bound to make restitution, and to what extent*

Furthermore, according to the principles which in general terms we have elsewhere set forth, those persons are bound to make restitution who have brought about the war, either by the exercise of their power, or through their advice. Their accountability concerns all those things, of course, which ordinarily follow in the train of war; and even unusual things, if they have ordered or advised any such thing, or have failed to prevent it when they might have done so.

Thus also generals are responsible for the things which have been done while they were in command; and all the soldiers that have participated in some common act, as the burning of a city, are responsible for the total damage. In the case of separate acts each is responsible for the loss of which he was the sole cause, or at any rate was one of the causes.

Sylvester, word *bellum*, 1, nos. 10, 11 and 12; Covarruvias, *On Sext*, V. ult. 4, pt. 11, § 2, no. 8; Lessius, II. xiii, dub. 4. Add *Dig.* XLVII. ii. 21. § 9.

V.—*Whether things taken in an unjust war are to be restored by him who took them*

1. I should not think that we ought to admit the exception, which some introduce with regard to those who furnish their services

Sylvester, *loc. cit.*, no. 10.

[1] *Numbers*, v. 6 [and 7]. Jerome, *To Rusticus*, says: 'The pronouncement of vengeance is not cancelled unless the whole is restored.' Augustine, in a letter to Macedonius, which is liv [*Letters*, cliii. 20], writes: 'If the property of another, for the sake of which the sin was committed, can be returned, and it is not returned, repentance is not felt but pretended.' This is cited by Gratian, in the *Decretum*, II. xi. 6 [II. xiv. 6. 1].

[2] There is a significant passage in *Isaiah*, lviii. 5, 6 and 7. You find it in Greek in Justin Martyr, *Dialogue with Trypho* [xv].

[3] See the penitential canons of Moses Maimonides, ii. 2. Also Moses de Kotzi, *Precepts Bidding*, 16.

[4] See Leunclavius, *Turkish History*, V and XVII.

to others, in case some blame should attach to them. Fault without evil intent is in fact sufficient to warrant restitution. There are some who seem to think that things captured in war, even if there was not a just cause for the war, should not be restored. The reason they allege is that those who fight with one another, in entering upon war, are understood to have given these things to the captors. But no one is presumed to risk his property rashly; and war of itself is far removed from the nature of contracts.

Vázquez, *Controversiae Illustres*, I. ix. 17; Molina, *disp.* 118, § *ut vero*.

However, in order to give to peoples that were at peace a certain rule to follow, that they might avoid being involved in war against their will, it was sufficient to introduce the idea of legal ownership (*externum dominium*) of which we have spoken, which may exist along with the moral obligation (*interna obligatio*) of restitution. The writers themselves seem to enunciate this in connexion with the law
IX [i. 5]. of the captivity of persons. Thus in Livy the Samnites say: 'We have restored the property of the enemy taken in the spoil, which seemed to be ours by the law of war'; 'seemed', he says,
VIII [xxxix. 10]. because that war had been unjust, as the Samnites had previously acknowledged.

2. A not unlike case is that arising from a contract entered
See above, II. xi. into without fraud, in which there is an inequality. In such a case by universal common law there arises a power of some sort to compel him who has made the contract to fulfil his agreements; nevertheless, in accordance with the duty of an upright and honourable man, he who has contracted for more than is right is none the less bound to reduce the transaction to an equality.

VI.—*Whether things taken in an unjust war are to be restored by him who holds them*

1. But he who has not inflicted the loss himself, or has inflicted loss without any fault of his own, and has in his possession a thing
See above, II. ix. taken from another in an unlawful war, is under obligation to return it, because there is no naturally just reason why the other should go without it [511] —neither his consent, his deserving of evil, nor
VI. v. recompense. In Valerius Maximus there is a story which bears on this point:

> After Publius Claudius had sold at auction the people of Camerina, captured under his leadership and auspices (he says), the Roman people, although they saw that the treasury had been enriched with money and their land increased by an accession of territory, nevertheless with the greatest care sought out and redeemed these people, and assigned to them a site on the Aventine to dwell upon, and restored their estates,[1]

[1] Antony compelled the Tyrians [512] to restore all that they held belonging to the Jews. He ordered that the men whom they had sold should be set free, and that goods should be restored

because it seemed that the good faith of the commander in this exploit was not beyond reproach.

In like manner by a decree of the Romans the Phocaeans received back both their freedom as a state and the lands which had been taken from them. Afterward the Ligurians,[1] who had been sold by Marcus Pompilius, recovered their liberty through the return of the purchase price to their buyers, and care was taken to restore their possessions. The Senate passed a similar decree with regard to the people of Abdera, adding as a reason that an unlawful war had been waged against them.

Livy, XXVIII [XXXVIII. xxxix. 12].

Livy, XLII [viii. 7].

[Livy,] LXIII [XLIII. iv. 13].

2. Still, in accordance with the principles which have been elsewhere explained, it will be possible, if the person who holds the thing has incurred any expense or labour, to deduct as much as the thing was worth to the owner, to recover the possession of which he had despaired. But if the possessor of the thing has, through no fault of his own, consumed or alienated it, he will not be held responsible except in so far as it may be held that he has been thereby enriched.

[II. x. 9.]

to their owners; Josephus, *Antiquities of the Jews,* XIV [XIV. xii. 5]. To the Parthians Macrinus restored the prisoners and booty, because there had been no reason for the Romans breaking the peace; Herodian, Book XIV, end [IV. xv. 6]. The Turk Mahomet ordered the liberation of those who had been in the city of St. Mary in Achaia; Chalcocondylas, Book IX [=p. 479, ed. Bekker].

[1] See Diodorus Siculus, *Excerpta Peiresciana* [p. 298].

CHAPTER XI

MODERATION WITH RESPECT TO THE RIGHT OF KILLING IN A LAWFUL WAR

I.—*In a lawful war certain acts are devoid of moral justice ; a condition which is explained*

1. Not even in a lawful war ought we to admit that which is said in the line,

Lucan [*Pharsalia*, I. 349].

> He, who refuses what is just, yields all.

On Duties, I [xi. 33].

Cicero's point of view is better : 'There are certain duties which must be performed even toward those from whom you have received an injury. There is in fact a limit to vengeance and to punishment.'[1] The same writer praises the ancient days of Rome, when the issues of wars were either mild or in accordance with necessity.

On Duties, II [viii. 26].

On Clemency, II. iv. [i = p. 94 A.]

Seneca calls those persons cruel who 'have a reason for punishing, but observe no limit'. Aristides, in his second speech *On Leuctra*, says : 'Men may, men may indeed be unjust in avenging themselves, if they carry vengeance beyond measure. He, who in punishing goes so far as to do what is unjust, becomes a second wrongdoer.' Thus, in the judgement of Ovid, a certain king,

From the Pontus, IX [I. viii. 19 f.].

> Avenging himself to excess,
> And slaughtering the guilty, guilty himself became.

[*Plataic*, viii = p. 298 B.]

2. In a speech of Isocrates the Plataeans ask, 'Whether it is just to exact so severe and unjust penalties for so trivial wrong-

[1] [525] See what has been said above, II. xx. 2 and 28, and the passages of Augustine, which we have just cited [on III. x. 2. 2], on the benevolence of Christians even in warfare. Aristotle, *Politics*, V. vi, relates penalties harsher than was just, which 'as a consequence of partisan zeal' were exacted at Thebes and Heraclea. Thucydides, III [III. lxxxii], mentions 'punishments greater than was just'.

Tacitus, *Annals*, III [III. xxviii], says : 'Pompey did more harm with his remedies than did the wrongs which he tried to correct.' The same writer in the same book [chap. xxiv] blames Augustus because, in his punishment of adultery, he transgressed ancestral clemency and his own laws. Juvenal [*Satires*, x. 314 ff.] writes :

> Sometimes, again, resentment more exacts
> Than any law to it concedes.

Quintilian declares [*Declamations*, VI. x] : 'It is only from the extreme parricide that punishment is exacted beyond human measure.' The Emperor Marcus [Aurelius] Antoninus, according to Vulcacius in the *Life of Avidius Cassius* [chap. xi], said : 'I shall write to the senate to prevent any too serious proscription or too cruel punishment.' Ausonius said [*Cupido Cruci Affixus*, II. 93, 94] :

> And greater than his crime
> His punishment appeared.

Ammianus, XXVI [XXVI. x. 6], writes : 'Vengeance was meted out to many more bitterly than their errors or their crimes demanded.' There is a similar passage in Agathias, Book III [IV. vi].

doings?' The same Aristides, whom we have cited above, in his second oration *On Peace*, says: 'Do not merely consider the causes for which you are going to exact punishment, but also who they are from whom the punishment is to be exacted, [513] who we ourselves are, and what is the just limit of punishments.' Minos is praised in Propertius because, [=p. 77 A.]

> Although a victor, just to the foe he was;[1]

[*Elegies*, III. xix. 27 f.]

and also by Ovid:

> Lawgiver most upright,
> He laws imposed upon his conquered foes.

[*Metamorphoses*, VIII. 101 f.]

II.—*Who may be killed in accordance with moral justice*

When it is just to kill—for this must be our starting point—in a lawful war in accordance with moral justice (*iustitia interna*) and when it is not just to do so, may be understood from the explanations which were given by us in the first chapter of this book.

Now a person is killed either intentionally or unintentionally. No one can justly be killed intentionally, except as a just penalty or in case we are able in no other way to protect our life and property; although the killing of a man on account of transitory things, even if it is not at variance with justice in a strict sense, nevertheless is not in harmony with the law of love. However that punishment may be just, it is necessary that he who is killed shall himself have done wrong, and in a matter punishable with the penalty of death on the decision of a fair judge. But we shall here say less on this point, because we think that what needs to be known has been sufficiently set forth in the chapter on punishments. Victoria, *On the Law of War*, nos. 36 and 45.

III.—*No one may rightly be killed because of his ill-fortune; for example, those who take sides under compulsion*

1. Previously, in discussing suppliants—for there are suppliants in war as well as in peace—we distinguished 'ill-fortune' (ἀτύχημα) and 'wrong' (ἀδίκημα). Gylippus, in the passage of Diodorus Siculus which we then quoted in part, asks in which class the Athenians should be placed, in that of the unfortunate or that of the unjust. He declares that they cannot be regarded as victims of ill-fortune, seeing that, of their own accord, and unprovoked by any wrong, they had waged war upon the Syracusans. He [II. xxi. 5. 1.] [XIII. xxix.]

[1] Ovid, *Tristia*, I. viii [I. ix. 35]:

> Even to the wretch is justice due, and toward a foe
> 'Tis praised.

concludes that, since of their own initiative they had undertaken the war, they must also in their own persons endure the evils of the war.

An example of the victims of ill-fortune are those who are in the ranks of the enemy without hostile intent, as the Athenians were
II [xxiii]. in the time of Mithridates. Of these Velleius Paterculus speaks thus:

> If any one blames the Athenians for this period of rebellion, when Athens was stormed by Sulla, he is indeed ignorant both of the truth and of antiquity. So steadfast was the loyalty of the Athenians to the Romans, that at all times and in every matter the Romans declared that whatever was carried out in good faith was done with Attic loyalty. But at that time, oppressed by the forces of Mithridates, the men of Athens were in a most pitiable condition. While they were in the grasp of the enemy, they were besieged by their friends, and they had their hearts outside the walls while their bodies, by constraint of necessity, were within.

The end of the quotation may seem to have been adapted from
XXVI [XXVII. xvii. 13]. Livy; in this author the Spaniard Indibil says that, although his body was with the Carthaginians, his heart was with the Romans.

For Quintius [ii. 6]. 2. 'Beyond doubt', as Cicero says, 'all men whose lives are placed in the power of another more often think what he, under whose authority and sway they are, is able to do, than what he ought
[ii. 5.] to do.' The same author, in his speech *For Ligarius*, declares: 'There is a third time, when he remained in Africa after the arrival of Varus; but if that is criminal, it is a crime of necessity, not of will.' The principle was applied by Julian in the case of the Aquileians, as we
XXI [xii. 20]. learn from Ammianus. This author, after recounting the punishment of a few persons, adds: 'All the rest departed unharmed; necessity, not intention,[1] had driven them into the madness of strife.'

[1] Shortly after he adds: 'For so the mild and kindly emperor, considering what was fair, had decided.' Thucydides, Book III [III. xxxix], in the speech of Cleon, says: 'I pardon those who deserted us under pressure from the enemy.' This is called a consideration of extreme necessity by Paul, in his *Sententiae*, V. i [V. i. 1]; for surely, as Synesius says, 'Necessity is something strong and violent.' Juvenal says of the Calagurritani [*Satires*, xv. 103 f.]:

> For who of men or gods forgiveness would refuse
> To men who had such dire and dreadful sufferings endured?

On the necessity imposed by famine, see Cassiodorus, [*Variae*,] IX. xiii. Pertinax says of Laetus and others: 'They obeyed Commodus unwillingly, but, when they had the opportunity, they revealed what they had always wished' [Capitolinus, *Life of Pertinax*, v]. Cassius Clemens in Xiphilinus's narrative of Severus [LXXIV. ix] declares: 'I knew neither you nor Niger; but, being left in the region which he had seized, I did what was necessary; I obeyed the actual ruler, not with the intention to make war upon you, but to drive out Julian.' When Aurelian entered Antioch, where many had sided with Zenobia, he issued an edict 'attributing what had transpired rather to the necessity imposed upon unwilling persons than to their real desires' [Zosimus, I. li].

In Procopius, *Vandalic War*, I [I. xx], Belisarius says: 'For all the Africans were subject to the Vandals against their will.' In the same writer, *Gothic War*, III [III. vii], Totila says to the Neapolitans that he knows that they have been unwillingly subject to the enemy. Moreover, Nicetas, or the continuator of his history, in speaking of [526] Henry, the brother of Baldwin, writes [*Urbs Capta*, xii]: 'He gave orders that the inhabitants of the city be slaughtered, as though they were cattle or sheep, and not Christians who were being put to death, and particularly such as had yielded to the Blachi under constraint and not by persuasion, and who had not voluntarily obeyed them.'

On the passage of Thucydides regarding the Corcyraean prisoners who had been sold, an ancient commentator remarks: 'He reveals a clemency worthy of the Greek character; for it is cruel to kill prisoners after a battle, especially slaves, who do not wage war of their own will.' In the speech of Isocrates, already mentioned, the Plataeans assert: [514] 'We served them' (the Lacedaemonians) 'not willingly, but under compulsion.' The same writer says of others of the Greeks: 'These were compelled to follow their side' (that of the Lacedaemonians) 'in body, but in spirit they were with us.' Herodotus had previously said of the Phocians: 'They sided with the Medes, not willingly, but by force of necessity.' I [lv]. [*Plataic*, xii = p. 299 A.] IX [xvii].

As Arrian relates, Alexander spared the Zelites 'because they had been compelled to serve on the side of the barbarians'. In Diodorus, Nicolaus of Syracuse says in his speech on behalf of the prisoners: 'The allies are compelled to take the field by the power of those who have authority over them; therefore, as it is fair to punish those who do wrong with intention, so it is right to pardon those who do wrong against their will.' Similarly, in Livy the Syracusans, in clearing themselves before the Romans, say that they had broken the peace because they were confused by fear and treachery. For a like reason Antigonus declared that he had been at war with Cleomenes, not with the Spartans. I [xvii]. XIII [xxvii]. XXV [xxix. 3]. Justin, XXVIII [iv. 13.]

IV.—*No one may rightly be killed on account of a fault that is intermediate between ill-fortune and deceit; the nature of such a fault is explained*

1. But it must be observed that between absolute wrong and unmitigated ill-fortune a mean may often intervene which is composed, as it were, of both elements. In such a case the action cannot be called purely that of a man having knowledge and intent, nor purely that of a man not having knowledge or acting against his will.

2. To this class of actions Aristotle applied the term 'fault' (ἁμάρτημα), which may be rendered in Latin by *culpa*. Thus, in the fifth book of the *Ethics*, the tenth chapter, he speaks as follows: [*Rhetoric*, I. xiii.]

> Of those things which we do of our own accord, some we do deliberately, others without premeditation. Those are said to be done deliberately which are done after a certain previous mental consideration; what is done otherwise is done without premeditation. Since, therefore, in human intercourse the infliction of injury may occur in three ways, that which proceeds from ignorance is called a mistake; as when a person has done something not against him whom he had in mind, or has done what he did not have in mind, or not in the way he thought, or not with the expected result; as if some one thought that he was striking not with this instrument, nor this man, nor for this cause, but there happened what he had not intended. An example would be if a man wished to prick, not to wound, or not to do it to this man, or not in this way.

Now when the hurt is done contrary to expectation it will be a mishap. But if the injury could have been in any way expected, or foreseen, and yet is not inflicted with evil intent, there will still be a degree of fault; for he is very near to a fault who has in himself the origin of the action, while he is unfortunate if the origin is outside of him. Whenever a person acts with full consciousness of what he does, yet not after deliberation, we must admit the presence of wrong, as in the acts which men are wont to commit under the influence of anger and similar natural or unavoidable emotions. For those who inflict injury when stirred by anger, and admit their fault, are not cleared from wrong, but yet they are not said to be unjust or wicked. But if any one commits the same act deliberately he will rightly be styled wicked and unjust.

3. Consequently, what is done under the influence of anger is correctly held not to have been done with premeditation. For it is not he who does something from anger, but he who has caused the anger, that started the trouble. Hence it often happens that in trials of this sort the inquiry is directed not to the facts but to other rights of the parties; for anger arises from that which any one thinks has been wrongfully done to him. Therefore the question under discussion is not whether this or that has been done, as in dealing with contracts—for in the case of a contract, unless there has been forgetfulness, the one of the two parties who has not fulfilled his obligation is clearly in the wrong—but the purpose is to discover whether what has been done has been done justly.

Now a person who first plotted treachery did nothing in ignorance; wherefore it is not strange if the one should think that he has been wronged, and the other should not think so. Nevertheless, it is possible that he who in turn inflicts an injury on such a ground should be considered unjust, particularly if he exceeds the rule of equality and proportion in his reprisal. Therefore he is just who acts justly from deliberate purpose, although any one may act justly [515] if he merely acts voluntarily, without deliberation.

4. But of the things which are not done on the spur of the moment, some are deserving of pardon, and others not. Deserving of pardon are those which are not only done by ignorant persons, but also done in consequence of their ignorance.[1] If something is done by ignorant persons, yet not because of their ignorance, but from such a diseased mental state as goes beyond the common limits of human nature, it is not deserving of your pardon.

This passage, which is truly notable and has been much used, I have rendered into Latin in its entirety, because in most cases it is not correctly translated and therefore not adequately understood.

On the Nicomachean Ethics, VII. ii.

5. In interpreting this passage Michael of Ephesus gives as an example of that which could not have been expected the case of one who injured his father when opening a door, and of one who wounded somebody when training himself in throwing the javelin in a deserted spot. As an example of what could have been foreseen, but happens without malice, is the case of him who has thrown his javelin on a public road. The same writer gives as an example of what is done under necessity the case of him who is compelled to do something by hunger or thirst; of what is done from natural emotions are cases of love, grief, fear. He says that something is done through

[1] Dionysius of Halicarnassus, I [I. lviii], says: 'Everything that is not done voluntarily is worthy of pardon.' And Procopius, *Gothic War*, III [III. ix]: 'If any persons have caused trouble to others, either because they have been under the domination of ignorance, or by reason of some forgetfulness, it is right that those very persons who have suffered the injuries should grant them forgiveness.'

ignorance when one is ignorant of a fact, as if some one should not know that a woman is married. Something is done by one who is ignorant, but not through ignorance, when one is ignorant of the law. However, to be ignorant of the law is at times pardonable, at times unpardonable; and this agrees very well with the sayings of the jurists. *Digest*, XXII. vi. *Code*, I. viii.

A passage not unlike this Aristotle himself has in his book on the art of oratory: 'Justice demands that we should not treat alike wrongs and faults, nor faults and misfortunes. Now misfortunes are things which could not have been foreseen, and are not committed with evil intent; faults, things which could have been foreseen, yet are not done with evil intent; wrongs, things done purposely and with evil intent.' The ancients also noted these three things, and in the verse of Homer on Achilles, in the last book of the *Iliad*, we read: [*Rhetoric*,] I [xiii.] [XXIV. 157 and 186.]

> Not ignorant is his mind, nor evil, nor imprudent.

6. Marcianus makes a similar division: *Digest*, XLVIII. xix. 11 [§ 2].

> Men do wrong either purposely, or on impulse, or by accident. Robbers, who form a band, do wrong purposely; those who resort to blows or to weapons when intoxicated do wrong on impulse; and when in hunting a missile cast at a wild beast kills a man the wrong is done by accident.

The two former classes of wrongs, those done purposely and those done on impulse, are distinguished by Cicero in the following manner: 'But in every act of injustice it is of the greatest moment whether the wrong is done from some mental excitement, which is usually brief and temporary, or designedly and upon reflection.[1] For what happens from some sudden impulse is less serious than what is inflicted after meditation and preparation.' Philo,[2] moreover, in his interpretation of the *Special Laws*, speaks thus: 'The crime is lessened by half where it has not been preceded by long deliberation.' *On Duties*, I [viii. 27].

7. In this class are, in particular, those things which necessity, if it does not justify them, at least excuses.[3] In fact, as Demosthenes

[1] Seneca, *On Anger*, I. xvi [I. xix], says: 'He frequently discharges [the culprits] if he perceives that their wickedness does not dwell in the depths, as they say, of the heart, but on the surface.' And then: 'Sometimes he punishes great crimes more leniently than lesser ones, if the great crimes have been oommitted from error and not from cruelty, while in the lesser crimes there is ingrained cunning, both secret and open.'

The same author says also: 'A crime will not affect people in the same way in the case of two persons if the one has done wrong through carelessness, and the other has laid plans for his guilty deed.'

[2] *On Special Laws*, II [III. xvii].

[3] Add what is above in II. xx. 29, and in this chapter, III. xi. 3, above. In Thucydides, Book III [III. xxxii], the Samians said to Alcidas the Lacedaemonian, when he put to death the Chian prisoners, that 'he did not speak the truth in saying that he had come to set Greece free, seeing that he put to death men who did not actively oppose him, and were not hostile in spirit, who were in fact allies of the Athenians, but had been driven to that course by necessity'.

Chrysostom, *On Providence*, V, says: 'Private enemies know how to pardon private enemies, and public enemies public enemies, whenever these commit some wrong, however serious, against them

[xxiii. 148 = pp. 668–9.] says, *Against Aristocrates*: 'Impulses arising from necessity prevent deliberation regarding that which ought or ought not to be done. Wherefore these actions must not be judged with too much strictness by those who would judge fairly.' This view is expressed at even greater length by the same orator in his speech on false testimony, [xlv. 67 = p. 1122]. *Against Stephanus*. Thucydides, Book IV, says:

[IV. xcviii.] We may well believe that with [516] deity also there is pardon ready[1] for those who do wrong under the constraint of war or some similar necessity. For the altars of the gods are open as a refuge for unintentional faults; and the term injustice is applied to those who are wicked of their own volition, not to those who are driven by extremity to desperate deeds.

VII [xx. 5]. In Livy the people of Caere say to the Romans: 'They should not term counsel what should be called compulsion and necessity.' VIII [i. 10]. Justin writes: 'The act of the Phocians, although it was condemned by everybody on the ground of sacrilege, nevertheless aroused greater animosity toward the Thebans, who had reduced them to this extremity, than toward themselves.' Similarly, in the opinion of [Porphyry, *On Abstaining*, III. xviii.] Isocrates, the person who, to save his life, commits an act of plunder, 'has necessity as a cloak for his wrongdoing'. Aristides, in his [= p. 145 c.] second speech *On Leuctra*, says: 'Hard times give some excuse to those who revolt.'

Regarding the Messenians who had been accused of not having [*Lives of the Sophists*, II. xv. 2.] received the exiles from Athens, Philostratus writes as follows: 'Their defence rests on a request for pardon; their excuse is Alexander, and the fear of him which was felt by every part of [*Nic. Eth.*, VII. xi.] Greece.' Such is the man whom Aristotle describes as 'half bad, but not unjust; for he plotted no evil'.[2]

[*Orations*, vii = p. 93.] In his praises of the Emperor Valens, Themistius applies these distinctions to the requirement of our subject as follows:

You have distinguished between wrong, error, and misfortune.[3] Although you are not learning the words of Plato, nor perusing Aristotle, nevertheless in fact you are following their precepts.[4] For you did not hold that equal punishment was deserved

unwillingly and contrary to their own desires.' In Agathias, III [IV. xx], the Misimiani declared that 'they were not altogether unworthy to be spared and pardoned, when, after having suffered a multitude of wrongs, they had consequently been impelled to take revenge with true barbaric vehemence'.

[1] *Deuteronomy*, xxii. 26; Moses Maimonides, *Guide of the Perplexed*, III. xli.

[2] 'On this charge Cleon attacks the cause of the Mityleneans, in Thucydides, III [III. xl]: 'They did not injure us unwillingly, but they plotted against us purposely. That alone is deserving of pardon which one does against his will.' Philo, in his book *De Constitutione Principis* [xiii], says: 'If he must proceed to take vengeance, he knows how to distinguish between those who lead a life of intrigue and those who are of a far different spirit. For to proceed to slaughter all, even those who have committed the least sins [or none at all], is characteristic of a fierce and savage mind.'

[3] [527] Seneca, *Natural Questions*, II. xliv, where he discusses thunderbolts, says: 'They wished to warn those, whose duty it is to thunder against the sins of men, that all things are not to be struck in the same way; some ought to be demolished, some shattered and separated, and some warned.'

[4] Such a one was Trajan, one of the notable Roman emperors: 'He was not master of that exact learning which is expressed in words, but its content he both knew and practised'; Xiphilinus [LXVIII. vii. 4].

Herodian [I. ii. 4] writes of Marcus Aurelius: 'He was the only one of the emperors to reveal

by those who had advocated war from the first, those who were later caught in the rush to arms, and those who submitted to him who seemed already to be master of the situation; but the first you condemned, the second you reproved, and the last you pitied.

8. The same author, in another connexion, expresses the desire that an emperor in his youth should learn, 'What is the difference between misfortune, error, and wrong; and how a king should pity the first, correct the second, and visit with vengeance the last alone.' Thus, in Josephus, Titus punishes the single leader in a criminal act 'in reality', and his following 'in speech', with mere verbal castigation. [ix = p. 123.] *Jewish War*, V [iii. 5].

Mere misfortunes neither deserve punishment nor create a liability to restoration of damage. Unjust actions do both. Fault, lying between the two, although it renders the responsible party liable for restitution, yet often does not deserve punishment, especially capital punishment. To this the lines of Valerius Flaccus are applicable: [III. 391 ff.

If fortune cruel, kin to fault, o'ertakes
Those ill-starred ones whose hands are stained with blood
Against their will, their conscience vexes them
In divers ways, and in their idle hours
Their deeds torment them.

V.—*Those who are responsible for a war are to be distinguished from those who follow them*

The counsel of Themistius, who warns us that we must distinguish between those who were responsible for a war [1] and those who followed the leadership of others, is supported by numerous historical examples. Herodotus relates that the Greeks exacted punishment from those who instigated the Thebans to desert to the Medes. So too, as Livy relates, the leaders of the revolt of Ardea were beheaded. In the same author, Valerius Levinus, 'after the capture of Agrigentum, scourged and executed the leaders, [517] but sold the rest of the people and the booty'. In another passage Livy says: 'The surrender of Atella and Calasia was accepted; and there also those who had been in control were punished.' In still another passage: 'Since those responsible for the revolt have received the punishment they deserved from the immortal gods and from you, conscript Fathers, what do you wish should be done with the innocent populace?' 'At length they were pardoned, and were IX [lxxxviii]. IV [x. 6]. XXVI [xl. 13]. [XXVI. xvi. 5.] [VIII. xx. 11.]

his wisdom, not by words or the knowledge of doctrines, but by sound morality and a life of moderation.' Of Macrinus, Xiphilinus [LXXVIII. xi. 2] writes: 'His conscientiousness in the execution of the laws surpassed the accuracy of his knowledge of them.' Grant, O Lord, such princes to our time!

[1] See Gail, *De Pace Publica*, II [II. ix], no. 18.

XXVIII [xxvi. 3]. granted citizenship, with the purpose', no doubt, as he elsewhere says, 'that the punishment might remain where the guilt arose.'

[*Suppliants*, 878 ff.] In Euripides, Eteocles the Argive is praised because—

> When he was judge, the culprit bore the blame,
> And not his native city, which ofttimes
> Bears the reproach for misdeeds of the ruler.

III [xxxvi]. The Athenians, according to Thucydides, repented of their decree against the inhabitants of Mitylene, 'that they should put to death the whole city rather than merely the instigators of the revolt'. [XXI. x.] Diodorus relates that Demetrius, after taking Thebes, executed only the ten persons responsible for its defection.

VI.—*With regard to those who are responsible for a war we must distinguish between causes which may be and those which may not be approved*

1. Further, in considering those who are responsible for a war, Victoria, *On the Law of War*, no. 59. we must distinguish between the causes of their action; for there are some causes which are not indeed just, but still are such that they may deceive persons who are by no means wicked. II [xvii. 25]. The author of the *Ad Herennium* suggests this as a perfectly equitable reason for pardoning: when any one has done wrong not from hatred or cruelty, *On Clemency*, II. vii. but moved by a sense of duty and righteous zeal. Seneca's wise man 'will dismiss his enemies safe and sound, at times even with praise, if they have taken the field on honourable grounds, on behalf of loyalty, a treaty obligation, or liberty'.

VII [xx. 2]. In Livy the people of Caere seek pardon for their error [1] because [Appian, *Syrian Wars*, iv. 21.] they gave aid to their kinsmen. The Phocians, Chalcidians, and others, who had supported Antiochus on the ground of a treaty, received pardon from the Romans. [= p. 135 B C.] Aristides, in his second speech *On Leuctra*, says that the Thebans, who had followed the leadership of the Lacedaemonians against the Athenians, 'had shared in an action unjust indeed, but one which they could cloak with some plea of justice, that of loyalty to the heads of their league'.

[I. xi. 35.] In his first book *On Duties* Cicero says that we must spare those who were not cruel, not inhuman, in war; then, that wars, in which [Plutarch, *Demetrius*, v = p. 891 A.] the prize is glory of empire, should be waged with less bitterness. In this sense King Ptolemy informed Demetrius that 'They were fighting not for existence, but for empire and glory'. III [vi. 4]. In Herodian [2]

[1] 'Sometimes one should pardon a ruler who has been conquered, if he did not know what was just.' Copied from Isocrates by Ammianus, Book XXX [XXX. viii. 6].

[2] The Greek words are these: *καὶ Νίγρῳ μὲν πολεμοῦντες οὐχ οὕτως εὐλόγους εἴχομεν αἰτίας ἔχθρας, ὡς ἀναγκαίας. οὐ γὰρ παρ' ἡμῖν πρυυπάρχουσαν ἀρχὴν ὑφαρπάζων μεμίσητο, ἐν μέσῳ δὲ ἐρριμμένην καὶ ἀμφήριστον οὖσαν, ἑκάτερος ἡμῶν ἐξ ἰσοτίμου φιλοτιμίας εἰς αὐτὸν ἀνθεῖλκεν.* Excellently said.

Severus says: 'When we waged war against Niger, we had not in fact such specious grounds for enmity; for each of us with equal ambition sought to secure for himself the principate, which lay open to all and was still an object of dispute.'

2. Often there occurs what we find stated in Cicero regarding the war between Caesar and Pompey: 'There was some uncertainty; there was a contest between the most eminent generals; many were in doubt as to what it would be best to do.' The same author says elsewhere: 'Even if we are guilty of some fault arising from human error, we are certainly guiltless of crime.' Evidently, as in Thucydides, those acts are said to deserve pardon which are done, 'not from wickedness, but rather from an error of judgement'. *For M. Marcellus* [x. 30]. [v. 13.] [I. xxxii.]

Cicero says also of Deiotarus: 'He did not act from hatred of you, but he went astray through a common error.' Sallust writes in his *Histories*: 'Of the rest of the crowd, after the fashion of a mob rather than prudently, the one followed the other as wiser than himself.' What Brutus wrote with regard to civil wars might, I should think, well be referred to most other wars: 'More zeal should be shown in preventing them than in giving vent to wrath against the vanquished.'[1] [*For King Deiotarus,* iii. 10.] [*To Caesar on Public Administration,* I. ii. 4.] Cicero, *Letters to Brutus,* ii [I. ii a].

VII.—*Punishment may often be remitted justly even to enemies who have deserved death*

1. Even where justice does not demand the remission of punishment, this is nevertheless often in conformity with goodness, [518] with moderation,[2] with highmindedness. 'The greatness of the Roman people has been augmented by pardoning,' says Sallust. From Tacitus we have: 'We ought to make use of as great kindness towards suppliants as tenacity against an enemy.' Seneca says: 'It is characteristic of wild beasts, though not of the higher types, to bite and worry those that have been struck down. Elephants and lions pass by what they have thrown over.' These words of Virgil are often timely, [*Speech of Philip,* vi.] *Annals,* XII [xx]. *On Clemency,* I. v. [*Aeneid,* X. 528 f.]

> Not here undone the Trojan's victory,
> Nor will one life decide so great an issue.

2. On this point there is a notable passage in the fourth book of the *Ad Herennium*: [IV xvi. 23.]

> Our ancestors did well in establishing this practice, not to put to death any king whom they had made prisoner in war. Why so? Because it was unjust to take advantage

[1] Bembo, IX.

[2] King Theodoric in Cassiodorus, [*Variae,*] II. xli: 'Those wars have turned out successfully for me which have been terminated without resort to extreme measures; for he conquers effectively who knows how to exercise moderation in all things.'

of the opportunity which fortune had given us for the punishment of those whom that same fortune had but shortly before placed in a most exalted station.

What of the fact that he led an army against us? I cease to recall it. Why so? Because a brave man holds as enemies those who strive for victory, but considers as men those who have been conquered, in order that courage may lessen war, and humaneness enrich peace. But if he had conquered, he would not have done the same, would he? Why then do you spare him? Because I have been accustomed to despise such folly, not to imitate it.

If you take this with reference to the Romans (a point that is uncertain, since this writer uses foreign and imaginary examples), it is in direct opposition to what we find in the panegyric addressed to Constantine, the son of Constantius:

[Eumenius, *Panegyric*, vi. 10.]

He may be more prudent who binds his adversaries to him by pardon, but he is stronger who tramples upon those that are angry. You, Emperor, have received that ancient trust of the Roman Empire, which was wont to exact the vengeance of death from the captured leaders of the enemy. In those days captive kings, after having adorned the chariots of those celebrating triumphs, from the city gates to the forum, as soon as the victorious general began to turn his chariot toward the Capitol were dragged off to prison and put to death. Perseus alone, at the personal intercession of Paulus, who had received his surrender, escaped the severity of this law. The rest, chained in dark dungeons, furnished an object lesson to other kings,[1] that they would find it preferable to cultivate the friendship of the Romans rather than to rouse their sense of justice.

See Plutarch, *Aemilius Paulus* [xxxvii = p. 274F].

[*Jewish War*, VII. v. 6.]

But this writer also speaks too sweepingly. Josephus, in his account of the death of Simon Barjoras, makes the same point regarding the severity of the Romans, but he is speaking of leaders like Pontius the Samnite, not of those who had the title of king. The substance of his narrative in translation is as follows:

The end of the triumph came after the arrival at the temple of Jupiter on the Capitoline hill; for the ancient custom of the state required that victorious generals should wait there until the death of the leader of the enemy should be reported to them. This leader was Simon, son of Joras, who was led among the captives in the triumphal procession; then, with a noose about his neck he was dragged into the forum, being meanwhile scourged by his guards. It is the Roman custom to exact punishment in this place from those who have been condemned of capital offences. When it was reported that Simon was dead, there followed the announcement of favourable omens and then sacrifices.

[1] I should not like to have this custom resurrected. Nevertheless even Joshua put captured kings to death; Josephus, *Antiquities of the Jews*, V. i [V. i. 19]. Dio Cassius [XLIX. xxii. 6] says of Sossius: 'He crucified Antigonus and scourged him with rods'; but he takes pains to add: 'a thing which no other king had suffered at the hands of the victorious Romans.' The same story is in Josephus, Book XV [*Antiquities of the Jews*, XV. i. 2].

Eutropius, Book X [X. iii], says of Maximian Herculius [rather of Constantine I]: 'When the Franks and Alemanni had been slaughtered, and their kings taken prisoner, he cast the kings to the wild beasts, in a magnificent spectacle which he had prepared as a distinction of his office.' See Ammianus, XXVII [XXVII. ii. 9], on the king of the Alemanni who was hung from a gibbet. Theodoric, king of the Visigoths, beheaded Athiulf, king of the Suevi, in Spain, as is recorded by Jordanes, *History of Goths* [xliv].

Verily, these instances furnish proof to kings that they should practise moderation, and that they should reflect that they too are subject to human vicissitudes, if God so wills; and that, according to the saying of Solon, which Croesus remembered when in like peril, one cannot pass judgement upon a man's good fortune until he is dead.

Cicero gives an almost identical account in the passage on punishments in his speech *Against Verres*. [V. xxvi. 66.]

3. Of commanders who met such a fate we have numerous examples; of kings, a few, as Aristonicus [Aristobulus],[1] Jugurtha, Artabasdus. But yet, besides Perseus, Syphax,[2] Gentius, Juba, and, in the time of the Caesars, Caractacus, and others, escaped such punishment, so that it appears that the Romans took into account both the causes of war and its manner of conduct, although Cicero and others admit that when victorious they were unjustly severe. [*On Duties*, I. xi; III. x.] So in Diodorus Siculus, Marcus Aemilius Paulus, in the case of Perseus, gives good advice to the Roman senators when he says: 'If they had no fear of men, yet they should fear the divine vengeance which hangs over those that make too insolent a use of victory.' [*Selections* [xxxi. 2].] [519] Plutarch records [3] that in the wars among the Greeks even the enemies of the Lacedaemonians did no violence to their kings, through respect for the royal dignity.

4. An enemy therefore who wishes to observe, not what the laws of men permit, but what his duty requires, what is right from the point of view of religion and morals, will spare the blood of his foes; and he will condemn no one to death, unless to save himself from death or some like evil, or because of personal crimes which have merited capital punishment. Furthermore, from humanitarian instincts, or on other worthy grounds, he will either completely pardon, or free from the penalty of death, those who have deserved such punishment.

The same Diodorus Siculus, whom I have mentioned, has an excellent statement: 'The storming of cities, the winning of battles, and all other successes in war, are more often due to fortune than to valour. But for those in the highest authority to show mercy to the vanquished is the work of wisdom alone.' XXVII [XVII. xxxviii]. In Curtius we read: 'Although Alexander could justly have been angry with those who were responsible for the war, still he gave pardon to all.' [IX. i. 22.]

VIII.—*One must take care, so far as is possible, to prevent the death of innocent persons, even by accident*

Again, with regard to the destruction of those who are killed by accident and without intent, we must hold fast to the principle which we mentioned above. It is the bidding of mercy, if not of justice, that, except for reasons that are weighty and will affect the

[1] See Appian, *Mithridatic Wars*, at the end [xvii. 117].

[2] Historians differ in regard to him. Many relate that he died in the neighbourhood of Rome before the triumph; Polybius [XVI. xxiii], that he was led in the triumph; Appian [*Punic Wars*, v. 28], that he died of disease, while his fate was under consideration.

[3] [528] *Agis* [xxi = p. 804 E].

safety of many, no action should be attempted whereby innocent
[V. xi.] persons may be threatened with destruction. Polybius is of the same opinion as ourselves, and in his fifth book speaks thus: 'It becomes good men not to wage a war of annihilation even with the wicked, but to proceed only so far that crimes may be remedied and corrected; and not to involve the innocent in the same punishment as the guilty, but even to spare those who are guilty for the sake of the innocent.'

IX.—*Children should always be spared; women, unless they have been guilty of an extremely serious offence; and old men*

1. With these principles recognized, the defining of provisions to cover the more special cases will not be difficult. 'Let the child
[*On Anger.*] III. xxiv. be excused by his age, the woman by her sex,'[1] says Seneca in the treatise in which he vents his anger upon anger. In the wars of the
Deut., xx. 14. Jews God himself desired that women and children be spared even after peace had been offered and rejected—apart from a few peoples that were excepted by a special law, and against whom the war was not a war of men, but of God, and was so called. When He desired
Numbers, xxxi. 18. that the women of the Midianites should be put to death because of their particular crime, he excepted the maidens who were virgin.
Jonah, iv. 2 [iv. 11]. Indeed when He had sternly threatened the Ninevites with destruc-

[1] Pliny, *Natural History*, VIII. xvi: 'When the lion is enraged, he attacks men before women, and children only when very hungry.' On these lines of Horace, *Odes*, IV. vi [IV. vi. 18 ff.], describing Achilles:

> Children as yet untaught to speak would he consume
> In the Achaeans' fires, even those that lay
> In their mother's womb,

the Scholiast comments thus: 'He bitterly inveighs against the cruelty of Achilles, who, if Apollo had permitted him to live, was so cruel that he would have spared neither infants nor babes still unborn.'

Philo, *De Constitutione Principis* [xiii], says: 'But let maidens and women go free,' and gives as the reason: 'It is cruel to make women the accessories of men, who devise wars.' The same author, *On Special Laws*, II [III. xx], writes: 'For against men of ripe age there may be found a thousand reasonable pretexts for differences and quarrels. But against children, who have just come into the light and life of men, not even calumny has anything to say, for they are clearly innocent.'

Josephus, *Antiquities of the Jews*, Book IX [IX. xi.], says of Manahem: 'By not even sparing infants he reached the extreme of cruelty, or rather ferocity. For he committed against his fellow countrymen acts which would not deserve pardon if they had been done to foreigners conquered in war.' Josephus also relates [*Antiquities of the Jews*, XII. viii. 3 and 5] that Judas Maccabeus, upon taking Bosra and Ephron, slew 'all males and those capable of fighting'. And elsewhere [*Antiquities of the Jews*, XIII. xiv. 2] he calls the penalty which Alexander, surnamed the Thracian, exacted from the women and children of the Jews, 'an inhuman vengeance'. Agathias, III [IV. xix], says: 'Since indeed it was impious thus to give vent to anger and to rage against newborn infants ignorant of their fathers' crimes, these deeds of theirs did not go unpunished.'

Nicetas, or the writer who continued his history to the times of King Henry, in speaking of the Scythians, who had taken Athira, says [*Urbs Capta*, xiv]: 'Not even infants still at the breast escaped destruction, but even these were so to speak harvested in their early growth, or withered as a flower, through the deeds of men untouched by pity, and who knew not that he who stretches his anger beyond the conquest and subjugation of his enemies sins against nature and violates the moral law of men.'

Add what Bede has in Book II, chap. xx, on the ferocity of Caraevolla; and the good law of the Swiss in Simler [Book II, p. 302, ed. Elzevir]; and the pious ordinances of Queen Elizabeth, in Camden on the year 1596.

tion for their very heinous crimes He suffered Himself to be diverted by compassion for the many thousands of the age which would be ignorant of the distinctions of right and wrong.

In Seneca there is a point of view which resembles this: 'Does any one become angry with children whose age is not yet able to comprehend distinctions?' Also in Lucan: *On Anger*, II. ix [II. x]. [II. 108.]

For what crime could little ones have deserved death?

If God has so done and so ordained—He who is able to kill justly any persons of whatever age or sex without cause, seeing that He is the Giver and Lord of life—what right have men, to whom He has assigned no right over men, to do anything not necessary for the preservation of human safety and human society?

2. In the first place, with regard to children we have the judgement of those peoples and ages over which moral right has exerted the greatest influence. [520] 'We have arms', says Camillus in Livy, 'not against that age which is spared even when cities are taken, but against men in arms.' He adds that this has a place among the laws of war, that is the natural laws. Victoria, *On the Law of War*, no. 36. [V. xxvii. 7.]

In dealing with the same incident Plutarch says: 'Among good men even war has certain laws.' Note here the phrase 'among good men', that you may distinguish this law from the law which is based on custom and impunity. Thus Florus says that a certain course of action was inevitable, if honour was not to be violated. In another passage of Livy we read: 'An age from which even enraged enemies would withhold their hands'; in still another, 'Their cruel rage led them to slay even the infants.' *Camillus* [x=p. 134 B]. I [xii]. XXIV [xxvi. 11]. [XXVIII. xx. 6.]

3. Again, that which is always the rule in respect to children who have not attained to the use of reason is in most cases valid with regard to women. This holds good, that is, unless women have committed a crime which ought to be punished in a special manner, or unless they take the place of men. For they are, as Statius says, 'a sex untrained and inexperienced in war'. When Nero in the tragedy calls Octavia a foe, the prefect replies: [*Silvae*, I. vi. 53.] [Seneca,] *Octavia* [864].

Does a woman receive this name?[1]

In Curtius Alexander says: 'I am not accustomed to wage war with prisoners and women; he whom I am to hate must be in arms.' Gryphus, in Justin, declares that 'None of his ancestors, in all their numerous civil and foreign wars, had after a victory ever displayed cruelty to women, whose very sex exempts them from the V [IV. xi. 17]. XXXVIII [XXXIX. ii. 7].

[1] And so Tucca and Varus thought that we should delete from the second book of the *Aeneid* the verses [567–88] in which Aeneas deliberates whether he shall kill Helen.

[*Annals*, I. lix.] dangers of war and the savagery of the victors.' In Tacitus another says that 'He is not waging war against women, but openly against armed men.'

IX. i [IX. ii. 4]. 4. Valerius Maximus calls the cruelty of Munatius Flaccus against infants and women ferocious, and intolerable even to hear about. In Diodorus it is related that the Carthaginians at Selinus slew old men, women, and children, 'uninfluenced by humane feelings'; elsewhere he calls this conduct 'cruelty'. Latinus Pacatus refers to women as 'the sex which is spared by wars'. Papinius [Statius] has a similar statement about old men:

XIII [lvii]. XIV [XIII. lvii]. [*Panegyric of Theodosius*, xxix.] [*Thebaid*, v. 258 f.]

Old men, a throng
Inviolate in war.

X.—*Those also should be spared whose occupations are solely religious or concerned with letters*

Victoria, *On the Law of War*, no. 36. XXVIII [xxiii. 1]. *Antiquities of the Jews*, XII. iii [1]. Livy, V [xxi. 13].

1. The same principle is in general to be applied to men whose manner of life is opposed to war. 'By the law of war armed men and those who offer resistance are killed,' as Livy says; that is, by that law which is in harmony with nature. Thus Josephus says that it is right that in war those who have taken up arms should pay the penalty, but that the guiltless should not be injured. When Veii was stormed, Camillus gave orders that the unarmed should be spared.

In this class must be placed first, those who perform religious duties. From ancient times among all nations it has been customary that such men should abstain from the use of arms; and so in turn men refrained from violence toward them. Hence the Philistines, the enemies of the Jews, did not harm the school of the prophets [1] which was at Gaba, as one may see in *1 Samuel*, x. 5 and 10. And so David in company with Samuel fled to another place where there was a similar school, that was removed, as it were, from all harm at the hands of armed forces (*1 Samuel*, xix. 18). The Cretans, Plutarch tells us, when engaged in internal strifes, refrained from doing any harm to priests,[2] and to those in charge of cremating the dead, whom they called 'cremators'. This explains the force of the Greek proverb, 'Not even a fire-bearer was left.' Strabo notes [3] that in

Greek Questions [xxi = p. 296 B–D]. VIII [iii. 33].

[1] [529] Hyrcanus, while besieging Jerusalem, sent victims to the Temple, as the Jews relate. The Goths are likewise praised by Procopius, *Gothic War*, II [II. iv], because they spared the priests of Peter and Paul outside the walls of Rome. See the supplement of Charles the Great to the *Bavarian Law* [no. 2], and the *Lombard Law*, I. xi. 14.

[2] Servius, *On the Aeneid*, VII [VII. 442], says: 'For he was excluded from war, if not by his age, at least by the sanctity of his priesthood.'

[3] Also Polybius, Book IV [IV. lxxiii], and Diodorus Siculus in the *Excerpta Peiresciana* [p. 225]. In like manner also those who went to compete at the Olympic, Pythian, Nemean, and Isthmian Games in time of war enjoyed 'safe conduct and security'. This we learn from Thucydides, V [V. xlix] and VIII [VIII. x]; and Plutarch, *Aratus* xxviii = p. 1040 B].

olden times, when the whole of Greece was ablaze with war, the Eleans, as sacred to Jupiter, and those enjoying their hospitality, lived in deep peace.

2. In the same class with the priests are deservedly ranked those who have chosen a similar manner of life, as monks and novices, that is, penitents; these the canons, in accordance with natural justice, order men to spare just the same as priests. [521] *Decretals* I. xxxiv. 2.

To priests and penitents you may properly add those who direct their energies to literary pursuits, which are honourable and useful to the human race.

XI.—*Farmers should be spared*

In the second place farmers, whom the canons also include, should be spared. Diodorus Siculus relates with praise of the inhabitants of India that 'in wars indeed enemies kill one another, but they leave the tillers of the soil unharmed, for the reason that these render a common service.' Of the ancient Corinthians and Megarians Plutarch says: 'No one harmed the farmers in any way.' Cyrus ordered that notice be given to the king of the Assyrians 'that he was ready to release those who tilled the soil, and not to harm them'. Of Belisarius Suidas says: 'He spared the tillers of the soil to such a degree, and exercised so great care for them, that when he was in command none of them at any time suffered injury.'

Library, II [xxxvi].

[*Greek Questions*, xvii = p. 295 c.] Xenophon, *Training of Cyrus*, V [iv. 24]. [On the word Βελισάριος.]

XII.—*Merchants and like persons should be spared*

The canon adds merchants; and this provision is to be taken as applicable not only to those who make a temporary sojourn in hostile territory, but also to permanent subjects; for their life also is foreign to arms.

Under this head are included at the same time artisans and other workmen, whose pursuits love peace, not war.

XIII.—*Prisoners of war also should be spared*

1. To come to those who have borne arms, we have already mentioned the remark of Pyrrhus in Seneca, who says that a sense of shame, that is, respect for what is right, forbids us to deprive a prisoner of his life. We have adduced the similar view of Alexander, which included prisoners with women. We may present also this statement of Augustine: 'Let necessity, not inclination, cut off[1]

[III. x. 1.]

[III. xi. 9. 3.] Letter i, *To Boniface* [*Letters*, clxxxix. 6].

[1] Gratian suggested *deprimat* (let it crush). Plutarch says in his *Marcellus* [*Comparison of Pelopidas and Marcellus*, i = p. 316 D]: 'Epaminondas and Pelopidas never put any one to death after a victory, nor reduced states to slavery; and it is believed that, if these men had been present, the Thebans would not have acted as they did to the people of Orchomenos.' Marcellus followed the same practice at the

the enemy who is fighting. Just as violence is done to him who fights and resists, so pity is now due to the vanquished or captive, especially in the case of him from whom no disturbance of the peace is feared.'

[*Agesilaus* i. 21.] Xenophon writes of Agesilaus: 'He instructed his soldiers not to punish prisoners of war as guilty of crime, but to guard them as men.' In Diodorus Siculus we find: 'All [the Greeks] fight those who resist, but spare the vanquished.' In the judgement of the same writer, the Macedonians who were under Alexander 'treated the Thebans more harshly than the law of war allowed'. (XIII [xxiv]. XVII [xiii].)

[xci. 6–7.] 2. In his history of the *Jugurthine War* Sallust, having related that youths had been killed after surrendering, says that that was done contrary to the law of war; this is to be interpreted as against the nature of justice and the usage of more civilized peoples. In Lactantius we read: 'The vanquished are spared, and room is found for mercy in the midst of strife.' Tacitus praises Antonius Primus and Varus, the Flavian generals, because they had vented their rage on no one except in battle. Aristides says: 'It befits men of our character to constrain with arms those who resist, but to treat leniently those who have been overthrown.' (V [ix]. *Histories*, IV [xxxix]. *On Peace*, ii [=p. 80 c].)

2 Kings, vi [22]. In regard to prisoners the prophet Elisha addresses the king of Samaria as follows: 'Wouldst thou smite those whom thou hast taken captive with thy sword and thy bow?' In the *Children of Hercules* by Euripides, when the herald inquires: [line 965.]

> Then does your law forbid to slay a foe?

the chorus replies:

> Yes, one whom Mars has suffered to survive the fray.

[line 1011.] [522] In the same play the captive Eurystheus says,

> The hands which me shall slay will not be guiltless.

capture of Syracuse, as Plutarch says in the same passage [xix = p. 308 D]. See the same writer in his life of *Cato of Utica* [lviii = p. 787 C D].

'When Cabades, the Persian king, had taken Amida by storm, and had caused a great slaughter, an aged priest told him that it was not befitting for a king to kill those who were already prisoners.' This is told by Procopius, *Persian War*, I [I. vii], who also says in the *Persian War*, II [II. ix]: 'It is contrary to piety to be cru to prisoners.' In the same writer there is a notable speech of Belisarius to his soldiers at the capture of Naples; *Gothic War*, I [I. ix].

To one who advised him to kill his Scythian prisoners, the Emperor Alexius in Anna Comnena [VIII. vi] replied: 'Even though they are Scythians, still they are men; even though they are enemies, still they are deserving of pity.' Gregoras, Book VI [VI. viii], says: 'Those deeds which are done in battle and actual warfare, whatever they may be, secure pardon for the doer, on the ground that his mind is beset at such a time, and that his hand in a fit of intoxication does not take reason as the guide and controller of its actions. But when the extreme danger is over, when the mind has the time freely to examine and decide everything, surrender of the control of action to the hand indicates a man's base purpose, if anything unseemly occurs.'

Add the other passage from the same Gregoras, which we included in the notes at the end of Chapter VII, of this book, and Chalcocondylas, Book V [=p. 259, ed. Bekker], on a laudable custom of the Poles. Julian, in the second panegyric on Constantius [*Orations*, ii = p. 86 C], in his person describes the good ruler: 'Once victorious in battle he put an end to the work of the sword, thinking it a crime to take the life of a man who has ceased to defend himself.'

In Diodorus Siculus, the Byzantines and Chalcedonians, because they had put to death a large number of prisoners, are branded with this characterization: 'They perpetrated crimes of extraordinary cruelty.' The same writer elsewhere speaks of sparing prisoners [1] as 'a law common to all'; those who do otherwise, he says, beyond question do wrong. To spare prisoners is commanded by the nature of goodness and justice, as we just now heard Seneca say in his philosophical treatises. We see that in history those are praised who, when they might have been burdened or endangered by an excessive number of prisoners, preferred to release all rather than kill them.

XII [lxxxii]. [XIII. xxvi.] *On Benefits*, V. xviii [*On Clemency*, I. xviii].

XIV.—*The surrender of those who wish to yield upon fair terms should be accepted*

1. For the same reasons the surrender of those who yield upon condition that their lives be spared ought not to be rejected, either in battle or in a siege.[2] Thus Arrian says that the slaughter by the Thebans of persons who had surrendered was not in accordance with Greek custom, 'not a Hellenic killing'. Likewise Thucydides in his third book says: 'You have taken us into your power willingly and with outstretched hands. It is the Greek custom not to kill such persons.' In Diodorus Siculus, the senators of Syracuse declare: 'It is worthy of a noble mind to spare the suppliant.' Similarly Sopater: 'It is customary to spare suppliants in times of war.'

[*Anabasis of Alexander*, I. ix. 10.] [III. lviii.] [XI. xcii.]

2. In the case of besieged cities the acceptance of surrender was the rule among the Romans before the battering-ram had shaken the wall. Caesar informed the Adratuci that he would save their city if they would surrender before the ram should have touched the wall. The custom even now obtains in the case of unfortified places, before cannon fire is opened; and, in the case of more strongly fortified places, before an assault is made upon the walls. But Cicero, looking not so much to what is done as to what is right according to nature, declares himself upon this point as follows: 'You must both be merciful to those whom you have overcome by force, and accept the surrender of those who lay down their arms and take refuge in the good faith of generals, even though the battering-ram has already battered the wall.'

Gallic War, II [xxxii]. *On Duties*, I [xi. 35].

The Jewish interpreters note that it was a custom among their

[1] Capitolinus says in his *Marcus* [*Aurelius*] *Antoninus* [xxiv]: 'He observed justice, even with regard to prisoners taken from the enemy.'

[2] [530] In [Procopius,] *Gothic War*, IV [IV. xii], the Romans say to the Persians, who were in the citadel of Petra: 'We, however, pity you who cast the yoke from your necks, and we wish to spare you who seek death, and to save you although you lightly despise life, as becomes Christians and citizens of the Roman Empire.' See De Serres in his *Life of Francis I* and *Life of Henry II*.

ancestors that, when they were besieging a city, they would not completely encircle it, but would leave a sector open for those who wished to escape,[1] in order that the issue might be determined with less bloodshed.

XV.—*Those also who have surrendered unconditionally should be spared*

The same sense of justice bids that those be spared who yield themselves unconditionally to the victor, or who become suppliants. *Annals*, XII [xvii]. 'To butcher those who have surrendered is savage' is the judgement of Tacitus. Likewise in the case of the Campsani, who had surrendered to Marius, Sallust, after relating that those who had reached *Jugurthine War* [xci. 6–7]. the age of puberty were slain, adds that this was a crime against the law of war, that is, the law of nature. *On Public Administration*, I [iv. 1]. The same author says elsewhere: 'Not armed men were slain in battle, according to the law of war, but suppliants, after battle.'

[XXVIII. xxiii. 1.] XLV [XLII. xxi. 3]. In Livy, as we have said already, 'By the law of war armed men, and those who resist, may be slain'; in another passage we read, 'who, contrary to law and right, had made war upon those that had surrendered.' Effort should be directed to this, that men should rather be driven to surrender through fear, than that they should [Plutarch, *Brutus*, xxvi = p. 996 A.] be slain. Praise is given to the conduct of Brutus, who 'did not permit a charge to be made upon his opponents, but surrounded them with cavalry, ordering that they be spared, on the ground that they would soon be on his side.'

XVI.—*What has been stated is true, provided that no serious crime has preceded; how this is to be understood*

1. Against these precepts of justice and the law of nature frequently exceptions are offered, which are by no means just; as, for example, if retaliation is required, if there is need of inspiring terror, if too determined a resistance has been offered. Yet he who recalls what has previously been said in regard to valid reasons for putting to death will easily perceive that such exceptions do not afford just [523] grounds for an execution.

See Victoria, *On the Law of War*, nos. 49 and 60. There is no danger from prisoners and those who have surrendered or desire to do so; therefore in order to warrant their execution it is necessary that a crime shall have been previously committed, such a crime, moreover, as a just judge would hold

[1] So Scipio Aemilianus, when about to destroy Carthage, proclaimed: 'Let those who wish, flee'; Polybius [Appian, *Punic Wars*, xix. 130].

punishable by death. And so we sometimes see anger vented upon prisoners or upon those who have surrendered, or a surrender upon guarantee of life refused, if any who were convinced of the injustice of a war have still remained in arms; if any have injured the good name of their enemies with monstrous slanders; if they have violated their plighted word, or another right of nations, such as that of ambassadors; if they were deserters.

2. But nature does not sanction retaliation except against those who have done wrong. It is not sufficient that by a sort of fiction the enemy may be conceived as forming a single body; this may be understood from our foregoing discussion on the sharing of punishments. II. xxi. 18. In Aristides we read: 'Is it not absurd to wish to imitate, as if they were right, the things which you attack and say it is wicked to do?' *On Peace*, ii [=p. 75 c]. Plutarch accuses the Syracusans on this ground, that they slew the wives and children of Hicetas for the sole reason that Hicetas had killed the wife, sister, and son of Dion. Plutarch, *Timoleon* [xxxiii = p. 252 c]; *Dion* [lviii = p. 983 E].

3. Even the advantage, which is anticipated for the future from frightfulness, does not suffice to give the right to kill; but if the right already exists it may be among the reasons for not waiving the right.

4. Furthermore a quite obstinate devotion to one's own party, provided only that the cause is not altogether dishonourable, does not deserve punishment, as the Neapolitans claim in Procopius. *Gothic War*, I [x]. Or, if such devotion is punished in any way, the penalty should not be carried so far as death; for no just judge would so decide. When, in a certain town, which had resisted with unusual fierceness, Alexander had ordered that all above the age of puberty should be slain, he seemed to the Hindoos to be waging war after the manner of brigands; and dreading the effect of such a reputation the king began to make a milder use of victory.

The same Alexander did better in wishing to spare certain inhabitants of Miletus, 'because he saw that they were noble and faithful to their cause', to cite the words of Arrian. Polyaenus, IV [iii. 30]. [*Anabasis of Alexander*, I. xix. 8.] Phyto, the commander of the people of Rhegium, when hurried to torture and death by Dionysius because of his too obstinate defence of the city, cried out that he was being punished for refusing to betray the city and that the deity would in a short time exact retribution for the mistreatment. Diodorus Siculus calls this punishment wicked, 'lawless punishment'. [XIV. cxii.]

I am greatly pleased with the prayer which is found in Lucan: [VII. 312 ff.]

> Be he the conqueror, who sees no need
> To draw the ruthless sword against the vanquished,
> Who does not think an impious deed was done,
> Because his countrymen took arms against him,

provided, nevertheless, that under the name of countrymen we understand not those of this or that district, but fellow-citizens of that common society which embraces all mankind.

5. Much less even is slaughter justified by resentment at some loss that has been sustained, as we read that Achilles, Aeneas, and Alexander avenged their friends with the blood of prisoners or of those who surrendered. Appropriately, therefore, Homer chants this verse: [*Iliad*, XXIII. 176.]

An evil deed he pondered in his heart.[1]

XVII.—*It is right to spare those who are guilty, if their number is very great*

Even where the crimes are such that they may seem worthy of death, it will be the part of mercy to give up something of one's full right because of the number of those involved. Such clemency, we see, began with God Himself; for He desired that the Canaanites [*Deut.*, xx. 10.] and their neighbours, by far the most wicked of peoples, should have the offer of a peace, [524] which would grant them their lives upon condition of their payment of tribute. Here applies the saying of Seneca: 'The severity of the general is directed against individuals, [*On Anger*, II. x.] but pardon is necessary where the whole army has deserted. What takes away a wise man's anger? The crowd of wrongdoers.'[2] Pertinent also are these verses of Lucan: [II. 198 ff.]

Famine, the frenzy of the sea, and swift disaster,
Or pestilence of earth and sky, or war's slaughtering,
Have oft laid low so many youths in hateful death,
But never punishment.

'The drawing of lots was devised that an undue number might not suffer punishment,' says Cicero. Sallust says to Caesar: 'Let [*For Cluentius* [xlvi. 128].] no one summon you to cruel punishments or harsh judgements, [*On Public Administration*, I. vi. 4.] by which the state is more afflicted than remedied.'

XVIII.—*Hostages should not be put to death unless they have themselves done wrong*

1. What decision according to the law of nature should be rendered in regard to hostages may be gathered from what we have

[1] That to later ages this seemed cruel is noted by Servius, *On the Aeneid*, X [X. 519].

[2] 'The sin that is committed by many goes unpunished,' says the Scholiast on Juvenal [ii. 46], citing Lucan [V. 260]. In Xiphilinus, who quotes from Dio [LV. xx], Livia says: 'If any one wishes to punish all such deeds rigorously, he does not see that he is thereby led to slay the great majority of men.' Augustine writes in his *Letters*, lxiv [xxii. 5]: 'Rather by admonition than by threats. In this way in fact one must deal with a multitude of sinners; but severity is to be exercised against the crimes of a few.'

Add Gail, *De Pace Publica*, II. ix. 36 [II. ix. 37].

said already. In former times it was commonly believed that each person had over his own life the same right which he had over other things that come under ownership, and that this right, by tacit or expressed consent, passed from individuals to the state. It is, then, not to be wondered at if we read that hostages who were personally guiltless were put to death for a wrong done by their state, either as though done by their individual consent, or by the public consent in which their own was included. But now that a truer knowledge has taught us that lordship over life is reserved for God, it follows that no one by his individual consent can give to another a right over life, either his own life, or that of a fellow-citizen.

Victoria, *On the Law of War*, no. 43.

Consistently with this point of view Agathias relates that to the good general Narses it seemed atrocious to exact punishment from innocent hostages. Other writers say the same of other generals. They cite also the example of Scipio, who said that he would not be severe with innocent hostages, but with the individuals themselves who had been guilty of defection,[1] and that he would exact punishment not from an unarmed foe, but from a foe in arms.

I [xii].

Livy, XXVIII [xxxiv. 9].

2. Furthermore some of the modern jurists, men not without standing, say that such agreements are valid if they are confirmed by custom. This I admit, if by right they mean mere freedom from human punishment, which in the discussion of this subject often passes under such a name. If, however, they consider that those who take the life of any one on the justification of an agreement alone are exempt from wrongdoing, I am afraid that they are both deceived themselves and by their dangerous authority deceive others.

Menochio, *De Arbitrariis Iudicum Quaestionibus*, vii.

It is clear that if he who comes as a hostage is, or previously was, of the number of great criminals, or has subsequently broken his pledge given in an important matter, it may be that his punishment will not be unjust.

3. But when Cloelia, who had come as a hostage, not of her own accord[2] but by the command of the state, made her escape by swimming the Tiber, her 'courage was not only pardoned, but even honoured by the Etruscan king', to use the words of Livy in his account of the incident.

II [xiii. 9].

XIX.—*All useless fighting should be avoided*

This remains to be added, that all engagements, which are of no use for obtaining a right or putting an end to a war, but have as their

[1] Julian says the same in Eunapius, *Selections on Embassies*, ix [=*Fragmenta Historicorum Graecorum*, IV, § 12, p. 18].

[2] Cf. the story of the hostages who tried to withdraw from this obligation, and were therefore punished, in Nicetas, Book II [*Isaac Angelus*, II. vi].

Acr. V [Arrian, *Anabasis*, I. xxii]. purpose a mere display of strength, that is, as the Greeks say, 'an exhibition of strength rather than a combat against the enemy', are incompatible both with the duty of a Christian and with humanity itself. Consequently rulers, who must render account of the useless shedding of blood to Him in Whose name they bear the sword, should strictly forbid such combats. [*Jugurthine War*, xcii. 4.] In fact, Sallust praised the generals who achieved victory without staining their army with blood. [*Germany*, xxx.] Tacitus says of the Chatti, a people of known courage: 'Raids and chance encounters [1] are rare among them.'

[1] Plutarch censures Demetrius [*Demetrius*, xl = p. 908 c], 'because he thrust his soldiers into danger, and exposed them to battles, rather from zeal for fame than for the sake of a real advantage.'

CHAPTER XII

MODERATION IN LAYING WASTE AND SIMILAR THINGS

I.—*What devastation may be lawful, and in what degree*

1. In order that any one may be able to destroy another's property without doing wrong, it is requisite that one of these three conditions should precede:

A necessity, such as should be understood to have been excepted in the first institution of ownership. An example would be that a person in order to escape imminent danger should cast into a river the sword of a third party, which a madman is about to use. In this case, however, we have elsewhere said that, in accordance with II. ii. 9. the better view, there remains an obligation to make good the loss.

Or, a debt arising from an inequality, it being understood that the thing destroyed is reckoned as received for that debt, since otherwise the right would not exist.

Or, a deserving of evil, for which such punishment may be an equivalent, or the measure of which is not exceeded by the punishment, [531] for, as a theologian of sound judgement observes, equity Victoria, *On the Law of War*, nos. 52 and 56. does not suffer a whole kingdom to be laid waste because flocks have been driven off or some houses burned. This was recognized also by Polybius, V [i.] who does not wish punishment in warfare to be carried beyond all bounds, but only so far as necessary that crimes may be expiated in a just way.

These reasons, which are applicable only within proper limits, cause the absence of wrong in the destruction of another's property.

2. But, unless a motive of utility commends such a course, it would be foolish to injure another without securing any good for oneself. Those, therefore, that are wise are usually influenced by considerations of utility. Of such considerations the most weighty is that which was pointed out by Onesander: 'Let him remember *Strategicus*, vi. to ruin the enemy's country, to burn and devastate it. For a lack of money and crops causes war to slacken [1] as much as an abundance causes it to flourish.' In accord with this is the saying of Proclus: [*On Plato's Republic*, III. iii.] 'It is the duty of a good general to weaken the resources of the enemy

[1] Philo, *On the Contemplative Life* [ii = p. 891 D]: 'Enemies are accustomed to lay waste hostile territory and to denude it of trees, in order that the enemy may yield the more readily through lack of necessities.' The same writer says in his *On Curses* [i]: 'They bring upon themselves a twofold misfortune, want for their friends, abundance for their foes.'

[IV. ix. 8.] in every way.' Curtius says of Darius: 'He believed that an enemy, who had nothing except that which he had seized by pillage, could be defeated by lack of supplies.'

3. In fact that kind of devastation must be tolerated which compels the enemy to sue for peace in a short time. This method of warfare was employed by Alyattes against the Milesians, by the Thracians against the Byzantines, by the Romans against the Campanians, the Capenates, the Spaniards, the Ligurians, the Nervii, and the Menapii.

Herodotus, I [xvii]. Polybius, IV [xlv]. Frontinus, *Strategemata*, III. iv. Livy, V [xii. 5]; VII; XXXIV [xvii]; XL [xxxviii]. Caesar, *Gallic War*, VI [iii and vi].

Nevertheless, if you examine the matter aright you will find that such depredations are ordinarily committed from motives of hatred rather than from considerations of prudence. It usually happens either that those conditions which justify devastation are lacking, or that there are other more cogent reasons which advise against it.

II.—*Devastation should be refrained from if the area is profitable for us and out of the power of the enemy*

1. This will happen, first, if our occupation of fruitful ground is such that it cannot yield produce for the enemy. That is the particular point of the divine law, which ordains that wild trees be employed in making walls and military structures, but that fruit-bearing trees be preserved for purposes of food, with the explanation that trees, unlike men, cannot rise up against us in battle; a restriction which Philo,[1] by similar reasoning, extends to fields under cultivation, adding to the law these words:

[*Deut.*, xx. 19, 20.]

On the Creation of Magistrates [xiii].

Why will you be angry with inanimate things, which are both mild and productive of wholesome fruits? Do trees, like men who are enemies, show signs of hostility, so that they must be uprooted for the things which they are doing or threaten to do? On the contrary, they are of use to the victors, and furnish them with a supply of the things which necessity demands, yes even those things which contribute to their pleasure. It is not man alone that pays tribute, for trees at fixed seasons bear richer tribute, such that without it man cannot live.

[1] Another passage of the same writer, *De Humanitate* [*De Caritate*, xx f.], is also worthy of being transcribed here:

[537] Moses, in dispensing justice even more freely, makes a very ample and liberal use thereof, in descending from persons endowed with reason to dumb animals, and from dumb animals, again, to the things which spring from the ground; and of these we must now speak, since we have already discussed men as being of the most importance, and other creatures which are capable of feeling. Moses wisely forbade the cutting down of cultivated trees, or the ruinous cutting down of crops before they are ripe, or the destruction of any products of the soil whatsoever, to the end that the human race may be supplied with an abundance of food; and not only an abundance of necessities but also of the things which contribute to a more luxurious life. The crops of the field are in fact a necessity, designed for the nourishment of men; while all the varied fruits of the trees contribute to their luxuries, although these often, when other things fail, take the place of nourishing foods.

Proceeding further, Moses refuses to sanction even the devastation of hostile territory; especially does he command enemies to refrain from cutting down trees, because he considers it unjust that the anger which has been aroused against men should be expended upon those things which are the cause of no evil. By this very thing he teaches us not to have regard to the present time only,

Moreover, in discussing the same passage, Josephus says that, if trees could speak, they would cry out that since they are not the cause of war it is wrong for them to bear its penalties. Unless I am mistaken, this is the source of the Pythagorean maxim in Iamblichus: 'Let it be unlawful to injure or cut down a cultivated and fruitful tree.' [*Ant. of the Jews*, IV. viii. 42.] [*Life of Pythagoras*, xxi. 99.]

2. Furthermore, in describing the customs of the Jews, in the fourth book of his work *On Abstaining from Animal Food*, Porphyry [1] extends this rule (interpreted, as I think, in the light of custom) even to living things employed in agricultural work. He says that Moses commanded that these too should be spared in war; the writings of the Talmud and the Hebrew interpreters add that this law is to be extended [2] to anything whatever which may be destroyed without cause, as touching the burning of buildings, or the destruction of supplies which can be eaten or drunk.

In harmony with this law is the wise moderation of the Athenian general Timotheus, who, as Polyaenus relates, 'did not permit a house or a homestead to be destroyed, or [532] a fruit-bearing tree to be cut down'. [III. x. 5.] There is also the law of Plato, in the fifth book of the *Republic*: 'Let not the land be ravaged, nor the houses set on fire.' [V. xvii = 471 A.]

3. Still more binding will this restriction be after a complete victory. Cicero disapproved of the destruction of Corinth, even *On Duties*, I [xi. 35]. *On His House* [xxiii. 60].

for the reason that nothing remains in the same condition, but all things are subject to vicissitudes and changes; hence it may easily happen that those, who are at present enemies, may again become allies, after they have joined in conferences and treaties. But it is a harsh thing to deprive friends of the necessities of life, when, in view of the uncertainty of the future, those things which may be useful should have been preserved for them.

It has been most truly said by the ancients that friends should be treated as though it were thought that no enmities could arise, and that offences should be so dealt with that friendship may be hoped for; that is, that each one should have in his mind, for his own protection, some measure of reserve, and not be obliged soon to repent of his excessive violence, through having revealed his purposes too openly in words and deeds; [538] and not be obliged to accuse himself, when the matter can no longer be remedied.

This wise saying, furthermore, should be observed by states, that in time of peace they should prepare the things which are necessary for war, but in time of war the things necessary for peace; and that they should neither place excessive confidence in their friends, as if these could not be diverted to the opposite side, nor utterly distrust their enemies, as if these could never be restored to friendship. But even if nothing ought to be done for an enemy in the hope of effecting a reconciliation, certainly none of the things which the soil bears is hostile, but all are friendly, and all are useful; indeed the cultivated plants are particularly necessary, seeing that their fruits are either nutritive or take the place of something nutritive.

War should not be waged on things that have nothing to do with war; one should not cut, nor burn, nor tear up by the roots the things which nature has tenderly reared with its streams of water and its summer skies, that they might bear tribute to men as to kings. For she, as the excellent and common ruler of all things, has taken care to secure undamaged force and vigour not only for animals, but also for the offspring of the soil, especially for cultivated plants, because they require greater care, and are not so prolific as wild plants, but require skilled cultivation to attain a vigorous growth.

[1] His words are [*On Abstaining from Animal Food*, IV. xiv]: 'The law also commands us to spare animals that are man's associates in toil, even on the land of the enemy; so that it is not permitted to kill them.'

[2] But, on the other hand, they wish to restrict it by adding the exception: unless trees situated in the suburbs should interfere with the javelin-throwers.

though Roman ambassadors had been shamefully treated there; and he also characterizes as horrible, criminal, and steeped in the depths of hatred, a war which is waged against walls, roofs, columns,
XXVI [xvi]. and doors. Livy praises the leniency of the Romans after the conquest of Capua, because they did not by fire and destruction vent their
Trojan Women [285 ff.]. anger upon innocent buildings and walls.[1] In Seneca, Agamemnon says:

> For my part I will confess (thy pardon, Argive land!),
> I wished to see the Phrygians brought low and undone;
> But Troy destroyed and razed to earth—such fate
> I should have censured.

Joshua, vi. 4. It is true that sacred history teaches us that certain cities were doomed to destruction by God, and that even contrary to the
2 Kings, iii. 19. general law it was ordered that the trees of the Moabites should be cut down. This, however, was not done out of hatred of the enemy, but to show a just abhorrence of their crimes, which were either publicly recognized as such, or in the judgement of God were worthy of such punishment.

III.—*Devastation should be refrained from if there is good hope for a speedy victory*

1. In the second place, what we have said will hold good even where the possession of land is in doubt, if there is good hope of a speedy victory, of which the prize will be both the land and its
XI [vi. 1]. fruits. Thus, as Justin relates, Alexander the Great prevented his soldiers from devastating Asia, 'saying that they must spare their

[1] On this subject there is a notable letter of Belisarius to Totila [in Procopius], *Gothic War*, III [III. xxii]:

> Previously it was thought that to construct works of beauty was characteristic of wise men and those versed in civilized life; that to destroy them, after they had been erected, was the act of fools and persons who did not blush to leave to posterity marks of their stupidity. It is agreed that Rome is the greatest and most worthy of admiration of all the cities which the sun beholds. This pitch of greatness and splendour it has not attained by the labour of one man alone, nor in a brief time; but very many kings and emperors, a vast line of eminent men, many centuries, and a marvellous accumulation of wealth, have brought together here, among other conditions, the leading workmen; and so by the gradual construction of so great a city [539] they have left monuments of their worthiness to succeeding generations. To destroy this city, therefore, would be to do a wrong to the human race of all ages, by taking from those who have gone before the memory of the praise that is due to them, and from those who are to come the pleasure of this spectacle.
>
> Since this is so, reflect that one of two things is inevitable, either you will be conquered by the Emperor in this war, or your fortune will be the better. If you are victorious, and the city has been destroyed, you will have lost what is not another's but your own. If it has been saved, you will enjoy the most beautiful of all possessions. If the lot has been cast against you, and Rome, through your efforts, is safe, a feeling of gratitude toward you will remain with the victor; but if Rome shall have been destroyed your lot will lie beyond hope of mercy. Not only will you gain nothing by the act, but the reputation which it deserves from all men will follow you. Such reputation is ready for you, according to your choice; for the repute enjoyed by those in power corresponds with their actions.

See also the law of Frederic I in Conrad, Abbot of Ursperg; and, with regard to Frederic Count Palatine, the *Chronicles* of Melanchthon.

own property,[1] and not destroy the things which they had come to take possession of.' So Quintius, when Philip was traversing Thessaly with a band engaged in plundering, for his part exhorted his troops, as Plutarch says, to pursue their march as though through a district which had been given up and already made their own. When urging Cyrus not to turn Lydia over to his soldiery to lay waste, Croesus said: 'You will not plunder my city, nor my possessions, for in no way do these things now belong to me; they are yours—yours are the things they will destroy.'

Flaminius [v = 371 D].

Herodotus, I [lxxxviii].

2. To those who do otherwise, the words of Jocasta to Polynices in Seneca's *Women of Thebes* are not ill suited:

[*Phoenician Women*, 558 ff.]

Seeking to win your country you destroy it;
To make it yours, you wish to make it nothing;
Your cause is harmed by this, with hostile arms
You burn the land, lay low the ripened crops,
And terror spread
Through all the fields. No one so wastes his own.
What you bid ruin with fire, with sword to reap,
You hold to be another's.

There is a similar thought in these words of Curtius: 'Whatever they had not ruined, they confessed belonged to the enemy.' Not far different are the arguments urged by Cicero in his *Letters to Atticus* against Pompey's plan of destroying his own country by starvation. On this ground Alexander the Aetolian censures Philip in the seventeenth book of Polybius, whose words, according to the Latin version of Livy, are as follows:

[IV. xiv. 2.]

IX. vii [4], ix [2], x [3].

[XVII. iii.]

XXXII [xxxiii. 11–13].

In war he (Philip) does not fight in the open field, nor engage in pitched battles, but he burns and plunders cities as he flees, and when vanquished spoils the victor's prizes. Such was not the custom of the ancient kings of Macedon; they were wont to fight on the field of battle, and to spare cities, so far as they could, in order that they might have a wealthier empire. What sort of a policy is it, to destroy the things the possession of which is at stake, and to leave for himself nothing except the war?

[533] IV.—*Devastation should be refrained from if the enemy has means of subsistence from other sources*

1. In the third place, the same thing will happen if the enemy can have means of subsistence from another source, for instance,

[1] When Gelimer and the Vandals were besieging Carthage, they neither plundered nor laid waste the land, but took care of it as of their own; Procopius, in the opening of the second book of the *Vandalic War* [II. i].

I read in Helmold, I. lxvi: 'Is not the land which we lay waste our land, and the people whom we assail our people? Why, therefore, are we found to be our own enemies, and wasters of our own revenues?'

With this agrees what Bembo has in Book IX, fol. 149 verso. See Paruta, again, against the Germans, *History*, Book VI.

if the sea, or if other boundaries, shall be open. According to Thucydides, Archidamus, in the speech in which he tried to dissuade his fellow Lacedaemonians from war against the Athenians, asks what hopes they have in waging war: Do they perhaps hope that, because they enjoy military superiority, it is easy for them to lay waste the land of Attica? But, he said, the Athenians have other lands under their sway (meaning Thrace and Ionia) and can obtain what they need through importations by sea.

[I. lxxx and lxxxi.]

Under such conditions, therefore, it is best to leave agriculture undisturbed even along the common frontier. This we see in recent times was the arrangement for a considerable period in the war of the Netherlands against the Empire, with the payment of tribute to either party.

2. This is in accord with the ancient custom in India, where, as Diodorus Siculus[1] says: 'The farmers are undisturbed and, as it were, held sacred; in fact even in the vicinity of camps and armies they pursue their tasks secure from danger.' He adds: 'Men neither burn the enemy's fields, nor cut down the trees.' Later: 'No enemy inflicts harm upon any farmer, but this class of men, as being common benefactors, is accorded protection from all wrong-doing.'

[*Training of Cyrus*, V. iv. 24.]

3. Xenophon says that it was agreed also between Cyrus and the Assyrian king that 'there should be peace with the farmers, war with those who bore arms'. So Timotheus[2] rented the most fertile part of the land to husbandmen, as Polyaenus relates; nay more, as Aristotle adds, he even sold the crops to the enemy, and paid his soldiers with the money. Appian bears witness that this was done also by Viriathus in Spain. As we have seen, in the war of the Netherlands and the Empire which we have mentioned, this arrangement was carried out with the highest degree of reason and profit, and evoked the admiration of foreigners.

[III. x. 5 and 9.] *Economics*, II [ii. 23]. [*Spanish Wars*, xi. 64.]

Decretals, I. xxxiv. 2.

4. The canons, teachers of humanity, established these practices for the imitation of all Christians, as those who ought to exercise and who profess a greater degree of humaneness than others; and so they seek to protect from the perils of war not merely the farmers, but also the animals which they use in cultivation and the seeds which they keep for sowing. The reason is assuredly the same as that for which the civil laws forbid that things useful for ploughing

Code, VIII. xvi. 7.

[1] Book II [II. xxxvi].

[2] Plutarch gives the same information with regard to the Megarians, in his *Greek Questions* [xvii = p. 295 B C.]. Of Totila, when he was besieging Rome, Procopius says, *Gothic War*, III [III. xiii]: 'In the meantime he did no harm to the farmers throughout the whole of Italy, but ordered them to till their lands continuously, without fear, just as they had been accustomed, provided that they paid tribute to him.'

Cassiodorus says, [*Variae*,] XII. v: 'It is the chief glory of the defenders if, while they seem to be protecting the appointed districts, the farmers do not cease to cultivate their inherited possessions.'

be taken as a pledge. In ancient times among the Phrygians and Cyprians, and later among the Athenians and Romans,[1] it was considered a crime to kill a plough-ox.

Nicholas of Damascus [frag. 19, p. 148, edit. Dindorf]. Aelian, [*Var. Hist.*,] V. xiv; Dio Chrysostom, *Orations*, lxiv [=p. 592].

V.—*Devastation should be refrained from if the thing itself is of no use in furnishing resources for war*

In the fourth place, it happens that certain things are of such a nature that they are of no value for making or waging war. Such things reason wishes us to also spare, during the continuation of the war. Here applies the speech of the Rhodians to Demetrius,[2] the taker of cities, on behalf of the portrait of Ialysus, at it appears in the Latin translation of Gellius:

[*Attic Nights*,] XV. xxxi.

> What is your reason for wishing to destroy that likeness by setting fire to the temple? If you conquer us all, and take this whole city, by your victory you will obtain that portrait also, safe and intact. But if you prove to be unable to conquer us, we ask you to consider, lest you incur the bad repute of having waged war against the dead Protogenes because you were unable to conquer the Rhodians.

Polybius says it is a sign of an infuriated mind to destroy those things which, if destroyed, do not weaken the enemy, nor bring gain to the one who destroys them; such things are temples, colonnades, statues, and the like. Marcellus, whom Cicero praises, 'spared all the buildings of Syracuse, public and private, sacred and profane, just as if he had come with his army to defend them, not to capture them.' The same author later says: [534] 'Our ancestors left to them the things which seemed agreeable to the vanquished, but of small value to us.'

V [xi].

Against Verres, Act II [IV. liv. 120]. IV [lx. 134].

VI.—*The principle stated is particularly applicable to things that are sacred or connected with things that are sacred*

1. While what has been said holds true of other things of artistic value, for the reason which we have already given, there is a particular reason in the case of those things which have been devoted to sacred uses. Although such things also, as we have said elsewhere, are public in their own way, and so, according to the law of nations, are violated with impunity, nevertheless, if there is no danger from them, reverence for divine things urges[3] that such buildings and [III. v. 2.]

[1] Also in the Peloponnesus; Varro, *On Farming*, II [II. v. 4]; Columella, VI, beginning. To these add Pliny, [*Natural History*,] VIII. xlv; Aelian, *History of Animals*, II, last chapter; Porphyry, *On Abstaining*, II [II. xxviii]; Vegetius, *On the Veterinary Art*, III [prolegomena, vi].

[2] See on this topic Pliny, *Natural History*, VIII. xxxviii [VII. xxxviii], and XXXV. x; and Plutarch, *Demetrius* [xxii = p. 898 E]. The same idea is found in the letter of Belisarius which we have just quoted [III. xii. 2. 3, note].

[3] Polybius says in the *Excerpta Peiresciana* [p. 45]: 'It is a mark of supreme folly to act impiously toward the gods because you are angry with men.' Rightly, beyond question; for Severus also, as Lampridius reports [*Life of Alexander Severus*, xlix], declared in a rescript: 'It is better that God

their furnishings be preserved, particularly among those who worship the same God, in accordance with the same law, even if perhaps they disagree in respect to certain doctrines or points of ritual.

Sylvester, word *bellum*, III, no. 5.

[IV. xcvii.] 2. Thucydides says that it was the law among the Greeks of his time 'that those, who made an attack upon hostile territory, should refrain from doing harm to sacred places'. When Alba was destroyed by the Romans, Livy says that they spared the temples of the gods. Of the Romans at the taking of Capua, Silius, in his thirteenth book, speaks thus:

[I. xxix. 6.] [XIII. 316 ff.]

> Lo, through their breasts there creeps a silent feeling
> Of sudden awe, and soothes their savage hearts,
> That they wish not for fire and torch, nor now
> That temples fall in ashes in one pyre.

XLII [iii. 9]. Livy recounts that it was said in criticism of Quintus Fulvius the censor, 'That he involved the Roman people in irreverence by building temples with the ruins of temples, as though the immortal gods were not everywhere the same, but some were to be worshipped and adorned with the spoils of others.' But Marcius Philippus, upon arriving at Dium, ordered his encampment to be laid out in the shadow of the temple itself, in order that nothing in the sacred place might be profaned. Strabo relates that the Tectosages, who with others had carried off the treasures from Delphi, consecrated these at home with an addition, in order to appease the deity.

[Livy,] XLIV [vii. 2].

IV [i. 13].

II [i]. 3. To come now to Christian peoples, Agathias records that the

should be worshipped there in any way at all, than that the place should be turned over to keepers of cook-shops.'

Pliny, *Natural History*, XVI. xi [XVI. xl], says of Hannibal: 'He was led by a feeling of reverence to spare the temple of Diana of Saguntum.' 'And we have not deprived our foreign foes of their temples,' is a remark found in Appian, *Civil Wars*, II [II. xix. 140].

The Latin author of the life of Agesilaus [Nepos, *Agesilaus*, iv] says of him: 'Not only on Greek soil did he make it a practice to maintain the sanctity of the temples of the gods, but even in the country of the barbarians he preserved the images and altars with the greatest reverence. He used to say that he wondered [540] that those who harmed their suppliants were not included in the number of the sacrilegious, or that those who caused reverence to decline were not punished more heavily than those who plundered temples.'

Regarding the scrupulosity of Agesilaus in this matter see also Plutarch [*Agesilaus*, xix = p. 606 A]. The same writer, in his *Sulla* [xii = p. 459 CD], accords this praise equally to many Romans: 'Some called to mind Flaminius, others Manius Aquilius and Aemilius Paulus; of these the former, when he had driven Antiochus from Greece, and the latter, when they had subdued the kings of Macedon, not merely spared the temples of the Greeks, but enriched them with gifts and increased their reputation and sanctity.'

Add also Vitruvius, Book II [II. viii. 8]; Dio Cassius, XLII [XLII. xlviii]; Plutarch, *Caesar* [xxvi = p. 720 E]; Brodeau, *Miscellanea*, V [V. xxix]. Gabaon, the Moor, although not himself a Christian, wished honour to be shown to the churches of the Christians; this was contrary to the conduct of the Vandals, with whom he hoped that the God of the Christians, whoever He might be, would be angry. This is vouched for by Procopius, *Vandalic War*, I [I. viii], who says also, *Persian War*, II [II. ix], that Chosroes, a Persian and not a Christian, spared the church of the Christians of Antioch.

Even Justinian, as the same author relates, *Vandalic War*, II [II. ix], did not dare to keep in his possession the objects which Vespasian had carried off to Rome from the Temple at Jerusalem, and which Genseric had found in Rome and transported to Africa. Benjamin the Jew, in his *Itinerary*, bears witness to the reverence which was manifested by the Mohammedans for the place in which the bones of Ezechiel and the three companions of Daniel had been interred.

Franks spared the temples, seeing that they were of the same religion as the Greeks. In fact it has been customary also to spare men on account of religious edifices, conduct which (not to mention pagan peoples, which afford many examples, since, in fact, writers call this custom 'a law common to the Greeks') in the case of the Goths who captured Rome [1] is praised by Augustine as follows: Diodorus, XIX [lxxiii]. *City of God*, I [i].

To this [2] the places of the martyrs and the basilicas of the Apostles, which in the midst of the sack received the vanquished that fled to them, both Christian and pagan, bear witness. So far the gore-stained enemy raged; there the madness of butchery was stayed. Thither were led by pitying enemies those whom (for 'those whom (*quibus*)' I should prefer 'who (*qui*)',[3] for he distinguishes the milder from the more savage) they had spared outside these places, that they might not be attacked by those who did not have the same feelings of mercy. Nevertheless, after those, who themselves elsewhere were savage and raged in the manner of enemies, came to these places [4] where that was forbidden which was elsewhere permitted by the law of war, all their savage frenzy was checked, and their desire to take captives was assuaged.

VII.—*The principle is applicable also to consecrated things*

1. What I have said of sacred things must also be understood of consecrated things, also of structures erected in honour of the dead; for these cannot be violated without contempt for human feeling, even though the law of nations does accord impunity to the venting of anger against them. The jurists say that that is the highest reason which acts in defence of religion. The pious utterance of Euripides in his *Trojan Women* relates as much to consecrated as to sacred things: *Dig.* XI. vii. 43. [lines 95 ff.]

Mad is the man who cities devastates,
[535] With temples and the Manes' consecrated seats.
For him there waits the doom of like destruction.

Apollonius of Tyana thus interpreted the fable of the giants assaulting the sky [5]: 'That they did violence to the temples and seats of the gods.' In Statius, Hannibal is termed sacrilegious because 'he set torch to the altars of the gods'. [Philostratus, *Life of Apollonius*, V. xvi.] [*Silvae*, IV. vi. 82.]

[1] Under the Arian Alaric. The following notable deed is recorded of him by Cassiodorus, [*Variae*,] XII. xx: 'When King Alaric had received the vessels of the Apostle Peter from his men who brought them, he held an inquiry; having learned the state of affairs, he ordered that they should be carried back to the sacred portals by the hands of those who had carried them off, that the greed, which from lust of plunder had committed the crime, should expiate its excess by the most lavish devotion.'

[2] Isidore has quoted this passage in his *Gothic Chronicles*, on the year 447.

[3] Orosius, in relating the story, VII. xxviii, shows conclusively that this should be the reading [in which case the English should be: 'Thither they were led by pitying enemies *who* had spared,' &c.].

[4] These same churches of the Apostles were spared by the Goths under Witiges, when they were besieging Rome, as Procopius testifies, *Gothic War*, II [II. iv]. Even for barbarians and non-Christians flight to such places brought protection; see Zosimus, IV [IV. xl], on the barbarian Tomitani.

Add the Swiss law in Simler [p. 302, ed. Elzevir]; Nicetas, *Alexis*, son of Manuel [v]; and the same author, *Andronicus*, I [I. ix], where he blames the Sicilians for having violated the churches of Antioch.

[5] As Diodorus Siculus [*Excerpta* from Book VII] also interpreted another fable regarding Epopeus.

2. Scipio, having taken Carthage, bestowed gifts upon his soldiers, 'excepting', says Appian, 'those who had sinned against the temple of Apollo'. As Dio relates, Caesar 'did not dare to overthrow' the trophy erected by Mithridates, 'because it was consecrated to the gods of war'. Marcus Marcellus, being restrained by religious scruples, did not touch the things which victory had made profane, says Cicero in his fourth *Against Verres*; and he adds in the same passage that there are some enemies who in time of war observe the laws of religion and custom. The same author elsewhere said that the war waged by Brennus against the shrine of Apollo was wicked.

Punic Wars [xx. 133]. XLII [xlviii]. [IV. lv. 122.] [*On Divination*, I. xxxvii 81.]

The action of Pyrrhus, who plundered the treasures of Proserpina, is called by Livy disgraceful and insulting to the gods. Diodorus characterizes a similar act of Himilco as 'impiety' and 'a crime against the gods'. Again, Livy calls the war of Philip wicked, as though waged against the gods of the upper and the nether worlds; also madness, and an aggregate of crimes. Of the same war Florus says: 'Philip exceeded the rights of the victor in his violence to temples, altars, and tombs.'[1] Touching the same affair, Polybius adds this judgement: 'Who will deny that, to set to work to destroy what will neither prove useful to us in waging war, nor disadvantageous to the enemy, particularly temples and the statues and similar ornaments which they contain, is the work of a mind that is wicked and maddened with rage?' In the same passage he does not accept the excuse of revenge.

[XXIX. xviii. 4.] XIV [lxiv]. [XXXI. xxvi. 11; xxx. 4; xxxi. 3.] [II. vii.] [V. xi.]

VIII.—*The advantages which follow from such moderation are pointed out*

1. It is, in truth, not strictly a part of our purpose to inquire at this point what is advantageous; we desire rather to restrict the unrestrained licence of war to that which is permitted by nature, or to the choice of the better among the things permitted. Nevertheless virtue itself, in low esteem in the present age, ought to forgive me if, when of itself it is despised, I cause it to be valued on account of its advantages.

In the first place, then, such moderation, by preserving things which do not delay the war, deprives the enemy of a great weapon, despair. There is a saying of Archidamus in Thucydides: 'Think of the enemy's land as nothing else than a hostage, the better the more it is cultivated; therefore it must be spared, so far as is possible, that despair may not make the enemy harder to conquer.' The

[I. lxxxii.]

[1] A similar act of Prusias is censured by Polybius, whose words are preserved by Suidas on the word *Prusias*, and in the *Excerpta Peiresciana* [*De Virtutibus et Vitiis*, I, p. 290].

same policy was followed by Agesilaus [1] when, contrary to the view of the Achaeans, he let the Acarnanians sow their crops in freedom, saying that the more they sowed the more desirous of peace they would be. This is what the satire says: 'For those, who have been plundered of everything, weapons still remain.' Livy, in relating the capture of the city of Rome by the Gauls, says: 'The chiefs of the Gauls had decided that all the houses should not be burned down, in order that what remained of the city might serve them as a pledge to break the morale of the foe.'

Xenophon, *Affairs of Greece*, IV [vi. 13].

[Juvenal, viii. 124.]

[V. xlii. 1–2.]

2. There is the further consideration that, in the course of a war, such moderation gives the appearance of great assurance of victory, and that clemency is of itself suited to weaken and to conciliate the spirit. According to Livy, Hannibal did no damage in the territory of Tarentum: 'It appeared', he says, 'that this course was pursued not because of the moderation of the soldiers or their general, but [536] in order to conciliate the feelings of the Tarentines.'

XXXIV [XXIV. xx. 10].

For a similar cause Augustus Caesar refrained from pillaging the Pannonians. Dio gives the reason: 'He hoped that in this way he would win them over to him without compulsion.' Polybius [Polyaenus] says that Timotheus, with that care of which we have already spoken, above all else 'sought to win great good-will from the enemy themselves'. Regarding Quintius [2] and those Romans who were under his orders, Plutarch, having narrated what we have said above, adds: 'Not long afterward he received the fruit of this moderation; for, when he arrived in Thessaly, the cities went over to him. Then in fact the Greeks who dwelt within Thermopylae also ardently longed for Quintius; and the Achaeans, renouncing the friendship of Philip, entered with the Romans into an alliance against him.'

XLIX [xxxvii].

III [x. 5].

[*Flamininus*, v = p. 371 D, cited above, III. xii. 3. 1.]

The state of the Lingones escaped the devastation which they had dreaded in the war waged by the general Cerealis, under the authority of Domitian, against Civilis the Batavian and his allies; regarding it, Frontinus narrates the following: 'Because the state had not lost any of its possessions, owing to the fact that contrary to expectation it had not been laid waste, when brought back to its allegiance it furnished to him seventy thousand armed men.'

V. iii [*Strategemata*, IV. iii. 14].

3. Opposite results have attended the opposite policy. Livy gives an example in the case of Hannibal: 'His spirit, inclined to avarice and cruelty, was prone to despoil what he could not protect. This policy was destructive both in its inception and in its result. For it alienated the minds not only of those who suffered undeserved

XXVI [xxxviii. 3–4].

[1] This is recorded also by Plutarch, *Agesilaus* [xxii = p. 608 B].

[2] Naturally Titus Quintius Flaminius [Flamininus].

wrong, but of others also, since more persons were affected by the example than by the disaster.'

Aegidius Regius, *De Actibus Supernaturalibus*, disp. 31, dub. 7, no. 127.

4. Moreover, that which has been observed by certain theologians I hold to be true, that it is the duty of the highest authorities and commanders, who wish themselves to be regarded as Christians both by God and by men, to forbid the violent sack of cities and other similar actions. Such actions cannot take place without very serious harm to many innocent persons, and often are of little consequence for the result of the war; so that Christian goodness almost always, and bare justice very often, shrinks from them.

Surely the bond which unites Christians is greater than that which united the Greeks of old, in whose wars a decree of the Amphictyons provided against the blotting out of a Greek city. And the ancients relate that Alexander of Macedon repented of nothing that he had done more than that he had completely destroyed Thebes.

[Plutarch, *Alexander*, xiii=p. 671 B.]

[541]

CHAPTER XIII

MODERATION IN REGARD TO CAPTURED PROPERTY

I.—*The property of enemy subjects which has been captured in war is to be held, up to the amount of their debt*

1. THE capture of enemy property in a lawful war is not to be thought devoid of wrong, or exempt from the obligation of restitution. In fact, if you consider what may justly be done,[1] it is not permissible to take or to hold property of greater value than the equivalent of the enemy's indebtedness, with this exception, that over and above that amount one may retain things necessary for a guarantee. When the danger is over, however, there should be a restoration, either of the things themselves or of their value, according to our discussion in the second chapter of Book II. What would be permitted in the case of property of persons at peace is much more permissible in regard to the property of enemies. There is, then, a certain right of seizure, without a complete right of ownership.

Victoria, *On the Law of War*, nos. 55, 56.

2. Now since a debt may be due to us either because of an inequality of possessions, or as the result of a punishment,[2] the property of enemies may be acquired for either reason, but still with a distinction. For we have previously said that by a debt of the former sort not merely the property of the debtor, but also that of his subjects, according to the accepted law of nations, is made liable, as though in the case of surety.

This right of the law of nations, indeed, we hold to be of another kind than that which exists in mere impunity or the external power of courts of law. For just as he with whom we have completed a transaction by our private consent acquires not only a legal but also a moral right to our property, so also a right is acquired by a kind of common consent, which through a certain force contains in itself the consent of individuals, in the sense in which a law is called 'a common agreement of the state'. It is the more credible that such a basis of right was approved by nations in the kind of affair under consideration because the law of nations was introduced not only for the sake of avoiding greater evil but also to secure to each one his right.

Cajetan, *Summula Peccatorum*, words *belli damnum*; Covarruvias, *On Sext*, V. ult. 4, previously cited, pt. II, no. 11; Victoria, *On the Law of War*, nos. 39 and 41; Molina, tract. ii, disp. 117.

[1] [543] See the decision of Pope Innocent, in Bembo, I.
[2] The Romans ordered Prusias both to make restitution to Attalus and to pay a penalty in addition.

II.—*The property of enemy subjects which has been captured in war is not to be held as punishment for the crime of another*

But in the other form of indebtedness, which is penal, I do not see that by the agreement of the nations such a right has been extended to the property of subjects. Such an obligation imposed upon the property of others is hateful, and consequently ought not to be extended further than the practice has clearly been. The advantage, furthermore, is not the same in the latter as in the former kind of indebtedness; for the former consists in goods, but the latter does not, and so its exaction can be omitted without loss.

III. ii [3]. This position is not controverted by what we said above about the Attic law. For according to its provisions men were held liable not in reality because the state could be punished, but rather to compel the state to do what it ought to do, that is, to render judgement against the guilty. This obligation arising from duty is to be referred to the former, not to the latter, sort of indebtedness. For it is one thing to be under an obligation to punish, and another to be subject to or liable to punishment, although the latter condition usually results from failure in respect to the former, but in such a way that one is distinctly the cause and the other the effect. Therefore the property of the subjects of enemies cannot be acquired on the ground of punishment, but only that of those who have themselves done wrong; among these are included also the magistrates who fail to punish the crimes.

III.—*Here we must understand as debt also indebtedness which arises in time of war. Examples*

Moreover the goods of subjects may both be seized and acquired, not only [542] for the exaction of the original debt which gave rise to the war, but also for the exaction of indebtedness which develops subsequently; this is according to what we said at the beginning of this book. In such a sense we must take what certain theologians write, that captures in war are not to be set off against the principal debt; for it is to be understood that such captures are an offset up to the point where, according to a sound judgement, satisfaction has been obtained for the loss occasioned by the war itself.

Sylvester, word *bellum*, no. 10; Victoria, no. 51; Bartolus, *On Digest*, XLIX. xv. 28.

XXVII [XXXVII. xxxv. 7]. Thus in the dispute with Antiochus the Romans, as Livy relates, held it to be just that the king should pay all the expense which had been incurred for the war,[1] since it was through fault of his that the

[1] This is mentioned by Polybius, *Selections on Embassies*, xxiii. And the Asiatics were condemned in the same way by Sulla, as Appian records in his *Mithridatic War* [ix. 61 ff.]. The King of Poland

war had arisen. In Justin is the phrase, 'ready, according to a just law, to assume the expenses of the war.' In Thucydides the Samnians are condemned 'to pay the expenses of the war'. And so, frequently, in other instances. However, what is justly imposed upon the conquered may also be justly exacted by a war. XXXIII [i. 5]. [I. cxvii.]

IV.—*In this matter it is an obligation of humaneness not to make the fullest use of one's right*

1. But we must keep in mind that which we have recalled elsewhere also, that the rules of love are broader than the rules of law. He who is rich will be guilty of heartlessness if, in order that he himself may exact the last penny, he deprives a needy debtor of all his small possessions; and even much more guilty if the debtor has incurred the debt by his goodness—for instance, if he has gone surety for a friend—and has used none of the money for his own advantage, 'for', as Quintilian the Father says, 'the peril of a bondsman is worthy of commiseration'.[1] Nevertheless so hard a creditor does nothing contrary to his right according to a strict interpretation. [*Declamations*, cclxxiii.]

2. Therefore humanity requires [2] that we leave to them that do not share in the guilt of the war, and that have incurred no obligation in any other way than as sureties, those things which we can dispense with more easily than they, particularly if it is quite clear that they will not recover from their own state what they have lost in this way. Here applies what Cyrus said to his soldiers after the capture of Babylon: 'What you have, you will hold not unjustly; but if you do not take away anything from the enemy that will be an evidence of your humanity.' [Xenophon, *Training of Cyrus*, VII. v. 73.]

3. This also is to be observed. The right over the goods of innocent subjects has been introduced as a subsidiary means; and as long as there is hope that we can obtain what is ours with sufficient ease from the original debtors, or from those who by not rendering justice voluntarily make themselves debtors, to come to those who are free from blame, even though it is granted that this is not in conflict with our strict right, nevertheless is to depart from the rule of human conduct. Aegidius Regius, *De Actibus Supernaturalibus*, disp. 31, dub. 7, no. 117.

4. Instances of such humanity are found everywhere in history,

claimed this custom in his favour, according to De Thou, LXXIII [LXXIII. ix], for the year 1581. So in Homer, *Iliad*, III [III. 286], the word τιμὴν is interpreted by the Scholiast as 'an estimation of the war; namely half of the property which was in the city.'

[1] He adds that a creditor can honourably approach a bondsman only in case he cannot recover from the debtor. The 'honourably' is well said; for it seems that there was a certain 'stigma' attached to calling on bondsmen, as Cicero says, *Letters to Atticus*, XVI. xv.

[2] Ptolemy returned to Demetrius, the son of Antigonus, his tent and other things which served his personal use, and also the money he had captured, saying that they were not fighting with one another for objects of all sorts, but for empire and glory. The story is told by Plutarch, *Demetrius* [v = p. 891 A]. See also the act of Sancho, king of the Basques, in Mariana, XI. xvi.

Dig. XLI. i. 16. *Dig.* XLI. i. 16; *Dig.* VI. i. 15. § 2; Victoria, *On the Law of War*, no. 40; Sylvester, word *bellum*, pt. I, § x, ¶ 3. [Livy, I. xv. 5.] Arrian, [*Anabasis*,] III [xvii].

particularly in the history of Rome. Examples are when lands have been ceded to the conquered enemy on the condition that they should pass to the state, that is, that they should fall to the conquered state; or when a part of the land was left to the ancient possessor [1] as a mark of respect. Thus Livy records that the inhabitants of Veii were penalized by Romulus with the loss of part of their land. Similarly Alexander the Macedonian granted to the Uxii under tribute the lands which they had possessed.

So you may often read that surrendered cities were not sacked; and we have said above that it is praiseworthy, and in accordance with the pious precepts of the canons, to spare not only the persons, but also the property, of the tillers of the soil, subject at any rate to tribute. Upon condition of a similar tribute, immunity from war is usually granted to merchandise also.

[1] Appian, *Civil Wars*, II [II. xix. 140], says: 'Not even from conquered enemies did the ancient Romans take all their territory, but they divided it with them.' The historians inform us that the Vandals in Africa, and the Goths in Italy, did likewise.

CHAPTER XIV

MODERATION IN REGARD TO PRISONERS OF WAR

I.—*To what extent, in accordance with moral justice, it is permissible to take men captive*

1. IN those places where custom sanctions the captivity and slavery of men, this ought to be limited primarily, if we have regard to moral justice, in the same way as in the case of property; with the result that, in fact, such acquisition may be permitted so far as the amount of either an original or derivative debt allows, unless perhaps on the part of the men themselves there is some special crime which equity would suffer to be punished with loss of liberty. To this degree, then, and no further, he who wages a lawful war has a right over the captured subjects of the enemy, and this right he may legitimately transfer to others.

Victoria, *On the Law of War*, no. 41; Decio [Lessius], II. v, dub. 4; Covarruvias, *On Sext*, V. ult. 4, pt. II, § 11; Molina, disp. 120 and 121; Valentia, *Disp.*, iii, qu. xvi.

2. Furthermore in this case also it will be the task of equity and goodness to employ those [544] distinctions which were noted above, when we discussed the question of killing enemies. Demosthenes, in his letter *For the Children of Lycurgus*, praises Philip of Macedon for not having enslaved all who were among his enemies.[1] 'For', said Demosthenes, 'he did not consider the same punishment for all either fair or right, but, examining the case in the light of what each had deserved, he acted in such matters as a judge.'

[*Letters*, iii. 12.]

II.—*What is permissible against a slave according to the moral power of justice*

1. Now in the first place it must here be noted that that right, which originates in a kind of surety on behalf of the state, can nowhere extend so widely as the right which arises from a crime against those who become slaves as a penalty. Hence a certain Spartan said that he was a prisoner, not a slave[2]; for, if we regard the question properly, this general right against prisoners captured in a lawful war is equiva-

[Plutarch, *Laconic Apothegms*, xl=p. 234 c.]

[1] His son Alexander, after capturing Thebes, exempted from slavery both the priests and those who had not assented to the decrees published against him; so Plutarch records in his *Alexander* [xi=p. 670 E].

[2] Philo [*That Every Virtuous Man Is Free*, vi] says: 'For both fathers have often paid a ransom for their sons, and sons for their fathers, who had either been violently carried off by brigands or captured according to the custom of war, but whom the laws of nature, more valid than those which are made upon earth, declare free.' In fact, as Helen said in the play of Theodectes [in Aristotle, *Politics*, I. vi]:

> Who would dare to call me slave,
> Me, child of the gods by either line?

lent to that right which masters have over those who, under constraint of poverty, have sold themselves into slavery; only the misfortune is even more to be pitied of those who have met this fate not by their own particular act, but through fault of their rulers. 'To be captured by the law of war is a most bitter fate,' as Isocrates bore witness.

Plataic Oration [xviii = 300 A].

2. This servitude, then, is a perpetual obligation of services for maintenance that is likewise perpetual. The definition of Chrysippus well suits this class of slaves: 'A slave is a perpetual mercenary.' The Hebraic Law expressly compares to a mercenary the man who has sold himself under constraint of want (*Deuteronomy*, xv. 18, 40, 53), and in case of his redemption the law wishes his services to be credited to him just as crops gathered from land that has been sold would be credited to the former owner (*Deuteronomy*, xviii. 50).

Seneca, *On Benefits*, III. xxii.

3. Therefore that which may be done to a slave with impunity according to the law of nations differs widely from that which natural reason permits to be done. From Seneca we previously quoted this: 'Although against a slave all things are permissible, there are some things which the common law of living things forbids to be done against a human being.' This saying of Philemon is to the same effect:

On Clemency, I. xviii.

[Stobaeus, lxii. 28.]

> He, Master, who is born a man, though he may serve
> In slavery, still ceases not to be a human being.

Elsewhere Seneca says also: 'They are slaves, nay rather men; they are slaves, nay rather comrades; they are slaves, nay, humble friends; they are slaves, nay rather fellow slaves.' What you may read in Macrobius has clearly the same sense as the saying of the Apostle Paul: 'Masters, render unto your servants that which is just and equal, knowing that ye also have a Master in heaven.' In another place the apostle wishes masters not to deal threateningly with their slaves, for the reason which we have just stated, that they also have a Master in heaven, who pays no regard to such differences of status. In the *Constitutions*, which are usually ascribed to Clement of Rome, we read: 'Beware of commanding a slave or a handmaid in bitterness of heart.' [1]

Letters, xlvii [1].

[*Saturnalia*, I. xi.]

Colossians, iv. 1.

Epistles [*Ephesians*], vi. 9.

VII. xiv.

Clement of Alexandria wishes us to treat our slaves as second selves, since they are human beings no less than we are. He is following the saying of the wise Jew: 'If you have a slave, treat him as a brother, for he is such as you are.'

The Instructor, end [III. xii. 92]. [*Son of Sirach*, xxxiii. 31.]

[1] So also we read in the *Epistle of Barnabas* [chap. xix]: [549] 'Command not harshly thy slave nor thy handmaid, who hope in Christ, lest thereby thou show that thou dost not fear the Lord who is common to thee and to them.'

III.—*It is not permissible to kill an innocent prisoner*

Therefore the right, which is called the right of life and death over the slave, causes the master to have domestic jurisdiction, which, indeed, is to be exercised with the same conscientiousness as public jurisdiction. This is what Seneca meant when [545] he said: 'In the case of a slave you must consider, not how much he can suffer with impunity, but how much is permitted to you by the nature of justice and goodness, which bids you to spare even prisoners of war and those who have been bought for a price.' *On Clemency*, I. xviii.

Elsewhere Seneca says: 'What does it matter by what power any one is held, if he is held by a power that is absolute?' In this passage he compares a subject to a slave, and says that on different grounds it is permissible to treat them alike; a statement that is certainly most true in respect to the right of taking away their life, and whatever approximates this. 'Our ancestors', says the same Seneca,[1] 'considered our household to be a diminutive state'; and Pliny writes: 'For slaves the household is a sort of republic, and, as it were, a state.' Cato the Censor, in Plutarch's account, did not inflict punishment upon a slave, who appeared to have committed a capital crime, until after he had been condemned, and that by the judgement of his fellow slaves. With this should be compared the words in *Job*, xxxi. 13, and following. *On Benefits*, III. xviii. *Letters*, xliii [xlvii. 14]. [*Letters*, VIII. xvi.] [Plutarch, *Cato the Elder*, xxi = p. 349 A.]

IV.—*It is not permissible to punish with severity*

But in regard to minor punishments also, as the beating of slaves, we must apply fairness, and further, clemency. 'Thou shalt not oppress him, thou shalt not rule him harshly,'[2] says the divine law in regard to the Jewish slave—a rule which should now be extended to all slaves, through extension of the force of relationship (*Deuteronomy*, xv. 17, 45, 53). On this passage Philo[3] comments thus:

Slaves in respect to fortune, indeed, are inferior, but by nature they are equal to

[1] Seneca, *Letters*, xlvii [xlvii. 14].

[2] See Moses de Kotzi, *Precepts Bidding*, 147, 175 and 178, and the *Collatio Legum Mosis et Romanorum*, tit. iii. Priscus, in the *Selections on Embassies* [*Fragmenta Historicorum Graecorum*, IV, p. 88], where he puts the Romans above the barbarians, says:

> 'The Romans treat their slaves in a much better fashion, and act toward them as fathers or teachers; for to turn them from the things which, according to their customs, are forbidden, they punish them when they do wrong, like their own sons. And they have not the right to kill them, as do the Scythians. Moreover there are very many kinds of liberty which the masters bestow upon them, not only when living, but also at the moment of their death; whatever disposition they make of their property when dying has the force of law.'

Add the *Law of the Visigoths*, VI. i. 12.

[3] *On Special Laws*, II [III. xxxv].

Cyprian writes *To Demetrianus* [chap. viii]: 'Unless you are served according to your caprice, unless you are obeyed in compliance with your pleasure, imperiously, and with excessive demands for subservience, you scourge, you beat, you afflict with hunger, thirst, nakedness, frequently with fetters and imprisonment, and, wretch that you are, you do not recognize that God is your Lord, since you yourself so exercise your authority over man.'

their masters; for in the divine law the rule of justice is not that which accords with fortune, but that which accords with nature. Hence masters ought not to use their power over slaves wantonly, nor in consequence of the possession of such power to indulge in pride, insolence, and savage wrath. For these are manifestations of a spirit that is not calm, but is ill-controlled and rages against those subject to it with a sort of tyrannical despotism.

[*On Clemency*, I. xvi. 4.] 'Is it in fact right', asks Seneca, 'that orders should be given to a man with greater severity and harshness than to dumb animals? Now a groom who is a skilful tamer does not frighten a horse with repeated blows; for the horse will become timid and balky unless [I. xvii. 1.] you stroke him with a caressing touch.' And soon after: 'What is more foolish than to blush to vent one's anger upon yoke-animals and dogs, while the worst condition is that of man?'

Exodus, xxi. 26, 27. Whence it comes that by the Hebraic law liberty was owed to a male or female slave not only for the loss of an eye, but also for that of a tooth,[1] wrongfully injured, of course.

V.—*It is not permissible to impose upon slaves tasks that are excessively severe*

1. But services also are to be exacted with moderation[2] and the health of slaves is to receive humane consideration. Besides *Exodus*, xx. 10; xxiii. 12; *Deut.*, x. 14 [xvi. 14]. other things the Hebraic law aimed to accomplish this result through the institution of the Sabbath, presumably in order that slaves might have some time to rest from their labours. There is also a letter of Gaius Pliny to Paulinus, which begins thus: [*Letters*, V. xix.] 'I see how leniently you handle your slaves, therefore I will the more frankly admit to you with what indulgence I treat mine. I have always in mind that [*Odyssey*, II. 47 and 234.] saying of Homer, "But the stepfather was as kind as a father," and this is our term for the father of the household (*paterfamilias*).'

2. In connexion with the same word Seneca also notices the *Letters*, xlvii [14]. humanity of the ancients: 'Do you not even see this, how our ancestors protected masters from all ill-will, and slaves from all insolence? They called the master the father of the household (*paterfamilias*), the slaves members of the household (*familiares*)'.[3] [*Orations*, i=p. 5.] In describing a most excellent king, Dio of Prusa says: 'So far is he from usurping the title of master over free men, that he refrains from the use of it even in relation to slaves.'

[1] Philo, in the passage cited [*On Special Laws*, III. xxxv], says: 'Thus he will pay a twofold penalty for his act, in losing both the services and the value of the slave; in addition to these there is a third penalty, more severe than these two, that the master is forced to benefit in the highest degree one whom he hates, and whom he had hoped that he could always abuse. But the other will have a twofold solace for the wrong which he has suffered, not only in obtaining his freedom, but also in being freed from so fierce and savage a master.'

[2] See chap. xiv, in the letter of the bishops to King Louis, which is included in the *Capitulary* of Charles the Bald [*Mon. Germ. Hist.*, *Leges*, II, vol. II, p. 437]. Seneca, *Letters*, xlvii [xlvii. 5], says: 'We abuse them, not as men, but as though they were oxen.' However, with regard to the leniency of the Athenians towards slaves see [Pseudo-]Xenophon, *On the Constitution of Athens* [I. ix ff.].

[3] Epicurus called them friends; Seneca, *Letters*, cvii [cvii. 1].

In Homer Ulysses[1] says that the slaves whom he found faithful will have in his house the same place as if they were brothers of Telemachus, his own son. Tertullian declares: 'The name of piety is more gracious than that of power[2]; the heads of households [546] are called fathers rather than masters.' Jerome or Paulinus writes to Celantia: 'So rule and order your household that you may wish to appear the mother rather than the mistress of your slaves, and from these exact respect by kindness rather than by severity.'

. *Odyssey*, V [XXI. 215 ff.]. [*Apology*, xxxiv.] [Jerome, *Letters*, cxlviii. 25.]

Augustine says:

City of God, XIX. xvi.

> The peace of the household was in olden times so directed by just fathers that with regard to these temporal goods they distinguished the lot of sons from the status of slaves, but in the worship of God they consulted with equal care the interests of all members of their household. This is in accordance with the prescription of the order of nature, so that from this source the name 'father of the household' arose and became so widely current that even those who rule unjustly are glad to be called by this name. However, those who are true fathers of the household aid all in their household just as sons to worship and propitiate God.

3. In commenting on the verse of Virgil, 'Now, boys, close up the rivulets', Servius observed a similar instance of piety in the use of the word 'boys' (*pueri*), which men applied to slaves. In the same spirit the Heracleots called their Mariandynian slaves 'gift-bearers (δωροφόροι)',[3] thus 'sparing the bitterness of the name', as the ancient interpreter Callistratus remarked in a note on Aristophanes. Tacitus praises the Germans, because their slaves were treated as tenant farmers. Theano says in a letter: 'This is the just way to use slaves; not to let them be worn out with toil, nor be too weak to endure labour because of poverty.'

[*On Eclogues*, VI. 14.] [Germany, xxv.] [*Letters*, iii. pr.]

VI.—*Under what circumstances the savings of a slave belong to the master, and under what circumstances to the slave*

1. As we have said, maintenance is due to the slave[4] for his work. Cicero says: 'Those make wise suggestions who bid us use slaves just as men who serve for hire, declaring that work is to be

On Duties, I [xiii. 41].

[1] Whose fatherly kindness toward himself Eumaeus proclaims, *Odyssey*, XIV [XIV. 138 ff.].

[2] This is also observed by Cyprian, *Testimonies*, III [III. lxxii], *To Quirinus*: 'Masters should be more gentle to their slaves, when they have embraced the faith'; and he proves this by the words of the Apostle Paul to the Ephesians [vi. 9]. Lactantius, V. xv, writes: 'There is no reason why we mutually apply to one another the name of brothers other than this, that we believe that we are equals. For if we measure all human beings not according to the body, but according to the spirit, although their bodily condition may be different, yet [550] they are not slaves to us; but we both consider them, and call them brothers according to the spirit, fellow slaves in religion.'

Augustine, *On the Customs of the Catholic Church*, X. xxx [I. xxx. 63], says: 'You teach slaves to cleave to their masters, not so much from the necessity imposed by their condition, as from delight in their duty. You make masters easily appeased by their slaves, from regard to the supreme God, who is indeed their common master, and more prone to advise than to coerce.'

Add also Isidore of Pelusium, *Letters*, I. cccclxxi. Refer to what we have just quoted from Priscus [p. 763, n. 2].

[3] Athenaeus, VI. xviii [VI. lxxxiv].

[4] *Son of Sirach* [*Ecclesiasticus*], xxxiii. 25, says: 'Bread, discipline and toil, are for the slave.'

required of them, but that they are to be furnished with what they deserve.' Says Aristotle: 'The slave's pay is his maintenance.' And Cato: 'Let him see to it that his slaves fare well, that they are neither cold nor hungry.'

Economics, I. v. [*On Farming*, V. ii.] *On Benefits*, III [xxi. 2]. [*On Terence's*] *Phormio*, I. i [43]. *Dig.* XV. i. 40. Thucydides, VII [lxxxvii]; Diodorus, XIII [xix]. [*On Benefits*, III. xix.]

'There are some things', says Seneca,[1] 'which a master should furnish to his slave; as rations and clothing.' The rations included four bushels of grain monthly, which, according to Donatus, were supplied to slaves. Marcianus the jurist says that there are some things which it is necessary for the master to supply to a slave, as tunics and the like. The cruelty of the Sicilians,[2] who killed the Athenian prisoners by starvation, is condemned by historians.

2. Seneca, moreover, in the passage cited proves that in relation to certain matters the slave is free, and that he has also the means of conferring a benefit, if he does something which exceeds the measure of his duty as a slave, something which is tendered not at a command, but voluntarily, where there is a transition from the obligation of service to the affection of a friend; this Seneca explains at length. It is in harmony with these ideas that if a slave, as in Terence,[3] in his leisure hours, has saved something by cheating his own soul, or by his industry, this is in some way his own.

Institutes, IV. vii.

Dig. XV. i. 5. § 1.

Theophilus does not do badly to define the slave's savings (*peculium*) as 'a natural patrimony',[4] as you might define 'the union of slaves (*contubernium*)' as 'a natural marriage'. Ulpian also calls the slave's savings a diminutive patrimony. It does not matter that the master can at his discretion take away or lessen the patrimony, for if he does this without cause he will not do what is just. By cause, however, I understand not only punishment, but also the master's necessity; for the advantage of the slave is subordinate to the advantage of his master, even more than the interests of citizens are subordinate to that of their state. On this point

[1] The same author, *On Tranquillity* [viii. 8], writes: 'The slaves ask for clothing and food.' In Procopius, *Gothic War*, III [III. xvii], the Romans say to Bessas: 'At least give us food, since we are your captives, I shall not say sufficient food, such as our need demands, but enough to ward off death.'

Chrysostom comments, *On Ephesians*, v. 21 [*Homily* XIX, v]: 'When he performs his bodily services, you indeed feed him, and see to it that, in addition to his food, he has clothing and shoes, and this, too, is a sort of servitude; for unless you also perform this service of yours, he will not render his, but will be free, and no law will compel him to render his services, if he is not nourished.'

[2] Also that of Isaac Angelus to the Sicilian prisoners, as is recorded by Nicetas, Book I [*Isaac Angelus*, I. iii], who quotes also the letter of the king of Sicily to the Greek emperor on this subject.

[3] *Phormio*, I. i [I. i. 44].

[4] Eumaeus in the *Odyssey*, XIV [XIV. 63 f.], says:

> Such things as a generous master gives to a bondsman,
> The ties of wedlock, land, and a habitation.

Ulysses himself, *Odyssey*, XXI [XXI. 214 f.], says to Eumaeus and Philaetius:

> To each of you shall I give wives and possessions,
> And houses near to my own.

Varro [*On Farming*, I. xvii. 7] says of slaves: 'They are rendered more zealous in their work by more generous treatment, by greater liberality in respect to food or clothing, or by the remission of a task, or by the permission to pasture on the estate some cattle of their own.'

Seneca [1] appositely remarks: 'It is not true that the slave has nothing merely because he will have nothing if his master is unwilling that he should have anything.' *On Benefits*, VII. iv.

3. Hence it is that a master does not seek to recover anything which was owed to a slave during slavery, and which was paid to the slave after emancipation. The reason, as Tryphoninus says, is that the ground for indebtedness or non-indebtedness is seen naturally in the claim of restitution; the master may naturally be indebted to his slave. And so we read that, just as clients [547] have made contributions for the use of patrons, and subjects for the use of kings, so slaves have made contributions for the use of their masters, as on the occasion of giving a dowry to a daughter, or ransoming a captive son, or some similar occurrence. *Dig.* XII. vi. 64. Dionysius, II [x].

Pliny, as he himself records in his letters, even allowed his slaves to make wills of a sort, that is to divide, donate, and leave their belongings within the household. We read that among some peoples slaves were allowed an even fuller right of acquiring property, just as we have elsewhere said that there are several degrees of slavery. *Letters*, VIII. xvi. II. iii [II. v. 27 ff.].

4. Among many peoples the laws have reduced even the external right of masters to this moral justice, which we are explaining. For among the Greeks slaves who had been too harshly treated were permitted 'to demand their sale', and at Rome to take refuge at statues, or to seek the aid of the magistrates against cruelty or starvation or intolerable wrong. Furthermore it will happen, not from a strict interpretation of law, but from humanity and kindness, that at times a slave will be given his freedom, which is due to him on the ground of long or very great services. *Institutes*, I. viii. § 2.

5. After slavery was introduced by the law of nations, there followed the benefit of emancipation, says Ulpian. Let us take as an example the lines of Terence: *Dig.* I. i. 4. [*Andria*, I. i. 10 f.]

> From a slave I made you my freedman,
> Because like a free man you served.[2]

Salvianus says that it was a frequent custom for slaves to be given their liberty, even when their service had not been of the best, at any rate if it had not been wicked; he adds, 'and they are not forbidden to take from their masters' house those things which they have acquired when in a servile condition'. Many instances of this sort of kindness appear in the martyrologies. [*Against Avarice*,] III [vii].

[1] In the same passage of the same author is this: 'Is there any doubt that the slave, along with his savings, belongs to his master? But yet he can give a gift to his master.'

[2] Thus the manuscripts, correctly. Varro [Servius, *On the Aeneid*, VIII. 564] relates that in the grove of Feronia it was customary to say to slaves: 'Let the well-deserving slaves be seated. Let them arise free.' In certain places it was the custom to set slaves free when they had acquired eight times their purchase price.

Deut., xv. 13. In this respect also we must praise the lenity of the Hebraic law, which ordained that the Jewish slave should be completely emancipated after the lapse of a fixed time, and not without gifts.[1]

[*Cato the Elder*, v = p. 338 E.] The prophets bitterly complain of the disregard of this law. Plutarch censures Cato the Elder for selling slaves who were worn out from old age, unmindful of that common nature in which all men share.

VII.—*Whether it is permissible for slaves to attempt to escape*

Sylvester, word *servitus*, § 3; Fortunius, *On Dig.*, I. i. 4; Aegidius Regius, De *Actibus Supernaturalibus*, disp. 31, dub. 7, no. 119.

The question here arises, whether it is right for a person who has been made a prisoner in a just war to attempt to escape; we are not dealing with him who has deserved this penalty by his own crime, but with him who has come into such a condition by a public act. The sounder view is that it is not right, because, as we have said, by the common consent of nations such a captive owes his services on behalf of his state.

This view nevertheless is not to be understood as valid in a case where intolerable cruelty imposes the necessity of escape upon the captive. On this subject one may consult the response of Gregory of Neocaesarea, xvi.

VIII.—*Whether the children of slaves are bound to the master, and to what extent*

II. v [29]. Lessius, II. v, dub. 5.

1. In another connexion we raised the question, whether and to what extent the offspring of slaves are bound to the master by moral justice. This question should not be passed over here, because it particularly concerns prisoners of war. If the parents had merited death by their own crimes, then for the preservation of their lives the offspring which was expected of them could be bound to slavery, because otherwise these would not be born. As we have said elsewhere, parents may in fact sell their children into slavery if

Deut., xv. 13 [xx. 14]. otherwise they would face starvation. Such is the right which God granted to the Jews over the descendants of the Canaanites.

2. However, children that were already born, no less than their parents, as part of the state could have been made liable for a debt of the state; but with regard to those who have not yet been born this reason does not seem sufficient, and another appears to be required. Either the obligation in question may arise from the express consent of the parents, along with the necessity of supporting the children, and then it may exist without end; or it may arise from the mere furnishing of sustenance, in which case it exists only up to the time

[548] when their services shall have cancelled all that has been expended for them. If any further right over the children is given

[1] Custom interpreted this as requiring a gift of not less than thirty shekels; see *Precepts Bidding*, 84.

to their master, apparently it arises from the civil law, which to masters is more generous than just. [Reading *largiente* for *largientibus*.]

IX.—*What is to be done in countries where the enslavement of prisoners of war is not customary*

1. Among those peoples who do not avail themselves of the right of slavery which arises from war, the best course will be to exchange prisoners; the next best, to release them at a price that is not unfair. What that price is cannot be set forth in exact terms; but humanity teaches that it should not be raised to the point where its payment would place the prisoner in want of the necessities of life. Such indulgence is in fact granted by the laws of certain countries to many who have fallen into debt by their own acts.

In some places the price put upon captives is fixed by agreements or by custom; as the sum of a mina among the Greeks of antiquity,[1] and at present among soldiers at a month's pay. Plutarch relates that formerly wars between the Corinthians and Megarians were waged 'humanely and as became peoples of the same race'. If any one were taken prisoner, he was treated by his captor as a guest and, upon his promise to pay his ransom, dismissed to his home; and from this arose the name 'war-guests (δορύξενοι)'. *Greek Questions* [xvii = p. 295 B].

2. The saying of Pyrrhus, which is praised by Cicero, reveals a nobler spirit: [*On Duties*, I. xii. 38.]

> I ask for myself not gold,[2] nor shall you pay me a ransom; [. . .]
> With steel, not with gold, on each side fight we for life. [. . .]
> To them whose valour the fortune of war has spared,
> Their liberty I am resolved to grant.

There is no doubt that Pyrrhus believed that he was waging a just war; yet he thought that he ought to spare the liberty of those whom worthy reasons had led into war.

Xenophon lauds a similar act of Cyrus; Polybius, the course taken by Philip of Macedon after his victory at Chaeronea; Curtius, the conduct of Alexander in relation to the Scythians; Plutarch, that of King Ptolemy and Demetrius, who rivalled each other fully as much in their kindness toward prisoners as in military operations. Dromichaetes, king of the Getae,[3] made Lysimachus, who had been taken prisoner, his guest, and by causing him to witness at the same time both the poverty and the civility of the Getae he induced Lysimachus to prefer to have the friendship of such people rather than their enmity. *Training of Cyrus*, II [III. i. 28 ff.]. [Polybius, V. x.] [Curtius, VII. ix. 18.] [Plutarch,] *Demetrius* [v = p. 891 A]. Strabo, VII [iii. 8].

[1] [551] In the war between the French and Spaniards in Italy, a cavalryman was ransomed for a quarter of a year's pay. But this did not include leaders of detachments or higher officers, nor those who fell into the enemy's power in a pitched battle or in the storming of a city; Mariana, XXVII. xviii.

[2] Menander Protector [frag. 60, p. 115, edit. Dindorf] praises the like generosity of the Christian Emperor Tiberius toward the Persians; Mariana, that of Sisebut [VI. iii], and also of Sancho, king of Castile, Book XI [XI. v].

[3] This is also recorded by Diodorus Siculus, in the *Excerpta Peiresciana* [pp. 257 and 258].

CHAPTER XV

NODERATION IN THE ACQUISITION OF SOVEREIGNTY

I.—*To what extent moral justice permits sovereignty to be acquired*

Victoria, *On the Law of War*, nos. 38 and 59.

THE equity which is required, or the humanity which is praised, in respect to individuals, is so much more required and praised in respect to peoples or parts of peoples in the degree that wrong or kindness toward a large number of persons becomes more notable. As other things may be acquired in a lawful war, so there may be acquired both the right of him who rules over a people and the right which the people itself has in the sovereign power; only in so far, however, as is permitted by the measure of the penalty which arises from a crime, or of some other form of debt.

To these reasons should be added the avoidance of extreme danger. But this reason is very often confused with the others, although both in establishing peace and in making use of victory it deserves particular attention for its own sake. It is possible to forgo other things from compassion; but, in case of public danger, a sense of security which exceeds the proper limit is the reverse of compassion. Isocrates wrote to Philip: 'The barbarians must be subjugated to a point which will enable you to make your country perfectly secure.'

[*Letters*, II. iv = p. 409.]

II.—*It is praiseworthy to abstain from the exercise of the right to acquire sovereignty over the vanquished*

Jugurthine War [*Conspiracy of Catiline*, xii. 4]. [*On Pub. Ad.*, I. vi. 2.] *Republic* [*Politics*], VII. xiv and xv; *Nic. Eth.*, X. vii. *On Duties*, I [xxiii. 80]. [I. xi. 35.] Thomas, II. i, qu. 40, art. 1, ad 3; Wilhelmus Matthaei, *De Bello*, § *requis.*, qu. 7. [Justin, I. i. 3.]

1. Sallust says of the ancient Romans: 'Our ancestors, being most scrupulous persons, used to deprive the vanquished of nothing save the power to do harm.' This is a view which could worthily have been uttered by a Christian; and with it accords another sentence of the same writer: 'Wise men wage war to secure peace, and endure toil in the hope of ease.' More than once Aristotle said: 'War was originated for the sake of peace, and business for the sake of leisure.' Cicero supports the same idea, and his is this exalted maxim: 'Let war be so undertaken that nothing else than peace may seem to be sought after.' From the same author comes this similar saying: 'So wars are to be undertaken for this reason, that men may live in peace without being wronged.'

2. These views differ in no respect from those which theologians of the true faith set forth to the effect that the end of war is the removal of the things which disturb peace. Before the time of Ninus, as we began to say elsewhere, following Trogus, it was the custom

to protect rather than to advance[1] the frontiers of one's empire; each one's realm was limited to his own country; kings sought not empire for themselves but [552] glory for their peoples, and, being content with victory, they abstained from acquiring dominion.

So far as he can, Augustine recalls us to this condition: 'Let them see to it, nevertheless, that it may not concern good men to delight in the extent of their dominion.'[2] He adds also this: 'It is a greater good fortune to live in harmony with a good neighbour than to subdue a bad neighbour who wages war on us.' Furthermore, the prophet Amos severely reproves in the Ammonites this zeal for extending their borders by armed force. *City of God*, IV. xv. *Amos*, i. 13.

III.—*Either by mingling them with the conquerors*—

To this ideal of old-time innocence the closest approach is in the wise moderation of the ancient Romans. 'What would our empire be to-day', says Seneca, 'had not salutary foresight mingled the vanquished with the conquerors?' 'Our founder Romulus', says Claudius in Tacitus, 'displayed so much wisdom that on the same day he had many peoples as enemies, and then as citizens'. He adds that the cause of the downfall of the Lacedaemonians and Athenians was nothing else than the exclusion, as foreigners, of those whom they had conquered. Livy says that the Roman power grew through the admission of enemies into the state. Examples are to be found in the history of the Sabines, Albans, Latins, and other Italian peoples; until, at last, *On Anger*, II. xxxiv [4]. *Annals*, V [XI. xxiv]. I [VIII. xiii. 16].

> Caesar in his triumph led the Gauls, and into the Senate, too. [Suetonius, *Caesar*, lxxx.]

Cerialis, in his speech to the Gauls, which is found in Tacitus, declares: 'You yourselves often command our legions; you yourselves govern these and other provinces; there is nothing shut off from you or closed to you.' And shortly after: 'Then love, then cherish, the peace and life which we, conquerors and conquered, enjoy by the same right.' At length came that most admirable step; in accordance with a constitution of the Emperor Antoninus [Caracalla] all those within the Roman world were made citizens of Rome, as Ulpian says. In consequence, as Modestinus declares, Rome became the common fatherland. And of Rome Claudian wrote: [*Histories*, IV. lxxiv.] *Dig.* I. v. 17. *Dig.* L. i. 33.

> To the peace-promoting customs of this city, . . .
> Due it is that we are all one people.

[*On the Consulship of Stilicho*, III. 154, 159.]

[1] The Emperor Alexander said to Artaxerxes the Persian: 'Each one should remain within his own borders, causing no disturbance, and no one, elated by an uncertain hope, should undertake wars, but each should rest content with his own possessions' [Herodian, VI. ii. 4].

[2] See Cyril, *Against Julian*, Book V, where he praises the Jewish kings for the reason that they were content with their own frontiers.

IV.—*Or by leaving the sovereign power to those who had held it*—

1. Another form of moderation in victory is to leave to conquered kings or peoples the sovereign power which they had held. So Hercules with Priam:

Seneca, *Trojan Women* [725 ff.].

> Vanquished by his young foe's tears,
> 'Take up', he said, 'the ruler's reins;
> Sit elevated on your father's throne,
> But with better faith the sceptre wield.'

Aelian, [*Various History*,] IV. v. Herodotus, VII [III. xv]. [Xenophon, *Training of Cyrus*, III. i. 33 ff.] [Seneca.] *On Clemency*, I. xxi [3]. [Polybius, V. ix.]

Hercules, also, after conquering Neleus, committed the kingdom to Neleus's son, Nestor. Similarly the Persian kings used to leave the royal authority to conquered kings; thus Cyrus to the Armenian king. Thus Alexander left royal power to Porus.[1] Seneca[2] praises this practice of 'taking nothing but glory from a vanquished king'. Polybius celebrates the goodness of Antigonus, who, although he had Sparta in his power, left the Spartans 'their ancestral constitution and their freedom'; and by this act, it is narrated in the same passage, Antigonus obtained the highest praises throughout Greece.

Livy, XXXII [XXXVII. liv. 26]. *Mithridatic Wars* [xvii. 114]. [Livy, XXXIII. xii. 9.] *Annals*, XII [xix].

2. In the same way the Romans allowed the Cappadocians to use whatever form of constitution they wished, and to many peoples their freedom was left after a war. 'Carthage is free and has its own laws,' say the Rhodians to the Romans after the second Punic War. Pompey, says Appian, 'left some of the conquered peoples free'.[3] When the Aetolians declared that there could be no sure peace unless Philip of Macedon were driven from his kingdom, Quintius said that they had stated their opinion without thinking of the Roman custom of sparing the vanquished. [553] He added: 'Whoever is mildest to the conquered has the loftiest mind.' In Tacitus we read: 'From the vanquished Zorsines nothing was taken away.'

V.—*Sometimes by the imposition of garrisons*—

Sometimes, with the concession of sovereign power, provision is made for the security of the victors. Thus Quintius ordered[4] that Corinth should be restored to the Achaeans, yet upon the condition that there should be a garrison in Acrocorinthus; also

[1] And so Pepin to Aistolf the Lombard.

[2] The whole passage deserves examination. It contains also this notable saying: 'This is to triumph even in accordance with one's victory, and to bear witness that one has found nothing among the vanquished which was worthy of the victor.' Pompey left to Tigranes a part of his realm; Eutropius, VI [VI. xiii].

[3] For a knowledge of their condition see Polybius, *Selections on Embassies*, vi [xix]; Suetonius, in his life of Caesar, where he discusses Gaul [*Divus Julius*, xxv]. Guilleman has also something worth reading in his history of Switzerland [I. viii].

[4] Nevertheless this was afterwards remitted; Polybius, *Selections on Embassies*, xi; Plutarch, *Flaminius* [*Flamininus*, x=p. 374 c].

that Chalcis and Demetrias should be retained, until the anxiety with regard to Antiochus should be over.

VI.—*Or even by tributes and similar burdens*

Often the levying of tributes also has for an object not so much the restitution of the expenses that have been incurred as the security, in the future, of both victor and vanquished. Cicero says of the Greeks: 'At the same time let Asia reflect on this, that if it were not held by this Empire there is no disaster of foreign war or domestic strife that would fail to assail it; and since, moreover, this Empire can in no way be maintained without taxes, let Asia with a part of its produce contentedly purchase for itself eternal peace and rest.' *Letters to his Brother Quintus*, I. i [II. § 34].

In Tacitus Petilius Cerealis speaks to the Lingones and other Gauls on behalf of the Romans in the following words: 'Although we have been so often provoked, this is the only burden we have laid upon you by right of victory, wherewith we might keep the peace; for there is no quiet for the nations without armed forces, and armed forces cannot be had without pay, and pay cannot be had without tribute.' *Histories*, IV [lxxiv].

To this same problem apply also the other conditions which we mentioned when discussing unequal treaties—the surrender of arms, of a fleet,[1] of elephants, not to maintain an army ready for battle nor an armed force. II. xv. 7.

VII.—*The advantage derived from such moderation is pointed out*

1. Moreover to leave to the vanquished their sovereign powers is not only an act of humanity, but often an act of prudence also. Among the institutions of Numa there is praised that which aimed to exclude any shedding of blood from the rites of Terminus, indicating that nothing is more useful in securing quiet and a sure peace than to remain within one's own frontier. Florus well remarks: 'It is more difficult to keep provinces than to win them; they are won by force, they are retained by justice.' Plutarch, *Roman Questions*, xv [= p. 267 c]. [IV. xii.]

Not unlike this is the comment in Livy: 'It is easier to gain things one by one than to hold all together'; also, the remark of Augustus in Plutarch: 'A greater task ... than winning a great empire is the governing of an empire already in existence.' The ambassadors of King Darius said to Alexander: 'A foreign empire is a dangerous thing; it is difficult to hold what you may not be able to take. Some things it is easier to conquer than to defend; by Hercules, how much more readily do our hands receive than retain!' XXXVII [xxxv. 6]. [*Apothegms*, p. 207 D.] [Curtius, IV. xi. 8.]

[1] Regarding the Persians, see Agathias, Book IV [IV. ix].

[Aristides, *In Praise of Rome*, p. 353 f.] Livy, XXVIII [XXXVI. xxxii. 6]. [III. x = 690 E.] [*Preface*, vii.] Valerius Maximus, IV. i [10].

2. This difficulty of holding an empire together is what Calanus of India [1] and, before him, Oebares the friend of Cyrus explained by the comparison of a dried hide, which rises up in one spot as soon as you press another spot with your foot; and Titus Quintius in Livy by comparison with a tortoise,[2] which is immune to blows when gathered into its shell, but exposed and weak as soon as it has thrust out a part of its body. Plato, *On Laws*, Book III, applies to this situation the saying of Hesiod: 'The half is better than the whole.'

Appian observes that not a few peoples who wished to come under the rule of the Romans were rejected by them; while for other peoples kings were appointed. In the judgement of Scipio Africanus, in his time Rome already possessed so much that it would be greedy to seek for more; and she would be richly fortunate if she lost nothing of what she held. The formula for making the lustral sacrifices, in which the gods were entreated to make the resources of Rome better and greater, he altered in such a way that he prayed that they might preserve Rome's resources in safety forever.[3]

VIII.—*Examples; with a discussion of a change in the form of government among the vanquished*

Thucydides, I [xix]; Isocrates, *Panathenaic Oration* [p. 243]. Demosthenes, *On the Chersonesus*; Diodorus, XIII and XV. [Stobaeus, xliii. 27.]

The Lacedaemonians, and, at first, the Athenians, claimed for themselves no sovereignty over the cities they had captured. They wished merely that these should use a form of government modelled on their own; the Lacedaemonians, in fact, a government under the influence of the aristocrats, the Athenians one subject to the will of the people, as we learn from Thucydides, Isocrates, Demosthenes, and even from Aristotle himself in the fourth book of his *Politics*, [554] chapter xi, and the fifth book, chapter vii. This very thing is indicated in a comedy by Heniochus, a writer of those days, in the following manner:

> Then drew near to them two women,
> Who turned all things to dire confusion;
> The one called Aristocracy, Democracy the other,
> Through whose solicitation the cities were driven to madness.

Annals, VI [xlii].

A similar course is that which, according to Tacitus, was pursued by Artabanus at Seleucia: 'He placed the commons under the aristocracy', he says, 'in accordance with his own interest: for the

[1] Plutarch has this in his *Alexander* [lxv = p. 701 E].

[2] Plutarch [*Flamininus*, xvii = p. 378 D] relates it thus: 'When he wished to dissuade the Achaeans who were seeking the island of Zacynthus, he said that they would run into danger if, like a tortoise, they extended their heads beyond the Peloponnese.'

[3] [556] The consul Claudianus Julianus makes use of this story in his letter to Pupienus and Balbinus [Capitolinus, *Life of Maximus and Balbinus*, xvii]. It was imitated by Augustus, who, as Dio [LIV. ix] says, 'was praised because he wished to acquire no new territory, but thought that that, which was already held, was enough.'

rule of the people is close to liberty, but the despotism of the few is nearer to the licence of a king.' But the question whether changes of this sort make for the safety of the conqueror does not belong to our investigation.

IX.—*If sovereignty is to be assumed, it is right to leave a part of it to the conquered*

If it is not safe to refrain from assuming any dominion over the conquered, the action may still be limited in such a way that a portion of the sovereign power may be left to them or to their kings. Tacitus calls it the practice of the Roman people 'to have kings also as instruments of subjection'. To the same author it seemed that 'Antiochus was the richest of the subject kings'. 'Kings subject to the Romans' is the phrase in the *Commentaries* of Musonius; also in Strabo, near the end of Book VI. Lucan writes: [*Agricola*, xiv.] *Histories*, II [lxxxi]. [Stobaeus, xlviii. 67.] [VI. iv. 2.]

> And all the royal purple which serves the Latin sword.[1]

[*Pharsalia*, VII. 228.]

Thus among the Jews the sceptre remained in the Sanhedrin, even after the confiscation of Archelaus. Evagoras, king of Cyprus, as we read in Diodorus, said that he was willing to be subject to the Persian king, but as one king to another. Alexander at different times offered to the conquered Darius this condition, that Darius should rule over others, but should obey Alexander.[2] XV [ix]. [Diodorus,] XVII [liv].

We have elsewhere spoken of the ways of dividing the sovereign power. To some peoples a part of their governmental power has been left, as to former possessors a part of their lands. I. iii. 17; III. viii. 3.

X.—*Or, certainly, some degree of liberty should be left to the conquered*

But when all sovereignty is taken away from the conquered with respect to their private affairs and minor public matters it is still possible to leave to them their own laws,[3] customs, and officials. Thus in the pro-consular province of Bithynia the city of Apamaea had the privilege of governing itself as it pleased;[4] we are so in-

[1] See the *Panegyric* addressed to Maximian [Eumenius, chap. x].

[2] Such were also in Italy, in former times, the kings under the authority of other kings; Servius, *On the Aeneid*, X [X. 655]. So in the *Persians* [24] of Aeschylus there are mentioned:

> Kings, subjects of the great king.

So also among the Turks, on the authority of Leunclavius, Book XVIII.

[3] Philo, in the *Embassy to Gaius* [xxiii], says: 'Augustus gave no less attention to preserving the laws peculiar to each people than to those of the Romans.'

[4] See Pliny, *Letters*, xciii, and the following letter of Trajan in Book X [X. xcii and xciii]. Under the Persians Sinope had a democratic form of government; Appian, *Mithridatic Wars* [xii. 83, but referring to Amisus, not Sinope]. Such was the shadow of liberty among the Greeks under Roman rule. See Cicero, *Letters to Atticus*, VI. i; Pliny, *Letters*, VIII. xxiv. The Cypriots could not be summoned out of their island; Cicero, *Letters to Atticus*, V. xxi [V. xxi. 6].

Letters, X. lvi, lxxxiv, cxi and cxiii [X. xlvii, lxxix, cxii and cxiv]. *Ibid.*, xciii [X. xcii]. formed by the letters of Pliny, who says also that the Bithynians have their own officials and their own senate. And so in Pontus the state of the Amiseni [Amisus] enjoyed its own laws through the kindness of Lucullus. The Goths left the Roman law to the conquered Romans.

XI.—*Some degree of liberty should be left to the conquered, especially in the matter of religion*

1. A part of this indulgence is not to deprive the conquered of the exercise of their inherited religion,[1] except by persuasion. This [*Embassy to Gaius*, xxxvi.] Agrippa, in his speech to Gaius, which Philo quotes in his report of his embassy, proves to be as devoid of harm to the victor as it is gratifying to the vanquished. [*Jewish War*, V. ix. 4; VI. ii. 1.] In Josephus, both Josephus himself and the Emperor Titus reproach the rebels of Jerusalem with the fact that, through the generosity of the Romans, the rights they enjoyed in the exercise of their worship were so complete that they could exclude foreigners from the Temple, even upon pain of death.

2. If, however, a false religion is practised by the vanquished, the victor will do right in taking steps to prevent the oppression of the true faith, as Constantine did, when he crushed the faction of Licinius, and, after him, the Frankish and other kings.

XII.—*At any rate the conquered should be treated with clemency; and why*

1. Last of all is this word of caution. Even under the fullest and, as it were, despotic sovereignty, the conquered should be treated with clemency, and in such a way that their advantage should be combined with that of the conquerors. Xenophon, *Training of Cyrus*, IV [iv. 10]. Cyrus bade the conquered Assyrians be of good cheer, saying that their lot would be the same as it would have been if they had only changed [555] their king; that they would retain their houses, their lands, their rights over their wives and children, which they had had up to that time; indeed, if any one should wrong them, he and his men would be their avengers.

[*Jugurthine War*, cii. 6.] In Sallust we read: 'The Roman people thought it better to gain friends than slaves; and held it safer to rule over willing than over compulsory subjects.[2] *Agricola* [xiii]. The Britons, in the time of Tacitus,

[1] 'It is better that some God should be worshipped there than none,' as we have just said [III. xii. 6. 1, note] in the words of Severus. So the Goths, in Procopius, *Gothic War*, II [II. vi], say that they have constrained no one to join their faith.

[2] In Thucydides, V [IV. xix], the Lacedaemonians say: 'And so we think that great enmities may thus be transformed into lasting concord, not if any one, in avenging himself and making use of a more favourable situation, imposes upon others the necessity of swearing to unequal terms, but if, when he could do this, he handles the matter as temperately as possible, displaying not less justice than courage in conquering.'

would patiently have endured the levy and tribute and the additional burdens of the Roman domination if they had not been subjected to wrongs; these they bore impatiently, for they were subdued to the point of obedience, but not yet to that of slavery.

2. The ambassador from Privernum, when asked in the Roman senate what sort of a peace the Romans were to expect from his people, said: 'If you should have given to them a good peace, then you may expect it to be reliable and perpetual; if a bad one, brief.' As the reason, there was added: 'Do not believe that any people, or any man, will remain longer than is necessary in a condition with which he is dissatisfied.' Livy, VIII [xxi. 4].

Similarly, Camillus said that that authority was the most secure with which those who obeyed were pleased. The Scythians said to Alexander: 'There is no friendship between master and slave; even in time of peace the rights of war are maintained.' Hermocrates, in Diodorus, declares: 'It is not so glorious to conquer as to make a mild use of victory.' Tacitus has a wholesome opinion regarding the use of victory: 'Wars have noble endings, whenever they are terminated by pardoning.' In a letter of the dictator Caesar are the words: 'Let this be a new method of conquering, to fortify ourselves with mercy and generosity.' Livy, VIII [xiii. 16]. Curtius, VII [viii. 28]. XIII [xix]. [*Annals*, XII. xix.] [Cicero, *Letters to Atticus*, IX. vii c.]

CHAPTER XVI

MODERATION IN REGARD TO THOSE THINGS WHICH BY THE LAW OF NATIONS HAVE NOT THE RIGHT OF POSTLIMINY

I.—*Moral justice requires that the things which our enemy has taken from another in an unlawful war shall be restored*

1. We have explained above to what extent things become the property of the captors by a lawful war. From such things we must deduct those which are recovered by right of postliminy; [557] for these are regarded as not having been captured.

But we said that that which was taken in an unlawful war must be restored, not only by those who took it, but also by others to whom the thing has come in any manner whatsoever. For no one, the authorities of the Roman law declare, can transfer to another more right than he himself has. This Seneca briefly explains thus: 'No man can give what he does not have.' The person who first took the thing did not have moral ownership (*dominium internum*), therefore the person who obtains his right from him will not have it; hence the second or third possessor takes an ownership which, for the sake of explanation, we call legal (*externum*), that is, an ownership which has the advantage of being everywhere protected by the authority and power of the courts. Nevertheless, if the possessor uses this advantage against him from whom the thing was taken by an act of injustice, he will not act rightly.

Dig. IX. iv. 27, § 1. *Dig.* XLI. i. 20. *On Benefits*, V. xii.

2. We may here cite as pertinent the opinion which the worthy jurists gave with regard to a slave who had been captured by robbers and had afterward reached the enemy; it was true that he had been stolen, and neither the fact that he had been in the power of the enemy nor that he had returned by postliminy nullified the right of the original owner. On the basis of the law of nature a similar opinion must also be rendered with regard to him who was captured in an unlawful war, and afterward, through an unlawful war, or from other causes, came into the power of another; for in moral justice there is no distinction between an unlawful war and brigandage. Gregory of Neocaesarea [1] gave answer in conformity with this opinion when he was consulted regarding the fact that certain men of Pontus had acquired goods of their fellow citizens which had been captured by barbarians.

Digest, XLIX. xv. 27.

Aegidius Regius, *De Actibus Supernaturalibus*, disp. 31, dub. 7, no. 122.

[*Epistola*] *Canonica*, X.

[1] [559] He is followed by Petrus, *De Potestate Principis*, chapter iii, qu. 4, and Bruningius, *De Homagiis*, concl. 241.

II.—*Examples*

1. Such things, then, must be restored to those from whom they were taken; and we often see that this has been done. Livy, III [x. 1]. after relating that the Volscians and Aequians were defeated by Lucius Lucretius Tricipitinus, says that the spoil was exposed in the Campus Martius, in order that each might take home what belonged to him within three days. The same author, having told of the rout [IV. xxix. 4.] of the Volscians by the dictator Posthumius, adds: 'Part of the booty was given back to the Latins and Hernicans upon their recognizing what was theirs; part the dictator sold at auction.' Elsewhere [V. xvi. 7.] he has: 'Two days were allowed to the owners for identifying their property.' Livy, again, after describing the victory of the Samnites X [xx. 15]. over the Campanians, writes: 'What most delighted the victors was the recovery of seven thousand four hundred prisoners of war, and a huge booty belonging to their allies; and the owners were summoned by proclamation to identify and recover their belongings on an appointed day.' Afterward he recounts a similar act on the part [X. xxxvi. 16 ff.] of the Romans:

The Samnites attempted to seize the Roman colony of Interamna, but did not take the city. After pillaging the fields, they were thence driving off another booty composed of both men and cattle and also the captured colonists, when they fell in with the consul returning from Luceria, and not only lost their spoil, but, owing to being in disorder in a long and encumbered column, they were themselves cut to pieces. The consul by proclamation called together the owners of Interamna to identify and recover their property, and leaving his army there, he set out for Rome because of the meeting of the assembly.

In another passage, dealing with the spoil which Cornelius Scipio [XXXV. i. 12.] had taken at Ilipa, a city in Lusitania, the same writer speaks thus: 'This was all set out outside the town, and owners were given the right to identify what was theirs. The rest was turned over to the quaestor to be sold; what was realized therefrom was divided among the soldiers.' After the battle fought by Tiberius Gracchus near Beneventum, we further read in Livy: 'All the booty, except the XXIV [xvi. 5]. prisoners, was given to the soldiery; there were also excepted such cattle as their owners should identify within thirty days.'

2. Of Licius Aemilius, who conquered the Gauls, Polybius *Histories*, II [xxxi]. writes: 'He restored the booty to those from whom it had been seized.' Plutarch and Appian relate that Scipio did likewise,[1] when Plutarch, *Apothegms* [=p. 200 B]. upon capturing Carthage he found there many temple offerings Appian, *Punic Wars* [xx. 133].

[1] Also Diodorus Siculus, in the *Excerpta Peiresciana* [p. 345].

Valerius Maximus, I. i. 6 [V. i. 6]: 'The humanity of the later Africanus also was notably and widely in evidence. For when he had taken Carthage he sent letters around to the cities of Sicily, that they might send representatives to recover the ornaments of their temples which had been carried off by the Carthaginians, and to see that these should be restored to their former places.'

which the Carthaginians had carried thither from the cities of Sicily and other places.

[II. xxxv. 86.] Cicero in his oration *Against Verres*, dealing with the administration of justice in Sicily, says: 'The Carthaginians had at one time taken the town of Himera, which was a particularly famous and rich city of Sicily. [558] When the war was ended, Scipio, who thought it worthy of the Roman people that our allies, in consequence of our victory, should recover what was theirs, took pains that, so far as possible, what had been taken by Carthage should be restored to all the Sicilians.' The same writer gives a sufficiently lengthy discussion of this act of Scipio when treating of the statues in his oration [IV. xxxiii. 73.] *Against Verres*.

Livy, XXXI [xv. 5]. The Rhodians restored to the Athenians four of their ships which had been taken by the Macedonians and recaptured. So Phaneas the Aetolian thought it right that what the Aetolians had Livy, XXXIII [xiii. 11 f.]. had before the war should be returned to them; Titus Quintius did not deny that this would be just, if it were a question of cities taken in war,[1] and if the Aetolians had not broken the terms of the Strabo, XIII [XIV. i. 26]. alliance. The Romans even restored to their ancient condition the treasures once dedicated at Ephesus, which kings had made their own.

III.—*Whether anything may be deducted from that which is restored*

1. If a thing of the sort under consideration has come into any one's hands by way of trade, will he be able to charge the person from whom it was originally taken the price which he has paid?

II. x. 9. It is consistent with what we have said elsewhere that the possessor may charge as much as the recovery of the thing despaired of would have been worth to him who had lost it. But if such an outlay may be recovered, why not also an evaluation of the labour and danger, just as if by diving some one had recovered another's property which was lost in the sea? Pertinent to this question, it seems to me, is the story of Abraham, when he returned to Sodom as victor over the Genesis, xiv. 16. five kings. 'He brought back all the goods', says Moses; that is, the goods which, as he had previously related, had been captured by the kings.

2. Again we are not to attribute to any other cause the arrangement which the king of Sodom proposed to Abraham, that he should restore the prisoners, but keep the other things for himself in return

[1] Pompey restored Paphlagonia to Attalus and Pylaemenes; Eutropius, VI [VI. xi].
In the alliance of the Pope, the Emperor Charles V, and the Venetians against Soliman, it was agreed that each party should recover what had been his; Paruta, VIII [IX=p. 650, ed. 1605]. In consequence, when the Spaniards had taken Cephallenia, they restored it to the Venetians.
Pertinent to this question is also a passage in Anna Comnena [XI. vi], dealing with Godefroy.

for his toil and danger. Abraham, however, being a man not only of a pious but also of a lofty mind,[1] wished to take nothing at all for himself; but from the things that were recovered (for this narrative, as we have said, relates to them) as though by his own right he gave a tenth to God, deducted the necessary expenses, and desired that a share be assigned to his allies. Verses 20–4 [*Genesis*, xiv. 20–4].

IV.—*Even subject peoples or divisions of peoples are to be restored to those to whom they belonged, if they have been unjustly taken over by the enemy*

Furthermore, just as goods are to be restored to their owner, so peoples also,[2] and divisions of peoples, are to be restored to those who had the right of dominion over them, or even to themselves, if they had been independent prior to suffering the unjust violence. Thus we learn from Livy that, in the time of Camillus, Sutrium was recovered and restored to the allies of the Romans. (Livy, VI [iii. 10].) The Lacedaemonians restored the Aeginetans and the Melians to their cities. (Livy, XXXIII [xxxii].) The Greek states, which had been invaded by the Macedonians, were restored to freedom by Flaminius. (Xenophon, *Affairs of Greece*, III [II. ii. 9].)

Flaminius also, in a conference with the ambassadors of Antiochus, declared it was right to set free the cities of Asia, which bore Greek names and which had been captured in war by Seleucus the great-grandfather of Antiochus, which had been lost and recovered by the same Antiochus; 'for', he said, 'the colonies were not sent to Aeolia and Ionia to be subject to a king, but to increase the race, and to spread a very ancient people throughout the world.' XXXIV [lviii. 13].

V.—*At what time the obligation to make restoration ceases*

Usually the question is raised also regarding the period of time in which the moral obligation to restore a thing may cease. But in

[1] This observation is well made by Iacchiades, *On Daniel*, v. 17. Sulpicius [Sulpicius Severus, *Sacred History*, I. v] says of Abraham: 'He restored the rest to those from whom it had been seized.' Ambrose, on the Patriarchs, I [*On Abraham*, I. iii], writes: 'And so, since he sought not for himself a reward from men, he received it from God.'

Very similar to this was the conduct of Pittacus and Timoleon. 'Pittacus of Mitylene, when with the consent of all he was offered the half of the territory recovered, turned his mind away from the gift, because he deemed it unworthy to dim the glory of his valour by the greatness of the spoil'; Valerius Maximus, VI. v. i. Of Timoleon Plutarch [*Comparison of Timoleon and Aemilius Paulus*, ii = p. 277 B] says: 'Under such circumstances it is not base to receive, but it is better not to receive; such self-restraint implies a certain superabundance of virtue, which shows that it can do without those things which are permitted.'

Cf. what was previously said, in II. xiv. 6 and III. iv. 1.

[2] The exiles from Saguntum after six years were restored by the Romans. Antony ordered that all those who had been made slaves in the war with Cassius should be liberated, and that property should be restored to its owners. Likewise Calatrava was restored by the king of Castile and others to the soldiers from whom it had been taken by the Moors; Mariana, XI [XI. xxv]. Cf. what is above in III. x. 6.

the case of citizens under the same government the question is answered according to their laws, provided that these admit a moral right and do not consist in a legal right only; this may be gathered from the language and scope of the laws by a careful examination. In the case of those, however, which are foreign in relation to one another, the question is to be answered in accordance with conjecture as to abandonment, which we have discussed elsewhere, so far as our purpose requires.

II. iv.

VI.—*What is to be done in a doubtful case*

Cicero, *On Duties*, II [xxiii. 82].

If, however, the lawfulness of the war is seriously open to question, the best course will be to follow the counsel of Aratus of Sicyon,[1] who on the one side persuaded the new possessors to accept payment and to give up what they held, and on the other persuaded the former owners to consider it more advantageous to have paid to them the value of their property than to recover it.

[1] This was done by King Ferdinand, as Mariana records, XXIX. xiv.

CHAPTER XVII

ON THOSE WHO ARE OF NEITHER SIDE IN WAR

I.—*From those who are at peace nothing should be taken except in case of extreme necessity, and subject to the restoration of its value*

It might seem superfluous for us to speak of those who are not involved in war, since it is quite clear that no right of war is valid against them. But since in time of war on the pretext of necessity many things [560] are done at the expense of those who are at peace, especially if they are neighbours, we must briefly repeat here what we have said elsewhere, that the necessity which gives any right II. ii. 10. over another's property must be extreme; furthermore, that it is requisite that the owner himself should not be confronted with an equal necessity; that even in case there is no doubt as to the necessity more is not to be taken than the necessity demands; that is, if retention is sufficient, then the use of a thing is not to be assumed; if the use is sufficient, then not the consumption; if consumption is necessary, the value of the thing must then be repaid.

II.—*Examples of self-restraint and precepts*

1. When Moses and his people were pressed by the extreme [*Numbers*, necessity of passing through the land of the Edomites, he said, first, xx. 17 ff.] that he would pass along the royal road, and would not turn off into the ploughed fields or vineyards, and if he should have need of their water he would pay its price. Famous Greek and Roman generals assumed the same obligation. In Xenophon, the Greeks who were [*Anabasis*, with Clearchus promised the Persians that they would march through II. iii. without causing them any damage; and if they would have supplies 23 ff.]. for the Greeks to purchase these latter would not seize things to eat or drink from any one.

2. Dercyllides, as the same Xenophon relates, 'led his forces [*Greek* through peaceful territory in such a way that his allies suffered no *History*, loss.' Livy says of King Perseus: 'He returned to his kingdom III. i. 10.] [XLI. through Phthertis, Achaia, and Thessaly, without causing damage or xxii. 6.] injury to the lands through which he marched.' Of the army of Agis of Sparta, Plutarch says: 'They were a marvel to the cities as they [*Agis*, xiv. traversed the Peloponnesus quietly, without injury and almost without =p. noise.' [1] 801 D.]

[1] Plutarch offers the same testimony to Titus Quintius Flaminius [*Flamininus*, v=p. 371 D].

II [xxv]. Velleius says of Sulla: 'You would think that he had come into Italy not to avenge in war, but to establish peace, with so great quiet did he lead his army through Calabria and Apulia into Campania, showing exceptional care for crops, fields, cities, and men.' Of Pompey the Great Cicero [1] affirms that 'his legions came to Asia in such a way that not only the hands of so vast an army, but even its footprints could be said to have done no harm to any one at peace'. Of Domitian Frontinus thus speaks: 'When he was establishing forts in the lands of the Ubii, he ordered that the value should be paid for the crops of the places which he incorporated in the fortifications; and by the report of this act of justice he bound to himself the allegiance of all.'

For the Manilian Law [xiii. 39]. *Strategemata,* II. xi [7].

[*Alexander Severus,* l.] Of the Parthian expedition of Alexander Severus, Lampridius writes: 'He conducted it with so great discipline, demanding so high respect for himself, that not soldiers, but senators, might be said to be passing by; wherever the soldiers were on the march, the tribunes were under arms, the centurions respectful, the soldiers gentle. Himself, however, the provincials received as a god, because of these great and numerous benefits.' Of the Goths,[2] Huns, and Alans, who were in the service of Theodosius, the Panegyrist says: 'There was no rioting, no disturbance, no plundering, as is usual with barbarians; indeed, whenever there was a shortage of supplies they bore the want with patience, and by their abstinence they augmented the grain which they diminished by their number.'

[Latinus Pacatus, *Panegyric,* xxxii.]

[*On the Consulship of Stilicho,* I. 163 ff.] Claudian attributes the same conduct to Stilicho:

> So great the peace, so great the fear, the guardian of right,
> 'Neath your command, that no plundering of vineyard nor of grain field
> Cheated the farmer of his harvest.

Similar conduct is attributed by Suidas to Belisarius.[3]

[1] Also Plutarch [*Pompey,* x = p. 624 A]: 'When he heard that his soldiers were acting too licentiously on the march he put a seal on their swords; and, if any one broke this, he was punished.'

[2] With regard to the moderation of this people we find much in Cassiodorus, as in [*Variae,*] V. x, and II. xiii [V. x, xi and xiii]. Besides, in letter xxv of the same book [V. xxvi] is this: 'Lay waste neither the fields nor the meadows of the landholders, but hasten with all self-restraint, that your coming may cause us delight. Because for this we willingly undergo the expenses imposed by the army, that civilization may be preserved intact by those under arms.' Also in IX. xxv: 'No losses to the owners were occasioned by his arms.'

[3] This virtue in Belisarius is often acclaimed by Procopius, the companion and witness of his actions. See his noble speech, which is pertinent here, delivered to his soldiers in Sicily when he was on the way to Africa, and the description of his march through Africa, in the *Vandalic War,* I [I. xii and xvii]. I shall cite in full the following passage from the *Gothic War,* III [III. i]:

> He acted with such care and forethought toward the peasants that none of them suffered violence while Belisarius led the army. On the contrary, all became rich wherever he arrived with a large body of troops; [563] for they sold their goods to the soldiers at their own price. And when the crops were ripe he took anxious care that they should not be spoiled by the cavalry; in addition, no one at all was allowed to touch fruit hanging on the trees.

See the similar praise of the Germans in their expedition to the Holy Sepulchre, in Nicetas, *On Manuel Comnenus* [I. iv]. Gregoras also lauds the same conduct in the Venetians, IX [IX. v]: 'There was no one who was not struck with admiration for the discipline of the Venetians, and their

3. This condition was brought about by scrupulous painstaking
in providing for necessities [1] by the regular payment of troops, and
by vigour in enforcing discipline, a rule of which you hear in Am- XVIII
mianus [2]: 'The lands of those at peace must not be trampled upon.' [ii. 7].
In Vopiscus, *Life of Aurelian*, we read: 'Let no one seize another's *Aurelian*
fowl; let no one touch a sheep; let no one carry off a bunch of grapes, [vii].
let no one destroy grain, let no one requisition oil, salt, or wood.'
Likewise in Cassiodorus: 'Let them live with the provincials under [*Variae*,
the civil law; [561] let not the spirit of him, who feels that he is VII. iv.]
armed, become insolent, because our army as a shield should guarantee
quiet to the Romans.' These rules may be supplemented by the
saying of Xenophon, in Book VI of the *Anabasis*: 'A friendly [VI. ii. 6.]
city should not be compelled to give anything against its will.'

4. In the light of these sayings you would aptly interpret that
admonition of a great Prophet, nay, a greater than a Prophet: *Luke*, iii.
'Extort from no man by violence, neither accuse any one wrong- 14.
fully; [3] and be content with your wages.' [4] Similar to this is the
order of Aurelian in the passage of Vopiscus which has been cited: [*Aurelian*,
'Let each one be satisfied with his allowance, let him live by the vii.]
spoil of the enemy, not by the tears of the provincials.'

No one should think that, while it is fine to say these things,
they cannot be carried into effect; for neither would the Divine
Man urge them, nor the wise authors of laws prescribe them, if they
believed that such rules could not be enforced. In fact, we must
grant that that can be done which we see done.[5] Therefore we have
adduced examples, to which may be added the notable example
which Frontinus records of Scaurus,[6] that an apple-tree, which the IV. i [*Stratege-mata*, IV. iii. 13].

magnanimity combined with justice. For no one of their army wished to go out and take anything without paying the price.'

[1] Pliny, *Natural History*, XXVI. iv: 'Else why have the Roman generals always devoted their first attention to commerce when waging war?'

Cassiodorus, [*Variae*,] IV. xiii: 'Let him have something to buy, that he may not be compelled to think of what he can carry off.' He has something similar in V. x and xiii.

[2] See also Book XXI [XXI. v. 8].

[3] You might translate 'from pillage', in which sense this word is taken in the Greek version in *Job*, xxxv. 9; *Psalms*, cxviii. 121 [cxix. 122]; *Proverbs*, xiv. 33 [xiv. 31], xxii. 16, cxviii. 3 [xxviii. 3]; *Ecclesiastes*, iv. 1; and also *Leviticus*, xix. 11. The Vulgate translator of *Luke*, xix. 8, renders the same Greek word by *defraudare* ('defraud').

[4] On this passage of *Luke*, Ambrose [*On Luke*, II. lxxvii] says: 'For this purpose pay was instituted for military service, that the soldier, in seeking his subsistence, might not act as a robber.' This is copied by Augustine in his sermon xix, *On the Words of Our Lord according to Matthew* [*Sermones*, lxxxii. 1, really not the work of Augustine; see *Appendices*, V. lxxxvii. 1, Migne].

On this subject there are notable edicts in Gregory of Tours, II. xxxvii; in the *Capitularies* of Charles and his successors, V, tit. clxxxix; in the *Councils of France*, II; in the *Capitularies* of Louis the Pious, II. xiv, and in vol. III; in the *Council of St. Macra*.

Add the *Bavarian Law*, II. v. Gunther [*Ligurinus*, VII. 299 ff.] thus reports a law of Frederic I:

If one has burned the farms or homes of folk
At peace, with shaven head he will be marked,
And after many blows from camp will he be chased.

[5] And so Guicciardini states, in Book XVI.

[6] On the severity of Niger, because of the theft of a cock, see Spartianus [*Pescennius Niger*, x].

survey had included in the lines of the camp, was left on the following day, when the army had marched off, with its fruit untouched.

XXVIII [xxiv. 9]. 5. Livy, after relating that the Roman soldiers in the camp at the Sucro had behaved themselves with too great licence, and that some of them had gone at night to pillage in the neutral land about them, adds that everything was done through the greed and licence of the soldiers and nothing according to regulation and discipline. XL [xxii. 10–11]. There is another notable passage of the same writer, when he describes the march of Philip through the land of the Denseletae:

> They were allies, but from lack of supplies the Macedonians plundered their territory just like that of the enemy; for, plundering on all sides, they first devastated homesteads, and then even some villages, to the great shame of the king, when he heard the voices of his allies calling in vain upon the gods, who are the guardians of treaties, and upon his own name.

Annals, XII [xlix]. *Histories*, III [ii]. In Tacitus, the reputation of Pelignus is one of shame, since he plundered allies rather than enemies. The same author observes that the soldiers of Vitellius were in idleness throughout the Italian municipalities, and a source of dread to their hosts alone. Also, in [I. xxi. 56.] Cicero's passage on the city praetorship, in his *Against Verres*, is this accusation: 'You gave your attention to the plundering and harassing of the peaceful towns of the allies, and of our friends.'

Aegidius Regius, *De Actibus Supernaturalibus*, disp. 31, dub. 7, no. 95. 6. At this point I cannot pass without mention the opinion of the theologians, which I think is very true, that a king, who has not paid what he owes to his soldiers, is responsible for the losses which in consequence have ensued, not only to the soldiers, but also to his own subjects and their neighbours, whom the soldiers under pressure of want have treated badly.

III.—*What the duty of those at peace is towards belligerents*

1. On the other hand it is the duty of those who keep out of a war to do nothing whereby he who supports a wicked cause may be rendered more powerful, or whereby the movements of him who III. i. wages a just war may be hampered, according to what we have said above. In a doubtful matter, however, those at peace should show themselves impartial to either side in permitting transit, in furnishing supplies to troops,[1] and in not assisting those under siege. In I [xxxv]. Thucydides the Corcyreans say that it is the duty of the Athenians, if they wish to be impartial, either to prevent the Corinthians from hiring troops on Attic soil, or to allow them the same privilege. Philip, king of Macedon, was charged by the Romans with having violated his treaty in two ways, both in having done injury to the

[1] See the noble example in Paruta, Book VIII.

allies of the Roman people, and in having aided the enemy with soldiers and money.

The same points are stressed by Titus Quintius in a conference with Nabis: [Livy, XXXIV. xxxii. 14.]

> 'Still', you say, 'I have not, strictly speaking, done violence to you and your friendship and alliance.' How many times do you wish me to prove that you have done this? I do not wish to do so at greater length, and I shall sum up the gist of the matter. By what things, then, is friendship violated? In very truth by these [562] two things, by treating my allies as enemies, and by allying yourself with the enemy.

2. In Agathias we read that an enemy is one who does what the enemy wishes; and in Procopius, that he is counted in the ranks of the enemy[1] who supplies a hostile army with what is directly useful for war. Demosthenes long ago said: 'He who creates and devises the means whereby I may be captured is my enemy, even if he does not strike me nor hurl a javelin at me.' Marcus Acilius told the Epirotes, who had not supported Antiochus with troops, but were accused of having sent him money, that he did not know whether he should class them as enemies or those at peace. The praetor Lucius Aemilius censured the people of Teos for having aided the fleet of the enemy with supplies, and for having promised them wine; adding, that he would treat them as enemies unless they gave the same to the Roman fleet. And there is recorded a saying of Caesar Augustus: 'A state, which receives an enemy, loses the right of peace.' [III [IV. iv]. *Gothic War*, I [iii]. *Philippics*, III [ix. 17 = p. 115]. [Livy,] XXXVI [xxxv. 9]. XXXVII [xxviii. 2]. Plutarch, *Brutus* [v = p. 1011 D].]

3. It will even be of advantage to make a treaty with either party that is waging war, in order that it may be permissible to abstain from war while retaining the goodwill of either, and to render to each the common duties of humanity. We read in Livy: 'Let them desire peace with either side, as befits impartial friends; let them not intervene in the war.' Archidamus, king of Sparta, when he saw that the Eleans were leaning to the side of the Arcadians, wrote a letter containing only this: 'It is a good thing to remain quiet.' [XXXV [xlviii. 9]. [Plutarch, *Apoth.*, p. 219 A.]]

[1] On the other hand he rightly says that we must call ally and friend not only him who takes his post beside us in battle, but also him who openly supplies all the things necessary for waging war; this is in the letter of Amalasuntha to Justinian [Procopius, *Gothic War*, I. iii].

[564] CHAPTER XVIII

ON ACTS DONE BY INDIVIDUALS IN A PUBLIC WAR

I.—*The question whether it is permissible for individuals to do harm to a public enemy is discussed with special regard to the law of nature, the law of nations, and municipal law*

1. WHAT I have heretofore said applies chiefly to those who either possess the supreme command in war or are carrying out public orders. We must also consider what is permissible for an individual in war, not only according to natural and divine law, but also according to the law of nations.

[I. xi. 36.] In his first book *On Duties*, Cicero says that the son of the Censor Cato had served in the army of the general Pompilius, but that the legion in which he was serving was disbanded; nevertheless, since the youth from love of warfare remained in the army, Cato wrote to Pompilius that he ought to oblige the young man to take the military oath a second time, if he wished him to remain in the army. Cato gave as a reason that after the first oath had been cancelled his son could not lawfully fight with the enemy. Cicero adds the very words of Cato from a letter to his son, in which he warns the youth to avoid engaging in battle, for the reason that it is not right for one who is not a soldier to fight with an enemy.

Plutarch, *Roman Questions*, xxxix [= p. 273 F], and *Marcellus* [*Comp. of Pelopidas and Marcellus*, iii = p. 317 D]. *On Anger*, ix [I. x. 2]. III. vi.

Similarly we read that Chrysantas, a soldier of Cyrus, received praise because, in an attack on the enemy, he drew back his sword as soon as he heard the signal for retreat.[1] Also Seneca said: 'He who disregards the signal for retreat is called a worthless soldier.'

2. But those are deceived who think that the principle thus stated has its origin in the law of nations. This becomes clear if you consider that, just as any one is permitted to seize the property of an enemy, so also, as we have shown above, it is permissible to kill an enemy. For according to the law of nations enemies are held to be entitled to no consideration. The advice of Cato, therefore, comes from Roman military discipline, which, according to Modestinus, contained the provision that one who had not obeyed orders should be punished with death, even if what he had done turned out successfully. But one who had fought an enemy outside the ranks and without the command of the general was understood to have disobeyed orders, as the instructions of Manlius teach us. The reason is that, if such disobedience were rashly permitted, either the outposts might be abandoned or, with increase of lawlessness, the

Digest, XLIX. xvi. 3. § 15.

Livy, VII [VIII. vii. 22].

[1] See Xenophon, *Training of Cyrus* [IV. i. 2].

army or a part of it might even become involved in ill-considered battles,[1] a condition which ought absolutely to be avoided.

Consequently Sallust, describing the Roman discipline, says: 'In war punishment is more often inflicted on those who have fought against the enemy contrary to orders than against those who have withdrawn from battle too slowly when recalled.' A certain Spartan, who was on the point of slaying an enemy, heard the signal for retreat and held back his stroke, giving as the reason, 'It is in fact better to obey the commander than to kill an enemy.' The reason why a discharged soldier cannot kill an enemy is thus stated by Plutarch: he is not bound by the military laws, by which those who are going to fight ought to be bound. According to Arrian, Epictetus, referring to the deed of Chrysantas just mentioned, said: 'It seemed to him so much better to obey the will of his commander than his own.'

[*Catiline*, ix. 4.] [Plutarch, *Apoth.*, lxxi = p. 236 E.] [*Roman Questions*, xxxix = p. 273 E.] II. vi [15].

3. If, however, we regard the law of nature and moral justice, it is apparent [565] that in a lawful war any person is allowed to do whatever he trusts will be of advantage to the innocent party, provided he keeps within the proper limits of warfare; nevertheless he is not allowed to make captured property his own, because nothing is due to him, unless indeed he is enforcing a legal penalty according to the common law of mankind. From our previous discussion we can understand how this last right has been restricted by the law of the Gospel.

II. xvii [II. xx. 10].

4. Now, a command may be either general or particular. A general command is exemplified in the words which the consul was accustomed to utter in the presence of the Romans in case of an uprising: 'Let those who wish the safety of the state follow me.' Individual subjects, moreover, in addition to the right of self-protection, are sometimes given the right to kill in case this is to the advantage of the state.

Servius, *On the Aeneid*, VIII [line 1]. *Code*, III. xxvii. 1 and 2.

II.—*What in respect to the enemy is permitted by moral justice to those who are serving in the army, or fitting out ships, at their own expense*

1. A special command may be given not only to those who receive pay, but also to those who serve at their own charges; and —a more important consideration—to those who support a part of the war with their own expenditures, such as those who fit out and maintain ships at private cost. Such contributors, in lieu of pay, are generally allowed to hold captured property as their own, as we have said elsewhere. How far this practice may be extended without

III. vi [24].

[1] Thus Avidius Cassius gave, as a reason for the sentence he imposed, 'that there might have been an ambuscade'; so Vulcacius [*Avidius Cassius*, iv].

the violation of moral justice and love, is a proper question for discussion.

2. Justice has regard either for the enemy or for the state itself with which an agreement is made. We have said that possession of all things, which can support war, may be taken from the enemy for the sake of security, but under the condition of making restitution. Indeed absolute ownership may be acquired in compensation for that which is due to a state waging a lawful war, either from the beginning of the war or from a later act, whether the property belongs to the hostile state or to individuals, even though the individuals themselves be guiltless; the property of the guilty may be taken away and acquired by the captors as a means of imposing a penalty. Enemy goods will therefore become the property of those who are conducting at their own expense a part of the war, so far as this affects the enemy, provided that the limit which I have mentioned be not exceeded; whether the limit has been reached ought to be decided by a fair-minded judgement.

III.—*What in respect to their own state is lawful for those who are serving in the army, or fitting out ships, at their own expense*

As regards their own state the arrangement with such contributors will be just, according to the standard of moral justice, if there shall be equality in the contract, that is, if the expenses and dangers shall be as great as the chance of booty. For if the expectation of booty shall be much greater, whatever shall be acquired in excess ought to be restored to the state. The case is like that of a man who has bought at a very low price a cast of the net, which is, indeed, of uncertain value, but is easy to make and warrants the expectation of a great catch of fish.

IV.—*What the rule of Christian love demands of such persons*

Even when justice, strictly speaking, is not violated, one may sin against the duty which consists of loving others, especially the duty prescribed by the Christian law. A case of this character might arise if it should be apparent that plundering by such persons would not be especially harmful to the enemy as a whole, nor to the king, nor to those who are in fact guilty, but would harm innocent persons, and in fact to such an extent that it would plunge them into the greatest misfortunes, into which it would be the negation of mercy to cast those who are privately indebted to us. Now if to this is added the consideration that such plundering will have no notable effect in ending the war, or in weakening the public strength of the enemy, then gain acquired solely in consequence of the unhappy

Sylvester, word *bellum*, no. 8, verse 5.

condition of the times[1] ought to be considered unworthy of a just man, and especially of a Christian.

V.—*How a private war may be mingled with a public war*

Sometimes it happens that a private war arises in connexion with a public war; as, for example, if a person has fallen among enemies and his life or property is endangered. In such cases the rules should be observed which we have elsewhere stated in regard to the limit permissible in self-defence. II. i [3].

Public authority, again, is wont to be joined with private advantage; a case would be if a person who had suffered a great loss at the hands of the enemy [566] should obtain the right of collecting damage from the enemy's property. The right in that case must be defined in accordance with the principles stated above in regard to the taking of security. III. ii [2].

VI.—*The obligation resting upon a person, who has done harm to the enemy without orders, is set forth with a distinction*

But if a soldier or any other person, even in a just war, has burned houses belonging to the enemy, has devastated fields, and caused losses of this character without orders, when, furthermore, there was no necessity or just cause, the theologians rightly hold that he is bound to make good the losses. I am, however, justified in adding, what was omitted by them, 'when there was no just cause'; for if there is such a cause he will perhaps be answerable to his own state, whose laws he has transgressed, but not likewise to the enemy, to whom he has done no legal wrong. Sylvester, word *bellum*, pt. 1.

This is not unlike the reply made by a certain Carthaginian to the Romans who were demanding the surrender of Hannibal: [Livy, XXI. xviii. 6.]

> I consider that the question at issue is not whether Saguntum was attacked in accordance with a decision of an individual or of the state, but whether it was attacked rightfully or wrongfully. For the question whether our citizen acted in accordance with our decision, or his own, is our business, and to us belongs the punishment of a citizen of ours. The subject of discussion between you and us is merely, whether under our treaty the attack was permissible.

[1] Plutarch accuses Crassus also on this account [*Crassus*, ii=p. 543 B]: 'Most of this property he amassed through fire and war, taking advantage of the common misfortunes as his greatest means of gain.'

CHAPTER XIX

ON GOOD FAITH BETWEEN ENEMIES

I.—*Good faith is to be kept with enemies of every description*

1. WE have said that, in respect to character and extent, what is permissible in war is considered either absolutely or with reference to a previous promise. The first part of the subject has now been finished; there remains the latter part, which concerns the good faith of enemies with one another.

XXV [XIV. 169 ff.]. Silius Italicus, a Roman consul, has well said:

> [567] And best is he
> In military service, who from first to last
> Maintains good faith in wars.[1]

[iii. 5.] Xenophon in his oration *On Agesilaus* says: 'So great and excellent a thing it is in all men, to be sure, but especially in the case of generals, to be and to be considered respecters of good faith.'

[=p. 184 c.] In his fourth speech *On Leuctra* Aristides says: 'Those who are devoted to justice are especially revealed in the maintenance of peace and other public agreements.' As Cicero, in fact, rightly declared in [V. xxii. 63.] his *On Ends*, there is no one who does not approve and praise the quality of mind by which not only is no advantage sought but good faith is kept even to one's disadvantage.

[*Declamations*, cclxvii.] 2. Public faith, as Quintilian the father remarks, makes truces between armed foes and preserves the rights of states that have [cccxliii.] surrendered. In another passage the same author says: 'Good faith is the strongest bond in human affairs; good faith is held in [*On Duties*,] II. xxix [I. xxix. 140]. *Letters*, ccv [clxxxix. 6], *To Boniface*. sacred esteem between enemies.' Similarly Ambrose also: 'Therefore it is clear that even in war good faith and justice ought to be preserved.' Again, Augustine[2] declares: 'When faith is pledged, it must be kept even with an enemy against whom war is being waged.'

Those who are enemies do not in fact cease to be men. But all men who have attained to the use of reason are capable of posses-[V. xxvii. 6.] sing a right which has its origin in a promise. In Livy Camillus says that he had such an alliance with the Faliscans as nature had produced.

[1] According to Appian, *Civil Wars*, IV [IV. ix. 68], Archelaus the philosopher said: 'You have sworn to the treaties and have given the pledge of your right hands, which even enemies hold inviolate.' Diodorus Siculus, in the *Excerpta Peiresciana* [p. 342=XXXII. vii], praises Africanus the Younger on account of this virtue.

[2] He treats extensively of the same subject in *Letters*, ccxxv [cxxvi].

3. From the association of reason and speech arises that binding force of a promise with which we are dealing. Because we have previously said that, in the opinion of many, lying to an enemy is either permissible, or free from wrong, it must not be thought that this view can be extended with like reason to pledged faith. For the obligation to speak the truth comes from a cause which was valid before the war, and may, perhaps, in some degree, be removed by the war; but a promise in itself confers a new right. [III. i. 18.]

Aristotle recognized this distinction when, treating of veracity, he said: 'We are not speaking of the person who is truthful in agreements and in those matters which have to do with justice and injustice. For these belong to a different virtue.' *Nicomachean Ethics*, IV. xix [IV. xiii].

4. Of Philip of Macedon Pausanias says: 'No one would rightly call him a good general who habitually disregarded oaths, broke treaties at every opportunity, and dishonoured good faith more than all other men.' [VIII. vii. 5.] Valerius Maximus has this characterization of Hannibal: 'He declared war openly on the Roman people and Italy, but he waged war more bitterly against good faith herself, having delight in lies and deception as if in noble virtues. For this reason it has come to pass that, though otherwise he might have left the memory of a noble name, it is doubtful whether he ought to be considered an extraordinarily great or extraordinarily bad man.' [IX. vi. ext. 2.] According to Homer the Trojans, troubled in conscience, thus accuse themselves: *Iliad*, X [VII. 351 ff.].

Now breaking sacred pledges
And sworn good faith we fight; for us a crime is war.

II.—*Refutation of the view that faith ought not to be kept with pirates and tyrants*

1. Already in our previous discussion we have said that we ought not to accept the principles laid down by Cicero: 'We should have no relations with tyrants, but rather the most absolute separation'; again, 'A pirate [568] is not classed in the number of regular enemies; with him there is no bond of good faith, and he does not respect a common oath.' II. xiii. 15. [*On Duties*, III. vi. 32; xxix. 107.] Seneca, too, said of a tyrant: 'When the relationship of human rights was broken off, every bond, that bound him to me, was severed.' *On Benefits*, VII [xix. 8].

From such a source arose the error of Michael of Ephesus, who in his commentary on the *Nicomachean Ethics* said that the violation of the wife of a tyrant did not constitute adultery.[1] [V. x.] By a like error

[1] Seneca in the *Excerpts* [*Controversies*], IV. vii, says: 'Not thinking it adultery to debauch the wife of a tyrant, as it is not murder to kill a tyrant.' Julius Clarus in the section *Homicidium*, no. 56, believes that adultery could with impunity be committed with a banished woman.

certain teachers of the Jews [1] have made a similar statement about foreigners, whose marriages they considered void.

[Plutarch, *Pompey*, xxvii = p. 633.] 2. Nevertheless Gnaeus Pompey finished the war with the Pirates in great part by means of treaties,[2] promising to them their lives, and places in which they might live without plundering. Sometimes also tyrants have restored liberty after having agreed to immunity. In the [III. xix. 2.] third book of the *Civil War* Caesar writes that the Roman commanders made an agreement with the brigands and deserters who were in the Pyrenees mountains. Who will say that, if an agreement of any sort had been made, no obligation would have arisen from it?

Such agreements do not in fact share in that special community of legal obligations which the law of nations has introduced between enemies engaged in a formal and complete war. But because their authors are human beings they have a common share in the law of [III. xxv = p. 322.] nature, as Porphyry has rightly maintained in his work *On Abstaining from Animal Food*. From this follows the consequence that the [XXXVI. i.] agreements must be kept. Thus Diodorus relates that Lucullus kept faith with Apollonius, a leader of runaway slaves, and Dio writes that LVI [xliii]. Augustus, in order not to violate good faith, paid to the brigand Corocotta, who had delivered himself up, the reward placed on his head.

III.—*Answer to the argument drawn from the fact that such persons deserve punishment, and the proof that this is not taken into account when they have been treated with*

[Above, III. xix. 2, 1.] 1. But let us see if a more plausible view can be presented than that expressed by Cicero.

[II. xx. 8.] The first consideration is that, as we have elsewhere explained, if we take into account the law of nature, atrocious criminals, who do not belong to any state, can be punished by any person whatsoever. But those who can be punished with the loss of life can also be deprived *On Duties*, III [vi. 32]. of their property and rights, as the same Cicero rightly said: 'It is not contrary to nature to despoil, if you can, the person whom it is lawful to kill.' Among the rights of such a person is the right arising from a promise. This right, therefore, can also be taken from him as a penalty.

I answer that the reasoning would hold good if one had not treated with the person in question as a malefactor; but if at any time we have treated with such a person as such [3] we ought to consider

[1] Rabbi Levi Ben Gerson and Rabbi Salomon, *On Leviticus*, xx. 10.

[2] So there was disapproval of the faithlessness of Didius towards the Celtiberians, who lived by plunder [Appian, *Spanish Wars*, xvi. 100].

[3] Terence, *Adelphi* [II. i. 34 f.], says:

> I own I am a pander, a common bane of youths,
> A perjured wretch, a pest; yet you I have not wronged.

On this subject refer to the author, who has written on the terms of peace between the princes and orders of the [Holy Roman] Empire.

that we have been treating in regard to the remission of the punishment belonging to his condition. The fact is, as we have said elsewhere, that that explanation must always be assumed which prevents an act from becoming without effect. [II. xvi. 6.]

2. According to Livy, Nabis made an apt reply when Quintius Flamini[n]us reproached him with being a tyrant: 'As regards this title, I can reply that, whatever I am, I am the same that I was when you yourself, Titus Quintius, made the alliance with me.' Later he says: 'I had already done these deeds, whatever they are, when you made the alliance with me.' He adds: 'If I had changed in anything, then I ought to offer an explanation of my lack of consistency; but since you are changing, you ought to offer an explanation of your inconstancy.' [XXXIV. xxxi. 12, 13, 15.]

In an address of Pericles to his fellow-citizens, according to Thucydides, there is a passage of similar purport: 'We shall permit the allied states to be free, if they were so at the time when the treaty was made.' [I. cxliv.]

IV.—*The fact that a promise has been extorted through fear presents no obstacle, if the fear was not felt as a personal fear by him who made the promise*

Next, the objection, which I mentioned elsewhere, may be brought forward, that the person who has caused a promise to be made through fear is bound to free the promisor, for the reason that he has caused the loss unjustly; that is, by means of an action opposed to the nature both of human liberty and of an act which ought to be free. II. xxi [II. xi. 7].

Though we admit that this is sometimes the case, yet it does not cover all promises made to brigands. For in order that the person, to whom a promise has been made, should be bound to free [569] the promisor, it is necessary that he himself should have caused the promise by an unjust fear. If therefore any one has promised a ransom in order to release a friend from captivity, he will be bound to pay; for the fear did not affect the person who came of his own free will to make the agreement.

V.—*Or, if an oath has been given, the fact that a promise has been extorted through fear presents no obstacle, although in the case of a brigand such an oath is violated with impunity so far as men are concerned*

There is the further consideration that a person who has made a promise under the compulsion of an unjust fear can be obligated if the sanction of an oath has been added. For, as we have said elsewhere, a man is thereby bound not only to man but also to God, and in relation to Him fear makes no exception. Nevertheless it is true that the heir of the promisor is not held by such a bond alone, because, according to the primitive law of ownership, those things which belong to the commercial relations of life pass to the heir, but these do not include a right sought from God, as such.

III. iv. 10 [II. xiii. 15]. This, again, must be repeated from an earlier statement, that if any one violates a sworn or unsworn pledge given to a brigand he will not on that account be liable to punishment among other nations. For because of the hatred of brigands the nations have decided to overlook illegal acts committed against them.

VI.—*The same rules are applicable in relation to rebellious subjects*

What shall we say regarding wars of subjects against their kings and other sovereign authorities?

I. iv. That subjects do not have the right to employ force, even though they have a cause which in itself is not unjust, we have shown elsewhere. Sometimes even the injustice of their cause, or the baseness of their resistance, may be so great that they may be punished severely. Nevertheless, if they have been treated with as one would treat deserters or rebels, punishment cannot be inflicted contrary to a promise, as we have just stated.

Aelian, [*Various History*,] VI. vii [4]. XI [lxxxix]. In their scrupulousness the ancients held that faith must be kept even with slaves; in fact it was believed that the Lacedaemonians had drawn down upon themselves divine anger because they had killed the Taenarians, their slaves, contrary to agreement. Also Diodorus Siculus notes that the faith pledged to slaves at the shrine of the Palici had never been violated by any master. Moreover it will be possible to nullify here also the exception allowed in case a promise was made by reason of fear, if the promise has been confirmed by an oath; so the plebeian tribune, Marcus Pomponius,[1] kept the promise which had been made to Lucius Manlius under the influence of fear, because he was bound by an oath.

VII.—*The special difficulty presented by promises made to subjects under the right of eminent domain*

At this point, in addition to the difficulties previously met with, a special difficulty is presented by the right of passing laws and the right of eminent domain over the property of subjects; this right

[1] 'The tribune took the oath and did not practise deception, but gave to the assembly this reason for dropping the accusation [action]. No one else has been permitted to restrain a tribune with impunity'; Seneca, *On Benefits*, III. xxxvii.

belongs to the state, and is exercised in its name by the one who holds supreme authority. If in fact this right covers all the possessions of subjects, why does it not cover also the right arising from a promise in war? If this be conceded, it appears that all such agreements will be void, and therefore there will be no hope of ending a war excepting through victory.

But, on the contrary, we must note that recourse is had to the right of eminent domain, not indiscriminately, but only in so far as this is to the common advantage in a civil government, which, even when regal, is not despotic. But in most cases it is to the common advantage that such agreements be kept; and what we have said elsewhere about the preservation of the existing government applies here also. An additional point is that, when circumstances demand the enforcement of this right, compensation ought to be given, as will be explained later.

VIII.—*It is shown also that such promises may be confirmed by an oath of the state*

1. Moreover treaties may be sanctioned by an oath taken not only by a king or a senate, but also by the state itself. Thus Lycurgus made the Lacedaemonians take oath to his laws, and Solon the Athenians; and in order that the oath might not become invalid on account of the change of persons it was repeated annually. [Plutarch, *Lycurgus*, xxix = p. 57 E; *Solon*, xxv = p. 92 B.]

If such repetition is in fact kept up, there will be no necessity of withdrawal from the promise, even for the sake of the public advantage; for not only may a state yield its own right, but [570] words can be made so clear as to admit of no exception. Valerius Maximus thus addresses Athens: 'Read the law which holds you bound by oath.' This kind of laws, by which the Roman people was itself in conscience bound, as Cicero explains in the speech *For Balbus*, the Romans called 'sacred'.[1] [V. iii [ext. 3].] [xv. 35.]

2. A rather obscure discussion bearing upon this subject is found in the third book of Livy, where he says that in the opinion of many interpreters of the law the tribunes were inviolable, but not likewise the ediles, judges, and decemvirs; yet, if harm should be done to any of the latter, an unlawful act was committed. The reason for the distinction is that the ediles and the others were protected by the law alone; moreover, what the people had voted last prevailed, and so long as the effect of the law lasted no one could lawfully act in opposition to it. The tribunes, on the contrary, were protected by a public religious obligation of the Roman people; for an oath had been taken which could not be annulled by those [III. lv. 6–7.]

[1] See Manutius, *De Legibus*.

who had sworn it, without violating religious scruple. Dionysius of
[VI. lxxxix. 2.] Halicarnassus says: 'Brutus summoned an assembly and advised the citizens to make this magistracy inviolable, not only by law but also by an oath, and all so voted.' That is the reason why the law is called sacred.

In consequence good men disapproved of the act of Tiberius Gracchus[1] when he removed Octavius from the tribuneship, though he declared that the tribunician power received its inviolability from the people and not against the people. Therefore, as I have said, both a state and a king can be bound by an oath, even in the case of subjects.

IX.—*Or, promises are binding if a third person, to whom the promise is made, enters into the case*

But also a promise will be made with binding force to a third person, who has not inspired fear. We shall not investigate how or to what extent he may be interested in the promise; these are subtle distinctions belonging to the Roman law. By nature, in fact, it is
Livy, XXXIX [xxiii. 6]. important for all men to have regard for other men. Thus we read that by the peace made with the Romans Philip was deprived of the right of visiting cruelty upon those Macedonians who had revolted from him in war.[2]

X.—*How the political character of a state may be changed*

I. iii. 17 ff. Further, we have shown elsewhere that states of mixed character sometimes exist; and just as by agreement states may pass from one pure form into another, so they may pass also into a mixed form. Similarly those who had been subjects may begin to hold sovereign power, or at any rate some part of it, together with the free right to defend that part by force.

XI.—*Fear does not justify an exception in respect to a war that is formal according to the law of nations*

1. A formal war, that is a war publicly declared on both sides, has not only other characteristics in respect to legal right but also this characteristic in particular, that all promises made in the course of the war, or for the purpose of terminating it, are valid to the extent that they cannot be made void by reason of a fear unjustly inspired, except with the consent of the party to whom the promise has been made. For just as many other things, though they may not be devoid of

[1] See Plutarch, in his life [*Tiberius Gracchus*, xv–xvi = p. 831 D], for this story in full.
[2] There is a similar example in Paruta, Book VI.

fault in some degree, are considered lawful according to the law of nations, so also the fear which in such a war [1] is inspired on both sides.

Unless this rule had been adopted, no limit nor termination could have been fixed for such wars, which are extremely frequent. Yet it is to the interest of mankind that such bounds be set. This may be understood to be that law of war which Cicero says must be observed with an enemy. Elsewhere Cicero declared that an enemy retains rights in war, obviously referring not only to rights arising from the law of nature, but also to certain rights which have arisen from the general consent of nations. *On Duties*, III [xxix. 107]. *Against Verres*, IV [lv. 122].

2. From this nevertheless it does not follow that the party who has extorted some such promise by an unlawful war can retain what he has received without violating the honour and duty of a good man, or even can compel the other to hold to the agreement, whether sworn to or not. For essentially and in its [571] nature the transaction remains unjust. This essential injustice of the action cannot be removed except through a new and absolutely free consent.

XII.—*What is to be understood regarding such a fear as the law of nations recognizes*

But my statement that the fear inspired by a formally declared war is considered lawful ought to be understood of such a fear as is not disapproved by the law of nations.[2] For if anything has been extorted by the fear of rape, or by terrorizing of any other sort which involves violation of pledged faith, it will be nearer the truth to say that the case has been brought within the scope of the law of nature; the force of the law of nations does not extend to such a fear.

XIII.—*Faith must be kept even with the faithless*

1. I have previously said, in the general treatment of promises, that faith must be kept even with the faithless. Ambrose, too, holds the same opinion; he thinks that beyond question the maintenance of good faith should be extended even to treacherous enemies, such as the Carthaginians, with whom the Romans kept faith inviolably. On this point Valerius Maximus remarks: 'The Senate did not take into consideration those to whom the obligation was being discharged.' Sallust, again, says: 'In all the Punic wars, although the Carthaginians both in time of peace and in periods of truce had II. xiii. 16. [*On Duties*, I. xxix.] VI. vi [3]. [*Catiline*, li. 6.]

[1] See the writer as referred to above, on the treaty of peace.
[2] So a promise extorted from a captured ambassador is of no value to the one extorting it; Mariana, XXX [XXX. xii and xix].

committed many atrocious wrongs, the Romans themselves never took advantage of an opportunity to do such deeds.'

[*Spanish Wars*, x. 60.] 2. Of the treaty-breaking Lusitanians, whom Sergius Galba had deceived by a new treaty and then slaughtered, Appian says: 'In avenging perfidy with perfidy he imitated the barbarians in a manner inconsistent with the dignity of Rome.' On this charge the same Galba was afterward accused by the plebeian tribune Libo. VIII. ii [VIII. i. 2]. In giving an account of the matter, Valerius Maximus says: 'Pity and not justice ruled [1] that trial, since the acquittal, which could not have been granted to innocence, was given out of regard for his Cicero, *On the Oration*, I [*On the Orator*, I. liii. 228], and *Brutus* [xx. 80]. children.' Cato had written in the *Origins* that Galba 'would have been punished if he had not made use of his children and his tears'.

XIV.—*Faith does not have to be kept if the condition changes; and this takes place if the other does not keep his part of the agreement*

At the same time the fact should be recognized that in two ways one may be free from breach of faith and yet not do what was promised—if the condition ceases, and if compensation is given. The cessation of the condition does not in reality free the promisor, but the result shows that there is no obligation, since this was entered into only under the condition.

To this principle we must refer the case which arises if the other party has not fulfilled what he on his part was bound to carry out. For the individual items of one and the same agreement seem to be related in respect to the two sides after the manner of a condition, as if it had been stated in this way: I will do thus and so if the other [Livy, I. xxii. 7.] does what he has promised. Thus Tullus, replying to the Albans, 'calls the gods to witness, which of the two peoples first rejected and dismissed the envoys demanding restitution, in order that they may *Digest*, XVII. ii. 14. visit on that people all the losses of the war'. Ulpian says: 'He will not be liable as a partner who has renounced a partnership for the reason that a certain condition, on which the partnership was formed, is not complied with in relation to him.' For this reason, whenever the intent is different, it is usually expressly stated that if anything is done contrary to this or that provision the others nevertheless will remain valid.

XV.—*Faith does not have to be kept in case a just compensation is tendered in return*

I. vii. 2 [II. vii. 2]. The origin of compensation I indicated elsewhere,[2] when I said that if anything is ours or is due to us, and we cannot otherwise obtain

[1] *Texit* (covered) is a typographical error for *rexit* (ruled).

[2] II. vii. 2. Tertullian, *Scorpiace* [vi], says: 'No one should object to compensation, in which regard is had alike for favour and for injury.'

it from him who has it or owes it to us, we can accept an equivalent amount in something else. From this it follows the more clearly that we may keep what is in our possession, whether it be corporeal or incorporeal. Therefore what we have promised will not have to be fulfilled if the value involved is no greater than that of our property which is wrongfully in the possession of the other.

In the sixth book *On Benefits* Seneca says: [1]

> So a creditor often loses his suit to his debtor when on another account he has taken more than he tries to secure from the debt. For the judge sits between the creditor and the debtor to say, 'You have loaned him money; what then? . . . You have possession of a field which [572] you did not buy; after an adjustment of values, you, who came as a creditor, depart as a debtor.'

XVI.—*Faith does not have to be kept in case a just compensation is tendered in return, even if this is on another contract*

The same principle will hold if the party with whom I have dealings owes as much or more under another agreement, and I am not able otherwise to secure what is due to me. In the law courts, as the same Seneca says,[2] different actions are separated, and the causes of action are not mixed. But, as noted in the same passage, those cases are guarded by definite statutes which it is necessary to observe: a law must not be mixed with a law; we must go whither we are led. The law of nations does not recognize those distinctions; in the cases which fall within its scope there is no other hope of acquiring one's right.

XVII.—*Faith does not have to be kept in case damage has been done*

The same principle will have to be applied if the party who insists on the fulfilment of a promise has not carried out his part of the agreement, but has inflicted damage. In the passage just cited Seneca says: [3] 'A landowner who has trampled down the crop or cut down the trees of his tenant has no legal right over the tenant, even though the lease is uncancelled, not because he has received what had been agreed upon, but because he himself was the cause of his not receiving it.' Presently Seneca adds other examples: 'You have driven away his cattle and killed his slave.' And again: [4] 'It is permissible for me to compare how much each one has assisted me, how much he has injured me, and then to declare whether he is more indebted to me or I to him.'

[1] Seneca, *On Benefits*, VI. iv. 4. [2] *Ibid.*, vi, vii [v. 6, 7]. [3] *Ibid.*, iv. [4] *Ibid.*, vi.

XVIII.—*Furthermore, faith does not have to be kept when something is due as a penalty*

Finally, what is due as a penalty can be taken in lieu of what has been promised. This is explained at length in the passage already
[*On Benefits*, VI. v.] quoted: 'On the one hand favour is due for a benefit, on the other vengeance for an injury. Gratitude is not due to him from me, nor punishment to me from him; the indebtedness on both sides is cancelled.' Presently Seneca adds:[1] 'After a comparison has been made between the favours and the injuries, I shall see whether anything more is due to me.'

XIX.—*How these principles become applicable in war*

1. Just as in case an agreement has been made between contesting parties, while the suit is in progress, neither the action which gave rise to the suit, nor the losses and damages of the suit, can be used as an offset for what was promised, so, while a war lasts, compensation cannot be given for what originally caused the war, nor for what is customarily arranged in accordance with the laws of war among nations. For the nature of the business, that it be not void of effect, shows that the agreement was made without consideration of the controversies which led to the war. Otherwise, in fact, there would be no agreement which could not be lightly set aside.

To this conclusion I may not inaptly apply the observation of the same Seneca,[2] whom I have several times quoted: 'Our ancestors accepted no excuse, in order that men might know that good faith must by all means be preserved. It was in fact better that even a just excuse from a few should not be accepted, than that any sort of an excuse should be tried by all.'

2. What, then, can be used as an offset to that which was promised? Undoubtedly whatever the other party owes, even under the terms of another agreement entered into during the war; or, it may be reckoned as an offset if he has caused damage during a truce, or has failed to respect the inviolability of ambassadors, or has done anything else which the law of nations condemns between enemies.

3. Nevertheless the observation should be made that the adjustment is arranged between the same parties, and in such a way that the right of a third party is not infringed; yet so that the goods
II. ii [11]. of subjects, as we have said elsewhere, are held by the law of nations to be liable for the debt which the state owes.

4. We add this also, that it is characteristic of a noble mind to abide by treaties even after an injury has been suffered. For this

[1] *Ibid.*, vi.

[2] *Ibid.*, VII. xv [VII. xvi. 2].

reason the wise Hindu Iarchas praised the king who, although wronged by an allied neighbour, 'did not withdraw from his sworn pledge, saying that he had sworn in so holy a manner that he would not harm the other even after suffering wrong'. Philostratus, III. vi [*Life of Apollonius of Tyana*, III. xx].

5. Almost all the questions which are wont to arise concerning the faith accorded to an enemy can be settled if we follow the rules already laid down in our discussion not only of the force of promises II. xi ff. of all kinds, or of a special oath, or of a treaty and sponsions, but also of the rights and obligations of kings, and the interpretation of ambiguous statements. Nevertheless, in order that the application of the foregoing principles may be more plain, and that our discussion may be extended to cover whatever else is in dispute, [573] I shall not hesitate to touch on the special questions which are more common and which more generally demand attention.

[574] CHAPTER XX

ON THE GOOD FAITH OF STATES, BY WHICH WAR IS ENDED; ALSO ON THE WORKING OF PEACE TREATIES, ON DECISION BY LOT, ON COMBAT BY AGREEMENT; ON ARBITRATION, SURRENDER, HOSTAGES, AND PLEDGES

I.—*Division of good faith between enemies, according to the order of what follows*

[575] UNDERSTANDINGS between enemies rest upon a promise expressed or implied.

An express promise is either public or private. If public it is imputed either to the supreme authority or to subordinate powers. That which is imputed to the supreme authority either puts an end to war or maintains its force while the war lasts.

Among the factors which terminate a war some are looked upon as principal, others as accessory. Those are principal which themselves end the war by their own action, as treaties, or by the consent to refer to something else, such as the drawing of lots, the issue of combat, or the decision of an arbitrator. Of the last three the first rests on pure chance, while the other two combine chance with strength of mind or body, or with capacity of judgement.

II.—*In a monarchy the right to make peace belongs to the king*

See II. xv. 3.

Those who have the right of initiative in conducting a war have the right to enter into treaties for the purpose of ending it. Each, in fact, is the manager of his own affairs. From this it follows that in a war which is public on both sides the right to end it belongs to those who have the right to exercise supreme power. In a true monarchy, therefore, this will belong to the king,[1] provided also the king has unrestricted power.

III.—*What if the king is an infant, insane, a captive, or in exile?*

See I. iii. 24.

1. A king who is of such an age that he does not possess maturity of judgement (in some kingdoms such an age is defined by law, elsewhere it will have to be determined by a more probable estimate) or a feeble-minded king cannot make peace.

The same principle will apply to a king in captivity,[2] provided he possesses a kingly authority which had its origin in the consent

[1] Mariana, XXI. i.
[2] See Guicciardini, Books XVI and XVIII; more than a single reference.

of the people. It is, in fact, not credible that sovereignty was conferred by a people on such terms that it could be exercised by one who is not free. Therefore in this case also not the undivided sovereignty indeed,[1] but the exercise, and, as it were, the guardianship of it, will belong to the people, or to the one to whom the people has entrusted it.

2. Nevertheless, if a king even in captivity has pledged anything of his own private possessions, the pledge will be valid, in accordance with the principle set forth in what we shall state concerning private agreements.

But if a king shall be in exile,[2] will he be able to make peace? Surely so, if it be established that he is not living under constraint; otherwise his condition will differ too little from that of a captive, for there are captives also who are loosely guarded. Regulus refused to give his opinion in the senate, saying that he was not a senator so long as he was bound by an oath to the enemy. Cicero, *On Duties*, II [III. xxvii.100].

IV.—*In an aristocracy or a democracy the right of making peace belongs to the majority*

In accordance with what we have said elsewhere, in aristocratic or democratic governments the right of making treaties will belong to the majority; in the former case, the majority of the public council, in the latter, the majority of the citizens who according to custom have the right to vote. II. v. 17.

Accordingly, treaties so made will be binding even on those who have voted against them. Livy says: 'When a treaty has once been voted it will have to be defended as a good and advantageous treaty by all, even by those who were previously opposed to it.' Dionysius of Halicarnassus states the case thus: 'What the majority has voted must be obeyed.' Appian says: 'All, without admitting any excuse, are bound to obey the decree.' Says Pliny: 'All had to observe what the majority had approved.' Peace, moreover, is of advantage also to those whom it obligates, if they so wish. XXXII [xx. 6]. XI [lvi]. VI [Polybius, V. xlix. 7]. *Letters*, VI. xiii [4].

V.—*Now the sovereignty, or a part of the sovereignty, or the property of the realm may be validly alienated for the sake of peace* Vázquez, *Cont. Ill.*, I. iv, cites many, and v. See above, II. vi. 3 ff.

1. Let us now see what the things are which may be made subject of a treaty.

[1] Arumaeus in his *Discourses on the Golden Bull* says: 'Rudolph of the Palatinate had fled to England in fear, and Henry of Mayence had been expelled by force from Trèves; yet they did not lose their votes as Electors.'

[2] Lucan says [V. 28 f.]:

And while Camillus dwelt in Veii's walls,
There too was Rome.

See Chassanaeus in the *Catalogus Gloria Mundi*, pt. v, consid. 89 [49].

Kings, such as the majority now are, are not able to alienate by treaty either the whole sovereignty or a part of it, since they hold their royal authority not as a patrimony, but as if in usufruct. [576] Even before they receive the kingship, while the people are still superior to them, such acts can be rendered entirely void for the future by a public statute, so that they cannot give rise to any obligation in the king's interest. And it is to be believed that the people have so willed; for otherwise, if the act were binding on the contracting party to his interest, the goods of subjects might be taken for the king's debts, and it would follow that the provision against the alienation of the sovereignty would be in vain.

2. In order, therefore, that the undivided sovereignty may be transferred in a valid manner, the consent of the whole people is necessary. This may be effected by the representatives of the parts which are called the estates.

In order to validly alienate any part of the sovereignty there is need of a twofold consent, that of the whole body, and in particular the consent of that part of which the sovereignty is at stake, since without its consent it cannot be separated from the body to which it has belonged. Yet in case of extreme and in other respects unavoidable necessity the part itself will probably transfer the sovereignty over itself in a valid manner without the consent of the whole people, because it is to be believed that that power was reserved when the body politic was formed.

3. In patrimonial kingdoms, however, there is nothing to prevent a king from alienating his crown. Yet it may happen that such a king would not be able to alienate a part of the sovereignty, if indeed he has received the kingdom as his property on the condition of not dividing it. But the property described as royal may be included in the patrimony of the king in two ways, either separately, or indivisibly united with the kingdom itself. If included in the latter way, it may be transferred, but only with the transfer of the crown itself; if separately, it may be transferred separately.

II. xiii [II. vi. 13]. 4. But kings who do not hold their kingship in patrimony seem hardly to have been granted the right of alienating the property of the realm, unless this right plainly appears as arising from some early law, or has never been considered contrary to custom.

VI.—*How far the people, or his successors, are bound by a peace made by a king*

II. xiv. 10 ff. Vázquez, aforementioned, I. v, no. 9. We have elsewhere stated how far the people, and at the same time also the successors of the king, are bound by his promise, to wit: so far as the power of creating binding obligations was included in his sovereignty. This ought neither to be given unlimited range, nor to be confined within too narrow limits,[1] but ought to be so understood that what is based on good reason may be accepted as valid.

The case will plainly be different if a king is at the same time the absolute master of his subjects, and has received a sovereignty akin to that of a household rather than to that of a state. Such are kings who have reduced to slavery people conquered in war; or a king who does not indeed have ownership of persons but of their property, as Pharaoh in the land of Egypt, in consequence of purchase; and others, who have taken strangers into their private possession. For here the right added to the royal power establishes the validity of that which could not be maintained as valid by the right of the king alone.

Above, III. viii. 2.

VII.—*In arranging peace the property of subjects can be given up for the sake of the public advantage, but with the obligation of making good the loss*

1. This question also is frequently discussed: in the effort to secure peace, what conclusion regarding the property of subjects may be adopted by kings who have no other right over the property of their subjects [2] than that inhering in the royal power?

I have said elsewhere that the property of subjects belongs to the state under the right of eminent domain; in consequence the state, or he who represents the state, can use the property of subjects, and even destroy it or alienate it, not only in case of direct need, which grants even to private citizens a measure of right over others' property, but also for the sake of the public advantage; and to the public advantage those very persons who formed the body politic should be considered as desiring that private advantage should yield.

2. But, we must add, when this happens, the state is bound to make good at public expense the damage to those who lose their property; and to this public levy the person himself who suffered the loss will contribute, if there is need.

The state, furthermore, will not be relieved of this burden if perchance it is not equal to the payment at the time; but whenever the means shall be at hand the obligation will reassert itself as if merely held in suspense.

Vázquez, I. v [15]. Romanus, *Consilia*, 310. Sylvester, word *bellum*, I. 43.

[577] VIII.—*What in regard to property already lost in war?*

I do not admit without modification the statement of Fernando Vázquez, that the state ought not to take upon itself the loss already

Cont. Ill., III. iii. end [I. iv. end].

[1] See Reinkingk, Book I, class III, chap. v, no. 30 [I. v. iii. 19]. See also above, II. xiv. 7 and 12.
[2] Gail, II, obs. 57.

caused by a war, for the reason that the law of war permits such damages. For that law of war has reference to other peoples, as
III. vi. 2 and x. 5. I have explained elsewhere, and in part applies to the relationships of enemies but not to those of citizens with one another. Since citizens of a state are associates, it is right that they should share the common losses which are suffered by reason of their association.
Digest, XVII. ii. 52. § 4. Obviously, also, the municipal law may expressly provide that there shall be no right of action against the state for property lost in war, to the end that each individual shall defend his property with greater energy.

IX.—*No distinction is here made between property acquired under the law of nations and under the municipal law*

Some make a broad distinction between property which belongs to citizens by the law of nations and that which belongs to the same persons by municipal law; in consequence they grant to the king a more unrestricted right over property owned under the law of nations, even to the extent of taking it away without cause and without compensation, while they admit no such right in the case of property held by the law of nature.

This distinction is wholly erroneous, for ownership, no matter from what cause it has arisen, always has effects originating in the law of nature; consequently it cannot be taken away except as the result of causes which are inherent in ownership by its very nature, or arise from an act of the owner.

X.—*From the point of view of foreigners public advantage is presumed*

Now this doctrine, that the property of individuals should not be given up except for the public advantage, has reference to the king and his subjects, just as the other doctrine regarding compensation for loss has reference to the state and individuals. The act of the king is in fact sufficient for foreigners, who make agreements with him, not only by reason of the presumption established by the dignity of his person, but also in accordance with the law of
III. ii. nations, which permits the property of subjects to be made liable by the act of the king.

XI.—*General rule for the interpretation of peace covenants*

1. In the interpretation of peace covenants the observation
II. xv. 12 [II. xvi. 12]. should be made that, as we have previously stated, the more favourable a condition is, the more broadly it is to be construed, while the

further a condition is removed from a favourable point of view the more narrow is the construction to be placed upon it.

If we have in view the law of nature, the most favourable condition seems to rest on this principle, that each shall obtain what belongs to him, which the Greeks have expressed by *ἕκαστον ἔχειν τὰ ἑαυτοῦ*; hence the interpretation of ambiguous clauses ought to be directed to the end that the party who had a just cause of war should obtain that for which he took up arms, and should likewise recover for damages and costs, but that he should not also recover anything by way of penalty, for that would arouse more hatred.

2. Since, however, it is not customary for the parties to arrive at peace by a confession of wrong, in treaties that interpretation should be assumed which puts the parties as far as possible on an equality with regard to the justice of the war.

This is usually accomplished in one of two ways; either the possession of property, which has been disturbed by war, is adjusted in accordance with the former right of ownership[1] [*status quo ante bellum*], the expression used in the speech of Menippus where he discusses the different kinds of treaties; or, things remain as they are [*uti possidetis*], and this the Greeks call 'holding what they have'. Livy, XXXIV [lvii. 8].

XII.—*In doubtful cases it is believed that the understanding is that things remain as they are; how this ought to be interpreted*

1. Of the two ways mentioned, in case of doubt the presumption is in favour of the second, because it is easier and does not introduce a change. Hence the rule laid down by Tryphoninus, that in peace the right of postliminy applies only to those captives who have been expressly mentioned in the treaty, as we have stated above, where it was shown by sound arguments that Faber's emendation of the text was correct. So also deserters will not be surrendered unless that is in the agreement. For we receive deserters by the law of war;[2] that is, according to the law of war we are allowed to admit and enrol on our side the one who changes allegiance. Under such an agreement the other things remain in the hands of the possessor. *Digest*, XLIX. xv. 12. Above, III. ix [4]. *Dig.* XLI. i. 51.

2. In such cases, however, the word possession is understood not according to municipal law but according to the law of nature. For in wars the fact of possession suffices, and nothing else is considered. Moreover we have said that lands are so held if they have been enclosed by fortifications; for temporary possession, as in the Above, III. vi. 4. Decio, *Consilia*, III. lxxiv.

[1] See Paruta, Book V.

[2] See above, III. i. 22. In peace this agreement is generally made, that deserters shall not be received; see the peace of Justinian with Chosroes in Menander Protector [frag. 11, p. 10, edit. Dindorf].

case of a stationary camp, is here not to be taken into account. [578] In his speech for Ctesiphon Demosthenes says that Philip hastened to seize what places he could, knowing that, as matters stood, after the conclusion of peace he would retain what he held.

[*On the Crown*, xviii. 26 = p. 234.]

Incorporeal possessions are not retained except through the things to which they belong, as the servitudes of lands, or through the persons who possess them, provided that the rights do not run with land which formerly belonged to the enemy.

Above, III. vii. 4.

XIII.—*What if an agreement has been made, that all things are to be restored to the condition in which they were before the war?*

In the first kind of agreement, in which possession disturbed by the war is restored, we must note that the last possession, which existed before the war, is meant; nevertheless with the understanding that private persons who have been dispossessed may institute legal proceedings either by possessory action or by a claim for damages.

XIV.—*In such cases those who previously were free and of their own accord became subject to another are not restored*

But if any free people has of its own will yielded to one of the belligerents, restitution will not be applicable to it; for restitution applies only to those things which are accomplished by force, or fear, or in other ways through deceit permissible only against an enemy. So when peace was made among the Greeks the Thebans retained Plataea,[1] saying 'that they held that place not by force, nor by betrayal, but by the free choice of those to whom it belonged'. With equal right Nisaea remained in the possession of the Athenians. Titus Quinctius made use of the same distinction in relation to the Aetolians, saying 'That is the rule for captured cities; of their own accord the cities of Thessaly came under our sway'.

Livy, XXXIII [xiii. 12].

XV.—*In case of doubt damages caused by war are considered as remitted*

If no other agreement has been made, in every peace it ought to be considered settled that there shall be no liability on account of the damages which have been caused by the war. This is to be understood also as to damages suffered by private persons; for such damages also are the result of war. In case of doubt it is presumed that the belligerents intended to make such an agreement that neither would be condemned as guilty of injustice.

[1] This passage is from Thucydides, V [V. xvii]; a similar one had preceded in III [III. lii]: 'That Plataea ought not to be given back, since the men of that city had yielded of their own accord.'

XVI.—*The principle stated does not apply to what was owed to individuals before the war*

Nevertheless we ought not to consider that debts, which were owed to individuals at the outbreak of war, have been cancelled. For cancellations of debts are not obtained by the law of war, but their collection has only been hindered by the war. When, therefore, the hindrance has been removed, they retain their full force. Although we should consider that no one ought easily to be deprived of the rights which he possessed before the war (for, as Cicero rightly says, commonwealths and states were established especially on this account, that individuals might be secure in holding what belonged to them), yet this must be understood in the case of those rights which arise from the inequality of things.

Decio, *Cons.*, lxi.

On Duties, II [xxi. 73].

XVII.—*In case of doubt also punishments, which were publicly due before the war, are considered as remitted*

The same principle does not apply to the right to inflict punishment.[1] For this right, in so far as it concerns kings or peoples, ought to be considered as held in abeyance, from fear that the peace will not be a perfect peace if it leaves the old causes for war.

Wherefore acts not known will also here be included under the general terms, as the case of the Roman traders who, as Appian relates, were drowned by the Carthaginians without the knowledge of the Romans. Dionysius of Halicarnassus declares that the best reconciliations are those which do away with the anger and the remembrance of the injuries. In his *Plataic Oration* Isocrates says: 'In peace it is not fitting to follow up former wrongs.'

[*Punic Wars*, i. 5.]

[III. viii. 4.]

[xiv = p. 299 B.]

XVIII.—*What of the right of private persons to inflict punishments?*

As to the right of private persons to inflict punishment, the reason is not so strong for thinking that it should be held in abeyance, because it can be enforced through the courts without war. Nevertheless, since this right is not so clearly ours as that which arises from inequality, and punishments always cause hatred, a slight extension of the scope of the words will suffice to suggest that this right also may be understood to have been given up.

XIX.—*A right, which was publicly alleged before the war, but was in dispute, is easily understood to be in abeyance*

What I have said, that a right which existed before the war ought not easily to be considered annulled, should be firmly main-

[1] Gail, *De Arrestis*, chap. xiv, no. 7.

tained with respect to the rights of individuals; [579] but as to rights of kings and peoples it is easier to understand that some condonation has occurred, if only statements, or not improbable inferences, are in evidence. This is above all the case if the right in question was not clear, but had been in dispute. It is, in fact, the part of kindness to believe that the right was suffered to fall into abeyance in order that the seeds of war might be eradicated.

III [ix. 3]. The same Dionysius of Halicarnassus, whom I quoted above, says: 'We ought not so much to consider the renewing of our friendship for the present, as to take care that we may not be involved in war a second time; for we have come together for the purpose not of putting off the evils but of putting an end to them.' The latter part of this statement was taken almost word for word from the oration of Isocrates *On Peace*. [xxv = p. 164 c.]

XX.—*Things captured after the making of peace must be restored*

It is well established that things which have been captured after the conclusion of a treaty of peace must be restored. The right of war had, in fact, already expired.

XXI.—*Some rules bearing upon the agreement to restore things captured in war*

Alciati, *Responsa*, V. xvii. In treaties which deal with the restitution of things captured in war, first, those provisions which apply equally to both sides ought to be interpreted more broadly than those which are one-sided. Again, the provisions that are concerned with persons are construed more favourably than those that treat of things. Among provisions treating of things those that deal with land are construed more favourably than those dealing with movables, and those dealing with public property more favourably than those that treat of private property. Also among provisions treating of private possessions those which order the return of things possessed under a saleable title allow greater latitude than those possessed under a burdensome title, as property held under bills of sale or as dowry. Cicero, *On Duties*, II [xxiii. 81].

XXII.—*Regarding income*

A person to whom a grant of property is made on the conclusion of a peace is entitled to receive the income of it also from the time of the grant, but not before that time. This principle was rightly maintained by Caesar Augustus against Sextus Pompey who, after the Peloponnesus had been granted to him, at the same time claimed also the taxes which were due for the previous years. Appian, *Civil Wars*, V [ix. 77].

XXIII.—*On the names of regions*

The names of regions must be accepted according to the usage of the present time,[1] and according to the usage of experts rather than of the common people; for such matters are usually treated by experts.

XXIV.—*Concerning reference to a former treaty; and concerning him through whom the failure to perform has come*

The following rules also are of frequent application. As often as reference is made to a former or ancient treaty, the qualifications or conditions of the former agreement are in each case considered as repeated. Also the party, who was willing to do an act, must be considered as having done it, if he was hindered from doing it by the other party with whom the dispute occurred. Quintilian, *Declamations*, ccxlviii [cccxliii].

XXV.—*Concerning delay*

However, the statement of some writers, that delay for a brief period is excusable, is not true unless an unforeseen necessity has proved a hindrance.[2] It is, in fact, not strange that some canons favour the excusing of such delay, since it is their duty to influence Christians to that view which is consistent with love for one another. But in this investigation concerning the interpretation of treaties we are not now inquiring what is the better course nor what religion and honour demand of each, but to what limit the application of a principle, based wholly on that right, which we have called legal, can be carried.

XXVI.—*In case of doubt that interpretation should be adopted which is contrary to the interest of the party that made the terms*

In case the meaning is doubtful, an interpretation is preferably to be adopted contrary to the interest of him who dictated the conditions,[3] because ordinarily he belongs to the stronger party. Hannibal says that the dictation of the terms of peace belongs to the [Livy, XXX. xxx. 24.]

[1] See Guicciardini, Book V [on the contest for Capitanata between the French and Spaniards; the former insisted it was a part of the Abruzzi, the latter, of Apulia].

[2] See Albert of Strassburg.

[3] Plautus, *The Persian* [line 586]:

The merchandise is yours, so you must price it.

In a matter of this sort the one who is more powerful generally speaks first; but when terms are being sought the one who is weaker is wont to speak first. Plutarch, *Sulla* [xxiv=p. 467 C], says: 'It is their part to speak first who have need of peace; it is sufficient for the victor to be silent.'

man who grants peace and not to the one who asks for it. So likewise
Dig. II. xiv. 39. an interpretation is adopted against the seller; for he has himself to blame for not speaking more plainly.

The other party, however, could rightly accept, to his own advantage, a condition which admitted of several interpretations.
[*Nicomachean Ethics*, VIII. xv.] [580] This is in harmony with what Aristotle said: 'Where friendship exists for the sake of advantage, there the advantage of the one who receives is the measure of what is due.'

XXVII.—*Distinctions are drawn between furnishing a new cause for war and breaking a treaty*

Of daily occurrence is the discussion of the question, when should a treaty of peace be considered broken? This the Greeks call a 'breach of faith'. It is, in fact, not the same thing to furnish a new cause for war and to break a treaty; but there is a great difference as regards both the penalty incurred by the one at fault and the relieving of the innocent party from his pledge in other matters.

A treaty of peace is broken in three ways: by acting either contrary to what is involved in every peace, or against what was expressly stated in the treaty of peace, or against what ought to be understood from the nature of every peace.

XXVIII.—*How a treaty of peace may be broken by acting contrary to what is contained in every peace*

A violation of what is involved in every peace will take place if a warlike attack is made, especially when no new cause is presented. If the fact can be alleged with probability, it is better to believe that the wrong was committed without faithlessness than with it.
[I. cxxiii.] This statement of Thucydides hardly needs mention: 'Not those who ward off force with force break the peace, but those who are the first to make the attack.'[1]

Having established this point, we must see by whom, and against whom, the armed attack which breaks the peace is made.

[1] See Ammianus Marcellinus, beginning of Book XXIX [XXIX. i. 3]. He speaks thus of the Romans: 'Intentionally retreating, that they might not be the first to do hurt to any one of the enemy with the sword and be judged guilty of having broken the treaty, they joined combat only under the stress of absolute necessity.'

According to Procopius, *Persian War*, Book II [II. iii=p. 94 B], the Armenians said in their speech to Chosroes: 'They do not destroy peace who are first in arms, but they who, in time of peace, are first detected plotting against the others.' In the same author, *Vandalic War*, Book II [II. xi= p. 259 C], the Moors say: [590] 'They do not break treaties of peace who have been oppressed by injuries and after making complaint openly transfer their allegiance to others, but they who do violence to those that wish to live as allies. If under such conditions any take their possessions and go over to the other side, they do not make God their enemy; but those do who seize the property of others and force the owners into the perils of war.'

XXIX.—*What if allies have made an attack?*

I see that there are some who think that if those, who have been allies, make such an attack, the treaty of peace is broken. And I do not deny that an agreement can be made on such terms, not, to be sure, that one people should be subject to punishment for another's act, but that peace should not seem to have been finally made, but should remain subject to a condition depending partly on intention, partly on chance.

We ought not, however, to believe that a peace has been made in this way, unless the fact is perfectly clear. Such an arrangement is irregular, and not in harmony with the common desire of those who are making peace. Therefore those who made the attack without the aid of others will be responsible for breaking the treaty, and the right to wage war will exist against them and not against the others. In opposition to this view the Thebans formerly spoke against the allies of the Spartans. Pausanias, IX [i. 5].

XXX.—*What if subjects have so acted? How their action should be considered as approved*

If subjects do anything by armed attack without public orders, it will be necessary to see whether the act of individuals can be said to have been publicly approved.

From what we have said above, it can easily be understood that to show public approval three requisites are necessary: knowledge of the act, power to punish, and neglect to punish. Knowledge is shown by the fact that the acts are manifest, or have been made subject of complaint. Power is assumed, unless the lack of it is apparent. Neglect is evidenced by the expiration of the period of time ordinarily taken for the punishment of crimes in each state. Such neglect is equivalent to a decree; and in this sense the statement of Agrippa in Josephus should be taken, 'that the king of the Parthians would consider the peace broken if his subjects should take up arms against the Romans'. II. xxi. 2 ff. [*Jewish War*, II. xvi. 4.]

XXXI.—*What if subjects should engage in warfare under the command of others?*

The question is frequently raised, whether the rule just given holds if subjects do not take up arms on their own account but serve under others who are carrying on war. Certainly according to Livy the people of Caere, in offering an excuse for themselves, say that their citizens did not serve with the public consent. Also the Rhodians had the same defence. VII [xx. 5]. Gellius, VII. iii [VI. iii. 5].

It is nearer the truth to consider that such service ought not to be permitted, unless it is made apparent, by plausible arguments, that a different point of view has been adopted. This sometimes happens now in accordance with the ancient example of the Aetolians,
XVII [iv. 5]. who held it right to take plunder from a plunderer.[1] Polybius[2] says that the force of this custom was that, though they were not themselves at war, but others, their friends or allies, were warring, it was nevertheless [581] lawful for Aetolians without a public decree[3] to serve on both sides and to take plunder from both. Of
[XXXII. xxxiv. 5.] the same people Livy says: 'They permit their young men to serve against their own allies, omitting merely the public authorization; and often opposing armies have Aetolian auxiliary troops on both
Livy, V [xvii. 9]. sides. Formerly the Etruscans, though refusing aid to the Veientes, did not hinder any of their youth from going as volunteers to that war.'

XXXII.—*What if harm has been done to subjects? Herein a distinction is made*

1. Again, a treaty of peace ought to be considered broken, not only if an armed attack is made on the whole body of the state, but also if such an attack is made on its subjects, of course without a new cause. For peace is made in order that all subjects may be safe. Peace, in fact, is an act of the state on behalf of the whole body and on behalf of its parts. Even more, if a new cause arises, by the peace it will be permissible for them to defend themselves
Digest, XLIII. xvi. 1. § 17. and their property. For, as Cassius says, it is natural to repel arms with arms. Consequently among equals it is not to be thought easy to give up this right. But it is not permissible to punish, or to recover stolen property, by force, except after judgement has been refused; for these matters admit of delay, while self-defence does not.

2. But if subjects commit wrongs so continuously,[4] and in a manner so contrary to the law of nature, as to warrant the belief that they are acting wholly without the approval of their rulers, and if they cannot be brought into court, as in the case of pirates, it will be lawful both to recover property from them and to take vengeance on them, as if on persons who had been surrendered to us. But it is in truth contrary to the conditions of peace on that account to attack others who are innocent.

[1] Plautus, *Truculentus* [line 567]:

Plunder from plunder I take.

[2] See the same author in the *Excerpta* [*Excerpta de Virtutibus et Vitiis*, 6=IV. iii. 1–2].

[3] Agathias, Book IV [IV. xiii], tells the same of the Sabirian Huns in his own time.

[4] So Augustus decided on behalf of Herod against Syllaeus; Josephus, [*Antiquities of the Jews*,] XVI. xvi [XVI. x. 8].

XXXIII.—*What if harm has been done to allies? Herein likewise a distinction is made*

1. Also an armed attack made upon allies breaks a treaty of peace,[1] but only an attack upon those allies who have been included in the terms of peace, as I showed in examining the controversy over Saguntum. On this principle the Corinthians insisted in the speech which is found in the sixth book of Xenophon's *Affairs of Greece*: 'We have all taken oath to all of you.' II. xvi. 13. [VI. v. 37.]

Further, if the allies themselves have not made the compact, but others for them, the same rule will nevertheless have to be applied, after it is fully settled that those allies have ratified the treaty of peace. For so long as it is still uncertain whether they wish to ratify it they are to be considered as enemies.

2. The case is different with other allies, such as those united by ties of blood and marriage, who are neither subjects nor named in the treaty of peace. Yet it does not follow, as I have said above, that war cannot be undertaken on that account, but it will be a war from a new cause. Caepolla, *Consilia*, dcxc. Deciò, *Consilia*, dxxxi.

XXXIV.—*How a treaty of peace may be broken by acting contrary to what has been stated in the peace terms*

As I have said, a treaty of peace is broken also by acting contrary to what has been stated in the peace terms. Under action, moreover, is included the failure to do what one should, and when one should.

XXXV.—*Whether a discrimination ought to be made between the articles of the treaty of peace*

I shall not here admit a differentiation of the terms of peace into those that are of greater and those that are of less importance. For everything that has been included in the treaty of peace ought to seem important enough to be kept. Goodness, nevertheless, and especially Christian goodness, will more easily pardon lighter faults, especially if repentance is added, so that the following is in point: Seneca, *Agamemnon* [243].

Who sin regrets, is almost innocent.

But in order that peace may be still more securely safeguarded it will be wise to add to the topics of minor importance[2] the provision that the treaty of peace is not to be broken by anything done in violation of these, or that arbitration should be tried before it is permissible to take up arms, as was provided, according to Thucydides, in the Peloponnesian treaty. See above, II. xv. 15. VII [V. lxxix].

[1] De Thou, Book LXV, year 1578. There is also something pertaining to this in Haraeus, in his history of Brabant, vol. II, for the year 1556.

[2] See an excellent example in the peace treaty of Justinian, between Justinian and Chosroes. Menander Protector has it [frag. 11, p. 10, edit. Dindorf].

XXXVI.—*What if a penalty has been added?*

And I am fully of the opinion that this seems to have been the intention, if any special penalty [582] has been added;[1] not because I do not know that a contract can be so made that the one, to whom the injury has been done, may have a choice, whether he prefers the penalty or withdrawal from the agreement, but because the nature of the business requires what I have said. This principle indeed is agreed upon, and has both been stated by us above and approved by the authority of history, that a treaty of peace is not broken by the party who fails to stand by it after the other has broken it; for he was only bound conditionally.

III. xix. 13–14.

XXXVII.—*What if necessity has hindered fulfilment?*

But if necessity is the cause why one party has not fulfilled his promise, as, for example, if the thing has been destroyed or lost, or the act rendered impossible by some chance, the treaty of peace will not be considered as broken; for, as I have said, a treaty is usually not dependent on a chance condition. But the other party will have his choice, whether he prefers to wait, if there is any hope that the promise may be carried out later, or to receive an equivalent in estimated value, or to be freed from mutual engagements corresponding with that item or of equal value.

XXXVIII.—*Peace continues, if the one injured so desires*

See above, III. xix [13 ff.].

Certainly even after a broken agreement it is within the power of the injured party to preserve peace, as Scipio did after many treacherous acts of the Carthaginians; no one frees himself from an obligation by acting contrary to it. And if the provision has been added, that the treaty of peace should be considered broken by such an act, this provision ought to be considered as added merely for the benefit of the innocent party, in case he wishes to take advantage of it.

XXXIX.—*How peace may be broken by acting contrary to what belongs to the special nature of every peace*

Lastly we said that a treaty of peace is broken by doing what is contrary to the special nature of the peace.

XL.—*What falls under the term friendship?*

1. Accordingly, acts that are contrary to friendship break a treaty of peace which was entered into under the terms of friendship.

[1] As in the treaty of the Goths with the Franks; see Procopius, *Gothic War*, I [I. xii=p. 342 B].

For whatever the duty of friendship by itself demands of other men ought by the right of the agreement to be performed in such a case as this also. To treaties of friendship (since Pomponius teaches us that there is also a kind of treaty not made for the sake of friendship), and not to every kind of treaty, I refer many matters arising out of injuries inflicted without force of arms, and insults, which are frequently discussed by legal experts; and to such treaties I refer the statement of Cicero: 'If any wrong has been committed after a return to friendly relations, it should be thought not due to neglect but a violation, and imputed not to imprudence but to faithlessness.' But in such cases also the motive of ill-will should as far as possible be eliminated from the act.

Digest, XLIX, xv. 5.

For Gabinius [see Jerome, *Apology against Ruf.*, I. i].

2. Consequently, if a wrong has been done to a person intimately connected with the party with whom the peace was made, or to a subject, it will not be considered as done to the party himself unless the wrong was done openly as an affront to him.

This principle of natural justice is followed by the Roman laws in cases of cruelty in the treatment of slaves. Adultery, also, and violation of chastity, will be referred rather to lust than to rupture of friendly relations, and the seizure of another's property will make the aggressor guilty of a new act of greed rather than of the breaking of faith.

Digest, XLVII. x. 15 § 35. *Inst.*, IV. iv. § 3. Alexander, *Consilia*, II, no. 3.

3. When no new cause is presented, threats that are truly savage are inconsistent with friendly relations. To this head I shall refer also the building of fortresses on the boundaries, not for defence but for the purpose of inflicting harm; and an unwonted levying of troops, if it shall be apparent, from satisfactory indications, that these are being levied against no one else than the party with whom the peace has been made.

XLI.—*Whether it is contrary to friendship to receive subjects and exiles*

1. It is not contrary to friendship to admit individual subjects [1] who wish to migrate from one government to another. Such liberty in fact, as I have said elsewhere, is not only natural but also advantageous.

II. v. 24.

[1] Solon says [Plutarch, *Solon*, xxiv=p. 91 F]: 'He did not allow any strangers to be enrolled in the list of citizens except those who had been banished for ever from their own country, or had moved to Athens with their entire household in order to practise some trade.' According to Appian, *Selections on Embassies*, no. xxv [=*Macedonian Affairs*, xi. 6], Perseus said: 'I have done this in accordance with the common right of mankind, as you also receive those who have been expelled from other places.' This common right is usually confirmed and strengthened by treaties.

See the peace of Antiochus in Polybius, *Selections on Embassies*, no. xxxv [=XXI. xlii. 18], and in Livy [XXXVIII. xxxviii]; the peace between the Romans and Persians in Menander Protector [frag. 11, p. 10, edit. Dindorf]; and Simler concerning the treaties among the Swiss. Strabo, Book XVI [XVI. ii. 14], bears witness: 'While the kings of Syria were fighting with each other, the Aradians obtained the right to admit fugitives, but not to permit their departure.'

Under the same principle I include the granting of asylum to exiles. For over exiles the state has no right, as I have noted elsewhere, quoting Euripides. In Livy Perseus rightly inquires: 'What is accomplished by sending any one into exile, if there is not going to be a place anywhere for the person exiled?' In the second speech *On Leuctra*, Aristides says: [583] 'It is a common right of mankind to admit exiles.'

[II. v. 25.] XLII [xli. 7]. [i=p. 105 c.]

2. As I have said elsewhere,[1] it is clearly not permissible to admit towns or large aggregations, which constitute an integral part of a state. It is equally unpermissible to admit those who, by reason of an oath or in some other way, are under an obligation of service or of slavery. Moreover we have previously stated that among certain peoples the same rule has been introduced by the law of nations concerning those who are slaves by fortune of war. But also we have treated elsewhere of the surrender of those who, though not driven into exile, are seeking to escape a justly deserved penalty.

[III. vii. 8.] II. xxi. 3 ff.

XLII.—*How war may be ended by drawing lots*

The result of a war cannot in all cases be made subject to the chance of drawing lots, but only in those cases in which the issue is one over which we have full power. For the obligation of the state to protect the life, chastity, and other rights of its subjects, and of the king to protect the welfare of the state, is too great to permit the disregard of those considerations which stand in the most natural relation to the defence of themselves and others. Nevertheless, if on a careful estimate the party attacked in an unjust war is so far inferior that there is no hope of resistance, it is apparent that a decision by lot can be offered, in order that a certain peril may be avoided by recourse to an uncertain one. This, in fact, is the least of the evils.

XLIII.—*How war may be ended by a set combat; and whether this is lawful*

1. There follows a much disputed question concerning combats which are agreed upon with definite numbers, for the sake of ending a war; such combats, for example, with one on each side, as that of Aeneas and Turnus, or Menelaus and Paris; with two on each side, as that between the Aetolians and the Eleans; with three on each side, as that between the Horatii, who were Romans, and the Curatii, who were Albans; or with thirty on each side, as that between the Lacedaemonians and the Argives.

Pausanias, V [iv. 2]. [Livy, I. xxiv.] [Stobaeus, *Florilegium*, vii. 67.]

[1] II. v. 24. See also Bizarri, Book XII.

2. If we consider only the law of nations, in a strict sense, there should be no doubt that, according to it alone, such contests are lawful; for this law permits the killing of enemies without distinction. If, again, the opinion of the ancient Greeks and Romans, and of other nations, were true, that each man is the master of his own life without restriction, then such combats would not lack moral justice also. But I have already several times said that this opinion is in conflict with true reason and the precepts of God. Elsewhere I have shown, both by reason and by the authority of the Sacred Writings, that whoever kills a man on account of things which we can do without sins against the law of love for his neighbour.

II. xix. 5 and xxi. 1 [xxi. 11]. II. i. 12 ff.

3. Let us now add that a man sins also against himself, and against God, who values so cheaply the life which was granted to him by God as a great favour. If the issue at stake, such as the safety of many innocent persons, is worthy of war, we must strive with all our strength to win. To use a set combat as an evidence of a good cause, or as an instrument of divine judgement, is unmeaning, and inconsistent with the true sense of duty.

Thomas, II. ii. qu. 95, art. 8, and Cajetan thereon.

4. There is only one condition which can render such a combat just and patriotic, from the point of view of one side merely; that is, if otherwise the expectation is in all respects warranted that the party supporting the unjust cause is going to be the victor with great slaughter of innocent persons. He, in fact, should be subject to no censure who prefers to fight in the way that will give to him the greatest probability of success. But this also is true, that some acts, which are not done rightly, are not approved as right by others, but are held permissible for the avoidance of more serious evils which cannot otherwise be escaped; as in many places base usurers and prostitutes are tolerated.

Cajetan, as cited above.

5. Therefore, as I previously said, when it is a question of avoiding war, if two persons, who are striving for the sovereignty, have prepared to contend with arms against each other, the people can allow such a combat in order that a greater calamity, otherwise imminent, may be avoided; so the same thing will have to be said when it is a question of ending a war. Thus [584] Cyrus challenged the Assyrian king;[1] and, according to Dionysius of Halicarnassus, Mettius said that it would not have been an unfair thing for the leaders themselves of the peoples[2] to decide the question

II. xxiii [10].

Aegidius Regius, disp. 32, dub. 2, no. 18.

[Xen., *On the Training of Cyrus*, V. iii. 5.]

III [xii. 3].

[1] Long before that time Hyllus challenged Eurystheus. See Euripides, *Children of Hercules* [800 ff.].

[2] Such is the reply which the inhabitants of Adrianople made to Mahomet, referring to him and to Musa Zeleb; Leunclavius, Book XI. So Cunibert, king of the Lombards, challenges Alachis; Paul Warnefrid, V [V. xl]. Thus Pharnacus wished to fight with the leader of the Sauromatae for the fortress of Cherso, in order that the populace might not be subjected to peril on account of their dispute, as Constantine Porphyrogenitus relates in the chapter on the fortress Cherso [*De Administrando Imperio*, liii, p. 150].

See Pontanus, *Danish History* [Book V, p. 151], for an example of a single combat [591]

by fighting with each other, if the contest had been for their own power or rank and not for that of their peoples. So we read that the Emperor Heraclius[1] fought in single combat with Chosroes, the son of the Persian king.

XLIV.—*Whether the act of kings in such cases binds their peoples*

On the other hand, those who thus refer a controversy to the outcome of a combat can indeed deprive themselves of whatever right they themselves possess, but in those kingdoms which are not patrimonial they cannot also give a right to another who does not possess it. In such cases, therefore, in order that a treaty may be valid, it is necessary to add the consent both of the people and of those persons, already born, who have the right to the succession. In fiefs which are not free the consent of the lord or seigneur of the fief also is required.

XLV.—*In such combats who is to be judged the victor?*

1. Often in such combats the question is raised, which of the two should be considered the victor.[2] Only those can be considered vanquished on whose side all have either fallen or taken to flight.
III [ii. 3]. So, according to Livy, withdrawal to one's own territory or towns is a sign of defeat.[3]

2. In three famous historians, Herodotus, Thucydides, and Polybius, three disputes about victory are presented, and of these the first refers to a set combat. But if any one views the evidence correctly he will find that in all these contests the parties separated
Herodotus, I [lxxxii]. without a true victory. For the Argives were not put to flight by Othryades, but had gone away at the coming of night, thinking that they were victors, and intending to report the victory to their people.
Thucydides, I [li and liv]. Neither had the Corcyraeans put to flight the Corinthians, who, after having fought successfully, had perceived a strong Athenian fleet and had gone away in good order without making any test of strength with the Athenians. Philip of Macedon had indeed captured a ship belonging to Attalus, after it had been deserted by its men, but he had completely failed to put the fleet to flight; and so, as
XVI [i]. Polybius remarks, he conducted himself, rather than considered himself, as a victor.

for the kingdom. See also what the historians relate concerning the challenges between the Emperor Charles V and Francis I, king of France.

[1] See Aimoin, IV. xxi, and Fredegarius, lxiv.

[2] Ennius [frag. 330, in Servius, *On the Aeneid,* XI. 307]:

> Who conquers is not victor, if the vanquished owns it not.

See Scaliger on the words of Festus, *herbam do.*

[3] And in Guicciardini, Book II.

3. The other evidences—the collecting of spoils, the giving up of dead for burial,[1] and challenging to battle a second time, which in the passage cited and in Livy you sometimes find mentioned as signs of victory—prove nothing in themselves, excepting in so far as, in connexion with other signs, they bear witness to the flight of the enemy. Surely in case of doubt the one who has retired from the field of battle may be presumed to have fled. When, however, there are no sure proofs of victory, the issue remains in the same condition as before the battle, and must be referred either to battle or to new agreements. XXIX and XL.

XLVI.—*How war may be ended by arbitration; and here arbitration is understood to be without appeal*

1. Proculus teaches us that there are two kinds of arbitrators. One is of such a sort that we ought to render obedience, whether he is just or unjust; and this kind of arbitration, he says, is found when the parties resort to an arbitrator under mutual promises to abide by his decision. The other deals with matters of such a kind that they ought to be referred to the decision of a just man; and of this type we have an example in the reply of Celsus: 'If a freedman', he says, 'has sworn to give as many services as the patron has judged proper, the decision of the patron will not be valid, unless the freedman has thought it fair.' *Digest*, XVII. ii. 76. *Digest*, XXXVIII. i. 30.

While it was possible for this interpretation of an oath to be introduced by the Roman law, it is not in harmony with the simple meaning of the words viewed by themselves. Nevertheless this remains true, that an arbitrator can be chosen in either of two ways. Either he is charged with the task of reconciliation only, as we read that the Athenians were when selected as arbitrators between the Rhodians and Demetrius; or he serves as one whose decision must be absolutely obeyed. It is the latter class with which we are here dealing, and of which we said something above, when we spoke of the methods of avoiding war. II. xxii [II. xxiii. 8].

2. Although municipal law may make provision for arbitrators to whom resort is had under promises on both sides, [585] and in some places has provided that it shall be lawful to appeal from them and to make complaint of injustice, nevertheless such a procedure cannot become applicable in relation to kings and peoples.[2]

[1] Plutarch, *Agesilaus* [xix=p. 606 B], says: 'But after the enemy had sent to ask permission to bury their dead he granted it, and having in that manner obtained a testimony of victory he went away to Delphi.' Likewise in the *Nicias* [vi=p. 527 AB]: 'And yet according to established and accepted custom those who had received permission to bury their dead were thought to have given up all claim to the victory, and those who had obtained such a request did not have the right to set up a trophy.'

[2] Mariana, XXIX. xv; Bembo, IV [fol. 62]. There are many examples of peace made by arbitration in Kromer's *Poland*, Books X, XVI, XVIII, XXI, XXIV, XXVII, XXVIII. There is one also in the second book of the *Danish History* by Pontanus. Cf. also above, II. xxiii. 18 [II. xxiii. 8].

For here there is no higher power, which can either hold fast or loosen the bond of the promise. Under such conditions, therefore, the decision of arbitrators, whether just or unjust, must stand absolutely, so that one may rightly apply here the saying of Pliny: 'Each makes the man whom he chooses the supreme judge of his case.' It is, in fact, one thing to make inquiry concerning the duty of the arbitrator, and another to inquire concerning the obligation of those who promise.

Natural History, preface [19].

XLVII.—*In case of doubt it is understood that arbitrators are bound to decide according to law*

1. In respect to the duty of an arbitrator, the point must be considered, whether he has been chosen in the place of a judge, or with somewhat larger powers. Seneca seems to think the latter characteristic of an arbitrator, when he says:

On Benefits, II. vii [III. vii. 5].

> The condition of a good case seems to be better if it is referred to a judge rather than to an arbitrator; for the rules of law apply to the former and set certain limits, which he may not pass. In the case of the arbitrator, a religious scrupulousness, free and unchecked by restraints, can both take away and add to, and direct the decision not as the law or justice advises, but as humanity and pity move.

Rhetoric, I. xix [I. xiii. 19].

Aristotle also says that 'it is the part of a fair and kindly man to prefer to have recourse to an arbitrator rather than to go to law'; and he adds as the reason, 'For the arbitrator has regard to what is fair, but the judge follows the law. Indeed the arbitrator was brought into existence for this very purpose, that equity might prevail.'

2. In the passage just quoted equity does not properly mean, as elsewhere, that division of justice which interprets more narrowly the general import of law according to the intention of the lawgiver, for such interpretation has been committed to the judge also; rather it means everything which is better done than left undone, even outside of the rules of justice properly so called.

Such arbitrators, however, as are common between private persons and citizens of the same country are especially recommended also to Christians by the Apostle Paul (*1 Corinthians*, vi). Yet in a case of doubt it ought not to be understood that so great power has been granted; in doubtful cases, in fact, we follow the narrowest interpretation. But this statement is especially in point in respect to those who hold sovereign power; for since they have no common judge, we must consider that they have restricted the arbitrator by those rules by which the office of a judge is usually restricted.

XLVIII.—*Arbitrators ought not to decide concerning possession*

Nevertheless this observation should be made, that arbitrators chosen by peoples or by sovereigns [1] ought to render a decision regarding the main point at issue, but not in regard to possession. For decisions regarding possessions belong to municipal law; by the law of nations the right of possession follows ownership. Consequently, while the case is under advisement, no change ought to be made, not only to avoid prejudice, but also because recovery is difficult. In his account of those who served as arbitrators between Carthage and Masinissa, Livy says: 'The commissioners made no change in the right of possession.' [XL. xvii. 6.]

XLIX.—*What is the force of surrender pure and simple?*

1. The acceptance of an arbitrator is of a different sort when any one entrusts the decision regarding himself to an enemy; for this is pure surrender, which makes the one who surrenders a subject, and confers the sovereign power on him to whom the surrender is made. The Greeks call this 'yielding the power over oneself'. So we read that the Aetolians were asked in the senate, whether they would leave the decision regarding themselves to the Roman people. According to Appian the advice of Publius Cornelius Lentulus in regard to the Carthaginian state at the end of the Second Punic war was as follows: Livy, XXXVII [xlix. 4]. XIV [Appian, *Punic Wars*, XIV. ix. 64].

> Let the Carthaginians entrust themselves to our decision, as conquered peoples are accustomed to do, and as many have done heretofore. We shall then look into the matter, and if we shall have granted anything to them they will be grateful to us; [586] for they will not be able to call it a treaty.
>
> That, furthermore, makes a very great difference. So long as we make treaties with them they will always be finding pretexts, as if wronged in respect to some point of the treaty, in order that they may break it. For openings for controversy always remained, since many points are of doubtful interpretation. But when we have taken away their arms from them as having surrendered, and have brought their very persons under our power, then at length they will understand that they have nothing that is their own; then they will lose heart, and whatever they may have received from us they will gladly accept as if bestowed from another's bounty.

2. But here we ought also to distinguish what the conquered ought to endure; again, what the victor can do lawfully, what even in conformity with the full discharge of duty, and finally, what it is most fitting for him to do.

After the surrender there is nothing that the vanquished may not have to suffer. He is, in truth, already a subject; and, if we consider only the strictly legal rights of war, he is in such a position that

[1] The Duke of Savoy said this in the contest about Saluzzo. See de Serres [or rather, his continuator] on Henry IV.

everything can be taken from him—his life, his personal liberty, and the property not only of the state but also of individuals.

XXXVII [vii. 1]. In another passage Livy says: 'The Aetolians, having surrendered at discretion, were afraid that vengeance would be wreaked III. viii. 4. upon their persons.' Elsewhere I have cited the following: 'When all things have been surrendered to him who is the more powerful in arms, it is for the victor to judge, and to decide, what he wishes the conquered to have, what he wishes them to give up by way of VI, 11 [XXVIII. xxxiv. 7]. punishment.' The following statement of Livy bears upon the same point:

> It was an ancient custom of the Romans not to assume sovereignty over a people as conquered—a people with which they were not united in friendship either by treaty or by common laws—until all things, divine and human, had been surrendered, hostages had been accepted, arms taken away, and garrisons placed in the cities.

III. xi. 18 [16]. Also we have shown that the putting to death of those who had surrendered was sometimes lawful.

L.—*What is the duty of the victor toward those who make an unconditional surrender?*

1. But in order that the victor may not do anything unjustly he ought first to see to it that he kill no one, unless this fate is deserved by the prisoner's own act; again, that he take nothing from any one except as a lawful penalty. Moreover within this limit,[1] so far as one's own safety allows, it is always the part of honour to incline to clemency and generosity; sometimes, in consideration of the circumstances, such a course is even made necessary by the rule of custom.

III. xv. 12. 2. As I have said elsewhere, wars are well ended when they XIII [xxi. 6]. terminate with pardoning. According to Diodorus, Nicolaus of Syracuse says: 'They surrendered themselves with their arms, relying on the clemency of the victor. Therefore it would be shameful for them to be deceived in their expectation of humane treatment [XIII. xxiii. 5.] on our part.' Afterward he adds: 'Who of the Greeks ever thought that those ought to be punished relentlessly who entrusted themselves to the clemency of the victor?'

[*Civil Wars*, V. v. 45.] In Appian Octavius Caesar, addressing Lucius Antony, who had come in order to surrender, says:

> If you had come to make a treaty, you would have found me both a conqueror and a man incensed by wrong-doing. Now, since you yield yourself, your friends, and your army to my decision, you take away my anger, you take away also that power which you would have been forced to yield to me in a treaty. For now I am obliged to take into

[1] See the famous example of Ferdinand, king of Leon, in Mariana, XI. xv. Also recall what I have said above, III. xi. 14–15.

account, along with what you ought to suffer, also a second consideration, what it is right for me to do; and I shall give preference to the latter.

3. In the Roman histories the expression 'to surrender oneself to the good faith', or 'to surrender oneself to the good faith and clemency', is often found. So in Livy, Book XXXVII: 'In a kindly [ix. 7.] manner he listened to the embassies from neighbouring peoples surrendering their states to his good faith.' Also in Book XLIV, [iv. 7.] where the narrative concerns [587] King Perseus, we read: 'Since Paulus was insisting that he should surrender himself and his possessions to the good faith and clemency of the Roman people.' Still the fact should be recognized that by these words nothing else is understood than absolute surrender; and the word translated good faith [1] in these passages does not suggest anything else than the probity of the victor, to which the vanquished commits himself.

4. In Polybius and Livy there is a famous story [2] about Phanaeas, the ambassador of the Aetolians, who in his speech to the consul Manius yielded as far as to say: 'Therefore the Aetolians have resolved to surrender themselves and their possessions', as Livy states, 'to the good faith of the Roman people.' In response to a question of the consul, he affirmed this a second time; then the consul demanded that certain persons who had stirred up the war should be surrendered to him without delay. Phanaeas took exception to this and said: 'We have surrendered ourselves to your good faith, and not to slavery,' adding that what was ordered was not consistent with Greek custom. The consul replied that he did not care what the custom of the Greeks was; that according to Roman custom he had power over those who had surrendered to his discretion; and he gave orders that the ambassadors be put in chains. In the Greek author is the question: 'Are you here discussing duty and propriety, when you have already surrendered yourselves to our good faith?' [Livy, XXXVI [xxviii. 1.]]

From these words it is clear with how great impunity, and without violating the law of nations, he can act to whose good faith a people has surrendered. Yet the Roman consul did not take advantage of this power, but both dismissed the ambassadors and gave to the council of the Aetolians an opportunity of deliberating anew.

Similarly the Romans are said to have replied to the Faliscans, that they had been given to understand that the Faliscans had surrendered themselves not to the power, but to the good faith of the [Valerius Maximus, VI. iv [VI. v. 1].]

[1] Polybius says [*Selections on Embassies*, xiii=XX. ix]: 'Among the Romans the same force is found in the expressions "to entrust oneself to another's faith" and "to give to the victor unrestricted power of deciding concerning oneself".'

The Greeks say, 'to surrender themselves to justice', as in Thucydides, Book III [III. lxvii], or 'to yield the power over themselves', as in Diodorus Siculus, Book XIV [XIV. cxi].

[2] *Selections on Embassies*, no. xiii [=XX. x].

Livy, VIII [ii. 13]. Romans. We read also of the Campanians, that they had come into the good faith of the Romans not by treaty, but by surrender.

5. You would, in truth, not ineptly apply to the duty of him to whom a surrender has been made this passage of Seneca: *On Clemency*, II. vii [4]. 'Clemency possesses unlimited right of decision. It judges not according to the letter of the law, but according to what is just and good; and it may acquit, or assign a penalty as great as it will.' And I do not think that it makes any difference whether the one who surrenders says that he surrenders himself to the wisdom, or to the moderation, or to the mercifulness of the victor. All these words are merely gracious expressions. The fact remains, that the victor becomes absolute master.

LI.—*Concerning conditional surrender*

Nevertheless there are also conditional surrenders. These either safeguard the interests of individuals, that the safety of their lives, or the freedom of their persons, or even certain property may be reserved; or they make provision for the whole body of the people. Such surrenders in some cases may even introduce a sort of mixed I. iii. 17. sovereignty, as I have explained elsewhere.

LII.—*Who can, and should, be given as hostages?*

Hostages and pledges are accessories of treaties. I have said that hostages are given[1] either of their own will, or by him who holds the power and authority. For in the supreme civil authority is included the right over the acts as well as over the property of the subjects. But the state or its ruler will be obligated to compensate the person who suffers, or his relatives, for the inconvenience.

If there should be several persons, and it should make no difference to the state which of these should go as a hostage, it seems clear that pains should be taken to have the choice settled by lot.

The lord of a fief does not possess the right to select a vassal as a hostage unless the vassal is also a subject. For the fealty and duty, which the vassal owes, do not go so far.

LIII.—*What the right over hostages is*

I have said that according to the strict law of nations a hostage can be put to death; but that is not also in accord with moral justice, unless there is a fault on the part of the hostage meriting such punishment. Hostages, moreover, do not become slaves. Furthermore, by the law of nations they can both hold property and leave it to their

[1] In this work, III. iv. 14; see also III. xi. 18.

heirs; although the Roman law provided that their property should go to the state treasury. *Digest,* XLIX. xiv. 31.

LIV.—*Whether a hostage may lawfully escape*

Is the question raised whether a hostage may lawfully make his escape? It is agreed that he may not, if [588] at the beginning, or afterward, he gave a pledge, in order that he might have more liberty. Under other conditions it seems to have been the intention of the state not to bind its citizen not to try to escape, but to give to the enemy the power to guard him as it might wish.

Thus the deed of Cloelia can be defended. But, although she had not herself done wrong, yet the state could not receive and retain the hostage.[1] So Porsenna said: 'If the hostage is not surrendered, the treaty will be considered as broken'; then we read: 'The Romans restored the pledge of peace in accordance with the treaty.' Livy, II [xiii. 6 ff.].

LV.—*Whether a hostage may be lawfully detained for any other reason*

The obligation arising from the use of hostages, moreover, is distasteful, not only because it infringes liberty, but also because it arises from the act of another. Consequently, a narrow interpretation is here in point. Hence it follows that hostages given on one account cannot be detained on another. This is to be understood as applying in case some other promise has been made without the addition of hostages.

If, however, good faith has already been violated in another matter, or a debt contracted, the hostage can then be retained, not as a hostage, but in accordance with the law of nations, according to which subjects can be detained 'by reprisal' (κατ' ἀνδροληψίαν) on account of an act of their rulers. Nevertheless provision may be made that this should not happen, by adding an agreement regarding the return of the hostages when the matter on account of which they were given has been closed up. See above, I, v. III [III. ii. 3].

LVI.—*A hostage is set free at the death of the one for whom he came as hostage*

One who has been given as a hostage, merely to take the place of a captive or hostage, is set free at the death of the latter. For Ulpian says that at the moment the latter dies the right of pledge

[1] See Plutarch, *Publicola* [xix = p. 107 A] on this matter. To the verse of Virgil [*Aeneid,* VIII. 651]:

And Cloelia broke her bonds and swam,

Servius adds, 'bonds of the treaty'.

Digest, XLIX. xv. 15. is destroyed, as in the case of a ransomed captive. Therefore, as in Ulpian's inquiry the ransom, which was to take the place of the person, is not due, so here the person who was made the substitute of another will not remain bound.

Syrian Wars [viii. 47]. Thus according to Appian Demetrius not unjustly demanded that he be released by the Roman senate, since he had been given as a hostage in the place of Antiochus, and Antiochus had died. XXXIV [iii. 6]. Justin, following Trogus, says: 'Demetrius, a hostage at Rome, having learned of the death of his brother Antiochus, came before the senate saying[1] 'that he had come as a hostage when his brother was living, but, now that his brother was dead, he did not know for whom he was a hostage.'

LVII.—*Whether a hostage may be retained after the death of the king who gave him*

The decision whether a hostage may still be held after the death of the king who made the treaty is dependent on the question treated II. xvi. 18 [II. xvi. 16]. by us elsewhere, whether the treaty should be considered personal or real. For accessories cannot cause us to withdraw from the rule in the interpretation of the main articles, the nature of which the accessories themselves ought to follow.

LVIII.—*Sometimes hostages are under obligation as principals, and one is not bound for the act of the other*

It should be added, in passing, that sometimes hostages are not mere accessories to the obligation, but are in fact the principal party. This would be the case, for example, when any one has promised under contract to perform an act not his own, and because he is bound for the resulting damage, if the act is not performed, his II. xv. 18 [II. xv. 16]. hostages are bound in his place; and I have said elsewhere that this seems to have been the decision regarding the Caudine treaty-Alberico Gentili, *De Iure Belli,* II. xix. compact. On the other hand the opinion of those who hold that hostages without their consent can be mutually bound for each other's acts is not only severe but also unjust.

LIX.—*Of what sort is the obligation arising from pledges of property?*

Pledges of property have certain points in common with hostages, and certain points peculiar to themselves. It is a characteristic common to both, that they are retained even on account of another debt, unless faith has been pledged to the contrary. It is a characteristic peculiar to pledges of property that an agreement made

[1] This word needs to be restored in the text to make the sentence grammatical.

concerning them is not taken as strictly as one concerning hostages. For the matter is not equally distasteful, since things are made to be held, but men are not.

LX.—*When the right of redemption is lost*

This also I have mentioned elsewhere, that no length of time can bring it about that a pledge of property should not be redeemable, if that is performed for which the pledge was given. For an act, which has an old and familiar cause, is not supposed to arise from a new cause. Thus the patience of the debtor should be ascribed to the old contract, and not to the abandonment of ownership, [589] unless inferences that are warranted suggest another interpretation; as if a person, prevented at the time when he wished to redeem a pledge, had allowed the matter to pass without mention for so long a time that it might warrant the presumption of consent. II. iv. 17 [II. iv. 15].

[592] CHAPTER XXI

ON GOOD FAITH DURING WAR; HEREIN ALSO CONCERNING A TRUCE, THE RIGHT OF SAFE-CONDUCT, AND THE RANSOM OF PRISONERS

I.—*What a truce is, and whether this interval is to be considered as peace or war*

1. EVEN during a war the sovereign authorities are accustomed to grant certain rights, which, with Virgil and Tacitus, I may call 'intercourse of war', or with Homer, 'solemn agreements'. Among these are included the truce, the right of safe-conduct, and the ransom of prisoners.

[*Aeneid*, X. 532.] *Annals*, XIV [xxxiii], and *Histories*, III [lxxxi]. [*Iliad*, XXII. 261.] [VIII. i. 4.]

A truce is an agreement by which warlike acts are for a time abstained from, though the state of war continues. I say, 'though the state of war continues', for, as Cicero says in the eighth *Philippic*, there is no middle ground between war and peace. War, furthermore, is the name of a condition which can exist even when it does not carry forward its operations.

Nic. Eth., [I. iii;] VIII [vi].

Aristotle says: 'It may happen that a man may be endowed with virtue, and either sleep or pass his life in inactivity.' Elsewhere the same author says: 'Distance between places does not destroy friendship, but hinders the exercise of it.' Andronicus of Rhodes remarks: 'An accomplishment may so exist that it accomplishes nothing.' Eustratius comments thus on the sixth book of the *Nicomachean Ethics*: 'Skill considered in relation to power simply is spoken of as potentiality; but if compared with the action itself or its exercise it is called a power, as the surveyor's art in a sleeping surveyor.'

[*On Nic. Eth.*, I. xiv.] [VI. i.]

Horace, *Satires*, I. iii [129–32].

Just as Hermogenes, though silent,[1] yet remains
A singer and the best of players; and Alphene,
Sly fellow, when his tools of trade were cast
Aside, and closed his shop, was still a cobbler.[2]

[I. xxv. 4.] [ix.]

2. In like manner, then, as Gellius also says: 'A truce is not peace, for, though [593] fighting ceases, the war continues.' Also in the *Panegyric* of Latinus Pacatus we read: 'A truce suspends the acts of war.' This I say that we may know that, if an agreement has been made which is to be valid in time of war, this will be valid also in a truce, unless it is clearly apparent that the agreement applies not to the state of war but to its acts.

[1] [599] Seneca, *On Benefits*, V. xxi [IV. xxi. 4]: 'He is even eloquent who is silent.'

[2] In the passage just cited, Seneca says: 'He also is an artisan who is not supplied with the tools for practising his trade.'

On the contrary, if anything has been said in regard to peace, this will not be applicable in time of truce; although Virgil spoke of a truce as a mediatress of peace, and Servius, on the same passage, as a temporary peace. So the Scholiast on Thucydides calls a truce 'an ephemeral peace in travail of war'; and Varro, a respite of military operations, lasting a few days. All these are not definitions but descriptions, and that, too, figurative. In the same class also is the characterization of Varro, when he called a truce the vacation of war; he might likewise have called it a slumber of war. Thus Papinius Statius called the holidays, which were free from lawsuits, peace. Aristotle called sleep the chain of the senses, and following his example you may rightly call a truce a chain of war.

[*Aeneid*, XI. 133.] [I. xl.] [Aulus Gellius, I. xxv. 1.] [*Silvae*, IV. iv. 40.] [*On Sleep and Vigil*, i, iii.]

3. Gellius rightly criticizes the explanation of Marcus Varro, which Donatus also follows, because Varro added the words 'lasting for a few days'; he shows that truces are frequently given also for hours, and I may add likewise for twenty, thirty, forty, and even for one hundred years. There are examples of such truces in Livy, and they disprove the following definition of Paul the jurist also: 'A truce exists when, for a brief period and for the present time, an agreement is made that the two sides refrain from attacking each other.'

I. xxi [I. xxv]. *On Terence's Eunuch*, I. i. [line 60]. *Digest*, XLIX. xv. 19. § 1.

4. Nevertheless, if it shall be apparent that the sole and only determining cause of an agreement was the cessation of warlike acts, it may happen that what has been said of a time of peace will in that case apply during the truce, not from the force of the word, but from a sure inference as to the intention, regarding which we have spoken elsewhere.

III. xvi. 20 [II. xvi. 20].

II.—*The derivation of the word*

Moreover, it seems clear that the word *induciae* (truce) is not, as Gellius thinks, derived from *inde uti iam* (then as now); nor from *endoitu*, that is, *introgressu* (an entering in), as Opilius proposes, but [from *inde otium*] because *inde*, that is, 'from a certain time', there may be *otium* (rest), just as the Greeks call a truce ἐκεχειρία (a holding of hands).

It is, in fact, apparent, even from Gellius and Opilius, that the ancients wrote this word with the letter *t* and not *c*; and, though now used as a plural, it was formerly without doubt also a singular. The old spelling was *indoitia*, for then they pronounced *otium* as *oitium*, from the verb *oiti*, which we now spell *uti*, just as from *poina* (now written *poena*) *punio* [1] is derived, and from *Poinus* (now *Poenus*) *Punicus* comes.

Gellius, XIX. viii [13].

[1] See Servius, *On the Aeneid*, X [X. 24], on the word *moerorum*.

Just as from the plural *ostia*, *ostiorum* has been derived the singular *Ostia*, *Ostiae*,[1] so from *indoitia*, *indoitiorum* has come *indoitia*, *indoitiae*; hence *indutia*, the plural of which, as I have said, is now in use. Formerly, as Gellius notes, it was also used in the singular number. Donatus was not far out of the way when he wished to explain *induciae* from the fact that a truce furnished a rest for some days.

XIX. viii. *On Terence's Eunuch* [line 60].

A truce, then, is a period of rest in war, not a peace. And so the historians use the term properly in saying, as they frequently do, that a peace was refused, a truce was granted.

Livy [X. xlvi. 14], Plutarch, Justin.

III.—*A new declaration of war after a truce is not necessary*

In consequence, after a truce there will be no need of a new declaration of war. For when the temporary obstacle is removed the state of war, which was not dead but sleeping, asserts itself, just as the right of ownership and the power of the father assert themselves in a man who has recovered from insanity.

Angelus, *On Dig.*, II. xiv. 27. § 1. Martinus Laudensis, [*De Bello*,] qu. 29.

Nevertheless, we read in Livy that, in accordance with the decision of the treaty priests, war was declared upon the termination of a truce. The fact is, however, that the ancient Romans wished by those unnecessary precautions to show how much they loved peace, and how just the causes were by which they were drawn into war. This is implied by Livy himself:

IV [xxx. 14].

> They had fought recently near Nomentum and Fidenae with the Veientes. [594] A truce, not a peace, had been made, the limit of which had expired, but before that date of expiration the Veientes had again taken up arms. Nevertheless heralds were sent, but when on oath they demanded restitution, in the manner of our ancestors, their words were not listened to.

IV.—*How the period of time fixed for a truce ought to be reckoned*

1. The duration of a truce is commonly made either a continuous period, as for one hundred days, or with the designation of a fixed limit, as up to the first of March. In the former case the calculation must be made exact to the minute. This, in fact, is in accord with nature; for the reckoning of time by civil days arises from the laws and customs of peoples. In the other case doubt is generally raised, whether the day, the month, or the year, which has been fixed for the duration of the truce, should be understood as reckoned inclusively or exclusively.

Dig. L. xvi. 134.

2. By nature, at any rate, there are two kinds of boundaries, one within the thing, as the skin is the boundary of the body, and

[1] And *ostrea, ostreae,* was formed from *ostrea, ostreorum.*

the second outside of the thing, as a river is the boundary of a country. Boundaries which are fixed according to choice can be established by both methods. But it seems more natural that the boundary, which is a part of the thing,[1] should be assumed. Aristotle says: 'That is called the boundary which is the extreme part of each thing.' *Metaphysics*, V. xvii [IV. xvii].

Such an assumption, furthermore, is not inconsistent with practice. 'If any one has said that something will happen before the day of his death, that day also, on which he has died, is counted.' *Dig.* L. xvi. 133. Spurina warned Caesar of a danger which would not be delayed after the fifteenth of March. When accosted on the fifteenth, he said that the day had come, but had not yet passed.[2] Suetonius, *Caesar*, v [lxxxi]. This interpretation, then, is all the more to be adopted when the extension of time contains an advantage in itself, as in the case of a truce, which spares human bloodshed.

3. But the day 'from' which a certain measure of time is said to begin will not be included in the measure, for the force of that preposition is to separate, not to unite.

V.—*When a truce begins to be binding*

Incidentally I may add this, that a truce, and everything else of the kind, is binding on the contracting parties immediately after the agreement is completed. The subjects on both sides, however, begin to be bound as soon as the truce has taken the form of a law, and this requires some sort of publication abroad. As soon as the publication has been made, it begins to have a binding force on the subjects. Nevertheless, if the publication has been made in one place only, that force does not manifest itself at the same moment throughout the whole area under governmental control, but only after a sufficient time for carrying the news to the different places. Therefore if in the meantime subjects have done anything contrary to the truce, while they will not be liable to punishment, the contracting parties will, nevertheless, be bound to make good the loss.[3] Bartolus, *On Dig.*, I. i. 9, Panorm., *On Decretals*, I. ii. 2 (?), and thereon, Felinus, no. 7.

VI.—*What is lawful during a truce*

1. What is lawful, what is not lawful in a period of truce, may be understood from the very definition. For all acts of war are unlawful, whether against persons or against property, that is, what-

[1] Baldus, *De Statutis*, on the word *usque*; Bartolus, *On Digest*, XXXII. iii. 35, and *On Digest*, I. ix. 12. Archidiaconus, *On Decretum*, II. xiii. 1. 1; Hieronymus de Monte, in his book *De Finibus*, chap. xxiii.

[2] Dio Cassius [XLIV. xviii] quotes the saying: 'It is here, but has not yet passed.' Appian [*Civil Wars*, II. xxi. 149]: 'The Ides are here, but have not yet passed.'

[3] As in the case of Scion in Thucydides, IV [IV. cxxii]. Therefore what Mariana (XXVIII. vii) relates was done by the Spaniards in Italy cannot be defended.

ever is done by force against the enemy. In a period of truce, in fact, all such acts are contrary to the law of nations; it was thus, according to Livy, that Lucius Aemilius explained the matter in a speech to his soldiers. [XL. xxvii. 9.]

2. Even property of the enemy, which has come into our hands by chance, will have to be restored, although it had been ours before. For as regards the legal right, according to which such matters have to be judged, the property in question has become theirs.

[*Digest*, XLIX. xv. 19. § 1.] This is what Paul the jurist had in mind when he said that in a time of truce the right of postliminy does not exist; for postliminy requires, as antecedent, the right of capture in war, but this right does not exist in a truce.

3. On both sides it is lawful to go and to return, but with such equipment only as does not suggest peril. This was noted by Servius on the verse of Virgil,[1]

> And with impunity the Latins mingled.

There Servius also relates that when Rome was besieged by Tarquin a truce was made between Porsenna and the Romans; and during the celebration of the Circensian games in the city [595] the leaders of the enemy entered and contended in the chariot race, and were crowned as victors.

VII.—*Whether during a truce it is lawful to retreat and repair walls, and the like*

It is not inconsistent with a truce to withdraw with the army further inland, as we read in Livy that Philip did. Again, a truce does not prevent the rebuilding of walls, nor the enrolment of soldiers, unless some special agreement has been made.[2]

XXXI [xxxviii. 10]. Frontinus, [*Strategemata*,] II. xiii [8].

VIII.—*A distinction regarding the seizure of places in time of truce*

1. Without doubt it is a violation of a truce to bribe garrisons of the enemy and seize places which they were holding. Such an acquisition, in fact, cannot be lawful except by right of war. The same principle must be applied in case subjects wish to revolt to the enemy. There is an example in Livy, Book XLII: [XLII. xlvi. 9.]

> The people of Corona and Haliartus, who had a kind of natural predilection for kings, sent envoys into Macedonia asking for a garrison with which they might be able to defend themselves against the unrestrained arrogance of the Thebans. To this embassy the king made answer, that he could not send a garrison to them on account of his truce with the Romans.

[1] Servius, *On the Aeneid*, XI [XI. 134].

[2] As in Paruta, Book III.

According to Thucydides, Brasidas in time of truce received the city of Mende, which revolted from Athens to Sparta; but the excuse is added, that he in turn had charges to make against the Athenians. [IV. cxxiii.]

2. It is indeed lawful to take possession of ownerless property, provided this has been really abandoned, that is, with the intention that it should no longer belong to those to whom it had belonged; but it is not lawful if the property is merely unguarded, whether the guard was removed before the truce was made, or afterward. Continuance of ownership in one renders possession by another unlawful. And by this rule the quibble of Belisarius against the Goths is refuted; for under such a pretext he had seized places which had been stripped of their garrisons[1] in time of truce. Procopius, *Gothic War*, II [vii].

IX.—*Whether, at the end of the truce, one can return who has been detained by* force majeure

1. The question is raised, whether a person, who has been hindered by *force majeure* from returning, and is arrested within the territory of the enemy after the expiration of the truce, has the right to return.

If we consider the strict law of nations, I do not doubt that this person is in the same position as one who, although he had come in time of peace, by his own misfortune is caught among the enemy by a sudden outbreak of war. We have noted above, that such a person remains a captive until the conclusion of peace. Nor is moral justice opposed to this, since the property and acts of the enemy are liable for the debt of the state and are taken in payment. The case in question does not in reality furnish more ground for complaint than that of so many other innocent persons upon whom the misfortunes of war fall. III. ix [4].

2. In this connexion, moreover, no comparison can be made with merchandise in a case of confiscation, nor with the illustration given by Cicero in the second book *On Invention*; he there speaks of a war vessel as having been driven into port by a storm, which the quaestor wished to confiscate according to law. In such cases *force majeure* frees from the penalty. But in the case of the person forcibly detained after a truce it is not, properly speaking, a question of penalty, but of a right, which was suspended during a certain time only. Nevertheless, there is no doubt that the releasing of such a person is a more kindly, yes, also a nobler, act. *Digest*, XXXIX. iv. 15 and 16. § 8. [II. xxxii. 98.]

[1] Portus, Centumcellae, Albanum.

X.—*Of special agreements in truces and the questions wont to arise therefrom*

Certain acts are unlawful during a truce on account of the special nature of the agreement; for example, if a truce has been granted only for the purpose of burying the dead, no deviation from that condition ought to be made. So if a truce has been given to those who are besieged, with the provision merely that they are not to be attacked,[1] it will not be lawful to admit auxiliary forces and supplies. For, while such a truce is advantageous to the one side, it ought not to make the situation harder for the other side which granted it.

Sometimes also the agreement is made, that it shall not be lawful to go back and forth. Sometimes, again, provision is made for persons and not for things.[2] In the latter case, if persons are injured while property is being defended, the truce will not be violated. For since it is permissible to defend property, then personal safety must be referred to the main provisions, and not to what is derived from the consequences of some one provision.

XI.—*When the terms of a truce have been violated by the one side, the other may begin war*

If the good faith of the truce has been violated by the one party, it should not be doubted that the party injured [596] is free to take up arms even without declaring war. For the main points of the agreement are implied in the manner of a condition in the agreement, as I have said a little above.

III. xix. 19 [xix. 14] and xx. 36.

In the histories you may indeed find examples of those who have endured wrongs till the end of the truce. But you may also read that war was declared against the Etruscans and others, because they had acted contrary to the truce. This difference is proof that the law is as I say, but that it is at the option of the injured party to use, or not to use, the right which he has.

Livy, IX [xli. 7] and XI [X. xxxvii ff.].

XII.—*What if a penalty, in case of violation of the truce, has been added?*

This is established, that if the penalty agreed upon is demanded, and is paid by the one who has done the wrong, the right to make war no longer remains. The penalty, in fact, is paid with this in view, that all else may remain in safety. On the contrary, if war is begun, it is necessary to consider that, since the choice was given, the idea of paying the penalty has been abandoned.

[1] Such as was given to the people of Naples by Totila, in Procopius [*Gothic War*, III. viii].

[2] See *Decretals*, V. vi. 11. There are examples of truces with exception of places in Procopius and Menander Protector.

XIII.—*When the acts of private citizens break the truce*

Private acts do not break a truce unless in addition there is a public act, that is, through command or approval.

Private acts are understood to be in accordance with public command or approval if the guilty parties are neither punished nor surrendered, and if restitution is not made.

XIV.—*What interpretation ought to be put on the right of safe-conduct outside of the period of truce*

The right of safe-conduct outside of the time of truce is a kind of privilege. In its interpretation, therefore, the rules which are laid down in regard to privileges ought to be followed. This privilege, however, is neither harmful to a third party nor very burdensome to the one who grants it. Consequently, within the natural meaning of the words a loose rather than a strict interpretation ought to be admitted, and so much the more in case the favour has not been granted in response to a request, but has been offered voluntarily; so much the more, also, if a public advantage of some sort is connected with the business outside of private gain. A strict interpretation, therefore, even according to the meaning of the words, ought to be rejected, unless otherwise some absurdity would ensue, or very probable inferences as to intention seem to require it.

See above, II. xvi. 12.

On the other hand, a freer interpretation than is afforded by the natural meaning of the words will be in point, in order that a like absurdity may be avoided, or because of very cogent inferences.

XV.—*Who may be classed under the term combatants*

From what has been said we draw the inference that the right of safe-conduct granted to combatants extends not only to inferior officers but also to officers of the highest rank; for the natural meaning of the word admits of this interpretation, although there is another interpretation that is narrower. Similarly a bishop is included under the term clergy.

Canon in *Decretals*, I. vi. 7. § 1.

Sailors also, who are serving in fleets, are understood to be combatants, and in fact all are who have taken the military oath.

Digest, XXXVII. xiii. 1. § 1.

XVI.—*How, in this connexion, we are to understand the terms go, come, and depart*

A provision in regard to going is considered to cover also the return, not from the meaning of the word, but to avoid an absurdity; for a favour ought not to be void of use. And a safe departure should be understood to hold good until the person has reached a place

Diodorus Siculus, XVII [lxxxiv].

where he is in safety. For this reason the good faith of Alexander[1] was under accusation; for he had ordered that those to whom he had granted the right to depart should be killed on the way.

However, a person to whom permission has been granted to depart cannot also return. Again, a person who has received permission to come himself will not be able to send another; and the reverse of this also holds. Such, in fact, are different matters, and in such cases reason does not compel us to go beyond the meaning of the words. Nevertheless, this principle is applicable with the understanding that, though an error confers no right, it at any rate relieves from the penalty, if a penalty formed a part of the agreement.

Also the person who has received permission to come will come only once, and not a second time unless the allocation of time supplies a different interpretation.

XVII.—*On the extension of this to persons*

Digest, XLIII. xxvi. 21.

The son does not follow his father, nor the wife her husband, otherwise than in accordance with the right of residence. For we are accustomed to live with our family, but to travel abroad without it. Nevertheless it will be understood, even if not expressly stated, that one or two servants are included in the case of a person for whom it would be unbecoming to travel without such attendance. For he who grants a favour grants that which of necessity follows. However, in such cases, necessity must be understood in a moral sense.

Abbas, *On Decretals*, V. vi. 10.

[597] XVIII.—*On the extension of safe-conduct to baggage*

Similarly, not all kinds of goods will be included in the safe-conduct, but only such as are ordinarily taken on a journey.

XIX.—*Who are included under the terms attendants and nationality*

If the term attendants is used, those ought not to be understood whose case is more provocative of hatred than that of the one for whom the safe-conduct is arranged. Such are pirates, brigands, deserters, and fugitives. The designated nationality of the attendants indicates clearly enough that the right is not extended to others.

[1] Plutarch, *Alexander* [lix = p. 698 c]: 'This remained as a blot upon the warlike exploits of the king, who in other warlike deeds was accustomed to act both justly and in a manner befitting a king.' You find in Leunclavius, Book VI, a similar deed of Bayezid against the Vidynenses in Servia.

XX.—*Whether a right of safe-conduct is annulled by the death of the grantor*

Since the right of safe-conduct is derived from the force of authority, in case of doubt it is not annulled by the death of the one who granted it. This is in accordance with the rules which I have stated elsewhere in regard to favours granted by kings and other rulers. II. xiii [II. xiv. 11–12].

XXI.—*What if a right of safe-conduct has been granted subject to the pleasure of the grantor?*

There is usually a discussion regarding a safe-conduct granted with the restriction, 'so long as I wish'.

The opinion of those is nearer the truth who think that a favour of this kind continues even if no new act of will occurs; in case of doubt the presumption is that that remains in force which is sufficient for the validity of the right. But the force of the safe-conduct does not continue when the one who granted it has ceased to be able to wish it,[1] a condition brought about by death. When in fact the person is removed, the assumption of continuance also will cease, just as the accident ends with the destruction of the substance. Canon in *Sext*, I. iii. 5.

XXII.—*Whether security outside of the territory also is due*

Moreover, safe-conduct is due to the person to whom it has been granted even outside of the territory of the grantor. For it is granted in derogation of the right of war, which in itself is not confined to a territory, as we have said elsewhere. III. iv [8].

XXIII.—*The favour of ransoming captives*

The ransoming of captives is in large measure an act of favour, especially among Christians, to whom the divine law especially commends this kind of compassion. 'The ransoming of captives is a great and glorious function of justice,' says Lactantius. The ransoming of captives, especially from a barbarous enemy, is called by Ambrose a characteristic and supreme generosity. Likewise he defends his own act and that of the Church, because they had broken up even the consecrated vessels of the Church[2] in order to redeem *Matthew*, xxv. 36, 39. VI [xii]. *On Duties*, II. xxviii [II. xv. 71]. *On Duties*, II. xviii [II. xxviii].

[1] *Digest*, XXXIX. v. 32, as corrected by the eminent scholar Antoine Favre, substituting *voluero* for *volueris* [*Conject. Jur. Civ.*, Book II. xix].
Add *Digest*, XIX. ii. 4; see Cardinal Toschi, *Practicae Conclusiones*, 751, lit. p; Reinkingk, Book II, class II, viii. 30.

[2] Augustine imitated this act of Ambrose, as Possidius relates [*Life of Augustine*, xxiv]; he says that this was done against the worldliness on the part of some persons. Deogratias, a bishop in the same Africa, also imitated the act of Ambrose, as Victor of Utica relates, I [Victor Vitensis, I. viii].
Hincmar, in the *Life of Remigius* [chap. v], relates that a consecrated vessel, which had belonged

captives. 'The ransom of captives is the adornment of sacraments,' he says, and he uses many other expressions to the same effect.

XXIV.—*Whether ransom may be forbidden by law is explained with the help of a distinction*

1. These considerations lead me not to venture to approve without discrimination the laws which forbid the ransom of captives, such as existed, we read, among the ancient Romans. Some one said in the Roman Senate, 'In no state are captives rated more cheaply than in our own.' The same state is said by Livy to have had the least consideration for captives, even from early times. There is a familiar ode of Horace which touches on this subject, in which he calls the ransoming of captives disgraceful terms and a precedent dragging ruin with it, a loss added to disgrace.

Livy, XXII [lix. 1–2]. Livy, XXII [lxi. 1]. [*Odes*, III. v. 14–16.]

What Aristotle criticizes in the institutions of Sparta is likewise ordinarily held to be faulty in those of the Romans. As a matter of fact all their energies were directed to matters of war, as if on these alone the safety of the state depended. But if we should only have regard for considerations of humanity it would in many cases be better that a right which is sought in war should be lost, than that a great many men,[1] our relatives, in fact, or fellow countrymen, should be left in the most pitiable condition.

[*Politics*, II. ix; VII. xiv.]

2. Such a law, therefore, does not seem just, unless the need of such severity is plain, with the purpose in view that greater evils, or the largest possible number of evils, which are otherwise with moral certainty inevitable, may be avoided. In case of such necessity, since the captives themselves, in accordance with the law of love, ought to bear their lot with resignation, the injunction not to set themselves in opposition can be laid upon them and upon others in accordance with the principles which we have laid down elsewhere in regard to the surrender of a citizen for the public good.

I. xxv. 3.

XXV.—*Can the right to a captive be transferred?*

According to our customs, it is true, those who are captured in war are not slaves. Yet I do not doubt that the right to collect the price of ransom from [598] a captive can be transferred from the party who holds the captive to another. For nature allows a transfer of ownership, even in things which do not have corporeal existence.

to Remigius, was given to ransom captives from the Norsemen. A similar act of Rimbert, archbishop of Bremen, is praised by Mark Adam of Bremen in his *Ecclesiastical History*, chap. xxxii. The sixth General Council of the Church approved this in a decree inserted in *Decretum*, II. xii. 2. This ought to be added to what I have said above, III. v. 2.

[1] [600] See Zonaras [XIV. xiii. 77–8] on the very late repentance of the Emperor Mauritius for such a deed.

XXVI.—*A ransom can be owed to several by one person*

Further, the same person can owe a ransom to more than one person if he has been let go by the first and captured by another before the first ransom has been paid. Such, in fact, are different debts, arising from different causes.

XXVII.—*Whether an agreement can be annulled on the ground that the wealth of the captive was unknown*

An agreement in regard to the amount of ransom cannot be annulled on the ground that the captive is understood to be richer than was believed. By the strict law of nations, which we are investigating, no one is compelled to make good what he has promised in a contract at less than a fair price, if there has been no deception. This can be understood from the explanations previously made concerning contracts. II. 26 [II. xii. 26].

XXVIII.—*What goods of the captive belong to the captor*

From what we have said, that captives are not our slaves, it follows that there is no room for the complete acquisition which, as we have said elsewhere, is the essential condition of ownership over the person. No other property, therefore, will be gained by the captor than what he has actually taken. III. vii. 4.

In consequence, if the captive has something concealed on his person, it will not be acquired, since it has not been taken. Just so Paul the jurist made answer, in opposition to Brutus and Manlius, that a man, who has taken possession of a farm, has not taken into his possession a treasure which he does not know is on the farm; for a person cannot possess what he does not know of. The conclusion from this is that property concealed on the person of a captive can be used in paying the price of the ransom, since ownership has in effect been retained. *Dig.* XLI. ii. 3. § 3.

XXIX.—*Whether the heir owes the price of ransom is explained, with the help of a distinction*

1. This question is also commonly raised, whether a ransom agreed upon, but not paid before death, is due from the heir.

The answer seems to me void of difficulty. The ransom is not due if the captive died in prison. There was, in fact, a condition attached to the promise, that the captive should be set free; but a dead man is not set free. On the contrary, if the captive died when at liberty, the ransom is due; for he had already gained that in return for which the ransom had been promised.

2. I admit that obviously the agreement can be made also with different conditions, so that the ransom may be unreservedly due from the very moment of the contract, the captive being retained no longer as a prisoner of war, but as security for himself. On the contrary, the contract can be so drawn up that the payment of the price shall only be made if on the appointed day the captive is alive and free. But these conditions, as being less natural, are not to be assumed without clear proofs.

XXX.—*Whether a person, who has been released in order to free another, ought to return if the other has died*

Again, the question is proposed for discussion, whether a return to prison is obligatory for a man who has been released under the agreement that he should cause another to be freed, where the other has anticipated release by dying.

II. xi. 22 and xv. 16. III. xx. 58. I have said elsewhere that the act of a third party, if fairly promised, is satisfactorily performed if nothing on the part of the promisor is omitted, but that in the case of burdensome promises the promisor is obligated only to an equivalent amount. So, in the question under discussion, the one who has been released will not be bound to restore himself to custody; for this was not the agreement, and the presumption in favour of liberty does not allow a tacit agreement to be understood. But the person who has been released ought not to get his freedom as clear profit; he will pay the estimated value of what he cannot furnish.[1] For this is more in accord with *Dig.* XIX. v. 5. § 1. *Dig.* XII. iv. 16. natural simplicity than what the interpreters of the Roman law set forth in an action according to prescribed formulas and on a formal claim for restitution of a thing given for a cause, when the cause did not follow.

[1] Paul Balioni did not do this, when released on the condition that he restore to liberty Carvajal, since Carvajal died before being set free. On this account he is criticized by Mariana, Book XXX [XXX. xxi]. But Paruta, Book II, relates the circumstances of the deed somewhat differently.

CHAPTER XXII

ON THE GOOD FAITH OF SUBORDINATE POWERS IN WAR

I.—*The kinds of military leaders*

As ONE form of public agreement, Ulpian reckons this: 'Whenever the leaders of the war make agreements with each other.' *Dig.* II. xiv. 5.

I have said that after considering the good faith pledged by the highest authorities I must treat of that which subordinate officials pledge to one another, or to others. Either the subordinate officials are next to the highest authority, such as have properly been called generals, to whom this expression of Livy must be applied, 'And we recognize as a general only the officer under whose auspices the war is waged'; or they are officers of lower rank, whom Caesar distinguishes as follows: 'A lieutenant-general (*legatus*) has one set of duties, a commander-in-chief (*imperator*) another. The one ought to carry out orders; the other, to deliberate freely on the conduct of the whole campaign.' IV [xx. 6]. *Commentary*, III [*Civil War*, III. li. 4].

II.—*How far an agreement made by military leaders is binding on the supreme authority*

In dealing with the promises of military leaders the subject must be viewed under two aspects; for the question is raised whether such promises impose a binding obligation on the supreme authority, or only on the leaders themselves.

The first point should be settled in accordance with the principle which I have elsewhere stated,[1] that an obligation is imposed on us also by the person whom we have chosen as agent to execute our wishes, whether our wishes have been stated in express terms or are inferred from the nature of the responsibility. For the one who grants a power grants the means necessary for the exercise of that power, so far as he possesses them; and this ought to be understood morally in matters pertaining to morals. In two ways, therefore, subordinate authorities will be able to bind the supreme authority by their actions, either by doing that which is thought on probable grounds to lie within their field of duty, or even outside their field of duty, in accordance with a special responsibility, known to the public, or to those whose interest in the matter is at stake. II. xi. 12.

[1] See Camden [p. 630], on the year 1594, relative to the sentence of Count Miranda in the case of Hawkins.

III.—*How far such an agreement furnishes occasion for an obligation*

There are also other ways in which the supreme authority is obligated by a previous act of its agents, but not in such a way that this act should be, properly speaking, a cause, but rather an occasion, of obligation. This may happen in two ways, either by consent, or by reason of the act itself. Consent is revealed by ratification, not only express but also implied, that is, when the supreme authority knew what had been done and permitted the accomplishment of the acts, which cannot with probability be referred to another cause.
II. iv. 5 and xv. 17. We have explained elsewhere how this matter proceeds.

By reason of the thing itself states are bound to this extent, that they should not become richer through another's loss, that [601] is, that they should either carry out the agreement, from which they wish to acquire gain, or renounce the gain. In regard to this prin-
II. x. 2. ciple of equity, also, I have spoken elsewhere. And to this extent, and not beyond, can we accept the maxim, that whatever has been done to our advantage is valid. On the contrary those cannot be acquitted of injustice who disapprove of the agreement and yet retain what they would not have had without the agreement. Such
IX. xvi [IX. vi. 3]. a case arose when, as Valerius Maximus relates, the Roman senate was unable to approve of the act of Gnaeus Domitius, and yet was not willing to disavow it. Many such instances occur in history.

IV.—*What, if anything, has been done contrary to instructions? Herein distinctions are presented*

II. xi. 12 and 13. 1. Also we must repeat what has been said above, that whoever has appointed an agent is bound, even if the agent, while yet within the limits of his public function, has acted contrary to secret instructions.

This rule of equity was rightly followed by the Roman praetor in an action relating to agents, that not everything done by an agent is, in fact, binding on the one who appointed him, but only that which, within the limits of his responsibility, was done in the interest of the principal. If now public notice has been given, that agreements should not be made with him, then he will not be considered as an
Dig. XIV. iii. 5. § 11; iii. 11. §§ 2, 3, 4. agent. If, however, the notice has been given, but is not generally known, the one who appointed the agent is bound.

Also the conditions of the appointment must be observed. For if any one has wished that an agreement be made under a certain condition, or with the intervention of a certain person, it will be most fair that the conditions under which the agent received his appointment shall be observed.

2. The consequence of this is, that some kings or peoples are put under greater obligation by the agreements of their military leaders, others under less, in case their laws and customs are adequately known. But if there is doubt on these points we must follow the line of inference, in such a way as to understand that that is conceded without which there can be no proper discharge of responsibility on the part of the official.

3. If a lesser official has exceeded the limit of his instructions, in case he is unable to make good what he has promised, he will himself be liable for the equivalent of the loss, unless such recovery is precluded by some law sufficiently well known. But if in addition there is deceit, that is, if the official pretended to have greater power than he did have, he will then both be liable for the loss caused by his fault and also, on account of his criminal conduct, he will be subject to a penalty commensurate with the crime. In the former case his property is liable, and, if that is not sufficient, also his work, or the liberty of his person. In the second case his person, or his property, or both are liable, according to the magnitude of the crime.

Moreover, what we have said regarding deceit will be in point, even if any one has declared beforehand that he is unwilling to make himself liable, because the debt due both for the loss occasioned and as a just penalty is associated with the offence by a natural and not by a voluntary connexion.

V.—*Whether in such a case the other party will be under obligation*

But since either the supreme authority, or its agent, is always bound, this also is certain, that the other party to the agreement is under obligation, and it cannot be said that the agreement is one-sided.

We are done with the relation of lesser officials to their superiors.

VI.—*What generals or magistrates are able to do with regard to those of lower rank, or on behalf of them*

Let us see also what higher officials are able to do with regard to those of lower rank.

We ought not, I think, to doubt that a general may place a binding obligation on his soldiers, or magistrates on their fellow townsmen, within the limits of those powers which they are accustomed to exercise; beyond those limits, consent would be necessary.

On the other hand, a compact of a commander or of a magistrate will, in general, be advantageous to those of lower rank in respect to matters merely expedient; such arrangements, in fact, are suffi- Alciati, *Consilia*, VIII. xl.

ciently understood as in their power. In respect to conditions which have a burden attached, the obligation is absolute within those rights which they are accustomed to exercise, but, beyond those, only if accepted.

II. x. 11 [II. xi. 14]. These provisions are in accord with the principles which we have elsewhere discussed, growing out of the law of nature regarding a stipulation in behalf of a third party. The general statements will now be made clearer by the presentation of particular instances.

VII.—*Generals do not have the power to make peace*

It does not fall within the province of the general to conduct negotiations with regard to the causes or the consequences of a war;[1] [602] the terminating of war is, in fact, not a part of the waging of it. Even though the general has been placed in command with absolute power, that must be understood to apply only to the conduct of the war. [Plutarch, *Agesilaus*, x = p. 601 B.] The reply of Agesilaus to the Persians was: 'The right of decision regarding peace belongs to the state.' Sallust says that the senate rescinded the peace which Aulus Albinus had made with king Jugurtha, because he had made it without the authority of the senate. *Jugurtha* [xxxix. 3].

XXXVII [xix. 2]. Also we find in Livy: 'How will that peace be valid which we shall have concluded without the authority of the senate, without the decree of the Roman people?' For that reason the Caudine agreement and the agreement in regard to Numantia did not bind the Roman people, as I have explained elsewhere. [II. xv. 16–17]. And up to this point the statement of Posthumius is correct: [Livy, IX. ix. 7.] 'If there is anything which can be made a binding obligation on the people, all things can'; that is to say, things which do not belong to the conduct of warfare. That this is the meaning is shown by the preceding statements concerning surrender, concerning an agreement to abandon or to burn a city, and concerning a change in the form of government.

VIII.—*Whether generals may make a truce; herein a distinction*

Not only generals in command but also officers of lower rank have the power to make a truce,[2] but only with those against whom they are fighting, or whom they are holding in a state of siege. This applies only to themselves and to their troops; for other officers of equal rank are not bound by such a truce, as is clear from the story of Fabius and Marcellus in Livy. XXIV [xix]

[1] Belisarius said to the Goths [Procopius, *Gothic War*, II. vi = p. 403 A]: 'For I do not have the right to manage the affairs of the Emperor.'

[2] See Paruta, Book V.

IX.—*What security of persons, and what property, can be given by generals*

1. Likewise it is not within the province of generals to dispose of men, dominions, and territories taken in war.

In accordance with this law Syria was taken away from Tigranes, although Lucullus had given it to him. In regard to Sophonisba, who had been captured in war, Scipio said that the judgement and will of the senate and the Roman people would decide; and so freedom could not be given to her by Masinissa, the general by whom she had been captured. Over other matters, which fall under the head of booty, we see that some rights are granted to commanders, not so much by reason of the strength of their authority as by the customs of each people. But in regard to that subject we have said enough previously.

Justin, XL [ii. 3]. Livy, XXX [xiv. 10]. Castrensis, *De Iust. et Iure,* I. i. III. vi. 15.

2. However, it is quite within the power of generals to grant things which have not yet been taken, because in many cases towns and men surrender in war on the condition of preserving their lives, or of keeping also their liberty or even their property. In such matters circumstances generally do not afford opportunity to request the decision of the sovereign authority.

For a like reason this right ought to be granted also to commanders not of the highest rank, within the limits of the matters entrusted to their administration. When Hannibal was far away, Maharbal had promised to certain Romans, who had escaped from the battle near Trasimenus, not only their lives—'their safety', as Polybius too concisely remarks—but also, if they should have given up their weapons, the privilege of departing with one suit of clothes each. But Hannibal detained them, alleging that 'it was not in the power of Maharbal, without consulting him, to give to those who surrendered his pledge that he would leave them uninjured and unharmed'.[1] The judgement of Livy on this act is, 'The pledge was kept by Hannibal with Punic faith.'

[III. lxxxiv. 14.] [XXII. vi. 12.]

3. Consequently, in the case of Rabirius we ought to consider Cicero as a lawyer and not as a judge. He maintains that Rabirius had rightly killed Saturninus, whom the consul Gaius Marius had persuaded to leave the Capitol by giving a pledge to him. 'How could a pledge be given', says Cicero, 'without a decree of the senate?' And so he treats the matter as if that pledge bound Marius only. But Gaius Marius had received authority by a decree of the senate to see to it that the sovereignty and majesty of the Roman people should be preserved. In this power, which according to

[*For Rabirius,* x. 28.]

[1] No more plausible was the evasion used in a similar case by Bayezid against the Servians of Crattovo, as Leunclavius relates, Book VI.

Roman custom was the highest,[1] who would deny that the right of granting immunity was included, if in that way every peril might be warded off from the state?

X.—*Such agreements should be interpreted narrowly; and why*

For the rest, in dealing with the agreements made by generals, because these are concerned with a matter outside their field, the interpretation must be restricted so far as the nature of the agreement allows, lest indeed [603] by their act either the sovereign power be obligated to a greater degree than it wishes, or they themselves suffer injury in the discharge of their duty.

XI.—*How a surrender accepted by a general is to be interpreted*

In consequence, one who is received in unconditional surrender by a general is considered to have been received on such terms that the decision in regard to him belongs to the victorious people or king. There is an example of this in the case of Genthius, king of Illyria, and in that of Perseus, king of Macedonia; the former surrendered to Anicius, the latter to Paulus.

[Appian, *Illyrian Wars*, ii. 9.] [Livy, XLV. vi. 10.]

XII.—*How to understand the proviso, 'if the king or the people has approved'*

Thus the added proviso, 'Let this be valid, in case the Roman people shall have ratified it', which is often found in treaty compacts, will have the effect that, if the ratification does not follow, the general will himself in no respect be bound, unless in some way he has thereby been made richer.

XIII.—*How to understand the promise to surrender a town*

Livy, XXIV. iv [i.].

Also those who have promised to surrender a town can allow the garrison to withdraw, as we read that the Locrians did.

[1] See Sallust, *Catilinarian War* [xxix. 3]. Not unlike this Ciceronian sophistry is that of Gonsalvo against the Duke of Valentinois; Guicciardini, Book VI [p. 339, edit. Genev., 1645].

CHAPTER XXIII

ON GOOD FAITH OF PRIVATE PERSONS IN WAR

I.—*Refutation of the opinion, which holds that private persons are not bound by a pledge given to the enemy*

SUFFICIENTLY well known is this statement of Cicero: 'Also if, under the pressure of circumstances, individuals have promised anything to the enemy, faith must be kept in that very matter.' Whether the individuals are combatants or civilians—it matters not as regards keeping faith. [*On Duties*, I. xiii. 39.]

It is strange that legal authorities have been found who would teach that the obligation was binding when an agreement was made publicly with the enemy, but that agreements made by private persons were not binding in like manner. For since private citizens have private rights, which they can place under obligation, and enemies [604] are capable of acquiring right, what can stand in the way of the obligation? Add that, unless this rule is established, opportunity is given for slaughter, an impediment is set to liberty. For captives in many cases will not be able to guard against the former, or to obtain the latter, if the good faith of private persons has been done away with. Bartolus, *On Dig.*, II. xiv. 5; Zasius, *Apology against Eck.* III. xix. 2.

II.—*It is shown that private persons are bound even to a pirate and a brigand; and to what extent*

Still further, not only is a pledge, which has been given to an enemy, recognized by the law of nations, but also a pledge to a brigand or to a pirate, just as we have said above in regard to public faith. II. xi. 7 and III. xix. 5. There is this difference, that if an unjust fear inspired by the other has induced the promise the promisor can demand restitution, or if the other party is unwilling to make restitution he can take it; such a procedure has no place in case of a fear arising from a public war, according to the law of nations. Oldradus, *Cons.*, vii.

If an oath also has been added to the promise, then what has been promised will have to be made good by the promisor, if he wishes to avoid the crime of perjury. If such a perjury has been committed against a public enemy, men are accustomed to punish it; but if against brigands or pirates, it is overlooked, because of the hatred of those whose interest is at stake. Covarruvius, *De Matrimonio*, II. iii. 4, no. 21.

III.—*No exception is here made for a minor*

Also in this aspect of the good faith of private persons we shall make no exception for a minor who has sufficient intelligence to understand his act. For the privileges which favour minors arise from municipal law, but we are treating of the law of nations.

IV—*Whether an error gives release*

II. xi. 6. Also as regards an error, we have said elsewhere that it gives the right to withdraw from an agreement only if that which was erroneously believed had the force of a condition in the mind of the promisor.

V.—*Answer to the objection raised from the point of view of public advantage*

1. It is more difficult to decide how far the power of individuals may extend in making an agreement. That public property cannot be alienated by an individual is well established. For if this right
[III] xxii. 7. is not permitted even to generals in war, as I have just shown, still less will it be permitted to private citizens. But in regard to their own acts and property the question can be raised because it is evident that these also cannot be put at the service of the enemy without some degree of damage. For this reason such agreements on the part of citizens may seem unlawful on account of the state's right of eminent domain, and on the part of enrolled soldiers on account of their military oath.

2. It must be understood, however, that agreements which avoid a greater or more certain evil ought to be considered advantageous rather than harmful to the public interest, because a lesser
Punic Wars [xiii. 94]. evil assumes the appearance of an advantage. 'Of evils one ought to choose the lesser', a certain speaker says in Appian. In fact neither an act of sincere good faith, by which one does not yield absolute power over himself and his possessions, nor the public advantage without the authority of law, can render void and deprive of all legal effect that which has been done, even if it is granted that this was done contrary to duty.

3. A law may indeed deprive either permanent or temporary subjects of such power. But the law does not always do this, because it spares the citizens; and it cannot do this in all cases, for the reason
I. iv. 7, 21 [I. iv. 7. 2–3]; II. xiv. 12. that human laws, as I have said elsewhere, have the power of imposing obligation only if they have been passed in a humane manner, and not if they impose a burden which is plainly inconsistent with reason and nature. And so special ordinances and orders, which openly claim some such right, ought not to be considered as laws. Moreover, general laws ought to be received with so benevolent an interpretation as to exclude misfortunes arising from extreme necessity.

4. But if the act of the private person, which had been forbidden by law or by an order and prevented from becoming valid, could rightly have been forbidden, then the act of the individual would be void. Nevertheless he could be punished on this account, because he promised what was not within his right; and especially, if he promised it on oath.

[605] [1]VI.—*The previous statements are applied to a pledge given of return to prison*

The promise of a captive to return to prison is properly allowable; for it does not render the condition of the captive worse. Therefore Marcus Atilius Regulus did not merely act nobly, as some think, but also as his duty required. Cicero says: 'It was the duty of Regulus not to disturb by perjury the conditions and agreements of war.' And no obstacle to his return was presented by this consideration: *On Duties*, III [xxix. 108].

> But yet he knew what tortures
> The barbarous executioner was making ready;

Horace [*Odes*, III. v. 49–50].

for he had known when he made the promise that this might happen. Likewise, also, of the ten captives, as Gellius tells the story from ancient authors, 'Eight replied that they had no right to postliminy, since they were bound by oath.' [2] VII. xviii [VI. xviii. 8].

VII.—*The pledge not to return to a certain place; the pledge not to serve as a soldier*

1. It is also customary for prisoners to promise not to return to a certain place, and not to take up arms against the one who had them in his power. An example of the former kind of pledge is found in Thucydides, where the people of Ithome promise the Lacedaemonians that they will leave the Peloponnesus never to return. [I. ciii.]

Instances of the second kind of pledge are now frequent. An ancient example is to be found in Polybius, where the Numidians are released by Hamilcar on the condition that none of them will bear hostile arms against the Carthaginians. Procopius [3] in the *Gothic War* records a similar agreement. I [lxxviii. 14]. III [xxxvi = p. 552 c].

2. Some writers declare such an agreement void, because it is contrary to the duty due to the country of allegiance. But whatever is contrary to duty is not at once also void, as I have said just above and elsewhere. Then, too, it is not contrary to duty to obtain

[1] [In the 1646 edition, sections 6, 7, 8, 9, 10 and 11 are numbered 7, 8, 9, 10, 11 and 12, and section 12 is run in in the last of those here enumerated.]
[2] That is, lacking civil rights, as Horace [*Odes*, III. v. 42] says of Regulus.
[3] *Gothic War*, II [II. xiv], about the Herulians.

liberty for oneself by promising what is already in the hands of the enemy. The cause of one's country is, in fact, none the worse thereby, since he who has been captured must be considered as having already perished, unless he is set free.

VIII.—*The pledge not to run away*

Some prisoners also promise not to run away. Contrary to the opinion of certain writers, such a pledge is binding on them, even though they made the promise when in chains. For in this way either lives are ordinarily saved, or milder captivity secured. If, however, the prisoner shall be put in chains afterward, then he will be released from the promise, if it was made on the condition that he should not be put in chains.

IX.—*One who has been captured cannot surrender to another*

Rather foolishly the question is raised, whether one who has been captured can surrender to another.

It is quite certain that no one by his own agreement can take away a right gained by another. But the captor has gained a right, either by the law of war alone, or partly by the law of war and partly III. vi. 23 ff. by the consent of him who is waging the war, as I have explained above.

X.—*Whether private persons should be compelled by their rulers to carry out what they have promised*

Regarding the effect of agreements an important question is, whether private persons, in case they are negligent, ought to be compelled by their rulers to fulfil their promises.

It is nearer the truth to say that they should be compelled to do so only in regular warfare, on account of the law of nations by which those who wage war are bound to render justice to each other, even in regard to the acts of individuals; a case in point would be if envoys of the enemy should be injured by private citizens.

VIII. viii [VI. xviii. 11]. Thus, according to the statement of Gellius, Cornelius Nepos wrote that many in the senate voted[1] that those of the ten captives who were unwilling to return should be put under guard and taken back to Hannibal.

[1] In like manner already earlier the senate had obliged those to return whom Pyrrhus had released conditionally; Appian, *Selections on Embassies*, vi [=*Samnite History*, x. 5].

XI.—*What kind of an interpretation ought to be applied in agreements of this sort*

In the matter of interpretation, the rules should be observed which have already been mentioned several times, to wit: that we should not depart from the natural meanings of the words except in order to avoid an absurdity, or from some quite satisfactory surmise as to the intention; and that in case of doubt we should be more inclined to interpret the words against the one who made the condition. II. xvi. 2; III. xx. 26.

XII.—*In what way we are to interpret the terms life, clothing, and the arrival of aid*

One who has made an agreement regarding his life does not have the right to liberty also.

Arms are not included under the term clothing; for these are different things.

Aid is rightly said to have arrived if it is in [606] sight, although it is doing nothing; for its very presence has an influence.

XIII.—*Who ought to be said to have returned to the enemy*

One who has returned secretly, so as to depart immediately, will not be said to have returned to the enemy. For returning ought to be understood as coming a second time under the power of the enemy.

Cicero held the opposite interpretation to be disingenuous and foolishly crafty, since it involves deceit and perjury. Gellius called it fraudulent cleverness, branded with disgrace by the censor; and he characterizes those who had practised it as odious and detestable. *On Duties*, III [xxxii. 113]. VIII. xix. [VI. xviii. 10].

XIV.—*What are adequate reinforcements in the case of a surrender made conditionally?*

In the case of an agreement to surrender,[1] which shall not hold if adequate reinforcements have arrived, the reinforcements ought to be understood to be such as will cause the danger to cease.

[1] There are four examples of a treaty of this kind in the *Gothic War* of Procopius, III [III. vii, xii, xxx, xxxvii]. There is another in Agathias, I [I. xii=p. 23 A], concerning Luca. Another concerning a castle in Corsica is in Bizarri, *History of Genoa*, Book X; others in Book XVIII and in the war against the Moors. Kromer, Book XI, also has a similar instance.

XV.—*Whatever pertains to the execution of an agreement does not constitute a condition*

This also must be noted, that if any covenant has been made regarding the method of execution this adds no condition to the agreement. The case is as if they said that payment is to be made in a certain place, which afterward changed ownership.

XVI.—*Regarding hostages given for such agreements*

In regard to hostages the position must be maintained which
III. xx. 58. we stated above, that in most cases they are merely accessory to the principal act. Nevertheless the agreement can be so made that the obligation shall present an alternative, that is, either that something shall be done, or that the hostage shall be retained. But in case of doubt we must maintain what is most natural, that is, that the hostages shall be believed to be only accessory.

CHAPTER XXIV

ON IMPLIED GOOD FAITH

I.—*How good faith may be tacitly interposed*

It was well said by Javolenus, that certain things are agreed to by silence; and this is found to be the case in public agreements, in private agreements, and in mixed agreements. *Digest*, XIX. ii. 51.

The reason is that consent, no matter how indicated and accepted, has the power of transferring a right. But there are also other signs of consent besides spoken and written words, as we have already more than once indicated. And certain signs by nature form a part of the act. II. iv. 4; III. ii. 8 [III. i. 8].

II.—*An example, in the case of a person who desires to be received under the protection of a people or a king*

An example may be found in the case of the person who comes either from the enemy or from a foreign country and entrusts himself to the good faith of another people or king. For there ought to be no doubt that such a person tacitly binds himself to do nothing against that government under which he seeks protection.

[607] Consequently we ought not to follow those who say that the act of Zopyrus was free from blame; for his faithfulness toward his king did not excuse his treachery toward those to whom he had fled. The same should be said of Sextus, the son of Tarquin, who fled to Gabii. About Sinon Virgil says: [Herodotus, III. cliv.] [Justin, I. x. 15.] Livy, I [liii. 5]. *Aeneid*, II [65–6].

> Hear now the plots of Greeks, and from the crime of one
> Learn to know all Greeks.

III.—*An example, in the case of one who asks or grants a parley*

Likewise the person who asks or grants a parley tacitly promises [1] that it will be without hurt to those who take part in it.

Livy declares that the law of nations is violated by doing harm to the enemy under the pretence of a parley; he adds, that the good faith of a parley was treacherously violated (for the reading 'through faith' (*per fidem*) in that passage is faulty), because Gnaeus Domitius placed in chains Bituitus, king of the Averni, after Domitius had invited him to a pretended conference and had received him XXXVIII [xxv. 8].

[1] [608] Deservedly Agathias, Book II [II. xiv=p. 50 c], censures the Hun Ragnaris, because he tried to kill Narses with a spear as Narses was going away from a conference.

X. vi [IX. vi. 3]. in hospitality. This judgement is passed on Domitius by Valerius Maximus: 'His excessive desire for fame made him treacherous.'

Wherefore one must wonder why the writer of the eighth book [VIII. xxiii. 3.] of Caesar's *Gallic War*, whether Hirtius or Oppius, in referring to a similar deed of Titus Labienus adds, 'He judged that the faithlessness of this man', that is, Commius, 'could be suppressed without any act of treachery,' unless the explanation is that this is the opinion of Labienus rather than of the writer.

IV.—*Nevertheless he who asks or grants a parley is not hindered from promoting his own interests, provided that he does not harm the other party to the conference*

But that implied consent must not be extended beyond what I have said. For, provided that the parties to the conference suffer no harm, it is not treacherous, but reckoned among honourable artifices, to divert the enemy from warlike plans by the pretext of a parley, and in the meantime to promote one's own advantage.

Livy, XLII [xlvii. 1 ff.] Those, therefore, who maintained that King Perseus was deceived by the hope of peace, took into consideration not so much right and good faith as highmindedness and warlike glory; and this can III. ii. 6 ff. [III. i. 6 ff.] be well understood from what we have said concerning stratagems in war. Of the same general character was the ruse by which Hasdrubal saved his army from the Ausetanian defiles, and that by which Scipio Africanus the Elder learned the location of the camp of Syphax; Livy, XXVI [xvii] and XXX [iv]. both of these instances are related by Livy. Their example was followed by Lucius Sulla [1] also in the Social War, near Esernia, as I. v [17]. we read in Frontinus.

V.—*Of mute signs which by custom have some meaning*

There are also certain mute signs which have a significance arising from custom. Such were in ancient times the use of fillets and olive branches; among the Macedonians the raising of spears, among the Romans the placing of shields over the heads,[2] all signs of a suppliant surrender,[3] which in consequence imposed the obligation to lay down arms. But whether one who indicates that he

[1] Also the Dictator Caesar against the Tencteri and Usipetes; Appian, *Selections on Embassies*, xvi [= *Gallic History*, xviii].

[2] Appian, *Civil Wars*, II [vi. 42].

[3] Among the Persians the hands were clasped behind the back; Ammianus Marcellinus, Book XVIII [XVIII. viii. 4]; see also the notes of Lindenbrog on this passage. The same Ammianus, Book XXVI [XXVI. ix. 7], notes that the shields and standards were reversed among the Romans. Latinus Pacatus, *Panegyric* [xxxvi], says that they lowered the flags.

The ancient Germans and others, following their example, offered grass, as Pliny states, Book XXII [XXII. iv. 8]. Servius, *On the Aeneid*, I [I. 487], says that those who surrender themselves as conquered lay down their arms as suppliants.

accepts such a surrender is under obligation, and how far, should be inferred from what I have said above. III. iv. 12 and xi. 15.

At the present time white flags [1] are the implied sign of a request for a parley; they will, therefore, be no less binding than if the parley had been requested by word of mouth.

VI.—*On the implied approval of a treaty compact*

How far a treaty compact made by generals ought to be considered as impliedly approved by the people or king, I have already stated above, to wit: when both the action was known and something was done or not done for which no other cause could be assigned except the wish to ratify the treaty. II. xv. 17 and III. xxii. 3.

VII.—*When a punishment is impliedly remitted*

The remission of a penalty [2] cannot be inferred from the sole fact of its being disregarded. There is need, besides, of some such act as either in itself may show friendship, as a treaty of friendship, or such as will express so high an opinion of the virtue of the party subject to punishment that his previous deeds ought deservedly to be pardoned; whether that opinion is expressed in words, or through acts, which customarily have such significance.

[1] Among the northern peoples the lighting of a fire was a sign that a parley was requested, as Johan Magnus and others state. Pliny, in Book XV. xxx [XV. xxx. 133], says of the laurel: 'It is itself the bringer of peace, so that, when it is presented, it becomes also a sign of cessation of hostilities between armed foes.'

[2] Polybius, in a passage preserved in the *Selections on Embassies*, xxii [=XXIII. vi], discusses the question whether punishment is remitted to those who committed the act at the same time that it is remitted to the instigators. I do not think that it is, for individuals are answerable for their own misdeeds.

CHAPTER XXV

CONCLUSION, WITH ADMONITIONS ON BEHALF OF GOOD FAITH AND PEACE

I.—*Admonitions to preserve peace*

At this point I think that I can bring my work to an end, not because all has been said that could be said, but because sufficient has been said to lay the foundations. Whoever may wish to build on these foundations a more imposing structure will not only find me free from envy, but will have my sincere gratitude.

Yet before I dismiss the reader I shall add a few admonitions which may be of value in war, and after war, for the preservation of good faith and of peace; just as in treating of the commencement of war I added certain admonitions regarding the avoidance of wars, so far as this can be accomplished.

And good faith should be preserved, not only for other reasons but also in order that the hope of peace may not be done away with. For not only is every state sustained by good faith, as Cicero declares, but also that greater society of states. Aristotle truly says that, if good faith has been taken away, 'all intercourse among men ceases to exist'.

On Duties, III [II. xxiv. 84]. *Rhetoric*, I. xv [22].

Rightly the same Cicero says that 'it is an impious act to destroy the good faith which holds life together'. To use Seneca's phrase, it is 'the most exalted good of the human heart'. And this good faith the supreme rulers of men ought so much the more earnestly than others to maintain as they violate it with greater impunity; [609] if good faith shall be done away with, they will be like wild beasts,[1] whose violence all men fear. Justice, it is true, in its other aspects often contains elements of obscurity; but the bond of good faith is in itself plain to see, nay more, it is brought into use to so great an extent that it removes all obscurity from business transactions.

For Quintus Roscius [vi. 16]. *Letters*, lxxxviii [29].

It is, then, all the more the duty of kings to cherish good faith scrupulously, first for conscience's sake, and then also for the sake of

[1] According to Procopius, *Persian War*, II [II. x], the ambassadors of Justinian thus address Chosroes:

> Unless, O king, this address were being made to you in person, we should never have believed that Chosroes, son of Cabades, would have entered Roman territory in arms after first scorning the sworn oaths, which are believed to be the highest and strongest pledge of truth and good faith among men; and besides, after breaking the treaty, in which rests the only hope left for those who are not living in safety on account of the evils of war.
>
> What else should we say that this is, than to exchange the life of men for the life of wild beasts? For when treaties have been done away with it will follow that all peoples will wage unending wars with one another. But unending wars have the effect, that they keep men continuously estranged from their own nature.

the reputation by which the authority of the royal power is supported. Therefore let them not doubt that those who instil in them the arts of deception are doing the very thing which they teach. For that teaching cannot long prosper which makes a man antisocial with his kind and also hateful in the sight of God.

II.—*In war peace should always be kept in view*

Again, during the entire period of administration of a war the soul cannot be kept serene and trusting in God unless it is always looking forward to peace. Sallust most truly said, 'The wise wage war for the sake of peace.' With this the opinion of Augustine agrees: 'Peace is not sought that war may be followed, but war is waged that peace may be secured.' Aristotle himself more than once condemns those nations which made warlike pursuits, as it were, their end and aim. Violence is characteristic of wild beasts, and violence is most manifest in war; wherefore the more diligently effort should be put forth that it be tempered with humanity, lest by imitating wild beasts too much we forget to be human.

To Caesar On Pub. Admin. [I. vi. 2]. *Letters,* i [clxxxix. 6], *To Boniface. Politics,* VII. ii [9] and xiv [11].

III.—*And peace should also be accepted even at a loss, especially by Christians*

If, then, it is possible to have peace with sufficient safety, it is well established by condonation of offences, damages, and expenses; this holds especially among Christians, on whom the Lord has bestowed His peace. And His best interpreter wishes us, so far as it is possible and within our power, to seek peace with all men. It is characteristic of a good man, as we read in Sallust, to be unwilling to begin war, not gladly to pursue it to the bitter end.

Romans, xii. 18.

[= Cicero, *Letters to Friends,* IV. vii. 2.]

IV.—*The consideration stated is useful to the conquered*

This one consideration ought to be sufficient. However, human advantage also often draws in the same direction, first, those who are weaker, because a long contest with a stronger opponent is dangerous, and, just as on a ship, a greater misfortune must be avoided at some loss, with complete disregard of anger and hope which, as Livy has rightly said, are deceitful advisers. The thought is expressed by Aristotle thus:[1] 'It is better to relinquish something of one's possessions to those who are stronger, than to be conquered in war and perish with the property.'

[VII. xl. 19.] [*Rhetoric to Alexander,* ii.]

[1] Philo, *De Constitutione Principis* [*On Justice,* xiii], says: 'Peace, even though with great loss, is better than war.'

V.—*The consideration stated is also useful to the conqueror*

Again, human advantage draws in the same direction also the stronger. The reason is, as the same Livy no less truly says, that peace is bounteous and creditable to those who grant it while their affairs are prosperous; and it is better and safer than a victory that is hoped for. It must be kept in mind that Mars is on both sides. As Aristotle says, 'In war men ought to consider how many and how unexpected changes are wont to occur.' In a certain oration for peace in Diodorus Siculus those are censured who magnify the greatness of their exploits, as if it were not evidently customary for the fortune of war to bestow favours alternately. And especially must the boldness of the desperate be feared;[1] wild beasts bite most fiercely when dying.

[XXX. xxx. 18.] [*Rhetoric to Alexander*, ii.] [XIII. liii.]

VI.—*The consideration stated is useful likewise to those whose fortunes are in doubt*

Civil War, I [III. x].

But, if both sides seem to be equal to each other, this in truth, as Caesar says, is the best time to treat of peace, while each has confidence in himself.

VII.—*Peace, when made, must be kept with the utmost scruple*

Moreover peace, whatever the terms on which it is made, ought to be preserved absolutely, on account of the sacredness of good faith, which I have mentioned; and not [610] only should treachery be anxiously avoided, but everything else that may arouse anger. What Cicero said about private friendships you may apply to public friendships no less correctly: not only should all friendships be safeguarded with the greatest devotion and good faith, but especially those which have been restored to goodwill after enmity.

[*For Gabinius*, frag., in Jerome, *Apology against Rufinus*, I. i.]

VIII.—*A prayer, and the end of the work*

May God, who alone hath the power, inscribe these teachings on the hearts of those who hold sway over the Christian world. May He grant to them a mind possessing knowledge of divine and human law, and having ever before it the reflection that it hath been chosen as a servant for the rule of man,[2] the living thing most dear to God.

[1] [Plutarch, *Marius*, xlv=p. 432 c:]

We even have to fear the dying lion's den.

[2] So Chrysostom in his sermon *On Alms* [beginning]: 'Man is the being dearest to God.'

APPENDIX

FROM THE LIFE OF ST. LOUIS, KING OF FRANCE, BY JOINVILLE, CHAPTER LXXXIX

THOSE who were in the Great Council of the king would often reprove him because he expended so much labour upon the restoration of peace among those outside his realm, saying that he was making a mistake in not permitting them to wage war, and that later this would result in their being dealt with more easily.

The king would reply that they were wrong. 'If', he said, 'the princes and rulers, who are my neighbours, should see that I readily allowed them to wage wars with one another, they would say to one another, "The king of France allows us to wage war with evil intent", and in consequence they would conceive a hatred of me and at some time would attack me; and from this source misfortune would result for my kingdom. Besides, it could happen that I should bring upon myself the wrath of God, since God says that those are blessed who strive to recall the hostile to peace and harmony.'

I am able to affirm that the Burgundians and Lotharingians, perceiving the goodness and justice of the king, were so devoted to him and so respected him, that they settled in his presence the causes of controversy which arose between them. I saw them often coming, now to Paris, now to Rheims, now to Melun, and again to other places, where the king was.

FROM THE LIFE OF THE SAME, IN CONNEXION WITH THE INJUNCTIONS OF ST. LOUIS THE KING GIVEN TO HIS SON

From the records of the Collegium Rationalium in the city of Paris

If any suit or action at law is commenced against you, inquire as fully into the truth against you as for you.

If you perceive that you have anything belonging to another, which it is established that you or your ancestors have taken, cause it to be restored immediately.

Do not wage war against any Christian except on the advice

of many, and only if you cannot avoid war. But if you are at war, refrain from injuring the clergy and those who have done you no harm.

If war or quarrellings arise among your subjects, bring them back to harmony, as soon as this can be done.

Examine often, what your bailiffs, prefects, and other officials are doing, and inquire into their acts, in order that you may correct whatever ought to be corrected. See to it that no disgraceful sin hold sway in your kingdom.

COMMENTARY

OF

HUGO GROTIUS

ON

THE EPISTLE OF PAUL THE APOSTLE TO PHILEMON

[612] THE PRINTER TO THE READER

SINCE about this time there came into our hands the commentary of the same author on the Epistle of Paul to Philemon, we thought best to give it a place here, not only that it might be preserved along with the larger work, but also because it contains some matter not foreign to the subjects which are treated in that work, in Book I, chapter ii, and Book III, chapters vii and xiv.

[NOTES

ON

THE EPISTLE OF PAUL TO PHILEMON]

1. Παῦλος δέσμιος Χριστοῦ Ἰησοῦ, 'Paul, a prisoner of Jesus Christ'.—At Rome, living under guard of a soldier, who was bound with the same chain; *Acts*, xxviii. 16. The genitive here indicates cause; so also below, verse 9, *Ephesians*, iii. 1, and *2 Timothy*, i. 8. In *Ephesians*, iv. 1, δέσμιος ἐν Κυρίῳ, 'prisoner in the Lord', instead.

καὶ Τιμόθεος ὁ ἀδελφός, 'and brother Timothy'.—The Christians called one another 'brother' because of a common regeneration. Timothy—almost always a companion of Paul, as may be seen in *2 Timothy*, iii. 10—was with him also in Rome; *Ephesians* [*Philippians*], i. 1, *Colossians*, i. 1.

Φιλήμονι τῷ ἀγαπητῷ, 'to Philemon dearly beloved'.—The name Philemon is Greek. This was the name also of a poet of merit, and of a writer on natural history who is mentioned by Pliny. Philemon seems to have lived at Ephesus, where Onesimus afterward held the office of bishop, as Ignatius in his *Letters* and other writers bear witness. Paul calls him 'dearly beloved', or 'most dear', because he considered Philemon, as an exceedingly devout man, in a relation of more intimate friendship.

καὶ συνεργῷ ἡμῶν, 'and our fellow-worker'.—That is, as one of the presbyters, of whom there were several at Ephesus; *Acts*, xx. 17. The Apostles applied the term 'fellow-workers' to all the presbyters (πρεσβύτεροι) and also to the elderly women (πρεσβύτιδες) who sought to bring women to Christ; *Romans*, xvi. 3, 9, *Philippians*, ii. 25, *Colossians*, iv. 11.

2. καὶ Ἀπφίᾳ τῇ ἀγαπητῇ, 'and to Appia dearly beloved'.—The name Appia is Roman, π being changed to φ according to Hebrew usage.

καὶ Ἀρχίππῳ τῷ συστρατιώτῃ ἡμῶν, 'and to Archippus our fellow-soldier'.—He seems to have served as an evangelist, now at Ephesus, now at Colossae [613]; *Colossians*, iv. 17. The testimony of Ambrose indicates that Archippus afterward took up his residence at Colossae, and so was made a bishop. Paul was wont to call his helpers 'fellow-soldiers' on account of the burdensomeness of the task, as may be seen by referring to *Philippians*, ii. 25.

καὶ τῇ κατ' οἶκόν σου ἐκκλησίᾳ, 'and to the church which is in thine house'.—The reference must be to Philemon, to whom this epistle is chiefly addressed. In his house there were several Christians. According to Tertullian even three Christians constitute a church. Similarly, those who were in the house of Aquila and Priscilla are called a church, *Romans*, xv. 15 [xvi. 5], and *1 Corinthians*, xvi. 19; also, those who were in the house of Nymphas, *Colossians*, iv. 15.

3. *χάρις ὑμῖν, καὶ εἰρήνη ἀπὸ Θεοῦ πατρὸς ἡμῶν, καὶ Κυρίου Ἰησοῦ Χριστοῦ*, 'grace to you and peace from God our father, and the Lord Jesus Christ'.—He prays for the favour of God and of Christ on their behalf, and for prosperity in all things, which the Jews are accustomed to designate by the word 'peace'. Paul frequently uses this prayer, as *1 Corinthians*, i. 3, *2 Corinthians*, i. 2, *Galatians*, i. 3, *Ephesians*, i. 2, *Colossians*, i. 2, *1 Thessalonians*, i. 1.

4. *Εὐχαριστῶ τῷ Θεῷ μου*, 'I thank my God'.—We ought to give thanks to God for gifts conferred not only on ourselves but also on others; *Romans*, i. 8, *1 Corinthians*, i. 4, *Ephesians*, i. 16.

πάντοτε μνείαν σου ποιούμενος ἐπὶ τῶν προσευχῶν μου, 'always making mention of thee in my prayers'.—We find the same words in the verse last referred to, *Ephesians*, i. 16; whence we may learn that under *προσευχαί*, 'prayers', here are included all utterances addressed to God, even those in which no petition is offered but thanks are given.

5. *ἀκούων σου τὴν ἀγάπην καὶ τὴν πίστιν*, 'hearing of thy love and faith'.—He states the reason for the giving of thanks, such as you will find also in the verses already referred to: *Romans*, i. 8; *1 Corinthians*, i. 4; *Ephesians*, i. 16. Here a noble pair is named, love and faith. See *1 Corinthians*, xiii; *Galatians*, v. 6; *Ephesians*, vi. 23; *1 Thessalonians*, iii. 6; *1 Timothy*, i. 14 and vi. 11; *2 Timothy*, i. 13 and ii. 22.

ἣν ἔχεις πρὸς τὸν Κύριον Ἰησοῦν, 'which thou hast toward the Lord Jesus'.—This has reference to faith.

καὶ εἰς πάντας τοὺς ἁγίους, 'and toward all the saints'.—This has reference to love. All Christians are called 'saints', as *Ephesians*, i. 1, and frequently elsewhere.

6. *ὅπως ἡ κοινωνία τῆς πίστεως σοῦ ἐνεργὴς γένηται ἐν ἐπιγνώσει παντὸς ἔργου ἀγαθοῦ τοῦ ἐν ὑμῖν εἰς Χριστὸν Ἰησοῦν*, 'that the fellowship of thy faith may become effectual in the knowledge of every good work which is in you unto Christ Jesus'.—First, there is a transposition here. For the words *εἰς Χριστὸν Ἰησοῦν*, 'unto Christ Jesus', relate to the preceding words *τῆς πίστεως σοῦ*, 'of thy faith'. Then, *κοινωνία τῆς πίστεως*, 'the fellowship of faith', was put in place of 'the faith which was common' to Philemon and the other Christians. And *ἐν ἐπιγνώσει*, 'in the knowledge', is here to be taken *παθητικῶ*[ς], 'in a passive sense', and carries the

signification of becoming known. The meaning, then, is: Thy love had this in view, that the faith, which thou hast in common with the other saints, should become effectual, and thus should be made known through the good works which proceed from thee and from others. Ἐνεργὴς γένηται, 'should become effectual', is here used with the same implication as πίστις δι' ἀγάπης ἐνεργουμένη, 'faith working through love', *Galatians*, v. 6. Thence follows ἐπίγνωσις, that is, the making known of the same faith; for faith is shown through works, *James*, ii. 18.

7. Χαρὰν γὰρ ἔχομεν πολλὴν καὶ παράκλησιν, 'For we have great joy and comfort'.—Justly, he says, we thank God for those virtues of yours, because from that source come to us our greatest joy and [614] a solace in the evils which we endure for the sake of the Gospel. So also *2 Corinthians*, vii. 4, 13; *1 Thessalonians*, iii. 7.

ὅτι τὰ σπλάγχνα τῶν ἁγίων ἀναπέπαυται διὰ σοῦ, ἀδελφέ, 'because the bowels of the saints have been refreshed through thee, brother'.—Σπλάγχνα, 'bowels', is here used instead of the word for 'soul', as *Sirach* [*Ecclesiasticus*], xxx. 7, xxxiii. 5. Consequently, ἀναπέπαυται τὰ σπλάγχνα, 'the bowels have been refreshed', and ἀνάπαυσόν μου τὰ σπλάγχνα, 'refresh my bowels', in verse 20 below, have a meaning similar to ἀνέπαυσαν τὸ ἐμὸν πνεῦμα, 'they refreshed my spirit', in *1 Corinthians*, xvi. 18. The poor, he says, are of tranquil mind, because they have learned by experience that in thy riches a resource has been provided against their necessities.

8. Διὸ πολλὴν ἐν Χριστῷ παῤῥησίαν ἔχων ἐπιτάσσειν σοι τὸ ἀνῆκον, 'Wherefore, though I have much boldness in Christ to enjoin that which is thy duty.'—The calling of an Apostle laid upon me by Christ gives me this right, to be able to enjoin upon thee and other Christians the things that it is your duty to do. The word παῤῥησία, 'boldness', went over from Greek speech to Syrian with a broader meaning, so that it often signifies 'right', 'authority'.

9. διὰ τὴν ἀγάπην μᾶλλον παρακαλῶ, 'on the ground of love rather I beseech'.—I prefer to entreat as a friend, by reason of the close relation of our friendship.

τοιοῦτος ὢν, 'since I am such'.—That is, I have recourse to entreaty, since I am such as you know me to be.

ὡς Παῦλος, 'Paul, to be sure'.—Founder of so many churches.

πρεσβύτης, 'an old man'.—One already advanced in years, to whom even strangers concede many things.

νῦν δὲ καὶ δέσμιος Ἰησοῦ Χριστοῦ, 'and now moreover a prisoner of Jesus Christ'—that is, a prisoner on account of Christ, as we said above [note on verse 1]. Great consideration is due to those who suffer hardships for very honourable causes; *Colossians*, iv. 18; *Ephesians*, iv. 1.

10. *παρακαλῶ σε*, 'I beseech thee'.—Παρακαλῶ σε here has the connotation of entreating, or rather of interceding. If slaves had committed any fault they were wont to arrange for an intercessor on their behalf, as Donatus suggests in a note to Terence [*On Terence's Phormio*, line 140]. Similar to this intercession is that of Pliny on behalf of a freedman of Sabinianus; *Letters*, IX. xxi.

περὶ τοῦ ἐμοῦ τέκνου, ὃν ἐγέννησα ἐν τοῖς δεσμοῖς μου, 'on behalf of my child, whom I have begotten in my bonds'.—Whom here at Rome, while I was a prisoner, I made a Christian. The rebirth of a man is the work of God. But so great is His goodness that He admits His servants to a participation in His name; *1 Corinthians*, iv. 15; *Galatians*, iv. 19. So likewise the Apostles are said 'to save', *σώζειν*, *Romans*, xi. 14, and elsewhere, and *1 Corinthians*, vii. 16.

[11.] *τόν ποτέ σοι ἄχρηστον*, 'who once was of no use to thee'.—It is the practice of intercessors to soften the harshness of the offence by words. Onesimus had not merely been 'of no use' to Philemon, he had also caused a loss to him. Flight and theft are commonly associated. Thus in the *Code* of Justinian the title *On runaway slaves* [VI. i] is followed by that *On thefts* [VI. ii]. Says Martial [*Epigrams*, XI. liv. 5–6]:

> The froward hands from feet have learned to sin;
> No marvel is the thief who was a runaway.

And those who were offering a slave for sale were accustomed to give assurance that he was not a thief nor a runaway; [615] *Digest*,[1] XVIII. i. 13 and 34. 3; XLVII. vi. 1 and 3; XIX. i. 11. 7 and 13. 1; Varro, *On Farming*, Book II [II. x. 5]; Seneca, *Controve sies*, III. xxi [VII. vi. 23].

12. *νυνὶ δέ σοι, καὶ ἐμοὶ εὔχρηστον*, 'but now 1 seful to thee and to me'.—Because he was useful to Paul, he was useful also to Philemon. For 'the possessions of friends', *τὰ τῶν φίλων*, are in common. There is a word-play on the name Onesimus [the Greek name Ὀνήσιμος means 'profitable', 'helpful'].

ὃν ἀνέπεμψα, 'whom I have sent back'.—Doubtless with this Epistle.

σὺ δὲ αὐτόν, τουτέστι τὰ ἐμὰ σπλάγχνα, προσλαβοῦ, 'do thou, then, receive him that is mine own bowels'.—Προσλαμβάνεσθαι has various meanings, all of which refer to kindly feeling and acts of kindness, as is clear from *Acts*, xviii. 26, *Romans*, xiv. 1, 3, and xv. 7. Here I should take it in the sense to receive kindly into one's house, as in *Acts*, xxviii. 2. Τὰ ἐμὰ σπλάγχνα, 'mine own bowels', that is, as dear to me as my own bowels. So in Plautus [*Casina*, line 837], 'my little heart'.

[1] [Grotius gives eight references to the *Digest*; two are correct, but the others appear to be mistakes. The references given above are to the passages he evidently had in mind.]

13. ὃν ἐγὼ ἐβουλόμην πρὸς ἐμαυτὸν κατέχειν, 'whom I was wishing to keep with me'.—The indicative mood is here used in place of the subjunctive, in accordance with Greek usage. I should have wished to keep him with me, if indeed other considerations, which will now follow, had not opposed. In regard to this manner of speaking, see what I have said *On Matthew*, xxvi. 39.

ἵνα ὑπέρ σου διακονῇ μοι, 'in order that he might minister to me in thy place'.—That he might render to me in all things the service which thou wouldst be rendering if thou wert here.

ἐν τοῖς δεσμοῖς τοῦ Εὐαγγελίου, 'in the bonds of the Gospel'.—In these bonds, which I bear for the sake of the Gospel. The manner of speaking is the same that we found above in verse 9.

14. χωρὶς δὲ τῆς σῆς γνώμης οὐδὲν ἠθέλησα ποιῆσαι, 'but I wished to do nothing without thy consent'.—I was unwilling to make use of him except with thy full approval.

ἵνα μὴ ὡς κατὰ ἀνάγκην τὸ ἀγαθόν σου, ἀλλὰ κατὰ ἑκούσιον, 'that thy goodness might not be as it were from constraint, but from free will'.—If Paul should have kept him, the desire of Philemon would not have become so apparent as it would be if he should have been sent to Philemon, and Philemon should send him back to Paul; Seneca, *On Benefits*, II. iv: 'If you wish to know whether I am willing, make it possible for me to be unwilling'. Ἑκούσιον, 'of free will', and ἀναγκαῖον, 'necessary', or, τὸ κατ' ἀνάγκην, 'that which is from constraint', are used in contrast, as in *1 Peter*, v. 2. So Paul the jurist sets over against each other performance from free will and from constraint, *Digest*, III. v. 18. 2. Praise, moreover, is not due except to free actions.

15. Τάχα γὰρ διὰ τοῦτο, 'For perhaps on this account'.—As if he were to say, 'Perchance that was the plan of God, when He permitted him to run away'. Compare *Genesis*, xlv. 5.

ἐχωρίσθη, 'he went away'.—Here also you see what we said above, that a thing harsh in reality is softened in statement; he said 'went away', ἐχωρίσθη, instead of 'ran away'. Such expressions the Greeks call εὐφημισμοί, 'euphemisms'.

πρὸς ὥραν, 'for a time'.—That is, for a short time. The same type of expression is found in *2 Corinthians*, vii. 8; *Galatians*, ii. 5; and *1 Thessalonians*, ii. 17.

ἵνα αἰώνιον αὐτὸν ἔχῃς, 'that thou mayest have him back forever'.—That, reformed by me, he may be permanently useful to thee. Αἰώνιον, 'forever', is here used as in Horace, 'will serve forever' [*Epistles*, I. x. 41].

Evangelical teaching does not remove differences of status and the authority of masters over slaves, as is clear from *1 Timothy*, vi. 1, 2; *Titus*, ii. 9; *1 Peter*, ii. 10 [ii. 18]; *Ephesians*, vi. 5, 6; *Colossians*,

iii. 22. [616] There is therefore no reason why a Christian, who as a master is able to have full authority over slaves, may not as a ruler have full authority over subjects. Similar are the master in his house, the king in his kingdom. Says Seneca, *On Benefits*, III. xviii: 'If a slave is hindered from attaining merit [as a benefactor of his master] by necessity, and the fear of suffering to the utmost, the same obstacles will hinder both him who is subject to a king and him who is under a commander, since, although under different names, they are similarly subject to authority.' And so Peter places on an equality the authority of kings and that of masters. For without having recourse to a magistrate masters were able to torture slaves who had misbehaved, and even to put them to death; *Digest*, I. vi. 1; *Institutes*, I. viii. 1. This, moreover, was the law not only at Rome but also in Greece; see Seneca, *Controversies*, V. xxxv [X. xxxv]. This in fact came from the law of nations, as we learn from the texts of law just cited.

In what way masters ought to apply this law, from the time that they became Christians, Paul taught them; and he would have said the same things to kings if at that time kings had been Christian, as many of the masters were. Both Nicodemus and Joseph of Arimathea were councillors, possessing authority and power to punish. For the public council of the people as well as that of the city of Jerusalem had the right of scourging, as is clear from *Matthew*, x. 17; *Acts*, v. 48 [v. 40]; *2 Corinthians*, xi. 24. Furthermore, it had also the right of punishing with death, if the Romans at any time should permit this, as the Jews had a general permission to kill a foreigner who should enter the enclosure of the Temple. Nevertheless, Christ never bade these councillors, His disciples, to withdraw from that office. If He had done so, He would undoubtedly have broken a law by which those that had been in a lawful manner called to this office were ordered to discharge its duties. But such procedure was far from Him. While He passed the life of a mortal, He was 'under the law', *Galatians*, iv; and He did not break the law in any particular Himself, nor instigate others to break it.

16. *οὐκ ἔτι ὡς δοῦλον*, 'not now as a slave'.—Supply 'merely', as is indicated by what follows. Frequently in the speech of all peoples, but especially in Hebrew, this particle is understood. Again, *προσλαβοῦ*, 'receive', is to be repeated from what has gone before.

ἀλλ' ὑπὲρ δοῦλον, 'but as more than a slave'.—Belonging to thee not by the law of the master alone, but etc.

ἀδελφὸν ἀγαπητόν, 'a beloved brother'.—Assuredly to all Christians.

μάλιστα ἐμοί, 'especially to me'.—To me who have made trial of his faithful service.

πόσῳ δὲ μᾶλλον σοί, 'but how much more to thee'.—He ought to be much more dear to thee than to me, because he will be always in thy service, so long as thou shalt desire.

καὶ ἐν σαρκί, 'both in the flesh'.—The body of Onesimus belongs not so much to himself as to thee, *κτήσει καὶ χρήσει*, 'in respect to possession and use'. In Aristophanes, Cario says [*Plutus*, 6–7]:

> Mastery of the body Fortune gives not to the master,
> But to him who by a purchase makes it his.

Σάρξ, 'flesh', and *σῶμα*, 'body', are often used one for the other, as is clear from the Hebrew; *Zephaniah* [*Sophoniah*], i. 17; *Ezekiel*, x. 12; and other passages, with comparison of the Greek and Latin translations.

[617] 17. *εἰ οὖν ἐμὲ ἔχεις κοινωνόν*, 'if, then, thou countest me a partner'.—If thou countest me a friend, and as such sharing in thy concerns.

προσλαβοῦ αὐτόν, 'receive him'.—Not only refrain from the punishment which by thine own right thou wert able to inflict, but also receive him kindly. 'You received into your house, unto your heart', said Pliny in regard to a matter quite similar; *Letters*, IX. xxiv.

ὡς ἐμέ, 'as myself'.—For since Onesimus was a friend of Paul, whatever was done for him seemed to be done for Paul himself.

18. Εἰ δέ τι ἠδίκησέ σε, 'Moreover if he hath wronged thee in any respect'.—If he carried off something when he ran away.

ἢ ὀφείλει, 'or owes [thee]'.—Or if according to thy accounts he was a defaulter. A general term is here used instead of the particular term.

τοῦτο ἐμοὶ ἐλλόγει, 'charge this to me'.—Charge that to my account. Make me instead of him thy surety.

19. Ἐγὼ Παῦλος ἔγραψα τῇ ἐμῇ χειρί, 'I Paul have written with my own hand'.—That thou mayest be certain, thou hast here my handwriting. Thou wilt be able to bring action against me at any time by reason of the autograph. This is what the Scholiast on the *Digest*, XX. iii. 4, calls 'to write a note of hand'. Add *Digest* [*Code*], IV. ii, and *Digest*, XXXIV. iii. 3.

ἐγὼ ἀποτίσω, 'I will repay'.—This, in Latin, is said to constitute a pecuniary obligation, and there is a title on the subject in the *Digest* [XIII. v]. The formula itself is contained in the words *ἐγὼ ἀποτίσω*, or *satisfaciam tibi*, 'I will satisfy you', as *Novels*, cxv. 6, has it; this is ordinarily inserted in the *Code*, under the title 'On constituting a pecuniary obligation' [IV. xviii]. Similarly in *Digest*, XIII. v. 5. 3, this formula is found: 'I have written in accordance with the commission of Seius, that if any debt to you has been approved I will guarantee it to you and will pay it without controversy.' And there is another formula in the same title, *Digest*,

XIII. v. 26: 'The ten [pieces of money] which Lucius Titius had received as a loan from your money-chest you have, Sir, in my possession, with full reckoning of interest.'

Moreover, an obligation can be created even in respect to money which is owed only according to the law of nature (*Digest*, XIII. v. 1. § 7). Slaves can owe their masters, not indeed by municipal law, but by natural law (*Digest*, XLV. iii. 1). So also a surety is rightly accepted for an obligation arising by nature (*Digest*, XLVI. i. 8. § 3).

ἵνα μὴ λέγω σοι ὅτι καὶ σεαυτόν μοι προσοφείλεις, 'not to say to thee, that thou owest to me thy very self'.—It is a 'figure', σχῆμα, of 'passing over in silence', παρασιώπησις, or of 'keeping silent', when we say that we wish to omit that which we are saying with the utmost emphasis. I could say, Paul remarks, that thou art in debt to me not only for what thou hast but also for thy very self; with reason, for without Paul Philemon would have been, and would have remained, in dense darkness and in sin, far from the hope of salvation.

20. Ναί, ἀδελφέ, 'Yes, brother'.—Ναί is here the utterance of one entreating, as in Hebrew.

ἐγώ σου ὀναίμην ἐν Κυρίῳ, 'Let me have joy of thee in the Lord'.—That is, may it be permitted to me to rejoice by reason of thy progress in Christ. Compare *Sirach* [*Ecclesiasticus*], xxx. 2, ὁ παιδεύων τὸν υἱὸν αὐτοῦ, ὀνήσεται ἐπὶ αὐτῷ, 'whoso teacheth his son shall have joy in him'. Ignatius, *To the Magnesians* [ii], says: διακόνου Σωτίονος, οὗ ἐγὼ ὀναίμην, 'of the deacon Sotion, in whom may I have joy'; and *To the Ephesians* [ii. 2]: ὀναίμην ὑμῶν διὰ παντός, 'May I have joy of you always'.

ἀνάπαυσόν μου τὰ σπλάγχνα ἐν Κυρίῳ, 'refresh my bowels in the Lord'.—That is, for Christ's sake cause me to be at peace in regard to this matter.

21. Πεποιθὼς τῇ ὑπακοῇ σου ἔγραψά σοι, 'Having confidence in thine obedience I have written unto thee'.—My confidence has been inspired by the knowledge of that obedience of thine which thou renderest to the Gospel. [618] So ὑπακοή, 'obedience', is taken in *Romans*, i. 5, xv. 18, xvi. 19 and 26; *2 Corinthians*, vii. 15, x. 5 and 6; *1 Peter*, i. 14 and 22.

εἰδὼς ὅτι καὶ ὑπὲρ ὃ λέγω ποιήσεις, 'knowing that thou wilt do even beyond what I say'.—I count it certain that thou wilt do more than I should dare to demand.

22. Ἅμα δὲ καὶ ἑτοίμαζέ μοι ξενίαν, 'At the same time moreover prepare me also a lodging'.—Prepare a lodging; so ξενία, 'lodging', is used in *Acts*, viii. 23 [xxviii. 23], and by Josephus and others.

ἐλπίζω γὰρ ὅτι διὰ τῶν προσευχῶν ὑμῶν χαρισθήσομαι ὑμῖν, 'for I hope that through your prayers I shall be granted to you'.—I hope that in answer to your prayers God will vouchsafe me to you, that is my coming to you. Some think that this hope of Paul was fulfilled and that, freed from his bonds, he went to Asia; that he returned to Rome.

23. Ἀσπάζονταί σε Ἐπαφρᾶς, 'There salute thee Epaphras . . .'—The full name is Ἐπαφρόδιτος (Epaphroditus); *Philippians*, ii. 25; iv. 18. The contracted form Ἐπαφρᾶς is found in *Colossians*, i. 7; iv. 12. Many contracted names of this sort, in ᾶς, we have brought together at the beginning of *Luke*.

ὁ συναιχμάλωτός μου, 'my fellow-prisoner'.—One of those of whom mention is made in *Acts*, xxvii.

ἐν Χριστῷ Ἰησοῦ, 'in Christ Jesus'.—That is, on account of Jesus Christ, as in verse 20 above.

Μάρκος, 'Mark'.—He of whom mention is made in *Acts*, xii. 12 and 25; xv. 37 and 39; *Colossians*, iv. 10.

24. Δημᾶς, 'Demas'.—Whose full name was Demetrius. He is mentioned in *Colossians*, iv. 14; *2 Timothy*, iv. 10.

Λουκᾶς, 'Luke'.—A physician who gave to us the *Gospel* and the *Acts*. See *Colossians*, iv. 14; *2 Timothy*, iv. 11.

οἱ συνεργοί μου, 'my fellow-workers'.—See on verse 1 above.

[25.] Ἡ χάρις τοῦ Κυρίου ἡμῶν Ἰησοῦ Χριστοῦ, 'the grace of our Lord Jesus Christ'.—The favour of Christ.

μετὰ τοῦ πνεύματος ὑμῶν, 'with your spirit'.—That is, be with you. The same phrase is used in *Galatians*, vi. 18. Elsewhere in place of this phrase he said: μεθ' ὑμῶν, καὶ μετὰ πάντων ὑμῶν, 'with you', 'and with you all'.

Ἀμήν, 'Amen'.—This is the word with which the Church made response after the reading of the Epistles. In consequence it began to be added to all the Epistles of Paul. See what I have said *On Matthew*, vi. 13.

LIST OF EDITIONS AND TRANSLATIONS OF THE DE JURE BELLI AC PACIS[1]

1. Hvgonis Grotii de ivre Belli ac Pacis libri tres. In quibus ius naturæ & Gentium : item iuris publici præcipua explicantur. Parisiis ; Apud Nicolavm Bvon, in via Iacobæa, sub signis S. Claudij, & Hominis Siluestris. M. DC. XXV. Cvm Privilegio Regis. 4°. [Not all the copies of this edition are alike, in consequence of changes made by Grotius during printing.] Paris 1625.

2. Hvgonis Grotii . . . explicantur. Moeno-Francofvrti, Typis & Sumptibus Wechelianorum, Danielis & Dauidis Aubriorum & Clementis Schleichii. Anno M. DC. XXVI. 8°. Frankfort-on-the-Main 1626.

3. Hvgonis Grotii . . . explicantur. Editio secunda emendatior, & multis locis auctior. Amsterdami, Apud Gvilielmvm Blaevw. CIↃ IↃC XXXI. Cum privilegiis S. Cæsareæ Maj. & Christianissimi Galliarum Regis. fol. Amsterdam 1631.

4. Hugonis Grotii . . . explicantur. Editio tertia emendatior, & multis locis auctior. Amsterdami, Apud Ioannem Iansonium. CIↃ IↃC XXXII. 8°. Amsterdam 1632.

5. Hvgonis Grotii . . . explicantur. Editio nova ab Auctore ipso recognita & correcta : de qua vide pagina sequenti. Amsterdami, apud Gvilielmvm Blaev. CIↃ IↃC XXXII. Cum privilegiis S. Cæsareæ Majestatis, & Christianissimi Galliarum Regis. 8°. Amsterdam 1632.

6. Hvgonis Grotii . . . explicantur. Editio nova cum Annotatis Auctoris. Accesserunt et Annotata in Epistolam Pauli ad Philemonem. Amsterdami, apud Ioh. & Cornelivm Blæv. CIↃ IↃ C XLII. 8°. Amsterdam 1642.

7. Hvgonis Grotii . . . explicantur. Editio nova cum Annotatis Auctoris, Ex postrema ejus ante obitum cura multo nunc auctior. Accesserunt & Annotata in Epistolam Pauli ad Philemonem. Amsterdami, apud Iohannem Blaev. M D C XLVI. 8°. Amsterdam 1646.

8. Hugonis Grotii . . . Philemonem. Amsterdami, sumptibus Henrici Laurentii. M D C XLVII. fol. Amsterdam 1647.

[1] Reprinted in summary form, by permission of Jacob ter Meulen, Librarian of the Peace Palace at The Hague, from his elaborate bibliographic list in the *Bibliotheca Visseriana*, volume v (Leyden, 1925), pages 159–99. No. 34a was discovered by Dr. ter Meulen after the publication of his list.

Amsterdam 1650. 9. Hvgonis Grotii . . . Philemonem. Amstelædami, apud Ioannem Blæv. MDCL. 8°.

Amsterdam 1651. 10. Hvgonis Grotii . . . Philemonem. Amstelædami, apud Ioannem Blæv. MDCLI. 8°.

Amsterdam 1651. 11. Hugonis Grotii . . . Philemonem. Amstelodami, Apud Ioannem Janssonium. CIↃ IↃC LI. 8°.

Amsterdam 1660. 12. Hvgonis Grotii . . . Philemonem. Amstelædami, Apud Ioannem Blaev. M DC LX. 8°.

Amsterdam 1663. 13. Hvgonis Grotii . . . Philemonem. Amstelædami, Apud Ioannem Blaev. MDCLXIII. 8°.

Amsterdam 1667. 14. Hvgonis Grotii . . . Philemonem, et Dissertatio de Mari libero. Amstelædami Apud Ioannem Blaev. M D C LXVII. 8°.

Amsterdam 1670. 15. Hvgonis Grotii . . . Mari libero. Amstelædami, Apud Joannem Blaev. M DC LXX. 8°.

Jena 1673. 16. Hugonis Grotii . . . explicantur, Cum ejusdem I. Annotatis ex postremâ ante obitum curâ, II. Commentatione in Epistolam Pauli ad Philemon et III. Dissertatione de Mari Libero Publicè ad Disputandum propositi, novis Animadversionibus illustrati, Indiceque Rerum ac Verborum locupletissimo adornati, Dirigente Johanne Georgio Simone, . . . Jenæ Apud Johann. Theodor. Fleischern. Typis Samuelis Adolphi Mülleri. M.DC. LXXIII. 4°.

Amsterdam 1680. 17. Hugonis Grotii . . . explicantur. Editio novissima cum Annotatis Auctoris, ex postrema ejus ante obitum cura. Accesserunt Annotata in Epistolam Pauli ad Philemonem, Dissertatio de Mari libero, & Libellus singularis de Aequitate, Indulgentia & Facilitate, quem Nicolaus Blancardus Belga Leidensis è codice Autoris descripsit & vulgavit. Nec non Joann. Frid. Gronovii V. C. notæ in totum opus de Jure Belli ac Pacis. Amstelædami, Apud Janssonio-Wæsbergios, M DC LXXX. 8°.

The Hague 1680. 18. Hugonis Grotii . . . explicantur. Editio novissima . . . vulgavit. Nec non Joann. Frid. Gronovii V. C. notæ in totum opus de Jure Belli ac Pacis. Hagæ Comitis, Apud Arnoldum Leers, M DC LXXX. 8°.

Jena 1680. 19. Hugonis Grotii . . . explicantur. Cum ejusdem I. Annotatis ex postremâ ante obitum curâ, II. Commentatione in Epistolam Pauli ad Philemon. III. Dissertatione de Mari Libero, IV. Epistola de Studiis instituendis, ad Benjaminum Maurerium, Legatum Regis Galliæ &, V. Excerpto ex alia de juris studio. Publicè olim ad Disputandum propositi, nunc vero novis Animadversionibus & adjectionibus locorum concordantium illustrati, allegatione Scriptorum distinctiori, Indicéqve pariter Rerum ac Verborum locupletissimo adornati, Dirigente Johanne Georgio Simone, ... Jenæ, Sumtibus Johannis Theodori Fleischeri, Bibliopol. Rudolphstadii, Literis Christophori Fleischeri, Anno MDC LXXX. 8°.

20. Hugonis Grotii . . . explicantur. Cum Annotatis Auctoris, ex postrema ejus ante obitum cura. Accesserunt Annotata in Epistolam Pauli ad Philemonem, Dissertatio de Mari Libero, & Libellus singularis de Aequitate, Indulgentia & Facilitate quem Nicolaus Blancardus Belga-Leidensis è codice Auctoris descripsit & vulgavit. Nec non Joann. Frid. Gronovii V. C. Notæ in totum opus de Jure Belli ac Pacis. Amstelodami. Sumptibus Janssonio-Wæsbergiorum, M DC LXXXIX. 8°. Amsterdam 1689.

21. Hugonis Grotii . . . explicantur. Cum Annotatis . . . vulgavit. Nec non Joann. Frid. Gronovii V. C. Notæ in totum opus de Jure Belli ac Pacis. Amstelodami. Sumptibus Abrahami à Someren, M DC LXXXIX. 8°. Amsterdam 1689.

22. Hugonis Grotii . . . explicantur, cum Annotatis Autoris ex postrema ejus ante Obitum cura: Accesserunt Excerpta Annotationum Variorum Virorum Insignium in totum Opus, edente Joh. Christoph. Becmano. . . . Francofurti ad Viadrum, Impensis Jeremiæ Schrey / M.DC.XCI. 4°. Frankfort-on-the-Oder 1691.

23. Hvgonis Grotii de Jure belli et pacis libri tres, cum annotatis Ipsius Autoris, & clarissimi Gronovii; tum noviter accuratis commentariis perpetuis Joh. Tesmari JCti Celeberrimi. Opus vt mvltorvm annorvm, ita Academiis, Aulis, Dicasteriis, diu multumque desideratum; Theologis, Jure-Consultis, Philosophis, Oratoribus, omnibusque adeo solidæ eruditionis studiosis perquam utile & necessarium; quippe in quo textus Grotianus fideliter exhibetur, obscuriora perspicuè illustrantur, dubia rationibus & auctoritatibus tam veterum quam recentium Scriptorum solide confirmantur, Paradoxa modestè diluuntur, omissa sedulò supplentur, aliorumque interpretationes solicitè perpenduntur & inter se conferuntur. Ad calcem operis accessere Ulrici Obrechti, JCti Excellentissimi, Observationes ad eosdem Libros, cum Indicibus plenissimis. Francofurti ad Moenum Sumptibus Joan. Davidis Zunneri, Typis Joannis Baueri, M DC XCVI. fol. Frankfort-on-the-Oder 1696.

24. Hugo Grotius de Jure belli ac pacis In quibus Jus Naturae & Gentium, item Juris publici praecipua explicantur. Cum annotationibus Auctoris, & Notis eruditissimis Variorum. Ex accuratissima recensione & cum animadversionibus viri Leyden 1696.

desideratissimi Gothofredi Spinaei, In Academia Lugd. Batava, (dum viveret) Professoris ordinarii. Editio plane nova. Lugduni Batavorum, Ex Officina Johannis du Vivié, Bibliopolae 1696. 4°.

Utrecht 1696–1703. 25. Hugonis Grotii . . . explicantur, Cum commentariis Gulielmi vander Muelen . . . Accedunt Et Authoris Annotata, ex postrema ejus ante obitum cura nec non Joann. Frid. Gronovii V. C. Notæ in totum opus. Ultra Jecti, Prostant apud Gulielmum vande Water [Gulielmum Broedelet], Bibliopol. CIƆ IƆC XCVI [MDCC] [MCDCIII]. 3 v. fol.

Frankfort-on-the-Oder 1699. 26. Hugonis Grotii . . . explicantur, Cum Annotatis Autoris ex postrema ejus ante obitum cura: Accesserunt Excerpta Annotationum variorum Virorum Insignium in totum Opus, edente Joh. Christoph. Becmano. Editio secunda correctior . . . Francofurti ad Viadrum, Impensis Jeremiæ Schrey / & Joh. Christoph. Hartmann / M.DC.IC. 4°.

Amsterdam 1701. 27. Hugonis Grotii . . . cura. Accesserunt Annotata in Epistolam Pauli ad Philemonem, Dissertatio de Mari Libero, & Libellus singularis de Aequitate, Indulgentia, & Facilitate, quem Nicolaus Blancardus Belga-Leidensis e codice Auctoris descripsit & vulgavit. Nec non Joann. Frid. Gronovii V. C. Notæ in totum opus de Jure Belli ac Pacis. Editio novissima, . . . Amstelodami, Apud Janssonio-Waesbergios. MDCCI. 8°.

Amsterdam 1701. 28. Hugonis Grotii . . . ostendit. Amstelodami, Apud Viduam Abrahami à Someren. MDCCI. 8°.

Amsterdam 1702. 29. Hugonis Grotii . . . ostendit. Amstelædami, Apud Henricum Wetstenium, ut & Rodolfum & Gerhardum Wetstenios, H. FF. CIƆ IƆ CC II. 8°.

Amsterdam 1704. 30. Hugonis Grotii . . . explicantur. Cum Commentariis Gulielmi vander Muelen, Domini d'Oudt-Brouckhuysen, Decani D. Mariæ, Aggerum, qui inferiorem Leccæ partem coërcent, Præfecti; &c Accedunt Et Auctoris Annotata, ex postrema ejus ante obitum cura; & Joan. Fred. Gronovii Notæ in totum opus. Amstelædami, Apud Janssonio-Waesbergios & Wetstenios. CIƆ IƆ CCIV. . . . 3 v. fol.

Amsterdam 1712. 31. Hugonis Grotii . . . explicantur. Cum Annotatis Auctoris, ex postrema ejus ante obitum cura. Accesserunt ejusdem Dissertatio de Mari libero, & Libellus singularis de æquitate, indulgentia, & facilitate, Nec non Joann. Frid. Gronovii V. C. Notæ in totum opus de Jure Belli ac Pacis. Editio novissima, . . . Amstelædami, Ex Officina Wetsteniana. CIƆ IƆ CCXII . . . 8°.

32. Hugonis Grotii . . . ostendit. Amstelædami, Apud Janssonio-Waesbergios. CIƆ IƆ CCXII. . . . 8°. Amsterdam 1712.

33. Hugonis Grotii . . . cura. Accesserunt Excerpta Annotationum variorum virorum insignium in totum opus edente Joh. Christoph. Becmano. Editio Secvnda Correctior. . . . Francofurti ad Viadrum Apvd Jeremiam Schrey. MDCCXVIII. 4°. Frankfort-on-the-Oder 1718.

34. Hugonis Grotii . . . cura. Accesserunt ejusdem Dissertatio de mari libero, & Libellus singularis de æquitate, indulgentia, & facilitate, Nec non Joann. Frid. Gronovii V. C. Notæ in totum opus de Jure Belli ac Pacis. Editio novissima [n.p.]. Anno CIƆ IƆ CCXIX. . . . 2 v. 4°. Place unknown 1719.

34a. Hugonis Grotii . . . cura. Accesserunt ejusdem dissertatio de mari libero, et libellus singularis de æquitate, indulgentia, et felicitate, nec non Joann. Frid. Gronovii V. C. notæ in totum opus de jure belli ac pacis. Editio novissima. Augustae 1719–1723. 2 v. 4°. Place ? 1719–23.

35. Hugonis Grotii . . . explicantur. Cum Annotatis Auctoris, ejusdemque Dissertatione de Mari libero, ac Libello singulari de Aequitate, Indulgentia, & Facilitate: Nec non Joann. Frid. Gronovii V. C. Notis in totum opus de Jure Belli ac Pacis. Editionem omnium, quæ hactenus prodierunt, emendatissimam, ad fidem priorum & optimarum recensuit; . . . Notulas denique addidit Joannes Barbeyrac, . . . Amstelædami, Ex Officina Wetsteniana CIƆ IƆ CCXX. . . . 8°. Amsterdam 1720.

36. Hugonis Grotii . . . addidit Joannes Barbeyrac, JC. & Publici Privatique Juris Antecessor Groninganus. Amstelædami, Apud Janssonio-Waesbergios. CIƆ IƆ CCXX. . . . 8°. Amsterdam 1720.

37. Hugonis Grotii . . . cura, et Præfatione Christiani Wolfii. Marburgi Cattorum, Apud Phil. Casimir. Müllerum. M DCC XXXIV. 8°. Marburg 1734.

38. Hugonis Grotii . . . explicantur. Cum Annotatis Auctoris, ejusdemque Dissertatione de Mari libero; Ac Libello singulari de Aequitate, Indulgentia, & Facilitate; Nec non Joann. Frid. Gronovii V. C. Notis in totum opus de Jure Belli ac Pacis. Ex altera recensione Joannis Barbeyracii, . . . Cum Notulis ejusdem nunc auctioribus, pluriumque locorum, ex Auctoribus quibusvis laudatorum, adcuratiori indicatione. Amstelædami, Apud Janssonio-Waesbergios. CIƆ IƆ CCXXXV. 2 v. 8°. Amsterdam 1735.

Amsterdam 1735. 39. Hugonis Grotii . . . indicatione. . . . Amstelædami, Sumptibus Gasparis Fritsch. CIϽ IϽ CCXXXV. 2 v. 8°.

Breslau 1744, 1746, 1747, 1752. 40. Henrici de Cocceji Sacræ Regiæ Majestati Borussicæ quondam a consiliis secretioribus Grotius illustratus seu Commentarii ad Hugonis Grotii de Jure belli et pacis libros tres in quibus Jus Naturæ & Gentium, item Juris Publici præcipua explicantur. Adduntur Annotata Authoris ex postrema ejus ante obitum cura. In commentario id præcipue agitur, ut Grotius ex ipso Grotio illustretur, defectus circa principia Grotiana notentur; et vera juris naturæ principia, inprimis quatenus ad interpretationem juris romani pertinent, proponantur. Accedunt Observationes S. d. C. H. F. . . . Wratislaviæ sumtibus Johannis Jacobi Korn. Bibliopol. Anno 1744, (1746), (1747), (1752). 4 v. fol. [The title-page of the fourth volume enumerates other writings of Grotius.]

Lausanne 1751–2. 41. Hugonis Grotii de Jure belli ac pacis libri tres, Cum Annotatis Auctoris, nec non J. F. Gronovii Notis, & J. Barbeyracii Animadversionibus; commentariis insuper locupletissimis Henr. L. B. de Cocceii . . . insertis quoque observationibus Samuelis L. B. de Cocceii Henrici filii . . . Adduntur tandem ipsius Grotii Dissertatio de Mari libero, ac Libellus singularis de Aequitate, Indulgentia et Facilitate. Lausannæ, Sumptibus Marci-Michaelis Bousquet, & Sociorum. MDCCLI, [MDCCLI] [MDCCLII] [MDCLII]. 5 v. 4°.

Lausanne 1758, 1759. 42. Hugonis Grotii . . . Facilitate. Cum quibusdam notis criticis. Lausannæ. Sumptibus Marci-Michaelis Bousquet, & Sociorum. MDCCLVIII. [MDCCLVIII] [MDCCLIX] [MDCCLIX] [MDCCLIX]. 5 v. 4°.

Leipzig 1758. 43. Hugonis Grotii . . . explicantur. Cum Annotatis Auctoris eiusdemque Dissertatione de Mari libero; Ac Libello singulari de Aequitate, Indulgentia, et Facilitate; Nec non Jo. Fr. Gronovii v. c. Notis in totum opus de Jure belli ac pacis. Ex altera recensione Joannis Barbeyracii. . . . Cum Notulis ejusdem nunc Auctioribus, pluriumq. locor. ex Auctorib. quib. laudat. adcuratiori indicatione. . . . Lipsiæ Impensis Ioannis Pauli Krausii bibliop. Vienn. MDCCLVIII. 2 v. 8°.

Utrecht 1773. 44. Hvgonis Grotii de Ivre belli ac pacis libri tres, cum adnotationibus selectis Joann. Frid. Gronovii, & auctioribus Ioannis Barbeyracii. Accedit H. Grotii Dissertatio de Mari libero; Et Libellus singularis de Aeqvitate, Indvlgentia, & Facilitate. Edidit atque præfatus est Meinardvs Tydeman.

Traiecti ad Rhenvm. Ex officina Ioannis a Schoonhoven & Soc. CIↃ IↃ CC LXXIII. 2 v. 8°.

45. Hugonis Grotii de jure belli et pacis libri tres accompanied by an abridged translation by William Whewell . . . Edited for the Syndics of the University Press. Cambridge: M. DCCC. LIII. John W. Parker, London. 3 v. 8°. Cambridge 1853.

46. Hugonis Grotii . . . Philemonem. Volume one. Reproduction of the Edition of 1646, Carnegie Institution of Washington, 1913. 4°. [For Volume Two see No. 76, *post.*] Washington 1913.

47. Hugonis Grotii . . . explicantur. Cum annotatis auctoris edidit P. C. Molhuysen. Præfatus est C. van Vollenhoven. Lugduni Batavorum Apud A. W. Sijthoff. MCMXIX. 4°. Leyden 1919.

Translations

Dutch

48. Drie boecken Van Hvgo de Groot, Nopende het Recht des Oorloghs Ende des Vredes. In dewelcke het Recht der Natuere, der Volckeren, mitsgaders de principaelste stucken van 't Burgelijcke Recht verklaert werden. Eerst in 't Latijn uytgegeven, Ende nu ten dienste van alle Bedienaers vande Bancken der Justitie / ende andere weet-suchtige Lief-hebbers onses Vaderlands / In 't Neder-duyts vertaelt Door H. V. Ghedruckt te Haerlem, by Adriaen Roman / Boeckdrucker, woonende inde Groote Houtstraet, inde Vergulde Parsze. Anno 1635. 4°. Haarlem 1635.

49. Drie Boecken Van 't Recht des Oorloghs en Vredes. . . . overgheset Door B. D. Seer . . . t' Amsterdam, Gedruckt by Iacob Colom, Boeckverkooper op het Water, in de vyerighe Colom, Anno 1651. 4°. Amsterdam 1651.

50. Drie Boecken Van 't Recht des Oorloghs en Vredes . . . overgheset Door B. D. Den tweeden Druck. Seer . . . t' Amsterdam, By Ian Hendricksz En Willem van Beaumont, Boeck-verkoopers. 1657. 4°. Amsterdam 1657.

51. Hugo de Groot Van 't Regt des Oorlogs en Vredes, . . . met de beste verklaringen en tegenwerpingen van de Hr. Joh. Frid. Gronovius, en anderen: nooit op die wijze in onze spraake aan 't ligt gebragt. Door Jan van Gaveren. Met een zeer wijdloopig register. t' Amsterdam, By François van-der Plaats, Boekverkoper in de Gaper-steeg, by de Beurs. 1705. 4°. Amsterdam 1705.

Amsterdam 1732. 52. Hugo de Groot van 't Regt des Oorlogs en Vredes, . . . Tweeden druk. t' Amsteldam, By Salomon Schouten, Boekverkooper in de St. Luciesteeg. 1732. 4°.

French

Paris 1687. 53. Le Droit de la guerre et de la paix, par M. Grotivs: divisé en trois livres, Où il explique le Droit de Nature, le Droit des Gens, & les principaux Points du Droit public, ou qui concerne le gouvernement public d'un Etat. Traduit du Latin en François, par Monsieur de Courtin. . . . A Paris, Chez Arnould Seneuze, . . . M. DC. LXXXVII. . . . 2 v. 4°.

Amsterdam The Hague 1688. 54. Le Droit de la guerre et de la paix, . . . Traduit du Latin en François, par Monsieur De Courtin. . . . A Amsterdam, Chez Abraham Wolfgang; et à la Haye, Chez Adrian Moetjens. M. DC. LXXXVIII. 3 v. 12°.

The Hague 1703. 55. Le Droit de la guerre et de la paix, . . . Traduit du Latin en François, par Monsieur De Courtin. Augmenté dans cette Edition de la Dissertation de la Liberté de la mer, &c. A La Haye, Chez Adrian Moetjens. M. DCCIII. 3 v. 12°.

Amsterdam 1724. 56. Le Droit de la guerre et de la paix. Par Hugues Grotius. Nouvelle traduction, par Jean Barbeyrac, . . . Avec les Notes de l'Auteur même, qui n'avoient point encore paru en François; & de nouvelles Notes du Traducteur. A Amsterdam, Chez Pierre de Coup. MDCCXXIV. 2 v. 4°.

Amsterdam 1729. 57. Le Droit de la guerre et de la paix; par Hugues Grotius. Nouvelle traduction; Par Jean Barbeyrac, . . . A Amsterdam, Chez Pierre de Coup. M. DCCXXIX. 2 v. 4°.

Basel 1746. 58. Le Droit de la guerre et de la paix. . . . A Basle, Chez Emanuel Thourneisen, MDCCXLVI. 2 v. 4°.

Leyden 1759. 59. Le Droit de la guerre et de la paix par Hugues Grotius. . . . A Leide, Aux Dépens de la Compagnie. MDCCLIX 2 v. 4°.

Basel 1768. 60. Le Droit de la guerre et de la paix par Hugues Grotius. Nouvelle traduction, Par Jean Barbeyrac, . . . A Basle, Chez Emanuel Tourneisen, MDCCLXVIII. 2 v. 4°.

Leyden-Lyons 1768. 61. Le Droit de la guerre et de la paix, . . . A Leyde, chez J. de Wetstein: Et se trouve, A Lyon, Chez Jean-Marie Bruyset, Imprimeur-Libraire. MDCCLXVIII. 2 v. 4°.

Paris 1865–7. 62. Le Droit de la guerre et de la paix . . . Nouvelle traduction Précédée d'un Essai biographique et historique sur Grotius et son temps accompagnée d'un choix de notes de Gronovius, Barbeyrac, etc. complétée par des notes nouvelles.

Mise au courant des progrès du Droit public moderne et suivie d'une table analytique des matières par M. P. Pradier-Fodéré, ... Paris Guillaumin et Cie. ... 1865 (1867) (1867). 3 v. 8°. 12°.

German

63. Hugonis Grotii Drey Bücher vom Rechte des Krieges und des Friedens / darinnen das Recht der Natur und der Völcker / wie auch die vornehmsten Sachen desjenigen Rechtes / welches von der Regierung eines Staates handelt / erkläret / und die Anmerckungen des Verfassers hinzugefüget werden. Aus dem Lateinischen ins Deutsche übersetzet durch P. B. S. g. Schütz / .... Leipzig / verlegts Friedrich Groschuff / im Jahr Christi / 1707. 4°. Leipzig 1707.

64. Hugonis Grotii Drey Bücher von Kriegs- und Friedens-Rechten ... Ins Teutsche übersetzet und herausgegeben von J. N. S. ... Franckfurt am Mayn / Zu finden bey Notar. Fischern / neben dem Schonburger Hof. Und daselbst gedruckt bey Johann Bauern / MDCCIX. fol. Frankfort-on-the-Main 1709.

65. Hugonis Grotii Drey Bücher von Kriegs- und Friedens-Rechten, ... Ins Teutsche übersetzet und herausgegeben von J. N. S. ... Franckfurt am Mayn, Zu finden bey Wolffgang Christoph Multzen. Den Laden gegen dem neuen Caffee-Haus über. MDCCXXI. fol. Frankfort-on-the-Main 1721.

66. Hugonis Grotii Drey Bücher von Kriegs- und Friedens-Rechten, ... Ins Teutsche übersetzet und herausgegeben von J. N. S. ... Franckfurt am Mayn, Zu finden bey Wolffgang Christoph Multzen MDCCXXVIII. fol. Frankfort-on the-Main 1728.

67. Des Hugo Grotius drei Bücher über das Recht des Krieges und Friedens, ... Aus dem Lateinischen des Urtextes übersetzt ... von J. H. v. Kirchmann. Berlin, 1869. Verlag von L. Heimann. 2 v. 8°. Berlin 1869.

English

68. The illustrious Hvgo Grotius of the Law of Warre and Peace with annotations. III parts. And Memorials of the Author's Life and Death. ... London, Printed by T. Warren, for William Lee, And are to be sold at his shop, at the signe of the Turks-head in Fleet-street, M. DC. LIV. 8°. London 1654.

69. idem, M.DCLV. 8°. London 1655.

70. The most excellent Hugo Grotius his three Books Treating of the Rights of War & Peace. ... Translated into London 1682.

English by William Evats, B.D. London, Printed by M. W. for Thomas Basset at the George in Fleetstreet, and Ralph Smith at the Bible under the Piazza of the Royal Exchange in Cornhill. MDCLXXXII. fol.

London 1715. 71. H. Grotius of the Rights of War and Peace, In three volumes. . . . Done into English by several Hands; . . . London: Printed for D. Brown in Exeter Exchange in the Strand; T. Ward in the Inner-Temple Lane; and W. Meares at the Lamb without Temple Bar. MDCCXV. 3 v. 8°.

London 1738. 72. The Rights of War and Peace, in three books. . . . London: Printed for W. Innys and R. Manby, J. and P. Knapton, D. Brown, T. Osborn, and E. Wicksteed. MDCCXXXVIII. fol.

Pontefract 1814. 73. The Rights of War and Peace, including the Law of nature and of nations, translated . . . by the Rev. A. C. Campbell. Pontefract: Printed by B. Boothroyd, and sold by F. and C. Rivington; Gale, Curtis, and Co., Paternoster Row; Cadell and Davies, Strand; and Stockdale, Piccadilly, London. 1814. 3 v. 8°.

Cambridge 1853. 74. Grotius on the rights of war and peace: an abridged translation. By William Whewell . . . Edited for the Syndics of the University Press. Cambridge: MDCCCLIII. John W. Parker, London. 3 v. 8°.

Washington, London 1901. 75. The rights of war and peace . . . translated . . . by A. C. Campbell, A.M. With an introduction by David J. Hill, . . . M. Walter Dunne, Publisher Washington & London. [1901.] 8°. [An abridged reprint of No. 73.]

Oxford 1925. 76. De Jure Belli ac Pacis Libri tres by Hugo Grotius. Volume Two: The translation by Francis W. Kelsey with the collaboration of Arthur E. S. Boak, Henry A. Sanders, Jesse S. Reeves and Herbert F. Wright and an introduction by James Brown Scott. Oxford: at the Clarendon Press, 1925. 4°. [Publication of the Carnegie Endowment for International Peace, Division of International Law. For Volume One see No. 46, *supra*.]

Spanish

Madrid 1925. 77. Del Derecho de la Guerra y de la Paz de Hugo Grocio. Versión directa del original Latino por Jaime Torrubiano Ripoll . . . Editorial Reus (S.A.). Madrid, 1925. 4 v. 16°.

INDEXES

NOTE

An attempt has been made to give the full name, date of birth and death or *floruit*, nationality, and field of labour of each author and the title of each work referred to by Grotius. The translated title is given first where the English translation helps to disclose the subject-matter of the work, in which case it is followed by the original title in parentheses. If the original title is in some other language than Latin, it is omitted or the Latin title under which it is commonly cited is substituted. The Loeb Classical Library and the Oxford Classical Texts have been used to verify the references where available. Otherwise a place and date is added inside the parentheses to indicate the edition used to verify Grotius's citations. Where the former were not available and no other edition has been specified, the reference has not been verified in the original. References to the authors and works contained in the *Corpus Iuris Civilis* or the *Corpus Iuris Canonici* are listed only under the particular part of the *Corpus* unless mentioned specifically by Grotius under their own name. Grotius almost invariably cites examples in support of his statements; references to these will be found under the subject which they exemplify. In the verification of the references and in the preparation of the indexes, invaluable assistance has been rendered by Mr. Walter H. Zeydel of the Division of International Law of the Carnegie Endowment.—H. F. W.

INDEX OF AUTHORS CITED

SUBJECT INDEX

THE CLASSICS OF INTERNATIONAL LAW

This series, which includes the classic works connected with the history and development of international law, was undertaken by the Carnegie Institution of Washington in 1906, at the suggestion of Mr. James Brown Scott, then Solicitor for the Department of State, under whose supervision as General Editor the series has since been published. On January 1, 1917, the project was transferred to the Carnegie Endowment for International Peace and the publication of the series is being continued by the Endowment's Division of International Law, of which the General Editor of the Classics is the Director.

The republication of these classics has been undertaken principally on account of the difficulty of procuring the texts in convenient form for scientific study. The text of each author is reproduced photographically, so as to lay the source before the reader without the mistakes which creep into a newly printed text. An introduction is prefixed to each work, giving the necessary biographical details concerning its author and stating the importance of the text and its place in international law. Tables of errata in the original are added when necessary, and notes to clear up doubts and ambiguities or to correct mistakes in the text are supplied. Each of the Classics is specially edited by an expert in international law and is accompanied by an English version made expressly for the series by a competent translator.

The following works have appeared and are now on sale. The price is indicated for each work. They can be obtained by remittance to the publishers, either the Clarendon Press, Oxford, England, or the Oxford University Press, American Branch, 35 West 32nd Street, New York, N.Y., who are the regular selling agents for the Clarendon Press in the United States.

Ayala, Balthazar: De jure et officiis bellicis et disciplina militari. Edited by John Westlake. 2 vols. Washington, 1912. [No. 2 of the series.] Price, $7.00.

Vol. I. A Photographic Reproduction of the Edition of 1582, with portrait of Ayala, Introduction by John Westlake, &c. xxvii + 226 pages.

Vol. II. A Translation of the Text, by John Pawley Bate. xii + 250 pages.

Bynkershoek, Cornelius van: De dominio maris. 1 vol. New York, 1923. 108 + 80 pages. [No. 11 of the series.] Price, $2.00.

1. Introduction by James Brown Scott.
2. A Translation of the Text, by Ralph Van Deman Magoffin.
3. A Photographic Reproduction of the Edition of 1744.
4. An Index of Authors Cited and a List of Errata in the 1744 edition, by Herbert F. Wright.

Gentili, Alberico: De legationibus libri tres. 2 vols. New York, 1924. [No. 12 of the series.] Price, $5.00.

Vol. I. A Photographic Reproduction of the Edition of 1594, with an Introduction by Ernest Nys, and List of Errata. 38a + xvi + 233 pages.

Vol. II. A Translation of the Text, by Gordon J. Laing, with Translation (by E. H. Zeydel) of Introduction by Ernest Nys, and an Index of Authors Cited by Herbert F. Wright. 38a + x + 208 pages.

Gentili, Alberico: Hispanicae advocationis libri duo. 2 vols. New York, 1921. [No. 9 of the series.] Price, $5.00.

Vol. I. A Photographic Reproduction of the Edition of 1661, with an Introduction by Frank Frost Abbott and a List of Errata. 44a + xvi + 274 pages.

Vol. II. A Translation of the Text, by Frank Frost Abbott, with an Index of Authors by Arthur Williams. 12a + x + 284 pages.

Grotius, Hugo: De jure belli ac pacis libri tres. 2 vols. [No. 3 of the series.] Price, both volumes, 2½ guineas in Great Britain, $12.50 in United States; Vol. II only, 1½ guineas in Great Britain, $7.50 in United States; Vol. I not sold separately; Vol. II consists of three books, each bound separately.

Vol. I. A Photographic Reproduction of the Edition of 1646, with a portrait of Grotius. Washington, 1913. xxiv + 663 pages.

Vol. II. A Translation of the Text, by Francis W. Kelsey, with the collaboration of Arthur E. R. Boak, Henry A. Sanders, Jesse S. Reeves, and Herbert F. Wright, with an Introduction by James Brown Scott, Indexes, and List of Editions and Translations. Oxford, 1925.

Legnano, Giovanni da: De bello, de repraesaliis et de duello. Edited by Sir T. Erskine Holland. 1 vol. Oxford, 1917. xxxiii + 458 pages. [No. 8 of the series.] *Out of print.*

1. Collotype of the Bologna Manuscript of *circa* 1390, with Extended and Revised Text of Same, Introduction, List of Authorities Cited, &c., by Sir T. Erskine Holland, together with Photograph of Legnano's Tomb.
2. A Translation of the Text, by J. L. Brierly.
3. A Photographic Reproduction of the First Edition (1477).

Rachel, Samuel: De jure naturae et gentium dissertationes. Edited by Ludwig von Bar. 2 vols. Washington, 1916. [No. 5 of the series.] Price, $4.00.

Vol. I. A Photographic Reproduction of the Edition of 1676, with portrait of Rachel, Introduction by Ludwig von Bar, and List of Errata. 16a + x + 335 pages.

Vol. II. A Translation of the Text, by John Pawley Bate, with Index of Authors Cited. 16a + iv + 233 pages.

Textor, Johann Wolfgang: Synopsis juris gentium. Edited by Ludwig von Bar. 2 vols. Washington, 1916. [No. 6 of the series.] Price, $4.00.

Vol. I. A Photographic Reproduction of the First Edition (1680), with portrait of Textor, Introduction by Ludwig von Bar, and List of Errata. 28a + vi + 148 + 168 pages.

Vol. II. A Translation of the Text, by John Pawley Bate, with Index of Authors Cited. 26a + v + 349 pages.

Vattel, E. de: Le droit des gens. 3 vols. Washington, 1916. [No. 4 of the series.] Price, $8.00.

Vol. I. A Photographic Reproduction of Books I and II of the First Edition (1758), with portrait of Vattel and Introduction by Albert de Lapradelle. lix + 541 pages.

Vol. II. A Photographic Reproduction of Books III and IV of the First Edition (1758). xxiv + 376 pages.

Vol. III. A Translation of the Text, by Charles G. Fenwick, with Translation (by G. D. Gregory) of Introduction by Albert de Lapradelle. lxxxviii + 398 pages.

Victoria, Franciscus de: Relectiones: De indis and De iure belli. Edited by Ernest Nys. 1 vol. Washington, 1917. 500 pages. [No. 7 of the series.] Price, $3.00.

1. Introduction by Ernest Nys, and Translation of Same, by John Pawley Bate.
2. A Translation of the Text, by John Pawley Bate.
3. Revised Text, with Prefatory Remarks, List of Errata, and Index of Authors Cited, by Herbert F. Wright.
4. A Photographic Reproduction of Simon's Edition (1696).

Zouche, Richard: Juris et judicii fecialis, sive juris inter gentes, et quaestionum de eodem explicatio. Edited by Sir T. Erskine Holland. 2 vols. Washington, 1911. [No. 1 of the series.] Price, $4.00.

Vol. I. A Photographic Reproduction of the First Edition (1650), with Introduction, List of Errata, and Table of Authors, by Sir T. Erskine Holland, together with portrait of Zouche. xvi + 204 pages.

Vol. II. A Translation of the Text, by J. L. Brierly. xvii + 186 pages.

(*In Press*)

Pufendorf, Samuel von: De officio hominis et civis juxta legem naturalem libri duo. 2 vols. [No. 10 of the series.]

Vol. I. A Photographic Reproduction of the Edition of 1682, with an Introduction by Walther Schücking.

Vol. II. A Translation of the Text, by Frank Gardner Moore, with Translation of Introduction by Walther Schücking.

Wolff, Christian von: Jus gentium methodo scientifica pertractatum. [No. 13 of the series.]

1. Introduction by Otfried Nippold, and Translation of Same by Francis J. Hemelt.
2. A Translation of the Text, by Joseph H. Drake.
3. A Photographic Reproduction of the Edition of 1764.

Address orders to

THE CLARENDON PRESS
OXFORD, ENGLAND

or

THE OXFORD UNIVERSITY PRESS
AMERICAN BRANCH
35 WEST 32ND STREET, NEW YORK, N.Y.